MW01630089

WILLIAM BECKFORD, 1760–1844

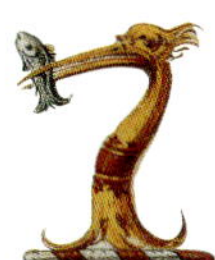

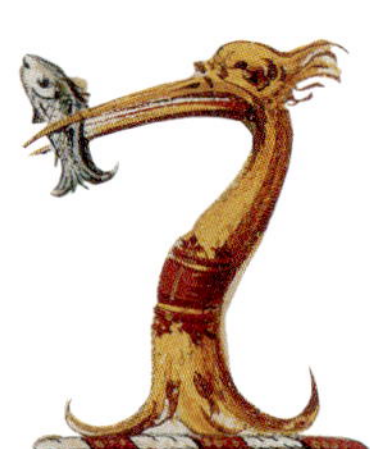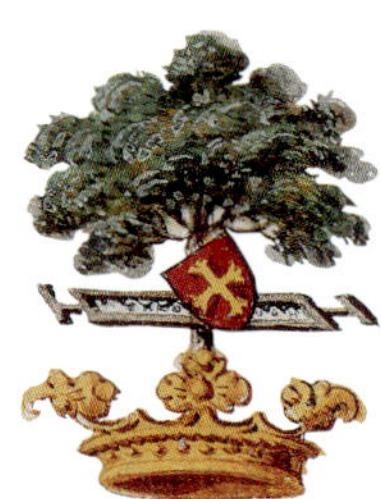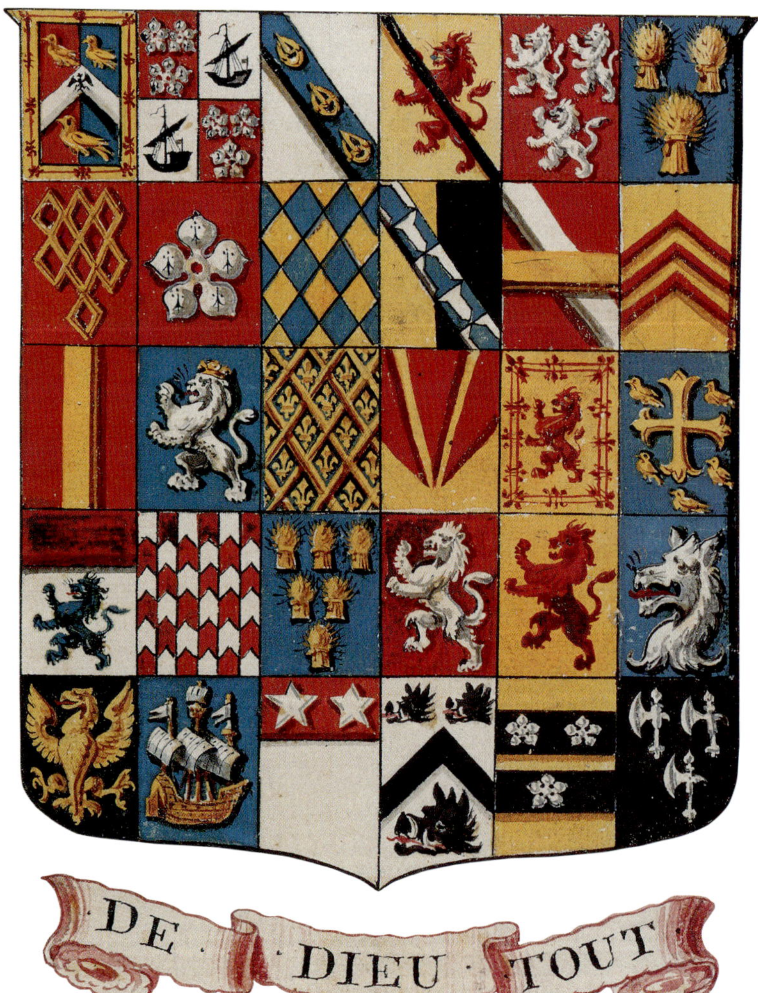

DE · DIEU · TOUT

WILLIAM BECKFORD, 1760–1844:
AN EYE FOR THE MAGNIFICENT

Philip Hewat-Jaboor

Bet McLeod

Megan Aldrich

Sidney Blackmore

Jeannie Chapel

Anne Eschapasse

William Hauptman

Oliver Impey

Malcolm Jack

Alexander Marr

Timothy Mowl

Michael Snodin

Adriana Turpin

David Watkin

John Whitehead

Christopher Woodward

Derek E. Ostergard, Editor

Published for The Bard Graduate Center for Studies in the Decorative Arts, Design and Culture, by Yale University Press, New Haven and London

This catalogue is published in conjunction with the exhibition
"William Beckford, 1760–1844: An Eye for the Magnificent"
held at The Bard Graduate Center for Studies in the Decorative Arts, Design and Culture
from October 18, 2001, through January 6, 2002.

Exhibition tour:
The Dulwich Picture Gallery, London, England
February 5 through April 14, 2002

Project director: Derek E. Ostergard
Exhibition curators: Philip Hewat-Jaboor and Bet McLeod
Project assistants: Ron Labaco and Olga Valle Tetkowski
Catalogue production: Martina D'Alton, New York; Sally Salvesen, London

Director of Exhibitions: Nina Stritzler-Levine

Copyright © 2001 The Bard Graduate Center for Studies
in the Decorative Arts, Design and Culture. The individual essay copyright
is held by the author and The Bard Graduate Center for Decorative Arts, Design and Culture.
All rights reserved. This book may not be reproduced in whole or in part, in any form
(beyond that copying permitted by Sections 107 and 108 of the U.S. Copyright Law
and except by reviewers for the public press), without
written permission from the publishers.

Library of Congress Catalog number: 2001095102
ISBN: 0 300 09068 4

Jacket design: Derek E. Ostergard
On the front: *William Beckford* (detail) by John Hoppner, ca. 1800. Oil on canvas.
City of Salford Art Gallery, Salford, England.

On the back: *Objects of Vertu* by Willes Maddox, 1844. Oil on canvas.
Beckford Tower Trust, Bath (Sole Trustee Bath Preservation Trust) (1986/44). *Cat. no. 156*.

Half title page: Detail of frontispiece. The heron, a heraldic device of William Beckford.

Frontispiece: The Beckford coat of arms. From left, beginning at the top row: row 1—Beckford,
Hamilton, Lesly, Abernethy, Ross, Comyn; row 2—Quincy, Bellomont, Mellent, Gwadyr, Fitz
Osborne, Yvery; row 3—Grantesmesnil, Galloway, Morville, Scot, Scotland, Saxon Kings; row 4—
Waltheof, Aldred, Kevelioc, Gernons, Meschines, Lupus; row 5—Algar, Caithness, Douglas of
Dalkeith, Reading, Coward, Hall. The College of Arms, London, MS. Norfolk 2, p. 176.

William Beckford, 1760–1844: An Eye for the Magnificent is made possible with the support of

Constance and Harvey Krueger

New York Design Center

The Samuel H. Kress Foundation

Mrs. Charles Wrightsman

Martin P. Levy

Mrs. Frederick M. Stafford

CHRISTIE'S

Promotional support has been provided by **nest** magazine.

CONTENTS

FOREWORD

Our knowledge of the decorative arts has been greatly enhanced over the past decade by studies of public and private collections that have examined both the material culture and connoisseurial aspects of the field. *William Beckford, 1760–1844: An Eye for the Magnificent* is the Bard Graduate Center's first contribution to this important body of work. Both the exhibition and the catalogue shed light on the world of a great collector and his extraordinary collection.

Using the privilege of great wealth, Beckford amassed one of the finest private collections of the late eighteenth and early nineteenth centuries. He had an uncanny eye for quality and an endless passion for the fine arts, the decorative arts, and architecture. The scope and diversity of his collecting interests extended from the decorative arts of China, England, France, Greece, and Turkey to contemporary paintings by J. M. W. Turner, Benjamin West, Jean-Honoré Fragonard, Andrea Casali, and others. His love of Old Masters is clearly seen in his distinguished collection, which included major works by Bellini, Mantegna, de Hooch, and Rembrandt. This exhibition brings together one of the largest assemblages of objects from Beckford's collection to be on public view since the nineteenth century. The exhibition and catalogue afford the opportunity to better understand Beckford's pervasive influence on nineteenth-century taste and style. The essays and text that follow present the results of much new research, accompanied by a stunning array of works of art.

In this catalogue, Beckford's formidable talents as a collector have been paid tribute by the many scholars and experts who have contributed their skills to illuminating his collection. I am especially grateful to Philip Hewat-Jaboor, who first approached the Bard Graduate Center about William Beckford. I want to thank Philip and his collaborator Bet McLeod for their curatorial effort and tireless quest to document Beckford's collection. Derek E. Ostergard, associate director of the Bard Graduate Center, served as the director of this complex endeavor, which has benefited substantially from his broad knowledge of the decorative arts and related fields.

I am indebted to our sponsors whose financial support has helped to make this project possible: Constance and Harvey Krueger, New York Design Center, the Samuel H. Kress Foundation, Mrs. Charles Wrightsman, Martin P. Levy, Mrs. Frederick M. Stafford, and Christie's. I am also appreciative of the in-kind contribution of Nest magazine.

We are privileged to have the Beckford exhibition travel to the Dulwich Picture Gallery, London, one of the great art museums of Beckford's time and a premier institution today. I am grateful to Desmond Shawe-Taylor for his enthusiasm for this project and to his staff at the gallery for helping to make the exhibition tour possible.

Numerous other institutions and private collectors have participated in this major effort to locate the works in Beckford's collection, now dispersed throughout the world. We are fortunate to have received loans from the following institutions and private collections: Art Gallery of Ontario, Toronto; Ashmolean Museum, Oxford; The Barber Institute of Fine Arts, The University of Birmingham, UK; Beckford Tower Trust, Bath; Bolton Museum and Art Gallery; The British Museum, London; The Burghley House Preservation Trust, Ltd., Lincolnshire; The Detroit Institute of Art; The Edward James Foundation, Chichester; Fitzwilliam Museum, Cambridge; Mrs. Jerome T. Gans; Gilbert Collection, Somerset House, London; Glasgow Museums, Glasgow; Hall & Knight Ltd., USA; The Hamilton Collection, East Lothian; Hanns Schell Collection, Graz; The Holburne Museum of Art, Bath; Sir Edmund Fairfax Lucy, Charlecote Park; The Metropolitan Museum of Art, New York; The Montreal Museum of Fine Arts; the Honorable Lady Morrison; The Museum of Fine Arts, Boston; The National Gallery, London; National Gallery of Art, Washington, DC; National Galleries of Scotland, Edinburgh; The National Museums of Scotland, Edinburgh;

The National Trust, Charlecote Park and Upton House; National Trust for Scotland, Brodick Castle; Professor Bernard Nevill, Fonthill Abbey; The Trent Parish Council, Trent; the Honorable Philip Smith; Sterling and Francine Clark Art Institute, Williamstown; Sudeley Castle, Gloucestershire; Tate Gallery, London; Thyssen-Bornemisza Foundation, Lugano; The Toledo Museum of Art; Victoria and Albert Museum, London; David Vyvyan-Robinson; Marian Walecki; The Walters Art Museum, Baltimore; The Whitworth Art Gallery, University of Manchester; Yale Center for British Art, New Haven; Margitta Zachert; and eleven anonymous private collectors.

This project has benefited greatly from the contribution of many scholars and curators who gave generously of their time and shared their knowledge with us: Megan Aldrich, Sidney Blackmore, Jeannie Chapel, Anne Eschapasse, William Hauptman, Philip Hewat-Jaboor, Oliver Impey, Malcolm Jack, Alexander Marr, Bet McLeod, Timothy Mowl, Michael Snodin, Adriana Turpin, David Watkin, John Whitehead, Christopher Woodward for their important catalogue essays. I would also like to acknowledge the contributions of the authors of the catalogue entries: Megan Aldrich, Ellenor M. Alcorn, Fabienne Audebrand, Sidney Blackmore, Barbara Drake Boehm, Maureen Cassidy-Geiger, Stefano Carboni, Charles Cator, Jeannie Chapel, Rachel E. Church, Aileen Dawson, Layla S. Diba, Rachel Layton Elwes, John Hardy, Christopher Hartop, William Hauptman, Henry Hawley, Philip Hewat-Jaboor, Malcolm Jack, Ian Jenkins, Ulrich Leben, Martin P. Levy, Jon Millington, Bet McLeod, Elisabeth Mitchell, Jeffrey Hoyt Munger, A.R.E. North, Julia E. Poole, Henry Potts, Anna Somers Cocks, Timothy Schroder, Jeanne Sloane, Eleanor Tollfree, Beth Carver Wees, Annette Wickham, and Christopher Woodward.

Martina D'Alton has done a magnificent job with the copy-editing of this publication, and designer Michael Shroyer has created a beautiful book. I also want to thank John Nicoll and Sally Salvesen at Yale University Press for their support of this project, as well as Carol Liebowitz for typesetting and Roberta Fineman for proofreading.

The staff of the Bard Graduate Center has made immeasurable contributions both to the publication and to the assembly of the exhibition. Working under the directorship of Nina Stritzler-Levine, members of the exhibition department staff have been diligent in seeing this complex project to its conclusion. Olga Valle Tetkowski, curator of exhibitions, Ron Labaco, curatorial assistant, and Han Vu, digital technology designer, assisted with numerous details involved in the production of the catalogue and the organization of the exhibition. Linda Stubbs, exhibition registrar, did a marvelous job in attending to the object loans and logistics for the exhibition tour, in addition to many related matters. Working with Derek Ostergard, Susan Loftin, exhibition designer, created an inspired installation. Lisa Podos, director of public programs, assisted by her committed staff, organized an extensive and informative series of events that have aimed to introduce the public to William Beckford. Susan Wall, director of development, and Tara D'Andrea, assistant director of development, managed a successful fundraising campaign, and Tim Mulligan, director of communications, assisted by Angela Washington, organized the press campaign. I appreciate the assistance of Lorraine Bacalles, director of finance and administration, as well as John Donovan, facilities manager, who oversees the operation of the gallery with a wonderful security and maintenance team. I am grateful to the entire staff of the Bard Graduate Center for their hard work and effort in making our exhibition program a success.

Susan Weber Soros
Director

INTRODUCTION

A life lived as long as William Beckford's (1760–1844) would be difficult enough to document in any depth had it been focused and singular in its achievements. Beckford's life, however, was exceedingly complex, and while he pursued a wide range of interests, his accomplishments were legendary. His lifelong passion for music, travel, literature, the arts, and design defy ready catagorization — he was both an active participant in the events of his age and a thoughtful observer of them. Beckford himself further complicated any perception of his life, by being invariably as much aware of his own achievements as he was of their presentation. As has been acknowledged by Beckford's many biographers, his own tendency to both erase and embroider his past has confounded not only the merely interested, but also the scholars who have sought significance in Beckford's life.

Self-awareness, generated to some degree by self-preservation, was engineered into Beckford from birth. Born to ambitious parents, who were already middle-aged by the standards of the eighteenth century, Beckford was the late, but necessary by-product of a marriage of convenience. As the heir to his parent's dynastic aspirations, he was eventually thrown into the competitive atmosphere of eighteenth-century England, propelled by his parent's economic, social, and political ambitions, which would come to shape his own. The focus of their hope, centered as it was on Beckford as the sole legitimate male heir, would be intensified during Beckford's youth through the defense of his future against the challenge of illegitimate children, the threat of his father's political and business rivals, and parental guidance that often was misguided. Any manner of overprotection accorded to Beckford especially by his mother was compounded by his own personality, which often acted as a barrier to achievement. Precocious, intelligent, and vain, Beckford often recognized his worth long before others might and then through his actions let them know that he had.

In 1784 Beckford's overweening, but fragile sense of self was shattered by rumors about him that suddenly placed his own homosexual inclinations on view in a society whose favor he sought, whether he chose to acknowledge his need for his fellow man's approval or not. The challenge that this scandal brought to his personal dignity, to his acceptance within society, and to his aspirations for a peerage, would focus much of the course of the remainder of his life. With his own sensitivities under siege, and simultaneously shunned by society, Beckford increasingly took refuge in a far more private domain than the one he had known as a young man. This world would be governed by travel in foreign countries, friendships with a limited group of individuals, and most importantly, through an intensely personal connection with works of art, building projects, and books. Seen for the remainder of his life as an eccentric and recluse, Beckford withdrew from the life of promise he had come to believe would be his in his early years. This retreat was not without its benefits. It gave him an opportunity to develop his considerable intellectual and aesthetic sensibilities in solitude, something that might not have occurred had his life progressed as planned. In many respects, something positive came from his exile from society.

It is precisely this reclusive aspect of William Beckford, and his desire to protect himself from the scrutiny of others, that has hampered the efforts of many scholars to understand this enigmatic individual. The scholars who produced the sixteen essays in this catalogue have overcome this handicap and put together a substantial body of new historical and statistical evidence through interdisciplinary studies that broaden the interpretation of William Beckford and his significance not only to his own era, but also to later generations. The essays concentrate on important but often neglected aspects of Beckford's life. The essay authors are joined by a group of specialists who have written about the objects in the exhibition, many of which are as enigmatic as their former owner. The catalogue entries reflect new research and provide fresh insights into Beckford and his wide-ranging collections and motivations as a collector.

This publication does not focus on the private life of William Beckford. That particular area has been addressed in the past century and a half through the many biographies of Beckford, many of which reveal as much about their subject as they do the era in which they were written. Beckford's seemingly overriding interests such as design, objets d'art, and residential architecture have received comparatively little attention overall in the literature devoted to his life. Most authors in this publication also chose to avoid psychological interpretations for Beckford's actions or motives. With a life such as Beckford's, the margin for error in such an approach is inordinately high. The introductory chapter does address his complex personality, however, and many of the situations in his life that defined it. Timothy Mowl has provided an intimate portrait of Beckford's own desires, both public and private, and situated them against the mores of his times and those later periods whose authors sought to examine Beckford.

As a collector and man of considerable learning, as well as someone consumed by an interest in style and taste, Beckford can be numbered among the great collectors of his time, including Thomas Hope, Sir John Soane, and to a lessor degree, the Prince Regent himself, later George IV. David Watkin's revisionist essay for this publication presents the parallel lives and interests of these well-known figures, as well as the places where their lives intersected through social interaction and correspondence. Beckford, traditionally seen as an outsider in late-Georgian society, was actually less of an anomoly than viewed by most of his biographers.

Beckford's oftentimes overriding interest in the realm of architecture and design was nurtured from his childhood. Born into great wealth derived from Jamaican sugar plantations, Beckford saw a portion of this income lavished on Fonthill Splendens, the remarkable house his father built and in which Beckford spent a considerable portion of his youth. Philip Hewat-Jaboor has painstakingly re-created the complex history of the house over its brief, fifty-odd years of existence, detailing the decorating schemes later applied by Beckford to its interiors. Most of these would be lost, however, leaving little documentation, when all but a portion of the house was demolished in the early nineteenth century.

The education that Beckford received at Fonthill was furthered by his mother who, in a gesture ususual for her generation, sent him to study to Geneva, Switzerland, when few Englishmen did the same. The remarkable intellectual life of that capital, the pursuits of William Beckford, and the sublime landscape that inspired him have been captured in William Hauptman's essay, which also discusses the long-term repercussions that this period would have upon Beckford and many of his later endeavors.

Beckford's three extended stays in Portugal, lasting until he was nearly forty, were among the happier periods of his life. Malcolm Jack's essay explores the somewhat somnolent world of Lisbon and Sintra during those years and Beckford's response to the landscape, the architecture and the people – all of which he saw as exotic. Portugal, still the center of a vast colonial empire, clearly made an indelible impression on Beckford, and he would revisit that period of his life many years later in some of his most successful travel writing.

Paris was far more constant in Beckford's interests, as an urban learning ground. Beckford came of age in Paris in the decade prior to the Revolution. As Anne Eschapasse has shown in her essay, Beckford largely developed his remarkable eye for works of art during his many stays in the city. Of great significance to his later development would

be his interaction with artists, designers, and artisans in Paris. From these individuals he learned the language of design that would increasingly hold his attention as he pulled away from an active engagement with his peers.

Without doubt, the single greatest achievement of Beckford's life was the design and construction of Fonthill Abbey, which survived for an even shorter period than had its predecessor, Fonthill Splendens. Despite its secure position in the mind of many historians, the details of the history of this house have remained controversial. Megan Aldrich has reconstructed the rapid evolution of the Abbey that was, in effect, a laboratory for Beckford's experiments in interior space, color, light, and ornament. Contradictory statements have been reconciled through a close examination of documentation including letters, models, and paintings.

Alexander Marr has reconstructed the grounds that comprised the Fonthill estate, which have been until now, placed on the margins of Beckford scholarship. Beckford took an active interest in the purchase of plantings for the estate, their placement within the grounds, and their impact on the rare visitors to the property. He was equally attentive to walkways, bridle paths, and carriageways that provided a view to the complexities of the grounds. Beckford's extensive knowledge of the various flora and fauna, both native and exotic, was remarkable for a man of his position during his generation.

Above all else, this publication and exhibition are concerned with Beckford as a collector of the decorative arts. The greater part of his life can be said to have been spent within the realm of works of art —again, quite unlike any other individual of his background or generation. Bet McLeod has examined the vast extent of his interests but focused on certain areas of his collections. This essay reveals Beckford's interest in a variety of types of objects, how his purchases were made through agents, dealers, and auctions, and of paramount importance, the manner in which these pieces were installed and arranged within his residences.

The essay on Beckford and furniture reveals the devlopment of Beckford's aesthetic and intellectual interests in terms of furniture. Adriana Turpin has charted Beckford's growth from a patron of contemporary neoclassical furniture and of boulle furniture in the late eighteenth century, to a collector of seventeenth-century pieces during the Regency period. Arguably, Beckford's most interesting period came in the final twenty years of his life, when he was increasingly involved with the design of furniture. Of additional interest are the charts that accompany the text and reconstruct the strengths of various currencies during this era.

Metalwork and the mounting of hardstones and porcelain were highly important interests of Beckford. Michael Snodin has built upon his earlier research in this area to discuss the largest body of objects that have retained their Beckford provenance. From the earliest pieces commissioned for Beckford's coming-of-age in 1781, to works commissioned in the final year of his life, it is evident that Beckford was deeply involved in every aspect of this area. In particular,

Beckford's own participation in the design of historicist works of art, many of which anticipated later trends in design, remains a distinct component of his life, setting him apart from his contemporaries.

Beckford's remarkable holdings in rare lacquer began when he lived in Paris. Pre-Revolutionary France saw the development of a tradition of collecting lacquer and among the important French collectors were Marie Antoinette and Madame de Pompadour. Following in this tradition, Beckford assembled one of the most significant collections of rare lacquers in the West during the late eighteeth and early nineteenth centuries. Oliver Impey and John Whitehead have reconstructed the elusive history of the major sales of the period, from which Beckford most likely purchased his pieces. They also discuss Beckford's use of rare lacquer boxes that were disassembled and integrated as elements in contemporary pieces of furniture.

Although this is a catalogue devoted to the history of Beckford's collections of the decorative arts, Beckford himself would never have isolated this work from the paintings which he collected. He saw his ownership of this wide array of works of art as all inclusive, and the interiors of his several residences expressed the spirit of a total work of art. Jeannie Chapel has written her essay on Beckford and his paintings and drawings in much the same spirit. She has shown how he might have found and purchased his paintings, how he saw them together in an installation, and how he oftentimes divested himself of valued works of art.

Sidney Blackmore has taken on the double responsibility by producing two essays, linked by their focus on the common subject of place and time. Although scholars have focused on Fonthill Abbey and Beckford's isolated existence there, he actually spent a considerable amount of time in London throughout his long life. Blackmore has located Beckford's various residences in London and provided a telling picture of each neighborhood or district when Beckford lived there, while adding a small diary of the daily activities that consumed Beckford's interest. By the same token, Beckford's relocation to Bath after selling the Abbey in 1822 has remained an area of little research. Sidney Blackmore has answered the question of why Beckford chose to move to Bath after years of splendor at the Abbey, while reconstructing additional elements of Beckford's daily routine and the decoration of his quarters.

It has often been assumed that the last two decades of Beckford's life were lackluster in comparison to the years he spent either traveling or building the Abbey. Christopher Woodward, however, focuses on that last great commission of Beckford's life, Lansdown Tower, and shows how Beckford intimately participated in this commission, as remarkable for its architecture as it was its interiors and the manner in which Beckford used this building. With the confidence of a man deeply involved in the design of objects and interiors over a past half century, Beckford made this last great commission also his most personal.

The catalogue section of this publication has been designed on two levels: for the general reader, uninitiated to Beckford studies, and for the specialist for whom the close examination and interpretation of objects remains highly significant. The objects in the exhibition have not been presented chronologically; instead they are grouped in nine sections relating to significant aspects of Beckford's life. Each of these sections includes a brief introduction that provides the logic for the selection of objects which follow. As much as possible, these groupings were meant to augment the essays in a substantial manner while focusing on specific aspects of the individual object, including the source of a design, the construction or fabrication, the particulars of the maker or material, the object's location in Beckford's interiors, provenance when known, and even the way Beckford may have used the piece.

An international team of specialists, including several essay authors, contributed to this important aspect of the project, and I am grateful to them all for working under tight deadlines and for adding considerably to the Beckford literature with their work. Our sincere thanks to all the entry authors: Megan Aldrich, Ellenor M. Alcorn, Fabienne Audebrand, Sidney Blackmore, Barbara Drake Boehm, Maureen Cassidy-Geiger, Stefano Carboni, Charles Cator, Jeannie Chapel, Rachel E. Church, Aileen Dawson, Layla S. Diba, Rachel Layton Elwes, John Hardy, Christopher Hartop, William Hauptman, Henry Hawley, Philip Hewat-Jaboor, Malcolm Jack, Ian Jenkins, Ulrich Leben, Martin P. Levy, Jon Millington, Bet McLeod, Elisabeth Mitchell, Jeffrey Hoyt Munger, A. R. E. North, Julia E. Poole, Henry Potts, Anna Somers Cocks, Timothy Schroder, Jeanne Sloane, Eleanor Tollfree, Beth Carver Wees, Annette Wickham, and Christopher Woodward.

The bibliography prepared by Jon Millington will add considerably to Beckford studies. He has done an exceptional job of research, pulling together a wide range of sources. The size of the catalogue ultimately required reducing the length of the bibliography, but it still offers a great deal of newly identified sources for Beckford scholars.

The assembly of such a huge project invariably requires the work of a large group of individuals. First and foremost in the history of this project, a profound note of appreciation must be extended to Philip Hewat-Jaboor, one of the two curators of this exhibition. He first presented the idea of having the Bard Graduate Center host an exhibition and symposium on Beckford. The general reputation of Beckford as a collector of the first rank, especially in the field of the decorative arts, and the wealth of objects bearing a Beckford provenance indicated that Beckford as a topic would be an ideal exhibition, especially for an institution based on the study of the decorative arts. Philip readily participated in every stage of the project, from retrieving information, to bringing Dulwich Picture Gallery into this project, to locating authors, and writing his own essay as well as several catalogue entries. His generosity has been noted by all individuals who were involved in this project. He has been involved in the many decisions, large and small, necessary to bring such a complicated project to a successful conclusion.

Philip was joined enthusiastically in this endeavor by co-curator, Bet McLeod, a scholar with considerable experience in Beckford studies. Along with Philip she helped to shape the principal checklist that formed the basis of this exhibition and catalogue. Bet also was responsible for the assembly of the sizable body of data that was used by many of the authors working on this publication. She contributed an essay and several entries to the catalogue and made herself available for consultation on aspects of this project.

At The Bard Graduate Center the exhibition department deployed its considerable talents and resources to bring this project to completion. A special thanks to Nina Stritzler-Levine, director of exhibitions, for her support and organization of numerous individuals who helped to prepare this exhibition and catalogue. Ron Labaco, curatorial assistant, kept the flow of information and contact between various individuals and institutions while maintaining an all-important log of such activities. Olga Valle Tetkowski, curator of exhibitions, supervised the complicated process of photography scheduling and coordinating the compilation of data for the catalogue entries. Linda Stubbs, registrar, supervised the assembly of all key information regarding lenders and gracefully conducted all negotiations with shippers and couriers. Han Vu provided significant technical support for the catalogue, especially the preliminary checklist, and for a special audio/visual presentation on William Beckford. Additional thanks go to Edina Deme, Brandy Culp, Lisa Skogh, Maria Fragopoulou, and especially John Woodhull, who assisted with a wide variety of details. Considerable thanks to Susan Loftin, exhibition designer and chief preparator, who, along with Ian Sullivan and Dante Brebner, supervised the key work to bring the exhibition installation to fruition.

Sincere thanks to the other important individuals at The Bard Graduate Center who helped to complete this project: Lorraine Bacalles, director of finance, who contended with the numerous financial details that accompany an exhibition and catalogue like this and has been ably assisted by Dianora Watson and Lisa Bright; Lisa Podos, director of public programs, who arranged many of the important educational programs that accompany the exhibition and worked on the special symposium along with Jill Gustafson, Lee Talbot, and Leslie Klingner; Susan Wall, director of development, and Tara D'Andrea did a remarkable job of fundraising for this project; Tim Mulligan, director of communications, and his assistant, Angela Washington, handled all the marketing elements crucial to the success of this exhibition; Greta Earnest, chief librarian, and especially Heather Topcik as well as Erin Elliot and Khadidja Fykes, who helped confirm so many important bibliographical references; Danika Volkert and Ayesha Abour-Rahman in the slide department; Miao Chen who helped with all technical support for the computer systems; especially John Donovan, who with Greg Negron, Orlando Diaz, Jose Olivera, Adel Mohamed, and Oualid Bel Haj Larbi, keep our buildings in impeccable order; and Jorge San Pablo, Terence Lyons, and Chandler Small. Thanks also to Helen Aravantinos and Rigmor Newman at the Leeman Agency who helped with so many of the travel arrangements.

This catalogue would not have been possible without the remarkable editorial organization that Martina D'Alton brought to the project. Her attention to detail, and fine skills as an editor and diplomat, as well as her willingness to work under challenging deadlines is deeply appreciated. Thanks to Michael Shroyer for his superb catalogue design, which is both visually pleasing and easy to use. Deep appreciation must be expressed to Sally Salvesen for her support of this project and contribution to the design of the catalogue cover.

I would also like to thank the funders of this exhibition—Constance and Harvey Krueger, James P. Druckman at the New York Design Center, the Samuel H. Kress Foundation, Mrs. Charles Wrightsman, Martin P. Levy, and Mrs. Frederick M. Stafford. We are also indebted to Christie's and Nest magazine.

I am grateful to individuals at many institutions. At the Art Gallery of Ontario: Felicia Cukier, Tim Hardacre, Katharine A. Lochnan, Michael Parke-Taylor, Brenda Rix, Barry Simpson, Faye van Horne. At the Ashmolean Museum: Christopher Brown, Geraldine Glynn, Anna Taylor, Timothy Wilson, Angela Woodcock. At the Barber Institute of Fine Arts: Paul Spencer-Longhurst, Richard Verdi. At Bard College: Michael Elrod, Victoria Mayes, George Pattison, Ginger Shore. At the Beckford Tower Trust: Michael Briggs, Ela Francis, Kathy Perry, Jesca Verdon-Smith. At the Bodleian Library, Oxford: Colin Harris and the staff of the Modern Papers Reading Room. At the Bolton Art Gallery: Tony Hughes, Lucy Whetstone, Mark Wisbey. At the Bridgeman Library: Nancy Blum. At the British Museum: Robert G. W. Anderson, John Cherry, Amy Clarke, Lucy Dixon, Antony Griffiths, Sovati Lounden-Smith, Karen Perkins, Judy Rudoe, Tracy Ryan, Evelyn Wood. At Brodick Castle: Bill Cowell, Kenneth Thorburn, Helen Thorburn, for all that they did to make the collections of the house available for study and photography, and thanks to all the staff. At the Burghley House Preservation Trust: Jon Culverhouse. At Christie's, London: Lucy Campbell, Charles Cator, John Hardy, David Llewellyn, Orlando Rock. At Christie's, New York: Richard Francis, George McNeely, and especially, Jeanne Sloane. At the Cincinnati Art Museum: Scott Hisey. At the Cleveland Museum of Art: Carol Ciulla. At the College of Arms: R. C. Yorke. At Dalmeny Castle: Rt. Hon. the Earl of Rosebery, the Countess of Rosebery, Linda Edgar. At the Detroit Institute of Art: Graham W. J. Beal, Alfred Ackerman, Silvia Inwood, Michelle Peplin, James Tottis, Mary Anne Wilkinson. At the Dulwich Picture Gallery: my sincere thanks to Desmond Shawe-Taylor for his support of this project and to Victoria Norton and Kate Knowles. At the Edward James Foundation: Christopher Gibbs, Sharon Michi-Kusunoki. At the Fitzwilliam Museum: Robin Crighton, Diane Hudson, Duncan Robinson, Thyrza Smith, Suzanne Wynne. At Fundación Coleccion Thyssen-Bornemisza: Maria Eugenia Alonso. At the Gilbert Collection: Timothy Stevens, Guy Turner. At the Glasgow Museums & Art Galleries: Mark O'Neill, Rosemary Watt, Jeff Dunn. At Hall & Knight Ltd.: Nicholas Hall, Richard Knight, Anne Varick Lauder, Sheri Lawson. At Hamilton and Kenneil Estates: the Duke and Duchess of Hamilton, John Mutch, Lyndsay J. Stuart. At the Hanns Schell Collection: Hanns Schell, Ewald Berger, Martina Pall. At the Holburne Museum of Art: Christopher Woodward, Polly Hawkes, Lisa White, Fiona Salvesen. At the Huntington Library, Art Collections, and Botanical Gardens: Shelley Bennett, Edward J. Nygren, Robert Skotheim. At the Indianapolis Museum of Art: Ellen W. Lee, Barry L. Shifman. At the J. Paul Getty Museum: Jacklyn Burns. At the John and Mable Ringling Museum of Art: Heidi Taylor. At the London Silver Vaults: Michael Koopman, Timo Koopman, Anthony Sefton, Lewis Smith. At the Louvre Museum: Daniel Alcouffe. At Madresfield: the Honorable Lady Morrison and Janet Sinclair. At The Metropolitan Museum of Art: Peter Barnet, Barbara Drake Boehm, Christine E. Brennan, Jeffrey Hoyt Munger, Olga Raggio, Deanna Cross, Everett Fahy, Dorothy Kellett, William Rieder, Francis Wallace, Julie Zeftel. At the Montréal Museum of Fine Arts: Danielle Blanchette, Anne-Marie Chevrier, Guy Cogeval, Linda-Anne D'Anjou, Marie-Claude Saia. At the Museum für Angewandte Kunst: Elisabeth Schmuttermeier. At the Museum of Fine Arts, Boston: Tracey Albainy, Christopher Atkins, Kim Pashko, George T.M. Shackelford, Gillian Spencer. At the National Gallery, London: Susan Foister, Rosalie Cass, Margaret Daly, Sarah Frances, David Jaffé, Neil MacGregor, Carol Plazzotta, Michael Wilson. At the National Galleries of Scotland: Tim Clifford, Anne Buddle, Michael Clarke, Deborah Hunter, Valerie Hunter, Stephen Lloyd, Janice Slater, Katrina Thomson. At the National Gallery of Art, Washington DC: Earl A. Powell III, Franklin Kelly, Nancy Stanfield, Alicia B. Thomas. At the National Library of Scotland: Iain Brown. At the National Museum of Ireland: Niamh Deegan, Dierdre Power. At the National Museums of Scotland: former director Mark Jones, Godfrey Evans, Rosalyn Clancey. At the National Trust, Charlecote Park and Upton House: a special note of appreciation to Simon Jervis and Martin Drury, and thanks to David Adshead, Sara Bertrand, Dudley Dodd, Ed Gibbons, Linda Griffin, Jeffrey Haworth, Sarah Hickey, Alastair Laing, Oliver Lane, Kate Turner. At the National Trust for Scotland, our principal lender: we are deeply grateful to Trevor Croft, Ian Gow, Katharine Mitchell, Bruce Mackie, Isla Robertson, Diana Stevens. At the Nemours Mansion and Gardens: Paddy Dietz. At the New York Design Center: James Druckman, Samantha Nestor. At the Parliamentary Estates Directorate: Janet McLean. At Payne Hicks Beach Solicitors: Graham S. Brown, Margaret Lawson. At the Royal Collection Trust: Caroline de Guitaut, Hugh Roberts, Matthew Winterbottom. At the Royal Ontario Museum: Peter Kaellgren, Cindy Brouse. At the Salford Museum and Art Gallery: a special thanks to Carolyn McDermott, Judith Sandling. At Sotheby's Brussels: Chantal de Spott. At Sotheby's London: Mario Tavella. At Sotheby's New York: Ian Irving, Mia Johnson, Tish Roberts, Kevin Tierney. At the Sterling and Francine Clark Institute: Michael Conforti, Alexis Goodin, Kris Walton, Mattie Kelley. At the Sudeley House/ Dent-Brocklehurst: Timothy C. Baylis, Gill Jerden. At the Tate Gallery of British Art: Sir Nicholas Serota, Alison Miles, Catherine McFarlane, Catherine Clement, Nicola Moorby. At the Thyssen-Bornemisza Foundation: Baron Hans Heinrich Thyssen, Christine Bader Nicoli, Tomàs Llorens. At the Toledo Museum of Art: Roger M. Berkowitz, Lawrence W. Nichols, Nicole Rivette, Karen Serota, Patricia Whitesides. At the Trent

Parish Council: Captain Lionel A. Bird. At the Victoria and Albert Museum: former director Alan Borg, Marian Campbell, Katherine Coombs, Judith Crouch, Helen Dobson, Richard Edgcumbe, Emily Howe, Rose Kerr, Susan Lambert, Rachel Lloyd, Francesca Vinti, Christopher Wilk, and the staff of the Metalwork Department, Janet Skidmore, Anne Steinberg, David Wright, Hilary Young. At the Victoria Art Gallery: Victoria Barwell, Jon Benington. At the Waddesdon Estate: Phillippa Glanville, Robert Selbie, Ruth Smith. At the Wallace Collection: Rosalind Savill, Andrea Gilbert, Peter Hughes, Robert Wenley. At the Walters Art Museum: Gary Vikan, William R. Johnston, Laura Graziano, Kate Lau, Marianna Shreve Simpson. At the Whitworth Art Gallery: Alistair Smith, David Morris, Penny Haworth. At the Worshipful Company of Ironmongers: Michael Pearson. At the Yale Center for British Art: Martha Buck, Melissa L. Gold, Timothy Goodhue, Patrick McCaughey, Scott Wilcox.

My thanks also to the Honorable Nicholas Assheton, James Berry, Mrs. Andy Blum, Graham Brown, Ken Cohen, John Culme, Lord Dalmeny, Angela Delaforce, Meredith Etherington-Smith, Edmund Fairfax-Lucy, Ronald Freyburger, Deborah Gage, Mrs. Jerome T. Gans, Pedro Girao, Philippa Glanville, Gale Glynn, Charles Hind, Anthony Hobson, Linda Homfray, Leon Horowitz, Elizabeth Jamieson, Rodney Keenan, Diana Keith-Neal, Sir Edmund Fairfax Lucy, Lord and Lady Margadale, Duncan McLaren, Fiona McLeod, Simon Metcalf, the Honorable Lady Morrison, the Honorable Alastair Morrison, Lucy Morton, Bernard Nevill, Angus Patterson, Annick Perceval, Kimille Pisane, Henry Potts, Nigel Ramsay, Antonia Reeve, Orlando Rock, Adrian Sassoon, Mr. and Mrs. Philippe Saverys, Kim Sloan, Susan Sloman, the Honorable Philip Smith, David Vyvyan-Robinson, Betsy Barlow Rogers, the late Clive Wainwright, Jane Wainwright, Marion Walecki, Duncan Walker, George Warrington, Giles Waterfield, Bruce White, David Wiltshire, The Countess of Wemyss, Lucy Wood, Andrew Wyld, Margitta Zachert.

Finally, as with all exhibitions at the Bard Graduate Center, the most important words of appreciation are for Susan Weber Soros, whose profound interest in the ideas and design history of nineteenth-century Britain has fueled this project. With the considerable number of exhibitions proposed to this institution, and the fact that so few can be shown annually, it is an honor to have *William Beckford, 1760–1844: An Eye for the Magnificent* in the center's galleries. This exploration of the life and pursuits of William Beckford completes, in a manner, something of a trilogy of exhibitions and catalogues on nineteenth-century Britain prepared by the Bard Gaduate Center, the other two being *A. W. N. Pugin: Master of Gothic Revival* (1995) and *E. W. Godwin: Aesthetic Movement Architect and Designer* (1999). It is my hope that both the exhibition and this catalogue will carry forward the tradition of excellence that the Bard Graduate Center has established.

Derek E. Ostergard
Associate Director

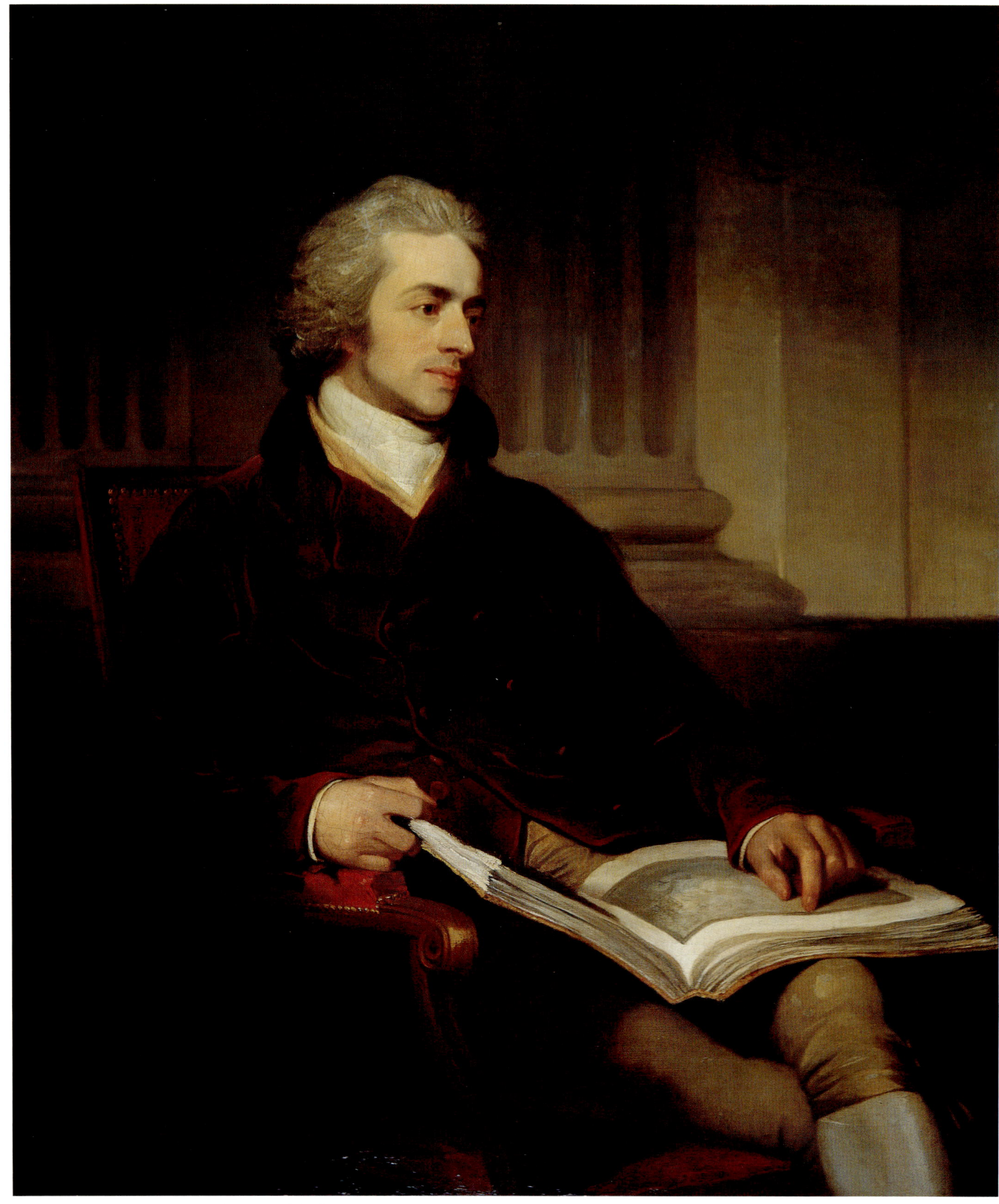

Fig. 1-1. John Hoppner. *William Beckford*, ca. 1800. Oil on canvas. City of Salford Art Gallery, Salford, England.

CHAPTER I

WILLIAM BECKFORD: A BIOGRAPHICAL PERSPECTIVE

TIMOTHY MOWL

The positive way to approach William Beckford's life and works is with a mixture of warm appreciation and cool caution. It is, for instance, unlikely that as a result of "modulating" his voice "in the most opposite tones,"[1] Beckford endeared himself to a lioness in a Paris zoo to such an extent that the keeper invited him into the cage to play with her claws. It makes a tremendous story, however, and he told it so well that it still comes over as credible. Similarly King Carlos III of Spain could hardly have been so charmed with Beckford's company in Madrid in 1788 that he commanded him, "Ask me a favour and it will be granted," because in harsh fact neither man ever set eyes on each other.[2] What does matter is Beckford's magnificent response, both scholarly and romantic, to a command that was never given: "Prise open the marble tomb of the Emperor Charles V in the Escorial that I may check whether Titian's portrait of the Emperor was a good likeness." Again, even though it did not happen, it should have.

Nor is it important that Beckford's most celebrated building, Fonthill Abbey, collapsed a mere twenty-seven years after he had begun it, or that the English text of *Vathek*, his best-known writing, is not Beckford's text at all, but that of his literary advisor, the Rev. Samuel Henley, who translated it from Beckford's original French text, now lost. Beckford's aristocratic indifference to the fine tuning of who really wrote the book is impressive. His atmospheric twenty-first birthday party in 1781 at Fonthill Splendens over Christmas may have been no more sensational than the effects of a few magic lanterns. That too is irrelevant sniping. Beckford projected the event, not once but twice, in his quivering violet-tinted prose-poems, and a legend was launched.

Beckford (fig. 1-1) is largely legend, yet truly legendary. He was, by his taste and by his flamboyant lifestyle, the ice breaker in the frozen sea of eighteenth-century English classicism and the morning star of the English Romantic movement. As a boy of seventeen he was already writing like a Firbankian angel. At eighteen in Protestant Geneva he had grasped the spirit of Goethe's emotional intensity and was prepared to practice it. His literary talent would always be far more limited than that of his German model, but for extended periods in his life his monetary wealth would be virtually unlimited. When he traveled the Continent his entourage was mistaken for that of the Holy Roman Emperor journeying incognito to meet the Pope. He was able, therefore, to make a little talent go a very long way.

In one person Beckford combined Wordsworth's appreciation of the integrity of peasant simplicity, Byron's confident amorality, Shelley's revolutionary sympathies, and a modicum of Keats's gift for negative capability. That he achieved nothing lasting in any of these four personae is unimportant because he was rich. By his intensely individual lifestyle he created a mood and tasted possibilities, becoming, long before his death, an icon of defiance for more hesitant fellow Romantics.

Beckford has not, however, been fortunate in his biographers. Of the authors of eight major pre-1980 studies: Cyrus Redding (1859), Lewis Melville (1910), J. W. Oliver (1932), Guy Chapman (1937), H. A. N. Brockman (1956), Boyd Alexander (1962), James Lees-Milne (1976), and Brian Fothergill (1979), only Lees-Milne in his cautious, detached approach seems actually to have liked his subject. This consistency of unease is no accident; Beckford remains a contentious figure.

Few men have collected as much potential autobiographical material around them as Beckford did without delivering an autobiography. Is it possible that he came in the end to disapprove of himself? There are fascinating scraps and insights in his papers, but eventually every biographer comes up against two massive sources of letters—if they are true letters and not simply cunning inventions later devised by Beckford to deceive future biographers. One set was written to Alexander Cozens, his drawing master, the other to his indiscreet cousin by marriage, Louisa Beckford. Neither correspondence can be ignored, as both are so revealing, yet both are characterized by whining self-pity and tearful emotionalism poured out over William Courtenay, a boy eight years younger than Beckford. Not by any standards of morality, then or now, was Beckford's attachment to

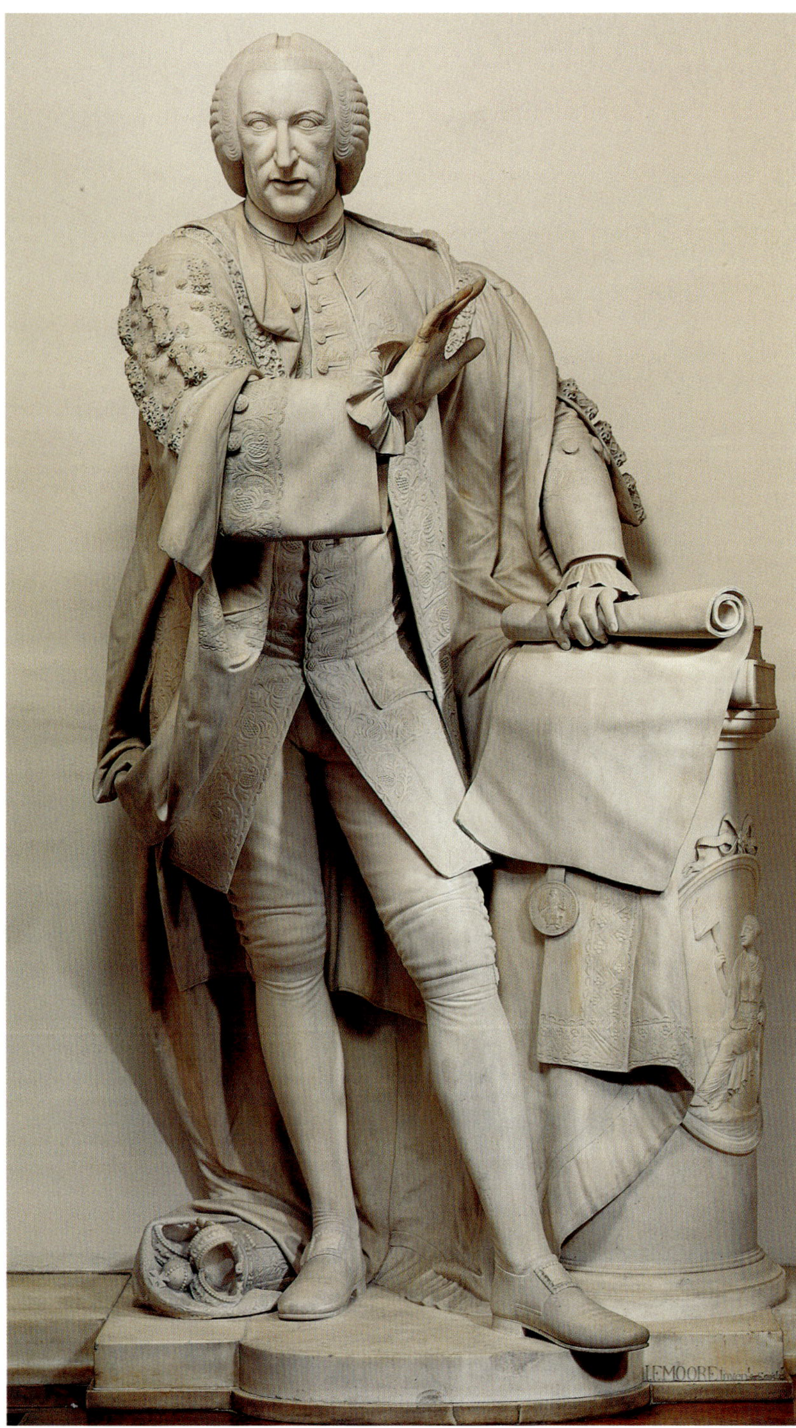

Fig. 1-2. John Francis Moore. *Alderman William Beckford*, 1767. Marble. Courtesy of the Worshipful Company of Ironmongers of the City of London.

the other six because they were writing post–Oscar Wilde, in a country paralyzed by the second-hand sexual traumas of the Wilde trials.

Once it is accepted that Beckford was a brilliant manipulator who revised some details of his own life in a reflective old age, it is best to let him speak for himself which, from his seventeenth year onward, he was well able to do. Before that year, 1777, there were seven factors that contributed to his upbringing. Four were people. There was his father, the great Alderman Beckford (fig. 1-2), a hero figure of Whig politics, who died when his only legitimate son William was not quite ten years old, leaving him an impossible example of bawdy populism to live up to. Then there was his narrowly conventional, sternly Christian mother (fig. 1-3), "the Begum": Beckford explained that he called her that "on account of her strong tendency to a sort of oriental like despotism,"[3] and his half sister Elizabeth, sophisticated, competitive, disloyal, and twelve years his senior. "Instead of crossing the Kennet to do me service," Beckford once wrote of her, "she wd swim across 20 common sewers to complete my ruin."[4] Nevertheless, in happier days she did translate improper stories from *Ariosto* to fire her young half brother's interest in magic realism. Last of the four was the Rev. John Lettice, Beckford's kind, permissive tutor and friend, the one emotional constant in his long life. When they were both old men they were still discussing poetry together.

As for the other three factors, they centered on place. There was the palace Beckford was born and brought up in, Fonthill Splendens, which he loved and then demolished. There was Fonthill Park, which his father had filled with enchanting but frightening grottoes in the manner of the Savage Picturesque. Finally, there was Fonthill parish and neighborhood, which had a strong "old" Catholic ethos quite unlike that of most English villages. This would have given Beckford an early sympathy for Catholicism, a delight in its ceremonial and an interest in comparative religion with a consequent sense of apartness in an England still militantly Protestant. If Beckford had a hobby, apart from fine and decorative arts, building, and boys, it was religion— studied from an inconstant viewpoint of instant emotionalism and mocking detachment. When music played he was always lost. At evensong in York Minster, 1779:

> Half an hour passed away, I believe, whilst I leaned against one of the great columns absorbed in legendary ideas & quite transported, by the Harmony which filled the place, to those Regions inhabited by Saints, whose images appeared glowing between every Arch & terminating every Aisle. It was impossible in such a situation not to be affected with the most religious Sensations. For my own part I was filled with Awe and looked up to the Range of Cloisters dimly seen above the Arches with peculiar veneration.[5]

When staying in 1777 as the house guest of a Catholic village curé in Switzerland, however, he wrote cynically in his epistolary diary:

> The old Bigot, imagining he had a most zealous Catholic for his

Courtenay either moral or sensible. The implications of it are unavoidable and, if less had been written about it in the Beckford archive, would be irrelevant. As well as being a courageous minor genius of Romanticism, Beckford was a bisexual, but more physically attracted to youths than to women. Those eight biographers, however, with the honorable exception of Lees-Milne, tried to write away from that obvious fact, Redding because he was a Victorian and knew Beckford well,

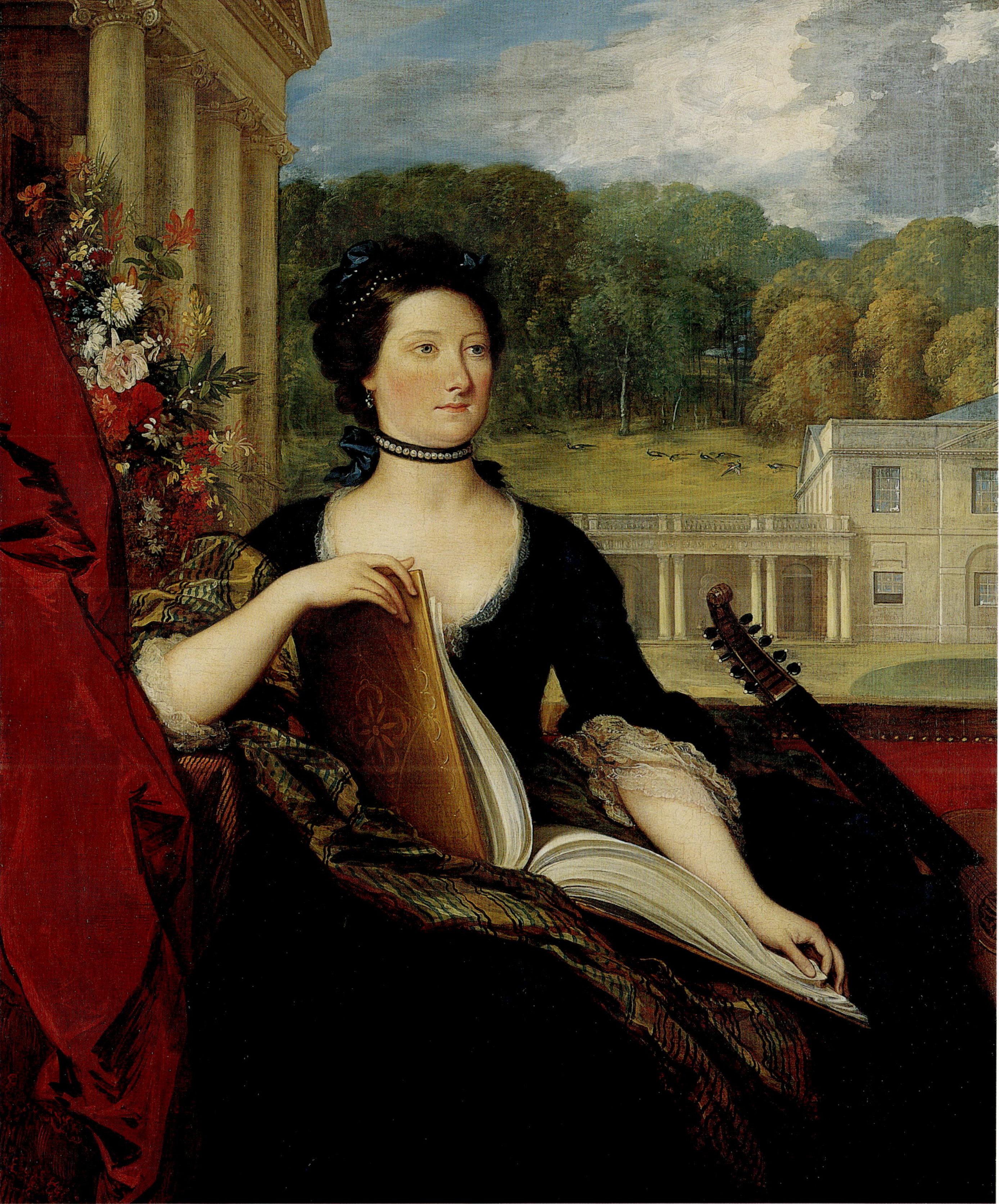

Fig. 1-3. Benjamin West. *Maria Hamilton Beckford (Mrs. William Beckford)*, 1799. Oil on canvas. The National Gallery of Art, Washington, Andrew W. Mellon Collection. *See cat. no. 2.*

guest, began a long conversation about the perverse heretical disposition of my country…I began a pathetic harangue upon the separation of England from the Mother Church…not to mention Thomas à Becket & fifty more sufferers on the like occasion.[6]

Neither emotional nor aesthetic consistency is a quality to be looked for in William Beckford. In his youth he ridiculed the talents of Gerard Dou; in old age he paid a fortune to purchase one of Dou's paintings, *The Poulterer's Shop*. He wrote sensitive paeans of praise for the welcoming beauty of "the peaceful palace" of Fonthill Splendens before he pulled it down and sold its contents, and, as well as being a predatory deviant, he was a much-loved husband and often an affectionate father.

In 1776 and 1777, immediately before he was sent off to Switzerland with Lettice, to complete his education and, as his mother hoped, to establish his Protestant faith, Beckford was simultaneously writing two very different books. One, which Lettice, as the fellow of a Cambridge college, contrived to get published in 1780, was *Biographical Memoirs of Extraordinary Painters*. It would be republished in 1824 and 1834. The other, which would not be published, was "L'Esplendente," a semi-autobiographical fantasy thrown off when Beckford, under the influence of Alexander Cozens, still believed he might become a great painter himself. This last is a most original and unpredictable work to come from a young man of seventeen.

The protagonist, L'Esplendente, who is obviously Beckford himself, is a Muslim boy living in sixteenth-century Christian Spain. Deserted by his father in a grotto-valley suspiciously like the east bank of the lake at Fonthill, he goes to sleep and "the forms of Eblis and Harnt were in his dreams": evil angels of Muslim folklore.[7] Beckford would use Eblis, the beautiful young Lord of Evil, in the last chapter of *Vathek*. In a second dream he sees Houris:

> Their dark eyes melted with felicity—they were walking amidst roses while a soft harmony proceeding from the shades—infused into his soul the most voluptuous ideas & transports unknown before.[8]

Eventually L'Esplendente leaves home to study art with a kindly old Jew, an Alexander Cozens figure.

Cozens, an artist and occasional drawing master at Eton College, is the mystery character in the Beckford story, a silent witness. Despite all the letters supposedly written to him by Beckford, none from him have survived. What is certain is that he was never able to teach Beckford to draw with any facility and that he was initially a malign influence on Beckford's critical taste, persuading him to despise all the artists he would come later to admire for their craftsmanship and the precision of their finished works. Cozens was known in his time as "the dirty digit" from his method of throwing a large blot on a paper, folding it to create an interesting arbitrary shape, and then using that as the center of a composition of some mountain or tree.[9] Under his influence Beckford spent his next two continental visits looking for

broad general effects, sunsets, and shadows. It was his tutor Lettice who brought him back to appreciate detail in painting and in architecture. In addition Beckford would use Cozens, as he used Louisa Beckford, as a convenient courier for passing forbidden letters to the boy William Courtenay, but it is unlikely that Cozens had any moral influence. In a rare comment, but one in keeping with Beckford's mercurial behavior, Beckford referred scornfully to the artist at Christmas 1782: "Cozens creeps about like a domestic animal. T'would be no bad scheme to cut a little cat's door in the great portals of the saloon."[10]

That mocking detachment is very much the mood of his second teenage writing, *Biographical Memoirs*. This book could be dismissed as crude adolescent humor, but in the hard-hitting style of a modern satirical magazine it remains both funny and shrewdly aimed at a number of painters, most of them Flemish, who were then currently fashionable. Beckford invented six fictional artists, all closely modeled on real painters who were, in Beckford's opinon, which was influenced by Cozens, artistic disasters because they observed real life too closely.

One of them, Salvator Rosa, is attacked under the name of Blunderbussiana, whose father, Rouzenski, is the leader of a group of Croatian bandits living in a huge Dalmatian grotto and whose mother is a Turkish captive. A first inspiration comes from "gloomy caverns hollowed in craggy rocks, which threatened every instant to fall on his head." But then, "his father's band frequently bringing bodies to their cave, he amused himself with dissecting and imitating the several parts, till he attained such a perfection in muscular expression as is rarely seen in the works of the greatest masters." In Friuli Blunderbussiana dissects a cat, corrects a painting by Joseph Porta, and is taken by Porta to Venice. There he specializes in "Clair Obscure" (a grayish, melancholy tint) and paints "vast perspective caverns red with the light of fires, round which banditti were carousing; or else dark valleys between shaggy rocks strewed with the spoils of murdered travellers. . . . If he represented waters, they were dark and troubled, if trees, deformed and withered." After going grave robbing at night Blunderbussiana falls ill, goes mad, and dies, bequeathing his body "with all his anatomical designs to the college of surgeons," his paintings "still terrify the tender hearted."[11] All juvenile wit perhaps, but fair comment on a painter over-praised at the time, and at least Beckford was critically involved, reacting against his dead father's taste as exemplified on the walls of Fonthill Splendens. Few things commit a writer to a life of authorship so much as the publication of a first effort, and in 1780 Lettice secured that for *Biographical Memoirs*.

Beckford's mother was not as pleased by these precocious talents as his tutor was. Her son was intended to become a politician like his father, not an art critic. Another potentially dangerous distraction from his career prospects loomed when, in 1776 on November 1, All Saints Day, the first solemn High Mass to be held outside London since 1538 was celebrated with seductive pomp in the splendid new chapel, described as a "basilica," at Wardour Castle in the parish next to Fonthill. The eighth Lord Arundell of Wardour had two resident

Jesuit chaplains, one of them Father Fleury, a persuasive young Frenchman. Catholicism was in the air, like incense, but in eighteenth-century England all Catholics were considered "recusants," hopeless outsiders in any political process. If he turned Catholic, Beckford would destroy his prospects in Parliament. Consequently Mrs. Beckford may have been relieved to get her impressionable seventeen-year-old son off in June 1777 to sternly Calvinistic Geneva to pursue the university stage of his education. By not sending him to Oxford or Cambridge Mrs. Beckford ensured that her son would never see himself as a patriotic Briton but always as an outsider, a patronizing European sophisticate, who would later anticipate eagerly a successful invasion of his country by Napoléon and the French. As for her prescribed Calvinistic inocculation against the evils of Catholicism, in less than a year Beckford's mother would be traveling out to Geneva in person to drag her son and his obliging tutor back to England, after hearing from Elizabeth Marsh, Beckford's half-sister, that the pair had made a pilgrimage to the Carthusians' mother house of the Grande Chartreuse, high in the mountains of Savoy.

Beckford had traveled to Switzerland intent on sampling the simple Theocritan pleasures of the peasant life as portrayed in the *Idylls*, prose poems written by Salomon Gessner of Zurich. These had been coming out in English translations since 1762.[12] Beckford, whose feeling for wholesome goodness and authentic, simple living was as acute as his appreciation of things forbidden and sybaritic luxury, was anxious to enjoy the Swiss pastoral. Hoping to control him, his mother had arranged for him to stay with her half-Swiss cousin, a middle-aged bachelor, Colonel Edward Hamilton, ex-East India Company army. The colonel was a Freemason and Freemasonry, usually anti-Catholic in mood, was a strong tradition on Mrs. Beckford's side of the family, the Hamiltons.

As usual, where Beckford was concerned, events went as he, with his enormous wealth, dictated. Instead of settling down to lectures on law, physics, and natural sciences, he whisked his new guardian off to Évian-les-Bains, a spa resort down the lake, for Gessner-style Theocritan revelry. On August 22 he wrote a triumphant letter to his aunt, Lady Effingham, one of the "Methodistical dowagers" who had cramped his youthful style, flaunting his new freedom. He was enjoying an hour of dancing every day before breakfast "in a long mall or alley of noble trees. . . . in short the company was so good & agreeable the weather so excellent and every circumstance so favourable that Colonel Hamilton resolved to give a Fête in the wood at Blonay."[13]

Skirting quickly over the improbability of that middle-aged bachelor having taken any such an initiative, Beckford went on to describe the fête in a scene straight out of Fragonard: "Colonel H and myself had arrived long before & had the pleasure of seeing the whole company clambering a natural terrace which forms a steep bank about 30 feet perpendicular to find green damask cushions laid out under the chestnut trees," a hidden orchestra playing, and a cold collation waiting to be eaten. Dancing began and "two Chanoinesses with their long robes of lawn waving with the Gale, looked as they stood on a green promontory which impended over the plain like Genie of the Wild." Inspired, Beckford presented his partner with the panache of a tall green fern to wear in her headdress, the other gentlemen following his lead. As Madame la Baronne de Montailleur "wished to walk amongst the lovely woodlands it was impossible not to accompany her quite in a Pastoral manner....then we returned," he added archly, "which was about in an hour."[14] Confident that Aunt Effingham would now be fuming at these hints of sexual impropriety, he turned lyrical and gave her a burst of Cozens's artistic diction. Night fell, the moon came out and,

> That luminary shortly moved to the mid heaven above the mouldering Towers of the Castle of Blonay, and in a few minutes cast a track of silver which quivered like the scales of a China fish on the waters. The firelight and the lustre of the full moon occasioned some noble effects of the Chiara Oscura.[15]

The letter ended with one sincere sentence: "It may be the happiest day of my life, such another may never return."[16] At Évian he had found his ideal Arcadia, an unimpressive, even insignificant little town on a dull stretch of the lake, yet he would escape there again and again in the crisis times of his youth. At heart he was at least as much a gentleman dandy of the late Rococo period as a wild romantic Goth.

Back in Geneva for a winter of studies Beckford fell into a confusion of literary and emotional experiences. Aubry's 1777 French translation, *Les Passions du jeune Werther*, of Goethe's thunderbolt of adolescent despair, *Die Leiden des jungen Werthers* (1774), was the scandal and the delight of Geneva's educated young middle class. Uninhibited emotionalism, love, honor, and noble suicide were suddenly fashionable in educated circles of Western Europe. Daniel Malthus's English translation, entitled *The Sorrows of Werter*, would hit England in 1779. Beckford, one of the book's natural victims, absorbed it there in Geneva in 1777. A slim epistolary novel that still reads well more than two centuries later by its winning emotional openness, it follows sympathetically the despair of Werther, an honorable, well-intentioned youth, who falls in love with Charlotte, the wife of his best friend. Werther shoots himself and dies, still gasping out sensitive reflections on life.

Essentially Goethe's book exalts and romanticizes forbidden love and encourages an extrovert expression of it. Beckford would soon, and disastrously, be looking around for his own forbidden love to dramatize and, instead of choosing a mature young woman, would light upon an aristocratic schoolboy. An epistolary novel is one thing, passionate Werther-like love letters to a schoolboy that then fall into the hands of a hostile lawyer are quite another. Goethe infected Beckford with Romantic expressionism, an emotional illness from which he would not begin to recover until 1822, when he abandoned Gothic Fonthill Abbey and retired to build a neoclassical tower on Lansdown in Bath.

This was not the only problem. Werther cries out in one of his reflections: "Ossian has taken the place of Homer in my heart and imagination. To what a world does the illustrious bard carry me! To wander in heaths and wilds, surrounded by impetuous whirlwinds in which, by the feeble light of the moon, we discover the spirits of our ancestors."[17] *Ossian* and *Fingal* were two fraudulent prose-poems, epics claiming to be translations of Gaelic poetry, stories of ghosts and bloodshed in the Dark Ages that had caught the jaded attention of an effete generation. The impressionable Beckford absorbed their theatrical ethos on Werther's recommendation. For the next few years he too would be listening for the voices of spirits to underwrite his Romantic credibility. As if that were not psychic confusion enough he was apparently initiated into Freemasonry in Geneva, delighting in the ritual if disappointed by the actual revelation of its mysteries.[18]

His response, while still enjoying amateur dramatics with a group of new young friends and exploring the Bernese Oberland with Jean Daniel Huber, a Genevan artist of good family, was to write an epic prose poem himself in which the mysteries would be finally made clear.[19] Beckford called it "Nouronihar" after the sinister spirit woman who leads him through various naked lustrations and vague erotic thrills. Another figure out of Swedenborg, an old man with a long beard and a white gown called Moisasour, commands him to "Gaze at the abode of purity and wisdom, old as creation, unshaken by four dreadful revolutions, fixed by the Supreme Power immovable, unalterable."[20] It reads like an eighteenth-century anticipation of twentieth-century fantasy fiction, but experienced underground.

While it is all tedious nonsense, it has an importance. Nouronihar was to reappear as the Caliph's bride in *Vathek*, while "The Fragments of Nouronihar," which were not published in 1930, include a memorably horrifying account of the cavern under Mount Caf (the Caucasus) where the sixty-one pre-Adamite Sultans—semi-human monsters whom Beckford had taken from Barthélemy d'Herbelot's 1697 *Bibliothèque Orientale*—sleep the dreadful slumbers of the undead. That theme would obsess Beckford for the rest of his life. At one time he was planning to be buried two stories up, in the Lancaster Chamber of Fonthill Abbey; at another he was considering interment under the floor of a corridor in the Lansdown Tower. The possibility of continued consciousness in the grave explains his insistence on being buried, as he still is today, above ground on Lansdown in a comfortable tomb with a good view of the Avon valley. As for the Sultans,

these wretches, tho' seeming sunk in the repose of death & exhibiting to all appearances the most loathsome images of corruption, still retain a sense of life & are conscious to all the horrors which surround them. Nay, those who have been permitted to view this melancholy place pretend to have perceived a languid motion in their eyes, to have noticed, ever & anon, a convulsive start, even to have heard a feeble moan spring from coffers of incorruptible cedar.[21]

With a Calvinistic severity Beckford turned to describe the Last Judgment:

the day when these rocks, these mountains, and even Caf itself will pass away like the clouds of the morning. 'Tis then they believe all punishments will be remitted, all Sins forgiven & the light of Heaven restore each being to his former happiness—then again disclaim this notion! When the last Earthquake arrives, Aherman [Eblis] may claim them for his own & awake them to keener torments.[22]

For all their crude effects of gnawing toads and "noxious birds," Beckford's adolescent writings contain some resounding rhetoric and genuine terror. The famous last chapter of *Vathek* would be set in this same cavern under Mount Caf. Beckford's own grim version of eternity and the equal relationship between God and the devil was already taking shape. For some sinners there could be no forgiveness; they were Aherman's forever. Yet this same doom-laden young man who had, by his seventeenth year, sifted out the most depressing elements of Hindu, Buddhist, Islamic, and Zoroastrian mythology, had just come from innocent pastoral frolics in the woods of Blonay and would soon, in the company of Jean Daniel Huber, be behaving more like a modern back-packer than an introverted religious pessimist.

The two young men made regular, often dangerous, expeditions by horse and on foot up into the mountains. In one of his unsent "letters" Beckford described how they climbed a sheer cliff in the valley of the Drance to explore yet another cave, the Grotte des Fées: "I began ascending and hung for a second or two between the craggs above and the Woods and Valley below. Had I dropped I should have fallen plump into the clear winding Rivulet whose appearance now for the first time began to alarm me."[23] Under Jean Daniel's tuition, however, his appetite for the Savage Picturesque increased. On another occasion the two tackled the tremendous precipices behind Leukerbad, and Beckford's little Green Note Book records:

The Mount Gemmi, a terrifying path—Bulwarks of Rock misshapen masses. After we had mounted 3 leagues we began to discern the glaciers of Savoy & the Vallais shooting up their white spires into the deep blue sky, we quit the frightful edge of the precipices & enter a savage desert. Beds of snow, ramparts of ice, and rugged rocks, shewed all over in the wildest confusion.[24]

This was yet another aspect of Beckford to add to the rococo exquisite of the select spa town of Évian-les-Bains.

Driven partly by religiosity and partly by this new interest in the Picturesque, Beckford determined to pay his respects to Saint Bruno, founder of the Carthusian order, at the Grande Chartreuse. Saints, first Thomas à Becket, then Saint Bruno, and finally Saint Anthony, were always more accessible to him than the Godhead or the Trinity. In that mood of febrile overreaction to every sight and every event, acquired from reading *Werther* and which would characterize his reactions for the next hectic years of his life, Beckford approached the monastery: "I travelled the valley with a thousand sensations I despair of describing, and stood before the gate of the convent with as much awe as some novice or candidate newly arrived to start the holy retirement of the order."[25]

The monks were captivated by Beckford's wealth and his enthusiasm. As usual, when he was with Catholic priests, Beckford gave the impression that he was on the edge of a conversion. He wandered their forests where the laboring brothers "desired me by signs to refresh myself with bread and milk and returned with some strawberries very neatly inveloped [sic] in fresh leaves."[26] It was Theocritus again but in a Christian context, a monkish pastoral. When, after three days on a vegetarian diet, he had to leave, the Coadjutor and two other fathers "declared that if ever I was disgusted with the World here was an Asylum. I was in a melancholy mood when I traced back all the windings of the road."[27] The idea of an abbey, high among wooded hills but with William Beckford as the Abbot, not a novice, had been implanted in his mind.

Mrs. Beckford, horrified when news of this Catholic flirtation reached her, traveled to the city to enforce his obedience. "My mother has taken alarm," he wrote to his sister, "I expect her to be here today, bag & baggage. Think how overjoyed I shall be!"[28] He returned with her to Fonthill, resentful and in a state of increasingly nervous excitement, to find that she had planned a political tour of England to prepare him for taking a seat in Parliament. Next year he was to study agriculture and industry and meet the great landowners whose support might advance him to a position in government. In one of many "letters" written at the time, as if for an epistolary novel, he declared: "I will exclude myself if possible from the World, in the midst of its Empire and conserve many hours every day with you Moisasour and Nouronihar. . . . all my consolation is centred on Fingal and the wild music of the winds."[29]

It was at this intensely impressionable and self-indulgent period of his life that one area of Fonthill Splendens became spiritually significant to him. This was the "rustic" or ground floor containing the chamber which he called "the Hall of the Pyramid" for its Egyptian qualities, and another room lined with tall porcelain vases. Porcelain to the young Beckford was not simply decorative art, it was the home of Ossianic spirits and semi-sacred. Those epistolary, unsent letters return again and again to the theme:

I entered the peaceful Palace where Silence and Solitude reign undisturbed. One glimmering lamp directed me to my apartment, 'twas all I desired: more Light might have alarmed those ancient and venerable Spirits who reside in Vases ranged mysteriously around the Cell. Having prepared a short prayer to those concealed Intelligencies I stretched myself out on Indian carpets and drank my tea.[30]

And again he wrote:

Think how we should exult at finding ourselves in arched Chambers glowing with yellow light—amidst Vases formed in

another Hemisphere and cabalistic Mirrors where Futurity is unveiled. . . . It is in vain these Vases are ranged in the loveliest Order—and filled with the perfume of Roses, in vain this whole Apartment is spread with the richest carpets and glows with the softest lights,—those Eyes are not destined to survey it, on whom I could gaze forever. . . . There is a book called the Sorrows of Werther, read it and tell me if every line is not resplendent with Genius. Fonthill, Friday 8 o'clock Eve, Dec 3 1779.[31]

Goethe, Werther, Ossian, spirits, and vases were twisted together in an adolescent fantasy world; Beckford was literally "mad about porcelain." Later in life he would employ Jean Boileau to redecorate this "Turkish" room in Fonthill's "rustic," but he had inherited it with its exotic Eastern contents from his father, the Alderman, and it was a significant influence on the aesthetic development of an emotional nineteen-year-old: "What are the Indian apartments to me now I am afraid you cannot view them—the animated trivets and footstools that amble round me."[32] He was withdrawing into a world of literary fantasies just as his mother, with the best of intentions, was pushing him out into the real world and so precipitating disaster on a scale worthy of *Werther*.

The autumn, winter, and spring of 1778–79 was the time when Beckford, brooding and intense, almost turned himself into a Romantic poet, ten years before Wordsworth and Coleridge began writing. By December 4 he had written a fantasy of remarkable boldness and sensitivity in which he imagined himself as one of a flock of rooks flying about the elms at Fonthill. In the spring he produced "Satyr's Range," a prose-poem transforming those woods and grottoes on the east bank of the Fonthill lake into a place of water nymphs, sly satyrs, altars for holy sacrifice, and finally a home for the great god Pan himself.

The text opens as he sets out early in the morning, rowing himself across the lake in a skiff, followed by swans and water-fowl, congratulating himself that "Never are they alarmed with Guns, scared with stones or pursued by malicious dogs and their more cruel Masters."[33] He lands and then his self-conscious prose almost limps into real poetry as,

I ran lightly along the alley where spreading boughs cast a
   chequered shade and, applying my horn (the horn a Satyr
   gave me in the groves of Savoy) to my lips
Blew an inspiring air that Dale and thicket rang
The Hunter's call to Faun and Dryad known
The oak-crowned sisters and their chaste-eyed Queen
Satyrs and sylvan Boys were seen
Peeping from forth their alleys green.
Do I behold ye then I exclaim. O ye rural powers—Deities I
   have worshipped from my earliest youth—on whose altars
   I have often heaped produce of a garden I cultivated with
   my infant hands. As I speak methinks I hear the musick of
   a distant reed.[34]

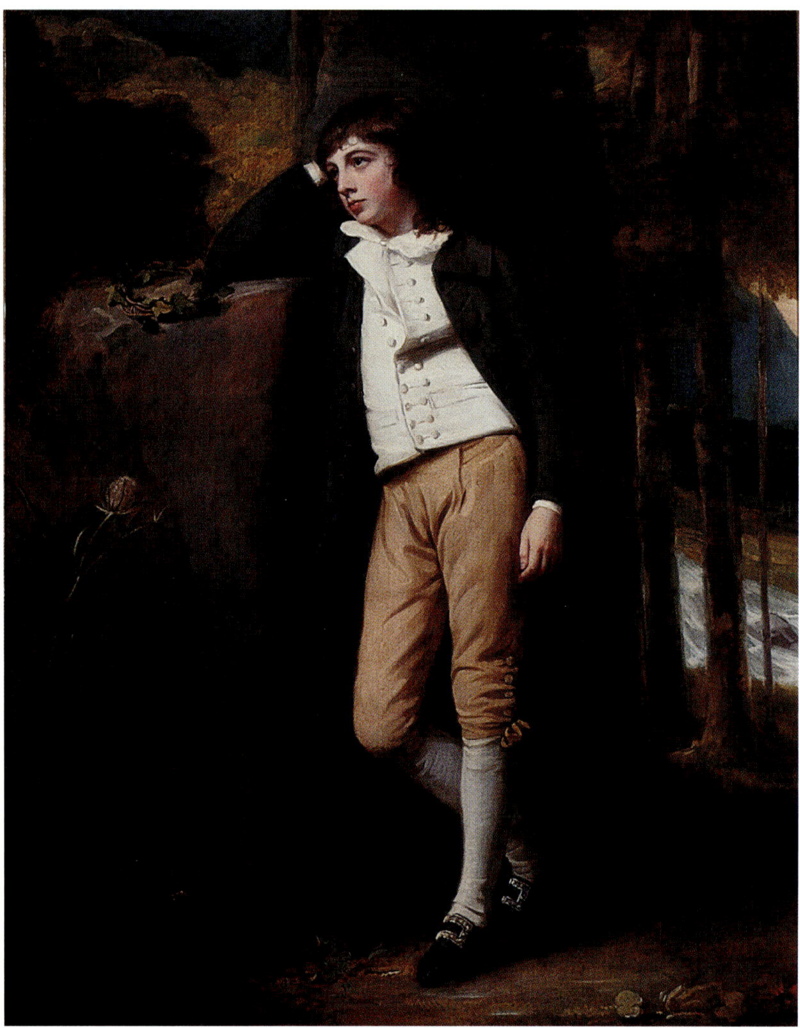

Fig. 1-4. George Romney. *William ("Kitty") Courtenay*, ca. 1782. Oil on canvas. The Nemours Foundation, Wilmington, Delaware.

that he was in love with the boy (fig. 1-4). He wrote of their parting in the spirit of Werther's first separation from Charlotte. Werther recalled:

> She went down the walk: I stood and followed her with my eyes, then threw myself on the ground in a passion of tears; I got up again and ran to the terrace, and there I still saw, under the shade of the lime trees, her white gown waving near the garden gate. I stretched out my arms and she was gone.[35]

Beckford wrote:

> Why did we experience that sudden love for each other? Did it not increase each hour and when I quitted his native castle— what expressive melancholy looks were cast after one down the long avenue—the solemnity of which was increased by the dusk—for it was dusk—when I parted from all my soul doted upon. During the whole journey that evening no other object filled my soul.[36]

Had he the ability to see into the future he could have changed that last sentence to: "During the next three years"; from that time onward all Beckford's travel-writing, art criticism, and letters to his friends are blighted by self-pitying, lovelorn laments at the misfortune of being separated from his beloved William. A sugary tone and quavering sentimentality were a constant feature:

> Fonthill, March, 1780. My situation is sad and solitary—I stray disconsolately on the Rocks by the Caves of the Sleepers scarcely knowing which way to bend my steps. My imagination roams to other Countries in search of pleasure it no longer finds at Home—This evening it has been transported to those immense unfrequented plains of Tartary which are covered with Herbs and Flowers. Amongst these I fancied myself reposing and thought the one I loved best in the Universe was gathering Roses by my side....Such Delusions as these form my present felicity.[37]

Theocritan raptures had turned to whimsical complaints. Between them, Werther and William Courtenay had stifled the poet in Beckford and sidetracked him into becoming a writer of lachrymose letters, which he would remain until *Vathek* released him in 1782.

Realizing the danger, Mrs. Beckford acted fast and, unlucky as ever, made matters much worse. She introduced him to two sisters, the daughters of Lord Rivers, intending him to form an attachment to Harriet, who was unmarried. Instead the other sister, Louisa, married to Beckford's cousin Peter, fell hopelessly and dangerously in love with Beckford, while Harriet remained politely uninterested. Beckford never loved Louisa intensely, but she flattered him, reflected his moods, and encouraged his lusts for Courtenay as a way of gaining his confidence. At one stage she offered to pander her own small son to him, though he, to be fair, never encouraged this. Throughout their intense, if largely epistolary, relationship Louisa was slowly dying of tuberculosis, and this has to be seen as some excuse for her infamous behavior.

The young Keats would not have been ashamed of "Satyr's Range" as a first effort. It would remain unpublished and unacknowledged, a dead end of creativity.

In June 1779, Beckford set off, with Lettice as usual in attendance, on his political tour of great houses in the West Country. One of their early stops was Powderham Castle, south of Exeter, the seat of the wealthy, indolent second Viscount Courtenay who had married a pretty barmaid and raised a family of twelve daughters and one son, William, then aged eleven. As they drove up the drive Beckford caught his first glimpse of William playing with his sisters among the deer, a good looking, confident schoolboy, home for the holidays from Westminster School. Beckford stayed only three days at the castle, but when he left he was already emotionally intoxicated with the certainty

Mrs. Beckford's next move, when Louisa and Harriet failed her, was to pack her son and his tutor off on a Grand Tour of Italy. This lasted from June 1780 to March the following year and proved a delightfully comic episode in Beckford's life. He set out intending to write a travel book with passages of description based on Cozens's theories of light and shade. In London, however, he heard the castrato Pacchierotti sing and this transformed him into a melomane. The entire Italian tour henceforth was dictated by the need to listen to the unpredictable improvisations and inhuman voice range of Pacchierotti wherever he was performing. As a natural counter tenor Beckford felt a sensitive bonding with castrati. The travel book was not abandoned, but it took second place to the drug of music. Frequent hints in the text to his sorrowing love for Courtenay made, in any case, the book unsalable. Five hundred copies of it would be pulped, on lawyers' advice, in 1783.

In Venice Beckford fell heavily but briefly in love with a son of the noble Cornaro family, a boy with "fine eyes." At Lucca he sat through ten performances of Bertoni's *Quinto Fabio*, in order to enjoy Pacchierotti's coloratura improvisations in Act Two. Rome was dismissed in three days, but in Naples he met his soul mate, a woman as precious and as uninhibitedly sensitive as himself, and as besotted by music. She was the Welsh wife of his distant cousin, the British ambassador to Naples, Sir William Hamilton. Beckford confessed his Cornaro affair to her, vowed to reform, and then began to pine for Fonthill. A letter to Cozens of November 16 throws an interesting light on his previous life in Wiltshire, more wholesome and innocent than might be expected.

> We shall inhabit our Huts on the borders of the Lake and sometimes our vast range of solemn subterranean Chambers visible by the glow of Lamps and filled with cabalistic images [these broken garden statues still lie in a quarry cave at Fonthill]. Another moment will find us encamped upon the green Desert we were so fond of, drinking our coffee in open Tents and dreaming ourselves in Yemen—Next day perhaps we shall repair to the stone of power, Stonehenge, where, to speak in the language of Fingal, Spirits descend by night in dark red flames of Fire.[38]

He set off for home, promising Lady Hamilton that he would avoid the Cornaro boy in Venice where Pacchierotti would be performing again. "But I almost fear attending to it," he wrote, "Such Musick—O Heaven, it breathes the very soul of voluptuous effeminacy."[39] Lady Hamilton replied encouragingly: "Take courage, My dear Friend, you have taken the first step. Continue to resist, and every day you will find the struggle less."[40] From Germany Beckford reported that "the gulph into which I was on the point of being precipitated has disappeared." He was composing again: "Did you ever read," he asked Lady Hamilton, "in some Lapland history, of certain gnomes who lurk in mines and chasms of tremendous mountains? The music I have been composing was exactly such, I should imagine, as elves and pygmies dance to—brisk and humming—moody and subterraneous."[41] Lady Hamilton wrote back: "Thanks to all Gracious Heaven you are escaped. I begin to take breath, for I have been in an agony about you."[42] She need not have been so disturbed. Beckford had reached Paris, where he was flirting with both the Duchess of Berwick and Georgina Seymour. He wrote with mock sadness to his friend in Naples: "I fear I shall never be half so sapient, nor good for anything in this world, but composing airs, building towers, forming gardens, collecting old Japan, and writing a journey to China or the moon."[43] All those prophecies would be fulfilled apart from the China voyages—Portugal would have to be a substitute—and he had begun seriously to collect Japanese lacquer.

The official, almost feudal, celebrations of his coming-of-age went off in tremendous style at Fonthill between September 28 and 30, 1781. Two castrati sang, Pacchierotti and Giusto Tenducci. Mrs Beckford contrived to include in one Pacchierotti recitative the ominous warning: "rather than any Circumstances should induce you to commit one base Action, Die first my Son, and your Death will be a Subject of Envy."[44] To Beckford in his Werther role that was merely an additional temptation. Disgrace and death were, in his present mood, actual incentives. Enjoying his new adult freedom, he took a townhouse in London where he could entertain William Courtenay, who was still at Westminster School, very easily. There he wrote:

> I never loved Winter before—don't you know how much I used to hate it & shiver when ever the north wind blew. At present I love its murmurs, even the dark fog that consumes vegetation. Never shall I see my breath exhale in a nippy frost without thinking of the little blue vapour that comes from Wm. and that I used to attempt appropriating with such avidity. Don't talk to me of Spring.[45]

The suppressed physicality of the writing is as clear as the breath vapor. Another draft, dated December 8, 1781, records the inevitable conclusion of a successful seduction:

> From the theatre I carry him to my bed. Nature, Morality and Fame are all forgotten, confused and swept away. Oh God! I wish I could die in these embraces and my soul dive down with his into eternal bliss or eternal punishment.[46]

Now, having sinned outrageously against accepted morality, he would need to write out his emotions and that "eternal punishment" in the text, in French like the draft above, of *Vathek*.

There followed, apart from his official coming-of-age, the famous delayed birthday party at Fonthill Splendens that Christmas. As Beckford wrote it up, long afterward:

> I still feel warmed and irradiated by the recollections of that strange, necromantic light which Loutherbourg had thrown over what absolutely appeared a realm of Fairy, or rather, perhaps, a Demon Temple deep beneath the earth set apart for

tremendous mysteries; and yet how soft, how genial was this quiet light. Whilst the wretched world without lay dark and bleak and howling, whilst the storm was raging against our massive walls and the snow drifting in clouds, the very air of summer seemed playing around us; the choir of low-toned melodious voices continued to soothe our ear; and, that every sense might in turn receive its blandishment, tables covered with delicious viands and fragrant flowers glided forth by the aid of mechanism at stated intervals, from the richly draped and amply curtained recesses of the enchanted precincts.[47]

It was here that Beckford met the Rev. Samuel Henley, an amateur scholar in Eastern literature, and it was in conversations with Henley at this birthday party that Beckford roughed out the plot for *Vathek*. Beckford supplied the necessary fusion of irresponsible gaiety and guilt, Herbelot's *Bibliothèque Orientale* supplied the characters, and Henley trimmed them into a taut, dramatic whole.

The first half of *Vathek*, written over the next four months, covers the Caliph Vathek's extravagant follies at his capital, Samarah. Beckford's text parallels his own foolish boasting about his current popularity in the London season:

All London, notwithstanding ten thousand malevolent insinuations, is at my feet, and all the Misses in array whenever I show myself.…if I promise to sing at such and such a place on such and such a night the rage and intriguing to be one of the party is truly ridiculous. Our holy Aunt saw me in the zenith of this sort of glory last Saturday at Marlborough House—where I contrived to dance, and by song and by frolic to produce a vivid sensation.[48]

The jilted Georgina Seymour wrote sourly to him reporting: "I heard you called one of the greatest coxcombes that exist—which I could not bear to hear."[49]

The shocking conclusion of *Vathek* reflects Beckford's second Italian visit, which he began with a vainglorious retinue, including a resident artist and a resident musician, in May. He quarrelled with his artist, the watercolorist John Cozens, Alexander's son. His musician, the talented John Burton, died of a fever, cursing his patron. Beckford himself fell very ill with the same fever, and when they reached Naples, a sickly caravansery, they found Lady Hamilton dying of tuberculosis, like Louisa. Beckford had a gift for singling out women friends with limited lifespans. He and Lettice made their subdued way back to England. Lettice had begun to translate a little of the French text of *Vathek*, a memorable masterpiece, which enclosed, symbolically, Beckford's sins, joys, loves, and guilt of the past six months.

Surprisingly, on their return to England, Beckford registered no storm of protest when his formidable mother dragooned him into marriage with Lady Margaret Gordon, a niece of her friend, Lady Euphemia Stewart. Lady Margaret was a pretty, good-natured blonde, an outdoor girl with few illusions about her proposed husband. As a

true bisexual Beckford would have seen nothing illogical in continuing a long-standing male love affair when he had a wife. The wedding was quiet, and a long honeymoon followed in Switzerland, the couple staying for part of the time with the Hubers on the lake shore at Geneva, but also touring energetically. Lady Margaret acquitted herself admirably. They had met an American on their trip to Chamonix to explore the glaciers, and the trio drove up through pine woods. In his Green Note Book Beckford wrote that evening:

Abandoning our carriage we emerged into a chaos of shattered fragments—there the American & myself climbed like Chamois—& Lady M. to my no small surprise—boldly followed us—we leaped several rapid branches of the torrent & advancing between huge masses of crystalline ice—saw the enchanted Grot of the Aveyron full before us—It had not been open according to the acct of our guides—above ten days—and was widening every hour—large glittering drops were trickling from the vault—& every now & then a fragment detatching itself, fell with the sound of thunder—into the Torrent—We were too much absorbed in contemplating the celestial blue of the grotto for some time to notice the rapid increase of the waters around us—half stunned with their roar—we made a precipitate retreat.[50]

Everything was going remarkably well. The young couple held a second, even more lavish fête in the woods at Blonay; Lady Margaret was pregnant and, enclosing a letter to Courtenay, in a letter to Cozens, Beckford told the old man: "You will be surprised and delighted to hear, that Lady M. has not the least jealousy & in the letter I inclose, and which I entreat you take care of, she assures . . . with her own hand of her affections."[51] Lady Margaret had decided to handle her bisexual husband by humoring him. In September, however, she had a miscarriage and then in May was delivered of a dead son, putting real strains on the relationship. After a holiday in Scotland they were invited to spend a fortnight at Powderham Castle. Mrs. Beckford advised against it, but Lady Margaret and William Courtenay were good friends, and the visit seemed to go off well. They were back in Fonthill by October 13.

It was then that the rumors began to spread. By December the press had begun to pick them up and print knowing references to "the detestable scene lately acted in *Wiltshire* [the wrong county] by a pair of fashionable *male lovers*."[52] Nothing more exact was ever printed and charges were never brought, but the whispers and insinuations were enough. Courtenay's uncle, Lord Loughborough, the Chief Justice of Common Pleas, had possession of passionate, whimsical letters that Beckford had written. Read aloud in court they would have reduced him to a national laughingstock. The peerage, which had been offered, making him Baron Beckford of Fonthill, was withdrawn. Society began to shun the young couple, and when, in April 1785, their first daughter Maria was born, even Lettice urged a strategic retreat to Switzerland until the scandal had died down.

A romantic little harborside castle at La Tour de Peilz was

rented, on the other side of Lake Geneva but in full view of beloved Évian, and there in July they settled to make a new life. Beckford's sister had urged Lady Margaret to leave her husband, but she remained loyal, even devoted. A letter that Beckford wrote next February to a friend, Robert Pigott, shows how hard he was working to reestablish his reputation as a sexually normal man:

> Our Balls continue quite amusing—a fine shew of young innocent Tits in the first heyday of Spirits & tender Inclinations….A long range of Appartments, animating Musick, flowing drapery, snug corners in the Windows—four feet deep! Rare work for young fellows you must allow & nice hotbeds for expanding the hearts of these lovely Blossomes.[53]

Another child was expected, Lettice and Lady Euphemia both came across the Continent to offer support. Susan Euphemia was born safely, but then two weeks later, on May 26, 1786, Lady Margaret died in agony of puerperal fever, unable even to recognize her much loved Aunt Phemy.

Always terrified of death, Beckford was devastated. Frantic with grief he took flight and, with Lettice as his only companion, ranged the country trying not to remember his wife's terrible last days. While he was away his two baby daughters were taken to England for Mrs. Beckford to bring up, her son being considered unsuitable. Worse still, it was intimated that he should not be present at Lady Margaret's funeral when her embalmed body was laid to rest at Fonthill.

At that point, to rouse him to a healthy, distracting fury, came the news that Henley, who had been translating *Vathek* into English with scholarly footnotes, had published the book with no mention of Beckford's authorship, its only title, "An Arabian Tale from an Unpublished Manuscript with Notes Critical and Explanatory." To make a bad situation even worse the Beckford fortunes from the Jamaican plantations were dwindling, and he was called back to London, a nervous, uncertain figure, to discuss the complexities of finance, which he had never troubled to grasp. Hard and unsympathetic, his mother told him that a spell in Jamaica was called for, and, after waiting several weeks in Falmouth for a favorable wind, he set sail in the *Julius Caesar* for an island of yellow fever from which his mother may have expected him never to return. Now that she had granddaughters in her care the Beckford estates would still be safe even if her son died. Her son had other ideas.

After a tempestuous crossing of the Bay of Biscay the *Julius Caesar* called in at Lisbon in May 1787, and Beckford, who had been seasick for several days despite the geranium leaves in his cabin, got off to savor this city, so recently ravaged by the earthquake of 1755. He had already determined never to go back on board. Lisbon was the city where Saint Anthony, Beckford's favorite saint, had been born, and for Beckford Portugal was a delightful Ruritania with strong devotional overtones. His travel diaries were never published in his lifetime, but they are a winning portrait of Beckford at his most vulnerable. Half delighted by the lemon blossom and the church ceremonial, half

embarrassed and bemused by Portuguese efforts to marry him off to a young girl, angered by the hostility of the British ambassador and by the reluctance of the queen to receive him at court, he wrote humorously, sensitively, and even honestly. After *Vathek*, the *Journal* is his best writing, and his failure to publish it while publishing instead a pompous and overwritten version of it, *Italy with Sketches of Spain and Portugal*, in 1834, is a mark of literary bad judgment.

Initially he was still downcast by the memory of his wife: "once so lovely and blooming, now lying cold and ghastly in the dark vaults at Fonthill, the loveliest and most unaffected of beings who doted on her poor William with such excessive fondness, and pardoned with such a sweet endearing cheerfulness his childish errors."[54] The novelty of it all, the Baroque pomps of an untrimmed Catholicism, were, however, a distraction and a delight. On Corpus Christi in Lisbon he stood in the Palace Square to watch as

> A shower of aromatic herbs and flowers announced the approach of the Patriarch bearing the Host under a regal canopy surrounded by grandees and preceded by vast numbers of saintly mitred figures, their hands joined in prayer, their scarlet vestments sweeping the ground, their attendants bearing croziers, silver reliquaries and other insignia of pontifical grandeur.[55]

And in the evenings there was exotic song, the Brazilian *modinhas*: "an original sort of music, different from any I ever heard, the most seducing, the most voluptuous imaginable, the best calculated to throw saints off their guard and to inspire profane deliriums. I was in high spirits and danced with a parcel of young tits till two in the morning."[56] He soon attracted the congenial company of aristocratic youths:

> We dined at five and drank champagne and burgundy till Bezerra, after spinning round the room like a moth on the point of singeing itself, fell down dead drunk and was carried off to bed. Don Pedro and I were wild with spirits. I could have sat up all night.[57]

The next morning Beckford was up to his old games with young men, recording gleefully: "Tomorrow! Tomorrow! He loves me, I have tasted the sweetness of his lips; his dear eyes have confessed the secret of his bosom."[58] Don Pedro, however, as the heir to a marquisate, was too aristocratic to be a long-term lover but Beckford had collected a choirboy and pianist, Gregorio Franchi, who would be his male companion and general factotum for life. After one unhappy night in a Lisbon brothel Beckford concluded: "I have need of some young sweet breathed animal to enliven my spirits, to run into the citron thickets and bring me flowery branches, to arrange my prints, transpose my songs, and write down the musical ideas which rush into my mind in happy moments."[59] There would be no more desperate infatuations, no second William Courtenay.

Beckford made his way home to England. Over the next few restless years he made return visits to Portugal and Switzerland. Back

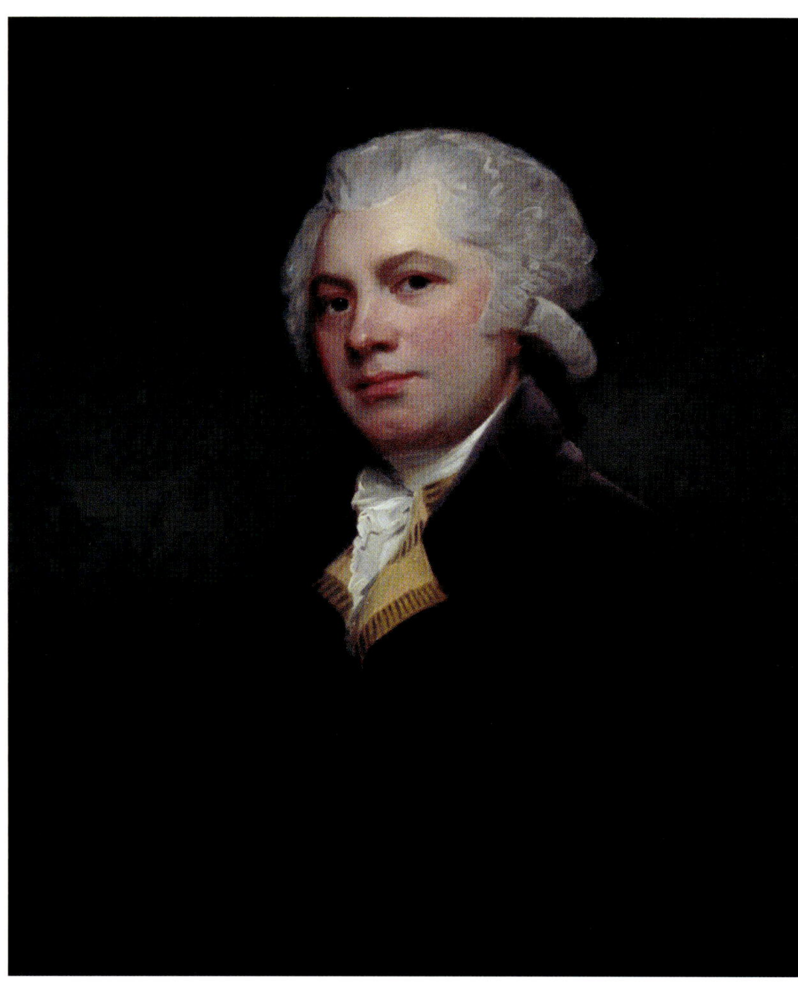

Fig. 1-5. George Romney. *Thomas Wildman*, n.d. Oil on canvas. ©Payne Hicks Beach.

in Paris in 1792 and part of 1793 he survived several months of the Terror and later tried to negotiate a peace treaty between the venal Directory in Paris and Pitt's government in London. This failed because his reputation still told against him. If the British were ever to forget the scandal of 1784 Beckford would have to become associated in the public mind with some impossible building project.

Earlier, in 1779, he had fantasized in a letter to Cozens, "I hope to erect a Tower dedicated to meditation."[60] Then there was the memory of the Grande Chartreuse among its woods and, more recently, that of another monastery, Batalha in Portugal, where he had marveled at "a group of richly parapeted walls, roofs and towers, detached chapels and isolated spires . . . in appearance it was not merely a church or a palace I was looking at, but some fair city of romance."[61] Fonthill Abbey never began as an entire, formal concept. It grew like an obsession, from a convent pleasure house in the woods, through two collapses and the improvisations of James Wyatt, its neg-

ligent architect, to become the most newsworthy house in England. Its construction led to the demolition of his beloved Fonthill Splendens. Even his lawyer, Thomas Wildman (fig. 1-5), a lifelong ally, had initially advised him against pulling down the old house.

As early as 1797, when Beckford feasted 700 gentry, tenants, and workers on his lawns at Splendens, followed by a well-attended football match, the Abbey project was succeeding. In response to the mayor of Salisbury's toast that evening Beckford replied in robustly patriotic and entirely insincere terms: "May the ears of John Bull never be insulted by the gypsy jargon of France!"[62] Cheers resounded inside the house and without. While still in middle age, he was becoming a living legend.

The Abbey grew erratically within its scaffolding. Beckford loved building it, but he never enjoyed living in it. By instinct and conditioning he was a classicist, not a Goth. Of the two towers that he built—the Abbey, 276 feet tall, and Lansdown Tower on the hills above Bath, 145 feet tall—it is the Lansdown Tower that still stands, that best represents his taste, and where he was happiest.

He would have to wait for Bath and Lansdown until 1822, by which time his tottering Abbey had become a financial impossibility for him. He had by then lived "Gothic" for a mere fifteen years, from 1807 to 1822, in an eighty-four-year lifespan spent otherwise in classical houses. He had chosen the Gothic for its wild profile, its drama, and because grand classical houses were commonplace. The various styles of Gothic were a mystery to him, and he despised what he considered their crudity. "Would to God," he wrote to Franchi on February 7, 1811, "that the Turks, Moors and Arabs had been not merely circumcised but castrated before inventing their pointed saracenic—gothic architecture—the cause of my ruin. The devil take them."[63] Yet when the Octagon was going up in 1808 he had been delirious with excitement: "It's really stupendous, the spectacle here at night—the number of people at work, lit up by lads; the inumerable torches suspended everywhere, the immense and endless spaces, the gulph below; above the gigantic spider's web of scaffolding."[64]

It was not until the outrageously dysfunctional structure was completed that a realization of its gloom, its chills, and its instability began to sink home:

> The dampness of this sublime abode is so great that everything will rot. . . . this place makes your flesh creep as soon as night falls . . . the horrible din of the winds last night. I didn't sleep a half-hour in succession. . . . Really this habitation is deathly in the stormy season. . . . My resolution to abandon the theatre of so much useless labour is fortified every hour that I stay here . . . blasts of cold, blasts of rheum and financial blasts in this uninhabitable place—uninhabitable for more than six months of the year at least.[65]

Throughout these Gothic tribulations, Beckford always retained a London townhouse where the capital, with its art dealers, bookshops, and galleries, offered occasional relief:

Alas, I was seduced by certain little Saxon tazza, certain sea-green bottles incredibly decorated with bronze, gilded in hell-fire—so bright and stony their colours. Two words breathed in my ear would have made me buy two fantastic Buhl armoire-like cabinets, magnificent, of a Solomonian richness, 400 the pair, and not dear at that.[66]

"I think," he confessed in a letter to Franchi, who was acting as his London agent, "of little agate vases, and little eggshell tazza!"[67] Paintings brought out a more critical response: "Here we spend our life putting up and taking down pictures. The Berchem and the Turner are in the large room, where they are not too bad. The Brueghel looked terrible and is now back where it was in the Lancaster Gallery. The de Cort has replaced the Berchem and is passable above the van Huysum."[68]

Isolated for most of the year on his windy hilltop, he lived out a curious, companionable existence with a Turkish servant, Ali Dru, for company and the constant rearrangement of his collections for consolation. On June 27, 1817, "I profited by the lack of sun to bathe with the Turk [in a woodland pond, the Bitham Lake; Beckford never bathed when the sun was shining]. The ivory cabinet is enchanting with its splendid hinges etc. It is a pity to let the mosaic table, bought years ago from Fogg, remain buried. I must have it made capable of bearing the ivory cabinet—black with few or no bronzes; it will do well in my room."[69]

Eventually it all became too much and he did abandon that "theatre of so much useless labour." Even its scale was a disappointment: "The miserable Fonthill sanctuary does not satisfy me. In vain they tell me, and think, that it is fine—I don't believe a word of it!"[70] The Sanctuary is the one wing of the Abbey to have survived demolition, and Beckford was right. It is a quite modest structure, thin in its detail, a rather fragile-looking structure of greenish gray stone, lost in the middle of a wood. Nevertheless rumor and myth had worked together. He had created the best-known, most talked-about building in Britain. "The craze for seeing the Abbey grows like the Tower itself," he noted in 1815[71]; and in the summer and autumn of 1822 he satisfied that craze abundantly. Announcing a sale of all the Abbey's contents on October 8, he opened his house to visitors for the inspection of his treasures. The great and the good arrived in their carriages, 7,200 of them, including half the British peerage. It was the sensation of the social season, and it was all a trick. There was to be no sale that year. With all the publicity Beckford had no trouble in selling his much-admired prodigy for a stunning £300,000 to a gunpowder millionaire. A year later the auctioneer Harry Phillips would hold a sale of some of Beckford's possessions, judiciously salted with other artworks that would gain in value by their supposed Beckford provenance. Such was the star quality of the Beckford name that the gunpowder millionaire, an old gentleman named John Farquhar, talked of leaving the entire monstrous edifice back to Beckford again in his will.

That was before the entire central tower of the Abbey col-lapsed into a pile of compo-cement dust, stone fixings, and timber bracing, bringing the Great Western Hall down with it. It was a ruin so gentle and unsensational that Mr. Farquhar, resting after lunch at the far southern end of the Abbey, slept on undisturbed by the event though one of his servants was propelled thirty feet along a corridor by a blast of compressed air. When it happened, on the afternoon of December 21, 1825, Beckford was safely settled in Bath, living in Lansdown Crescent and deciding on the design of his next tower, which would house those choice art treasures that he had retained and bought back out of the Phillips sale in 1823.

By this time Beckford was entirely purged of medieval romanticism and was deciding on the strictly severe shaft of his Lansdown Tower, rejecting all Henry Goodridge's suggestions of the Saxo-Norman with scorn. Instead he directed his new, young, biddable architect in the design of an eminently civilized structure, half chaste Italian, half cast-iron Greek, based on the Choragic Monument of Lysicrates, that was the true realization of his "Tower dedicated to meditation." There, on Lansdown, his life could be orderly, rich, and refined: a ride each morning up a picturesque strip garden, then a time to arrange flowers, enjoy his art treasures and survey the wide landscape, before another calm return, escorted by his grooms, to a late breakfast.

The strip garden was, in effect, a linear park of eclectic delights including a Romanesque-style gateway and an Italianate cottage. It offered widening views over a landscape of green hills while preserving anyone riding along it from the public gaze by underpass tunnels, quarry gardens, and grottoes. Old Vincent, Beckford's devoted gardener, persuaded an arboretum of exotic foreign conifers to grow on what had been bare hillside; scented herbs flowered in sheltered folds of land, and a dripping wall of ferns rose above the longest grotto.

From 1827 until the end of his life, Beckford's first duty each morning on arriving at his new Lansdown Tower was to climb to its plate-glass belvedere and enjoy a view of six counties and the Bristol Channel. Then he would rearrange his treasures in rooms draped in his favorite purple and scarlet cloths, their floors equally oppressive with Turkish carpets. After a brief phase of neoclassical furnishings he had ordered Goodridge to design new furniture and cabinets with a motif of round arches. Ahead of his time as usual, he was assisting in the evolution of the decorative style of the Victorians. Pleased by the rich gloom, he had his house down on Lansdown Crescent draped in the same colors.

This introverted period of Beckford's life was interrupted in 1832 with the arrival of a book, *Contarini Fleming: A Psychological Autobiography*, the latest romantic novel written by the young Benjamin Disraeli, who would soon become a successful politician, the greatest and most improbable Conservative Prime Minister of Britain's nineteenth century, and the cunning flatterer who persuaded Queen Victoria, reluctantly, to become Empress of India. At this time Disraeli was no more than an up-and-coming writer of flashy romantic novels, written in an aureate prose curiously like Beckford's own style, as if the younger man had consciously modeled himself on the older. A chain-smoking, high-camp dandy with greasy curls, a sharp wit, and an indeterminate sexual identity, Disraeli had sent Beckford the book because, or so he told his sister, "I like to do astonishing things."[72] Certainly Beckford was astonished, as *Contarini* was very close to being his own biography. Its hero, an aristocrat with a politician father, began by falling in love with a young boy, then traveled to Geneva and Italy, wrote a sensational first novel, married in haste a girl who died tragically early, and then climaxed a life of adventure by building, in Naples not Bath, a tower a mere five feet higher than that on Lansdown. "Here," the Contarini-Disraeli-Beckford composite concluded, "let me pass my life in the study and the creation of the Beautiful."[73]

Beckford was not simply astonished, he was delighted. This was recognition at last and from a fellow spirit. Now he too must not only study in his tower, but create "the Beautiful." When Disraeli followed up with a second present, a piece of marble from the Parthenon with a note—"I think it very unfair that I shd. hear of (the *great*) Beckford only from my friends, and that I am not permitted personally to express to him how very much he has obliged—Disraeli"[74]—Beckford was completely won over, and a meeting between hero and hero worshipper was swiftly arranged. It took place during a performance of Rossini's *Semiramide* at London's King's Theatre. "He amused me very much," Disraeli wrote to his sister Sarah, "Beckford's feeling for the fine arts is beyond all conception. His sight is marvellous; he can detect without a glass a picture that has been painted over; and he is a perfect musician, deciding on the merits of an Opera by reading the score."[75]

The admiration was mutual. Beckford's letter of thanks for *Contarini Fleming* had been brief but rapturous: "How wildly original! How full of intense thought! How awakening! How delightful!"[76] So

delightful in fact that over the next three years Beckford would bring out his notebooks and publish two new books: *Italy; with Sketches of Spain and Portugal* (1834) and *Recollections of an Excursion to the Monasteries of Alcobaça and Batalha* (1835). On these his Victorian reputation as a writer of stature would be largely based. By simply living long enough he had evolved in a prime old age, not only into a Victorian writer, but, in the furnishings of his new tower and the art he was collecting, into an arbiter of eclectic Victorian taste: a remarkable cultural evolution in a man born in 1760, the first year of the reign of George III. Rococo, neoclassical, Gothic Revival, and Italianate, William Beckford had worked in all of them and now was opening up by his example the floodgates of nineteenth-century eclecticism with all its perils and adventures.

There was still one last, great tribute to be paid to his architectural daring and inspiration. Fonthill Abbey had fallen ignominiously, but its even wilder, nobler, and unlikely child would rise beside the Thames, though there is no record that Beckford ever registered this final honor. It was the British nation, not William Beckford, that had caught the Gothic infection. Without the legend of that astonishing structure high on a windy Wiltshire hillside and the images of it, exaggerated by a full third in the perspective of George Cattermole's illustrations for John Rutter's *Delineations of Fonthill Abbey*, it is unlikely that an educated public or the Building Committee of 1836 would ever have risked Charles Barry's proposals for a new Palace of Westminster. But the decision to go Gothic was taken, and, in a morally quite inappropriate and unintentional tribute to the memory of the profoundly undemocratic Beckford, the home of the nation's democratic institutions would rise from 1840 to 1860, with Fonthill's axis and a skyline of "roofs and towers, detached chapels and isolated spires," more memorably fantastic than anything the youthful Beckford had dreamed of that day he stood marveling at Batalha.

1. MS Beckford c.18, fol. 59. The majority of Beckford papers have been collected and deposited in the Bodleian Library, Oxford, Department of Western Manuscripts.

2. Robert Liston, British ambassador to Spain, reluctantly refused to present Beckford at the Spanish court. In neither his 1788 nor his 1834 accounts of his time in Madrid does Beckford claim a meeting with Charles III. "His library contained a *Book of Hours* in which he wrote that it was presented to him by the King on his leaving Spain. But such a statement from Beckford is not evidence" (Guy Chapman, *Beckford* [London: Jonathan Cape, 1937]: 221, n).

3. MS Beckford c.18, fol. 17.

4. Mrs Hervey to Beckford, 15 January 1790, scribbled footnote, MS Beckford c.32.

5. MS Beckford d.3, fol.23.

6. MS Beckford c.32, fol.89.

7. MS Beckford d.11, fols. 20–21.

8. Ibid., fol. 24.

9. Alexander Cozens, *A New Method of Assisting the Invention in Drawing original Compositions of Landscape* (London, n.d.).

10. MS Beckford e.1, fol.10.

11. William Beckford, *Biographical Memoirs of Extraordinary Painters, by the author of "Vathek"* (London: R. Bentley, 1834): 101–11. Beckford was still sufficiently pleased by his youthful writing to have it republished in his old age.

12. Salomon Gessner, *Rural Poems* (London, 1762); idem, *Select Poems*, translated by Ann Penny (London, 1762); idem, *Daphnis, a Poetical Pastoral Novel*, translated by Charlotte Butler (London, 1768). On a Grand Tour of 1780–81 Beckford took a copy of Gessner's *New Idylles*, translated by W. Hopper (London: S. Hooper, 1776).

13. MS Beckford c.29, fol. 1.

14. Ibid., fol. 2.

15. Ibid.

16. Ibid.

17. J. W. von Goethe, *The Sorrows of Werter*, translated by D. Malthus (London, 1779): letter 57.

18. There is considerable circumstantial evidence for Beckford's initiation into Freemasonry. William Beckford's great-uncle on his mother's side, James Hamilton, seventh Earl of Abercorn, was Grand Master of the first Grand Lodge of England. Freemasonry was introduced to Geneva by John Hamilton. George Hamilton was a Provincial Grand Master in Geneva. Beckford lived

with Col. Edward Hamilton at Geneva. Beckford was a close friend of the Hubers, and Jean Huber, Col. Hamilton's first cousin, was a prominent Freemason. When Beckford had been a few months in Geneva he began writing a story about initiation ceremonies of water and fire with tremendous revelations of mysteries about the nature of creation that never get explicitly related. His chosen companion for two years in Portugal and Spain, his personal physician, was Dr. Verdeil, a prominent Freemason and political activist who became Grand Master of the Grand Orient Lodge of the National Helvetique Roman. See Timothy Mowl, *William Beckford: Composing for Mozart* (London: John Murray, 1998): 59–61.

19. This would not be published in full. For a shortened version, see *The Vision, Liber veritatis, by William Beckford of Fonthill,* ed. with an introduction and notes by Guy Chapman (London: Constable and Company, 1930).

20. Ibid., p. 39.

21. MS Beckford c.48, fol. 59.

22. Ibid., fol. 61.

23. Beckford to Mrs Hervey, 1778 (rough copy), MS Beckford c.32. Also quoted in Lewis Melville, *The Life and Letters of William Beckford of Fonthill* (London, W. Heinemann, 1910): 55–56.

24. MS Beckford e.2, fol. 3.

25. MS Beckford c.35, fol. 85.

26. MS Beckford d.2, fol. 20.

27. Ibid., fol. 32.

28. MS Beckford c.32, fol. 107.

29. MS Beckford e.1, fol. 38.

30. Ibid., fol. 43.

31. Ibid., fol. 33.

32. Ibid., fol. 82.

33. MS Beckford c.47, fol. 1.

34. Ibid., fols. 6–7.

35. Goethe, *Sorrows of Werter* (1779): letter 35.

36. MS Beckford e.1, fol. 98.

37. Ibid., fol. 29.

38. Ibid., fols. 65–67.

39. MS Beckford c.14, fol. 4.

40. MS Beckford c.31, fol. 35.

41. Ibid., fol. 37.

42. Ibid., fol. 39.

43. Ibid., fol. 77.

44. *Il Tributo, A Pastoral Cantata from the original Italian of Sig. Girolamo Tonioli, performed September the 29th 1781 at Fonthill in the County of Wilts, on the celebration of the Birthday of William Beckford Esq.* (Salisbury, 1781): 6. Pacchierotti playing Philenus sang: "often have I heard, from his earliest days, the Mother thus instructs her excellent son: 'Suffer me, my dear Son, to point out to you your chief Good . . . in vain does Man pretend to conceal his Actions from the Eye of Heaven'."

45. Letter with no addressee, dated 11 November 1781, MS Beckford c.14.

46. Translated from the French of a draft letter to Countess Rosenberg, quoted in Boyd Alexander, *England's Wealthiest Son* (London: Centaur, 1962): 265.

47. Draft letter written by Beckford on the flyleaf of Waagen's *Works of Art and Artists in England,* quoted in Chapman, *Beckford* (1937): 105. There are other versions of this event, all written around 1835.

48. Fair copy of a letter to Georgina Seymour, dated 17 March 1782, MS Beckford c.18.

49. MS Beckford c.35, fol. 7.

50. MS Beckford e.2, fols. 43–44.

51. MS Beckford e.1, fol. 91.

52. *Morning Herald*, 8 December 1784, Bath City Library.

53. MS Beckford c.37, fol. 15.

54. *The Journal of William Beckford in Portugal and Spain 1787–1788*, ed. with an introd. and notes by Boyd Alexander (London: Hart-Davis, 1954): 62.

55. Ibid., p. 69.

56. Ibid.

57. Ibid., p. 241.

58. Ibid., p. 242.

59. Ibid., p. 208.

60. MS Beckford d.10, fol. 4.

61. William Beckford, *Recollections of an Excursion to the Monasteries of Alcobaça and Batalha* (Philadelphia: Carey, Lea and Blanchard, 1835): 107.

62. *Bath Journal*, 23 January 1797, Bath City Library.

63. *Life at Fonthill, 1807–1822, with interludes in Paris and London, from the correspondence of William Beckford*, trans. and ed. Boyd Alexander (London, R. Hart-Davis, 1957): 97.

64. Ibid., p. 81.

65. Ibid., pp. 173–228.

66. Ibid., p. 152.

67. Ibid., p. 202.

68. Ibid., p. 305.

69. Ibid., p. 213.

70. Ibid., p. 218.

71. Ibid., p. 183.

72. Disraeli to Sarah Disraeli, 26 May 1832 (John Matthews, ed., *Benjamin Disraeli Letters*, vol. 1, *1815–1834*, ed. J. A. W. Gunn [University of Toronto Press, 1982]: 280, letter 193).

73. Benjamin Disraeli, *Contarini Fleming: A Psychological Romance* (London, 1927): 363.

74. Disraeli to Sarah Disraeli, n. d., (*Letters*, vol. 1 [1982]: 410, letter 327).

75. Disraeli to Sarah Disraeli, 16 June 1834 (ibid., p. 411, letter 329).

76. Quoted by Disraeli in a letter to Sarah Disraeli, 26 May 1832, (ibid., p. 280, letter 193).

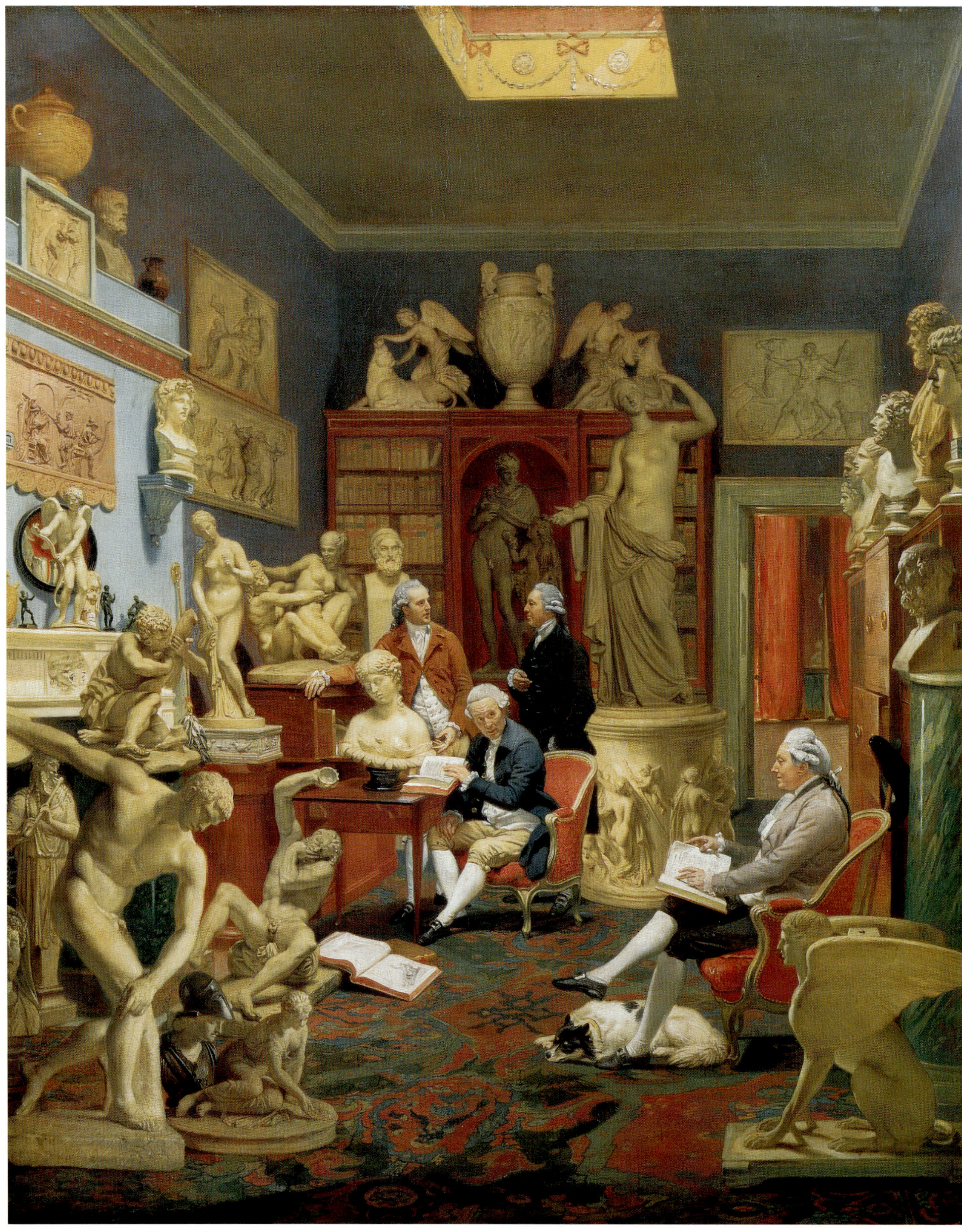

Fig. 2-1. Johann Zoffany. *Charles Towneley in his Library at 7 Park Street, Westminster*, 1781–83. Oil on canvas. Depicted are antiquarians and collectors who influenced Beckford, Soane, and Hope: Charles Towneley (seated, right), "Baron" d'Hancarville (seated, center), Thomas Astle (standing, center), and the Honorable Charles Grenville, nephew of Sir William Hamilton, Beckford's cousin and friend. Towneley Hall Art Gallery and Museum, Burnley.

Chapter II

BECKFORD, SOANE, AND HOPE
The Psychology of the Collector

David Watkin

It is customary to consider William Beckford as a unique and exotic creature, a brilliant but bizarre eccentric who occupied a private fantasy world insulated from contemporary society and culture. The reality is very different: parallels are offered by other collectors and designers who were his near contemporaries (fig. 2-1), and especially John Soane and Thomas Hope. Like Beckford, all were outsiders in some ways, facing real or imaginary opposition. Beckford suffered years of social isolation after the Powderham scandal. Soane believed that he had been the victim of professional persecution throughout his architectural career. Hope, the ugly opinionated Dutchman who told the English how to design their "household furniture," was ostracized by the Royal Academicians for behavior that they found presumptuous. All three sought escape in the private self-contemplation characteristic of the obsessive collector. Beckford, Soane, and Hope lived in houses that they themselves wholly or largely designed, which were, in effect, museums rather than settings for domestic sociability.

The Enlightenment Inheritance

These creative form-givers experienced varieties of alienation, but a contributing factor—the trauma experienced by men of taste at finding themselves at war with France, a country that they regarded as the most civilized in Europe—has often been overlooked in accounts of British society and culture in the late eighteenth and early nineteenth centuries. That men with backgrounds as varied as Hope, Beckford, and Soane admired Napoléon as a romantic hero and artistic patron was merely one disquieting aspect of a world in which their "hero" had assembled an army of 80,000 French troops at Boulogne ready to invade England.

Beckford, Soane, and Hope—all well-known to each other and serious figures intellectually—were united in their cultural identification with eighteenth-century France, in particular with the Enlightenment belief in returning to the twin primary sources (reason and nature), as well as in extending sympathy to non-European cul-

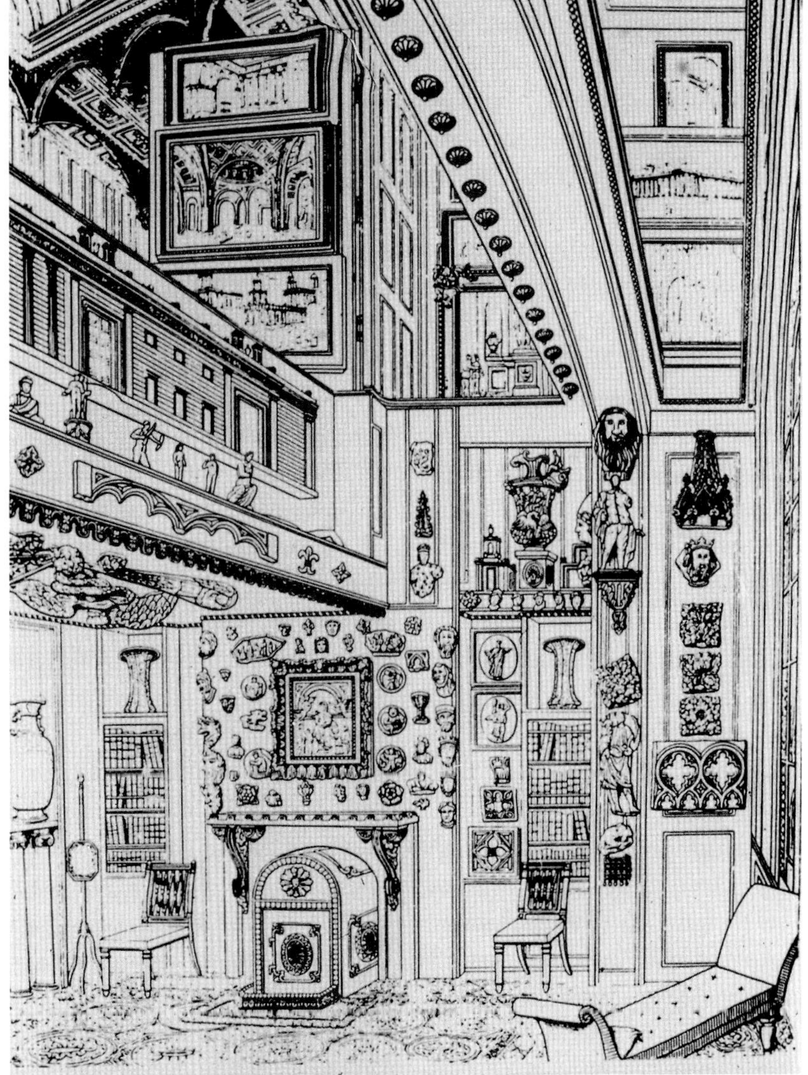

Fig. 2-2. Monk's Parlour and picture room, 13 Lincoln's Inn Fields; designed by John Soane, 1824. From John Britton, *The Union of Architecture, Sculpture and Painting* (London, 1827). Trustees of Sir John Soane's Museum, London.

ture. This last is expressed in the oriental novels by Beckford (*Vathek*) and Hope (*Anastasius*). Soane's admiration of *Vathek* is evident in his account of the Monk's Ruins at Lincoln's Inn Fields where he refers to the "inimitable humour by the author of 'Vathek'."[1] Hope owned a copy of the first edition of *Vathek* of 1786, as well as the French translation of 1816. *Vathek* and *Anastasius* were both originally written in French, suggesting the international character of Enlightenment Europe and the cultural dominance of France. The pan-European character of Enlightenment culture meant that the Anglican church was to exercise little appeal for men such as Beckford, Soane, and Hope. Hope largely abandoned Christianity for deism, while his posthumously published book, *An Essay on the Origin and Prospects of Man* (1831), containing a proto-Darwinian view of evolution, was suppressed by his executors as latitudinarian. Hope was intrigued by Islam, while Beckford and Soane were familiar with Freemasonry, which, as the religion of the Enlightenment in continental Europe, was seen as a survival of the religion of antiquity. Roman Catholicism exercised a powerful appeal to Beckford, partly because the English establishment, which had been responsible for his persecution, so strongly disapproved of it, and partly because it was an historical romantic force beyond contemporary Protestantism. Accordingly, he became "abbot" of Fonthill, while Soane similarly created a reclusive monk called "Padre Giovanni" with whom he identified emotionally. For this fictive monk he created, only half ironically, a cell or "monk's parlour" in the crypt of his house and museum in Lincoln's Inn Fields, where he could withdraw from the real world into that of the imagination (fig. 2-2).

It has been claimed that in *Vathek*, "through the rich texture of oriental imagery . . . Beckford was in fact exploring deeply emotional themes and was casting into dramatic form his feeling of rebellion against the adult world of respectability and convention."[2] Thomas Hope's interest in Islam is clear from *Anastasius: Memoirs of a Greek*, written at the close of the eighteenth century, a Byronic novel that Beckford admired.[3] In the guise of writing the life of Anastasius, a romantic scoundrel at odds with society, Hope painted a vivid portrait of the Ottoman Empire on the verge of collapse. Well-qualified to write a descriptive account of life, manners, politics, and architecture in that empire, Hope understood that, though it included Turks, Greeks, Arabs, Armenians, Kurds, and Jews, its power structure was so fluid that anyone, regardless of origin, could rise within it, provided he was prepared to adopt the Muslim faith—as Hope's Anastasius does. The biggest dividing point in the empire as portrayed in Hope's novel was thus not racial but religious: the distinctions between Christians and Muslims. Anastasius was married three times, had two mistresses and two illegitimate children, and died at the age of thirty-five, exhausted, a condition to which most readers are reduced by the end of the book.

Beckford, Soane, and Hope also shared the complex psychology of the collector, which provides a clue to understanding their complicated personalities. Interior design and furnishing before the eighteenth century had been largely created for kings and princes as an

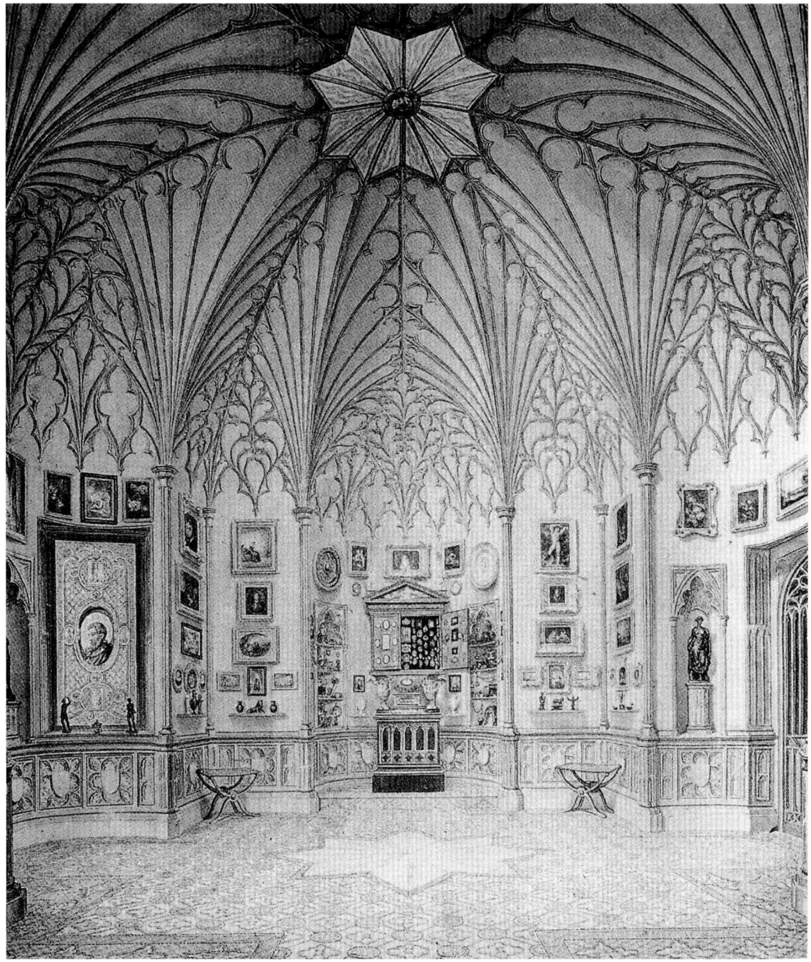

Fig. 2-3. Edward Edwards. The Tribuna or Round Room at Strawberry Hill, 1774–80. Watercolor. Room designed by John Chute and Horace Walpole, ca. 1759. The Lewis Walpole Library, Yale University, New Haven.

expression of the magnificence of the state and the reality of power. By contrast, as an educated and wealthy middle class developed in early-eighteenth-century England, the domestic interior and its furnishings became expressions of the personality of an individual, often a woman. The flowering of this new sensibility can be seen in the intensely personal interiors of Hope, Soane, and Beckford, none of whom was of aristocratic birth and all of whom had inherited commercial wealth in the 1780s, enabling them to indulge their visual passions by collecting and by creating personal settings of immense aesthetic individuality.

The father figure of these men was Horace Walpole, who created Strawberry Hill as a portrait of his personality, and commissioned watercolors of its interiors which are among the earliest records of their kind (fig. 2-3). Soane and Hope followed by writing illustrated accounts of their houses: Soane's *Plans, Elevations and Views of Pitzhanger Manor-House* (1802) was probably the first book by an

English architect on his own house. Five years later Hope issued an illustrated account of his mansion in Duchess Street, *Household Furniture and Interior Decoration Executed from Designs by Thomas Hope* (1807), copies of which both Beckford and Soane owned. Beckford actively encouraged the publication of three finely illustrated books on Fonthill Abbey in 1822–23, two by John Rutter and one by John Britton. It has been suggested that, "If the text of Rutter's *Delineations* was not actually dictated by Beckford, it certainly represents his views very closely."[4] Britton followed his book on Fonthill with *The Union of Architecture, Sculpture and Painting . . . with descriptive accounts of the House and Galleries of Sir John Soane* (1827), while Soane produced his own elaborate monograph on the museum in 1830, revising it in 1832 and 1835–36. Printing this book privately, he sent unsolicited copies to numerous men of distinction and influence in the arts. Hope, meanwhile, owned Britton's *Fonthill Abbey* (1823), as well as two copies of Britton's book on the Soane Museum.

Recalling biographies of living persons, these monographs on houses in which the new emphasis was on interior design and its promotion through publication, were accompanied by the birth of the confessional novel. Both Goethe's *Sorrows of Werther* (1774) and Rousseau's *Confessions* (1781–88) were admired by Beckford and Soane. The libraries of Hope and Soane also contained copies of Bernadin de Saint-Pierre's *Paul et Virginie* (1788), a Rousseau-esque image of idyllic childhood on a tropical island. Napoléon admired Goethe's *Werther*, choosing to discuss it with the author when he met him. Napoléon also honored Bernadin with decorations and a pension, believing that he spoke "the language of the soul."

Beckford, Soane, and Hope were all bibliophiles who formed important libraries of architecture, archaeology, and travel[5]; each built more than one house and private museum for himself; each was a creature of the Enlightenment, at home in the world of the eighteenth-century philosophes. Hope and Soane owned Diderot's *Encyclopédie*; Beckford met Voltaire, while Soane read his work assiduously, and Hope owned Voltaire's writings in seventy-two volumes and those of Rousseau in thirty-eight. Beckford and Soane identified with Rousseau as the victim of organized persecution and as a justification for self-obsession; psychologically, both suffered from persecution, real in Beckford's case, largely imaginary in Soane's. Alain-René Le Sage's picaresque novel of the failings and absurdities of human nature, *Gil Blas* (4 volumes, 1715–35), was a favorite of Beckford and Soane who seem to have regarded Gil as an alter ego.

Persecution and Self-regard

In a draft of his autobiographical novel, *L'Esplendente* (ca. 1780), Beckford described the duc d'Arcas, patron of the arts, as a character with whom both he and Soane could identify: an architect and collector who had been forced into retreat as a result of being "disliked and dreaded."[6] This is paralleled in a manuscript that Soane drafted as a personal and explosive history of his own house and museum in Lincoln's Inn Fields. It was written in August and September 1812 at

one of the numerous moments in his career when he was weighed down by a sense of failure and persecution. This mood was related to his disastrous relationship with his sons, the suspension of his lectures at the Royal Academy, and the attack on the design of his own house by William Kinnard, the district surveyor. Even while the house was being built, Soane imagined it as a future ruin inspected by visitors speculating on its function—as a convent, the home of a magician, or an architectural museum. He described himself as someone who "had raised a nest of wasps about him sufficient to sting the strongest man to death," and added that "Melancholy, brooding constantly over an accumulation of evils [had] brought him to a state little short of mental derangement. . . . They smote his rock and he fell as many had done before him and died, as was generally believed, of a broken heart."[7]

Soane's sense of himself as a tragic, persecuted genius was echoed, with far more justification, by Beckford who chose to live in complete isolation at Fonthill for nearly thirty years, some time after the scandal at Powderham Castle in 1784. The accusation that at the age of twenty-four he had a sexual liaison with the sixteen-year-old William Courtenay was doubtless engineered and was certainly publicized by his political enemy, Lord Loughborough, whose wife seems to have been in love with Beckford. Loughborough could think of no better way of punishing both his wife and Beckford than by promulgating this accusation. The fact that there was no proof against Beckford is suggested by Loughborough's not taking him to court where, if found guilty, he could have been sentenced to death.

Though spared this ordeal, Beckford instantly lost hope of obtaining the title, Lord Beckford of Fonthill, which he had virtually been promised earlier in 1784 by the Lord Chancellor, Lord Thurlow. Moreover, no book would ever again appear under Beckford's name, hence the publication of his books after *Vathek* (1786) as "by the author of Vathek."[8] Worse, for the rest of his life he not only bore the grievance of having been unjustly accused and condemned without a hearing, but was also blamed publicly for the death of his beloved wife in 1786. Once again, there is a striking emotional similarity with Soane who managed to convince himself that his wife had been all but murdered by the behavior of their younger son, George. This conviction was a result of the vicious attacks on Soane's architecture and personality that George published anonymously in *The Champion* in 1815. When Soane's wife died within weeks of their publication, Soane described them as "Death Blows." Not that he was unfamiliar with such criticism. *The Modern Goth* (1796) had condemned his "pilasters scor'd like loins of pork," and there was a sustained attack on his "Sixth or Boetian Order of Architecture" in *Knight's Quarterly Magazine* (1824).[9]

The connections between Beckford and Hope include the facts that Beckford's illegitimate brother John had been trained in the counting house of Hope and Company in Amsterdam and that Hope courted Beckford's daughter Susan unsuccessfully in 1805–6. Hope, also like Beckford, grew increasingly isolated from his peers. In 1804 he had been struck off the list of those invited to the annual Royal Academy dinner for two reasons. Firstly, the Academicians were

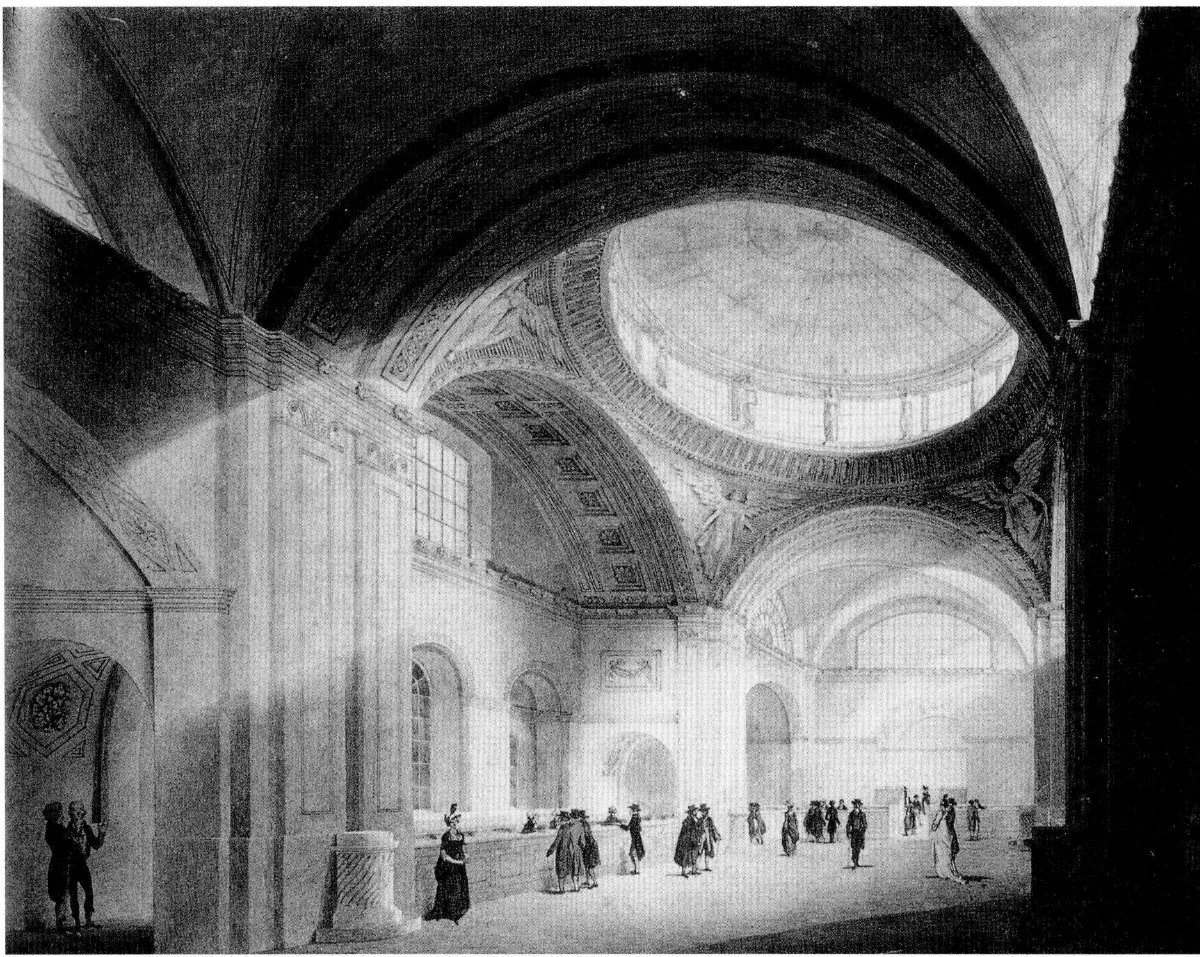

Fig. 2-4. John Michael Gandy. Sketch of the Consols Transfer Office, Bank of England; designed by John Soane, 1798. Trustees of Sir John Soane's Museum, London.

annoyed by the tickets Hope had sent them to view his house, feeling they had been invited "not to meet company but as professional men to publish his fine place."[10] Secondly, Hope had attacked James Wyatt, who would shortly become president of the Royal Academy, in a pamphlet, *Observations on the Plans . . . for Downing College* (1804). It is an extraordinary coincidence that just four years later Soane should also have been ostracized by the Royal Academy for attacking a work by a living architect—Covent Garden Theatre, built by Robert Smirke, whose father was a leading Academician. In each case the opposition was partly provoked by the difficult characters of the two men: Hope was the short unattractive Dutchman, and Soane the prickly paranoid son of a bricklayer.

As wounded figures, Soane and Beckford seem in particular to have been made for each other. Both were indebted to the confessional writings of Rousseau, the popularity of which is insufficiently appreciated in accounts of British eighteenth-century patrons, architects, and collectors. Beckford's Rousseau-esque belief in childhood, for example, is expressed in the emotional pederasty of his adoration of the eleven-year-old William ("Kitty") Courtenay: "how firmly am I resolved to be a Child for ever!,"[11] he wrote at the age of twenty to Alexander Cozens. The twelve-foot-high wall with which he surrounded Fonthill was not only to keep out the prying eyes of those who had ostracized him after the Powderham scandal, but also to prevent others from hunting and shooting on his land. Beckford's sentimental affection for youth was associated with his passion for untrammeled nature. "Early in life," he explained, "I gave up shooting because I consider we have no right to murder animals for sport. I am fond of animals. The birds in the plantations at Fonthill seemed to know me—they continued their songs as I rode close to them—the very hares grew bold."[12] He was able to express the notion of genius, imagination, humanitarianism, and spiritual enlargement, in the deep, secluded valley of Fonthill where he re-created Rousseau's wild Elysium.

In their different ways, Beckford and Soane responded to Rousseau's disturbing doctrines, which celebrated the primitive, passionate nature of the persecuted, suspicious individual, warring with convention.[13] "The heart," Beckford declaimed, "the heart is everything."[14] As Rousseau, the romantic egoist, began his *Confessions* with the claim that, "I dare to believe I am not made like anyone else who exists,"[15] so the nineteen-year-old Beckford wrote a letter to Alexander Cozens in December 1779, ending with the question, "Am I not the strangest of Beings?"[16] Moreover, as Soane sketched Rousseau's tomb at Ermenonville in one of his copies of Rousseau's *Confessions*,[17] so Beckford owned numerous editions of Rousseau's works, including *A Tour in France with Rhapsody composed at the Tomb of Rousseau* (1789).[18]

After Rousseau, Goethe was the most important figure in the history of the new confessional literature of the eighteenth century, which celebrated the romantic hero driven through self-contemplation and despair to the point of suicide. Beckford and Soane both owned copies of Goethe's immensely influential novel, *Die Leiden des jungen Werthers*, in its English translation, *The Sorrows of Werter* (1780). Beckford wrote to a friend: "There is a Book called the Sorrows of Werter; read it and tell me if every Line is not resplendent with Genius."[19] Soane, meanwhile, gave a copy of the book to Lady Elizabeth Yorke, for whose husband, Philip Yorke, he had designed the primitive Rousseau-esque dairy at Hammels, Hertfordshire, in 1783.

By a curious coincidence, both Beckford and Soane noted in 1818 the suicide of the legal and political reformer, Sir Samuel Romilly, an important early follower of Rousseau.[20] Romilly had been despondent over his wife's death in November 1818. Beckford's attitude toward Romilly was characteristically ambiguous because, though he shared some of Romilly's radical attitudes, he opposed his advocacy of the abolition of slavery which would have adversely affected Beckford's sugar plantations. "No one ever sold justice more than this 'honest' man," Beckford wrote ironically of him, "—this excellent Jacobin, this good Calvinist, this perfect Genevan."[21] To Soane, at the same time, Romilly was a mirror image of himself as a man cast into despair by the death of his wife. Soane drew this analogy in notes made in the course of copying out passages from Rousseau's *Confessions* in November 1818, exactly three years after his own wife's death.

"THE POETRY OF ARCHITECTURE"

The Gothic Fonthill, although the most famous, was not the only expression of Beckford's architectural tastes. Throughout his career he envisaged an architecture of light, shadow, and mystery, independent of style, frequently subterranean and incorporating mirror-glass. This vision corresponds closely to the poetry of architecture, the "*lumière*

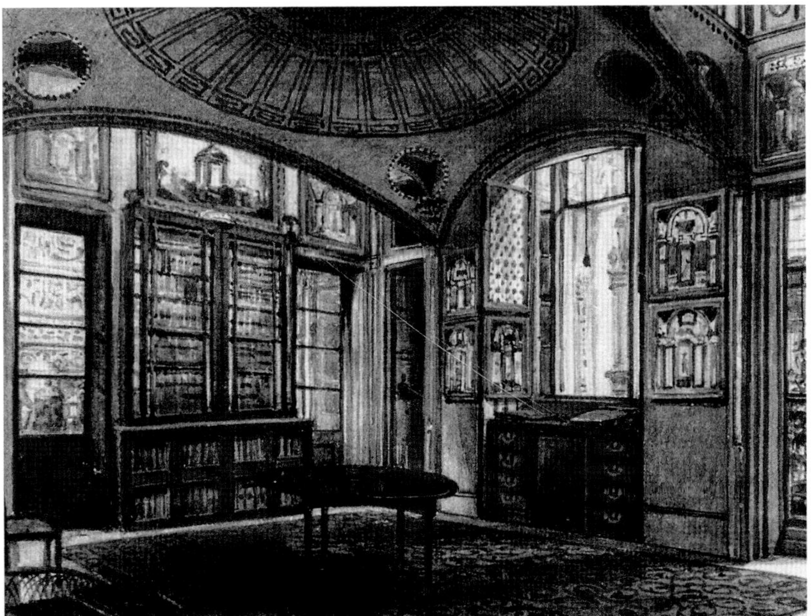

Fig. 2-5. Breakfast Parlour, 13 Lincoln's Inn Fields; designed by John Soane, 1812–13. Drawn in 1825. Trustees of Sir John Soane's Museum, London.

mystérieuse," which Soane found adumbrated in *Le Génie de l'architecture: ou l'analogie de cet art avec nos sensations* (1780), by Le Camus de Mézières, a key work of French theory that Soane translated for himself.[22] The lavish celebrations for Beckford's coming-of-age at Fonthill Splendens struck a chord within Beckford. Fonthill, he claimed, "was admirably calculated for the celebration of the mysteries." He explained how, "under the direction of Loutherbourg, himself a mystagogue . . . [a] world of decorated chambers . . . [was bathed in] that strange, necromantic light which Loutherbourg had thrown over what absolutely appeared a realm of Fairy, or rather, perhaps, a Demon Temple deep beneath the earth set apart for tremendous mysteries."[23] Later, when visiting the convent of Mafra in Portugal in 1787, Beckford explained how, "It was growing dark, and the numerable tapers burning before the altars and in every part of the church, [seemed] to diffuse a mysterious light."[24]

In his romantic tale of 1777, *The Long Story*,[25] Beckford had earlier described a subterranean palace with

> stately halls decorated with colonnades of slender pillars inconceivably striking. The lesser order of pillars was formed of a clear white crystalisation, exquisitely beautiful. They supported neither frieze or cornice, nor any ornament in the least degree consistent with the rules of architecture we observe on the surface of the earth.[26]

Anticipating the floating and disembodied vaulted interiors that Soane began designing at the Bank of England over twenty years later (fig. 2-4), Beckford also described "an immensely spacious concave, unsupported by any visible cause and glowing with a refulgence."[27] This mood was maintained in *Vathek*, Beckford's essay in Burkean sublimity and beauty, owing much to the sensationalist psychology of Locke which Beckford studied from a early age. Beckford wrote about the subterranean palace of the Devil, with domed and vaulted ceilings, "rows of columns and arcades, which gradually diminished, till they terminated in a point radiant as the sun . . . halls and galleries, that opened on the right hand and left; which were all illuminated by torches and braziers." Nearby was a mausoleum in the form of "a hall of great extent and covered with a lofty dome. . . . A funereal gloom prevailed over the whole scene."[28]

As early as December 1779, Beckford envisaged a room that seems strangely close to the domed and mirrored Breakfast Parlour which Soane created over thirty years later at Lincoln's Inn Fields (fig. 2-5). "Think," Beckford wrote, "how we should exult at finding ourselves in arched Chambers glowing with yellow light—amidst Vases formed in another Hemisphere—and Cabalistic Mirrors where Futurity is unveiled."[29] A few years later Beckford seems to anticipate Soane's acquisition of the sarcophagus of Pharaoh Seti I. In January 1783, Beckford wrote to William Hamilton, "You cannot imagine the solemn appearance of the Hall [at Fonthill Splendens] with its expiring Lamps towards midnight. I often fancy myself in the Catacombs of Egypt and expect to stumble over a Mummy."[30]

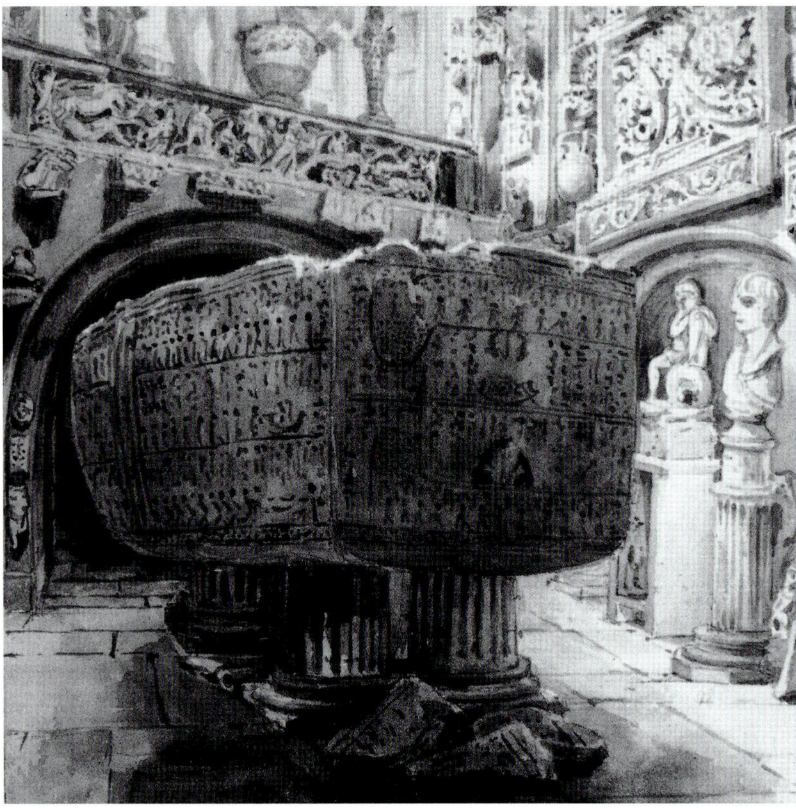

Fig. 2-6. Sarcophagus of Seti I in the crypt at 13 Lincoln's Inn Fields, 1825. Trustees of Sir John Soane's Museum, London, "Sketches and Drawings," vol. 82/46.

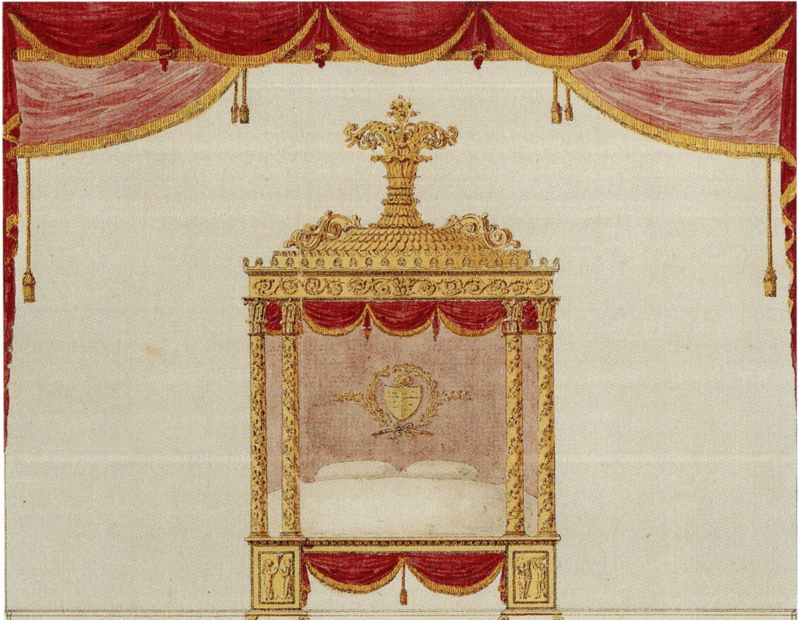

Fig. 2-7. John Soane. Design for the state bed at Fonthill House, 1788. Watercolor. The Bodleian Library, University of Oxford, MS Beckford c.84, fol. 122r.

Soane acquired the prize of his collection in 1825 and celebrated it with a series of remarkable evening parties.[31] Lit with numerous lamps, some inside the sarcophagus of Seti I, which Soane housed,

characteristically, in the crypt of his museum (fig. 2-6), the scene must have recalled Joseph Gandy's visionary painting, *The Tomb of Merlin* (1815), which Gandy offered to Soane in 1816. Beckford, meanwhile, had even earlier, in November 1780, written to Alexander Cozens from Naples imagining a future with him in which, "Every month we shall invent some new Ornament for our Apartments and add some exotic rarity to its treasures . . . ; sometimes we shall inhabit . . . our vast range of solemn subterraneous Chambers visible by the glow of Lamps and filled with Cabalistic images."[32]

Staying with his cousin Sir William Hamilton at Naples in 1780, Beckford visited the Temple of Isis at Pompeii, of which Soane had made drawings on his visit a couple of years before. Beckford described the "covered cloister," "the pediment of the chapel [sic] with a symbolical vase in relief; ornaments in stucco on the front of the main building, consisting of the lotus, the sistrum, representations of gods, Harpocrates, Anubis, and other objects of Egyptian worship."[33]

SOANE AND FONTHILL SPLENDENS

Between the composition of *Vathek* and the design of Soane's early interiors at the Bank of England, Beckford had commissioned Soane to transform a seventy-foot-long corridor on the second floor at Fonthill Splendens into a top-lit, picture gallery. Soane was chosen on a visit that Beckford made to Fonthill in January 1787, before leaving in March for his long stay in Spain and Portugal. Lit from two shallow, oval domes with ribbed pendentives, the gallery was a key design in Soane's early career, forming an important link between the similar Guildhall Council Chamber of 1778 by his master, George Dance, and Soane's Yellow Drawing Room at Wimpole of 1791. Soane visited Fonthill in April 1787, taking drawings of the gallery with him[34] which he showed to Beckford's mother in London in the following month.[35] He was intending to incorporate plaster reliefs of the ancient Roman wreathed eagle at SS Apostoli in Rome, with which he was also to adorn the front of Pitzhanger Manor.

It has recently been shown that Soane's gallery was not executed.[36] Beckford's idea for hanging prints of the Vatican logge frescoes in the gallery, however, was probably adopted, for John Britton described in 1801 that an adjacent room was "decorated with illuminated prints from the Loggias of Rome, coloured by Francesco Pannini in a very superior manner, and also [with] original drawings of the cielings [sic] and ornaments still remaining amongst the ruins on the Palatine."[37] In the Tapestry Room on the *piano nobile*, Soane designed the decoration for the apses of two niches which he filled with 140 "pannels of mosaic work run in with double squares, Vitruvian scrolls, flowers, and water-leaves."[38] He also designed a chimneypiece adorned with cornucopia for the same room which was executed by Thomas Banks in June 1787.[39] Soane employed Banks for various chimneypieces at Fonthill between 1787 and 1792, and for the Bank of England in 1790. Soane designed another chimneypiece for the southeast parlor, and in 1788 a sumptuous state bed (fig. 2-7).[40] In the form of a *lit-en-alcove*, both the bed and the arch above it are girt with scarlet hangings trimmed with gold fringes. At the foot, two pairs of gilded foliate columns with lotus capitals support a vast domical superstructure inspired by the Choragic Monument of Lysicrates as published in James Stuart and Nicholas Revett's *Antiquities of Athens* (1762). It is a piece of archaeological spectacle, untypical of Soane who was not noted as a furniture designer but who here responded to Beckford's flamboyant side. An alternative, unexecuted design, more Soanean, had an octagonal form based on the Tower of the Winds in Athens.

Soane's work at Fonthill Splendens was executed by his old friend Edward Foxhall, a fellow student at the Royal Academy. A decorator, carver, furniture-maker, and purveyor of pictures, furniture, and fittings, Foxhall was subsequently employed by Beckford at Fonthill Abbey. Soane's master mason at Fonthill Splendens, James Nelson, also worked for him at the Bank of England and at Holwood, which he was remodeling for William Pitt the Younger.[41] Though Beckford would not have seen Soane's work at Fonthill Splendens until his return from his travels in October 1789, Soane had the advantage of seeing Beckford's picture collection. It must have made a deep impression on him as he was subsequently to make important purchases from it: when the contents of Fonthill Splendens were dispersed in 1802, he bought Hogarth's *Rake's Progress* which was then hanging in the second-floor corridor, the remodeling of which he had proposed in 1787. At the six-day sale at Fonthill Abbey in 1807, Soane bought a major work by Canaletto, known as "Venetian Scene."[42]

The House as Museum

After Beckford's collection, Hope's was one of the most important and influential ever assembled in Britain. Formed in the Napoleonic era (1795–1803), it was the last great British collection to be assembled on and from the soil of Italy. Soane's, by contrast, was formed in England, not shipped back from the Continent in the established manner of the Grand Tour.[43] Hope's mansion in Duchess Street, which he bought in 1799 and remodeled with galleries in 1800–1804, was not spatially interesting in disposition.[44] In contrast, if somewhat later (1808, 1812, and 1824), Soane created the spatially complex Soane Museum in Lincoln's Inn Fields, although in a plan of 1812 he was considering creating a series of rectangular galleries close to those of Hope, whose collection he admired as an example of Enlightenment civic virtue. He wrote to Hope in March 1804 to thank him for "the high gratification in viewing again some days since your collection," which he described as "a lasting monument of your civic spirit and classical taste." He added that he would be "happy on further occasions to avail myself of your kindness and taste."[45]

When Hope finished his house and opened it to the public in 1804, visitors would have been struck on arrival by Sir William Beechey's romantic portrait of Hope in Turkish dress, which hung on the staircase. Seeing one civilization through the eyes of another, this was an expression of Hope's vision of Greece as a living place. This cumulative effect was close to Soane, who was happy to mingle Egyptian, Greek, Indian, and Gothic objects.

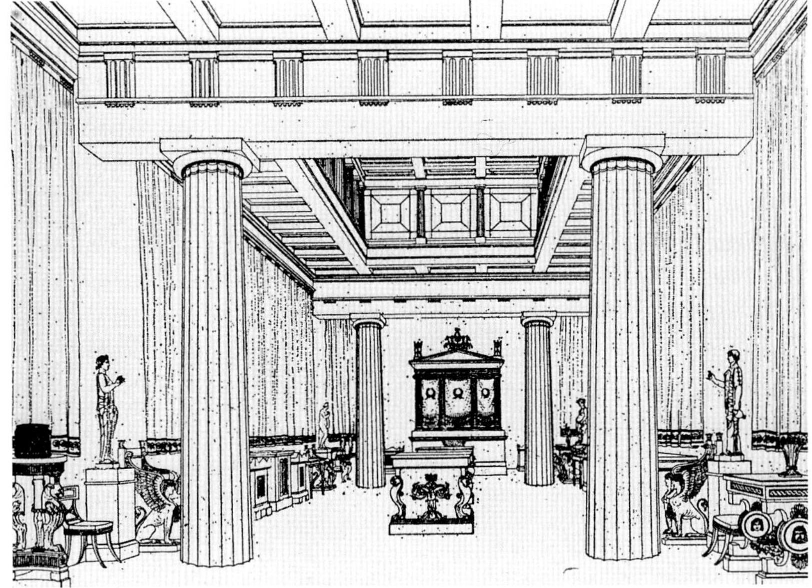

Fig. 2-8. Picture gallery, Duchess Street; designed by Thomas Hope, 1800–1804. Engraving by Edmund Aiken and George Dawe. From *Household Furniture and Interior Decoration executed from Designs by Thomas Hope* (London 1807).

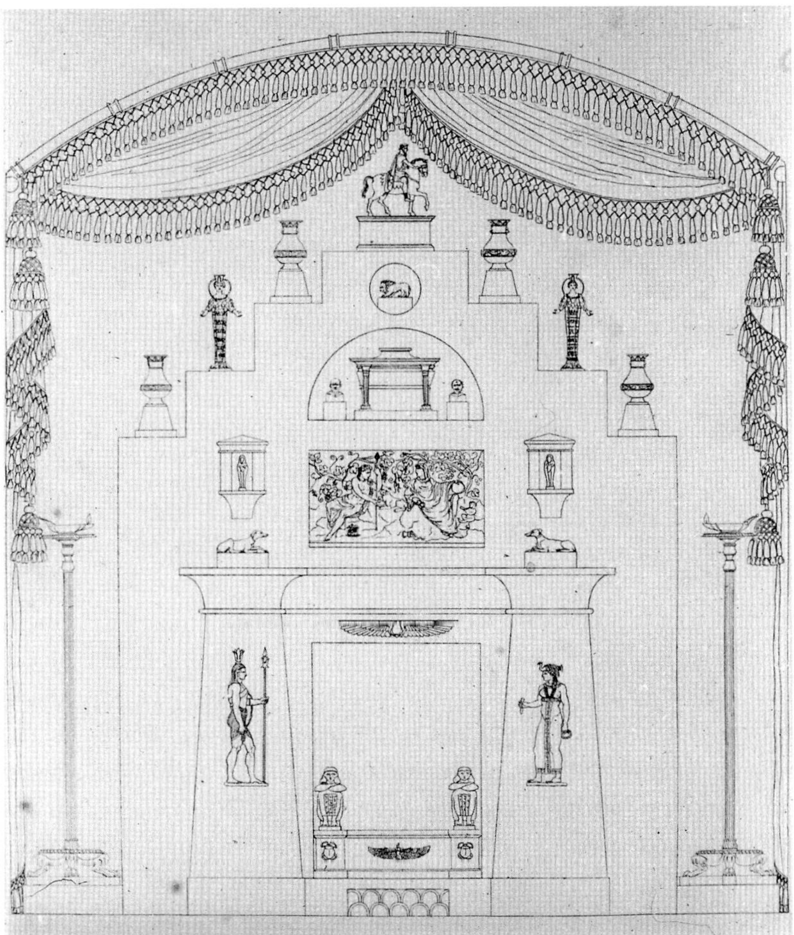

Fig. 2-9. The Lararium, Duchess Street; designed by Thomas Hope, 1800–1804. Engraving by Edmund Aiken and George Dawe. From *Household Furniture and Interior Decoration executed from Designs by Thomas Hope* (London 1807).

Hope conceived his picture gallery (fig. 2-8) as a kind of temple of the muses, symbolically guarded by statues of priestesses of Isis. Aware that the ancient Greeks intended art not for private but for public and religious display, Hope created a version of the Greek *mouseion*, the Greek term for a cult-center built for the cultivation and worship of the Muses of the arts and sciences, not necessarily a temple, but an open portico with an altar. Stressing the sacred character of his picture gallery, Hope explained that the inclusion of an organ, which he provided with a front in the form of a pedimented portico, "gives it the appearance of a sanctuary."[46] Here are parallels with Fonthill, a monastery dedicated no longer to God but to the arts, yet focused on the Chapel of Saint Anthony.

The Lararium (fig. 2-9), or room of the household gods, described by Hope as a "tabernacle . . . fitted up for the reception of a few Egyptian, Hindoo [sic], and Chinese idols and curiosities,"[47] contained objects representing the different religions of the world. These expressed the belief in the common origins of religious symbolism as explained in the writings of the scholar Pierre François Hugues, normally known as "baron d'Hancarville." Hope's objects included a pair of statues after the celebrated many-breasted Diana of Ephesus, of which Soane acquired a more important version. Hope said that the chimneypiece in "the shape of an Egyptian portico" was "placed against a back ground of looking-glass," thus recalling Soane's use of mirror in the Soane Museum. The room was roofed with bamboo lathes hung with "cotton drapery . . . in the form of a tent." This may have been inspired by A.-C. Quatremère de Quincy's opinion that the tent, along with the cavern and the hut, was one of the three principal types of primitive architecture,[48] a interpretation adopted by Soane in his Royal Academy lectures. Hope also pointed out that the ceiling beams in his statue gallery "imitate a light timber covering."

The elaborately iconographical decoration of Hope's Flaxman Room at Duchess Street and its furnishings referred to the religious symbolism of the ancients. This was inspired by the uncovery of the symbolical language of antiquity by scholars such as d'Hancarville, whom both Soane and Hope studied carefully. On either side of Flaxman's statue, *Aurora Abducting Cephalus at Dawn on Mount Ida*, were strange rarities preserved in glass showcases rather like relics of saints in a Catholic church. In one case was a male arm, long thought to be from a Lapith on one of the Parthenon metopes. Hope, unlike Soane, had been in Athens, so this fragment may have had a genuine Athenian provenance, though its whereabouts is now unknown. Hope unexpectedly displayed it as a counterpart to a stalactite from the grotto on the Greek island of Antiparos in the opposite showcase. This juxtaposition was clearly adopted to show the characteristic Enlightenment belief, which Soane shared, in the origin of Greek design in nature.

Beckford, Soane, and Hope are linked in their knowledge, unusual in England at that time, of the advanced architecture of Claude-Nicolas Ledoux, the most brilliant architect of late-eighteenth-century France. Hope owned engravings of Ledoux's Hôtel de Thélusson, while in 1784 Beckford visited Ledoux's atelier in Paris where he looked through the French architect's startling designs for public and private buildings, including the *barrières* and the visionary Ideal Town of Chaux. The catalogue of the sale of Beckford's library in 1882 contains a lot described as "M. Le Doux, plans des édifices, 54 plates, n.d.,"[49] which must have been part of Ledoux's visionary publication, *L'architecture considérée sous le rapport de l'art, des moeurs, et de la législation* (1804). One of the few other copies of this work in England in Beckford's lifetime was eagerly acquired by Soane on its publication in 1804. Soane annotated his copy briefly and made extensive notes on it,[50] clearly impressed by Ledoux's romantic and obscure prose, rich in Orphic and Freemasonic rhetoric, and outlining a speaking architecture of character and desire. Soane may have identified with the self-pitying, sentimental tone of a book largely written while Ledoux, who was a victim of persecution as much as both Beckford and Soane, had been in prison.

The links between Beckford, Ledoux, and Soane need to be set in the context of Soane's obsession with French architectural theory and practice of the Enlightenment, and Beckford's parallel devotion to the cultural and social life of Paris. After his first formative visit in 1777, Beckford spent much of the years between 1787 and 1793 in Paris, paying further extended visits in 1801–2 and 1814. He moved in an intellectual and social circle close to that of Ledoux, which included the painter and garden designer, Hubert Robert; the Comte de Buffon, son of the great naturalist; the financier, Jean-Joseph, Marquis de Laborde, creator from 1784 of Méréville, near Paris, one of the greatest Picturesque gardens in France; the literary hostess and writer, Madame Necker; and the Emperor Joseph II, a subscriber to Ledoux's book. From 1784 onward, one of Beckford's principal reasons for visiting Paris was to buy books and works of art.[51] Through the services of a Dutch dealer, he acquired porcelain from Sèvres, carpets for Fonthill Splendens from the Savonnerie factory, and neoclassical silver designed by Jean-Guillaume Moitte and made by Robert-Joseph Auguste, goldsmith to the king from 1778.[52]

Writing to Hamilton about Auguste in 1792, Beckford asked, "will your man ever be able to complete the Herculaneum drawings, a volume of which he sold me last summer? If he could, I might treat with him. Pray reserve a fine copy of your new work for me; I am continually asked when it will make its appearance."[53] The "new work," on Hamilton's vases, was *A Collection of Engravings from Ancient Vases* (1791), a copy of which Beckford, Hope, and Soane each acquired. From Auguste, Beckford acquired four ewers and, in 1788, a set of twelve dessert plates, while Lady Ann Hamilton recorded in 1803 that a statue of Saint Anthony of Padua on an altar at Fonthill Abbey "was surrounded by 36 wax lights in gold branches and candlesticks (f[ro]m) Auguste at Paris."[54] In all these activities, Beckford reveals himself as no Goth, but as an advanced classicist, buying and commissioning works from artists such as Auguste and Moitte, who were central figures in the development of the Empire style.

In a letter inviting Hamilton to stay with him in Paris in April 1791, written in a state of euphoria at the atmosphere of liberty then prevailing in the capital, Beckford explained that, "I have the pleasantest appts [sic] imaginable either in Paris or in the most beautiful part of the country near it." He tempted Hamilton further by explaining that, "The reign of grim Gothic prejudices is nearly over, & people begin to serve God and themselves in the manner they like best."[55] It is striking that Beckford should be ready to use "Gothic" as a term of abuse. On his continental travels, too, he enthused over classical buildings such as Palladio's Redentore in Venice, which he described as "a structure so simple and elegant, that I thought myself entering an antique temple."[56]

Freemasons and Symbols

Beckford's interest in hermeticism and in cabalistic signs was paralleled by the preoccupation of Hope and Soane with the symbolical language of ancient ornament. All three men, for example, were in touch with the arcane scholar, James Christie, who gave each of them a copy of his remarkable book, *Disquisition upon Etruscan Vases; displaying their probable connection with the shows at Eleusis, and the Chinese Feast of Lanterns* (1806). Beckford acquired two copies of this work, annotating one to draw attention to its somewhat risqué subject matter: "Is it not rather strange that such an acknowledged and exemplary a Purist as Mr. Christie should have given the public at large a free translation of these passages."[57] Hope and Soane owned Christie's *Essay on that Earliest Species of Idolatry, the Worship of the Elements* (1814), which Soane annotated, while Beckford, Soane, and Hope all owned copies of the rare and far more risqué work by Payne Knight, *An Account of the Remains of the Worship of Priapus . . . to which is added a Discourse on the Worship of Priapus and its connexion with the Mystic Theology of the Ancients* (1786).

Soane annotated his copy of Christie's *Essay on that Earliest Species of Idolatry*, a book that provided him with many explanations of ornament and symbolism. Beckford owned a book referred to in an inventory as *A Dissertation on the Eleusinian and Bacchic Mysteries*. This is probably to be identified with Christie's *Essays on the Mysteries of Eleusis* (1817) which Christie sent to Soane in 1817 and doubtless to Beckford. Christie subsequently wrote to Soane that Soane's lamplit reception for the sarcophagus of Seti I coincided with his own views that the paintings on Greek vases "were copied from transparent scenes" at occasions such as the Eleusinian mysteries.[58]

Both Soane and Hope owned d'Hancarville's *Recherches*, a work that Soane studied constantly, while Hope acknowledged d'Hancarville's *Vases* in the bibliography to *Household Furniture*.[59] When Hope wrote about his Vase Room at Duchess Street (fig. 2-10), he explained that his reading of his Greek vases was influenced by his study of d'Hancarville. Thus, in a "Room containing Greek fictile vases . . . [the] vases were all found in tombs . . . [and] relate chiefly to the Bacchanalian rites, which were partly connected with the representations of mystic death and regeneration." The terms on the cases were accordingly "surmounted with heads of the Indian or bearded Bacchus."[60] Hope's furniture and interiors were an early attempt to re-

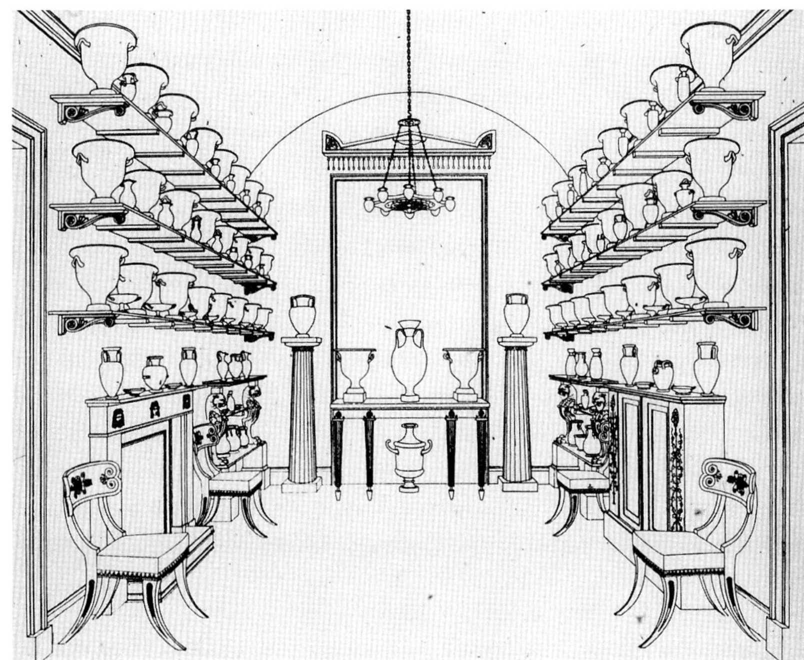

Fig. 2-10. The Vase Room, Duchess Street; designed by Thomas Hope, 1800–1804. Engraving by Edmund Aiken and George Dawe. From *Household Furniture and Interior Decoration executed from Designs by Thomas Hope* (London 1807).

create the kind of symbolical ornament along lines envisaged by d'Hancarville in his *Recherches*.

Both Beckford and Soane owned a strange work by Antoine Court de Gébelin, *Monde primitif, analysé et comparé avec le monde moderne, considéré dans son génie allégorique et dans les allégories auxquelles conduisit ce génie* (1773–84), which shed further light on this mysterious world of light and symbolism. Believing that symbolism and allegory were the keys to historical interpretation, Gébelin was preoccupied by the sublime horror and drama of initiatory rituals. Beckford and Soane were similarly intrigued by the ceremonies of initiation in Freemasonic ritual which were often seen in the eighteenth century as survivals from antiquity. Soane, of course, became an enthusiastic Freemason, while Beckford, after meeting Ledoux, who was in close touch with that world, accompanied the French architect in 1784 to the bizarre ceremonies of a secret society, linked to the Mesmerists and Freemasons. These took place in an unidentified château near Paris which Ledoux had dramatically remodeled for the purpose. Having renounced all right to knowledge of the locality and nature of the premises, Beckford was conducted there in a closed carriage. He left a lengthy account of his extraordinary experiences, describing a path of initiation from avenues of woodpiles like thatched cottages, through a salon with a coved ceiling "richly painted with mythological subjects," and designed by Ledoux, up a staircase reminding Beckford of the Scala Regia in the Vatican, and so into a tribune overlooking a chapel which was in darkness though "suddenly a stream of light, such as might be supposed to emanate from the tapers of an altar, shone forth through the perforations of a lofty screen of carved work."[61]

Beckford had been selected for the honor of this visit partly because he was thought to possess certain hermetic powers: he had, apparently, "mesmerized" a lion in the Jardin des Plantes, and charmed animals in the grounds of Fonthill. Moreover, the artist Jacques de Loutherbourg, who had staged Beckford's theatrical coming-of-age party at Fonthill, was known as a disciple and friend of Count Alessandro Cagliostro, the alchemist and forger, and eventually claimed powers of healing and prophecy.[62] Here, too, Soane joins the strange web of connections that links him to Beckford, for he too was a friend of Loutherbourg who was, in turn, a friend of Soane's patron, Sir Francis Bourgeois. Loutherbourg even sent Soane one of his healing recipes, and Loutherbourg's widow asked Soane to design a monument over her husband's tomb in the Chiswick churchyard in 1812.[63]

Collectors of Books

Given the artistic and intellectual parallels drawn between Beckford, Hope, and Soane, it is not surprising that their libraries should overlap, a point already noted. It is revealing to compare the mentality of these three men as obsessive, but professional book collectors. Beckford collected for sixty years, beginning at the age of nineteen, and Soane for over fifty years. Hope, Beckford, and Soane were among the numerous visitors to post-Revolution Paris, Hope in 1815 and 1816, Beckford and Soane in 1814. Soane, in particular, scoured the leading Parisian bookshops. British interest in and, to some extent, sympathy for Napoléon was expressed by Soane's acquisition in Paris of the sumptuous edition of Percier and Fontaine's *Palais, maisons, et autres édifices modernes déssinés à Rome* (1798), with hand-colored plates, which its authors had inscribed and presented to the future Empress Joséphine. Soane and Hope also owned Percier and Fontaine's illustrated books on their decorations for Napoléon's coronation in 1804 and wedding to Marie-Louise in 1810.

Beckford rented a house in London for the season each year, spending much time with his bookdealers. Like Soane, he had the mentality of the true book collector, acquiring more than one copy of the same book, attracted by special editions such as those extra-illustrated with proof or colored plates, as well as by books with associations to previous owners.[64] Hope owned the *Cabinet du Roi*, twenty-three volumes of engravings celebrating the reign of Louis XIV, whose arms and monogram were stamped on the bindings. One of Soane's many association copies was Beckford's copy of Gray's poems illustrated by Richard Bentley. Soane, like Beckford, used many booksellers and binders, the best of the binders employed by both of them being the German immigrant, Christian Samuel Kalthoeber. They were not aesthetes who bought books to admire them: they bought them to read them, both making extensive annotations or notes on them. Despite the great fortune which Soane spent on his library, he unwisely enclosed his books in glazed bookcases which deprived them of air. Beckford, by contrast, looked after his books far more meticu-

lously, denying them access to light but not to air.

Both Beckford and Soane collected the great French works of archaeology and travel,[65] as well as all the standard architectural and archaeological works of eighteenth- and early-nineteenth-century Britain.[66] Beckford owned Soane's *Plans, Elevations and Sections of Buildings* (1788), to which he was a subscriber, his *Sketches in Architecture* (1793), and an inscribed copy of *Designs for Public Improvements in London and Westminster* (1828), given to him by Soane.[67]

The libraries of Beckford and Soane were also rich in works by Leon Battista Alberti, Sebastiano Serlio, Athanasius Kircher, Johann Bernard Fischer von Erlach, Francesco Bianchini, Pietro Santi Bartoli, Johann Joachim Winckelman, and Scipione Maffei. Soane owned fourteen folio volumes of works by Piranesi, Beckford at least eighteen, and Hope twenty-three.[68] Soane also owned objects from Piranesi's own collection, as well as an antique capital, adorned with dolphins, and a cinerary urn, both of which had been illustrated by Piranesi, respectively, in *Della Magnificenza* (1761) and in *Vasi* (1778). The importance of Piranesi's plates to Soane's crowded and evocative display of casts and antiquities can hardly be exaggerated. The libraries of Beckford and Soane also contained the key texts by British, French, and German authors on the philosophy and practice of Picturesque gardening.[69] Beckford's signed and dated presentation copy of William Chambers's *Dissertation on Oriental Gardening* (1772), presumably given to him at a time when he may have been Chambers's pupil, is dated "19th March 1773."[70] It was at exactly this time that Soane was a student at the Royal Academy where he was also under the influence of Chambers.

One singular study of Gothic that united Beckford and Soane was *Plans, Elevations, Sections, and Views of the Church of Batalha in the Province of Estremadura in Portugal, with the History and Description by Fr. Luis de Sousa . . . To which is prefaced an Introductory Discourse on the Principles of Gothic Architecture* (1795), by the Irish architect and antiquary, James Murphy. Following Beckford's visit to Batalha in June 1794, this work was used by Wyatt in his designs for Fonthill Abbey.[71] Before publication, the book was issued in parts to subscribers, including Beckford, from 1792 to 1795 .[72] Soane valued his copy of this book, which he bought as early 1796, annotated, and, after 1802, inserted into it a list of the plates.[73] A second and rare edition of 1836 was dedicated to Soane who acquired a copy of it.[74]

A Shift from Gothic to Classic

In their complicated attitudes to Gothic, Beckford and Soane had much in common.[75] It was not Gothic to which Soane was totally opposed, but its cheap, flimsy, and incongruous contemporary imitation. Both men admired the "delirium" provoked by Gothic at its most sensational. Indeed, the passages in Soane's Royal Academy lectures on Gothic are written in the language of Edmund Burke's *Sublime and Beautiful* and the opium dreams of Beckford and Samuel Taylor Coleridge.

Beckford and Soane, though admiring genuine Gothic, came to have the same low view of James Wyatt, the architect of Fonthill.

According to the diarist, Joseph Farington, Beckford told Benjamin West as early as 1804 that, "He [Beckford] is much disatisfied with Wyatt who perpetually disappoints Him."[76] Beckford also complained: "if Wyatt can get near a large fire, and have a bottle by Him He cares for nothing else."[77] Moreover, ten years later, following a visit to Longleat where James Wyatt's nephew, Jeffry Wyatt (later Wyatville), was working, Beckford wrote that: "Throughout the building one recognises the hall-mark of Bagasse [James Wyatt]—his poor lazy methods, his eternal vulgar architraves and his false arches etc—a plague of Wyattiana. That infamous style will corrupt all England and like mice and bugs will riddle beds, tables, roofs, walls etc, etc."[78]

Beckford was impressed by Thomas Hope's criticism of Fonthill in 1804 that, "had the Grecian orders been employed, a mansion might have arisen, unrivaled in the most distant parts of the island, [but] a style had on the contrary been adopted, which subjected every one of its details to disadvantageous comparisons with the Cathedral at Salisbury, whose proud spire arises in its very sight."[79] Having read this passage in March 1804, Beckford told Benjamin West that, "Tom Hope was right in His remarks.—He said He felt the force of what He observed of the Abbey at Fonthill being a Gothic design ill placed within view of Salisbury Cathedral."[80] Soane also agreed: in lecture notes of 1810 he wrote ironically of "The rich abbey of Fonthill with its lofty tower aping the spire of Salisbury."[81]

Though admitting the justice of Hope's criticism of Fonthill, Beckford defended himself by explaining, rather improbably, that his choice of Gothic for Fonthill was partly dictated by the fact that "Gothic windows & compartments afforded him opportunities to blazon and introduce the arms of the various great families . . . from which His daugtrs. are descended or to which they are allied."[82] Though Soane also thought that architecture should be capable of commemorating great men and events through painting and sculpture, he complained of Gothic that "notwithstanding the blaze of its architectural beauties, this system was not calculated to call forth the energies of the painter and sculptor. Painting would have been confined to little more than portraits, and sculpture to busts and single statues." He explained that "the costly abbey at Fonthill which, being partly finished and the mansion house [Fonthill Splendens] in consequence pulled down, the pictures by ancient and modern masters were sold, being found too large, and unsuitable to the decoration of a modern Gothic abbey."[83] Since Soane knew Beckford, and bought at his sales, it is possible that this explanation of Beckford's dissatisfaction with Fonthill derived directly from Beckford.

BECKFORD AND SOANE IN LONDON AND BATH

Hope and Soane are recorded as having visited Fonthill.[84] In a letter from John Britton to Soane, written from Fonthill on August 29, 1822, Britton made arrangements for Soane's forthcoming visit, anticipating that they would "have some delightful strolls through the most enchanting grounds imaginable."[85] Soane is also known to have been on calling terms with Beckford in London from at least as early as

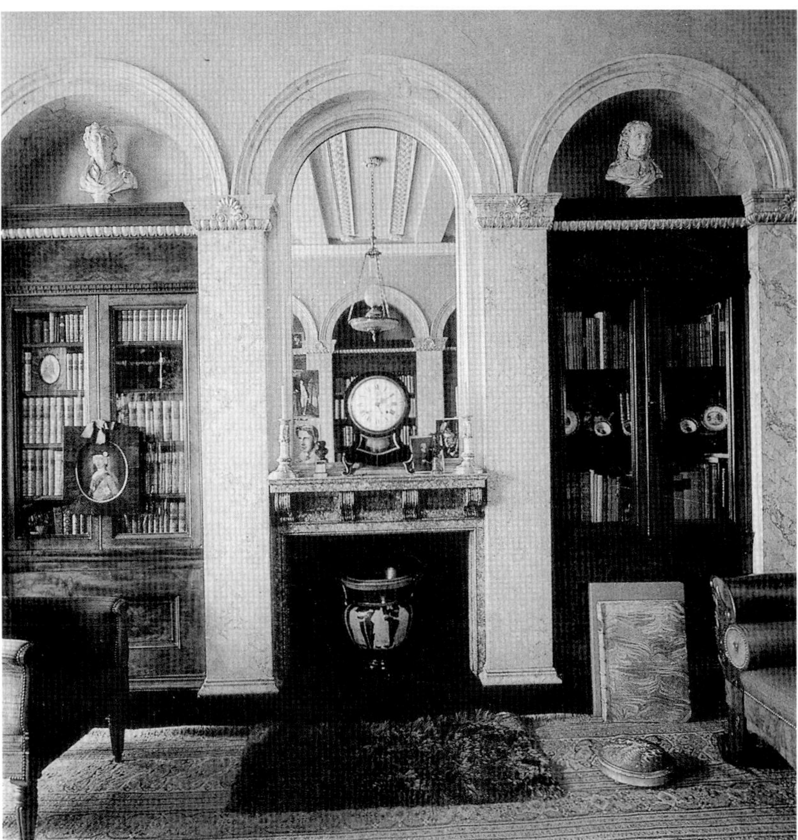

Fig. 2-11. The library, 19 Lansdown Crescent, Bath; designed by Henry Edmund Goodridge, 1837. Photographed in 1986. Trustees of Sir John Soane's Museum, London.

1813.[86] There are further references in Soane's notebooks to his meeting Beckford in April and May 1829, and in the following autumn when he was taking a cure in Bath. On September 19, after a walk to Beckford's house at 20 Lansdown Crescent, Soane wrote in his note book, "Left card for Mr Beckford," and two days later, "Mr B called early. Saw Mr Beckford home."[87] The late-Georgian terraced houses in Bath and London of these two curious old gentlemen—Beckford, now nearly seventy, and Soane, seventy-six—had certain features in common. Apart from the general limitations as to the narrow width of Georgian row houses, the reasons that prompted the two men to occupy at different times, sometimes at the same time, parts of three adjacent terraced houses—Beckford in Bath and Soane in London, are hard to discern.[88]

In 1823, having sold Fonthill, Beckford acquired two recently completed houses in Bath: 20 Lansdown Crescent and the adjacent building, 1 Lansdown Place West. He linked them curiously with a bridge, probably designed by Henry Edmund Goodridge, a gifted local architect stylistically influenced by Soane.[89] By 1832 Beckford had sold 1 Lansdown Place West, though retaining the bridge, and by 1837 had bought 19 Lansdown Crescent, again remodeled for him by Goodridge who filled one end wall of his bridge library with a huge looking glass

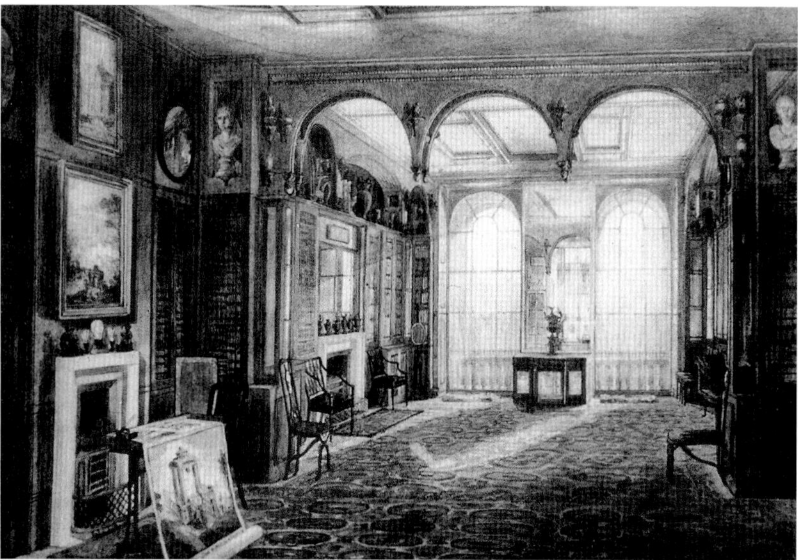

Fig. 2-12. Library and dining room, 13 Lincoln's Inn Fields; designed by John Soane, 1812–13. From Joseph Michael Gandy, "Composite View of Lincoln's Inn Fields . . . ," 1822. Trustees of Sir John Soane's Museum, London, ref. P.86.

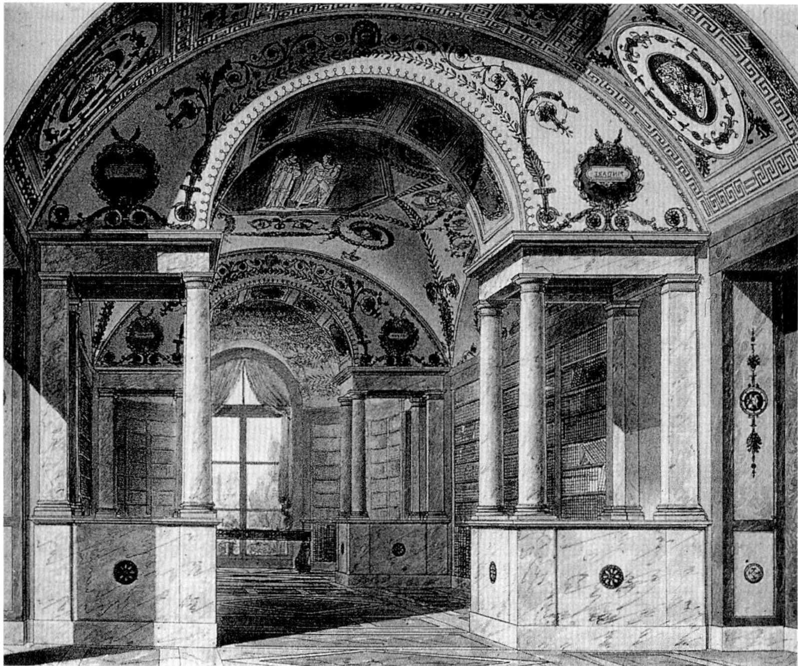

Fig. 2-13. Charles Percier and P. F. L. Fontaine. The Library at Malmaison, ca. 1800. From P.F.L. Fontaine, *Journal 1799–1853* (Paris: Ecole nationale supérieure des beaux-arts: Institut français d'architecture, Société de l'histoire de l'art français, 1987).

from floor to ceiling, rather like the mirrors in Soane's library. At the same time, Goodridge created another handsome library, always described by Beckford as his "Grecian Library," on the ground floor of 19 Lansdown Crescent (fig. 2-11). Formed in 1837, the year of Soane's death, and today the only surviving Beckford interior in any of his three adjacent houses, it is surely a room in which Soane would have been at home. A beautifully articulated space, defined by mirrored arches and scagliola Siena marble pilasters, it contains fitted bookcases of red mahogany veneer over walnut.[90]

Staying in Bath in December 1832, Soane sent a letter to Beckford, which indicates the considerable intimacy between them and the high regard in which he held Beckford's contribution to the arts, as well as his admiration for the Lansdown Tower:

Accept my dear Sir, my best thanks for your obliging attention. I regret very much that indisposition has prevent[e]d me [having] the pleasure of seeing you which circumstance will also cause me to lose the opportunity of your permission to view your truly classical mansion and noble Tower—objects which once seen can not be easily be [sic] forgotten. I hope to revisit Bath in the Spring and to have opportunity to assure you in person of the sense I have of what you have done for the advancement of the Fine Arts. I have the honour to be,
Dear Sir,
Your very ob[e]d[ient] and obliged Serv[t] John Soane.[91]

It is interesting to speculate on the topics of conversation during their visits to each other: architecture and literature, illustrated books, certainly, and perhaps in addition, France, Freemasonry, politics, persecution, and Napoléon, for whom both had a romantic admiration. Beckford had visited Malmaison in 1814, and Soane five years later. Soane noted that he was "much interested . . . [in] those things which once had the care and attention of Josephine."[92] Both Beckford and Soane were able to bring back souvenirs of Napoléon and Joséphine from their visits to Paris.[93] Soane acquired Joséphine's copy of Percier and Fontaine's *Palais, maisons, et autre édifices modernes déssinés à Rome* (1798), while at the sale of Malmaison in 1816, Beckford bought a magnificent circular table with a top then believed to be formed from a slab of marble brought from Egypt by Napoléon and given to Joséphine.[94] Afforded pride of place in the Grand Drawing Room at Fonthill Abbey, the table rested on a neoclassical Savonnerie carpet from the château de Saint-Cloud, made for Napoléon in 1814. Indeed, Beckford's neoclassical acquisitions and his consistent patronage of neoclassical silversmiths—his favorite silver designer, Auguste, had, incidentally, provided the goldsmith's work on Napoléon's crown—preclude casting Beckford in the role of a Romantic Goth rather than as a figure akin to Hope or Soane.

A curious link between the collections of Soane and Beckford is that they both acquired objects associated with the Sultan of Mysore, known to the English as Tippoo Sahib. By 1823 Soane had bought a set of ivory furniture of around 1790 from southern India: he described it as among the belongings of Tippoo that were captured at the siege of Seringapatam in 1799 when Tippoo was killed. Beckford proudly displayed what he claimed to be Tippoo's hookah on the Malmaison table in the Grand Drawing Room at Fonthill.

Soane's arched library and dining room in Lincoln's Inn Fields (fig. 2-12) are not without similarities to Napoléon's library at Malmaison (fig. 2-13). After his visit to these interiors in 1814, Beckford wrote: "I like the gallery at Malmaison well enough and am pleased by the vault, the general colouring and the not too great height of the walls; it is Imperial-like, Italianate and comfortable . . . The marble columns at each end of the room give an air of grandeur and the perspective discovered through them of another apartment beyond is enchanting."[95]

It seems likely that Beckford took Soane to see progress on Lansdown Tower (see fig. 16-1) in September 1826, or that Soane saw it in 1829, two years after its completion. A drawing of September 1826 shows the tower without its tall crowning cupola of iron columns which, according to tradition, was added by Beckford as an afterthought. Certainly, the building was originally conceived as a castellated tower with round-headed windows in a sort of "Saxon" manner. Beckford made sketches in this style, which he gave to Goodridge, who seems to have persuaded him to adopt classical, though still asymmetrical forms.[96] To that extent, the tower, as built in 1825–27, may also be seen as Beckford's response to Hope's criticisms of the shoddy Gothic of Fonthill, criticisms shared by Soane who doubtless made them clear to Beckford. In view of the links between Beckford and Hope, it is interesting to note that a visitor to the Lansdown Tower recorded seeing in a glass case

> a little ivory reliquior [sic], four or five hundred years old. It was given to Mr Beckford by the late Mr Hope. It is in the shape of a small chapel; on opening the doors, the fastenings of which were two small dogs or monkeys, you found in a recess the Virgin and Child, surrounded by effigies, all carved in the most astonishingly minute manner.[97]

The Picturesque quality that unites Hope, Beckford, and Soane is further underlined by the fact that John Britton was responsible for producing illustrated books on the homes of all three — Hope's Deepdene in 1821–26, Fonthill in 1823, and "the House and Galleries of John Soane" in 1827 — stressing their relation to the theory and psychology of the Picturesque. The exteriors of the Lansdown Tower are not especially Soanean, but the Italianate tower is certainly close to that of around 1818 at Thomas Hope's Deepdene (fig. 2-14). In a European context it can be related to the contemporary work of Karl Friedrich Schinkel in Berlin and Potsdam: Schloss Glienicke (1832) and Schloss Charlottenhof (1829), especially the nearby Guest House and Court Gardener's House complex of 1829–33. Schinkel expressed his belief in "architecture as the continuation of nature in her constructive activity," capable of growth and expansion. To that extent, Schinkel's work was like Fonthill, which had been altered considerably between

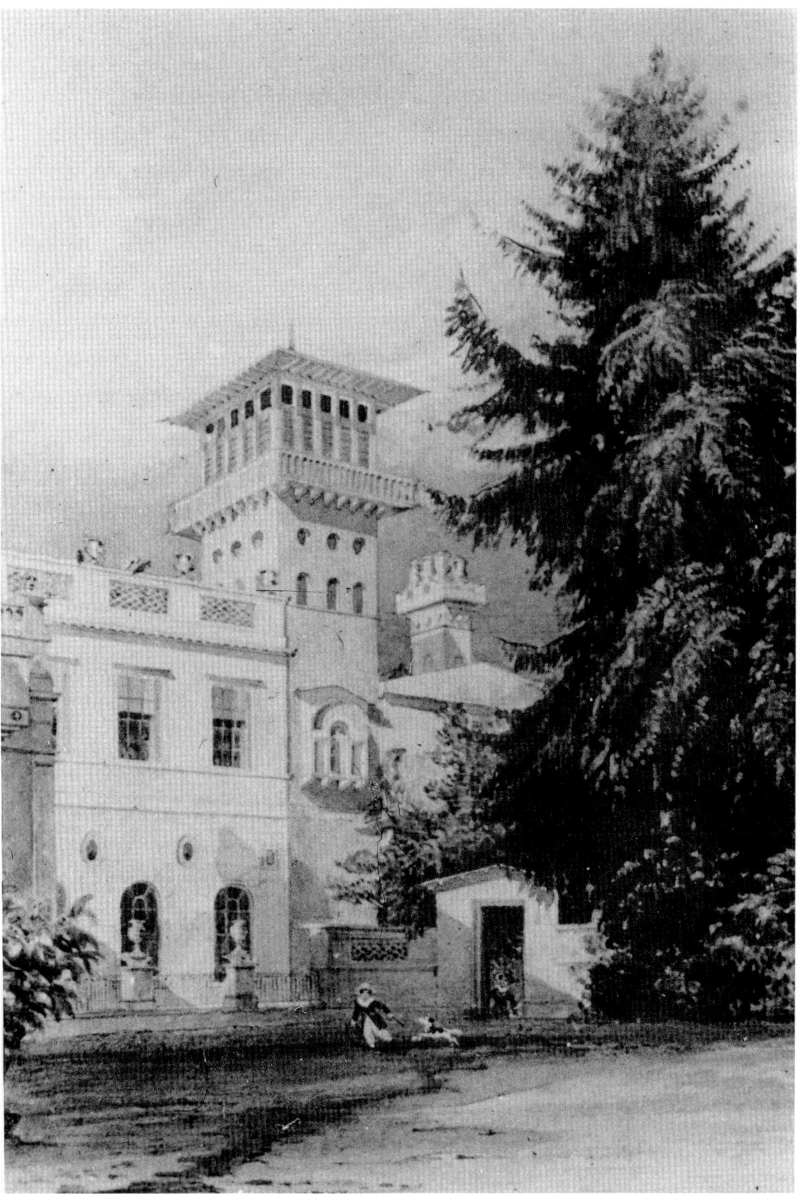

Fig. 2-14. William Henry Bartlett. Exterior and tower, Deepdene, Surrey; designed by Thomas Hope, ca. 1818–23. Watercolor. From John Britton, "Illustrations of the Deepdene, Seat of T. Hope Esqre., 1825–26," Minet Library, Brixton

1796 and 1818, and also like the Lansdown Tower, which similarly grew and changed as the building rose. Like Schinkel's work, the Lansdown Tower combined Grecian scholarship with asymmetrical forms in an expression of that eighteenth-century Enlightenment belief, shared by Soane, in the origins of Greek architecture and ornament in nature and natural forms.

The finial of the crowning lantern of the Lansdown Tower is directly based on that of the Choragic Monument of Lysicrates in Athens, as restored by Stuart and Revett. Schinkel was to use the same source a year or so later for the Belvedere at Schloss Glienicke, known as the Grosse Neugirde, the "great curiosity." Soane, as we have seen, had adopted the same form for the domed canopy of the state bed that he designed for Beckford at Fonthill Splendens in 1788. It was subsequently used by Goodridge in his unexecuted design of 1817 for a monument to Princess Charlotte.[98] Goodridge also followed the example of both Beckford and Soane by buying recent architectural books in Paris: a copy of Percier and Fontaine's *Recueil de décorations intérieures* (1812) bears Goodridge's inscription and notes which indicate that he bought it on a visit to Paris in or before 1818.[99] Moreover, the rather heavy forms of the entrance gateway built by Goodridge in 1848 in the grounds of the Lansdown Tower, which had become a cemetery in 1847, may be indebted to Soane's ponderous monument to his wife in Saint Pancras Gardens (1816).[100]

Unfortunately, there is no record of what the interiors of the Lansdown Tower were like in the 1820s when Soane would have seen them, for they were completely redecorated and refurnished by Beckford and Goodridge in an early-Victorian manner between 1841 and Beckford's death in 1844 (see chap. 16). The forms and lighting of rooms such as the sanctuary, however, are close to late interiors by Soane such as his gallery of 1830–31 for Sir Francis Chantrey at 30 Belgrave Place (fig. 2-15). The Soane Museum is recalled by the very small scale of the rooms at Lansdown Tower and their rabbit-warren-like quality. Here, the two men, both given to dreams and reverie, could have indulged in melancholy and poetic reflections, for the view north from the summit of Lansdown Hill reminded Beckford of the Roman Campagna which he had first visited in 1780, two years after Soane. For Beckford, it was a "land of solemn recollections, of perished nations, the memento of an approaching eternity." In going on to add that, "I shall never forget how I first passed over that land of the Dead, strewed with . . . ruined sepulchres and shattered columns,"[101] he showed how totally he had entered into Soane's mind.

Beckford becomes more comprehensible by being set in the context of his near contemporaries who, like him, were authors, designers, and collectors, aware of the psychology of interior design. He might be compared with the Prince Regent who was constantly criticized for extravagance by his father and was thought ridiculous by many of his subjects. Children of the pan-European vision of the eighteenth-

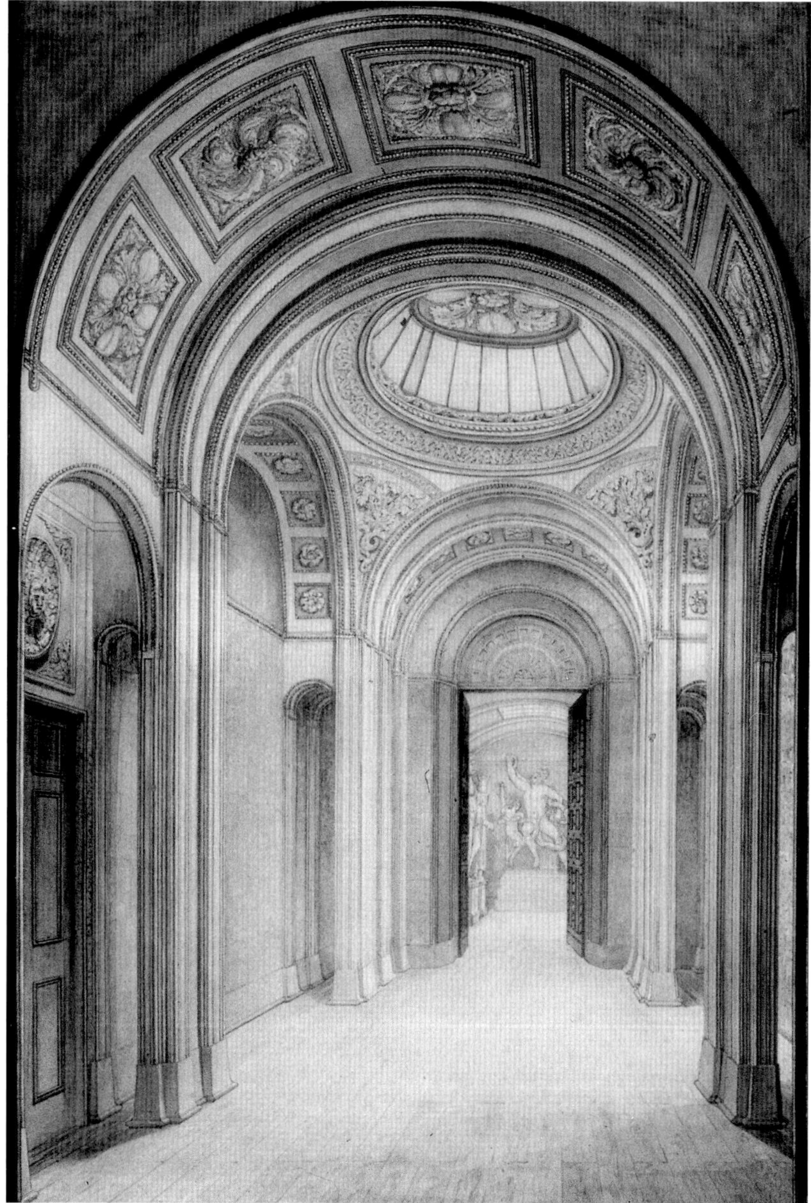

Fig. 2-15. "Ante-Room" to Sir Francis Chantrey's gallery, 30 Belgrave Place; designed by John Soane, 1830–31. Trustees of Sir John Soane's Museum, London.

century Enlightenment, they were all rancophiles who had to decide what attitudes to adopt toward revolutionary and Napoleonic France. Part of the international community of men of taste, promoted by Quatremère de Quincy, they found themselves in a cultural world in which the Protestant Church of England seemed to have little relevance, especially in comparison with Continental Freemasonry and Roman Catholicism. Moreover, the preoccupation with self and personal sensations, which had been encouraged by the associationalist philosophy of Locke and Burke, and by the confessional literature of Rousseau and Goethe, led them to live in a world of the imagination.

1. John Soane, *Description of the House and Museum on the north side of Lincoln's Inn Fields* (London: privately printed, 1835): 28.

2. Malcolm Jack, Introduction, *Vathek and Other Stories: A William Beckford Reader* (London: Penguin Books, 1995): xix–xx. Hereafter cited as *Beckford Reader*.

3. Lewis Melville, *The Life and Letters of William Beckford of Fonthill* (London: Heinemann, 1910): 283.

4. Timothy Mowl, *William Beckford: Composing for Mozart* (London: John Murray, 1998): 266.

5. Hope's library is known from the auction sale. See *Catalogue of the Valuable Library of Books on Architecture, Costume, Sculpture, Antiquities, etc., formed by Thomas Hope . . . being a Portion of the Hope Heirlooms removed from Deepdene, Dorking*, sale cat., Christie, Manson & Woods, London, 25–27 July 1917. Despite the claim that the collection was formed by Hope, it contains some works published after his death.

6. Cited from Boyd Alexander, "The Decay of Beckford's Genius," in *William Beckford of Fonthill, 1760–1844: Bicentenary Essays*, ed. Fatma Moussa Mahmoud (1960; reprint, Port Washington, N.Y.: Dover, 1972): 20.

7. "Crude Hints . . . ," AL Soane Case 31, fols 53–56, Soane Museum, London. See also Christopher Woodward, ed., *Visions of Ruin* (London: Sir John Soane's Museum, 1999): 61–74.

8. Alexander, "Decay of Beckford's Genius" (1960; 1972): 20.

9. Gillian Darley, *John Soane: An Accidental Romantic* (New Haven and London: Yale University Press, 1996): 278.

10. Quoted from David Watkin, *Thomas Hope (1769–1831) and the Neo-Classical Idea* (London: John Murray, 1968): 10.

11. Melville, *Life and Letters* (1910): 96.

12. Ibid., p. 216.

13. For Soane's emotional debt to Rousseau, see David Watkin, *Sir John Soane: Enlightenment Thought and the Royal Academy Lectures* (Cambridge University Press, 1996): 114–15, 206–10.

14. Quoted in Guy Chapman, *Beckford* (London: Jonathan Cape, 1952): 187.

15. Jean-Jacques Rousseau, *Les Confessions,* vol. 1 (Geneva 1781): 1. [Author's translation.]

16. Melville, *Life and Letters* (1910): 78.

17. Reproduced in Watkin, *Sir John Soane* (1996): pl. 2.

18. This title was among the books sold in the 1823 sale: see *The Valuable Library of Books in Fonthill Abbey*, sale cat., Phillips, London, 1823, lot 2085.

19. Melville, *Life and Letters* (1910): 76.

20. For Beckford, see Beckford to Gregorio Franchi, 5 November 1818, quoted in *Life at Fonthill 1807–1822 . . . From the Correspondence of William Beckford*, ed. and trans. Boyd Alexander (London: Rupert Hart-Davis, 1957): 253. For Soane, see AL Soane Case 164, fol. [179], Soane Museum.

21. Alexander, *Life at Fonthill* (1957): 253.

22. AL Soane Case 160, Soane Museum.

23. Quoted in John W. Oliver, *The Life of William Beckford* (Oxford University Press, 1932): 89–91.

24. Beckford, "The Portuguese Journal," in *Beckford Reader* (1995): 232.

25. Written in 1777, it was first published by Guy Chapman as "The Vision" see William Beckford, *The Vision, Liber Veritas*, ed. with an introduction and notes by Guy Chapman (London: Constable, 1930).

26. Beckford, "The Long Story," in *Beckford Reader* (1995): 22.

27. Ibid., p. 23.

28. Beckford, "A History of the Caliph Vathek," in ibid., pp. 91–93.

29. Melville, *Life and Letters* (1910): 77.

30. Ibid., p. 165. The hall referred to is the Egyptian Hall at Fonthill Splendens.

31. See Helen Dorey, "Sir John Soane's Acquisition of the Sarcophagus of Seti I," *Georgian Group Journal* 1 (1991): 26–35.

32. Melville, *Life and Letters* (1910): 96–97.

33. Beckford, "Dreams," in *Beckford Reader* (1995): 218.

34. Soane, Miscellaneous drawings and architectural designs, no. 11, ff. 30–37, Soane Museum.

35. Soane, Journal 1781, no. 1, 25–26 April, 28 May, 5 June, Soane Museum.

36. A point established in Christopher Woodward, "William Beckford and Fonthill Splendens: Early Works by Soane and Goodridge," *Apollo* (February 1998): 31–40. I am indebted to Christopher Woodward for helpful comments on the first draft of this essay.

37. John Britton, *The Beauties of Wiltshire*, vol. 1 (London 1801): 238.

38. Soane, Miscellaneous drawings and architectural designs, no. 11, ff. 30–37, Soane Museum.

39. Soane, Journal 1781, no. 1, 25 June, Soane Museum.

40. For the subsequent history of this remarkable bed, executed from Soane's designs, which are signed and dated January 1788, see Woodward, "William Beckford" (February 1998): 31–40. For Soane's designs, see MS Beckford, c.84, fols. 111–12, 122, and MS Beckford b.8, fols. 1–2, Bodleian Library, Oxford. For related designs see 81/1/29 and 32, Soane Museum.

41. Surviving bills for Soane's work for Beckford include payments of £36.14.4. for Willmott, plasterer; £93.6. to Banks, sculptor; and £135.5.4.to Nelson, mason (Ledger A 1787, Soane Museum). See also a bill from Soane to Beckford for designs of interiors and journey to Fonthill, totaling £284.14.4, and a receipt from Soane of 2 December 1788 for £284.14.10 for surveying and for designing chimneypieces for Beckford (B388 and S823Bb, respectively, Beinecke Rare Book and Manuscript Library, Yale University).

42. Soane maintained a close interest in Fonthill Splendens, acquiring catalogues of the sale of its building materials and contents in August and October 1801. He annotated his copy of the *Catalogue of the Valuable Building Materials of the Two Wing erections and colonnades of Fonthill Mansion with sundry Household Furniture . . . 8 magnificent statuary chimneypieces*, sale cat., Phillips, London, 7–9 October 1801, which included the pair of statuary marble chimneypieces in the Picture Gallery "enriched by emblematic figures of exquisite sculpture." The sale catalogue of the contents in August 1801 contained the bed designed by Soane for the state bedchamber, with "feet posts richly carved and gilt, crimson velvet furniture, inside and outside of tester and valance, richly ornamented with carved and gilt ornaments."

43. See Cornelius Vermeule, "Sir John Soane, His Classical Antiquities," *Archaeology* 6 (1953): 68–74, and idem, "Catalogue of Antique Sculpture in Sir John Soane's Museum," typescript, 1951–53, Soane Museum.

44. Peter Thornton and David Watkin, "New Light on the Hope Mansion in Duchess Street," *Apollo* (September 1987): 162–77.

45. Drafts of Soane's correspondence, Soane Museum.

46. Thomas Hope, *Household Furniture and Interior Decoration* (London: Longman, Hurst, Rees & Orme, 1807): 24.

47. Ibid., p. 38.

48. For a development of Laugier's stress on the primitive hut, see A.-C. Quatremère de Quincy, *De l'architecture égyptienne* (Paris 1803): 229.

49. *Hamilton Palace*, sale cat., Christie's, June 1882, lot 1617.

50. For a full account of these, see Watkin, *Sir John Soane* (1996): 220–25.

51. For the risk of such travel to Beckford during the Revolution, see John Whitehead, *The French Interior in the Eighteenth Century* (London: Laurence King, 1992): 33.

52. Beckford claimed that Auguste's "talents equal if not surpass those of the first artists of antiquity. I think you will be enraptured with the furniture I am having made under his direction in the true spirit of Corinth & Athens; the bronze friezes &c,. finished as highly as the gold vase you saw at Fonthill" (Beckford to Sir William Hamilton, Paris, February 1792, reprinted in *The Hamilton and Nelson Papers*, vol. 1, *1756–1797* [1893], The Collection of Autograph Letters and Historical Documents formed by Alfred Morrison, 2d ser. [Privately published, 1882–93]: 165, letter 205).

53. Ibid.

54. Lady Ann Hamilton, MS Journal, p. 4, Beckford Papers, Bodleian Library (quoted in Michael Snodin and Malcolm Baker, "Beckford's Silver," *Burlington Magazine* [November 1980]: 740).

55. *Hamilton and Nelson Papers* (1893): 153, letter 191.

56. *The Travel-Diaries of William Beckford of Fonthill*, ed. with a memoir and notes by Guy Chapman, vol. 1 (London: Constable, 1928): 85.

57. Howard Gotlieb, *William Beckford of Fonthill: Writer, Traveller, Collector, Caliph, 1870–1844*, exh. cat., Yale University Library (New Haven: Yale University Press, 1960): 61.

58. James Christie, *A Disquisition upon Etruscan Vases* (London, 1806): iv.

59. Watkin, *Sir John Soane* (1996): 256–71; Hope, *Household Furniture* (1807): [141].

60. Ibid., p. 24.

61. Oliver, *Life of William Beckford* (1932): 176, 168, respectively. Some of Beckford's biographers have doubted the authenticity of this account, but for a defence of its accuracy from an authority on Ledoux and eighteenth-century secret societies, see Anthony Vidler, *Claude-Nicolas Ledoux: Architecture and Social Reform at the End of the Ancien Régime* (Cambridge, Mass., and London: Massachusetts Institute of Technology, 1990): 337–40.

62. See James Stevens Curl, *The Art and Architecture of Freemasonry* (London: Batsford, 1991): 172.

63. Giles Waterfield, ed., *Soane and Death*, exh. cat. (London: Dulwich Picture Gallery, 1996): 100–101.

64. See Eileen Harris, "Sir John Soane's Library," *Apollo* (April 1990): 246.

65. For example, Antoine Desgodetz, *Edifices antiques de Rome* (Paris: Jean Baptiste Coignard, 1682); Antoine Le Pautre, *Oeuvres d'architecture* (Paris: Jombert, 1682); Claude Perrault, *Ordonnance des cinq éspèces de colonnes* (Paris: Jean Baptiste Coignard, 1683); Jean-François Félibien des Avaux, *Maisons . . . de Pline* (Paris 1699); Augustin-Charles d'Aviler, *Cours d'architecture* (Paris: Jean Mariette, 1710); Corneille Le Brun, *Voyage au Levant* (Paris 1714); Bernard de Montfaucon, *L'antiquité expliquée* (Paris: E. Delaune, H. Foucault, M. Clousier, J.-G.Nyn, E. Ganeau, N. Gosselin, P.-E. Giffart, 1729); Engelbert Kaempfer, *Histoire naturelle . . . du Japan* (The Hague 1729); Frederic Louis Norden, *Voyage d'Egypte et de Nubie* (Copenhagen 1755); Julien-David Le Roy, *Ruines des plus beaux monuments de la Grèce* (Paris: H. L. Guerin, L. F. Delatour, Jean-Luc Nyon, and Amsterdam: Jean Neaulme, 1758); Pierre Patte, *Monumens érigés en France à la gloire de Louis XV* (Paris: the author and Desaint and Saillant, 1765); Nicolas Ponce, *Description des Bains de Titus* (Paris: the author and Barbou, 1786); Cornelius De Pauw, *Recherches philosophiques sur les Chinois et les Egyptiens* (Paris 1773); and Denis Vivant Denon, *Voyage en Egypte* (Paris: P. Didot, 1802). I have drawn these parallels by comparing Soane's library with the sale catalogues of Beckford's books in 1804, 1808, 1817, 1823, and 1882.

66. For example, *Vitruvius Britannicus*, and books by Giacomo Leoni, William Kent, Robert Castell, Matthew Brettingham, Isaac Ware, James Paine, William Chambers, James Stuart, Thomas Major, Charles Cameron, Robert Adam, Charles Heathcote Tatham, Thomas Hope, William Wilkins, Benjamin Wyatt, and, of course, Soane himself.

67. *Hamilton Palace,* June 1882, lot 2080.

68. Two plates of antique marble vases in Piranesi's *Vasi, Candelabri, Cippi* (Rome 1778) bear fulsome dedications to William Beckford, presumably the Alderman, though he had died in 1770 (see vol. 1, pl. 24, and vol. 2, pl. 78). His son was eighteen in 1778 but had not yet visited Rome.

69. These are principally by Christian L. Cay Hirschfeld, René–Louis, Marquis de Girardin, Thomas Whately, William Chambers, Uvedale Price, and Richard Payne Knight.

70. *Hamilton Palace,* June 1882, lot 1788; and see Robert J. Gemmett, *William Beckford* (Boston: Twayne Publishers, 1977): 35. For Beckford as Chambers's pupil, see Brian Fothergill, *Beckford of Fonthill* (London: Faber and Faber, 1979): 25–26.

71. Though Beckford later referred to "that dull draughtsman Murphy" (Beckford, *Recollections of an Excursion to the Monasteries of Alcobaça and Batalha* [London: Richard Bentley 1835]: 136–37).

72. See Clive Wainwright, "William Beckford, his Collection and the Influence of his Excursion to Alcobaça and Batalha in 1794," in *Portugal e o Reino Unido: A Aliança Revisitada*, exh. cat., (Lisbon: Fundaçao Calouste Gulbenkian, 1994–95): 99.

73. I am indebted to the late Clive Wainwright for drawing my attention to the fact that copies of some of Murphy's letters, as well as all his drawings for this book, survive in the collection of the Society of Antiquaries, London, bound in an album as MS 260.

74. It is possible that Sir William Chambers, who knew Murphy, was responsible for introducing him to both Beckford and Soane. Murphy mentioned that Chambers had told him that when he had been in Paris, Soufflot had shown him drawings he had made of Gothic buildings (James Cavanah Murphy, *Plans . . . of Batalha* [London: I. & J.Taylor, 1795]: 12.) Soufflot had prepared these as part of his aim in the church of Sainte Geneviève of "uniting in one of the most beautiful forms," as his pupil Brébion put it in 1780, "the lightness of construction of Gothic churches with the purity and magnificence of Greek architecture": an ambition of which Beckford and Soane would have approved.

75. Beckford even criticized the flamboyant Gothic of the mausoleum at Batalha, which he compared to "Saxon crinklings and cranklings . . . the preposterous long and lanky marrow-spoon-shaped arches of the early Norman . . . and the Moorish horse-shoe-like deviations from beautiful curves." He went on to wonder "how persons of correct taste could ever have tolerated them, and batten on garbage when they might enjoy the lovely Ionic so prevalent in Greece, the Doric grandeur of the Parthenon, and the Corinthian magnificence of Balbec and Palmyra" (*Recollections of an Excursion* [1835]: 137).

76. *The Diary of Joseph Farington*, ed. Kenneth Garlick and Angus Macintyre, vol. 5 (New Haven and London: Yale University Press, 1979): 2283, entry dated 29 March 1804.

77. Ibid.

78. Beckford to Gregorio Franchi, 12 September 1813, quoted in Alexander, *Life at Fonthill* (1957): 157.

79. Thomas Hope, *Observations on the Plans and Elevations designed by James Wyatt, Architect, for Downing College* (London: D. N. Shury, 1804): 15.

80. *Diary of Joseph Farington* (1979).

81. Cited from Watkin, *Sir John Soane* (1996): 336.

82. *Diary of Joseph Farington* (1979).

83. Watkin, *Sir John Soane* (1996): 556.

84. Melville, *Life and Letters* (1910): 238.

85. Private correspondence III.B.1.26, Soane Museum.

86. He noted that Beckford called on him on 5 December 1813 and that he called on Beckford in his London house on 17 December (Notebook, 1813, Soane Museum).

87. A point noted in Dorothy Stroud, *Sir John Soane: Architect* (London: Faber and Faber, 1984): 60.

88. Beckford enjoyed teasing his neighbors by claiming that he had only bought no. 19 so that he would not be disturbed by anyone when sitting in his library next door (Oliver, *Life of William Beckford* [1932]: 292).

89. In 1829, Goodridge altered Hardenhuish House, Wiltshire, incorporating suggestions by Soane.

90. James Lees-Milne, "Beckford in Bath," *Country Life* 29 (April 1976): 1106–9.

91. MS Beckford c.35, fols. 52–54. The date is very faint but it is almost certainly 7 December 1832. I am indebted for assistance with this previously unpublished letter to Timothy Rogers, Department of Western Manuscripts, Bodleian Library.

92. Notebook of Soane's visit to Paris, August–September 1819, Soane Museum.

93. On Soane's Napoleonic acquisitions, see Peter Thornton and Helen Dorey, *A Miscellany of Objects from Sir John Soane's Museum* (London: Laurence King, 1992): 123.

94. See Clive Wainwright, *Romantic Interiors: The British Collector at Home, 1750–1850* (New Haven and London: Yale University Press, 1989): 141.

95. Alexander, *Life at Fonthill* (1957): 166–67.

96. See Philippa Bishop, "Beckford in Bath," *Bath History* 1 (1986): 85–112.

97. Henry Venn Lansdown, *Recollections of the Late William Beckford* (Bath, 1893): 24.

98. The drawing is in the Victoria and Albert Museum. I am indebted to Christopher Woodward for bringing it to my attention.

99. *Architecture of the Continent of Europe*, cat. 44 (London: B. Weinreb Architectural Books, 1981): no. 355.

100. For further information on Goodridge and on his villas in Bath, see Christopher Woodward, "Aerial Boudoirs of Bath," *Country Life* 4 (September 1997): 68–71.

101. Boyd Alexander, *England's Wealthiest Son: A Study of William Beckford* (London: Centaur Press, 1962): 226–27.

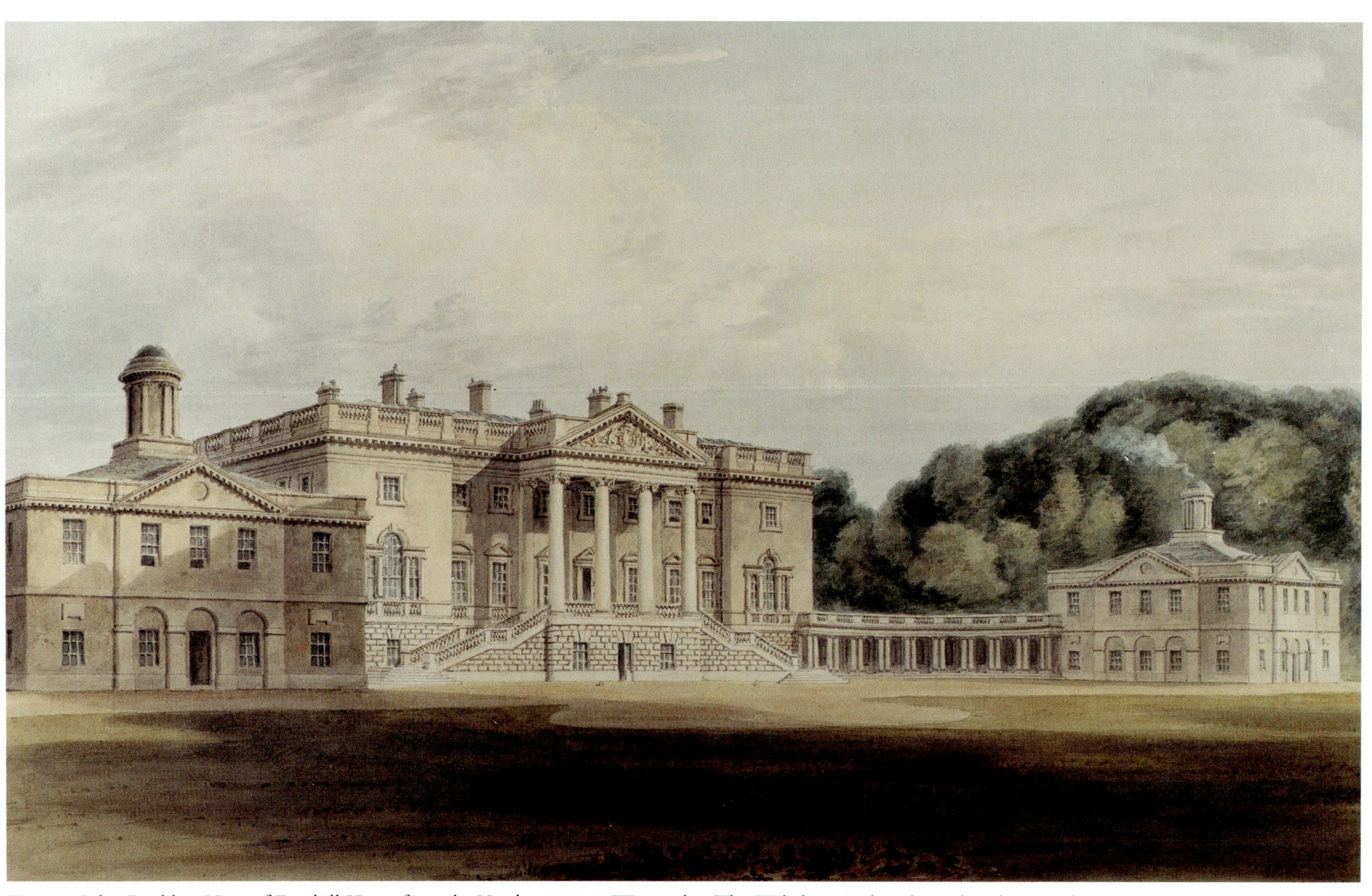

Fig. 3-1. John Buckler. *View of Fonthill House from the North,* ca. 1806. Watercolor. The Wiltshire Archaeological and Natural History Society, Devizes.

Chapter III

FONTHILL HOUSE: "ONE OF THE MOST PRINCELY EDIFICES IN THE KINGDOM"

Philip Hewat-Jaboor

William Beckford was born and raised at Fonthill House in Wiltshire, in a setting that was to play an unusually significant role in his life. This great estate was not merely the site of his upbringing, but it served a critical role as an anchor in his turbulent life while helping to shape his precocious taste and restless intellect. Surviving for only two generations in a family that rapidly rose from mercantile beginnings, this "princely edifice" stood for fewer than fifty years.[1] Almost inexplicably, Beckford demolished it in 1807, removing himself and his collections to Fonthill Abbey, his greatest achievement, which was then rising on the estate as the most legendary house of Regency England.

Fonthill House is now generally known as "Fonthill Splendens" (fig. 3-1), a sobriquet that was only first used with an engraving issued in 1829.[2] As the political base of his father, Alderman William Beckford, "the great Beckford," as he is usually styled,[3] Fonthill was a magnificent seat surrounded by an extensive park, landscape gardens, and grottoes. The house itself had lavish and fashionable interiors of the 1760s, furnished with carved and gilded furniture, richly colored damasks, a catholic picture collection, and splendid library. Those interiors, however, would be short-lived. A little more than a decade after his father's death in 1770, Beckford would begin to transform the English Palladian interiors into some of the most fashionable examples of neoclassical taste.

Family Background

Alderman Beckford (fig. 3-2) was the third generation of the Beckford clan of buccaneering sugar potentates and was the most influential among a powerful group of Jamaican merchants who dominated this trade. His grandfather Peter had settled in Jamaica in the 1660s, becoming a plantation and slave owner, and was appointed lieutenant-governor of the island during the reign of William III (1689–1702). His son, also named Peter, was speaker of the Jamaican Assembly, and during a particularly uproarious session members drew swords against him

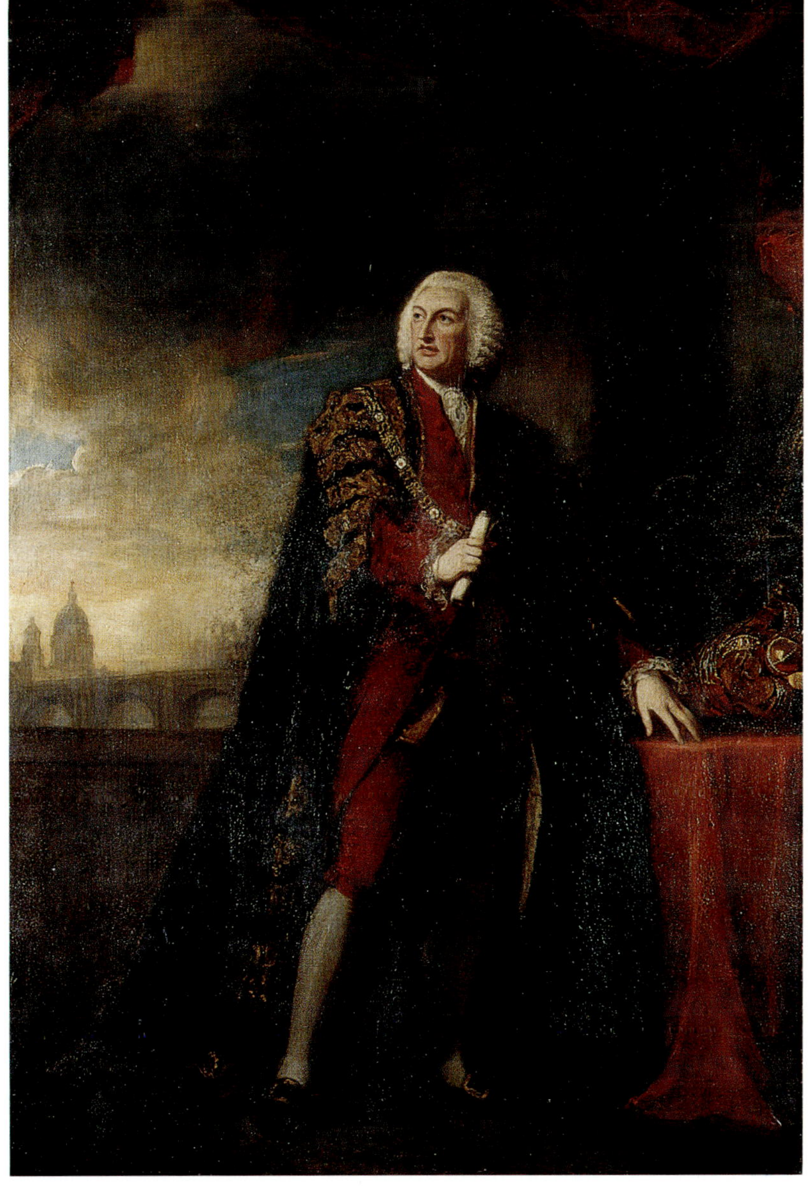

Fig. 3-2. Sir Joshua Reynolds. *Alderman William Beckford,* ca. 1770. Oil on canvas. Courtesy of the collection at Parham Park, West Sussex.

to prevent its closure. The lieutenant-governor, coming to his son's aid, tripped down a staircase and fell to his death. The younger Peter Beckford married Bathsua—daughter of Colonel Julines Hering, a member of another leading Jamaican family—and had a family of twelve children. The Alderman was the second son and succeeded as head of the family after the unexpected death of his elder brother, another Peter, in 1737. The Alderman certainly inherited his family's strong temperament and irascible habits. Sent from Jamaica in 1723 to be educated at Westminster School, London, and Balliol College, Oxford, he excelled in the classics, an interest later reflected in the richly iconographic interiors of Fonthill House when it was rebuilt after 1755.

Alderman Beckford lived in London in a house in Soho Square, adjoining that of his younger brother Richard, with whom he controlled the family sugar empire, along with his eldest and favorite bastard son, Richard.[4] As the most dominant of the West Indian traders, the Alderman sought to protect the family's interests by becoming a Member of Parliament for London Petersfield (1754–70) and for the City of London (1761). His election as Lord Mayor of London, twice, in 1762 and 1769, was a considerable achievement and a position of immense power at this time of Britain's greatest prosperity.[5] The Alderman's life was complicated by the existence of three mistresses and a bastard family of seven children. It was not until his prestigious marriage in 1756 to Maria Marsh, *née* Maria Hamilton (see cat. no. 2), the youngest granddaughter of the sixth Duke of Abercorn, and widow of a fellow Jamaican trader, that he produced a legitimate heir.[6] Maria's eight-year-old daughter, Elizabeth Marsh,[7] had to wait four years for the arrival of her half-brother, William Thomas, who was born on September 29, 1760, at Fonthill, where he was christened; William Pitt the elder, first Earl of Chatham acted as godparent.[8]

The Alderman was extremely active politically, a patriot and hero in the defense of liberty as well as a great supporter of the arts. A poor speaker in the House, hindered by his strong West Indian accent, he was nonetheless a skilled politician, prompting even Horace Walpole later to comment: "it looks as if Beckford had been the firebrand of politics, for the flame has gone out since his death."[9] A dedicated Whig, close political ally to and friend of the first Earl of Chatham, he was a strong supporter of John Wilkes and his Cause for Liberty, which advocated greater freedom of speech. In pursuit of this goal he famously petitioned King George III and was twice received in astonished silence before making a third protest at St. James's Palace on May 17, 1770, arguing with the king, in a breach of court etiquette. His speech was immediately published, and the Alderman became a national hero, although soon thereafter he fell ill and within the month, on June 21, died at Fonthill House.[10]

THE ALDERMAN'S FONTHILL

The Fonthill Estate had been purchased by Alderman Beckford in January 1744 from Francis Cottington.[11] The existing Elizabethan house had been altered by Cottington's father in 1715, and its exterior

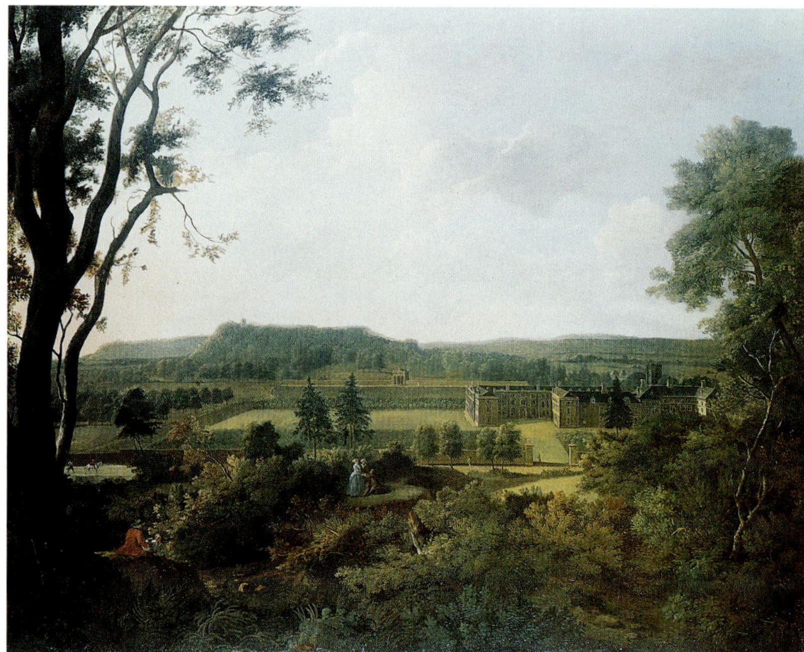

Fig. 3-3. George Lambert. *Fonthill House,* 1740. Oil on canvas. The house is shown as it was at the time of its purchase by Alderman William Beckford. Crown copyright UK Government Art Collection.

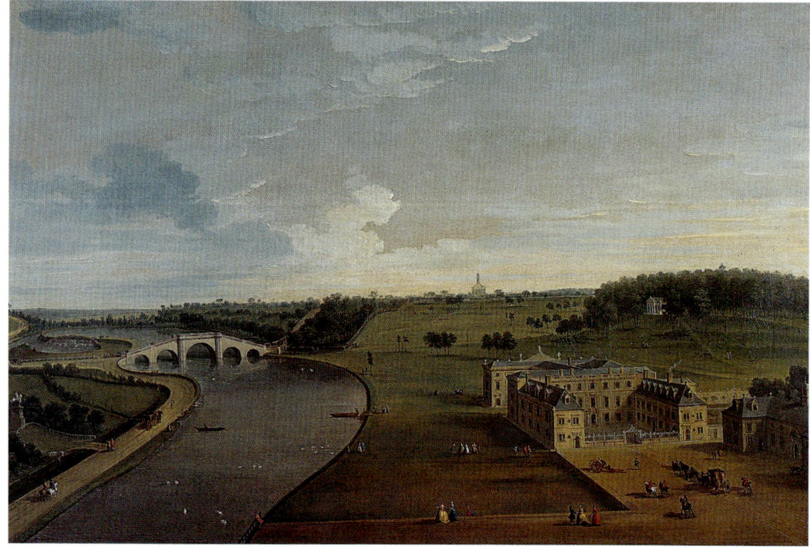

Fig. 3-4. Arthur Devis. *Fonthill House from the North,* ca. 1750–55. Oil on canvas. Painted after alterations made by the Alderman and before the fire of 1755. Private collection.

refaced in the classical style (fig. 3-3). By 1740 the formal gardens surrounding the house had been landscaped in the Picturesque manner, the canal removed, and the east gatehouse replaced by eagle-capped piers.[12] Grander north and south entrances were built for the Alderman between 1745 and 1753 in the "Roman" manner of Inigo Jones, when further substantial additions were made to the grounds as well as to the house (fig. 3-4).[13] To improve the landscape planning, the old Parish

Church was demolished around 1747–49 and rebuilt on a new site, its "Roman" temple replacement provided with a Tuscan porticoed facade facing Fonthill House. A stream was dammed to create a wider river; a bathhouse and pagoda were constructed; and a series of grottoes built by Josiah Lane all served to aggrandize and diversify the charms of the park.[14]

Alderman Beckford's papers have vanished and little is known of his acquisitions of works of art for the house. He is known, however, to have purchased from artists' sales. He acquired the two great series of paintings by William Hogarth—*The Rake's Progress* and *The Harlot's Progress*—as well as important landscapes by Claude Lorraine.[15] He evidently lived in a magnificent style even before his marriage; the house was described by contemporaries as having been "finished with much expence [sic], and there are many modern paintings all over it as well as on the ceilings, and a handsome library; but what makes it most curious is a very fine large organ in the hall, which plays thirty tunes without a hand, and cost around £1500."[16]

In the early hours of February 13, 1755, while the Alderman was in London, a devastating chimney fire, accidentally started by craftsmen, broke out at Fonthill House.[17] It was an hour before assistance came, and by then the Great Hall and all the north apartments had been destroyed, although much of the furniture from the south apartments was salvaged.[18] Widely reported in the local press, the disaster prompted Horace Walpole to comment on the loss of "Beckford's fine house in the country, with pictures and furniture to a great value. He says 'Oh! I have an odd fifty thousand pounds in a drawer: I will build it up again: it won't be above a thousand pounds apiece difference to my thirty children."[19]

Undaunted and determined to rebuild using the safest and most up-to-date construction, the Alderman took advice from Peter Wyche, a fellow of the Royal Society, who in turn consulted Felix François d'Espie, the French military engineer responsible for developing new methods for fireproofing buildings. The Alderman's close interest in these novel building techniques led to a publication on this subject being dedicated to him.[20] The choice of brick roofs with flat arch construction, made with brick, mortar, and plaster, and without wood or iron, led not only to a safer building than was possible with then current building practices, but also one that was "more durable and less expensive."[21] French workmen, including an inspector, appear to have been brought over to Fonthill House in April 1756 to supervise the work.[22]

The Alderman's marriage into the aristocracy in 1756, as well as the loss of the original house, encouraged the construction of a building of increased grandeur, more suited to his higher social standing and political aspirations. The new house (see cat. no. 4) was built of brilliant white limestone quarried from the hill across the river. It was approached from the north via a graveled drive through an imposing rusticated gateway. To the west lawns rose to a hill on which stood an open rotunda.[23] A public road passed through the great arched northern entrance lodge that had been built in the Palladian manner

for the Alderman's earlier house in the 1740s .[24] The new building was situated a little south of the old one in a hollow close to the west bank of the stream. A visitor in the late 1760s commented: "The House is a Large and Handsome Stone Building with two Wings but it is Situated much too near the Road & confin'd on one side by a Common." [25] Its proximity to water led to endless complaints of damp, not only from the Alderman but also his son, and was probably one of the many reasons for William Beckford eventually moving from the house.[26] Stretching 390 feet from pavilion to pavilion, the house consisted of a central block of nine bays with a portico supported on four giant-order Ionic columns. The projecting bays had Palladian tripartite windows, the northeast bay being blind, and the house was flanked by quadrant colonnades leading to pavilions surmounted by cupolas.

Fonthill House was modeled closely on Houghton Hall, the residence built by Sir Robert Walpole as a monument to political merit. Its north and south fronts correspond to the west and east fronts of Houghton, respectively. No prominent architect appears to have been involved in Fonthill's design and construction, although the Alderman, dedicated as he was to the support of the nation's arts, must have consulted prominent architects. The house seems to have been built with either James or George Hoare as contractor, both London bricklayers.[27] Sir Charles Farnaby commented: " there is one Hoar a Builder in the City of whom I have heard good Character he built Beckford the present Lord Mayor's house in Wiltshire."[28]

The house took fifteen years to build and furnish, a considerable though not excessive time, and there seems to have been no impediment in its progress when the Alderman commissioned Robert Adam to design a second house at his nearby estate of Witham (fig. 3-5), which had been purchased from Charles Wyndham, the second Earl of Egremont, at some point before the latter's death in 1763.[29] The exterior of this second house was substantially completed.[30] Lady Shelburne, who lived at the neighboring Bowood House, stayed at Fonthill House in 1769 and visited "Witham where Mr Beckford has executed a very beautiful Shell of a House design'd by Mr. Adams as I never comprehend an unfinish'd House I can give no Opinion of this but the Country & Situation I think give it much more the Properties of a

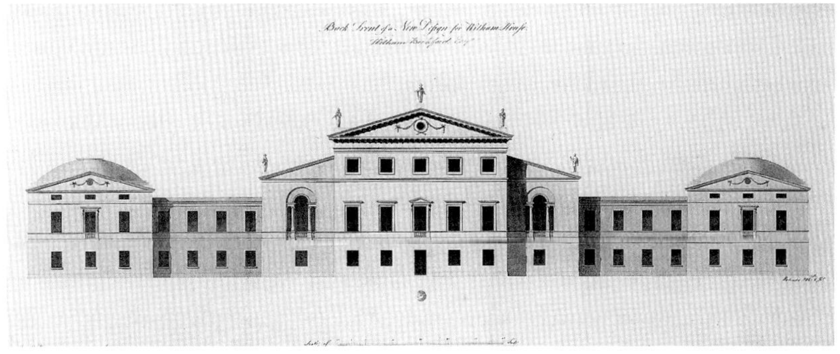

Fig. 3-5. Adam office. Design for Witham Park, Somerset, 1762. Inscribed: "Front of a New Design for Witham House / William Beckford Esq." Signed and dated Robt. Adam Architect, 1762. Pen and monochrome washes. Trustees of Sir John Soane's Museum, London.

Great place than can be found at Fonthill & if there was not a complaint of the wetnefs of the soil at Witham I shou'd very much wonder he had not turn'd his Expence there we din'd in a part of Sir William Wyndham's Old House wch Mr Beckford keeps up till his own is habitable."[31] The motives of the Alderman in commissioning such a substantial new house at his estate of Witham while in the midst of construction and furnishing at Fonthill House are uncertain. Lady Shelburne in her diary implies the house was soon to be ready for the Alderman's occupation.[32] She also suggests that the site of Witham, though not perfect, was an improvement over the poorly situated Fonthill House.

The shell of Fonthill House was completed by 1760. By the mid-1760s work was well underway to complete the interiors,[33] which were mostly finished at the time of the Alderman's death in 1770, with the exception of the delivery of a magnificent state bed and Gobelins tapestries.[34] The Alderman, who spent much of his time in London, was most likely living there throughout the latter part of the 1760s, judging from the surviving correspondence which was written from the house. Certainly by the time of Robert Drysdale's appointment as tutor to the young William Beckford in June 1768, the family was in residence.

The Interiors Under the Alderman

The Alderman's choice of furnishings and the opulent interiors conformed with contemporary taste, even though the structure of the building was somewhat old-fashioned for the time. The state rooms, for example, had richly coffered ceilings inset with paintings by Andrea Casali, while the walls were clothed with rich crimson and multicolored velvets and blue damask.[35] The rooms were lavishly furnished with gilded seat furniture in the rococo taste.

The Alderman's promotion of the nation's art of architecture was demonstrated by his having his house included in the 1767 supplement to *Vitruvius Britannicus.* Of typically Palladian layout (fig. 3-6), the plans resemble those of other houses, such as Wanstead House and Houghton Hall, which were built for the Alderman's Whig friends.[36] These enlightened Protestants, drawn from the wealthy mercantile landowning class, generally eschewed the Continental baroque style of architecture and interior decoration, instead favoring an earlier taste based on ideal classical forms derived from Andrea Palladio and expressed in England by Inigo Jones.[37]

Although thoroughly educated in the classics, the Alderman did not benefit from the experience of a Grand Tour and thus, unlike many of his aristocratic contemporaries, lacked the usual collection of pictures, statuary, and works of art with which to embellish a new house. This may account for the absence of such a collection at Fonthill House in which, seemingly, the only pieces thought to be antique were two porphyry busts in the Grand Entrance Hall.[38]

Fonthill House boasted an impressive library, complex iconographical decorative schemes painted by Casali, as well as a collection of mainly Dutch, Flemish, and some Italian paintings, documented in

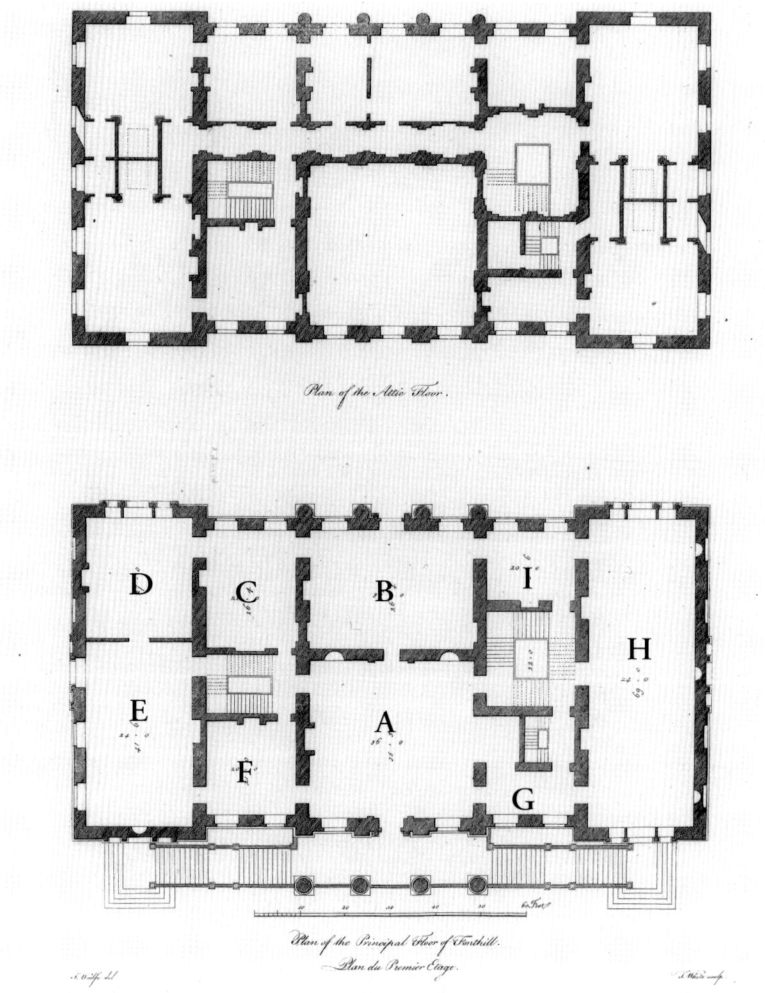

Fig. 3-6. Plan of the principal and bedchamber floors of Fonthill House. The "letter" key has been added: A, Organ Hall or Grand Entrance Hall; B, Grand Saloon; C, State Bedchamber before ca. 1801 and "Sattin" Drawing Room by 1807; D, State Dressing Room before ca. 1801 and Morning Drawing Room by 1807; E. Great Dining Room; F, Tapestry Room before ca. 1801 and Music Room by 1807; G, Cabinet Anteroom; H, Picture or Great Gallery before ca. 1801 and divided into two rooms by 1807, one of which may have been the Vatican Chamber; I, Small Anteroom. From *Vitruvius Britannicus* by J. Wolfe and J. Gandon, vol. 4 (1767), fol. 83. Trustees of Sir John Soane's Museum, London.

later sale records and visitor's accounts. Similar collections could be found in other Whig country houses and show the Alderman to be conservative in his acquisitions and, no doubt, anxious to ensure that his collection conformed with those of his peers. The picture collection would have provided the inspiration for his son William's first literary publication, *Biographical Memoirs of Extraordinary Painters,* published in 1780. The Alderman's patronage of Hogarth and his obvious enjoyment of the satirical is echoed in the two low-relief carved chimney-

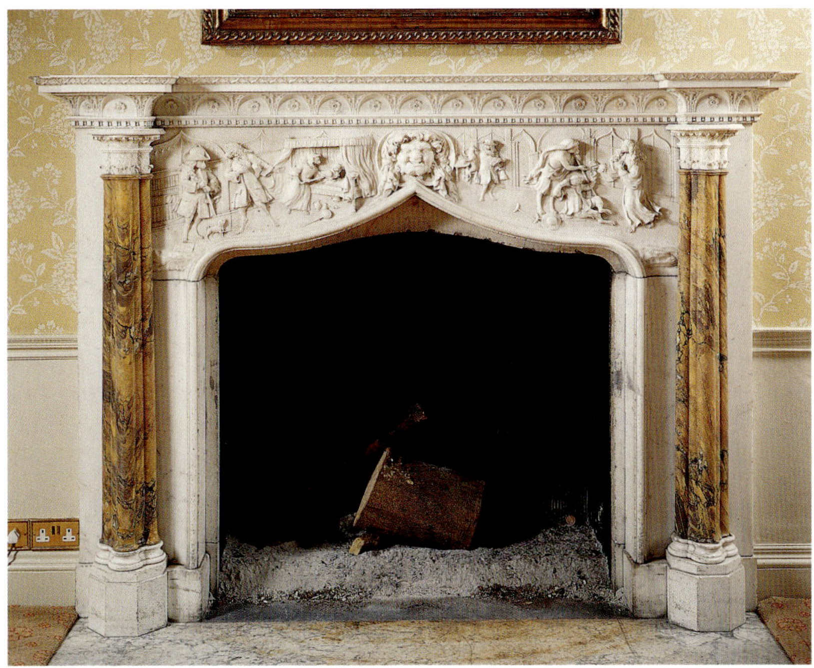

Fig. 3-7. Chimneypiece carved with vignettes satirizing physicians and lawyers, from the corner library, Fonthill House, ca. 1755. White and siena marble. Private collection.

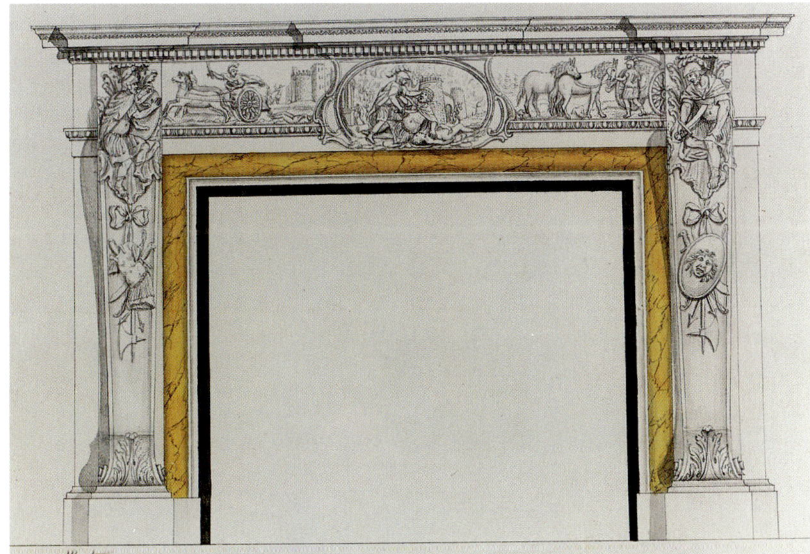

Fig. 3-8. John Francis Moore. Design for the Grand Saloon chimneypiece, ca. 1765. Watercolor. The actual fireplace is now in the Manor House, Beaminster. The Wiltshire Archaeological and Natural History Society, Devizes.

pieces rescued from the burnt house. One chimneypiece, the relief carved with a moralizing tale reminiscent of Hogarth, was reinstalled in the dining parlor on the ground floor.[39] The second was to be found in the corner library (fig. 3-7).[40]

Fonthill's new chimneypieces were much celebrated and in the vanguard of fashion. Derived from William Chambers's *Book of Archi-*

tecture, published in 1758, the most spectacular of these "caryatic" chimneypieces were executed by the sculptor John Francis Moore, who is first recorded working at Audley End in 1761.[41] A French visitor to London in the spring of 1765 visited the sculptor's studio, where he described the Alderman's Grand Saloon chimneypiece in the process of being carved (fig. 3-8).[42] Moore also supplied a chimneypiece for the Grand Entrance Hall, as well as a fountain and another chimneypiece for the Great Dining Room,[43] and in 1767 he carved a heroic statue of the Alderman (see fig. 1-2) for the niche in the picture gallery.[44]

The paucity of records make it difficult to identify the leading craftsmen and artists whom the Alderman would have patronized. Apart from one remaining piece of silver, a tea kettle of 1742 by George Wickes, none of his silver is known to survive.[45] It was presumably melted down by his son and reused for the plate made in 1781 to celebrate his coming-of-age, or it has lost its identity by having had the armorials erased. No furniture-makers have been identified, although the organ from the Grand Entrance Hall may have been made to the designs of William Chambers, either by John Linnell or by William Vile and John Cobb.[46] A pair of magnificent bureau–dressing-tables lavishly mounted in gilt-bronze and almost certainly made for Fonthill House would confirm the Alderman's sophisticated patronage and the extraordinary quality of the furnishings .[47]

One artist who figures prominently, and for whom Fonthill House must have been a very extensive English commission, was the Roman artist Andrea Casali who arrived in England in 1741. Known for his small easel paintings and portraits of the Grand Tourists for whom he acted as *cicerone* in Rome, he was commissioned in 1743 to produce six large history paintings for Wanstead House, Essex, the influential Palladian house built for the Whig financier Sir Richard Childe. Casali had a wide artistic circle, which included Hogarth and Robert Adam.[48] At Fonthill House Casali painted mythological and allegorical works for the rooms on the principal floor. It is quite possible that in his capacity as a dealer he advised the Alderman on purchases of other paintings. Casali's departure from England in 1766 was marked by two sales in London, mainly of his own works but also of paintings that formed part of his trading stock. The Alderman then purchased further paintings, including *The Story of Gunhilda* and *The Murder of Edward Martyr* to complete his picture gallery.[49]

An insight into the interiors of the Alderman's Fonthill can be gleaned from a letter written from William Beckford's elder half-sister, Elizabeth Marsh, to her young friend Miss Cathcart. She describes the detail and extravagance of the fittings: "I must here remark that all the doors of the Grand Apartment (of which there are at least 40) are all of the finest mahogany. The floors are of fine oak and the panes of the window sashes of large plate glass with very neat brass frames covered with mahogany."[50] The doors were similarly praised at the time of their sale in 1807 and the use of brass for glazing bars is unusual and costly.

Lady Shelburne's diary for July 1769 gives an idea of life at Fonthill.[51] As was usual in such a house most activities of daily life took place on the ground, or rustic, floor; the *piano nobile* or prinicipal floor was reserved for the most important visitors and events. From the exterior the rustic floor was reached from doors beneath the sweeping outside stairs that led to the entrance on the principal floor. The stone-lined hall, like that at Houghton, stretched the full depth of the building, the vaulted ceiling supported by immense stone buttresses. Two chimneypieces carved with trophies of game stood on the same wall, opposite urn-shaped stoves. The family dining room and parlor occupied the southeast corner. Lady Shelburne wrote: "it surpris'd me that with so fine an Appartment we shou'd always breakfast dine & sup in the Rustick Story…,"[52] while in the southwest corner were two adjoining libraries that were later altered by James Wyatt.[53] These housed an extensive collection of literature devoted to the classics, travel, and the Orient, which had a significant influence on the young Beckford, who would make additions to his father's library from the age of eleven.[54] Off the library was a large bedroom which later became the celebrated Turkish Room; Robert Drysdale commented on the libraries and bedroom beyond: "Hark, Sir, I cannot ask you to follow the young Lady into a fine bed-chamber even tho' you have to go through a library containing upwards of a thousand and 500 volumes. However, I want you just to give a glance en passant to that Highlandlike man. It is Regent Earl of Murray's picture drawn to the life, inconceivably well executed."[55]

The principal floor contained the state rooms, with the bed-chamber floor above. Guests were generally put up in the attic or second floor, as Lady Shelburne recalled: "We Slept in the Atticks which are very handsomely furnish'd & commodious our Appartment consisted of a Large BedChamber, two drefsing rooms, & a Light Closet; the two first hung with red damask'd & pictures Lord Shelburne's with Blue."[56]

The Principal Floor

The principal floor, above the ground floor, was similar in plan to earlier Palladian houses, such as Houghton and Wanstead. It consisted of nine intercommunicating rooms arranged in a circuit around two top-lit staircases, flanking a double-height central hall. This planning is particularly close to that of Hagley Hall built around 1754–60.[57]

That music played an important part at Fonthill is evident from the description of the organ at the old Fonthill[58] and of the magnificent new instrument (fig. 3-9) installed by Crang in the Grand Entrance Hall. The stone-colored hall, scaled as a 36-foot cube, was paved in checkered black and white marble. Used as a banqueting room and a reception room, it also became the focus of musical life at the new Fonthill House. Lady Shelburne commented: "I saw nothing I admir'd so much as a noble Organ that stands in the Hall & which we made great use of every evening & to which Master Beckford sung," and again "Mrs Beckford lighted up the Gallery wch looked very fine Master Beckford after having sung & acted one of Lovattini's Songs was drefsed like a Girl & acted his part very well & looked very pretty."[59]

Dominating the room, the organ was of serpentine form with gilded pipes, its stone-colored case carved with musical trophies, floral garlands, palm, laurel, and oak branches, and rose bushes supporting

a book of music inscribed with the national anthem, the whole surmounted with a figure of Fame blowing a trumpet.[60] Flanked by porphyry busts of Pompey and Vitellius, set on elaborately inlaid pedestals, the organ stood opposite one of the celebrated white and siena marble chimneypieces carved by Moore with appropriate musical figures and reliefs.[61] The musical iconography was continued in the painting of a classical subject by Casali, set above the chimneypiece within a pedimented tabernacle frame flanked by columns.[62] On a bracket above the painting stood a marble bust, possibly of the Alderman, with further busts of Socrates and other philosophers placed above the doors.[63] Grisaille panels, also by Casali, in imitation of bas reliefs were set in the upper levels of the walls. The coved ceiling of the hall was filled by Casali with another allegorical painting, Apollo and Muses in Grand Concert; Apollo with his harp, Fame her trumpet and the Muses with instruments of ancient and modern music.[64]

A large hexagonal gilt-bronze lantern was suspended from the ceiling by "a gilt chain…in which are five boys or cherubims entwining a Garland and a wave of Linnen."[65] The walls were stuccoed and had raised decoration of musical elements, painted in white on a pale brown ground simulating stonework.[66] Wall-niches, flanking the mahogany double doors leading into the Grand Saloon, held white marble statues of Venus and Apollo symbolizing lyric poetry. These replicas of the Apollo Belvedere and the Venus de Medici were executed by John Wilton.[67] Wilton was the most prominent sculptor of his time

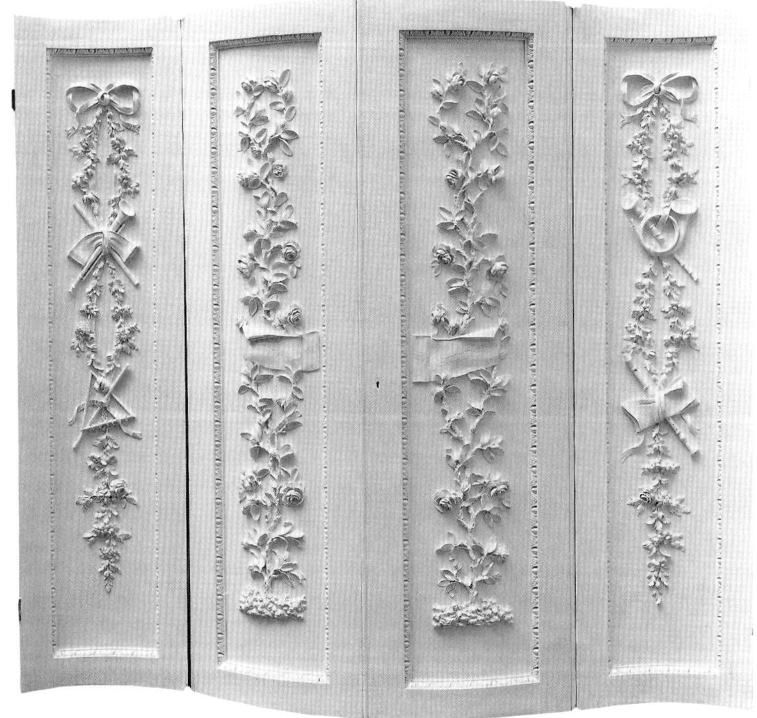

Fig. 3-9. The four central panels from the organ by John Crang, originally installed in the Grand Entrance Hall, Fonthill House, ca. 1760–65; restored in 2000. Carved and painted pine. Trustees of the Victoria and Albert Museum, London, acc. no. W.13–1980.

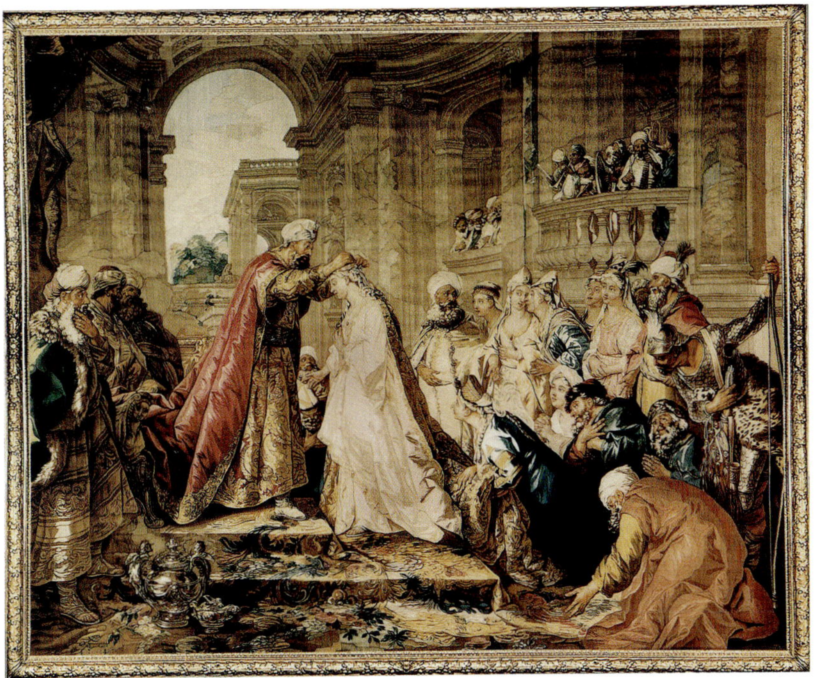

Fig. 3-10. *La Couronnement d'Esther*, 1765–70. Designed and made by the Gobelins Manufactory, Paris. Musées de France, on display at the Château de la Roche-Guyon.

and a leading proponent of classical taste; these sculptures were typical of the reproductions of classical antiques he supplied to William Pitt and other Whig patrons on his return from Italy, with William Chambers, in 1755.[68] The close relationship between patrons, designers, and craftsmen in the eighteenth century makes it possible that while working at nearby Witham, Robert Adam recommended artists and craftsmen, such as Wilton and Casali, who were preferred by Whig patrons, including the Alderman.

Lady Shelburne and other visitors were then taken "thro a Saloon hung with red Damask & Pictures."[69] While the sun-god Apollo was the ruling deity of the Grand Entrance Hall, the adjoining Grand Saloon was presided over by his sister the dawn-goddess, Aurora. Occupying the center of the southern side of the house, the focal point of this room was another spectacular chimneypiece, this one celebrating Homer's Iliad (see fig. 3-8), illustrating "most of the famous actions at the taking of Troy, etc."[70]

Lady Shelburne, who was shown the adjacent State Bedroom by Mrs. Beckford and Elizabeth Marsh, described a "Bed Chamber hung with red Velvet and gold in wch is a Magnificent State Bed." [71] Both Robert Drysdale and Elizabeth Marsh commented on the bed.[72] It was later borrowed by the Herbert family at nearby Wilton House for a forthcoming royal visit, although in the event it was unused by the royal party.[73] The statuary marble chimneypiece in this room was carved by Thomas Banks.[74] Adjoining the State Bedchamber, in the southeast corner of the house was the State Dressing Room, with its

Palladian window overlooking the park. It housed part of the collection of Dutch and Flemish paintings and also met with the admiration of Lady Shelburne, who called it "one of the prettiest Drefsing rooms I have seen furnish'd with crimoisen damask & small pictures."[75] This room, with its portrait of the young William Beckford incorporated within an oval medallion in the giltwood overmantel mirror (see cat. no. 1), was described by an admiring Elizabeth Marsh: "The hangings, settees and chairs are crimson damask, but the room is almost covered over with a prodigious fine collection of pictures by several of the greatest masters. An excellent Portrait of my Brother in an Oval of an elegant ornamental Glass. Casali had taken the strongest resemblance of my Brother, and it is a sweet pretty picture."[76]

The Great Dining Room was located on the east side of the house, with its windows overlooking the river. The iconographic tradition of the house was continued with bacchic allusions, but these were also combined with a display of family portraits. It was described carefully by Elizabeth Marsh: "the walls of this Stucco painted white. On the north side is a white marble fountain representing the four elements finely executed by Moore, my Papa and Mama's portraits by Casali are on each side of it, and opposite to these are my Papa's mother's and Lady Effingham, his sister's. And either side of the Chimney are those of my Papa's Father and Grandfather by Hoare. The feast of the gods is very finely painted on the ceiling; and also Ceres, Pan, Pomona and Morpheus at each corner in ovals. The tablet of the Chimney piece is a conversation between Apollo and Diana; the supporters Daphne and Arethusa. The chairs and curtains are of cut flowered velvet of different colours intermixt. The marble tables, the glasses and frames are remarkably elegant and the gilding extraordinarily well done. But all the carved work here is exquisite and greatly resembles lace. The frames of the tables and glasses are inconceivably beautiful; the glass frames are vines, by which also the tables seem to be supported growing from the ground under the tables, where are pretty little boys playing with goats. Vauxhall was the ingenious carver."[77]

The Alderman clearly appreciated costly and luxurious materials; the use of lavish multicolored velvets was the height of conspicuous consumption and was in accordance with other, slightly earlier, Palladian interiors such as Holkham Hall and Houghton Hall. The written descriptions suggest that the tables and mirrors in this room were related to designs by both Thomas Chippendale and Thomas Johnson. They also recall earlier furniture of the 1740s and may have been pieces salvaged from the previous house.[78]

The Great Dining Room led to the Grand Entrance Hall through a smaller room which was "to be furnish'd with Goblin tapestry but is now fitted up with pea Green paper."[79] The Alderman's knowledge of the latest fashionable taste is evident by his commissioning from Gobelins sumptuous tapestries depicting the Old Testament story of Esther for this room (fig. 3-10).[80] This subject seems to have appealed to him; he also possessed a painting by Claude on the same theme, which had survived the earlier fire, and perhaps this encouraged the choice of subject.[81] Although there is no firm evidence,

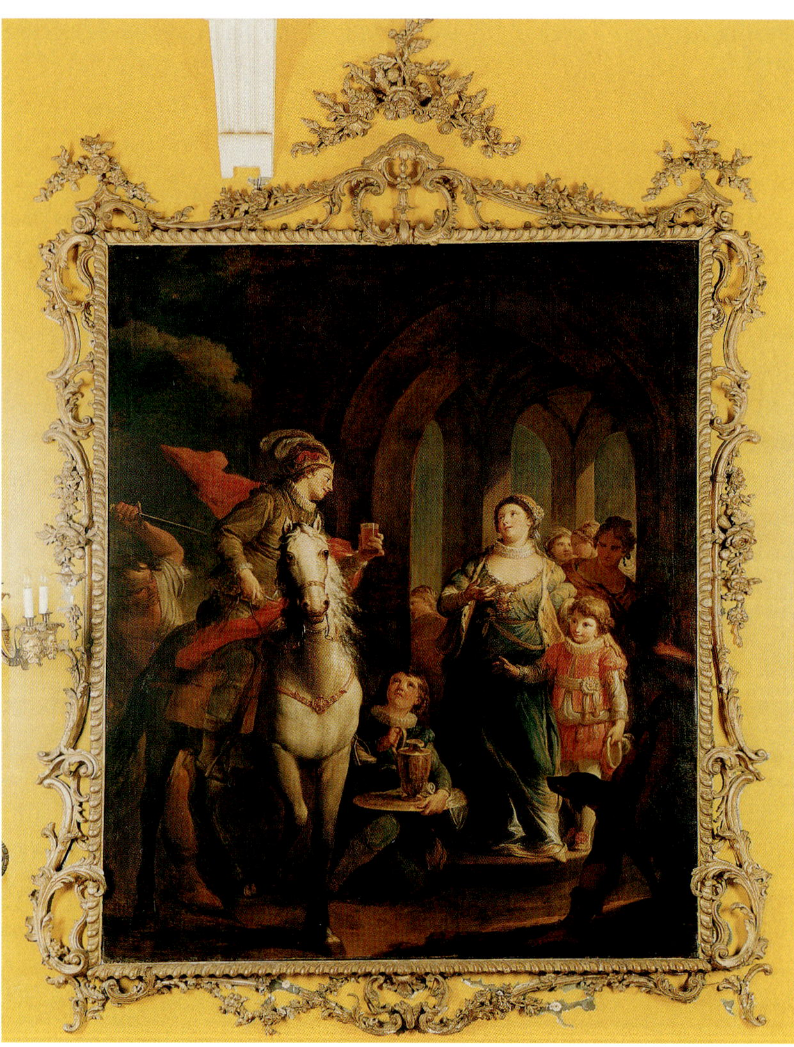

Fig. 3-11. Andrea Casali. *The Murder of Edward Martyr,* 1761. Oil on canvas; 18th-century gilded papier-mâché frame made for the picture gallery at Fonthill. The Burton Constable Foundation, Hull.

these tapestries may have been ordered through Robert Adam, who was at that time creating other interiors specifically for Gobelins tapestries. It is possible that the Fonthill tapestries were intended to form part of an, as yet unknown, furnishing scheme for the new house at Witham, and that a change of circumstance led to their installation at Fonthill House. Certainly by July 1769, when Lady Shelburne visited, the tapestries were anticipated at Fonthill. In any event, they were only delivered after the Alderman's death in 1770, with a further delivery to complete the order being sent in 1771.[82] This second delivery might have been for upholstery for seat furniture, although no appropriate upholstered furniture can be identified in the sale catalogues or the descriptions of the house.

The entire west side of the house was given over to a picture gallery: "a very fine Gallery the depth of the House the furniture is Large Pictures on Blue Damask in a nich in the middle of one side of the room is a White Marble Statue of Mr Beckford when Lord Mayor, with an Inscription under it—The Furniture is but just put up the Gilding all new & bright and the Ceilings being painted by Cafsali give the whole a magnificent & brilliant appearance."[83] The description suggests that the furnishings were newly supplied. Emphasizing the Alderman's promotion of the nation's trade and commerce, and his advocacy of the art of history painting, the gallery was presided over by the statue of the Alderman in mayoral robes (see fig. 1-2), which was placed in a niche on the windowless west wall. The gallery was dominated by a series of history paintings by Casali: five ceiling panels emblematic of the arts and sciences, a pair of paintings over the chimneypieces, and four enormous depictions of historical subjects.[84] Certain of these had been exhibited at the Royal Academy in 1760 and 1761 (fig. 3-11) and were purchased by the Alderman in the artist's sale of 1766.[85] Hung against blue damask, the fashionable color to hang pictures against in the 1760s, the pictures had richly sculpted, gilded papier-mâché frames, rather than standard gilded wooden ones, presumably more as a matter of temporal expediency than of economy.[86] There would have been little room on the walls to hang additional paintings, and some of the large Casalis must have been moved at a later stage to accommodate the numerous smaller paintings acquired and hung in the picture gallery by the younger Beckford.[87]

The Blue Staircase, with its fine, wrought-iron balustrade painted in blue and highlighted with gilding, had walls with a "buff coloured ground with Landskips, Bustos, and Trophies painted in shades of blue."[88] It was top lit by a large skylight and hung with large-scale classical paintings by Casali. The staircase rose to a corridor where Hogarth's series, *The Rake's Progress*—purchased by the Alderman from the artist's sale in 1745 and saved from the 1755 fire—was installed certainly at the end of the eighteenth century.[89] Topographical views of earlier Fonthill houses were displayed along the corridor, together with a group of fourteen family portraits, which served to show the Alderman's establishment of a dynasty and the honoring of his ancestors.[90] The corridor, which was later intended to be remodeled by John Soane for William Beckford, led to the prinicipal bedrooms. Predominantly designed with recesses for beds in the grand contemporary French manner, the bedrooms were elegant and luxurious. One visitor commented, for example, that "Mrs. Beckford's dressing room has in it numbers of superb and elegant nick-nacks."[91] It would have been in these rooms that stood the pair of mahogany bureau–dressing-tables already mentioned.

The Alderman's sudden death in 1770, left his son William the owner of this imposing house. The Alderman, while seemingly abreast of current fashions and undoubtedly employing the most prominent craftsmen, was never as deeply involved in collecting and furnishing as was his more cosmopolitan son. The Alderman's political ambitions necessitated the establishment of an appropriate seat. With his relatively new and enormous wealth, he must have sought to project an image suitable to his stature and consistent with the aesthetic validated by his circle of Whig friends. There can be no doubt that the opulent and ostentatious interiors of Fonthill House also contributed to the aesthetic taste of the Alderman's son. While Beckford later reacted against this, in part with his simpler but no less opulent francophile taste, his recurrent use of luxurious materials—such as the scarlet and crimson velvets chosen for the interiors of Fonthill Abbey, Lansdown Crescent and Lansdown Tower—was surely inspired by the lavish use of these materials by the Alderman. Purporting to despise his father's Dutch and Flemish paintings, Beckford must nonetheless have been stimulated and influenced by the Alderman's collection. Unlike his father, however, Beckford became totally immersed and involved in his collections and their display. This passion, fueled by his broader and more international outlook, would be manifested in the future alterations to Fonthill House.

Fonthill House Under William Beckford

William Thomas Beckford was educated in the luxurious setting of the Alderman's Fonthill. Isolated and removed from the outside influences so feared by his mother, he was tutored at home, first by Robert Drysdale and later by others.[92] From the summer of 1777 Beckford traveled extensively between England and the Continent. On one visit home, on April 14, 1781, either at his house on Wimpole Street, London, or at his mother's house at West End, Hampstead, he sat for the great full-length portrait commissioned from George Romney to

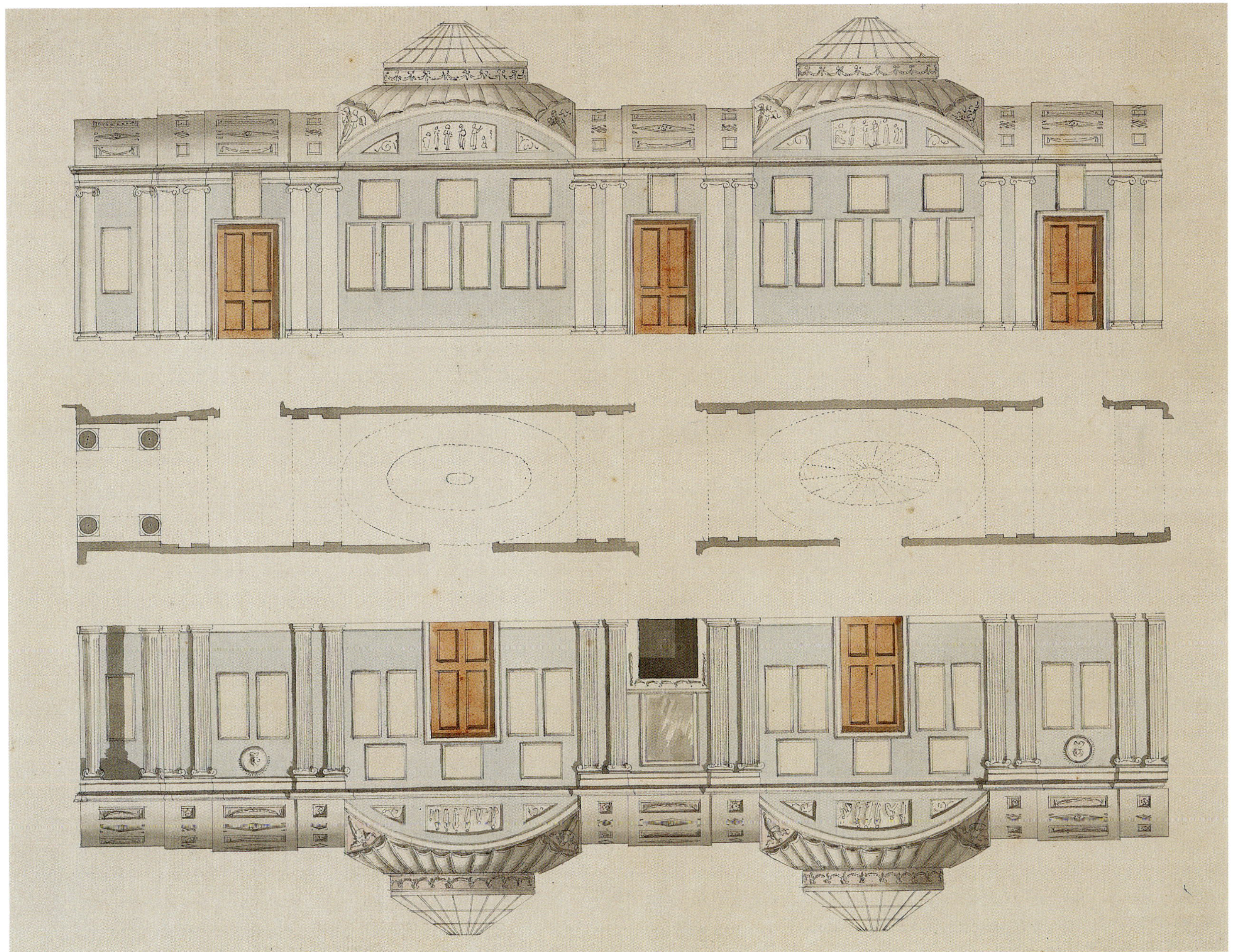

Fig. 3-12. John Soane. Final design for the picture gallery at Fonthill, 1787. Watercolor. Trustees of Sir John Soane's Museum, London.

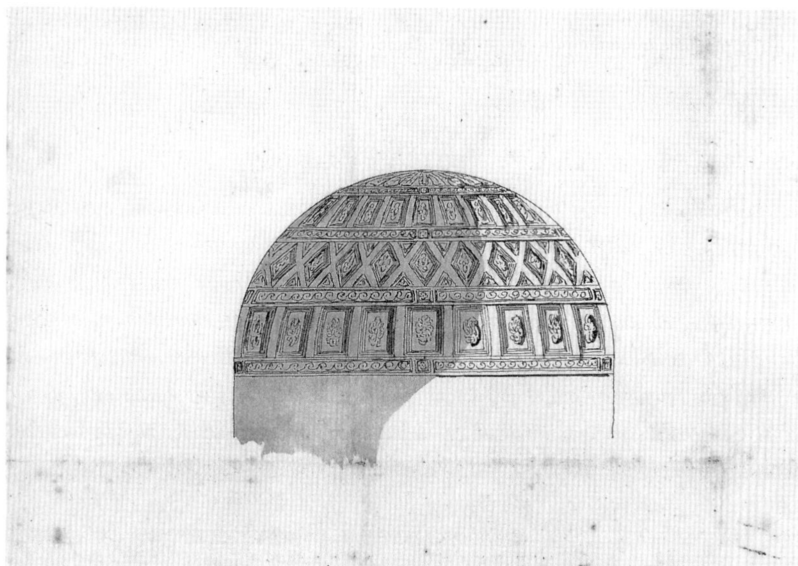

Fig. 3-13. John Soane. Design for the coffered niches in the Tapestry Room, Fonthill House (detail), 1787. Pen and ink. The Bodleian Library, University of Oxford, MS Beckford c.84, fol. 122r.

record his coming of age (see cat. no. 8). Early in July he returned to Fonthill to prepare for these festivities.

In spite of his absences on the Continent, Beckford was almost constantly initiating alterations to Fonthill House and the surrounding park. During May of 1783, the month of his marriage to Lady Margaret, excess furniture from the house was sent to London for their new residence in Portman Square.[93] Further shipments of his father's furniture, presumably considered old-fashioned, continued to be sent to other of his properties during the 1780s. After a shipment in 1787 to his residence in Lisbon, Fonthill House must have looked somewhat empty, and this would have necessitated later refurbishing schemes.[94]

Throughout this period Beckford constantly worried about his finances, and some idea of this concern can be gleaned from his letters. Writing on January 18, 1786, from the Château de la Tour de Peilz in Switzerland[95] to Thomas Wildman, his lawyer, Beckford talks of financial problems and his irritation that funds accruing from the sale of some of the Alderman's dated furniture were being diverted for use elsewhere: "the money I allow for one thing is taken without ceremony for another as in the case of the old furniture…."[96] The shortage of funds is stressed in a second draft of this letter: "full powers you have from me of felling timbers, leasing upon lives, even stripping Fonthill."[97] This is one of the earliest known indications of his waning attachment to the house. Living in Switzerland with his wife, Lady Margaret, in an attempt to escape the scandal of his liaison with William Courtenay, he most likely viewed the prospect of an early return to England as impossible. To use Fonthill House and its contents as a financial resource would have seemed a good short-term solution to his financial problems.

The second draft of this letter also refers to Beckford's connections with Edward Foxhall, his general factotum, cabinetmaker, upholsterer, and furnisher, who played such an important role in the furnishing of both Fonthill House and, subsequently, Fonthill Abbey.[98] Foxhall may well have been a capable designer of furniture, but his significant role was that of "upholder" who had the vital task of coordinating the supply of furniture and furnishings in Beckford's frequent absences. He was also well known as a picture-frame maker.[99] "Vauxhall," the ingenious carver mentioned in Elizabeth Marsh's description of the dining room, must in fact refer to Edward Foxhall rather than the eponymous glass manufactory.[100] It is unlikely that Marsh was referring to the glass manufactory as she specifically mentions "Vauxhall" as a carver. Foxhall may not have been old enough, however, in the mid-1760s to have carved these mirror frames, but it seems likely that there was a Foxhall family business employed by both the Alderman and his son. Interestingly, Foxhall was married to a daughter of the sculptor Moore, who was closely involved with earlier work for the Alderman.[101] Foxhall may have been introduced to Beckford through his family connections with Moore rather than through an introduction from John Soane, with whom Foxhall had collaborated since as early as 1781 and who was employed by Beckford in 1786.[102] Foxhall's role has, perhaps, been underestimated. His importance is highlighted by Beckford's lament after Foxhall's death in 1815: "I haven't failed to perceive and feel the horror of the loss of Foxhall."[103]

Soane and Beckford

On a brief trip home in the autumn of 1786, before leaving for Portugal, Beckford commissioned a variety of work from the twenty-three-year-old architect John Soane. Soane visited Fonthill House in April 1787, although Beckford was abroad, and in London the following month Beckford's mother was presented with final designs for a proposed new gallery (fig. 3-12).[104] A picture gallery, top lit by a circular dome flanked by two oval ones, was to be inserted into the long corridor gallery on the bedchamber floor.[105] Intended to display either Beckford's fine collection of colored engravings after Raphael's *grotteschi* in the Vatican *logge*,[106] or possibly his father's Hogarths, this pioneering scheme for a top-lit gallery was not carried out.

There was a considerable amount of activity at Fonthill House during the summer of 1787. Beckford wrote: "I learn from Foxhall that painting and furnishing goes on briskly at Fonthill."[107] Soane designed a marble chimneypiece for the southeast parlor on the ground floor and on the principal floor a further chimneypiece for the Tapestry Room, in which he also inserted coffered niches (fig. 3-13).[108] A new state bed was also designed by Soane (see fig. 2-7). Elaborately carved and gilded, it was designed in a monumental "Greek" style, the canopy surmounted by a finial derived from the Choragic Monument of Lysicrates in Athens. Sumptuously hung with elaborate, crimson velvet draperies, it had a headboard embroidered with a large heraldic cartouche. The bed, placed in a recess behind additional elaborate crimson and scarlet draperies, was complemented by carved giltwood seat furniture upholstered in the same crimson velvet. It is also possible that the six mahogany hall settees (see cat. no. 29) with their double heraldic backs were also designed by Soane for the Grand Entrance Hall.

Simultaneously with the Soane commission, Beckford received two views of Wales, one of the ruins of Conway Castle, the other of Grassmere Mill, commissioned from Phillippe Jacques de Loutherbourg for the apartment or anteroom off the picture gallery on the principal floor.[109] Chimneypieces were also sculpted by John Bacon and Thomas Banks.[110]

THE LAST PHASE OF FONTHILL HOUSE

The most important period of refurbishment was carried out at Fonthill during the 1790s, when William Beckford spent a great deal of time in Paris as well as in Lisbon and Madrid. He developed a keen appreciation for the latest Parisian trends, and indeed he commissioned silver and other works of art in a refined and restrained neoclassical style from several notable makers including the goldsmith Henri Auguste.[111] He also commissioned two small carpets from the Savonnerie factory in 1792–93, which were probably destined for his London residence.[112] He was personally acquainted with the revolutionary architect Claude-Nicolas Ledoux and was aware of, and excited by, the many new, severely neoclassical buildings being erected in the 1780s and 1790s.[113] He had employed in 1790 the avant-garde architect Joseph Ramée to construct a tent in oriental style.[114] Ramée had been apprenticed to François-Joseph Bélanger and was, therefore, acquainted with the latest developments in the new classical style. Beckford may well have seen the comte d'Artois' highly unusual and influential neoclassical interiors at the Château de Bagatelle in Paris, although at this date they were no longer in the vanguard of fashion.[115] The combination of this exposure and the influence of the exotic atmosphere of Lisbon strongly influenced his highly sensitive imagination and encouraged his passion for the severely elegant, rich interiors that he sought to recreate at Fonthill House.[116]

In Lisbon during 1794 and 1795 Beckford spoke of endless economies at Fonthill. In spite of the great increase in the price of sugar between 1796 and 1799, several factors—legal claims challenging the ownership of Beckford's plantations in Jamaica, slave revolts on other Caribbean islands, the effects of the French Revolution, and Beckford's extensive borrowing of funds from the Wildman brothers—contributed to a sense of financial insecurity.[117] By 1794 Beckford had begun to consider demolishing the house and building a more manageable structure. In a letter written to him by Wildman in September 1794, however doubts were raised: "as to pulling down the House, there is no possibility of agreeing to it, the price would, be assured, be trifling compared with the expence of putting up furnishing."[118] James Wyatt, already employed to redesign the ground floor libraries, was asked for his advice on replacing Fonthill House with a smaller house, either on the same site but facing the water, or on a new site across the lake. Naturally, Wyatt encouraged the idea of a new building.[119] It was felt that this could not be accomplished for less than £50,000, and ulti-

mately Wildman wrote: "I have concluded to offer you my advice that the house should stand some time longer without further Conson [concern] about pulling it down as I am convinced from everything I hear on the Subject that you would never put 10,000 clear into your pocket and I very much doubt whether on half of that money."[120] Nothing came of these proposals, but again, in November 1797, Beckford told Wyatt that he was thinking of taking down Fonthill House and that now he wished to enlarge the future Abbey as "His Mansion House."[121]

In 1796 construction had begun on the Abbey, which would, in effect, sound the final death knell for Fonthill House. However, in spite of this and Beckford's growing dissatisfaction with the poor situation of Fonthill House and the high cost of its maintenance, the 1790s still saw the most extensive period of refurbishment. Wyatt was perhaps more involved with this work than has previously been supposed. By 1791 he was certainly employed by Beckford.[122] In 1795 a letter from Foxhall describes giltwood stools designed by Wyatt: "I have begun six stools for you from the sketches of Mr. Wyatt—they were quite plain and the only gilding is the legs which are in the form [sketch of x-framed, upholstered stool]. I would thank you sir in your next letter to send me a small piece of the straw colour silk for a pattern & then I can get any quantity made that you may please to order."[123] On July 15, 1799, the Hon. Ann Rushout visited Fonthill House and recorded in her diary: "there is an Armoury where are Musquets for 150 men, the number of Mr. Beckford's troop and there is a band of twenty-four Musicians belonging to it." Describing the two-room library on the ground floor, she noted: "we now went round the appartments on the rustic floor, here Mr. Wyatt has exerted all his genius for he has united to the appearance of the greatest comfort, the most perfect elegance, there is a Library consisting of two rooms, with the ceiling gothic-ised, in one room there is a curious chimney Piece which was the only thing saved from the fire of Mr. Beckford's first House, it is a burlesque upon Physicians and Lawyers" (see fig. 3-7).[124] Beckford's insatiable book collecting and the increasingly large numbers of books would also have required, no doubt, more extensive accommodation.[125]

In April 1796, underlining his intention to modernize the Alderman's interiors, Beckford wrote "harmony is everything in pictures, furniture &c. I have been trying to harmonize Fonthill—no easy attempt, I can assure you—wealth having done a confounded deal of mischief."[126] This redecoration is again confirmed in a letter to his mother, written from Fonthill, mentioning "the painting & new fitting up of several rooms in the House."[127] Around this time, in July 1796, Foxhall offered Beckford a pair of large French mirror glasses, which he proposed to suitably frame and hang in the piers of the Tapestry Room and of the anteroom between the picture gallery and the saloon.[128] Beckford's response is not known, but pier mirrors of similar size were sold in the sale of 1801, suggesting that he accepted Foxhall's proposals, and his sale catalogues bear out the renown of Fonthill House's extravagant and costly mirror glass.[129]

Before Christmas of 1799 the two paintings by Claude had

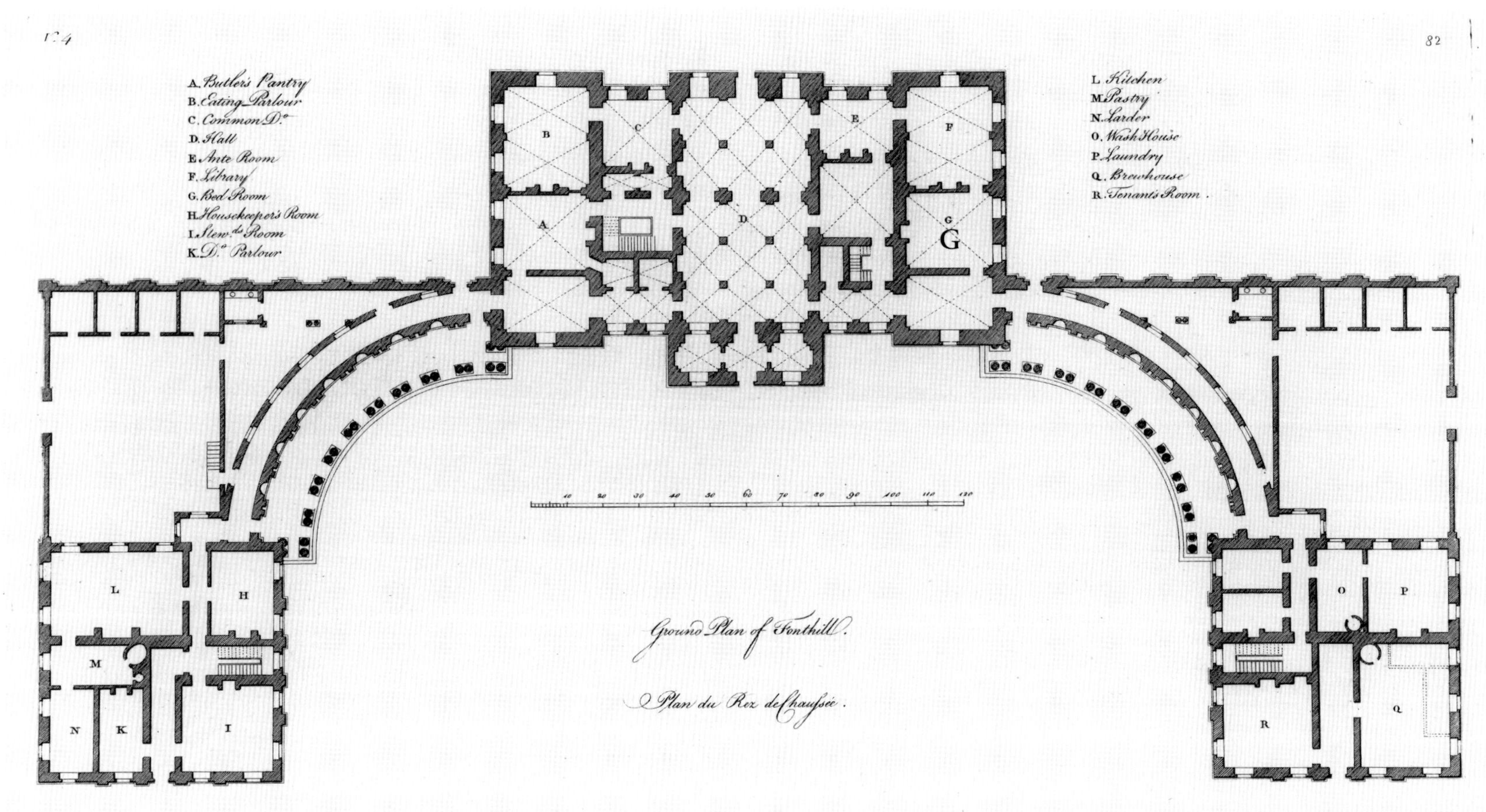

Fig. 3-14. Plan of the ground floor of Fonthill House. The bedroom (G) later became the Turkish Room. From *Vitruvius Britannicus* by J. Wolfe and J. Gandon, vol. 4 (1767), fol. 82. Trustees of Sir John Soane's Museum, London.

been delivered: "I am warming myself by the Altieri Claudes which have found their way to Fonthill, and being magnificently framed, well-placed, and tenderley washed by Tresham, appear in the utmost glory and perfection."[130] These hung above a splendid pair of alabaster-topped tables in the Grand Saloon. Their elaborate frames had been designed by Wyatt but have now vanished.[131] They are known to have been made specifically for the large-scale landscape paintings with wide borders and projecting corners. They are referred to as of "the old pattern," which might suggest that there was an earlier style of "Beckford" frame (although it is not known whether Beckford had his pictures framed in a uniform style) or that these new frames were inspired by the ones in which the paintings were presumably purchased.[132] This "old pattern" might refer to the frame supplied in 1789 by Foxhall for a portrait of the Alderman by Romney.[133]

During the mid-1790s William Beckford most likely employed "those distinguished French artists" John James Boileau and Feuglet to carry out extensive decorative schemes and to design furniture.[134] Boileau arrived in London from Paris around 1787. Although known primarily for his silver designs,[135] he is recorded as working, with

Feuglet (about whom little is known), for the Chelsea Paper Manufactory.[136] Later Boileau was the preeminent "decorator" for the Prince Regent at Carlton House, where he and Feuglet were employed by 1792.[137] It is possible that Boileau met Beckford through Auguste, who made silver for Beckford and acted as his agent for purchasing works of art in Paris. Boileau's designs reflect a deep knowledge of Auguste's work as well as that of other artists who worked in this archaeologically inspired, neoclassical style.[138] Equally, Beckford probably knew of Boileau's work for the Prince Regent and the Carlton House set, from which he was ostracized. Despite this, employing the prince's designers would have strongly appealed to him. Tantalizingly, in a letter from Portugal on September 5, 1787, discussing his house Ramalhão, Beckford wrote that "Not one of Boileau's chanoines ever sunk into a sofa more voluptuously," which intimates that he may have met Boileau earlier in Paris or at least knew of his work.[139] The apparent longevity of Boileau further suggests that there might in fact be two craftsmen of that name, one a silversmith, the other a decorator.

The Prince of Wales and his entourage visited Fonthill House in Beckford's absence in September 1794 and expressed their admiration, an event relayed to Beckford by Wildman: "the Prince most highly commended the Place and your taste in the furniture."[140] Boileau's work at Fonthill House included the ceiling decorations for the Turkish Room as well as designs for numerous pieces of furniture, including a pair of Turkish-style giltwood tripods and an extraordinary suite of case furniture for the Tartarian Room.

Beckford's exposure to Eastern literature inspired a lifelong interest in all things Oriental and exotic. At the Château de Bagatelle or at the comte d'Artois' official Paris residence, Le Temple, Beckford may have first seen a Turkish-style interior.[141] At Ramalhão he constructed a mirrored room hung with draperies,[142] and at Fonthill House a tent in the Turkish style was erected for the Twelfth Night festival of January 6, 1797. Boileau may have assisted with the tent's production, as he was working for William Beckford at this time. In October of the same year, however, Boileau was dismissed by Beckford, if only temporarily.[143] Quite conceivably, however, Beckford might have reused the "oriental" tent that he had ordered from Ramée only a few years earlier for use in Geneva.

The genesis of the Turkish Room is uncertain, but it did not exist as such during the Alderman's lifetime.[144] The west side of the ground floor consisted of three rooms (fig. 3-14), the two southernmost of which comprised the library. The third room, which was to become the Turkish Room, was used in 1768 as a bedroom and was described by Elizabeth Marsh.[145] By 1799, when Ann Rushout visited Fonthill, the transformation had taken place. She wrote, "adjoining to this room,[the library] is the Turkish Room, with this I was enchanted, opposite to the door at which we entered was a looking glass down to the ground with drapery hanging over it, the hangings were of an Orange colour, the Carpet Persian and Ceiling, Cabinets and all the ornaments were painted in the most exquisite style."[146]

These two descriptions provide the evidence necessary to establish that it could only have been William Beckford who created the Turkish room and not the Alderman. John Britton's *Beauties of Wiltshire* (1801), a publication describing the architecture and interiors of some of the most important estates in the county, gives a detailed account of this room:

Adjoining the library in an apartment called the Turkish room, as splendid and sumptuous as those magical recesses of enchanted palaces we read of in the Arabian Nights Entertainments. The ground of the vaulted ceiling is entirely gold, upon which the most beautiful arabesques and wreaths of flowers are delineated, in the vivid colours of nature, by the pencil of the distinguished French artists, Boileau and Feuglet. The whole room is hung round with ample curtains of the richest orange satin, with deep fringes of silk and gold. Between the folds of this drapery, mirrors of uncommon size appear as openings leading to other appartments. The carpet, of reddish etruscan brown, contrasts admirably with the tints of the hangings. The windows are screened by blinds of orange silk, admitting a warm glow of summer light. Opposite to these apertures, an altar of the finest verd-antique contains the fireplace, secured by a grate-work of gilded bronze. One each side are two cabinets of an elegant and novel form, sculptured and gilt in a very magnificent style. The upper panels, painted by Smirke, are very inferior to the generality of this artist's productions; but the drawers by Hamilton, in imitation of antique cameos, are designed with the utmost grace, and executed with spirit and correctness. Candelabra, vases of japan, cassolets, and piles of cushions, are distributed about the appartment, which combines more splendor, singularity and effect, than any room of its size in the kingdom. The space is not large, not above twenty-six by twenty-three; but the whole is managed, by the aid of mirrors, as to appear boundless, and to seize most powerfully on the imagination.[147]

The cabinets mentioned were those formerly standing in the niches designed by Soane for the Tapestry Room and which were sold in 1802.[148] They were painted by Richard Smirke, from whom Beckford commissioned other work in 1797,[149] and by William Hamilton, who also supplied designs for a window for the new Abbey and later was appointed drawing master to Beckford's daughters.[150]

The room also made a striking impression on a German visitor named Goede, who commented: "The so-called Turkish room can serve as a vivid example. This room is very bright, and of considerable size. All the surroundings have the objective of giving the whole the glow of Asian magnificence, improved by European taste."[151]

The demolition of the east wing of Fonthill House precipitated an auction held by Phillips in 1801, which included the luxurious contents of this room.[152] From the sale catalogue it can be determined that heavily trimmed, satin-upholstered ottoman sofas stretched around three sides of the room, while full-length French plate glass mirrors were placed between the windows facing the door and over the chimneypiece and were partially concealed by silk. The window soffits were carved, gilded, and painted by Feuglet. The room also contained a pair of Turkish-style giltwood tripods, designed by Boileau, who was also responsible for the four ceiling paintings.[153] The effect of light filtered through colored silks would have enhanced the exotic and luxurious feeling of this interior, which to a modern eye, however, may not have appeared to be so obviously "Turkish."[154]

This passion for atmospheric Eastern interiors appears again on the bedchamber floor. One visitor described "the Tartarian Room, which is quite beautiful, all sorts of things used by the Tartars and painted about the Room in the very best manner, some elegant Cabinets and there is a most ingenious contrivance for the fireplace, it is on one side of the room, being summer it was shut up, and looked like an elegant cabinet, but by opening the doors we saw the fireplace and the smoke is conveyed up the Chimney on one side."[155] This extraordinary fire surround or enclosure took the form of a pier table with doors, divided from the end panels by carved giltwood quivers of

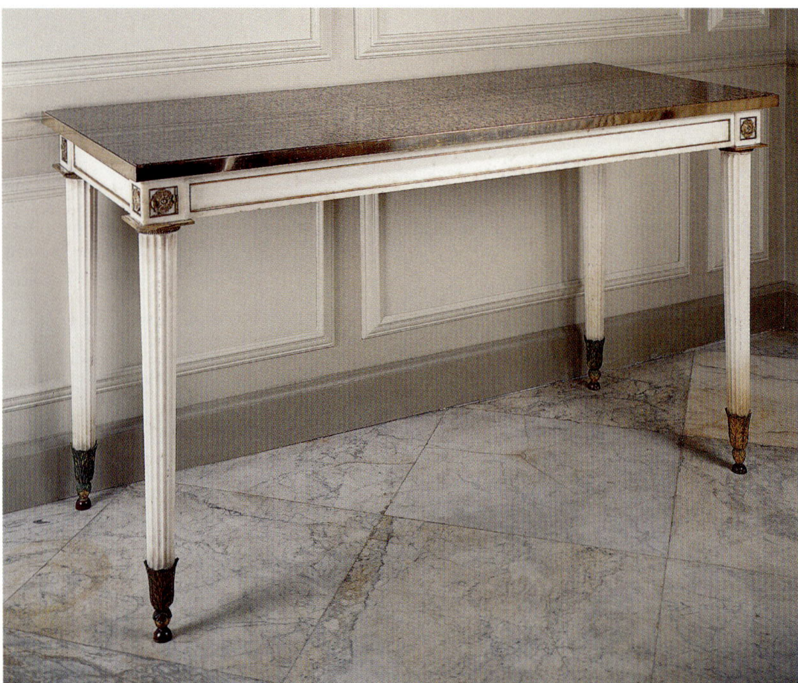

Fig. 3-15. One of a pair of tables from the dining room at Fonthill House, ca. 1795–1800. White marble and red Egyptian granite with gilt-bronze mounts probably supplied by Vulliamy. Private collection.

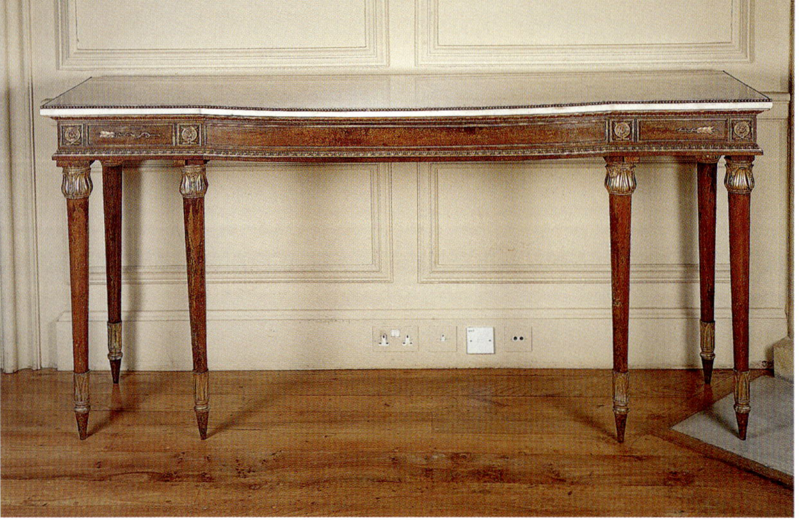

Fig. 3-16. Side table from the State Dressing Room at Fonthill House, ca. 1795–1800. Giltwood and purpleheart. Private collection.

arrows. It may have been designed to balance the pier commode, which, together with a large china press, formed the major furnishings of this room. The commode had open ends to display china and is reminiscent of those made by Adam Weisweiler for the Chinese Drawing Room at Carlton House which had arabesque wall panels painted by Boileau.[156] These three pieces of unusual furniture were described as carved and gilded, painted by Boileau, and mounted in ormolu, the commode and pier table having granite tops.[157] The pieces were pur-

chased at the 1801 sale by a Mr. H. Jeffrey who ran a gallery in Salisbury. They reappear in an exhibition catalogue of the Jeffrey gallery in 1809, together with other pieces from Fonthill and elsewhere as well as pieces from differing sources.[158] The Jeffrey catalogue describes them as being "highly ornamental to the Boudoir of any Lady of Fashion."[159]

The Tartarian Room also had a pink silk-lined door, pink silk window curtains, and a suite of giltwood stools and ottomans upholstered in pink silk.[160] The window shutters, as in all the rooms on this floor, were mirrored. The dazzling effect of light reflecting off the silks, the mirrors and the unusual mirrored shutter cases contributed to the exotic atmosphere of both the Tartarian and the Turkish rooms.[161]

Beckford's grand scheme of redecoration was still in progress at the time of the Reverend Richard Warner's visit to Fonthill House in September of 1800.[162] The State Bedchamber and Dressing Room were in the process of being transformed, the former as a music room. According to Warner: "The music room is not yet finished, but the same splendour of decoration is intended to be bestowed upon it as the other apartments have had. It is coved, and contains, *The Fifth Plague of Egypt*, by Turner."[163] The dressing room, by then the morning drawing room, appeared to retain the same wall and window decoration unaltered from the Alderman's day, with the addition, hung over the fireplace, of Romney's *Indian Woman* illustrating an episode from *A Midsummer Night's Dream*.[164] The style and composition of this painting may anticipate Beckford's interest in William Blake. Opposite this, below one of the largest mirrors, a white marble table "designed with singular taste from the antique, richly carved and gilt, supported by a pedestal and a statuary marble top"[165] held a selection of "vases and cups of gold, designed after the purest antique models, and chased by the famous Auguste, of Paris."[166] The heavy use of gilding and the glittering effect of the gold and silver reflected in the three plates of the immense mirror glass in its "rich carved frame gilt to imitate or-molu," would have conveyed the atmosphere of a sophisticated Parisian interior.[167] The mirror glass would no doubt have been imported from France which remained the main and much admired source for this component of interiors.[168]

The Great Dining Room also underwent considerable changes in the 1790s. Britton welcomed some improvements: "the eating room, forty-three feet by twenty-four feet; which is lightsome and well proportioned; but disfigured by a ceiling and chimney-piece in the heavy taste that prevailed when the house was built, and which we are sorry to see Mr. Beckford has not yet removed. He has added two tables of solid granite supported by frames and fluted legs of white marble, with gilt-bronze, in style of much elegance."[169] These tables (fig. 3-15), with their combination of rare red Egyptian granite slabs and carved white marble frames, with lavishly gilded mounts probably supplied by Vulliamy, London's leading supplier of fine bronzes, maintained the refinement of the morning-room furniture .[170] Two landscapes, copies of paintings by Claude, hung above the marble tables.[171] In what would appear to be a bardiglio marble niche, replacing the earlier marble fountain, Beckford installed an antique marble sculpture, recently

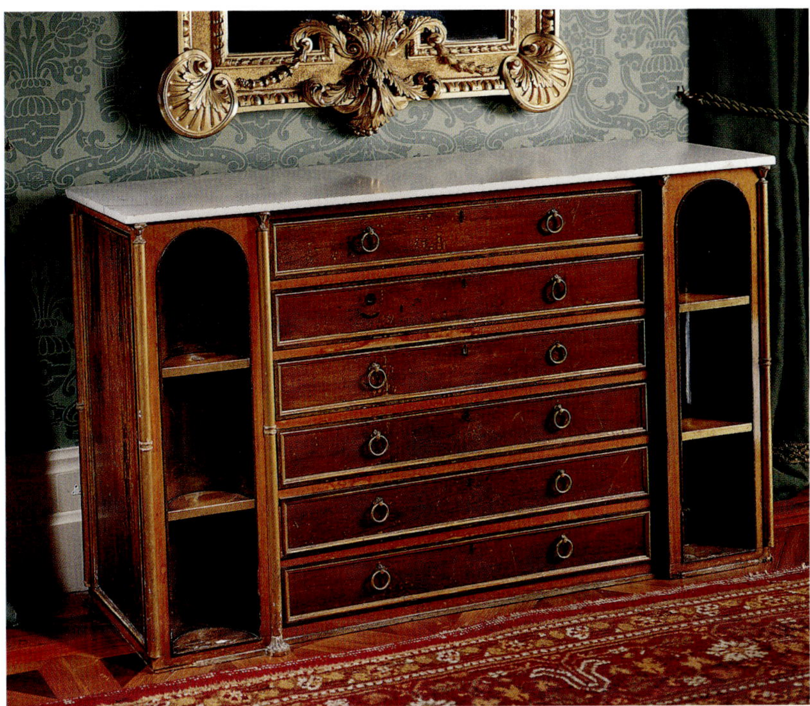

Fig. 3-17. Cabinet from the Tapestry Room at Fonthill House, ca. 1795–1800. Giltwood, purpleheart, mahogany, and white marble. The original white marble base and one drawer pull are now missing. Private collection.

acquired from his great-uncle Charles Hamilton's collection.[172] Warner describes it as a "noble antique statue of Bacchus, the arms and left foot modern. The nebris, or leopard's skin, is flung across his shoulder, a panther stands at his side, and he supports himself on the trunk of a vine with grapes, etc. and leaves at his foot."[173] The importance of this antique marble was reinforced by the artist and diarist Joseph Farington: "The Statue of Bacchus, which was bought for Mr. Beckford, is 7 or 8 feet high. The Trunk & Head of the figure only are original—all the other parts are added. Nollekens, for himself, would not have given 90 guineas for it—to Conoisseurs it might be worth 200 or £250—Ld. King bid for it—Beckford had it for 400. Bonomi said that Mr. Hamilton told him that He bought this Statue in Rome in the year 1727 and gave £2000 for it. Nollekens does not believe it was sold at such a price."[174]

In front of the niche in which this statue stood was an imposing carved, giltwood side table with an ormolu-banded, specimen marble top. In the center of the room, around a large mahogany dining table unusually banded with satinwood and tulipwood, stood satinwood dining chairs, in a classical style, unusually upholstered in yellow morocco leather.[175] The curtains had elaborate valances and were made from straw-colored silk, which helped to lighten the earlier decorative scheme. Much of the furniture was sold in 1801, while the dining table and the chairs reappeared in the auction of 1807.[176]

The furniture made for Beckford at this period was in a severely refined style inspired by late eighteenth-century French neoclassical design promoted by Henry Holland and his team of artists and craftsmen who were employed at Carlton House. Many of these craftsmen had earlier worked with Bélanger and his brother-in-law Jean Desmothenes Dugourc in France. Beckford's new furniture must have been very similar to that being supplied for Carlton House by Nicholas Morel and Tatham, Bailey and Sanders.[177] Also close in spirit was the furniture made almost contemporaneously by Marsh and Tatham for Southill Park, Bedfordshire.[178] A recently discovered group of furniture from Fonthill House is unusual in the extensive use of contrasting panels of purpleheart and satinwood enriched with gilding (figs. 3-16 and 3-17).[179] This combination of materials seems to have been a speciality of a little-known cabinetmaker called Thomas Brownley, who supplied furniture to Vulliamy for Beckford.[180] Beckford had been commissioning furniture in Paris, "in the true spirit of Corinth and Athens," made under the direction of Auguste which probably influenced these novel English pieces.[181] The prevalent use of white marble, whether for tops, plinths, or even solid marble furniture, is characteristic of Beckford's Parisian taste, promoted by Henry Holland under the Prince Regent at Carlton House and at Brighton Pavilion and with the Carlton House set. The presence of neoclassical white marble sculpture must have added to the overwhelmingly French taste of these chaste, yet opulent interiors at Fonthill.[182]

The Vulliamy day books reveal that the firm was heavily involved in the provision of furniture for Fonthill House. Beckford was a client of Vulliamy at least as early as 1798, and the name of Beckford's primary coordinator of furnishings, Edward Foxhall, frequently appears in the Vulliamy records.[183] Beckford owned Vulliamy mantel clocks and used the firm to clean and mend his plate.[184] There is a tantalizing description of an extraordinary pair of semicircular gilt-bronze tables with chimera supports ordered by Beckford from Vulliamy in 1801 and converted a year later into a single circular library table.[185] Lady Ann Hamilton's diary and sketchbook illustrate a table with chimera-like supports, the design derived from the late-eighteenth-century French sources that were so influential in nineteenth-century England, which must be close in style to these converted tables.[186]

A pair of elaborately inlaid satinwood cabinets, commissioned by Beckford, were described in the Vulliamy day books on December 10, 1800. Like most of Beckford's commissioned work, these cabinets were planned with exacting attention to detail. The cabinet doors were subcontracted to Thomas Brownley[187] with detailed specifications: "For making a pair of large Mahogany Cabinet doors Veneered with Sattin wood Purple Wood Ebony and White Holly inlaid with Metal Bands and Corner ornaments Gilt and very highly burnished and fixed into the doors with a great number of small screws after which they were Gilt in such a manner that all the Metal Work may be taken out to be Regilt whenever necessary and fixed in again in the same perfect manner as it is at present al the fastenings of the Metal Work are concealed by a Mahogany Veneer which is screwed upon the inside of the doors the woodwork is very highly polished and is executed as well as the Metal Work in the very best manner the Workmanship of these two doors including the brass work Engraving & gilding comes to 45."[188] The cabinets were destined for the piers in the Grand Saloon to replace those that were sold in 1801.[189] Foreshadowing the display of works of art at Fonthill Abbey, they held Beckford's collection of gold plate from the private oratory of King Louis XVI, as well as other rare works of art.[190]

During the summer of 1801 a severely reduced income and Beckford's need to economize resulted in his decision to demolish part of Fonthill House: "Beckford has ordered the colonnade, & wings of Fonthill to be pulled down. The body of the House is to remain & to be the residence of his daughters who are to have an establishment of £10,000 a year."[191] Only the east wing was demolished, however, leaving the remaining structure unbalanced. Part of the contents of both wings and the majority of the contents of the rooms on the ground and principal floors of the main house were offered at auction in August 1801. The event received much acclaim.[192] Shortly afterward Beckford made Fonthill Abbey his principal residence. Since the death of Beckford's mother on July 25, 1798, his daughters, when not in London, had been living at Berwick-in-the-Park, a house on the Fonthill estate. Writing from Fonthill Abbey on July 4, 1802, to Sir William Hamilton, Beckford stated: "My young are just arrived at their new chateau, a very snug, convenient habitation; extremely well done up and feathered by Mr. Williams."[193] The daughters must have first resided that summer at Fonthill House, which had by now been reduced in size and refurbished in what could be considered a more feminine and domestic fashion. From a correlation of the various descriptions of the interiors with an examination of the auction catalogues of 1801 and 1807, it can be deduced that the sequence and arrangement of some of the principal rooms had been altered to reflect the new inhabitants. The function of some of the rooms had also changed; for example, in 1800 the State Bedchamber had been turned into a music room, and the Tapestry Room had become the "satin" drawing room. The picture gallery on the principal floor lost its collection, consigned to auction in 1802, and was divided; one room became the Vatican Chamber.

These changes and the introduction of new furnishings strongly imply that as early as 1800 the house was being made ready for use by his daughters, who had not yet married but who had reached an age and status that required a more suitable residence. Lady Ann Hamilton provides the sole contemporary account at this period of a visit to both Fonthill House and the Abbey. She described her visit in 1803:

Sept 2 Friday—a low sociable [carriage] abt a foot from the Ground, painted wt 2 Greens stuffed with green cushions, drawn by 4 Beautiful Grey poneys wh were rode by two little boys in scarlet & gold—4 attendants upon 4 other grey poneys conveyed us to Fonthill House. Here we beheld the finest house of 50 years standing, except the lower appartments which are

fitted up, to set off abt 50 of the finest pictures ever seen! A fine organ stands in the Hall. Above stairs are rooms full of antique images, miniature pictures, valuable rings, curious cut ivory &C. The bed chambers were magnificent! The most simple and most elegant was one fitted up in the Turkish stile, something like a tent, with linen drawn full all round from the top so that the corners of the room made excellent closet behind the hanging. The bed was in a recess—but the whole looked very cool and comfortable [included here a sketch of the shape of the room].[194]

The bedroom referred to would have been the tented bedchamber. Farington confirmed the daughters' residency by 1804: "Mr. Beckford at Fonthill resides at the Abbey, but His two daughters live at the Great House as it is called, from which they go every day to dine with him at the Abbey at 5 oClock—it is 3 miles distant."[195] Curiously, however, on October 16, 1806, Farington also reported that "the Miss Beckfords did not then reside at the Abbey or at the old House at Fonthill, but at a House in a neighbouring village."[196] They may, temporarily, have moved back into Berwick-in-the-Park while further refurbishing was going on at Fonthill House, or may have moved as plans for the sale of Fonthill House began to be formulated.

Certainly a sale was being contemplated by this time. Beckford was in correspondence with his future son-in-law, Alexander, Marquess of Douglas, later tenth Duke of Hamilton. Douglas had a longstanding and deep affection for Fonthill House and attempted to persuade Beckford not to sell: "Let me begin by interceding for poor old Fonthill. I cannot forget my old & favourite abode."[197] Beckford's reply assures him that he will take Douglas's feelings into account, suggesting that hearing Wyatt's point of view and seeing the model for Fonthill Abbey (see cat. no. 79) would persuade Douglas not to jeopardize the completion of the Abbey for the sake of "a good common house in an uncommonly bad situation."[198] Beckford and his future son-in-law, only seven years apart in age, had been close friends in their youth and shared an all-consuming passion for works of art. This would help explain Douglas's intervention. Beckford's concern over the costs, his declining income and increased indebtedness, together with the added fear that the "cloud of taxation, blacker than hell hangs over us,"[199] encouraged him to proceed with an auction and the subsequent demolition of Fonthill House.

Beckford agreed with Phillips', the auctioneers, to sell the contents of Fonthill House in August 1807.[200] In a foretaste of the events of 1822 when, at the last minute, he arranged to sell the Abbey and its contents privately before the scheduled auction, Beckford attempted to induce Foxhall to purchase Fonthill House and its contents.[201] The private transaction foundered, however, and the auction with Phillips' went ahead as planned. As the frontispiece to the 1807 catalogue suggests, the auction included furniture made since the previous auction of 1801, "most of which NEW within the last Four Years."[202] This may not have been strictly true for furniture was being commissioned almost continuously. The 1807 auction also included many pieces that Beckford either repurchased, or that did not find buyers, in the 1801 sale. Finally, in September 1807, Fonthill House, with the exception of one pavilion, was demolished, its architectural elements sold off in lots at a second auction comprising "massive and valuable material."[203] Much of this material was incorporated, and can still be seen, in other buildings. The partially gilded ironwork from the main staircase, for example, was purchased, altered, and installed at Dodington Park, Gloucestershire, on the advice of Wyatt.

There is now no trace of the house, apart from the empty but evocative site above the lake. The northern gateway and some piers to the south side of the old park still stand, as do the bath or boathouse and the bridge at the northern end of the lake. The landing site on the eastern edge of the lake leading to the grottoes, and its four enormous urns with bands of vermiculation still remain.

Fonthill's interiors undoubtedly made a great impression on visitors. One of the earliest references to the art of interior decorating reports that "Fonthill has put all previous images of splendid decoration in the shade, . . . unsurpassable elegance, . . . extraordinary magnificence, . . . an astonishing splendour is shown here, combined with the finest taste, and one can say without exaggerating that those who are in the business of decorating for the great and rich, to perfect their art would find in Fonthill the most excellent examples."[204] From the house's inception as a political reflection of the Alderman designed to underscore his position, to its francophile apotheosis and final destruction by his son, there is no doubt that Fonthill House and its splendid interiors richly deserved the appellation, Fonthill "Splendens."

Acknowledgments: With thanks to Sidney Blackmore, Jonathan Bourne, Charles Cator, Elisabeth Einberg, Gale Glynn, John Hardy, Eileen Harris, John Harris, Rodney Keenan, Norman Kitz, Tim Knox, Alexander Marr, Bet McLeod, Lynda McLeod, Jon Millington, Tony Mitchell, Dr. David O'Connell, Derek Ostergard, Celeste Ponzellini, Henry Potts, Rose Sanguinetti, Michael Snodin, Peter Thornton, and the staffs at the Modern Papers Room, Bodleian Library, Oxford; Beinecke Rare Book and Manuscript Library, Yale University, New Haven; picture library at the Victoria and Albert Museum, London; as well as Helen Dorey, Susan Palmer, and Stephen Astley at The Sir John Soane Museum, London; and Lorna Haycock and the staff at the Wiltshire Archaeological and Natural History Society, Devizes—P.H-J.

1. Thomas Wildman to Beckford, 30 September 1794, MS Eng. Lett., c. 501, fols. 10v., 11, Bodleian Library, Oxford. Wildman wrote: ". . . with all its imperfections it certainly is the most Princely Mansion or at least one of the most Princely Edifices in the Kingdom."

2. "Journal of a Five Day's Tour, in a Letter to a Friend, 1776," in *Passages from the Diaries of Mrs. Philip Lybbe Powys of Hardwick House, Oxon*, ed. Emily J. Climenson (London: Longmans, Green and Co., 1899): 166–67.

3. John Buckler, *Fonthill Splendens Ao 1805*, engraved by Thomas Higham, published by Sir R. C. Hoare Bart, January 1829.

4. The house, no longer in existence, was rented. For a list of Alderman Beckford's properties see Boyd Alexander, *England's Wealthiest Son* (London: Centaur Press, 1962): 289, n 6. See also chap. 14, by Sidney Blackmore, in this volume.

5. For details of the political career of the Alderman Beckford., see Alfred B. Beavan, *Aldermen of the City of London* (London 1908): 198. Beckford had also become a Master of the Ironmonger's Company in 1753.

6. See chap. 1, by Timothy Mowl, in this volume.

7. The future romantic novelist Mrs. Elizabeth Hervey.

8. The Alderman's brother-in-law Lord Effingham stood proxy for the Earl of Chatham.

9. Walpole to Mann, 26 July 1770, in *The Yale Edition of the Correspondence of Horace Walpole*, ed., W. S. Lewis et al., vol. 23 (New Haven: Yale University Press, 1937–84): 234.

10. This speech is commemorated in a sculpture by John Francis Moore that was erected in the Alderman's memory in the Guildhall in the City of London. See Samuel Redgrave, *Dictionary of Artists of the English School from the Middle Ages to the nineteenth century . . .* (1878; photographic reprint, Amsterdam: G. W. Hissink, 1970).

11. Deed of Covenant to produce Title Deeds, 413/277, 20 January 1744, The Wiltshire Record Office, Trowbridge. For a full chronology of the Fonthill Estate, see D. A. Crowley, *A History of Wiltshire* (Oxford University Press, 1987): vol. 13, pp. 155–69.

12. For a full description, see J. Harris, "Fonthill Wiltshire—1. Alderman Beckford's Houses," *Country Life* 140 (24 November 1966): 1370–74.

13. R. Pococke, *The Travels through England of Dr. Pococke* (London, 1888–89): vol. 2, p. 4. Visiting Fonthill on 3 July 1754, Dr. Pococke declares: "the house here was very much improved by this gentleman, and fronted in the Italian taste, to the west it is two half H's, one to the South-East, and the other the grand front to the East, one side of which there is a large wing of stable offices."

14. The grottoes were later embellished by the young William Beckford. For further discussion of the park see chap. 8, by Alexander Marr, in this volume. For a discussion of the landscape, see Timothy Mowl, *William Beckford: Composing for Mozart* (London: John Murray, 1998): 32–37. Mowl suggests the park was further and later improved, probably with the help of Richard Woods, a landscape gardener working at the nearby estate at Wardour Castle from 1764 to 1768. The structure known as the boathouse is believed by Tim Knox to be a bathhouse (personal communication, 2000).

15. *The Rake's Progress* is in the Soane Museum, London, P40–47. This series was thought, until recently, to have been destroyed in the Fonthill fire of 1755, but two paintings have been rediscovered. Claude Lorrain's *Sermon on the Mount* (The Frick Collection, New York, 60.1.162) and its near pendant, *Queen Esther Approaching the Palace of Ahasuerus* (Collection of the Earl of Leicester) were also damaged in the fire, *Queen Esther* severely. See *The Frick Collection: An Illlustrated Catalogue*, vol 11, *Paintings* (Princeton University Press, 1968): 50–55.

16. Pococke, *Travels* (1888–89): vol. 2, p. 47.

17. According to the *Salisbury Journal*, 24 February 1755, the fire "in three hours consumed the whole building and most of its rich furniture except the two North wings, the great kitchen and the brewhouse" (Beckford Papers, Box 8, Beinicke Rare Book and Manuscript Library, Yale University, New Haven).

18. "however, the neighbours, now to a considerable number, were got together, and with utmost hazard to their lives, saved most of the rich furniture in the South Appartments by four o'clock when the whole house was in a blaze" (ibid.).

19. Horace Walpole to Richard Bentley, 23 February 1755, Walpole, *Correspondence* (1937–84): vol. 35, p. 211.

20. Felix François, Le comte d'Espie, *The Manner of Securing all Sorts of Buildings from Fire, Or A Treatise upon the construction of arches made with bricks and plaister, called Flat-Arches, and of a roof without timber call a bricked-roof..*, trans. L. Dutens (London, [after 1755]).

21. Peter Wyche to comte d'Espie, 11 May 1755, in ibid., pp. 48–52.

22. Comte d'Espie to Peter Wyche, 27 May 1755, ibid, pp. 54–58: "I shall be able to send these very Men to you, and that will be about the beginning of April next."

23. Pococke, *Travels* (1888–89): vol. 2, p. 47: "There is a large lawn that way, and plantations to the west, an open temple on the side of the hill, and an open rotundo is building higher up on the hill. To the east is a broad serpentine river, with a very handsome bridge of free stone built over it of three arches, with a stone baluster. To the North is a grand gateway near the village, from which there is a gravel walk to the great front about a furlong in length."

24. Mowl, *William Beckford* (1998): 28. Mowl suggests the involvement of John Vardy.

25. Unpublished diary of Sophia, Countess of Shelburne (1746–1771), vol. 5, 14 July 1769 to 15 September 1770, pp. 4–9. This section of the diary records her visit to Fonthill House from 25–30 July 1769, together with her husband, Lord Lyttelton, and others. With thanks to Kate Fielden for bringing this diary to my attention and to the Earl of Radnor for his kind permission to reproduce these extracts. Hereinafter referred to as Shelburne diary.

26. Beckford to Her Serene Highness the Margravine of Anspach, Fonthill, 19 January 1797, MS. Beckford, c.16, fol.11: "this wretched climate whether on the banks of the Thames or on those of

the humble river Nadder which be vapourous Fonthill is equally abominable."

27. Harris, "Fonthill Wiltshire"(24 November 1966): 1373. John Vardy and James Paine have also been suggested as architects. With thanks to Tim Knox for pointing out that at this time the word *bricklayers* meant a speculative builder (personal communication, 2000).

28. Ibid.

29. Rev. J. Collinson, H*istory and Antiquities of the Count of Somerset*, vol. 2 (Bath, 1791): 234–45. Charles Wyndham, b. 1710, succeeded to title 1750.

30. Robert Wilson-North, "Witham: From Carthusian Monastery to Country House," *Current Archaeology* 13, no. 148 (June 1996): 151–56; see also Michael McGarvie, *Witham Friary*, 3d ed., rev. (Society for Local Study, 1989): 34; and Shelburne diary.

31. Shelburne diary.

32. Ibid.

33. Joyce Godber, ed., *The Travel Journal (1744–63) of the 2nd Earl of Hardwicke*, Bedfordshire Historical Record Society Publications, vol. 47 (Bedfordshire: Historical Record Society, ca. 1968): Ac 8081. A journal entry dated August 1760 states: "Took a view of Mr. Beckford's new house at Fonthill (the shell of which is finished but no part of the inside fitted up)."

34. P. J. Grosley, *Londres*, vol. 3 (Lausanne, 1770): 22–23. Grosley describes an almost-finished chimneypiece in 1765, which implies the interiors were nearing completion. Correspondence from Robert Drysdale to the Rev. James Nairne, now again lost, was discovered by Sir James Balfour Paul C.V.O. in an Edinburgh house and published in 1924 in a series of extracts in the *Wiltshire Gazette* (copies in the Wiltshire Archaeological and Natural History Society, Devizes): part 1, "A Scots tutor and William Beckford: Interesting unpublished letters come to light," 14 February 1924; part 2 "The young Scots tutor of William Beckford," 21 February 1924; part 3, "William Beckord's first tutor," 28 March 1924; part 4, "Robert Drysdale, Scotch Tutor," 6 March 1924; part 5, "Beckford's first tutor: Last of the Edinburgh letters," 13 March 1924. The first letter, dated 13 October 1768, tells of Drysdale's new position; the second (undated, but probably October–December 1768) quotes from a detailed description of Fonthill's interiors written by Elizabeth Marsh, Beckford's half-sister, to her friend Miss Cathcart, elder daughter of Lord Cathcart; and the third is dated 9 December 1769. References to these letters are hereinafter cited as Drysdale 1768–69 and Marsh 1768.

35. For further information on Casali, see Jane Turner, ed., *The Dictionary of Art*, vol. 5 (London: McMillan, 1996): 906–7; and E. Croft-Murray, *Decorative Painting in England, 1537–1837*, vol. 2, *Eighteenth and Early Nineteenth Centuries* (London: Country Life, 1970): 181.

36. J. Wolfe and J. Gandon, *Vitruvius Britannicus*, vol. 4 (London,1767): fol. 83.

37. For general discussion on this subject, see George Hussey, *English Country Houses: Early Georgian 1715–1760* (London: Country Life, 1955): 10–12; James Stevens Curl, *Georgian Architecture* (London: David & Charles, 1993); Giles Worsley, *Classical Architecture in Britain* (New Haven and London, Yale University Press, 1995).

38. These were purchased by Thomas Hope on the third day of the Phillips 1801 auction. See *A catalogue of part of the superalatively elegant and magnificent household furniture…of William Beckford…*, sale cat., Phillips, Fonthill, Wiltshire, 19–22 August 1801, lot 56: "A porphyry bust of Pompey, on an inlaid marble pedestal"; and ibid., lot 57: "A ditto of Vitellus on a ditto pedestal for the sum of sixty three pounds." This catalogue is hereinafter referred to as Phillips 1801.

39. Drysdale 1768–69 and Marsh 1768: "come into a low Dining Room, turn your eyes toward the chimney piece, which you will observe is marble, and Astraea will point to you thereon carved 'A poor (I transcribe with as much exactness as I was wont to mark the absent on Sundays) lean poet sitting in his wretched garrett in a very pensive mood. He holds a pen in his hand with his elbow leaning on the table, racking his brains for verses to gain a little sustenance. Want and thought are strongly expressed in his countenance. His dress is perfectly negligent, for his stockings hang over his shoes. The whole furniture of the room is suitable to the miserable appearance of its guest. A shirt sleeve hanging out of a cupboard on the top of which stands a little treasure, viz., the scanty remains of his last meal; a broken chair and window; linens hung across the room to dry, being the few things that are off his back. But, above all a half-starved cat (unfortunate animal to belong to a poet) greedily falling upon some papers dropt from her Master's table and perhaps a composition that has cost him no small pains. The poor poet seems ignorant of the injury he is receiving."

40. Unpublished diary of the Hon. Ann Rushout, 19 July 1799, p. 51 (description of chimneypiece). Hereinafter referred to as Rushout diary. By kind permission of Nicholas Robinson.

41. J. D. Williams, *Audley End: The Restoration of 1762–1797*, Publication No. 45 (Chelmsford: Essex Records Office, 1966): 19, 36. See John Hardy, "Fonthill Splendens: An Iconographic Chimneypiece Rediscovered," *Apollo*, n.s., 133, no. 329 (July 1989): 40–42, 70.

42. Grosley, *Londres* (1770): 22–23: "J'ai vu dans l'atelier du second [Moore] un morceau auffi fingulier par le fini de l'execution que par la fingularite de l'idee fur laquelle it etoit execute. C'etoit un chambranle de cheminee en marbre blanc, pour une maifon de campagne de M. Beckford, ancien maire de Londres. Tous les meurtres les plus les plus fignales de L'Iliade y etoient reprefentes dans des grouppes correfpondans, en figures faillantes & prefque detachees; & ces grouppes etoient meles de bas-reliefs reprefentant let meurtres les moins importans. Ajax fe tuant lui-meme, Priam poignarde par Pyrrhus au pied des autels, Hector traine par Achille autour des murs de Troye, Rhefus affaffine par Ulyffe & par Diomede, brilloient au premier rang. Ce chambranle etoit paye d'avance 60000 livres." This chimneypiece is now at the Manor House, Beaminster.

43. For a watercolor inscribed "Chimney piece of Musik room of William Beckford esq. Fonthill Wiltshire John Moore Statuary," see Arundell Papers, fol. 20. drawing no. 34b, The Wiltshire Record Office, Trowbridge. The chimneypiece itself is in a private collection in London. See ibid., drawing no. 54a, inscribed "Chimney piece for Saloon of William Beckford esq. Fonthill Wiltshire."

44. The statue was presented in 1833 by his son William to the Ironmongers' Company in the City of London, where it remains. See E. Glover, *A History of the Ironmongers' Company* (London: The Worshipful Company of Ironmongers, 1991): passim.

45. *Beckford and Hamilton Silver from Brodick Castle*, exh. cat. (London: Spink and Son, 1980): no. H 43, ill.; and *Argenteries, Le Trésor du National Trust for Scotland: La Collection Beckford et Hamilton du Château du Brodick*, exh. cat. (Brussels: Banque Bruxelles Lambert, 1992), no. H 46, ill.

46. The organ is now in the Victoria & Albert Museum, London, acc. no. W. 13-1980. With thanks to Timothy Miller of the museum, who was responsible for the organ's restoration and made the connection to the drawings of William Linnell, whose son John is more likely responsible for the cabinetwork itself. See Michael I. Wilson, *The Chamber-Organ in Britain, 1600–1830* (London, Ashgate Publishing, 2001). I am grateful to the author for allowing me to see the relevant extract from the book before publication. See also Howard Schott, "Part 1, Keyboard Instruments," in *Catalogue of Musical Instruments in the Victoria and Albert Museum* (London, Victoria & Albert Publications, 1998): 83, no. 28, ill., fig. 28a.

47. See Christopher Gilbert and Tessa Murdoch, *John Channon and Brass-Inlaid Furniture, 1730–1760* (New Haven and London: Yale University Press in association with Leeds City Art Galleries and the Victoria and Albert Museum, 1993): 91, 94, and 154n21, and figs. 106–9. One dressing table is in the Victoria and Albert Museum, London (W. 4-1956), its pair, from the collection of Mr. & Mrs. Saul Steinberg, sold Sotheby's New York, 26 May 2000, lot 205, and is now in a private collection. Their authorship is still uncertain. John Hardy has identified them as almost certainly those referred to as being on the bedroom floor at Fonthill House. See John Britton's manuscript notes on Fonthill House, MS Eng. Misc., d. 222, Bodleian Library. Britton's notes form the basis for his descriptions published in *The Beauties of Wiltshire* (London, 1801), vol. 1, pp. 208–52. The manuscript notes are hereinafter referred to as Britton Manuscript.

48. Casali gave Hogarth his *Adoration of the Magi* for the collection at the Foundling Hospital in London. For information on the Foundling Hospital and Hogarth's role in procuring paintings for it, see Martin Postle, "A Display of Charity," *Art Quarterly* (Winter 2000): 38–40. Almost contemporaneously with his work at Fonthill, Casali was producing similar chiaroscuro *bas reliefs* for the dining room at Syon House under Robert Adam's direction. See *Syon*, guidebook (Derby, 1979): 6.

49. *Collection of Pictures of Chevalier Andrea Casali*, Prestage, 18 April 1766, Lugt 1524. This sale comprised fifty canvases by Casali. Alderman Beckford acquired, among others, *Susannah and the Elders* (lot 48), its companion, *Edward the Martyr, on horseback when stabbed by order of Elfrida his step mother* (lot 49), and *The Empress Gunilad, being accused of adultery, and her Innocence being to be tried by a single combat, the champion or the accusater (a man of gigantic stature) is slain by her papa* (lot 50).

50. Marsh 1768.

51. Shelburne diary.

52. Ibid.

53. Adam Drawings, vol. 11, fols. 91–92, and vol. 50, fols. 31–32, Sir John Soane's Museum, London. Robert Adam's unexecuted designs of 1763 show alternative library and ceiling designs.

54. Beckford's first recorded purchase was Pétis de la Croix's *Mille et un Jour, Contes Persianes* (R. J. Gemmet, ed., *The Consummate Collector, William Beckford's Letters to his Bookseller* [Norwich: Michael Russell Publishing, 2000]: 14). For Beckford as a bibliophile, see Anthony Hobson, "William Beckford's Library," *Connoisseur* 151 (April 1976): 298–303.

55. Drysdale 1768–69. Painted by John Michael Wright, the portrait was sold at Christie's London, 14 June 2000, lot 2. See chap. 13, by Jeannie Chapel and Giles Waterhouse, in this volume.

56. Shelburne diary.

57. My thanks to Tim Knox for this information. While not identical in plan to Houghton or Wanstead, they both have similar double staircases, which are also found at Nostell Priory and at Hagley Hall.

58. Pococke, *Travels* (1888–89): vol. 2, p. 47.

59. Shelburne diary.

60. Britton Mansucript. The manuscript describes the organ surmounted by an eagle.

61. Marsh 1768: "The chimney piece here is prodigiously fine. The Tablet represents Apollo and the Muses. The friese: N.E, Mercury and Amphion S.E. Orpheus, who has allured by his ravishing music Musick the wild beasts and trees to gather round him to listen to his sweet harmony; the supporters are two fine large figures of the Muses."

62. Ibid.: "Io is being transformed into a white cow, whilst Argus lies asleep lulled by Mercury's pipe before his head is struck off by Mercury's sword." Derived from Ovid's "Metamorphoses," the painting celebrates the triumph of Music in its depiction of Mercury, Jupiter's messenger, playing Pan-pipes to charm the giant Argus to sleep. I am indebted to John Hardy for this information.

63. Britton Manuscript, fol. 26

64. Ibid., fol. 25

65. Ibid. This recalls lanterns designed in the French style by Thomas Chippendale, Thomas Johnson, and others.

66. Marsh 1768.

67. When sold, these sculptures were also described as having dove-colored and veined marble bases. See Phillips 1801, 21 August, lots 50 and 51.

68. My thanks to Dr. Joan Coutu for information regarding Joseph Wilton. See Joan Coutu, "Wilton and William Chambers," in *William Chambers, Architect to George III*, ed. Michael Snodin and John Harris (London: Courtauld Gallery, 1996): 175–85

69. Shelburne diary.

70. Drysdale 1768–69: "Achilles pursuing Hector and afterwards dragging his dead body by the heels, Pyrrhus killing old Priam on the dead body of his son; the head of the wooden horse higher than the walls; Aeneas fleeing with Anchises on his back and Julius in his hand and Creusa just behind him between the sides of the gate etc." For a description of this chimneypiece also see Grosley, *Londres*, vol 3 (1770): 22–23

71. Shelburne diary.

72. Drysdale 1768–69: "the principal thing which remains to be finished is a bed, which they way will be the finest in England. The room in which it is to be put is hung with crimson velvet. I heard Mr Beckford say that the article of painting had cost him about £10,000" (14 February 1924). Marsh 1768: "Adjoining to this is the State Bedchamber 18 feet long by 26, has two windows to the south, hangings, &. Crimson velvet. The bed is not yet finished, but it is said that it will be the finest in England.—Hark, again, Sir, I am glad to have the honour of telling you that the bed is now up, and if you will believe the upholsters neither the King of B. nor the King of E. has anything like it" (21 February 1924).

73. Lord Herbert, ed., *The Pembroke Papers (1734–1780)*, 1938 (reissued 1942): 139; Dr Eyre to Lord Herbert, I January 1779: "to accommodate their Majesties with a good Bed, I made interest with Mr Hill, Mr Beckford's Steward, to lend us his Superb State Bed, which we brought to Wilton, slung on the Carriage of a Wagon."

74. Purchased by Thomas Johnes of Hafod. See *A catalogue of the magnificent and costly household furniture…*Phillips, Fonthill, Wiltshire, 17–23 August 1807, lot 477. (Hereinafter referred to as Phillips' 1807). See C. F. Bell, ed., *Annals of Thomas Banks* (Cambridge University Press, 1938): 87, 90. He also purchased looking glasses, now presumed burnt, for the octagonal library at Hafod. Dibdin, visiting Hafod in 1815, commented on "the looking glasses bought at the Fonthill sale"; see T. F Dibdin, *The Bibliographical Decameron*, vol. 3 (London: W. Bulmer and Co., Shakespeare Press, 1817): 360.

75. Shelburne diary.

76. Marsh 1768.

77. Ibid.

78. A console table dating from 1745–48, in the collection of the Thomas Coram Foundation for Children, does sound strikingly similar. See *Rococo Art and Design in Hogarth's England,* exh. cat., London: Victoria & Albert Museum, 1984), cat. no. L.155.

79. Shelburne diary.

80. *La Toilette* and *La Couronnement* are part of a series supplied by Neilson, after designs by Jean-François de Troy and made in the workshops of Cozette and Audran. These tapestries were included Phillips' 1801, third day, lot 68: "Two pieces of TAPESTRY, the history of the preparation, and Marriage of Queen Esther, of the Gobelins Manufactory, in fine preservation, 12 feet high and 11 feet 4 wide, 189 pounds." The next lot was for the gilt molding that framed them.

81. Claude's *Queen Esther at the Palace of Asahuerius* is now in the collection of the Earl of Leicester at Holkham Hall, Norfolk. While its arrival at Holkham is not recorded, it is mentioned in an inventory prepared for the Countess of Leicester in 1759/60 (MS 765, fol. 37, Holkam Hall archive). Fire-damaged and, according to the fifth earl of Leicester, from Fonthill, this would

imply an as-yet-unrecorded sale of surviving contents from the pre-1755 Fonthill House. My thanks to M. Daley esq., at Holkham Hall. Also see n. 15.

82. Letters from Neilson, to the Duc de la Vrilliere and the Comte de Guiche, 1771, informing them he wished to send to England several pieces of tapestry completing the sets already delivered to Lord Coventry, Chevalier Bridgman and the late Mr. Beckford. See M. Fenaille, *État général des tapisseries de la manufacture des Gobelins depuis son origine jusqu'à nos jours, 1600–1900*, vol. 4 (Paris: Imprimerie Nationale, 1903–23): 265.

83. Shelburne diary.

84. Three of these, *Architecture, History,* and *Music* are now incorporated in the ceiling of the Great Hall, Dyrham Park. See Christopher Woodward, "William Beckford and Fonthill Splendens," *Apollo,* n.s., 147, no. 432 (February 1998): 31–40.

85. This would imply that these paintings, at least, did not form part of a commissioned scheme of decoration. *Gunhilda, Empress of Germany, and the Emperor, her Page with the head of her Accuser* was exhibited at the Royal Society of Arts (RSA) in 1760 and won the second prize of 50 guineas. *Edward Martyr being stabbed in the back in the presence of Elfredo at Corfe Castle* was exhibited at RSA in 1761 and won first prize. Both were engraved by Jean Ravenet. For sale record, see n. 49.

86. My thanks to Tim Knox regarding the use of colored damasks. See Jacob Simon, *The Art of the Picture Frame* (London: National Portrait Gallery Publications, 1996): 40–41.

87. Rev. R. Warner, *Excursions from Bath* (Bath: R. Crutttwell, 1801): 123. Letter 2, dated 5 September 1800, describes a large collection of paintings (but not the Casalis) in the picture gallery.

88. Marsh 1768.

89. Britton, *Beauties* (1801): 237, "the celebrated series of pictures by Hogarth, representing *the Rake's Progress*." The series was purchased for 570 guineas by John Soane. See *A catalogue of the most superb, capital, and valuable collection of Italian, French, Flemish, and Dutch pictures…sale cat.,* Christie's, London, 27 February 1802, lot 86.

90. Woodward, "William Beckford" (February 1998): 31.

91. Powys, *Diary* (1899): 167.

92. Drysdale 1768–69: "This home, or palace if you will, which is his principal residence, is exceedingly grand, but I cannot at present enter into a particular description of it. It has been 14 years in building and is not yet quite finished."

93. "The arrival of my caravans from Fonthill laden with furniture and superfluities of all kinds has already made quite a stir in the neighbourhood" (Beckford letter, May 1783, Gen MSS 102, Series I, Box 1, William Beckford Collection, Beinicke Library).

94. See J. W. Oliver, *The Life and Letters of William Beckford of Fonthill* (London: Oxford University Press, 1910): 106.

95. Beckford and his wife, Lady Margaret, lived at this modest medieval château at the remote east end of Lake Geneva from July 1785 until her death in May 1786. See chap. 4, by William Hauptman, in this volume.

96. MS. Beckford, c.37, fols. 3–6. No doubt Edward Foxhall was instrumental in arranging the sale of this furniture, but there are no records of any sales of furniture at all, from Fonthill House, during the eighteenth century.

97. Ibid., fols. 5–6.

98. Foxhall's firm was Foxhall & Fryer, Old Cavendish Street, London. See Geoffrey Beard and Christopher Gilbert, eds., *The Dictionary of English Furniture Makers, 1660–1840* (Leeds: Furniture History Society and W. S. Maney & Sons, 1986).

99. Simon, *Art of the Picture Frame* (1996): 122, 126

100. I thank Bet McLeod for raising this issue and for subsequent discussion on this matter

101. *The Diary of Joseph Farington*, ed. K. Garlick and A. Macintyre, vol. 3 (New Haven and London: Yale University Press, 1978): 909. "Byrne spoke of Foxhall's insolent manner. —He married a daughter of Moore the Statuary" (27 October 1797). Farington also refers to Foxhall as a "framemaker."

102. Woodward, "William Beckford" (February 1998): 31. Foxhall had studied at the Royal Academy and was also a neighbor of Soane, who in turn had worked for a cousin of Beckford's mother, the Hon James Hamilton, seventh earl, later created first Marquess of Abercorn. It was Foxhall who introduced Lord Arundel, of nearby Wardour Castle, to John Soane. Mowl points out the great Roman Catholic chapel at Wardour Castle, with its altarpiece by Giacomo Quarenghi, was inaugurated on 1 November 1776, and this may have encouraged Beckford's fondness for Catholic pomp and ceremony (*William Beckford* [1998]: 43–44).

103. *Life at Fonthill, 1807–1822, with interludes in Paris and London, from the correspondence of William Beckford*, trans. and ed. Boyd Alexander (London: Rupert Hart-Davis, 1957): 187, letter dated 11 November 1815.

104. "28 May 1787: Mr. Soane went to Mrs Beckford to shew her the Section," Soane, Journal

1787, no. 1, vol. 57, fol. 36, Soane Museum. See also Woodward, "William Beckford" (February 1998): 32; and, for expenses incurred by Soane from April 1787 until January 1788 and details of some of the craftsmen involved, see Series III, Folder 109, William Beckford Collection, Beinecke Library.

105. Woodward, "William Beckford" (February 1998): 32–33

106. These engravings were sold. See Phillips 1807, sixth day, lot 596: "An unique coloured set of the Loggie of the Vatican, comprising forty-two impressions—This set has ever been esteemed the finest and most precious extant; the colouring equal in execution to the most exquisite miniature, and the varied tints vivid and unfaded, heightened by gold embossments and pencilling by F. Panini, and in high preservation, sumptuously framed, and glazed with plate glass."

107. *The Journal of William Beckford in Portugal and Spain*, ed. with an introduction and notes by Boyd Alexander (London: Rupert Hart-Davis, 1954): 123–24, letter dated 6 July 1787.

108. Woodward, "William Beckford" (February 1998): 34. Each niche contained "a superb and most elegant carved and gilt Secretaire, the Compartments exquisitely painted from the Fable of Cupid and Psyche, by that ingenious and most admired Artist, Mr. Smirke; and bas reliefs in Chiaro Oscuro by the late Mr. Hamilton, forming a magnificent Specimen of Genuine Taste and Elegance" (*A catalogue of the most superb, capital, and valuable collection of Italian, French, Flemish, and Dutch pictures…*sale cat., Christie's, London, 27 February 1802, lots 51–52.

109. Beckford, *Journal…in Portugal* (1954): 124. The two paintings by de Loutherbourg seemed to have fallen out of favor fairly quickly, for they were to be sold by Christie's (see *A catalogue of the most superb, capital, and valuable collection of Italian, French, Flemish, and Dutch pictures…*sale cat., Christie's, London, 27 February 1802, lots 49, 50).

110. Woodward, "William Beckford" (February 1998): 32, 39n18. See Beckford, *Journal…in Portugal* (1954): 124

111. See the catalogue section and chap. 11, by Michael Snodin, in this volume. See also Michael Snodin, "J. J. Boileau: A Forgotten Designer of Silver," *Connoisseur* (June 1978): 124–33; idem and M. Baker, "William Beckford's Silver," parts 1 and 2, *Burlington* 122, no. 932 (November 1980): 735–48; no. 933 (December 1980): 820–34.

112. For a full discussion, see Pierre Verlet, *Savonnerie, The James A. de Rothschild Collection at Waddesdon Manor* (Fribourg: Office du Livre, 1982): 124 and passim. If the carpet delivered to Beckford was in fact for his London residence it would help explain its absence from any of the sale catalogues

113. For a full discussion of Beckford and Le Doux, see Anthony Vidler, *Claude-Nicolas Le Doux* (Cambridge, Mass.: MIT Press, 1990): 337–40. For the revolutionary new palaces being built in Paris, see Jean Charles Krafft and Nicholas Ransonnette, *Les Plus Belles Maisons Et Hotels Construit A Paris Et Dans Les Environs* (1801–12; reprint, Nördlingen: Verlag. Dr. Alfons Uhl, 1992).

114. See Paul V. Turner, *Joseph Ramée* (Cambridge University Press, 1996): 36–38. I thank Derek Ostergard for bringing this publication to my attention.

115. Designed by F-J Bélanger in 1777, the château contained both Turkish and tented rooms in neoclassical style. The majority of the craftsmen who worked on these interiors were later to be employed at Carlton House. Bélanger had also visited Fonthill House in 1762 on his trip to England. See Bélanger's sketchbook "Croquis d'un voyage en Angleterre," pp. 134, 136, Bibliothèque des Beaux Arts, Paris. My thanks to Dr. Hans Ottomeyer for help with this. See also, Jean Stern, *A l'ombre de Sophie Arnould: François-Joseph Belanger, architecte des Menus Plaisirs, premier architecte du comte d'Artois* (Paris, 1930). I thank Derek Ostergard for bringing this publication to my attention.

116. Jacques-Henri Meister, *Letters Written During a Residence in England, translated from the French of Henry Meister* (London, 1799): 295. Meister's letter 19 gives us some idea of this, "I know of nothing of the kind in France of superior grandeur" and goes on to mention that "the fireplaces have all of them noble vases of the rare old japan china, filled with the gayest flowers of the season."

117. For the oscillations of Beckford's fortune, see Boyd Alexander, *England's Wealthiest Son* (London: Centaur Press, 1962), chap. 16. For information on the Wildman family, see Rosalys Coope, "The Wildman Family and Colonel Thomas Wildman of Newstead Abbey, Nottinghamshire," *Transactions of the Thoroton Society* 95 (1991): 50–66.

118. Wildman to Beckford, 30 September 1794, MS Eng. Lett., c. 501, fols. 10v., 11r. and v., Bodleian Library.

119. Ibid.

120. Ibid.

121. Farington, *Diary* vol. 3 (1978): 916, entry dated 6–7 November 1797.

122. See chap. 7, by Megan Aldrich, in this volume.

123. Foxhall to Beckford, MS Beckford c.30, f. 169, Bodleian Library. These stools may have been the "six stools, gilt in burnished gold" that were sold from the Turkish room (Phillips' 1801, third day, lot 21.

124. Rushout diary, p. 51. In one of these two library rooms stood the renowned amber cabinet. The Vulliamy records detail its packing and shipping from London: "Made a strong packing case for the amber cabinet" (P.R.O., Chancery Masters Exhibits, C.104/58, Part I, Day Book no. 29, Bill dated 12 August 1798). This would not necessarily imply that Beckford had recently purchased the cabinet; he could already have owned it and kept it at his London residence.

125. For a comprehensive discussion of the library see Anthony Hobson, "William Beckford's Library," *Connoisseur* 191, no. 770 (April 1976): 298–305.

126. Beckford to Wyatt, April 1796, reprinted in *The Hamilton and Nelson Papers*, vol. 1, *1756–1797* (1893), The Collection of Autograph Letters and Historical Documents formed by Alfred Morrison, 2d ser. (Privately published, 1882–93): 218, no. 279.

127. MS Beckford c. 16, fol. 7, Bodleian Library.

128. Ibid., c. 30, fol. 168.

129. A sale catalogue title page lists near the top of its offerings, "Noble French Plate Glasses, of singular Magnitude, Perfection, and Beauty…" (Phillips' 1807).

130. Beckford to Sir William Hamilton, Fonthill, 23 December 1799, reprinted in *Hamilton and Nelson Papers*, vol. 2, p. 78, no. 438.

131. "Wyatt described the 2 frames which He designed for the Altieri Claudes now Mr. Beckfords. They are 12 inches wide—project 10 Inches, and at the corners 12 Inches. The pattern is something of the old pattern. He supposes they will cost £400" (Farington, *Diary,* vol. 4 [1978]: 1320, entry dated 7 December 1799).

132. Ibid.

133. Romney Ledger 1786–96, under 6 October 1789, Archive, National Portrait Gallery, London, cited in Simon, *Art of the Picture Frame* (1996): 203, n.47.

134. Britton, *Beauties* (1801): 213.

135. Snodin, "Boileau" (1978): 124–33.

136. Croft-Murray, *Decorative Painting*, vol. 2 (1970): 172. Dorothy Stroud, *Henry Holland: His Life and Architecture* (London: Country Life, 1966): 73–74.

137. *Carlton House: The Past Glories of George IV's Palace*, exh. cat.,(London: The Queen's Gallery, Buckingham Palace, 1991–92): 22, 218, 220. See also Geoffrey de Bellaigue, "Furnishings of the Chinese Drawing Room, Carlton House," *Burlington* 109 (September 1967): 526–27.

138. One such artist was Jean-Desmothenes Dugourc, Bélanger's brother-in-law. For a general discussion of Dugourc, see *De Dugourc a Pernon: nouvelles acquisitions graphiques pour les musées: 1890–1990 centenaire du musée des Tissus* exh. cat. (Lyon: Musée historique des tissus, 1990). I thank Derek Ostergard for bringing this publication to my attention.

139. Beckford, *Journal…in Portugal* (1954): 199.

140. Wildman to Beckford, 30 September 1794, MS Eng. Lett., c. 501, fols. 10 and 11v., Bodleian Library.

141. The Palais du Temple (1776–77) contained a Turkish room designed by Boullée and furnished by Jacob. See Jean-Jacques Gautier, "Le goût du Prince: La Folie d'Artois," in *L'Objet d'Art*, exh. cat., Château de Bagatelle, Paris (1988): 80–142; Christian Baulez, "Le Goût Turc," *L'Objet d'Art* (December 1987): 34–45.

142. For a full discussion of tented and fabric-draped interiors, see John Morley, *Regency Furniture and Design* (London: Zwemmer, 1993): 261–72.

143. Farington, *Diary*, vol. 3 (1978): 911, entry dated 31 October 1797.

144. Modern accounts have erroneously credited the Alderman with its creation. See, e.g., Mowl, *William Beckford* (1998), and others.

145. Marsh 1768.

146. Rushout diary, p. 51.

147. Britton, *Beauties* (1801): 213–14.

148. *A catalogue of the most superb, capital, and valuable collection of Italian, French, Flemish, and Dutch pictures…*sale cat., Christie's, London, 27 February 1802, lots 51, 52.

149. Farington, *Diary*, vol. 3 (1978): 836, 840.

150. Ibid., p. 1047; vol. 4, pp. 1570–71.

151. C. A. G. Goede, *England, Wales and Ireland*, vol. 5 (Dresden 1805): 116. His description continues: "The ceiling of the room is vaulted, and the surface of the same heavily gilded. On its golden ground, delicate arabesques and garlands have been painted in bright colours. The floor of the room is laid out with one of the finest and richest carpets, of a chocolate brown colour, which pleasantly contrasts with the golden glow of the ceiling and other decoration. The room is hung all around with curtains of the richest orange-yellow Atlas (a smooth silk), which are folded with artistic perfection and hang down to the floor. Behind these curtains the wall is covered with very large, valuable mirrors which are as high as the room itself, where one cannot see where they were joined, and which therefore appear as openings to other rooms, and greatly

enhance the size and magical glow of the whole. The magnificently decorated windows have been fitted with blinds of orange-yellow silk, through which the light that enters into the room itself has a golden glow. The oven consists of a very delicate altar of an antique shape, of 'verde antice', and is surrounded by a finely worked, richly gilded bronze fireguard. Large vases of the finest Japanese porcelain, beautiful candelabras, and two richly decorated Ottomans stand around the walls of the room." The Turkish room was dismantled in 1801, and Goede's travels took place in 1802–3, which would imply he did not actually see the Turkish room. However, his description has detail lacking in other published sources (primarily Britton, *Beauties* [1801]) which might infer that he had first-hand knowledge of this room. I thank Jeannie Chapel for bringing this publication to my attention and Mona El-Mamoun for her translation.

152. Phillips' 1801, third day, lots 18–29.

153. "A pair of superlatively elegant tripods, formed a la turque, exquisitely carved and gilt in an expensive stile, designed by Boilieu [sic]" (ibid., lot 22).

154. Michael Snodin has pointed out the title page to Thomas Hope's *Household Furniture and Interior Decoration* (1807), with its supposed Turkish ornament, is not immediately apparent as such.

155. Rushout diary, p. 50.

156. Morley, *Regency Furniture* (1993): 336–38. See also *Carlton House* (1991–92).

157. Phillips' 1807, second day, lots 162–63.

158. *A Catalogue of a Valuable Collection of Paintings,…. now on sale, Jeffrey's Gallery, Market Place, Salisbury*, 1809. The only known copy of this catalogue is in the collection of the author.

159. Ibid., pp.28–29.

160. Rushout diary, p. 50: "we went next into the Tartarian Room, which is quite beautiful, all sort of things used by the Tartars and painted about the Room in the very best manner, some elegant Cabinets and there is the most ingenious contrivance for the fireplace, it is on one side of the room, being summer it was shut up, and looked like an elegant Cabinet, but by opening the doors we saw the fireplace and the smoke is conveyed up the Chimney on one side." For a description of the mirrored shutters, see *A Catalogue of the whole of the massive and valuable materials of that noble and modern stone mansion called Fonthill, near Salisbury…*, sale cat., Phillips, Fonthill, 16 September 1807, first day, lot 163. (Hereinafter referred to as Phillips Demolition Sale, 1807).

161. With thanks to Peter Thornton for information on the the use of mirrored shutters.

162. Warner, *Excursions from Bath* (1801): 119–27.

163. Ibid., p. 125.

164. Painted in 1793, it might, however, only have been purchased by Beckford in 1797. "Beckford also gave Romney the other day 300gs. for a picture" (Farrington, *Diary,* vol. 3 (1978): 840, entry dated 15 May 1797). This was sold Phillips 1807, sixth day, lot 582.

165. Phillips 1807, fourth day, lot 430.

166. Britton, *Beauties* (1801): 231. See also Snodin and Baker, *"William Beckford's Silver,"* part 1, *Burlington* 122, no. 932 (date?): 735–48.

167. It measured 13 feet, 6 inches by 4 feet, 2 inches (Phillips 1807, fourth day, lot 429).

168. For a British visitor's opinion of the Parisian glass makers, see John Lough, *France on the Eve of the Revolution: British Travellers' Observations, 1763–1788* (London: Croom Helm, 1987): 77–78. I thank Derek Ostergard for bringing this publication to my attention.

169. Britton, *Beauties* (1801): 233–24.

170. Vulliamy Records, P.R.O. Chancery Masters Exhibits, C104/58, Part I: Day Books 1798–1800, 25 November 1799. The entry perhaps refers to these tables.

171. Britton, *Beauties* (1801): 29.

172. The Hon. Charles Hamilton was a youngest son of the 6th Earl of Abercorn and therefore Beckford's mother's uncle.

173. Warner, *Excursions from Bath* (1801): 126. Britton writes that it was "brought from Rome about seventy years ago by the Hon. Charles Hamilton. The arms, and part of the torso, are restored; the head is of the finest Greek sculpture. The statue is advantageously placed in a spacious niche, lined with dove-coloured marble very highly polished, and gives an air of dignity to the appartment" (*Beauties* [1801]: 223–24). This statue was purchased by Beckford on 23 October 1797 from Bond Benjamin Hopkins, who had purchased Painshill and its collections from Beckford's uncle Charles Hamilton. The sculpture was later purchased by Thomas Jones of Hafod (Phillips 1807, sixth day, lot 623); it appears that the statue was sold by Christie's at Hafod and may possibly be that now in the collection at Anglesey Abbey.

174. Farington, *Diary,* vol. 3 (1978): 921, entry dated 10 November 1797.

175. The use of yellow morocco was uncommon at this date. Dr. Geoffrey Beard, personal communication, 2000.

176. Phillips 1801, third day, lots 81–110; Phillips 1807, third day, lots 317–33. Presumably, some

of this furniture was either unsold, or characteristically, Beckford purchased some pieces back. In the 1807 sale the chairs still retained their tufted yellow morocco upholstery, but the curtains had been replaced by others of scarlet camblet and buff morine, rather more in the style of the new Fonthill Abbey which was being furnished at the same time.

177. For further information on the royal furniture suppliers, see *Carlton House* (1991–92).

178. Southill Park, Bedfordshire, built 1796–1803 for Samuel Whitbread, by Henry Holland. See Christopher Hussey, *English Country House, Late Georgian, 1800–1840* (1955; reprint, London: Antique Collectors Club, 1984): 27–40. Also Gervase Jackson-Stops, "Southill Park, Bedfordshire," *Country Life* (28 April 1994): 64–67.

179. Discovered by the author in a private English collection, this small group was purchased at Phillips 1807.

180. R. Smith, "Benjamin Vulliamy's painted satinwood clocks and pedestals," *Apollo* n.s. 141, no. 400 (June 1995): 25–30.

181. "I think you will be enraptured with the furniture that I am having made under his [Auguste's] directions in the true spirit of Corinth and Athens; the bronze friezes, & C., finished as highly as the gold vase you saw in Fonthill" (Beckford to to Sir William Hamilton, Paris, 27 February 1792, reprinted in *Hamilton and Nelson Papers*, vol. 1 [1893] 165, no. 205). See also chap. 6, by Anne Eschapasse, and chap. 10, by Adrianna Turpin, in this volume.

182. Beckford owned two marble sculptures by Moitte of Ariane and Hebe (ordered but not delivered in 1794). For the sale of *Hebe*, see Phillips 1807, sixth day, lot 624. For further details of Beckford's patronage of Moitte, see Gisela Gramaccini, *Jean-Guillaume Moitte,* vol. 1 (Berlin: Akademie Verlag, 1993): 270 and passim.

183. See Helen Clifford, "The Vulliamys and the Silversmiths, 1793–1817," *Silver Society Journal* (Autumn 1998): 96–102.

184. For example, Phillips 1807, seventh day, lot 648.

185. Beckford was charged £67 4s for each of them (Vulliamy Records, P.R.O. Chancery Masters Exhibits, C104/57, Part I, Bill Book 30, 21 June 1801); for details for their conversion into a large bronze circular library table, see ibid., 3 December 1802. This sounds strikingly similar to the table illustrated in the center of the drawing room at Fonthill Abbey although that table only has three legs (see cat. no. 000). See also chap. 10, by Adrianna Turpin, in this volume.

186. Lady Ann Hamilton (1766–1846), nicknamed "the Macaw," was guardian to and cousin of Susan and Margaret Beckford. Her notebook (1788–1835) describes both Fonthill Abbey and Fonthill House in 1803, around the time that Susan and Margaret were living there. See MS Beckford e. 4, fol. 49, Bodleian Library.

187. Smith, "Benjamin Vulliamy's painted satinwood" (June 1995): 30–32.

188. See Vulliamy Records, P.R.O. Chancery Masters Exhibits, C104/58, Part I, Day Book No. 29, p. 266, account dated 10 December. The description goes on to mention a further pair of smaller doors for this cabinet and two further sets for the second cabinet.

189. Phillips' 1801, fourth day, lot 149.

190. Britton, *Beauties* (1801): 227. See also See also Snodin and Baker, "William Beckford's Silver," part 1, *Burlington* 122, no. 932 (November 1980): 735–48.

191. Farrington, *Diary*, vol. 4 (1978): 1573, entry dated 4 July 1801.

192. *The Sun*, 27 July 1801, no. 2761, previews the Phillips 1801 sale.

193. Beckford to Sir William Hamilton, from Fonthill Abbey, 4 July 1802, reprinted in *Hamilton and Nelson Papers*, vol. 2 (1894): 193–94, no. 674.

194. Lady Ann Hamilton, notebook, MS Beckford e. 4, fol. 49, Bodleian Library.

195. Farrington, *Diary*, vol. 6 (1978): 2250, entry dated 1 February 1804.

196. Ibid., vol. 8, pp. 2887–88, entry dated 16 October 1806.

197. Beckford to Douglas, 27 November 1806, MS Beckford c.20, fols. 14–15, Bodleian Library. I thank Bet McLeod for bringing this correspondence to my attention.

198. Beckford to Douglas, 28 November 1806, MS Beckford c.21, fols. 6–7, Bodleian Library.

199. Ibid.

200. Phillips' 1807.

201. The aborted Christie's sale of 1822. For the agreement for the private sale to Foxhall, dated 31 July 1807, see MS Beckford c. 37, fol. 175.

202. Phillips' 1807.

203. Phillips' Demolition Sale, 1807. For a full discussion of the Fonthill estate after its sale by Beckford, see Jon Millington, "Fonthill after Beckford," *The Beckford Journal* 2 (1996).

204. Goede, *England*, vol. 5 (1805): 116.

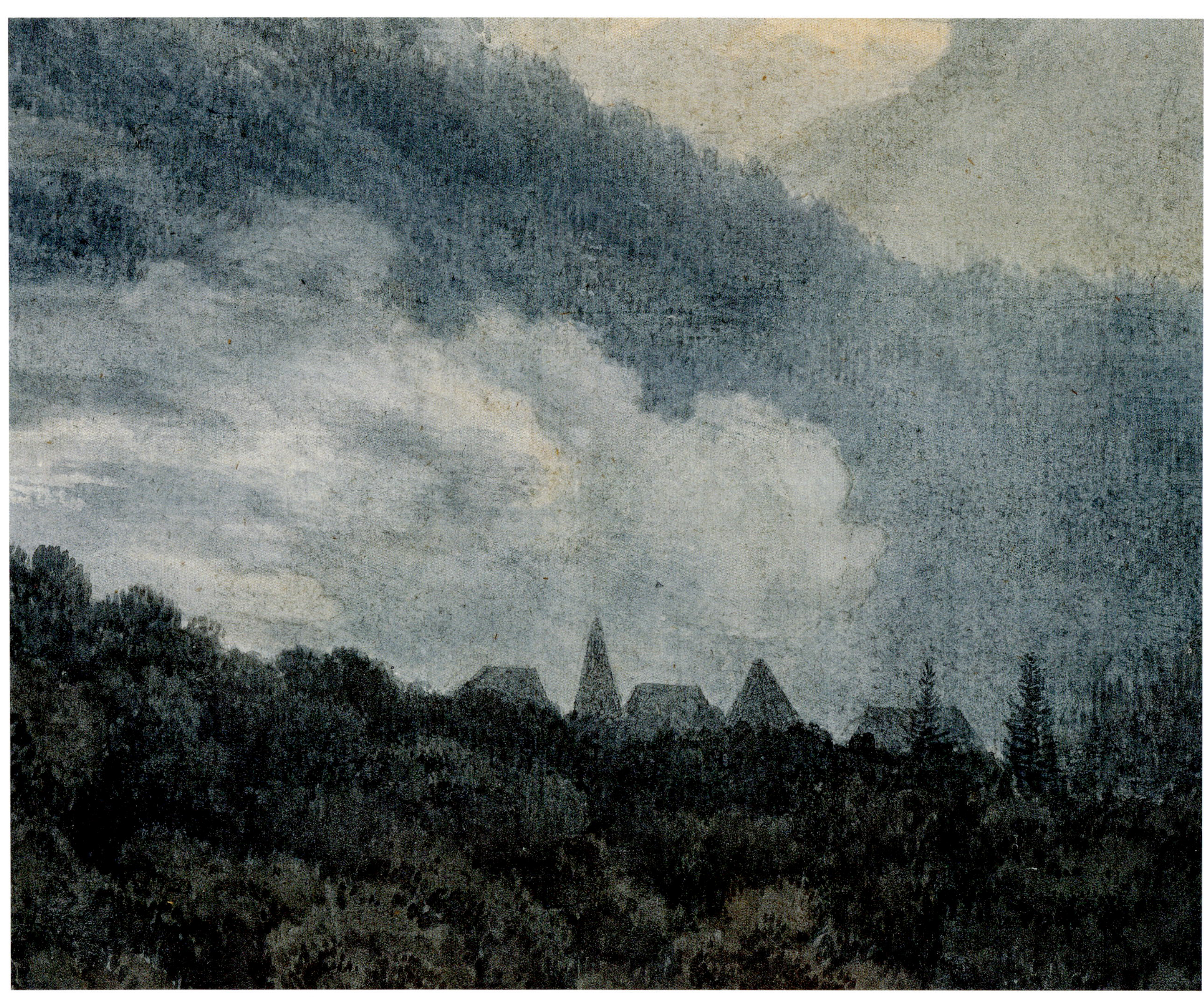

Fig. 4-1. John Robert Cozens. *La Grande Chartreuse* (detail), ca. 1783–85. Watercolor. Private collection. *See cat. no. 13.*

WILLIAM HAUPTMAN

CHAPTER IV

CLINGING FAST "TO MY TUTELARY MOUNTAINS": BECKFORD IN HELVETIA

As the passionate nomad who zealously pursued assorted quests and aesthetic landscapes, William Beckford was as much linked with various European cultures as he was with his own. While his most ardent thoughts found expression in the stimuli of Italy, France, Germany, Spain, and especially Portugal, the Beckford compass also pointed to Switzerland where, for the most part, he found a place of refuge, a province of enlightenment, and an unfailing source of philosophic reflection. The prominence of Beckford's many Swiss visits has received less notice in the extensive Beckford bibliography, certainly because few letters explore his thoughts here, and no diary or comprehensive travel notes record his observations on Helvetic soil.[1] Consequently, even establishing the number of his Swiss voyages, their regularity, and their exact dates is difficult. Yet from Beckford's adolescence until his mature years, a number of visits to the Swiss cantons can be accounted for, some as a respite between trips to other lands, others as stable points within his peripatetic existence, but each maintaining a persistent hold on Beckford's sentiments throughout his European wanderings.

Beckford's attachment to Switzerland matured at a time when that sovereign state was one of the least familiar in Europe.[2] This nescience was clearly expressed by 1714, when Abraham Stanyan, the British Envoy to the Swiss Cantons, remarked on the fact that "a Country situated almost in the Middle of *Europe*, as *Switzerland* is, should be as little known" beyond its borders.[3] Stanyan's assertion indicated that the confederation remained singularly out of the sphere of European attention, but the situation would change rapidly, so that by the time Beckford made his early sojourns there in the late 1770s, British voyagers in increasing numbers were beginning to explore the uncommon peculiarities of the country (fig. 4-1). The reasons why the British were drawn to Switzerland, more than the French or the Germans, are innately tied to common cultural kinships, long-standing commercial ties, mutual foundations in democratic doctrines, and the reassuring fact of shared Protestant convictions, points frequently underscored in eighteenth-century literature and early guides.[4] Prospective British travelers also noted that Switzerland was the only European nation with which Great Britain had never fought, either as an ally or an enemy.

The British discovery of Switzerland during much of the late eighteenth century was generally confined to specific geographical loci. With the exception of Geneva, Bern, Basel, and Zurich, there was little inducement to explore farther afield, except along routes to select mountain passes and southern destinations. By the mid-1740s, British explorers had indeed penetrated some of the most daunting Alpine regions,[5] particularly the valley of Chamonix, describing the intimidating peaks and vast glaciers with awe and alarm, earmarks of the Sublime that Burke would set down in 1756. These were still the expeditions of unusual navigators and not yet the domains of private travel, but when Beckford set out on his first Swiss visit in 1777, the stage was already set for the substantial numbers of British tourists who began to perceive the Alpine tour as pertinent for the cultivation of the Sublime as the Grand Tour was a prerequisite for the development of the aesthetic palette. By Beckford's time, the Swiss had already responded to this growing British flux by establishing accommodations in strategic centers and importing various amenities, including the latest issues of popular London journals. Beckford's two longest stays were his first, made in 1777–78 as an adolescent, and a few years later, in 1785–86, when scandal forced his exile from a hostile England.

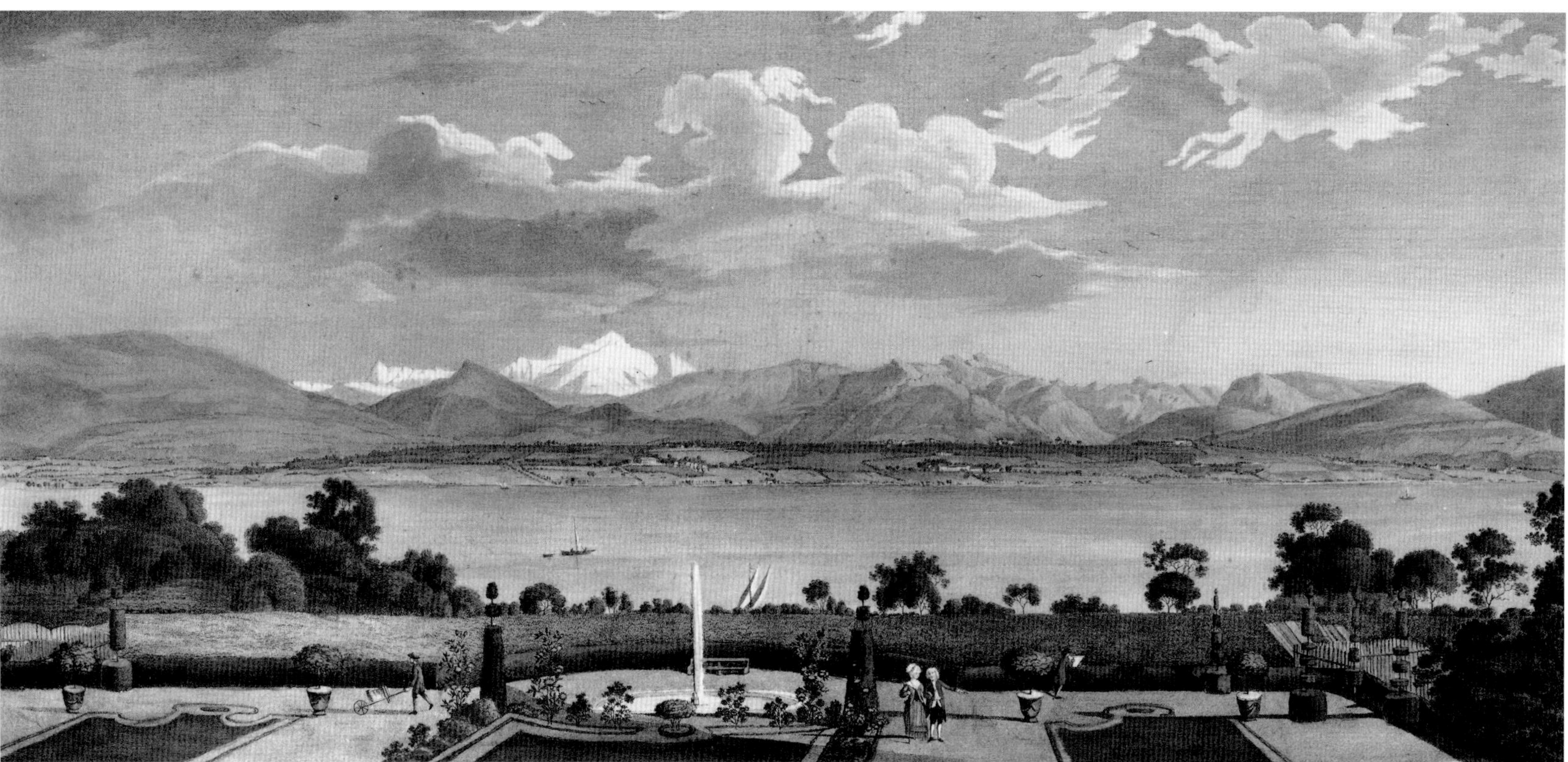

Fig. 4-2. Simon Malgo. View across Lake Léman toward Mont Blanc, from Charles Bonnet's villa north of Geneva, 1781. Engraving. Geneva, Bibliothèque publique et universitaire, Centre iconographique genevois.

"The strange Animals of Geneva": 1777–78

There is no certainty which itinerary Beckford took in the summer of 1777, when he left London to pursue his instruction in Geneva or how long the voyage took. The route taken by the botanist Thomas Blaikie in 1775 may be considered typical for the age and is no doubt a reflection of Beckford's own course two years later.[6] Blaikie left London on April 15, crossing the Channel in two days because of inclement weather, although the sailing could be made in several hours under favorable conditions. He traveled from Boulogne to Paris in a public carriage in six days—this on one of the best roads in France—while two additional days were spent in another coach from Paris to Chalons, where a boat took yet another seven days to reach Lyon. From there a private *chaise-poste* was hired to bring Blaikie to Geneva four days later. Not including the necessary rest stops, the total time spent in actual travel from London was twenty-one days.

Since Beckford had the privilege of affluence, his voyage was certainly speedier and undeniably more comfortable than Blaikie's. There is no reason to assume that Beckford relied on public transport, which was frequently noted as being particularly uncomfortable and often untrustworthy. Beckford would have had a private carriage, as he did when traveling within Switzerland, contracting for changes of horses at established linking posts. It is equally unlikely that Beckford would have lodged in public inns or the widely spaced country *auberges*, as his coach would have been equipped with a traveling bed.[7] It is also to be presumed that Beckford did not dine at the post inns, which in France were notoriously ill-stocked and almost universally disparaged by British travelers of all classes. Like many of his affluent compatriots, Beckford, and his tutor and companion John Lettice, were able to supply their own provisions at designated stops, as did Beckford's cousin when he traveled to Italy several years later.[8]

When Beckford arrived in Geneva in September, 1777—the

precise date cannot be determined because foreigners were not required to provide travel documents or even register their presence on Swiss soil[9]—he found the city to be still a relatively small enclave of about 1,300 dwellings, housing about 25,000 inhabitants.[10] Beckford's stay was intended only as a provisional one, lodging with his distant relative Edward Hamilton, who owned two houses in the area: his principal residence was in the city itself; the other, a country estate in Chênes, about three miles to the southeast. Beckford, but not Lettice, was domiciled in the Geneva house; the estate in Chênes was still within the domain of the Duke of Savoy and would not be officially annexed by Geneva until 1816.

The predilection of Beckford for Geneva as a site for his early education followed an established paragon among Europeans, who came here because of its reputation as a leading center of liberal studies. This is already clear in one of the earliest descriptions of the city published by a British writer, Gilbert Burnet, who repeatedly noted the stimulation of local men of letters, the general enlightenment of its citizenry, and the "universal Civilite" of its population.[11] John Moore, a distinguished Scottish physician, also underlined these points five years before Beckford's arrival. Moore noted that a majority of Genevans enjoyed the unprecedented counsel of "a great number of men of letters," so much so that he found the level of instruction of both sexes significantly higher than in England.[12]

Burnet's and Moore's esteem for the intellectual character of Genevan life was based on their encounters with members of the Collège de Genève, founded by Calvin in 1559 and later designated as the Académie.[13] In Beckford's age, lectures were entrusted to a faculty of eleven permanent professors,[14] but there is no record that Beckford ever enrolled here officially, although certain classes were open to the public at large.[15] It may be concluded that Beckford pursued his education in an independent manner through the guidance of Lettice and Hamilton and the extensive contacts of the latter with prominent individuals who set the intellectual tone of the city.

This aspect of Beckford's Geneva life has always been sketched in very general terms and remains difficult to document accurately. The Beckford biographies mention several savants who in their own way were said to have contributed to Beckford's instruction if only indirectly. Many are renowned outside the Swiss context and need only be mentioned in passing. Foremost were Charles Bonnet and Horace-Bénédit de Saussure, both of whom received many students privately in their respective houses in nearby Genthod on the northern shore of the lake.[16] Bonnet was a celebrated naturalist and forefather of modern biology, whose work and philosophical writings would be acknowledged by all major European scientific institutions.[17] His melding of science, reason, and art as essential components in comprehending the physical and spiritual aspects of nature must have particularly enticed Beckford's early secular interests. At the time of meeting Beckford, Bonnet maintained a sumptuous villa with a direct view of the Salève and Mont Blanc (fig. 4-2), a dramatic sight that Beckford surely knew well from repeated visits with the naturalist.

De Saussure, Bonnet's nephew, was one of the pioneering figures in Swiss Alpine studies. His brilliance was recognized when he was awarded the chair of philosophy in Geneva at the age of twenty-two.[18] It was at this time that De Saussure began his comprehensive examination of the Mont Blanc range, compensated by diverse European scientific societies.[19] De Saussure's major writings were published after Beckford was in Geneva,[20] but given Beckford's immediate passion for the mountains, he and De Saussure must have discussed them, engendering to an extent Beckford's own passion for the Sublime. Beckford, whose fascination with fine books was now also developing, may have been further stimulated in his bibliophilic course by De Saussure's reputable library which was eagerly shown to guests.[21]

In addition to Bonnet and De Saussure, there were other figures in the Geneva intellectual community from whom Beckford probably benefited. It is thought that Beckford instructed himself on aspects of civic law under the guidance of François-André Naville,[22] as indeed he was said to have been impressed by the publications of Jean-Louis Delolme.[23] The latter became a respected lawyer, whose radical politics had forced him to leave Geneva in 1769 for London, where he produced an exceptionally erudite study of the English constitution that remained a standard study for generations to come.[24] Beckford was said to have read Delolme's work, but there appears to be no documentary evidence to establish whether they actually met, although Delolme had returned to Geneva just before Beckford's stay.

This was not the case with Paul-Henri Mallet who is one of the few Genevan savants directly mentioned in Beckford's writing.[25] In 1752 he was appointed professor of belles-lettres in Copenhagen, where he composed his greatest work, *Histoire de Dannemarc* [sic]. Mallet's examination of Nordic history gave rise to his even more celebrated publication, *Northern Antiquities*, the first significant study to propose an alternative to the entrenched dogma of a Greco-Roman mythological orientation.[26] The importance of these volumes in the European sphere may be gauged by the fact that an extraordinary range of writers were influenced by their contents: Gibbon, Walpole, and Voltaire were fervent admirers, as indeed Blake, Coleridge, and Scott would find new objectives from Mallet's writing that nourished their prevailing Romantic sensibilities.

How much Beckford was influenced by Mallet's work in his youth can only be conjectured, but a letter of November 24, 1777, testifies to its impact. In musing on the exploration of the "polar Climates," with their "sublime horror which overwhelms you on first beholding this mysterious Light," Beckford was led to ruminate on the "Country of *Odin*," and "the Gigantic *Valkyriur* [sic] shooting along with the Souls of the Brave to his *Valhalla*."[27] Beckford noted that further sources on the Valkyries could be found in Thomas Gray's poem, "The Fatal Sisters,"[28] but to assimilate the concept of Valhalla, the predominate work was unequivocally Mallet, "with whom I am very intimate," wrote Beckford. Indeed, of the Geneva savants associated with Beckford's youth, the works of Mallet appeared to have a particularly dominant place in his library.[29]

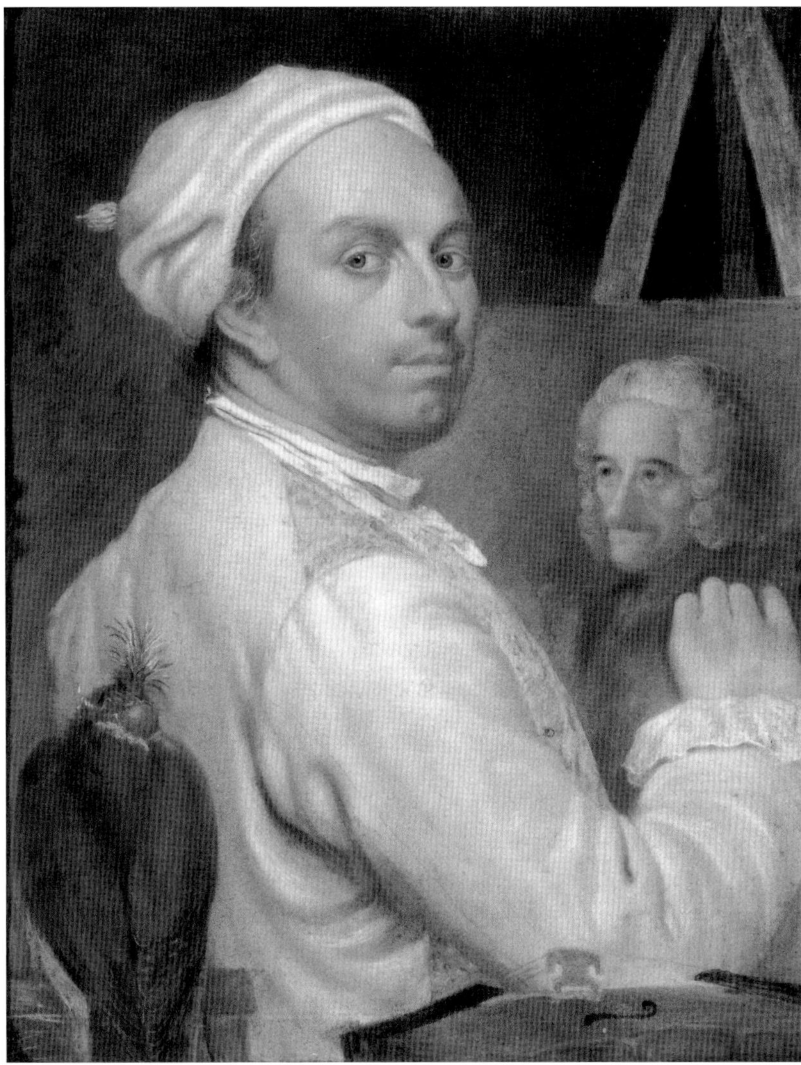

Fig. 4-3. Jean Huber. *Self-Portrait,* painted while working on a portrait of Voltaire, ca. 1773. Pastel, from a larger work, inv. 1890–7. Lausanne, Musée historique de Lausanne.

If Beckford's Genevan enlightenment can only be surmised from probable contacts or texts absorbed, his early interest in the arts likewise affords a cloudy picture, but one with a fixed point in his friendship with the distinctive artist, Jean Huber (fig. 4-3), who would remain one of his most enduring Swiss colleagues.[30] Having already created an indelible link to Alexander Cozens, Beckford was particularly prone to artistic stimulation and thus profited from the Hamilton's family connections with Huber to amplify this aspect of his refined interests. In befriending Huber, Beckford chose a singular figure in the Genevan milieu, one with an exceptionally distinguished and cultivated background. Before establishing himself in the Genevan artistic environment in 1746, Huber had served in the military in Cassel and later Sardinia, had amused diverse princes and monarchs with his remarkable wit and erudition, and had individually elevated

the folk craft of *découpage* into an singular art form.

Beckford's interest in Huber was fostered not only by his extraordinarily polymath talents, but also by the quirks of his picturesque temperament. Beckford described Huber's eccentric, meteoric genius in a letter of January 19, 1778, to his half-sister, in which he noted that he was saved from perpetual ennui by these "strange animals of Geneva," among whom "shines my Friend Huber whose particular excellence would be very hard to discover, as he is as changeable as the wind and sometimes as boisterous." These talents extended to falconry, as they did to solitary reflections "on the nature of the Universe and the first principle of all things." Beckford informed his half-sister that Huber had that remarkable capacity to adapt himself equally to designing deft caricatures, composing accomplished choral Misereres, or even writing "a dissertation upon the nature of Cats' whiskers."[31] Huber also exulted in Voltaire's writing, but was equally passionate about Shakespeare and Ariosto, thus forming a perfect foil for Beckford's youthful literary interests. It is little wonder that Huber's prismatic qualities were also commented on by Goethe during a visit shortly after Beckford had left Geneva.[32]

Beside sharing Beckford's concerns for literature and art, Huber was also responsible for Beckford's introduction to various dignitaries, including Voltaire, then aged eighty-four and living on his property at Ferney, only several miles from Hamilton's Genevan residence (fig. 4-4). In seeking out the Sage of Ferney, Beckford was following a British tradition whereby dozens of respectful voyagers habitually made the pilgrimage to pay their respects, gape obligingly at the heroic figure, or exchange philosophical musings.[33] When Beckford visited Voltaire, he was no more than "a mere skeleton—a living anatomy," who nevertheless gave Beckford a tour of his garden, spoke to him of his family, discussed Ariosto, and at the end of the visit offered his blessings on a clearly appreciative adolescent.[34]

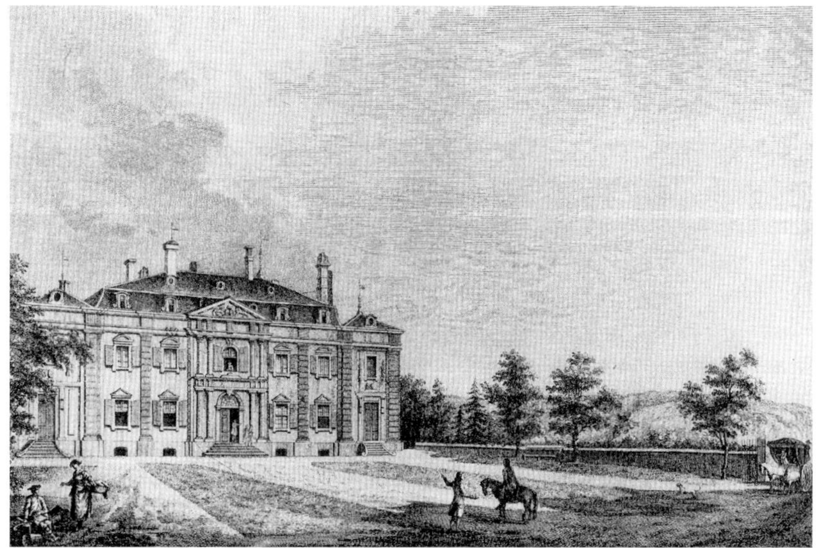

Fig. 4-4. Michel-Vincent Brandoin. The Château de Ferney. From Jean Benjamin de la Borde, *Tableaux topographiques, pittoresques littéraire de la Suisse,* vol. 2, *Tableaux de la Suisse, ou voyage pittoresque fait dans les treize cantons* (Paris: Imprimerie de Clousier, 1780), plate 155.

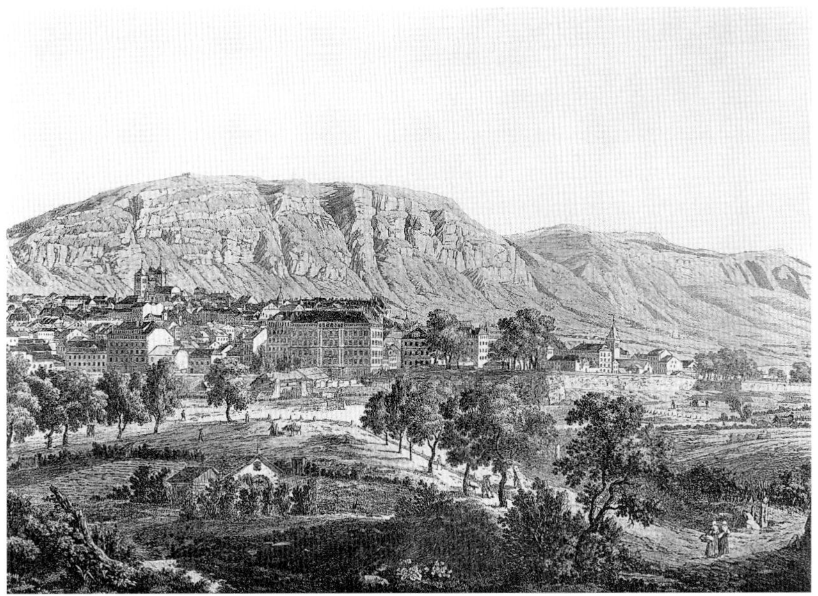

Fig. 4-5. Jean-Philippe Linck. View of Geneva, with the Grand-Salève in the background, ca. 1805. Colored engraving, the right section of a panorama. Geneva, Bibliothèque publique et universitaire, Centre iconographique genevois.

Beckford does not record whether Huber introduced him to the various artistic depositories of the city.[35] There was as yet no public museum in Geneva, but one of the most remarkable private galleries was to be found at the residence of François Tronchon. Although trained as a banker, Tronchin amassed two collections in his lifetime, the most prominent arrays of paintings in the region.[36] Despite Huber's decades-old acquaintance with Tronchin, and Beckford's inherent sensibility for the pictorial arts, there is no record that Beckford had any knowledge of these works.

All biographies of Beckford note that his Genevan stay of 1777–78 was punctuated not only with academic application, however indeterminate and perhaps capricious, but also with various forms of social amusement and diverse travel within the area.[37] On September 13, 1777, Beckford climbed the Salève, which was clearly visible throughout the city (fig. 4-5), and to which he would return several times as a fetish site.[38] Beckford was again following an established tradition, since the proximity of the mountain to the urban area, and its relatively facile path to the summit, made it one of the first Alpine peaks most British travelers ascended.[39] Beckford recorded his impressions after a pre-dawn trek up the Salève, noting first the precise time of his writing as 9 o'clock in the morning. In bursting enthusiasm on his inaugural Alpine crest, about 3,000 feet above the lake and the Geneva basin, Beckford exalted in the impressive views with "Assemblage of substantial Vapours" and "Volumes of grey cloud" that

reminded him of "a declining volcano," sensations that both incited and bewildered his adolescent sensibilities.[40] He envisioned himself in the romantic guise of "an ancient Helvetian in defense of his Liberty," whose letter was literally cast from "the rugged fragment, mouldered from the peak of the Mountain." When he made his descent courageously after eight in the evening, his enthusiasm gave way to the terrors of "horrid forms" emerging in the haze, "like crucified Malefactors," who metamorphosed themselves into "the Shape of weather beaten Oaks," branches of which "have stood the brunt of Tempests for ages."[41]

The "Land of freshness and verdure": 1782 and 1783

When Beckford left Geneva in the fall of 1778, he was no longer the youthful student, but now a proto-Romantic who was "determined to enjoy my dreams, my phantasies and all of my singularity."[42] These desires were augmented in England by his discovery of Goethe's *Werther*, which he strongly advised Cozens to read,[43] but offset by the constrictive rigors of life at Fonthill Splendens.[44] Beckford's state of mind was for the most part subdued by the gloomy thoughts and petulant fits of despair that marked the boredom he felt on his return to the confines of family and obligation. These were relieved in June 1780 when Beckford set off on his first Grand Tour, but in returning to England—"this vile Country"—he decided that he needed to travel to Italy again to "joyfully creep" in its culture and lack of restraint.[45] Traveling by way of Geneva in mid-October 1782, he again renewed his friendship with Huber and enjoyed the pacification the "Land of freshness and verdure" provided.[46]

During Beckford's Italian wanderings, he penned some of his thoughts on the nature of the Swiss and his admiration for their national ideals.[47] Beckford's comments fall within the habitual British view of Swiss traditions and life as had been expressed by numerous travelers before and after. He noted that while many nations surpass "Swisserland" in "riches, splendor, and magnificence," the imbued ethical codes here "dispute the palm" with any country in Europe. Beckford signaled in particular the ideals of "Liberty, patriotism, toleration, economy, justice, and simplicity of manners" as the guideposts by which the Swiss distinguished themselves from their autocratic European neighbors. Beckford then explained the nature of each of these points, stressing in particular "the liberal spirit of toleration" in which "the cordial confederacy" easily accepted peaceful cohabitation among opposing religions, one of the guiding canons of peaceful synergy. He would have reason to doubt the notion a decade later, when in politically charged times he attempted to seek refuge on Swiss soil.

While Beckford's philosophic exhalation of the Swiss was sincere, his sentiments at this time were not always untroubled. They would in effect take a sour note when Beckford, now in the company of new bride, Lady Margaret Gordon, again passed through Geneva in the summer of 1783. Huber was already prepared to receive Beckford and his wife, having been notified by Lettice in May of the marriage.

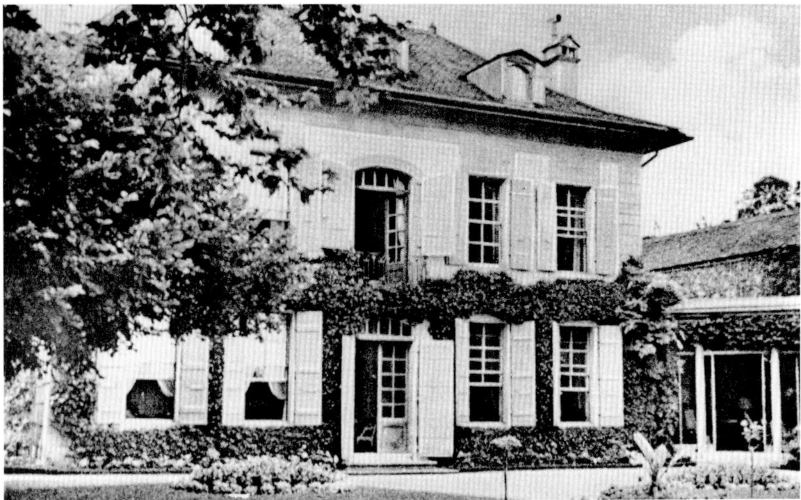

Fig. 4-6. Garden front of the "Villa Beckford" at Collogny, facing Lake Geneva. Photographed before 1970; from a postcard. Geneva, Bibliothèque publique et universitaire, Centre iconographique genevoise.

Beckford had apparently enlisted Huber to find adequate lodgings, to which Huber responded that he would seek a house near his own in Collogny on the fashionable southern outskirts of the town. Before Beckford left England, Huber informed him that he had negotiated the lease of an appropriate dwelling belonging to the Cramer family.[48] Huber was referring to a country estate built before 1760 by the banker Pierre Cramer, which subsequently became known locally as the "Villa Beckford" (fig. 4-6), and which still stands at 39 Route de la Capite, Collogny.

Beckford wrote Cozens that "I lead a quiet uniform stupid sort of life on the banks of the Lake" that only Huber seemed to comprehend. Beckford's thoughts were again devoured by "Strange hopes and as strange fears," and he wondered "Why am I not happy?—Is it not my fault that I am miserable?"[49] Even a voyage to the "Region of Ice and Crystal" in the Chamonix valley, where Beckford was guided by the village doctor, Michel Gabriel Paccard,[50] or the exploration of the ice caves at the source of the Arveyron, did not mollify Beckford's brooding thoughts.[51] By autumn, however, he again found reconciliation in the Swiss landscape, with the "Woods, the Mountains, the wild flowery hills" delighting his eye and restoring his fleeting sense of serenity. Evenings were often spent in the convivial company of Huber who regaled his guest with readings of Goldoni comedies, while Beckford entertained with music.[52] By late October, Beckford could write that "I seem to walk in light and tread in Air. My happiness is inexpressible."[53]

During this time, Beckford had occasion to participate in various social salons of which the one at the château de Prangins, near

Coppet, is the best documented.[54] The château was then the domain of Louis-François Guiguer, recently married to his English bride, Mathilda Shore Cleveland, whose portrait by the Danish painter Jens Juel was painted at about this time (fig. 4-7).[55] Just after their marriage the couple began jointly recording their daily activities in a written journal which noted no fewer than four citations of Beckford in a period of a year.[56] None of these entries indicate how Beckford was introduced to their select company, although it may be surmised that the nationality of Guiguer's wife played a role. Beckford's first recorded visit was on Friday, October 18, 1782, when it was noted that "We saw Mr Beckfort [sic] on his way to England from Italy."[57] The Prangins hosts were somewhat alarmed to see him arrive in a stunning retinue of horses, carriages, and servants, the sight of which astonished the neighbors as an overly flamboyant manner of exhibiting the guest's reputed wealth.[58] The impression made by Beckford himself, however, was apparently more favorable since Guiguer wrote, "We judged his destiny as brilliant…his supposed talents marvelous…nothing as yet will stop his progress."[59] As one who is young, extraordinarily gifted, and master of himself, he caused them also to worry about his direction and wondered what sort of life awaited him.

On June 7, 1783, news of Beckford's passage in Nyon reached

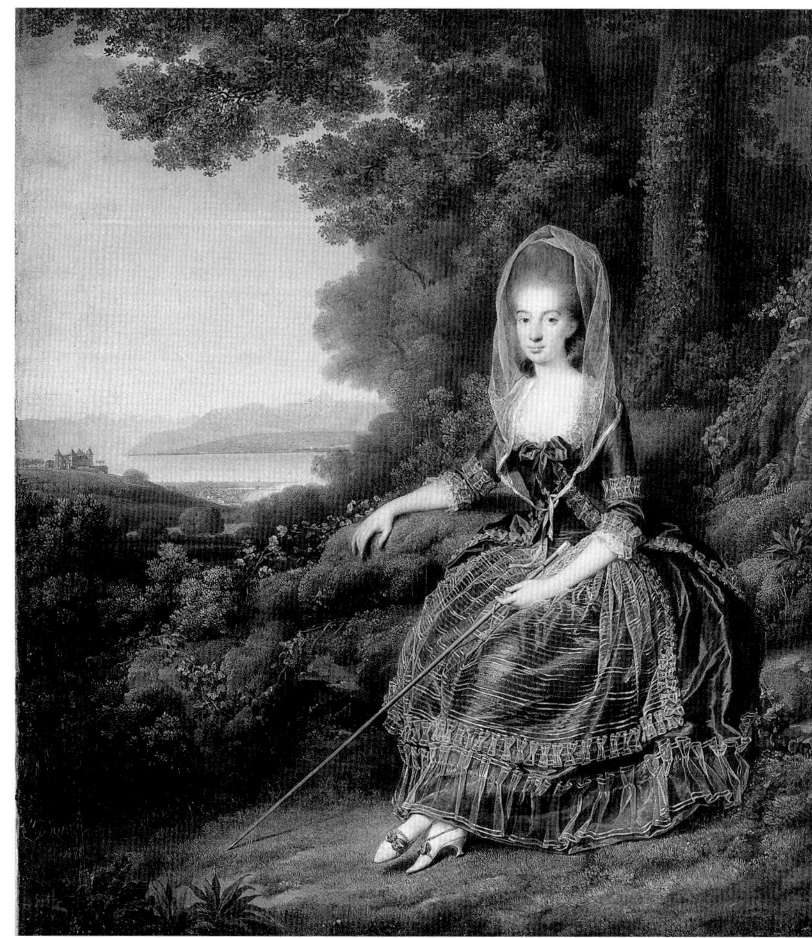

Fig. 4-7. Jens Juel. *Madame de Prangins in Her Park*, 1779. Oil on canvas. The Château de Prangins is seen in the distance. Copenhagen, Statens Museum for Kunst.

the Guiguers in regard to a visit to the château de Coppet where the Necker family lived. Guiguer noted at this time that Beckford "is the man of the hour, and is in good health, which we hardly expected."[60] Beckford, now accompanied by his wife, did not meet with the Guiguer family, but apparently asked his hosts in passing of news of their welfare.

But on August 9, the Guiguers themselves were invited to a musical soirée at the château de Coppet, where among the guests of the Necker family, were twenty-two "Anglois," including Beckford. Little is actually mentioned of the evening except that Beckford had met Charles D'Espinasse here, the latter joining the instrumentalists in a final performance at the end of the evening.[61] The Guiguers' entry in the diary also noted that Beckford proposed to continue the soirée in the early hours of the morning across the lake at Evian. There are no descriptions of the Evian portion of the party, as many of the exhausted guests refused to attend because of the lateness of the hour; according to Guiguer, Beckford expected to hire a boat at three in the morning and continue the revelry through the next day.

In the following months, there must have been some dissension between Beckford and the Guiguer family about which they provided no details. The last reference to Beckford in their journal is a curiously apathetic entry for October 15, 1783. Beckford arrived unexpectedly in mid-week without a prior invitation, but curiously announced his desire to dine and then spend the night. He was received neither coldly nor in a friendly manner, and it is clear from the wording in the diary that Beckford's hosts neither encouraged his welcome nor his lodging for the night. Guiguer only noted that Beckford acted suitably with no further commentary. The implication is that Beckford's gregarious manner was seen by them as inappropriate to their staid standards.

As the Guiguers' journal indicates, Beckford had by this time also developed his contacts with the Necker family at Coppet.[62] In this instance, there is no doubt that Huber was Beckford's intermediary because of his particular links to the family: in 1747 Huber had married Marie-Louise Alléon, Madame Necker's cousin. Beckford's meeting with Louise Necker, the future Madame de Staël, was recalled late in his life as having occurred in Coppet in 1783,[63] a fact corroborated by the entry in the Prangins journal. Other than the musical evening noted here, there is no information of Beckford's actual meeting with Louise Necker at this time, nor her impressions of Beckford's expansive character. Nevertheless, their paths would cross several weeks later in Paris when Beckford lent her a copy of his newly published *Dreams, Waking Thoughts and Incidents*. Louise's letter to Beckford contained the customary homage to his writing—although it is not clear that she had read the entire work—as well as an invitation to dine.[64] Beckford spent an afternoon and evening dancing in the company of the composer Piccini and discussing science with the naturalist Georges-Louis Buffon. It seems that the gaiety of the evening was spoiled when Beckford made a social faux pas by awkwardly spilling a glass of water on Louise. A further letter from her to Beckford eased his discomfort,

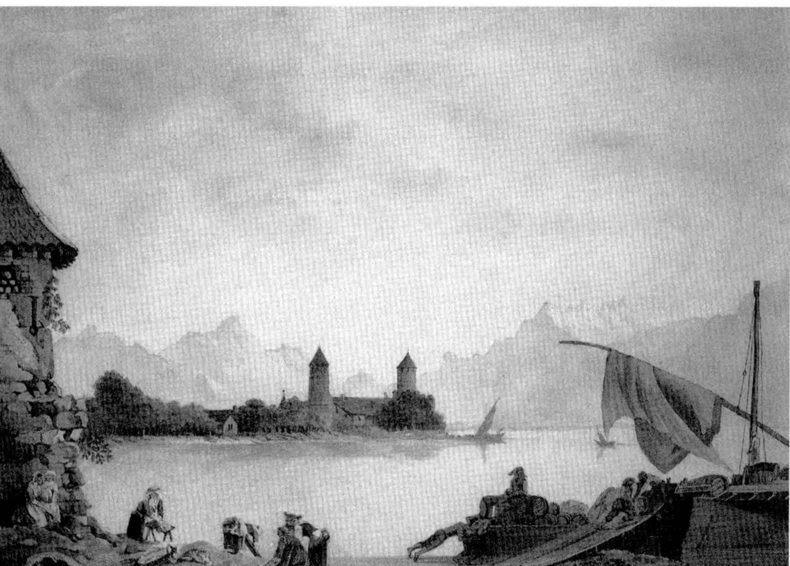

Fig. 4-8. Michel-Vincent Brandoin. The Château de la Tour-de-Peilz, viewed from the port of Vevey looking east, ca. 1782. Watercolor. The château is now the Musée suisse du jeu. Vevey, Musée historique du Vieux-Vevey.

and contained another offer to dine that same evening.[65] Beckford declined and returned to England shortly afterwards.

"…UN SUJET POUR UN MORALISTE": LA TOUR-DE-PEILZ, 1785–86

One of Beckford's most arresting Swiss respites occurred in the aftermath of the Courtenay affair. Fearing the torrent of scandal, Beckford left England in the summer of 1785, establishing himself by September in La Tour-de-Peilz, a hamlet adjoining Vevey.[66] The choice of this remote site may seem especially odd, as it was composed only of two parallel streets adjacent to the lake and housed a population of 800 inhabitants in fewer than 150 permanent buildings.[67] Beckford rented the only substantial lodging available to him here, the château de La-Tour-de-Peilz, directly on the water's edge (fig. 4-8). In ruin by the middle of the eighteenth century, it had been restored by its owner, Jean Gressier, a retired French military officer, who added a central court, small private chapel, and living quarters where Beckford took up his expatriate residence.[68] The citadel created the allusion of a "melancholy castle," as Lord Camelford described it when he passed here in September 1786,[69] and many visitors to the area thought that from the outside it was uninhabitable.[70]

Beckford's decision to rent this imposing dwelling could not have been not an arbitrary one. There must have been some correspondence, now seemingly lost, detailing the negotiations with the owner or an intermediary, as had been the case earlier when Huber secured the Cramer residence for him in Collogny.[71] In this case,

Beckford probably had relied upon his relationship with the powerful de Blonay family, whose domains extended from Vevey to Evian.[72] Beckford had known the local branch of the family for years, having attended *fêtes* in Evian since 1777, held in the forest near the summer estate. English tourists favored lavish dancing parties in the Bois de Blonay, and it was here that two years earlier Beckford had proposed to continue a soirée hosted by the Necker family.[73] When Beckford installed himself in the château, it had only recently been incorporated into the de Blonay holdings. Gressier died on May 4, 1785,[74] and the château had passed to his daughter, Anne-Catherine, who had married J.-R.-F. de Blonay, known commonly as Major de Blonay in homage to his military escapades. He bore the official title of Seigneur de La Tour-de-Peilz until his death in 1789 and would play an active role in defending Beckford against adverse criticism. De Blonay must have been informed of Beckford's requirement for exile in 1785 and offered his newly acquired residence as a suitably cloistered temporary sanctuary.[75]

Beckford remained there about eight months, occupying himself with the *Episodes*, which would become an integral part of *Vathek*, and otherwise "calmly resigned to my present situation. I cling fast to my tutelary mountains."[76] Beckford's solitude seemed assured, and in old age he would recall the stay at La Tour-de-Peilz as a particularly soothing experience, while burdened by the "bitter domestic calamity."[77] There seemed to be little to disturb his seclusion, and he apparently maintained the image of a model resident of the commune. The archives of the municipality record his name only once in 1785, a request to local officials to cut overlapping branches on the road leading to the property so that "his carriage could easily pass."[78]

Beckford did not isolate himself completely. He continued to communicate with Huber and his son, Jean-Daniel Huber, who supposedly had made some illustrations—now lost—for *Vathek*. When the younger Huber visited Beckford in October 1785, his father related the visit in a letter to Madame de Staël, noting that Beckford was conspicuously in need of consolation and encouragement—presumably Huber was aware of the scandal in England—and that Beckford had made certain unnamed "connaissances" in the region who could provide him with intellectual stimulus in his isolation. Huber *père* knew Beckford well enough, however, to tell Madame de Stäel that his extravagances, which he described as, "more quixotic than depravity," would in effect be the reason for his downfall no matter how exemplary his later life would prove to be.[79] It was not surprising that Huber described the twenty-five year old Beckford as "a subject for a moralist," a fact that perhaps the Guiguer family already felt when they cooled their relationship with him.

On May 26, 1786, Beckford's tranquility was upset by the death of his wife after complications in childbirth.[80] Beckford acted in an official manner concerning established procedures when a foreigner died on Swiss soil. Two days after Lady Margaret's death, local government officials were called upon to act on a demand Beckford made to have his wife temporarily buried in the local church until her body could be embalmed to be sent to London. The city council, meeting in a *session extraordinaire* under the leadership of de Blonay, unanimously granted the request the same day.[81]

There were no further actions by the council in regard to Beckford until July 1786, when news circulated from an article in the June 9 issue of the *Morning Chronicle* that Beckford was in some manner responsible for Lady Margaret's death. In response to the accusation, on July 24, 1786, twenty-eight leading dignitaries, again headed by de Blonay, provided Beckford with an "Attestation des bonnes mœurs."[82] Such documents are very unusual in Swiss communal records and are generally given to citizens who wish to establish themselves in other municipalities. In this case the matter must have been a private one between de Blonay and Beckford—as no mention of it is recorded in the local archives—and can only be regarded as an unprecedented circumstance afforded to a favored resident and friend. The document categorically rejected notions that Beckford was in some way accountable for his wife's death, affirming his good will in all matters and pronouncing him a man of honor, charity, and upstanding morals.

The death of Lady Margaret put Beckford into contact with the painter Michel-Vincent Brandoin in nearby Vevey.[83] The first instance in which Beckford's name appears in the Brandoin correspondence occurs as Brandoin was supervising the final aspects of the sepulchral monument of Catherine Orloff he had been commissioned to design.[84] Brandoin at this time inquired of Orloff's Lausanne agent charged with the details of the commission, Maximilien de Cerjat, about the payment he was due, adding a postscript to the letter, "Is it true that M. Beckford is coming to Lausanne?"[85] Although a landed Swiss nobleman, Cerjat had been active in English affairs since the 1750s, and after his return to Lausanne, he enticed various English friends to stay for prolonged holidays, entertaining them in his house. Associated as he was with the Necker and Guiguer families, it seems likely that Cerjat not only knew Beckford personally, but also was aware of his travels in Switzerland.

It is not known whether Beckford came to Lausanne in 1783 or, if he did, whether he was introduced to Brandoin through Cerjat, but Beckford's long association with the artist materialized after his wife's death. Beckford, grief stricken by the tragedy, was advised to alleviate his anguish with travel, this time engaging Brandoin to record the sojourn in watercolor sketches. They were known to have gone to the areas around Zurich and Bern, as well as to the Salève, and in Beckford's account, Brandoin's name was cited.[86] There is, however, no trace of sketches by Brandoin made during this trip, as indeed no works by the artist in any form were noted in the sales of Beckford's collections.

After their brief tour in the summer of 1786, Beckford and Brandoin corresponded for several years. The most revealing letter is dated March 20, 1789. Brandoin wrote to Beckford in Paris, addressing his patron in an unaccustomed intimate form as "mon cher"; Beckford replied ten days later, as he noted directly on the letter.[87] The familiar nature of Brandoin's salutation connotes a particular affinity

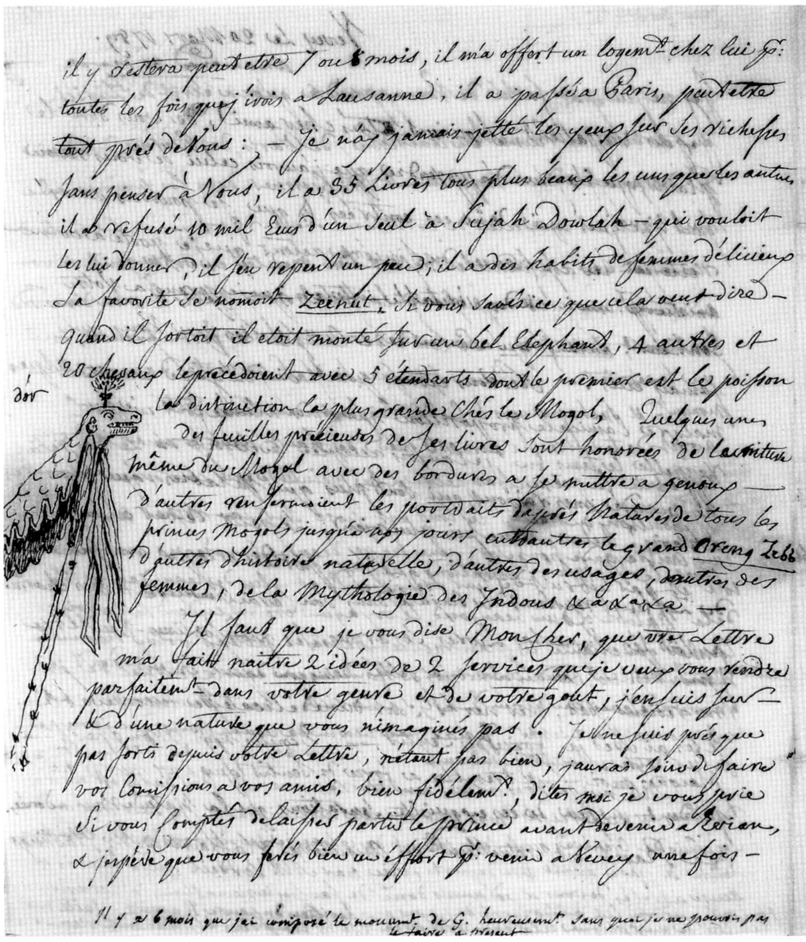

Fig. 4-9. Letter from Michel-Vincent Brandoin to Beckford, March 20, 1789. Oxford, Bodleian Library, Ms Beckford, c. 27, fol. 2v.

piqued by Brandoin's enthusiastic description of several remarkable illuminated manuscripts, unusual fabrics, and a plethora of objects, including "five standards of which the first is the Golden Fish, the highest distinction among the Mogul,"[90] which Brandoin thoughtfully illustrated in the margin of his letter (fig. 4-9). In later years, Beckford acquired some of the actual objects Brandoin described, which were eventually sold by the Hamilton heirs in 1882.[91] Whether Brandoin acted as an agent with Polier before his death in 1795 is not certain, but it is unlikely that Beckford could have made these acquisitions without Brandoin's assistance.

Beside the relationship with Brandoin, Beckford's Swiss friends included two physicians, both of whom had literary interests and who would attach themselves to Beckford's service. Probably the most privileged of these was François Verdeil, who studied with and eventually succeeded the eminent Dr. Auguste Tissot. Verdeil was also a friend of Brandoin, who mentioned him in the 1789 letter cited above.[92] An ardent protagonist of political liberties, Verdeil was a conspicuous free-thinker among conservative Swiss factions, a leader of the Masonic movement in the area, and one of the first Swiss physicians who dared endorse vaccination. He was Beckford's personal physician for several years, attending to Lady Margaret and then to Beckford's depression after her death,[93] remaining in Beckford's service until the late 1780s. Beckford's appreciation of Verdeil's friendship and medical advice was acknowledged in a life pension of £100 a year.

Also close to Beckford was Frédéric Scholl who kept an active medical practice in Vevey until 1788. Scholl, it seems, was the only one of Beckford's Swiss devotees to whom Beckford continually corresponded well into old age. He too was at one time an associate of Tissot and later became the personal physician of Gibbon. Scholl's intimacy with Beckford was underscored when he designated Beckford to be the godfather of one of his daughters. Scholl also acted on Beckford's behalf in other services, including evaluating some aspects of his book and manuscript collection; the sale of one item in Beckford's collection, previously belonging to Polier, seems to have been made on Scholl's appraisal.[94]

Also important in Beckford's Swiss entourage during the stay at La Tour-de-Peilz was Jean-David Levade (fig. 4-10), a notable figure in local theological circles. Levade, who had worked in London, was an overt Anglophile who developed a reputation as a sycophant of wealthy British travelers.[95] Like Scholl, Levade had been associated with Gibbon and other notables, who met regularly in the wooden pavilion Levade had built at the foot of the cathedral for the purpose of philosophic and political discussions in which Beckford was said to have participated. One of reasons why Levade attracted Beckford's attention may well have been his penchant for bizarre habits, in the same way that Huber's eccentricity had proven to be an irresistible bond between the two.[96] Levade translated the English text of *Vathek* into French for the Lausanne publication by Isaac Hignou after Henley's pirate publication in London; it is likely that Verdeil also had a hand in correcting the second Paris edition.[97]

between the two that induced Brandoin to discuss various aspects of his current projects, the nature of which prevented him from accepting Beckford's invitation to join him in France. Brandoin detailed, for example, diverse commissions associated with a spectacular collection of Indian manuscripts and objects he had examined near Lausanne. The collection had been assembled in India and then exported to Switzerland by Antoine-Louis de Polier, known locally as the "Rajah" or "Polier l'Indien."[88] In associating himself with Polier, possibly through the intervention of Cerjat, who knew the Polier family well, Brandoin in fact was given access to one of the leading figures of Indian studies at the end of the eighteenth century.[89]

It is unlikely that Beckford would have known of Polier before Brandoin's wrote about him, but Beckford's interests were most likely

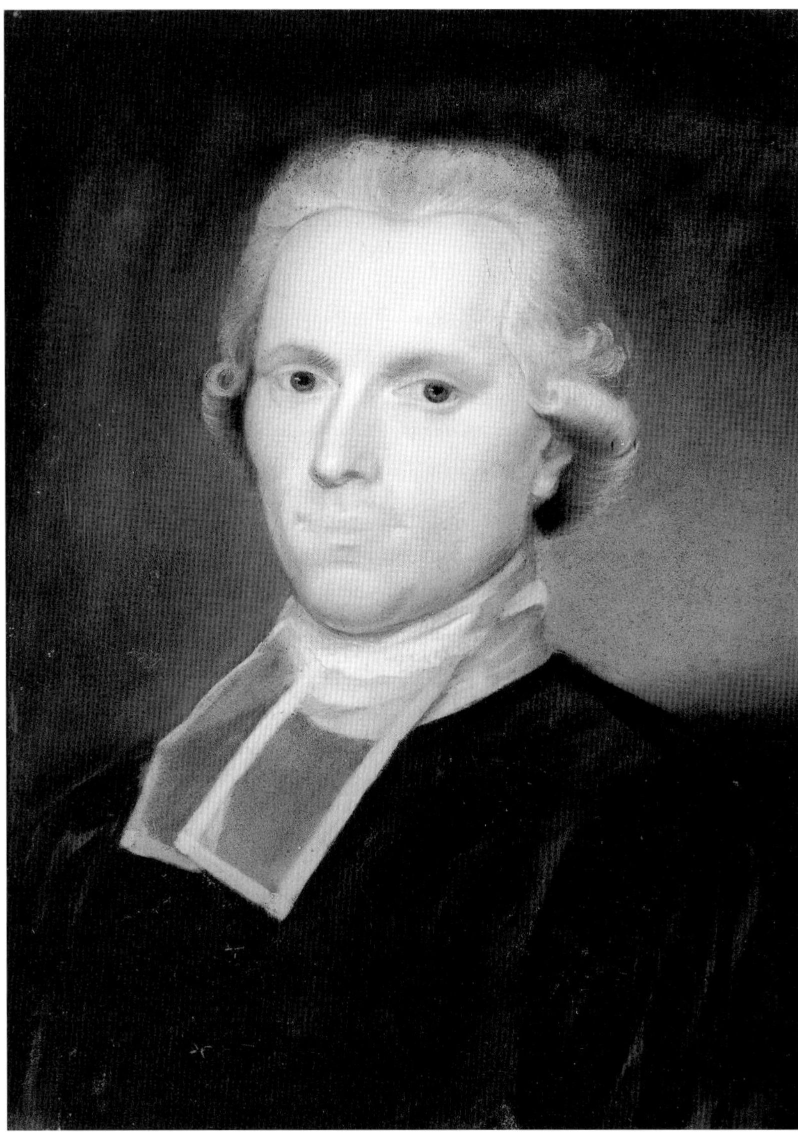

Fig. 4-10. Artist unknown. *Portrait of David Levade*, ca. 1775. Pastel on paper. Lausanne, Fondation de l'Hermitage.

"…LES DÉSAGRÉMENTS QUE VOUS AVEZ ÉPROUVÉS": LAUSANNE, 1792

After Beckford's stay at La Tour-de-Peilz, he again traveled extensively, taking Verdeil with him, until the start of the French Revolution, when the latter decided to remain in Paris. Beckford's sojourns to Switzerland at this time are exceedingly difficult to trace, although he is known to have been in Evian in 1789, a fact mentioned in the writings of Madame Gauthier.[98] Beckford's wanderings a few years later began when he left Paris in July 1792, fearing that as an English aristocrat, he might be in danger. He first sought refuge in Evian during the summer, but by September the encroaching Jacobin fervor in the area

forced him to seek further sanctuary,[99] this time crossing the lake to Lausanne. Even though Swiss officials had required foreigners, particularly those escaping the political situation in France,[100] to register for passports and entrance visas, there is no record that Beckford applied for one, although the German musicians he had engaged in Evian, who had accompanied him, were required to do so.[101]

The difficulties Beckford encountered in Lausanne are recorded in the well-known account of Thomas Whaley, who wrote that Beckford, said to have rented a house in Lausanne, was apparently expelled the day after his arrival on orders from the Bernese bailiff of the city, Baron Gabriel Albert d'Erlach de Spiez.[102] Whaley explained that Beckford was suspected of having favored the escape of a prisoner condemned to more than twenty years for his role in a conspiracy in Rolle, in other words advocating local freedom over Bernese control. Whaley's chronicle seems on the surface to be specious for several reasons: the accusations of political intervention in local affairs is incongruous with Beckford's nature, and indeed, this extraordinary event was never mentioned by him in any of his later correspondence or memoirs.

In order to comprehend the curious circumstances Whaley described, and to either verify or dismiss them, it is first necessary to understand the political climate in Lausanne and surrounding region. With the news of the French Revolution, the local citizenry under autocratic Bernese rule since 1536, accepted its ideals of liberty.[103] The Bernese authorities were thus especially wary of the propagandist movement that the French stimulated, imposing censures to preserve their political supremacy. By August 1789, a rigid restraint of travel by most foreigners had been enacted at border crossings, with the requirement of registration through passports and certified visas. By late 1790, Baron d'Erlach was not only limiting immigration further, but also censoring the publication or importation of all political leaflets and tracts.[104]

The reaction of the Vaudois to these prohibitive programs was to show their solidarity with the French through public civic manifestations, innocently called "banquets," but in fact no less than political meetings. The most impassioned of these occurred in Lausanne on July 14, 1791, in the garden of Charles D'Apples, Gibbon's respected banker,[105] while a second manifestation took place in Rolle the following day.[106] These provocations caused the Bernese authorities to prohibit all public gatherings and to establish an organized spy network to report on questionable political movements and figures.[107] A committee was created in Bern to punish those involved in the Lausanne and Rolle "banquets," and twenty-seven participants were placed under arrest, including D'Apples, who was sentenced to two years of house arrest.[108]

It was precisely this ambience of fear, political insurrection, and Bernese suppression, which Gibbon humbly called "this very awkward crisis,"[109] that Beckford unwittingly discovered in September 1792, observing that Lausanne was "in sad confusion, its government half crazy with alarms, suspicions, etc."[110] On September 24, 1792, the Bernese Conseil in Lausanne issued an exacting directive to prevent further social disturbance, dictated particularly by the substantial number of foreigners coming from the Savoy, presumably including Beckford. Owners of all accommodations were compelled to furnish daily records of occupants while paid informants kept track of foreigners who had already been permitted into the country.[111]

With such sophisticated spy channels in place, Beckford's arrival in Lausanne could not have gone unnoticed, but in the profusion of official documents, oddly it is never mentioned. Finally, there is no official record of his forced expulsion either by d'Erlach or any other administrative officer in the régime.[112] This lack of documentation may have various explanations. Beckford, already sensitive to the dangers in Paris and Evian, could have entered Switzerland under a false name, or he could have left the area in an unofficial manner before an actual order was issued. Maximilien de Cerjat, for example, was on intimate terms with D'Erlach,[113] and might have warned Beckford of the situation.

Was Beckford indeed thought by the Bernese to be politically menacing, and if so why? Beckford's nationality, wealth, and social class were not a priori factors in suspecting his intentions of asylum in Lausanne. In the summer of 1792, many notable English aristocrats were either visiting Lausanne or in temporary residence; some were even greeted by d'Erlach in September 1792 at a dinner given by Gibbon.[114] Whaley makes some intriguing points, however, that should not be dismissed out of hand. The prison escape allegedly condoned by Beckford refers clearly to the incarceration of Ferdinand-Antoine Rosset and Georges-Albert Muller de La Mothe, political prisoners who escaped in October 1792.[115] There is no hint that Beckford was aware of their situation upon his arrival in Lausanne.[116] Furthermore, it seem unlikely that Beckford, already conscious of his delicate position, would have aroused further suspicions by speaking out on their behalf. Whaley must have erred here, as indeed he may have been mistaken concerning the issuance of an order of expulsion.

Nevertheless, Beckford's culpability could have been generated by his association with known local radicals. In the paranoia of the times, the very publication of *Vathek* in Lausanne several years earlier might have been perceived as suspicious because its publisher, Isaac Hignou, was himself considered a reactionary literary figure. As a prominent printer and bookseller, Hignou was closely watched even before the events of 1789, and the manuscripts he published and their readers were scrutinized by a committee of censors.[117] Beckford's relationship with Verdeil was even more damaging. Verdeil had openly subscribed to the Lausanne "banquet" of 1791—signing his name as "Werdeil, docteur"—and was condemned to three months of prison.[118] He went into hiding before he could be apprehended, however, which is why Beckford did not meet with him while he was in Lausanne. In the distrusting climate of 1792, such connections alone would have persuaded the Bernese officials to consider Beckford too dangerous to permit his residency.

Whatever the truth behind the affair, Beckford apparently wished to have no confrontation with the local authorities and in fact abandoned the idea of refuge in Lausanne. He decided to leave Switzerland altogether, but there is no way of knowing whether his decision was forced or voluntary. He traveled through Bienne on September 26, 1792, and then went to Neuchâtel in the company of Lord Coleshill and Viscount Cloncurry.[119] News of Beckford's hasty departure from Lausanne was known to his friends. Huber *fils* wrote Beckford that he regretted the "unpleasantness which you experienced in Lausanne" which made him renounce further excursions in Switzerland.[120] Huber suggested a political motive in the decision by noting that should Beckford entertain notions of returning to Switzerland, the area around Lugano could be recommended because the government was more liberal.

Beckford, however, did return to Lausanne, but years later, when the region achieved its independence from Bernese authority. At the end of 1799, he was recorded as being in the city to assist in the baptism of his goddaughter, Henriette Scholl. By this time, he had further reason to meet with Scholl, who had negotiated Beckford's purchase of Gibbon's considerable library three years earlier, but Beckford had yet to take possession of it. Containing about six thousand volumes, the library had been transferred from Gibbon's house to Scholl's barely a hundred yards away where visitors were allowed to inspect it.[121] Beckford intended to ship the most prized volumes to Fonthill, but apparently never did.[122] In 1802, on another trip to Lausanne, Beckford shut himself in Scholl's house and "read myself nearly blind,"[123] but he left the books with Scholl who eventually disposed of them to several buyers in later sales.[124] Although continuing to correspond with Scholl for years, Beckford apparently had no reason for further excursions to Switzerland and remained ensconced in England, in the isolation of the "vile country" from which as a youth he seemed to have continually sought to escape.

Acknowledgments: Valuable assistance in preparing this essay was provided by Paul Bissegger, Archives cantonales vaudoises (Lausanne); Lionel Breitmeyer, Bibliothèque publique et universitaire (Geneva); Albert Curchod, Archives de La Tour-de-Peilz (La Tour-de-Peilz); Susan Palmer, Sir John Soane's Museum (London); Olivier Pavillion, Musée historique de Lausanne (Lausanne); and Chantal de Schoulepnikoff, (Château de Prangins). Additional acknowledgement is made to the present owners of the unpublished Prangins journal for permitting the citation of verbatim extracts concerning Beckford's visits.

Abbreviations. ACV: Lausanne, Archives cantonales vaudoises; *RHV: Revue historique vaudoise.*

1. Beside the standard literature on Beckford which cite his Swiss excursions briefly, see Henri Perrochon, "Un ami de Gibbon," *Gazette de Lausanne,* 1 May 1932, p. 1; Edmond Jaloux, "Beckford," ibid., 24 November 1945, p. 1; idem, "Lettres de Beckford," ibid., 8 December 1945, p. 1. Most important, however, are Gavin R. De Beer, "Anglais au pays de Vaud. V. William Beckford," *RHV* 59 (December 1951): 165–80; and Silvio Corsini, ed., *Un calife à Lausanne: William Beckford et 'Vathek',* exh. cat. (Lausanne: Bibliothèque cantonale et universitaire, 1987).

2. For an useful anthology of European voyagers in Switzerland, see Gavin R. De Beer, *Travellers in Switzerland* (Oxford: Oxford University Press, 1949), which includes a chronological list but no texts. For extracts of important texts, see Claude Reichler and Roland Ruffieux, eds., *Le voyage en Suisse: Anthologie des voyageurs français et européens de la Renaissance au XXe siècle* (Paris: Robert Laffont, 1998). The introduction (pp. 3–19) discusses the genesis and diffusion of the Swiss image in Europe.

3. [Abraham Stanyan], *An Account of Switzerland. Written in the Year 1714* (London: 1714), unpaginated. The citation is the opening line of the preface.

4. For a focused study on the subject, see John Wraight, *The Swiss and the British* (Salisbury: M. Russell, 1987). On British travels in the Swiss cantons and early travel guides, see William Hauptman, "Gli artisti britannici visitano la Svizzera: *recits de voyage,* racconti icastici e prime guide di viaggio," in *Itinerari sublimi. Viaggi d'artisti tra il 1750 e il 1850,* exh. cat. (Lugano: Museo cantonale d'arte, 1998): 93–100.

5. See Jeremy Black, *The British Abroad: The Grand Tour in the Eighteenth Century* (Gloucestershire: Sutton Publishing, 1997): 33f. Noteworthy were the voyages of Walter Chetwynd, William Windham, and Richard Pockocke, the latter two of whom published well-known accounts. On the early interest in the Alps and its expression in a variety of literary forms, see Claire-Eliane Engel, *La littérature alpestre en France et en Angleterre aux XVIIIe et XIXe siècles* (Chambéry: Dardel, 1930).

6. Blaikie's account was first published as *Diary of a Scotch Gardener at the French Court at the End of the Eighteenth Century,* ed. F. Birrell, (London: G. Routledge, 1931). I have used the somewhat abbreviated French translation, *Journal de Thomas Blaikie: Excursions d'un botaniste écossais dans les Alpes et le Jura en 1775,* ed., Louis Seylaz (Neuchâtel: Éd. La Braconnière, 1935): 17–31.

7. For the appalling accommodations, see Black, *British Abroad* (1997): 137–43. Many aristocratic travelers equipped their coaches with traveling beds, as was the case with Lady Craven when she sojourned to the Balkans; see Elizabeth Craven, *A Journey Throught the Crimea to Constantinople* (London: n. p., 1789): 368.

8. Peter Beckford, *Familiar Letters from Italy, to a Friend in England* (Salisbury: J. Easton, 1805): vol. 1, p. 17.

9. Such travel documents were not mandatory until after the French Revolution. Blaikie, *Journal* (1935): 32, noted that at the entrance gate to Geneva, all foreigners were simply questioned as to their intentions in visiting the city and especially where they were to be housed. If a reservation in an inn or an hotel was produced, an entrance visa was automatically granted.

10. Within this population, 58 percent were considered lawful bourgeois of the city, those who could legitimately call themselves *citoyens de Genève.* Of the remaining populace, 26.6 percent were established foreigners with residence permits, while 15.4 percent were migrant employees. See Alfred Perrenoud, *La population de Genève du seizième au début du dix-neuvième siècle: Etude démographique* (Geneva: Société d'histoire et d'archéologie, 1979): 9 and 242.

11. Gilbert Burnet, *Some Letters Containing an Account of What Seemed Most Remarkable in Switzerland, Italy, etc.* (Rotterdam: Abraham Acher, 1686): 258–60. Burnet passed through Geneva twice in late 1685. There is a very substantial literature on foreign descriptions of Geneva, but see especially Jean-Daniel Candaux, *Voyageurs européens à la découverte de Genève: 1685–1792* (Geneva: Imprimerie populaire, 1966).

12. John Moore, *A View of Society and Manners in France, Switzerland, and Germany* (London: n. p., 1780), vol. 1, pp. 158–59. Moore had resided in Geneva from June 1772 to September 1774. Moore noted that education in all social classes was more developed than elsewhere, so that one heard "mechanics in the intervals of their labour amusing themselves with the works of Locke, Montesquieu, Newton, and other productions of the same kind."

13. For an overview of the Académie, see Henri Stehle, ed., *Le Collège de Genève, 1559–1959: Mélanges historiques et littéraires* (Geneva: A. Jullien, 1959); and Marco Marcacci, *Histoire de l'Université de Genève, 1559–1986* (Geneva: Université de Genève, 1987): esp. 41f.

14. These were noted in Thomas Pennant, *Tour on the Continent 1765,* ed. G. R. de Beer (London: B. Quartich, 1948): 68.

15. The most important source recounting the British contribution to the Académie is Adrien Chopard, "Genève et les Anglais (XVe–XVIIIe siècle)," *Bulletin de la Société d'histoire et d'archéologie de Genève* 7 (1939–42): 179–213; for a list of dozens of English students associated with the academy through the end of the eighteenth century, see ibid., pp. 215–74. The official registration of students is contained in the "Livre du Recteur," but Beckford is not found in the records of June 1777 or later. See Sven Stelling-Michaud, ed., *Le Livre du Recteur de l'Académie de Genève, 1559–1878* (Geneva: Droz, 1959), vol. 1, pp. 317–18, but without Beckford's name. Nor is Beckford noted in any of the known "Liber amicorum," a series of student yearbooks, nor in the "Livre des anglois," Geneva, E. C., Communautés diverse, 2, Archives de l'Etat.

16. For a description of both houses, see Guillaume Fatio, *Histoire de Genthod et son territoire* (Genthod: Mairie, 1943): 73–86.

17. On Bonnet, see, for example, Georges Bonnet, *Charles Bonnet, 1720–1793* (Paris: M. Lac, 1929); Raymond Savioz, *La philosophie de Charles Bonnet de Genève* (Paris: J. Vrin, 1948); Jacques Marx, *Charles Bonnet contre les Lumières,* (Oxford: The Voltaire Foundation, 1976); and Lorin Anderson, *Charles Bonnet and the Order of the Known* (Dordrecht and Boston: D. Reidel, 1982).

18. There is no notable modern biography of De Saussure, but see Jean Senebier, *Mémoire historique sur la vie et les écrits de Horace Bénédict Desaussure* (Geneva: J. J. Paschoud, [1801]); and Douglas William Freshfield, *Horace-Bénédict de Saussure,* trans. M.-L. Plan, (Geneva: Ed. Atar, 1924). For analyses of his contributions to Alpine studies, see Alphonse Favre, *H.-B. De Saussure et les Alpes* (Lausanne: G. Bridel, 1870); Albert V. Carozzi, *Horace-Bénédict De Saussure: Forerunner in Glaciology* (Geneva: Éd. Passé Présent, 1995); idem, ed., *Les plis de temps: mythe, science et H. B. De Saussure,* exh. cat. (Geneva: Musée d'ethnographie, 1998–99).

19. For a summation of his work on the Mont Blanc range in particular, see *De Saussure e il Monte Bianco,* exh. cat. (Courmayeur, 1987). For De Saussure's reception in London, see Claire-Eliane Engel, "Horace-Bénédict De Saussure à Londres," *Alma Mater* 11–12 (1945): 329–40; and Gavin R. De Beer, "H.-B. De Saussure's Election Into the Royal Society," *Notes and Records of the Royal Society of London* 7, no. 2 (1950): 265–67.

20. Foremost was *Voyages dans les Alpes, précédés d'un essai sur l'histoire naturelle des environs de Genève,* vol. 1 (Neuchâtel: Samuel Fauche, 1779); vol. 2 (Geneva: Barde Manget & Compagnie, 1786); vols. 3 and 4 (Neuchâtel: Louis Fauche-Borel, 1796).

21. The contents were catalogued; see Albert V. Carozzi and Gerda Bouvier, *The Scientific Library of Horace-Bénédict De Saussure (1797): Annotated Catalogue of an 18th-Century Bibliographic and Historic Treasure* (Geneva: Société de physique et d'histoire, 1994).

22. There is no monograph on Naville. He was a member of a prominent Genevan family, played a substantial role in local government, becoming *procureur général* of Geneva, and also lectured regularly at the Académie. His most important book was *Etat civile de Genève* (Geneva: Barde Manget & Compagnie 1790).

23. For Delolme, see Albert Choisy et al., eds., *Receueil généalogique suisse: Genève* (Geneva: A Jullien, 1902), vol. 1, pp. 204–18, which includes a genealogical chart of the family. He came from the French branch, which spelled the last name Delorme.

24. Jean-Louis Delolme, *Constitution de l'Angleterre, ou état du gouvernement anglois comparé avec la forne républicaine et avec les autres monarchies de l'Europe* (Amsterdam: n.p., 1771); the first English translation, with no translator indicated, was entitled *The Constitution of England* (London: G. Kearsly, 1775).

25. For the earliest biography of Mallet, see Jean Charles De Sismondi, *De la vie et des écrits de Paul Henri Mallet* (Geneva: J. J. Paschoud, 1807). Information in this essay is taken from Hélène Stadler, *Paul-Henri Mallet, 1730–1807* (Lausanne: Imprimerie commerciale, 1924). Beckford, however, is not mentioned in either publication. On the history of the family, see Albert Choisy, *Notice généalogique et historique sur la famille Mallet de Genève* (Geneva: Atar, 1930).

26. *Northern Antiquities, an Historical Account of the Manners, Customs, Religion and Laws, Maritime Expeditions and Discoveries of the Ancient Scandinavians,* translated into English by Thomas Percy (London, 1770). For remarks on the significance of the work as a major source for pre-Romantic literature, see the introductory notes in Paul Henri Mallet, *Northern Antiquities,* ed. Burton Feldman (New York and London: Garland Press, 1979), vol. 1, pp. v–vii.

27. Lewis Melville, *The Life and Letters of William Beckford of Fonthill* (London: W. Heinemann, 1910): 36–40.

28. The poem, written in 1761 and first published in 1768, paraphrased a section of *Njal's Saga;* see Herbert W. Starr and John R. Hendrickson, eds., *The Complete Poems of Thomas Gray* (Oxford: Oxford University Press, 1969): 29–31, for the poem, and 211–15 for the editors' commentary.

29. Mallet's books are listed in *Catalogue of the Second Portion of the Bedford Library Removed From Hamilton Palace* (London: J. Davy, 1882): 150. There is no way of knowing whether Beckford had purchased Mallet's works while in Geneva, or whether he had acquired them later in his other

library acquisitions.

30. The three major sources on Huber are G. Jean-Aubry, "Un original du XVIIIe siècle: Jean Huber ou le démon de Genève," *Revue de Paris* 3 (1 June 1936): 593–626; and ibid. (15 June 1936): 807–821; Garry Apgar, "The Life and Work of Jean Huber (1721–1786)," Ph.D. diss., Yale University, 1988; and idem, *L'art singulier de Jean Huber. Voir Voltaire* (Paris: Adam Biro, 1995).

31. Melville, *Life and Letters* (1910): 47–51. See also Beckford's letter to Edward Thurlow, May 22, 1778, published in J. W. Oliver, *The Life of William Beckford of Fonthill* (London: Oxford University Press, H. Milford, 1932): 16–17, in which Huber's originality is likewise extolled.

32. Goethe met Huber on 3 November 1779, as noted in his *Briefe aus der Schweiz*, in J. W. Goethe, *Gedenkansgabe der Werke, Briefe und Gespräche*, ed. Ernest Beutler (Zurich: Artemis-Verlag, 1949), vol. 12, p. 21: "…[Huber], dem Geist, Imagination, Nachahmungsbegieder zu alle gliedern heraus will, einen der wenisen ganzen Menschen, die wir angetroffen haben!"

33. Several accounts contemporary with Beckford's visit provide lively descriptions of Voltaire's receptions, his daily routines, and his animated conversation, which as Thomas Pennant recalled, was in fractured English ("By G- I do lov de Ingles G-d dammee, if I don't lov them bettre dan de French by G-."); see Pennant, *Tour* (1948): 76.

34. Melville, *Life and Letters* (1910): 26–27. In Beckford's letter to his sister of 19 January 1778, he mentioned that Voltaire had "asked me to spend two or three Days at Ferney," but there is no documentary evidence of Beckford actually having done so. The same letter attests to his discussions of Ariosto.

35. See Mauro Natale, *Le goût des collections d'art italien à Genève du XVIIIe au XXe siècle* (Geneva: Musée d'art et d'histoire, 1980).

36. The major reference on Tronchin is Henry Tronchin, *Le Conseiller François Tronchin et ses amis Voltaire, Diderot, Grimm, etc. d'après des documents inédits* (Paris: Éd. Plon Nourrit, 1895). For the importance of his collection, see Renée Loche, *De Genève à l'Ermitage: Les collections de François Tronchin*, exh. cat. (Geneva: Musée Rath, 1974). By 1770, Tronchin's collection numbered ninety-five works, which he then sold to Catherine II through the counsel of Diderot and Huber. Almost immediately afterward, however, he began a second collection which, when Beckford was in Geneva, amounted to well over a hundred paintings. Tronchin was an especially erudite connoisseur, and in that capacity was asked to evaluate the sumptuous collection of Pierre Crozat de Thiers, also purchased by Catherine; see Margret Stuffmann, "Les tableaux de la collection de Pierre de Crozat," *Gazette des Beaux-Arts* 72 (July-September 1968): 35.

37. Boyd Alexander, *England's Wealthiest Son: A Study of William Beckford* (London: Centaur Press, 1962): 61f; Brian Fothergill, *Beckford of Fonthill* (London: Faber and Faber, 1979): 47f.

38. For the historical and scientific situation of the Salève, see Alphonse Favre, *Considérations géologiques sur le Mont Salève et sur les terrains des environs de Genève* (Geneva: J.-G. Flick, 1843).

39. Blaikie, *Journal* (1935): 53–56, found that his inexperience made the ascent more hazardous than he was led to believe, and indeed he was told that two similarly inexperienced climbers had perished recently. On the other hand, when Mme Roland came to Geneva in 1787, she found the mountain a disagreeable sight which she described as more fatiguing than inspiring; see M[anon]-J[eanne] Roland, *Voyage en Suisse en 1787* (Geneva: Slatkine, 1989): 17.

40. The following descriptions are noted in Melville, *Life and Letters* (1910): 30–34.

41. It is noteworthy in this context to correct an error that has persisted in the Beckford literature for generations. There are several letters from Beckford's early months in Geneva that bear the curious heading "Thun"; three of these are reproduced in Melville, *Life and Letters* (1910): 29f. These inscription headings have been seen as evidence for various trips to the city of that name in central Switzerland, well over a day's ride from Geneva. But Beckford's sojourn here is improbable as the evidence of the correspondence itself indicates. The first letter bearing this inscription was dated by Beckford 12 September 1777, the day before he climbed the Salève, which, considering the distances between Geneva and Thun—more than a day's ride—cannot be correct. The logical explanation is that Beckford's letters were in fact written in Thônex, only a few miles from the center of Geneva, which Beckford continued to abbreviate, or confuse, in this fashion. Thônex was a sensible site for him to have drafted his correspondence, as it was near the path where the climb or the descent would have originated. Placing Beckford here in the early autumn of 1777 explains the otherwise odd geographical context of the correspondence in which the topography he described is unmistakably of the Geneva region and not of the city of Thun. Further evidence may be found in a letter of 3 October 1777, where Beckford noted that he had "descended the Mountain [the Salève] and arrived in 3 hours at Thun," a timing that corresponds closely to a descent to Thônex from the summit. To verify the timing, I made the descent Beckford probably used, assuming that the path downward toward Geneva had not changed considerably from that frequently used in the late eighteenth century.

42. Melville, *Life and Letters* (1910): 65–66, Beckford to Cozens, December 4, 1778.

43. "There is a Book called Sorrows of Werter [sic]: read it and tell me if every line is not resplendent with Genius." Melville, *Life and Letters* (1910): 76, Beckford to Cozens, 3 December 1778.

44. This included the mundane task of seeing his book on painters' lives into print, for which

see William Beckford, *Biographical Memoirs of Extraordinary Painters*, ed. Robert J. Gemmett (Rutherford/Madison/Teaneck: Fairleigh Dickinson University Press, 1969): 11–31.

45. Melville, *Life and Letters* (1910): 148–49, Beckford to Lady Hamilton, 26 March 1782.

46. Ibid., pp. 163–164, Beckford to Cozens, 18 October 1782.

47. These were embodied in his travel diaries, *Dreams, Waking Thoughts and Incidents*, Letter 27, in which Beckford considered political aspects of the major European systems. These notes are reproduced in *The Travel-Diaries of William Beckford*, ed. Guy Chapman (London: Constable and Co., 1928): 243–48.

48. Jean-Aubry, "Un original" (1936): 812. The family was related to the celebrated mathematician Gabriel Cramer; see Lucien Cramer, *Une famille genevoise. Leurs relations avec Voltaire, Rousseau et Benjamin Franklin-Bache. Documents inédits* (Geneva: E. Droz, 1952).

49. Melville, *Life and Letters* (1910): 166–67, Beckford to Cozens, 8 June 1783.

50. For Beckford being guided by Paccard, see Alexander, *England's Wealthiest Son* (1962): 104. Paccard, or his father or both, also guided Blaikie in 1775; see Blaikie, *Journal* (1935): 116 and 121. Paccard would become celebrated later as one of the first to scale Mont Blanc when he made the ascent in 1786 with Jacques Balmat; the question of who reached the summit first was disputed. See *Les Anglais à Chamonix aux 18ème et 19ème siècles*, exh. cat., La Résidence, Chamonix, 1984, unpaginated.

51. Melville, *Life and Letters* (1910): 167–68, Beckford to Cozens, 28 July 1783.

52. Alexander, *England's Wealthiest Son* (1962): 106, Lady Margaret to Lady Gower (later Lady Stafford), 20 October 1783.

53. Melville, *Life and Letters* (1910): 169, Beckford to Cozens, 21 October 1783.

54. Beckford's visit to Prangins is noted in Cyrus Redding, ed., *Memoirs of William Beckford of Fonthill, author of "Vathek,"* (London: C. J. Skeet, 1859), vol. 1, p. 132; and Melville, *Life and Letters* (1910): 25, but both date the visit incorrectly to his first Geneva trip in 1777. Alexander, *England's Wealthiest Son* (1962): 103, on the other hand, provides the correct date of 1782, but does not note additional visits.

55. She was introduced to the family through her aunt, who was married to the Swiss banker Louis Girardot, and arrived at Prangins on 16 July 1776 with her aunt and sister Salina. For the portrait by Juel, see Ellen Poulson, *Jens Juel Katalog* (Copenhagen: Ejlar's Forlag 1991), vol. 1, pp. 75–76, no. 192, which reviews the prior literature on Juel's stay in Geneva and his relationship to the Guiguer family.

56. The "Prangins journal," begun on 31 March 1771, and terminated with the baron's death in 1786, is still in the possession of the family, although a copy is deposited at the Musée national suisse, Château de Prangins, Pringins. The manuscript includes entries in three separate handwritings, two belonging to Guiguer and his wife, and the third to the valet Christophe-Daniel Renz, who filled in the events the other two left out. There is no study of the full contents of the journal, but for an overview, see Chantal de Schoulepnikoff, "Le journal de Louis-François Guiguer, baron de Prangins," *Rapport annuel du Musée nationl suisse* (Zurich: Musée national suisse, 1988), pp 57–73. All references to Beckford, in the Guiguer's hand, occur in volume 5 and are cited as "Prangins Journal," by date with the original spelling. The translations are by the author.

57. "Nous avons vu repasser d'Italie pour l'Angleterre, M. Beckfort [sic]" ("Prangins Journal," 18 October 1782).

58. This description concurs with another one in 1792. See below, n. 115.

59. "On a jugé sa destinée brillante,…Ses talens supposés merveilleux…rien jusques ici n'arrête ses progrès" ("Prangins Journal," 18 October 1782).

60. "[Beckford] est bien de l'honneur, il est très bien portant, C'est que nous n'attendions guère" (ibid., 7 June 1783).

61. The journal noted that Charles d'Espinasse, along with the musicians, "…ont executé differens morceaux, ala grande satisfaction de La Cour" ("…played different morsels [of music], to the grand satisfaction of the Court"). This note alters somewhat the relationship Beckford was supposed to have had with D'Espinasse, as the latter is usually mentioned in the Beckford literature in the context of lecturing on experimental physics either at Prangins or Coppet; see Redding, ed., *Memoirs* (1859): vol. 1, p. 132; Oliver, *Life of William Beckford* (1932): 15–17; Guy Chapman, *Beckford* (London: Jonathan Cape, 1937): 41; Fothergill, *Beckford* (1979): 64.

62. For the history of the château and the Necker family's part in its ownership—from the de Thelluson family—see Monnique Fontannaz, "Du château fort à la résidence seigneuriale," in Monique Bory, ed., *Coppet. Histoire et architecture* (Yens-sur-Morges: E. Cabédita, 1998): esp. pp. 109f.

63. Redding, ed., *Memoirs* (1859): vol. 2, p. 353.

64. Madame de Staël, *Correspondance générale. Lettres de jeunesse*, ed., Béatrice W. Jasinski (Geneva: Klincksieck, 1962): vol. 1, pp. 19–20; and described in Oliver, *Life of William Beckford* (1932): 187–88.

65. Madame de Staël, *Correspondance* (1962): 21–22.

66. On the village itself, see Albert Naef, *Notes déscriptives et historiques sur la ville de La Tour-de-Peilz* (Lausanne: B. Benda, 1892). As was the case with Geneva, no official permission was necessary to obtain residence, and thus there are no communal documents pertaining to Beckford's arrival.

67. The figures are for the pre-1824 population and published in Louis Levade, *Dictionnaire géographique, statistique et historique du canton de Vaud* (Lausanne: Frères Blanchard, 1824): 310.

68. Albert de Montet, *Histoire de la ville de Tour-de-Peilz*, 2d ed. (Vevey: Säuberlin et Pfeiffer, 1977): 30–37. The plans for Gressier's renovations, with the living quarters Beckford would occupy, are in ACV, GB 347b/LTP 5089.

69. Camelford to John Soane, 26 September 1786, in Private Correspondence, IV.P.2.8, Sir John Soane's Museum, London. For Beckford and Soane, see Christopher Woodward, "William Beckford and Fonthill Splendens: Early Works by Soane and Goodridge," *Apollo* 147 (February 1998): 34.

70. [Mme de Gauthier], *Voyage d'une française en Suisse et en Franche-Comté depuis la Révolution* (London and Neuchâtel: n.p., 1790): vol. 2, p. 47.

71. From 1784 to 1786 Huber was living in Lausanne but was known to have made trips to Vevey. See the notes compiled by the editor and documentalist Georges Bridel in dossier "William Beckford," Archives Bridel, Musée historique de Lausanne.

72. See Société vaudoise de généalogie, *Recueil de généalogies vaudoise* (Lausanne: G. Bridel, 1923): vol. 1, 6ᵉ fasicule, p. 3. On the de Blonay domains, see Frédéric Gingins-La Sarra, "Note sur l'origine de la Maison de Blonay," *Mémoires et documents publiés par la Société d'histoire de la Suisse romande* 20 (1857): 249–57.

73. On the site, see Camille Perroud, *Histoire de la ville d'Evian* (Thonon-les-Bains: Dubouloz, 1927): 248f. Evian was still a village at the time, with a population in 1785, including the surrounding areas, of slightly over 1,700; no post office was installed until 1790. The village was under the reign of the Savoys and would not be ceded to the French until 1792.

74. The date of Gressier's death is noted in "Manuel du Conseil de La Tour-de-Peilz, 1783–1788," May 5, 1785, A 26, p. 163, La Tour-de-Peilz, Archives.

75. De Blonay, however, sold the château in 1789 to a Genevan banker. It remained in private hands until 1979 when it was purchased by the commune and transformed into the Museé suisse du jeu; see Daniel de Raemy, "Le Château de La-Tour-de-Peilz," masters thesis, Université de Lausanne, 1983.

76. Oliver, *Life of William Beckford* (1932): 171–72, Beckford to Robert Pigott, 26 February 1786.

77. Redding, ed., *Memoirs* (1859): vol. 2, p. 350.

78. "…pour que sa voiture puisse aisément passer" (so that his carriage could easily pass). The demand was noted in the "Manuel," A 26, September 14, 1785, p. 194, La Tour-de-Peilz, Archives. The council decided to review the situation and commented on it no further, meaning that the request was granted. See too Louis Seylaz, "William Beckford en Suisse," *Gazette de Lausanne*, 28 August 1932, p. 1.

79. Jean-Aubry, "Un original" (1936): 819.

80. The death of Lady Margaret was inscribed in the cantonal records (Eb 129⁵, pp. 150–51, ACV), with a note under "Monsiueur Guillaume Beckfort" reading: "1786 mai 26. Sa femme, Lady Marguerite Gordon, âgée de 24 ans, meurt à La Tour de Peiz [sic]. Elle a été emmenée en Angleterre pour y être ensevelie" (1786 May 26. His wife, Lady Marguerite Gordon, aged 24 years, died at La Tour-de-Peilz. Her body was sent to England to be buried). The latter, however, was not effectuated immediately, as in the following note.

81. "Manuel," A 26, 28 May 1786, p. 250, La Tour-de-Peilz, Archives.

82. The "Attestation" is in Beckford MS., c. 84, fols. 5r and 5v, Bodleian Library, Oxford, and reproduced in Oliver, *Life of William Beckford* (1932): 198.

83. The outlines of the relationship are recorded in William Hauptman, "Beckford, Brandoin, and the 'Rajah'," *Apollo* 142 (May 1996): 30–39, from which the following material is drawn.

84. Brandoin's work for Orloff, sometimes noted as Orlov, is discussed in Paul Bissegger, "Une dynastie d'artisans vaudois: les marbriers Doret," *Zeitschrift für Schweizerisches Archäologie und Kunstgeschichte* 37 (1980): 104f.; and Marcel Grandjean, *Les monuments d'art et d'histoire du canton de Vaud. Lausanne: ville, hameaux et maisons de l'ancienne campagne*, vol. 4 (Lausanne and Basle: Éditions Birkhäuser, 1981), p. 414. The sepulchre, perhaps the most admired work in Lausanne at the end of the eighteenth century, was noted by most writers who visited the cathedral. Orloff had various Swiss connections, including the doctor Louis Levade, whom he took to Russia with him in 1774; he was the brother of the theologian Jean-Daniel Levade who would become one of Beckford's associates during the stay in La Tour-de-Peilz.

85. "Est il vrai que M. Beckford vient à Lausanne?" (Brandoin to Cerjat, P Orloff, 1, ACV). Although the letter is undated, the contents suggest a date around November 1783, when the project for the sepulchre was terminated and just weeks after Beckford's last visit to Prangins. For Cerjat, see Maxime Reymond, *Cerjat* (Lille: L. Danel, 1938), pp. 132f; and Ernest Giddey, *Anglais à Lausanne au XIXᵉ siècle*, exh. cat. (Lausanne, Musée historique de l'Ancien-Èvéché, 1978): 21–23.

86. In Beckford, *Travel-Diaries* (1928): vol. 1, p. 313; and Oliver, *Life of William Beckford* (1932): 198. Redding, ed., *Memoirs* (1859): vol. 1, pp. 272–273 notes that Beckford traveled with Lettice and a friend—this was Brandoin—to the southern areas near the Lake of Neuchâtel and then to Zurich and Bern, but with no mention of the trip to the Salève.

87. The letter is in Beckford MS. c.27, fols. 2–3, Bodleian Library.

88. For literature on Polier and his importance in early Indian studies, see Constantin Regamey, "Un pionnier vaudois des études indiennes: Antoine-Louis de Polier," in *Mélanges offerts à Monsieur Georges Bonnard* (Geneva: Droz, 1966): 183–209. Brandoin's commission from Polier was to make copies of some of the manuscripts and miniatures. Brandoin, it might be noted, became known locally as Polier's painter, as is indicated in the unpublished journals of Polier's cousin, Jean-Henri Polier, in Fond René Monod, P 131, 536, ACV. Under the date 16 February 1789, it is noted that "…all dined [in English]; Le Polier indien & Brandoin son peintre."

89. Polier was acclaimed by such figures as Sir Joseph Banks, to whom Polier presented the first Western copy of the sacred *Vedas*; these are now in the British Library (Add. Ms. 5346–56), for which see Cecil Bendall, *Catalogue of the Sanskrit Manuscripts in the British Museum* (London: British Museum, 1902): 1. Polier sent these volumes to Banks on 20 May 1789, as is noted in a letter from Polier to Banks appended to Add. Ms. 5346, fol. 3, British Library. Sir William Owens, a leading Orientalist of the late eighteenth century, described Polier as "one of the best-disposed and best informed men, who ever left India"; see G. Canon, ed., *The Letters of Sir William Owens* (Oxford University Press, 1970): vol. 2, p. 735.

90. "5 étandarts dont le premier est le poisson d'or, la distinction la plus grande ches [sic] le Mogul" (Brandoin to Beckford, 20 March 1789, MS. Beckford, c.27, fols. 2–3, Bodleian Library).

91. These were later dispersed in German collections, including twenty albums of Indian miniatures bearing the Polier–Beckford provenance, which are split between the Islamische Kunstabteilung and the Museum für Indische Kunst in Berlin. For their history, see Hauptman, "Beckford" (1996): 30f.

92. On his career, see Edmond Jomini, *Dr François Verdeil, un grand vaudois, 1747–1832* (Lausanne: Jordan, 1950), which emphasizes his medical, humanist, and political interests, but with no mention of his relationship to Beckford.

93. Oliver, *Life of William Beckford* (1932): 205.

94. There is a reference in Beckford's journal for 2 April 1817 that specifies Scholl's services: "We are selling the whole of Polier's *Natural History*, valued in the list by Scholl at 8,000…" The reference is certainly to an anthology of natural history designs once owned by Polier, now in Orme 4769, India Office Library, London.

95. In a manuscript entitled "Tableau de l'Académie" (Ms. IS 4086a, Bibliothèque cantonale et universitaire, Lausanne), the following poem was inscribed: "Le Professeur Levade, habile courtisan / Encense lâchement tout ce qui est riche et grand / Il n'épargna jamais ses humbles révérences / Surtout aux grands seigneurs de britannique engeance" (Professor Levade, clever flatterer / cowardly compliments everyone who is rich and grand. / He never spares his humble admiration / Especially the grand breed of English lords). For a list of Levade's activities with the Lausanne Académie, see Philippe-Cyrice Bridel's 1828 manuscript, "Matériaux pour une histoire littéraire de l'Académie de Lausanne et du Canton de Vaud," B 801, Bibliothèque cantonale et universitaire, Lausanne. Levade's work for Beckford, however, is not noted here.

96. Meredith Read noted that Levade apparently enjoyed sleeping in his own coffin and was once discovered there by his astonished daughter (*Historic Studies in Vaud, Berne, and the Savoy: From Roman Times to Voltaire, Rousseau, and Gibbon* [London: Chatto and Windus, 1897]: vol. 2, p. 493).

97. For the best summary of the *Vathek* publications and their respective intrigues, see John Carter, "The Lausanne Edition of Beckford's *Vathek*," *The Library* (17 March 1937): 369–94; For Levade and Verdeil's roles, see ibid., pp. 385–89.

98. Gauthier, *Voyage d'une française* (1790), vol. 2, pp. 64–65. In the late summer of 1789, Beckford presumably crossed the lake from the Swiss side to Evian. In August of that year, Madame de Gauthier noted that a company of musicians from Geneva had been imported for the season, by "un Anglois nommé Becfort [sic]." She went on to describe the announced plans for a party in the Bois de Blonay.

99. For the Jacobin incursions in Evian, see Louis-Etienne Piccard, *Thonon, Evian-les-Bains et le Chablais moderne: Etude historique depuis la Révolution jusqu'à nos jours* (Annemasse: J. Chambet, 1889).

100. For documentation on how the French émigrés were tightly controlled by Swiss authorities, see Jean-Paul Cavin, "L'émigration française dans le Pays de Vaud aux débuts de la Révolution (1789–1793), d'après les Actes et les Manuax du Conseil secret de Berne," *RHV* 53 (1972): 49–101.

101. The passport requests for the musicians are noted under 26 September 26 1792, in "Livre pour y inscrire les noms de personnes qui demanderont de Passeports, 1792," D488, fol. 7ᵛ, Archives

de la Ville de Lausanne. The musicians were "Srs Miller, Welch, Rhin, Kerschner [or Kirchner], Galai, Schmuck, et Schwendt, allemands, musiciens de Mr Beckfort, allant on Italie."

102. Thomas Whaley, *Buck Whaley's Memoirs…*, ed. Sir Edward Sullivan (London: Alexander Moring, 1906): 304–305. Whaley's souvenirs were written in 1797. For d'Erlach's importance in local politics, see Hans Ulrich von Erlach, *800 Jahre Berner Erlach: die geschichte einer familie* (Bern: Benteli, 1989).

103. For a concise history from of the Swiss reaction to the French Revolution, which much of the following material is based, see *La Suisse et la Révolution Française*, exh. cat., (Musée Historique de Lausanne, 1989).

104. The order of censure was issued on 3 September 1790 in a seven-page ruling, "Ordonnance de la chancellerie de Berne sur la censure," P48/91/8, Archives de la Ville de Lausanne.

105. For the clearest account of the Lausanne "banquet," see Louis Monnet, *Rapport présenté au Conseil communal de Lausanne* (Lausanne: C. Pasche, 1897). The report, which was intended to document the patriotic aspects of the event as justification for erecting a monument to the participants, is in dossier 244, Archives Bridel, Musée historique de Lausanne.

106. The Rolle manifestation is described from contemporary documents in G. Favey, "Deux documents des années 1790 et 1791," *RHV* 11 (1903): 175–76.

107. The spy network is outlined in "Lettres de Conseils de Berne à Gabriel-Albert d'Erlach et Louis de Biren, baillis de Lausanne, concernant la surveillance des émigrés," Bu 23^{2}, ACV, Lausanne. See also C.-R. Delhorbe, "Le service de renseignenemnts de LL.EE en juillet 1791," *RHV* 63 (1955): 125–38; the designation "LL.EE," (Leurs Excellences) was the traditional manner of the Vaudois in referring to the Bernese authorities. The acts of the commission established to study the events are recorded in "Actes du Conseil, secret XIV," Staatsarchiv, Bern.

108. The condemnation is noted in a decree by d'Erlach on 21 May 1792, Archives Bridel, dossier 244, Musée historique de Lausanne. The originator of both demonstrations, Amédée de la Harpe, was sentenced to death, but escaped to France. De La Harpe was the cousin of the more celebrated Frédéric-César de La Harpe, who in fact would become the prime artisan of the Vaudois Revolution against the Bernese in 1798. For the former, see Édouard Secretan, *Le général Amédée de La Harpe* (Lausanne and Paris: Corboz and A. Chevalier-Marescq, 1899): esp. 22–26, for his activities in Rolle and Lausanne. See also, for others who likewise fled Swiss territory to avoid prosecution, M. G. Dutoit, "Après les banquets de 1791, d'après la correspondance inédite de quelques fugitifs," *RHV* 42 (1934): 342–58.

109. Gibbon, *Letters*, vol. 3, p. 278.

110. Fothergill, *Beckford* (1979): 219.

111. "Regître des délibérations du Conseil de Lausanne, 6 avril 1790–25 janvier 1793," D 103, p. 277^v, Archives de la Ville de Lausanne.

112. The major documents of the political acts in Lausanne for the year are housed in the Stasstsarchiv, Bern, with copies in ACV, Lausanne. These include "Onglets baillivaux, Lausanne," Bb, 25bis; "Cour baillivale," Bg 4/34, where court actions such as expulsions were recorded; "Affaires politiques, personnalités, princes et princesses," Bu 25; "Etrangers divers non Français ou Genevois," Bu, 23^4; "Manuaux du Conseil secret, X," R 302/3; and "Actes du Conseil secret de Berne," R 300/15. None mention Beckford, although other English names are noted.

113. Reymond, *Cerjat* (1938): 134f.

114. Among the English nobility known to be in Lausanne at this time were Charles Blagden, head of the Royal Society, the Duchess of Devonshire, Frederick William Hervey and his retinue, Lady Palmerston, who would be joined by her husband, Lady Duncannon, and others. See Gavin R.

De Beer, "Anglais au pays de Vaud. VI. La Duchesse de Devonshire," *RHV* 59 (1951): 180–94. The dinner at Gibbon's house with d'Erlach is noted on p. 190.

115. Two Lausanne officials took part in the "banquet" at De la Harpe's residence, Ferdinand-Antoine Rosset and Georges-Albert Muller de la Mothe, both of whom were given twenty-five year prison terms; see Paul Maillefer, *Le Pays de Vaud de 1789 à 1791* (Lausanne: C. Viret-Genton, 1892): 114f. Both, however, escaped under curious circumstances on 30 October 1792, for which see Louis Junod, "Une évasion de prisonniers d'état au Château d'Aarbourg en 1792," *RHV* 60 (1952): 1–27. Muller de la Mothe fled to England and would return to region after 1797 when, under French pressure, amnesty was accorded all of the participants; Rosset, on the other hand, died in Philadelphia in 1795. See Eugène Mottaz, "Un prisonnier d'état sous le régime bernois: Muller de la Mothe," *RHV* 5 (1897): passim.; and "Le mémoires de Muller de la Mothe," *RHV* 13 (1905): 97–104 and 129–38.

116. News of the imprisonment was widely known even though the investigations and sentences of the committee in regard to lesser figures was not always made public. Gibbon, who had friends in high places, including d'Erlach, noted in a letter of 9 November 1791 that "we hear nothing of the proceedings of the Commission"; see Gibbon, *Letters*, vol. 3, p. 235.

117. See Jean-Jacques Eggler, "Entre deux révolutions: Le temps des pamphlets politiques," in Silvio Corsini, ed., *Le Livre à Lausanne: Cinq siècles d'édition et d'imprimerie, 1493–1993*, exh. cat. (Musée historique de Lausanne, 1993): 70–74. For the surveyance of the chief printers and publishers, see also Eugène Mottaz, *Dictionnaire historique, géographique et statistique du canton de Vaud* (Lausanne: F. Rouge, 1911), vol. 1, pp. 850–51.

118. For an account of Verdeil's activities, see in Auguste Verdeil, *Histoire du canton de Vaud*, 2d ed. (Lausanne: D. Martignier and Corboz, 1854), vol. 3, pp. 172f. The author was François Verdeil's son. Verdeil was not actually condemned until 23 January 1793, for which see R. M., 424/104, Staatsarchiv, Bern. He was fined, however, when he returned in 1794 and would be watched continually from that time. He became of the leaders of the independence movement in 1798 that created a free canton. See Monnet, *Rapport* (1897): 26; and Jomini, *Verdeil* (1950): 23f.

119. For his arrival in Neuchâtel with thirty horses, four carriages, and dozens of servants, see Valentine Browne Lawless, Baron Cloncurry, *Personal Recollections of the Life and Times, with Extracts From the Correspondence, of Valentine, Lord Cloncurry* (Dublin: n.p., 1849): 8; see also Chapman, *Beckford* (1937): 242.

120. "…les désagréments que vous avez éprouvés à Lausanne" (the unpleasantness that you suffered in Lausanne); Huber *fils* to Beckford, 4 April 1794, Ms. IS 3963/4bis, Bibliothèque cantonale et universitaire, Lausanne.

121. See Mary Berry, *Extracts of the Journals and Correspondence of Mary Berry From the Year 1783 to 1852*, ed., Lady Theresa Lewis, 2d ed. (London: Longmans and Company, 1866), vol. 2, p. 260. She recorded that she had gone to the house of Scholl to inspect the books. Le Comte de Vaublanc, *Mémoires de M. Le Comte de Vaublanc*, ed. F. Barrière (Paris: Firmin-Didot, 1857): 350, noted that while he was exiled temporarily in Lausanne in 1796, he became a friend of Scholl who lent him books in Italian before his trip to Italy.

122. See Read, *Historic Studies* (1897): vol. 2, p. 505. Read had received his information from Henriette's sister Fanny who told him that Beckford in fact only took several volumes with him, leaving the rest in Scholl's care.

123. Melville, *Life and Letters* (1910): 180.

124. Louis Seylaz, "La bibliothèque de Gibbon," *Gazette de Lausanne*, 11 September 1932, pp. 1–2.

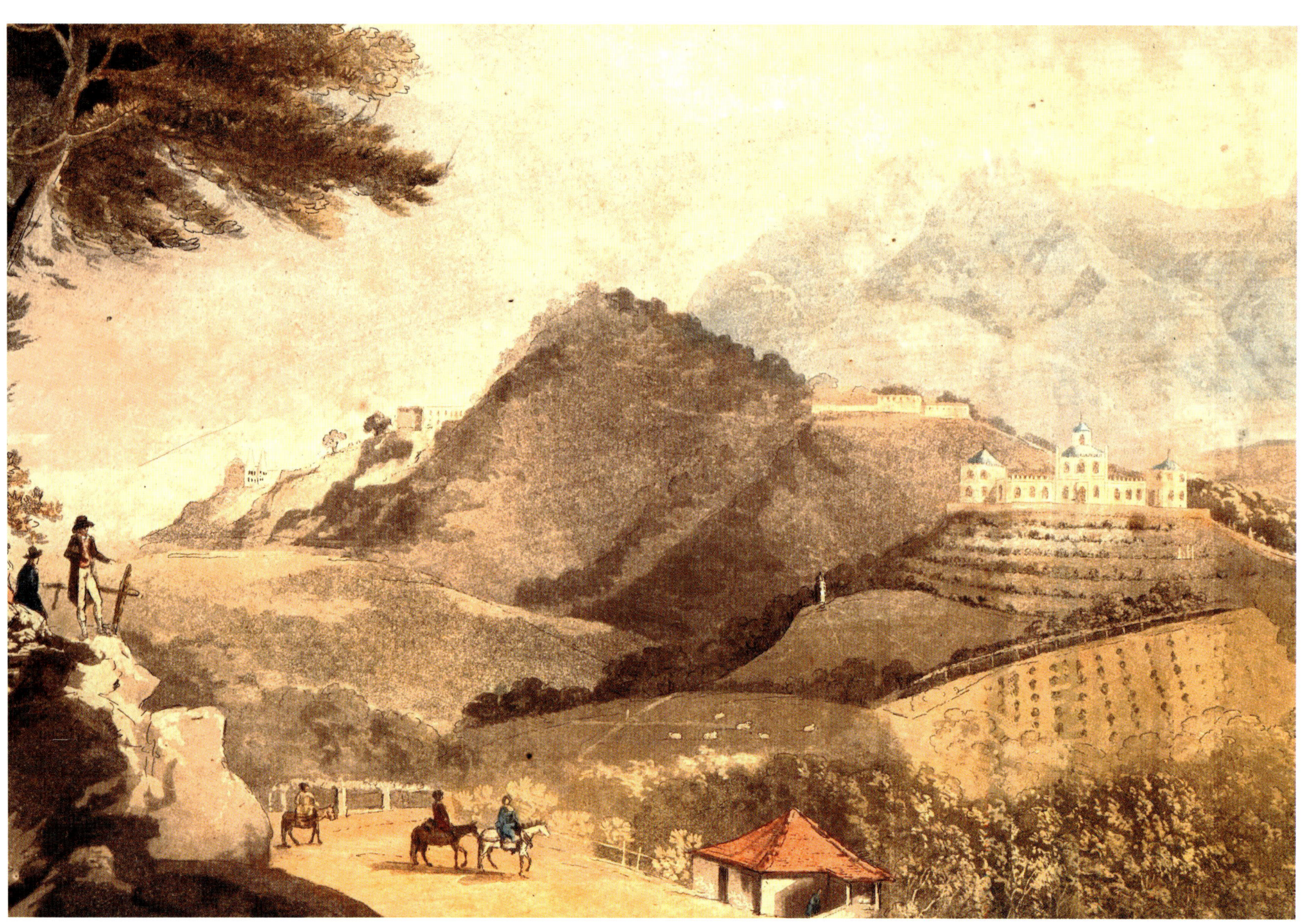

Fig. 5-1. "View of Sintra," 1829. Lithograph by D. Esquioppetta. Sintra, Historical Archive, Municipal Archive.

Chapter V

THE WORLD OF BECKFORD'S PORTUGUESE PALACES

Malcolm Jack

William Beckford was a young, dashing man of twenty-six when he made his first appearance in Portugal in the summer of 1787. Although he cultivated a seigneurial, somewhat aloof manner he was not a man at peace with himself. During the heady years between his writing of *Vathek* in the early months of 1782 and this visit, Beckford had experienced every kind of emotional trauma, which included public shame, the death of his wife, plagiarism of his literary work, and ostracism from English society. Lady Margaret's death cast a dark shadow over him; painful memories of her are recorded in the otherwise sunny pages of his private diary. Of all these cruel strokes of fortune, his exclusion from what he regarded as his rightful, rather grand place in English society, left him most bitter. It colored his attitude toward his fellow countrymen for the rest of his life and explains his contempt for the majority of Englishmen he met or saw at a distance, in Portugal or elsewhere. Beckford's hauteur was also brought on by his enormous wealth, however, which made him contemptuous of anyone who had to earn a living from trade. The only category of people whom he respected despite their indigence were artists, craftsmen, and worthy practical men, like his long-serving gardener, Vincent, although he cultivated titled people.

Beckford's arrival in Lisbon in May 1787 may have been unplanned, but it was certainly not unnoticed. Among the lively, gossipy diplomatic society of Lisbon was the French ambassador, the marquis de Bombelles, who observed in his *Journal*:

The arrival of one of the richest men in England, who put into port with three boats that belonged to him, caused a considerable public stir among the inhabitants of Lisbon. The person in question is Mr Beckford, a young man of twenty-five years of age, son of the famous Alderman and Lord Mayor who, in his time had played a prominent part in parliamentary debates in Great Britain. Even though this gentleman [the Alderman] had spent much of his fortune in keeping a number of illegitimate

children, his legitimate son still inherited ten thousand pounds sterling in income and fifty thousand pounds sterling [in addition] as well as huge and superb possessions on the island of Jamaica. It is said that Mr Beckford had a disposable net income of thirty thousand louis a year.[1]

Nor did the young Wiltshire gentleman in any way play down his wealth and position. He arrived, as Rose Macaulay records, with a retinue of some twenty to thirty servants as less would not have given the impression he intended to make. As she tartly puts it:

he did not see why he should not have a biscuit properly made, with his glass of sherry, nor couriers to arrange his goings out or comings in, nor valets to see to his clothes, nor lackeys to run his errands, nor a few grooms to mind his horses and chaise, nor a footman to run behind them; in fact all the attendants, including doctor, tailor, halter, barber, musicians and chef, of whom a travelling gentleman might find himself in need.[2]

Beckford was indeed no ordinary traveler, rather one who intended to live in a princely style wherever he went, whether to Lisbon or the Sintra countryside (fig. 5-1), however short his stays. He relates, with more than a hint of condescension, that the Portuguese admired the "elegant" and "antique" English furniture, described as well varnished and ancient, which he brought to Lisbon with him.[3] They exuded an air of opulence and grand taste, which would have impressed Lisbon society. Traveling with magnificent pieces of furniture was also a sign of Beckford's princely style. In the age of the Grand Tourist, such a milordly gesture would have inspired respect and envy in equal share.

If the furniture showed Beckford's *fidalgo* pretensions, his library of books indicated that an unusual Grand Tourist had arrived in Lisbon, one who was well read and learned. It is known from Beckford's own accounts that he brought a considerable selection of travel literature with him to Portugal. He had already read much of the

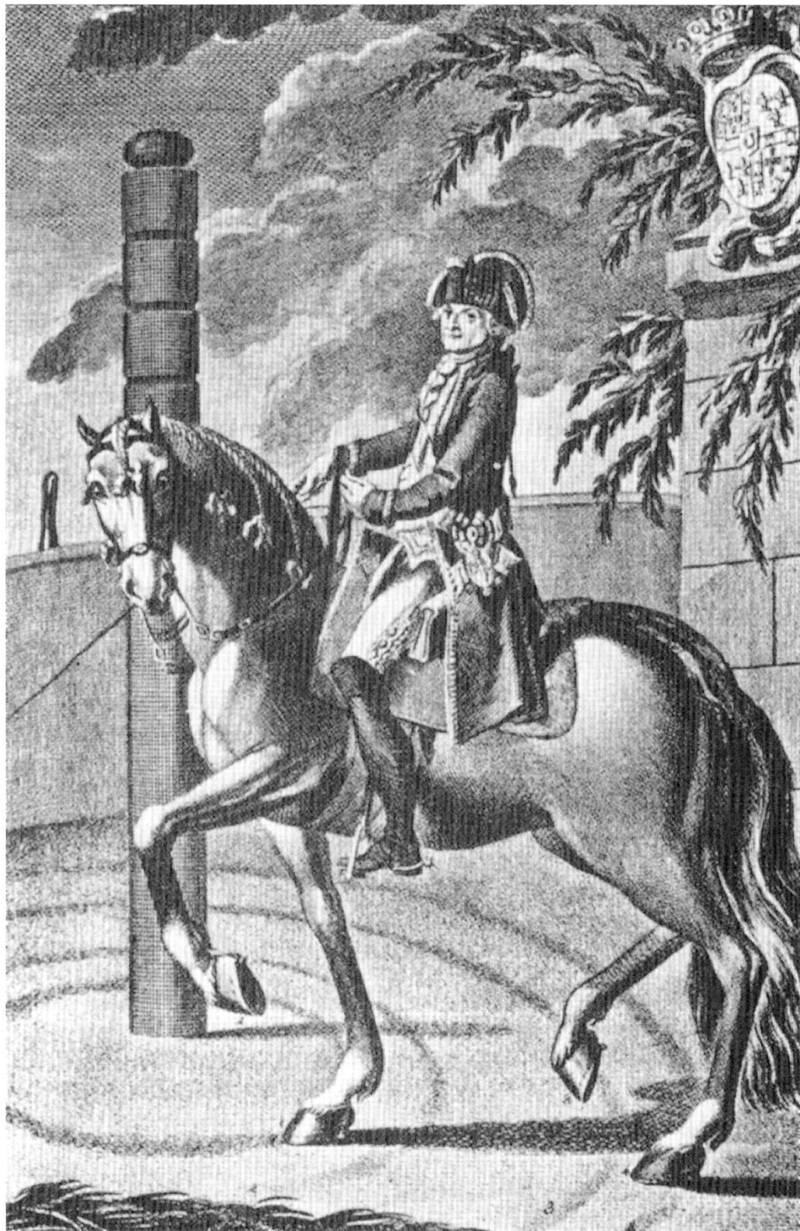

Fig. 5-2. Dom Diogo, fifth Marques of Marialva, 1790. Engraving. Sintra, Historical Archive, Municipal Archive.

early accounts of the Portuguese explorations of the sixteenth century including Luís de Camões's great epic, the *Lusiads,* about Vasco da Gama's voyage to India.[4] When Beckford came to Lisbon in 1787, he had with him, among other tomes, the six volumes of J. A. de Colmenar's *Délices de L'Espagne et de Portugal* (1715) and Udal ap Rhys' *Account of the most remarkable Places and Curiosities in Spain and Portugal* (1749). Schooled in this background, the young aristocratic Beckford had a good idea of what to look for in grand, impressive mansions and whom to cultivate among the Portuguese *fidalgos.* When he tired of Iberia itself he could read C. Cullen's new translation of the Abbé Clavigero's *History of Mexico,* containing controversial criticism of

the iniquities of Spanish colonialism. When he tired of serious history altogether and was inclined to a more entertaining read, there was Frances Brooke's tragic tale, *The History of Lady Julia Mandeville,* whose chilling pages provoked a vicarious reaction in a young man whose own life had been marred by setbacks and disasters.[5] In a country of the Inquisition, however, the arrival of large consignments of foreign books aroused suspicion. Two months later, due to the "negligence of the Customs House Officers," they had still not been delivered.[6]

The most significant event that occurred shortly after Beckford's arrival in Lisbon was his meeting the Abbade Xavier, a nonagenarian cleric and family friend of the Marialvas, one of the best-placed aristocratic families in Portugal. On May 25, the first day in which he began his diary, Beckford went from his own house nearby to the Marialvas' palace at Belém, just beyond Saint Jerónimos, where the Abbade Xavier "was upon the watch at the door."[7] Beckford found this residence, despite its long facade with pointed turrets, "meanly furnished with English coloured prints and indifferent drawings of saints and madonnas,"[8] hardly the home he imagined of a personage as grand as the Marquês de Marialva, the Queen's Equerry (fig. 5-2). Being introduced to Dom Diogo, the fifth marquis, however, he made sure that the Portuguese aristocrat would be pleased by his manners and bearing.

Although Beckford was amazed by the semifeudal manner of living of the Marialvas whose table was always attended by a troupe of hangers-on that included priests, clowns, and street artists, he never put aside his first impression of the lack of refinement and comfort in the physical world of the Portuguese *fidalgos.* Some of his condescension toward them may have been put on to impress his English middle-class readers who were buying his books as travel writing when they came out in the 1830s. When he visited the villa of the Barão de Quintela, in Lisbon, he implied that the taste was rather nouveau riche despite the finely polished floors of Brazilian wood and pretty Chinese paintings on glass, which caught his eye. Here, as elsewhere, the proportions of the rooms displeased him; rarely did he find interiors in Portugal to satisfy his extremely demanding eye.[9]

Beckford himself had taken up residence not far from the royal palace, on the rua Cova da Moura. This westerly part of the city had been made fashionable by that grand royal patron of Lisbon, King João V, who had built the Necessidades Palace there between 1742 and 1750. Beckford lived in a house of wooden construction, probably the property of his agent Thomas Horne, which he describes as being composed of planks from America, offering little protection against the summer heat. Thousands of such houses had been erected after the earthquake of 1755, on the orders of the dictator Pombal, who was determined to rebuild the city as quickly as possible. Their existence must have given Lisbon a frontier air to a man of Beckford's classical tastes, and his prejudice was confirmed by his notion of a lack of comfort and embellishment in Portuguese aristocratic homes and his apparent unwillingness to take into account the extent of destruction done to the city only some decades before his visit.

The first royal palace he was taken to was that of Palhavã, the residence of the bastards of the King João V, known for his amorous courting as well as his lavish patronage of the arts. Beckford—once again wanting to shock the middle-class audience for whom he was writing in 1834 when he published his *Sketches*—describes the tawdriness of the approach to the house. A road bordered by unkempt gardens, mosquito-infested ponds and filthy bands of beggars did not inspire him, and his description was meant to unsettle his reader.[10] Inside the palace, things were no better. Heavy crimson damask curtains created a gloom; there were no mirrors or pictures to catch the eye. Indeed, decorations of all sorts were lacking and tables were "concealed by velvet flounces, in the style of those with which our dowagers used formerly to array their toilets."[11] If the Palhavã palace did not impress the future owner of Fonthill, nor did the royal palace of Ajuda which he dismissed as a shabby, low barnlike edifice, spread with greasy Persian carpets and hung with the coarsest tapestries.[12]

Despite the scathing remarks that are repeated throughout his diaries, some objects in the physical world of the Portuguese *fidalgos* did attract Beckford. He was particularly struck by the tableware of Portuguese aristocratic homes, for their ostentatious display of both silver (*prata*) and exquisite porcelain from China, which the Portuguese had been among the first to import into Europe through their colony of Macau on the Pearl River estuary. He remarks upon "silver canteens of extraordinary magnitude"[13] at the Marialvas' table and the glittering array of plate at Gildemeester's palace of Setéais in Sintra. Among the Portuguese silver, Beckford would have noticed unusual items such as fish-slicers and duck-shaped tureens from China. Indigenous items included highly decorated pieces, such as ewer and basin sets for washing hands, which were essential components of the dinner table. These could be highly ornate pieces, decorated with mythological figures and sophisticated chasing in high relief in the Italian style.

The highest quality French work had also been imported, particularly during the reign of the sybaritic king, Dom José I. Among the royal collection were elaborate pieces from François-Thomas Germain, including highly stylized oval tureens, standing on scroll feet, decorated with acanthus leaves, palm fonds, and oak sprigs. The Portuguese royal coat of arms is embossed on this service, with oak leaves and laurels as decoration. Bunches of fruit and flowers drape over the tops. Numerous dishes, with highly ornate covers, sometimes decorated with cabbage leaves, formed part of the royal collection. The sumptuousness of tableware and silver symbolized the unassailable, feudal nature of Portuguese society, something that appealed immensely to Beckford's conservative belief in a hierarchical social order.

The Marialvas' table also included imported china, known as Companhia das Índias. Because the Portuguese Crown itself retained the prerogative over this trade, an East India company was never actually set up as it had been in Holland, England, and Sweden.[14] The royal pieces of this imported china were specially commissioned and bear the coat of arms of the House of Bragança, but the nobility and the higher clergy had the opportunity to order their own sets, emblazoned with their own coats of arms. The porcelain was produced in many different styles, white with red and gold being the court favorite. Traditional blue and white, sometimes with classical scenes, which nevertheless betray an oriental touch, was also popular. Portraits of the patrons were sometimes reproduced; other pieces were decorated with familiar Chinese floral decorations that included chrysanthemum and lily. One set, commissioned in 1775–76 by Paulo Fernandes Viana, Baron São Simon, known as the "*Meninos de Palhavã*" (the Palhavã boys) commemorates the two bastard princes whose palace was so scorned by Beckford. Primarily in blue and white, with a gray band in the center oval-shaped plates, the set shows the two princes as guards, facing the inscribed initials of the Barão São Simon, topped by a crown indicating their royalty and perhaps the patron's connection with the court since he later became comptroller of the treasury when the court fled to Brazil during the Napoleonic period. Considerable portions of this export china remained in South America after the Court returned to Lisbon in 1821.

Like so many other foreigners, when Beckford wanted to escape the heat and humidity of Lisbon, he made for umbrageous Sintra where, in 1787, he rented the house of a Luso-Irish lawyer, José Street Arriága Brum da Silveira, known as the palace of Ramalhão (fig. 5-3), just on the outskirts of the town and a short ride from the Marialva villa in the village of São Pedro. The house, which had already had a long history by Beckford's time,[15] was started in the early eighteenth century. By 1707, soon after it was completed, the owners were consulting lawyers about its redevelopment; by 1748 the colonial hero, Luis Francisco Garcia de Bivar was living in it. By then it had assumed its existing longitudinal dimensions. Damage caused by the Lisbon earthquake of 1755 may have benefited Beckford; the airy suite of rooms he so admired, with their outside terrace giving vistas eastward across the plains to the sea, were built after that time. The mansion, thereafter assuming a grand aspect, was built on a raised terrace, which meant exposure to strong winds blowing in from the sea. Beckford noticed an absence of fireplaces auguring chilly winter days. Behind the house lay the dark, craggy peaks of the mountain (*serra*), which then, as now, could suddenly be enveloped in swirling mists even on a high summer's day. Beckford's extraordinary ability to furnish and redecorate houses in which he lived, even for short periods, took on an extravagant form at Ramalhão. He decorated one of the suites of the eastern wing as a great oriental salon, a lanternlike apartment decorated with chintz and deep, comfortable sofas, and Persian carpets. Heavy damask curtains added to the atmosphere of eastern opulence. In this exotic setting, Beckford, the "Caliph of Sintra," provided his guests, extravagantly dressed in oriental apparel, with musical entertainment arranged by Jerónimo Francisco de Lima, a leading Portuguese composer of the day, who eventually presented an exorbitant bill for his services. On other, quieter occasions Beckford retreated into solitude, playing out a plaintive tune on the pianoforte, the curtains drawn to keep the wind from rattling through the drafty salons.

Beckford had reservations about the nearby Marialva villa in

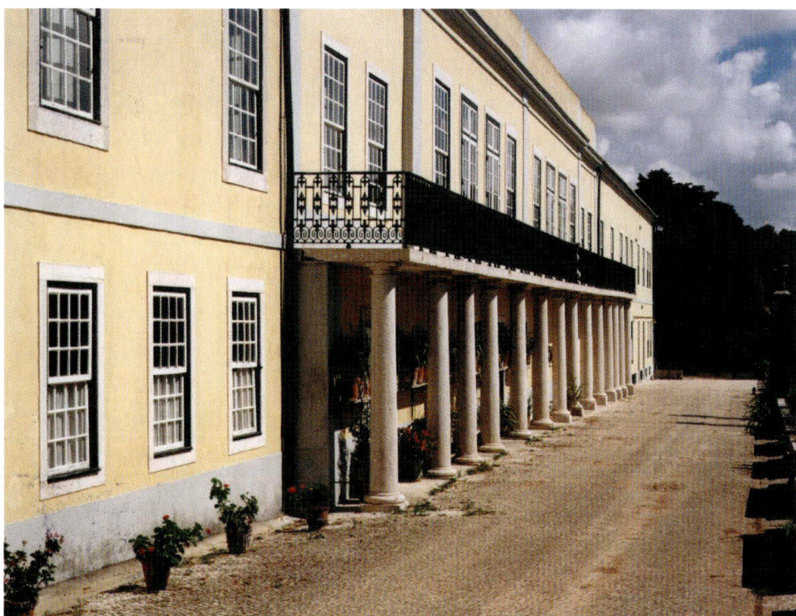

Fig. 5-3. Palace of Ramalhão, Sintra. Photographed ca. 1960. Sintra, Historical Archive, Municipal Archive.

São Pedro because of its position, which was similar to wind-swept Ramalhão. Nevertheless, he said that the villa had a gay pavilion decorated by the Lyonnaise artist Jean-Baptiste Pillement, with a parterre with fountains, which was romantically set in a "hill strewed over with stones and fragments."[16] Thick alleys of laurel, bay, and laurustine and cascades of plants and greenery already gave the house, with its balustraded stone patio, an artificially well-established look.[17] This mixture of the civilized and the sublime greatly appealed to Beckford's developing aesthetic of landscape. Sintra represented in microcosm the uncontrollable grandeur of nature with the civilized appurtenances of an aristocratic living, unchecked by middle-class restraints. Gazing out from the Marialvas' terrace it was delightful, he records lyrically, to watch the night descend upon it through "a bower of fantastic trees mingling their branches."[18]

On the other side of the hill, in a location more to Beckford's taste was Setéais, the neoclassical mansion which the wealthy Dutch consul, Daniel Gildemeester was building for himself (fig. 5-4). Here too one could stare at Pillement friezes, though this time in more elegant interiors of French taste. Pillement visited Lisbon on a number of occasions in 1750, and from 1780 to 1786, when he was also in Oporto.[19] Pillement was quintessentially a landscape painter who, following Rousseauesque precepts, gave scale to nature by inserting human figures, peasants, fishermen, or sailors into his compositions. Idealized in the manner of Claude Lorraine, his scenes sometimes depict landscapes in a pastorally romantic manner with shepherds and domesticated animals in a tranquil rusticity. Trees and flowers also

interested him and figure in the pastoral, bucolic scenes that he produced both in pastel and in oil. Rustic hermitages with spiky towers, rivers, brooks, and streams abound in his landscapes. Pillement could also be touched by the sublime; wild scenes of storms at sea, shipwrecks, or bleak, mountain landscapes formed alternatives to his calmer, Arcadian vision of countryside. Even in his landscape compositions, his attention to water, whether in the form of cascades or falls, is one of his strongest features.

Pillement was also a decorator of neoclassical designs and motifs. While he could paint scenes of classical serenity, bordered by curtains or columns, there is a touch of oriental delicacy about much of his work, as well as exotica in his liking for rare tropical fauna and flora. He also took to outright chinoiserie, introducing a style that was then popular in France, to a sympathetic Portuguese aristocracy whose country had had long and enduring experience of the art and culture of the Far East. His illustrations, published in London in 1758 in his *Livre de Chinois*, consisted of delicate engravings of a romanticized daily life in China. The extent of work attributed to Pillement in *quintas* and palaces in Portugal suggests that he must have had a thriving school of followers. At Ramalhão, after Beckford's time, exotic tropical frescoes reminiscent of Pillement's style, were commissioned by Queen Carlotta Joaquina on her return from Brazil (fig. 5-5).

If Beckford tired of the social swirl of Sintra society, he could take solitary rides in his Elysian valley of Colares, which Sacheverell Sitwell later called, in some aspects, the most Italian corner of the Peninsula.[20] Here the vines descended on the slopes, camellias bloomed in profusion, the roads were lined with oleander and aloe, the fields were fertile with olive and thick chestnut trees. Colares was a northerner's joy, with its balsamic air alternating with sudden sea mists and a secluded, ancient feeling.

By contrast, Lisbon offered more worldly attraction in the form of the spectacular and exuberant Catholic ritual of the court of Queen Maria. Beckford chose to entice his reader into this exotic world by a description, early in his diary, of the procession held on the feast day of Corpus Christi. All of Lisbon has been tented and festooned with red damask and multicolored tapestries, with satin coverings glittering with gold. The front of the patriarchal church was magnificently curtained; in due course the highly colorful procession of Yeoman Guards, priests and flocks of sallow monks added to the pageant. Within the church, High Mass was celebrated in full glory, with incense ascending in clouds, thousands kneeling and the light of innumerable tapers blazing on the diamonds and rubies of the ostensorium elevated, with trembling hands, by the sumptuously dressed Patriarch himself. Later the procession, with numerous mitered and scarlet figures, left escorted by attendants bearing crosses and silver reliquaries.[21] Many other occasions of similar pomp and circumstance are described by Beckford, whose reputation as a devotee of Saint Anthony, patron saint of Lisbon, helped, for the while, to consolidate his status in the capital.

Beckford's second and third visits to Portugal, in 1793 and

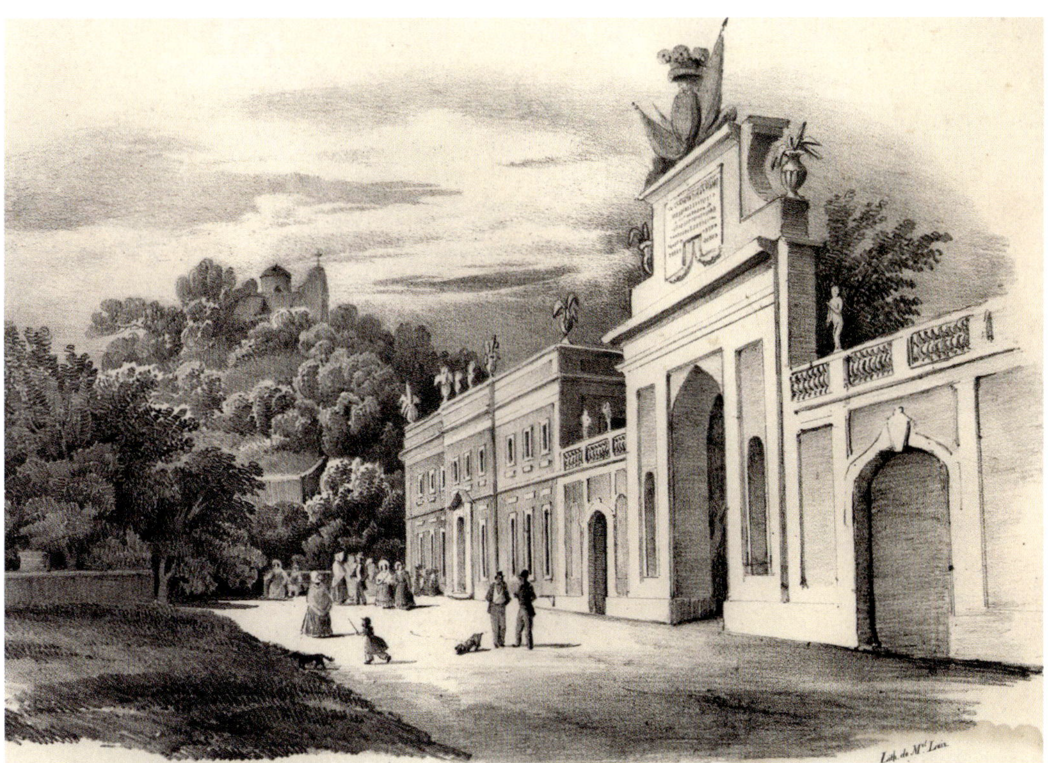

Fig. 5-4. Palace of Setéais, Sintra, mid-ninetenth century. Lithograph by Manuel Luiz. after C. Brelaz. Sintra, Historical Archive, Municipal Archive.

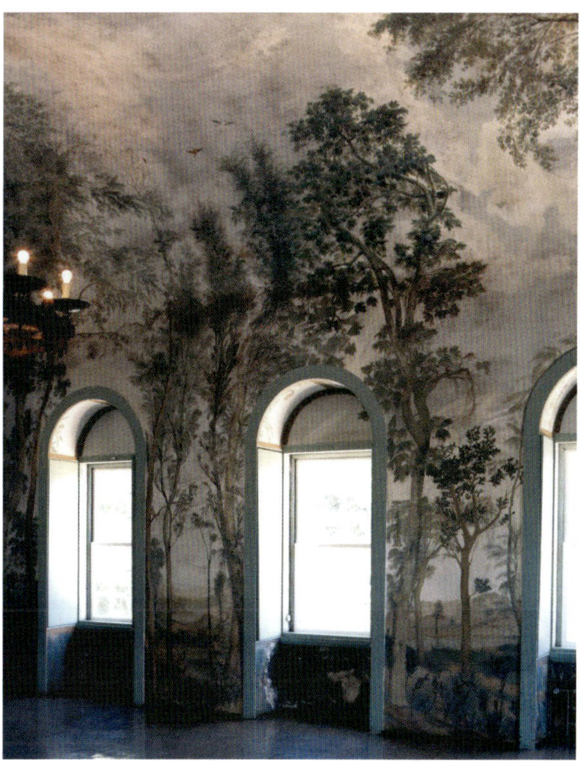

Fig. 5-5. Frescoes in the present-day Refectory, Palace of Ramalhão, Sintra. Photographed ca. 1960. Sintra, Historical Archive, Municipal Archive.

1798, are closely associated with the monasteries of Alcobaça and Batalha on the one hand and Sintra's "glorious Eden" on the other. Having been away for six years he was tempted back to the *fidalgo* life for a second time, lured once more by the prospect of taking up a privileged position in this socially secure, still feudal land. Nor was there anything to hold him at home: the much-longed-for rehabilitation had not come about. When Beckford returned to Lisbon in 1793 he took up residence along the coast at the villa of São José de Ribamar, while work was being done to convert the wooden house he had previously stayed in at the rua Cova da Moura. This house had belonged to Beckford's agent, Thomas Horne who bequeathed it to his nephew Joseph Sill, from whom Beckford bought it. A plan in Beckford's own hand gives a clear idea of what he wanted to do with the house. The plan shows a series of apartments in a long, open suite. From the ante-room at one end of the main wing, there is a long vista through the entire length of the house. The viewer's eye would traverse a Grand Drawing Room toward the central octagon, then beyond to a Turkish salon (presumably in imitation of the room at Fonthill Splendens) toward a sanctuary at one end, no doubt to be dedicated to Saint Anthony of Padua.[22] As Boyd Alexander observed, this plan is the prototype for the great north/south wing of Fonthill Abbey, with the same octagonal center and the saint's sanctuary at the northern most extreme.[23] It illustrates the highly dramatic way in which Beckford designed the interior of his houses, whether in Lisbon or later at Fonthill and at Bath.

Meanwhile from his villa, with its fine prospect of the Tagus estuary, Beckford was planning his great excursion to the monasteries of Alcobaça and Batalha, a journey that he captured with enduring joy and high spirits in his memoir of the trip not published until 1835.[24] The book is a celebration of many sorts, but it highlights two themes in its lush, graphic prose. The first is the Portuguese landscape, with its contrasts, surprises, and irregularities, the salty Atlantic never far away; the other is in his delighted enthusiasm for Batalha, a Gothic masterpiece of the fifteenth century.

Beckford's love of the countryside was guided by a landowner's careful assessment of its use, as well as by a Romantic's appreciation of color, light, and shade. The countryman's concern is much in evidence in *Recollections*, where with his keenly observant eye, he makes much of the exotic fauna and flora of Portugal, enticing his reader with views of "canes knotted like bamboo, bulrushes of enormous size and osiers, the tallest I had ever seen."[25] The exuberance of the southern clime is conveyed in a scene of a "boundless vineyard in full luxuriant leaf, divided by long broad tracts of thyme and camomile" leading to a cluster of "plum, pear, orange and apricot trees."[26] These are the joys of an English country gentleman, happily transferred to a land of abundance where the blue skies, sunny days and invigorating air invite good spirits and provide a sparkle to daily life. Although Beckford enjoyed cavorting with the Marialvas, he was most enthusiastic, most Rousseauesque about nature, when he was rambling on his own. Nothing pleased him more than to rise early, as he habitually did at

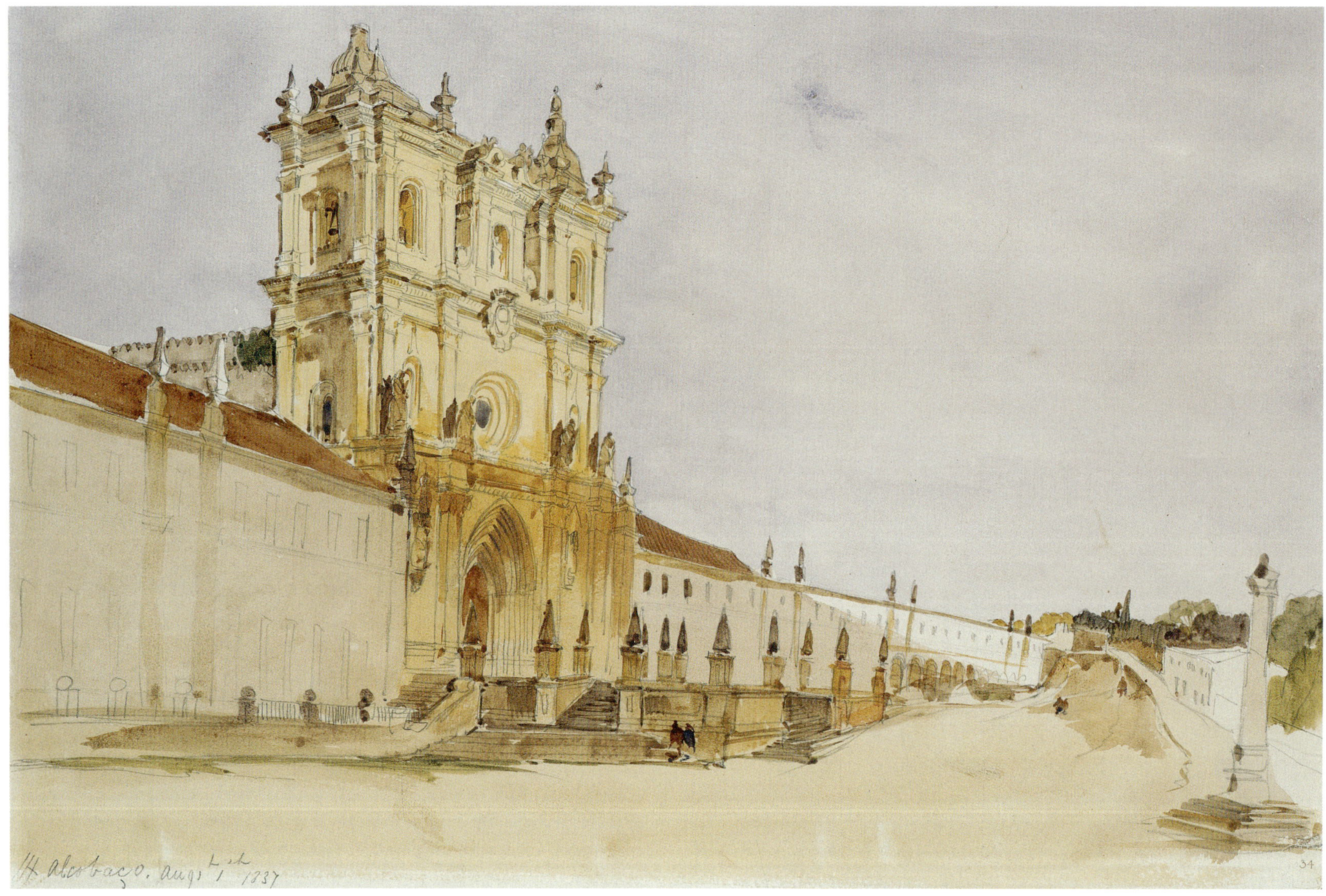

Fig. 5-6. James Holland. *Monastery of Alcobaça,* 1837. Watercolor. Trustees of the Victoria and Albert Museum, London.

Fonthill, and to ride out into the gentle, morning air, leaving his companions still deep in their slumbers.

On the fifth day of the excursion to the monasteries, he relates:

Not long after daybreak, whilst all the dews of the morning were still waiting to be dried up, I took a ramble over the hills, and, on one of their level summits, discovered an irregular opening with rude steps leading down to a little cavern hewn out of pumice rock, blessed with a tinkling spring, and mantled all over with the deliciously-scented flowers of the Lonicera tribe in wild profusion—exactly the sort of grotto described in Gil Blas as the resort of Algerine pirates.[27]

This Romantic recreation, always with a suggestion of human cultivation and sensibility, is a characteristic tone of Beckford the wanderer: in *Recollections* it reaches a highly fluent level of expression. Just at the point when the reader feels that Beckford is about to cross the line of exuberance into the merely gushing, the prose becomes restrained, even taut; an observation about well-cultivated fields surveyed by the practical eye of the landowner restrains the aesthetic from overpowering the reader. Sometimes the two elements are cleverly combined. Returning from Alcobaça, after noting the system of irrigation used on the land, Beckford adds, "Every cottage, apparently the abode of industrious contentment, had its well-fenced garden richly embossed with gourds and melons, its abundant water spout, its vine, its fig-tree and its espalier of pomegranate."[28]

A self-sufficient rustic existence, based on properly regulated

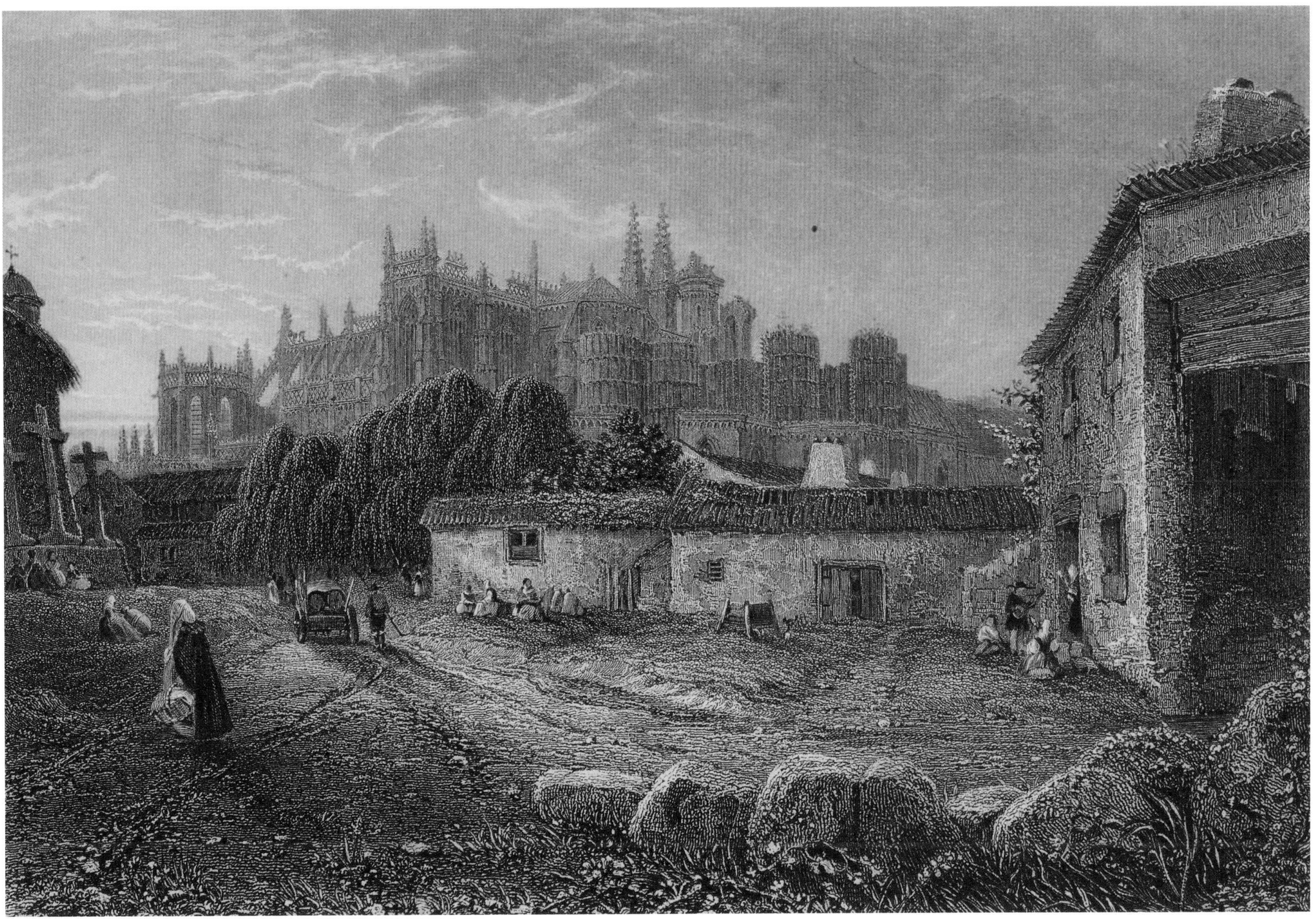

Fig. 5-7. Monastery of Batalha, 1837. Engraving by H. Adland after James Holland. Trustees of the Victoria and Albert Museum, London.

agriculture, was close to Beckford's social ideal. He was never a city man and had little sympathy with or understanding of the commercial and preindustrial urban development in his own country. At home in Fonthill, he lived the patrician existence of an old Whig landowner whose sense of social hierarchy was satisfied by the structured arrangements of local society. Beckford was no democrat, as he himself attested, but he had some feeling and concern for the livelihood of the community around him. He also had a true love of nature, understanding the benefits that could accrue from careful cultivation and husbandry. After he had moved to Bath in 1822 his former Wiltshire tenants missed his patriarchal protection.

Recollections is also a journal of shared joys—Beckford relied upon the good humor of the Grand Prior of Aviz, a friend from the languid and snug Sintra days of 1787.[29] Ehrhart, his new physician, provided a sane, scientific presence in the same way as Dr. Francis Verdeil had done before, while Gregorio Franchi was always at hand to play the guitar to him should Beckford become bored. Simon, the chef, provided their food, though it soon transpired that Beckford's Portuguese hosts were more fond of "gourmandizing" than he was himself.

When it came to buildings, it was Batalha that delighted Beckford. Alcobaça he had found gloomy and "Saxon," although he had been impressed by its bulk (fig. 5-6), but Batalha (fig. 5-7), from the first sight, filled him with awe:

My eyes being fairly open, I beheld a quiet, solitary vale, bordered by shrubby hills; a few huts, and but a few, peeping out of dense masses of foliage; and high above their almost level surface, the great church, with its rich cluster of abbatial buildings, buttresses, and pinnacles, and fretted spires, towering in all their pride and marking the ground with deep shadows that appeared interminable, so far and so wide were they stretched along.[30]

This is the enjoyment of a building as spectacle, a vision of a kind of medieval picturesque, which was to inspire him in his pursuit of Fonthill's rising spires. Some of the features of Batalha, its long nave, supports for the ceiling, and stained glass reminded him of Winchester, a building that he had always admired. It is significant that Beckford could make this English identification with Batalha, for it meant that he was more likely to think of transferring aspects of its architecture to a home setting. He noticed differences as well as similarities between the two buildings. The walls at Batalha are plainer than those at Winchester; its vaulted roof less intersected. Even so there is enough in common to make him speculate on whether any of William of Wykeham's disciples were in the entourage that accompanied Philippa of Lancaster when she became Queen of Portugal toward the end of the fourteenth century. When evening came again, Beckford was fascinated by the play of light and shadow through the stained-glass windows. The effect reminded him of the undulating shadows of a tree's leafy branches. There is a special solemnity to hearing a simple Mass celebrated in these surroundings.

In this whimsical, highly sensitized mood, Beckford came upon the chapel containing the tomb of João I and Queen Philippa, "linked hand in hand in death as fondly as they were in life."[31] The chapel dates from 1434 during the early Manueline period. Its decoration was restrained compared to the full, flamboyant style that Beckford found too exaggerated for his purist taste. The king and queen are surrounded by their distinguished offspring, including Prince Henry who played a prominent role in directing the Portuguese exploration of the Atlantic islands (Madeira, the Azores, and Cape Verde) and the West African coast. Around the king and queen were the marks of the Lancastrian royal house—the garter, leopards, and fleur-de-lis, symbols familiar to an Englishman—which gave the place a special feeling of familiarity. The impression that the royal chapel made on Beckford never faded and had a strong impact on his plans for Fonthill Abbey.

Although the chapel was the part of Batalha that Beckford most enjoyed, he also found other parts of the complex to his taste. He remarked that the stately chapter house, with its impressive sixty-foot-high ceiling, appeared to be entirely unsupported but was held up by beams that sloped gradually toward its center. A stained-glass window added a dignified effect to the lofty chamber. The only part of the monastery that displeased Beckford was the Founder's Mausoleum, but, diplomatically, he did not let his hosts know of his disappointment. What particularly offended him was the strange jumble of styles in which the mausoleum had been built, an incongruous mixture of Norman and Moorish.

Beckford's last Iberian dwelling was the palace of Monserrate, set in the idyllic lush vale that slopes down from the Sintra mountain ridge.[32] Monserrate, like Ramalhão, had already had a long history by the time Beckford took up residence there. Francisco Costa relates that in 1540 a chapel was erected on the site by one Gaspar Preto who was influenced in his choice of name by an image of our Lady of Monserrate in Catalonia. By the beginning of the eighteenth century, a country house (*quinta*) had been built by the family of Mello e Castro who had become the owners of the site. One of this tribe, with the flowery name of Dona Francisca Xavier Marianna de Faro Mello e Castro (a connection with great Jesuit missionary saint and Goa showing in her name) sold the house to Gerard de Visme.[33] Monserrate was built in mock-Gothic style, the long front facade interrupted by a central tower, with two turrets at each end embellished with angular, tapering windows and capped by pointed roofs. Its castellated front lent it a feigned medieval appearance, perhaps suited to the retreat of an Englishman gentleman like de Visme who sought to escape from the bustle of Lisbon. According to Cyrus Redding, Beckford later described the house as being "barbarous Gothic."[34] He was not amused by Byron's mocking description of it as a ruin in *Childe Harold*.[35] Nevertheless, he seems to have liked it enough to take on a long lease, returning to live there on his third visit to Portugal in 1798.

The most evocative description of the house was given years later by an itinerant English lady, Mariana Baillie, in 1821.[36] By then the palace was completely in ruins; she describes it as an English villa with elegant apartments, one in the classical style with fine mirrors and precious crystal glass doors still in situ. There was a spacious central room that opened out onto the lawn, where rare shrubs and flowerbeds reflected the interior design. In another room, with a rotund cupola one could practice echoes, an authentic Beckfordian contrivance.[37]

The setting of Monserrate was idyllic. Sunk somewhat in the lush valley, the house had been built on a mound. Beyond it towered the craggy heights of the Sintra hills, capped by the ancient Moorish castle. All around were rolling vales giving panoramas in all directions. In this setting Beckford conducted his experiments in landscape gardening, trying to create a total picture of a natural setting that was improved but not overwhelmed by human cultivation. Vistas were opened by clearing thickets and brambles so that trees could extend their branches unrestricted. Straight lines and the formalities of Continental gardening were avoided: the rolling hills and dips were used to emphasize the shape of trees. Cultivated areas were left to merge "naturally" into wilder ones. Wherever possible, shrubs and trees native to the area were cultivated. In these experiments Beckford carried on the English tradition of landscape gardening begun in the seventeenth century by Sir William Temple[38] and still flourishing when Horace Walpole produced his *History of the Modern Taste in Gardening* (1771). Walpole confidently dismissed the French or Italian penchant for formal terraces and raised waterfalls. Instead a more subtle art had to be developed: classical, Claudian scenes had been "interpreted" by William Kent at Rousham and by Charles Hamilton, Beckford's uncle, at Painshill in England. Monserrate was the ideal location to try out these ideas: the irregularity of the setting and its sense of ancient feeling could be intensified by the provision of temples or ruined walls, usually near running water and with a view, perhaps of the house or one of its turrets. From the terraces of the house, vistas opened out so that a distant ruin or folly came into view. A waterfall was blended into a natural setting. All about, trees and bushes abounded: the glades and paths provided endless tours of visual joy.

Beckford's last stay in Monserrate and indeed in Portugal was from late 1798 to the middle of the following year. This visit was over-shadowed, however, by the growing turmoil that was spreading across the Continent. It was not much longer before Napoléon's armies invaded the Peninsula, causing immense physical destruction and hindering the economy of Portugal for decades. Moreover, Beckford had left England after the death of his mother and in Portugal, favorites like the Abbade had died, so in a personal sense too the shadows had descended. Yet the grandeur of its Gothic buildings and the possibilities of landscape that Sintra had suggested remained in his imagination and in his nostalgia and inspired his grandest, princely project at home in the deepest recesses of Wiltshire.

1. L'arrivée d'un des plus riches particuliers de l'Angleterre qui vient de relâcher dans ce port à bord trois bâtiments qui lui appartiennent, occupe beaucoup l'attention du public de Lisbonne. Ce particulier est M Beckford, jeune homme de vingt-cinq ans, fils du fameux alderman et lord-maire qui, dans son temps, a joué un grand rôle dans les débats parlementaires de la Grande Bretagne. Quoique ce personnage ait diminué considérablement sa fortune en établissant celles de ses nombreux bâtards, son fils légitime a encore hérité de dix milles livres sterling de rente en Angleterre et de cinquante mille livres sterling également de rente et immenses et superbes possessions dans l'île de la Jamaique. On assure que, toutes charges déduites, M Beckford a en espèces sonnantes trente mille louis à manger annuellement. Marc de Bombelles, *Journal d'un Ambassadeur de France Au Portugal, 1786–1788*, ed. Roger Kann (Paris: Presses Universitaires de France, 1979): 117. Author's translation.

2. Rose Macaulay, *They Went to Portugal.* (London: Jonathan Cape, 1946): 110.

3. *The Journal of William Beckford in Portugal and Spain,* ed. Boyd Alexander, (London: Rupert Hart-Davis, 1954): 52.

4. Beckford claims to have discussed a sonnet of Camões, which surpassed the *Lusiads,* with Maria Manuel du Bocage, greatest of eighteenth-century Portuguese satirists. See Malcolm Jack, *Vathek and Other Stories* (London: Pickering & Chatto, 1993): 258–59.

5. Beckford, *Journal* (1954): 239 and 256.

6. Ibid., p. 153.

7. Ibid., p. 37.

8. Ibid.

9. Ibid., pp 253–54.

10. *The Travel-Diaries of William Beckford of Fonthill,* ed. G. Chapman (London: Jonathan Cape, 1928): vol. 2, p.19.

11. Beckford, *Journal* (1954): 50.

12. Ibid., p. 262.

13. Beckford, *Travel-Diaries* (1928): vol. 2, p. 19.

14. For a detailed account of Companhias das Índias porcelain, see R. T. Leite, *As Companhias das Índias e a Porcelana Chinesa de Encomenda* (San Paulo: Cerámica Aruan, 1986).

15. See Malcolm Jack, "Ramalhão: Beckford's First Sintra House," *Beckford Journal* (Spring 1997): vol. 3, pp. 20–24.

16. Beckford, *Journal* (1954): 128.

17. Francisco Costa, *Beckford em Sintra no verão de 1787* (Sintra: Câmara Municipal, 1982): 24.

Costa, for many years in charge of the Sintra archives, contributed greatly to local history, including a series of meticulously researched and charming monographs on particular subjects (the Charter of 1154) or buildings (Ramalhão, Monserrate, and Setéais), as well as a detailed bibliography of books on Sintra.

18. Beckford, *Journal* (1954): 130.

19. See do Espírito Santo Silva, *Jean Pillement and Landscape Painting in 18th Century Portugal* (Lisbon: Foundation Ricardo do Espírito Santo Silva, 1997).

20. Described as "a little enclave of Italy" by S. Sitwell, *Portugal and Madeira* (London: B.T. Batsford, 1954): 101.

21. Beckford, *Journal* (1954): 68.

22. Boyd Alexander, *England's Wealthiest Son* (London: Centaur Press, 1962): facing p. 118.

23. Ibid., p. 160.

24. William Beckford, *Recollections of An Excursion to the Monasteries of Batalha and Alcobaça,* ed. B. Alexander (London: Centaur Press, 1972).

25. Ibid., p. 124.

26. Ibid., p. 29.

27. Ibid., p. 31–32.

28. Ibid., p. 164.

29. "Snug," a favorite word of Beckford's, is used throughout his *Journal* (1954) and *Recollections* (1972).

30. Beckford, *Recollections* (1972): 66.

31. Ibid., p. 85.

32. See Malcolm Jack, "Monserrate: Beckford's Second Sintra House" in *Beckford Journal* 4 (Spring 1998): 48–51.

33. Francisco Costa, *História da Quinta e Palácio de Monserrat* (Sintra: Câmara Municipal, 1985): 9.

34. Cyril Redding, *Memoirs of Beckford of Fonthill* (London: Charles J. Skeet, 1859): vol.1, p. 279.

35. Lord George Byron, *Poetical Works* (Oxford: University Press, 1979): 74.

36. Costa, *História da Quinta* (1985): 28.

37. Ibid.

38. See Malcolm Jack, *William Beckford: An English Fidalgo* (New York: AMS Press, 1996): 116ff.

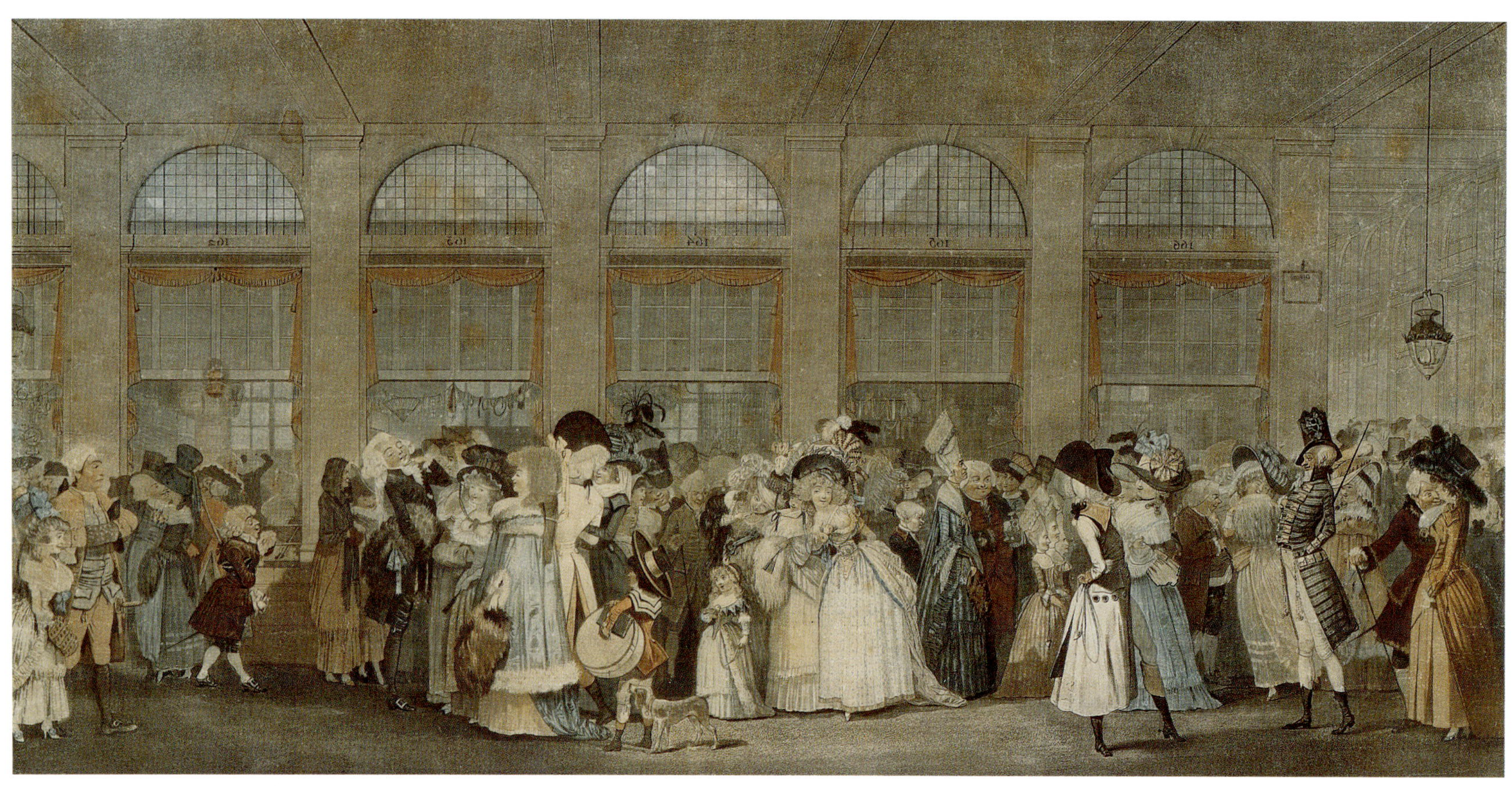

Fig. 6-1. "The Morning Walk at the Palais-Royal, Paris," ca. 1788. Engraved by Philibert-Louis Debucourt. Musée Carnavalet, Paris.

WILLIAM BECKFORD IN PARIS, 1788–1814: *"LE FASTE SOLITAIRE"*

A N N E E S C H A P A S S E

No other city in William Beckford's life better aided in the development of his complex personality, idiosyncratic artistic sensibility, and hedonistic lifestyle—aptly labeled *"le faste solitaire"* (solitary magnificence)—than Paris during his prolonged visits between 1777 and 1814 (fig. 6-1).[1] Indeed, throughout much of Beckford's life, Paris remained a recurrent destination. Unlike any other European capital he visited, he maintained a residence there intermittently between 1788 and 1803. During this period in particular, as an ambitious and enterprising man, Beckford not only actively sought to benefit from the city's immense artistic riches to acquire priceless works of art, but also to cultivate his eye as a nascent collector and connoisseur (fig. 6-2). The later visit in 1814, however, was marked by a more detached and dispirited attitude toward the capital, which clearly reflected a shift in his priorities, a disregard for the French post-revolutionary society, and possibly a symptom of his age.

Beckford had first visited Paris with his mother, Maria Marsh Beckford, a devout Protestant Scot, in 1777. He returned to the French capital in 1781 on his way back to England from his Grand Tour of Italy, and visited for a third time in 1783–84 with his bride, Lady Margaret Gordon. On none of these trips had he truly indulged in the French *douceur de vivre* celebrated by Frenchmen and foreigners alike. In 1788 during his first residency, however, as a young widower in a self-imposed exile and with a substantial but fluctuating annual income, Beckford had all the leisure and ambition to enjoy the best of Paris. If Portugal's natural beauties and warm climate pleased him particularly, Paris with its exquisite art, excellent opera, fine food, and rich mix of people offered a widely entertaining and cosmopolitan society, despite emerging signs of social and political unrest and, later, manifest danger during the French Revolution.

Paradoxically, in spite of a privileged position from which he observed the epic political events unfolding around him, Beckford rarely spoke of his times in Paris during this crucial period and, if at all, only in laconic and evasive words.[2] What were undoubtedly inspirational

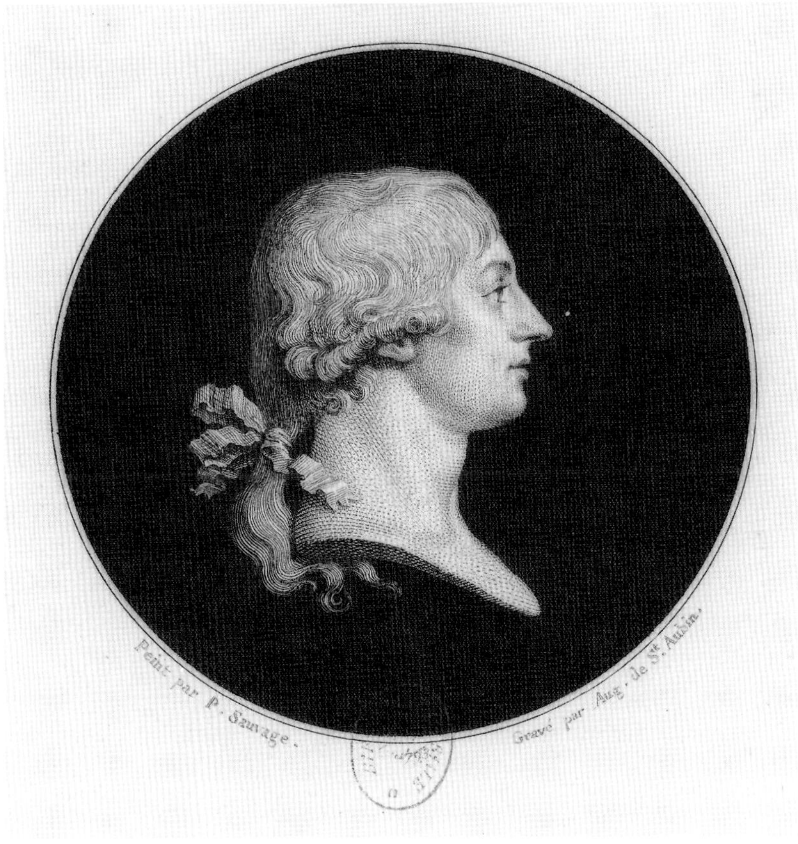

Fig. 6-2. Piat-Joseph Sauvage. "Portrait of William Beckford," 1801. Engraved by Augustin de Saint-Aubin. Cabinet des Estampes, Bibliothèque Nationale de France, Paris.

and significant years were kept shrouded in mystery. In light of Beckford's later tendencies to forge self-promoting half-truths and rewrite unflattering or insignificant personal recollections into an idealized past, this concealment of his Parisian activities and the scarcity of his correspondence on the subject are bewildering.[3] It is only by carefully weaving together biographical elements with historical events

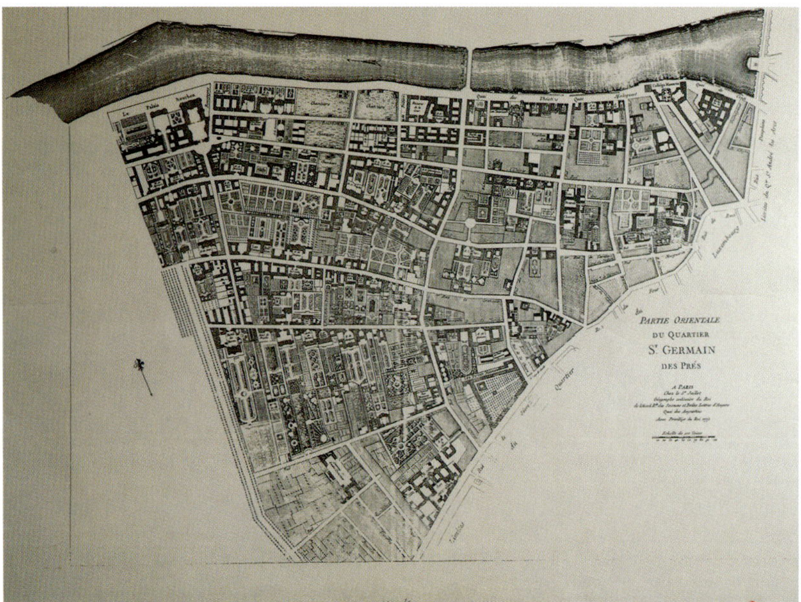

Fig. 6-3. Jean-Baptiste-Michel Renou de Chevigné called Jaillot. Map of Faubourg Saint-Germain, 1775. Bibliothèque Historique de la Ville de Paris, Paris.

that some light can be shed on Beckford's daily activities, aesthetic quests, and political predicament during this obscure yet formative interval.

THE FORMATIVE YEARS, 1788–93

Paris had long exerted a powerful fascination on Beckford who reveled in its bustling and liberal atmosphere. In the summer of 1788, on his return to the French capital from Spain, Beckford, finally, took up residence in Paris accompanied by his young lover Gregorio Franchi, the dwarf Pierre de Grailly, and a large retinue.[4] The entourage first settled in the Hôtel du Prince de Galles near the church of Saint-Sulpice, before renting the furnished Hôtel d'Orsay (formerly the Hôtel de Clermont) on the rue de Varenne in the Faubourg Saint-Germain in September of that year.[5] The Faubourg Saint-Germain (fig. 6-3) was a closed community, stronghold of the French aristocracy, and, as a contemporary noted, a difficult area of the capital to settle in: "The faubourg Saint-Germain did not admit anyone new into its ranks. In order to be part of it, one had to be born there, have a family there, or else be a wealthy foreigner with impressive credentials. Wealth was more important than a recommendation."[6] Pierre-Gaspard-Marie Grimod, comte d'Orsay, who had moved to Germany a year earlier with his second wife, Marie-Anne of Hohenlohe and Waldenbourg-Bartenstein, daughter of the crown-prince of Hohenlohe-Waldenbourg, was fortunate to have found in Beckford one of the rare visitors in Paris at the

time who could both afford to rent his luxurious residence and appreciate its refined interiors.[7]

It is not surprising that Beckford chose to live in the Hôtel d'Orsay. Designed by the architect Jean-Baptiste-Alexandre Le Blond between 1708 and 1714 for the marquise de Saissac (born Albert de Luynes), it had been acquired by the comte d'Orsay from the duc de Chaulnes in 1768. A wealthy and ambitious young man from the bourgeoisie, d'Orsay, who had contracted a powerful alliance in his first marriage to Marie-Louise-Albertine-Amélie, princess of Croÿ–Molembais, in 1770, had undertaken immediately to make it one of the most elegant houses of the capital. The much-admired *salon doré* (part of which has been rebuilt at the Corcoran Gallery, Washington, D.C.) had been furbished for the princess, under the supervision of the architect Jean-François-Thérèse Chalgrin, in a white and gold *à l'antique* scheme celebrating conjugal love. D'Orsay also commissioned distin-

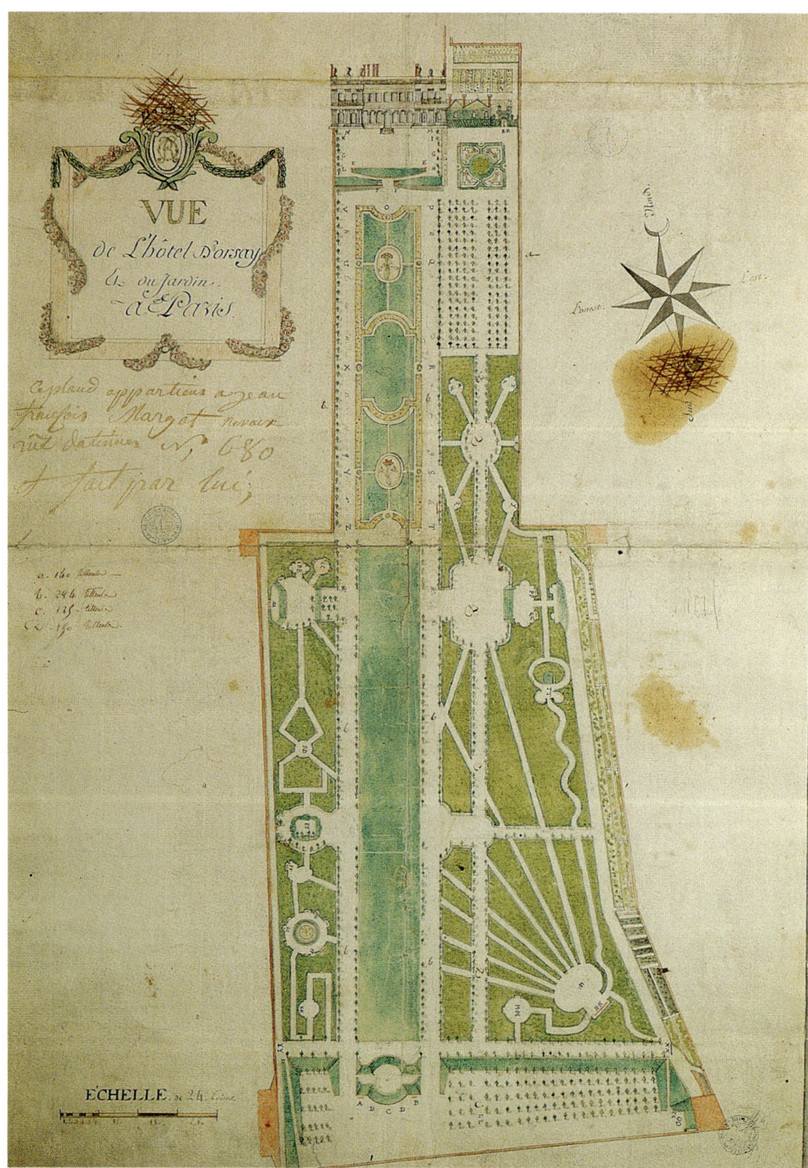

Fig. 6-4. Jean-François Margat. Topographical view of the grounds of the Hôtel d'Orsay, ca. 1785. Margat was the gardener at the time. Bibliothèque Historique de la Ville de Paris, Paris.

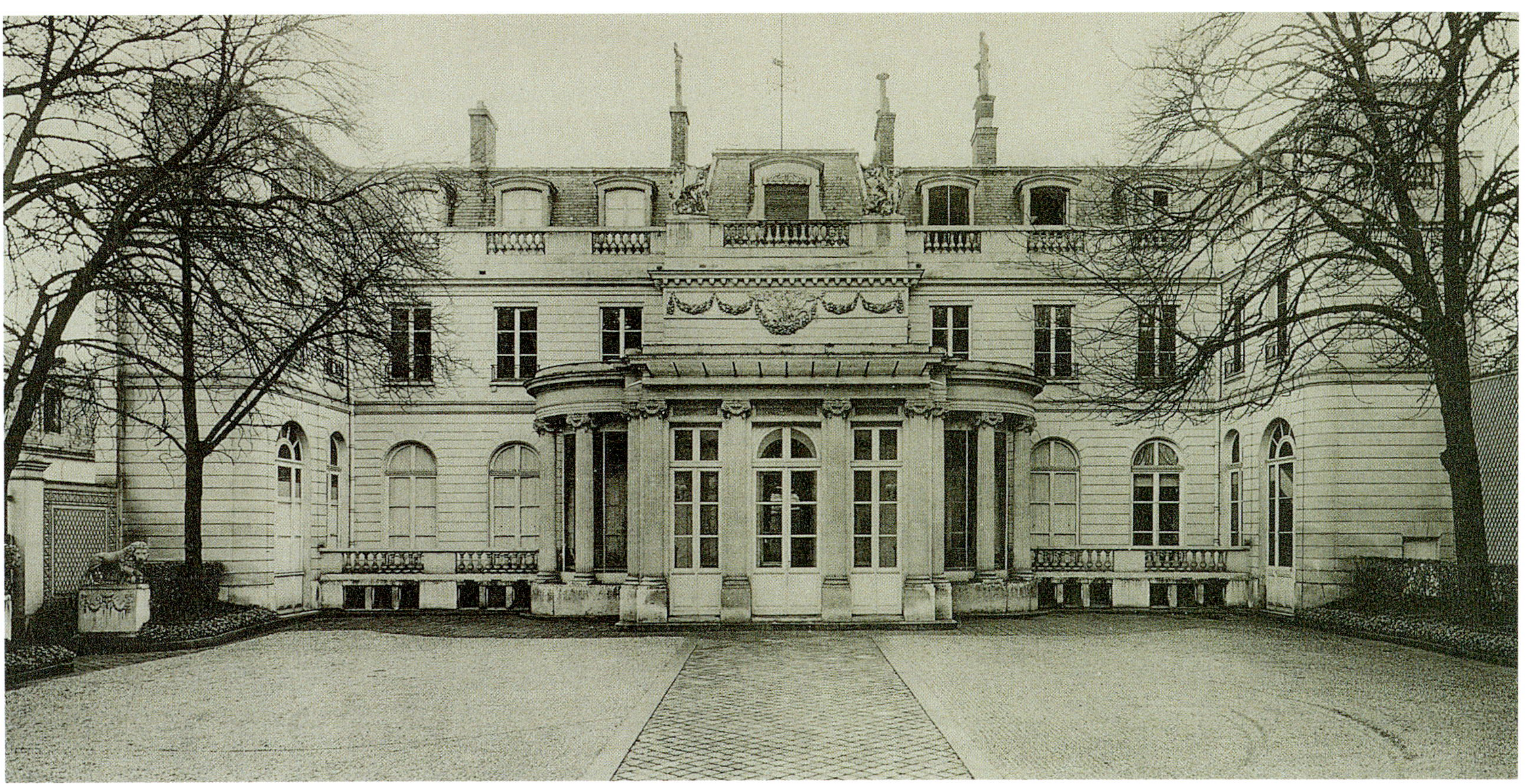

Fig. 6-5. The Hôtel d'Orsay from the main courtyard. Photographed ca. 1910. From Paul Jarry, *Les vieux hôtels parisiens. Le Faubourg Saint-Germain,* vol. 3 (Paris: F. Contet, 1910): plate 3.

guished craftsmen to supply the furniture and furnishings, while actively purchasing paintings, sculptures, and antiquities. This most recent renovation campaign had been completed by the architect Charles-Joaquim Bénard (or Besnard) and the painter Tassaerd in 1785 at a staggering cost of 126,801 *livres*,[8] about which a contemporary chronicler had remarked. "This son of a financier has indulged in the arts and possesses indeed one of Paris's most striking residences to be seen for the richness, taste, luxury and idiosyncrasies it contains."[9]

It was an entirely renovated, richly decorated, and celebrated residence, therefore, that Beckford, in keeping with his highly developed sense of self, style, and decorum, rented in portion for over a year at the considerable annual cost of eight thousand *livres*, according to the lease.[10] Both parties had the right to terminate the lease at anytime, notwithstanding a six months notification. The estate included a large garden of six *arpents* (approximately six acres), a stable for fifteen horses, three carriage bays, as well as numerous other facilities (fig. 6-4). A noteworthy mention was made in the rental contract of the furniture and furnishings left behind by d'Orsay. It stated that nothing

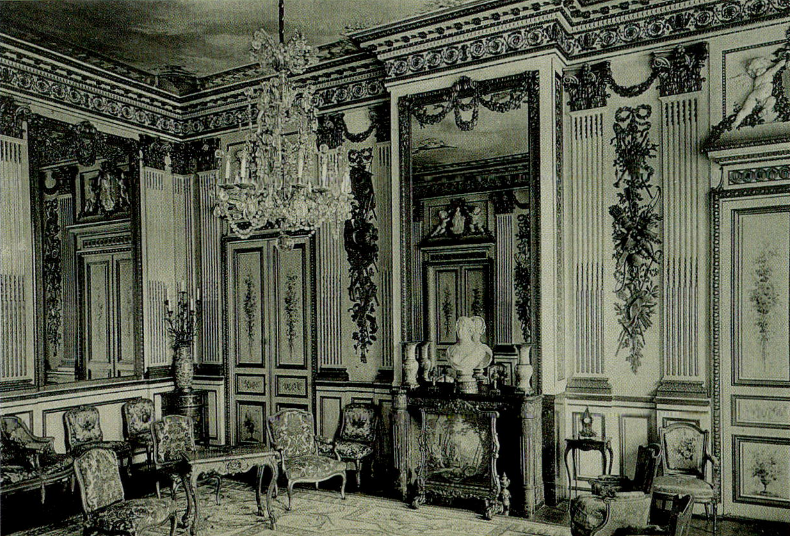

Fig. 6-6. The great saloon of the Hôtel d'Orsay, with its original paneling. Photographed ca. 1910. From Paul Jarry, *Les vieux hôtels parisiens. Le Faubourg Saint-Germain,* vol. 3 (Paris: F. Contet, 1910): plate 4.

could be removed from the residence and specified that great care be taken by Beckford to "enjoy the premises . . . and especially the furnishings like a responsible individual," clearly underscoring their significance and value in the eyes of its owner.[11]

The main building, flanked by two side wings housing small *appartements*, was centered, on its garden facade, on a half rotunda supported by eight Doric columns in *portor* and *verde antico* marbles that flanked tall doors (fig. 6-5). The garden facade looked onto a terrace leading to a series of formal gardens filled with classical sculptures and antique vases and several modest pavilions scattered about. The interior was comprised of a succession of grand *appartements* profusely decorated with precious materials, giltwood furniture in the neoclassical style, and allegorical paintings (fig. 6-6).[12] This taste for ostentatious interpretations of the antique in the decoration chosen by d'Orsay coincided with Beckford's sensibility and may have later served as a source of inspiration for the lavish neoclassical redecoration of Fonthill Splendens in the 1790s.

Beckford's time in Paris was occupied by assiduous visits to esteemed artists, craftsmen, and manufactories, including royal institutions such as the Sèvres porcelain works and the Savonnerie tapestry manufactory, and private ones like Dagoty, another Parisian porcelain manufacturer. Unlike most foreigners visiting the capital, Beckford favored going directly to the workshops to place orders himself, rather than through the services of a *marchand-mercier*, such as Philippe Julliot or Dominique Daguerre, whose rates he castigated. Beckford's decision to bypass an intermediary who could counsel and assist him was motivated not only by his genuine interest in personally commissioning and buying pieces for his interiors and collections, but also perhaps by his private nature. Although he certainly sought to partake in the creative process—even possibly offering suggestions for designs, as he later did in his life for pieces he ordered from famous craftsmen—he also profited from the savings made by going directly to the suppliers. Beckford was a demanding customer, repeatedly inquiring about the state of his orders and concerned with bargaining prices down, even refusing to pay for finished work if found unsuitable.

In June 1791, for instance, he went to the Savonnerie manufactory to order a carpet described in the firm's accounts as

> a piece of 7. feet wide by 3. feet 6. *pouces* in height [length] representing a bouquet, on a favorable ground to make the flowers stand out and framed by a border with moldings imitating gold intertwined with green oak leaves, the whole of the most perfect execution.[13]

The royal manufactory, whose production had been essentially reserved for the Crown since 1673, was in such a precarious state following the Revolution's outbreak and the subsequent loss of royal patronage that it was eager to take an order from a private citizen. While numerous distinguished foreigners, such as Emperor Joseph II, Grand Duke Paul of Russia, or Richard Cosway (the miniature painter), had received Savonnerie carpets as state gifts from the king of France, purchases from private individuals at the Savonnerie manufactory were rare. The third Duke of Richmond had been the only British citizen to buy a carpet directly from the manufactory when he was ambassador to France in 1765–66, until Beckford's 1791 order.[14]

This small carpet on order, based on a cartoon by the famous flower painter from the Gobelins, Laurent Malaine, took six months to weave at a cost of 1,126 *livres* 16 *sous*. Upon receipt of the piece, Beckford thanked Guillaumot, comptroller of the Savonnerie and Gobelins manufactories, for the "financial sacrifice granted to him in recognition of his love for the arts" since he only paid 600 *livres* for it. Guillaumot justified this substantial loss to his supervisor Delaporte by remarking that this export would certainly promote the manufactory's reputation in England, noting that Beckford was "an amateur very eager to gather at his place all that is the most perfect in the productions of the arts and from the manufactories ("amateur très curieux de réunir chez lui tous [*sic*] ce qu'il ÿ à [*sic*] de plus parfais [*sic*] en production d'arts et de manufactures"). Upon delivery of the carpet in late March 1792, Guillaumot further reported that Beckford had been delighted with the carpet when delivered to him in Paris, and indeed, Beckford ordered a second one of almost the same pattern shortly afterward. He also chose a third piece from the manufactory's inventory, which was brought to him in the summer of 1792, but returned it because while its dimensions were accurate, its colors did not blend well with his white and gold saloon. A pendant of the first model ("un tapis d'un simple fond ver [*sic*] avec bordure sans rien et un autre d'un fond mordoré ou lac et des fleurs dessus") was ordered in its place for his London residence, and this was completed in February 1793. Though almost equal in size to the first carpet, its decoration varied slightly in its flower composition.[15]

Later that year Beckford purchased a set of plates (see cat. no. 48) with a decoration of "Chinese Parasols and Arabesques" from the Sèvres manufactory, and he benefited from a 12 percent discount, an exceptionally high discount granted by the manufactory.[16] While clients at this time never paid the full price requested by a retailer in a store or by a craftsman for the invoice submitted for payment (*mémoire*), private individuals were generally charged the full price at Sèvres. Only accredited customers, like *marchands-merciers* or specially favored clients such as the banker Jean-Frédéric Perregaux, enjoyed rebates. Beckford's privileged treatment (also noted at the Savonnerie manufactory) suggests that, in fact, despite his enormous wealth, Beckford looked for substantial bargains or expected them through negotiation. The vast expenses in buying artwork did not preclude a sense of parsimony. He not only enjoyed searching for unique objects that met both his criteria of superior technical execution and aesthetic refinement, but he was also animated by the desire to get a fair—if not good—deal. The negotiation that followed the find of a rare object or the placement of a new order was a necessary evil in order to persuade himself that he was not being robbed or defrauded. A discerning buyer with a practiced eye, his pleasure resided as much in the quest for the ideal item—unique, skillfully crafted and aesthetically pleasing—as in the feeling of paying an advantageous price for it. This matter remained an on-going concern throughout his life, whether at Fonthill Abbey or later in Bath.

The context of the political crisis leading to the French Revolution in 1789 and its detrimental impact on the manufactories certainly served Beckford well. Not only was Paris the center in the Western world that offered the creativity, quality, and sophistication he was seeking in artistic productions, but his patronage was eagerly courted, as reflected by the substantial discounts he was granted. Following one of his visits to the Savonnerie in 1792, for instance, the comptroller of the Civil List, Delaporte, reported to a colleague that "M. Beckfort [*sic*], who is a very wealthy Englishman and amateur of artistic productions, gathers around him in London a great number of distinguished people."[17] While the statement about his social circle was more of erroneous impression than reality on the part of an administrator eager to promote his goods, Beckford's readiness for spending profusely on artistic productions was clearly notorious. It is apparent that in those times of economic hardship, he was received as a savior who might help keep the French manufactories afloat thanks to his orders, like Paul I of Russia who exported vast quantities of furniture and artwork to furnish his newly built Mikaelovsky Palace in the years 1791–95.[18]

Although Beckford generally conducted most of his purchases as his own agent, he sometimes relied on the services of the famous silversmith Henri Auguste whose work he had discovered while visiting Madrid in 1787.[19] Beckford had noted in his diary upon seeing Madame d'Aranda's *toilette* designed by Jean-Guillaume Moitte and executed by Auguste that it was "by far the most exquisite *chef d'oeuvre* of the kind I ever saw."[20] Upon befriending Auguste in Paris around 1788, Beckford entrusted him with numerous projects over the years, from the commissioning of important pieces of silver, to the handling a number of trivial transactions, such as the payment and collection of goods purchased at Sèvres. Though Auguste, whose father Robert-Joseph Auguste had been royal goldsmith to Louis XVI, enjoyed an honorable reputation, he was not yet the celebrated craftsman he was to become under the Empire. Therefore, it was quite enterprising of Beckford to trust him with significant commissions.

The most unusual aspect of their relationship certainly lay in their collaboration on exceptional pieces of furniture, which Beckford greatly prized and praised. In February 1792, he enthusiastically wrote to his cousin residing in Naples, Sir William Hamilton:

> If the K[ing of Naples] is desirous of having really good work in gold, silver or bronze, he should apply to Auguste, whose talents equal if not surpass those of the first artists of antiquity. I think you will be enraptured with the furniture I am having made under his directions in the true spirit of Corinth & Athens (. . .)[21]

Generally, each piece produced for or acquired by Beckford during his visits to Paris around that time, and still extant, unmistak-

ably reflect his quest for exquisite works of art in the classical vein: harmony, elegance, and exceptional skill presided over his choices for silver by Auguste or Moitte.[22]

If the neoclassical style emerged as a constant throughout these years, from its most restrained and simplified manner in the early 1780s to a more opulent and intricate form by the mid-1790s, the pursuit of excellence in workmanship remained the sole impulse behind Beckford's long-lasting patronage of contemporary craftsmen, quite independently from the ebb and flow of fashion. As such, he distinguished himself from his contemporaries who rarely ventured out of a circuit of established manufacturers or craftsmen publicized through indispensable travel guides to Paris, such as Thiéry's *Guide des amateurs et des étrangers voyageurs à Paris* (1787). It is noteworthy, for example, that the prominent Russian amateur Nicolas Demidoff commissioned a gueridon-table with gilt-bronze mounts by Auguste in 1806, more than a decade after Beckford had first employed Auguste.

Beckford did more than just accumulate precious objects. His passion for literature and fine books complemented his collecting, and in light of the fact that Paris was a rich source for bibliophiles, he took every opportunity to enhance his impressive library. Valued by French authorities in 1794 at the staggering sum of "200,000 *livres*, it comprised "all the masterpieces of typography whether Greek, Latin or French."[23] This is not surprising, considering that already in 1784, when only twenty-four, he had attended the sale of the duc de la Vallière's famous collection and had successfully bid, despite fierce competition from Louis XVI and Joseph II's agents.[24] The books amassed from various sources were stored in a house rented on the rue de Grenelle between 1791 and 1793, before being shipped to England where they formed the core a formidable collection of over 10,000 volumes, each bound with the utmost care.

The Parisian bookseller Charles Chardin (established since 1779) served as Beckford's principal supplier, advisor, agent, and librarian in Paris. During the Revolution Chardin's close ties with Beckford caused him to be accused by the local revolutionary council of having appropriated Beckford's library and horses, and of being an English agent. He was arrested but released shortly after, stating in his defense that he had turned down Beckford's full-time employment offer carrying a generous yearly salary of 15,000 *livres* "out of his fervent love for his homeland."[25] After the Revolution and until his death in 1826, with a lifetime annuity of 2,400 francs, Chardin continued to act as Beckford's agent, most notably at auctions.[26] Beckford relied over the years on Chardin's acumen as a fellow connoisseur, as much as on his experience in the art market and his unfailing devotion, in order to secure the best possible purchases. These qualities were indeed indispensable in the embroiled context of the Revolution and post-Revolution art and book markets.

By the years 1791–92, opportunities on the Parisian art market for collectors like Beckford abounded. The seizure and sale of assets owned by fleeing aristocrats, wealthy individuals and members of the clergy had thrown massive quantities of luxury goods on the market.

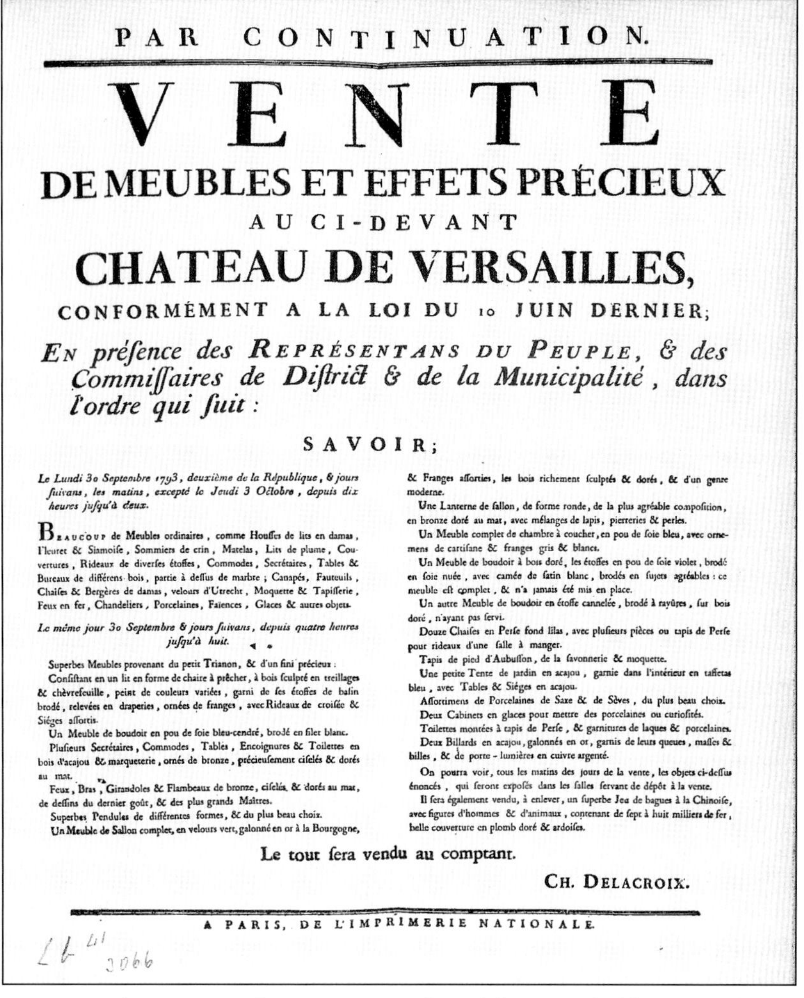

PAR CONTINUATION.

VENTE
DE MEUBLES ET EFFETS PRÉCIEUX
AU CI-DEVANT
CHATEAU DE VERSAILLES,
CONFORMÉMENT A LA LOI DU 10 JUIN DERNIER;

En présence des REPRÉSENTANS DU PEUPLE, *& des Commissaires de District & de la Municipalité, dans l'ordre qui suit :*

SAVOIR;

Le Lundi 30 Septembre 1793, deuxième de la République, & jours suivans, les matins, excepté le Jeudi 3 Octobre, depuis dix heures jusqu'à deux.

BEAUCOUP de Meubles ordinaires, comme Housses de lits en damas, fleuret & Siamoise, Sommiers de crin, Matelas, Lits de plume, Couvertures, Rideaux de diverses étoffes, Commodes, Secrétaires, Tables & Bureaux de différens bois, partie à dessus de marbre ; Canapés, Fauteuils, Chaises & Bergères de damas, velours d'Utrecht, Moquette & Tapisserie, Feux en fer, Chandeliers, Porcelaines, Faïences, Glaces & autres objets.

Le même jour 30 Septembre & jours suivans, depuis quatre heures jusqu'à huit.

Superbes Meubles provenant du petit Trianon, & d'un fini précieux :
Consistant en un lit en forme de chaire à prêcher, à bois sculpté en treillages & chèvrefeuille, peint de couleurs variées, garni de ses étoffes de balin brodé, relevées en draperies, ornées de franges, avec Rideaux de croisée & Siéges assortis.
Un Meuble de boudoir en pou de soie bleu-cendré, brodé en filet blanc.
Plusieurs Secrétaires, Commodes, Tables, Encoignures & Toilettes en bois d'acajou & marqueterie, ornés de bronze, précieusement ciselés & dorés au mat.
Feux, Bras, Girandoles & Flambeaux de bronze, ciselés & dorés au mat, de dessins du dernier goût, & des plus grands Maîtres.
Superbes Pendules de différentes formes, & du plus beau choix.
Un Meuble de Sallon complet, en velours vert, galonné en or à la Bourgogne,

& Franges assorties, les bois richement sculptés & dorés, & d'un genre moderne.
Une Lanterne de sallon, de forme ronde, de la plus agréable composition, en bronze doré au mat, avec mélanges de lapis, pierreries & perles.
Un Meuble complet de chambre à coucher, en pou de soie bleu, avec ornemens de cartisane & franges gris & blancs.
Un Meuble de boudoir à bois doré, les étoffes en pou de soie violet, brodé en soie nuée, avec camée de satin blanc, brodés en sujets agréables : ce meuble est complet, & n'a jamais été mis en place.
Un autre Meuble de boudoir en étoffe cannelée, brodé à rayûres, sur bois doré, n'ayant pas servi.
Douze Chaises en Perse fond lilas, avec plusieurs pièces ou tapis de Perse pour rideaux d'une salle à manger.
Tapis de pied d'Aubusson, de la savonnerie & moquette.
Une petite Tente de jardin en acajou, garnie dans l'intérieur en taffetas bleu, avec Tables & Siéges en acajou.
Assortimens de Porcelaines de Saxe & de Sèves, du plus beau choix.
Deux Cabinets en glaces pour mettre des porcelaines ou curiosités.
Toilettes montées à tapis de Perse, & garnitures de laques & porcelaines.
Deux Billards en acajou, galonnés en or, garnis de leurs queues, masses & billes, & de porte-lumières en cuivre argenté.
On pourra voir, tous les matins des jours de la vente, les objets ci-dessus énoncés, qui seront exposés dans les salles servant de dépôt à la vente.
Il sera également vendu, à enlever, un superbe Jea de bagues à la Chinoise, avec figures d'hommes & d'animaux, contenant de sept à huit milliers de fer, belle couverture en plomb doré & ardoises.

Le tout sera vendu au comptant.

CH. DELACROIX.

A PARIS, DE L'IMPRIMERIE NATIONALE.

Fig. 6-7. Advertisement for an auction of royal furniture held at Versailles on September 30, 1793. Bibliothèque Nationale de France, Paris.

This movement was further accelerated when the National Convention voted to disperse the nationalized property of the royal family (*Liste Civile*) and the *Garde-Meuble*'s holdings on June 10, 1793.[27] Over 200,000 objects were auctioned at Versailles alone between August 25, 1793, and August 11, 1794, and similar sales took place at other royal residences, such as Saint-Cloud, Rambouillet, Bellevue, Compiègne, and Fontainebleau (fig. 6-7). By this time, however, if the exemption of any taxes for the exportation of works of art and the continuous depreciation of the paper money known as *assignats* rendered these auctions particularly attractive, the political and economic environment's uncertain state made bidding a perilous art, even for foreign buyers. Most of the buying was carried out by shrewd Parisian dealers (often *marchands-tapissiers*) or intermediaries acting on behalf of foreign clients and often working in collusion. Their dealings continued unabated well into the Directoire period (1795–1799). François-Louis

Godon, royal clockmaker to the king of Spain since 1787, for example, actively bought at auction on behalf of Charles IV during this time.[28] Speculators like Treuttel, Hébert or the brothers Eberts, on the other hand, sought to attract clients by advertising in foreign publications their services to bid at these auctions.[29] Beckford observed knowingly, that these individuals bought "on behalf of clients rich and informed enough to appreciate the opportunities offered to them by the Revolution."[30]

This situation was further compounded following the short-lived abolition of the auctioneers' monopoly on holding auctions. As a result, anyone could act as an agent between a consignor and a buyer, and upholsterers, retailers of all sorts, and even innkeepers soon began to administer sales, charging a 6 percent commission on the hammer price. A lucrative under-the-counter business, especially with foreign agents, flourished, with the resale of merchandise purchased inexpensively at auction due to the lack of competition, the constant depreciation of the *assignats*, and the absence of any form of legal control.

The clandestine nature of most transactions, added to the fact that British citizens, with few exceptions, were forbidden entry to French territory between February 1793 and 1801, accounts for the difficulty in tracing important acquisitions made at that time by Beckford and other collectors. He could either have resorted to a still unidentified agent who was present at the sales (his usual agent Chardin's name does not appear in the minutes of the royal auctions), or he may have purchased pieces in Paris upon his subsequent visits or through a London dealer, such as Robert Fogg of Warwick Street.[31] Fine objects and furnishings of French origin also frequently came up for sale at auction in London, most notably through the association of the *marchand-mercier* Daguerre and the auctioneer James Christie.[32]

BECKFORD'S SOCIAL LIFE IN PARIS

The flood of goods entering the art market at that time, often sold at historic lows, and the ongoing exile of the aristocracy and wealth around 1791–93, rendered Beckford's living conditions ever more pleasing and comfortable. The nature of his lavish Parisian life can be grasped from a particularly complacent letter written to his solicitor Thomas Wildman on 29 November 1791:

> The finest linen which ever Flanders and Saxony produced is scarcely thought worthy to garnish my sideboards, or be spread under my boots—when I return—in all the majesty of mud, from dashing in the most invincible manner thro' the sloughs of the Bois-de-Boulogne attended by half-a-dozen Captains & Lieutenants of the Garde Nationale.[33]

Paris had always greatly entertained Beckford who compared the city's boisterous and unbridled social life to "Lucifer's own metropolis."[34] This was a compliment coming from a man who celebrated all forms of sensual pleasures and every kind of luxury and had been ostracized in England for these conspicuous penchants. Following the disarray of the French monarchy and thanks to seemingly unlimited funds,

Beckford succeeded in securing some kingly amenities, such as several of Louis XVI's former cooks and the opera box of the exiled prince de Condé. Like the Irish tycoon Quintin Crawford ("Make your wealth where you live but enjoy it in Paris"),[35] he proceeded to make Paris an endless pleasure ground, boasting to Wildman:

> Happy—aye—thrice happy are those who in this good Capital & at this period have plenty of money—their Kingdom is come, their will is done upon Earth, if not in Heaven—By St. Anthony, my dear friend—I never was better amused since I existed.[36]

Paradoxically, despite all the amenities available to entertain on a large scale, Beckford's social circle is difficult to reconstruct. Contemporary memoirs or journals never mention his name, even though it is unlikely that his presence went unnoticed, especially after the publication of his Arabian tale *Vathek* in French in 1787. It remains uncertain, for instance, if the Powderham Castle scandal of 1784 thwarted his socializing, causing prominent members of the large Paris-based British community, such the Duke of Dorset or Lord Malmesbury, as well as fashionable Parisian social circles, to shun him. The Duchess of Devonshire engaged in a scandalous *ménage à trois* with her husband and her friend Lady Elizabeth Foster, as well as having extraconjugal affairs, and had a notorious gambling habit, yet she never experienced any form of ostracism while staying in Paris during these years. A friend of Queen Marie-Antoinette, she visited Versailles in June 1789, a privilege which must greatly have hurt Beckford's pride who longed for acceptance at court.[37]

In reading Beckford's own impassioned accounts of his 1783–84 trip, it does appear that he led a much more discreet social life on his subsequent visits to the French capital: his assiduous socializing during the latter trip had more to do with his status as a newlywed than with his genuine reclusive personality. One longtime English resident in Paris commented on Beckford's early predisposition to be extremely selective about whom he chose to see, to a point of being disrespectful, even before the Powderham scandal:

> called on Mr Beckford to enquire about my Nephew at Naples, but for some reasons I cannot divine he did not chose to be seen. He is a little impertinent.[38]

This attitude was by no means reserved for Beckford's compatriots. Even the famed architect Claude-Nicolas Ledoux—"this most singularly high-flown personage"—whose work Beckford admired greatly, had experienced an initial rebuff.[39]

This reluctance to socialize was not specific to his times in Paris. Indeed, while in England or abroad, Beckford almost never entertained on a large scale, preferring to enjoy the company of a few chosen acquaintances in intimate settings or on outings. The extravagant celebration given on his twenty-first birthday at Fonthill Splendens was said to have been truly exceptional. Over time, his inclination toward singular personalities led him away from conventional social gatherings or protocol, to almost complete seclusion in his final years in Bath. Among the many British aristocrats in the French capital, the outlandish Lady Craven and Lady Clargues were his most intimate friends:

> I cannot quit them—they are no every day copies of every day people—originality marks them for her own, and they act as that glorious power dictates without submission to any rules that were ever established—so do I—no wonder we agree so perfectly.[40]

He also kept in touch with the acquaintances he had met during his 1783–84 Paris trip and his subsequent trips to Portugal and Spain. The musically talented and cosmopolitan dowager Duchess of Berwick (a sister of Princess Louise of Stolberg, the estranged wife of Prince Charles Stuart), whom he had met in Madrid, the Necker family, and the duc and duchesse de la Vallière were some of the few people he saw in Paris on a regular basis around that time. Among the artists he visited were the British painter Maria Cosway—who had painted a miniature portrait of Beckford's wife—as well as Hubert Robert and Jacques-Louis David, soon to become one of France's most celebrated painters.[41] Of his Portuguese and Spanish acquaintances residing in Paris, he socialized with Count and Countess Souza de Couthinho and the eccentric Casimir Pignatelli, Count Fuentes y Egmont, the latter relationship facilitated by their common interest in artwork and men.[42]

In the last decades of the ancien régime Paris offered a more tolerant society for homosexuals than England, and Beckford must have felt unfettered to yield to his quests for male romances. As an anonymous French observer noted in 1784:

> Homosexuality has always been in fashion amongst women, as has pederasty amongst men; but one has never displayed these vices with such scandal and flair as today.[43]

While homosexuality and cross-dressing were considered morally reprehensible acts, their public exposure, widespread among the privileged classes, did not constitute a cause for repression, despite the existence of a special police squad in Paris dedicated to the surveillance of homosexuals since the early eighteenth century. At that time, public order castigated this manner of behavior performed with violence, threat, or abuse. In keeping with the philosophy of the Enlightenment, however, if violence was perceived as an abnormal and socially disruptive occurrence, homosexuality was looked upon as a weak and rather harmless—albeit disgraceful—manifestation of the senses, which therefore did not call for prosecution: it was only condemnable if it prevented an individual from fulfilling his or her conjugal and parental responsibilities. As the Marquis de Condorcet observed in 1786, the crime of sodomy, in effect passable of death penalty, was disproportionate to the little damage it caused to public order:

> Sodomy, when it is not performed with violence, should not fall under the jurisdiction of criminal laws. It does not violate the

right of any other man. It only has an indirect influence on the good order of society, like drunkenness, the love of gambling. It is a base vice, disgusting, for which the only punishment should be contempt.[44]

Consequently, infamous acts perpetrated by members of the royal family or aristocrats, such as the Marquis de Villette's relationship with an Italian actor, did not stir public passions beyond amusement, mockery, or insults. The prosecution of Lenoir and Diot, which led to their public execution at the stake in 1750 for the crime of sodomy, constituted an exception to the general leniency shown by the French authorities toward homosexuals. By the Revolution's onset, homosexuality, although officially equated with the decadence of the ancien régime, became even more open as a result of the decriminalization of the act of sodomy performed in private between consenting partners. Furthermore, according to several pamphlets published around that date to denounce this tolerance, the National Convention was full of homosexuals: the notorious Marquis de Villette, a leader of the National Club and member of the Foreign Affairs Commission, was one among many homosexuals seated at the Convention.[45] In this context of clemency and openness Beckford could have given free rein to his amorous activities, possibly within the revolutionary circles he was known to have frequented.

BECKFORD AND THE FRENCH REVOLUTION

The extent to which Beckford actually embraced the French Revolution remains difficult to assess. His early enthusiasm for the new regime, characteristic of his spirited temperament but equally shared by many Englishmen,[46] seem to have quickly waned as the Revolution and its violent exertions progressed:

> at first [I] felt all the enthusiasms of the time in favour of liberty, an enthusiasm quickly checked by subsequent events.[47]

Whereas his compatriots' reactions closely correlated the Revolution's various political phases, from fervor, curiosity, and disillusionment to horror, Beckford very rapidly entertained no illusions about the true nature of events unfolding under his eyes. As early as 1784, he had astutely remarked upon the country's precarious political future:

> The reality of these liberal wishes & good will to the people at large is so problematical that I am more than persuaded this [illegible] milk of human kindness would turn to the deadliest poison at the first evident assurance of a patriotic thunderstorm —that such a tempest is brewing requires no inspiration to foretell.[48]

Regrettably Beckford left few observations on his stay in Paris during July 1789 when crucial revolutionary events such the fall of the Bastille and the Oath of the Tennis Court in Versailles occurred.[49] In a rare testimony on this period, he reported to a friend from Lausanne later in the summer on how deeply shocked he had been at the sight of violence:

> I still shudder at the recollection of the Kalends of July; and when I think of the midnight processions on the eve of my departure, I am transported in imagination to the Temple of Vitzlipochtli [Mexican war god] rather than the Dome of St. Geneviève [church dedicated to the patron-saint of Paris].[50]

It is improbable that Beckford radically turned his back on the ancien régime at the Revolution's outbreak. For the past decade he had enjoyed both the pomp and glory tangential to several continental courts (although both the British envoys in Madrid and Lisbon later refused to introduce him to the respective courts they served), and the social and economic privileges inherent to his aristocratic standing. How could he relate to the lackluster decorum established by the new government when all he had ever cared for was rank, magnificence, pleasure, the arts, and artistic genius? Although he certainly profited from the intense trafficking of artworks to enhance his personal collections, his sensibility must have been particularly harmed by the revolutionaries' repeated assaults against the national patrimony and human creativity in general: the random destruction of churches, the public bonfires of books, the methodical and unfair confiscation of the *émigrés*' possessions, and the massive meltdown of silverware and tapestries with silver and gold thread may have contributed to his growing dissatisfaction with the new regime. From another perspective, his considerable commercial interests in Jamaica may well have predisposed him to oppose the newly proclaimed equalitarian principles and antislavery laws in the French possessions, which would have threatened his own financial situation had the British government not severely muzzled any form of social uprising in the colonies.

A curious account published in Paris in 1802 offers a rare insight into Beckford's opinions on revolutionary events, though the source's reliability is subject to interpretation and caution. It consists of a collection of casual observations made by Beckford during August 1792 while he was visiting the capital accompanied by the author Pierre-Joseph-Alexandre Roussel d'Epinal.[51] The tour began with a visit to the Tuileries Palace and proceeded with visits to the Café Valois, National Convention, Convent of the Petits-Augustins, and Palais-Royal among other places of interest. Through this source, Beckford emerges as a highly knowledgeable yet inquisitive observer, admiring Marie-Antoinette's lacquered furniture abandoned in her former apartments, looking for clues to the personalities of royal family members in their furnishings, pondering the causes behind the fall of the monarchy, and lamenting the loss of brilliance of the ancien régime. From the militant *sans-culottes*' miserable-looking uniforms to the manifest lack of spirituality at a wedding ceremony he observed, nothing escaped Beckford's sharp comments. He delighted in the formal beauty of the Jardin des Plantes, but deplored the merging of the social classes into one faceless mass. Although the book's anecdotal content yields little information on Beckford's actual political views, it reveals—if it is factual, as the author affirms in the introduction—Beckford's rare ability to mingle with all types of individuals and immerse himself at the core of action, while maintaining an objective and secure position in the most unusual situations. He wrote in 1790: "What care I for Aristocrates or Democrates. I am an—Autocrate—determined to make the most of every situation."[52]

Throughout his time in Paris until the spring of 1793 (interspersed with a few excursions to Switzerland), Beckford made no effort to dispel doubts on his political convictions, preferring to maintain an equivocal position that certainly better served his interests. His situation was indeed a delicate one, as he had to play a prudent game on two fronts: reassure the French authorities that he did not pose a political threat to the new regime and prove to his fellow countrymen that he was not a revolutionary tied to the Jacobins. Several documents, however, unquestionably establish that he was courted by some members of the Convention to settle in France at a time when the government held all foreigners in distrust and spy reports on counter-revolutionary activities led by Englishmen abounded.[53] In a letter of December 1791 Beckford informed Sir William Hamilton, for instance, that he had recently entertained a group of deputies from the National Convention at home. They may have responded to his invitation in the hope of convincing him to settle in France as an undated letter sent by Beckford to Wildman infers. Both a report issued by the government on Beckford's eligibility for French citizenship and an investigation drafted by a local political assembly in 1793 undoubtedly confirm that his presence in France was indeed looked upon favorably by French officials:

> . . . this Englishman was generally esteemed for his revolutionary principles . . . Inspired by the love of freedom, he then sought to purchase a national domain in order to settle altogether in France, but having not found something that suited his fancy, he was forced, by the fate of circumstances, to return to England. He left the country, with the regrets of the *sansculottes* and the esteem of the authorities in place in Paris.[54]

The reference to Beckford's attempts to buy a national domain may refer to negotiation led by his banker Perregaux and friends Auguste and Chardin to acquire the Hôtel de Boulogne in 1791 in his name and as a gesture to shield some of his assets from seizure.[55] The transaction fell through for unknown reasons, but Beckford's longtime acquaintance with Jacques Necker, his undisguised dislike of France's utmost enemy, William Pitt, as well as the lasting prestige enjoyed in revolutionary circles by his father, Alderman Beckford, must have served as satisfying proof of Beckford's loyalty to France and French revolutionary principles and, therefore, the nonthreatening nature of his residency.

Evidently, in the uncertain climate of 1792–93, only Beckford's effective if not sincere republican alliances could have saved him from persecution. Unlike countless foreigners perceived by the revolutionary regime either as likely spies or potential agitators, he never endured any

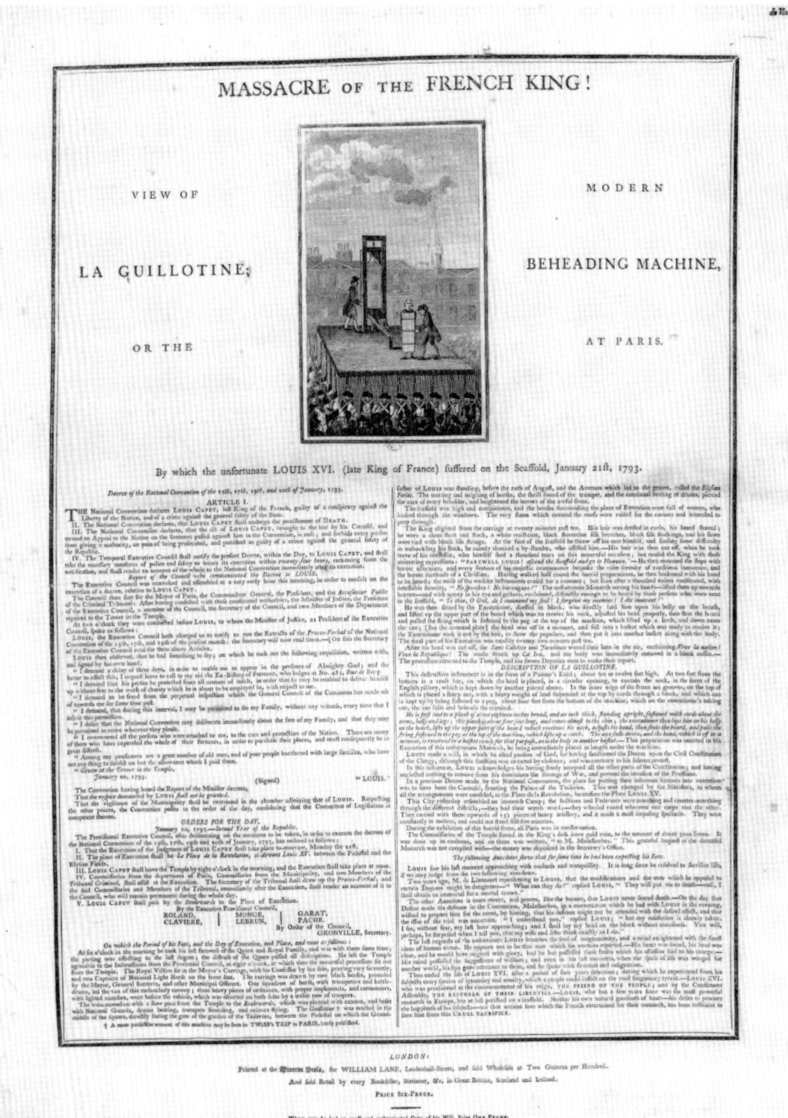

Fig. 6-8. English broadside reporting the execution of King Louis XVI on January 21, 1793. Cabinet des Estampes, Bibliothèque Nationale de France, Paris.

form of arrest or threat against his person or fortune. Thomas Billington, for example, who had been residing in France since 1790, "out of choice and love for the arts and Liberty," very much like Beckford himself, had been one of the new regime's victims, as had been Elizabeth and Anne Whitherhill and John Davies who were all arrested and sent to jail around 1792.[56] Rank and wealth did not prevent political trouble. The wealthy landowner Louis Disney-Ffichte, the Whig Quintin Crawford, the Scottish banker Walter Boyd and his business partner John William Ker, also suffered the drastic consequences of the legislation against foreigners, rigorously enforced following England's declaration of war against France on February 1, 1793. All managed to escape the country in time, but the property they left behind was "confiscated for the benefit of the Republic . . . seized and handed over to the commissars of the National Domain" (decree of October 10, 1793), never to be fully recuperated or compensated for by the Napoleonic regime.[57] Longtime residents in France, such as Lord and Lady Kerry, Henry Seymour (nephew of the first Duke of Somerset), Louis Disney-Ffitche, and Casimir Pignatelli were proclaimed *émigré*, a classification signifying the death penalty for those returning to France from abroad during revolutionary exactions. It is noteworthy that Beckford was also listed as an *émigré* but only subsequent to his departure in May 1793.[58] Unlike his fellow compatriots, direct threats against his person and possessions did not appear to have materialized before then.

However esteemed by the Jacobins Beckford may have been, he was fully aware of the dangers of his position. Ironically, the immediate threat came from England. The Tory cabinet led by Pitt had adopted the Traitorous Correspondence Act in April 1793, on the recommendation of the newly appointed Lord Loughborough, Lord Chancellor and Beckford's personal enemy in the Powderham Castle scandal. This bill made it high treason, punishable by hanging, beheading, quartering, or the forfeiture of all possessions, to have any correspondence with the French or to enter into any political arrangements. While Beckford attempted to reassure Wildman that "there never existed in Paris a single scrap of my writing in which my political opinion was conveyed. I cannot therefore be accused of traitorous correspondence,"[59] England had declared war against France following Louis XVI's execution on January 21, 1793 (fig. 6-8). Beckford was still in Paris three months later, although by then feverishly seeking a visa. Thanks to pressure from an unidentified source applied to the administration, the visa was finally granted to him only ten days after his initial request, whereas some less-fortunate travelers had been waiting for more than three months. Beckford hastily left Paris and sailed to England in May 1793. On his passport was inscribed the unambiguous mention "foreigner which Paris regrets to see leave."[60]

Beckford reached Fonthill Splendens after an arduous journey through the strife-ridden French countryside and various administrative setbacks. He had abandoned some three thousand fine paintings, amassed for his collection.[61] Some of his horses had been seized on the way, and he had been arrested in Arras for having his footmen wear green liveries, a color considered a "symbol of feudalism."[62] Furthermore, forty-five cases containing rare books, fine porcelain, furniture, and silverware were held at Calais in 1794 by order of the National Convention. By attempting to export such vast quantities of precious possessions, Beckford had overestimated his good standing in France. Several decrees adopted by the National Convention that year forbade exports, whether commercial or personal, to countries at war with France: the goods were confiscated and dispatched to the appropriate administrations. Consequently, in strict observance of the law, Beckford's silver was sent to the mint and his books were dispatched to the newly founded Bibliothèque Nationale.[63]

BECKFORD AND HIS PARISIAN AGENTS

Over the following years, while at Splendens, Fonthill Abbey, or traveling, Beckford kept close contact with France, regularly inquiring about the French state of affairs and instructing his agents, such as Chardin and Auguste, on property claims, purchases, and ongoing commissions. The sale of de Calonnes's painting collection advertised in the *Morning Chronicle* on February 1795 tantalized his imagination:

> Where will people find money or confidence at this critical period big with invasion and bankruptcies to bid for such high-priced capital pictures ?[64]

In order to avoid missing any outstanding opportunities while away from France, Beckford extended his network of reliable agents to Jean- Frédéric Perregaux who had been his banker in France since the mid-1780s. By a proxy dated February 20, 1796, Beckford entrusted Perregaux with all due powers to represent him under all circumstances in his French affairs.[65] His choice was perfectly legitimate and sensible: Perregaux had not only been the official banker of the English community in France since 1781 (a 1791 police report concluded that "he is the damned soul of all the English people"), but he also maintained close personal ties with leading artists and craftsmen known to Beckford, which must have facilitated certain transactions.[66] Members of the English aristocracy, such as the Duchess of Devonshire, the Duke of Dorset, and Lord Elgin, as well as manufacturers such as Josiah Wedgwood and bankers such as Thomas Coutts, all maintained accounts at Perregaux & Co. They took advantage of his incomparable ability to obtain almost anything. Together with Chardin and Auguste, Perregaux worked to defend Beckford's interests in France in close collaboration with Beckford's trusted agent, Captain Nicholas Williams.

Williams was dispatched to Paris in 1797 on a multifold mission, which would last for five months. The presence alone of an agent acting on his behalf in France when all foreigners were at risk of imprisonment is indicative of Beckford's commented and lasting privileged status in France. Williams himself commented to one of his friends:

> You . . . will be gratified to hear that whatever party prevail'd, M. B[eckford] has ever been held in the same estimation and his interest remained undiminished, and tho' every other Englishman has been sent out of Paris, I remain with the most positive assurance of his protection in secure possession of his property. This friendship has arisen from his known abilities and moderation, and the great encouragement he gave to Arts and Manufactories while he was in the Country.[67]

One of Williams's key missions lay in his attempt to negotiate a secret agreement with the Directoire representatives, which Beckford secretly hoped would establish him as a sagacious if not brilliant politician. While Williams was gathering information and making preliminary inquiries in France, Beckford actively worked behind the scene, exchanging correspondence with the Duke of Portland, Lord Thurlow, and William Pitt. Commenting on these efforts, Williams wrote:

I sincerely hope the English Government will wisely listen to reason and incline for peace . . . Great indeed would be the merit and praise due to that man who could avert from mankind the horrid devastation that is about to overspread the face of Europe . . .[68]

Ultimately Beckford's ambitious diplomatic scheme failed, arguably because of Pitt's personal reluctance to consider a project submitted by his former childhood friend whom he had come to despise. The genuine motivation behind the project, however, was probably Beckford's high hopes that Williams would be able to retrieve his Parisian assets confiscated by the French government following the decree of October 10, 1793, and to locate the containers seized at Calais in 1794. His correspondence with Williams abounds with instructions on the repatriation of his possessions. He was particularly keen on the return of a "certain China bason [sic] mounted on 3 griffins of gilt bronze . . . ranked amongst the first specimens of porcelain in Europe," as well as that of "two small Japan cabinets . . . , one in the shape of a sort of baby House with galleries and sliding doors &c.; the other with rich folding Doors inlaid with Mother of pearl and gold Mosaic" which he had recently acquired.[69] His risky and ambitious scheme soon paid off. Thanks to the joint efforts of Williams and the painter Piat-Joseph Sauvage, another of Beckford's valuable French connections, the seals on his possessions in Calais and Paris were removed in June 1797. In light of the fact that France and England were still at war, this outcome was particularly fortunate. These holdings were probably repatriated to England later that year.[70]

Williams also took the opportunity to make sure that new acquisitions made by Chardin were shipped back to England, and that several ongoing furniture commissions were progressing as planned. Among the pieces on order was a unique jewel cabinet ("meuble de boudoir pour servir de cabinet") executed in part by the famous cabinetmaker Adam Weisweiler under the supervision of Sauvage. This spectacular piece had been ordered by Beckford in April 1793, right before his departure for an eight-year hiatus. It was completed in 1801, and advertised in the *Journal de Paris*.[71]

THE NAPOLEONIC YEARS, 1801–14

With the signature of the Amiens preliminary peace agreement between France and England in 1801, Beckford, along with countless foreigners, flocked to Paris in the fall of that year.[72] According to Catherine Wilmot, Paris was becoming "a little England," with over five thousand British visitors.[73] Reasons for this invasion were as diverse as the tourists' interests, ranging from sheer curiosity and excitement to rediscovering the capital after a decade of exile and turmoil (fig. 6-9) and to shopping for fine furnishings and artwork, commented on by an English tourist:

> The modern furniture of highest price is very beautiful, and in admirable taste: Marble is much used, and blended well with

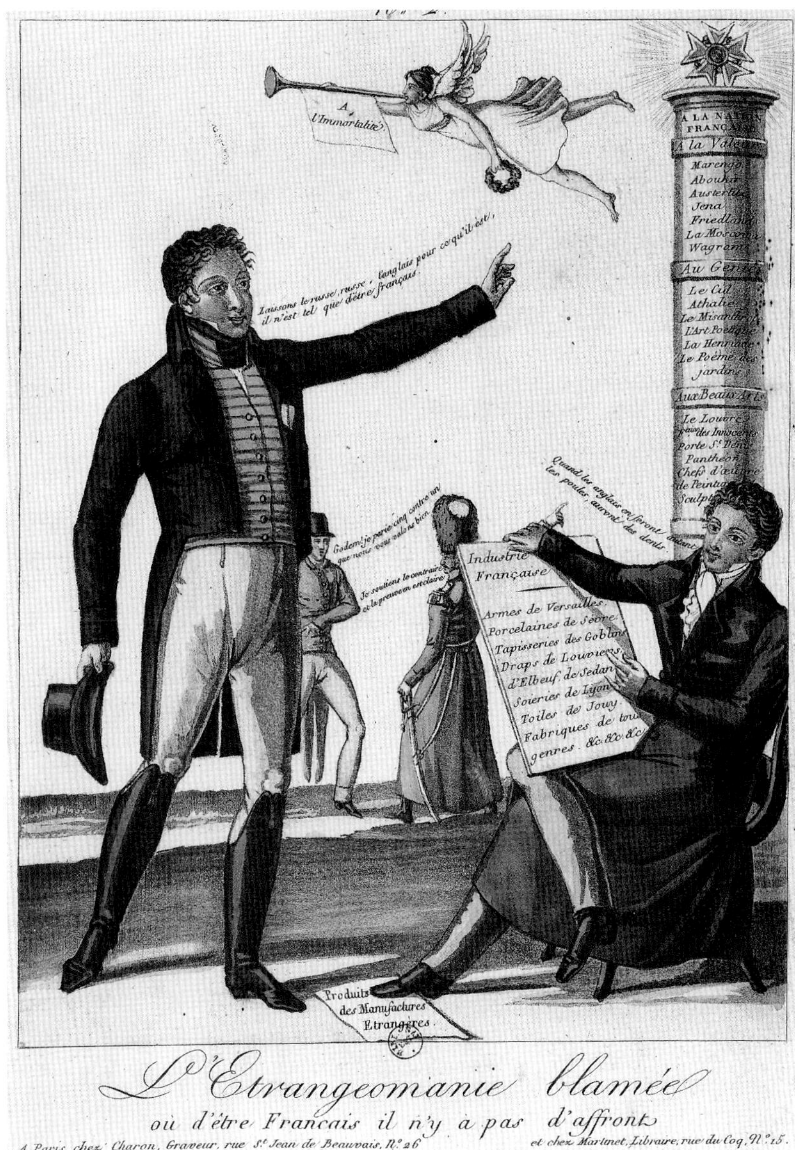

L'Etrangeomanie blâmée
ou d'être Francais il n'y a pas d'affront
A Paris chez Charon, Graveur, rue S.t Jean de Beauvais, N.º 26   et chez Martinet, Libraire, rue du Coq, N.º 15.

Fig. 6-9. A French nationalist engraving celebrating the prestige France and French goods still enjoyed among foreigners after a decade of political turmoil. Cabinet des Estampes, Bibliothèque Nationale de France, Paris.

> wood and bronze, which is really excellent. In the shops the women beat ours both in manners and dress.[74]

England's strong currency against the franc rendered shopping and traveling in France particularly attractive in those days.

A visit to Paris was also an opportunity for many former residents whose possessions had been seized during the Revolution to reclaim them. Indeed, in accordance with a provision of the agreement (article 14), private property illegally confiscated during the Revolution was to be returned to the rightful owner. While some resorted to direct

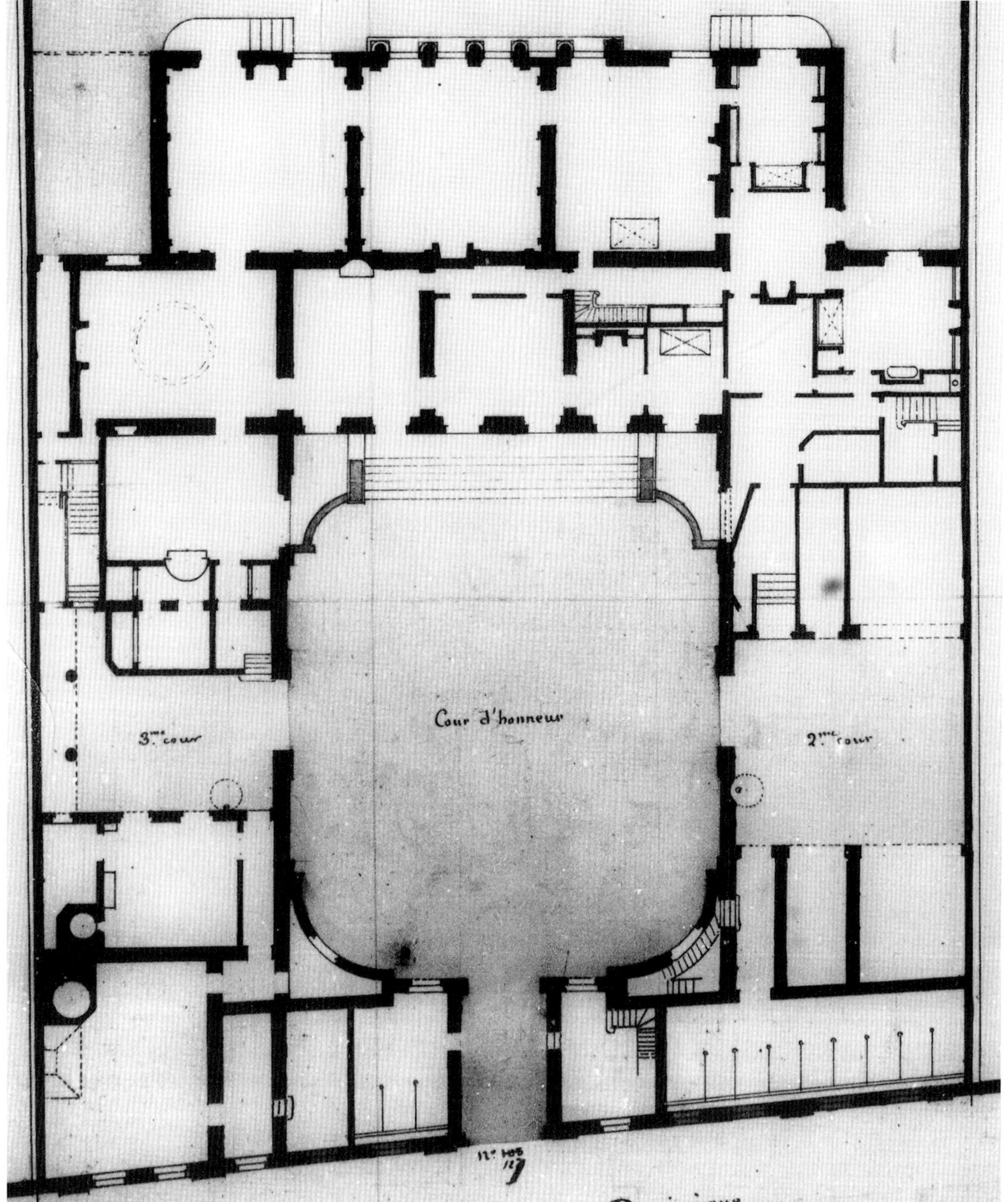

Fig. 6-10. Floor plan of the Hôtel Kinsky, 1823. The plan is almost unchanged from the time of Beckford's residence, 1801–03. Archives Nationales, Paris.

and personal appeals to the Consulate regime, Beckford, who still had some unsettled claims despite Williams's decisive efforts, chose the diplomatic channels. In 1802–3 he petitioned the Minister of Foreign Affairs Charles-Maurice de Talleyrand-Périgord for compensation through the English ambassador in France, Lord Whitworth.[75] Unfortunately, it is impossible to assess how much of an indemnity Beckford was granted or how much of his property was still being held or was returned to him.[76]

Beckford seems to have approved at first of the new Bonapartist regime. Feelings about this government were mixed among English visitors, as a police report of 1802 clearly conveys:

The English people in Paris do not all share the same feelings: most part praise the First Consul, but they are some, who in the reading cabinets and cafés where their compatriots usually assemble, are only preoccupied with censoring the new French government spread bad news and repeat that war will break out soon.[77]

Uncertainty about the future of Franco-English relationships still prevailed, and many visitors to the French capital felt compelled to remain cautious about their opinions. Beckford, on the other hand, may have shown his support for the Bonapartist regime by viewing a grandiose procession held in honor of the First Consul's birthday in 1802. More than anything, he commended the decorum and splendor associated with the restoration of power. Disillusionment was soon in coming, however, as Bonaparte's repeated military campaigns and irreversible march toward European domination revealed to Beckford unmistakable signs of brutality. Beckford's forced departure with thousands of visitors in 1803, after the renewal of hostilities between the two countries dealt a severe blow to his initial enthusiasm. Writing to his friend Count Egmont-Pignatelli in 1805, he despaired over the dreadful circumstances that kept him away from France, and begged the count to intercede to the authorities on his behalf.[78]

Significantly Beckford, after a short stay at the famous Hôtel de l'Empire on the rue Cerutti, chosen to settle again in the Faubourg Saint-Germain, renting the Hôtel Kinsky (or de Kinsky, formerly known as the Hôtel de Gourges and Lamoignon) on rue Saint-Dominique (see fig. 6-3).[79] Indeed, as the Francophile chronicler Mary Berry observed during her visit to Paris in 1802,

> the hotels of the F. St. Germain are no longer the fashion, as they used to be. The brilliant *quartier* is the one we left [the Chaussée d'Antin], and is so far convenient that it is now near all the theaters, and in the Hôtel de l'Empire there are certainly the most elegant apartments . . .[80]

Real estate speculation and urban development led by the architect Samson-Nicolas Lenoir in the early 1780s and newly found prosperity among leading members of the Bonapartist government eager to move to an animated neighborhood with a cleaner air had contributed to make the Chaussée d'Antin (also called the *quartier* Poissonnière), situated in the north of Paris, the most desirable district of the capital with its impressive coterie of luxurious residences that had been built shortly before the Revolution.[81] The celebrated beauty Mme Récamier, Général Moreau, Perregaux, and Madame Mère were among the privileged set that enjoyed the proximity of bustling cafés (Bal du Prado), theaters (Théâtre de la Porte Saint-Martin, de Vaudeville), amusement parks (Bains Chinois), and concert halls (Concerts Français). The Portuguese ambassador Count Souza de Couthinho and Lord Kerry had been among the first foreigners to settle in this new neighborhood, each renting splendid houses on the rue d'Artois (renamed rue Cerutti from 1792 to 1814, now rue Lafayette).[82]

Why Beckford, who possessed the ample means to settle wherever he wanted and mingle with the most fashionable sets in the new society, chose the Faubourg Saint-Germain over the Chaussée d'Antin well illustrates his genuine snobbery and quest for beauty and sophistication over the mere dictates of fashion. Whereas most of his fellow contemporaries rejected any artistic or historical associations with the ancien régime, Beckford actively sought to recapture its glorious evocations and patrimony. The Hôtel Kinsky, with one of the few interiors to have survived the Revolution almost intact, perfectly embodied the formal lifestyle of the ancien régime in which Beckford had thrived. Its former owner, Princess Kinsky, a Hungarian aristocrat *née* Marie-Léopoldine-Monique Pàlffy, had devoted herself to decorating the residence with the most luxurious productions from skilled craftsmen, famous *marchands-merciers*, and royal manufactories almost up to her death in 1794. Coincidentally its refurbishment had been completed in 1792 by the architect Charles-Joaquim Bénard who had supervised the Hôtel d'Orsay's renovation. The contents of the Hôtel Kinsky had been auctioned off in 1796, but most of the building and its architectural shell had survived untouched because it had never been confiscated by the revolutionary administration of the *Régie des domaines*.[83] In 1795, the house was advertised for sale by the princess's estate representative, Citizen Boilleau, as "large and attractive . . . very well planned-out and pleasant . . . with two very beautiful apartments with parquetry floors, decorated with mirrors and boiseries."[84]

Beckford rented the property for 5,000 francs from November 1801 until spring 1803 (fig. 6-10).[85] The townhouse was famed for its grounds, which had been landscaped in the Anglo-Indian taste by the gardener John Williams. The extensive facilities could comfortably accommodate Beckford's princely retinue of over sixty, and there was a stable for fifty horses. The right to undertake any construction, changes, and renovations had been granted, but in effect architectural projects remained minimal.[86] Only the conservatory filled with exotic plants and flowers and the orange house were torn down, and nothing was erected in their place.[87] Rather, Beckford, with the assistance of the architect Larsonneur, concentrated his efforts on refurnishing the *hôtel* in the most ornate fashion as publicized in a placard in the *Petites Affiches* announcing the auction of the *hôtel* upon the termination of the lease in spring 1803. Over 18,000 francs had been spent on mirrors alone![88]

Beckford, who disliked the rigid and masculine late manifestation of neoclassicism favored during the Empire period (1804–15), actively pursued masterpieces of eighteenth-century furniture, books, paintings, and Oriental wares.[89] While he had always appreciated lacquer objects, his taste had grown more eclectic and remarkable with time. His rejection of the monumental and rigid lines characteristic of the decorative arts produced in this style, may have restrained his commissioning of contemporary creations, and, thus, assisted in widening his interests as a collector. Fortunately, Paris continued to offer outstanding opportunities for collectors. The Duc de Bouillon sale held in June 1801, for instance, proved to be an exceptional source of delight for Beckford who still enjoyed comfortable revenues from his West Indies sugar plantations.[90]

War between France and England following the eighteen-month peace forced Beckford out of Paris in 1803, on an exile which would last for over a decade. His emotional correspondence with his French acquaintances during this period attests to his great affliction over this situation.[91] He, nonetheless, kept a close interest in the Parisian art market, regularly inquiring from Chardin about potential acquisitions or auctions. When he finally returned to Paris from October to December 7, 1814, he continued to purchase works of art, though not with quite the same panache and flair, as his ambitious building project at Fonthill Abbey was by then his true priority. He relied more heavily on his agents, such as Franchi and M. Constantin, to make discoveries. On the 1814 trip, however, he secured for Fonthill Abbey two sixteenth-century stained-glass panels "after or by Jean Cousin, from the chapel of Gaillon," though his academic interests in literature and fine arts seem to have prevailed overall.[92] He went to the Bibliothèque Nationale to look at Persian, Greek, and Arabic manuscripts, as well as to the Louvre where the director, Dominique Vivant Denon, showed him the Italian Primitive galleries. To his great dismay he found "the majority of the pictures before Raphaël [to be] miseries, regilded and repainted, without value and without authenticity," and the gallery to present "bad lighting, false daylight, no harmony or effect or mystery."[93] He also visited Malmaison, Joséphine and Napoléon's former private residence located west of the capital, which greatly pleased him. It may have been on this occasion that he discovered the large center table with an extraordinary marble slab presented by Napoléon to Joséphine, which he possibly acquired at the 1816 Malmaison sale (see cat. no. 88). It is uncertain whether he bought the table with its gilt-bronze dolphins or just its slab, but it was prominently placed in the Grand Drawing Room at Fonthill Abbey among other fine examples of French decorative arts acquired over the years (see fig. 7-10).[94] On this final visit in 1814, of which little is known, the magic and fascination he had experienced as a young man had vanished. Not only had French society lost the enchanting brilliance and refinement emblematic of the ancien régime, but, by then, his fortune and energy were beginning to dwindle. The financial problems that would be brought on by his ambitious building schemes and frantic purchases, as well as literary aspirations, would supplant his desire for continental travels and new experiences: Fonthill Abbey had become his preoccupation, but it too would fall from favor nearly a decade later.

A many-sided man, Beckford led a singular life, between Enlightenment and Romanticism, and Paris had occupied a crucial position in his early years. Whimsical yet rational, prodigal yet egotistical, avant-garde yet old-fashioned, effusive yet reclusive, Beckford had found in Paris a city that satisfied his endless quest for beauty, intellectual stimulation, and sensual pleasures, while serving as both a haven from his torments and a training ground for his artistic sensibility. A discriminating collector and connoisseur of both contemporary artwork and rare objects, Beckford undoubtedly trained his eye during his Parisian years, not only through extensive visits to salesrooms and museums, but also in his regular and personal communication with manufacturers and craftsmen. His enthusiasm for a wide range of art forms, styles, and provenances, and his constant personal involvement in the design process, resulting from his first-hand contact with numerous artists and artworks, were unique among his contemporaries. Other great francophiles of varying intensity such as John Soane, Thomas Hope, and the Prince Regent, for instance, never set foot in Paris, and their collections reflected a less eclectic and well-rounded sensibility.[95] Beckford's honing of his artistic expertise and constant preoccupation with his surroundings clearly set him apart as an true aesthete, and as such, his adventurous collecting foreshadowed that of future generations of amateurs, who included Lord Hertford, Richard Wallace, Anatole Prince Demidoff, and the Rothschilds. The successful dispersal of Beckford's possessions at auction throughout the nineteenth century well demonstrate the premium placed upon his discriminating eye and helped to establish him as one of the most unusual and visionary personalities of his time.

Acknowledgments: I am grateful to Ulrich Leben for his unfailing support and generosity.—AE

Archives: The Beckford Papers are kept largely in the Bodleian Library, Oxford. and are cited as "MS Beckford." The French archives consulted for the preparation of this essay include the Bibliothèque Nationale de France (BNF), Archives Nationales (AN), Archives de Paris, Archives du Ministère des Affaires Etrangères, all in Paris. Abbreviations are used in the citations below. All the translations are the author's own.

1. This expression was used by the French poet Stéphane Mallarmé, who had discovered William Beckford's literary production while visiting the British Museum's library in 1875; see preface to *Contes Cruels* by Villiers de l'Isle (Paris, 1876). It well captured the essence of Beckford's exceptional life and personality.

2. Remarkably Beckford scarcely discussed this period with the journalist Cyrus Redding who became his first biographer. Redding only commented that "Mr Beckford watched the events of the Revolution with a keen eye" (*Memoirs of William Beckford of Fonthill, Author of Vathek*, vol. 2 [London: Charles J. Skeet, 1859]: 42).

3. Beckford's puzzling silence on his French sojourns was underscored by the French scholar André Parreaux (*William Beckford, auteur de Vathek (1760–1844)* [Paris: A. G. Nizet, 1960]: 44). This situation was also noted by others, most recently, Timothy Mowl (*William Beckford. Composing for Mozart* [London: John Murray, 1998]: 201).

4. A police report of 1 August 1788 noted that "M. Beckford, English gentleman, member of Parliament for the town of Arundel in the county of Sussex, arrived here last week, and stayed at the hôtel Prince de Galles, rue du Colombier. This gentleman comes from Spain where he traveled for a almost a year: he will spend some time in this capital and will then go back to England" (AMAE, *Contrôle des étrangers*, vol. 69).

5. A *hôtel* or *hôtel particulier* is the name given by the French to a grand townhouse, seat of an aristocrat or wealthy owner and family. Unlike Bristish aristocrats, a French nobleman spent more time in his *hôtel* than in his country houses on his estates. The most important ones in Paris were built by famous architects in the second half of the seventeenth century until the Revolution. Many of these elegant buildings can still be seen in the Marais and the faubourgs Saint-Germain and Saint-Honoré.

6. ". . . le faubourg Saint-Germain n'admettait personne dans ses rangs. Pour en faire partie, il fallait y être né, y avoir de la famille, ou bien être étranger recommendé et riche. La recommendation est moins nécessaire que la richesse," in Comtesse Dash, *Mémoires des autres*, vol. 2 (Paris: A la librairie illustrée, [ca. 1870]): 199–200. "Comtesse Dash" was the pseudonym of Anne-Gabrielle de Cisternes de Courtiras, vicomtesse Poilloüe de Saint-Mars.

7. The *hôtel* is located at 69 rue de Varenne. For a detailed history and a biography of the comte d'Orsay, see *Le Faubourg Saint-Germain. La rue de Varenne*, exh. cat., Délégation à l'Action Artistique de la Ville de Paris (Paris: Musée Rodin, 1981): 64–74; and Bruno Pons, *French Period Rooms, 1650–1800* (Dijon: Editions Faton, 1995): 324–33. The cabinetmakers Pierre Roussel, Jean-

François Leleu, Jean-Henri Riesener, and Louis Delanois supplied most of the furniture.

8. AN, Z/1j/1125, 13 October 1784.

9. "Ce fils de financier a donné dans les arts et en effet possède une des maisons de Paris les plus curieuses à voir pour la richesse, le goût, le luxe et les singularités qu'elle renferme," quoted in *Le Faubourg Saint-Germain* (1981): 70.

10. AN, MC/ET/LVIII/554, 29 September 1788. "MC" stands for *Minutier central*, the French notaries public records's office kept in the Archives Nationales, Paris. It is subdivided in *études* ("ET"). Each *étude* corresponds to a notary's lifelong activity. All information hereafter in this paragraph have been gleaned from the consultation of the lease.

11. "jouir des lieux . . . et surtout du mobilier en bon père de famille," ibid.

12. Several descriptions of the Hôtel d'Orsay are available for this period, enabling an accurate reconstitution of the building and its interior at the time when it was rented by Beckford. The first document is the detailed statement submitted by Bénard and other contractors involved in its refurbishing (AN, Z/1j/1125); the second source is a report drafted by the *Régie des domaines*, the revolutionary administration in charge of confiscated properties (ADP, DQ10, 209); the last source is a report on the sports events (*jeux gymniques*) held in the *hôtel* between 1797 and 1802 (Jean-François Sobry, *Programme des Jeux Gymniques ouverts à Paris, rue de Varenne, numéro 667* [Paris: Imprimerie de J.-F. Sobry, 1797]: 33–8). The newly constructed dining room under the rotunda featured stuccoed walls, imitating colored alabaster inset with classical low-reliefs; gilt ceramic figures were arranged about the room. The billiard room's ceiling was painted with allegorical *grisailles* representing the seasons and the arts; the great gilt-paneled saloon was designed with Corinthian pilasters framing carved trophies and pier-glasses placed above richly gilt consoles (sold at Christie's London, December 10, 1992, lots 402–3); one of the bedrooms displayed a bed raised on an enclosed stage and placed in an alcove framed by four columns veneered in green porphyry; in the library was a large work table resting on fourteen marble columns and fitted with bookcases at each end; and the music room was adorned with massive doors carved with musical trophies. The only original elements remaining from the 1773 decorating scheme were Hugues Taraval's paintings, *Psyche's Apotheosis,* for the great saloon's ceiling and the composition in the billiard room. Taraval had also completed in the early 1780s the decor of a small boudoir painted with allegorical figures amid arabesques (see above, n. 7).

13. "un morceau de 7. pieds de large, par 3. pieds 6. pouces de hauteur, représentant un bouquet, sur un fond favorable pour en faire ressortir les fleurs, et encadré dans une bordure à moulures imitant l'or, mêlé de feuillages de chesne verd [*sic*] le tout de la plus parfaite exécution," AN, 01/2053/B, 17 June 1791. It measured 227 cm wide, 113 cm high (89 x 44½ in).

14. For a complete history of the Savonnerie manufactory, see Pierre Verlet, *The James A. de Rothschild Collection at Waddesdon Manor. The Savonnerie* (Fribourg: Office du Livre, 1982): esp. appendices B and C.

15. For correspondence on this commission, first published in ibid., pp. 520–23, see AN, O1/2052/B and O1/2057/A. A search through the records did not reveal the first names of Guillaumot and Delaporte.

16. This observation is based on an analysis of the Sèvres manufactory's ledgers which survive intact in the archives.

17. "M. Beckfort, qui est un homme fort riche et amateur de productions des arts, rassemble chez lui à Londres quantité de personnes distinguées," AN, O1/2057/A.

18. I am grateful to Derek E. Ostergard for bringing this important connection to my attention.

19. "Henry Auguste" and "Henri Auguste" are used interchangeably in the literature. M. Olivier Gaube du Gers, director of Souche-Laparra and former director of the Maison Odiot, has confirmed that while a number of Auguste's designs have survived, his order books, if still extant, have not been located (personal communication, 12 April 2001). When Auguste went bankrupt for the second time, in 1809–10 (first banckruptcy in 1806), a number of his designs were acquired by his competitor Jean-Baptiste-Claude Odiot. Part of this collection was sold by the Maison Odiot (Sotheby's, Monaco, 26 November 1979).

20. Entry dated 23 December 1787, *The Journal of William Beckford in Portugal and Spain,* ed. Boyd Alexander (London: Rupert Hart-Davis, 1954): 301.

21. *The Hamilton and Nelson Papers*, The Collection of Autograph Letters and Historical Documents formed by Alfred Morrison, 2d ser., vol. 1, *1756–1797* (Privately published, 1893): 165, February 27, 1792.

22. This conclusion was also reached by Micheal Snodin and Malcom Baker who have analyzed Beckford's extensive silver collection in "William Beckford's Silver," parts 1 and 2, *Burlington Magazine* 122, no. 932 (1980): 735–48; no. 933 (1980): 820–34.

23. "une bibliothèque évaluée à deux cents mille livres, composée de tous les chefs d'oeuvres de tipographie [*sic*] tant grecs que latin et français," AN, F7/4639, fol. 3, ca. 1793.

24. See Beckford's account of the sale to his cousin Louisa, 2 November 1784, MS Beckford c. 18, fols. 51–52.

25. Details of this affair can be found in AN, AF*/II/292, fol. 88 and F7/4639, fol. 3. Copies of several reports related to this case are kept in the Bibliothèque Nationale de France: *Rapport fait par Junius Dupérou . . .* (8-Lb40-1753); *Lettre du citoyen Leymerie . . .* (8-Lb41-1709); *Réponse du citoyen Chardin . . .* (8-Lb41-1214). See also Grégoire Morgulis, "Un épisode de la vie de William Beckford," *Revue de Littérature Comparée* 14 (1934): 690–94.

26. "This Chardin is the best consolation left to me, and for my part, I shall know how to give him all the proofs of friendship and trust he can want" (Beckford probably to Franchi, 22 July 1814, quoted in to come [Hart-Davies or Oliver or Boyd?,] 155).

27. The *Garde-Meuble*, founded in 1663, was the royal institution in charge of the administration and upkeep of the furniture and furnishings for royal use. At its head was the *intendant et contrôleur général des Meubles de la Couronne* who was appointed by the king. The *intendant's* principal mission consisted in receiving orders for new pieces from the royal family, and farming them out to the most talented craftsmen. He also supervised all the moves between the numerous royal residences. For more on the *Garde-Meuble*, see Pierre Verlet, *Le mobilier royal français. Meubles de la Couronne conservés en France, avec une étude sur le Garde-Meuble de la Couronne* (Paris: Librairie Plon, 1956): 9–41.

28. Dorothée Guilleme-Brulon, "François-Louis Godon, horloger et agent du roi d'Espagne," *L'Estampille* 185 (October 1985): 56–58. Godon also exported furniture to the Spanish Court on behalf of Parisian dealers.

29. Little research has been done on the art-market during the French Revolution, partly of scanty minutes of the revolutionary auctions kept in the Archives départementales des Yvelines. For a pioneering study of this topic, see Michel Beurdeley, *La France à l'encan 1789–1799. Exode des objets d'art sous la Révolution* (Paris: Tallandier, 1981); see also idem, "Lebrun, l'expert-marchand-aventurier," *Connaissance des Arts* (1989): 27–31; and Christian Baulez, "Versailles à l'encan, " ibid., pp. 34–42. For a study on Parisian furniture workshops during this period, see "Les ateliers parisiens dans la tourmente révolutionnaire," chapter 6 in Anne Forray-Carlier, *Le mobilier du musée Carnavalet* (Dijon: Editions Faton, 2000).

30. "pour des clients riches et suffisamment avertis pour apprécier les occasions que la Révolution leur offre," quoted in Beurdeley, *La France à l'encan* (1981): 33.

31. In 1814 Fogg may have sold to Beckford the imposing pair of armoires attributed to André–Charles Boulle (now in the Louvre Museum, OA 9518–9519), probably acquired on the Parisian art-market during the Revolution. For further discussion on this issue, see chap. 10, by Adriana Turpin, in this volume. Beckford's reluctance—or inability—to keep records of his acquisitions compounds the difficulty to trace the sources of many important pieces. Indeed, another puzzling provenance is that of the famous roll-top desk executed by Jean-Henri Riesener for the comte d'Orsay, now in the Wallace Collection, London (F102). Though Chardin is known to have attended Orsay's auction held on September 12, 1791, there are no grounds for assuming that the desk was purchased then. When the *hôtel* was confiscated during the Revolution, the dealer Jean-Baptiste-Pierre Lebrun seized the remaining furniture for the benefit of the Commission des Arts, which was stored at the hôtel de Nesles on the rue de Beaune. There representatives of the newly founded Muséum Central could select artworks deemed suitable for the national collections; see Marc Furcy-Raynaud, *Les tableaux et objets d'art saisis chez les émigrés et condamnés et envoyés au Muséum Central* (Paris: Daupeley-Gouverneur, 1913): 76–81. The *hôtel* was then occupied by the Commission de la Marine, and the remainder of its contents sold to a pawn-broker in 1799. Michel Beurdeley has suggested that the desk could have directly been purchased by Beckford in a private sale at the end of 1791 ("Paris 1790–1791. Ventes et saisies des collections du comte d'Orsay dans la tourmente révolutionnaire," in *Trois siècles de ventes publiques* [Paris: Tallandier, 1988]: 63–70).

32. A "capital and valuable assemblage of superb articles, in French or-moulu; comprising candelabra, girandoles, clocks, bronze vases . . . imported from Paris by Mons. Daguerre . . ." was sold by James Christie in Pall Mall on 25 March 1791. Christie auctioned Marie-Antoinette's paintings from the château de Saint-Cloud in 1793, the comtesse du Barry's magnificent jewels in 1795, as well the collections of a number of "Foreign gentlemen of Distinction" and other various "French noblement" in exile in England at the time.

33. Quoted in Lewis Melville, *The Life and Letters of William Beckford of Fonthill* (London: William Heineman, 1910): 179.

34. For his correspondence written during his 1784 stay in Paris, see MS Beckford c. 18, particularly fols. 47 and 53.

35. "Faites fortune où vous êtes mais jouissez-en à Paris," quoted in Pierre Robin, *Les séquestres des biens ennemis sous la révolution française* (Paris: Editions Spes, 1929): 13.

36. Letter dated 29 November 1791, quoted in Melville, *Life and Letters* (1910): 179.

37. For further reading on Georgiana, see Amanda Foreman, *Georgiana Duchess of Devonshire* (London: Harper Collins Publishers, 1998).

38. AN, T//779, Meek Papers (in English), 27 October 1782.

39. "He beset my door and my antechamber too for some time before I would grant him admittance. At last, he would take no denial—he rushed in—we met—mutually be-praised and be-flattered each other and became most intimate and confidential," letter to Louisa, 1784, quoted

in John W. Oliver, *The Life of William Beckford* (London: Oxford University Press, 1932): 173; in the same letter (ibid., pp. 171–82), Beckford recounted the bizarre events that occurred when Ledoux brought him to a magnificent residence he had built for a mysterious patron. The two men had first met that year at the comtesse de Souza de Couthinho's house. The architect was then age forty-eight and Beckford only twenty-four. In 1786, Beckford's banker in Paris Jean-Frédéric Perregaux won at a lottery the delightful *hôtel* designed by Ledoux in 1770—known as the Temple of Terpsichore—and put up for sale by the famed dancer Melle Guimard. On Ledoux's life and work, see Michel Gallet, *Claude-Nicolas Ledoux,1736–1806* (Paris: Picard, 1980).

40. Letter to Louisa, 1784, MS Beckford c. 18, fols. 57–58.

41. Beckford commissioned, through the painter Piat-Joseph Sauvage, a painting from Hubert Robert around 1792. He also commissioned a painting representing Saint-Bruno, at a cost of "320 *livres* including wrapping," from Louis Bouchet around that time (MS Beckford c. 26, fol. 153).

42. Beckford later proposed Count Fuentes y Egmont to his daughter Susan Euphemia as a suitable marriage prospect, but she married instead the Marquess of Douglas, future tenth Duke of Hamilton, another of her father's Parisian acquaintances and a distant relative. Another of Beckford's relatives residing then in France was his aunt on his mother's side, Elizabeth Cameron *née* Hamilton, wife of John Cameron. She lived in Saint-Germain-en-Laye, near Versailles, with her daughter Anne-Elizabeth-Charlotte, a pensioner at the royal abbey of Saint-Cyr. Upon John Cameron's death in 1787 Beckford granted his young cousin a life pension of 600 *livres* per year (AN, MC/ET/X/776, 19 May 1788). Elizabeth Cameron remarried a year later to Firmin-Henry, comte de Faÿ (AN, MC/ET/X/777, 22 July 1788).

43. "La tribaderie a toujours été en vogue chez les femmes, comme la pédérasterie chez les hommes; mais on n'avait jamais affiché ces vices avec autant de scandale et d'éclat qu'aujourd'hui," *Mémoires historiques, littéraires, politiques, anecdotiques et critiques de Bachaumont*, 2d ed., vol. 3 (Paris, 1809): 222.

44. "La sodomie lorsqu'il n'y a point de violence, ne peut être du ressort des lois criminelles. Elle ne viole le droit d'aucun autre homme. Elle n'a sur le bon ordre de la société qu'une influence indirecte, comme l'ivrognerie, l'amour du jeu. C'est un vice bas, dégoûtant, dont la véritable punition est le mépris," quoted in Claude Courouve, *Les assemblées de la manchette. Documents sur l'amour masculin au XVIIIe siècle* (Paris: Claude Courouve, 1987): 8. This excellent and concise study of homosexuality in eighteenth-century Paris draws extensively on police records in the Bibliothèque de l'Arsenal.

45. Ibid.; see also Jeffrey Merrick and Bryan Ragan, *Homosexuality in Modern France* (New York: Oxford University Press, 1996).

46. The English ambassador to the French Court, the Duke of Dorset, shared his enthusiasm with the Duke of Leeds in 1789: "Nothing could exceed the regularity and good order with which all this extravagant business has been conducted . . . Thus, my Lord, the greatest revolution that we know anything of has been effected with comparatively speaking—if the magnitude of the event is considered – very few lives. From this moment, we may consider France as a free country, the King a very limited monarch, and the nobility as reduced to a level with the rest of the Nation" (quoted in John Alger, *Englishmen in the French Revolution* [London: Sampson Low, Marston, Searle & Rivingston, 1889]: 25). A speech made by a deputation of Englishmen, Scots, and Irishmen to the National Convention further reveals how supportive of the new regime British residents were as late as 1792. It praised the revolutionaries for their military victories and fight against oppression (*Adresse des Anglois, des Ecossois, et des Irlandois Résidant & domiciliés à Paris, à la Convention Nationale*, Bibliothèque de la Ville de Paris, 604 384).

47. Quoted by Boyd Alexander from Redding, "Memoirs" manuscript, ii, 1.

48. MS Beckford c.18, fol. 54.

49. Mowl noted that Beckford, who was a "play-acting Jacobin," possibly witnessed Louis XVI's capital execution on 21 January 1793, if Beckford's allusions to his biographer Redding that he was the man on horseback represented in several contemporary illustrations are to be believed (*Composing for Mozart* [1998]: 211).

50. Quoted in Boyd Alexander, *England's Wealthiest Son. A Study of William Beckford* (London: Centaur Press, 1962): 142, 1 September 1789.

51. Pierre-Joseph-Alexandre Roussel d'Epinal, *Le château des Tuileries*, 2 vols. (Paris: Lerouge, 1802). The subtitle reads: "Avec des particularités sur la visite que le Lord Bedfort y a faite après le 10 Août 1792." Despite the misspellings (Lord Bedford or Bedfort), it undoubtedly William Beckford who stands behind this name. Not only was the Duke of Bedford in England at the time, but there was no "Lord Bedfort" in the English peerage. Furthermore, there is a reference in the preface to Chardin, Beckford's librarian. Finally, the overall tone of the remarks and type of observations seem consistent with Beckford's personality. This document was first mentioned in connection to Beckford by Didier Girard, *William Beckford. Terroriste au Palais de la Raison* (Paris: José Corti, 1993): 135–36.

52. Beckford to Lady Elizabeth Craven, future Margravine of Anspach, 29 November 1790, quoted in Oliver, *Life of William Beckford* (1932): 209.

53. On this topic, see, for example, a report by the Foreign Affairs Commission, ca. 1792, AN, AF/II/63.

54. "cet Anglais était généralement estimé pour ses principes révolutionnaires . . . inspiré par l'amour de la Liberté, il voulut par la suite acheter un domaine national, afin de se fixer entièrement en France, mais n'ayant pas trouvé sa fantaisie, il fut forcé, par une fatalité de circonstances, de retourner en Angleterre. Il partit accompagné des regrets des sans-culottes et de l'estime des autorités constituées de Paris" (*Rapport fait par Junius Dupérou . . .* , BNF, 8-Lb40–1753, 12–13). The report on Beckford's eligibility for French citizenship is in the Bodleian Library, Oxford.

55. Chardin to Beckford,. MS Beckford c. 27, fol. 93.

56. On Billington, see AN, AF*/II/282, August 18, 1792; on Whitherhill and Davies, see F7/4777.

57. AN, F7/6138/3. On Crawford's auctions, see AN, T//1610 and ADP, DQ10, 137, no. 3811. As in the case of other prominent foreign residents declared *émigré* (Egmont-Pignatelli, Kerry), Crawford's most precious pieces were seized and deposited at the Hôtel de Nesles, where representatives of the Muséum Central could select objects worthy of interest for the national collections (Furcy-Raynaud, *Les tableaux* [1913]: 76–81). Ker and Boyd, however, must have enjoyed some sort of protection. In 1796, the auction of their property was canceled, and their names were removed from the *émigrés'* list (AN, T//1679, no. 1541; for their files confiscated by the Bureau National des Domaines, see AN, T//1604 and AN, F7/4615); for an analysis of political measures taken against foreigners, see Robin, *Les séquestres des biens ennemis* (1929).

58. Beckford's name was removed from the *émigrés'* list on June 24, 1797 (MS Beckford c. 15, fol. 39).

59. Quoted in Oliver, *Life of William Beckford* (1932): 216, 3 May 1793.

60. "étranger que Paris voit partir avec regret," quoted in Parreaux, *William Beckford* (1960): 44. This mention was first recorded in A.V. Arnault, et. al., *Bibliographie nouvelle des contemporains,* vol. 2 (Paris: Librairie historique, 1821): 295. It is also referred to in Louis de Jullian, *Galerie historique des contemporains,* vol. 1 (Mons: Le Roux, 1817–20): 420–1.

61. MS Beckford c. 37, fols. 20–21.

62. AN, AF/II/288.

63. AMAE, *Correspondance politique*, vol. 601, 1802–3, 97. No accession records concerning Beckford's books have been located at the Bibliothèque Nationale. Notwithstanding, there are documented instances of books seized at the time of exportation, and sent to enrich the collections of the Bibliothèque Nationale founded in 1792 in replacement of the Bibliothèque du Roi (Marie-Pierre Laffitte, curator, Département des Manuscrits, Bibliothèque Nationale de France, letter to the author, February 9, 2001; for a history of the Bibliothèque Nationale during the French Revolution, see *1789: Le Patrimoine Libéré*, exh. cat. (Paris: Bibliothèque Nationale, 1989).

64. MS Beckford c. 37, fol. 22.

65. AN, MC/ET/X/826, 24 June 1797.

66. "Perregaux was Lord Malmesbury's bnker in 1790. He was the ambassador of England to France milord Fitzgerald's close friend and banker. . . . [He] is the friend of major Gall, a spy for England. . . . He is the damned soul of all the British" ("Perrégaux était le banquier de Lord Malmesbury en 1790. Il était l'ami intime et le banquier de milord Fitzgerald, ambassadeur d'Angleterre en France . . . [Il] est l'ami du major Gall, espion de l'Angleterre . . . Il est l'âme damnée de tous les anglais", AN, F7/6140, circa 1791. In 1793 Beckford had an overdraft at Perregaux & Co. of 9,032 *livres* and 12 *sous*, a large sum for the time in comparison to other privately held accounts which ran around 1,000 *livres* (AN, F7*/4774/68, 1793). For a study of Perregaux's strong connections with the British community, see Geoffrey de Bellaigue, "Jean-Frédéric Perregaux: The Englishman's Best Friend," *Antologia delle Belle Arti* 29/30 (1986): 80–90.

67. Letter to James Goddard, 9 September 1797, quoted in Melville, *Life and Letters* (1910): 191.

68. Ibid., p. 198.

69. Ibid., p. 247.

70. Williams to Beckford, 27 June 1797, MS Beckford c. 15, fol. 39. Unfortunately, export records detailing the nature of the pieces have not yet been discovered.

71. *Journal de Paris*, 29 September and 9 October 1801 (8 and 18 Vendémiaire *an* X). Details on this commission (AN, F17/1036/B, fol. T) were first brought to light by Christian Baulez; see Ulrich Leben, ed., *Bernard Molitor, 1775–1833*, exh. cat. (Luxembourg: Galerie d'Art de la Ville de Luxembourg, 1995): 86–87.

72. Beckford was granted His Majesty's license to travel to France by the Duke of Portland on 16 May 1801 (MS Beckford c. 34, fol. 79). A French police report recorded Beckford's arrival in the following terms: "Beckford, Gme [for Guillaume, French translation of William], 40 [Beckford was actually 42], Propriétaire, Londres, domicilié 8 rue Cerrutti [sic] à Paris, arrivé le 17 prairial an 9." He was issued a visa for two months (AN, F7/3501, 1802).

73. Catherine Wilmot, *An Irish Peer on the Continent (1801–1803)*, ed. Thomas U. Sadleir (London: Williams and Norgate, 1920): 77.

74. Bertie Greatheed, *An Englishman in Paris: 1803*, ed. J. P. T. Burry and J. C. Barry (London: Geoffrey Bles, 1953): 9.

75. Lord Withworth, Charles, first baron later earl, who had served as an ambassador in Poland,

Saint Petersburg, and Copenhaguen, presented his credentials to First Consul Bonaparte on 7 December 1802.

76. AMAE, *Correspondence politique, Angleterre*, 1802–3, vol. 601, 97. Neither evidence of a settlement for compensation, nor a ministerial clearance for repatriation was found in the French archives.

77. "Les anglais qui sont à Paris ne partagent pas tous les mêmes sentiments: la majeure partie se plait à faire l'éloge du Premier Consul, mais il en est d'autres qui, dans les cabinets de lecture et dans les cafés où se rassemblent ordinairement leurs compatriotes, ne s'occupent que de censurer le gouvernement français, de répandre des mauvaises nouvelles et de répéter que la guerre recommencera avant peu," AN, F7/3830, 1802.

78. MS Beckford c. 29, fols. 122–23, ca. 1805.

79. AN, MC/ET/X/844, 3 November 1801. The *hôtel* was rented from Jacques-Edme Bazin, the de Lamoignon family estate's representative. The de Lamoignons had rented the *hôtel* to Princess Kinsky in 1773, who purchased it in 1777. Upon her death in 1794, since she had no heir, the property returned to the de Lamoignons. The *hôtel*, still standing on 53, rue Saint-Dominique, houses the French administration in charge of music and theater (Direction de la Musique et du Théâtre).

80. Mary Berry, *Extracts of the Journals and Correspondence of Miss Berry, from the year 1783 to 1852*, 2d ed., ed. Lady Theresa Lewis, vol. 2 (London: Longmans, Green and Co., 1866): 132.

81. *Le Faubourg Poissonnière. Architecture, élégance et décor*, exh. cat., Délégation à l'Action Artistique de la Ville de Paris (Paris, 1986).

82. For a complete description of the house rented by Lord Kerry from the banker Jean-Jacques de la Borde, see AN, T//451. The Souza de Couthinho family, who had also rented a residence from de la Borde, moved from the rue d'Artois to the rue Basse-des-Remparts in 1784.

83. For documents on the *hôtel* and its suppliers since 1777, see AN, T//220; for the minutes of the auction held on 28 February 1796, see ADP, DQ10, 786.

84. "Grande et belle maison, très bien distribuée et agréable . . . deux très grands appartements parquettés, ornés de glaces et de boiseries," AN, AD/XXc/70, no. 128, 30 June 1795.

85. Rental contract, 3 November 1801 AN, MC/ET/X/844 (see above, n. 79). The *franc* replaced the old numeral system on April 7, 1795. It was later decreed that 5 silver *francs* equaled 5 *livres*,

1 *sous* and 3 *deniers* (law of April 14, 1796).

86 The lease stated that he "will be allowed to undertake in the house any extension, changes, or embellishments that suit him" ("aura la faculté de faire à la maison tout accroissements, changements et embellissements qui lui conviendront"), ibid.

87. For details on the garden executed by Williams, "entrepreneur et décorateur de jardins," see AN, T//202/5–7.

88. *Petites Affiches*, May 1803, 4291. The architect Larsonneur is not recorded in Michel Gallet, *Les architectes parisiens du XVIIIe siècle* (Paris: Mengès, 1995). Beckford's suppliers in this period are still unknown, as is the fate of the furnishings and works of art acquired to decorate this residence.

89. Didier Girard has inaccurately stated that the famous architect and proponent of the Empire style Charles Percier had designed a bed for Beckford, which is now in a private collection in New York (*William Beckford. Terroriste* [1993]:176–77). This bed was commissioned by his son-in-law, the Duke of Hamilton, when Percier was involved in the refurbishment of Hamilton Palace.

90. Through his agent Dumorth, Beckford purchased a number of important pieces, such as a very fine Japanese lacquer chest and box (now in The Victoria and Albert Museum, London). A year later he added to his Oriental collections a twelve-fold screen from China bought from one Doyen (MS Beckford c. 37, fols. 57, 69, 70–71). For the first mention of these documents, see Francis Watson, *Gazette des Beaux-Arts* (February 1963): 118–9, and *Apollo* (September 1969): 252. For Doyen's receipt, see MS Beckford c. 29, fol. 104.

91. See, e.g., Beckford to Pignatelli, ca. 1805, MS Beckford c. 29, fols. 122–23.

92. For example, "I managed to secure . . . two beautiful staned-glass pieces said to be after or by Jean Cousin from the de Gaillon chapel . . ." ("Je me suis procuré le tout conditionellement deux beaux vitrages soit disant d'après ou de Jean Cousin, provenant de la chapelle de Gaillon . . ."), 13 February 1815, MS Beckford c.37, fol. 113.

93. MS Beckford c. 15, fol. 63.

94. Clive Wainwright, *The Romantic Interior: The British Collector at Home, 1750–1850* (New Haven and London: Yale University Press, 1989): 141.

95. For further discussion of this issue, see chap. 2, by David Watkin, in this volume.

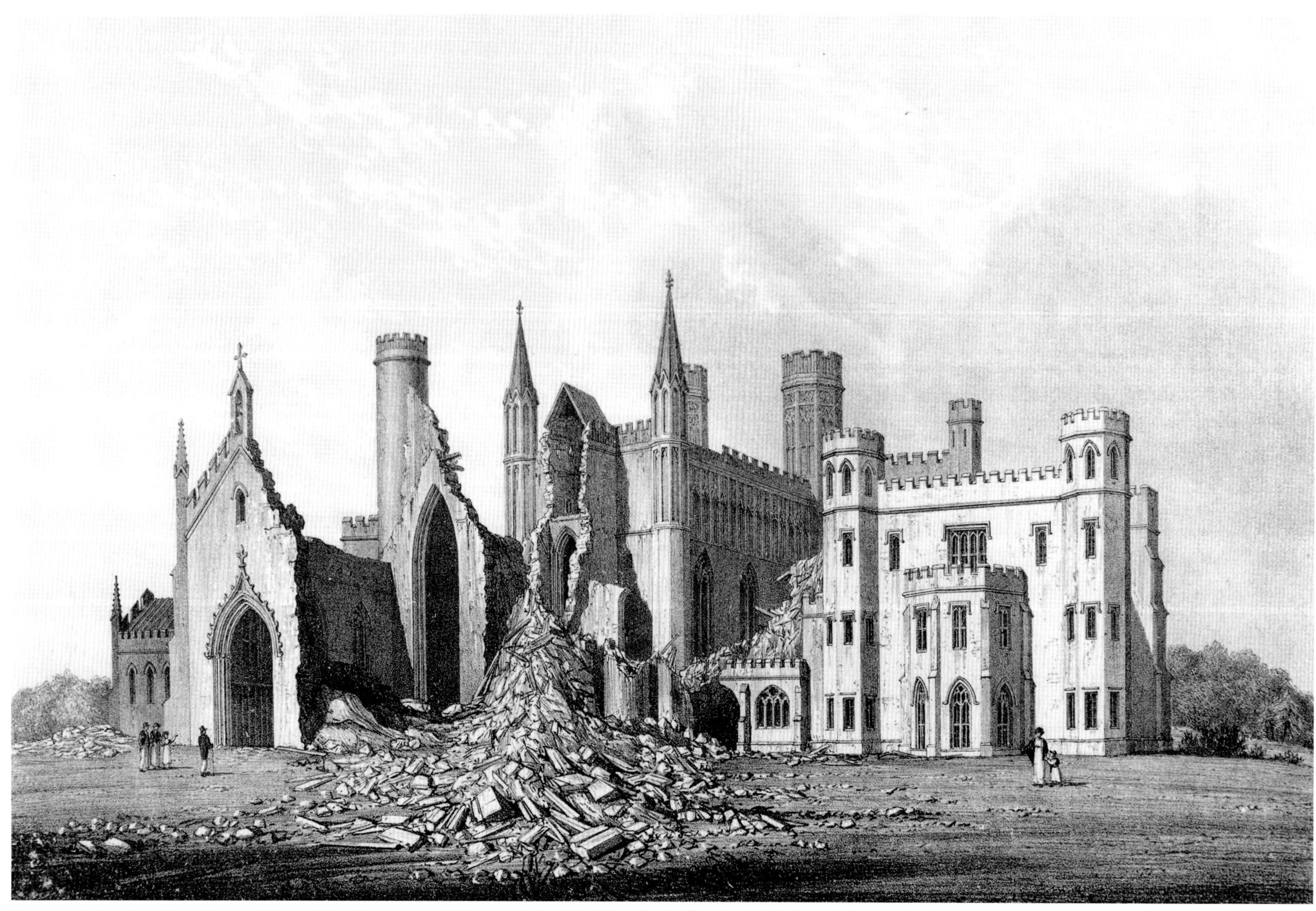

Fig. 7-1. John Buckler. *Ruins of Fonthill Abbey*, 1825. Lithograph by W. Westall. Collection of Sidney Blackmore.

Chapter VII

WILLIAM BECKFORD'S ABBEY AT FONTHILL: FROM THE PICTURESQUE TO THE SUBLIME

Megan Aldrich

Loss and memory are powerful themes in the life of William Beckford, and loss, especially, comes to the fore in a study of Fonthill Abbey, the creation of Beckford's mature years. While he chose to demolish his father's house at Fonthill in Wiltshire,[1] he was forced to sell the enormous Gothic Abbey and many of the treasures it contained owing to increasing financial difficulties. The purchaser was a self-made millionaire, John Farquhar. The sale was agreed late in 1822, just days before the abortive auction planned and advertised by the long-suffering Mr. Christie, who had spent considerable time cataloguing the Abbey and its contents.

Fonthill Abbey, Beckford's principal residence from 1807 to 1822, remains the most potent symbol of loss in his life, for having lost it once through its enforced sale, he lost it again when the central tower collapsed for the third and final time on December 21, 1825, damaging much of the building and fueling its already legendary status. So great was the public interest in this event that almost immediately a drawing of the collapsed tower by John Buckler was printed for public consumption (fig. 7-1).[2]

After the collapse of the central tower, which had been so lofty that Beckford claimed to have seen it from the site of his rising tower at Lansdown in Bath,[3] Beckford's solicitors wrote to him, expressing the view of many: "As a distinguished Monument in Architecture and of great national moment, as well as from other recollections, we learnt the News of the Fall of the Tower of Fonthill Abbey and the destruction of the Octagon etc. with great regret."[4] His solicitors, Fownes and White, continued the letter, however, by congratulating Beckford on his "happy fortune" in having disposed of the Abbey before the disaster.

Beckford must have experienced a pang or two at the destruction of so remarkable a building which closely reflected his tastes, prejudices, and ideas. He saw its ruins at least twice toward the end of his life—in 1838 and again in 1843, when he went to gaze upon it for the last time.[5] By then, despite the elapse of nearly twenty years since the fall of the tower, a substantial portion of the derelict Abbey remained, with some interior decoration intact. This was true especially of the sections of the north, south, and east ranges of the cruciform building which were farthest away from the tower.

In 1844, the year of Beckford's death and the year after his last visit to Fonthill, the Abbey was visited by an artist from Bath, Henry Venn Lansdown, who had known and admired Beckford. Venn Lansdown's description of the surviving building was eventually published in 1893, indicating the degree of continued public interest in the Abbey throughout the nineteenth century.[6] By the time his description appeared, however, only a small portion of the north range of the building remained. This exists today, with nineteenth-century additions.[7] Thus it was that Fonthill Abbey, originally intended as a picturesque "ruin" in the landscape of Beckford's princely estate, became an actual ruin, ensuring its fascination for posterity.

Like so many buildings of the early Gothic Revival, the concept of the Abbey had its origins in the eighteenth-century landscape garden. Beckford's rolling landscape was located in the west of England near monuments Stonehenge and Salisbury Cathedral, which were evocative of the distant British past. The park at Fonthill was replete with the picturesque elements of water, woods, hills, and vistas. Beckford's father, the Alderman, had begun a commemorative tower to form a focal point on the most elevated part of the estate, known as Stops Beacon, in about 1770.[8] The base, which is all that was built, shows it was a triangular design with turrets attached, similar to Alfred's Tower (referring to the ancient British king) in the nearby landscape garden of Stourhead. The tower at Stourhead had been designed in 1762 by the architect Henry Flitcroft, who had designed a similar monument in Yorkshire in 1748.[9] Even earlier was James Gibbs's triangular Temple of Liberty in the famous gardens of Stowe in Buckinghamshire, which paid homage to the signing of the Magna Carta. It was Gothic in style and can be dated to 1741.[10] Therefore, there was nothing particularly innovative about the Alderman's unfinished tower at Stops Beacon; rather, it was representative of a certain type of medievalism in the eighteenth-century landscape garden.

Around 1790 the Alderman's son began to develop ambitious plans for the Fonthill estate. Correspondence from William Beckford to the architect James Wyatt survives from 1791, and Beckford's letter implies their working relationship extended back even further.[11] Wyatt was designing interior fittings for Fonthill Splendens, as well as a fishing seat for the grounds, at about this time,[12] and it is not clear whether Beckford intended initially that Wyatt should finish the tower on Stops Beacon, or whether it was to be superseded by something altogether more up-to-date. Certainly, designs for picturesque garden structures at Fonthill were being actively considered by Beckford and Wyatt during the early 1790s.

One such idea was recorded in the richly informative diaries of Joseph Farington, a Royal Academician. A good friend to James Wyatt until a falling out toward the end of Wyatt's life, Farington provides much information on the relationship of the architect and Beckford, as most of Wyatt's papers have not survived. In a diary entry for July 20, 1796, Farington sketched a Gothic tower at Fonthill, based on a drawing Wyatt had shown him four years previously.[13] The design had three stages, surmounted by a lantern. Despite the exaggerated height of the tower design (some 175 feet) and Beckford's proposed burial chamber at the top of it, which Wyatt thought "not quite serious,"[14] it was otherwise in keeping with an established tradition of eighteenth-century garden structures. The eccentric architect Thomas Wright of Durham, for example, had designed a variety of garden towers, all medievalizing, in about 1750.[15] By 1796 Wyatt and Beckford's ideas were already evolving beyond the picturesque landscape.

In the early 1790s Beckford had been traveling on the Continent, initially in revolutionary France. From there he fled to Switzerland to avoid arrest, before settling on a lengthy stay in Portugal from 1793 to 1796. On April 10, 1794, Beckford wrote to James Wyatt: "My appetite for honouring Saint Anthony you see is still so keen that I cannot live without a little tidbit of a sanctuary till the moment arrives when by the permission of providence and Mr Wildman I may carry your magnificent plan for the chapel upon Stops' beacon into execution."[16] In this letter, Beckford requested Wyatt's assistance in designing "a sort of Tabernacle with curtains and Lamps" of bronze, with six altar candlesticks of carved (and presumably, gilded) wood, "provided you will settle the proportion and design." The tabernacle dedicated to Saint Anthony of Padua—the patron saint of Lisbon, whom Beckford adopted for his own—was for his house in the Portuguese capital,[17] and he had already sent Wyatt the dimensions of the available space and a rough plan containing a series of rooms with an octagon opening onto a "sanctuary," a theme that was to be developed at Fonthill Abbey. The "Mr Wildman" referred to by Beckford was Thomas Wildman, one of three brothers who grew rich from manipulating Beckford's business affairs until he dismissed them for fraud in 1801.[18] Beckford concluded his letter to Wyatt by writing, "we may still live to erect the buildings both grecian and gothic…you designed for Fonthill."

On June 4, 1794, Farington remarked in his diary that Wyatt, during dinner one evening at the Freemasons' Tavern, had spoken enthusiastically about his new client, shedding some light on his character: "Wyatt said a good deal to me abt. Mr. Beckford of Fonthill—He thinks him a man of extraordinary abilities.—Of unbounded expense. His income from Jamaica for the three last years has not been less than 120,000 a year. Wyatt believes that the greatest part of this enormous sum he expends. Beckford is easy to professional Men, but of consummate pride to people in higher situations."[19] Indeed, it was probably owing to feelings of insecurity, which ran deep in his personality, that Beckford behaved better to artists and tradesmen than to his social equals and superiors.

In 1794 Wyatt was nearly at the height of his busy career, immersed in work for George III and in his controversial cathedral restorations, whereas Beckford had lived abroad more or less for a decade in order to escape his personal scandals, sorrows and frustrations. In May 1786 Beckford's young wife, Lady Margaret Gordon, had died in Switzerland after giving birth to their daughter, Susan, depriving him of his most loyal supporter.[20] Beckford toured Switzerland as an outlet for his feelings before returning to Fonthill in January 1787. The visit was to be brief. His mother and Thomas Wildman were concerned for his reputation, as the effect of the Courtenay scandal lingered, mixing with fresh, malicious rumors that Lady Margaret had died of a broken heart. It was felt that Beckford should visit the family estates in Jamaica, the source of his fluctuating income, so he was dispatched to the Caribbean in March 1787 with feelings of loss and rejection uppermost in his mind.[21] Beckford made the journey as far as Lisbon, the first stop. Suffering from sea sickness, and perhaps other sensations, he disembarked and began something of a love affair with Portugal and its people, which was to have an influence on the design of Fonthill Abbey. At some point during his second Portuguese stay (1793–96),[22] and almost certainly at the suggestion of James Wyatt, Beckford visited the Dominican monastery at Batalha, one of the outstanding examples of Portuguese Gothic architecture and the subject of intense antiquarian interest during Beckford's stay. In 1795 the architect James Murphy, a native of Cork in Ireland, published a handsome folio volume with twenty-seven meticulously engraved plates entitled *Plans, Elevations, Sections and Views of the Church of Batalha*, which set new standards in publications on medieval architecture.[23] Both Beckford and Wyatt were subscribers to the volume. Murphy, who published *Travels in Portugal* at the same time, dedicated *Batalha* to "the Right Honourable William Conyngham: one of His Majesty's most Honourable Privy Council, Teller of the Exchequer in Ireland, Treasurer of the Royal Irish Academy, Fellow of the Society of Antiquaries, London, etc. etc." The dedication is dated May 3, 1792, and plates were issued from this year, thus predating Beckford's visit.

Conyngham was a prominent antiquary who amassed an important collection of topographical drawings recording Irish antiquities.[24] In 1783 he had traveled to Batalha in the company of Colonel Tarant and Captain Broughton to make his own drawings of the then unpublished convent and church.[25] These drawings inspired Murphy's visit to the site in 1789, under Conyngham's patronage, in order to prepare a publication. Most importantly for the purposes of Fonthill Abbey, James Wyatt would certainly have seen Conyngham's drawings when he began to rebuild his seat, Slane Castle, County Meath, Ireland, in 1785.

The building history of Slane is complex. The ruins of a late medieval tower and church stand near the site of the eighteenth-century house, which incorporates the remains of a medieval castle on the River Boyne.[26] In 1785 Wyatt had been called back to Slane by the second Lord Conyngham, recently returned from Batalha; he demolished the existing house to ground level and rebuilt it in the style of a castle.[27] Aside from a two-story Gothic library in the Round Tower with rich plasterwork tracery and Gothic bookcases, and a small Gothic arcade in the dining room, the interiors were neoclassical.[28] The exterior, however, was medievalizing in character and remains essentially as Wyatt designed it, with battlements and a varied silhouette, in which the large round tower was contrasted with smaller square towers.

The idea that Wyatt would have known of the Conyngham drawings of Batalha shortly after they were made in 1783, and at least ten years before Beckford visited the site, is evident when one considers Wyatt's other Gothic house of the 1780s, Lee Priory near Canterbury in Kent. Design work began around 1782, but the building took shape principally between 1785 and 1790, overlapping that at Slane.[29] There are some interesting similarities between the two designs for antiquarian houses. Wyatt had prepared both classical and Gothic designs for the owner of Lee Priory, the antiquary Thomas Barrett, a good friend of Horace Walpole.

Walpole's approbation of Wyatt's work at Lee Priory is well known.[30] In particular, Walpole praised the Gothic library, approached through a low, fan-vaulted corridor, which had battlemented bookcases very similar in design to those at Slane.[31] As at Slane, the library at Lee Priory was situated in the principal tower of the house. Significantly, at Lee Priory the central tower was octagonal in form, capped by a spire, and clearly foreshadowing Wyatt's early designs for Fonthill Abbey. The tower was based on the Mausoleum of King John I at Batalha (fig. 7-2), as drawn by Conyngham and later published by Murphy. As the house was finished by 1790, and as Wyatt never traveled to Portugal, he must have used Conyngham's drawings as the model.[32]

As at Slane, only some of the Lee Priory interiors—the library, entrance hall, and Strawberry Room (named in honor of Walpole's Strawberry Hill—were Gothic. The rest of the interiors at Lee Priory were classical. This mixing of styles was entirely in keeping with contemporary ideas of the Picturesque. While Slane Castle had a site with genuine medieval ruins, at Lee, "there were some monastic associations in the immediate district, and monasticism was all the rage."[33]

Thus it can be seen that, while Beckford was traveling on the Continent, Wyatt was sharpening and clarifying his ideas on the design of country houses and "ruins" in the Gothic style. In 1792 he had

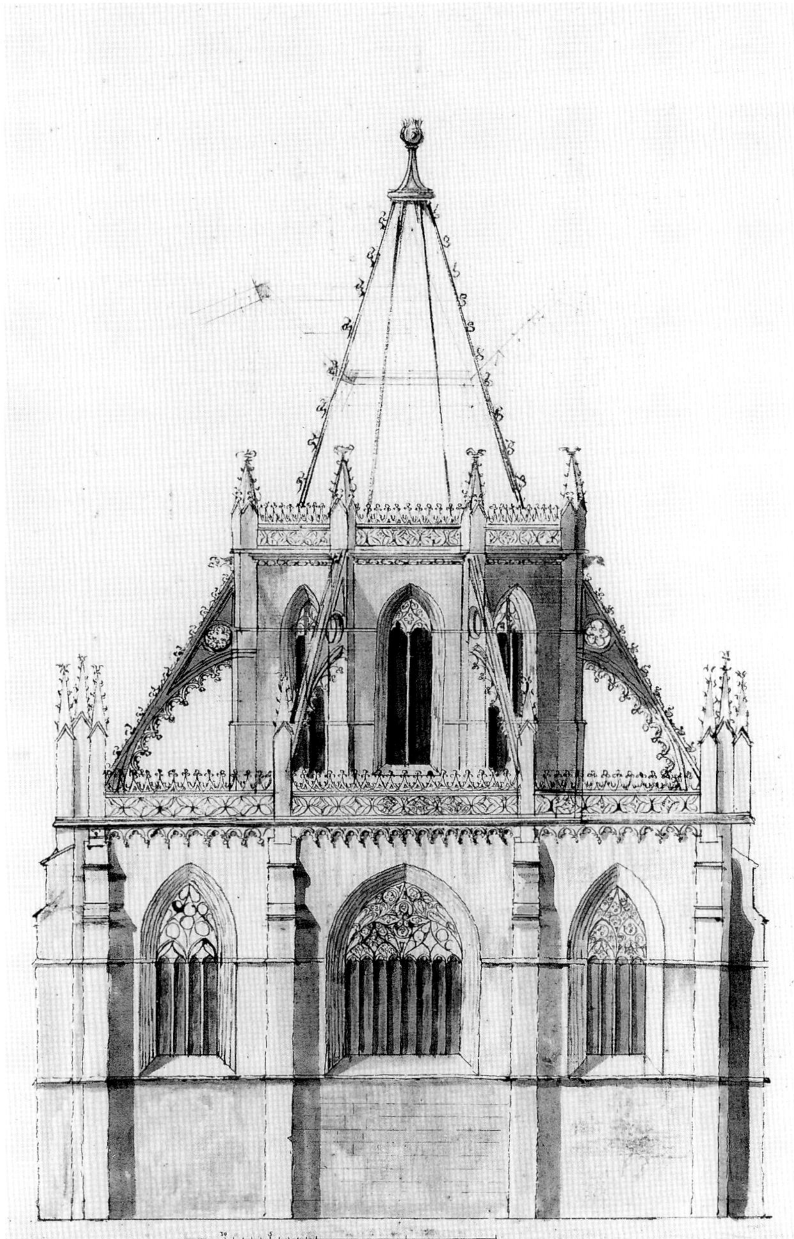

Fig. 7-2. James Murphy. Mausoleum of King John at Batalha Abbey, Portugal, 1789. Pen, ink, and wash. From "Sketches of Batalha," fol. 20. Society of Antiquaries, London.

designed the sham Gothic ruins in the garden of Frogmore House, the private residence of Queen Charlotte near Windsor Castle in Berkshire. These were praised by contemporaries.[34] John Rutter, writing in 1823 about Fonthill Abbey, plainly states that the original concept for the Abbey had been a garden building with a suite of rooms, to be designed like a ruined convent,[35] an idea probably arising from Wyatt's work for the queen.

In the summer of 1796, when Beckford returned from his travels in Portugal to Fonthill, design work began in earnest. In this year,

Fig. 7-3. J. M. W. Turner. Fonthill Abbey in progress, ca. 1799. Pencil. From the Fonthill Sketchbook. Tate Britain, London.

too, Wyatt received the supreme architectural accolade of being appointed Surveyor General to the Board of Works upon the death of Sir William Chambers. This ensured his status as the foremost British architect of his day. The appointment, moreover, was due to the clearly stated wishes of King George III.[36] If Beckford had entertained any doubts about whether to use James Wyatt as architect for his new abbey, such royal approval would have decided the matter for him. Wyatt was now entrusted with realizing Beckford's Gothic vision.

Many writers have remarked upon Beckford's fascination for Catholicism and its ritual, some tracing this back to a visit he made in 1778, when an impressionable teenager, to the Grande Chartreuse, the chief monastery of the Carthusians in Switzerland.[37] Antiquarians, such as Horace Walpole and his good friend John Chute, had flirted with Catholicism in the Gothic designs for Strawberry Hill and for Chute's

house, The Vyne, in Hampshire,[38] suggesting that an interest in Gothic architecture and the "old religion" went hand-in-hand.[39] The fact that the site of the future Fonthill Abbey was near to ruins of a medieval priory made it that much more natural that Beckford should adopt a monastic theme.[40]

When finished, the Abbey had become a large building in the shape of a cross, with the two axes of the cross meeting at a central octagon. The four ranges, or arms, of the design were composed of individual architectural units. Initially, however, just the south range, Western Hall, and the Octagon were built. Building work proceeded rapidly. By November 1796 Beckford wrote to his mother that the "Abbey," as he now called it, was nearly 200 feet in length, and much of the building had progressed up to the first floor; by February 1797 he wrote to his good friend and relative, Sir William Hamilton, in

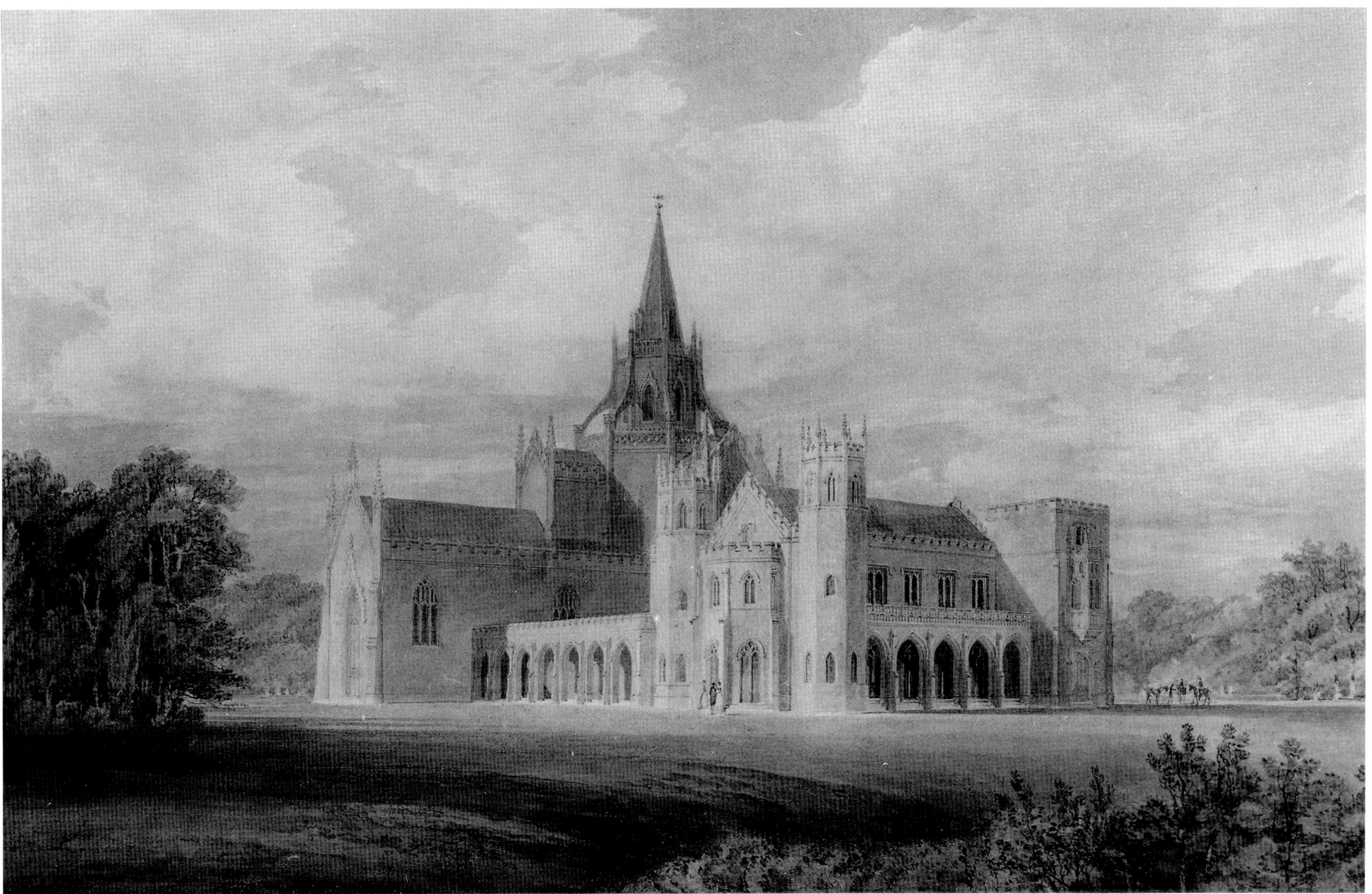

Fig. 7-4. J. M. W. Turner. *Perspective View of Fonthill Abbey from the South-West*, 1799. Watercolor and gouache. Bolton Museum and Art Gallery, Lancashire.

Naples, of his "little pleasure-building in the shape of an abbey, which is already half-finished. It contains apartments in the most gorgeous Gothic style with windows of painted glass, a chapel for Saint Anthony (66 feet diameter and 72 feet high), a gallery 185 feet in length, and a tower 145 feet high."[41]

One of the key ideas for the Abbey that Beckford had developed in Portugal was the idea of a dramatic sequence of rooms, culminating in a candlelit oratory/sanctuary/chapel to Saint Anthony. It is clear from the dimensions Beckford gave to Hamilton that the Octagon was intended as the Chapel of Saint Anthony in this early phase of building. The gallery referred to is Saint Michael's Gallery, and the tower was probably just at the foundation stage, and nowhere near the height quoted by Beckford. A sketch of around 1799 (fig. 7-3),

shows the tower to be still unfinished and surrounded by scaffolding two years after Beckford wrote to Hamilton.[42]

It is also clear from this letter to Hamilton that Beckford still thought of his Abbey as a "pleasure building" to ornament his estate, rather than as a residence. The building would have had a very asymmetrical, picturesque silhouette, and it was being constructed rapidly of timber and cement. This somewhat impermanent construction was standard practice for eighteenth-century garden architecture, and Wyatt had a particular interest in the use of cement.[43] He has been unfairly criticized for his choice of building materials and construction by later generations, but even flimsier materials were used in the eighteenth-century landscape garden, where the longevity of structures was not of prime concern. The famous Gothic "Cathedral" in Kew

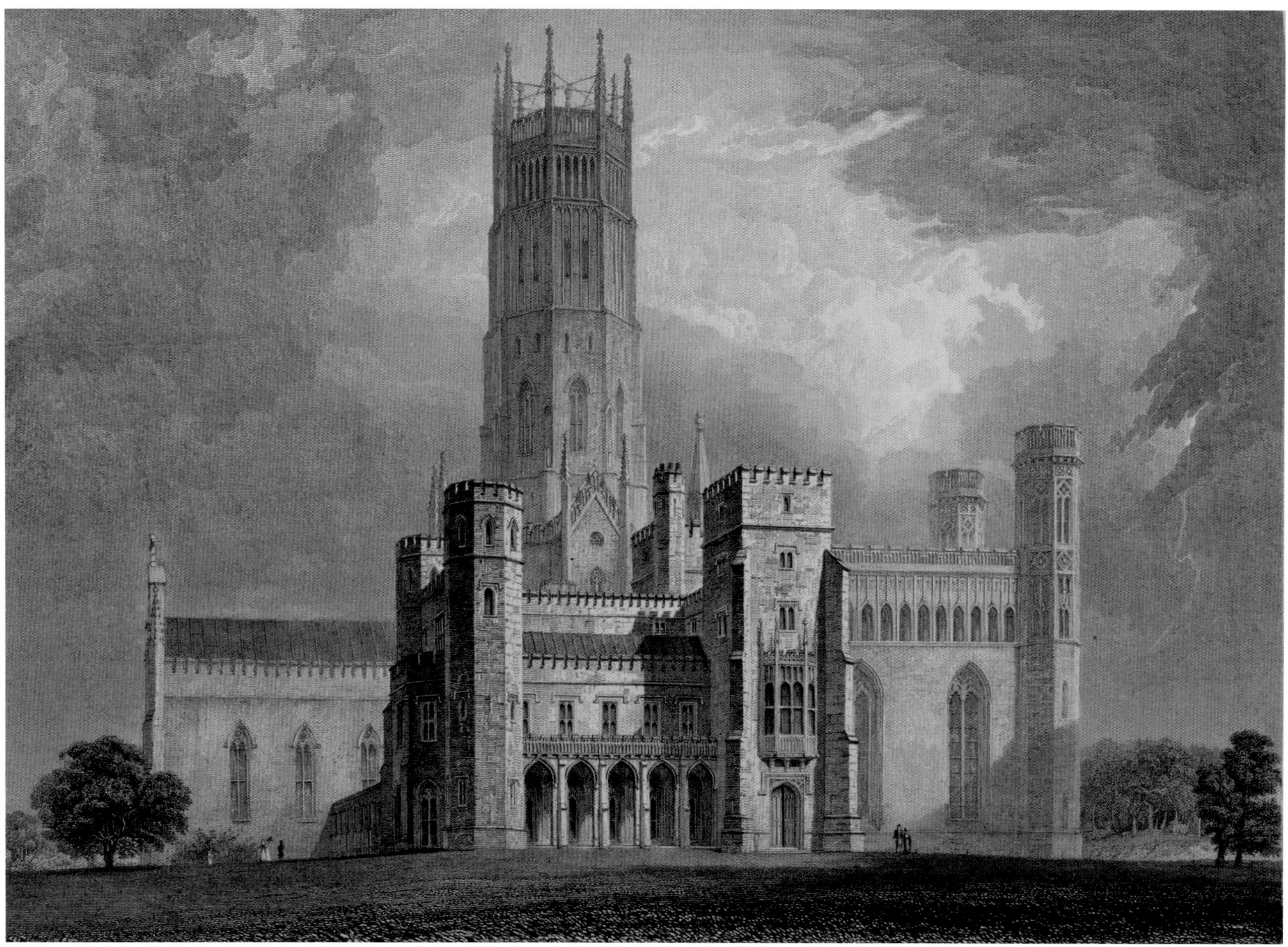

Fig. 7-5. "View of the South Front," Fonthill Abbey. From *Delineations of Fonthill and its Abbey* by John Rutter (1823), plate 12.

Gardens, for example, was designed in 1759 by Johann Heinrich Müntz, a member of the Strawberry Hill circle, and it was built of wood and painted plaster.[44] The scenic qualities of the Abbey at Fonthill, originally built as an ornament for Beckford's grounds, owe their origin to this very significant design tradition.

The three years from 1797 to 1800 were a period of feverish building activity, despite Beckford's third departure to Portugal in November 1798. Joseph Farington, in his diary for August 6, 1797, records a conversation with James Wyatt about "Beckford's Gothic building—which is now much enlarged—among the furniture are to be four Cabinets of £500 value each—all in Gothic taste—four Gothic statues to be executed by Nollekens, Flaxman, Rossi and Westmacot. The Tower is not proceeding with at present but in his will Beckford

has directed that it shall be finished shd. He die."[45] The expensive Gothic cabinets cannot be traced at present, but the remark reveals that, from the beginning, Beckford was planning a comprehensive scheme of furnishing and decoration for the Abbey.

Throughout the spring and early summer of 1797, Farington indicates that much negotiation between Beckford and the painter Richard Smirke regarding decorative schemes for the Abbey was taking place through the mediation of Edward Foxhall, a cabinetmaker, agent, and dealer whom Farington describes as "the frame maker."[46] It is revealing that Wyatt told Farington, "Beckford leans to [Benjamin] West on account of his situation with the King."[47] West was the leading history painter and president of the Royal Academy, and, as was undoubtedly the case with Wyatt himself, Beckford sought to use artists patronized by the royal circle. By November 1797, Beckford's plans for the Abbey had evolved to such an extent that he was already discussing with Wyatt the idea of demolishing Fonthill Splendens and enlarging the Abbey to be his principal residence, some years before this actually took place.[48]

Wyatt had exhibited his first designs for Fonthill Abbey at the Royal Academy in 1797, and subsequent designs were exhibited to acclaim in 1798 and 1799. Another exhibitor at the academy in 1799 was the young artist J. M. W. Turner, who was commissioned by Beckford to prepare a number of views of the Abbey, including a series of five large watercolors portraying the building in different lights during the day. In the autumn of 1799, Turner had spent three weeks sketching the building, as it took shape. Of particular interest is a Turner watercolor (fig. 7-4), taken from the southwest of the building, showing in some detail the southern arm of the Abbey, containing Saint Michael's Gallery, as well as the projecting Western Hall with the main door.[49] What is especially interesting about this view is that it demonstrates the extent to which the Mausoleum of King John at Batalha was still the model for the central octagon of the Abbey's design. As Turner's strengths did not lie in the detailed depiction of architecture, it has been suggested that he had access to Wyatt's architectural drawings and used them in completing his sketches and watercolors of Fonthill Abbey.[50]

The majority of published views of Fonthill Abbey depict it from the south or southwest. The view of the south elevation published by Rutter in 1823 (fig. 7-5) shows a square tower with stepped buttressing and a projecting, first-floor oriel that marks the southern extremity of Saint Michael's Gallery, which would have been finished by about 1803.[51] The arches of the cloister, to the immediate left of the tower, shaded the Oak Parlour on the ground floor of the Abbey. This was one of the principal living rooms, with an important program of stained glass and an oriel window on the west side of the building.[52] Above it were the Yellow Drawing Rooms and the Oak Library, known as the "Board of Works" because, in a practice reminiscent of Walpole and his designers at Strawberry Hill, Wyatt, Beckford, and the artists working at Fonthill Abbey used to gather here and consult the reference works and prints Beckford owned for inspiration in design.[53]

To the left, in the middle ground of Rutter's view, can be seen the tall, western entrance hall surmounted by a statue of Saint Anthony and a cross fleury, referring to Beckford's stated descent from the House of Lancaster. This functioned as a state entrance and, initially, as a banqueting hall. Between the south range and the Western Hall ran the western cloister, enclosing the fountain court. These are clearly marked on the plan published by Rutter in his book on the Abbey. To the right, in the middle ground, looms the towered Eastern Transept, which was to be the last phase of the building of the Abbey, still unfinished at the time of the sale in 1822.

The interiors of the southern range of the Abbey have been recorded in five principal sources: first, in accounts of the banquet held in honor of Admiral Nelson, hero of the Battle of Trafalgar, in December 1800; second, in the manuscript journal of Beckford's relative, Lady Ann Hamilton, who visited the Abbey in 1803; third, in James Storer's 1812 publication on the Abbey, the earliest of such accounts; and finally in the books by John Britton and John Rutter, published in 1823, after the sale of the Abbey to John Farquhar. It is thus possible to trace the evolution of Beckford's interiors over a period of nearly twenty-five years. The Nelson banquet was of great general interest partly because Beckford lived more or less in seclusion at Fonthill, aside from the company of artists and a few intimates, and because the architecture of the Abbey was already exciting great public curiosity.[54]

The Nelson banquet was the only grand entertainment ever held at Fonthill Abbey. Work on the building was intense during the autumn of 1800, as "nearly five hundred men were successively employed night and day."[55] The timber and cement tower had blown down during a gale in May 1800, but it was rebuilt in time for the December banquet.[56] On November 8, 1800, Farington recorded in his diary a conversation with the artist William Hamilton, who was designing stained glass for the Abbey: "Hamilton called—Has been at Fonthill near 4 months…One wing of the Abbey is finished and furnished—but Mr. Beckford has never slept in it…[The Abbey] fills the mind with a sentiment which is almost too much to support, certainly of too melancholy a cast to be long dwelt upon."[57]

The sublime, awe-inspiring character of the Abbey was very much in evidence at the Nelson banquet. In addition to Nelson, the party included Sir William Hamilton, Beckford's relative and the British envoy to Naples, and his notorious second wife, Emma, the mistress of Nelson; the artists Wyatt, West, Hamilton (no relation), Tresham, Smith, and others; "Madame Banti," and "several French emigrés" along with a "Portuguese nobleman."[58] The emigrés were French clerics Beckford had accumulated in his travels, who now lived at Fonthill, and the "Portuguese nobleman" was in fact a singer of Italian descent, Gregorio Franchi, whom Beckford had taken into service during his first trip to Portugal and who later became a Chevalier through Beckford's contacts with the Portuguese royal family.[59] Franchi was to play an important future role in the furnishing of the Abbey interiors.

The guests arrived at Fonthill Splendens, then Beckford's residence, on December 20. On the 23rd, they were driven by torchlight through the Fonthill woods to the Abbey, which loomed up among the trees, arriving in time for the six o'clock banquet. They entered through the Western Hall, with its massive 35-foot Gothic oak doors, attended by Beckford's resident dwarf in livery, and then proceeded to the Octagon where they were dazzled by Wyatt's tall, severe pointed arches and the height of the tower rising above their heads.

After their reception in the Octagon, the guests returned to the large timbered banqueting hall (that is, the Western Hall) for a sit-down dinner during which they were serenaded from the minstrel's gallery above the main entrance. They retired upstairs after dinner along a winding staircase that connected the banqueting hall to the Octagon Saloon, passing hooded servants holding torches. This highly theatrical scenario added to the overall medieval effect. The procession wound through the western Yellow Drawing Room (the eastern one was added later) and the Oak Library into Saint Michael's Gallery, then half-furnished, where Emma Hamilton entertained the party with her (classical) attitudes. The *Gentleman's Magazine* remarked that the interiors of the Abbey "recalled the grand chapel scenes and ceremonies of our antient Catholic times."[60] This was Gothic gloom, indeed.

Despite some refinements and changes, the principal interiors prepared for Nelson's visit remained more or less intact until the sale of the Abbey. Instead of continually pulling apart and redecorating his interiors, as the Prince Regent did at Carlton House and Brighton Pavilion, for example, Beckford was a serial builder who simply kept adding new interiors and new ranges to the Abbey, ending with the Eastern Transept. Beginning late in 1800 with the account of the Nelson banquet, the *Gentleman's Magazine* tells us that the Octagon functioned as: "the great saloon, called the cardinal's parlour, furnished with rich tapestries, long curtains of purple damask before the arched windows, ebony tables and chairs studded with ivory, of various but antique fashion; the whole room in the noblest style of monastic ornament, and illuminated by lights on silver sconces."[61] These long purple curtains remained a feature of the Octagon until Beckford sold the Abbey in 1822.

Certainly, the effects of drapery and light were two of William Beckford's major preoccupations as regards his contribution to the Abbey interiors. In his travel memoirs, *Italy, with Sketches of Spain and Portugal*, he commented on, "The powers of drapery…Nothing produces so grand and at the same time so comfortable an effect."[62] Venn Lansdown, in his *Recollections*, remarked upon the powerful impression made by the use of scarlet draperies at Beckford's house in Bath, to which Beckford replied that it "was nothing to what I had at Fonthill in the great octagon. There were purple curtains fifty feet long."[63] Draperies, he continued, were too often neglected in the design of interiors.

The *Gentleman's Magazine* also describes the furniture in the Octagon. It was colonial, probably made in Batavia in the seventeenth century for the Western market, and carved principally of solid ebony, with ivory accents and spirally turned uprights. A very similar suite of furniture was acquired in the nineteenth century by George IV for Windsor.[64] The description makes it clear that the tables and chairs did not all match, but were a variety of antique pieces of similar design that Beckford had acquired. Ebony furniture of both European and South Pacific colonial origin was used extensively throughout the Abbey interiors. The former, Beckford would have known through his travels in France; the latter had a long association with Gothic houses dating back to the 1730s, when the antiquary Henry Pelham had acquired some ebony chairs of Batavian origin for his country house, Esher Place in Surrey. He mistakenly believed them to have belonged to Cardinal Wolsey, a former resident of this house, to whose Tudor gateway William Kent added two battlemented wings around 1730.

Horace Walpole, who greatly admired Esher and its ebony furniture, acquired a sizable amount of ebony for Strawberry Hill, and continued its mistaken association with Tudor England, as evident in the so-called Holbein Chamber of Strawberry Hill, where the "state bedroom" was decorated around 1759 with colonial ebony chairs and a table, and "Cardinal Wolsey's hat," among other choice collectibles. Walpole combined contemporary ebonized furniture of Western origin in conjunction with his antique ebony furniture, as did his friend John Chute at The Vyne. This practice was continued at Fonthill. In the houses of antiquarian collectors, ebony furniture came to signify medievalism, or "the true black blood," as Walpole expressed it in an era when there was little understanding of real medieval furniture.[65]

A slightly later description of the Octagon and its furniture survives to give further useful information. In September 1803 Lady Ann Hamilton, a relative and guardian of Beckford's two daughters since 1798, visited Fonthill Abbey. She remarked, "One Angle only is finished" before describing the "Abbot's Parlour," or Octagon, its oak wainscoting decorated with tapestry, its purple curtains now contrasted with crimson draperies (a favorite Beckford color combination), and the stained glass in the upper portion of the windows, showing the "Kings and Saints from William the Conqueror to the Suppression of Monestrys—the Chairs are Ebony and Ivory coverd with Crimson Serge the Skreens the Same."[66]

As recorded by Storer eight years later, the Octagon remained much the same, with the addition of four north windows with stained glass copied from Batalha.[67] The height of the central tower was now 132 feet from the ground. By the time Rutter published his detailed account in 1823, however, the Octagon Saloon (as it was now known) was furnished with contemporary x-frame "chairs and bergères in recesses" and the purple curtains had been removed.[68] By 1812 some of this ebony and ivory furniture had found its way to the southern end of Saint Michael's Gallery, while other of the ebony and ivory furniture had been moved to the "Lancaster State Bedchamber" in the north range, a room decorated in crimson with contrasting black furniture. The Nelson party had visited the Western Hall when it was used as a banqueting hall. Storer describes it as "magnificent," and "in the ancient baronial style," with stained-glass windows on the south wall after originals at Canterbury Cathedral.[69] Rutter, who calls it the "Great Western Hall," gives considerably more detail concerning its appearance. The hall was paneled in oak wainscot with a splendid timbered roof grained in oak pattern and emblazoned with heraldic shields. One of Wyatt's design triumphs, the roof anticipates that at Ashridge, in Hertfordshire, a house finished by his nephew and son after his death.[70] On the north wall were Gothic niches with crimson drapery and a statue of Beckford's father, the Alderman. Rutter tells us that the walls were plaster, painted in imitation of stone.[71]

By the time of Rutter's description, the hall had been converted into a vessel for tremendous spatial and scenic effects. It connected the Western Avenue, an arrow-straight allée of cut lawn extending about a mile west from the house through the grounds (and perfectly aligned with the main entrance of the Abbey) to the Octagon, the central point of the building, thus linking the gardens with the architecture. Wyatt had added to the hall a broad, straight staircase of twenty-two steps by 1812,[72] by means of which the visitor was drawn up into the Abbey's interior. Rutter described the effect: "We ascend leisurely the spacious steps, watching the gradual developement of an architecture, which, from the stateliness of its parts, the masterly arrangement of the chiaro oscuro, the atmosphere of the coloured light, and the solemn brilliancy of the windows, produces an effect very little removed from the sublime."[73]

Fonthill Abbey began as a picturesque structure for the grounds of Beckford's estate, but by the time of James Wyatt's death in 1813 it had evolved into an example of the sublime in architecture. The combination of scenic effects, rich color, and overwhelming scale of its dimensions inspired awe in the minds of those who visited it and attempted to capture its effect on paper. Beckford and Wyatt were both highly imaginative, and Wyatt had an already-established reputation for designing buildings with marked scenic effects. Their talents came together in the creation of the Abbey interiors.

The *Gentleman's Magazine* account of 1801 and Lady Ann Hamilton's journal of 1803 both describe the furnishings of the south range of the Abbey in some detail. In a building remarkable for its Gothic gloom, the south- and west-facing rooms would have been the most cheerful, and it is not surprising that Beckford made these his principal living quarters when he moved permanently to the Abbey some time before February 1804.[74] The first interior both sources mention is the Yellow Drawing Room, which the *Gentleman's Magazine* described as: "A magnificent room, hung with yellow damask, and decorated with cabinets of the most precious japan…" and many other precious objects.[75] Lady Ann concurred: "An Easy Winding Stair Case conducts you into a small ante room full of the most beautiful Japan and China…." There were cabinets and boxes of Japanese black and gold lacquer, and "China jars," of porcelain, three feet high.[76]

Storer indicates that the "Yellow Damask Room," as he called it, had five windows, three of them in the west oriel, thus placing the room directly above the Oak Parlour. The China jars mentioned by Lady Ann were placed in the oriel, and Storer says they were gifts from the Prince of Brazil, one of Beckford's friends among the Portuguese royal family. In addition to Japanese lacquer cabinets, Storer describes fine "Buhl" cabinets: "one of the latter formerly adorned the apartments of Fontainbleau, and is remarkable for a beautiful medallion of Lewis the Fourteenth."[77]

Here we see a different use of "black" furniture to create a striking interior. Beckford, assisted by Franchi, who was deeply interested in ebony furniture and who would have seen it in Lisbon, mixed black lacquer objects with European ebony-veneered furniture that had gilt metal mounts, a type that came to the fore in the seventeenth century and was very much associated with the court of Louis XIV and with the workshop of André-Charles Boulle, in particular.[78] With its yellow walls no doubt chosen deliberately to contrast with the ebony and lacquer, the Yellow Drawing Room represents one of the neo-

Baroque interiors at Fonthill, a stylistic feature of a number of antiquarian and Gothic houses.[79]

By the 1822 sale the furnishing of this room had changed somewhat. Rutter, who distinguishes between a western Yellow Drawing Room (the room referred to by the *Gentleman's Magazine*, Lady Ann Hamilton, and Storer) and an *en suite* eastern Yellow Drawing Room, criticized the choice of yellow hangings for a room with a southwest aspect, and said the color clashed with the many crystal, amber, and stone objects that covered every surface and were also placed in "open armoires," almost certainly contemporary glazed display cabinets perhaps made with tortoiseshell in the manner of Boulle.[80] The Japanese lacquer was now placed in the eastern room. Rutter does mention "A carved ebony armoire, 8 feet high," which may be that referred to by Storer, as still in the western room; in the eastern Yellow Drawing Room were an "inlaid ebony table," a table with an alabaster slab, and "Three Persian (sic) cabinets and stands of ebony and ivory." Clearly, Beckford, with Franchi's active assistance, had bought a great many objects in the eleven years between Storer and Rutter's accounts.[81]

Decorated in a similar style to the Oak Parlour, the Oak Library had oak wainscoting, crimson damask curtains with interior scarlet moreen draperies, and a carpet of scarlet and black pattern to set off the simple black (i.e. ebonized) and gilt bookcases with a frieze of quatrefoils, probably designed by Wyatt and made by Edward Foxhall.[82] According to Lady Ann these contained manuscripts. Wyatt had long been involved in the design of furniture and interior fittings for his clients, and designed two frames for Beckford's "Altieri Claudes," as well as a Gothic altarpiece for the Abbey, later used as an overmantel mirror frame in the Grand Drawing Room. Foxhall's correspondence makes frequent mention of Wyatt as a designer of furniture.[83]

Lady Ann Hamilton relatess that Saint Michael's Gallery was unfinished when she visited in September 1803, though she was eloquent about the effects of lights and shade produced by the long, narrow gallery running from north to south. She wrote: "The Beauty of this Gallery must be seen to be Conceived….the Gradations of light is very fine."[84]

The oriel at the south of the gallery was of particular note. The *Gentleman's Magazine* had commented on the sparkle and reflections of the plate glass in the window at night, whereas Lady Ann spoke of the sun making the red hangings glow, and of the beautiful, elevated view over the surrounding countryside which was framed within the plate glass of the lower oriel. The four fathers of the Christian Church in stained glass occupied the upper part of the oriel window.

The ceiling of Saint Michael's Gallery was one of the glories of the Abbey. It was an exercise in Wyatt's richest fan vaulting (in plaster painted to look like stone), which he had used at Lee Priory in the library corridor in painted pine. The richness of the Fonthill "vaulting" may owe something to Horace Walpole—Wyatt would have seen the remarkably lavish ceiling of the Strawberry Hill Gallery when he worked there in 1790. Lady Ann describes two fireplaces, "well con-

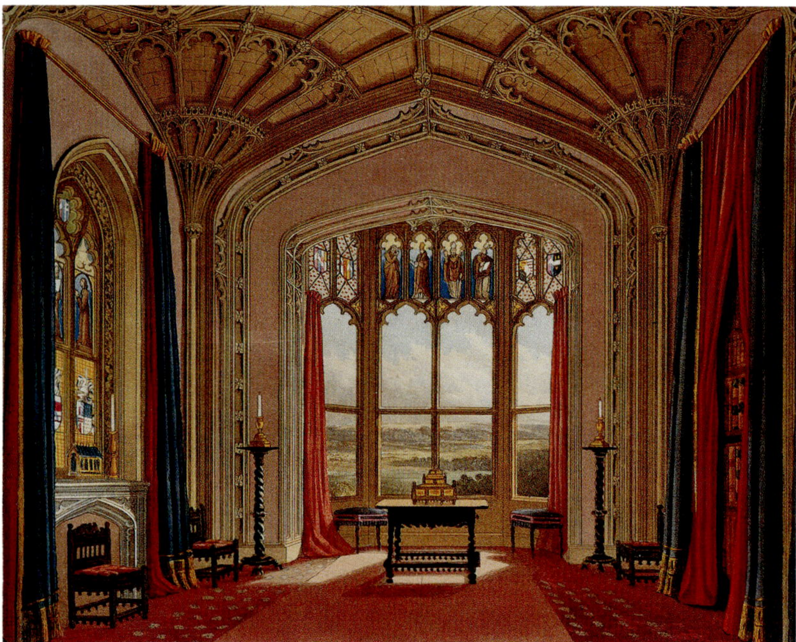

Fig. 7-6. "South End of Saint Michael's Gallery," Fonthill Abbey. From *Graphical and Literary Illustrations of Fonthill Abbey* by John Britton (1823), plate 9.

cealed," and recesses between the windows filled with rare books behind curtains. Storer, writing in 1812, tells us the fireplaces were superb Gothic specimens of marble placed under each of the windows, with tracery in the spandrels of the arches. These were doubtless to Wyatt's designs.[85] Of the gallery furniture, Lady Ann noted in her journal: "The Chairs and Stands for Candles are Ebony and Ivory To heavy as hardly to be lifted, and of the same Pattern as those below."[86] Thus the ebony and ivory furniture used in the Octagon was continued in the gallery, indicating Beckford owned a large group of these objects. It is interesting that candlestands are referred to, for these were normally Western in origin. Rare examples do exist of stands made in Europe in the seventeenth century of ivory and exotic timbers,[87] but the majority of these spirally turned stands were made in the first part of the nineteenth century for antiquarian interiors.

By the time Storer published his account of the Abbey, the furnishing of Saint Michael's Gallery was well advanced. In the space created at the south oriel he describes a large amber cabinet "once in the possession of the Queen of Bohemia, daughter of James the First," placed on a "table of ebony, with torsel feet, which formerly belonged to Cardinal Wolsey."[88] This arrangement was *in situ* when Britton published his book on the Abbey eleven years later (fig. 7-6). The mention of Cardinal Wolsey suggests a provenance from Esher Place, making it the same ebony furniture that had so excited Walpole in the 1740s.[89] Beckford would have treasured such a provenance, for, despite his occa-

sional denigrating remarks about Strawberry Hill, it is obvious that Walpole's ideas and enthusiasms were enormously influential on him. In Britton's view, the ebony table has been joined by six chairs, which, he asserts, came also from Esher. On the mantelpiece is a medieval enameled reliquary (see cat. no. 96), which Beckford believed to have been plundered from the Treasury of Saint Denis during the French Revolution.[90]

Many more precious objects in Saint Michael's Gallery were recorded by Rutter in 1823. Besides the ebony suite in the oriel, he described contemporary "glazed cabinets of buhl and tortoiseshell" on each side of the gallery, filled with small objects, and resting on eleven ebony tables with slabs of marble.[91] These tables are very likely those referred to in a letter by Foxhall to Beckford of December 1802: "The Ebony Tables are nearly finished and I have got the Drawing for the Gothic Table—which shall be finished making before your return and I expect to get the Drawing for the piece of Furniture for the red damask Room in a few Days."[92] In fact, the tables would probably have been made of ebonized wood and spirally turned elements to echo the design of the antique ebony furniture. That Wyatt was the designer for much of this furniture at the Abbey is strengthened by the representation of the furniture at a contemporary Gothic house he designed, Cassiobury Park in Hertfordshire (now demolished).

Wyatt designed Cassiobury late in the 1790s for the fifth Earl of Essex, and it was sketched by Turner after he had visited Fonthill. The exterior shows many similar features to the architecture of Lee Priory and Fonthill Abbey, most notably in the use of oriel windows, contrasting square and octagonal towers, and an octagon capped by a spire that derives from the Mausoleum of King John at Batalha.[93] A watercolor view of the interior of the Great Cloister is among the Turner drawings of Cassiobury (fig. 7-7), illustrating oak paneling on the walls, crimson drapery, and furniture of a very similar design to that in Saint Michael's Gallery at Fonthill.[94] At Cassiobury, the high-backed armchair placed against a window pier seems to be of late-seventeenth-century date, while the four chairs with broader, lower backs appear to date to around 1800. It is difficult to see the table clearly in this view, as it is covered by a cloth, but the spirally turned legs are certainly very close in design to tables in Saint Michael's Gallery at Fonthill Abbey. If this furniture is not antique, and if James Wyatt is the author of it, then it represents perhaps the earliest known examples of the "Tudor Revival" in furniture, a phenomenon principally associated with the 1830s, and one in which he may have played a pioneering role.

The pace of work at Fonthill Abbey slowed in the period 1802–05, when fluctuating sugar prices contracted Beckford's income.[95] In 1804 Farington recorded the first real rumbles of dissatisfaction on Beckford's part with his architect,[96] but the two had already worked together for fourteen years, and Beckford knew he was getting the best that Gothic Revival design could offer with Wyatt. This was recognized by King George III, who remarked of Wyatt that, "At Fonthill He had done a great work."[97] In October 1806, Farington recorded a conversation with the young Jeffry Wyatt about his uncle James's

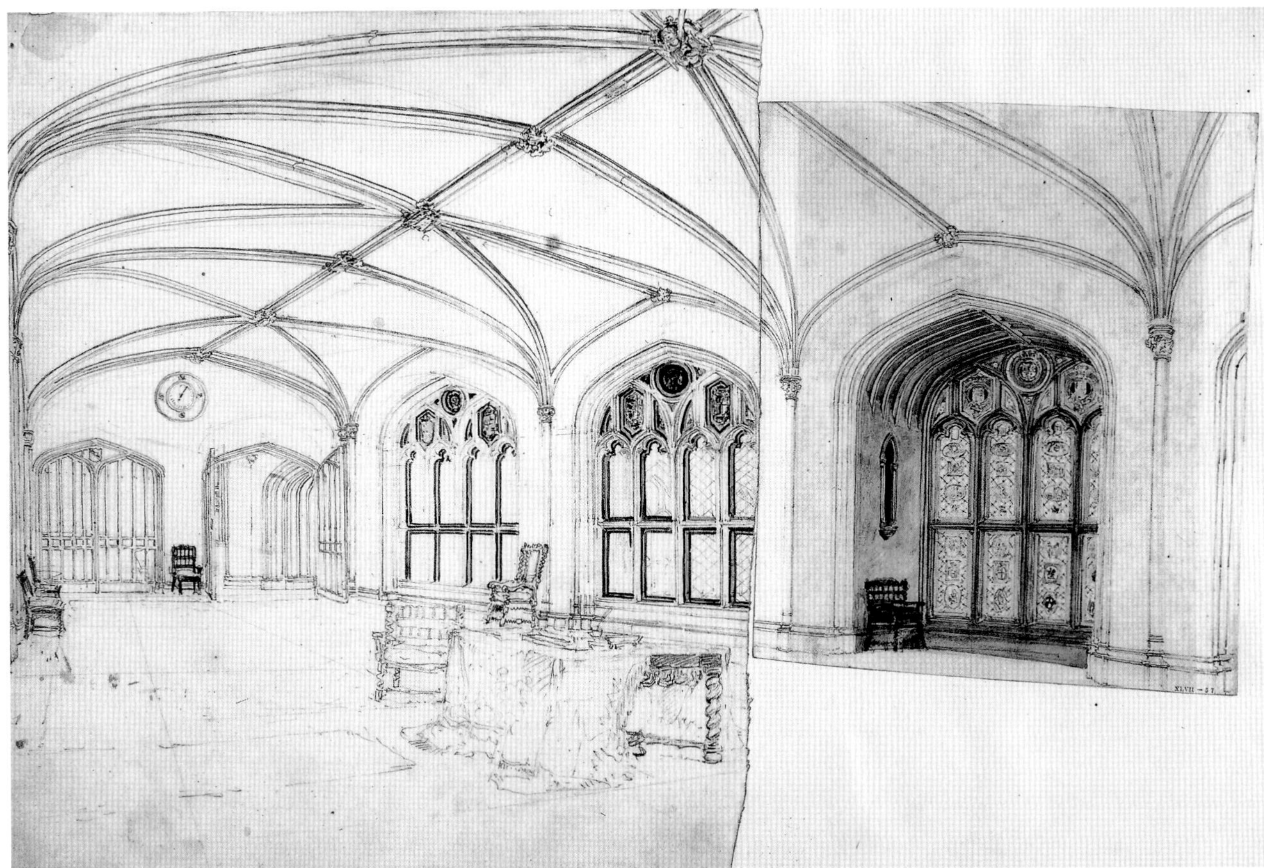

Fig. 7-7. J. M. W. Turner. Interior of the Great Cloister, Cassiobury Park, Hertfordshire, ca. 1800. Pencil and watercolor. From the Fonthill Sketchbook. Tate Britain, London.

"irregular habits." The younger Wyatt said his uncle would spend many hours on seemingly trivial problems or issues that interested him, neglecting larger issues, and that he was losing commissions because of his delay in executing them.[98] The truth was that Wyatt had so much work he could easily afford to lose a few commissions, and most clients, like Beckford, felt that the end result of his labors was worth waiting for.

During the busy years 1806 to 1807, the exterior of the Abbey was being faced in stone to replace the crumbling cement, and Beckford took the decision to demolish Fonthill Splendens, having demolished a wing in 1801.[99] The most exciting project, however, was the new northern "arm" of the cross on the Abbey's plan. In 1803 Lady Ann Hamilton had noted that a northern range was planned for the Abbey, and it was built between 1806 and 1812. In April 1806 Beckford wrote to his future son-in-law, later the Duke of Hamilton, "Wyatt has but just left me after displaying the greatest abilities and taking the greatest pains."[100] This must refer to the designing of the new part of the Abbey. On the plan of Fonthill Abbey published by Rutter in 1823, this unit appears at the top of the page. It consisted of a long gallery of some 150 feet, named King Edward's Gallery because of Beckford and his late wife's many ancestors who were supposedly descendants of Edward III.[101]

King Edward's Gallery opened northwards onto a smaller, "Vaulted Corridor" with nineteen heraldic shields documenting Beckford and his late wife's descent from Edward III,[102] and a magnificent ceiling decorated with numerous ribs in broad, Perpendicular Gothic, picked out in gilt. John Britton likened the pierced bronze doors on either side of the corridor to a "monastic confessional."[103] The Vaulted Corridor directed the eye into the Sanctuary, which had more of Wyatt's fan vaulting with gilt pendants and in which were placed two carved and pierced gilt chests.[104] Both the Sanctuary and the Oratory beyond were hung in crimson damask, and in the Oratory, the holy of holies of Fonthill Abbey, the theme of gilded fan vaulting was continued, creating the effect of "a net-work of burnished gold above our heads." The flickering gilt hanging lamp of Beckford's design illuminated the sculpture of Saint Anthony on his candlelit altar. As Rutter put it, "We believe that the sublimest feelings of our nature were never before raised by such a limited quantity of space and material."[105] In other words, Beckford and Wyatt together had achieved the effect of a Gothic cathedral by means of a lengthy, continuously unfolding vista at the northern extremity of the Abbey at Fonthill.

John Rutter's view illustrates the exterior architecture of this part of the Abbey very clearly (fig. 7-8). The seven Gothic windows of King Edward's Gallery, with double lancets and dripstone moldings, extend north from the Octagon. Rising out of the roof, above the battlements, are the five dormer windows of the Lancaster Gallery, located

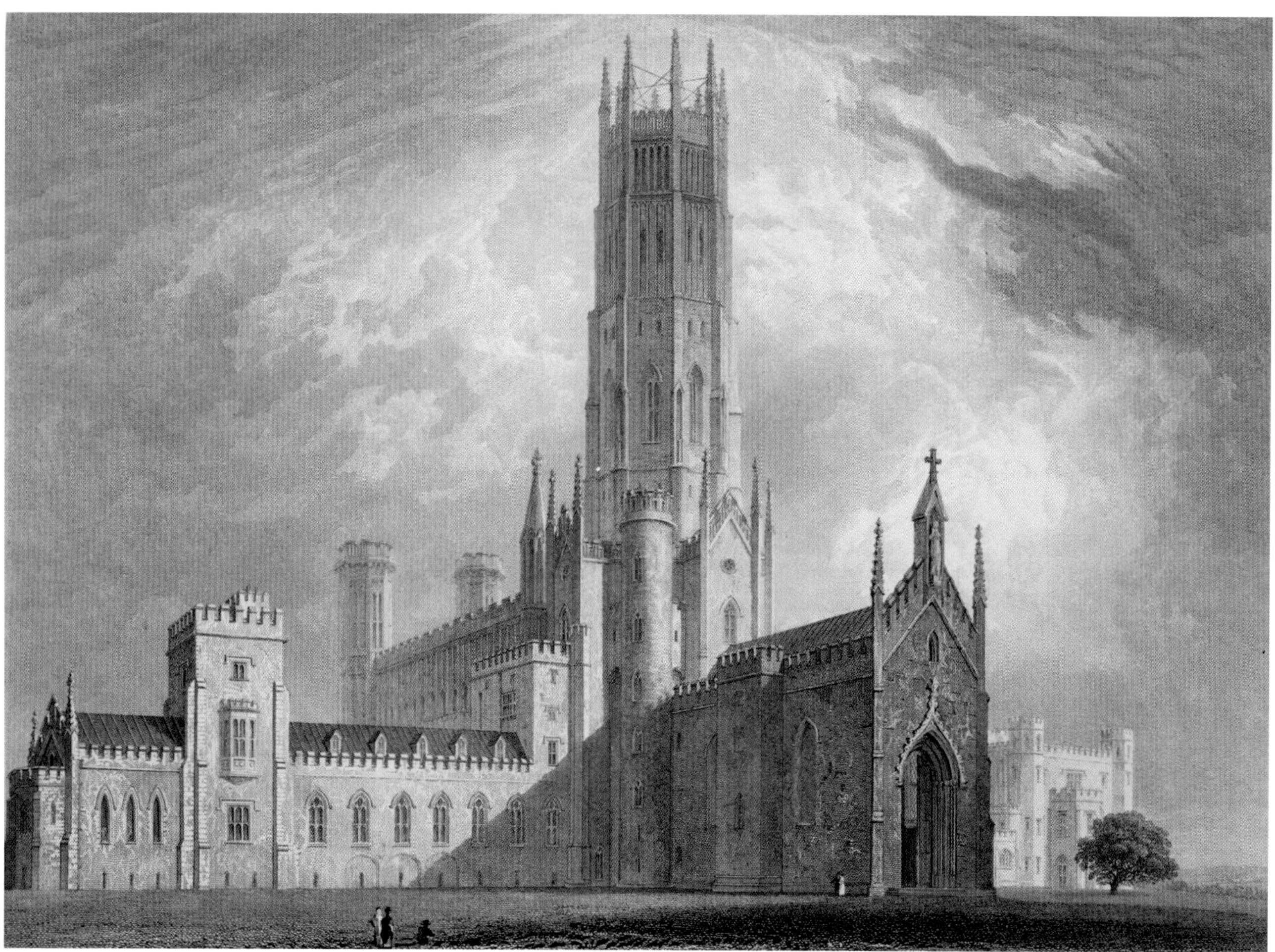

Fig. 7-8. "View of the West and North Fronts," Fonthill Abbey. From *Delineations of Fonthill and its Abbey* by John Rutter (1823), plate 11.

directly above King Edward's Gallery and leading to the Lancaster State Bedchamber. The iconography of this gallery, like that below, was intended to emphasize Beckford's ancestry—in this case, his descent from the medieval house of Lancaster. For designing the decoration of these interiors, Beckford used a specialist consultant in heraldry, Mr Beltz, who held the position of Lancaster Herald, and corresponded with Sir Isaac Heard, another expert on the subject.[106]

Farther north in Storer's view, is the square, battlemented, three-story Lancaster Tower, which survives today along with the remaining structure to the left (north) of it. The prominent oriel window in the Lancaster Tower was already a familiar feature of Wyatt's Gothic, and it lit the State Bedchamber. Immediately to the left of the tower are the three narrow pointed Gothic lancet windows of the Sanctuary, which opened off the Vaulted Corridor and served as the small ante-chamber to the Oratory, whose polygonal form marks the northernmost point of Beckford's Abbey.

Beckford had long toyed with a location for his sanctuary to Saint Anthony at Fonthill Abbey. The original candlelit chapel that Lady Ann Hamilton had described in 1803 was off the Octagon, and opened onto Saint Michael's Gallery, but now it was dramatically placed at the far end of his Abbey, in opposition to the southern oriel of Saint Michael's and more than 300 feet away. This new arrangement was complete by 1812, when Storer recorded it, and the spatial and per-

spectival qualities of it were among the most pronounced in the Abbey. An eyewitness account in the *Morning Herald*, published before the 1822 sale, described it as:

> …the most delightful fairy tale that imagination ever devised. Conceive, Sir, a perspective of 312 feet, through a vaulted gallery, with gothic mouldings overhead, and everything most costly and rich on either side, where the light is admitted chiefly through crimson draperies; but at the half-extent it plays on the enlarged floor of the octagonal opening, in all the varieties of tint that stained glass can impart.[107]

This breathless description of the magical effects of perspective, color, and light created by the two galleries in opposition, across the Octagon, is typical of contemporary opinion of the Abbey. In this central part of the Abbey's architecture, Beckford's interest in effects of light and color combining with Wyatt's genius for spatial effects and Gothic detailing are clearly evident. While few British country houses were of sufficient dimensions to offer such a perspective, this aspect of Fonthill Abbey's architecture was to re-emerge after the collapse of the tower in the design of the first major public building of the Gothic Revival, the New Palace of Westminster, designed by Charles Barry and A. W. N. Pugin after a disastrous fire in 1834.[108]

The two long galleries of Fonthill Abbey, which functioned as private art galleries-cum-libraries for Beckford's vast collections, were decorated differently, but what bound them together and created such a sense of spatial unity was their coloring. In both, hues of red were dominant. It is interesting to note, among contemporary descriptions of the Abbey, the number of different color terms used, principally in the following order: crimson, scarlet, and red, contrasted with purple or dark blue, and gilt. Crimson was a color with strong personal associations for Beckford, as, with his keen interest in heraldry, he knew it was the color connected with his mother's family, the Abercorn Hamiltons, of whom he was extremely proud.[109]

For example, the draperies of the Oak Library, as discussed, were described by Rutter as of crimson damask with inner draperies of scarlet moreen,[110] while the library table in the window recess was covered with purple velvet. Rutter described the draperies in the Oak Parlour as purple silk, alluding to Beckford's belief in his royal Scottish descent, with inner draperies again of scarlet moreen. In the late medieval period, purple and scarlet, originally terms applied to cloth, would have been recognized as belonging to the same family of colors, and distinctions between these colors were often blurred.[111] By the eighteenth century, the educated person would have distinguished between crimson and scarlet as different hues of the color red — scarlet perhaps being considered the warmer red.[112] The purple and crimson theme was continued in the stained glass and draperies of the Octagon, while shades of red dominated Saint Michael's Gallery. Rutter described the carpet there as crimson with cinquefoils of white, while he characterized the curtains as scarlet and deep blue. Britton, however, in his account of 1823, refers to them as scarlet and purple, which sounds more accurate, given Beckford's use of purple elsewhere in the Abbey because of its royal connotations.

In the later ranges of Fonthill Abbey, to the north and, finally, to the east, crimson dominated the interior coloring. Rutter reserves his highest praise for King Edward's Gallery, as "a magnificent apartment," "superbly furnished," with a portrait of Edward III over the Gothic alabaster chimneypiece and curtains of "deep blue" and scarlet.[113] Britton, again, refers to them as purple and scarlet, echoing the description of Storer. Britton tells us the walls were hung with "red" damask, and the frieze around the gallery bore the shields of the seventy-eight Knights of the Garter from whom Beckford claimed that he and his wife, Lady Margaret, were descended.[114]

King Edward's Gallery featured a portrait of Edward III, "copied by Mr. Matthew Wyatt, from a picture in the vestry of Saint George's Chapel, Windsor."[115] The Windsor chapel also provided the model for the lacelike ceiling design of lozenges carved into oak panels with Latimer crosses, painted in stone color. King Edward's Gallery contained some of Beckford's most important manuscripts and rare books, housed in six bookcases, three positioned either side of the chimneypiece, opposite the seven Gothic windows on the west wall. The furnishing continued the antiquarian theme of Saint Michael's Gallery with, in Britton's succinct words, cabinets on stands, "carved in imitation of the style of the Elizabethan age." Britton also wrote that

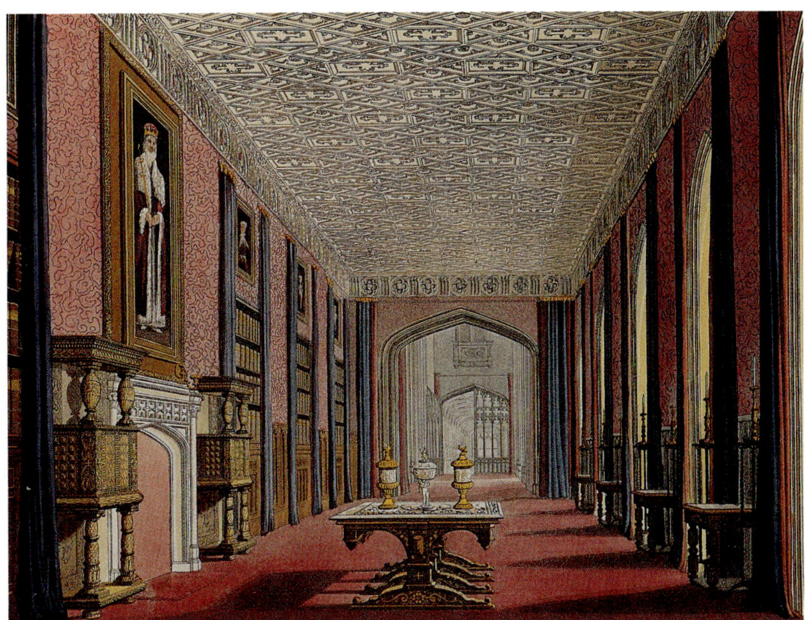

Fig. 7-9. "Interior of King Edward's Gallery," Fonthill Abbey. From *Delineations of Fonthill and its Abbey* by John Rutter (1823), plate 6.

"A series of black [ebonized] tables and candlelabras is on the side of the room, between the windows."[116] These furnishings are clearly visible in the view of the gallery published by Rutter in 1823 (fig. 7-9), which is dominated by the so-called Borghese table, in the center of the gallery, opposite the chimneypiece and under the gaze of Edward III. This is a magnificent slab of Roman late-sixteenth-century pietre-dure work on a carved oak and parcel gilt trestle base made for Beckford, as it displays the Latimer cross, the repeating motif of King Edward's Gallery.[117]

The question of the authorship and dating of the oak, "Elizabethan" or Tudor-style furniture in King Edward's Gallery is an extremely interesting one. This furniture departs in character from the emphasis on black furniture with spirally turned supports in the earlier parts of the Abbey, which can be associated with James Wyatt. The design of the trestle base of the "Borghese" table has classical elements, such as scrollwork carved in its spandrels, which differ in character from Wyatt's work. The bold silhouette, pendants, and bulbous supports of the pier tables and cabinets on stands likewise move beyond Wyatt's Gothic designs of the late eighteenth and early nineteenth century into new territory — that is, the Elizabethan Revival of the first half of the nineteenth century. In character, they anticipate designs for furniture at Ashridge House, Hertfordshire, which was unfinished at Wyatt's sudden death in 1813.

Storer doesn't mention this furniture in his account of 1812, and it is tempting to speculate that it was designed after the death of

James Wyatt, by his son, Benjamin Dean Wyatt, or his nephew, Jeffry Wyatt, who were designing similar carved oak furniture for Ashridge between 1813 and 1823.[118] For example, the octagonal Porter's Table designed by Jeffry Wyatt for the hall at Ashridge survives in the house today. It is Gothic, rather than Elizabethan, in detailing, yet shares a massive silhouette and the prominent use of spandrels found in the Borghese table at Fonthill Abbey. This suggests Jeffry Wyatt was the designer for Beckford's table, as well.[119]

The death of James Wyatt came abruptly and without warning, ending his twenty-three-year working relationship with Beckford. On September 4, 1813, he was traveling in a carriage with Christopher Codrington of Dodington Park, Gloucestershire, who, along with Lord Bridgwater of Ashridge, was one of the two clients most responsible for distracting Wyatt from Fonthill Abbey, greatly to Beckford's annoyance. The carriage suddenly met oncoming traffic and overturned, throwing Wyatt to the ground. Apparently a blow to the head rendered him unconscious, and he died shortly afterward.[120] He was sixty-two years old and still as busy as ever in his profession. Beckford, despite the snide comments he had occasionally made at Wyatt's expense, seems to have been genuinely shocked and grieved. He replied to a letter of condolence from his son-in-law:

> I have perused with sensibility, I might even say with tears, the lines you composed in honour of poor Wyatt in the consoling letter which I have just received from you. My dear friend, it will ever be a great loss for the building, should I take it into my head to finish it. But alas, my poor Bagasse [Beckford's unsavoury nickname for Wyatt] had already sunk from the plane of genius to the mire; for some years now he had only dabbled about in the mud, and I carried on my back the same burden that I carry now.[121]

The last half of this typically Beckford statement is amusing, but entirely untrue. Beckford was under no illusions as to his own limitations as an architect and as to how much he relied on Wyatt. In 1808 he had written, when lamenting another of Wyatt's absences, while the architect was seeing one of his many other clients, "I have some knowledge of my own, but not enough." In the summer of 1810, when Wyatt wasn't available to help him arrange porcelain, Beckford had fretted and remarked, "without Bagasse I'll lose heart. Enclosed is a note begging him to come."[122]

In fact, Wyatt had been much engaged in designing the last "arm" of the Abbey, the Eastern Transept, in the year before his death. Beckford's income from Jamaica had recently increased, allowing a new program of building, and the addition of a "choir" had been mooted since Wyatt's 1799 plan shown at the Royal Academy.[123] In an annotated, super-illustrated volume of his 1823 account of the Abbey, Britton mounted at the back of the book tracings of a series of drawings for architectural details of the Eastern Transept, including details of parapets, turrets, and window tracery. Two of these are clearly inscribed "from James Wyatt," implying that Britton had access to Wyatt's working drawings.[124]

It is not really clear who took over as architect of Fonthill Abbey after Wyatt's death, though his nephew Jeffry Wyatt, his eldest son Benjamin Dean Wyatt, and his youngest son Philip Wyatt, all vied for the copious projects left unfinished at James's death, including Ashridge.[125] Beckford made several coy references to "Sweetness" (Philip) in his correspondence, but does not seem to have used him to any degree at Fonthill. Britton criticized, with justification, the disparity of scale between the Eastern Transept and the rest of the Abbey, which it loomed over.[126] It was Beckford's most megalomaniac scheme of building, and the view Britton published of it illustrates this disparity clearly. Beckford's near-obsession with heraldry and his ancestry were continued in the interiors.

Prior to this last building phase, Beckford had taken all his meals in the Oak Parlour, which was not entirely satisfactory, so a Great Dining Room was included in the new range of the Abbey, as well as a Crimson Breakfast Room and a Crimson Drawing Room. This allowed for the conversion of the Western Hall into a state entrance, forsaking its earlier function as a banqueting hall. Upstairs in the Eastern Transept was an unfinished baronial hall whose theme was a display of the arms of all the barons who extracted the signing of the Magna Carta from King John I in 1215. Beckford and his late wife claimed descent from them all.[127]

The crimson and ebony theme established in Saint Michael's Gallery and in the north range of the Abbey was continued in the Great Dining Room, which boasted two large, upright armoires of ebony with tortoiseshell and brass marquetry and gilt bronze mounts. In Beckford's day they were considered to have been designed by Charles Le Brun, the court designer to Louis XIV, but they are now considered to be among the finest examples of the work of André-Charles Boulle in the Louvre.[128] There were an ebony commode and two further armoires in the Great Dining Room, the latter mounted with pietre dure. The Crimson Drawing Room, in Rutter's account of 1823, had six of the "Wolsey" chairs from Esher, plus three ebony cabinets and an armoire of "buhl and tortoiseshell, made for Lewis XV…from the king's cabinet at Versailles," and some notable pieces of black and gold lacquer, including the famous Van Diemen coffer now in the Victoria and Albert Museum, London.[129]

While Beckford had relied on James Wyatt for advice with purchases and the arrangement of the interiors at Fonthill, after Wyatt's death, Chevalier Gregorio Franchi emerged to fill the vacuum and to make a considerable contribution in his own right to the collections and their arrangement at Fonthill Abbey. In July 1814, Franchi wrote to Beckford from Paris, giving a small sketch of a cabinet he had purchased,[130] and a very interesting letter of September 1817 reports to Beckford on a visit to the "sancta sanctorum" of Gillow's, the leading furniture-making firm, in Hanover Street, London. Franchi reported seeing, "an immense quantity of ebony cabinets" and chairs, six "Italian cabinets" (presumably of pietre-dure technique) and lacquer, as well as a "Buhl cabinet of the old school, very picturesque." Between 1815 and

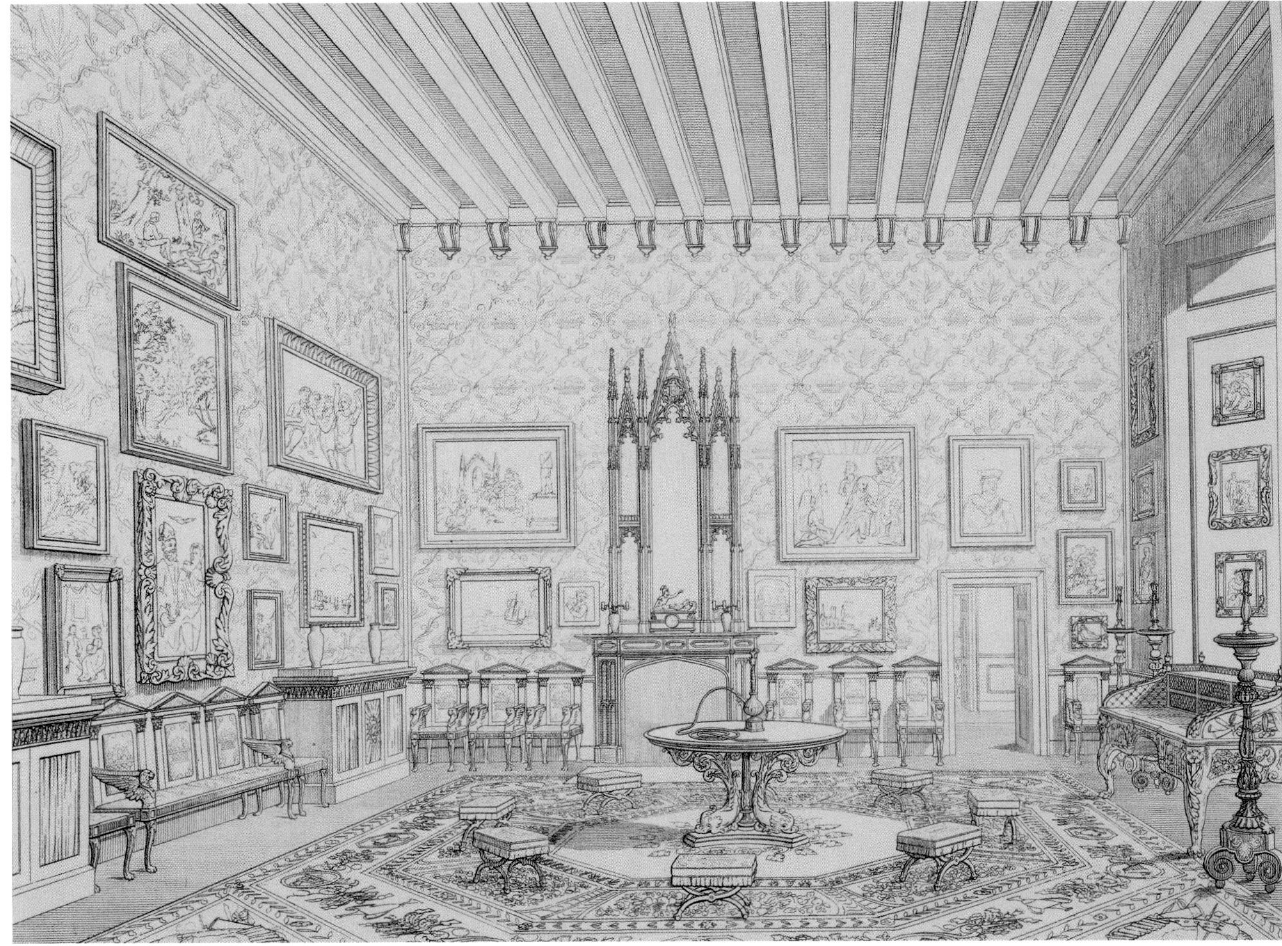

Fig. 7-10. "The Grand Drawing Room," Fonthill Abbey. From *Delineations of Fonthill and its Abbey* by John Rutter (1823), plate 5.

1816, a number of important objects were purchased from the dealer Robert Hume, including a pietre-dure cabinet, an ebony cabinet for the Lancaster Gallery, and the ebony table which was placed in the oriel of Saint Michael's Gallery, supposedly from Esher.

With the Grand Drawing Room of the Eastern Transept, the walls were hung with "garter-blue" silk damask rather than the crimson of earlier interiors, and there is an interesting shift of emphasis in this later interior. Rutter observes that the room had, "a higher degree of finish" than the other interiors of the Eastern Transept,[131] and he may be referring to the fact that the furnishings were more up-to-date and less antiquarian than the rest of the Abbey, and featured a far greater use of gilding. The famous bureau by Riesener made for the Comte d'Orsay, (around 1760) now in the Wallace Collection, London, is seen on the right side of the view published by Rutter in 1823 (fig. 7-10), while the center table of "Egyptian marble," as Rutter calls it, on dolphin supports supposedly came from Malmaison, the château of Napoléon's first empress, Joséphine (see cat. no. 88).[132] The highly classical suite of seat furniture came from the vast collections of Napoléon's uncle, Cardinal Fesch (see cat. no. 53). Even the Boulle-work *bibliothèques* seen against the left-hand wall in figure 7-10 are neoclassical in style and were probably made by the successor to the Boulle workshop, Etienne Levasseur, in the 1770s.[133] Despite the Wyatt-

designed Gothic altarpiece, reused as an overmantel mirror, the style of the Grand Drawing Room was essentially classical, leaving behind the Gothic tradition of the house and pointing the way that Beckford was to follow during the last period of his life, in Bath.

During the final decade of his residence at the Abbey, Beckford's complaints about his social isolation increased. He wrote to his son-in-law in August 1817: "But my dear Douglas I will die…If I vegetate here many more months in this state of solitary abandonment."[134]

In fact, others had tried to assist his transition back into society long before this letter was written, but Beckford seems to have acted as his own worst enemy. The highly sociable James Wyatt, for example, offered to smooth the way to an introduction to the king, but Beckford was too impatient and too proud to proceed with the caution that Wyatt thought necessary.[135] At about the same time, Beckford's agent Mr Wildman had arranged a country house party with several prominent men who wished to meet Beckford, but at the last minute Beckford refused to go. Farington observed, "He makes the difficulty greater."[136] The gloom and isolation of the Abbey certainly must have increased Beckford's sense of melancholy the longer he lived in it.

Eventually change was forced upon Beckford. The temporary expansion of his income in 1812, which allowed the Eastern Transept to proceed, did not last long. By 1818, Beckford and Franchi were aware of financial clouds looming on the horizon. In February 1821 Beckford wrote to his son-in-law that, "affairs in Jamaica go from bad to worse," and "I do not buy any more—I sell."[137] The following week he wrote a cover note to a detailed proposition sent by Franchi, opening negotiations for a private sale to the Duke of Hamilton, whose heir was Beckford's grandson. Doubtless the idea of keeping the Abbey and the Fonthill estates in the family was, initially, uppermost in Beckford's mind. Among the Beckford papers in the Bodleian library are the three-way correspondence between Beckford, Franchi, and Mr Brown, the duke's frugal and cautious agent in Scotland, who minutely dissected the financial proposals regarding the sale of the Abbey to the duke. In January 1822, when negotiations had gone nowhere for some time, the exasperated Beckford wrote directly to the duke, saying, "You are the master—B(rown) must obey you," and that he (Beckford) was "suspended between the sky and the earth—I implore you to release me from this insupportable position."[138] There is the sound of genuine torment in these words.

During the summer of 1822, however, Beckford realized the duke was not going to buy Fonthill,[139] and he quickly came to terms with the idea of a public auction and sale, and fixed his future residence in Bath. Indeed, by early September 1822, Beckford seemed to be positively enjoying the bustle, the international attention, and the extensive press coverage generated by the forthcoming sale of the Abbey and its contents. It was the faithful Franchi who oversaw the thousands of visitors to Fonthill during the sale preview, while Beckford stayed away and began his new life in Bath. On September 23, 1822, Franchi wrote to the Duke of Hamilton that he was in bed with fatigue, as he was welcoming 600 people per day to see the Abbey, including the dukes of Beaufort, Buckingham, and Wellington.[140] By October 8, 1822, it was all over—the Abbey and much of its contents were to be privately sold to the obscure millionaire Mr Farquhar for the princely sum of £300,000, and poor Mr Christie's sale was canceled.[141]

Since August 1822 there had been a frenzy of excitement among the national press, recording almost daily descriptions of the Abbey, its contents, the visitors to it, and the exciting atmosphere. The press coverage was overwhelmingly enthusiastic and was eagerly followed by Beckford, who must have felt he was at last receiving the attention and accolades for which he had longed. The *Times*, on October 1, 1822, cited the "variety of scenery, elegance of architecture, novelty of situation" of the Fonthill estate, adding "the furniture astonishes everyone."[142] On October 5 it reported, "The building, notwithstanding its Gothic character, is light and elegant in the highest degree," while the *Morning Post* reported on October 8 that the announcement of the private sale caused a public sensation.[143] After the sale to Farquhar, the *Morning Chronicle* of November 23, 1822, observed that it would be a matter of great regret if the Abbey were not kept in good order and its contents looked after.[144]

Beckford must have received an enormous boost to his confidence and morale from such glowing reports of his Abbey and his collections. Indeed, despite his departure from a building that had been his life's work up to then, in some respects the sale of Fonthill proved a liberation for him, not the least in financial terms. He wrote to his friend Schöll in Switzerland, "Not for twenty years have I found myself so rich, so independent, or so tranquil."[145] The new life he was forging in Bath was to prove the happiest chapter in his own remarkable story.

Perhaps it is the words of that greatest of Romantic poets and an admirer of Beckford, Lord Byron, that best capture the mood and the public perception of Fonthill Abbey in the days after Beckford had left it:

> Here didst thou dwell, here schemes of pleasure plan,
> Beneath yon mountain's ever beauteous brow:
> But now, as if a thing unblest by Man,
> Thy fairy dwelling is as lone as thou!
> Here giant weeds a passage scarce allow
> To halls deserted, portals gaping wide:
> Fresh lessons to the thinking bosom, how
> Vain are the pleasaunces on earth supplied:
> Swept into wrecks anon by Time's ungentle tide![146]

1. This came to be known as Fonthill Splendens in the nineteenth century. See chap. 3, by Philip Hewat-Jaboor, in this volume.

2. Published by J. Buckler, late December 1825, as a lithograph; see Jon Millington, *Souvenirs of Fonthill Abbey*, ex. cat. (Bath: Bath Preservation Trust, 1994): 22–23, L 12.

3. Cyrus Redding, "Redding's Recollection of Beckford," MS.Eng, misc.d.1459, p. 147, Bodleian Library. Beckford actually claimed to have seen the tower of Fonthill Abbey from his new tower at Lansdown, which would have been impossible in terms of chronology. He said he noticed its disappearance on the day it fell.

4. MS.Beckford, c.30, fols. 136–37, Bodleian Library.

5. Jon Millington, "Fonthill after Beckford," *The Beckford Journal* 2 (Spring 1996): 56.

6. Henry Venn Lansdown, *Recollections of William Beckford*, facs. ed. (Bath: Kingsmead Reprints, 1980).

7. The nineteenth-century history of the site is complex; it is addressed in Millington, "Fonthill" (1996). I am extremely grateful to Sir Charles Morrison, Diana Keith Neal, and Rose Sanguinetti for a memorable tour of the Fonthill estate and for providing a history of its buildings and gardens. Further information was kindly given me by the Hon. Alastair Morrison.

8. James Storer, writing in 1812, implies that the project was still current. See *A Description of Fonthill Abbey, Wiltshire* (London: Storer et al., 1812): 4.

9. Kenneth Woodbridge, *The Stourhead Landscape, Wiltshire* (London: The National Trust, 1995): 60.

10. See Michael McCarthy, *The Origins of the Gothic Revival* (New Haven and London: Yale

University Press, 1987): 30–31. These triangular towers may deliberately echo the design of the Elizabethan hunting tower that survives in the grounds of Chatsworth, Derbyshire.

11. Beckford to Wyatt at Windson, 23 October 1791, MS. Beckford, c.37, fols. 48–49, Bodleian Library. Beckford writes, "I have been waiting for you the *whole* summer" and waits for him to be "coming again to Fonthill." Beckford's most recent biographer, Timothy Mowl, suggests that Wyatt was consulted in 1790 about the walling in of the wooded hills on which the Abbey was to be sited (*William Beckford: Composing for Mozart* [London: John Murray, 1999]: 206). John Wilton-Ely has suggested that Wyatt may have met Beckford in the mid-1780s when working at Powderham Castle, Devon, the home of "Kitty" Courtenay ("The Genesis and Evolution of Fonthill Abbey," *Architectural History* 23 [1980]: 49n5.) However, most writers place Wyatt's work at Powderham in the mid-1790s. See Howard Colvin, *A Biographical Dictionary of British Architects, 1600–1840,* 3d ed. (New Haven and London: Yale University Press, 1995): 1118; and John Martin Robinson, *The Wyatts: An Architectural Dynasty* (Oxford: Oxford University Press, 1979): 245. A date of around 1790 for the start of Beckford and Wyatt's working relationship seems most likely.

12. Robinson, *Wyatts* (1979): 241.

13. See *The Diary of Joseph Farington,* ed. Kenneth Garlick and Angus Macintyre, vol. 2, Jan. 1795–Aug. 1796 (New Haven and London: Yale University Press, 1978): 612.

14. Ibid.

15. McCarthy, *Origins* (1987): 42–43.

16. MS. Beckford, c.37, fols. 50–51, Bodleian Library.

17. Michael McCarthy has suggested that, owing to Beckford's well-known hatred of hunting, he may have conflated the identities of Saint Anthony Abbott and Saint Anthony of Padua, perhaps having witnessed the annual blessing of animals in the Church of Saint Anthony Abbott in Rome (letter to author, 8 October 2000). For more on the subject of Beckford, Saint Anthony of Padua, and Lisbon, see Eric Darton, "William Beckford and Religion," *The Beckford Journal* 4 (Spring 1998): 34–35; and J. C. M. Nolan, "The Devotee Glances at the Glorious One," in ibid., pp. 39, 43; see also Malcolm Jack, "Monserrate: Beckford's Second Sintra House," in ibid., pp. 48–51.

18. William Beckford, *Life at Fonthill, 1807–1822,* ed. Boyd Alexander (London: Hart-Davis, 1957): 60n2.

19. Farington, *Diary,* vol. 1 (1978): 196.

20. Beckford, *Life at Fonthill* (1957): 12; see also Guy Chapman, *Beckford* (London: Jonathan Cape, 1937): 200. Chapman suggests, "His grief was natural and unaffected."

21. This part of Beckford's life is recounted in some detail in Mowl, *Beckford* (1999): 123–44. Correspondence in the Bodleian library attests to Beckford's feelings of dismay at being told the time was not ripe for him to return to England. See, for example, Thomas Wildman to Beckford, 14 April 1789, MS. Beckford, c.37, fol. 13–14, Bodleian Library.

22. Mowl casts doubt on the idea that Beckford visited Batalha in 1794 when he visited Alcobaça, despite his claims to have done so in *Recollections of an Excursion to the Monasteries of Alcobaça and Batalha of 1835.* He is, however, mistaken in suggesting that it was Beckford who introduced Wyatt to Batalha. (Mowl, *Beckford* [1999]: 217–18).

23. Murphy, *Plans…Batalha* (London: I and J Taylor, 1795); it was reissued in 1836, with a French edition in 1797, and an influential German edition published in Leipzig in 1813, translated by Johann Daniel Engelhard. For some of Murphy's preparatory drawings, see "Sketches of Batalha" (1789), bound album, ref. 189G, library of the Society of Antiquaries, London. I am most grateful to the late Clive Wainwright for bringing this album to my attention.

24. See Gabriel Beranger, *Drawings of the Principal Antique Buildings of Ireland,* ed. Peter Harbison (Dublin: Four Courts Press, 1998): 14. For further information on Beranger and Conyngham, see Sir William Wilde, *Memoir of Gabriel Beranger, and his Labours in the Cause of Irish Art and Antiquities, from 1760 to 1780* (Dublin: M. H. Gill and Son, 1880). Born William Burton, in 1781 he succeeded his uncle to the Barony of Mount Charles, inheriting Slane Castle, Co. Meath, and becoming the second Lord Conynham. See Alastair Rowan, "Georgian Castles in Ireland," *Bulletin of the Irish Georgian Society* 7 (January–March 1964): 16.

25. See Paolo Pereira, intro. to *James Murphy e o Mosteiro da Batalha,* ex. cat. (Lisboa: Instituto Portugues do Patrimonio Cultural, 1989). I am most grateful to Michael McCarthy for supplying me with an English translation by Oliver Condon.

26. Beranger, *Buildings of Ireland* (1998): 150–53. The first Lord Conyngham had engaged James Wyatt to make designs for neoclassical interiors early in the 1770s, as drawings by Wyatt for Slane dated as early as 1772 survive in the National Library in Dublin. This was at the beginning of Wyatt's architectural career, following close on the heels of his great success and first major commission, the Pantheon on Oxford Road, London. See four plans dated 1772 for "Major General Cunninghame," Wyatt Album, A.D. 3125–3138, and a design for the library ceiling at Slane Castle, 1773, Box 2, A.D. 3156, National Library, Dublin. I am grateful to Collette O'Daly for her assistance and ideas in interpreting the Wyatt drawings in Dublin. Further drawings by Wyatt for Slane, all neoclassical in style, are in the Wyatt Album/58.511, Department of Drawings, Prints and

Photographs, The Metropolitan Museum of Art, New York.

27. Rowan, "Georgian Castles"(1964): 17.

28. See Desmond Guinness and William Ryan, *Irish Houses and Castles* (New York: Viking Press, 1971): 262–67.

29. Colvin, *Biographical Dictionary* (1995): 1116. The house was demolished in the 1950s but is illustrated in, Anthony Dale, *James Wyatt* (Oxford: Basil Blackwell, 1956).

30. Ibid., pp. 133–38. It is worth noting that the gentleman-architect Thomas Pitt, who provided some designs for Strawberry Hill, visited and sketched Alcobaça, Batalha, and other Portuguese monuments in 1760. See McCarthy, *Origins* (1987): 17–19.

31. The anteroom and some of the bookcases from the Lee Priory library are now in the collection of the Victoria and Albert Museum, London. Walpole remarked of the library, in 1794, "a prior's library that does such honour to Mr Wyatt's taste" (Dale, *Wyatt* [1956]: 135).

32. Some modern accounts of the Abbey have erroneously credited Beckford, rather than Wyatt, with the choice of Batalha as a model. See Mowl, *Beckford* (1999): 218. This idea, no doubt, began to be encouraged by Beckford during his own lifetime. For example, the *British Press,* 11 October 1823, reported that Fonthill Abbey's architecture was inspired by "the convents of Mafra and Battaglia," and claimed this was at the suggestion of Beckford's friend the Marquis of Marialva (MS. Beckford, b.6., fol. 126, Bodleian Library). This sounds like pure Beckford and is a claim that doesn't stand up in the light of Wyatt's career and contacts.

33. Reginald Turnor, *James Wyatt, 1746–1813* (London: Art and Technics, 1950): 39.

34. Dale, *Wyatt* (1956): 180–81.

35. *Delineations of Fonthill and its Abbey* (Shaftesbury: by the author, 1823): 109.

36. See Farington, *Diary,* vol. 1 (1978): 162–63; and Dale, *Wyatt* (1956): 184–85. Dale tells us from 1796, Wyatt was, "almost continuously employed by George III" (p. 185). Wyatt had already held the post of Surveyor to the Fabric of Westminster Abbey for 20 years.

37. See John Wilton-Ely, "Beckford the Builder," *The William Beckford Exhibition,* Diana Keith Neal, organiser (Tisbury, Wilts: The Compton Press, 1976) p. 36; and Michael Snodin and Malcolm Baker, "William Beckford's Silver" I, *Burlington Magazine* CXXII (November 1980) p. 740. Timothy Mowl suggests the Catholic chapel nearby at Wardour Castle may have inspired Beckford (*Beckford* [1999]: 43).

38. Regarding Walpole's chapel, later called the Tribune, see McCarthy, *Origins* (1987): 85; and J. Mordaunt Crook, "Strawberry Hill Revisited" I, *Country Life* (June 7, 1973). Regarding the "Catholic air," as Walpole referred to it, of Chute's chapel and ante-chapel at the Vyne, see *The Vyne, Hampshire* (National Trust Guidebook, 1983) pp. 17–18.

39. The most obvious example of this is to be found in the career of A.W.N. Pugin, who asserted that true Gothic design could only be practiced by those who had the true ancient faith. The theme is recurrent in his most famous publication, *The True Principles of Pointed or Christian Architecture* (London: John Weale, 1841). See, for example, pp. 10 (note), 38, 50–51, and 54.

40. Wilton-Ely, "Beckford the Builder" (1976): 36.

41. Ibid., pp. 40–41.

42. JMW Turner, pencil sketch of Fonthill Abbey in progress, 1799, DO 2182/XLVII 5, Clore Gallery, Tate Britain.

43. In 1779, Wyatt had built one of the first London townhouses to be entirely faced in stucco, known as "Higgins cement." (See Turnor, *Wyatt* [1950]: 32) One of his earliest Gothic houses, Sheffield Place, Sussex (1775–77; 1780–90) was faced with "Roman cement" (Dale, *Wyatt* [1956]: 126). Moreover, his cousin, Charles Wyatt, was a cement manufacturer in London (Colvin, *Biographical Dictionary* [1995]: 1105).

44. McCarthy, *Origins* (1987): 57 and fig. 69.

45. Farington, *Diary,* vol. 3 (1978): 880.

46. Ibid., pp. 697 and 840–912, passim. This is the Edward Foxhall who was employed as a carver for Sir John Soane at Wimpole House, Cambridgeshire; and the cabinetmaker cited by Thomas Sheraton at Old Cavendish Street, Cavendish Square, London, a sometime partner in "Foxhall and Fryer." See Christopher Gilbert and Geoffrey Beard, eds., *The Dictionary of English Furniture Makers, 1660–1840* (Leeds: W.S. Maney & Son, 1986): 315. See also Clive Wainwright, *The Romantic Interior: The British Collector at Home, 1750–1850* (New Haven and London: Yale University Press, 1989): 120.

47. Farington, *Diary,* vol. 3 (1978): 912.

48. Ibid., p. 916.

49. See Andrew Wilton, *Catalogue of Turner Drawings in the British Museum: Watercolours, Part 2* (London: British Museum, date?): 337–39 (no. 332 illustrates the Bolton view); and A. J. Finberg, *A Complete Inventory of the Drawings of the Turner Bequest,* vol. 1 (London: HMSO, 1909): 120–24.

50. See Susan Morris, "'Two Perspective Views': Turner and Lewis William Wyatt," *Turner Studies*

2 (Winter 1983): 34–36. I am very grateful to Kim Sloan for bringing this article to my attention.

51. See the drawings for tracery on the oriel windows of Lee Priory, album of designs by James Wyatt for Lee Priory, ca. 1782–85, 92.D. 59, p. 25, Department of Prints and Drawings, Victoria and Albert Museum, London.

52. The stained glass in the Oak Parlour, which was still *in situ* at the time of Venn Lansdown's visit in 1844, was designed by the artist William Hamilton and made by Eginton's of Birmingham. For the thirty-two colored designs of standing figures of kings and knights from the Conquest to the Tudor period, see Box D.4.B/7888.1-32, Department of Prints and Drawings, Victoria and Albert Museum, London. Research by Sarah Baylis suggests that some of this glass may now be situated at Newstead Abbey, Nottinghamshire (electronic letter to the author, 22 January 2001).

53. Rutter tells us that, "On the shelves and armoires…Mr Beckford has deposited an extensive and costly collection of works in the fine arts for their information study" (*Delineations* [1823]: 14); see also Storer, *Description* (1812): 11.

54. For the original article, see *Gentleman's Magaine* 71 (April 1801): 297; reprinted at the time of Farquhar's sale in the *Morning Chronicle* (1822; b.6., fol. 34, Bodleian Library); and in John Britton, *Graphical and Literary Illustrations of Fonthill Abbey* (London: Longmans, Green and Co., 1823): 28–30. The probable author was Henry Tresham, a member of the Royal Academy who attended the Nelson banquet.

55. Britton, *Illustrations of Fonthill* (1823): 28.

56. This was the second time the tower fell; in 1799 the central tower had first fallen (MS. Beckford, c.37, fols. 54–55, Bodleian Library).

57. Farington, *Diary*, vol. 4 (1978): 1452.

58. Ibid., p. 1537. For further information on Sir William Hamilton, his circle, and the Beckford connection, see Ian Jenkins and Kim Sloan, *Vases and Volcanoes: Sir William Hamilton and his Collection* (London: British Museum Press, 1996).

59. See Mowl, *Beckford* (1999): 237; and Beckford, *Life at Fonthill* (1957): 28–30.

60. As quoted in Britton, *Illustrations of Fonthill* (1823): 30.

61. Ibid., p. 29.

62. Quoted in Mowl, *Beckford* (1999): 13.

63. Venn Lansdown, *Recollections* (1980): 19.

64. Six ebony chairs were presented to George IV by the Duke of York as "Cardinal Wolsey's" chairs. They were very likely Beckford's, acquired from Esher Place and sold in 1823. The king purchased a further eleven ebony and ivory chairs similar to Beckford's from the dealer Kensington Lewis in 1825. See Clive Wainwright, "Only the True Black Blood," *Furniture History* 21 (1985): 254. One chair is illustrated in Alexandre Pradère, *French Furniture Makers: The Art of the Ebéniste from Louis XIV to the Revolution* (London: Philip Wilson, 1989): 135.

65. Wainwright, "True Black Blood"(1985): 251, 254.

66. "Journal of Lady Ann Hamilton," 1803, MS. Beckford, e.4, fol. 4, Bodleian Library.

67. Storer, *Description* (1812): 17.

68. Rutter, *Delineations* (1823): 21.

69. Storer, *Description* (1812): 18.

70. It seems likely that James Wyatt's timbered ceiling at Fonthill was the model for that at Ashridge, executed posthumously by his nephew, Jeffry Wyatt (later Wyatville). It is illustrated in the guide to the house, *Ashridge* by Kay Sanecki and Michael Thompson (Norwich: Jarrold Publishing, 1998). Despite his denigration of "Wyatt the destructive," A. W. N. Pugin illustrates a very similar timbered roof design in *The True Principles* (pl. 6, fig. 1).

71. Rutter, *Delineations* (1823): 25.

72. Dale, *Wyatt* (1956): 153. The centralized, straight, lower level of steps was foreshadowed in Wyatt's Liverpool Town Hall of around 1795 (see Turnor, *Wyatt* [1950]: fig. 60).

73. Rutter, *Delineations* (1823): 24.

74. On 4 July 1801 Farington reported of Fonthill Splendens that, "Beckford has ordered the Colonnade and wings of Fonthill to be pulled down. The body of the House is to remain and to be the residence of his daughters" (*Diary*, vol. 4 [1978]: 1573) On 1 February 1804, Farington stated that Benjamin West, recently returned from Fonthill, told him, "Mr. Beckford at Fonthill resides at the Abbey, but His two daughters live at the Great House, as it is called, from which they go every day to dine with him" (*Diary*, vol. 4 [1978]: 2230).

75. Britton, *Illustrations of Fonthill* (1823): 30.

76. MS. Beckford, e.4, fol. 5, Bodleian Library.

77. Storer, *Description* (1812): 14. The spelling of "Buhl" for ebony veneered cabinets inspired by André–Charles Boulle (1642–1732) seems to be a phenomenon of the early nineteenth century. Storer, in 1812, is among the earliest writers to use this spelling. By the time of the Fonthill sale in 1822, "buhl" was a common term used by the newspapers to refer to European furniture with ebony veneer, regardless of date or the presence of tortoiseshell in the decoration. Colonial furniture tended to be called "ebony," but this was by no means systematic.

78. In 1813–15, Franchi was buying ebony furniture for Beckford (MS. Beckford, c. 37, fols. 73, 76, 79, Bodleian Library.) Payments are recorded to the dealers Hitchcock, E. H. Baldock, Prato, Jenkins, Lambeth, and Robert Hume (fols. 77, 79) At least some of these objects were shipped from across the Channel. (fol. 78) This was a period of great activity on the part of British purchasers of French antique furniture and luxury goods. For example, the Duke of Wellington, hero of the Battle of Waterloo and a great admirer of Fonthill Abbey, acquired over twenty pieces of Boulle-type furniture from Paris during the period 1814–16. See Megan Aldrich, "A Setting for Boulle Furniture: The Duke of Wellington's Gallery at Stratfield Saye," *Apollo* 147 (June 1998): 19–27.

79. For antiquarian houses combining Baroque and Gothic elements, see Wainwright, *Romantic Interior* (1989): esp. chaps. 6, 7, and 8.

80. Rutter, *Delineations* (1823): 51. Similar cabinets from Saint Michael's Gallery were purchased by George Hammond Lucy in 1823 and are now at Charlecote Park, Warwickshire, where a number of Beckford objects reside. See Clive Wainwright, "Beckford the Collector," *The William Beckford Exhibition*, organized by Diana Keith Neal (Tisbury, Wilts: Compton Press, 1976): 81. In the drawing room, Lucy used the same yellow silk on the walls as Beckford had done in order to set off his ebony furniture, including a handsome ebony and *pietre dure* cabinet on a stand made for Beckford. See *Charlecote Park, Warwickshire* (London: The National Trust, 1996): 24–25.

81. Clive Wainwright pointed out, however, that Storer's description of Fonthill Abbey is by no means as complete as that of Rutter in terms of recording the contents of the interiors at the time of publication ("Some Objects from William Beckford's Collection now in the Victoria and Albert Museum," *Burlington Magazine* 113 [May 1971]: 258). Nonetheless, a considerable quantity of objects and furnishings was acquired in the 1808–18 period.

82. For Lady Ann's sketch of the frieze of the bookcases, see MS. Beckford, e.4, fol. 5, Bodleian Library. For a detailed description of the Oak Library, see Rutter, *Delineations* (1823): 14.

83. As early as 1795 Foxhall wrote to Beckford in Lisbon that he was making six stools to Wyatt's designs for Splendens (MS. Beckford, c.30, fols. 169–70, Bodleian Library). See also ibid., fols. 171–74, dating to December 1802, discussing "ebony" and Gothic furniture for the Abbey, to Wyatt's designs.

84. MS. Beckford, e.4, fol. 6, Bodleian Library.

85. Storer, *Description* (1812): 16.

86. MS. Beckford, e.4, fol. 6, Bodleian Library.

87. See Christopher Wilk, ed. *Western Furniture, 1350 to the Present Day, in the Victoria and Albert Museum* (London: Philip Wilson, 1996): 56–57.

88. Storer, *Description* (1812): 15.

89. See note 64 regarding the probable sale of Beckford's "Wolsey" furniture to the Duke of York.

90. For a discussion of the objects in Saint Michael's Gallery and their provenance, see Wainwright, *Romantic Interior* (1989): 133–35.

91. Rutter, *Delineations* (1823): 53. Two of these glazed cabinets are now at Charlecote Park, Warwickshire. One table with a slab top was also purchased by Lucy in 1823 (Wainwright, "Beckford the Collector" [1976]: 81).

92. MS. Beckford, c.30, fol. 173–74, Bodleian Library.

93. These exterior views of Cassiobury come from the Fonthill Sketchbook (1799–1804), Box 320/DO 2221/XLVII 38-45, Clore Gallery, Tate Britain, London. I am grateful for the assistance of Sarah Taft in examining the Turner drawings.

94. For views of the stained glass and furnishings of the Great Cloister, Cassiobury, see ibid., DO 2220/XLVII 43 and DO 2234/XLVII 57.

95. Wilton-Ely, "Beckford the Builder" (1976): 45. Wilton-Ely suggests work "effectively ceased" between 1802 and 1805, but Wyatt was certainly at Fonthill in 1804 (see next note).

96. Late in October (?) 1804, Beckford was partly irritated, partly amused that Wyatt, "lately left him at the Abbey on pretence of being obliged to go immediately to town." In fact, Beckford discovered Wyatt stayed secretly with Foxhall for one and a half days at Splendens enjoying Beckford's food and hearth. Perhaps Wyatt found his client a bit intense and demanding on occasion (Farington, *Diary*, vol. 4 [1978]: 2283).

97. Ibid., p. 2214. George III had embarked on a new palace at Kew in the Gothic style, with Wyatt as architect. It was never finished owing to the onset of insanity in the unfortunate king. His son George IV demolished it, preferring to concentrate his energies at Windsor.

98. Ibid., vol. 8, ed. Kathryn Cave (1978): 2887.

99. Wilton-Ely, "Beckford the Builder" (1976): 45. Farington remarked that, "By taking down the House and selling the furniture Mr. Beckford will be relieved from an annual expense of £3000. …and probably receive £25,000 from what is sold" (*Diary*, vol. 8 [1978]: 3116). Foxhall was allowed

to remove materials salvaged from the wreck of the house, and paid £16,000 for its contents. See MS.Beckford, c.30, fol. 175–76, Bodleian Library.

100. Dale, *Wyatt* (1956): 150.

101. Britton, *Illustrations of Fonthill* (1823): 43.

102. Rutter, *Delineations* (1823): 39.

103. Britton, *Illustrations of Fonthill* (1823): 45.

104. See Wainwright, *Romantic Interior* (1989): 125. These chests are now in the Wallace Collection, London.

105. Rutter, *Delineations* (1823): 35. For the design of the hanging lamp, see chap. 11, by Michael Snodin, in this volume.

106. Regarding Beltz's role, see Britton, *Illustrations of Fonthill* (1823): 19; and Beckford, *Life at Fonthill* (1957): 337n1; regarding Heard, see MS. Beckford, b.8, fols. 10–11, 14–15, Bodleian Library. Beckford's correspondence with him concerned his attempt to claim a defunct peerage.

107. A Tourist, "Fonthill Abbey," letter to the ed., *Morning Herald*, 15 August, 1822, MS. Beckford, b.6, fol. 3, Bodleian Library. Beckford assembled a sizable collection of newspaper cuttings (some annotated in his own hand) on topics that interested him. Among the largest groups are those concerning Fonthill Abbey and Strawberry Hill, the pioneering Gothic house of Horace Walpole.

108. This has long been recognized. See Boyd Alexander, "Fonthill, Wiltshire—III: William Beckford as Collector," *Country Life* 140 (8 December 1966): 1576; and Clive Wainwright, "William Beckford, his Collection and the Influence of his Excursion to Alcobaça and Batalha in 1794," *Portugal e o Reino Unido: A Aliança Revisitada*, organized by Angela Delaforce (Lisbon: Gulbenkian Foundation, 1994): 100.

109. Boyd Alexander, "Fonthill and Portraits of William Beckford (1760–1844)," *Register of the Museum of Art, University of Kansas* 3 (Winter 1967): 8.

110. Damask was considered the principal luxury fabric for "elegant Drawing Rooms" during the Regency period, whereas moreen was a woven woollen cloth considered less expensive and desirable. See Frances Collard, *Regency Furniture* (Woodbridge, Suffolk: Antique Collectors Club, 1985): 283, 285.

111. For more on this complex and fascinating subject, see John Gage, *Colour and Culture: Practice and Meaning from Antiquity to Abstraction* (London: Thames and Hudson, 1995): esp. 80–83. Purple was considered problematic as a color for heraldry, and it was not really defined as a color until the seventeenth century.

112. John Gage to the author, 29 June 2000.

113. Rutter, *Delineations* (1823): 33–34.

114. Britton, *Illustrations of Fonthill* (1823): 45. Unlike Britton, Rutter does not use the color term *red* in his description of the Abbey interiors, referring instead to either scarlet or crimson.

115. The portrait of King Edward was "in a forward state" when Matthew Digby Wyatt wrote to Beckford on 2 October 1812 (Wyatt family MSS. 3143/10, Victoria and Albert Museum, London). There was a misunderstanding concerning the amount Wyatt expected to be paid; a similar situation had occurred with William Hamilton over tuition given to Beckford's daughters (Farington, *Diary*, vol. 4 [1978]: 1570–71).

116. Britton, *Illustrations of Fonthill* (1823): 45.

117. It is now at Charlecote Park, Warwickshire, where it occupies a prominent position in the Great Hall along with the small oak tables seen against the window piers of King Edwards' Gallery in Rutter's view. National Trust, Charlecote Guide, p. 13; and Clive Wainwright, *Romantic Interior* (1989): 117–18. Also at Charlecote is the "Lancaster State Bed" with its crimson hangings, using the backs of two seventeenth-century carved ebony settees as headboard and footboard. The uprights of the bed, which may have been supplied by Foxhall, have spirally turned supports above polygonal posts with Gothic arches reminiscent of Wyatt's architectural designs.

118. Designs for the Ashridge furniture and architectural fittings by Jeffry and Benjamin Dean Wyatt, dating between 1813 and 1823, are in the Drawings Collection of the Royal Institute of British Architects, London (see WyBD[1] 1–8; and WyJe [1] 1–92). I am most grateful to Sarah Day for a splendid tour of Ashridge, now Ashridge Management College.

119. Jeffry Wyatt would have learned the Elizabethan style on-site at several notable commissions during the early nineteenth century. In 1801 he executed work at the Elizabethan great house, Wollaston Hall, Nottinghamshire; in 1802–06 he built Nonsuch Park, Surrey, in the "Tudor" style; and 1806–13 he carried out extensive work at Longleat House, Wiltshire, one of the most famous of Elizabethan great houses. See Colvin, *Biographical Dictionary* (1995): 1130–31.

120. See Dale, *Wyatt* (1956): 193–95.

121. MS. Beckford, c.21, fols. 34–35, Bodleian Library; the translation from the French into English was published by Boyd Alexander in Beckford, *Life at Fonthill* (1957): 137.

122. Beckford, *Life at Fonthill* (1957): 90–93. In August 1812, Beckford was referring to his "angelic Bagasse" who labored tirelessly on the Eastern Transept, assisted by "Sweetness," Wyatt's youngest son, Philip, for whom Beckford clearly felt an attraction, and " Coxone," or Charles Hayter, Beckford's Clerk of Works.

123. Wilton-Ely, "Genesis" (1980): 47, 44.

124. These are 1982.3025 and 1982.3003, bound into the endpapers of Britton's *Illustrations of Fonthill* in the Wiltshire Archaeological and Natural History Society Library, Devizes. I am grateful to the librarian, Mrs Haycock, for her assistance, and to Philip Hewat-Jaboor for bringing this document to my attention. The original drawings by Wyatt for the Eastern Transept have not been located, and, indeed, few of Wyatt's drawings or professional papers survive, which is surprising given the size of his professional practice. Other pages in this volume include sketches and correspondence by Franchi and Beckford.

125. For details of the activities of the younger Wyatts who succeeded James, see Robinson, *Wyatts* (1979): chap. 4.

126. Britton, *Illustrations of Fonthill* (1823): 12. He also stated that the two prominent turrets at the east end of the wing were based on the gateway at Saint Augustine's, Canterbury (p. 11n1).

127. Ibid., p. 51. This is another fascinating way in which Fonthill Abbey may have influenced the design of the New Palace of Westminster, for this theme is echoed exactly in the iconography of the House of Lords, opened in 1847 and designed as a large, sumptuously decorated baronial hall by A. W. N. Pugin. Pugin and Wyatt's contemporary John Carter were the two most vociferous critics of James Wyatt, mainly on the basis of his cathedral restorations. Pugin called him "this pest of cathedral architecture," and "Wyatt the destructive" (see Clive Wainwright, introduction, *Recollections of Pugin* by Benjamin Ferrey [London: The Scholar Press]: 80, 85–86; and Pugin, *True Principles* (1841): 62. However Pugin, like every other architect of his generation, could not avoid the powerful influence of Wyatt and his career. Carter was formally reprimanded by the Society of Antiquaries of London for his public persecution of Wyatt, and Anthony Dale has convincingly established that most of Wyatt's contemporaries approved his work on the cathedrals (*Wyatt* [1956]: chap. 7). For more on the fanatical Carter, see J. Mordaunt Crook, *John Carter and the Mind of the Gothic Revival*, Occasional Papers of the Society of Antiquaries of London, 17 (Leeds: W. S. Maney, 1995).

128. For the d'Aumont armoires, see Wainwright, *Romantic Interior* (1989): 132–33, although the date given of 1630 is about seventy years too early; they are illustrated in Pradère, *French Furniture Makers* (1989): 80.

129. Rutter, *Delineations* (1823): 30.

130. MS. Beckford, c.12, fols. 46–47 and 53–54 (written in Portuguese), Bodleian Library. For further memoranda concerning the purchase of ebony, lacquer, and precious objects, see MS. Beckford, c.37, fols. 73, 74–75, 78–101; fol. 77v, in Beckford's hand, details the objects from Hume. For a list of the treasures that the dealer Fogg had, and what Franchi hoped to buy during his forthcoming trip to Paris in 1814, see MS. Beckford, c.39, fol. 72–73, and 74–75.

131. Rutter, *Delineations* (1823): 30.

132. For a discussion of Beckford's purchases in Paris after 1800, see Clive Wainwright, "In Lucifer's Metropolis," *Country Life* 186 (1 October 1992): 82–84.

133. Aldrich, "A Setting for Boulle" (1998).

134. MS. Beckford, c.21, fol. 86 (written in French), Bodleian Library.

135. Farington, *Diary*, vol. 3 (1978): 913–14.

136. Ibid., p. 1117.

137. MS. Beckford, c.21, fols. 99–100 (written in French), Bodleian Library.

138. Ibid., fols. 102a–b (in French).

139. "I have no hopes of the business…Mr Brown is the overruling providence in the Duke's affairs…Nothing remains…but to bring on the Great Sale" (Beckford to his solicitor Fownes, 17 August 1822, MS. Beckford, c.30, fols 112–13, Bodleian Library).

140. MS. Beckford, c.39, fol. 89, Bodleian Library.

141. Ibid., fols. 92–93.

142. MS. Beckford, b.6, fol. 6, Bodleian Library.

143. Ibid., fol. 11.

144. Ibid., fol. 18.

145. MS.Beckford, c.25, fols. 89–90, Bodleian Library.

146. Lord Byron, *The Works of Lord Byron* (Ware, Hertfordshire: Wordsworth Editions, 1994): 180, stanza 23. *Childe Harold's Pilgrimage* was written in 1817–18, and the number of similarities between the hero of the poem and Beckford's biography suggests Beckford was the model. The stanza quoted actually refers to the house in Sintra of "Vathek, England's Wealthiest Son," but the qualities of loss and melancholy apply equally to the Abbey at Fonthill. For the relationship of Byron and Beckford, see Jon Millington, "Beckford and Byron," *The Beckford Journal* 1 (Spring 1995): 41–46.

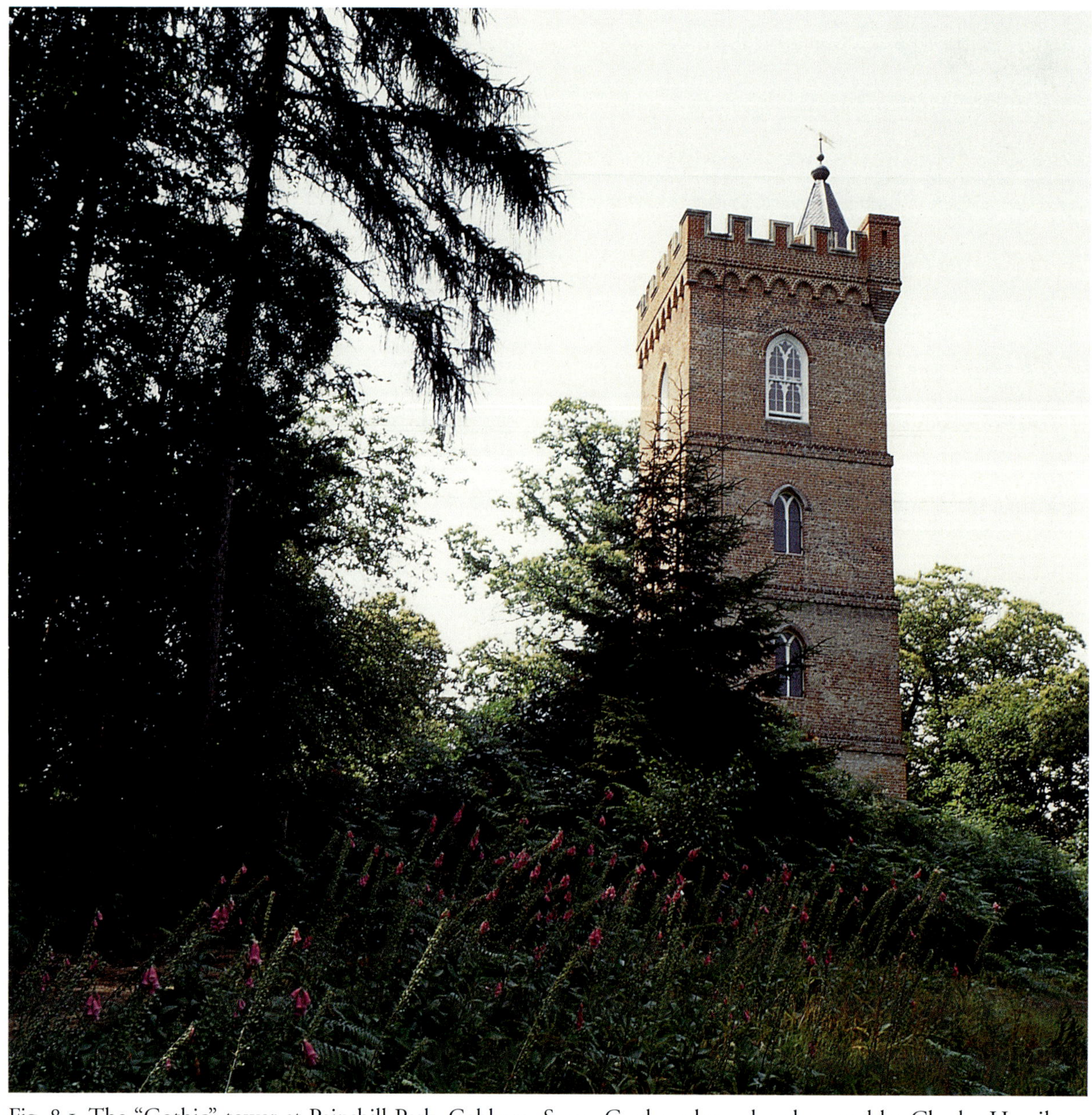

Fig. 8-1. The "Gothic" tower at Painshill Park, Cobham, Surry. Garden planned and created by Charles Hamilton, Beckford's great-uncle. Photographed in the 1990s.

Chapter VIII

WILLIAM BECKFORD AND THE LANDSCAPE GARDEN

Alexander Marr

The landscape and gardens created by William Beckford between his coming of age in 1781 and his departure from the Abbey in 1822 were, in true Beckford fashion, changeable, diverse, and frequently contradictory. The estate, made up of Fonthill Old Park, outlying plantations and the "walled enclosure" of grounds surrounding the Abbey , comprised almost 6,000 acres by the time it was sold.[1] The alterations and improvements that Beckford made during his time at Fonthill led commentators to proclaim the estate a veritable re-creation of Eden in the midst of the Wiltshire landscape.[2] To some the grounds were reminiscent of passages from Milton or the Elysium to which Julie retired in Rousseau's *La Nouvelle Héloise*.[3] To others it evoked Rasselas's "Happy valley" or the gardens of Armida.[4] Elements of the scenery of countries as diverse as Norway, Switzerland, and America were seen to be encapsulated within its boundary. For those concerned with the ever-changing fashions in landscape gardening, the grounds were a manifestation of the numerous varieties of "Picturesque" taste.

In *Graphical and Literary Illustrations to Fonthill Abbey* (1823), John Britton gave this description of the Fonthill estate:

> Immediately within the domain, and within the walled enclosure, there is much diversified, picturesque, beautiful, and romantic scenery—an alteration of hill and dale, of terrace and valley, of wood and lawn, of rugged wilderness and dressed parterres, with a sort of mountain lake, are the distinguishing features of the place. As variety is ever pleasing to the eye and mind, both must be gratified here: for the various inequalities of the ground have been rendered more intricate and mazy by the disposition of plantations and multiplicity of intersecting and winding drives.[5]

By the time Britton described Fonthill, the Abbey grounds, which were "covered with woods," contained many diverse features.[6] To the south of the Abbey was a much-admired American plantation, next to which a serpentine-edged lake was home to "Flocks of wild ducks, cootes, &c. with the long necked heron."[7] An undulating Great Avenue, the turf of which was irregularly planted with shrubs and trees, led to the Abbey building, around which were lawns containing nothing exotic "save an apricot and a fig tree."[8] To the southwest of the Abbey was "a small lawn, surrounded by Alpine shrubs and firs, and adorned with a Norway cottage."[9] A promontory called Knoyle Corner, situated to the northwest, boasted some moss houses. From this point the "*Great Terrace*, skirted by a belt of plantations to the north, and by a long narrow valley to the south"[10] conveyed the visitor eastward upon the north side of the grounds. Other areas included the Chinese Garden, Pine Lawn, and Clerk's Walk, where grew, during spring and summer, "a beautiful and fascinating display of flowers, luxuriant shrubs and variegated hollies."[11] Throughout the domain were "alternate masses of oak, beech, pine, &c." and countless "roads, paths, ridges, dells, knolls, woods, and lawns."[12] The landscape was so varied and complex that one visitor, Henri Meister, declared "fully to describe all its beauties it would have been necessary to have invoked the shade of Gessner."[13]

The Fonthill grounds, with varying degrees of success, were an intriguing combination of the natural and the artificial. Nature and art were at once consolidated and opposed, creating an exciting dialogue that was sensually and mentally stimulating, pleasing to both the "eye and mind." This dialectic was physically represented throughout the estate by devices such as the intermingling of different species of tree and shrub. Both the exotic and the native were to be found side by side at Fonthill, while the variety of landscape—"hill and dale," "terrace and valley," "wood and lawn"—ensured that the scenery remained "diversified." This eclectic mix of scenes also satisfied the painterly eye. Fonthill reminded Britton "alternately of Poussin and Ruysdael, of Salvator and Wilson, of Gainsborough and Turner."[14]

It is not surprising that a man famous for forging his own life, principally through the rewriting of letters and, simply, by lying, should have created a landscape that is difficult to define.[15] Britton, Beckford's contemporary, called the grounds "picturesque, beautiful"

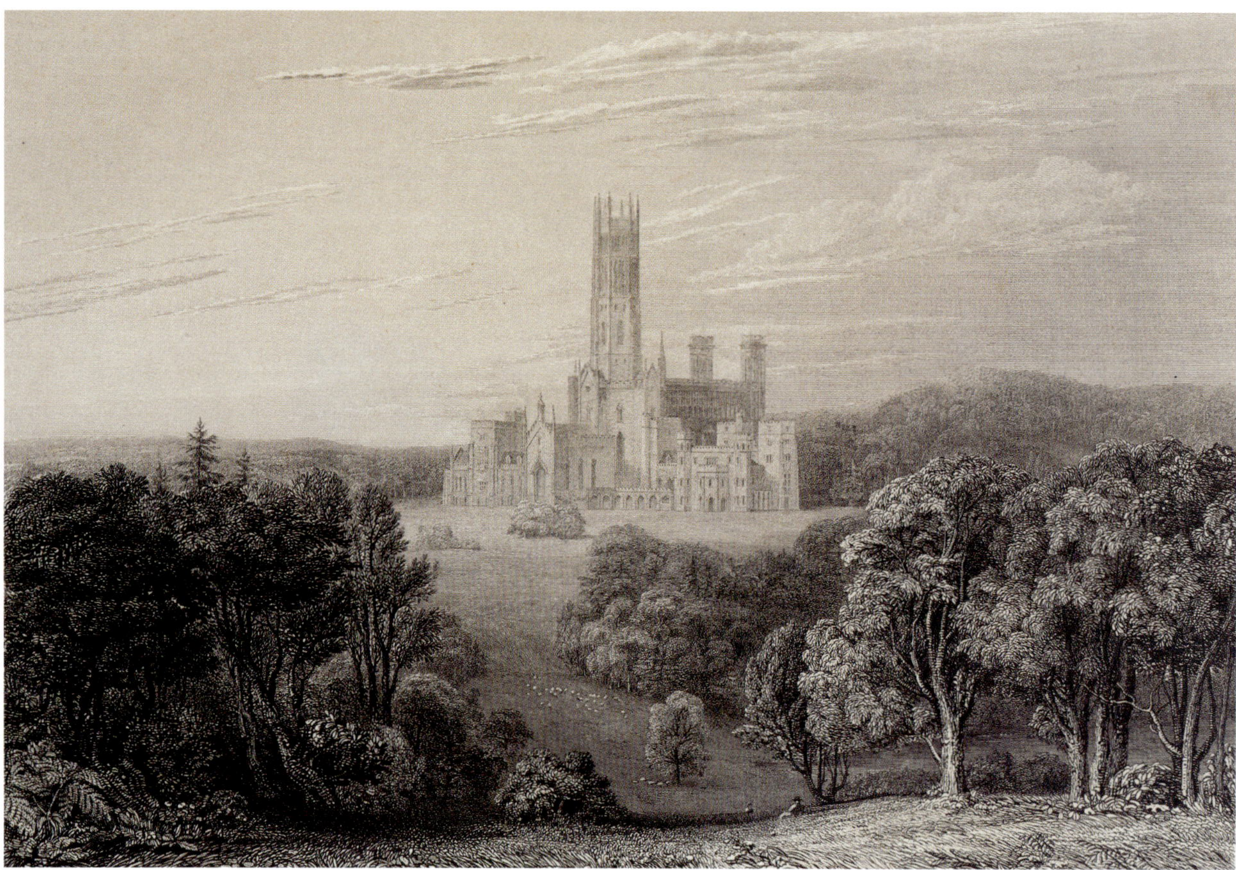

Fig. 8-2. "The West and South Fronts of the Abbey from Beacon Terrace." From John Rutter, *Delineations of Fonthill and its Abbey* (Shaftesbury and London, J. Rutter, 1823), between pages 90 and 91.

and "romantic." His statement that the grounds were "intricate and mazy" might well be applied to any study of the Fonthill landscape during Beckford's residence. Even though five books on the Abbey and its grounds, three of which were lavishly illustrated (fig. 8-2), were published, considerable confusion still remains concerning the exact dating of the differing areas of the grounds, their inspiration, and by whom the plans were executed. This confusion is partially due to the absence of primary documentation for much of the work undertaken on the landscape.[16] In his letters, Beckford was ambiguous about the exact role of his two main gardeners at Fonthill, James Vincent and J. Milne,[17] and rarely even mentioned the sources from which he acquired plants and trees.[18]

Equally problematic has been the erroneous belief that the entire Fonthill landscape was a homogenous work, presided over by a single designer—William Beckford. In fact two distinct landscapes existed at Fonthill. The first was Fonthill Old Park—the relatively flat, partially landscaped grounds inherited (along with Fonthill Splendens) by Beckford from his father, the Alderman. Beckford appears to have made some significant improvements to this part of the estate, principally after his coming of age in 1781. The second was the hilly woodland west of the Old Park to which Beckford turned his attention while constructing and living in the Abbey.[19]

The actual layout and appearance of this second phase of

Beckford's landscaping activities is well recorded, even if his motives and the exact dates remain obscure. Five books, published between 1812 and 1823—*A Description of Fonthill Abbey* (1812) by James Storer, *Graphical Illustrations* (1823) by Britton, and three by John Rutter, *Description of Fonthill Abbey* (1822), *New descriptive guide to Fonthill Abbey* (1823) and *Delineations of Fonthill Abbey* (1823)—devote a considerable amount of space to describing the Fonthill estate.[20] They provide an invaluable source for visualizing and understanding Beckford's landscape. Indeed, Rutter's *Delineations* even includes a foldout map of the entire Fonthill property (fig. 8-3).

Difficulties in understanding the Fonthill landscape may also partially be attributed to the neglect of landscape gardening as a subject in Beckford scholarship until relatively recently.[21] The majority of his biographers almost entirely ignored Beckford's landscape creations.[22] Boyd Alexander, for example, recognized the importance of the creation of the Fonthill landscape in the Beckford *oeuvre*, yet gave little attention to the grounds themselves.[23] He cites Cyrus Redding (Beckford's first biographer) as his source when telling us Beckford considered that "his greatest achievement was the creation of the flowering wilderness round the Abbey."[24] Unlike more recent studies, Redding's *Memoirs of William Beckford of Fonthill* (1859) abounds with references to his subject's fondness for "botany" and "planting."[25] Published some fifteen years after Beckford's death, the book addressed his reputation during the nineteenth century as a skilled landscape gardener, a man to whom botany and horticulture were esteemed as highly as the "liberal arts in general."[26]

In addition to Fonthill Beckford created a pleasure ground at Montserrate in Portugal, formed a garden in Paris, and extensively landscaped his grounds at Lansdown, Bath.[27] His commitment to creating landscapes and gardens equaled, if not exceeded, his dedication to building residences or acquiring works of art.[28] He was "to the highest degree fond of that on which he lavished years of personal attention."[29] This "personal attention" was attested to by Redding, who informs us that observation and supervision of the Fonthill grounds were regularly incorporated into Beckford's daily routine. An examination of the "works going on" would be followed by a walk to the garden or an hour's ride on horseback throughout the grounds. In November 1817 Beckford mentioned one of his frequent walks desig-

nating trees for felling, writing: "I have returned from an oak-marking walk, as usual towards half-past four."[30] A writer for the *European Magazine* observed as early as 1797 that "One of [Beckford's] principal amusements at Fonthill consists in attending and frequently directing the superior workmen in the execution of his schemes."[31]

Scattered throughout Beckford's correspondence are references to his intimate involvement with the rapid evolution of the Fonthill landscape. He often remarked on the progress made by certain plantations or offered eulogies on the scents and visual delights to be found among the gardens. A letter to Gregorio Franchi of 1814 serves as a typical example: "Yesterday there was sunshine, and Milne's paradise was all gilded and full of sweet smells of pine-apple, violet and cyclamen; the vine and the fruit trees are beginning to bud; every day this place becomes more immense and beautiful."[32] Toward the end of Beckford's residence at Fonthill this attachment was emphasized by Franchi who

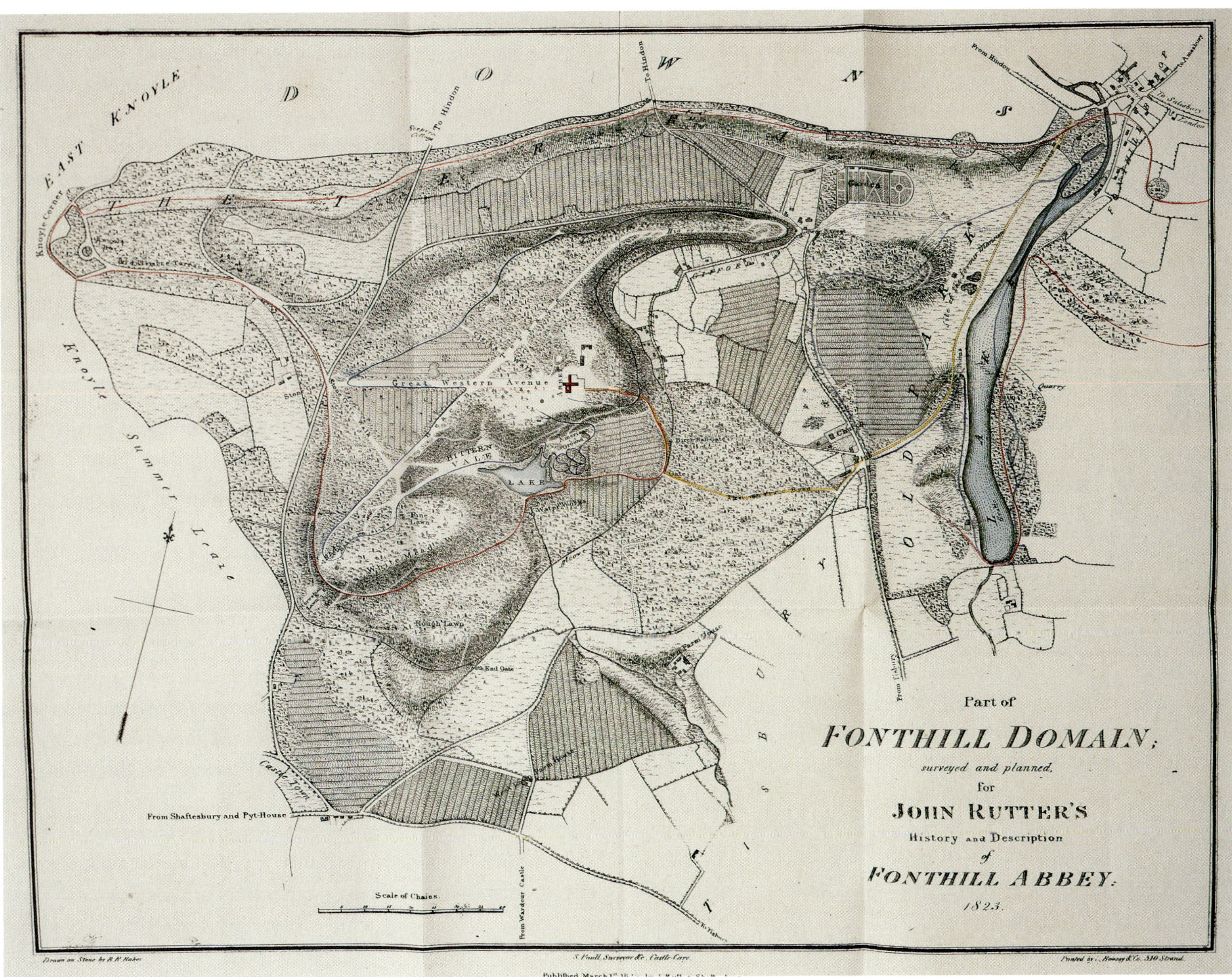

Fig. 8-3. A partial plan of the Fonthill estate. From John Rutter, *Delineations of Fonthill and its Abbey* (Shaftesbury and London, J. Rutter, 1823), foldout.

informed the Duke of Hamilton that "the only pleasure and liberty left" to Beckford was the planting and felling of trees.[33] Another contemporary, John Claudius Loudon, wrote: "One of the last things which Mr. Beckford did, after having sold Fonthill . . . was to mount his pony, and ride round with his gardener, to give directions for various alterations and improvements which he wished to have executed."[34]

Beckford's devotion to gardening paralleled the period's general enthusiasm for landscaping and dedication to debating methods of "improvement," which had become practically febrile in England. Beckford was well placed to enjoy the squabbling surrounding the Picturesque controversy, with the various propositions, contradictions, and amendments vociferously announced by figures such as William Gilpin, Richard Payne Knight, Uvedale Price, and Humphry Repton. Beckford's life coincided with a quick succession of changes in landscape vogue. At his birth the cultivated parks of Lancelot "Capability" Brown were reaching the peak of their popularity; when Beckford was thirty-five, Price and Payne Knight first published their treatises and poems on landscape; and by the time of Beckford's death, in 1844, the "gardenesque" movement of Repton and his followers was firmly entrenched. Beckford was thoroughly aware of the various vicissitudes in landscaping taste, and, although he never adhered fully to one particular exponent, these vogues informed and were reflected in his shaping of Fonthill.

Fonthill Old Park

Redding suggested that the "intense love of nature, before noted as so remarkable in Mr. Beckford's earlier years, was probably imbibed at Fonthill, where there were some places remarkable for their sequestered wild beauty."[35] Considerable disagreement exists concerning the roles taken in landscaping Fonthill Old Park by the Beckfords junior and senior. Various contemporary writers made clear distinctions between the Old Park and the Abbey grounds. Rutter, for example, in his proposed "walk without the barrier," stated: "We are about to quit those grounds which have been entirely created by the genius of their late possessor, to ramble through walks which were the appendage of a former mansion."[36] Storer completely ignored Fonthill Old Park in favor of the Abbey grounds, while Britton, referring to "Fonthill house *that was*"[37] devoted only a paragraph to the then-abandoned park, which he described as "diversified in surface and adorned by groves of fine old wood."[38] No account, however, clarifies which elements of this region were conceived by the Alderman and which by his son.

Fonthill Splendens, the residence in which Beckford spent most of his childhood, was not the first building to have been constructed on the Fonthill estate. It replaced the mansion originally bought in 1745 by the Alderman—Fonthill Redivivus—a Jacobean house that burned down, with all its contents, in 1755. It is in the grounds adjacent to Fonthill Redivivus that the first visual evidence of gardening activity at Fonthill is recorded. A painting by George Lambert, *Fonthill House* (see fig. 3-3), of 1740 (five years before the Alderman purchased the estate from Francis Cottington) illustrates, in

the background, a formal walled garden and a lawn.[39] Beyond the garden, on the left, is shown a regular plantation of deciduous trees, while in the foreground are what appear to be deliberate clearings or glades among the untended trees and shrubs, where figures can be seen walking or reposing. Interestingly, even in this early view some spots of "sequestered wild beauty" may be observed. Redding stated that glades comparable to those depicted in the foreground of the picture were also "formed and planted by his [Beckford's] father."[40]

The Alderman made quite extensive revisions to the Fonthill landscape before the 1755 fire. Some idea of his contribution may be gleaned from Richard Pococke's account of a visit to Fonthill in July 1754: "beyond the park, and opposite to the grand front, Mr. Beckford has built a Church, on the plan of Covent Garden, which is a good termination of the prospect. There is a large lawn that way, and plantations to the west, an open temple on the side of the hill, and an open rotundo is building higher up the hill. To the east is a broad serpentine river, with a very handsome bridge of free stone built over it of three arches, with a stone baluster."[41]

As may be gathered from this description, the Alderman's landscaping efforts were by no means confined simply to planting and clearing. Considerable emphasis was placed on the garden buildings that the Alderman constructed. The church, for example, which was probably built between 1747 and 1749[42] (in the "style of Inigo Jones") may have been intended more as a garden feature than as a practical place of worship.[43] This is attested to by its location far from the Alderman's mansion and the neighboring village of "new" Fonthill Gifford.[44] Its cupola, however, could be glimpsed among the trees from the garden front of the house.[45]

The "open temple" and "open rotundo" further enriched the landscape.[46] These buildings conformed to popular taste of landscape design in the mid-eighteenth century. Indeed it might be said that in his gardening tastes the Alderman was something of a "Squire Mushroom."[47] He was keen to enliven the landscape by including exciting views and glimpses of intriguing building throughout the foliage of the estate. This aim is attested to by Britton who wrote: "Views also on every desirable combination of objects, within or without the place, which could be gained are now commanded from different points. The whole is managed so as to present to the moving spectator a continual variety of scenes, each marked with a different, and generally some striking character, calculated to inspire that particular sentiment or emotion, intended in the plan of the last improver."[48]

One of the most striking features of the Alderman's landscape, in true Brownian fashion, was the "broad serpentine river" that he created to the east by damming the stream approximately one mile south of the house. A stone bridge with accompanying baluster, as Pococke tells us, further ornamented the river.[49] This bridge was to prove somewhat controversial. William Gilpin, recalling a visit he paid to Fonthill around 1775–78, was of the opinion that "If the bridge had been more simple, the scenes about it would have been more pleasing."[50] Similarly, the Irishman John Parnell "recoiled in disgust" from the edifice.[51]

William Beckford may have been of the same opinion as these visitors. When Britton visited Fonthill a few years later the bridge observed by Gilpin had been "removed twenty years ago."[52]

Pococke also mentions a "large lawn" and "plantations." The Alderman, like many of his generation, was spurred into the planting of trees for twin rewards: healthy profit from the sale of timber and the approbation of bodies such as the Royal Society of Arts (RSA). This society had, for some years, been awarding medals for planting, and in 1769 the Alderman was presented with a premium award (gold medal) for planting almost 62,000 Scotch pines.[53] This would have been a considerable addition to the park and would seem to substantiate that during this period the Alderman was landscaping Fonthill in earnest.[54]

At this date, however, there may have been "very little landscaping" at Fonthill.[55] On January 2, 1769, the minutes of the Committee of Agriculture of the RSA, reporting on the Alderman's plantations, listed Fonthill after the Somerset estate of Witham.[56] It is certainly possible that a sizable portion of the planting had taken place at Witham, partially because the house was not yet completed and was in need of landscaping, and also because, as Parnell recorded, the valley in which Splendens was situated was narrow and the clumps of Scotch pine planted around were young and puny. There were certainly enough mature trees at Witham for Beckford to note, on a visit there in the autumn of 1811, "I might have been in Norway such were the sights and smells; pine-wood huts; pines on the ground in a strange and splendid disorder."[57]

Beckford and the Landscape Garden

How extensive was Beckford's knowledge of landscape gardens? Was he, as were so many nobles and wealthy individuals of his age, commissioning others to design his grounds, or a mere copyist, imitating an "ideal" or "model garden" as an essential addition to any gentleman's abode? Fonthill Old Park was the first English landscape garden to which he was exposed; yet this was only one of many gardens, both in England and on the Continent, that Beckford saw and commented upon. His debt to the natural landscape of the Continent was recognized during his lifetime. Loudon remarked that the grounds of Fonthill owed something to the "mountainous regions of Catholic countries on the Continent."[58] While Beckford's travels in Europe had a profound effect on his attitude towards landscape, Loudon, writing in the 1830s, recognized that the Fonthill grounds also expressed a character "long since past in this country."[59] It seems probable that Loudon was referring to what he perceived as a general wildness about the grounds,[60] a rejection of artifice in favor of nature that he associated with attitudes to the Picturesque in the latter part of the eighteenth century.

No discussion of Beckford's gardening activities has considered Beckford's responses to the many landscape gardens that existed in England during his lifetime. Beckford was conversant with both the theory and practice of English landscaping of the late eighteenth and early nineteenth centuries. Fonthill was situated almost directly adjacent to one of the most admired gardens of the age: Stourhead, created by Henry Hoare and his grandson, Richard Coalt Hoare.[61] This garden, which Beckford always referred to as "Stourton," could be viewed from certain high spots of the Fonthill estate. Loudon recorded being able to see the Stourhead tower from Fonthill quite clearly,[62] as does Storer who wrote that from the northwestern boundary of Beckford's property, "the prospect ranges over a country extensive and delightfully diversified. Among the most prominent objects are Alfred's tower, and part of the grounds at Stourhead, the seat of Richard Coalt Hoare, Bart."[63]

Beckford, who visited Stourhead on numerous occasions, seems to have been competing with the neighboring landscape. His proposal to raise a tower that would doubtless have eclipsed that of his neighbor suggests a certain landscape-gardening rivalry.[64] Similarly, Beckford took evident pleasure in declaring that "the terrace at Stourton is no longer comparable to that at Fonthill: the lines too straight, the ground not undulating, a repetition of pyramids, larches planted everywhere like the fleur-de-lis on the royal robe which used to be at St. Denis. I don't like it, I can't admire it."[65] This proud belief in the superiority of Fonthill even extended to the quality of trees throughout the estate. When felling a number of pines in the spring of 1814 he wrote: "They're the finest in England—neither Stourton or Longleat have ever had anything comparable for quality and cleanliness of wood. Norway has produced nothing superior."[66] Rather than imitating the landscapes around him, Beckford was attempting to surpass them. Even though he admitted few visitors to the estate (which added to its notoriety), he seems to have desired fame and approbation for his creation, which helps to explain his encouragement of the publications by Storer, Rutter, and Britton.

Beckford does not seem to have been overly impressed with England's landscape gardens.[67] In the summer of 1779 he toured the country at the behest of his mother, accompanied by his tutor Lettice, and visited most of the major houses in the west of England. Beckford merely "glanced at the noble oaks and fine park" belonging to G. Yonge, while Lord Bathurst's woods, which "were at that time celebrated for their beauty, stateliness and extent," were scornfully received.[68] Redding tells us that "they were deemed dreary by the young traveller, who was eager to get away from them."[69] The reason given for this surprising judgment is that they "stood unfortunately upon level ground, near Cirencester, destitute of water, prospect, ruins, and any kind of diversity to relieve the eye."[70] These elements, that Bathurst's woods were so sorely lacking, are principal features of the Picturesque landscape. Beckford's bias towards the Picturesque is not surprising; the ideas of Alexander Cozens, his boyhood drawing master and aesthetic mentor, were freshly implanted in his mind.[71]

One possible reason for Beckford's derision of the Bathurst estate is that prior to his visit he had stayed with "'young' Mr. Hamilton, he who planted Pain's Hill."[72] At the time of Beckford's visit, Charles Hamilton, Beckford's great uncle, had retired to Bath, "purchased ten acres of land, and was creating on their face a thousand beauties."[73] This visit is a particularly interesting episode in the history of Beckford's interest in gardening. Although the conversations between these two relatives passed entirely unrecorded, they probably discussed landscape gardening, a topic close to Hamilton's heart and one that was becoming increasingly important to Beckford. Hamilton's grounds at Painshill included many features that were to be implemented at Fonthill (see fig. 8-1). There were American plants and a grotto that may have inspired those at Fonthill. Redding certainly implies that viewing Hamilton's new Bath grounds made a considerable impression on Beckford, writing: "It is probable the sight strengthened the love of rural economy and gardening which was afterwards so marked a trait in Mr. Beckford's history."[74]

Redding's choice of the word "strengthened" suggests that even by this date, Beckford, who was only nineteen, had developed a particular love of "gardening." Indeed, the idea that Beckford formed his tastes in landscape early on in life is attested to by Britton who, in *Beauties of Wiltshire*, wrote: "Mr. Beckford, in a very early stage of his minority discovered that feeling for the picturesque, for which he is so much celebrated."[75]

Beckford was also familiar with a number of gardens on the Continent. He praised the Electors of Bavaria for their preservation of natural woodland, saw the gardens of the Nymphenburg, and was unimpressed with the "artificial scenery" of the palaces lining the Mira.[76] Equally unsuited to his tastes were the Dutch gardens of "stiff parterres scrawled and flourished in patterns like the embroidery of an old maid's work-bag."[77]

In Italy the Boboli gardens were a favorite spot in which to walk or repose in the evening; he also ruminated on the ruins of grottoes in the Gonzagas' palace at Mantua.[78] He proclaimed the garden of the castle of Garzoni to contain "no great purity of taste," although in the Negroni garden in Rome he found what his "soul desired, thickets of jasmine, and wild spots overgrown with bay; long alleys of thick cypress totally neglected, and almost impassable through the luxuriance of the vegetation."[79]

Like other Englishmen of the late eighteenth century, Beckford disliked Bentinck's formal garden "with parterres and bosquets by no means resembling, one should conjecture, the gardens of the Hesperides."[80] His horror of obvious artfulness in gardens is further demonstrated perhaps by a visit to the Marques of Marialva's villa in Portugal, when he ignored a "grand artificial cascade" (the pride of the owner) in favor of gorging himself on the apples and plums of the nearby orchard.[81]

He was generally dismissive of Portuguese gardens, declaring the modern gardening tastes of the Portuguese "gaudy."[82] One of his few comments on Spanish gardens was reserved for a condemnation of Madrid's Royal Palace, which he proclaimed incapable of sustaining vegetation.[83] Although he rarely admired the artificial gardens of foreign climes, Beckford was often enamored of their natural scenery and tried to re-create this in the Fonthill landscape.

BECKFORD AND THE NATURAL WORLD: AN EDUCATION IN LANDSCAPE

The most significant influence on Beckford in the formulation of his gardening tastes and their subsequent implementation at Fonthill was his actual experience of landscape. In Beckford's case the distinctions between the imagined, read, and actual experience of landscape are decidedly blurred.[84] His attitude to landscape was one of association—in a sense he was never fully in one place at a time. A visit to Venice might spur the recollection of reading about a Chinese landscape in a volume of Jesuit's travels, which itself takes on the tone of a reverie in Beckford's description.[85] Even at Mount Edgcumbe he could write: "Here I am breathing the soft air of Mount Edgecombe . . . I cannot help thinking myself in an isle of the Atlantic Ocean."[86] This blending of real and imagined landscape,[87] a chain of geographical locations linked by common landscape features, might be said to have determined the Fonthill environment. Thus, it is not surprising to find Henri Meister, a traveler from Switzerland, remarking of Fonthill that the "views were continually changing to a new country, and I thought myself by turns in Switzerland, in France, in England, and in America."[88]

Beckford traveled extensively. Indeed, during his lifetime the fame afforded him by *Vathek* was equaled by that of his "travel writing," if the evocative descriptions of his responses to numerous tours may be defined as such. In 1834 John Gibson Lockhart (Sir Walter Scott's biographer) wrote that Beckford "is a poet, and a great one too, though we know not that he ever wrote a line of verse. His rapture amidst the sublime scenery of mountains and forests . . . is that of a spirit cast originally in one of nature's finest moulds. Some immortal passages in Gray's letters and Byron's diaries are the only things, in our tongue, that seem to come near the profound melancholy, blended with a picturesque description at once true and startling."[89]

Beckford explored and resided in many areas of northern and southern Europe. He visited France, the Low Countries, Switzerland, Germany, Italy, Portugal, and Spain. His experiences of these countries are recorded in several published volumes. The earliest of these was *Dreams, waking Thoughts and Incidents* (1783), the material for which was provided by a ten-month tour of Europe in 1780 and 1781. The second, *Italy, with sketches of Spain and Portugal* (1834), describes this and subsequent tours on the Continent. His expeditions to two Portuguese monasteries were recorded as *Recollections of an Excursion to the Monasteries of Alcobaça and Batalha* (1835). In addition to these accounts published in Beckford's lifetime, the journal he kept while in Portugal and Spain between 1787 and 1788 was published posthumously, but not until 1954.

The landscape of Fonthill recalled the scenery of these travels, yet also provided that of countries that Beckford would never see, such as America, Norway, and China. Beckford was as much a mental as an actual traveler. Those voyages that he could not physically undertake were experienced vicariously through reading books on travels, tours, and explorations. As the nineteen-year-old Beckford wrote in 1779:

"I have lately committed myself to the guidance of Voyagers and followed them over vast Oceans to distant climes where my exotic inclinations are satisfied."[90] This tendency in Beckford's character was recognized as early as 1930 when, in the preface to *The Vision*, Guy Chapman wrote that "volumes on Northern mythology, on travels in China, India and Mexico," were "more than enough to enflame his [Beckford's] active mind."[91]

This inclination was to continue throughout Beckford's adult life, and included a fascination for climes closer to home, in addition to the more "distant" and "exotic" lands. Thus Beckford's library contained volumes on tours in the British Isles, such as Gilpin's *Picturesque Tours to the Wye* (1789).[92] Not content with general explanations of these differing locations, he also acquired and consulted texts on natural history, such as Catesby's *Natural History of Carolina, Florida and the Bahama islands* or Hughes's *Natural History of Barbadoes*.[93] Sometimes he would compare a real landscape to a more fantastic one that he might have read about. While rambling in the valley of Collares, for example, he thought the walks and foliage "something like the groves of Tonga-taboo, as represented in Cook's voyages."[94]

Beckford collected many botanical texts, including some by Linnaeus, and rare items such as books by Gesner, John Gerarde's *Herball* (1597) and the *Hortus Floridus* of Charles de l'Ecluse and Rembert Dodoens. Furthermore he amassed a considerable collection of fine botanical illustrations and prints. At various stages in its development, the Fonthill library contained such rarities as a volume of *velins* by the celebrated Aubriette, a folio of drawings of tulips and 148 paintings of flowers and fruit from the "Van-Braam collection."[95] The library and grounds of Fonthill were an echo of each other. Both a paper and an organic landscape garden existed at Fonthill, and each was largely the product of the "superintending mind" of William Beckford.[96]

Beckford's fascination with the natural world thus took two forms. On one hand, his books of travels and natural history, many of which were lavishly illustrated, belong to the encyclopedism of Diderot and d'Alembert.[97] On the other, his emotive response to nature reflects a Rousseau-like longing for the pastoral life,[98] a desire to return to the simplicity afforded by the natural world. Encyclopedism was provided at Fonthill by its geographical diversity. As Ann Hamilton noticed while exploring the grounds: "the produce of every climate seems to flourish and abound."[99] Rousseau was present in the wildness of the "romantic wood" in which "the precipices are awful."[100]

Beckford's response to the countryside of the Sintra mountains in Portugal, the "almost irresistible impulse to fall down at worship in this vast temple of Nature" that he experienced, has the ring of Rousseau's philosophy.[101] He had a similar attitude toward the "consecrated foliage" of Fonthill, writing, for example, at a young age: "When the hurry was over and all desert[ed] and silent I ran across the lawn, mounted the Hill of Pan and addressed my vows to the Sylvan deities in the midst of their consecrated foliage. The reviving fragrance of the vegetation is not to be described nor need it to the Worshippers of Nature they know the perfume she diffuses when awakened from her Winter's repose."[102] In another example, Beckford's assertion, made while touring the English lake district, that he "should love to lead a wild and savage life in these primaeval regions and fish for sustenance" is also remarkably close to Rousseau's notions of noble savagery.[103] It has already been noted that Meister compared Fonthill to Julia's Elysium, and Beckford himself remarked that the pastoral huts near Salanche were "like the chalets to which Julia retired."[104]

In Switzerland Beckford extended his knowledge of nature through his acquaintance with the great naturalist Horace Bénédict de Saussure, whose "Apparatus and a Cabinet of Natural History" he saw.[105] He also knew Charles Bonnet, of whom he wrote: "This gentleman, since Linnaeus and Haller are gone, may perhaps justly claim the first rank in the walk of Natural History."[106] Beckford was not, by any means, an armchair naturalist, content only to attend the odd lecture or glance at the pages of a popular text. He made his own notes on the trees, flora and wildlife of the regions he visited. For example, the Green Note Book that Beckford kept during his stay in Switzerland, contains records of alpine vegetation.[107] Such notes are symptomatic of a delight in all things botanical, which led to the individual plant or flower playing a central role at Fonthill.

In 1807 Beckford was planning a trip to Malvern, which was to include botanical excursions. Among his retinue was the gardener, Milne, perhaps suggesting that such trips were intended as plant-gathering expeditions, a form of recognizance to choose which plants and flowers were to be introduced at Fonthill.[108] It was certainly more than natural providence that caused Ann Hamilton to remark of Fonthill: "a finer place for the botanist than this whole place is cannot be."[109]

The Grounds of Fonthill

In what manner did Beckford's varied experiences of landscape become manifest at Fonthill? From an early age he seems to have reacted against the then-popular Brownian landscapes, not least that of his father. Britton writes that "in a very early stage of his minority" Beckford began improving the landscape around Fonthill Splendens, particularly the area on the east bank of the river.[110] This he "planted with every sort of forest wood" in an attempt to fill in the barren areas that the Alderman had neglected to plant.[111] It seems probable that this planting began soon after the Alderman's death, although little documentation exists to be conclusive.[112]

It seems likely that between the Alderman's death and Beckford's concentration upon the grounds that were to surround the Abbey, considerable construction and planting took place. During this period Beckford may have built the suite of grotto buildings and follies that still exist on the banks of the lake—the "rocks, caverns, baths and grottoes in the taste of the earlier part of the century."[113] These consisted of two grottoes, a hermitage, the quarries (fig. 8-4), which had supplied stone for Splendens, and a "cromlech." The lake was Beckford's adaptation of the serpentine river that his father had created.

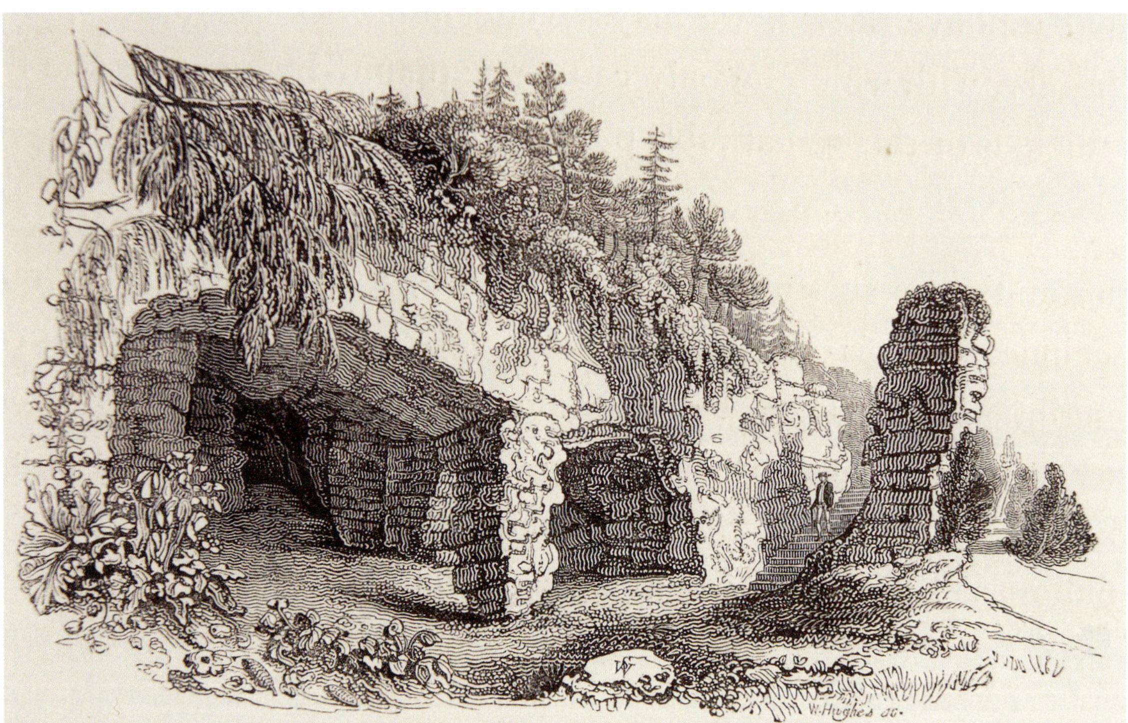

Fig. 8-4: "A Scene in the Alpine Gardens," showing the stone quarries. From John Rutter, *Delineations of Fonthill and its Abbey* (Shaftesbury and London, J. Rutter, 1823): chap. 5 vignette.

Beckford enlarged the riverbed by partially damming it, thus creating a broad undulating sheet of water—"a beauty of the superior order"—around which a thick wood was planted.[114] Beckford was evidently pleased with the effect, as by 1784 he invited Samuel Henley to Fonthill to "enjoy my new creation of wood and water."[115]

The other major improvement that Beckford made to the grounds around Fonthill Splendens was to devise walks and interesting scenes throughout the woods of the east bank. There were two stages in the development of these amendments. As Britton tells us, the first "walks and scenes of lawn, rocks etc., were opened in several parts, where the nature of the place suggested improvement."[116] These were created "some years" after the plantations had "attained a most luxuriant growth."[117] A further set of walks seems to have been implemented some years later. Redding tells us that soon after Beckford's return from Aranjuez, Lettice (by now Beckford's daughters' tutor) "suggested that walks should be made of nearly a mile in extent, in order to render that wild spot pleasanter for the ladies."[118] It is probable that Redding was referring to Beckford's second visit to Aranjuez, from which he returned in 1796, as this date tallies with Britton's assertion that by the time the new walks were added, "the wood had reached about five and twenty years growth."[119]

By this time the features of the wood were such that it earned the appellation "Alpine Garden." It is not certain at what point Beckford decided to impress an alpine character upon this area of the grounds. It is quite conceivable that his decision followed his experiences of mountainous scenery on the Continent. An alpine garden was certainly flourishing by 1791, as it was remarked upon by Baron Johan Frederick Willem van Spaen van Biljoen, in a visit of that year.[120]

Beckford had formed a taste for alpine scenery very early on in life. His first visit abroad, in 1777, was to Geneva, and his experience of Switzerland was the beginning of a life-long love of alpine landscape. As early as 1779 he could identify the kind of scenery to which he was particularly drawn: "My imagination delights in haunting the woody hills and valleys which lie concealed and sheltered at the top of the Alps."[121] Beckford ensured that his imagination was well provided for by the Fonthill landscape—an alpine character was one of the aesthetics most frequently associated with the grounds by those who visited during Beckford's lifetime.

Loudon noticed that at Fonthill the "solemn solitary grandeur of the scene" recalled "the associations we have formed of monasteries in Alpine countries."[122] As an example of this he pointed to the trees planted around the Great Avenue leading to the Abbey. These were "of the spiry-topped kind, which adds to the prevailing expression of alpine scenery."[123] Throughout Fonthill, firs, pines, and flowering shrubs reminiscent of the Alps were to be found. To the southwest of the Abbey was, Britton informs us, "a small lawn, surrounded by alpine shrubs and firs."[124] This spot, the "Norwegian Lawn"[125] (confusingly named since the plantings were alpine) included a "Norway cottage."

Rutter described this building, which he called the "Norwegian Hut" (fig. 8-5), as "a sort of log house, of very tasteful proportions, and altogether in perfect harmony with the general scenery."[126]

Such a building invokes those rural huts that Beckford had enjoyed and Cozens had sketched in Switzerland. Beckford seems to have transposed to Fonthill the pastoral idyll he experienced on his travels. This pastoral aesthetic was also to be found near the Grand Terrace, the scenery to the right of which was "said much to resemble the rural scenery of Switzerland."[127]

A further Swiss feature at Fonthill was Bitham Lake, of which Venn Lansdown exclaimed: "Never in happy England did I see a spot that so forcibly reminded me of Switzerland."[128] This "pellucid lake," as Storer called it, was created from what was originally a fishpond, dug by the former owners of the site in the seventeenth century.[129] Beckford repaired part of the dam and embellished its contours into irregular coves and inlets, so that by 1801 it was the last prominent feature of a circling tour of the Abbey.[130] Trees were planted around the borders of the lake, grouped with spaces so that the water could be "viewed from the Abbey, from various stations among the woods, or from different parts of its banks."[131] Beckford encouraged wild fowl to populate the lake, which served the dual purpose of making it appear more natural and increasing its "animation."[132]

Beckford was particularly proud of the lake's lack of artificiality, writing to Franchi: "The lake looks as if God had made it, it is so natural, without the least trace of art; I don't say it is marvellous for its banks are too flat, but it spreads itself grandiosely and the swans look as if they are in Paradise."[133] Unfortunately, the lake spread too far in 1817, when it burst its banks. Beckford had been aware this might occur, having agreed (though never being able to bring himself to execute the plan) to convert the lake to water meadows. After the disaster he wrote: "Now we must have meadows there or incur ruinous expense: the meadows would be more useful, but it would be cruel to destroy the noble features of Fonthill."[134]

One such noble feature was the remarkable "American Garden" (fig. 8-6)—an area of land on the eastern side of the lake, "fatiguing the senses with the colours and perfume of groves of rhododendrons and magnolias."[135] The American Garden was begun some time after 1801, and by 1810 it was flourishing, with Beckford pleased to record that "The Andromeda is doing fairly well and so are the American Plants. That rogue Milne says he has some magnificent magnolia shrubs, but I doubt it, like everything else he tells me."[136]

Beckford was by no means the first Englishman to introduce American species into Britain. In 1759 William Constable, of Burton Constable in East Yorkshire, was buying American plants, including magnolia, as well as thirty-seven varieties of holly—a plant that regularly featured among the woods and shrubberies of Fonthill. Constable's plantings have been compared to Charles Hamilton's at Painshill,[137] suggesting again that Hamilton's plantings may have exerted some influence over those at Fonthill. The grounds at Painshill contained the andromeda, arbutus, azalea (*Rhododendron viscosum* or

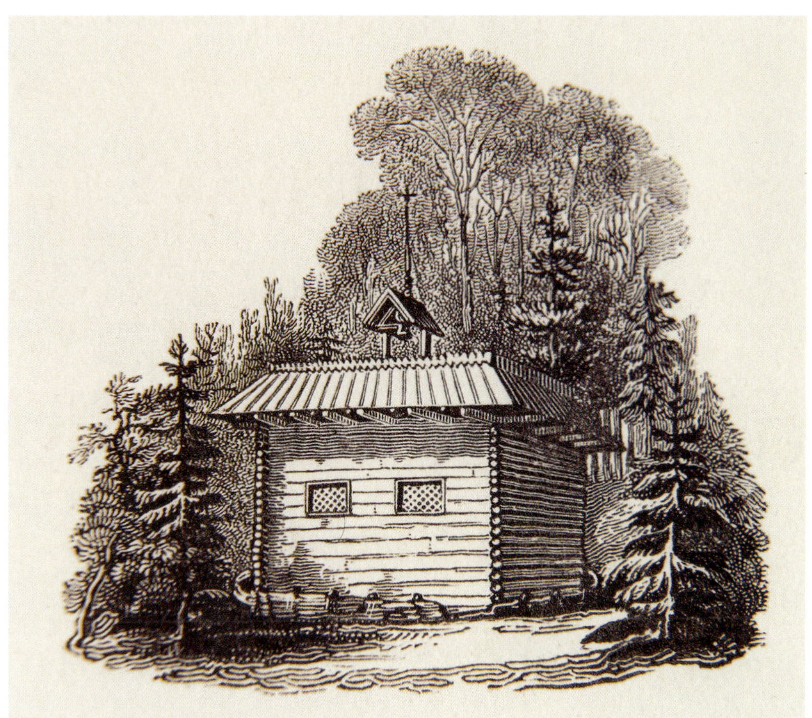

Fig. 8-5. "The Norwegian Hut." From John Rutter, *Delineations of Fonthill and its Abbey* (Shaftesbury and London, J. Rutter, 1823), page 92.

R. nudiflorum), Portugal laurel, rhododendron, tulip tree, fir, pine, and spruce, all of which were to be found at Fonthill.[138] Of the published descriptions of the American Garden, Rutter's *New descriptive guide* lists the plants in greatest detail:

The plantation is principally formed upon the declivity of a large knoll, and covers a considerable number of acres. On the west side is an island exhibiting every variety of the laurel leaved Tulip tree, *(Magnolia)* American Upright Honeysuckle *(Azalea)* and American Rose-bay, *(Rhododendron Ponticum)* which although they have been planted but a short time, have the appearance of spontaneous produce of the soil, flowering with all that kind of luxuriance, which they assume in their native land. Passing by the west side of the Lake towards the south, a complete underwood is reached, of the most choice varieties of Azaleas *(viz. Coccinea Auranteina, Coccinea Major Flammea)* and every other variety, flowering most magnificently, with some unique specimens of American and other trees towering above them. On the right is another grove of the *Rhododendron Ponticum* and *Maximum*, aspiring to the height of our common horse chestnut, and flowering to the very summits, intermixed with the Carolina Rose, *(Rosa Carolinensis)* growing most luxuriantly.

To the left, is a group of the Magnolia tribe, some of

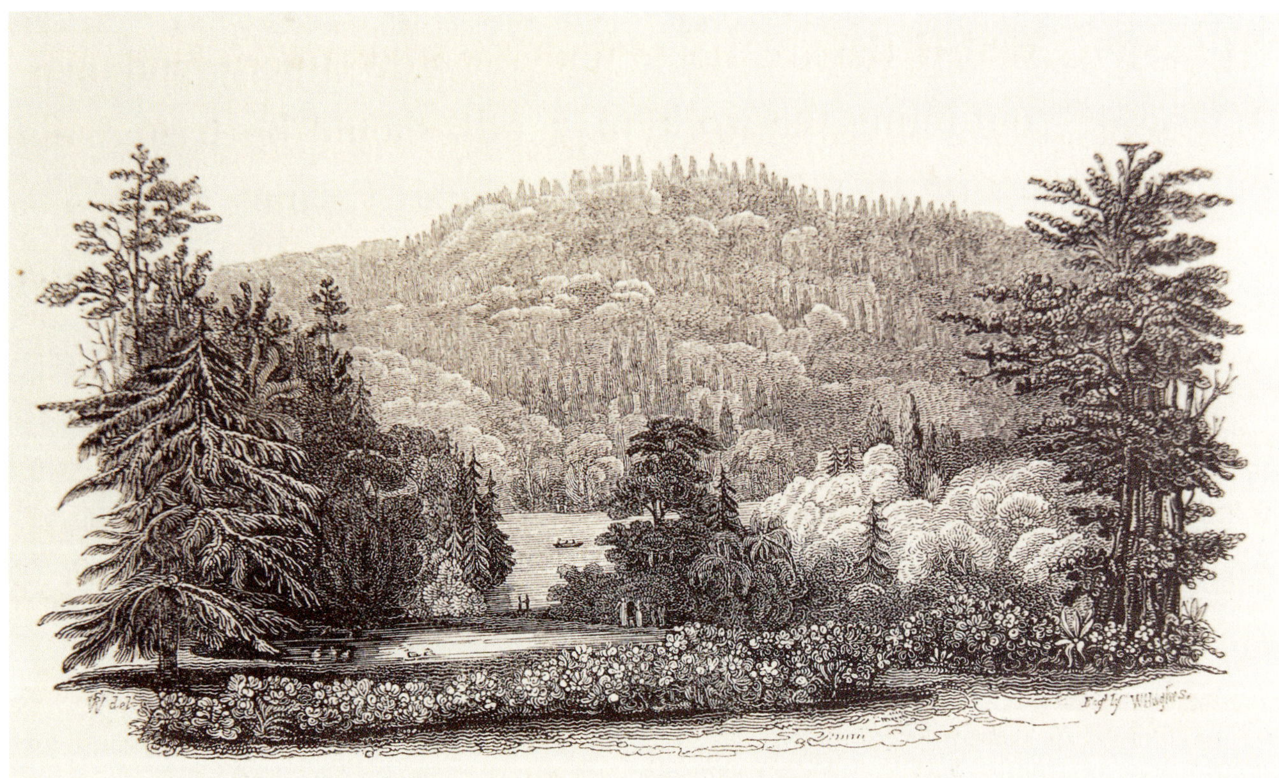

Fig. 8-6. "A View of the Scenery of the American Plantations." From John Rutter, *Delineations of Fonthill and its Abbey* (Shaftesbury and London, J. Rutter, 1823), page 82.

the specimens rising in luxuriance, with the beech and firs above them: near to this are some very fine specimens of Carolina Allspice, *(Calicanthus Floridus)* flowering in such abundance as to extend their perfume over the whole of the American Ground.

The American Rose Acacia, *(Robinia Latifolia* and *Augustifolia)* also grow here, with the different species of Andromeda, from Arborea down to the most diminutive kind. Likewise the Wild Rosemary, *(Loedum* and *Cloethra)* with all their varieties, and Wild Strawberry Tree *(Arbutus)* growing to the size of Portugal Laurel. At a short distance is a Basin of Water, with a fine spring, covered with White and Yellow Water Lilly, *(Nymphea Alba* and *Lutea)* with the banks thickly clothed with *Rhododendron Angelica* and other American plants, in their native splendour.[139]

The American Garden was a great success. At the time of the 1823 sale, when Beckford no longer lived at the Abbey, a newspaper article declared that the plantations "give an idea of as deep and wild a solitude for their extent as Pennsylvania itself could afford."[140] The plants, which were difficult to cultivate in a northern climate and English soil, continued to flourish even after Beckford's departure. Loudon explained in the *Gardener's Magazine* of 1826, that "One reason why the American plants grow so luxuriantly at Fonthill Abbey, is that they were interspersed among bushes of hazel, dog-wood, &c. and sheltered by firs, oaks, and other timber trees."[141] Their flourishing

is probably a testament to the skill of Beckford's gardeners, Vincent and Milne.

The American Garden offered not only the wonders of its plants but also a pleasing view of the Abbey, as did other areas in the grounds. Visitors would frequently, seemingly by accident, happen upon a stunning view of the Abbey building while traversing the many paths and carriageways throughout the grounds. The principal "circuit" of Fonthill was being planned in 1796 when Beckford wrote to his mother: "My Walk, which you will recollect is, according to the plan, to be carried considerably more than twenty Miles thro' and round the woods . . . has already proceeded to nearly the length of nine Miles."[142] This plan was brought to completion in the winter of 1800–1801, with a long carriage ride being added to the "Nine Miles Walk."[143] In fact, so "mazy and deceptive" were the paths of Fonthill that at the time of the sale visitors would "regularly lose themselves three times an hour."[144]

Ann Hamilton neatly summarized the intended effects of traversing these walks and rides, stating: "The variety of ground it is impossible to describe as the beauty of the distant country and the effect of the Grand Abbey rising in the midst of such stupendous woods which seem as endless as they are various."[145] This variety could be found in the different character of the trees, when the "dark and solemn pine is succeeded by the sparkling and feathery birch."[146] Similarly, Rutter wrote of how "woodbine and the jasmine not only interlace the thickets with their green and fragrant tendrils, but the rose and rhododendron bloom beneath the larch and the hawthorn, and the furze and the lily blossom in equal companionship."[147] He went on to explain that such appearances were sometimes concentrated in secluded spots, the famous "by-scenes" as Loudon called them, but that they were not confined to particularly favorable situations.

This is entirely typical of the planned informality that Beckford strove to create at Fonthill—a careful balancing act between natural incidents of beauty and the artful manipulation of landscape. Of course, even the "natural" elements of Fonthill were carefully orchestrated. Beckford admitted to Repton that although "nature has been liberal to Fonthill," some of its embellishments had been "received from Art."[148] Beckford's success in creating a seemingly natural environment at Fonthill is attested to by the opinion of one tourist who concluded: "Nature here prevailed over art."[149]

Beckford focused his attention on flowers as carefully as on the rest of his plantings.[150] In his travels he never failed to notice their presence, rhapsodizing over the "gay embroidery" of wild flowers, such as the "Beds of poppies, hollyhocks, scarlet lychins, and other flame-coloured flowers" that he encountered in Europe.[151] At Innsbruck he wrote that the grass was "enamelled, in the strict sense of the word, with flowers. Geraniums predominated, brighter than ultramarine; here and there auriculas looked out of the moss, and I often reposed upon tufts of ranunculus."[152] In Sintra he gathered Jasmine "brought from the garden of the Necessidades, and inhaling their soft perfume."[153] In Switzerland he enjoyed traversing a rocky, picturesque valley "overgrown with juniper. . . . blooming with cyclamens," and "clambered up several of these crags . . . to gather the flowers I have just mentioned and found them deliciously scented."[154]

Beckford included a quotation from Ariosto in this description, which is reminiscent of the culture of "association" promoted by figures such as William Mason, whose flower-filled garden at Nuneham was intended to remind visitors of passages from the poets or of antiquity.[155] Both Mason and Beckford could be seen as landscape gardeners who helped restore the virtues of individual flower and flowering shrubs to the garden. Flowers were a vital part of the Fonthill landscape— Beckford recognized that their diverse colors and scents would serve to enrich the landscape and increase its variety.[156] The areas on each side of the "Nine Miles Ride," for instance, were "broad spaces covered with flowers, which appear to be cultivated with peculiar care."[157]

As always with Fonthill, however, the introduction of these plants was not straightforward. Beckford cultivated both wild and exotic flowers at Fonthill. The "wild" flowers tended to be natives to the British Isles,[158] or at least those suited to a northern climate that would flourish naturally once planted throughout the woods, walks, and glades. The situation with exotics was rather more complicated. Redding suggested that exotics had been introduced in Fonthill Old Park, writing that at the sale of the old mansion in 1801 the gardens were "embellished with every European, American, and Asiatic tree or shrub that could be procured."[159] Britton had mentioned that the first walks in the Alpine Garden were "made of sufficient width to admit of borders of flowers and exotic shrubs."[160] In fact, exotics were intro-

duced quite liberally throughout the grounds. One of the great successes of Beckford's planting scheme was the grouping of native with non-native species.

Several sources attest to areas specifically dedicated to the cultivation of rare and non-native species at Fonthill.[161] In addition to the American Garden, a Chinese Garden, and a flower garden, as well as greenhouses, were included in the estate. The earliest experiments in exotics as part of the Abbey scheme were undertaken in 1796. In November Beckford wrote that "The Conservatory and flower Garden, which are to surround it [the Abbey] are begun."[162] A year later the *European Magazine* was describing the new kitchen and flower garden, developed from those of the old estate, approximately one mile north of the Abbey:

> Mr. Beckford's next undertaking was the formation of a new Kitchen and Flower Garden, contiguous to each other, in a more convenient scite, under a warmer aspect, and upon a scale four times larger than the old one. The Hot Walls, Pineries, Conservatories, quantities of glazed Frame-work, the Gardener's House, importation of soil for this extensive spot of many cares, with its plantations and nurseries, and an extensive enclosure of a handsome brick wall round the whole, have altogether concurred to render this work almost as unrivalled in magnitude and convenience, as it must have been in matter of expense.[163]

In 1821 this area was still being used, with "extensive hot and greenhouses, filled with the choicest and most luxurious fruits and flowers."[164] Rutter even gave the dimensions of these structures, writing that to the right of the Great Terrace were gardens "occupying many acres, enclosed with high walls, and containing a range of hothouses, four hundred and fifty feet long."[165] At first glance it is perhaps surprising to find such buildings and their cultivated "artificial" produce in an environment supposedly dedicated to the wildness of nature.[166] Yet Ann Hamilton tells us that, far from being an eyesore— a formal, artificial blot on the savage Fonthill landscape—the flower garden was "quite irregular and the enclosure not seen."[167] As Rutter reminds us "The great principal upon which this labyrinth of groves has been constructed, is that of exhibiting an union of the wildest and the most ornamented scenery."[168] It is not surprising, therefore, that Beckford included such a feature.

Another part of Fonthill that fostered exotics was the Chinese Garden. In 1812 Storer described a "small garden, surrounded by a light iron fence, which is called the Chinese Garden, particularly appropriated to the culture of the rarest flowers."[169] Situated at the end of the Nine Miles Walk, this small garden eventually became known, in 1823, as the "Dwarf's Garden." Loudon reports seeing in his visit of 1807: "a small hot-house, not much bigger than a cucumber frame," which may have been used in cultivating Asiatic plants.[170]

During the eighteenth century Chinese gardens had been erroneously thought of as grand parks, the result of William Chambers's *Dissertation on Oriental Gardening*, which had argued that there were many affinities between the Chinese approach and the new type of landscape garden fashionable in England at that time.[171] Chambers's book (of which Beckford owned a presentation copy) sparked a debate over the true nature of Chinese gardening.[172] Beckford demonstrated his awareness of this debate—and his own belief as to the dubious nature of Chambers's text—in a passage from *Recollections*. Quizzing a priest, who had been stationed at Peking and who had read Chambers's "most florid essay on Chinese gardening,"[173] Beckford enquired as to the truthfulness of the text:

> I asked him how many words of truth there might happen to be in all this luxuriant description? He answered . . . "There be ten-tousand-time-ten-tousand." "You don't mean to assure me," said I, that our famous architect's most wonderful account of the magical splendour of Yven-ming-Yven and Tchang-tchung-Yven is not exaggerated?" "It is not," answered the padre, "I have seen greater wonders than he—I have seen in the depth of winter a whole extent of garden warmed by a deliciously mild and scented vapour, and all the trees covered with silken leaves and artificial flowers.[174]

Beckford was in a strong position to question the validity of Chambers's book, as his knowledge of China was considerable.[175] Although he had never traveled to China, not only had he read most of the sources available on that country (in the form of travel writing, early accounts of the Jesuit mission, and natural history books) but he had also collected images of China. Several volumes of watercolor illustrations of zoological and botanical subjects formed part of Beckford's library at Fonthill.[176]

The Chinese Garden would, in fact, have been a most fashionable addition to the estate. Repton, for instance, had planned one at Woburn.[177] Such features were generally stocked with Chinese imports, and it is likely that Beckford cultivated such exotic blooms, fine images of which filled his library and which he had assiduously studied.[178] During the early years of the nineteenth century, the term *Chinese garden* was beginning to take on a new meaning in English minds. Travelers were reporting that "frequently-changed flowers in beds or pots, dwarf trees and plants, small rock-sculptures, trellises and creepers" formed true Chinese gardens.[179] The Chinese Garden at Fonthill may well have been of this type, such features being attuned to the formality creeping back into British garden design.[180]

The eclecticism of Fonthill makes it clear that Beckford was not a blind imitator. Rather, he was a *selective* imitator, responding to landscapes rather than styles of landscape, a subtle but vital distinction. There is never any suggestion that he set out to create a landscape with a stringent, formulaic aesthetic in mind. He was well read in the field of landscape and garden theory. Sir J. Murch, recalling a visit to Beckford at Lansdown, informs us that: "In my conversations with Mr. Beckford he was by no means reticent on topics mutually interesting. From the

works of planting and landscape gardening we were led to authors on such subjects and thence to other parts of literature."[181] Beckford's library contained Gilpin's complete works, Payne Knight's *Enquiry into the Principles of Taste*, Chambers's *Dissertation on Oriental Gardening*, several works by Repton (one of which, *On Landscape Gardening*, he annotated), and Loudon's *Observations on Landscape Gardening* (also annotated).[182]

Elements of Beckford's aesthetic coincided with, but were not determined by, the preferences of some of the major landscape theorists of his age. His was not a "Brownian" or a "Reptonian"[183] landscape, nor could Fonthill be called a Picturesque landscape, given the problematic nature of the term both in Beckford's age and our own. It has been suggested that "Beckford's record as a landscape gardener was one of response to changing fashion."[184] Beckford, however, formed his ideas about landscape parallel to those protagonists that it is believed he imitated. Beckford, in the company of John Robert Cozens, traveled to Switzerland only one year after Richard Payne Knight and Cozens had made a similar trip. The responses of both Beckford and Payne Knight to the alpine landscape were similar, and each incorporated alpinism into their landscape designs. Payne Knight's landscape garden at Foxley, for example, included an "Alpine bridge."

To classify Beckford as merely an imitator would be to rely too heavily on hindsight. While it is now certainly possible to perceive in Beckford's landscaping certain elements common to the numerous landscape theories of the age, this should not be mistaken as a direct and absolute response to such "fashions." Clearly, some aspects of the Fonthill grounds correlate to the aesthetics expressed in landscape treatises contemporary to Beckford. Certain passages from Uvedale Price's *Essay on the Picturesque* are particularly reminiscent of Fonthill and Beckford's approach to landscape.[185] This being said, the opinions and language of those commenting on and describing Fonthill (such as Rutter and Britton) would have been colored by a familiarity with such writings.

It has been claimed that Beckford's "conversion" to the so-called "Savage Picturesque" determined the layout of Fonthill. Fonthill certainly contained Savage Picturesque elements but it also included those that were the opposite, such as the Chinese Garden, the greenhouses, and the terraces. These should not be ignored when addressing the Fonthill landscape. The ideas of landscapists such as Mason and Repton might be read into the Fonthill grounds. Loudon even claimed that when complete, Fonthill would "probably contribute more to the establishment of my ideas of Picturesque Improvement, than any thing that I can write."[186]

Remarkably, although such a great variety of features could be found at Fonthill, the landscape still contrived to express "the most perfect unity of character."[187] Paradoxically, it was the variety of the Fonthill grounds that provided their unity—a complexity and diversity entirely characteristic of the landscape's creator. Indeed, as Redding noted: "No one understood the force of contrast better than Mr. Beckford."[188]

Acknowledgments: My thanks to Philip Hewat-Jaboor, Adriana Turpin, and Michael Symes for their generous assistance.—AM

1. Prompted by the intrusion of huntsmen into the estate, Beckford ordered the construction of a "barrier wall" in 1793. This extended for seven miles, enclosing 519 acres—the "sacred enclosure" in which he was to build the Abbey. The wall was "of considerable height and thickness, built of hewnstone," and "finished with a strong painted paling, inclined outwards, as a *chevaux de frize*" (*European Magazine and London Review*, 31 (1797):105).

2. Britton quoted the grounds as being "groves of Eden" (John Britton, *Graphical and Literary Illustrations of Fonthill Abbey, Wiltshire; with Heraldical and Genealogical Notes* [London, 1823]: 35), and explained that "some have bestowed unequalled praise on its '*paradisaical charms*'" (John Britton, *The Beauties of Wiltshire displayed in Statistical, Historical & Descriptive Sketches; Illustrated by Views of the Principal Seats &c, with Anecdotes of The Arts*, vol. 1 [London, 1801]: 209). One of Beckford's newspaper cuttings relating to the Abbey, an "extract of a private letter" of 1823 declared areas of the estate "a perfect Eden" (MS. Beckford, b.6, fol.49). On landscaping and the aspiration to re-create Eden in England see Max F. Schulz, *Paradise preserved: re-creations of Eden in eighteenth-and nineteenth-century England* (Cambridge: Cambridge University Press, 1985).

3. Both Rutter and Meister thought the Fonthill grounds might have been inspired by Milton's poetry. S*ee* John Rutter, *Delineations of Fonthill and its Abbey* (Shaftesbury and London, 1823): 84, 85, 90, 94; and Henri Meister, *Letters Written During a Residence in England, translated from the French of Henry Meister* (London, 1799), 303. This was a translation of the original French version of Meister's visit (in 1792 or 1793) entitled *Souvenirs de mes Voyages en Angleterre* (Zurich, 1795). There are several discrepancies between the French and English versions of these letters. The citations in this essay, taken from the English edition, contain no essential differences to the French original. Beckford himself included passages from Milton in his unpublished work *The Dome of the Setting Sun* (MS. Beckford.d.9, fols.1–32). On the "eighteenth century Miltonic" garden, *see* Schulz, *Paradise preserved* (1985): 9–29. Meister, when visiting Fonthill, thought himself in "Julia's Elysium" (*Letters* [1799]: 303).

4. One writer thought the grounds such "as we conceive in the imagination when we dream of the Happy Valley of Rasselas" (*Morning Herald*, 7 Oct 1822). Rutter, quoting from Fairfax's Tasso, compared the grounds to the "Faire trees, high plants, strange herbs and flowrets new" of the Armida gardens (*Delineations* [1823]: 83).

5. Britton, *Illustrations* (1823): 32. It is worth noting that Cyrus Redding appraised the Fonthill grounds in a similar manner, writing that there was "every kind of surface" in the designed landscape (Cyrus Redding, *Memoirs of William Beckford of Fonthill, Author of "Vathek,"* vol. 2 [1859]: 146–48).

6. Britton, *Illustrations* (1823): 33. The scale of planting at Fonthill was phenomenal. In some years Beckford planted "several hundred trees," in others "not less than a million" (*European Magazine* 31 [1797]: 104). For the purposes of this essay the term "Abbey grounds" includes everything except Fonthill Old Park. It has also been termed the "Abbey area"; see Laurent Chatel, "The Mole, the Bat and the Fairy or the Sublime Grottoes of 'Fonthill Splendens': A Brief Study of Beckford's Contribution to *Subterranea Brittanica*," *Beckford Journal* 5 (Spring 1999): 53–74, 54.

7. Britton, *Illustrations* (1823): 35, 36.

8. John Claudius Loudon, "Notes on Gardens and Country Seats, visited, from July 27. to September 16. 1833," *Gardener's Magazine* 11 (1835): 442.

9. Britton, *Illustrations* (1823): 34.

10. Ibid.

11. John Rutter, *A Description of Fonthill Abbey and Demesne, Wilts; the Seat of William Beckford, Esq. Including a List of its Numerous and Valuable Paintings, Cabinets, and other Curiosities* (Shaftesbury, 1822), 19.

12. Britton, *Illustrations* (1823): 35 and 33, respectively. Regrettably, Britton declined to describe these features in detail fearing that "it would be tedious and prolix to the reader" (ibid., p.33). This comment, rather than being a criticism of the grounds, might be read as an acknowledgment of their extent and intricacy.

13. Meister, *Letters* (1799): 311–12. Gessner, the great European naturalist, was particularly known for his descriptions of landscape. Indeed, Beckford records that when near Harlem "I promised myself a sentimental saunter in the groves, took up Gesner, and began to have pretty pastoral ideas as I walked forward" (William Beckford, *Italy; with Sketches of Spain and Portugal*, vol. 1 [London: Richard Bentley, 1834]: 33). Beckford himself owned a full edition of Gessner's work: "*Oeuvres Completes de Gessner*, 3 to. *gilt leaves*" (*Books, books of prints*, sale cat., [London: Leigh, Sotheby and Son, 9–11 June 1808], lot. 216). References to sale catalogues here and in subsequent notes are based on Robert Gemmett, ed., "Catalogue of the Principal Public Sales of Books, Prints, Pictures, Furniture, Objets d'Art, and other Valuable Possessions of William Beckford of Fonthill," in *Poets and Men of Letters*, vol. 3 of *Sale Catalogues of Libraries of Eminent Persons*, ed. A. N. L. Munby (London: Mansell Publishing and Sotheby Publications, 1972).

14. Britton, *Illustrations* (1823): 33. Beckford developed his visual senses in a painterly manner. Robert Gemmett suggests that Beckford's *Dreams, Waking Thoughts and Incidents* ". . . displays an eager eye for colour, lights and shades, surface textures, distant lines, perspectives, and picture-like views . . . Beckford cultivated seeing as though it were an art form" (Robert J Gemmett, *William Beckford* [Boston: Twayne Publishers, 1977]: 76). Gemmett further suggests that *Dreams* "remains one of the best illustrations of the 'literary picturesque'" and compares Beckford's writings to the aesthetics of William Gilpin (ibid., pp.75–76).

15. Timothy Mowl wrote that Beckford was "a fluent and seductive liar who had ample funds to pay secretaries to rewrite letters" (*William Beckford, Composing for Mozart* [London: John Murray, 1998], 1).

16. As Laurent Chatel wrote: "the paucity of material relating to Fonthill in the Bodleian and Yale archives has meant that biographers have relied on a number of indirect primary sources documenting the estate, such as diaries by contemporaries who actually saw Fonthill" ("Mole, the Bat and the Fairy" [1999]: 54).

17. Milne was with Beckford from 1807 to 1815. In June 1815 Beckford wrote that "The new gardener hasn't yet arrived (*Life at Fonthill* [1957]: 180). Vincent was Beckford's gardener at both Fonthill and Bath. Beckford referred to the Fonthill grounds as "Milne's Kingdom" rather than his own (ibid., p. 94). This implies that to some extent the purchasing of plants and the exact implementation of his landscaping plans was left to the gardeners, a notion borne out by the fact that we find Beckford being informed by Milne of plant purchases that the gardener had made.

18. For the earliest mention of Beckford's purchases for the grounds, see Beckford to Thomas Wildman, 9 March 1787: "the best opportunity to secure greenhouse plants offers next 23rd of April, when Princess Amelia's collection comes to market. Let me enjoin you, as you love Fonthill and believe in the excellence of its conservatory, to buy fifty or a hundred pounds' worth of the grandest orange, oleander and myrtle trees" (cited in Boyd Alexander, *England's Wealthiest Son: A Study of William Beckford* [London: Centaur Press, 1962], 18). In his correspondence with Franchi during the middle of November 1815, Beckford wrote of his impatient wait for some "piante" from one "Chandler." On the November 22 he informed Franchi that: "Le piante di Chandler son arrivati ignoro in quel state" (MS. Beckford, c.4, fol.110r). Beckford was probably referring to the firm Chandler and Son, who were nurserymen of Vauxhall (see John Harvey, *Early Nurserymen* [London and Chichester: Phillimore & Co., 1974], 130). In October of 1819 Beckford complains, "all I have to pay—it's horrible: £65 to Whitely for flowers and plants etc." (William Beckford, *Life at Fonthill, 1807–1822, With Interludes in Paris and London from the Correspondence of William Beckford,* ed. and trans. Boyd Alexander [London: Hart-Davis, 1957]: 324). It is likely that Beckford is here referring to the firm Whitely, Brames and Milne, nurserymen of New King's Road. Redding noted such "purchases at the suburban nurseries" in his biography of Beckford (Redding, *Memoirs*, vol. 2 [1959]: 371).

19. For the distinctions between Fonthill Old Park and the Abbey grounds see Robert J. Gemmett, "Beckford's Fonthill: The Landscape as Art," *Gazette des Beaux Arts* 80 (1972): 335–36.

20. Although each of these books describes the appearance of the grounds, their descriptions are not entirely objective. Beckford encouraged the production of each publication and may have offered advice on the texts. Rutter's work, in particular, has been perceived as being heavily influenced by Beckford's personal view of the Abbey and grounds.

21.The first serious appraisal of the Fonthill grounds was made by Robert J. Gemmett in his doctoral dissertation; for a summary see Gemmett, "Beckford's Fonthill" (1972). Discussions of the Fonthill landscape have appeared in wider surveys of eighteenth- and nineteenth-century landscape gardening; see especially David Jacques, *Georgian Gardens: The Reign of Nature* (London: Batsford, 1983); and David Watkin, *The English Vision: The Picturesque in Architecture, Landscape and Garden Design* (London: J. Murray, 1982). More recently, Mowl devoted several pages to Fonthill Park and the Abbey grounds (*William Beckford*, [1998]: 32–37, 265–68), while Chatel has written on the architectural embellishments to the Fonthill landscape in his doctoral thesis (which was unavailable for consultation during the writing of this essay): "Utopies paysagères: vues et visions de William Beckford—de la mise en fable à la mise en scènes d'espaces," Ph.D. diss., Université de la Sorbonne-Nouvelle, Paris.

22. Gemmett noted this fact: "While a great deal has been written in recent years concerning William Beckford's neo-Gothic building at Fonthill, Wilts., comparatively little has been said about the transformation of the 519 acre estate" (Gemmett, "Beckford's Fonthill" [1972]: 335).

23. For Beckford's gardening activities see Alexander, *England's Wealthiest Son* (1962): 172–80. The majority of Alexander's account, however, is presented in the form of quotations from texts such as Rutter's *Delineations* (1823).

24. Alexander, *England's Wealthiest Son* (1962): 172

25. Redding, *Memoirs,* vol. 2 (1959): 225.

26. Ibid.

27. Very little is known about Beckford's "paradise in Cintra" as Byron put it in *Childe Harold's Pilgrimage*. Maria Laura Bettencourt Pires has suggested (without citing any evidence) that Beckford "imported exotic flowers" for his Portuguese gardens and that at Monserrate he

". . . built some waterfalls that can still be seen there today" (*William Beckford and Portugal, an Impassioned Journey, 1787, 1794,1798* [Institutio Português do Patrimônio Cultural, Palácio de Queluz, 1987]: 15–16). Beckford wrote in a letter: "Monserrat with all the blooms and fragrances is at your absolute command . . . . I have been too much engaged with the royalty of Nature, with climbing rocks and cork trees, with tracing rills and runnels to their source and examining the recess of these lovely environs" (William Beckford to Isabel Sill Bezerra, Monserrate, 18 June 1795, quoted in ibid., p. 160). For Beckford in Paris see chap. 6, by Anne Eschapasse, in this volume; and see also Beckford to Lady Craven, November 1790: "No sooner had I taken possession of my Appartments than I waved my wand and behold—a garden as green as in the month of May— full of wall flowers and Laurustine, primroses started up on the terrace, upon which I go out *de plein pied* from the large glass door of my Saloon" (quoted in J. W. Oliver, *The Life of William Beckford* [London: Oxford University Press, Humphrey Milford, 1932], 209). For Beckford's landscape at Lansdown see Henry Venn Lansdown, *Recollections of the Late William Beckford of Fonthill, Wilts and Lansdown* (1893; reprint, Bath: Kingsmead Reprints, 1969).

28. Indeed, it might be argued that the Abbey building itself developed out of his landscaping plans, since Beckford's Gothic edifice evolved from the small ruined chapel that he had planned as a landscape feature.

29. Alexander, *England's Wealthiest Son* (1962): 172.

30. Beckford, *Life at Fonthill* (1957): 235. The felling of trees helped to provide Beckford with capital. In July 1814, for example, he sold "an immense amount of wood" in order to raise money for the purchase of drawings (ibid., p.154). In 1814 he wrote "there is no lack of buyers, of big prices and ready money . . . . The oak will fall—for nine guineas a pound," and for pine he was being offered "five guineas for each" (ibid., pp.175, 176).

31. *European Magazine* 31 (1797): 107.

32. Beckford to Gregorio Franchi, 31 January 1814, quoted in Beckford, *Life at Fonthill* (1957): 145.

33. Ibid., p.333. This letter was written during Beckford's attempt to secure funds from the duke in exchange for the Abbey reverting to Hamilton after his death. Given the evidence for Beckford's love of planting there is no reason to believe that Franchi's remark is not genuine, even though control of the estate was a contentious issue in the negotiations.

34. Loudon, "Notes on Gardens" (1835): 448. Although this story may be apocryphal, it serves to illustrate that during Beckford's lifetime he was perceived as being wholly dedicated to the improvement of the Abbey grounds.

35. Redding, *Memoirs*, vol. 2 (1959): 80. It seems likely that the grounds of Fonthill Splendens inspired the landscape descriptions in Beckford's unpublished work, "The Transport of Pleasure," one passage of which reads, "Many an hour have I already spent in this sequestered Forest which covers the side of the Hill" (MS. Beckford,d.10, fol.19v). He further describes this forest as a place where "my youthful fancy has met with such amusement" (ibid., fol.20v).

36. Rutter, *Delineations* (1823): 92.

37. Britton, *Illustrations* (1823): 26.

38. Ibid., p. 26. Britton earlier devoted several pages to describing the landscaping around Fonthill Splendens (*Beauties of Wiltshire*, vol. ? [1801]: 210–11 and 240–48).

39. This painting is now in the Government Art Collection, Ref. 7074. The house, seen by Richard Pococke in 1754, was described as "fronted in the Italian taste" (*The Travels Through England of Dr. Richard Pococke, Succesively Bishop of Meath and of Ossory during 1750, 1751 and later years*, vol. 2 [London: Camden Society, 1889]: 47. *See also* John Harris, *The Artist and the Country House: A History of Country House and Garden View Painting 1540–1870* (London: Sotheby's Publications, 1985), 262.

40. Redding, *Memoirs*, vol. 2 (1959): 80.

41. Pococke, *Travels*, vol. 2 (1889): 47.

42. *See* Jon Millington, *Souvenirs of Fonthill Abbey: An exhibition to commemorate the 150th anniversary of the death of William Beckford, Beckford's Tower, Lansdown, Bath, Easter–October 1994* (Bath: Bath Preservation Trust, 1994): 22.

43. The name of Inigo Jones has frequently been associated with Fonthill. Fonthill Redivivus has been thought to have been built by Jones, and Mowl noted that the "arched gate-lodge," which the Alderman built north of the house and which survives intact, stylistically evokes Jones' work. Mowl suggested that John Vardy, whose interest in Jones is attested to by his 1744 publication, *Some Designs of Mr. Inigo Jones and Mr. William Kent,* may have had a hand in designing this structure. *See* Mowl, *Wiiliam Beckford* (1998): 28; and Britton, *Beauties*, vol.1 (1801): 210.

44. The village was originally located close to Fonthill House and claimed its own medieval church. When the Alderman purchased Fonthill he demolished the village and rebuilt it (out of sight of his house) in a valley beyond the hill to the west of the mansion.

45. This effect was still apparent in 1823 when the west wing or "pavilion" was all that remained of Fonthill Splendens. For an illustration of this view see R. Ackerman, *Repository of the Arts* &c., Boosey & Co., August 1, 1823, no.8.

46. In 1801 Britton recorded that the Alpine Garden included "a rustic rotunda, called the Paliaro." This building was "thatched with straw, like the huts of the Calabrian shepherds; and supported by six rude unbarked firs as columns" (Britton, *Beauties*, vol.1 [1801]: 245).

47. Squire Mushroom was a satirical character devised to ridicule the gardening pretensions of the nouveau riche. He first appeared in an article by Francis Coventry for *The World*; see Alison Hodges, "Painshill Park, Cobham, Surrey (1700–1800): Notes for a History of the Landscape Garden of Charles Hamilton," *Garden History* 2, no. 1 (Autumn 1973): 44.

48. Britton, *Beauties,* vol.1 (1801): 242–43. Britton here seems to suggest that William Beckford continued to landscape Fonthill in a manner designed to fulfil his late father's intentions.

49. After creating the river, the Alderman rerouted the public road to the east bank so that it led away from the house, and the bridge was intended to bring this road back to its original course on the west bank. See Mowl, *William Beckford* (1998): 28.

50. William Gilpin, *Observations on the Western Parts of England Relative chiefly to Picturesque Beauty to which are added a few remarks on the picturesque beauty of the Isle of Wight* (London: T. Cadell Jun. & W. Davies, 1798): 116.

51. *See* Chatel, "Mole, the Bat and the Fairy" (1999): 57.

52. Britton, *Beauties,* vol.1 (1801): 248.

53. "A certificate of William Beckford's Esq. having planted in the Parishes of Witham Somerset and of Fonthill Wilts Sixty One Thousand eight Hundred Scotch Firs upon One Hundred and Seventy Five Acres of Land, was read. Resolved that the Certificates sent by Mr. Beckford are satisfactory. Resolved that Mr. Beckford is intitled to the first premium of a Gold Medal offered by the Society for that Article', archives of the Royal Society for the Encouragement of Arts, Manufactures and Commerce" (quoted in Chatel, "Mole, the Bat and the Fairy" [1999]: 72).

54. David Jacques suggests that the Alderman actually had no skill in planting matters, and that he may have been receiving assistance from his uncle by marriage, Charles Hamilton (*Georgian Gardens* [1983]: 90).

55. Chatel, "Mole, the Bat and the Fairy" (1999): 57.

56. Ibid. Chatel concluded that "the extent to which he had landscaped Splendens at all is not clear."

57. Beckford, *Life at Fonthill* (1957): 105.

58. Loudon, "Notes on Gardens" (1835): 442.

59. Ibid., p. 441.

60. It should be remembered that Loudon was writing his account partially from a visit in 1807 and partially from "its present state," i.e. a decade after Beckford had quit the property, during which time the grounds were "in such a state of neglect, as hardly to be recognised for what they were in 1807" (ibid., p. 444). As such the natural quality that Loudon so praised would have been due, in part, to the overgrown state in which he found Fonthill.

61. For Hoare's comments on Fonthill and environs see Richard Coalt Hoare, *The History of Modern Wiltshire* (London: John Bowyer Nichols and John Gough Nichols, 1822):44; Hundred of Dunworth: 23–28.

62. Loudon, "Notes on Gardens" (1835): 443.

63. Storer, *A Description of Fonthill Abbey, Wiltshire* (London, 1812): 3–4.

64. Rutter records in his *New descriptive guide* that the Alderman had designed such a tower to "correspond with Alfred's tower, at Stour-Head" (John Rutter, *A new descriptive guide to Fonthill abbey and demesne, for 1823, including a list of its paintings and curiosities* [Shaftesbury, 1823], 72). In the early 1790's, Beckford proposed raising a tower on the foundations of one begun by his father, but it was never built. The proposed tower was to be "280 feet high, with a lantern at the top, so that it will command a view of near 80 miles every way, and the lantern to be seen at night from a great distance. It is to be furnished as an observatory" (*Gentleman's Magazine* 61 [September 1796]: 784). The idea of building a tower may have been in his mind at least since he wrote "The Transport of Pleasure," in which a tower features prominently.

65. Beckford, *Life at Fonthill* (1957): 158.

66. Ibid., p.176.

67. However, in "The Transport of Pleasure," Beckford praises the English landscape, if not its gardens, writing ". . . there are Mountains in England to which we may resort and Woods as lovely as those I beheld from the peak there are rivers more limpid than those which flow from the Alps, on whose green Margin we may walk at midnight and trace the melancholy wanderings of the Moon" (MS.Beckford, d.10, fol.17v).

68. Redding, *Memoirs,* vol. 1 (1959): 148.

69. Ibid.

70. Ibid.

71. Cozens was influential in the formulation of Beckford's tastes in landscape and may well have

fostered his Orientalist tendencies. See Kim Sloan, *Alexander and John Robert Cozens: The Poetry of Landscape* (New Haven and London: Yale University Press, 1986); and Elizabeth Schaeffer, "'To Remind us of China'—William Beckford, Mental Traveller on the Grand Tour: The Construction of Significance in Landscape," in *Transports: Travel, Pleasure and Imaginary Geography 1600–1830,* ed. Chloe Chard and Helen Langdon (London and New Haven: Yale University Press for the Paul Mellon Centre, 1996): 207–42.

72. Redding, *Memoirs,* vol. 1 (1959): 148.

73. Ibid. Hamilton moved to from Painshill to Bath in 1773.

74. Ibid.

75. Britton, *Beauties,* vol.1 (1801): 242.

76. "Joy to the Electors of bavaria! For preserving such extensive woods of fir in their dominions" (Beckford, *Italy,* vol. 1 [1834]: 63); "We were driven in the evening to Nymphenburg, the Elector's country palace, the bosquets, jets-d'eau and parterres of which are the pride of the Bavarians" (ibid., p. 64); "We glided along by the Mira, a village of palaces, whose courts and gardens, as magnificent as statues, terraces and vases can make them, are far from composing a rural prospect" (ibid., p. 146).

77. Ibid., p.36.

78. Describing the Boboli gardens Beckford writes: "You would have been enraptured with the broad masses of shade and dusky alleys" (ibid., p. 183); on a later visit he states: "I went through a plat of vines to a favourite place of mine:- a little garden of the most fragrent roses, with a spring under a rustic arch of grotto work fringed with ivy. Thousands of fish inhabit here, of that beautiful glittering species which comes from China" (ibid., p.206). Visiting Mantua he noted: ". . . here nettles grow thick and rampant; there, tuberoses and jessamine spring from mounds of ruins, which during the elegant reign of the Gonzagas led to grottoes and subterranean apartments, concealed from vulgar eyes, and scared to the most refined enjoyments" (ibid., p.165).

79. For Garzoni and Negrone *see* ibid., pp.188 and 299 respectively.

80. Ibid., p. 22. It should be noted that previous English visitors had, in contrast to Beckford, admired the natural style of Bentinck's landscaping at Zorgvliet. See John Dixon Hunt and Eric de Jong, eds., The *Anglo-Dutch Garden in the Age of William and Mary,* special double issue of the *Journal of Garden History* 8, nos. 2 and 3, (April/September 1988): 164. His account continued: "The walks and alleys have all the stiffness and formality which our ancestors admired; but the intermediate spaces, being dotted with clumps and sprinkled with flowers, are imagined in Holland to be in the English style. An Englishman ought to behold it with partial eyes, since every possible attempt has been made to twist it into the taste of his country" (Beckford, *Italy,* vol. 1 [1834]: 23). These comments perhaps illustrate Beckford's awareness of the dangers inherent in a formulaic application of garden principles, the results of which he may have encountered in landscape gardens throughout England.

81. Beckford, *Italy,* vol. 2 (1834): 107. Beckford continues: "I paid it not half the attention its proprietor expected, and retiring under the shade of the fruit trees, feasted on the golden apples and purple plums that were rolling about me in such profusion." Beckford's behavior may also have been intended as a slight in the usual Beckford manner.

82. William Beckford, *The Journal of William Beckford in Portugal and Spain, 1787–88,* ed. Boyd Alexander (London: Rupert Hart-Davis, 1954), 111.

83. "They cover a vast extent of sandy ground in which there is no prevailing upon trees to flourish" (Beckford, *Italy,* vol. 2 [1834]: 359).

84. From an early age Beckford was rhapsodic about landscape. In 1778 he wrote *The Dome of the Setting Sun,* the "advertisement" to which reads: "The design of the following Rhapsody is to colect the beautiful ideas scattered about through the Greek and Latin classics on the subject of the setting sun, together with the antient notions about the fortunate isles and Elysium." This account included a selection of Greek and Latin passages on Arcadia translated by Beckford (*see* MS.Beckford, d.9, fols.1–32).

85. For example, while looking on a "round of turf peculiarly green," at Fonthill in December 1778, Beckford explains how "my thoughts were wandering into the interior of Africa and dwelt for hours in those countries I love" (MS. Beckford, e.1, fol.9v).

86. Ibid., fol.21r. At Mount Edgcumbe Beckford was, in fact, practcally on an island in the Atlantic, being situated between the Atlantic on one side and Plymouth Sound on the other. Michael Symes notes that it is a place where "there were Italian, French and English gardens constructed both as an exercise in contrast and as visitor education in garden styles" ("Gardens Picturesque and Sublime" in *The Picturesque,* ed. Dana Arnold [1994]). Similarly, referring to his travels in Portugal, Beckford wrote: "The mossy fragments of rock, grotesque pollards, and rustic bridges you meet with at every step, recall Savoy and Switzerland" (Beckford, *Italy,* vol. 2 [1834]: 213).

87. In *The Dome of the Setting Sun* Beckford linked imagination to the idea of Arcadia, writing: "In this remote region, Where Imagination may retire in security and give a loose to her caprices, flourish the loveliest groves waving with continual breezes" (MS. Beckord, d.9, fol.9r). He also

wrote: "I fear I shall stand self-convicted of having sacrificed a little too freely to Imagination." (Beckford to Thurlow, 22 May 1778, MS. Beckford, d.9, fol.35r).

88. Meister, *Letters* (1799): 302.

89. John Gibson Lockhart, "Italy; with Sketches of Spain and Portugal. In a Series of Letters written during a Residence in those Countries. By William Beckford, Esq., Author of 'Vathek'," *Quarterly Review* 51 (March–June1834): 429.

90. Beckford [probably to Alexander Cozens], 3 December 1779, MS. Beckford, e.1, fol.17v.

91. William Beckford, *The Vision, Liber Veritatis, by William Beckford of Fonthill,* ed. Guy Chapman (London: Constable and Co., 1930), xiii. More recently, Elizabeth Schaeffer has discussed Beckford's "mental travelling in the midst of real geographies" ("To Remind us of China,"). On Beckford's "paradis artificiel" see Geoffrey Bullough, "Beckford's Early Travels and his 'Dreams of Delusion'," in *William Beckford of Fonthill Bicentenary Essays,* ed. Fatma Mahmoud (Cairo: Costa Tsoumas & Co, 1960): 31–50.

92. *Books, books of prints,* sale cat., Leigh, Sotheby & Son, London, 24 and 26 May 1804, lot.179.

93. A copy of Catesby's book was also owned by Hamilton. Hughes's book is listed in *Books, drawings,* sale cat. Sotheby, London, 6–8 May 1817, lot.304.

94. Beckford, *Italy,* vol. 2 (1834): 214. Several volumes of Cook's voyages—"Captain Cookes Voyage in 1772–3-4 & 5, 2 vols." and "Cooke and Kings voyage to the pacific ocean in 1776-7-8–9 & 80— are recorded in an inventory of books in the Fonthill library, ca.1786–1803: MS.Beckford, b.1, 18r.

95. Similarly, Charles Hamilton had a case of drawings of flowers and shrubs. See Michael Symes, "Charles Hamilton's Plantings at Painshill," *Garden History* 11, no. 2, (1983): 113.

96. Rutter, *Delineations* (1823): 87.

97. It seems that Beckford associated the investigation of nature with a quest for encyclopedic knowledge. In "The Transport of Pleasure," he states that an observation of flowers and insects has provided "every hour some new insight into the great volume of the Universe" (MS.Beckford, d.10, fol. 21r). Numerous illustrations of and volumes on insects filled Beckford's library. For example, in the sale of 1817 were the following: lot 138, "Barbut's Collection of British Insects, the ORIGINAL DRAWINGS, *in red morocco*"; lot 149, "Martyn's English Entomologist, ORIGINAL DRAWINGS ON VELLUM, *with port. of the Author, in red morocco,* 1792"; lot 150, "Martyn's Natural History of Spiders, *coloured drawings after nature, with frontispiece,* 1793" (*Books, drawings,* sale cat., Sotheby, London, 6–8 May 1817). Similarly, the sale of 1823 contained: lot 761, "Swammerdamii (Joannis) Biblia Natura, sive Historia Insectorum, in Dutch and Latin, 2 vol. folio, *Leid.* 1737"; and lot 1809, "WILKE'S NATURAL HISTORY OF ENGLISH MOTHS and BUTTERFLIES, *illustrated by one hundred and twenty most beautiful coloured plates,* 4to *Lond.* 1773" (*Books, books of prints, pictures, miniatures, sculpture, furniture, silver, porcelain, glass, miscellaneous,* Phillips, Fonthill, 9 September–29 October 1823).

98. Beckford owned a rare copy of Rousseau's complete works: "ROUSSEAU (J.J.) OEUVRES, 25 VOL. VELLUM PAPER, 64 *plates by Dupréel after Moreau inserted, fine copy in blue morocco extra, silk linings, gilt edges by Lefebure, Paris* 1801. Very scarce, only 100 copies printed" (*Books,* Sotheby, Wilkinson & Hodge, London, part 3, 2–14 July 1883, lot.1551). Redding tells us that Beckford "openly declared how fondly he felt attached to the pastoral life" (*Memoirs,* vol. 1 [1959]: 207). Such inclinations are to be found scattered throughout "The Transport of Pleasure," as well as in his travel writing. In Innsbruck, Beckford commented upon the "huts which are scattered about for the shelter of herds" which Cozens was then sketching. He explained, "These edifices . . . excite those ideas of pastoral life to which I am so fondly attached" (*Italy,* vol. 2 [1834]: 289). Beckford himself partook of the vogue, fuelled by Gilpin, for sketching picturesque scenes. The Bodleian archives contain a very few landscape sketches by Beckford. He tells us that while viewing the mountains near Leiria: "I longed to transfer their picturesquely-varied outline to the leaves of my sketch-book" (William Beckford, *Recollections of an Excursion to the Monasteries of Alcobaça and Batalha. By the author of "Vathek"* (London: Richard Bentley, 1835), 121.

99. "Journal of Lady Ann Hamilton," MS. Beckford, e.4, fol.8v. For an itinerary, including her 1804 visit to Fonthill, see ibid., fol.61v.

100. Quotes are from, respectively, Britton, *Illustrations* (1823): 34; and MS. Beckford, e.4, fol. 8v.

101. Beckford, *Italy,* vol. 2 (1834): 181. While Beckford's relationship with Rousseau's thought (a subject that demands considerable further study) falls outside the scope of this essay, it should be noted that there are correlation's between Rousseau and eighteenth-century landscape gardening. See Christopher Thacker, *The History of Gardens* (London: Croom Helm, 1985), 224–25.

102. MS. Beckford, e.1, fol. 00?

103. Letter from Switzerland, MS. Beckford, d.3, fol.7r.

104. Notes and journal entries of travels, 1778–95, MS.Beckford, e.2, fol.39r; also see Meister, *Letters* (1799): 303.

105. Beckford owned two copies of Saussure's *Voyage dans les Alpes* (1789); see *Books,* sale cat., Sotheby, Wilkinson & Hodge, London, part 3, 2–14 July 1883, lot.1768. Beckford's near-Franciscan belief in the sanctity of all life would seem to preclude any interest in cabinets of nat-

ural history. In Switzerland, for example, when enjoying the vivid colorings of "Fratillarias, and the most gorgeous flies," he wrote: "I could not find it in my heart to destroy their felicity. . . . Had I been less compassionate, I should have gained credit with that respectable corps, the torturers of butterflies; and might, perhaps, have enriched their cabinets with a few unknown varieties" (Beckford, *Italy*, vol. 1 [1834]: 91–92). A month earlier, however, he wrote that the Prince of Orange's cabinet had restored him to his "sober senses," even though "the butterflies . . . were very near leading me another dance; I thought of their native hills and beloved flowers on the summits of Haynang and Nan-Hoa" (ibid., p.27). Later in his tour he had intended to visit "Count Eysenberg's cabinet, enriched with the rarest productions of the mineral kingdom, and a complete collection of moths and flies peculiar to the Tyrol" (ibid., p.81). In Paris he excused himself from an excursion to view similar cabinets in the company of Buffon, son of the great naturalist. Beckford seems to have been interested in the "curiosity" of earlier centuries, collecting books by figures such as Aldrovandi and and Conrad Gesner; see *Books*, sale cat., Sotheby, Wilkinson & Hodge, London, part 1, 30 June–13 July 1882, lot.140; and ibid., part 2, 11–23 December 1882, lots.129–13. A desire to acquire the kind of rare and unusual objects associated with the cabinet of curiosities is recorded in Italy. Near Leghorn, Beckford encountered a fisherman selling coral and recorded: "I eagerly made the purchase, and thought myself a favourite of Neptune" (Beckford, *Italy*, vol. 1 [1834]: 200).

106. Beckford to Thurlow from Geneva, 22 May 1778, MS. Beckford, d.9, fol.37r. Evidence for Beckford's considerable interest in Natural History is also provided in "The Transport of Pleasure," in which he wrote: "All the day we will consecrate to subjects of natural history we will explore Buffon whose animated eloquence deserves your admiration nor will you despise our Goldsmith tho he does but imitate him" (MS. Beckford, d.10, fol.26r). Beckford owned works by both Buffon and Goldsmith: "BUFFON HISTOIRE NATURELLE, 36 vol. 4to. *Par.* 1749, DE LA CEPEDE, HISTOIRE NATURELLE DES QUADRUPEDES, OVIPARES, ET DES SERPENS, et Histoire des POISSONS, *Paris*, 1798" (*Books, books of prints, pictures, miniatures, sculpture, furniture, silver, porcelain, glass, miscellaneous*, sale cat., Phillips, Fonthill, 9 September–29 October 1823, lot.2267); and "Goldsmith's Animated Nature, *plates*, 8 vol. *very scarce*, 1776" (*Books, books of prints*, sale cat., Leigh, Sotheby & Son, London, 24 and 26 May 1804, lot.175).

107. For Beckford's notations on "Lichen" and "Aconite" see the back of the Green Note Book, MS. Beckford. e.2.

108. ". . . my retinue will consist of . . . Milne, to accompany me on my botanical excursions" (quoted in Beckford, *Life at Fonthill* [1957]: 43).

109. MS. Beckford, e.4, fol.9r.

110. Britton, *Beauties,* vol.1 (1801): 242.

111. Ibid. Robert Gemmett suggests that this planting took place only after 1781, even though by this date Beckford had achieved his majority. See Gemmett, "Beckford's Fonthill" (1972): 336.

112. As Laurent Chatel points out, "it would be pretentious today to claim original research or even to attempt to trace the chronology of works at Splendens between 1769 and 1794 since so little material sheds light on the matter"("Mole, the Bat and the Fairy" [1999]).Chatel does, however, provide an account of some of the evidence for a chronology of works at Splendens.

113. Redding, *Memoirs,* vol. 2 (1959): 97.

114. Britton, *Beauties,* vol. 1 (1801): 240.

115. Beckford to Henley, 1784, quoted in Alfred Morrison, *Collection of Autograph Letters and Historical Documents,* vol. 1, 2d series (Privately printed, 1893): 192.

116. Britton, *Beauties,* vol. 1 (1801): 242.

117. Ibid.

118. Redding, *Memoirs,* vol. 2 (1959): 81.

119. Britton, *Beauties,* vol. 1 (1801): 242.

120. Evelyn Newby, trans., "A Dutchman's visits to some English Gardens in 1791: Extracts from the Unpublished Journal of Baron Johan Frederik Willem von Spaen van Biljoen, with a Biographical Introduction by Heimerick Tromp," *Journal of Garden History* 2, no. 1 (January–March 1982): 41–58.

121. Notes on English tour of 1779, MS. Beckford, d.3, fol.10v.

122. Loudon, "Notes on Gardens" (1835): 442.

123. Ibid.

124. Britton, *Illustrations* (1823): 34.

125. There is a "Norwegian" lawn in this area marked on Rutter's plan. It is worth noting that Beckford's library contained texts on the natural history of Norway, such as: "Pontoppidan's Natural History of Norway and Iceland with a Meteorological Table, folio, *Lond.* 1755" (*Books, books of prints, pictures, miniatures, sculpture, furniture, silver, porcelain, glass, miscellaneous* Phillips, Fonthill, 9 September–29 October 1823, lot.2389), and a "Voyage en Norwege trad de l'allemand de Fabricius, Paris, 1802" (MS. Beckford, b.1, fol.77r).

126. Rutter, *Delineations* (1823): 91.

127. Rutter, *New descriptive guide* (1823): 79.

128. Lansdown, *Recollections* (1893/1969): 47.

129. Storer, *Description* (1812): 5. As Mowl notes, "Bottom lake," as Bitham was originally called, was created by the Cottingtons in 1639 (*William Beckford* [1998]: 266).

130. Timothy Mowl is mistaken in suggesting that Beckford had no hand in shaping the lake. One of Beckford's letters of 1817 explicitly stated that the "sublime effect" of the lake was caused not only by "tree felling," but also by "the particular shape I have given to the shore on a grand scale" (quoted in Beckford, *Life at Fonthill* [1957]: 234).

131. Britton, *Illustrations* (1823): 36.

132. For example, Storer mentioned that "the woodcock has frequently chosen this sequestered valley for her nest" (*Description* [1812]: 5). Beckford may have been inspired by the theories of "animated nature" propounded by some picturesque theorists.

133. Beckford to Franchi, 16 June 1811, quoted in Beckford, *Life at Fonthill* (1957): 97–98.

134. Quoted in ibid., p. 234.

135. Unidentified newspaper, 16 June 1823, MS.Beckford, b.6, fol.49.

136. Quoted in Beckford, *Life at Fonthill* (1957): 90.

137. *See* Elizabeth Hall, "The Plant Collections of an Eighteenth Century Virtuoso," *Garden History* 14, no. 1 (spring 1986).

138. The Portugal laurel was mentioned by Beckford in a letter of 1810: "azerieri covered in flowers" (Beckford, *Life at Fonthill* [1957]: 90). Firs, pine and spruce were planted liberally throughout the grounds; for the other plants in this list see Rutter, *New descriptive guide* (1823): 74–75.

139. Rutter, *New descriptive guide* (1823): 74–77

140. Unidentified newspaper, Wednesday 10 September 1823, MS. Beckford, b.6, fol.67.

141. John Claudius Loudon, "Calls at the Nurseries," *Gardener's Magazine* 1 (1826): 214.

142. Beckford to his mother, 1796 (Lewis Melville, *The Life and Letters of William Beckford of Fonthill* [London: William Heineman, 1910]: 221–22).

143. Redding, *Memoirs,* vol. 2 (1959): 127. Storer explained that the Nine Miles Walk was "part of a journey of twenty-two miles which may be made within the grounds without retracing our steps" (*Description* [1812]: 3).

144. Respectively, Storer, *Description* (1812): 2; [London] *Times*, 3 October, 1822. The *Times* further reported that guides were ". . . stationed at different points of the demesne to bring back such ladies as happen (thus) to go astray."

145. "Journal of Lady Ann Hamilton," MS. Beckford, e.4, fol.8v. Mowl has suggested that the only saving grace of Beckford's plantations was that they afforded regular glimpses of the Abbey. This ignores the "variety" emphasized by Hamilton. See Mowl, *William Beckford* (1998): 266–67.

146. Rutter, *Delineations* (1823): 86.

147. Ibid., p.84.

148. Beckford to Humphry Repton, 24 July 1799, MS.Beckford, c.16, fol.19v.

149. *Morning Herald*, 15 August 1822, MS. Beckford, b.6, fol.3.

150. Redding recorded that Beckford arranged flowers at Fonthill daily before breakfast, and that "he could not live without having them about him" (*Memoirs*, vol. 2 [1959]: 271, 371).

151. Beckford, *Italy*, vol. 1 (1834): 64

152. Ibid., p.289.

153. On this occasion he revealed his interest in rare or unusual plants, noting: "Mr. Horne has a species of Cape Jasmine which bears double flowers the size of a common rose" (Beckford, *Journal* [1954]: 63). The Cape jasmine, *gardenia jasminoides* was first cultivated around 1750 and while thought to be a native of the Cape of Good Hope, it actually came from China and Japan. Beckford gathered flowers on numerous occasions, for example at Valombre he "visited every little cave in the ridges of the rock, and gathered large sprigs of the mezereon and rhododendron in full bloom" (Beckford, *Italy*, vol. 1 [1834]: 50).

154. Beckford, *Italy*, vol. 1 (1834): 91.

155. "Fra gli odoriferi ginepri (Ariosto Orlando Furioso—Canto 7, stanza 22)," ibid. Beckford also referred to Ariosto when enjoying the roses in the Pagliavam gardens: "You know how warmly every mortal of taste delights in these lovely flowers; how frequently and in what harmonious numbers Ariosto has praised them" (ibid., vol. 2, p. 24). He shows his awareness of Mason in a reading note (transcribed by Boyd Alexander) to Tours in Teesdale, 1804, in which he noted similarities between passages in the first book of Mason's English Garden and the grounds of Rokeby (MS. Eng. misc. d.1291, fol.224r). Beckford and Mason shared a common adherence to the "cult of flowers and sensibility" referred to by Mavis Batey ("William Mason, English Gardener," *Garden History* 1, no. 2 [February 1973]: 000). Batey further suggests that Mason's "feeling for the romantic past" was stimulated by writers such as Gray and Walpole, both of whom were of some interest to Beckford. Beckford referred to Gray as "our beloved poet," while an interest in

Walpole's writings is illustrated by several of Beckford's reading notes (see MS.Eng., misc, e.1236, fol.38r).

156. In 1798 he wrote to Issac Smeard: "I never remember such a summer—the flowers here are as vigorously and richly coloured as those of Portugal" (MS. Beckford, c.16, fol.13r).

157. Rutter, *Description* (1822): 19.

158. Elizabeth Hall has suggested that there was enthusiasm for British botany during the latter half of the eighteenth century ("Plant Collections,"). Although Beckford certainly admired and cultivated exotics at Fonthill, he complained, in July 1810, that "This craze for novelty always makes it impossible to have the good old plants (jasmin, gardenias etc) in the condition in which one ought to have them" (*Life at Fonthill* [1957]: 94).

159. Redding, *Memoirs,* vol. 2 (1959): 130.

160. Britton, *Beauties,* vol.1 (1801): 242.

161. Beckford provided some idea of the rarity of the flowers cultivated at Fonthill in a letter of July 1810. He describes "the most stupendous collection of flowers that have ever been gathered in that rogue Milne's kingdom, a certain very scarlet lily *(Fothergalia)* of rare beauty, and various other marvels, some of which have flowered for the first time in this island." In a typically Beckfordian self-contradiction, however, his enthusiasm for these plants is quickly negated— "if they don't flower again it will be little loss"—and he yearns for more traditional plants (*Life at Fonthill* [1957]: 94).

162. Oliver, *Life* (1932): 234.

163. *European Magazine,* 31 (1797), 105.

164. Britton, *Illustrations* (1823): 35.

165. Rutter, *New descriptive guide* (1823): 79.

166. Mowl suggests that Beckford could never free himself from the "culture of greenhouses," as though they were a nefarious influence (*William Beckford* [1998]: 265).

167. MS. Beckford, e.4, fol.9v.

168. Rutter, *Delineations* (1823): 83.

169. Storer, *Description* (1812): 6; for a verbatim copy from Storer, see Rutter, *Description* (1822): 23–24.

170. Loudon, "Notes on Gardens" (1835): 444. It is only in Rutter's *New descriptive guide* (1823) that its name first appears as Dwarf's Garden.

171. For example, in his attempt to present the Chinese as comparable to the English gardening lords he wrote that the Chinese were "not only Botanists, but also painters and Philosophers; having a thorough knowledge of the human mind, and of the arts by which its strongest feelings are excited" (William Chambers, *A Dissertation on Oriental Gardening,* 2d ed. [London, 1773]: 13).

172. In the sale catalogue the book is listed as "Presentation copy, from the Author, 19th March, 1773" (*Books,* sale cat. Sotheby, Wilkinson & Hodge, London, part 1, 30 June–July 1882, lot. 1788).

173. Beckford, *Recollections* (1835): 21.

174. Ibid., pp. 21–22.

175. In "The Transport of Pleasure," Beckford wrote: "To Day we will devote to wandering over those great empires of China, and Japan, which in my early years engrossed far too considerable a share of my attention" (MS. Beckford, d.10, fol.28v). It is likely that Alexander Cozens fostered the young Beckford's interest in all things oriental.

176. For example, lots. 208–20 of the 1817 sale comprised "thirteen volumes contain nearly 700 subjects of Zoology and Botany, painted in water colours with the greatest accuracy and truth: several figures in this rare collection are still unknown to European Naturalists" (*see Books, drawings,* sale cat., Sotheby, London, 6–8 May 1817). In the imaginary tower of "The Transport of Pleasure," Beckford described a room which contained "large folios of paintings which lie scattered on Tables representing those delightful Gardens where Cam=hi: Yong=Ching and Kien=Long used to unbend their minds" (MS. Beckford, d.10, fol.30r).

177. This garden was proposed in 1804, Repton was employed at Woburn until 1810. Beckford showed his interest in such additions in a reading note to Repton's *An enquiry into the changes of taste in landscape Gardening* (1806), where he noted the "chinese pavillion" and a series of "botanic, american, chinese and animated gardens" (MS. Beckford, c.56, fol. 92).

178. In "The Transport of Pleasure," Beckford wrote: "I shall rear the roses of China the Hiliatropes and variety of other flowers that remind me of their native Countries and bring a charming association of ideas into my imagination" (MS. Beckford, d.10, fol.29v). A number of Beckford's MS reading notes were on Chinese plants. For example, on the blossoming of the nenupha (lily): "Towards the end of May—the stalks shooting up from the waters—and in a few days are mantled with Leaves of the brightest green interspersed with vivid buds like Tulips that in expanding assume the same appearance of Enormous Roses" (MS. Beckford, c.55, fols.13 and 27).

179. Patrick Conner, "The Chinese garden in Regency England," *Garden History* 14, no. 1 (spring 1986): 43.

180. Mowl wrote that Beckford may have used sunken flowerpots in the grottoes at Fonthill (*William Beckford* [1998]: 265).

181. The Beckford Family, *Reminiscences of Fonthill Abbey* (London: Simpkin, Marshall & Co., 1898): 98.

182. For Payne Knight see *Books,* sale cat., Sotheby, Wilkinson and Hodge, London, part 1, 30 June–13 July 1882, lot.1342; for Gilpin see ibid., part 2, 11–23 December 1882, lot.170; for Chambers see ibid., lot.1788; for Loudon see ibid., lot.1882; for Repton see ibid., part 3, 2–14 July 1883, lots.1293–97.

183. Indeed, Beckford turned down an offer from Repton to improve Fonthill (Beckford to Repton, 24 July 1799, MS. Beckford, c.16, fol.19v).

184. Mowl, *William Beckford* (1998): 265.

185. For example: "Upon the whole, it appears to me, that as intricacy in the disposition, and variety in the forms, the tints, and the lights and shadows of objects, are the great characteristics of picturesque scenery; so monotony and baldness are the greatest defects of improved places" (Uvedale Price, *An Essay on the Picturesque as Compared with the Sublime and the Beautiful,* new edition [London: J. Robson, 1796]).

186. J. C. Loudon, *Observations on the formation and management of useful and ornamental plantations . . .* (Edinburgh: Constable, 1804): 167.

187. Idem, "Notes on Gardens" (1835): 441.

188. Redding, *Memoirs,* vol. 2 (1959): 147.

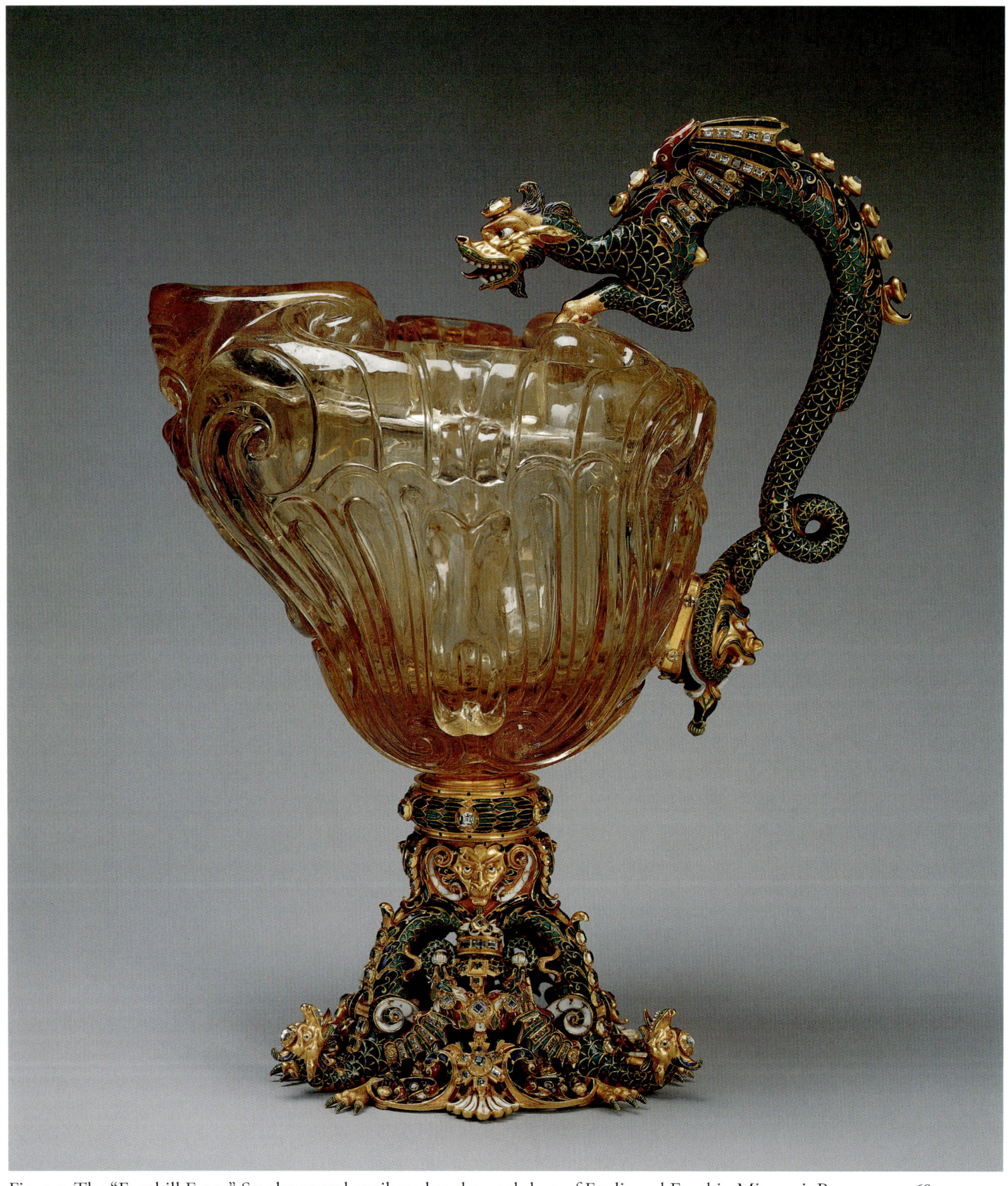

Fig. 9-1. The "Fonthill Ewer." Smoky crystal attributed to the workshop of Ferdinand Eusebio Miseroni, Prague, ca. 1680; enameled gold mounts set with diamonds, French, probably Paris, ca. 1814–17. The Metropolitan Museum of Art, New York, Jack and Belle Linsky Collection, 1982.60.138.

CHAPTER IX

A CELEBRATED COLLECTOR

BET MCLEOD

The name William Beckford ranks foremost among those of the distinguished English collectors of the late eighteenth and early nineteenth centuries. This "wayward child of fortune" assembled one of the most outstanding collections of works of art of the period, which included such magnificent objects as the "Fonthill Ewer" (fig. 9-1). He earned an exalted reputation, begun in his own lifetime, which endures through today, as a passionate collector and discriminating connoisseur. It is Beckford's legendary collection of paintings and works of art, sadly dispersed, with which his name is immediately associated.[1] A complex man of fierce intelligence and vivid imagination, Beckford differed from such contemporaries as the Prince Regent (later George IV) in his very personal engagement with his collection. It is this highly individual and romantic streak, coupled with his activities in commissioning works of art that sets Beckford apart from his peers.

Beckford himself did not produce an inventory, catalogue, or classifications of any sort of his collection. Nonetheless, the objects do speak for themselves: certain preferences are noticeable, and a number of areas stand out as having special significance for Beckford.[2] Two significant aspects of the wide-ranging collection are Beckford's holdings of objects typically found in *Kunstkammern* and his strong Francophile taste. Notions of connoisseurship and taste were particularly important to him, as was the disposition of his collection. The complex nature of Beckford's activities over a lifetime of acquisition reveals much about the works of art as it does Beckford's fascinating relationships with dealers and agents. Beckford's own voice resonates throughout the documentation, and both his correspondence and the surviving works of art bear witness to his extraordinary achievements as a collector and patron.

THE *Kunst-* UND *Wunderkammer* COLLECTION

A key area that dominated the collection is the works of art of the type found in German princely cabinets of the sixteenth and seventeenth centuries; Beckford's romantic taste quite consciously looked back to such traditions. The diverse nature of his eclectic collection encompassed the art of the goldsmith, jeweler, lapidary, and sculptor, and comprised a wide range of materials and styles.

The collection held a large number of items that would have conformed to such established classifications as *naturalia* and *artificialia;* principal among these were hardstones, shell, and ivory, generally richly carved or extravagantly mounted. Masterpieces of craftsmanship and the sumptuous use of precious materials exemplified Beckford's intense admiration for the virtuoso pieces of an earlier date, and many objects were reputed to have come from celebrated collections and thus may date to the seventeenth century or earlier. It is clear, however, that Beckford not only had some of these earlier pieces enriched to suit his own flamboyant aesthetic, but also collected or commissioned contemporary works of art that likewise fitted a broadly Renaissance concept of princely treasures.

Beckford's lifelong enchantment with small-scale, exquisitely crafted works of art and the esteem in which they were held by him can be seen by the large numbers he held back from the sale of Fonthill Abbey in 1822 and removed to his residence at Bath. Gregorio Franchi's "Accounts" of purchases made over the early decades of the nineteenth century, the Franchi "Packing Lists" of items to be shipped from the Abbey to Bath, the posthumous inventory of 1844, and the listings in the subsequent sales of 1845 and 1848 enumerate multiple objects of this kind.[3] Indeed, the sheer volume of this type of object may well be considered acquisitiveness rather than collecting. Descriptions and some extant pieces indicate that a good number of these can be classified as second rate. Even Beckford's anxiety about quality is evident in a letter to Franchi in 1813: "I see from the buying mania which dominates you that we are well on the way to ruin. Oh my God, so many things! I trust to the Saint that they are not junk and unworthy of this sanctuary and refuge of Good Taste."[4]

There are sufficient illustrations that indicate Beckford's marked preference for these works of art, whether they were genuine *cinquecento* objects, objects commissioned by Beckford in the

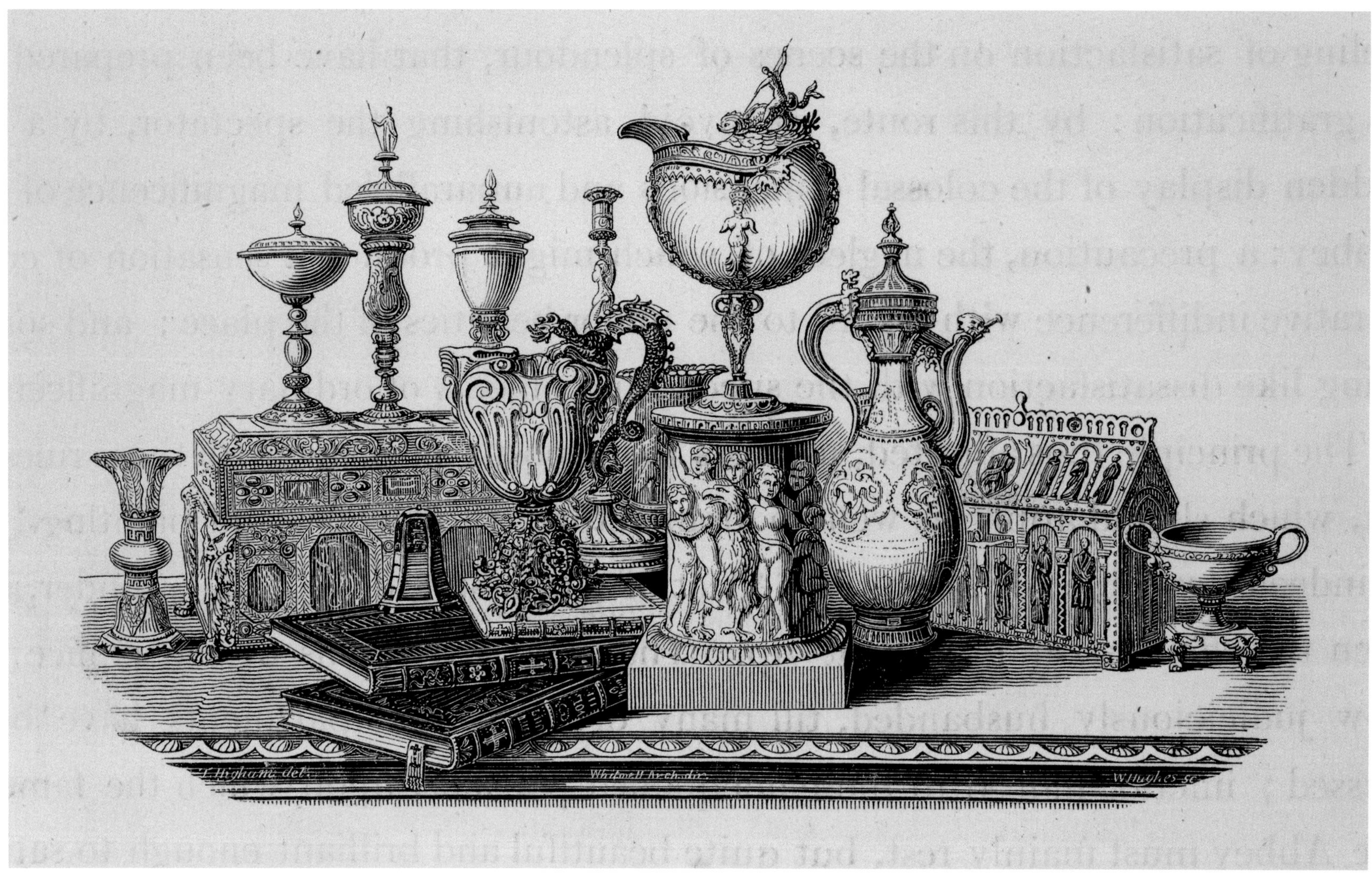

Fig. 9-2. "A Groupe of the Rarest Articles of Virtu." Woodcut vignette. From John Rutter, *Delineations of Fonthill and its Abbey* (Shaftesbury, 1823): 7.

Renaissance manner, or simply modern objects that attained the same high levels of extraordinary quality and virtuoso craftsmanship so sought after by Beckford. Many nineteenth-century patrons determined that there was no lessening of quality between Renaissance work and work carried out in the seventeenth, eighteenth, or nineteenth century: what remained significant was the taste for earlier styles, even though interpreted with a modern eye and executed in modern techniques. A wide range of differing objects of this type can be seen in the various illustrations of Fonthill Abbey and Lansdown Tower, as well as in John Rutter's "Groupe of The Rarest Articles of Virtu" (fig. 9-2). Objects can also be seen in the three successive issues of the *Illustrated London News* after the 1845 sale, and of course in Willes Maddox' paintings, each of which is entitled *Objects of Vertu* (see cat. nos. 155–57).[5] It has to be assumed that Beckford and his heirs were careful to include

in these illustrations objects of particular artistic significance or provenance or that had some personal resonance.

Hardstones were a lifelong passion for Beckford. No doubt first stimulated by the princely collections Beckford saw in his travels on the Continent, this passion was shared by Franchi, whose own love of hardstones and whose commercial trading in these items may itself have further encouraged Beckford's collecting activities in this field. Beckford's taste for hardstones was decidedly aristocratic: the majority of the sixteenth-century hardstones detailed in the several sale catalogues, for example, reputedly came from either French royal and noble collections or Italian ducal collections.

Documents do not reveal whether Beckford was consciously imitating the great hardstone collectors of antiquity or whether any of his hardstones were of antique origin, with one exception, the renowned "Rubens Vase" (fig. 9-3). There can be no doubt that Beckford was certainly aware of the historic intellectual fascination with hardstones and their associated properties, and above all, had an intense admiration for the technical skill required to work such difficult material. The Orient also had a significant and parallel influence on the formation of Beckford's taste for hardstones. Beckford had a number of examples of what were probably Mughal rock crystals, usually embellished with mounts and gems, one of which survives at Brodick Castle in Scotland.

In his overwhelming passion for hardstones, Beckford was quite unlike his collecting contemporaries in England, and this singularity in taste is a trait for which he was renowned even in his own time. A watercolor drawing of mounted and unmounted hardstones would appear to have been presented to Beckford, probably by a Parisian *marchand-mercier*, for his perusal and consideration of the objects depicted.[6] Beckford's commissioning and collecting of mounted hardstones have been the subject of several studies, as has his collection of hardstone-mounted furniture.[7] The surviving examples at Brodick Castle exemplify the wide-ranging depth and varying quality of his holdings, and are a touchstone for a reading of the documents. Of a number of mounted hardstones illustrated in 1845, however, only two have been identified to date—an agate cup and cover (see cat. no. 119) and a rock crystal vase and cover at Brodick Castle. It cannot be judged whether the remainder of the mounted hardstones are older objects, or objects contemporaneous with Beckford and mounted to his specification. A large series of unmounted hardstones also occur throughout the several sales and in the 1844 inventory. Again, it is not possible to determine the date or origin of these, although it is clear from their forms (cups, bowls, saucers and bowls for spoons) that many were intended to be mounted.

A reading of the documents shows that of the hardstones, quartz, either in its chalcedony or crystalline form, occurs most frequently. The variations in colors, occlusions, and transparencies of the different kinds of quartz, from many countries of origin, were highly prized by earlier collectors, and Beckford was no exception. He referred to quartz in some detail, and identified several members of the chalcedony group, such as agate, bloodstone, carnelian, jasper, and sardonyx. Beckford made a number of qualitative judgments on rarity, area of origin, clarity, and color. Rock crystal was also a material of particular importance to Beckford, again no doubt due to his appreciation of the purity and clarity of the stone and the virtuoso engraving with which most of his examples were decorated. Lapis lazuli and turquoise are found in some number among the hardstones, perhaps indicative of Beckford's interest not only in their color, but also in their associations with the Orient.

The two most distinguished hardstones in Beckford's collection were also two of the most celebrated objects in the collection, the "Fonthill Ewer" and the "Rubens Vase," which have been extensively published.[8] Beckford was not unique at the period for his propensity to "improve" objects, although in this case both the "Rubens Vase"

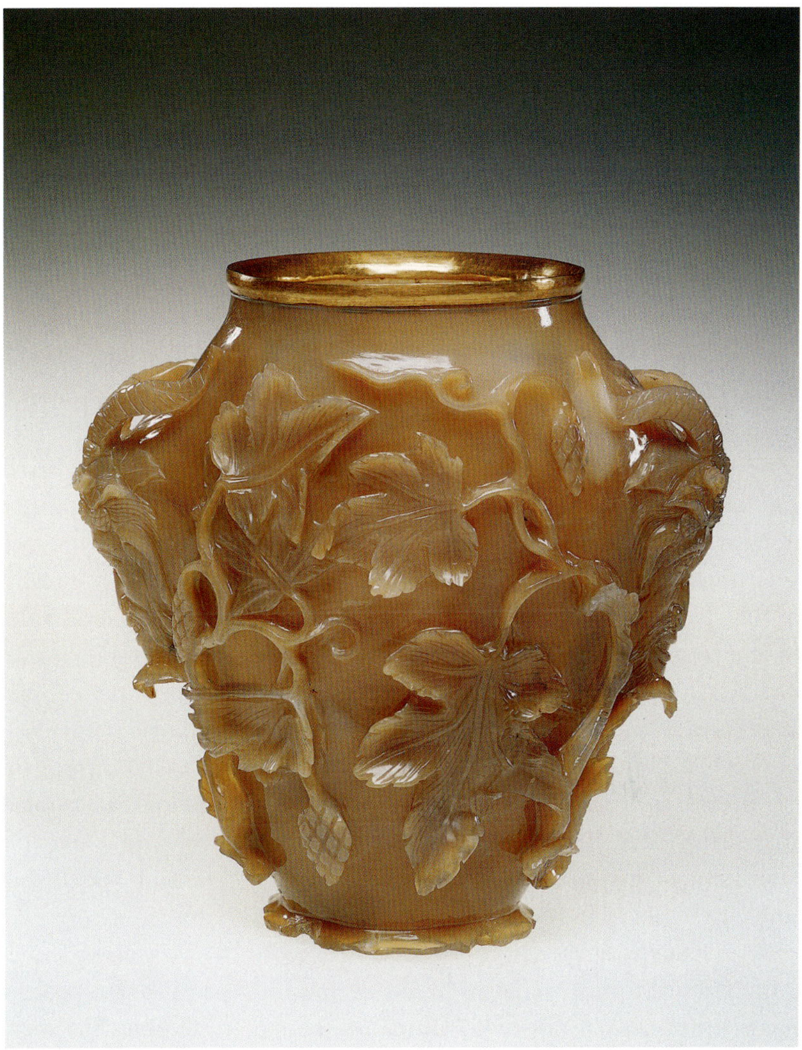

Fig. 9-3. The "Rubens Vase." Agate, 4th century A.D.; gold mounts, French, 1809–19. The Walters Art Museum, Baltimore, 42.562.

and the "Fonthill Ewer" were already mounted when he acquired them, but, acknowledging their rarity and superiority, he did not augment them in any way. Beckford belonged to a small, but recognized group of collectors in the early nineteenth century who employed to great effect the skills of goldsmiths and lapidaries to enhance objects in their collections. The retailers of the time were cognizant of this flamboyant and costly taste: it is thought that the "Fonthill Ewer" was among a number of objects mounted in the early nineteenth century with such a group of patrons in mind.

Beckford was one of the greatest British collectors of the time of nautilus cups, an essential part of any collector's cabinet. Of the nine in his possession, the present whereabouts of only two are known: one, supported by a silver-gilt triton (see cat. no. 152) is in a private collection and the other, mounted on a dolphin stem, is at Brodick Castle. Both have mounts contemporaneous in date to Beckford: those on the piece at Brodick Castle were almost certainly fitted to Beckford's instruction. The quality and type of mounts on the nautilus cups in the collection would appear to vary quite considerably, ranging from the finest silver-gilt set with gems and semiprecious stones, to the melange of engraved silver-gilt, coral, and entwined dolphin stem on the Brodick Castle example, to one described in a sale catalogue simply as "chased silver."

Two other nautilus cups previously in Beckford's collection are known from illustrations. One can be seen in John Britton's view of King Edward's Gallery at Fonthill Abbey.[9] This cup was sold in 1823 to another Maecenas, Richard Grenville, second Duke of Buckingham, and was later reproduced in the catalogue of the Buckingham collections at Stowe House which were sold in 1848.[10] The other, shown in a Westminster family portrait, is now in a private collection.[11] The esteem in which nautilus cups were held by Beckford is apparent not only by the large number he owned, but also by the inclusion of the Stowe nautilus in the very deliberate, staged disposition of objects in the illustrations by Rutter and Britton. The ivory sleeve vase on which the nautilus is placed in each of these illustrations was one of two mounted in gilt bronze as a pair. Both appeared in the 1882 Hamilton Palace sale, suggesting that Beckford's son-in-law, Alexander, tenth Duke of Hamilton or his son, William, Marquess of Douglas, purchased the single example from the Stowe sale.[12]

Beckford owned a number of ivory sleeve vases, some mounted prior to his acquisition, others mounted to his order, probably in emulation, if not direct imitation, of earlier examples. As with mounted nautilus shells, carved ivory met the criteria of both *naturalia* and *artificialia*, and it would seem that Beckford held ivory in even higher regard than nautilus. Ivory is one of the few areas in Beckford's collection where the artist is actually named in the sales catalogues. These may well be optimistic, or "generic," attributions to the maker rather than catalogue descriptions written with any certitude, although it was presumably Beckford himself who provided the information for the Fonthill Abbey sale catalogue of 1822. It is possible that the dealers who supplied these pieces deceived Beckford about the artists, only for Beckford to perpetuate the inaccuracies in the sale descriptions. If so, Beckford's connoisseurship might be questioned, but he may also have decided, whether out of malice or mischief, to deliberately mislead the cataloguer. Beckford commented at length on ivories:

"My dear Gregory, my Fiammingo is more important, as you know (I've told you so a thousand times), but for the grace and essence of the artist, his very spirit, where can you find a better example than the one which meets they eye of a true connoisseur on the vases of the Margravine? . . . I don't know what kind of thing this Tankard attributed (doubtless falsely) to Benevenuto Cellini will turn out to be, but one must remember, and I beg you to remember, that it is better to give a con-

siderable sum for things of undoubted authenticity, than to buy at a lower price carvings that are uncertain, problematic and second-rate.[13]

Relief scenes on several ivories are also listed in the sale catalogues, among which are "Battle of the Centaurs," "Triumph of Bacchus," and "Dance of Bacchante." Some of the ivories are described as being mounted as tankards or "plinths"; one is said to have "old mounting." In only one other instance are the mounts further detailed: the vase by "Strous" is described as being mounted in silver-gilt by the renowned goldsmiths Rundell and Bridge, but no description of the form or decoration is given. Unfortunately, the sparse, even laconic descriptions of the pieces and the generic nature of the scenes render it hazardous to attempt an identification of any extant Beckford ivories. It is impossible to verify whether any of the ivories are Gothic, Renaissance, or Baroque, or works that date from the eighteenth and nineteenth centuries. The carved bowl now at Brodick Castle, mounted by John Robins in 1820/21, is possibly of the late seventeenth century and Netherlandish in origin. Beckford also owned a number of carved figural ivories, which he clearly held to be of high import: the celebrated "Magnus Berg" cup, now in the Royal Collection, was given an especially prominent position in the theatrical, deliberate arrangement of objects seen in Rutter's view of King Edward's Gallery (see cat. fig. E), where the cup is shown flanked by the two ivory sleeve vases mounted by David Willaume. The significance of the three ivory pieces is clear; they are the only objects shown in this view of the gallery and were undoubtedly selected as being entirely appropriate in form and in date for the evocative antiquarian atmosphere.

In the manner of earlier princely collectors, Beckford owned a number of pieces of amber: two caskets and a freestanding figure group of the Adoration of the Magi. The three-tiered casket seen in Britton's view of the south end of Saint Michael's Gallery (see fig. 7–6) at Fonthill Abbey was one of the few items known to have been at Fonthill Splendens and in Beckford's possession since at least 1801. Described in some detail and said to have been made for the Princess of Bavaria or the Queen of Bohemia in 1665, this amber casket, now lost, was sold from Fonthill Abbey in 1823 and entered the collection of the second Duke of Buckingham. Of the other organic materials in the collection typical of a Renaissance cabinet are ostrich eggs, boxwood carvings, coral, pearls, and gourds. Two engraved gourds at Brodick Castle were mounted as miniature flasks by Beckford: one has a chalcedony stopper and enameled gold mounts in the same style as the mounted spoons; and the other, a favorite combination of silver-gilt mounts set with turquoise, carried out by Rundell, Bridge and Rundell in 1820/21.

It would appear that Beckford owned only one example of Limoges *champlevé* enamel, a "Crucifixion" chasse (see cat. no. 96). It is not known how or when he acquired this piece, which he erroneously described as having come from the abbey church of Saint-Denis, but it was no doubt acquired as much for its workmanship as for its reputed provenance. One example of medieval *champlevé* enamel does not a collection make, and in this particular respect, Beckford did not follow in the footsteps of a number of English antiquarian collectors.[14] What he did have in quantity, however, was sixteenth-century painted Limoges enamels, highly prized in the Renaissance and thereafter for their autographed workmanship, painterly technique, and decorative motifs. Beckford would also have responded to the dazzling, jewellike surface finish of painted enamel, and his admiration for this medium can be seen in the many oil paintings on copper in his collection. The surviving pieces known to have been in Beckford's collection are of an undisputed, extremely high quality (see cat. nos. 97–99).[15]

Historic Continental metalwork was a field in which Beckford seemed to have collected with caution rather than zeal, but the pieces he acquired were typical of the magnificent display pieces seen in *Kunstkammern,* and of these, two Nuremberg silver-gilt standing cups and covers can be readily identified by illustrations. The famed work by Hans Petzold (fig. 9-4) was retained by Beckford's descendants until 1973 and is now in the Thyssen-Bornemisza Collection, as is the superb example by Veit Moringer (see cat. no. 103).[16] Each cup is a brilliant tour de force, and the superb quality of these two quintessential Mannerist examples is a guide to an understanding of the rest of the collection. Though few in number, the pieces are executed with an absolute mastery of goldsmithing techniques. The significance of these is attested by their inclusion in Maddox's *Objects of Vertu* (see cat. nos. 155, 157). There has been speculation that it is the Petzold cup that appears in the deathbed portrait of Beckford (see cat. no. 150), but the actual silver-gilt cup and the silver-gilt ewer also seen in the shadows cannot be positively identified. Two other standing cups and covers, whose present whereabouts are unknown, are illustrated not only in Maddox's *Objects of Vertu,* but also in the lithograph entitled "Ornamental Furniture" in *Views of Lansdown,* and in the Hamilton Palace sale catalogue.[17] Beckford owned four silver-gilt beakers by Hans Uten, two of which remain at Brodick Castle, and the other two are at the Toledo Museum of Art.[18]

Cabinet bronzes were indispensable to a cultivated connoisseur and patron of the arts, and Beckford owned a small, but select group of these. Comprising Renaissance and later reductions after the antique, examples in the collection included a model of the "Gladiator Repellens," "Bacchus and the Infant Hercules," the "Piping Boy," and the "Nessus and Dejanira" model by Giambologna, now in the Henry E. Huntington Library.[19] Beckford also owned a cast from nature of a toad, and an inkwell in the form of a *putto* astride a dolphin. The impetus for the collecting of these small-scale bronzes may well have come from Beckford's visits to such Italian ducal collections as the Medici collection or from knowledge of the German princely *Kunstkammern,* but a French connection is equally pertinent. The cabinet bronze was an essential component of the refined, luxurious Parisian interiors of the eighteenth century.

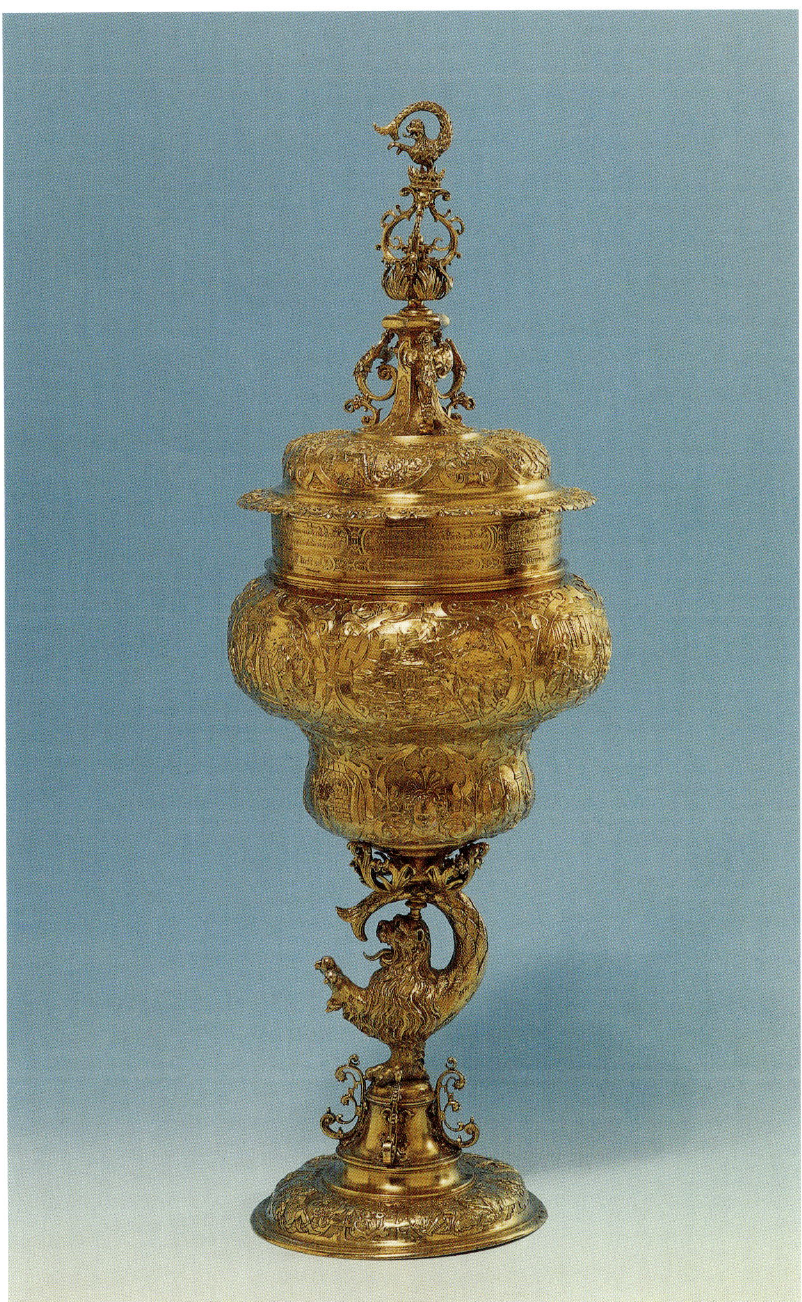

Fig. 9-4. The "Imhoff" standing cup, by Hans Petzold, Nuremberg, 1626. Silver gilt. The Thyssen-Bornemisza Collection, Lugano, Switzerland, K194B.

Beckford's Francophile Taste

Beckford's distinct Francophile taste was a significant influence upon the formation of his collection. This sophisticated, urbane sensibility, formed during his peripatetic travels on the Continent during the last years of the ancien régime, was also a major factor in the furnishing and decoration of both Fonthill House and what is known of his residence at Harley Street, London. Although only one room at Fonthill Abbey was decorated in a contemporary "French" style, it can be ascer tained that Beckford's own suite of rooms in the Abbey held a collection worthy of the greatest French collectors of the eighteenth century. A passion for France and the arts of France remained a constant factor in Beckford's life until 1822, the year he moved to Bath and demonstrated an abrupt change in direction, creating an entirely different aesthetic in Lansdown Tower.

Beckford's collecting of Dutch and Flemish cabinet pictures, of mounted porcelains, hardstones and marble, of magnificent gilt bronzes and cabinet bronzes, of the finest Japanese lacquer, and a passion both for Boulle and for giltwood furniture, all point to a French sensibility. Although he maintained a keen interest in the latest Parisian fashions, continuously acquiring works of art in the current taste, Beckford continued to purchase or commission, in the early decades of the nineteenth century, items that might have been considered old-fashioned and out-of-date, such as Boulle furniture and furniture mounted with lacquer panels or with pietre dure. The acquisition of this type of furniture, which was to feature so prominently in his collection, strongly reflects an eighteenth-century taste and for Beckford may possibly have been a means of romantic association with such archetypal French collectors of the eighteenth century as Pierre-Louis Randon de Boisset and Madame de Pompadour.

For many eighteenth-century connoisseurs, the Francophile taste was an aesthetic preference for such shimmering and exotic materials as pewter, brass and gilt, polychrome hardstones, and gold and silver details set into dark, rich surfaces. The startling contrast between colored grounds of porcelain and hardstone vases and their flamboyant gilt-bronze mounts would also have appealed to him for the same reason. Commenting on a cabinet at Stourhead reputed to have belonged to Pope Sixtus V, Beckford revealed his own appreciation of effect:

> Sixtus the Fifth's cabinet is divine, I know—the bronzes are of extreme delicacy and elegance, and those lovely agates, alabasters and cornelians, mingled with the glittering mother-of-pearl, produce a rich effect, agreeable and grateful to the eye. It will be difficult to surpass, but we must try, and produce something to make people doff their hats, whether they will or no.[20]

Although Beckford visited Paris in 1781, it does not appear that he was an active collector at that time, nor even on his subsequent visit with his wife in 1784, although he reports on his viewing some of the celebrated collections in Paris that year.[21] Although Beckford was not "received" by Parisian society in the accepted sense after 1784, he would certainly have known of the outstanding collections in Paris, either through guidebooks and pamphlets, or directly from tours around the *hôtels*. During his later visits, however, a collecting mania consumed him.[22]

Beckford was also clearly obsessed with owning French works of art with a princely or royal provenance, strengthening his romantic associations with the past. Items thus classified in his collection range from the chasse allegedly from the abbey church of Saint-Denis, to mounted hardstones, and to the numerous pieces of lacquer said to be from the collections of the Duc de Bouillon, Prince Charles of Lorraine, Madame de Pompadour, and Cardinal Mazarin. Furniture with royal provenance comprised lacquer, Boulle, and marquetry pieces. The romantic figures of Henri II and Diane de Poitiers are represented by a magnificent Limoges enamel salver and by stained glass. Other stained-glass panels in Beckford's collection reputedly belonged from the Montmorency family. Britton even describes some gold communion plate as having "belonged to Louis the sixteenth's private oratory at Versailles."[23]

Beckford's passion for the Louis XVI style continued throughout the decades, shifting somewhat in emphasis in the second decade of the nineteenth century as he flirted briefly with the severe Empire taste. Although not as republican a sympathizer as his son-in-law, Alexander, Marquess of Douglas, Beckford nonetheless acquired several works of art relating directly to the Bonaparte dynasty. In 1814, however, he complained vehemently about the latest trends in Paris: "No, my very dear friend, I cannot marvel at Paris. . . . Everywhere one discovers a sham style—false Roman of the false Empire which I no longer respect and which I like no better than Birmingham gold or Pinchbeck's masterpieces."[24]

The side cabinets and the torcheres in the Grand Drawing Room at Fonthill Abbey reflect a persistent attraction for the Boulle furniture, which was by then outdated.[25] The Reisener desk from the collection of the comte d'Orsay may well have been acquired out of sentimental reasons: Beckford had rented the Hôtel d'Orsay in Paris in 1788. Despite his own protestations at the Empire style's imitative aspirations, the suite of giltwood seat furniture once belonging to Cardinal Fesch and the Aubusson carpet reputedly from the château of Saint Cloud, both items directly associated with the Bonaparte family, represents this phase of Beckford's taste. This is the only illustrated room in Fonthill Abbey that approaches anything domestic in scale, and it must have been included as a deliberate contrast to the great vistas and imposing spaces of the other views. An instant recognition of the Louis XVI and Empire styles is in startling opposition to the other, decidedly antiquarian views illustrated.

Despite Beckford's entirely different aesthetic approach at Lansdown Tower, he did maintain an interest in the arts of France, as can be seen in the type of objects retained from the Abbey and taken to Bath. Gilt-bronze mounted porcelains and large-scale mounted hardstone vases, cabinet bronzes, and mounted objets d'art reflect his continuing interest in French taste, as did furniture mounted with pietre dure. Beckford retained in 1822, or bought back from the 1823 sale of Fonthill Abbey, many hardstone items and pietre-dure furniture. Not only did he continue to commission pietre-dure cabinets during his Bath years, but he also continued to acquire mounted hardstones almost until his death. Although Beckford's French taste did not play as prominent a role in his collecting as it had in earlier years, nonetheless a reading of the 1844 inventory reveals the legacy of a taste shaped by eighteenth-century French collecting traditions.

A significant, and enduring aspect of Beckford's Francophile taste is undoubtedly his acquisition of lacquer; he was one of the greatest European collectors of this rare and exotic material.[26] Beckford's "Japan-mania" can be explained not only by his strongly romantic taste for the Oriental culture that produced such delicate and technically superlative works, but also by his fascination with collectors and connoisseurs of the past. In 1815 he provided a connoisseur's critique of the great French collections and their dispersal:

> No lady of the old or new world has ever been a better judge of the rare, the beautiful and the fine than Mme de Pompadour. My Maria van Diemen [box] was presented to her by the Prince de Conti and bought at her sale by the Duc de Bouillon. The most beautiful lacquer which the Queen had was formerly hers, but for ages now all these treasures have been either moving about or lost sight of in Vienna, Russia and Poland; I doubt whether genuine pieces will ever come to light, but I can assure you that Mme de Pompadour was the finest connoisseur of *objets d'art* and curiosities in the whole of Europe."[27]

Beckford's personal suite in the Abbey, and the Yellow Drawing Rooms above, took on the character of his inner sanctum, only rarely shown to the infrequent visitors. In 1812 Beckford's bedroom was described as containing: "a large glazed cabinet, in which are the most exquisite pieces of japan."[28] It is significant that he kept some of the choicest pieces of lacquer here, housed solely for his own delight and appreciation. The Yellow Damask Room is also described as containing numerous pieces of lacquer.[29] When Beckford sold the Abbey and its contents in 1822 to the millionaire John Farquhar, he kept back a large quantity of lacquer, including some of those individual items that had already been divided into lots and were published in the 1822 sale catalogue. He also retained the most significant items, described as: "such specimens of Japan and other objects as are within the closet in the yellow room, and as have not been exposed in the Abbey during any part of the last three months."[30] The individual lots in both the 1822 and the 1823 sale catalogues reveal the wide range and differing quality of the enormous collection of lacquer. The catalogue descriptions themselves are of interest; provenance, when known, is listed, and the limitation of the contemporary state of knowledge of lacquer is evidenced in the literal descriptions of the objects.

Surprisingly, given Beckford's high regard for lacquer, it was not included in any of the interior views of the Abbey. Similarly, no lacquer is shown in any of the rooms of Lansdown Tower, although there is one isolated lithograph of a Chinoiserie cabinet containing Oriental porcelain jars and some small items of lacquer. Although Beckford retained the van Diemen box from the Abbey, his interest in lacquer would appear to have declined sharply after his move to Bath. Perhaps this essentially Rococo taste no longer suited the very different schemes for the interior spaces, or perhaps he could not compete with his only other real contemporary rival in the collecting of lacquer, his friend, cousin, and son-in-law, the Duke of Hamilton.

Like the Prince Regent and Watson Taylor, the Duke of Hamilton cherished royal French furniture of the eighteenth century incorporating lacquer panels. It appears, however, that he was also a significant purchaser of export lacquer objects. In this perhaps he was stimulated by Beckford, as the collecting of lacquer works of art is very much a French eighteenth-century taste and not one followed by such contemporaries in England as the Duke of Buckingham, for example. It is documented that the Duke of Hamilton purchased the Mazarin chest (see fig. 12-5) from the 1823 sale. He also acquired the Vulliamy cabinets (see fig. 12-1), made to Beckford's instructions from a seventeenth-century lacquer box known as the Buys box, at some stage prior to 1825, when they first appear in the Hamilton Palace inventory.[31]

The numbers of British collectors, as opposed to the plethora of tourists, on the Continent during the peace between Britain and France in 1802–3 and during and immediately after the Napoleonic wars, reveal that Beckford was certainly not unique in his taste for a wide-ranging collection of the arts of France, nor in his ability to acquire such objects. The Prince Regent, Lord Charles Stuart de Rothesay, and the tenth Duke of Hamilton are but three of Beckford's British contemporaries whose Francophile taste and collections of French works of art have been studied and published.[32]

TASTE AND DISPLAY

Beckford's principal residences offered ample opportunities for the display of his diverse collection. Regrettably there are no views of interiors of Fonthill Splendens, although a number of illustrations of furniture and window treatments survive. From an account written in 1797, it is clear that the arrangement of objects must have created a truly "splendid" impression: "During the Tuesday am & Monday pm were exhibited to us the endless Treasures of Mr Beckford in silver and gold, Diamonds—Coin, Cameos, Intaglios together with an endless collection of Manuscripts, rare prints scarce books etc etc as also his solid Gold Knives Forks Spoons Vases, curious China services, Salvers his Cabinets of rare antiques presented by Lady Hamilton."[33]

In the illustrations of the interiors of Fonthill Abbey, there is an interesting and obvious discrepancy between the large quantities of objects noted as being housed in the rooms, and the scarcity of objects on view. The sectional views of the Abbey do not contribute to a further understanding of the display of the collection; the depictions of objects provide little more than a sense of scale. The clear intention of the views of Saint Michael's Gallery and King Edward's Gallery was to depict the dramatic lengthy vistas of these immense spaces, and emphasize the sequence of bays as defined by ranges of bookcases, furniture, candlesticks, and garnitures of porcelain. A more realistic rendition of the actual contents of these rooms, showing a massed arrangement of relatively small-scale objects, would have upset the visual harmony and staged setting that work so successfully in portraying the grandeur and scale of the Abbey.

The view of the south end of Saint Michael's Gallery, by contrast, (see fig. 7–6) projects the idea of a much smaller and intimate

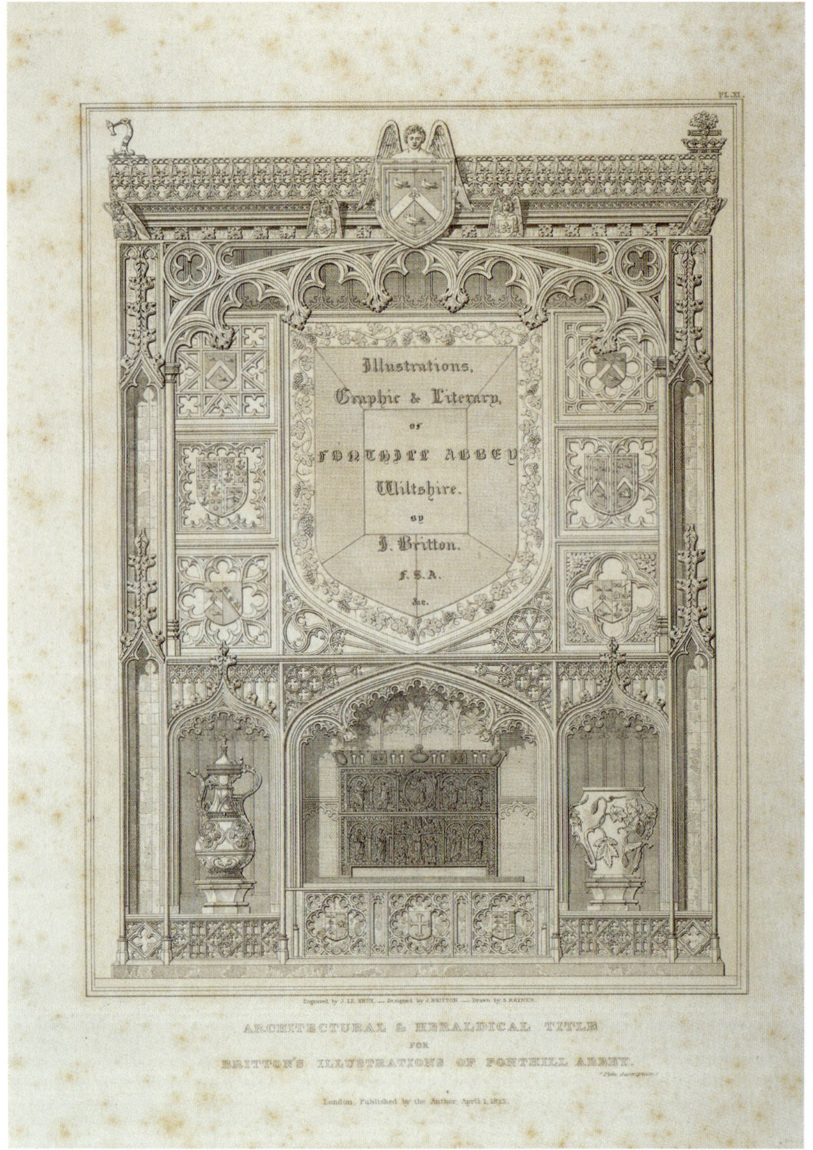

Fig. 9-5. Frontispiece to *Graphical and Literary Illustrations of Fonthill Abbey, Wiltshire; with Heraldical and Genealogical Notes* by John Britton (London: Longmans, Green and Co., 1823).

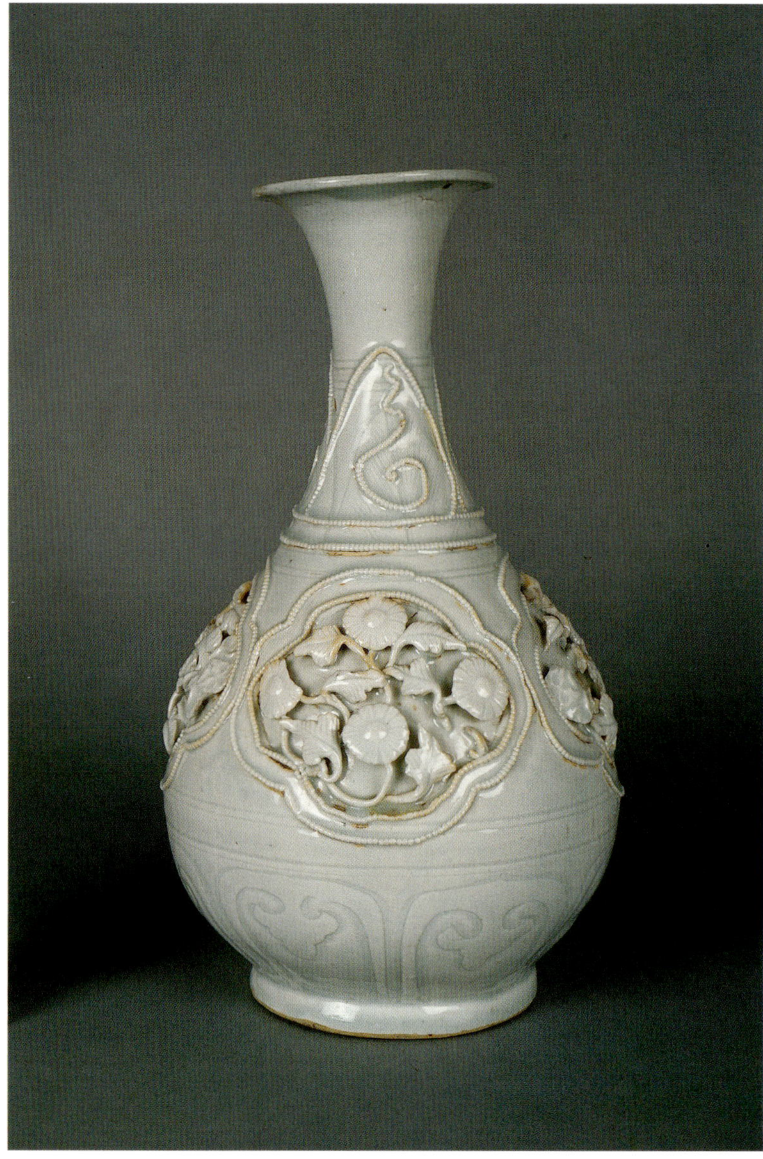

Fig. 9-6. The "Fonthill-Gaignières Ewer." Yuan dynasty, ca. 1300. Qingbai porcelain. National Museum of Ireland, Dublin.

interior space, which itself looks out upon a landscape extending to the horizon. In this view, an amber cabinet takes pride of place, arranged very deliberately in front of a sunlit window to emphasize the translucency of the material. The Limoges chasse is also singled out for attention. This piece was undoubtedly highly esteemed by Beckford, for it appears not only in the interior view of the Abbey, but also in Rutter's "Groupe" (see fig. 9-2) and, more significantly, was intended for the frontispiece to Britton's publication (fig. 9-5).

These respective illustrations suggest the breadth of the collection. Rutter's "Groupe" comprises a complex range of materials, styles, and manufacture. A Renaissance sensibility predominates:

nautilus, hardstone-mounted casket and vessels, standing cups, candlesticks, and carved ivories are exactly the type of item that could be seen in views or noted in accounts of earlier collectors' cabinets. The remaining items are a curious mix of medieval, "oriental" and "antique."

While the Limoges chasse and elements of the "Fonthill-Gagnières Ewer" (fig. 9-6) are medieval pieces, not everything else, however, is as it might seem. According to Rutter's text the "antique" bowl on stand is contemporary to Beckford, being a piece of silver-gilt designed by Jean-Guillaume Moitte and made by Henri Auguste in 1793. Similarly, the candlestick in the form of an archaic bronze is also contemporary.[34] The Fonthill bindings so prominently displayed in the illustration were commissioned by Beckford. The "Fonthill Ewer" is also a piece with contemporary mounts, and the ivory sleeve vases are probably early eighteenth century, possibly mounted in gilt bronze at the end of the same century. The standing cups, listed respectively as "onyx, striated agate, and calcedony" are almost certainly contemporary, fashioned for Beckford. The unusual, bell-shaped item placed on the books, is listed as being "an exquisite bit of old japan."

Both Rutter and Britton visited the Abbey during the preparation of their respective publications and spoke at length with Beckford, Franchi, the Abbé Ange Macquin (another of Beckford's companions at the Abbey), and, subsequently, Farquhar. It has to be assumed that Beckford directed both of them with regard to the illustrations and the text, and he presumably selected the works of art to be shown. The "Fonthill-Gagnières Ewer" and the chasse were again selected for inclusion in Britton's publication, accompanied by the "Rubens Vase." It is interesting to note that Britton, as a respected antiquarian, did not include any quasi-Renaissance or contemporary works of art for the frontispiece; perhaps he had persuaded Beckford that the "Rubens Vase" was the single most appropriate object to be shown with the other two masterpieces. It is also curious that the items selected for the frontispiece were all of, or purported to be of, Near East or Oriental manufacture: the chasse was believed to be Greek, the ewer was known to be from China, albeit with European mounts, and the "Rubens Vase" was acknowledged as being carved in "Asia Minor."

All three masterpieces were listed in the 1822 sale catalogue, but only the "Rubens Vase" was retained by Beckford, indicating the immense importance he attached to this piece.[35] This acknowledgment of the singularity of the vase was commented upon by Franchi in 1818, and by Hume in 1844, shortly before Beckford's death, who wrote: "I often think of his [George Gunn, the dealer from whom Beckford acquired the vase in 1818] Onix Cup, you now have a rare specimen of Antiquity there are few works of its class."[36] Its very real significance to Beckford, however, was demonstrated in 1841, when he bequeathed the vase to the Duke of Hamilton.[37] Although long been assumed that the "Rubens Vase" had been part of the Beckford estate inherited by his daughter Susan, Duchess of Hamilton, and subsequently passing into the Hamilton collections, it is now known that Beckford himself actually selected this one item above all others to give directly to the duke. Its importance is even recorded by the clerks preparing the various listings of items from Bath to go to Hamilton Palace—it is always referred to as "The" sardonyx vase.

The display of his collection exercised Beckford a great deal: "Everything depends on the way objects are placed, and where. Horrors in one place discount beauties in another."[38] The greatest treasures of Beckford's collection were dispersed throughout the Abbey, and there did not appear to be a set scheme or plan for the display of particular categories of art in rooms or suites especially set aside for that purpose. The various texts by John Storer, Rutter, and Britton reveal that the works of art were generally kept within cabinets, these being either glazed display cabinets, or, more frequently, closed cabinets with a number of interior shelves. The practice of housing in cupboards those small-scale objects or objects of special interest for close examination and contemplation, was probably equated with the traditions of the Renaissance *studiolo*.

Objects at Fonthill Abbey seemingly were mixed for deliberate effect:

> If anything could enchant a timid and religious soul, it would be the incredibly rich and sublime effect produced by Cellini's stupendous dragon alongside the conch in the Bouchardon cabinet: diamonds, topaz and enamel—everything glitters in a magical way. The little piece of scarlet leather, on which this sublime *objet d'art* rests, looks so well, and the height of the vase is so correct when it is grouped with the conch, that I see no need to dispatch the lapis-lazuli.[39]

Rutter enumerated at some length the contents of the several cabinets in the dining room in 1822; one of the Boulle armoires contained different examples of goldsmith's work, while the ebony cabinet in the same room appears to have held predominantly hardstone works of art and Limoges enamels. Beckford's bedroom is noted in 1812 as containing "two closets filled with curious specimens of carvings in ivory and other rarities."[40] Again in 1812 the housing of the collection was noted: "Numerous articles of japan, with a great variety of delicate gold vases, some enamelled and others enriched with gems, are arranged in cases, somewhat in the style of those ancient cabinets which were called Ambries."[41] This last, very deliberate reference to "Ambries" would no doubt have been supplied by Beckford, indicating quite clearly his own historical and romantic association with collectors' cabinets of the past and here particularly, the *Kunstkammer* of Archduke Ferdinand II, housed at Schloss Ambras.

Beckford commented upon contemporary English collectors of porcelain and in doing so directly expressed his admiration for French collections of the eighteenth century, while evaluating his own taste in comparison: "The porcelain collections of Sudley, Lascelles and Essex surpass a hundred times everything here. Sainte-Foix had some outstanding china, but almost everything of this quality, acquired from the famous cabinets of Gaignat, Conti, Pompadour and Mazarin, went to Vienna, Russia and Poland. But patience! In matters of true taste and real art there is sufficient consolation for the man who plans cabinets like my ebony and Florentine ones."[42]

When on display, objects were probably massed together on surfaces, mixed by material and date, the most fragile material either covered by a glass shade or a leather cloth. Despite these precautions, additional care needed to be taken:

> . . . the dampness of this sublime abode is so great that everything will rot. Today, visiting the tabernacles or cribs in the Lancaster Gallery . . . I found them all covered with lichen and stalactites like Fingal's cave; the lacquer was covered with a white beard and verdant. . . . I don't speak of the gilt stuff—this

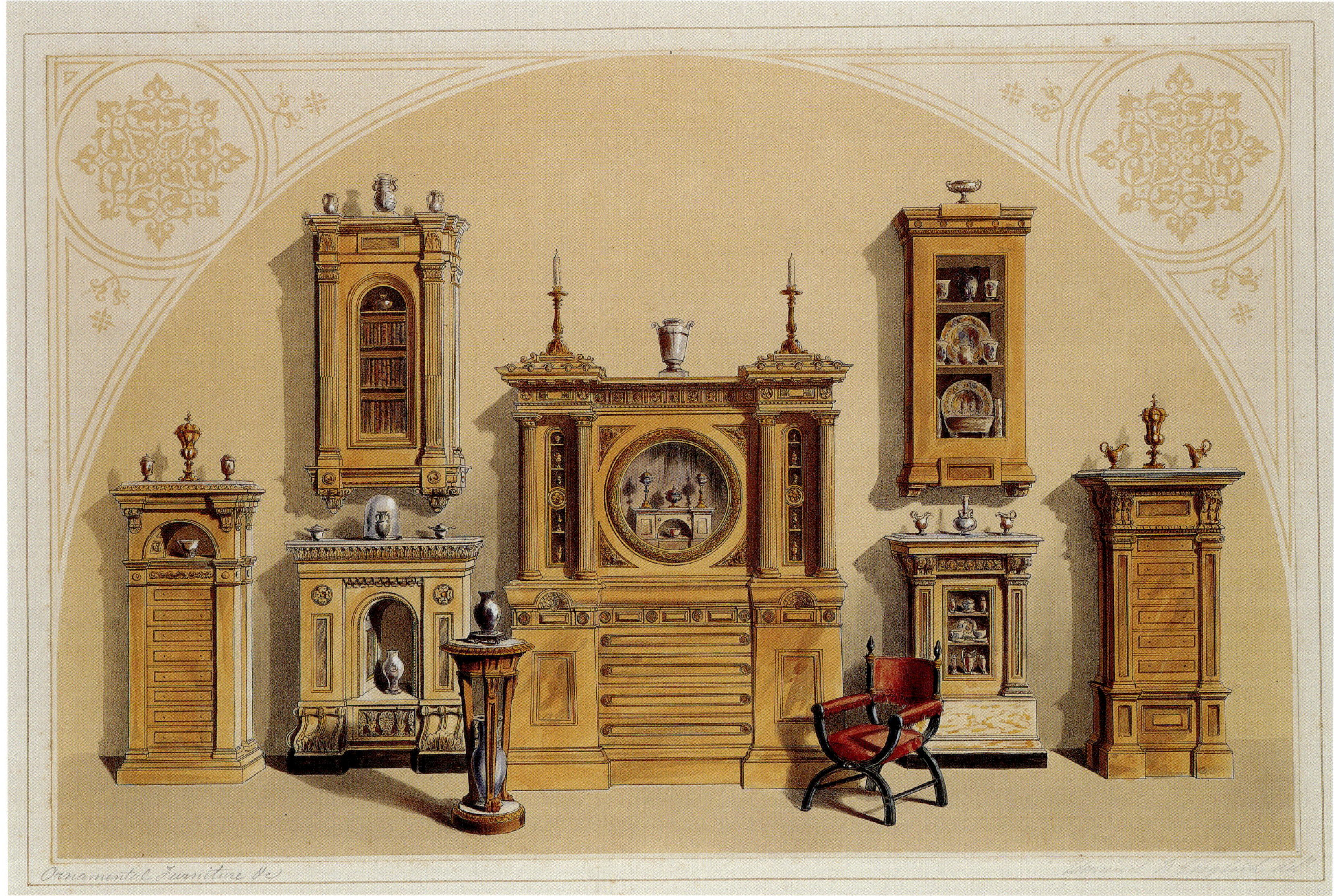

Fig. 9-7. "Ornamental Furniture from Mr Beckford's Collection." Chromolithograph. From Edmund F. English, *Views of Lansdown Tower, Bath,* (Bath, 1844): plate 14.

is already ash-colour like on the first day of Lent. Coxone says he is going to remedy it, but who can trust him — the remedy will be the breaking of ten of twelve pieces of china in the confusion of withdrawing the semi-putrid objects.[43]

Those objects held back from the 1822 sale to Farquhar reveal the predominance of mounted works of art, those works of art of the highest quality or rarity, and as would be expected, of objects commissioned by Beckford. Many of these can be seen in the interior views of Lansdown Tower. The views of the tower, although just as carefully

arranged and stage-managed as those of the Abbey, show, by contrast, a series of interiors where the objects dominate. Surfaces are covered, niches are filled, and the glazed display cabinets, crammed to overflowing, are presented in full view. This massing of objects was no doubt necessary, given the severe restrictions of space in the tower in comparison to the Abbey, but the contrast in aesthetic between the Abbey views and the tower views is considerable. Antiquities or works after the antique appear in most views of the tower, juxtaposed with Oriental porcelains and *Kunstkammer* objects. Beckford's collection of Etruscan vases and hardstone caskets and urns was seen in the interiors for the first time. The Etruscan Library contains only this type of material, admitting to no such fripperies as objets d'art.

Some notion of how Beckford displayed the "rarest gems" of his collection can be formed by examining the several views of the tower, especially a plate from *Views of Lansdown Tower* entitled 'Ornamental Furniture' (fig. 9-7). Works of the very smallest scale were housed in the differing shelf arrangements within the display cabinets; delicate items were kept beneath glass shades; and the larger, or heavier items were displayed either on the tops of the cabinets and tables, or on stretchers below. The arrangements were symmetrical and ordered as well as decorative, and comprised a melange of material: porcelains next to metalwork, which share space with hardstones and mounted works of art.

The elegiac text of *Views of Lansdown Tower*, published after Beckford's death, in fact echoes the views of Gustav Waagen, who visited the tower in 1838, prior to its final 1841 redecoration, and wrote: "But what especially pleased me was, that all these things bear a due proportion in size to the moderate apartments in which they are, and are likewise so arranged that they serve rightly to adorn each, without producing, as often happens, by overloading and confusion, the disagreeable effect of auction-rooms."[44]

BECKFORD AND THE ART MARKET

Although much is known of Beckford's life, comparatively little is known of the means by which he acquired his works of art. Unlike many of his contemporaries, Beckford seems not to have acquired many items as gifts, no doubt due to his isolated social position. Significantly, although he inherited a sizable fortune founded two generations earlier, Beckford was still considered *nouveau riche* and, unlike his aristocratic contemporaries, did not appear to have inherited any outstanding works of art. Instead, Beckford used a number of sources to acquire his collection. These were primarily his agents, or the antique dealers or "brokers," or the auction rooms. Several publications devoted to the study of dealers and the various sources of supply of antiques in the nineteenth century paint a picture of a thoroughly modern trade, not too dissimilar from contemporary practices.[45] Individual dealers or firms, whatever their title on a trade card or registration, sold all manner of works of art, ranging from antiquities and oriental art, to modern and antique furniture, different categories of works of art, and pictures. Most firms were involved to some degree in the supply of components and in the manufacture and restoration or "improvement" of their stock.[46]

Beckford's correspondence sheds light on his collecting activities and notes the significance of his agents and dealers in the process of acquisitions of works of art. His dependence on the eye and acumen of his agents was nothing out of the ordinary; his grandee contemporaries would have acquired their collections in much the same way, with the advice and encouragement of well-informed friends and agents. What sets him apart perhaps is the very real involvement, obsession often, he showed in the day-to-day transactions, and his interest

in commissioning works of art. Beckford's agents and dealers were closely briefed on, or quickly assimilated, his taste for objets d'art, and his concepts of interior decoration and appropriate furnishings. In addition to keeping constantly on the alert for new items coming on to the market, the agents were under instruction to buy particular objects from certain sales or private collections.

Beckford's agents Thomas Wildman and Nicholas Williams, and his upholder, Edward Foxhall, were responsible for much of the fitting out of Fonthill Splendens were also active in the acquisition of works of art.[47] Williams, for example, wrote to Beckford in 1788: "Your tea kettle will be sent you forthwith from Boulogne. Tell Berti if you please that Mons. Ducasnoy of Boulogne will pay the duty for me"; and "I have nothing now to detain me from Fonthill—but your Portugal cabinets.'[48] Beckford employed the services of, among others, two dealers named Delamotte and Gaudin in Paris for the acquisition of works of art.[49]

Much is known about the various smallworkers and goldsmiths used by Beckford, listing accounts and prices paid, often as sum totals as well as for specific objects.[50] Numerous other dealers are listed in the Beckford manuscripts—for example, Emmerson, Robert Hitchcock, Isaacs, Jenkins, Lambeth, William Newhouse, Smith, and Samuel Woodburn, among others—usually noted against sums for payment. Robert Hume, a dealer himself, jokingly referred to the stock-in-trade of some of these dealers: "You will have noticed Phillips have up for Sale for to morrow a matchless Colln. of Invalids and Incurables from the depots of Phillips, Emmerson and Co."[51]

On occasion the documents list payments for individual objects, as for example, to a dealer named Bentley, for the Nessus and Dejanira bronze, purchased in November 1814 for £20,[52] or £420 to the English dealer George Gunn, trading out of Paris and Amsterdam, for the renowned "Rubens Vase."[53] A reading of the correspondence sheds light on other sources of acquisition. Beckford ridiculed the dealer R. Davies, goldsmith and jeweler of York Street, Portman Square: "Enter 'Magnus Berg' Davies with a salver of beaten silver etc-la, la."[54] This must surely refer to the "Magnus Berg" cup now in the Royal Collection, which is now known not to be by Berg, although its origin remains uncertain. The magnificent "Borghese" pietre-dure tabletop, now at Charlecote Park, was acquired from Edward Holmes Baldock, who in turn was supplied by the priest and dealer, Abbé Celotti.[55] As Hume notes of the sale of 1823, "the Great Table of Florence work has sold to a Mr Lucy for the sum of *1800 Guineas* by which Mr Beckford will profit near one Thousand Pounds."[56]

Beckford was not unusual in his patronage of the established dealers of the time. Documentation shows he clearly not only spent a great deal of time with such major dealers as Robert Fogg and Baldock, but also paid substantial amounts of money for items they offered. Fogg, of Warwick Street, Golden Square, operated principally as a "China Man," a dealer in porcelains. Although Beckford complained about the high prices, the pieces in stock would appear to be irresistible:

I have returned from Fogg's; so far, little temptation, but two large bottles, rather beautiful seagreen with faint white, . . . perfect, pretty straight and with beautiful stoppers; price 140—cursèd pest of a Jew. The Saxon ware very so-so; other pieces of seagreen and seacoal, cleverly made (?) if you like and fine, but Pompadourised enough to make you vomit.[57]

Despite his caustic dismissal of what would appear to be the Rococo style of the mounts, two successive letters show just how attractive these must have been to Beckford:

This morning I fell right into Fogg's net. Alas, I was seduced by certain little Saxon tazza, certain sea-green bottles incredibly decorated with bronze, gilded in hell-fire—so bright and strong their colours. . . . I cannot say the other things are very attractive [illegible], but dear or cheap, here they are in this house, being packed up for Fonthill.[58]

Although the purchases from Fogg comprised mostly porcelains, Beckford also acquired furniture from him: "It is a pity to let the mosaic table, bought some years ago from Fogg, remain buried. I must have it made capable of bearing the ivory cabinet—black with few or no bronzes; it will do well in my room."[59] Fogg sold Boulle furniture to the Prince Regent and, no doubt, to other such Francophile collectors as Beckford.[60] In 1814 Beckford wrote: "Two words breathed in my ear would have made me buy two fantastic Buhl armoire-like cabinets, magnificent, of a Solomonian richness, 400 the pair, and not dear at that."[61] Beckford's protestations about prices or quality cannot always be taken on trust. What is said in one letter is often superseded by the next, announcing the acquisition of the very same items.

One of the brokers most frequently patronized by Beckford was Baldock.[62] Like Fogg, Baldock seems to have supplied Beckford primarily with porcelain, and it was from him that Beckford acquired the "Fonthill Ewer" in 1819. Beckford agreed to buy the piece for £285, no doubt enticed by the effusive language and extravagant claims of provenance, addressed to "The Connoisseur & Man of Taste."[63] Beckford anxiously attempts to verify the workmanship of the ewer:

. . . for my part I prefer the Cornaro—if it is the Cornaro; I've searched in vain so far for any information about this real marvel in the writings of Benvenuto Cellini. In his treatise on the goldsmith's art he talks a good deal about enamelling, but I can't see that he ever quotes this vase as an example.[64]

The desperate straits in which Beckford found himself that same year after massive purchases of works of art and a severe decline in his Jamaican income can be seen in another letter to Franchi: "Cups, goblets, the Queen's slaves, harpsichord, china for sweetmeats, massive objects from Ceylon, Cuttel, Coulson, Aldridge and Fogg—all are crying out 'Pay me! Pay me!'"[65] Franchi's witty, pictorial response to these pressing financial demands shows the "Fonthill Ewer" quite clearly among the drawings of objects. [66]

What is perhaps unusual about Beckford is his reliance upon the circle of architects, artists, designers, and agents in his employ. These specialist roles overlapped to a great degree, and Beckford moved seamlessly between the players. This continuum makes ascribing particular responsibility to any one individual very difficult. Beckford's architect James Wyatt was much more involved in the acquisition of works of art than had previously been realized. Wyatt exasperated Beckford beyond belief over the course of many years, but he also had an eye for high-quality works of art. Beckford wrote to Williams in 1796:

Wyatt has been buying a lot of curiosities for me—some very fine Japan—a pair of bronze tripods etc.—pay for and take possession of them all—he talks of a large coffer price 10 guineas—that should be sent to Fonthill—I have ample room for it—As for the Japan Box—he has a scheme of presenting it I do not quite approve—I should like to see it before anything is done, so bring it with you if you think you can answer for conveying it with perfect security; for Wyatt who looks upon it as unique and capital is extremely fearful it shd receive injury.[67]

It is entirely possible that the "Japan Box" could refer to either the van Diemen box or the Buys box, and perhaps it was actually Wyatt who first suggested to Beckford that either of these boxes be dismembered to form cabinets, as "a scheme of presenting it."

As no correspondence between Beckford and Franchi survives from Beckford's self-imposed exile on the Continent during the 1790s and early 1800s, it is not known exactly when Franchi began to act as an agent for Beckford in the acquisition of works of art.[68] It is likely, however, that in England at least he began acting in this capacity around 1800. When Beckford was either unwilling or unable to travel to London to view collections in salerooms or stock at dealers, Franchi would report to him, describing what was available, and make recommendations. That Beckford was an exacting patron is readily apparent: "What the devil are the plates anyway? Chinese or Japanese? God knows. Why not send one, or put them aside until I can see them? How can I judge without seeing them! What are the other trifles?"[69] In a similar vein he wrote: "What rage for trash governs you? How is it possible for you to tolerate this monstrosity—you who have an eye capable of perceiving beauty in the opposition of colours! . . . For the love of true taste, don't let yourself ever again be indoctrinated by Baldock! It is cruel to throw away so many shillings on the transportation of monstrosities."[70] The tone of these extracts reveal that these exchanges took place between client and agent; no matter what their personal relationship might have been, Franchi remained indebted to Beckford for his living. It is highly probable that Franchi and Wyatt collaborated in the design, supply, and acquisition of furniture and fittings for Fonthill Abbey, and, by the same token, it is more than likely that Franchi and Foxhall worked together.

The letters between Beckford and Franchi are full of gossip; they recount the goings-on in the salerooms and detail individual collections on the market. These letters identify extant objects and the methods and sources of acquisition, while the accounts and reports show how much Beckford relied on Franchi to act as his eyes and ears, and how much he trusted Franchi's judgment, both for quality and for acumen. He wrote on one occasion:

> I'm very impatient to know the result of the great sale at Christie's, especially whether Lord Yarmouth (who swallows up everything) has swallowed up the fine Leonardo da Vinci. From what you have written I don't doubt that this picture has very real merit—what a pity not to have seen it before my departure; that's what one gains by burying oneself away from London.[71]

Beckford had very few acquaintances with whom he could correspond about works of art, and he was decidedly isolated from contemporary collectors. He would not have been involved firsthand in examining pieces, nor in discussions or visits to collections, and was thus doubly reliant on agents. Despite the arrogant and presumptive tone he usually adopted in letters to Franchi as agent, by contrast he also frequently addressed Franchi as an equal when discussing works of art, cognizant of Franchi's own taste and connoisseurship: "This Philipine gem has bought treasures of the most capital Buhl, ebony carvings after your own heart and heaven knows what marvels; and there still remains a mine of sublime things and artistic marvels to be bought in Paris."[72] His reliance on Franchi's valued opinion is made plain in another letter: "The cupboards etc will be arranged under your supervision. When you are far away I haven't the spirit or the courage to think of anything."[73]

Franchi appears to have an equal, if not greater, appreciation and knowledge of hardstones and lapidary work than his patron. The two sales of Franchi's collection—in 1827 and after his death in 1829—show an astonishing quantity and variety of hardstones, suggesting that in all probability he acted as a broker in hardstones, either for mounting on furniture or in the creation of works of art. The hardstones described in the documentation appear to be either plaques or relief stones for mounting on furniture, uncut pieces of stone, or shaped bowls and cups ready for mounting as objets d'arr.

It is therefore not surprising to discover that an enormous shipment of hardstones was made from Paris during Franchi's buying trip there in the summer of 1814. Among the Franchi "Accounts" is a listing in francs of items acquired in France; the majority of the items are of agate, lapis lazuli, mosaics, rock crystal, jade, and cornelian, some of which are noted as mounted.[74] This listing can be better understood when read in conjunction with the accompanying letter from Franchi:

> I have bought several agates, some small lapis vases that I bought with my allowance and that we bought at Auguste's sale, of a beautiful shape similar to a Hanap and mounted on the cover; I bought you some rock-crystal vases, none of them broken, none of them ugly and among them there is one bought

for 25 louis and I have no doubt that if Your Excellency would see it in London you would pay 100 because it is superior to everything of this kind that I've seen; the others are larger and carved although they cost as much as a slice of bread; the agates are all cohesion and one in particular is of such high quality that I've never seen another in a particular collection for which I would change.[75]

The letter also discusses pietre-dure cabinets, revealing that Franchi was very much involved in the supply of hardstones for the manufacture of these cabinets.

> I told you already how much the Prince Regent would pay for two pietre dure cabinets like the ones you have in Harley Street. You know that all the mosaics made by Rafaelli, we can't find any others. I had to pay immediately for the ones I did buy and now the sellers are giving me 12% more to buy it back. Fogg did not buy it because it was expensive, and all those that can be found have gone to the Prince. . . . With the ones we have here and in London we can make many beautiful pieces of furniture in good taste. I also bought six stupendous columns of the most perfect scarlet flowery jasper. I've already told you about these.

The supply of hardstones for pietre-dure furniture would include thinly cut panels to be inset into a frame, decorative mosaic panels, relief fruits and ornaments, and such architectonic elements as pilasters, columns, and capitals.[76] The correspondence makes it clear that Franchi was acquiring hardstones not only in Paris, where he may have purchased some seventeenth-century elements from the Gobelins hardstone workshops, but also from Rome and Florence, where he may have obtained original elements from the Grand Ducal workshops.

Franchi's knowledge and connoisseurship of hardstones is apparent. He wrote:

> The sanguine jasper cup is good, although I have sent it to Cuttel to dismount the foot and clean it. The agatine jasper cup is magnificent although it has a small defect (I believe its natural) and it is of an incredible lightness. The green cup is curious and of a type that I've only seen once in a tobacco box. . . . The description that Chassogne makes of the green sanguine cup is that it is well-known in Kunstkammer cabinets (*alta curiosidade*) and that it was sold once for 1201 and another time for 1002 and another for 950 francs.[77]

At the end of this commentary, Franchi listed a number of the purchases referred to above, with prices; the sanguine jasper cup was priced at 601 francs, the total sum being 1,927. He added in brackets after the total: "I don't think that is expensive," and continued to discuss the merits and deliveries of hardstones:

> Between us, what Your Excellency has in the Abbey [sanguine jasper] is the best that I have seen. Durand's example is of a different quality, full of defects and undulations, I suppose a

much rarer species; the crystal is very good and we must make an enamelled circle around the foot in order for it to be perfect . . . the work is no doubt by Bolerius de Vicence.[78]

This last reference is to a rock crystal bowl (see cat. no. 104), from which the original enameled foot mount is missing.

Franchi settled the account for the "Rubens Vase" from Holland in 1818, and it is highly probable it was he who viewed it and negotiated the sale. Franchi wrote to the Marquess of Douglas in November: "Several days ago I wrote to the Marchioness to tell her about the purchase of the famous Nuremberg vase. It is truly beautiful and I repeat that it is the finest object in the Abbey—because of its curious workmanship, its antiquity and its size, besides which, a sardonyx of this magnitude is a unique object."[79]

Franchi acted as an agent for Beckford for all manner of items besides hardstones; ivories, lacquer, porcelain, pictures, and furniture, all fell within his remit. "Franchi has been for some days now in London, in the embrace of his porcelain dealers and cabinet makers," Beckford wrote to the Marquess of Douglas.[80] Franchi's artistic talents were often put to good use in describing a piece to Beckford. A drawing of the item accompanied the following account: "At Rotibus' is a small piece of lacquer, very curious in form and quality. Its perfect, in good taste, and of very similar quality to the piece with horses. The shape is [drawing] the price 10s. Lascelles is trying to get it."[81] Another extract reveals more of Franchi's aesthetic judgment:

> In connection with ivories, the socle [drawing] of Fiammingo is one of the best things known by him and is the copy of the Farnese vase with alterations in his own hand; the pieces of the Margravine are like this so they must be much superior to your [illegible]Tankard; the refinement, the delicacy and the softness and the spirit of this work is the most beautiful and most pleasant I have seen, the companion is not by the same hand but is good; and because they are a pair it would be worth paying 3000 francs for the two pieces, one of which is undoubtedly from the hands of that great man. I have another group of two boys also by him, and their stomachs don't have the stiffness of pieces that belonged to Grijoux.[82]

The description and the drawing suggest the pieces to which Franchi referred are the ivory sleeve vases mounted in gilt bronze, as seen in Rutter's "Groupe" and Maddox's *Objects of Vertu*.

Franchi was in Paris early in the summer of 1814, apparently to review collections prior to Beckford's visit in the autumn of the same year. He sent Beckford a lengthy report, dated July 13, 1814, on the collections he had seen, with descriptions and details of items either purchased or taken on approval. It is one of the most revealing documents in the correspondence, illuminating Franchi's activities in his role of agent:

> Your Excellency thinks that I have forgotten the things you asked of me, no sir, I never forget what you tell me when I know what interests you . . . about books, do not think I have forgotten; I intend to take to you a small collection that I am sure will please you. The collection of Aldos de Corogna is sublime, you will see some of it and judge for yourself; all your books not sent and bought are here in his house in a cupboard with everything else that Your Excellency has written. I've seen everything with my own eyes.[83]

In the letters dated after the milestone of 1822, when Beckford sold the Abbey and most of its contents to Farquhar, Franchi no longer appeared to be the principal agent for Beckford, who increasingly turned to Hume to act in that capacity. Whether this breakdown in patron–agent relationship occurred at the same time as, or is a consequence of, the breakdown of their personal relationship is hard to judge. It could merely reflect Beckford's concentration on the supply of newly made furnishings for Lansdown Tower, for which he needed Hume, rather than on the acquisition of works of art as previously. Franchi's letters dated after 1822 concerning works of art are mostly written from the Continent and show that Beckford continued to use him as an agent for foreign purchases.

Franchi reported on some of the private collections viewed in Paris in 1814, among them Baron Dominique Vivant-Denon and the merchant Julliot. Franchi wrote again about sales from Paris in 1823 and 1824 and from Florence and Rome in 1824 and 1825. In Paris again in 1826, he noted items he purchased for Beckford in the merchant Sallé's sale. This last report demonstrates not only the diversity of Oriental porcelains available on the Paris art market that were to Beckford's taste, but also the collaboration between patron and agent. Beckford, in England, clearly had a copy of the catalogue, while Franchi, attendant at the sale, noted the lot numbers for greater ease of reference.

What are of more significance in terms of types and quality of objects are Franchi's comments on and his listings from the Denon sale in 1826. Beckford had visited the Denon collection in 1814 and been given a tour of the Louvre by Denon himself. Beckford had earlier commented on Denon's collection in rather disparaging terms, and later described how he avoided any inducement to buy:

> If I did not flee from buying temptations I'd be down to my last farthing; for this reason I've left M. Denon in peace—I haven't taken a step in his direction, and since he hasn't given himself the trouble to come galloping to me, he's off my list. I can't help marvelling at this because when I last saw him he seemed to be afire with the liveliest enthusiasm for my accomplishments, and talked about his drawings, prints and pictures etc with those fervent encomiums which were obviously born of a great inclination to cede the said treasures to a dear friend, *for money of course*.[84]

Franchi's list of objects from the Denon sale included Limoges enamels, ebony, sandalwood and lacquer caskets, porcelains and jade.[85]

Lot numbers were noted, and prices enumerated against some items. The listings can be read in conjunction with an accompanying letter from Franchi to provide a better understanding of what was available on the market, the state of current prices, and the types of objects acquired by Beckford. Franchi described the lacquer in particular detail, and indicated which lots were acquired. Other lots purchased included porcelain, mounted porphyry vases, and jade. Clearly Beckford's expenditure at this sale was enormous, totaling 12,000 francs, and Franchi wrote with regard to settlement of the account: "Before I leave I will sign a letter to Lafitte for £500 and I will make all the arrangements to pay for the cabinets and stands over different periods to lighten the load."[86]

Franchi was not entirely Beckford's creature. It is clear that he also represented Beckford's daughter Susan Euphemia Beckford and the Marquess of Douglas from a very early date. Franchi and Susan would appear to have had an affectionate relationship, almost one of brother and sister, and this relationship was extended to the Marquess of Douglas after his marriage with Susan in 1810. Correspondence between Beckford and the marquess usually referred to Franchi in the most friendly of terms, to his activities and purchases, or to his health. One might conjecture that Franchi was astute enough to realize that his special relationship with the fickle Beckford would not last, and that he turned to Susan and the marquess as alternative patrons, while remaining within the family unit. Franchi of course visited Hamilton Palace on a number of occasions, which Beckford never did. Beckford jealously wrote in 1819: "I trust you will not be bestially benign enough to go to the Scottish Court in preference to that of Fonthill,"[87] and similarly, "Notwithstanding your lively desire to go to the Kingdom of the Cinquefoils."[88]

Franchi's role as an intermediary between Beckford and the duke in the last frantic attempts to save Fonthill Abbey has been commented upon in many biographies of Beckford. The Franchi correspondence has shed new light on several aspects of the proposed public sale by Beckford of the Abbey in 1822. When noting the throngs of people at the "View," Franchi added: "Christies has made many changes and there is no doubt that the second edition will be capital. What I regret is not having employed two or three draughtsman and engravers in copying all the vases, cabinets and other curiosities. And to sell it at the door as a pretty little book."[89] The next month Franchi comments on Britton's forthcoming publication: "Britton is very happy with the offer Your Excellency made to add to your book, which will have very pretty views of the interior and the exterior of the Abbey. The one with Sta Dada, the reliquary, the stool, the torcheres and the ebony chairs and roof is finished and is very beautiful."[90] This reference is to Britton's view of Saint Michael's Gallery (see fig. 7-6). The remaining correspondence between Franchi and Beckford concerning the sale of the Abbey covers the retention of objects from Farquhar and several listings and enquiries regarding items to be sent to Bath. These can be read in conjunction with Franchi's 'Packing Lists' to provide a reasonably comprehensive idea of which items Beckford took with him to Bath.

The other principal character that features highly in Beckford's collecting activities is Robert Hume. Much has been written about him, usually in connection with hardstone-mounted cabinets and the great collector George Watson Taylor, or with the work he undertook for the Duke of Hamilton at Hamilton Palace.[91] Unlike Franchi, Hume was not only an agent for Beckford, but also an established dealer in his own right and a renowned cabinetmaker in partnership with his father. Hume was therefore not as "tame" as Franchi. He had numerous other clients for whom he acted in a number of different capacities, many of whom were much wealthier and of greater significance than Beckford. Among these were the Lucy family of Charlecote, George Watson Taylor, and Lord Grosvenor. Hume also worked at Saint James's Palace and York Minister. Significantly, like Franchi, Hume was sufficiently adept at balancing the demands of both Beckford and the Duke of Hamilton, two equally demanding clients, while remaining on good terms with each.

The date of partnership between the Hume father and son, each called Robert, is not certain, nor is the date of Hume senior's retirement. Hume junior wrote to the Duke of Hamilton in 1841, thanking him for patronage to his father and himself for almost forty years,[92] suggesting that the duke had had dealings with Hume senior since around 1808, the date when he is first recorded in the London trade directories. Hume is recorded as being Beckford's agent at a picture sale in 1811, and this was probably also Hume senior.[93] As early as 1815, however, Beckford called upon "young Hume," who by then was clearly of sufficient stature and experience, to sort out proposed structural alterations to the Cabinet Room in the Eastern Transept of Fonthill Abbey, which would affect the ebony cabinet. Hume junior also acted for both Beckford and the Duke of Hamilton at the sale at Fonthill Abbey in 1823, notifying the duke: "My father will be glad to attend to any business your Grace may have in Town."[94] In 1824 Hume senior was still practicing, as Hume junior wrote to the duke: "My father is quite well and presents his respects. We are very busy with a large quantity of very inferior work for Saint James' Palace."[95] It is Hume junior who dealt with the matter of Franchi's death in 1827 and who continued to act for Beckford's daughter Susan in the settlement of her father's affairs until 1848.

As a cabinetmaker of the first order, it is not surprising that Hume was employed by Beckford to supply work at Fonthill Abbey. The renowned "Ebony Cabinet" was commissioned by Beckford from Hume in 1815, and its design and considerable expense caused great anxiety in Beckford:

Only the final stage of ruin will make me abandon the great Ebony Cabinet. It's better to pay tribute than to allow to go far from the Abbey a piece of furniture so august and colossal—an object calculated to bestow, of its own accord, splendour on any apartment, however imperial. I'm convinced of this without having seen it. This being so, it'll cost me something to deprive this place for ever of an object of this rank, planned for the

Abbey, decorated for the Abbey, conceived with all Hume's genius and ardour.[96]

This particular letter is revealing in a number of ways. It demonstrates Hume's own design skills, which were rarely acknowledged by Beckford, who usually claimed authorship of such matters. Hume clearly was well able to fully comprehend and realize Beckford's concepts for the interior furnishings of the Abbey and the desired effect of the totality. It is apparent, however, that Beckford appreciated the cabinet as a masterpiece in its own right, rather than perceiving it as one object, albeit splendid, making up part of the whole. The letter continues to discuss who might purchase it from Hume in Beckford's stead if he could not raise the funds; the Marquess of Buckingham is proposed, but rejected due to his dire financial straits, and Beckford tellingly states: "But to sell it on credit to the miserable, wrinkled Shepherd [the Marquess of Douglas] would be painful, cruelly painful to me."[97] Not only does Beckford seem unwilling to advertise to his son-in-law his own precarious financial position, but he also reveals his jealousy and bitterness at the marquess's more fortunate state. Beckford's serious patronage of Hume as a cabinetmaker would appear to have begun at this time, in all probability as a replacement for Foxhall, Beckford's previous cabinetmaker, who had died in the autumn of the same year.

In November 1815 Hume was first recorded in the Franchi "Accounts" in a list of "Items to be made by Mr Hume" which includes: "A Florentine cabinet, a cabinet for the Lancaster Gallery, a table for the amber cabinet, two oak side tables."[98] The Lancaster Gallery at Fonthill Abbey is known to have been furnished mostly with ebony, or ebonized furniture, which implies that the cabinet in this account could have been ebony. The different styles and materials of the furniture listed in the accounts show the capability of Hume to supply diverse articles of furniture in response to precise requirements from his patron.

The same listing further details items that Hume must have acquired in his capacity as an agent: "A small Persian cabinet, a plinth, an enamel dish."[99] The documents reveal that Hume also supplied the "Buhl" display cabinets and stands for Saint Michael's Gallery, two examples of which can be seen at Charlecote Park. Hume wrote in 1823, after the sale of the Abbey by Farquhar: "Some of the small Buhl cases and Tables in St. Michael's Gallery sold for Double what Mr Beckford paid us for them."[100] Because Beckford noted the gallery as being complete in October 1817, the furniture must have been delivered prior to that date. Hume was recorded as being paid £200 in the accounts signed and dated May 4, 1818, which might possibly have been for this suite of furniture.[101]

Hume's activities as an agent were not dissimilar to those of Franchi. On Beckford's behalf he viewed the sale of the collection of the late Queen Charlotte in February 1819, Beckford wondering, "who knows whether the little lacquer cabinet will come to light."[102] A short time later he mentioned the same lacquer cabinet: "In London I went with Hume to Christie's tabernacle where the Queen's trumperies were on show. I saw the jade which I detest and the Frogmore cabinet, which I still like but not as much as I thought; it is covered with smoky filth. I suppose it will be bought and will go to fulfil its destiny at Fonthill. Who the devil would have ever thought of such a thing: Not I. When one remembers that I had commissioned Bagasse [Wyatt] to offer a diamond in exchange!"[103]

Beckford also relied on Hume's good nature in the acquisition of works of art from the saleroom: "I was right in thinking I wouldn't escape a few little purchases. I trusted—I had a look and there already in a tiny corner of my cupboard at Jaunay's are the divine, gold-mounted little chest painted in the Hindu style (formerly at Gwennap's) and the most magnificent piece of engraving in silver I've ever seen (the Margrave's Wildercom—sublime). With all possible honesty and, one might say, friendship, Hume let me have them for what they cost him, by a happy chance, at that rogue Phillips'."[104]

Remarking upon debts Hume was owed, Beckford wrote: "The thought of owing him so much torments me night and day."[105] The torment felt was not sufficient, however, to stop Beckford from making further purchases: "Almost every day now I see Hume, and seeing him one sees objects of curiosity, and seeing them one always thinks them desirable; then one gives little commissions, and then one makes little purchases, and so piling up debts and deficits one marches towards an abyss as black as Death!"[106] Standing on the edge of this particular abyss, Beckford would appear to have been in considerable debt to Hume alone. In May 1823, with the proceeds of the sale of the Abbey to Farquhar, Beckford settled his account with Hume, in the extraordinary sum of £8,000.[107]

Hume's role in the negotiations with Christie in 1822 and in the drawing up of the catalogue of Fonthill Abbey remains uncertain, but his involvement in the subsequent negotiations with Phillips and Farquhar are well documented. He was present at the negotiations with Phillips and Farquhar, appearing to have acted as an intermediary between all three parties in 1822.[108] Hume's frequent correspondence with the Duke of Hamilton is most revealing about particulars of the 1823 sale.[109] It details not only the purchases he made for the duke and the means by which these were achieved, but also the purchases and commissions from Beckford, as well as Lord Grosvenor and Lord Belhaven. Hume's letters provide a narrative of the sale's progress and attendance, commenting further on prices realized and detailing certain underbidders. Taken together, the purchases Hume made for Beckford in 1823, Franchi's "Packing Lists," and the Franchi correspondence detailing items sent from the Abbey to Bath are invaluable in ascertaining exactly which items Beckford considered most precious and worthy of removal to Bath.

Hume continued to be active as an agent and cabinetmaker for Beckford when he lived in Bath. In April 1824 Hume noted that frames were ready, not specifying whether mirror or picture frames. He also wrote: "The Franks cabinet shall be finished without delay also the Michelangelo one."[110] If this "Michaelangelo" cabinet is the same cabinet for which the goldsmith James Aldridge was paid £11.14 in 1815 for producing two figures, it certainly was a long time in the making. Perhaps Hume would not proceed with completing the work until Beckford's debts had been settled, or perhaps Beckford himself had asked for the commission to be put on hold. In 1825 Franchi had commented upon the exorbitant price of a cabinet made by Hume and complained about the excessive time it took for Hume to complete orders; perhaps it was to this cabinet that Franchi was referring.[111] Evidence shows that in 1827 the cabinet was itself being altered: "Cuttel is already making the panels for the base of the Michelangelo. If he doesn't finish on time it doesn't matter, for we will put the cabinet in its place with its old panels and when the new ones are finished Obum or Obborn (or God knows what he's called) will replace it as the operation is not difficult."[112]

Hume recounted in 1830:

Mr B signified his wish to part [with] some few things to [illegible] his disappointment from Jamaica. . . . He then said there was Two of his Cabinets which he would also part with and that He would send them to me from Bath which has been done. One of them is the one called the Auguste Cabinet the other is an Ebony & Mosaic with Marble Top as the enclosed sketch. It is of *good* mosaic and most *Excellent Workmanship.* He tells me I may take £300 *ready money* for the Two which is moderate as he paid 18,000 Francs for the Auguste one. Before I offer them to anyone here I beg to submit them to Your Grace they are well worth the money."[113]

In the event, the duke paid the asking price for these two cabinets, and Hume further noted: "I have informed Mr B that I had sold them for Hamilton. He said it was pleasant & he was glad they were so well placed."[114]

Like Franchi, Hume wrote chatty, even gossipy letters, describing the travels and activities of the auctioneers, dealers, and purchasers. He noted viewing at sales from which he might acquire certain lots for Beckford, and generally kept Beckford up-to-date with the London art market. Hume also described his own travels to the Continent, apprizing Beckford of the picture collections. In a letter from the Continent, he wrote in jest, "I have waddled mit de brou Eggshell & Dem Her Van Lacquer through many Kamers & Magazyns."[115] References abound in the correspondence relating to Hume acting as banker to Beckford, advancing him money against government bonds, presumably because Beckford still had problems with cash flow. Hume noted in 1829 that the balance due from Phillips and Farquhar for the acquisition of the Abbey and contents was to be finally completed, but it would appear that even in 1830 there were still problems with this settlement.[116]

In 1824 Hume assured Beckford: "I have put some of the pieces of furniture in hand. They shall be produced with every attention and care," promising two days later, presumably in response to a letter from Beckford, "2 more chairs shall be made . . . the other furniture is advancing."[117] There is no indication as to what this furniture might be, nor any insight into whom might have been instrumental in the design. At this date the furniture referred to would have been for Beckford's residence in Lansdown Crescent.

The next reference to furniture made by Hume is in 1831; this is in fact the furniture made for Lansdown Tower. A letter in the summer of 1831 noted: "I hope tomorrow or the next day you will receive the three cases safe with the table slab and bookcases. . . . The ebony caskets and the commode are going forward."[118] That same winter, Hume wrote concerning the bookcases and cabinets, and this letter is annotated with drawings of a cabinet similar to that seen in Willis Maddox's "Ornamental Furniture." The letter also discusses the shipment of bronzes, tripods, and marble.[119] The next letter from Hume detailed at some length proposed designs for candelabra, which are sketched with units of measurements. The sequence of correspondence shows that Beckford was responsible for the initial design, Hume making suggestions for changes and alterations, such as: "I should prefer the small one therefore will not proceed until I hear again whether you will pronounce a Divorce from your first instruction."[120]

Although after the move to Bath Beckford does not appear to have acquired works of art in the same quantities as he did for the Abbey, he continued nonetheless to purchase at a steady rate. Hume wrote in 1823: "when I sent off the Dresden etc. etc. I had had hope of including the Sea Green Bottle & the Red Jar, also the Gold mounted Tumblers—the China is ready and I am awaiting the Tumblers which have been at Goldsmith's Hall these four days."[121] The porcelain appears to have been supplied by Baldock, but the correspondence also shows that Beckford was at the same time making major purchases through English & Son, the Bath auctioneers. The reference reveals that Beckford's interest in mounted porcelains continued unabated throughout his life, as did his fascination with the finest quality works of art. He wrote to Hume: "Your chastely beautiful oaken cabinets are filled with the rarest gems of art—few but excellent."[122]

Hume also supplied Beckford with hardstone vases: "I have sent by Coach this day the two long [illegible] vases. I hope they will give you satisfaction when placed in their places—they are more beautiful than I had expected to have been able to make them."[123] Beckford's reply was immediate: "The vases are recently arrived and most beautiful they are in every respect—charming specimens of the richest alabaster—I have nothing in true & colour & perfect in the execution—they leave nothing to wish me—if the cassettes turn out as happily you will have reason to be proud of and I likewise."[124] At several intervals in the correspondence Hume details different types of marbles, including porphyries and jaspers, and discusses the paucity of pietre-dure panels: "Florentine tablets are now scarce but I hope ere long may turn up for the purpose you desire."[125] Hume, one of the foremost makers of pietre-dure furniture, may have had his own lapidary workshop that produced hardstone works of art as well as panels for mounting on furniture, decorative tabletops, and solid slabs to be used for plinths and tops.

In 1837 Beckford was again in debt to Hume, in the sum of £14,200. Curiously, Hume suggested that the Marquess of Douglas, Beckford's grandson, might settle the account. Beckford had earlier reflected sadly: "Collecting is become so hopeless that I am strongly inclined to give it up in toto & limit my exertions to the production of picturesque effects in the open air."[126]

It was Hume who acted for Beckford on his last real flurry of buying, at the Strawberry Hill sale of 1842.[127] Beckford wrote to Hume two, sometimes three times daily about the sale, with regard to the catalogue, arrangements for his own private view, the lotting up, and the purchases made on his behalf. As he himself admits: "Waking or dreaming Strawberry Hill occupies all my thoughts."[128] There can be few more pathetic sights than Beckford, aged eighty-two, alone and isolated, obsessed by a sale of a long-dead rival collector. Ironically, in this aspect, he was not unlike Horace Walpole himself. Hume, in these dealings with Beckford over the Strawberry Hill sale, treats Beckford not only as a client and with the utmost professionalism, but seemingly with some measure of affection, which is clearly reciprocated.

Hume's involvement in Franchi's final illness and, subsequently, in the arrangements for the funeral and the settlement of the estate was extraordinary. Hume was a respected cabinetmaker and agent for a number of noble and important clients, and not in Beckford's sole employ. His very personal involvement, particularly in the retrieval of what has to be assumed were intimate Beckford–Franchi letters, coupled with the negotiations with Susan Beckford for the payment of the funeral accounts, make it clear that the relationship between Beckford and Hume was a great deal more significant than that of mere patron and agent/cabinetmaker. Despite Hume's obvious repugnance at Beckford's shameful treatment of Franchi during Franchi's many bouts of ill health and especially during his final illness and death, the dealings Hume had with Beckford over some thirty years appear to be of an amiable and personal nature, discussing at the end of Beckford's life the problems of Beckford's granddaughter, Beckford's hopes for his grandson, and the health and affairs of the Duke and Duchess of Hamilton. This relationship was conducted by Beckford with a professionalism and grace rarely shown to agents, not even Franchi, or cabinetmakers. One of Beckford's last letters to Hume, dated March 7, 1844, closes: "With equal constancy."

Although Beckford's properties of Fonthill Abbey and Lansdown Tower are undoubtedly antiquarian in their architectural style and commissioned fittings, Beckford's collection of works of art is decidedly romantic in nature. Items of archaeological or scientific interest were not for him, nor were the typical "souvenirs" collected on the Grand Tour. Beckford instead avidly collected works of art, mostly from the medieval and Renaissance periods, which formed a parallel with his commissioning of works of art or acquisition of contemporary pieces in the same spirit.

An insatiable collector, his passions were wide-ranging and whole-hearted, and he demanded pieces that engaged his emotions, as well as his intellectual and visual interest. Beckford acquired items often of great rarity and intense beauty, and it was of no special concern to him whether these pieces were authentic. Of the "Fonthill Ewer" he wrote tellingly: "I'll return to this research another day, though it matters little whether or not I find the answer—the object in itself deserves the most wholehearted eulogy."[129] What mattered to Beckford was the creation of an ensemble, the effect the collection produced: "It costs nothing to see things, and seeing them, few are the objects that one regrets. Everything unknown seems a treasure . . . - distance softens the sharpest rocks and lends enchantment to what, nearer, loses all value."[130]

For a man of such romantic sensibility, the power of association was overwhelming. Whether distinguished by precious material, virtuoso workmanship, or illustrious provenance, the works of art reflected the collecting traditions of the past, be it eighteenth-century France, sixteenth- and seventeenth-century European princely courts, the earlier ducal courts of Italy, the dynastic courts of India, or the Imperial courts of India, China and Japan. Beckford collected for the pleasure of possession as much as anything else, and he battled fiercely with rivals for the best works of art. Spite and malice would steer much of his enthusiasms, as would sheer greed or simply an eye for a bargain.

The well-publicized attack on Beckford and the contents of Fonthill Abbey by the art critic William Hazlitt is now seen very much as a product of its time. Hazlitt described the Abbey as "a Cathedral turned into a toy shop, an immense Museum of all that is most curious and costly and, at the same time, most worthless in the productions of art and nature. . . . Mr Beckford has undoubtedly shown himself an industrious bijoutier, a prodigious virtuoso, an accomplished patron of unproductive labour, an enthusiastic collector of expensive trifles; the only proof of taste (to our thinking) he has shown in this collection is his getting rid of it. . . . the specimens exhibited are the best, the most highly finished, the most costly and curious of that kind of ostentatious magnificence which is calculated to gratify the sense of property in the owner, and to excite the curiosity of the stranger who is permitted to see or even touch baubles so dazzling and of such exquisite nicety of execution."[131]

These disparaging comments have long clouded judgment of Beckford's taste, and it is only since the Hamilton Palace sale of 1882 that Beckford and his collections have come under renewed scrutiny and, subsequently, been reappraised. Hazlitt did indeed identify quite correctly that Beckford was trying to create a type of *Kunstkammer* worthy of princely collectors, and recognized that as a patron Beckford delighted in the exquisitely detailed, small-scale works of art so suited to collections of previous traditions. To historians of art in the twentieth and twenty-first centuries the same attributes that Hazlitt condemned are now considered worthy of praise and admiration. Considered by many to be a thoroughly dislikable man, to most Beckford is redeemed by his literary talents, his architectural vision, his collections, and his 'eye for the magnificent'.

Beckford once wrote: "I am just what I always was in that respect—an Amateur a Dilettante a Connoisseur perhaps but no Professor."[132] Written in 1795, at the age of thirty-five, to refute allega-

tions that he was about to convert to Roman Catholicism, this extraordinary insight might just as easily be applied to Beckford's own attitudes towards collecting.

Acknowledgments: I am grateful to Nicolas Bock, Marian Campbell, Philip Hewat-Jaboor, Martin Levy, and Hugh Roberts for their generous assistance —BM

1. The author dedicates this essay to the memory of Clive Wainwright, the first scholar to study Beckford as a collector of works of art. See *The Romantic Interior: The British Collector at Home 1770–1850* (New Haven and London: Yale University Press, 1989), 109–35. The author expresses her deep gratitude to Jane Wainwright for generously permitting access to research files and notes.

2. This essay does not address Beckford's collecting of books and pictures, and will refer only in passing to furniture, metalwork and lacquer. For furniture, see chap. 10, by Adriana Turpin; for metalwork, see chap. 11, by Michael Snodin; for lacquer, see chap. 12, by Oliver Impey and Jonathan Whitehead, in this volume. The term *works of art* hereafter refers to the decorative arts.

3. Franchi "Accounts," MS Beckford c. 37, fols. 73–83, Bodleian Library, Oxford (hereafter referred to as "MS Beckford"; Franchi "Packing Lists", MS Beckford c. 37, fols. 92–99.

4. *Life at Fonthill, 1807–1822, with interludes in Paris and London, from the correspondence of William Beckford,* trans. and ed. Boyd Alexander (London, R. Hart-Davis, 1957): 136–37, 18 September 1813. All quotations in this essay follow original documentation or publication: the author has not amended original spelling or grammar. Unless otherwise indicated, all translations are the author's own.

5. *Illustrated London News* 7 (1845): 324–25, 344–46, 364–65.

6. "Soane Cups," MS Beckford b. 8. One of the mounted hardstones in the drawing is now in the Musée du Louvre, OA 10907; see *Musée du Louvre: Nouvelles acquisitions du département des Objets d'art 1980–1984,* pp. 93–96.

7. Michael Snodin and Malcolm Baker, "William Beckford's Silver," parts 1 and 2, *Burlington Magazine* 122, no. 932 (1980): 735–48; no. 933 (1980): 820–34.; *Beckford and Hamilton Silver from Brodick Castle,* exh. cat. (London: Spink's, 1980); *Argenteries: Le Tresor du National Trust for Scotland*, exh. cat. (Brussels: Banque Bruxelles Lambert, 1992). See chap. 11, by Michael Snodin; for hardstone-mounted furniture, see chap. 10, by Adriana Turpin, in this volume."

8. For the "Fonthill Ewer" (New York, Metropolitan Museum of Art, The Jack and Belle Linsky Collection, 1982.60.138), see *The Jack and Belle Linsky Collection in The Metropolitan Museum of Art* (New York: Metropolitan Museum of Art, 1984): 179–80; R. E. Stone, "A Noble Imposture: The Fonthill Ewer and Early Nineteenth-Century Fakery," *Metropolitan Museum Journal* 32 (1997): 175–206; idem, "The Fonthill Ewer: Reconstructing the Renaissance," *Metropolitan Museum of Art Bulletin,* 55 (Winter 1997/98): 46–56. The author would like to thank Clare Vincent, European Sculpture and Decorative Art Department, The Metropolitan Museum of Art, for her generous assistance and her interest in this project. For the "Rubens Vase" (Baltimore, The Walters Art Gallery and Museum, 42.562) see M. C. Ross, "The Rubens Vase," *Journal of the Walters Art Gallery* 6 (1943): 9–39; J. M. Eisenberg, "The Rubens Vase in Baltimore: An Oriental Copy?", *Minerva* (March–April 1997): 20–25.

9. John Britton, *Graphical and Literary Illustrations of Fonthill Abbey, Wiltshire; with Heraldical and Genealogical Notes* (London: Longmans, Green and Co., 1823): pl. 8.

10. Christie's, 1822, 8th Day, lot 55; Phillips', 1823, lot 570, £63. See H. R. Foster, *The Stowe Catalogue* (London: the author, 1848): 5th Day, lot 570, purchased by Garrard for £67, ill. None of the catalogue descriptions note the shell as being carved or engraved; the detailed illustration in the Stowe catalogue does not indicate any carving or engraving of the shell.

11. Christie's, 1822, 8th day, lot 52; Phillips', 1823, 29th day, lot 1148, £6.6, purchased by Robert Hume for Robert, second Earl Grosvenor. Illustrated in a portrait by F. G. Cotman of Lady Elizabeth Mary Leveson-Gower, Dowager Marchioness of Westminster (private collection). Information kindly provided by Eileen Simpson, Archivist, Grosvenor Estate, and Mr. L. Clark.

12. Christie's, Hamilton Palace, 1882, lot 872, purchased by E. Radley for £556.10s; ibid., lot 873, purchased by G. Attenborough for £162.15s. The astonishing difference in price may perhaps be

accounted for by damage. One of the sleeve vases survives in a private collection, but has lost its mounts and has suffered extensive fire damage.

13. Alexander, *Life at Fonthill* (1957): 244–45, 24 July 1818.

14. S. Caudron, "Connoisseurs of Champlevé Limoges Enamels in Eighteenth Century England," *British Museum Yearbook* 2 (1977): 9–33. I thank Marian Campbell for her discussions with me on this subject, and her interest in the writing of this section.

15. For a further discussion on Beckford's Limoges enamels, see B. McLeod, "Some further objects from William Beckford's collection at the Victoria and Albert Museum," *Burlington Magazine 143* (June 2001): 367–70.

16. For the Petzold cup, see H. Müller, *The Thyssen-Bornemisza Collection: European Silver*, trans. P. S. Falla and Anna Somers Cocks (London: Sotheby's, 1986): 194–99, cat. no. 58; for the Moringer cup, see ibid., pp. 136–39, cat. no. 36.

17. Christie's, Hamilton Palace, 1882, lot 644, purchased by J & S. Goldschmidt, for £3,244. 10s, ill.; ibid., lot 645, purchased by J & S. Goldschmidt, for £740.5s. The wide discrepancy in price may possibly be explained by the fact that on the underneath of lot 644 is a portrait medallion inscribed "Georgen Roemer, año.1580."

18. Toledo Museum of Art, 65.179A–B.

19. Henry E. Huntington Library and Art Gallery, San Marino, California, Acc. No. 17–13.

20. Letter to Franchi about Stourhead, 14 September 1814, quoted in Alexander, *Life at Fonthill* (1957): 158.

21. Letter to Louisa Beckford from Paris, 19 January 1784, MS Beckford c. 18, fols. 52–3; also quoted in J. Oliver, *The Life of William Beckford* (London: Oxford University Press, 1932): 161–64.

22. Beckford's unique position at this time as an English collector and patron in France has been fully reviewed; he was well placed to acquire works of art during the turbulent last decades of the eighteenth century and was an exacting patron in the commissioning of works of art from the French luxury industries; see P. Verlet, *The James A. de Rothschild Collection at Waddesdon Manor: Savonnerie* (Fribourg: Office du Livre, 1982): 520–23.

23. J. Britton, *The Beauties of Wiltshire,* vol. 1 (London: the author, 1801): 227.

24. Letter from Beckford to the Marquess of Douglas, 7 November 1814, quoted in Alexander, *Life at Fonthill* (1957): 161.

25. For a thorough assessment of this room, see Wainwright, *Romantic Interior* (1989): 140–42.

26. See chap. 12, by Oliver Impey and Jonathan Whitehead, in this volume. A full account of Beckford's collecting of lacquer is given by F. Watson, "Beckford, Mme de Pompadour, The duc de Bouillon and the Taste for Japanese Lacquer in Eighteenth century France," *La Gazette des Beaux-Arts* 61 (February 1963): 101–27.

27. Alexander, *Life at Fonthill* (1957): 186, 18 October 1815.

28. J. Storer, *A Description of Fonthill Abbey* (London: the author, 1812): 12.

29. Ibid.

30. MS Beckford b. 8, fols. 19–20.

31. List of purchases made by the Duke of Hamilton at the 1823 Sale, National Register of Archives [Scotland], 2177, Bundle 602. All references to the Hamilton Muniments will hereafter be referred to as: NRA[S], followed by the index number. The author acknowledges with thanks the receipt of a grant from The Tom Ingram Fund to undertake research in the Hamilton Muniments. She is most grateful to The Trustees of the Hamilton and Kinneil Estates and His Grace The Duke of Hamilton and Brandon for permitting access to the Hamilton Muniments at Lennoxlove, and would especially like to thank John Mutch for facilitating the access with great patience and good humor. She also expresses her gratitude to Isabel Walker and the staff at Hamilton District Library.

32. *Carlton House: The Past Glories of George IV's Palace,* exh. cat. (London: The Queen's Gallery, Buckingham Palace, 1991–92); S. Medlam, et al., *The Bettine, Lady Abingdon Collection* (London: Victoria & Albert Museum, 1996); *French Connections: Scotland and the Arts of France,* (Edinburgh: HMSO & Royal Scottish Museum, 1985).

33. Ozias Humphrey's account of a visit to Fonthill Splendens, MS Beckford c.16, fol. 10.

34. Michael Clayton, *Christie's Pictorial History of English and American Silver* (Oxford: Phaidon, Christie's, 1985): 244–45, ill. p. 245.

35. MS Beckford b. 8, fols. 19–20.

36. MS Beckford c. 22, fol. 237.

37. MS Beckford c. 21, fols. 203–7.

38. Alexander, *Life at Fonthill* (1957): 126, 6 July 1822.

39. Ibid., pp. 324–5, 28 October 1819.

40. Storer, *Description of Fonthill* (1812): 12.

41. Ibid., p. 14.

42. Alexander, *Life at Fonthill* (1957): 191–92, 22 November 1815.

43. Ibid., p. 173, 7 February 1815.

44. G. F. Waagen, *Works of Art and Artists in England,* trans. H. E. Lloyd, 3 vols. (London: John Murray, 1838): 120.

45. Clive Wainwright was one of the foremost scholars in the study of the antique trade. A selection of his publications on this subject include "The Trade," in *Romantic Interior* (1989): 26–53; "Carlton House: George IV and Wheeling and Dealing in the Eighteenth Century," *Apollo* 134, no. 356 (October 1991): 246–50; "Curiosities to Fine Art: Bond Street's First Dealers," *Country Life* 179, no. 4632 (29 May 1986): 1528–29. At the time of his death, Wainwright was preparing a publication on the history of the antique trade in the eighteenth and nineteenth centuries. See also J. Culme, "Kensington Lewis: A Nineteenth-Century Businessman," *Connoisseur* 190, no. 763 (1975): 26–41; G. De Bellaigue, "Edward Holmes Baldock," parts 1 and 2, *Connoisseur* 189, no. 762 (1975): 290–99 and 190, no. 763 (1975): 25.

46. Examples can be seen in *The Dictionary of English Furniture Makers, 1660–1840,* ed. G. Beard and C. Gilbert (Leeds: Maney, 1986); London *Directories* of the period, and newspapers.

47. For further information on Wildman, Williams, and Foxhall, see chap. 3, by Philip Hewat-Jaboor, in this volume.

48. MS Beckford c. 37, fol. 8.

49. For a payment note drawn in francs upon Beckford's account, dated January–April 1804, listing Franchi, Delamotte, Chardin, and Gaudin, see ibid., fol. 72.

50. Snodin and Baker, "William Beckford's Silver" (1980).

51. Hume to Beckford, 17 July 1835, MS Beckford c. 22, fol. 153–54.

52. MS Beckford c. 37, fol. 74 v.

53. Ibid., fol. 83. For further information on Gunn, see Medlam, *Lady Abingdon Collection* (1996); 104, index.

54. Alexander, *Life at Fonthill* (1957): 272, 22 January 1819.

55. The inscription in the Charlecote copy of the Fonthill Abbey sale catalogue of 1823, signed by Celotti, reads: "The mosaic table was in Venice. . . . M. Celotti who has ceded this same table to Mr Baldock will be able to let you have this information" (Jane Wainwright, personal communication).

56. Letter from Robert Hume to the Duke of Hamilton, 30 September 1823, NRA[S], 2177, Bundle 602.

57. Alexander, *Life at Fonthill* (1957): 151–52, 30 June 1814.

58. Ibid., pp. 152–53, 4 July 1814.

59. Ibid., p. 213, 27 June 1817.

60. *Carlton House,* cat. no. 32.

61. Alexander, *Life at Fonthill* (1957): 152–53, 4 July 1814. It is not clear whether the cabinets referred to are the armoires from Fonthill Abbey now in the Louvre.

62. De Bellaigue, "Edward Holmes Baldock."

63. MS Beckford c. 26, fol. 22; MS Beckford b.8, fol. 7.

64. Alexander, *Life at Fonthill* (1957): 323–4, 29 October 1819.

65. Ibid.

66. Ibid., ill. opp. p. 323.

67. Beckford to Williams, 12 October 1796, MS Beckford c.37, fol. 42 v.

68. The relationship between Franchi and Beckford has been much discussed; see Boyd Alexander,

From Lisbon to Baker Street: The Story of the Chevalier Franchi, Beckford's Friend, (Lisbon: The British Historical Society of Portugal, 1977). For Franchi's role in the design of Beckford's metal-work, see: Snodin and Baker, "William Beckford's Silver" (1980). Many of the Portuguese letters between Beckford and Franchi have been recently translated, and reveal the very real significance Franchi had on the formation of Beckford's collection. These letters have been transcribed and translated by Pedro de Moura Carvalho for the PHJ/Beckford Database. These letters in translation shall be designated hereafter by "P." after their reference.

69. Alexander, *Life at Fonthill* (1957): 45, 27 September 1807.

70. Ibid., p. 84, 25 September 1808.

71. Ibid., p. 99, 22 June 1811.

72. Ibid., p. 295, 10 March 1810.

73. Ibid., p. 314, 20 July 1819.

74. MS Beckford c. 37, fol. 77.

75. Letter from Paris, 13 July 1814, MS Beckford c.12, fol. 46-v, P.

76. For a detailed study of Franchi and the design and manufacture of pietre dure cabinets, see Philip Hewat-Jaboor and Bet McLeod, [untitled article], *Furniture History Society Journal,* forthcoming.

77. Letter from London, 11 June 1818, MS Beckford c. 12, fol. 55, P.

78. Ibid., fol. 55v., P.

79. Alexander, *Life at Fonthill* (1957): 254–55, 26 November 1818.

80. "Franchi est depuis plusieurs jours a Londres dans les bras de ses porcelainiers et de ses ebenistes," letter in French from Fonthill Abbey to the Marquess of Douglas, 28 January 1814, MS Beckford c. 21, fol. 39v.

81. Letter from London, 15 December 1809, MS Beckford c. 12, fol. 31v., P.

82. Letter from Paris, 13 July 1814, ibid., fol. 46, P.

83. Ibid.

84. Alexander, *Life at Fonthill* (1957): 163, 13 November 1814.

85. MS Beckford c.37, fol. 99.

86. Letter from Paris, 15 June 1826, MS Beckford c.13, fol. 88v, P.

87. Alexander, *Life at Fonthill* (1957): 317, 30 September 1819.

88. Ibid., 1 October 1819.

89. Letter from Fonthill Abbey, 1 August 1822, MS Beckford c. 12, fol. 88.

90. Letter from Fonthill Abbey, 4 September 1822, ibid., fol. 92.

91. The most recent account is Christie's, London, 6 July 2000, lot 100, the 'Gerstenfeld' Cabinet. See also A. Tait, "The Duke of Hamilton's Palace," *Burlington Magazine* 125, no. 964 (July 1983): 394–402.

92. NRA[S], 2177, Bundle 753, August 1841.

93. Alexander, *Life at Fonthill* (1957): 103.

94. NRA[S], 2177, Bundle 602, 16 September 1823.

95. Ibid., 14 February 1824.

96. Alexander, *Life at Fonthill* (1957): 190–91, 18 November 1815.

97. Ibid.

98. "Objets que sont a faire Mr Hume"; "Un cabinet de Florence, un cabinet pour la Gallerie de Lancaster, Une table pour la Cabinet d'ambre, deux consoles de chene," MS Beckford c. 37, fol. 77 v.

99. "un petit cabinet de perse, un socle, un plat d'email," ibid.

100. Letter from Hume to the Duke of Hamilton, 29 October 1823, NRA[S], 2177, Bundle 602. The several sets of these Buhl display cabinets and stand sold for £80 on average.

101. MS Beckford c. 37, fols. 80–81.

102. Alexander, *Life at Fonthill* (1957): 284, 15 February 1819.

103. Ibid., pp. 307–8, 22 May 1819. Alexander notes that this was Queen Charlotte's sale, day 1, lot 97, purchased for Beckford for £20.9.6.

104. Ibid., p. 302, 22 March 1819.

105. Ibid., p. 298, 15 March 1819.

106. Ibid., p. 301, 20 March 1819.

107. MS Beckford c. 22, fol. 10b.

108. Ibid., fols.1–9.

109. See Bet McLeod, [untitled article on the dispersal of the Beckford collection], *Journal of the History of Collections,* forthcoming.

110. MS Beckford c.22, fols. 39–40, 28 April 1824.

111. Letter from Paris, 24 May 1825, MS Beckford c.13, fol. 63 v., P.

112. Letter from Franchi in London, 25 May 1827, c. 13, fol. 96 v., P.

113. Letter from Robert Hume to the Duke of Hamilton in Paris, 11 February 1830, NRA[S], 2177, Bundle 602.

114. Ibid.

115. Letter from Hume in Amsterdam, 14 June 1830, MS Beckford c. 22, fols. 113–14.

116. Ibid., fols. 104–5, 7 November 1829; ibid., fols. 117–8, 23 June 1830.

117. Ibid., fol. 50, 14 September 1824; ibid., fols. 51v.–52, 16 September 1824.

118. Ibid., fol. 119, 20 July 1831.

119. Ibid; fols. 130–131, 7 December 1831.

120. Ibid., fols. 132–3, 17 December 1831.

121. Ibid., fols. 135–36, 28 May 1832.

122. Ibid., fol. 175, 18 August 1837.

123. Ibid., fol. 146, 27 March 1833.

124. Ibid., fol. 147, 29–30 March 1833.

125. Ibid., fol. 165, 3 August 1836.

126. Ibid., fol. 177, 10 September 1832.

127. See Bet McLeod, [untitled article on the parallels between Beckford and Walpole as collectors and the Beckford and Hamilton acquisitions from Strawberry Hill], *Journal of the History of Collections*, forthcoming.

128. Draft in Beckford's hand, 23 February 1842, MS Beckford c. 22, fol. 200v.

129. Alexander, *Life at Fonthill* (1957): 136–37, 18 September 1813.

130. Ibid.

131 William Hazlitt, *Criticisms on Art* (London, 1843): 284–87.

132. Letter, Beckford to Thomas Wildman, 22 August 1795, MS Beckford c. 37, fol. 26.

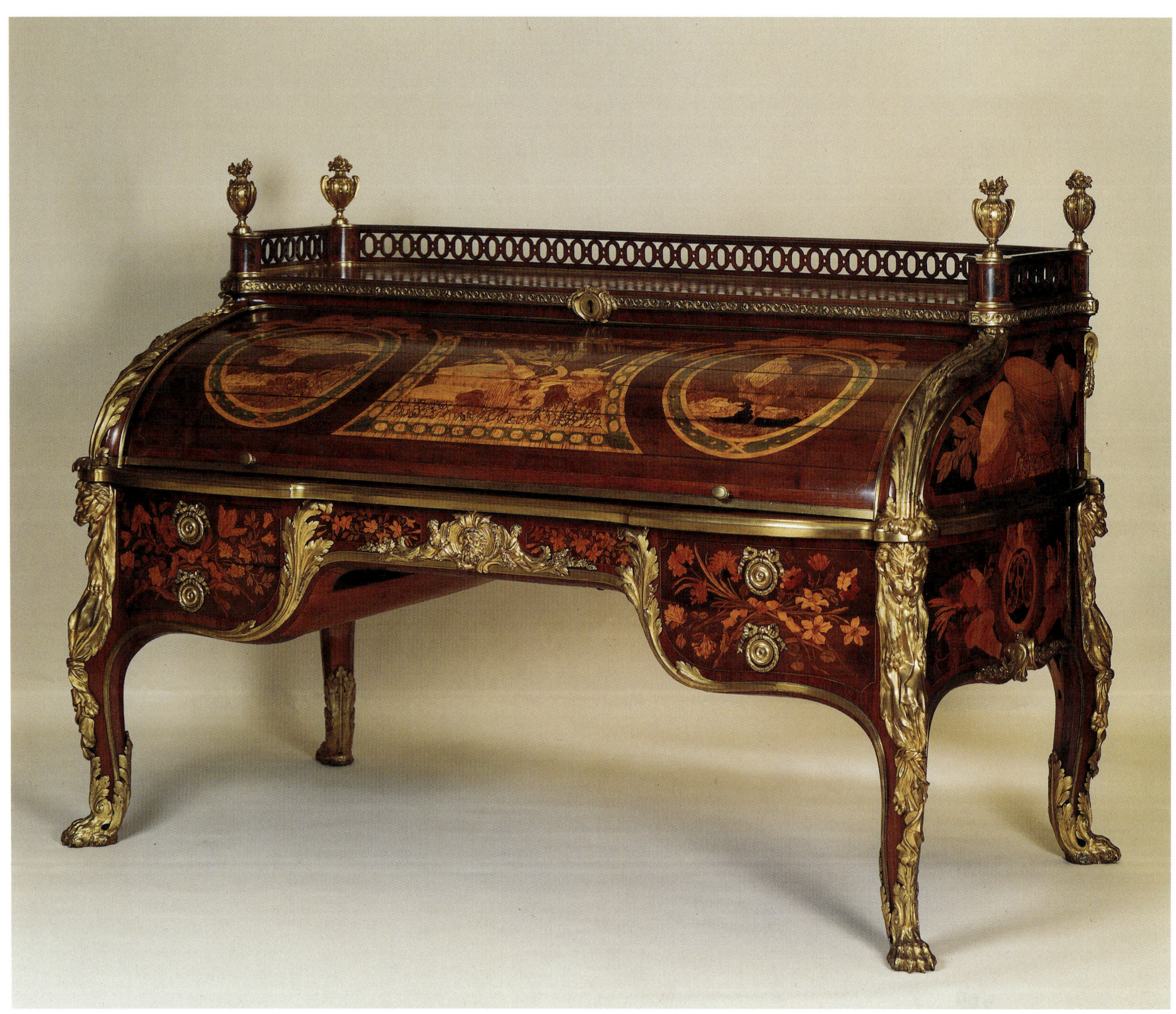

Fig. 10-1. Jean-Henri Riesener. Roll-top desk, ca. 1770. Holly, walnut, ebony, and boxwood in ground of sycamore, crossbanded with purpleheart. The Wallace Collection, London, F102.

Chapter X

FILLING THE VOID: THE DEVELOPMENT OF BECKFORD'S TASTE AND THE MARKET IN FURNITURE

Adriana Turpin

William Beckford spent much of his long life creating various assemblages of furniture "in such profusion as to dazzle and confound but for the order in which they were arranged."[1] This activity fell, broadly speaking, into three periods. Between 1781, when he gained his majority, and 1801, the date of the first sale from Fonthill Splendens, he was primarily influenced by contemporary French taste, which led to his interest in Boulle and Boulle revival furniture, furniture decorated with intarsia of pietre dure, pieces using Japanese lacquer, and pieces associated with the French aristocracy (fig. 10-1). At this time he also acquired English furniture in contemporary French taste, some commissioned in France, other pieces made for him. During the second period, from 1801 until his departure from Fonthill Abbey in 1822, he acquired furniture in a very different taste, combining his Francophile approach with what could be described as an English antiquarian taste. This led him to purchase and commission furniture in the Tudor and Elizabethan revival style, and to begin collecting seventeenth-century cabinets. Finally, in the third period, during his last years in Bath, between 1822 and 1844, he refined and developed his taste, divesting himself of much of his collection. Most importantly, he commissioned new works, which he combined with the choicest pieces from his earlier houses. Thus he began his career reflecting contemporary taste; by old age he had developed confidence in his own ideas, the result of a lifetime's experience in the pursuit and acquisition of a wide array of furniture, and of equal importance to him, their display and installation.

While it is impossible to determine exactly when Beckford acquired much of his furniture or identify its subsequent history, it is relatively easy, through his letters and the descriptions and sale catalogues of his houses, to recapture some parameters of his taste.[2] In addition, consideration of his purchases in the context of the contemporary art markets in London and Paris provides an insight into the complexity of his taste in furniture.[3] By examining what was available and at what prices, it is also possible to gain an understanding of the opportunities open to Beckford for purchasing furniture, the ways in which he might have acquired his pieces, and how his taste related to the interests of his contemporaries.

Beckford saw his furniture as an integral part of the interiors of his houses, in which the careful juxtaposition of objects created a visual unity through materials, form, and color. As one contemporary noted during the viewing of the sale at Fonthill in 1822: "The furniture astonishes everyone. It is indeed costly and superb beyond comparison. One peculiar beauty which strikes immediately is that the whole is excellent. Scarcely a meuble that is not formed of material prodigiously expensive or that does not bear about it in workmanship half the labour of a life; and all that is valuable — all magnificent — not a single mediocre article breaks the unity of design."[4] This perfection was sought after in each of his principal residences. As Beckford wrote in 1817, "Everything depends on the way objects are placed, and where. The Bernini cabinet in the Nunneries will not do without a picture, so see if the genuine Brueghel can be had. In that case, the Mantegna will hang above the cabinet."[5] Nonetheless, while aware of the requirements of the rooms he was furnishing, in certain areas — namely furniture of ebony, Boulle, pietre dure, or Japanese lacquer — he maintained a continuity of taste, commissioning and purchasing such furniture in both contemporary and historical styles.

Beckford's methods of acquisition

Two concepts dominate the study of Beckford's collecting activities — his great wealth and his "rapacious collecting activities" particularly in Paris.[6] How these questions relate to his purchases of furniture must be considered before analysing the development of his taste. With regard to his wealth, it has been estimated that until 1804 Beckford had an average income of about £27,000.[7] Thereafter it diminished greatly due to loss of estates in Jamaican lawsuits and, with the notable exceptions of 1813 and 1814, a permanent reduction in prices of sugar. An annual income of £27,000 in 1780 was equivalent to an income of about £2.25 million in the year 2000. By 1804, due to twenty-five years of mild inflation, an income of £27,000 was worth about £1.25 million in present-day terms. These conversions understate Beckford's purchasing power.[8] This is because Beckford was spending large sums on a considerable retinue of servants and on luxury goods involving "half the labour of a life." Costs of such goods and services have risen far more than that of bread. It follows that in 1780 Beckford had at his disposal an income well in excess of £2.25 million a year in terms of its potential to purchase personal service and goods of highest quality and labor-intensive craftsmanship. How much in excess it is not possible to say without constructing an index of prices relating to the basket of goods and services consumed by Beckford. This gives rise to insuperable difficulties, however, which are both practical and theoretical: the cost of data collection would be prohibitive; the current price of a coach-and-four or salary of a second footman, for example, are virtually unknowable since there probably are no precise modern equivalents. Another way to look at the income of the young Beckford is to compare it with that of his contemporaries. The only reliable data for English income in the early nineteenth century relates to 1801. Out of a population of 12 million only 1,020 (approximately one in 3,000 heads of household) paid tax on an income in excess of £5,000 per annum (equal to about £175,000 in 2000). Their average income was £9,975 per annum (equal to £340,000 in 2000).[9] With an income nearly three times that of the average for the top one-thirtieth of 1 percent, Beckford's reputation for having a high income was still well justified in 1801, yet his expenditures would eventually overwhelm his income.[10]

There is very little documentation as to what furniture Beckford might have bought during the pre-Revolutionary years in Paris. In 1787 he sent a box of porcelain home to England, which is the only indication of purchases getting to England, although it is quite possible that other shipments were made at the time.[11] Beckford certainly commissioned works of art while he was in Paris between 1791 and 1793, some of which later appeared in his sales in 1817 and 1823. How much furniture he bought in this visit or when it might have come to England is uncertain.

In July 1797 his agent, Nicholas Williams, was sent to Paris to collect Beckford's possessions, which had been left behind in 1793), and attempted to ship sixty boxes from France, presumably containing some of Beckford's earlier purchases, which had been impounded by French Revolutionary authorities. There is, however, no indication what was in the boxes, nor whether this consignment ever reached England.[12] Thus even if he did acquire some Boulle or other furniture in Revolutionary-period sales in Paris, he may have had to leave it behind. In a letter to his solicitor, Thomas Wildman, dated May 3, 1793, he wrote: "finding it impossible to send my pictures home I parted with 10 or 11 of them—and the money arising from this sale has enabled me to spare you—in a manner you little expected."[13]

As an Englishman, how would Beckford have been able to acquire furniture while in Paris during the Revolution? In August 1793, seven months after war had been declared with England and at least

three after Beckford left Paris, the Revolutionary government decided to sell the contents of the royal palaces by auction. Sales were held every day in the courtyard of the royal palace of Versailles, during which time it has been estimated that 20,000 lots were sold at often extraordinarily low prices.[14] The main purchasers at the year-long sales were Parisian dealers and some of the cabinetmakers such as Riesener and Georges Jacob. Among the dealers, Rocheux, the Treuttel family, and the family of Jean-Henri Eberts seem to have been the most prominent.[15] Certain dealers had specific connections with England. Dominique Daguerre, one of the most influential of the Parisian *marchands merciers*, had moved to London, but his partner, Martin-Eloy Lignereux, remained in Paris, acting on his behalf.[16]

Prices of works of art in 1793 and 1794, at the height of the Revolution, were not necessarily low.[17] On the contrary, Beckford paid 17000 livres[18] as part payment for "a piece of furniture for a boudoir to serve as a desk," which he commissioned in the autumn of 1792.[19] If this sum was required to be paid in specie, then it was equivalent to about £45,000 in 2000, but if it could have been paid in *assignats*, the paper currency introduced in 1789, then it was equivalent to £19,000. By 1795 any obligation which could be discharged by presentation of *assignats* to the required amount would have become negligible.[20] For an Englishman there was a lesser countervailing factor. Published rates of exchange showed the value of the pound sterling declining to one-third of its 1789 value by 1793, after which rates of exchange ceased to be published.[21] (These contradictory trends are plotted in chart 1, at 1792a and 1792b.) Perhaps the best guide to prices in this time of monetary turmoil is the bullion rate of exchange, based on the gold content of English and French coins and the cost of transferring bullion from England to France.[22] The rate is relatively stable (see chart 1, from 1780 to 1822), but its use, too, is problematic. By English law it was illegal to export gold bullion. Under French law it was illegal to demand payment in gold. If consignments of bullion were intercepted by the English authorities, they were confiscated. It is not certain, however, that everyone complied with these regulations.[23] The dealers could well have insisted on payment in specie, not in paper. For example, for many years bills of exchange drawn on Paris had been payable in gold, but it is not known whether this remained the practice throughout the Revolution.

Even if Beckford was able to take advantage of low prices, he probably would not have bought directly himself. His name does not appear in any of the sale catalogues of the time.[24] When Beckford bought various items of Japanese lacquer in Pairs in 1801, some of which came from the Duc de Bouillon's collection, the invoice he received was from a M. Dumorth, who had presumably bought the lacquer on his behalf, although Beckford and his agent, Nicholas Willliams, were both in Paris. The banker Jean-Frédéric Perrregaux was an important figure in Paris at this time, with contacts in the political and financial worlds, and connections with dealers and manufacturers. He acted as an agent for the Prince of Wales as well as the many English aristocrats buying in Paris before, during, and after the

Revolution.[25] He was also Beckford's banker both during Beckford's residence in Paris and upon his return to England. In 1788 Beckford was told by his lawyer, Thomas Wildman, that, "your tea kettle will be sent you forthwith from Boulogne tell Bertie if you please that Mons Ducarnoy of Boulogne will pay the duty . . . and that therefore M Perregaux need not advance any Money."[26] Beckford would continue to draw on the firm of Perregaux, or the firm of Lafitte as it would become after Perregaux's death, well into the 1830s. In a letter from Beckford of 1797, he sent his regards to Perregaux, who may have acted as an agent for Beckford as well as being his banker.[27]

After 1793 England and France were at war, limiting the opportunities for an Englishman to buy in Paris. This did not mean that sales of French works of art stopped; some were held in Hamburg, others in London.[28] One reason to hold these sales abroad was that the Commission des Substances, which was responsible for importing raw materials from abroad, found itself having to pay its foreign agents in works of art rather than bills of exchange, specie, or paper money.[29] Some of these agents were American, such as Colonel Swann, and others were French, such as Jacques de Chapeaurouge, who operated from Hamburg.[30] It has been suggested that the Prince Regent acquired some of his works of art as early as 1797 through the agency of Chapeaurouge.[31] Beckford bought at least once from Otterwald, a dealer in Hamburg.[32] The first sale in London took place in April 1798, and consisted of "Parisian elegances from the Palace of Versailles," mostly porcelain. Two years later Phillips held a sale of works of art "imported from Paris via Hamburg from the Queen of France's chateau at St Cloud."[33]

Beckford's next stay in Paris was from November 1801 to May 1803, but once again there is no documentation regarding his furniture purchases. When the Treaty of Amiens was signed in 1802, many English immediately set out for Paris, and there is some evidence of their purchases. The diaries of Bertie Greatheed, for example, specifically mentioned visits to Lignereux's shop.[34] "Nothing can be more beautiful or more costly," Greatheed wrote. "Tables and Secretaires of yew, with gilt and Bronze ornaments for 1000 louis (about £47,000). For 30 per Ct. advance he [Lignereux] will deliver them in England. He says the chief sale is there. . . . the china tables are all in the richest and best taste.'[35]

In the autumn of 1814, Beckford returned to Paris, as did many others, following the penultimate defeat of Napoléon and the intermediate restoration of the Bourbon monarchy. Although he did not describe his purchases in any detail, it is clear from his letters to Franchi from Paris that he was looking for works of art and paintings. Apart from one reference to a lacquer cabinet that he was determined to bring to London, there is no mention of furniture. He remained in Paris only a few months before returning to Fonthill. This may have been on account of his financial difficulties. It may also be that he was not part of the lively English community in Paris at the time.[36] He wrote to Franchi on November 29, 1814, that Paris was as sad for him as London.[37] Other English collectors, however, were buying furniture

in Paris in the years just after the final defeat of Napoleon at Waterloo in 1815. The Duke of Wellington and Charles Stuart, later Lord Stuart de Rothesay, were among those able to take advantage of the works of art flooding the market, as were many French and English dealers.[38] Frances, Lady Shelley, remarks in her diary that the duke showed her his purchases from Cardinal Fesch's sale, which took place in June 1816.[39] The duke bought his Boulle and Levasseur furniture while he was ambassador in Paris and shipped it to London in 1818 through the dealer Bonnemaison.[40] Charles Stuart acquired several items from the Hôtel de Saisseval, residence of Marechal Ney, probably privately sometime after 1817.[41] Beckford, however, limited his acquisition of French furniture in the contemporary taste of the early nineteenth century to a set of chairs from the sale of Cardinal Fesch and a large marble table, said to have come from Malmaison (cat. nos. 53 and 88). Both had connections with Napoléon; Cardinal Fesch was Napoléon's uncle and Malmaison was the principal residence of Napoléon's first wife Joséphine. Once again there is no documentation for these purchases; Beckford himself had left Paris by the time of these sales.

The London dealers also bought in Paris, presumably both for themselves and for clients. Thus the Prince Regent is known to have purchased a drop-front secrétaire from the dealer Robert Fogg, who had purchased it a few months earlier in Paris.[42] The prince also sent his own agents to buy there directly on his behalf. In London, after the resumption of trade in 1815, there was a dramatic increase of the number of sales of French works of art. Both dealers and private individuals were able to purchase furniture brought over from Paris, including many of the dispersed contents from the French royal palaces.[43]

In England, Beckford used agents and dealers both to purchase and commission his furniture. Although he discussed sales in his letters, there is less evidence that he bought his furniture at auction. Both James Wyatt, Beckford's architect at Fonthill, and Franchi, his closest companion between around 1796 and the 1820's, acted as advisors and agents. Franchi's importance as Beckford's advisor and agent is well-known, shown by the constant references to purchases in the letters between Beckford and Franchi from 1807 until Franchi's death in 1827, as well as from the regular sums of money sent by Beckford to Franchi in London.[44] James Wyatt purchased items for Beckford, and from quite an early date, to judge by the reference in Beckford's letter to Nicholas Williams on October 12, 1796, in which he wrote, "Wyatt has been buying a lot of commissions [illegible] for me—some very fine Japan[,] a pair of bronze tripods . . . he talks of a large coffer [illegible] price ten guineas—I have ample room for it."[45] A year later, he referred to a Japanese box in the style Wyatt had bought for him.

Beckford seems to have used Edward Foxhall, his cabinetmaker, until his death in 1815,[46] after which Beckford employed Robert Hume the younger,[47] who was also a cabinetmaker. Hume would seem to have taken over from Foxhall in carrying out tasks in London and providing furniture; he also acted as Beckford's agent after Franchi's death in 1827.[48]

In addition, Beckford used the leading London dealers, who

were beginning to emerge as important figures in the art market in the early nineteenth century.[49] In his correspondence with Franchi, Beckford refers to two of the best-known dealers in London, Robert Fogg[50] and Edward Holmes Baldock,[51] both of whom were known primarily as dealers in porcelains but had furniture in their shops. Although Beckford did not mention purchasing furniture from him, Baldock certainly sold the types of furniture Beckford was acquiring, although perhaps not until later. Baldock's name does not appear in the sale catalogues as a buyer until the 1820s. He seems to have become increasingly important as a dealer, and after 1830 he had among his clients many of the richest and most influential collectors of his day. At the 1823 Fonthill sale, one of the few items of furniture he bought was the great ebony cabinet designed around 1815 for the Abbey. Fogg probably began dealing in furniture at an earlier date; his name appears in auction sales at least by 1805. Beckford wrote to Franchi in 1815 about Buhl pieces he had seen at Fogg's and in 1817 he commented: "It is a pity to let the mosaic table, bought years ago from Fogg remain buried."[52] This at least implies that he had been buying furniture from Fogg for some time.

After moving to Lansdown in 1822, Beckford commissioned furniture from Hume, taking close interest in the design of each piece, as can be seen in their correspondence during those years.[53] The letters also show that Hume acted as an agent for his purchases of books and works of art, and perhaps for some furniture Beckford acquired as well.

The Formation of Beckford's Taste

Many factors contributed to the development of Beckford's taste in furniture. His travels abroad, especially in Italy, Portugal, and France, between 1780 and 1798, when he finally returned to settle in England at Fonthill, seem to have been of great significance. Letters from this period occasionally mention details of works of art or interiors that he found interesting, and these fragments reveal something of the disparate elements that would later be combined in the interiors of Fonthill Abbey and Lansdown Crescent.

Arguably his many visits to Paris and his observation of French collecting traditions were the most important influences on his taste. His early concepts regarding furniture and their arrangement in interiors were confirmed on his 1783 visit to Paris, when he likely visited the homes of the most modern and fashionable figures of Parisian society, such as the Neckers, Madame de Luyne, M de Briossac who are mentioned in his letters.[54] In the 1780s a great number of Parisian *hôtels* were being built, which Beckford might have visited, even if not mentioned in his accounts, as some were accessible to the general, affluent public; the famous interiors designed by François-Joseph Belanger, architect to the Comte d'Artois, for the actress Sophie Arnaud, or the many *hôtels* designed by Claude-Nicolas Ledoux, an architect Beckford mentions in his letters. The Hôtel Thélusson (1778) by Ledoux, for example, was one residence where tourists were admitted with tickets. Beckford was not completely enthusiastic about everything he saw. He described the Parisian interiors as cold, stating that nothing could

enliven them. About Ledoux, he also had mixed views, calling him "the very prince of pomposity,"[55] yet visiting and admiring some of his projects. It is thus not surprising that Beckford later commissioned furniture from designers who had worked on projects with Ledoux in Paris, especially Jean-Guillaume Moitte[56] and the architect Jean Arnaud Raymond.[57]

During these early years in Paris, Beckford no doubt was introduced to Boulle furniture, the Japanese lacquer furniture, and the concept of the French cabinet. In a letter of 1784 Beckford described "de Chablis' snug little appartments [sic] . . . which are lined from top to bottom with beautiful cabinet pictures and exhale an odour of old japan and spiced rose leaves perfectly delectable."[58] The descriptions of the cabinets of earlier Parisian collectors were very similar. In the *hôtel* of the famous collector, Blondel de Gagny, (d1776) in the Place de Louis le Grand (the Place Vendôme), one of the cabinet rooms contained a very fine bronze placed on a Boulle low wardrobe, while nearby on a table of Lumakel marble, were displayed a vase of black Egyptian marble with gilt-bronze mounts, two Chinese vases, and small classical bronzes.[59] A porphyry vase mounted by Auguste and a great quantity of Japanese lacquer were also listed in the room. The same ingredients were to be found in the sale catalogues of these late eighteenth-century French collectors: hardstone vases and tabletops, Oriental and Sèvres porcelain, Japanese lacquer and Boulle furniture.[60] As much part of the cabinet as the paintings or the sculptures and bronzes, boulle furniture not surprisingly, was sought after by Beckford, and the quality had to be the best.

Another important component of this French taste was the emphasis on hardstone and marble objects. Collections of marble and porphyry tabletops appeared in the sale catalogues, and during the late eighteenth century, the *marchands-merciers* invented the idea of decorating low ebony cabinets with plaques of pietre dure, or Florentine mosaic, as it was often called at the time.[61] In 1782 the compiler of the catalogue of the sale of the opera singer Marie-Joséphine Laguerre commented, "These pieces, enriched with the decoration of Florentine hard stones were highly sought after in the previous century and in many Parisian cabinets, took their place beside the furniture of Boulle."[62] The effect this had on the young Beckford may be gauged by his singling out these two types of furniture in a letter that he wrote, possibly in 1793, from Paris: "All around the room, on every side—in every recess—the most superb armoires of brass and tortoiseshell presented themselves, intermingled with cabinets rich in clustered gems and polished mosaic pannels, not exceeded, I am quite certain, in point of beauty and costliness by the most valuable specimens of this species of furniture secluded in the Palazzo Vecchio of Florence itself."[63]

In England, there was a long-established tradition, a result of the Grand Tour, of collecting Florentine cabinets-on-stands with drawers of pietre-dure panels. While in Florence Beckford visited the Tribuna in the Uffizi, which seems to have made an impression on him; it was one of the few sights he described during his first Italian tour: "we entered a small luminous apartment, surrounded with cases richly decorated and filled with the most exquisite models of work-manship in bronze and various metals, classed in exact order. . . . The morning was gone before I could snatch myself away from the Tribune."[64] He went on to comment on the collection of cabinets and curiosities of the Medici. The role of the north and south Tribune rooms and the Green Cabinet room at Fonthill Abbey, and of the tower at Lansdown, may have been based on associations with the Uffizi Tribuna as a form of *Kunstkammer*, a collection of works of art. This included not only bronzes, antiquities, and paintings, but also creations in hardstone and rock crystal, shells and other naturalia, all mounted in the finest goldwork that could be produced in Florence.[65] That the Uffizi Tribuna also contained a spectacular cabinet in ebony, pietre dure, and gilt bronzes would have given authority to Beckford's interest in collecting furniture of this type. This visit probably confirmed his taste for pietre-dure furniture, and his interest in seventeenth-century cabinets may also have had its origin in his visit to the Medici collections, although he never directly stated so.

He might also have been buying on these Italian travels: in 1782 he wrote about some of his discoveries of works of art, or of works in "old Japan," including a piece of rare lacquer he saw in the Medici collections.[66] After Florence, Beckford traveled to Naples, staying with his distant cousin Sir William Hamilton, but he makes no mention of any furniture that impressed him.

In the journals describing his several visits to Spain and Portugal between 1787 and 1797, Beckford also gave an account of what interested and impressed him, including observations on the furnishing of houses.[67] He noticed the fine work in marble and pietre dure, commented on the use of drapery in the interior, and praised a toilet service by Moitte.[68] Although he did not comment on it directly, furniture of exotic rosewood and ebony dating from the seventeenth century and carved ebony cabinets, now generally called Indo-Portuguese, may have had a profound influence on his taste. In this, more than in any other respect, Beckford differed from his continental peers, falling much more within the traditions of collecting in England. Ebony furniture had been acquired for Strawberry Hill by Horace Walpole who was among the first to be interested in it. This type of furniture has been identified since that time as coming from India, on the Coromandel coast, and Ceylon as well as from the Dutch colonies in Indonesia.[69] Walpole thought his chairs were Tudor, however, and there seems to have been little, if any, awareness in England of their foreign origin at that date.[70]

Parallels for Beckford's interest in French fashion can be found in England. There was a long-established tradition of buying works of art from the shops and dealers in Paris.[71] Moreover, in 1783 the Prince of Wales, later George IV, commissioned Henry Holland to design his residence, Carlton House. Not only was Holland greatly influenced by French architectural treatises but he was also instrumental in employing various French suppliers, craftsmen, and decorators in his buildings. Beckford does not comment in his letters on seeing Carlton House or other Holland interiors, but he certainly owned furniture and works of art in this taste, including several pieces designed by Boileau, who worked with Holland, which appeared in the 1801 sale of the furnishings of Fonthill.[72] Holland also collaborated with Dominique Daguerre to purchase contemporary French furniture, ceramics, and clocks for the prince.[73] Daguerre held a sale in 1791, which brought some of his stock onto the London market, and in general the London sales gradually showed an increase in the number of pieces of French furniture available at this date.[74] Thus the sale after the death of the Countess of Holderness in 1802 was described as having a "profusion of French furniture," most of which was contemporary in style.[75] In these purchases English collectors seemed not to be imitating French collecting traditions, but to be eager to own French porcelain or furniture in the latest fashion made in Paris. The taste for Boulle furniture and hardstones, which formed such an important part of the French cabinet, did not truly become prevalent in England until around the beginning of the nineteenth century. Horace Walpole, who prefigured Beckford in his buying of furniture and in his cabinet room, did not create the entirety of the French cabinet as Beckford seems to have done.[76]

Furniture in French taste

Some of Beckford's earliest acquisitions were pieces of English furniture inspired by French design. There is considerable evidence to show that he, like other members of fashionable society, purchased and commissioned such pieces and kept some of them in his collection at least until 1823. In 1801 he sold several pieces made by Boileau.[77]

There were also a number of French-made pieces—a marquetry pier table with ormolu mounts, as well as a French commode with three drawers, also of marquetry and with ormolu mounts.[78] Beckford had shown his taste for contemporary French design early in his travels, and some of the furniture he acquired may have been an attempt to re-create a Parisian interior.[79] He obviously also kept some furniture in this style long after; there is late-eighteenth-century French furniture in the 1817 sale from his London house in Lower Harley Street, among them a "beautiful cabinet with 9 drawers . . . of old Japan, with slab at top, and lower shelf of Brocadella marble" decorated with ormolu.[80] According to the catalogue it had belonged to the Comte d'Artois as part of the furnishings of his folly, Bagatelle, in the Bois de Boulogne.[81] Such a piece might have been collected by Beckford partly for its intrinsic interest as an example that incorporated Japanese lacquer, but possibly also partly for its association with a member of the French royal family.

Of commissioned pieces, while in Paris in the 1790s Beckford may have ordered at least two and probably three cabinets from leading Parisian designers and makers. One of these was described by the painter Piat Joseph Sauvage, who, in a petition to the Commission of Monuments in the autumn of 1793, declared that he had received 17,000 *livres* (equal to about £45,000 in 2000) from Beckford as part payment for a secretaire decorated with fifty-six paintings "in cameos and other forms."[82] This secretaire was designed by the architect Jean

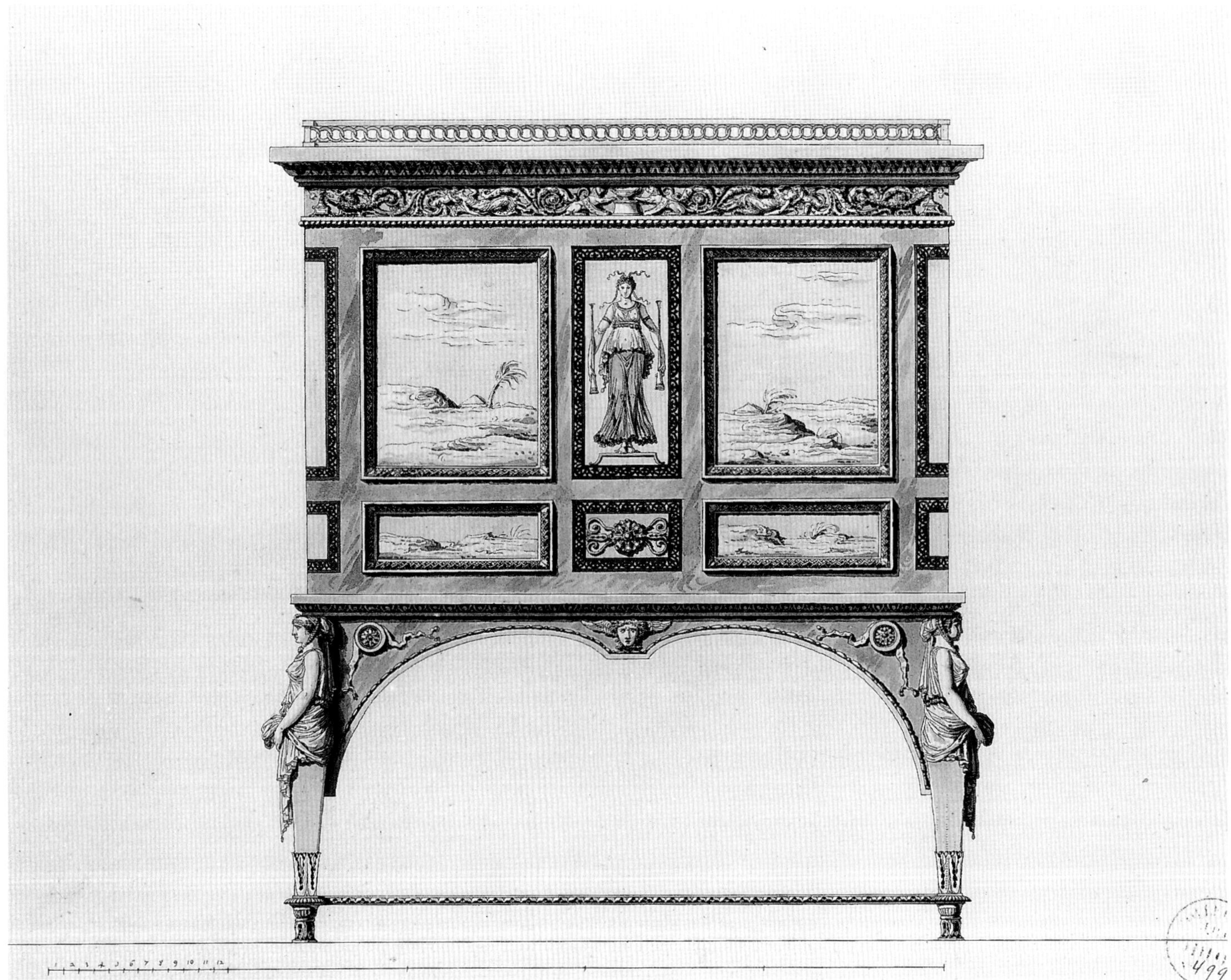

Fig. 10-2. Henri Auguste after Jean-Guillaume Moitte. Preliminary design for a jewel casket, ca. 1790–95. Pen and gray wash. Trustees of the Victoria and Albert Museum, London.

Arnaud Raymond, the mounts were executed by "Raimond" (thought to be François Rémond, *ciseleur*), and Adam Weisweiler was paid for the cabinetwork.[83]

In 1801 Sauvage wrote in the *Journal de Paris* on October 10 that he had completed a *secrétaire*, possibly the one mentioned in the previous commission as it was ascribed to the same makers. Ten days earlier in the same paper, he had described the piece as "all that the most renowned names can supply by way of the most precious marble, agate and crystal, all that a cabinetmaker can execute with the utmost delicacy, everything that a sculptor can provide by way of the rich and new bronze ornaments."[84] Thus either Beckford changed his mind from the 1793 commission or he had ordered a second *secrétaire*.

There is also a drawing for "un diamentaire de Lord Beckford" by Auguste to designs by Moitte (fig. 10-2), which suggests that

Beckford may have commissioned a jewel cabinet during his 1792–93 stay in Paris, although whether it was actually made is uncertain.[85] The design is similar to other works by Moitte at this date. The inscription, however, has also been read as "lord Bedford," suggesting an association with the fifth Duke of Bedford, who is known to have visited Paris in 1786.[86] A jewel coffer on a stand based on this design exists, arguably the one commissoned by Beckford.[87] The coffer, however, does not match the Moitte design, nor either of the descriptions in Sauvage's declarations of 1793 or 1801 making it difficult to assume it was Beckford's. The design may indeed reflect the type of furniture Beckford was commissioning in Paris; the fact that Beckford admired Auguste is well documented, and Auguste often worked to Moitte's designs.[88] The mounts and frieze of the stand of the jewel coffer are of the highest quality and give an indication of the standard of work being done by Auguste and Moitte for Beckford in furniture as well as in silver. Neither the *diamentaire* nor the *secrétaire* described by Sauvage appeared in any of the Beckford sales, nor in the inventory taken at Lansdown after Beckford's death; they may have disappeared from Beckford's collection at a fairly early date, if indeed they were ever delivered.[89]

The third cabinet associated with Beckford is a cabinet with Japanese lacquer, based on a drawing by Moitte.[90] There was a similar cabinet with lacquer panels described in the 1822 Christie's catalogue,[91] and, as no cabinet by Auguste was listed in the 1823 sale, it is possible that Beckford took it with him to Bath in 1822. There is a letter from Hume in 1830, suggesting that Beckford wanted to sell his Auguste cabinet, which might therefore be this piece.[92]

After his return to England in 1793, Beckford commissioned two lacquer cabinets with gilt-bronze mounts from the Vulliamy family; the mounts in particular are very similar to the designs of Moitte and Auguste.[93] These were supplied by Benjamin and Benjamin Louis Vulliamy in 1803 (fig. 10-3), and stood in the Octagon at Fonthill. The Vulliamy accounts give a detailed description of the manufacture of these secretaires, including the fact that a lacquer box was cut up and reused and that a "Very great number of Patterns were made for all the different parts of the Metal Work," the cost coming to the very great sum of 850 guineas (about £42,000).[94] These were not the only pieces of furniture ordered by Beckford from this firm, although they are the only examples known to have survived. The Vulliamy's were given two other equally important and innovative commissions by Beckford at much the same time. One of these commissions was for a large mahogany cabinet with veneers of satinwood, amarynth, and ebony, inlaid with metal stringing and decorated with gilt-bronze mounts and smaller cabinets to match.[95] The other was for a pair of metal pier tables, each with three legs in the form of chimera.[96] The use of metal for furniture had been among the innovations introduced by designers such as Dugourc; a number of such tables made by Weisweiler working for such designers still survive. The following year, Beckford had the pier tables joined as a library table with six legs.[97]

These two commissions not only show Beckford having furniture made for him in the latest taste, and again at quite an expense, but also show him as one of the first patrons who asked the Vulliamys to make furniture for him, possibly because of their knowledge of French style and craftsmanship.[98] It would seem, moreover, that he was among the first, if not the first, to order this type of furniture from the firm and was followed shortly afterward by the Duke of Bedford, who also had two bronze tables made in 1805 and 1811 (probably those now at Woburn Abbey),[99] and Lord Kinnaird, who ordered a pair of bronze candelabra with mahogany pedestals in 1807–8 (now at Brighton Pavilion).[100] The Vulliamy account books continue until 1815 but Beckford's name does not reappear after 1803. One explanation may be that it was because the Prince of Wales monopolized Vulliamys with his extensive requests[101]; it may also be that Beckford turned to smaller firms where he could control the design more closely and save costs.[102]

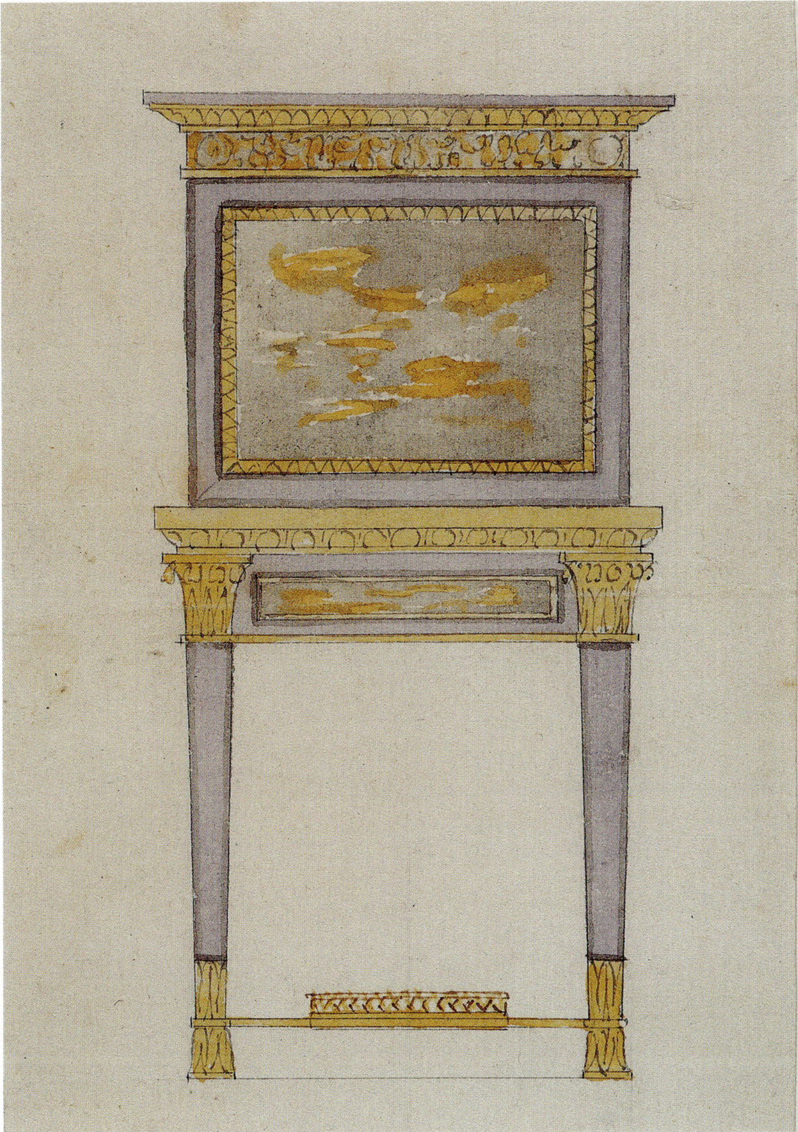

Fig. 10-3. Attributed to Benjamin and Benjamin Louis Vulliamy. Preliminary design for a secretaire, ca. 1803. Pen and watercolor. Bodleian Library, Oxford, MS Beckford c. 83, fol. 113.

Boulle furniture

In his taste for the brass and tortoiseshell furniture of the seventeenth-century cabinetmaker André–Charles Boulle, *ébéniste* to Louis XIV, Beckford came closest in spirit to the late-eighteenth-century Parisian collectors. The fashion for these sumptuous and formal pieces of furniture had never died out completely, even in the height of the rococo, and with the advent of the "true" or "antique" taste of the later eighteenth century, such furniture was even more fashionable. Thus in the sales of the great French collectors of the previous generation, from the 1770s onward, Boulle furniture appeared regularly.[103] Sometimes the catalogues from this period are explicit as to whether the furniture was made in Boulle's lifetime or merely used the techniques that bear his name. In the London sale catalogues, the descriptions refer to Buhl furniture, furniture in buhl and tortoiseshell; only occasionally were the pieces given a specific date or referred to as being antique. This

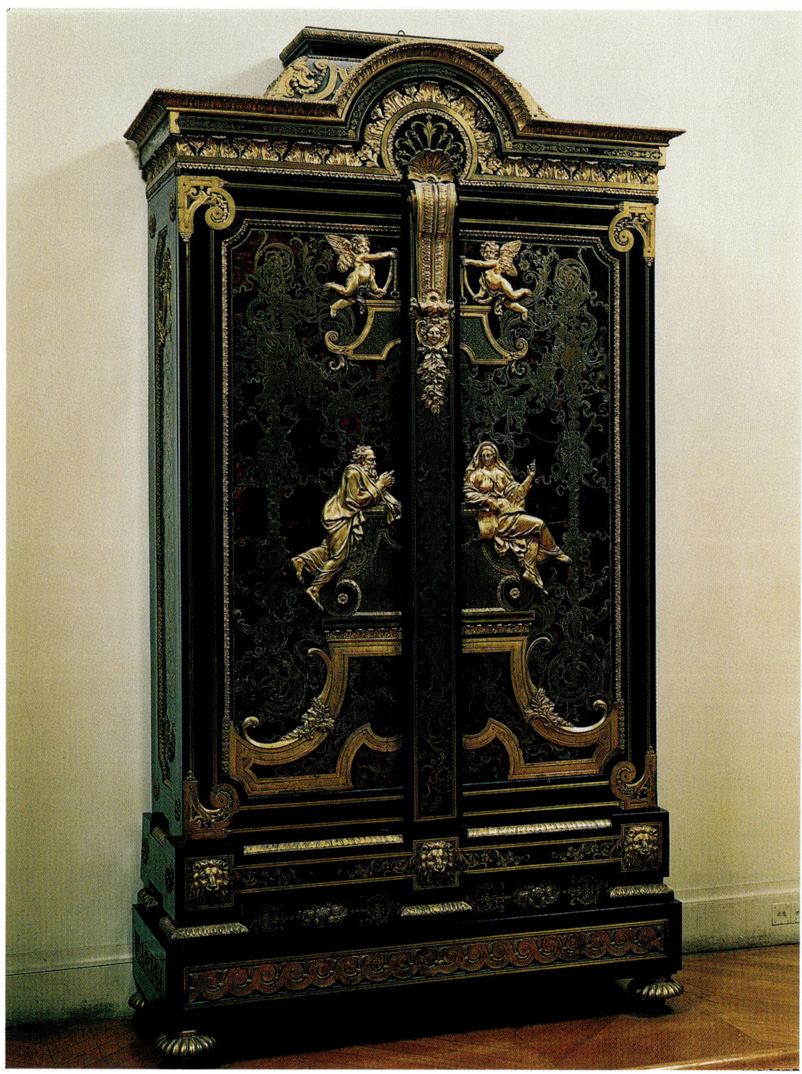

Fig. 10-4. André-Charles Boulle. Armoire. Tortoiseshell and brass (*première parte*) on oak, gilt-bronze mounts. Musée du Louvre, Paris, 88EE2128

reflects the difficulties attached to the term Boulle or Buhl, the English translation of Boulle. It could be used to mean furniture in tortoiseshell and brass made in the second half of the reign of Louis XIV (1648–1715) or furniture using the same materials from a later date, including contemporary pieces, which by 1800 were being made in both France and England. The term was even used for any furniture with metal, either in bands or in marquetry, often set into exotic wood veneers of rosewood, mahogany or, especially in Beckford's case, ebony. All of these types figured in Beckford's interiors and reflected the growing taste for original Boulle pieces as well as furniture in the Boulle technique. Beckford sold ten items described as "Buhl" in the 1817 sale, and there were nineteen itemized in the 1822 Christie's sale catalogue of Fonthill Abbey.

Some of Beckford's collection would seem to have been pieces of early, original Boulle furniture. In *Description of Fonthill* of 1812,

Storer wrote that the Yellow Damask Room contained "some of the finest cabinets of japan and Buhl work in Europe." One of them "formerly adorned the apartments of Fontainebleau, and is remarkable for a beautiful medallion of Lewes [sic] the Fourteenth." Another royal piece in Beckford's collection was a wardrobe of Boulle and red tortoiseshell in the Crimson Drawing Room, said to have been made for Louis XV's cabinet at Versailles.[104] Among the most celebrated pieces of Boulle furniture at Fonthill Abbey was the pair of wardrobes, claimed by Beckford to have come from the duc d'Aumont's collection (fig. 10-4).[105] These wardrobes appear in Rutter's book on Fonthill (1823), although not Storer's, suggesting that they were acquired after 1812. In fact Beckford's correspondence in the summer of 1814 mentioned that he was considering buying a pair of Boulle cabinets from Fogg.[106] They may later have replaced a Boulle cabinet sold in 1817, described as a "magnificent cabinet, the upper part with eleven drawers and central doors, . . . of Boulle work; a press underneath with folding doors, panelled with plate glass and lined with crimson silk."[107] This indicates perhaps that an original seventeenth-century French cabinet was combined with a later base. The description of the cabinet is very close to that of a cabinet-on-stand, with a crested top of intertwined initials, which was sold by George Watson Taylor from his London house in Cavendish Square in 1825.[108] Even if it is impossible to be certain that they were one and the same cabinet, it shows the close correlation in taste between certain collectors at that time.

Other examples of original seventeenth-century Boulle in Beckford's collection may have been the candlestands in the Grand Drawing Room at Fonthill. It is known that Boulle made these stands in some quantity and illustrated them in his published designs.[109] Beckford had already sold two pairs of candlestands in 1817, one in red tortoiseshell; the other was of ebony and tortoiseshell, "inlaid with steel [pewter] and brass."[110] There were three candlestands illustrated in Britton's view, and it is possible that two pairs described in the 1823 Phillips catalogue refer to these: "a pair of ancient Buhl tripods, designed with simple elegance, and enriched with BRONZE gilt."[111] According to the view of Saint Michael's Gallery in Rutter's, there was at least one other pair of similar stands at Fonthill. These had green marble tops and the shape, as rendered by Rutter, seems slightly different from the drawing room set.[112] It is worth considering, therefore, that this last pair could have been made to Beckford's order rather than being early Boulle work.

The imitation of these stands, closely following original Boulle models, is all the more interesting in the light of the Boulle revival of the early nineteenth century. The cabinets illustrated in Rutter's views of Saint Michael's Gallery were probably in this revival style. They were described as being made of "ebony, buhl & tortoiseshell" with crimson silk lining and tops of black marble.[113] Others, possibly those in the Yellow Drawing Room, were similarly in buhl and tortoiseshell but with green marble tops.[114]

In view of the many sales of Boulle furniture in Paris at the end of the eighteenth century, Beckford or any other English visitors could have acquired Boulle furniture while there, although at significant prices. There were thirty-seven pieces said to be in Boulle marquetry in the Randon de Boisset sale (1777) and nineteen in the Blondel de Gagny sale the same year, not including those said to be in the taste of Boulle.[115] There were not many collectors on this scale, and more typical in number were the five lots in the duc d'Aumont's sale in 1782. At this time the price for Boulle furniture could be extremely high. Of the type of Boulle furniture acquired by Beckford, there was a pair of cabinets-on-stand with the medallion of Louis XIV in the Randon de Boisset sale (lot 777), which sold for 3,001 *livres* (equal to £9,000 in 2000).[116] Candlestands in the sale ranged significantly in their prices; the highest being 10,000 livres (£30,000) for a pair (lot 795) while two other pairs, of similar size and description (lots 793 and 794) fetched 1,500 livres (£4,500) and 1300 livres (£3,900). There were not as many cabinets; one pair of low cabinets, of exceptional quality, was sold for 4,701 livres (£14,000). More typical no doubt were the several low cabinets sold in the Blondel de Gagny sale for about 950 livres (£2,900) to 1,000 livres (£3,000) each. Many of the lots were sold to intermediaries; some, such as Jean-Baptiste-Pierre Lebrun, were dealers and later auctioneers; others, such as Vincent Donjeux or Ph. F Julliot, were *marchands merciers* with fashionable shops, who also bought on their own account.[117] There is no evidence, however, that any English collectors were buying Boulle at this date.[118]

Although there seem to have been fewer sales in general at the beginning of the Revolution, Lebrun's sale in 1791 had several items of Boulle, including some stands identified from previous sales. Two stands (lot 767) bought for 1,605 livres (equal to £4,250 in 2000) in the Randon de Boissot sale were sold for 1,001 livres in 1791 (£2,700) while a pair of low cabinets (lot 769) with a satyr's masque were 1,220 livres (£3,200). During the winter of 1792 and spring of 1793 there were a number of sales with Boulle furniture.[119] Whether prices were significantly lower for Boulle pieces is difficult to determine, given the problems of comparing pieces of varying descriptions with each other. In the case of one lot, the evidence would suggest that prices had indeed fallen. A cabinet with a central mount of Apollo flaying Marsyas bought in 1777 for 2,003 livres (£6,000) sold for only 800 livres (£2,000) in 1793.[120] The Boulle furniture sold at the Choiseul-Praslin sale, which was also in 1793, on the other hand, reached much higher prices, with two very fine stands (*gaines*) 3 feet, 11 inches high (lot 243) fetching 1,260 livres (£3,200) and a sarcophagus commode (lot 240) 2,901 livres (£7,400).[121]

Beckford might have found it difficult to acquire original Boulle furniture of the quality he sought when he returned to Paris in 1814, although he wrote of his impatience to acquire more works of art. This may explain the mixed account in his letters regarding the possibilities of buying.[122] It may also explain why he bought the Boulle wardrobes from Fogg's in December 1814 (perhaps the same ones he failed to buy the previous summer), even at the high price of £400 (equal to £15,000 in 2000).[123]

There seem to have been fewer sales of Boulle furniture between 1803 and 1815, and certainly not on the scale of those held in the late eighteenth century.[124] During this period the market for Boulle may no longer have been found among Parisian collectors. In the 1814 inventory of the contents of Malmaison, taken after the death of the Empress Joséphine, there was no Boulle furniture,[125] and Boulle furniture of any significance was absent from the sales immediately after 1815. Two low armoires in Cardinal Fesch's sale in 1816, which were sold for 616 francs (equal to about £1,100 in 2000),[126] were the only Boulle items. The cabinets and armoires sold in sales during the following years generally reached a price in the region of 1000 francs or less and were seemingly not of great interest. An exception was the sale of the stock of the dealer, Madame LeRouge, in 1818, at which there were thirteen lots of Boulle furniture, most of which interestingly were sold to the painter Bonnemaison, who also acted as a dealer for the Duke of Wellington.[127] At the same sale a pair of cabinets (lot 118) fetched 3,805 francs (£6,200), and another small piece (lot 123) went to the dealer Perignon for 4,005 francs (£6,500). The furniture is titled "meuble de Boule," but descriptions make it more likely that the pieces were in the Boulle style rather than made by Boulle himself.[128] After this 1818 it was only not until the 1824 sale of the dealer Maelrondt, who also had dealings with London clients, that a significant number of Boulle pieces were to be found in Paris.[129]

By 1815 in London the taste for Boulle furniture may have made the prices higher but also have brought increasing quantities of Boulle furniture onto the market.[130] Earlier, at the sale of Beau Brummel in 1807, there were only three pieces: two jewel boxes, one of which was bought by Vulliamy for £112 16s (equal to £4,750 in 2000), and a commode with scagliola top, sold for an unspecified sum.[131] Lord Kinnaird, a friend of the Prince Regent, owned at least one piece Boulle furniture before 1815; a Boulle commode was offered in his sale in 1813 as part of a collection of fine French furniture.[132]

From 1816 onwards auctions with significant quantities of Boulle furniture began to take place. In each of the four sales of Parisian furniture held by Phillips in the following years, there were a number of Boulle pieces, some of which could well be from the seventeenth century, while others seem in a later style.[133] Although "Buhl" figures in the title, however, there were probably fewer examples than suggested, except for the first sale in 1816, which listed pieces with royal provenances. In a 1818 sale, there were only three pieces identified as being by Boulle: one medal cabinet and two armoires. The medal cabinet, seemingly estimated at £90, in fact sold for £58 16s (equal to £2,300 in 2000).[134] The two armoires, however, were much more highly priced at £100 (£3,900) for one and 275 guineas (£11,300) for the other; they came from the royal palace at Compiègne. The price paid by the Duke of Hamilton of £509 5s (£27,700) for each of the great wardrobes in 1823 reflects a similar awareness of rarity and provenance, as well as the likelihood of an increased market in Boulle furniture.[135]

By 1823 it was the English collectors who were seeking important pieces of Boulle furniture, whereas there seems to have been less interest in Paris for such ancien régime furniture. Beckford's collection, as represented at Fonthill Abbey, contained pieces of the highest quality. The extent of his acquisitions by 1812 indicates that he was among the first Englishmen to buy antique Boulle on this scale. From an analysis of the markets for Boulle furniture, it would seem that whether he bought in Paris or London, he probably paid dearly for the quality of furniture that he desired. The complexity of the market further indicates, that although prices might have dropped considerably during the first years of the French Revolution, when some of the Boulle furniture with royal provenance presumably came on the market, even that cannot be taken as certain. Moreover, although it seems as if French collectors were no longer prepared to pay large sums for Boulle furniture, the French dealers had a new market in England.

Furniture in pietre dure

In keeping with contemporary taste, Beckford furnished his interiors with furniture surmounted by marble or hardstone tops. One exceptional piece was the circular table with top of *brêche universelle* marble in the Grand Drawing Room at Fonthill Abbey, that came from Malmaison (see cat. no. 88).[136] Beckford was also influenced by the Parisian fashion for decorating contemporary low cabinets with plaques of what was often earlier Florentine work in pietre dure that coincided in the second half of the eighteenth century with the taste for reusing Japanese lacquer or inserting Sèvres plaques into furniture. The extent of his interest is attested by the number of low cabinets that appeared in his sales, two commodes with panels of pietre dure in his 1817 sale[137]; three cabinets as well as the small caskets said to have come from the Pitti palace in the 1822 catalogue.[138] The one in the cabinet room was described in the 1822 sale catalogue as "a singularly beautiful and costly armoire of ebony, centred between two fluted columns with capitals of ormoulu between which is a superb pannel (sic) of Florentine mosaic" with a vase of flowers and four small drawers with birds on each side.[139] This was sold for £252 (equal to £14,600 in 2000), which was less than some prices realized in late-eighteenth-century Paris, where the catalogues of sales give some indication of the high prices fetched at that date. Two cabinets, sold at the duc d'Aumont's sale in 1782 were bought by Paillet for Louis XVI at 5,708 livres (about £17,500), in comparison to two Boulle cabinets at 2,451 livres (£7,500).[140] In an anonymous sale of 1803 there was also one cabinet (lot 554), which was at 3,200 livres (about £6,500), by far the most expensive item sold. Once more it was a tripartite cabinet, decorated with Florentine mosaic panels, brass on ebony with gilt-bronze mounts, such as those cabinets cited in the late-eighteenth-century inventories and sales.[141]

In view of the great vogue for these low cabinets in the early nineteenth century both in England and France, it is perhaps surprising that Beckford did not buy more. They were certainly available on the market, at least in Paris. The Prince of Wales was particularly interested in such cabinets, and one or possibly two were bought as early as 1791 in the Daguerre sale, while others were bought later in Paris.[142] The appearance of such cabinets at this date on the London market,

however, seems to have been exceptional. It is not until 1816 that a similar cabinet appeared in the auction catalogues; in the sale of Sir Gerrard Noel it was described as "a beautiful cabinet, formed of tortoiseshell and ebony enriched with mosaic medallions of birds, fruits, and flowers" when it sold for 65 guineas (equal to £3,000 in 2000).[143] Two years later a cabinet inlaid with beautiful specimens of mosaic in birds and flowers and lapis lazuli and ormolu enrichments sold for 140 guineas (£5,800).[144] This was, moreover, a significant increase on the 1,255 francs (£2,500) the amount for which an ebony piece with Florentine mosaic sold in Paris, in the 1824 sale of the dealer Feuchère.[145] The difference in price and the relative scarcity of such cabinets in the later Paris sales would suggest that English collectors were most interested in acquiring these cabinets.

One of the most tantalizing descriptions in Storer's description of Fonthill was of "two tables of the rarest Florentine work, imitating shells, corals and pearls, upon grounds of lapis lazuli and oriental alabaster" in the green cabinet room. These were lots 1019 and 1020 in the 1823 sale and as the catalogue makes clear, one top depicted a design of shells while the other consisted of a more unusual design of flowers and insects, set into a background of Oriental alabaster. Apart from the fact that they are described as having twisted legs, the closest comparison that can be made is with the tabletops designed for the *Opificie delle Pietre dure* by Zocchi around 1765. The design of shells against a lapis lazuli ground was popular and was repeated throughout the second half of the eighteenth century, with later designers adapting rococo shapes to a more classical outlines. The second table of flowers and insects was much rarer, and only one example is known today, which is in the Louvre.[146]

These tables with their pictorial images are very different from those commonly found in England at that date.[147] They might indeed have been bought by Beckford in Paris, where there certainly was a growing taste for tabletops in pietre-dure mosaic after around 1800, inspired no doubt by the Florentine work that was sent to Paris from the Palazzo Pitti on Napoléon's orders. Seventeen pieces were listed in an inventory of 1801 taken in Paris of objects destined for the Louvre and more were to be sent later from Florence.[148] In general these were eighteenth-century tables with decorative scenes, Etruscan vases, or scenes of the four seasons. There were several depicting seashells as well as a pair with butterflies and insects on a ground of lapis lazuli divided into five compartments. It is certainly possible that Beckford saw these tables in his 1802–3 visit to Paris and was influenced by this new taste for mosaic tops in pietre dure. On the other hand, although such tabletops, with Florentine pietre-dure decoration, appeared on the Paris market, none can be identified with the Beckford tables. One of the most important sales of this period was that of L'Espinasse d'Arlet in 1803, in which there were a great many tables with tops of rare hardstones and marbles, such as commonly found in the great sales of the late eighteenth century. Of the thirty-nine lots of such pieces, four were described as of Florentine work.[149] The descriptions are brief and too vague to compare precisely with Beckford's tables: lot 102 was a large table with *echantillons,* or small patterns; lot 99 was a large table top of antique pietre dure, supported on a putto; while lot 109 consisted of fifteen panels of Florentine mosaic, suitable to decorate a piece of furniture. The fourth piece, was an ebony cabinet in the form of a *sécrétaire* with nine panels of early Florentine work depicting scenes of ruins and figures. Thus, even in this sale, out of so many items, there was only one table that could be said to be in the same taste as Beckford's tables decorated with intarsia of pietre dure.

The great table with a pietre-dure top (fig. 10-5 and 10-6) of around 1600, which stood in King Edward III's Gallery at Fonthill Abbey, was one of the most notable items in the 1823 sale. With its purported provenance from the Borghese Palace as well as its immense size, it sold for the considerable sum of £1,890 in 1823 (equal to £103,000 in 2000) to George Lucy, who outbid all the other contenders for it; and the top remains one of the most important examples of pietre dure in England. Of Oriental onyx, various jaspers, and other stones, it has geometric borders of arabesques typical of late-sixteenth-century and early-seventeenth-century Roman work, so that the Borghese attribution may very well be correct. It cannot be certain, however, where, when, or how Beckford acquired it.[150] It did not, significantly, appear in Storer's 1812 description and so must not have come into Beckford's possession after that publication.

It is possible that these tops were acquired in England rather than France, as the English were also trading directly with Italian dealers, although most of the evidence comes from later than the 1823 Fonthill sale.[151] In 1803 and again in 1804, however, two sales of paintings from the Borghese and Pitti palaces took place in London, which implies there might have been direct imports of Italian works of art into England. In this context, it is interesting that George Lucy bought a second tabletop, similar to Beckford's, in 1824, suggesting that pietre dure furniture of this date was becoming more available in England.[152]

An important figure in this trade was the Abbé Celotti who seems to have worked in both Paris and London specializing in importing Italian works of art. In 1819 he held a sale in Paris of cabinets, tables, and other small pieces of furniture.[153] He is mentioned again in connection with the dealer Swaby, to whom he sold a number of Italian chairs,[154] and he also seems to have specialized in Renaissance manuscripts.[155] From a letter written by Celotti in 1825, in which he gives a London address, he presumably maintained some sort of presence there.[156] It is possible, but there is no evidence, that Celotti supplied Beckford with some of his cabinets or tables in pietre dure, but none of the descriptions in his sales matched any of Beckford's furniture precisely. It is also curious perhaps that there is no mention of any of these tables in Beckford's correspondence with Franchi or Hume.

At Lansdown, Beckford had an equally important top in early pietre dure and marble. A "Parallelogram table of pietre commesse" was in Lansdown Tower, "the centre being a unique specimen of African marble, surrounded by arabesques of various costly and uncommon marbles, banded with an enriched ormolu moulding."[157] Thus at both Fonthill and Lansdown, tables of antique pietre dure were com-

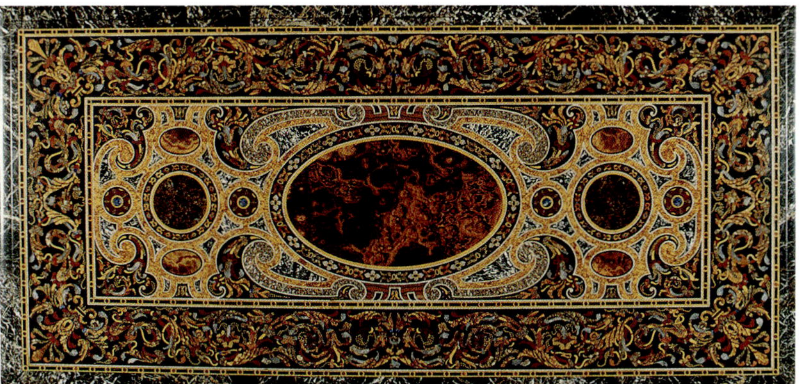

Fig. 10-5. Tabletop. Rome, 16th century. Pietre dure. The National Trust, Charlecote Park.

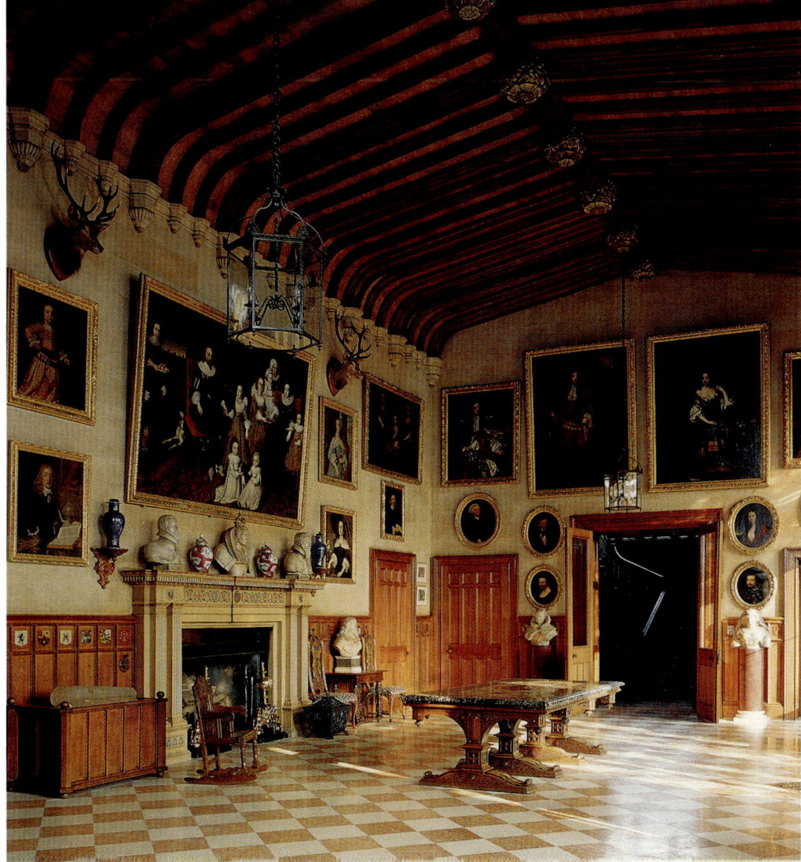

Fig. 10-6. Beckford's 16th-century tabletop, on a base made for him, in the Great Hall, Charlecote Park, Warwickshire. Photographed ca. 1999. The National Trust, Charlecote Park.

bined with lacquer and important Renaissance works of art to create the sumptuous effects of the *Kunstkammer*. Acquisition of this type of furniture was part of a new tradition—although possibly emerging from that of the late eighteenth century—and Beckford was integral to establishing the taste for bolder, more sumptuously rich, and strongly designed Italian tops inlaid in pietre dure and marbles made in the seventeenth and eighteenth centuries.

Riesener and French Royal Furniture

Several examples of furniture were attributed to the royal cabinetmaker, Jean-Henri Riesener in the 1823 Fonthill sale, thus linking Beckford's name indirectly with the purchase of eighteenth-century royal furniture, and Beckford has often been considered an important collector of French furniture that was historicist rather than contemporary in style. There is no certain proof, however, that he ever acquired these pieces.[158] Only one such piece can be confirmed as having belonged to Beckford, namely the comte d'Orsay desk now at the Wallace Collection (see fig. 10-1), illustrated in Rutters' *Delineations of Fonthill*; it sold for £179 15s (equal to £9,800 in 2000) in 1823 to Boss.[159] This desk was described in the 1822 catalogue as having come from the *Garde Meuble*.[160] In fact, it has been identified with a desk made for the comte d'Orsay, whose residence Beckford rented between 1788 and 1790. Various suggestions have been made as to when he might have acquired it, including the possibility that he bought it while renting the house.[161] The desk was listed in an inventory taken at the Hôtel d'Orsay in 1795, however, and Beckford was not in Paris at that date, so could not have bought it directly from the count.[162] Although it is conceivable that Nicholas William bought it before he left France in 1797, it is also possible that Beckford bought it at a later date, on a subsequent visit to Paris.

It is surprising that Beckford made no mention of the desk's correct provenance, assuming that he knew it; more importantly, whether it was his intention or not, the desk was considered a royal piece until recently. Ancien régime furniture was purchased avidly by the Prince of Wales from an early date, as shown in his acquisitions at the Daguerre sale of 1791. As furniture from the French royal palaces appeared on the market, the royal provenance became an essential part of the grand collections of the early nineteenth century, with the Marquess of Hertford, George Watson Taylor, or the Duke of Hamilton among the leading exponents. There was only one sale in London before the end of the century of French royal imports that included furniture. This sale, "Parisian Elegancies from the Palace of Versailles", held by Phillips in April 1798, consisted mainly of porcelain and small objects d'art. It also included, however, a library table of bronze figures supporting a marble top, and two writing tables, one in "the most choice wood" and one in mahogany, which because of their mechanical fittings were probably roll-top desks.[163] While one of these was valued at £105 (equal to £6,200 in 2000), the other was probably much less important, as a similar desk sold the following year for only £27 6s. (£1,400). It would seem that the high prices for ancien régime furniture were yet to come.

The name Riesener also appeared for the first time in London then, and by 1818 a Phillips sale of Parisian furniture scheduled for May 30, 1818, was described as "the most splendid assemblage of decorative furniture by Buhl and Reisner that has yet been imported."[164] "Riesener" seems to have been used in the catalogues of this period much as "Buhl" had been before, signifying a style rather than a firm attribution to Riesener. Sometimes the price may give an indication of authenticity, as for example, in the 1818 Phillips sale, a writing table in "marqueterie de Riesener" only sold for £8 15s (equal to £340 in 2000), as opposed to a "splendid secretaire and cabinet," which sold for 51 guineas (£2,100).[165] In these early sales, the Riesener furniture seems to be valued at marginally less than the Boulle furniture, but by 1825 at the Watson Taylor sale of furniture from his house in Cavendish Square, this had changed. A Boulle pier table in a sarcophagus form sold for £48 6s (£2,100 in 2000), even with its provenance given as having belonged to Louis XIV; the only piece firmly attributed to Riesener in the catalogue, a jewel cabinet made for the comtesse de Provence, wife of the comte de Provence, later Louis XVIII, was bought for the exceptional price of £514 10s. (£22,100) by George IV.[166] Without the Riesener attribution, a floral marquetry commode from Versailles was valued at only £58 16s (£2,500).[167] Beckford's purchase of the Riesener desk thus once again appears to anticipate a fashion that was to develop as a major trend among English collectors in the nineteenth century. Although he may not have bought Riesener on the scale that he has sometimes been credited with, which, given the sales from the Royal Palaces, would no doubt have been possible, nonetheless the desk was an important ingredient of the splendor of Fonthill Abbey.

Acquiring Historicist Pieces

Because of the importance of Fonthill Abbey in the history of the Gothic Revival, its furniture, made to complement these interiors, has been widely studied.[168] It has been argued that Beckford commissioned furniture for the Abbey in the newly fashionable Tudor revival style, rather than pure Gothic.[169] It was therefore in this spirit that Beckford acquired the historicist furniture for which he is so well-known. Among these is the famous "Holbein" cabinet, said to have been made for Henry VIII, which was one of the highlights of the 1823 Fonthill sale (fig. 10-7). This is not described in Storer's description of the Abbey in 1812, and may have been acquired by Beckford after that date.[170] Beckford had already acquired similar collectors' items and in 1817 had sold "a pair of ivory carvings in pear-tree wood about the time of Holbein."[171] Also in the sale was a small jewel chest, with historical figures in relief, which was said to have been made during the reign of Edward III, and bought at the sale of the Cardinal of York's effects in Rome.[172] In terms of furniture, there were several items that were either antique or purporting to be so. Among these were two robe chests, said to be from the time of James I, now in the Wallace Collection. They were bought at the 1823 sale by the dealer, Mr. Broadway, for £89 18s and £94 10s respectively (about £5,000 in 2000), presumably for the Duke of Buckingham, as they were sold from his collection in 1848 with a Fonthill provenance.[173] These were clearly modern commissions, as were the Elizabethan cabinets-on-stands that appear in Britton's illustrations of King Edward III Gallery.

The interest in Tudor and Elizabethan furniture is well documented in collections, but very few original examples appear in the furniture sales of the period. Items such as the "Holbein" cabinet may more often have been bought through the new breed of dealers, who specialized in such antiquities.[174] Equally, they may have been included in a different type of sale, closer to the antiquarian tradition of collecting works of art, rather than furniture. For Beckford, however, this facet of his collecting seems to have been primarily concerned with creating the desired character for his interiors at Fonthill, as the pieces were made up in imitation of seventeenth-century furniture. Much of the furniture designed for the Abbey had turned legs as supports, reminiscent more of English seventeenth-century furniture than of anything earlier. At the time, however, there was little distinction between such styles and Beckford may have bought "the ancient dressing table with drawer, turned legs of walnut, top inlaid with flowers" as an example of Elizabethan taste. He also bought many ebony chairs with turned and twisted legs and backs, following the example of Horace Walpole, who had bought examples for Strawberry Hill. The entire Lancaster bedroom at Fonthill Abbey was decorated with this ebony furniture, a cause for comment in the press.[175]

In the following years, Edward Holmes Baldock was to deal extensively in carved ebony furniture, most of which is now thought to have come originally from the Coromandel Coast, in India as well as Sri Lanka and Indonesia. Beckford's furniture, as with many of the pieces bought in the nineteenth century, was partly original seventeenth-century work, partly made up of older elements, and sometimes combined with newly made elements.[176] It is not known whether Beckford realized that they were not Tudor survivals, but were being found in large quantities, and were possibly purchased from Amsterdam.

Also in ebony, but with different historical connotations, were a number of seventeenth-century cabinets-on-stands, some of which are described by Storer and, therefore, must have been in Beckford's possession by 1812. In the Octagon there were ebony and ivory cabinets; in the dressing room was a cabinet covered with silver mounts, which no doubt was one of the Franco-Flemish ebony cabinets of this type.[177] Beckford bought these cabinets to complement the interiors at Fonthill. He may have also had them in his London house, as suggested by the 1817 sale, which contained a "magnificent cabinet of ebony, lined with rosewood, the doors ends & friezes covered with engravings of bacchanalian figures, fruit & foliage, with Corinthian pillars on the corners." The cabinet rested on a stand of twisted legs, the entire piece being 7ft high and 4ft 2" wide; it was sold in 1817 to Foster for £69 6s. (equal to £2,700 in 2000).[178]

Beckford was also interested in cabinets with decorated panels. The most elaborate was the Bouchardon cabinet, acquired by 1817 and described as a jewel cabinet decorated with rubies and diamonds, with panels of lapis lazuli and blood stones and with figures by Bouchardon.[179] He placed "Cellini's stupendous dragon alongside the conch" within this piece.[180] He also had several cabinets with pietra-dura panels, which were of particular significance to him; Beckford wrote after a visit to Stourhead, that he considered the sixteenth-century cabinet he had seen there to be one of the greatest examples of furniture.[181] Among the cabinets at Fonthill one was described as "sumptuous ebony cabinet composed of choice Florentine mosaic divided by

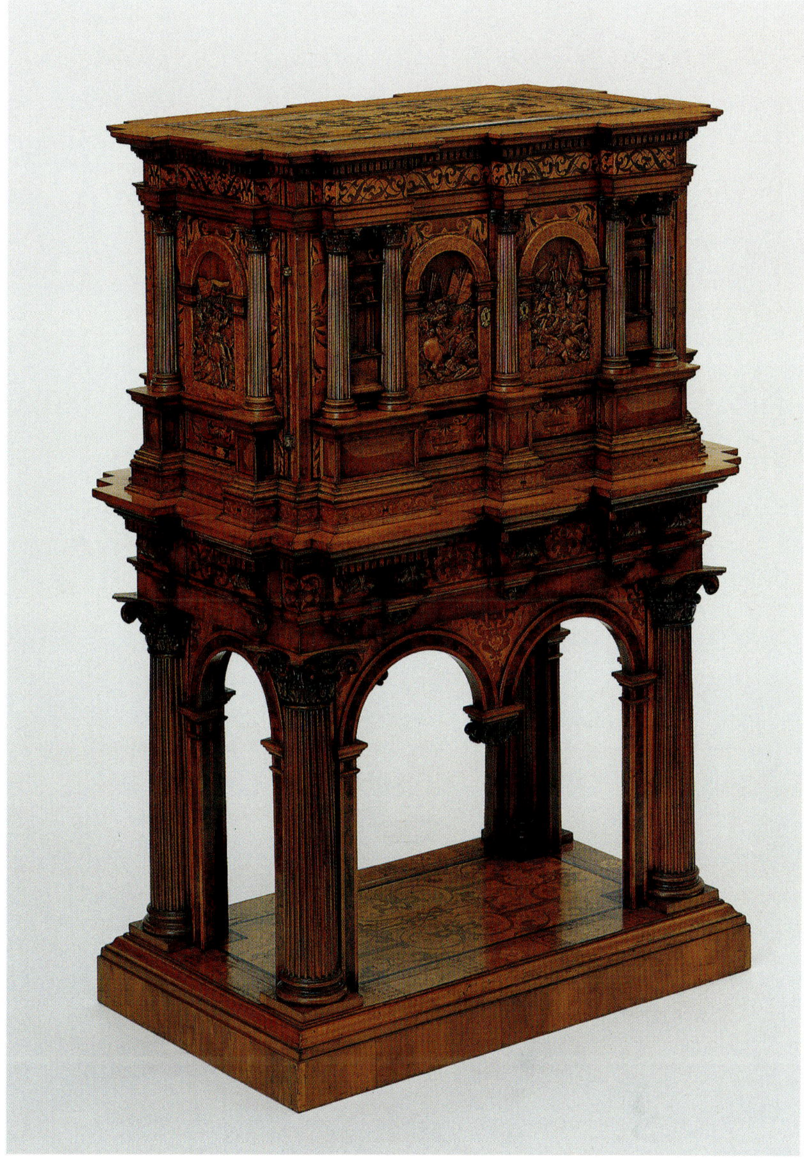

Fig. 10-7. The "Holbein" cabinet, late 16th century. Probably made in Augsburg, Germany. Oak base; marquetry of various woods; interior carved boxwood. The stand is of a later date, possibly made for William Beckford. Trustees of the Victoria and Albert Museum, London, 27-1869.

ebony columns having gilt bronze capitals and bases, also various rich mouldings, the whole finely chased and gilt, surmounted by a slab of fine Griotta marble."[182] The more famous "Bernini" cabinet, decorated in agates, jaspers and other precious materials was placed in the Octagon at Fonthill and later in Lansdown Tower.[183] Both of these rooms were dedicated to the collections of "pictures and curiosities," the great cabinet stood in both rooms, as in the Tribuna in Florence, an association that Beckford may have well intended.

Acquired after the Fonthill sale, and part of Beckford's collection at Lansdown, was a highly important ebony cabinet decorated with paintings by the Flemish artist, Frans Franken, and said to come from the Royal Palace at Madrid. Based on the letters between

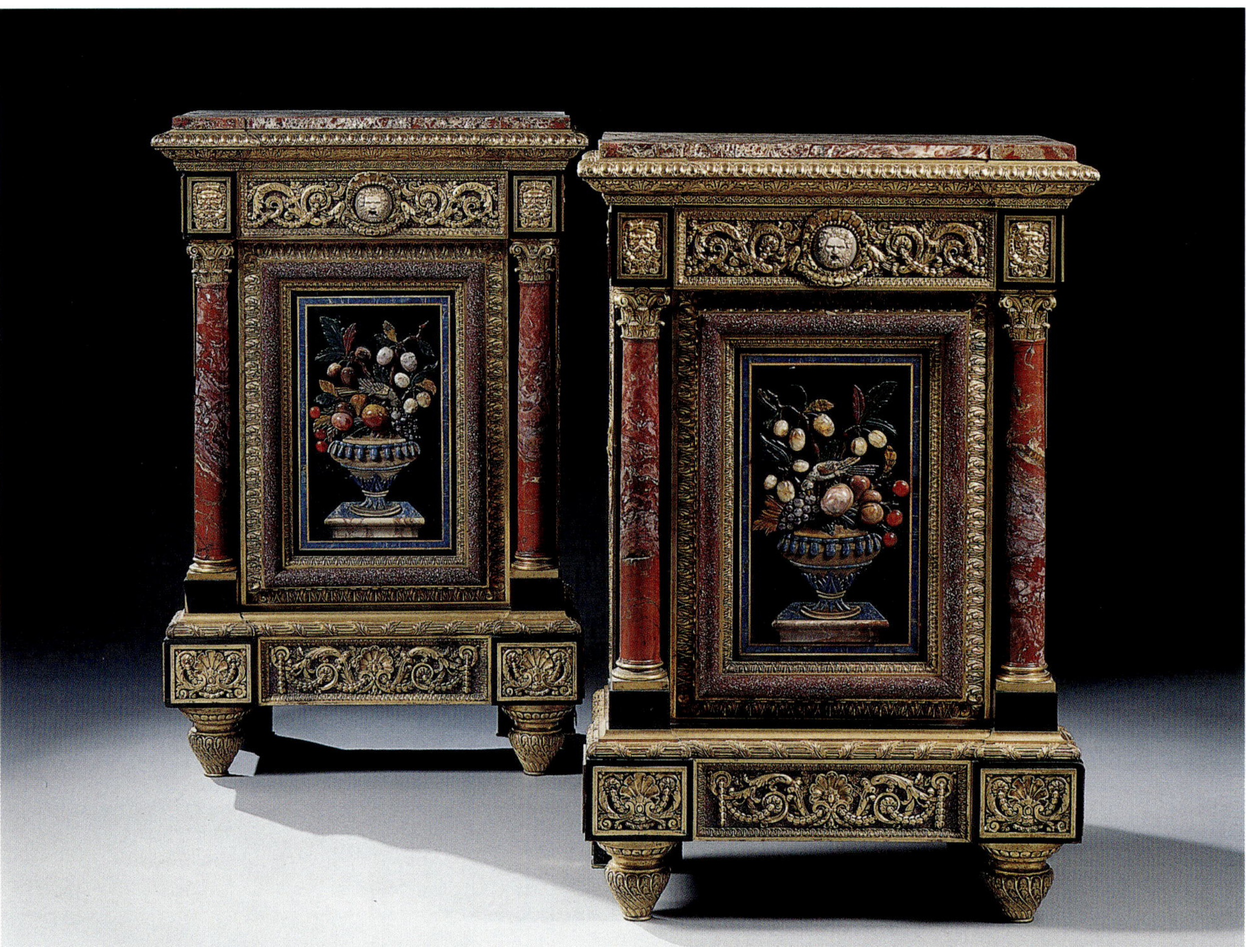

Fig. 10-8. Pair of cabinets, ca. 1825. Ebony, gilt-bronze mounts; 17th-century pietre-dure plaques probably made at the Gobelins manufactory. Christie's. *See cat. no. 160.*

Beckford and Robert Hume, it was probably acquired in 1824.[184] These seventeenth-century cabinets continued to play a role in Beckford's interiors, even when no longer required to complement the Tudor setting of Fonthill Abbey. Two ebony cabinets were offered in the 1841 Lansdown sale suggesting that Beckford had not completely abandoned this style.[185]

The collecting of such cabinets seems to be essentially an English phenomenon; there is very little evidence in the Paris sale catalogues for such works of art. There was an ebony cabinet, however, with paintings by "Old Frank" (Frans Francken), in an anonymous sale at Mr. Greenwood's, London, as early as 1790.[186] A considerable number of sales from 1800 onward offered cabinets with ebony, tortoiseshell, or ivory decoration, thus showing that such items were on the market and collected by, among others, James Wyatt and the Earl of Moira, or bought by dealers such as Crace, Greenwold, and Bentley.[187] Thus from an early date, Beckford could have found examples in the London sales of the type of ebony cabinet he acquired for Fonthill Abbey and for Lansdown Tower. An ebony cabinet with silver mounts was sold in 1803, while a cabinet on stand, sold at Christie's, on June 21, 1805, almost matched the description of Beckford's "Bernini" cabinet.[188]

This must have been exceptional, as it sold for 33 guineas (equal to £1,400 in 2000) as opposed to the £4 18s (£190) paid in the same sale for an ebony cabinet with Florentine marble.[189] This sale seems to have been an important one to judge from the number of dealers who made purchases, including Rundell, possibly of Rundell, Bridge and Rundell, one of the most prominent silver dealers. It is also one of the first occasions that Fogg's name appears repeatedly. After 1815 these cabinets appear with even less frequency, such is the overwhelming taste for Boulle furniture. None of the sales of French furniture in the 1820s included them; but in 1831, a cabinet of red tortoiseshell was sold for £18 18s (£900). Their scarcity in the sales of this period indicates a lack of interest by collectors.[190] Beckford, however, continued to display his Bernini and his Franken cabinets, and, to judge from the prices they fetched in 1844, English collectors followed suit. The Bernini cabinet, which sold for £27 6s (£1,500) in 1823, sold for 150 guineas (£7,200) in 1841.[191]

Beckford's interest in ebony and seventeenth-century cabinets may have encouraged him to collect a number of other objects in ebony, and in ebony and ivory.[192] The degree to which these pieces were described as "Indian," "Oriental" or "Persian" suggests that Beckford was acquiring furniture in a new vein, and of an exotic nature. Some of the cabinets were of carved ebony: "a cabinet of ebony . . . carved with foliage of oriental design" and twisted ebony moldings, or a "sumptuous cabinet with sixteen small drawers of Indian wood, flowered inlayings of ebony and brass mountings, supported on small table of ebony and oriental wood also with flower inlayings."[193] In 1817 the descriptions in the catalogue used either "Indian" or Oriental," interchangeably. In the 1822 catalogue, on the other hand, some of these pieces were defined as "Persian."[194] A small ebony coffer with its later stand, listed in the inventory at Lansdown and shown in a painting of Beckford on his death bed (see cat. no. 150), may indicate the type of furniture that was signified—namely, carved ebony work known as Indo-Portuguese. Beckford considered them to be Persian, however, writing to Franchi in 1813: "The Persia cabinet may be the world's wonder and worth all the jewels in Peru, but this said, it is hard and difficult to find seventy pounds [equal to £2,250 in 2000] for a superfluous trifle."[195] Unfortunately, it is not possible to ascertain what the differences were between those described as Persian, Indian, Oriental, or simply of ebony. The use of the term *Persian* does seem to be unusual at this date and may stem from Beckford's early orientalism, his writing of *Vathek*, and his lessons from Cozens, who was called "the Persian" by Beckford.[196]

It is not certain where Beckford acquired these cabinets and tables. In Franchi's account book, he listed a cabinet in "santo pao," purchased in June 1813.[197] In the same book, but two years later, Franchi also bought a small Persian cabinet with two ebony caskets and a small Persian ivory coffer,[198] which may have been similar to those described in the 1823 sales.[199] It is possible that these were bought in Portugal, as "pao santo" is a specifically Portuguese term for South American rosewood. It is difficult to assess how far Beckford considered these pieces to be part of the long-established tradition of collecting Oriental works of art, a substitute for the more conventional seventeenth-century lacquer cabinets still to be found in English collections in the eighteenth century. Nonetheless in his awareness of these items as exotic and in his interest in collecting such Oriental cabinets, Beckford had few counterparts among collectors of his day, at least not until the second quarter of the nineteenth century.[200] Most of these pieces were sold in the Fonthill sale, and there is little indication the Beckford wished to continue this tradition at Lansdown, except for the one small coffer he kept in his bedroom.

Creating a new style

Throughout his life, Beckford acquired his furniture for its variety, richness of materials, and excellence of workmanship. He often altered the furniture he bought and created new pieces in various historic idioms. Increasingly, as his taste matured, the furniture he commissioned for his interiors became more individual and possibly more avant garde. Among the earliest pieces he commissioned, both his French jewel cabinets and Vulliamy lacquer cabinets were designed in the most modern terms. At Fonthill, his furniture was as varied as the interiors—Elizabethan-inspired oak cabinets on turned stands in King Edward's Gallery or ebony cabinets with gilt brass decoration and crimson silk linings in Saint Michael's Gallery. These were commissioned in the same eclectic spirit and obsession for perfection and quality as he collected older works of art. In his third, final phase of creating ensembles of furniture in Bath, he turned increasingly to furniture in a new, bolder style, conceived in a unity both of design and material. During the twenty years he lived at Lansdown he worked closely with Robert Hume, Henry Edmund Goodridge, and Edmund English, participating in the design process to create furniture of a highly personal style.[201] This led to the abandonment of some of his former interests. It is particularly interesting that there was no Boulle furniture at Lansdown, showing the extent to which he had eliminated historical pieces from his furnishing schemes.[202]

For both acquiring and commissioning works, he considered "taste and real art" the essential qualities for "the man who plans cabinets like my ebony and Florentine ones."[203] This reference was to the great ebony cabinet, commissioned for Fonthill by 1815. The doors were of seventeenth-century work, depicting Quintus Curtius and Mutius Scaevola leaping into the gulf while the cabinet itself and the base with six legs designed in the shape of vases would seem to have been designed by Beckford and possibly Franchi.[204] It stood in the cabinet room at Fonthill, at least by 1822,[205] and was a source of great pride to Beckford: "Only the final stage of ruin will make me abandon the great Ebony Cabinet. It's better to pay tribute than to allow to go far from the Abbey a piece of furniture so august and colossal—an object calculated to bestow, of its own accord, splendour on any apartment, however imperial," he wrote to Franchi on November 18, 1815.[206]

Beckford also created new versions of pietra-dura cabinets. One such, a long low ebony cabinet with a central plaque of vase and flowers sold from Fonthill (now at Charlecote Park, see cat. no. 86) was possibly made for him by Robert Hume.[207] Derived from the French versions of the 1780s, this cabinet is simpler, with more classically correct friezes in the gilt bronze mounts. Beckford also owned a pair of hardstone cabinets (fig. 10-8 and see cat. no. 160a, b), very different in their rich decoration and ornate mounts.[208] A drawing in the Beckford papers sketching out the main lines of the cabinet (fig. 10-9) has been attributed to Franchi, who may thus have been involved in the design.[209] The cabinets were commissioned in 1825 and made in Paris, but it is probable that Robert Hume acted as Beckford's agent and supplied the seventeenth-century hardstones used to decorate the cabinets.[210] What is certain is that they were acquired by Beckford in emulation of his earlier pieces, continuing his Francophile taste, but with a new sense of weight and monumentality

Increasingly Beckford developed his interest in the execution of new furniture for his interiors at Lansdown, seemingly changing and adding to these rooms throughout the twenty years he lived in Bath, using his architect Goodridge to achieve a classical unity between his interiors and their furnishings. The inspiration behind his furnishing was now drawn from the antique, but it was combined with forms

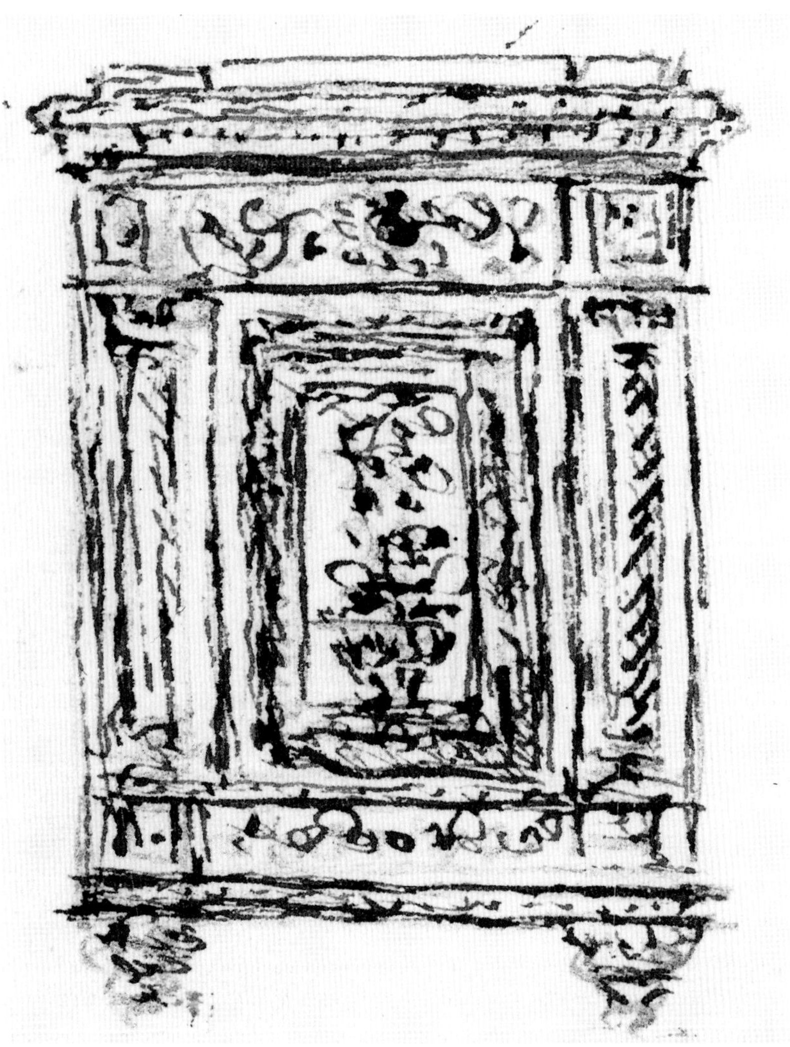

Fig. 10-9. Sketch for a cabinet. Pen and ink. Bodleian Library, Oxford, MS Beckford c.84, fol. 122.

taken from the Italian Renaissance, appropriate for his collections of *Kunstkammer* objects. The Crimson Drawing Room in Lansdown Tower held Beckford's prize works of art, many of them sixteenth century. The room was described in detail in Edmund English's *Views of Lansdown Tower by Willes Maddox* as: "A coffer composed of Florentine mosaic exceedingly beautiful once the property of the famous Cardinal Mazarin stands upon a table of fine mosaic. All the tables of the room are from classical designs, the tops of valuable Italian marble. Most of these splendid objects are of exquisite form, beautifully wrought."[211] On these tables were placed a salver by Cousins based on designs by Raphael, a bronze by Giovanni da Bologna, candlestands by Vulliamy in the manner of Holbein, and other objects worthy of the *Kunstkammer*.

The inspiration of the Italian sixteenth century was made explicit in English's text: the Crimson Drawing Room was of "a similarity closely in tone to that deep mellow richness remarkable in a fine picture by Titian . . . [and] is alike indescribable in language, while the

former [room] in contradiction would remind us of a daylight work by Veronese, more decisive in colour."[212] The furniture was described in similar terms. A large armoire for books, probably commissioned by Beckford, was described as being "in the style of many at the Escorial,"[213] while another pair were said to be in the style of Holbein.[214] As seen in the illustration of the Crimson Drawing Room at Lansdown Tower (see fig. 16-10) the furniture drew on Renaissance architectural forms such as rounded arches, triangular pediments, console supports and pilaster frames.[215] The frame and panel construction used was also a reference to Renaissance furniture. These new forms sought simplicity rather than decoration. Thus the cabinets were described in the catalogues as architectural with pediments or as having "circular-headed panelled doors." Two pairs of coffers on architectural stands created for Lansdown exemplify this new taste (cat. no. 148).[216] They were described as "sarcophagus-headed" and were decorated with boldly carved architectural decoration.[217] In keeping with the interiors at Lansdown, most of the furniture was in oak, although Beckford retained his love of ebony and marbles. His Escorial cabinet was in ebony as were the pair of pedestal cabinets with drawer fronts of Florentine mosaic.[218] Many of his cabinets had fine hardstone tops of sienna marble, jasper, or red porphyry. The "Michaelangelo" cabinet, acquired around 1819—when he first referred to it[219]—would have been in keeping with these concepts. He must have still had it at Lansdown, as it never appeared in the Fonthill sale catalogues and was the subject of discussion between Hume and Beckford in 1824.[220]

The correspondence between Hume and Beckford in the late 1820s, after Beckford's removal to Bath, shows that Beckford concerned himself with the details of the furniture he commissioned and that Hume consulted him with equal assiduousness. In December 1831 Hume wrote with detailed questions concerning changes in the design for bookcases and a sketch of his suggestions (fig. 10-10).[221] As the design shows, the architectural form seems to owe much to the seventeenth-century cabinets, which it may have accompanied, especially if, as a letter the following week suggests, they were to have been in ebony.[222] In another letter to Hume, dated July 5, 1837, Beckford enclosed suggestions for the gilt ornaments on the frieze of the cabinet being made by Hume. Further evidence of his interest in furniture of pietre dure is shown in a reference to another cabinet of ebony and mosaic with a marble top, which was described in a letter from Hume to the Duke of Hamilton.[223] Hume enclosed a drawing that shows it to have been a tall cabinet in two parts, seemingly quite plain, with drawers of pietra-dura panels. If Beckford sold this to the duke, then he must have made another in a very similar style; a "very handsome Ebony upright Cabinett (sic) inlaid with pannels (sic) of Florentine mosaic framed in water gilt mouldings" in the great drawing room at Lansdown Crescent," was listed in the 1844 inventory.[224]

Beckford developed and refined his taste throughout his life, always looking for the interesting and the exceptional object, although his taste was expressed different but overlapping ways at various points in his life. Beckford's collecting and furnishing can be defined by three principal stylistic phases. In broad terms he moved from a monostylistic approach prior to the building of Fonthill Abbey, through a polystylistic taste for the furnishing of the Abbey, returning once more to the monostylistic at Lansdown. In the first phase, based on the traditions of late eighteenth-century collectors, Beckford sought Boulle furniture and commissioned contemporary pieces in the taste appropriate for the French *cabinet*. In the period of his most avid collecting, he pursued a great variety of styles, which included exotic pieces and seventeenth-century cabinets. In his later years, however, his furniture was no longer eclectic, and the interiors at Lansdown Tower represent the summation of Beckford's achievements as a collector and patron. Here he used his own experience and observations in the imaginative realization of an ensemble evolved from the architecture of the Italian Renaissance, in which new forms of greater simplicity were combined with rich textures and materials. Edmund English, in his *Views of Lansdown Tower*, wrote: "In this collection whatever knowledge, influence, wealth and perseverance could command during the long term of seventy years" were brought together.

The patterns of Beckford's collecting, although sometimes reflecting the taste of his contemporaries, remained highly individual. In his early interest in late-eighteenth-century French furniture or in commissioning cabinetmakers to make furniture decorated with Japanese lacquer, comparisons can be made with the francophile taste of the Prince of Wales and his immediate circle—the Earl of Yarmouth (later fourth Marquess of Hertford) and Lord Kinnaird. Beckford's acquisition of Boulle furniture, although not unique, was exceptional in its range and quality in the early nineteenth-century. He shared the late-eighteenth-century passion for French cabinets of pietre-dure intarsia and sought out examples of this technique. In buying works such as the Borghese table, he seems to have anticipated others in England; such was its magnificence that this pietre-dure masterpiece was one of the most expensive items of any type sold in his lifetime. His taste for ebony furniture did have parallels in contemporary and earlier English interiors—Walpole's Strawberry Hill and Sir Walter Scott's Abbotsford—as did his interest in seventeenth-century cabinets, which were shown in period sales. To this tradition, however, he added Indo-Portuguese ebony furniture, with only James Wyatt in England acquiring similar "Persian" cabinets, presumably under Beckford's influence. By 1822, the variety and range of his furniture was unparalleled, combining the traditions of both France and England in one set of interiors. Finally, at Lansdown, he reversed this trend, and just as other collectors were amassing their eclectic and varied collections, filling the interiors with accumulations of works of art, Beckford refined his interiors to a greater simplicity.

After leaving Fonthill, Beckford no longer had any Boulle furniture, nor did he retain any French royal furniture. Instead, he had

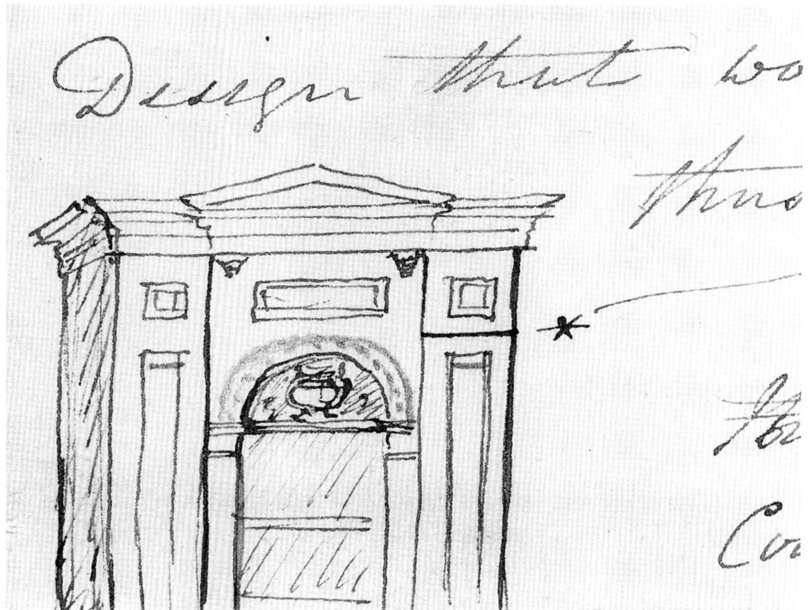

Fig. 10-10. Robert Hume. Sketch for a bookcase. From a letter to William Beckford, 7 December 1831. Bodleian Library, Oxford, MS Beckford c. 22, fol. 130.

Robert Hume made up furniture to his own designs, perhaps because of a genuine enthusiasm for his own taste, perhaps because he did not want and could not afford to compete with collectors such as the fourth Marquess of Hertford, George Watson Taylor, or even his own son-in-law. The collection of Watson Taylor, like Beckford a commoner of fabulous wealth built on the sugar trade, concentrated on the by-then more fashionable taste, acquiring French eighteenth-century furniture in floral marquetry or Japanese lacquer, Boulle furniture, and ebony cabinets with pietre-dure panels.[225] It is doubtful whether Beckford could or would have brought together such a sumptuous collection in the later period of his life. Instead, perhaps as he had always done, he concerned himself with creating an ensemble designed to impress, concentrating on a few choice items, such as the Bernini cabinet or the tables of fine marbles in the tower, the center of his *Kunstkammer*. Although less influential, the interior of Lansdown Tower might be regarded with admiration equal to that inspired by interiors created some thirty years earlier by Thomas Hope at Duchess Street.

The singular nature of Beckford's collections created a mystique that has lasted until the present day. The sale of Fonthill Abbey was one of the great events of its day, and attracted an unprecedented number of visitors, including the wealthiest and most influential collectors of the day. That the Beckford provenance was and is avidly sought stands as a testament to the reputation Beckford created for himself as an arbiter of taste.

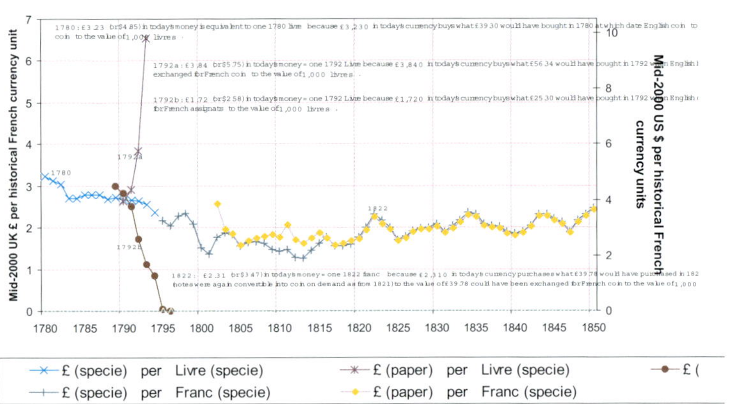

Chart 1. French currency values 1780–1850 in relation to contemporary UK pounds or US dollars. Charted by N. H. Morison.

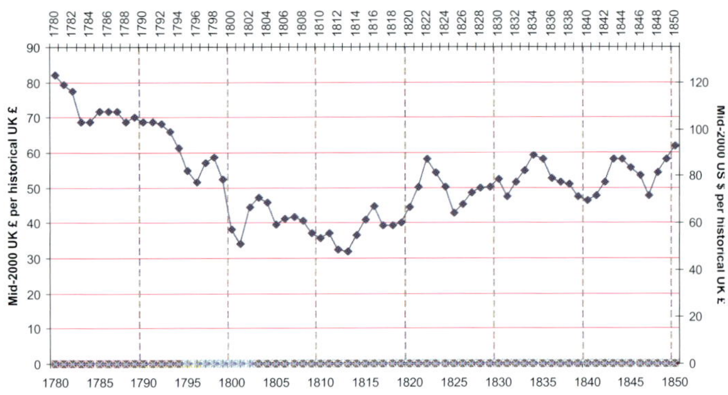

Chart 2. UK pound values 1780–1850 in relation to contemporary UK pounds and US dollars. Charted by N. H. Morison.

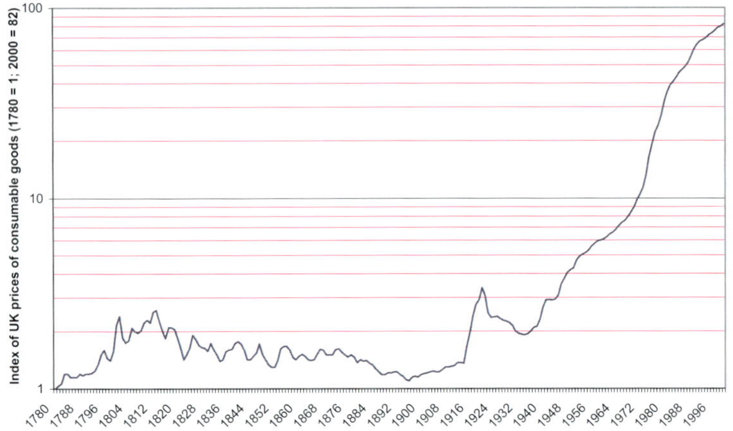

Chart 3. Index of UK consumer prices 1780–2000. Charted by N. H. Morison; information collated from the Office of National Statistics, London.

Acknowledgments: I would like to thank Daniel Alcouffe, Geoffrey de Bellaigue, Charles Cator, Alastair Clarke, Pierre Ennes, Carolyn Sargentson, and Mario Tavella for their generous assistance and advice. I have benefited from discussion with my fellow contributors and would like to thank Megan Aldrich, Anne Eschapasse, Philip Hewat-Jaboor, Martin Levy, Alex Marr, Bet McLeod, Michael Snodin, John Whitehead, and Christopher Woodward, and particularly Derek Ostergard for his comments and suggestions. I am very grateful to the archivists at the Wallace Collection and Christie's, London, for their help, and to Preston Fitzgerald for his perseverance in collecting information from the Christie's and Phillips' catalogues. My greatest debt is to Humphrey Morison, who researched and collated all the information on prices and exchange rates and who produced the three graphs in the article. —AT

1. William Beckford, *Vathek* (1786; reprint, London: Everyman, 1930): 196. Beckford was acutely sensitive to individual object and overall effect. This essay concentrates on his acquisition and sale of individual items of furniture (excluding lacquered furniture, for which see chap. 12, by Oliver Impey, in this volume). The word *collection* is problematic in that it seems to imply an approach that was not Beckford's; he treated both old and new furniture in the same way, subjecting both to needs of display in his interiors. Not only did he alter pieces, but he also often ignored their historical authenticity. The James I chests, now in the Wallace Collection, London, were sold as genuine, but had actually been made for Beckford, and are perhaps the most notable evidence of this attitude; see Peter Hughes, *The Wallace Collection Catalogue of Furniture* (London: The Trustees of the Wallace Collection, 1996): 249–53.

2. Given the lack of precise evidence, it is hazardous to identify specific pieces as having belonged to him. Moreover, the descriptions in the sale catalogues are often too general to guarantee individual pieces that have emerged since as belonging to Beckford. This is particularly the case with furniture from the 1823 sale. Evidence for Beckford's furniture relies on the sale catalogues of furniture in Phillips' sale from Fonthill Abbey in 1801; Christie's sale of pictures from Fonthill, 27 February 1802; Christie's sale of household furniture from Upper Harley Street in May 1817; the canceled sale of the contents of Fonthill Abbey by Christie's in October 1822; and the actual sale in September 1823 recatalogued by Phillips. The two accounts of the contents of Fonthill Abbey differ, with many more lots being offered in the Phillips' sale of 1823; see Clive Wainwright, "Some objects from William Beckford's Collection now in the Victoria and Albert Museum," *Burlington Magazine* 113, no 818 (May 1971): 254–57 For the purpose of this essay, only items from the Christie's 1822 catalogue, unless supported by further evidence, are considered definitely to have been owned by Beckford. Additional information is given in the following descriptions: for Fonthill Abbey, see James Storer, *A Description of Fonthill Abbey Wiltshire* (1812); John Rutter, *Delineations of Fonthill and Its Abbey* (1823); and John Britton, *A New Guide to Fonthill Abbey, Wiltshire* (London, 1822); and for Lansdown Terrace and Lansdown Tower, see the sale catalogues of 1841 and 1843 by Messrs English and Fasane (MS Beckford d. 27/2, Bodleian Library, Oxford); Robert Hume's 1844 inventory after Beckford's death (MS Beckford c. 58); as well as contemporary descriptions and the paintings by Maddox. Sources among the Beckford papers in the Bodleian Library, Oxford, are hereafter cited as "MS Beckford."

3. This evidence is piecemeal and imprecise, dependent on the survival of sale catalogues, which do not always include prices, particularly for the Paris sales. The English catalogues rarely give precise descriptions or dimensions. Thus it is not possible to make exact comparisons between the pieces of furniture in the different sales, only to mark general trends. The analysis in this essay is based on some 150 Paris sale catalogues between 1770 and 1830, taken either from the microfiche copies in *Art Sales Catalogues* (Microform Publications, Leiden, Netherlands), sale catalogues in the library of the Wallace Collection, London, or early nineteenth-century French catalogues in the British Library, London, most of which were annotated with prices. English sale catalogues are to be found in the Christie's Archives, London; Phillips' catalogues are in the library of the Wallace Collection; various miscellaneous sale catalogues are in the National Art Library, Victoria and Albert Museum, London. There were approximately ninety catalogues of London sales during the same period that contained what could be called collector's items. English sale catalogues also included household furniture at a much earlier date than in Paris, but most of those before ca. 1800 consisted primarily of English mahogany or satinwood furniture.

4. London *Times,* 1 October 1822.

5. Letter dated Monday 18 August 1817, in *Life at Fonthill, 1807–1822, with interludes in Paris and London, from the correspondence of William Beckford,* trans. and ed. Boyd Alexander (London, R. Hart-Davis, 1957): 217.

6. Clive Wainwright, *The Romantic Interior* (New Haven and London: Yale University Press, 1989): 110–11: "there is plenty of evidence of his collecting activities abroad . . . more importantly in France." Timothy Mowl, on the other hand, argues that Beckford only began serious collecting after he could no longer travel on the Continent; see Mowl, *William Beckford: Composing for Mozart* (London: John Murray, 1998): 270.

7. Boyd Alexander, *England's Wealthiest Son* (London: Centaur, 1962): 203–8.

8. Central Statistical Office, United Kingdom.

9. The nearest equivalent statistics for 1998 show the top one-quarter-of-one percent of UK taxpayers earning, on average, £445,000 per annum. The number of taxpayers involved is 62,000.

10. "There was not a single cause for Beckford's financial ruin. . . . [After] the economic decline of Jamaica and the dishonesty of his agents . . . came a series of expenditures [costs of litigation and parliamentary expenditure among them]. . . . Then, as a coup de grace, came the building of Fonthill" (Alexander, *England's Wealthiest Son* [1962]: 225.

11. A "box containing china belonging to Mr Beckford which was landed on 21st inst. out of Prince of Wales from Boulogne," item no 48, Cust 54/ 2 (Jan 1787), Public Record Office, Kew, London (hereafter cited as PRO). The file consists of the custom officers' notebooks and only concerns those items that, for one reason or another, had to be stored in the warehouse at Dover. I am most grateful to Sir Geoffrey de Bellaigue for this reference. I have found no other references to Beckford in the customs records at the PRO but many of these records were destroyed in the nineteenth century.

12. Letter from Beckford to Nicholas Williams, 11 July 1797, quoted in Lewis Melville, *The Life and Letters of William Beckford of Fonthill* (London: Heinemann, 1910): 247. Not all of these items were recent purchases, or even purchased in France, as Beckford asked Williams to make sure that a Japanese cabinet, a gift to him from the late Duke of Queensbury would be safe.

13. Letter to Wildman, 3 May 1793, MS Beckford c.37, fol. 20.

14. Michel Beurdeley, *Ventes du mobilier royal de Versailles, De Versailles a Paris: le Destin des collections Royalees* (Paris, Centre culturel du Panthéon) n.d.): 115–26; and idem, *La France à l'encan—Exode des objets d'art sous la Révolution, 1789–99: Les Arts Sous la Révolution*, (Fribourg: Office du Livre, 1981). The sales took place from 25 August 1793 until 11 August 1794, and fetched a total of 299,902 livres (about £0.75 million).

15. Michel Beurdeley, "Ventes" (n.d.): 116–18.

16. Geoffrey de Bellaigue, "Martin-Eloy Lignereux and England," *Gazette de Beaux Arts* 6, no. 71 (May–June 1968): 283–94.

17. Geoffrey de Bellaigue, "Jean-Frederic Perregaux, the Englishman's Best Friend," *Antologia di Belli Arti*, n.s. 29–30, *Mélanges Verlet . . .* 2 (1986): 80–90. In September 1792 Perregaux bought a Sèvres service for 1,539 *livres* (equal to about £4,050 in 2000). This price is not much lower than that of a service acquired in 1785 for 1,763 *livres* (about £4,900). The price of another service acquired at approximately the same date, 1786, for 5,486 *livres* (about £15,250) would seem to suggest that it was the lavishness of the service or number of parts that made the difference.

18. In order to facilitate comparisons, all prices of furniture have been translated into their modern equivalent, that is to say the number of pounds sterling which in June 2000 would buy the quantity of basic consumer goods that the price in question would have paid for in the year in which the furniture was sold. Prices were denominated in units of account (in England the pound; in France the *livre* replaced by the *franc* in 1803). Prior to the Revolution, trade was conducted using gold and silver coins ("specie") or promises to pay in coin ("bills of exchange") which, if payable in Paris, had to be settled in gold. Neither the *livre* nor the pound were coins. Settlement of debts with cash was complex, requiring a rate of exchange into *livres* for each gold and silver coin. Different mintings of the same coin could have different values. See Ferdinand Braudel, *The Identity of France* (London: Fontana, 1991): 610.

19. Translated as "un meuble de boudoir pour servir de *secrétaire.*" This would indicate that prices during the Revolution were still referred to in *livres*. Christian Baulez, "Tout Europe tire ses bronzes de Paris," in *Bernard Molitor, 1755–1833: Ébéniste Parisien d'Origine Luxembourgeoise*, ed. Ulrich Leben, exh. cat. (Luxemburg: Ville de Luxembourg,1995): 87.

20. In France the Revolution brought "monetary chaos." Specie was hoarded. The government issued paper currency denominated in *livres* (*assignats*). Their value fell catastrophically. By 1796, 43 *livres* in coin were equivalent to 10,000 *livres* in *assignats* and the paper money was worthless by the end of the year; see Braudel, *Identity of France* (1991): 618. It is not known to what extent it would in practice have been possible for an English purchaser of furniture to have benefitted from this circumstance by discharging any debt owed with *assignats*. According to Beurdeley, French dealers were expected to pay in *assignats*; see *La France à l'Encan* (1981): 99.

21. The English unit of account was the pound sterling: 240 *pence* (d) = 20 *shillings* (s) = 1 *pound* (£). Formerly worth 20 shillings of sterling silver, the pound was later defined in terms of the price of gold. From 1717 to 1931 an ounce of gold was held to be worth £3 17s 10 1/2d (i.e., £3.89375). This relationship was maintained by obligations of the Mint Office and Bank of England to mint gold into coin for a small fee; and to exchange bank notes for gold at the official rate. From 1792 this system broke down. There was a flight to cash (i.e., gold). In 1797 the bank ceased to "make cash payments" (i.e., exchange its bank notes for gold coin). The value of the pound became uncertain. Rates published by the government's official bullion broker were described at the time as being "either incorrect or arbitrarily stated." Only in 1821 were "cash payments" restored. Nevertheless, despite contemporary forebodings, the cessation of "cash payments" in 1797 took place without severe adverse effects on the value of paper money in England.

22. Rates of exchange between French and English units of account are not available for the period 1793 to 1802. Otherwise, information has been taken from reports to the British Parliament ("Report of the Secret Committee on Resumption of Cash Payments 1819"; "Report from Select Committee on Banks of Issue 1840"). Chart 1 has been based on the gold content of coins used to settle debt (the English *guinea* (£1.1s. ie £1.05) and *sovereign* (£1 introduced in 1821) and the French *louis d'or* and *20 franc piece*) together with contemporary estimates of the cost of transferring gold from London to Paris. This "bullion-based" rate of exchange is shown for the whole period 1780 to 1850 as a check on the published rates of exchange. This accords with contemporary comment that all trade was conducted thinking in terms of bullion including the cost of transporting gold to France and having it coined by the mint if the rates of exchange were unfavorable. In broad-brush terms, between 1780 and 1850, £1 was worth first 25 *livres* and later 25 *francs*. This fixed relationship was a consequence of the reliance on payment in specie. Variations from these means are plotted in chart 1.

23. Marcel Marion, *Histoire Financière de la France depuis 1715* (Paris: Rousseau et Cie., 1927); S. E. Harris, *The Assignats* (Cambridge: Harvard University Press, 1930); François Crouzet, *La Grande Inflation La monnaie en France de Louis XVI à Napoléon* (Paris: Fayard, 1993); all deal with the problems of finance in the Revolution but with no specific information on purchases of luxury goods during the Revolution.

24. I am most grateful to Anne Eschapasse, who kindly informed me that no one has yet found evidence of William Beckford or Nicholas Williams in the auction catalogues of records of Paris sales (oral communication, 2001).

25. De Bellaigue, "Jean-Frederic Perregaux" (1986): 86.

26. Letter from Wildman (in pencil answered Monday 13 October 88 [?], MS Beckford c. 37, fol. 8.

27. Lewis Melville, *The Life and Letters of William Beckford of Fonthill* (London: W. Heinemann, 1910): 249

28. Charles Davillier, *Vente du Mobilier du Chateau de Versailles pendant le Terreur* (Paris, 1887). In a Haarlem newspaper of 1794, there was an announcement of a sale from the French royal collections. Apparently the sale did not actually take place in Holland, and the prices quoted were in *livres*, but the implication was that they were sold for export.

29. F. J. B. Watson, "George IV as an Art Collector," *Apollo*, n.s., 83 (June 1966): 411.

30. P. Verlet, "Chapeaurouge et les collections royales françaises," *Festschrift fur Erich Meyer zum Sechzigsten Geburtstag* (1959): 286–94.

31. Among these were a bronze group by Lemoyne bought 28 September 1797 and the tapestries of Esther 1797. Ibid., p. 289.

32. MS Beckford c. 37, fols. 57–81. He submitted an invoice for paintings on 9 July 1801.

33. *Assemblage of Articles imported from Paris via Hamburg, from the Queen of France's Châteaux at St. Cloud*, sale cat., Phillips', 17 February 1800. Perhaps most interesting of the furniture was a pier glass of Gothic design, which sold for £22 1s (equal to about £850 in 2000); other items included a hookah and backgammon table of pierced ivory.

34. Bertie Greatheed, *An Englishman in Paris: 1803 The Journal of Bertie Greatheed*, ed. J.P.T. Bury and J.C. Barry (London: Geoffrey Bles, 1953), quoted in de Bellaigue, "Martin-Eloy Lignereux" (1968): 284.

35. Lignereux is known to have charged the Prince of Wales £190 (about £9,000) for a secretaire in *bois jaune* in 1803 (ibid., p. 285); Greatheed may have been referring to the cost of an entire suite of furniture.

36. He did not appear in any diaries written at the time by English travelers to Paris either in 1802 or in 1814–45. For example he does not appear in Bertie Greatheed's diary in 1802, in the letters of Mary Berry, or the diaries of Fanny Burnett, Mme d'Arbaly. Frances, Lady Shelley, wrote extensively about the English community in Paris after the fall of Napoléon, and again Beckford's name was not mentioned; see *The Diary of Frances, Lady Shelley, 1787–1817*, ed. Richard Edgcumbe, vol. 1 (London: John Murray, 1912).

37. Ms. Eng. Misc.d .1296, fol. 55, Bodleian Library, Oxford.

38. Sarah Medlam, *The Bettine, Lady Abingdon Collection, the Bequest of Mrs T. R. P. Hole* (London: The Victoria and Albert Museum, 1996): 34–35. The English dealer George Gunn continued to buy in Paris for Stuart, as letters from 1832 and 1834 show. Gunn had acquired premises at 64 rue Amulet and seems to have worked with a partner in England, James Nixon, who had premises at Great Portland Street (ibid., pp. 30–32).

39. Entry for 25 June 1816, *Diary of Frances, Lady Shelley* (1912): 203.

40. Megan Aldrich, "A Setting for Boulle Furniture: The Duke of Wellington's Gallery at Stratfield Saye," *Apollo* 147, no. 436 (June 1998): 21.

41. Medlam, *Lady Abingdon Collection* (1996): 48–51. The furniture was in the house after Ney's execution and, as there was no public sale of the contents of the hotel, it has been assumed that he bought it privately after April 1817.

42. The secretaire by Levasseur was sold to the Prince Regent by Robert Fogg for £367 10s (£12,000) and delivered in July 1812. It is thought that Fogg acquired it from the French dealer Maëlrondt, who had bought it earlier that year at the sale of the architect Villers (lot 154) in Paris; see *Carlton House: The Past Glories of George IV's Palace*, exh. cat., The Queen's Gallery, Buckingham Palace (London 1991): 80.

43. Phillips' held sales of French works of art from 1817 to 1822. The annotated sale catalogues between 1815 and 1830 show a repetition of names, many of which are known to have been dealers; see, e.g., *A Catalogue of Parisian Furniture . . . from the Palaces of Versailles . . . ,"* sale cat., Phillips', 8 June 1816; *A splendid Assemblage of French Furniture;* sale cat., 8 June 1819; *A Splendid Consignment of Parisian Furniture*, sale cat., 21 March 1821; *An Assemblage of Useful and Decorative Boule and Reisner (sic) Furniture,* sale cat., Phillips', London, 30 May 1818 (Wallace Collection London). See also Beurdeley, *La France à l'encan* (1981): 95.

44. Letters to Franchi, MS Beckford c. 1–11. They were translated and selected by Boyd Alexander in *Life at Fonthill* (1957). Instructions to Morlands, Aurtol and Co., Gen. Mss. 102, William Beckford Collection, Beineke Rare Book and Manuscript Library, Yale University, New Haven.

45. Letter to Mr. Williams, Grosvenor Square, October 12 1796, MS Beckford c.37, fols. 34–38.

46. Edward Foxhall had premises at Old Cavendish Street, Cavendish Square from 1799.

47. Robert Hume (active 1808–40) resided at 11 Crown Street, Saint Giles's (1808), 34 Great Titchfield Sreet, Cavendish Square (1809–11), 4 Great Portland Sreet (1817), 4 Little Portland Sreet (1820), and 65 Berners' Sreet (1837). He was probably registered as Robert Hume and Son, 53 Wigmore Sreet in 1820 and 56 Berners' Street in 1829; see Geoffrey Beard and Christopher Gilbert, eds., *Dictionary of English Furniture Makers, 1660–1840*, (Leeds: W.S. Maney & Son Ltd., 1986): 462.

48. Letters from Hume, 1823–42, MS. Beckford c.22.

49. Wainwright, *Romantic Interior* (1989): 26–53.

50. Robert Fogg and Son, Chinamen, were registered at 50 New Bond Street as early as 1793 (*Universal British Directory, 1793*, Guildhall Library, London) and remained there until 1800. In 1801 they had either moved or extended their premises to include 55 New Bond Street. On 24 March 1803 Robert Fogg junior of Bond Street purchased property in Warwick Street, Golden Square, from a certain Thomas Nash, who had gone bankrupt (PRO: Crest 38/1241) and the firm was certainly at that address by 1805, according to the Trade Directory of that date. The Post Office Directory of 1815 gives the address as 16 Warwick St. Golden Square. Fogg's name also appears in the Vulliamy accounts having mounts made for some china in 1811 (C 104/57, Box 1, Piece 4, PRO).

51. Geoffrey de Bellaigue, "Edward Holmes Baldock," parts 1 and 2, *Connoisseur* 189, no. 762 (1975): 290–9; 190, no. 763 (1975): 18–25.

52. Alexander, *Life at Fonthill* (1957): 213.

53. Correspondence with Hume 1822–44, MS Beckford c. 22.

54. Letter from Paris, 19 January 1784, quoted in J. W. Oliver, *The Life of William Beckford* (Oxford University Press, 1932): 161. He sent a copy of *Dreams, Waking Thoughts and Incidents* to Louise Necker, later to become Madame de Staël.

55. "Letter to Louisa," Paris 1784, quoted in Oliver, *Beckford* (1932): 173.

56. Moitte worked with Ledoux in 1787 on the projects for the *Barriéres*; see Gisela Gramaccini, *Jean-Guillaume Moitte: Leben und Werk* (Berlin: Akademie Verlag, 1993). He was elected a member of the Académie Royale de Peinture et de Sculpture in 1783 (ibid., p. 3).

57. Raymond was a member of the Académie as well and one of six reelected after the Revolution to the new Institut. He is most famous for the *hôtel* he designed for Charles and Louise Vigée Lebrun. He worked with Moitte on at least one occasion, on a statue of Rousseau (1789–99; see ibid., p. 232).

58. "Letter to Louisa," in Oliver, *Beckford* (1932): 177.

59. "Blondel de Gagny" in L.Courajod, ed., *Livre-Journal de Lazard Duvaux* (Paris: Societé des Bibliophiles François, 1873): 233–54. Excerpt from *Dictionnaire pittoresque et historique d'Hébert*, vol 1 (1766): 36–81.

60. The sale catalogue of the cabinet of the duc de Choiseul–Praslin, Paris, 18 February, 1793 (Lugt 5005) was typical in its contents: "Figures & Bustes en marbres, Goues & Figures de bronze, Vases, Colonnes & Coupes de marbres & matières rares de granit; de serpentin, porphyre rouge & noir; riches Meubles & Cabinets de marquetterie de *Boulle;* Porcelaines anciennes & rares du Japon & de la Chine; Tasses, coupes & Énchantillons précieux d'agate Orientale; Pendules, Feux & Bras dorés, Girandoles de grands modèles, Paravants de laque & autres objets, Bauges de pierres gravées, minatures de *Petitot* etc." In England, there are fewer examples of this type of collection at this date.

61. Carolyn Sargentson, *Merchants and Luxury Markets: The Marchands Merciers of Eighteenth Century Paris* (London and Malibu, California: Victoria and Albert Museum / J. Paul Getty Museum, 1996).

62. "Ces meubles enrichis d'ornements en pierres dures de Florence, étaient fort recherchés au siè-cle dernier, et dans plusieurs cabinets de Paris ils prenaient place à coté des meubles du Boulle," in Charles Davillier, *Une vente d'actrice sous Louis XVI, Mlle Laguerre de l'Opéra, son Inventaire, Meubles, Porcelaines etc. avec in introduction et des notes par Baron C. Davillier,* sale cat., Paris, 1870, lot 17. The history of this commode is discussed in A. Setterwall, "Some Louis XVI Furniture dec-

orated with pietre dure Reliefs," *Burlington Magazine* 101, no. 681 (December 1959)*:* 430–35.

63. "Letter to Louisa," in Oliver, *Beckford* (1932): 177. There is much disagreement as to whether this letter was written in 1784; it was copied and rewritten several times by Beckford in 1838–39.

64. Beckford, *Dreams, Waking Thoughts and Incidents 1783*, vol. 1 of *The Travel-Diaries of William Beckford*, ed. Guy Chapman (London: Constable and Co., 1928).

65. Francesco de Medici (Grand Duke, 1574–87) collected works of *naturalia, exotica,* and *artificialia* for his *Stanzina* or study, which were then transferred to the Tribuna in the Uffizi shortly before his death. See the "Inventory of the Wardrobe of the House and Palace of the Casino, under the custody of Piero Elmi, begun today, this eighth day of March 1587 . . . " in Anna Maria Massinelli and Filio Tuena, *Treasures of the Medici* (New York: Vendome Press, 1992): 230–33. Horace Walpole also had a collectors cabinet at Strawberry Hill called the Tribune, which housed his collection of coins, medals, miniatures, and enamels; see John Iddon, *Horace Walpole's Strawberry Hill* (London: St. Mary's University College, 1996); and Wainwright, *Romantic Interior* (1989): 71–107.

66. Letter to Sir W. Hamilton, Geneva, 12 October 1782, *The Collection of Autograph and Historical Documents Formed by Alfred Morrison Second Series, 1882–1893,* vol. 1, "Letters A-B" (London: privately printed, 1893).

67. Beckford, *Italy; with sketches of Spain and Portugal*, vol. 2 of *The Travel-Diaries* (1928). At Aranjuez, for example, he wrote, "Two Corinthian columns of a most beautiful purple and white marble, sustain a pediment, as highly polished and as richly mottled as any agate I ever beheld; the capitals are bronze splendidly gilt, so is the foliage of the consoles supporting the slab which forms the altar. The design, the materials, the workmanship, are all Spanish, and do the nation credit" (letter 17, Tuesday, December 1795). "I wonder that architects and fitters up of apartments do not avail themselves more frequently of the powers of drapery. Nothing produces so grand and at the same time so comfortable an effect. The moment I have an opportunity I will set about constructing a tabernacle, larger than the one I arranged at Ramalhaô, and indulge myself in every variety of plait and fold that can possibly be invented" (letter 16, Sunday, 23 December 1787, in Beckford, *Dreams* [1928]: 236).

68. Ibid., p. 236. In the letter as published by Boyd Alexander in *The Journal of William Beckford in Portugal and Spain 1787–88* (London: Rupert Hart-Davis, 1954): 301, Beckford discussed the toilet as a "chef d'oeuvre of chased work as well designed as executed" without mentioning Moitte.

69. Walpole developed a passion for this type of ebony furniture, writing in 1763, "As I came for ebony I am up to my chin in ebony; there is literally nothing but ebony in the house, . . . all made by the Hallet of two hundred years ago"; quoted in Amin Jaffer, *Furniture from British India and Ceylon* (London: Victoria and Albert Museum Publications, 2001): 130. I am most grateful to Amin Jaffer for being allowed to see this before publication.

70. Ibid.

71. G. de Bellaigue, "Daguerre and England," in *Bernard Molitor* (1995): 157–76. Clients such as the Spencers visited Daguerre in Paris; there are two cabinets with Japanese lacquer fronts by Weisweiler, which were sold by Daguerre (ibid.). London sale catalogues from at least 1790 mention items of French furniture, particularly mirror glass and pier tables.

72. See Chap. 3, by Philip Hewat-Jaboor, in this volume.

73. F. J. B Watson "Holland and Daguerre: French undercurrents in English Neo-Classical Furniture Design, *Apollo,* n.s. 96 (October 1972): 282–87.

74. Christie's, London, Friday 25 March 1791, (Lugt 4698, microfilm). Most of the French furniture found in the late-eighteenth-century London sales were chairs and pierglass mirrors. (Christie's Archives).

75. Christie's, 22 February 1802 and the four following days, Christie's Archives, London.

76. Walpole's Tribune contained coins and medals, as well as historical items. It was closer to the tradition of scientific collecting or collection of curiosities, which formed one stream of English taste. Beckford had no interest in this tradition, which was exemplified in the collection of the Duchess of Portland, whose collection of curiosities was inherited from the Earl of Arundel. The sale, 24 April 1786, included a few items of oriental work, and "artificial curiosities," but the bulk of the collection was entirely shells and such naturalia as corals, minerals, nests, eggs, insects, and vegetables in spirits. Among the only items of furniture were four ebony chairs, curiously carved with cane seats, sold for £6 (about £430), two India cane chairs with a cushion to each, sold with a writing stand for six guineas (£450), and a looking glass in a tortoisehell frame, sold for £2 (£140).

77. "Tripods, carved and gilt, burnished gold by Boileau" were sold for £47 5s (£1,600), Phillips' 1801, second day, lot 22; "A pair of superlatively elegant tripods formed *à la Turque,* exquisitely carved and gilt in a superior and expensive stile, designed by Boileau" sold for £40 10s. (£1,400).

78. Phillips' 1801, second day, lots 33 and 15. There is, of course, no way of proving whether these were bought in Paris, but given the rarity of French furniture in the London sales at that date, it is certainly possible.

79. See chap. 3, by Philip Hewat-Jaboor, and chap. 6, by Anne Eschapasse, in this volume.

80. Christie's 1822, third day, lot 77, was sold for £32 11s (£1,900) to Davies.

81. "Artois, Mecenat et Collectionneur," *La Folie d'Artois* (Antiquaires à Paris, n.d.): 73–81. The complete inventory is listed in the "Etat des objets d'arts provenant de l'emigré d'Artois, trouvés dans la maison du Temple et réservés par la Commission temporarier des Arts 19 Prairal an II" (7 June 1794), Archives Nationales, F 17 1269, no. 20; and in "Inventaire des objets trouvés au Temple provenant de l'emigré d'Artois 15 Fructidor an II" (1 September 1795) taken by Lebrun, Archives Nationales, R1 309, R1 310, R1 314. As the Prince Regent also bought pieces from the collection of the comte d'Artois, some pieces must have come on the open market and been bought by English collectors.

82. ["en camées et autres"]. Christian Baulez, "Tout Europe tire ses bronzes de Paris," in *Bernard Molitor* (1995): 87.

83. Ibid. Baulez quotes the payments to the different artists as follows: Rémond 3,800 livres (equal to around £10,000 in 2000) for the bronze work and the models, Weisweiler 1,000 livres (£2,600) for the work on the secretary and the architect J. A. Raymond 400 livres (£1,000) for two different designs. Sauvage himself was owed 2,400 livres (£6,100) for the paintings on ivory. Baulez also cites payments from Rémond's accounts, including one to "Damerat, modele de griffe 60 livres (£150); "Lebon les trois surmoulés des dites griffes 80 livres" (£200), which are probably similar to the mounts on a secrétaire with porcelain plaques, acquired "at the beginning of the Empire" by the queen of Spain, now in the Royal Palace, Madrid.

84. ["tout ce que les carrieres les plus renames fournissent de plus precieux en marbres, agathes & crystaux, tout ce que l'ebenisteries peut executee de plus delicat, ce que le ciseleur peut donner au bronzes d'ornementens riches & nouveaux"]. Ibid., pp. 87 and 108.

85. *Dessins d'Ornements et d'Orfeverie des XIIIe et XIXe Siècles*, Sotheby's Monaco, 22 February 1986, lot 181. The collection of designs was sold to the Maison Odiot by Auguste's grandson in 1810. The design illustrated in the catalogue is inscribed with Auguste's signature but attributed to Moitte on the basis of an identical stand in one of his engravings.

86. Richard Campbell, "Jean-Guillaume Moitte: The Sculptor and the Graphic Art, 1785–99," Ph.D. diss., Brown University, 1982 (University of Michigan, Ann Arbor, Microfilms, 1994): 193. The design is in a private collection and has not been available for study. The difficulty of reading the inscription might make either rendering possible, and there are occasions when the spelling of his name is confused. In all the Paris accounts, however, he is referred to as "Monsieur." The Duke of Bedford was not in Paris at the time and is not thought to have been commissioning French furniture at this date.

87. Sotheby's Monaco, 14 June 1997, lot 137, described as "An important jewel coffer made for William Beckford before 1801 under the direction of Henri Auguste after designs and models by Jean-Guillaume Moitte; the cabinet-work by Weisweiler; the pannels painted by Sauvage" (translated from the French by the author).

88. For Beckford's admiration for Auguste, see Michael Snodin and Malcolm Baker, "William Beckford's Silver," part 1 *Burlington Magazine* 122, no. 932 (1980): 739. For Auguste and Moitte working together, see Gramaccini, *Moitte* (1993); and Campbell, "J-G. Moitte" (1983).

89. There have been suggestions that a set of cabinets, made by Weisweiler with mounts by Auguste is still at Elton Hall, Cambridgeshire; see Sotheby's Monaco, 14 June 1997; and Lucy Morton, *Recent Acquisitions* (London: Partridge Fine Arts Ltd., 1998). The only pair of cabinets at Elton, however, is the pair by Vulliamy.

90. Beckford referred to a "cabinetto d'Auguste," which might refer to this cabinet; see letter to Franchi, 16 June 1812, MS Eng. Misc. d. 1295, Bodleian Library.

91. Christie's, 1822, day 9, lot 96, described as "a superb cabinet of gold Japan and various foreign woods on a stand ornamented with ormoulu, the frieze most exquisitely chased and gilt surmounted by an Egyptian granite slab, made by Auguste." There was a pair of cabinets attributed to Auguste in the Hamilton Palace sale, lots 172 and 173, as well as the above cabinet, lot 293; see *Catalogue of the collection of . . . the Property of His Grace the Duke of Hamilton . . . ,* sale cat., Christie, Manson and Woods, 18 June 1882. Hugh Roberts suggests that these were in fact the Vulliamy cabinets; see Roberts, "Beckford, Vulliamy and old Japan," *Apollo* 124, no. 296 (October 1986): 338–41.

92. Letter from Robert Hume, Hôtel d'Alberg, to the Duke of Hamilton, 11 February 1830, Hamilton Papers: bundles 602. I am most grateful to Bet McCleod for this reference and drawing.

93. Roberts, "Beckford, Vulliamy" (1986): 338–41.

94. Bill book 30, 31, London, 6 May 1803, C 104/58, PRO, London. Box 1, Daybook 1799–1803, C 104/58, PRO, London. Beckford is first mentioned in 1799, but he may have been a client before that date, as it was customary for firms to carry out repairs for established customers.

95. These may have still been in Beckford's possession in 1812 as he mentions a commode by Vulliamy in the Tempietto in his letter to Franchi, 5 July 1812, Ms. Eng Misc d.1295, 164, Bodleian Library.

96. Bill Book 30, C 104/58, PRO, London. On 21 June 1801 Beckford was charged £67 4s (£2,300)

for each of two pier bronze tables "in the form of a Chimera representing the heads and body of an Eagle with the Wings expanded the body is continued into a long Taper leg with a Large Claw to serve as a foot."

97. Entry for 3 December 1802, Bill Book 30, C 104/58, PRO London: "For Unmounting the six chimera Legs of the two Pier Tables and converting them into a very large Bronze Circular Table to stand in the center of a Library the top of the Table is formed of a large circular Metal band near 4 feet diameter worked into a reeded Moulding, the band is made in six parts which are screwed together with Cap pines to cover the joints the Metal Ring is fixed on a very strong Oak frame which to prevent it from casting is made of a great number of pieces of wood,[.] the six legs are fixed upon a Very strong Metal frame the principal part of which is a double circular frame enriched with Chased ornaments in the openings[.] from this principal part project six semicircular open parts [.] each part has a roller with a universal Motion concealed in for to roll the table upon the floor, the frame consists of a great number of pieces which are all fixed together steel screws and strong bolts[.] This part is enriched with antique rosettes, the whole of this Table is executed with great exactness and prepared in such a manner as to keep the parts of a proper size for Gilding and at the same time, strong enough to bear its own weight, the whole Table is one of the best pieces of Workmanship that has ever been made at 270 guineas" (£12,600).

98. Geoffrey de Bellaigue, "The Vulliamys and France," *Furniture History* 3 (1976): 45–53.

99. Box 1, Piece 142 and 143, C 104/57, PRO, London, has details of the bronze tables delivered to the Duke of Bedford, 15 March 1811.

100. Roger Smith, "Vullliamy and the Kinnaird Candelabra: Craftsmanship and Patronage in Regency London"' *Apollo* 145, no. 419 (January 1997): 30–34.

101. Geoffrey de Bellaigue, "The Crimson Drawing Room, Carlton House," *Furniture History* 26 (1990): 10–19; idem, "The Vulliamy's Chimney-pieces," *Furniture History* 33 (1997): 188–216; idem, " Samuel Parker and the Vulliamy's purveyors of gilt bronze," *Burlington Magazine* 139 (1997): 26–37.

102. Snodin and Baker, "William Beckford's Silver," part 2 (1980): 820–22. The authors argue that Beckford's patronage of individual craftsmen such as Aldridge gave him greater control over the design and execution.

103. Among these were the sales of the collections of: Lalive de July (1770), Blondel de Gagny (1777), his nephew, Blondel d'Azincourt (1770), Randon de Boisset (1777), the duc de Choiseul (1772, 1774, 1786, 1788 and 1793), the duc d'Aumont (1782) or the Comte de Ste Foix (1782), to mention only the most famous.

104. Rutters, *Delineations* (1823); and Phillips' 1823, lot 1155, where it is specifically mentioned as being in red tortoiseshell.

105. Although it is sometimes claimed that they were lot 312 in the sale of the Duc d'Aumont (see Wainwright, *Romantic Interior* [1989]: 132), they do not fit the descriptions of the wardrobes in the sale catalogue. In *Inventaire aprés deces du duc d'Aumont* (photocopy in Départment des arts décoratifs, Louvre) there is no mention of any wardrobes with a similar description. I am most grateful to M. Alcouffe for supplying me with this information and allowing me access to the department's archives. The wardrobes were acquired by the Duke of Hamilton for £506 5s each, and it is from the Hamilton Palace sale that they found their way to the Louvre.

106. Letter to Franchi, 4 July 1814, quoted in Alexander, *Life at Fonthill* (1957): 152. These might have been the pair at Fonthill; in a following letter on 6 July, however, it is implied that he did not acquire this pair at the time. (Boyd Alexander, "transcripts of letters to Franchi," MS. Eng. Misc. d.1296, fol. 22, Bodleian Library). Moreover, the correspondence hints at the fact that Franchi, who was in Paris at the time, was finding similar, perhaps more suitable items for Beckford to view when he came to Paris later that year. On 10 December, however, Beckford wrote that Fogg had promised to send the wardrobes, perhaps the same Boulle ones he had seen in July. (ibid., fol. 62). Reitlinger, on the other hand, argues that Beckford bought the two armoires in Paris in 1814 from the auctioneer, Lebrun; see Gerald Reitlinger, *The Economics of Taste*, vol. 3 (New York: Holt, Rinehart and Winston, 1963): 128. They did not appear in the sale, 23–29 May 1814, held by Paillet in Paris (British Library, London).

107. Christie's 1817, Second day, lot 112.

108. E. Lennox Boyd, "George Watson Taylor" in *The Gerstenfeld Collection* (London: Christie's, 1998): 157. The present cabinet, now in a private collection, was sold Christie's New York, Tuesday, 21 October 1997, lot 35. The dimensions were 86 feet high, 43 feet wide, 18? feet deep. It was probably lot 44 in the Watson Taylor sale at Erlstoke, which was described as "A superb cabinet of brass, steel and tortoiseshell (manufacture of Buhl) the lower part consisting of two plate Glass Doors, the upper part of eleven drawers fronted with Buhl work and or-moulu, and Pilasters with capitals of or-moulu, a central door opening discloses a Recess having Secret Drawers, fronted with various woods, inlaid; the Pediment contains a Disk, upon which the Royal French Cypher is inlaid in brass-work." The similarities are striking to the cabinet in the Beckford 1817 sale, except for the pediment in the Watson-Taylor cabinet, which makes it difficult to be certain that both entries refer to the same cabinet.

109. There were six in preparation in Boulle's workshop in 1715 and eighteen in stock in 1720; see

Jean-Pierre Samoyault, *André–Charles Boulle et Sa Famille* (Geneva: Librairie Dros, 1979); and *Nouveaux Desseins de Meubles et Ouvrages de Bronze et de Marqueterie Inventés et gravés par André Charles Boulle* (ca. 1707), reproduced in ibid., pp. 214–21.

110. A pair possibly these were sold recently, see *Magnificent French Furniture,* sale cat. Christies, New York, 2 November 2000, lot 34. They match the description, which included the measurments of the stands, 4 feet, 4 inches; the difference being attributed to a change in the feet.

111. It is interesting to note that there were no such candlestands listed in the Christie's 1822 catalogue.

112. Christie's 1822; Third day, lot 40; Phillips' 1823, lot 1359. The pair was sold to McQueen for £45 13 6 (£2,700 in 2000). Henry Hawley has pointed out that the depictions in Rutter of individual works coincide with the appearance of known surviving pieces, from which it can be surmised that the drawings may be renditions of Beckford's collections. On the other hand, there were more candlestands in the engraving than appear in the 1822 and 1823 catalogues, so the numbers may not have been correct. I am grateful to Derek Ostergard for this information.

113. Christie's 1822: Third day, lots 57, 58; Sixth day, lots 98, 99; Ninth day, lots 91 and 92; Tenth day, lots 91 and 92. Phillips' 1823, lots 1264, 1297, 1298, 1304, 1306, "Ebony & buhl tortoiseshell cabinet, with plate glass folding doors, ormolu, lined with crimson silk tabaret and slab of black marble" in Saint Michael's Gallery. The cabinets sold to different dealers for prices ranging from £40 to £54 (£2,200 to £2,900 in 2000). In addition there were a number of ebony cabinets mounted in ormolu, lined with rose-colored silk, which did not use tortoiseshell.

114. Christie's 1822, Third day, lots 43, 46. They do not seem to appear in Phillips' 1823.

115. Sale of the collection of Randon de Boisset, Remy and Julliot, Paris, 27 February to 25 March 1777 (Victoria and Albert Museum, London) and sale of the collection of Blondel de Gagny, Remy, Paris 10 to 14 December 1776 and 8 to 22 January 1777 (Victoria and Albert Museum London). Both are annotated with prices.

116. Sale of the collection of Randon de Boisset, Remy and Julliot, Paris 27 February to 25 March 1777 (Lugt 2652, Victoria and Albert Museum, London).

117. Le Baron Charles Davillier, *Le Cabinet du Duc d'Aumont: Catalogue de sa vente* (Paris: Aubry, 1870).

118. There is no Boulle furniture listed in English sales of the late eighteenth century and the Boulle furniture in the Royal Collections seems to have been acquired through dealers after 1802.

119. This is based on photocopies of Parisian catalogues listed in Lugt, *Art Catalogues*: the ci-devant duc de Choiseul, 18–15 February 1792 (Lugt 5005); the collection of Citizen Lareyniere, 3 April 1793 (Lugt 5025); and Lespignac d'Tricot, 22 May 1793 (Lugt 5069). These were all sold by Lebrun, with from four to six pieces of Boulle furniture in each. The collection of the cabinet of M M*** (Segur de Mal de Clesle de Beaudoin), Paillet, and L. F. J. Boileau, Paris, 9 April 1793 (Lugt 5028), ten lots listed. There were no prices in these catalogues.

120. Catalogue of the sale of Vincent Donjeux, Lebrun, and Paillet, Paris, 29 April 1793, lot 788 (Lugt 5049). The problems faced in determining the prices of Boulle furniture can be shown in the completely different prices fetched in this sale. Two wardrobes with clocks were sold: one for 2651 livres (equal to £6,800 in 2000) in contre partie (probably that now in the Wallace Collection (Hughes, *Wallace Collection* [1996]); the second, described as being just as grand, for only 1,201 livres (£3,100). A number of cabinets were much cheaper at 600 or 800 livres (approximately £1,750).

121. Sale of M.Choiseul-Praslin, 18 February 1793 (Lugt 5005), British Library, London.

122. " Everyone one discovers a sham style . . . ," letter to Franchi, 7 November 1814, quoted in Alexander, *Life at Fonthill* (1957): 161. A few days later he wrote, "If I did not flee from buying temptations I'd be down to my last farthing," ibid., p. 163.

123. Christie's 1817, Second day, lot 112; Alexander, "transcripts," p. 62.

124. The Choiseul-Praslin sale in 1808 included three pairs of low cabinets with the figures of Aspanasia and the Philosopher; in 1811 the sale of the cabinet of M Gamba included one lot of a Boulle marquetry table; the sale of M de L'Espinalle de Langeac, Comte d'Arlet, in 1815 listed one piece of furniture in the style of Boulle. There were no prices given in the available catalogues.

125. Serge Grandjean, *Inventaire après décés de l'Impératrice Joséphine à Malmaison* (Paris: Reunion des Musees Nationaux, n.d.).

126. Sale of the collection of Cardinal Fesch, lot 443 (British Library, London). The description of two "bas armoires" in partie and contrepartie, with marble tops is very brief; in addition they were described as "par Boulle" and this more general term might also be used for later versions of Boulle furniture. It is thus very difficult to assess their importance in relation to those in the previous sales.

127. Catalogue of the sale of the collection of Madame le Rouge, after her death, 27 April, 1818, Le Rouge, Le Neuve, Coquille and Chariot, Paris (British Library, London).

128. Thus the cabinets were are very low and had marble tops, and although most of the descriptions were brief, two lots (120 and 121) specifically mentioned octagonal medallions in the center, all of which are generally found on later eighteenth-century examples.

129. Sale of the stock of Maelrondt, 15 November, 1824 (Lugt 10760, British Library, London). There were two small cabinets between 1500 and 1725 francs (£3,000 to £3,400) and a third at 570 francs (£1,100).

130. The Levasseur secretaire bought by the Prince Regent in 1812 from Fogg for £367 10s (£12,000) had been bought earlier that year in the Villers sale for 1,100 francs (£1,900); see *Carlton House* (1991): 80.

131. *A Catalogue of the Genuine HOUSEHOLD FURNITURE . . . the property of a man of Fashion. which will be sold by Auction by Mr. Phillips on the premises, No. 18, Bruton Street, Berkeley Square on Wednesday 4 March 1807.*

132. *Lord Kinnaird's Rich and Costly Furniture, silk and cloth draperies, Buhl and Parisian Commodes, Seve China, Ancient Bronzes . . . ,* sale cat., Phillips', London, 17 February 1813 and eight following days, Second day, lot 195 (Microfiche, British Library, London). No prices are given but a similar one the previous year had fetched 70 guineas (£2,400).

133. *A Catalogue of Parisian Furniture . . . from the Palaces of Versailles . . . ,"* sale cat., Phillips', 8 June 1816; *A splendid Assemblage of French Furniture;* 8 June 1819; *A Splendid Consignment of Parisian Furniture;* 21 March 1821; *An Assemblage of Useful and Decorative Boule and Reisner Furniture,* Phillips', London, 30 May 1818. (Wallace Collection London). The catalogues made very little distinction as to whether the "Buhl" item offered for sale was considered old or not.

134. Phillips', London, 30 May 1818, lot 239. This can be compared to a similar cabinet in Beckford's 1817 sale, day 1, lot 72, a jewel chest and stand of tortoiseshell bought by Forster for £55 13s (£2,200).

135. Phillips', London, 30 May 1818, lots 779, 701.

136. Phillips' 1823, lot 1140. It was sold to Miles for £262 10s (equal to £14,000 in 2000). Although Beckford visited Malmaison while in Paris in 1814, there is no comparable table either in the inventory of Malmaison taken at Joséphine's death, or in the subsequent sales; see Denise Ledoux-Lebard, "La liquidation des objets d'art provenant de la succession de l'Imperatrice Joséphine à Malmaison," *Archives de l'Art Français* 22 (1959): 340–48; Serge Grandjean, "Les Collections de l'Imperatrice Josphine à Malmaison et leur dispersion," *La Revue des Arts* 4 (1959): 193–98; idem, *Inventaire après décès de l'Impératrice Joséphine à Malmaison* (Paris: Reunion des Musees Nationaux, n.d.).

137. For the two commodes, see Christie's 1817, First day, lot 70, "a superb commode of ebony, lined with oak, in 3 divisions, central door & those on the sides with pietre dure gems & oriental alabaster; top of black & yellow Italian marble"; and Third day, lot 47, a "capital pier commode with a door in front, 11 small pannels [sic] filled with medallions of pietre dure of birds and fruits of fine Italian workmanship, pannels at end of Buhl, twisted ebony columns at the angles; top of Scotch Garnet. It is tempting to identify it with one of two cabinets by Weisweiler at the Getty Museum, acc. nos. 76.D.A. 9.1–2, which came from Hamilton Palace; see Charissa Bremer-David, *Decorative Arts: An Illustrated Summary Catalogue of the collections fo J. Paul Getty Museum* (Malibu, California: The J. Paul Getty Museum, 1993). Lots 185 and 186 in the Hamilton Palace sale are, however, described as a pair, each one, "an oblong cabinet of ebony inlaid with brass, with fluted columns at the angles, inlaid with slabs of Florentine pietre-dure mosaic, with birds, fruit & flowers, richly mounted with friezes masks & mouldings of ormolu chased in high relief, black & gold marble slab." As Douglas had bought such pieces from an early date, had visited Italy himself, and had owned many examples, it is impossible to be certain that any piece of pietra-dura furniture from the Hamilton Palace sale might originally have belonged to Beckford.

138. Third day, lot 45, a cabinet of Florentine mosaic with ebony columns; Third day, lot 95, an ebony commode with mosaic panels, sold to Lucy.

139. Christie's, 1822, Fifth day, lot 53.

140. Davillier, *Cabinet du Duc d'Aumont* (1870): lot 313, "deux cabinets, premier partie decuivre et étain, avec panneaux à pierres de rapport, du plus parfait ouvrage de Florence, à sujets d'oiseaux, branchages, fleurs et fruits."

141. See A. Setterwall, "Some Louis XVI Furniture" (1959): 430–35, where a number of these pieces and the trade in pietre-dure panels are discussed.

142. Sale of M Daguerre, Christie's London, 25 March 1791, lot 59 (Lugt 4698): " an elegant ebony cabinet, the front curiously and beautifully inlaid with gems, comprised of precious stones from Florence, brocadella marble top, superbly mounted in or-moulu." The cabinet and others now in the Royal Collections are discussed in *Carlton House* (1991): 76–77.

143. *Household furniture etc from Exton park near Stamford, 15 April 1816 and ten following days,* Tuesday, 23rd April, 1816 [handwritten in ink].

144. *Sale of Parisian furniture, the most splendid assemblage of decorative furniture by Buhl and Reisner (sic) that has yet been imported,* Phillips', 30 May 1818, lot 439 (Wallace Collection Library, London).

145. Sale of the stock of Feuchere, père, sold by his son, 29 November 1824 (Lugt 10766 (British Library, London).

146. Alvar Gonzales Palacios, *Il Tempio del Gusto; Le Arti Decorative in Italia fra Classicismi e*

Barocco: Il Granducato di Toscana e gli Stati Settentrionali, (Milan: Longanesi and Co., Phillips'1986): 83.

147. There are no references to Florentine tabletops in the London sales at this date (1812). All the tops listed in the catalogues, of which there were many, were of different types of marble. Although there had been many Italian tabletops collected by those doing the Grand Tour, they were generally imitating antique forms, not the seventeenth-century pietra-dura tops from Florence or Rome. In England, although there were many examples of marble tops for sale in London, they were either antique or of marble. Collectors such as Count d'Adhemar (Christie's, 17–22 March 1788) or the Countess of Holderness (Christie's, 22 February 1802) had tables with hardstone tops, but not of Florentine mosaic. One of the first examples of this taste to appear in the London sales was a lady's work and writing table with a beautiful Florentine marble slab, which was sold in Phillips', 30 May 1818, lot 358 (Wallace Collection, London).

148. "Inventaire descriptif des Tableaux et autres objets d'arts, extraits du Palais Pitti et déposés au Musée le 21 Termidor par le *Cen.* Joseph Grégoire prépose du gouvernement pour les transports des dits objets" (Gonzales Palacios, *Tempio del Gusto* [1986]: 88–94).The inventory was taken in Paris, 9 August 1801 and included nineteen tables sent from Florence by the French Commissaire in Florence, Charles Reinhard (ibid., p. 94).

149. Sale of Lespinasse d'Arlet de Longeas, Paris, 11–19 July 1803 (Lugt 6668).

150. The base with its decoration of Latimer crosses was made later for Beckford, although it is not known by whom.

151. Wainwright, *Romantic Interior* (1989): 193 and 223.

152. However, one top brought from Florence to Paris was a sixteenth-century top designed by Ligozzi, possibly for Francesco de Medici. It was given a base by Jacob and installed at Malmaison (Serge Grandjean, "Une console de l'Impératrice Joséphine à Malmaison, *La Revue des Arts* 2 [1955]: 182–83). Interestingly, there are several tables described as Florentine in the sale of M. Feuchère, Paris, 29 November 1824: lot 265, with arabesque designs, which sold for 2911 francs (equal to £5,700 in 2000); and lot 260 with birds & animals, which sold for 2760 francs (£5,400). The same sale contained a guéridon designed by Percier and Fontaine with black marble top and rich mosaics by Belloni, sold to Jacob for 2220 francs (£4,400). This is one of the few to have Florentine pietra-dura tables.

153. Celotti sale, 1819 (British Library). One of these cabinets had paintings by Hans van Balen, another was with drawers paneled with stone scenes imitating ruins in landscapes and two were with pietre-dure panels of flowers and birds.

154. Anthony Coleridge, "Andrea Brustolon: Some Additions to his Oevre," *Apollo* 77 (1963): 209–12.

155. Add Mss 35, 254, British Library. The collection of miniatures acquired from Malcolm of Poltalloch includes several brought over by Celutti, which he claimed to have acquired from the Vatican.

156. Letter to Thomas Grenville (to whom the other letters seem to be addressed), August 1825, from 14 Brompton Row, MS BL 1859 fol 113, British Library. He writes offering Grenville a 1532 copy of Ariosto for £160 (£6,900) which cost him 4000 francs (£6,800).

157. *Sale of Valuable Paintings, Magnificent Cabinets and Splendid Furniture from Lansdown Tower,* sale cat., English and Fasana, Bath, 4 January 1841, lot 15, MS Beckford d. 27, fol. 2.

157. For Beckford as collector of French furniture, see Wainwright, "Some Objects" (1971): 29; Wainwright, *The Romantic Interior* (1989): 142; *The Collection of the Barons Nathaniel and Albert von Rothschild,* Christies, London, July 1999, p. 372. Phillips' 1823, lot 1579; a "lady's japan secretary & cabinet sumptuously mounted & enriched with ormulu, the interior lined with satinwood, marble slab top, formerly in the possession of Marie Antoinette, Queen of France" was sold to Scott for £40 8s 6d (£2,200). It has sometimes been associated with the secretaire and commode sold to Marie Antoinette for the Cabinet Intérieur de la Reine at the Château de Saint Cloud (now in The Metropolitan Museum of Art, New York). This set was acquired by George Watson Taylor and sold in the 1832 sale of his collection at Erlstoke to Robert Hume on behalf of the Duke of Hamilton; see Ronald Freyburger, "Eighteenth-Century French Furniture from Hamilton Palace," *Apollo* 94, no. 238 (December 1981). Similarly, a Riesener commode from the Hamilton Palace sale of 1882, formerly in the Rothschild collection, Vienna, and recently sold, could once again have been at Fonthill. If so it would be lot 1574 in the 1823 sale, "a matchless Riesener commode, inlaid and decorated with bronze cariatides, friezes, masks, highly gilt & sharply chased," which was sold to Wills for £120 5s. (equal to £6,500 in 2000). Again, however, Beckford's ownership cannot be substantiated by the 1822 catalogue or other evidence and has already been pointed out, there is evidence that Phillips included other important lots he wanted to sell in 1823.

159. Hughes, *Wallace Collection* (1996): cat. no. 191 (F102). This desk, based on the *bureau du roi* for Louis XV's study at Versailles, was until recently, thought to have been made for King Stanislaus of Poland and father-in-law to Louis XV. It was, however, probably sold to the comte d'Orsay, whose initials are on the side of the desk, ca. 1770, and it is the one listed in the 1774

inventory of the Hôtel d'Orsay. It appeared again in a Phillips', 1825 sale and the Marquess of Hertford is thought to have bought it soon after that.

160. The Garde Meuble de la Couronne was the name of the royal stores or wardrobe, housed after 1774 in the Place Louis XV; see Jean-Nérée Ronfort, "Le Mobilier royal à l'époque de Louis XIV et le Garde-Meuble de la Couronne," in *De Versailles à Paris* (n.d.): 35; and Jean-Jaques Gautier, "Le Garde Meuble de la Couronne sous Thierry de Ville d'Avray," in ibid., pp. 53–58. During the Revolution it was also used as a place of storage for other confiscated property; see Beurdeley, *La France à l'encan* (1981): 95.

161. Francis Watson, "The Tilsit Table and the Stanislas Bureau," *Burlington Magazine* (June 1950): 165–67; Reitlinger, *Economics of Taste,* vol. 3 (1963): 86; and Beurdeley, *Ventes* (n.d.): 120. Both authors argue that he bought it for 760 English pounds in 1792.

162. Hughes, *Wallace Collection* (1996): cat. no. 191 (F102).

163. The description of the library table may not be compatable with pre-Revolutionary royal pieces, and it is always possible that in this, as in later sales, items other than royal furniture had been added.

164. *An Assemblage of Useful and Decorative Boule and Reisner Furniture,* sale cat., Phillips', London, 30 May 1818. Although not common to find Riesener singled out in the Paris sales, he was mentioned at least once by name; e.g., Paillet & Delaroche, 10 July 1802, lot 319, "a secretaire à cylindre by Riesener, in parquetry, richly decorated with girandoles, and other mounts of or moulu." Interestingly the catalogue includes A. Lund in London among the three auctioneers. It seems to have been quite common to have an agent abroad after 1815, although it was sometimes the practice before then.

165. Phillips', 30 May 1818, lots 475, 541, attributed to Riesener with a very general description of "marqueterie de Riesener"; Phillips', London, 8 June 1819, lot 184, a ""richly inlaid Reisner commode with moulding and marble slab." The implication is that anything with marquetry might be considered "Riesener."

166. lot 76, *Sale of . . . Furniture . . . from the Late Very distinguished Town House of G. Watson Taylor . . . ,* Christie's, London, 28 May 1825.

167. Ibid., lots 31 and 58. There were three commodes in the sale; the two others sold: lot 27, for £34 2s 6d (equal to £1,500 in 2000), and lot 36, for £75 (£3,200).

168. See chap. 7, by Megan Aldrich, in this volume.

169. Wainwright, *Romantic Interior* (1989): 117–18. He also refers to Jeffrey Wyatt's espousal of the Elizabethan style, and the furnishing of Endsleigh in Devon and Longleat in Wiltshire in this taste.

170. Wainwright, "Some Objects"(1971): 257.

171. Christie's 1822. First day, lot 19; no buyer listed.

172. Ibid., Third day, lot 76, sold to Forster for £26 5s (equal to £1,500 in 2000).

173. Phillips' 1823, lots 69, 70. At the Stowe sale on 16 August, 1848 the cabinets were Second Day, lots 236, 237, sold for 20 guineas each (£1,150) to the Marquess of Hertford, and they are now in the Wallace Collection. They were sold as if original, but Beckford, who had commissioned them, must have known that they were modern (Hughes, *Wallace Collection* [1996]: 249–53).

174. Wainwright, *Romantic Interior* (1989): 44–45, shows that many of the pieces illustrated in H. Shaw, *Specimens of Antique Furniture* (1836) were owned by dealers such as John Swaby, Edward Hull, and John Webb.

175. [London] *Times,* 1 October 1822.

176. The Lancaster bed, for example, was created from different elements to create a convincing English "Elizabethan" bed. Among Baldock's patrons, Walter Francis, fifth Duke of Buccleuch acquired many such pieces. See de Bellaigue, "Edward Holmes Baldock" part 2 (1975): 21–22; and Jaffer, *Furniture from British India* (2001): 130–42.

177. A significant number of these ebony cabinets carved with mythological scenes were made ca. 1640–60 and are to be found in museums today. Many of the most elaborate were made in Paris, and the names of Jean Macé, Garbrand and Pierre Golle have been associated with them. See Reinier Baarsen, *Cabinets in the Rijksmuseum* (Amsterdam: Wanders Publishers, Rijksmuseum, 2000).

178. Christie's 1822, Third day, lot 15.

179. Ibid., sixth day, lot 46, " a superb jewel cabinet of ebony and other costly materials, in imitation of an architectural façade: the niches, in the centre, are filled with small groups by BOUCHARDON, being the original models, in miniature, by that distinguished French sculptor, for the embellishment of a public fountain constructed by him in Paris. They are placed within columns of Rosso Antico; the pannels of the drawers are of lapis lazuli and blood stone, set with 40 rubies and emeralds; the ornaments are richly chased and gilt and the stand is in correspondent taste." In the letter of 26 June 1817 Beckford wrote, "I have practically destroyed my nails in a vain effort to open the Bouchardon cabinet"; quoted in Alexander, *Life at Fonthill* (1957): 212.

180. Ibid., p. 323.

181. Wednesday, 14 November 1814, quoted in ibid., p. 158.

182. Christie's 1822, day 9, lot 63; it does not appear in the 1823 sale and may have been withdrawn by Beckford as it was later to be found at Lansdown.

183. This cabinet has recently been associated with a Roman ebony cabinet with panels of lapis lazuli, jasper, agate, and bloodstones, which was recently most recently sold in the *Sale of Highly Important Continental Furniture,* Sotheby's, London, 10 June 1998, lot 20. At an earlier sale (Sotheby's New York, 7 December 1991, lot 20), there was a stand with the Latimer cross, a heraldic device that Beckford often used. Because of this the cabinet and stand were associated with Beckford, and then with the Bernini cabinet. The measurements of the cabinet with its original stand were very close to those given in the 1844 description of the Bernini cabinet. The differences may reflect changes made to the mounts now on the cabinet, or the cabinet might be another owned by Beckford. Inside the lowest drawer are three labels: "Fossil shells," "Fossil wood," and "Fossil Coral," written in ink in an unknown hand.

184. Sale of 1841, lot 20, "A superb ebony cabinet, originally in the Royal Palace of Madrid enriched both in the interior and exterior with Paintings by old Franks, of exceeding interest and description of the life of Adam from the Creation of Woman to his expulsion from Paradise. . . ." In a letter to Beckford, 28 April 1824, Hume wrote: "The Francks cabinet shall be finished without delay and also the Michaelangelo one," which could refer to this cabinet but also implies that Hume made some alterations to it (MS. Beckford c. 22, fol 39).

185. Lansdown Tower sale 1841, lots 10 and 11.

186. *The Property of a Gentleman . . . sold by Auction by Mr. Greenwood, at his room in Leicester Square, on Friday the 12th March, 1790.* This would suggest that, were Beckford so inclined, he could have bought seventeenth-century cabinets such as this at the beginning of his collecting career.

187. For Wyatt, see Phillips', Foley Place, 6 June 1814. Wyatt had three ebony and ivory, ebony or tortoiseshell cabinets, even more Japanese lacquer pieces, some Boulle, and most interestingly a rosewood cabinet inlaid with tortoiseshell and ivory, with numerous drawers. For the Earl of Moira, see Phillips', London, 22 May 1813, an inlaid cabinet, silver mounted. For Crace, see Christie's, London, 27 May 1808. Crace bought an ivory and tortoiseshell jewel chest for £6 16s (equal to £275 in 2000) and a tortoiseshell and ivory cabinet on stand for £3 10s.(£140). For Greenwold, see Christie's, London, 17 October 1809. Greenwold bought an ebony jewel cabinet with various secret drawers for £6 15s. (£250). For Bentley, see ibid., lot 115 was an ebony cabinet bought by Bentley for £7 7s 6d.(£275).

188. " curious ebony cabinet inlaid drawers inside, with silver tablets" was sold by Mr. Farebrother, 16 Old Bond St, 23 July 1803, lot 144.

189. *A Catalogue of a collection of . . . Pictures . . . also some fine Cabinets, Old china, Bronzes, Marbles, Ivory Carvings etc. which will be sold by auction by Mr. Christie on Friday June 21, 1805 . . .*

190. It might, or might not, be significant that the Celotti sale in 1819, which had six cabinets of ebony and pietre-dure plaques took place in Paris. There may have been a growing interest in antique furniture among French collectors, which had previously been found mainly in England, as shown in some of the Parisian sale catalogues from 1820 onward.

191. *Highly Important Continental Furniture,* sale cat., Sotheby's, London, 8 June 1998, lots 20, 43.

192. Lansdown sale, 1841. On the second day, lot 10 was a large ebony armoire for books, lot 12 was four ebony chairs, lot 16 was a pair of ebony pedestal cabinets, lot 22 was a semicircular ebony cabinet with gilt mounts, and lot 23 was an ebony and beefwood console table. In the 1845 sale held by English and Son there was only one item of ebony: lot 600, a pair of ebony cabinets with folding doors (MS Beckford d.27).

193. Christie's 1817, day 3, lot 55, bought for 43 gns. (equal to £1,800 in 2000); day 1, lot 38, bought by Forster for £36 15s. (£1,400). Other examples of carved ebony were day 3, lot 60, an "Indian cabinet with 28 small drawers of Indian wood with flowered inlayings of ebony & brass mounts," bought by Boulleville for 34 guineas (£1,400); and day 1, lots 92 and 93, a pair of square work tables with drawer of Oriental woods and ebony on black and gold fluted legs, bought for £10 guineas (£400) each. In 1822, day 2, lot 53, was "a curiously inlaid cabinet of Oriental wood having nine drawers of ebony and ivory on a table to correspond, solid ebony legs and carved mouldings chased."

194. For two such entries: Christie's 1822, day 2, lot 44,"An elegant Persian Cabinet on stand of ebony & ivory, richly mounted with ormolu," and lot 45, "A Persian solid ebony table, with legs carved in scroll ornaments, with crimson silk velvet top, and drawer."

195. Letter to Franchi, September 1813, Ms Eng. Misc.d.1296, 57, Bodleian Library.

196. Kim Sloane, *Alexander and John Robert Cozens* (New Haven: Yale University Press 1986): 74. Cozens was called "the Persian" by Beckford.

197. A small account book in Portuguese in Franchi's hand from 1813 to 1815, MS Beckford c. 37, fols.73–90. On 1 June 1813 is listed "1 cabinete de pao Santo para a Salla de espera at £10 8s 0" (equal to £330 in 2000; fol. 73) In the same list, "duay cadieras de Ebano at £28 18s 0 (£920; 1815,

fol. 76) and 1 cabinete de Persia at £16 (£510). Customs payments from Lisbon to London (fol. 90) might indicate that some of the items listed on these pages had been imported from Lisbon, although the context of the notebook is not clear as there are also references to imports from Paris.

198. A "coffret d'ivoire persian avec 1 capoletta de Christal de roche—une petite coupe de jade blanc," MS. Beckford c.37, fol. 92.

199. Christie's 1822, day 2, lot 79,"an Ivory Jewel cabinet, elaborately carved with foliage, mounted with rich chasings and silver hinges", which was in the King Edwards Gallery, sold to Hume for £48 6s (£2,800 in 2000); Phillips' 1823, lot 545.

200. Jaffer, *Furniture from British India* (2001).

201. See Christopher Woodward, chap. 16, in this volume.

202. No Boulle furniture is listed in the sale catalogues of 1841 and 1844, English and Sons; nor in the inventory of Lansdown Crescent and Tower taken by Robert Hume, 1844 (MS Beckford c.58).

203. Letter of 22 November 1815, Alexander, *Life at Fonthill* (1957): 192.

204. The cabinet (Phillips' 1823, lot 1045) was sold for £572 6s (equal to £31,000 in 2000) to Baldock. In Baldock's sale of 21 July 1843, "a pair of ebony cabinet doors, richly engraved, the centre boldy carved in subjects, Mutius Scaevola and Quintus Curtius" was sold to Alexandre du Sommerard. (de Bellaigue, "Edward Holmes Baldock," part 2 (1975): 21. These might have been originally the doors from Beckford's cabinet. They are now part of a later cabinet in the Musée de la Renaissance, Ecouen. I am most grateful to M Pierre Ennes for allowing me to examine these panels and photograph them.

205. Rutter, *Delineations* (1823). Before it had been in the dining room and had probably been created to hold some of Beckford's works of art, as with his other cabinets (Michael Snodin, personal communication, 2000).

206. Alexander, *Life at Fonthill* (1957): 190.

207. Christie's 1822, day 3, lot 95; Phillips' 1823, lot 1138, an "ebony commode, with mosaic pannels [*sic*], architectural centre and wings, richly ornamented with ormolu," 5ft 3" long with a black marble slab. It was sold to Lucy for £133 10s. (equal to £7,250 in 2000).

208. Sotheby's sale of Important Continental Furniture, London, 10 June 1998, lot 86 and Phillips'sale of Important English Furniture, Christie's, 13 June 2001, lot 100. It has been suggested that they were probably intended for Beckford's London house in Park Place. The cabinets were recorded in the inventory of Stafford House, London, by 1839 and subsequently sold in 1913.

209. MS Beckford c.37, fol. 99.

210. Robert Hume had undertaken much the same role for the Duke of Hamilton as agent for a clock cabinet now in the Gilbert Collection at Somerset House. See Ronald Freyburger, "The Duke of Hamilton's Clock Cabinet", *Christie's International Magazine,* 8 (June 1991): 10–13; and Anna Maria Massinelli, *Hardstones* (London: Phillip Wilson, 2000): 49. The cabinets will be the subject of a forthcoming article by Philip Hewat-Jaboor and Bet McLeod in *Furniture History* (2002). I am most grateful to Philip Hewat-Jaboor for discussing their research with me.

211. Edmund English, *Views of Lansdown Tower, Bath, The Famous Edifice of the late William Beckford from Drawings by Willes Madox* (Bath and London, 1844). Although published after Beckford's death, the concepts are Beckford's. I am grateful to Derek Ostergard for suggesting this as a source and to Philip Hewat-Jaboor for the use of his copy.

212. Ibid., pl. 8.

213. Lansdown Tower sale 1841, lot 10 (MS Beckford d. 27/2).

214. Ibid., lot 24. These were of oak, and said to come from the King Edward's Gallery at Fonthill Abbey.

215. I am most grateful to Derek Ostergard for discussing this aspect of Beckford's taste with me and for his many valuable suggestions.

216. Lansdown Tower 1841, lot 26 (MS Beckford d. 27/2); and *Sale of the contents of Lansdown Tower,* English and Son, 1845, lots 520 and 521.

217. Lansdown Tower sale 1845, lot 26.

218. Lansdown Tower sale 1841, lot 16 (MS Beckford d.27/2).

219. Letter to Franchi, 5 February 1819, Ms Eng. 1296, Bodleian Library.

220. Letter from Robert Hume, London, 28 April 1824, MS. Beckford c.22, fol 39. It is interesting that a cabinet also said to have been by Michaelangelo appeared in the Hamilton Palace sale. A cabinet, probably the one in the Hamilton Palace sale, is now at Elton Hall, Cambridgeshire. This cabinet has a base with Hamilton devices and differs from the description of Beckford's cabinet, although it is possible that these are the result of subsequent alterations (Bet McLeod, personal communication, 2000).

221. Letter from Hume, 7 December 1831, MS Beckford c. 22, fol. 130.

222. Letter from Hume, 17 December 1831, ibid, fol 132.

223. Letter from Hume, Hôtel d'Alberg to the Duke of Hamilton, 11 February 1830, Hamilton Papers, bundle 602, Hamilton Archives. Hume wrote that Beckford would consider selling the cabinet as well as his Auguste one. This may be the cabinet sold at the Hamilton Palace Sale lot 293, or either of lots 172 or 173. I am most grateful to Bet McLeod for this reference and drawing.

224. Inventory of 1844, MS Beckford c. 58.

225. *A Catalogue of a Selection of Sumptuous Articles of Parisian and other Furniture . . . from the Late Very distinguished Town House of G. Watson Taylor . . .*, Christie's, London, 28 May 1825. The provenances quoted in this sale give an indication of the extraordinary quality of the pieces bought between around 1815 and 1824. See Hugh Roberts, "Quite Appropriate for Windsor Castle? George IV and George Watson Taylor," *Furniture History* 306 (2000): 115–37.

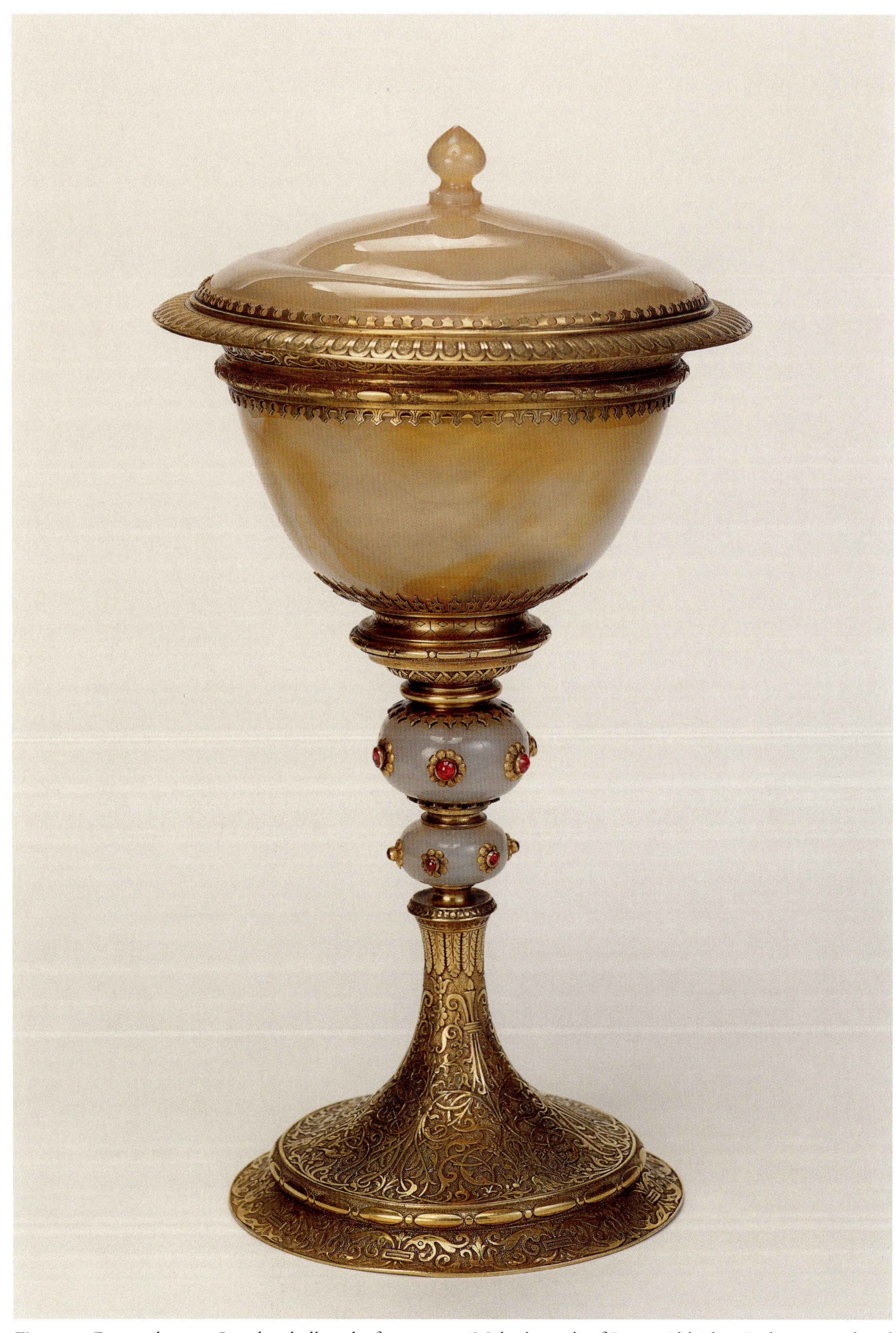

Fig. 11-1. Cup and cover, London hallmarks for 1815–16. Maker's mark of James Aldridge. Indian agate bowl and cover; chalcedony knops set with rubies in gold, mounted in silver gilt. Trustees of the Victoria and Albert Museum, London, M.428-1882.

Chapter XI

WILLIAM BECKFORD AND METALWORK

Michael Snodin

William Beckford's collection of metalwork forms a unique episode in European taste, including as it did the first metalwork in Europe to display a consistently applied historicism, marking the start of a century of revivalism.[1] Beckford's specially commissioned historicist pieces were made from 1800 onward (fig. 11-1), but both before and after this date he also acquired many magnificent, although entirely conventional neoclassical silver for more functional use. As with all Beckford's acquisitions, his metalwork needs to be put into its immediate and wider contexts to be fully understood. Both his new and antique metalwork were intimately linked to the changing interiors—at Fonthill House and Abbey and at his houses in Bath—as well as with their other contents. Metalwork was also part of a shift in avant-garde taste which lifted the applied arts from mere decoration or utility toward a level approaching fine art, a trend that culminated in the Victorian notion of the "Art Object."

For art critic William Hazlitt, Fonthill Abbey was "a desert of magnificence, a glittering waste of laborious idleness, a cathedral turned into toy-shop, an immense Museum of all that is most curious and costly, and at the same time, most worthless, in the productions of art and nature."[2] For Beckford, however, as for John Soane and Thomas Hope, architecture, and the fine and applied arts could be seen as forming a single significant aesthetic and intellectual whole, although Beckford never theorized his ideas as Hope and Soane did. The central idea was expressed by Hope as "the entire assemblage of the productions of ancient art and of modern handicraft, thus intermixed collectively, in a harmonious, more consistent, and more instructive whole."[3] Hope's mission to rescue the applied arts from the "mere plodding artisan" in order "to give some scope to the talent of the professor of the more liberal arts; the draughtsman, the modeller, the painter, and the sculptor"[4] was part of a general movement towards the greater involvement of fine artists in the applied arts.

Metalwork was particularly affected in the early days of this elitist movement. In particular, the royal goldsmiths Rundell, Bridge and Rundell employed a design studio of sculptors and painters that included John Flaxman, the leading sculptor of the day. Rundell's efforts paid off. The artistic value of their metalwork rose sharply after 1800 and was avidly acquired by many, led by the firm's chief client, the Prince Regent. Beckford's interest in metalwork was therefore not unusual, nor was he unique in his pursuit of historicism in that field.[5] He was unique, however, in his single-minded pursuit of his goals, with results more extraordinary than those of any of his contemporaries.

The Classical phase

The earliest surviving pieces of Beckford's silver are functional pieces made in the hallmarking year 1781–82, which were probably in Beckford's hands by the time of his coming-of-age in September of that year.[6] The tea wares, salvers, pieces for the dining table, and candlesticks made in that year are in the conventional neoclassical style of the day, with its characteristically pure forms and restrained ornamental repertoire; they would have fitted well into the interiors at Fonthill House.[7] They were made by leading London specialists of the day, such as John Scofield for candlesticks and the firm of Smith and Sharp for tableware, although they may all have been supplied through a single large retailer, such as Jefferys, Jones and Gilbert, appointed the royal goldsmiths in 1783.[8] Over the next fifty years, this early group of functional work was regularly augmented by pieces in the same style. Before 1796, the hallmark dates usually match the comparatively short periods that Beckford was in England, suggesting that much of his plate traveled with him. This idea is confirmed by matching pieces made in France and by a gold teapot and stand (see cat. no. 20), made by Smith and Sharp, which was hallmarked in May 1785. The teapot and stand went to Switzerland with Beckford in July of that year, indicated by a further mark for exported plate.[9] By 1800 many of these neoclassical pieces were in need of repair, as the surviving papers of Vulliamy and Company show.[10] The firm had begun working for Beckford by January 1797, during his long stay in England from June 1796 to

October 1798. Among other tasks, they set about regilding and repairing 287 pieces of plate in addition to much flatware. The work was carried out in two main campaigns, one in 1800, the other in June 1802, while Beckford was in Paris. It included mending Beckford's gold toasting fork (see cat. no. 25).[11]

During this first stage not all of Beckford's metalwork was in the English neoclassical style of the 1780s, as he purchased a remarkable group of silver and gold pieces from the royal (later, imperial) goldsmith Henri Auguste in Paris from 1788 onward. Many of these pieces were designed by the sculptor Jean-Guillaume Moitte, who, in his work for Auguste in the late 1780s, had laid the ground for the French Directory style of the next decade.[12] According to his journals, Beckford first came across pieces by the Moitte–Auguste partnership in Madrid, where in 1787 he was immensely impressed by a toilet service belonging to Madame d'Aranda.[13] A year later he made his first purchases from Auguste, a set of plates, a teapot stand, and some candlesticks.[14] In 1792 he praised Auguste's skill in metalwork, comparing furniture he was having made by him with a gold ewer he had acquired two years earlier.[15] He continued buying metalwork from Auguste up to 1802; the marks of the objects, or the dates inscribed on them, match his visits to Paris.[16] The Moitte-designed metalwork included three silver ewers, two of which were accompanied by basins, or tazze (see cat. no. 51), a gold ewer and two gold basins.[17] In addition to an ormolu-mounted lacquer cabinet by Auguste, Beckford also owned a pair of Moitte-designed silver candelabra and a silver-gilt jewel coffer carrying a sleeping figure of Morpheus, the last perhaps the most splendid of all Auguste's surviving plate (see cat. no. 52).[18] Most were in the extraordinarily pure and finely modeled style pioneered by Moitte, and a number match his surviving drawn designs. Beckford's own view of his Auguste pieces is probably conveyed by their entries in the sale catalogues, which not only mention Moitte as the designer, information that almost certainly came from Beckford himself, but also describe them in unusually great detail.[19] Their design and finish are variously eulogized in the sale catalogues as: "worthy of the best period of Grecian art" (silver tazze); "designed with infinite spirit" ("Morpheus" coffer); "executed with a truth and feeling unexampled" (silver-gilt ewer); and "finished with unrivalled excellence" (gold tazze).[20]

Just as Beckford was not unique among English collectors in acquiring Auguste silver,[21] so he was by no means alone in being attracted to advanced French styles in the late 1780s and early 1790s. The same design approach was employed by Henry Holland in the decoration of the Prince of Wales's Carlton House, where French craftsmen and decorators were employed. About 1790 Beckford used some of the same people at Fonthill House for its new decorations, which included pieces by Auguste. Among those people was the decorative painter Jean-Jacques Boileau, who also designed for Beckford a pair of tripods *à la Turque* in the Turkish Room. In the late 1790s Boileau went on to become one of the most influential designers of Regency-period silver, introducing a French or Empire element derived from Moitte's style of some ten years earlier.[22] The sale catalogues show that Beckford owned at least two examples of Boileau-designed silver.[23] The identification of Boileau as the designer, like that of Moitte, was provided almost certainly by Beckford. Among other probable Boileau-designed pieces in Beckford's collection were the lacquer cabinets made through Vulliamy's in 1802 and the remarkable wheat-ear cake baskets of 1797–98 (see cat. no. 26).[24] The latter were made by Paul Storr, who executed silver designed by Boileau and retailed by a number of different firms, including the royal goldsmiths Rundell, Bridge and Rundell and Jefferys and Gilbert.[25] The closest English parallels for Beckford's French metalwork, and English metalwork in the French style can be found in the metalwork apparently designed by Thomas Hope and made for him by Paul Storr.[26] Hope's silver included four silver-gilt baskets made a year before Beckford's pair, with which they share a number of features. The similarity of the detailed design treatment of Beckford's and Hope's baskets to drawings by Boileau suggest that all of them were designed by him.[27]

HISTORICISM AND ECLECTICISM

In comparison with the other applied arts, metalwork (the precious metals in particular) was a comparatively late arrival in the field of historicism. Pioneering Gothic interiors of the mid-eighteenth century, such as those at Horace Walpole's Strawberry Hill, contained little Gothic Revival furniture and even less Gothic Revival metalwork. In the 1770s silver candlesticks with Gothic stems were available with a neoclassical bases.[28] Compared with such playfulness, Beckford's first historicizing metalwork, in the form of the silver-gilt "Holbein" candlesticks, was not only highly serious, but also provided several significant pointers for the future (see cat. no. 107). Made by Paul Storr in 1800 but retailed through Vulliamy's, they were firmly linked to Fonthill Abbey by proud inscriptions on their bases: they would indeed have been ready for Nelson's famous visit to the house over Christmas of that year. The exquisite color and detail of their finish, carefully explicated in Vulliamy's bill, not only eventually led them to being described as made of gold, but also became a characteristic of Beckford's later metalwork.[29] In design they are copied, and perhaps in part directly cast from, a type of late seventeenth-century toilet-set candlestick. Examples of such candlesticks have survived carved in wood, imitating precious metal, although the wording of Vulliamy's bill suggests that Beckford's pair could have been taken from metal rather than wooden examples.[30] Beckford's attribution of the design to Holbein, must derive from the similarity of the ornament to that found on a type of late seventeenth-century Indian furniture of ebony which, thanks to Horace Walpole, was generally linked to Cardinal Wolsey,[31] who in turn was linked to Holbein.

Beckford's Holbein candlesticks were among the first expressions of a profound change in the general attitude to historical metalwork that would begin to emerge in the years around 1800. This change was in part due to a new interest in sculptural values in silver, and in part linked to the establishment of historicism as a legitimate approach to design.[32] Not only was Rococo silver being imitated, in

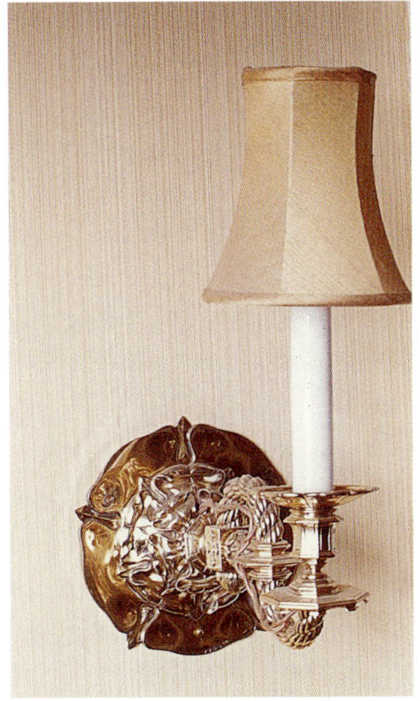

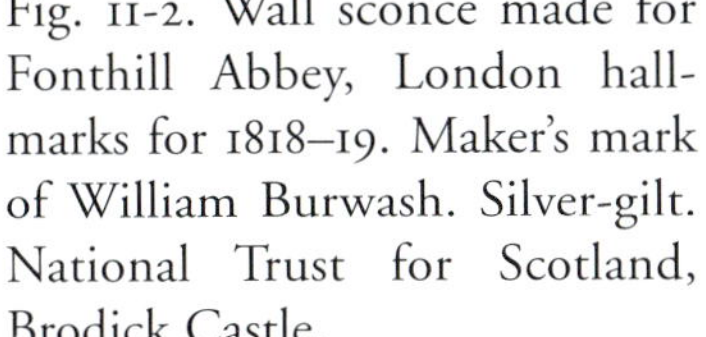

Fig. 11-2. Wall sconce made for Fonthill Abbey, London hall-marks for 1818–19. Maker's mark of William Burwash. Silver-gilt. National Trust for Scotland, Brodick Castle.

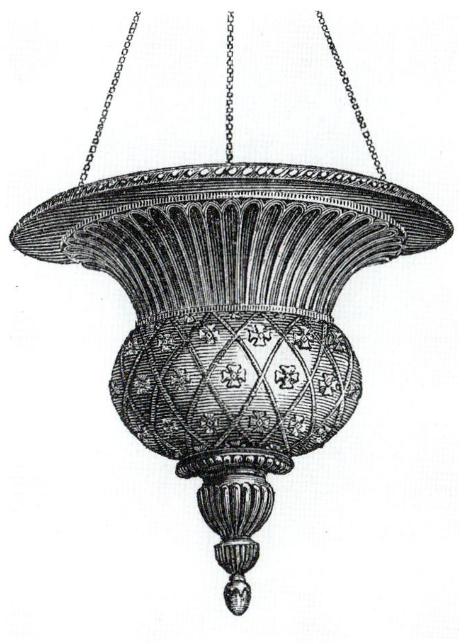

Fig. 11-3. The Oratory lamp, Fonthill Abbey. Woodcut. From John Rutter, *Delineations of Fonthill and its Abbey* (Shaftesbury and London, The Author, 1823): 65.

line with the collecting of French ancien régime mounted porcelain and other luxury objects, but baroque and Renaissance plate attracted increasing attention from connoisseurs and collectors. Baroque display silver was particularly favored, with its deeply embossed figurative work earning not only a place in Sir John Soane's collection of casts, but also the compliment of imitation in modern silver, most especially in pieces made by the chaser William Pitts from at least 1809, by Paul Storr from at least 1812, and the goldsmith Edward Farrell from 1814.[33]

Shifting attitudes to baroque silver were strongly indicated by the sale of some baroque plate in 1808 by Rundell, Bridge and Rundell. The firm had been sent this plate by the Crown for melting and conversion into new pieces, but sold them clandestinely instead. Among the purchasers was Beckford, who although thoroughly shocked by the expense, bought two late-seventeenth-century sideboard dishes and perhaps also the three pairs of sconces from the same period which were at the Abbey in 1822.[34] At that date the Abbey contained no less than thirty-three dishes and other examples of antique plate.[35] Beckford, although an admirer of real baroque plate, shunned its overblown modern imitations. When the time came to finding appropriate lighting for the expanding interiors of Fonthill Abbey he used old sconces and employed long rows of neoclassical candlesticks placed on stands for his dramatically candlelit galleries. The few new pieces for lighting included the earliest examples of Beckford's metalwork treating historicism in an imaginative manner. In King Edward's Gallery, a pair of sconces probably closely resembled a surviving pair of 1818–19 (fig. 11-2).[36] With their twisted branches, Latimer-cross ornament, cinquefoil rose-shaped backplates and polygonal elements, they clearly

share the same design idiom and use of heraldic references as the neo-Elizabethan furniture of the gallery.

The theme had been set somewhat earlier, however, in a group of lighting probably linked to the altar terminating Saint Michael's Gallery, which had so impressed Lady Ann Hamilton in 1803 with its "immense blaze of light."[37] Already in place was the oratory lamp, retailed by Green, Ward and Green. It was of classical form but linked in design to the gallery ceiling through its decoration of heraldic Latimer crosses within a Gothic diaper (fig. 11-3). A similar design vocabulary was used for two pairs of silver-gilt candlesticks on the altar, made by Henri Auguste, and probably ordered by Beckford during his visits to Paris between 1801 and 1803 (fig. 11-4).[38] They may already have had the ormolu branches with which they are now provided. Although the candlesticks (and the branches) are close in overall form to neoclassical ormolu examples, the bases are decorated with cinquefoils and Latimer crosses set within auricular-style cartouches. The lattice and rosette pattern on the lower stems, seemingly Gothic in this context, can also be found on neoclassical ormolu. At the top of the lower stem, however, is a ring of medieval crowned heads. Although the rest of the thirty-six lights seen by Lady Ann on the altar in 1803 may have been made up of neoclassical candlesticks, it is possible that they included the six pairs of ormolu candlesticks in a mixed Gothic and modern neo-classical style recorded at the Abbey in 1822 (see cat. no. 82).[39] These candlesticks are closely related in general form to the

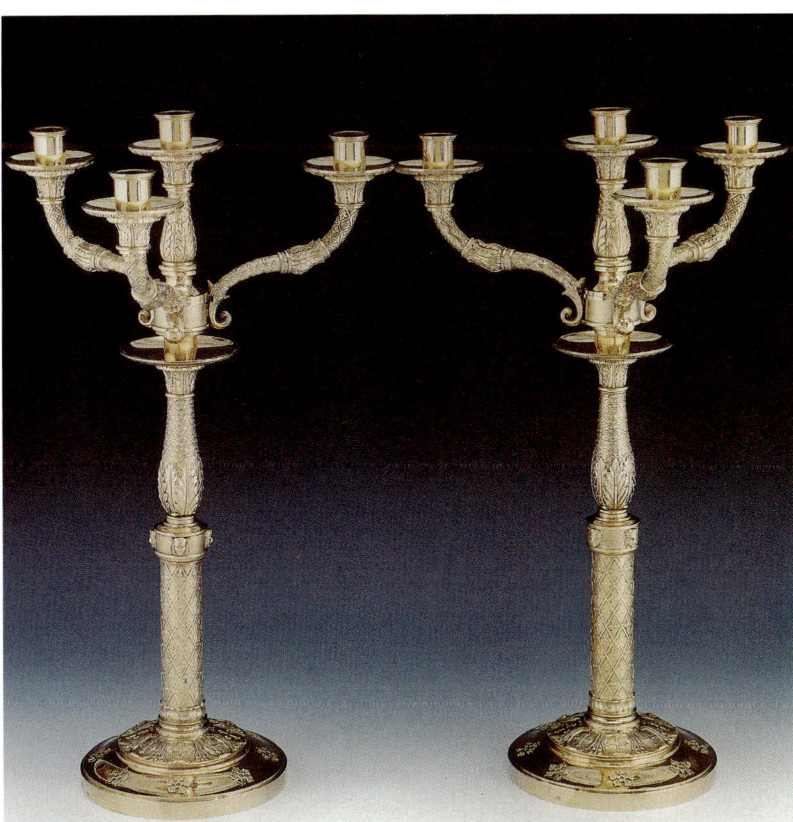

Fig. 11-4. Pair of candelabra, ca. 1801–3. Maker's mark of Henri Auguste. Arms possibly made by Vulliamy & Co. Candlesticks, silver-gilt; arms, ormolu. Private collection.

Auguste examples, but are much more coherent in design. The stem diaper is clearly heraldic and encloses crosses and cinquefoils. Their crisp foliage ornament and the characteristic chimeras at their bases, suggest that they were designed by Jean Jacques Boileau.

Useful silver for the Abbey

From 1812 Beckford went beyond lighting in his orders for useful silver specifically for Fonthill Abbey. Significantly, this date coincided with the Abbey's external completion as well as an upturn in Beckford's finances. The pieces are characterized by two features: they are all linked to the service of tea, and they greatly expand the range of historicist and heraldic treatments begun with the Holbein candlesticks twelve years earlier. Some of these pieces were more useful than others. Like the cream jugs with historicist mounts, many of them were probably used only occasionally. Some must have been used more regularly, such as the set made up in 1819–20, by adding a cream jug and sugar bowl to a teapot, stand and caddy of various earlier dates but of the standard neo-classical forms of the 1780s (see cat. nos. 40–44). The bodies of the new jug and bowl are in the Empire style, while their bases are formed as large cinquefoils carefully engraved with ermines to signal their heraldic meaning. The whole set is unified by an engraved heraldic checker pattern enclosing Latimer crosses and cinquefoils. This pattern matches that found on a set of Worcester porcelain cups and saucers of 1807–13, but carrying martlets instead of crosses (see cat. nos. 33–36).

The other pieces of Fonthill Abbey silver linked to tea can be divided into two groups. The first re-creates older objects, examples of which formed part of Beckford's collections. It includes a ladle of 1812–13 (see cat. no. 109), which, with its handle copied from a print by Heinrich Aldegrever of 1539, is the earliest neo-Renaissance object to be created for Beckford. Also in this group is a delicate bowl of 1812–13, imitating an eighteenth-century Chinese enameled example of the type collected by Beckford. Its surface is very carefully matted and burnished to suggest the different colors of the painted original.[40] As with all these pieces, the heraldry, here in the form of cinquefoils decoratively disposed on the inside, establishes its Beckfordian origin. The same Chinese pattern occurs on another Beckford bowl of 1813–14 (see cat. no. 68). Another bowl of 1812–13, possibly once part of a bigger tea service, imitates carved Chinese laquer, and a tea service of 1817–18 takes the forms of Yixing red stoneware (cat. no. 59–62). All these imitations must be seen in the context of a period in which silver was used to re-create famous objects in other media, including Homer's iron Shield of Achilles and a cup suggested by a wooden example described in the first idyll of Theocritus.[41]

The design of the second group of pieces linked to tea treats historic and other sources in a uniquely imaginative manner, which became the leading characteristic of Beckford's historicizing metalwork. The earliest, and most complex piece is an extraordinary teapot and stand of 1812–13 (see cat. no. 58). The overall shape of the body of the pot seems to be taken from a Chinese porcelain teapot, but its strongly

lobed formation and the relief handling of the foot suggest carved Indian and Mughal hardstones of a type in Beckford's collection. The whiplash tails at the bottom of the handle are very close to the split dragons' tails on Chinese bronze and porcelain vessels, but they might also have a Renaissance origin.[42] The straight spout, while of conventional neoclassical form, is decorated in a remarkable manner with bands of Chinese motifs wrapped around it. A similar treatment is given to a group of seemingly deliberately contrasted sugar tongs, all of 1812–13, perhaps survivors of once much larger sets of flatware (see cat. nos. 111–13). In spite of their diminutive size, all carry stylistic and heraldic messages linking them to the Abbey and are worth examining in detail. Two carry the type of curling moresque ornament seen on the furniture of King Edward's Gallery and later a major motif in Beckford's silver. In one case it is set out in applied wire. Eight years later this treatment was to be developed in an exquisite gold teaspoon in which a conventional fiddle-pattern stem is constructed out of wire which has been shaped into moresque pattern, the spoon's later date being shown by the moresque-engraved bowl.[43] In a second pair of tongs the moresque is shown in relief, but it is tightly constrained by heraldic bands, and the ends are shaped as Greek-style anthemia. In a third pair of tongs matching a set of fiddle-pattern teaspoons, the stems are still bound but have lost their arabesque ornament. A fourth set of tongs has interlaced stems of coral in the rococo manner.

The Renaissance style

The gradually emerging neo-Renaissance style reached its culmination in Beckford's experience in a large group of objects made from 1814 until several years after his move to Bath in 1822. The group contains all Beckford's most celebrated pieces of historicizing metalwork. The qualities already observed, notably Beckford's obsession with heraldry and a very close attention to finish and detail, are markedly present. Above all, although the objects are in the Renaissance style, they are never slavish imitations of originals, but imaginative exercises in the neo-Renaissance manner. This last quality is shown in the earliest object of the group, probably created to commemorate the birth of Beckford's grandson in 1814 (fig. 11-5). At first sight it seems to be a straight copy of a Renaissance display dish, but a closer examination reveals it to be an immensely subtle reconfiguration based on a profound knowledge of several different types of Renaissance objects, including printed sources. The overall form, with its armorial depression in the center to fit a ewer that was never made, is not derived from a silver example but from a base-metal "Veneto-Saracenic" dish of the sixteenth century.[44] The outer border is a continuous band of ornament of the type evident on Renaissance dishes, but in this case its precise pattern is very probably from an engraved design for a standing cup attributed to Matthias Zuendt.[45] The rest of the engraved decoration, however, which also seems to be in bands, in fact breaks with Renaissance precedent by radiating from the center in repeated elements of increasing size. The interlaced strapwork from which it is composed is usually found not on Renaissance dishes, but on late-sixteenth-century Flemish manner-

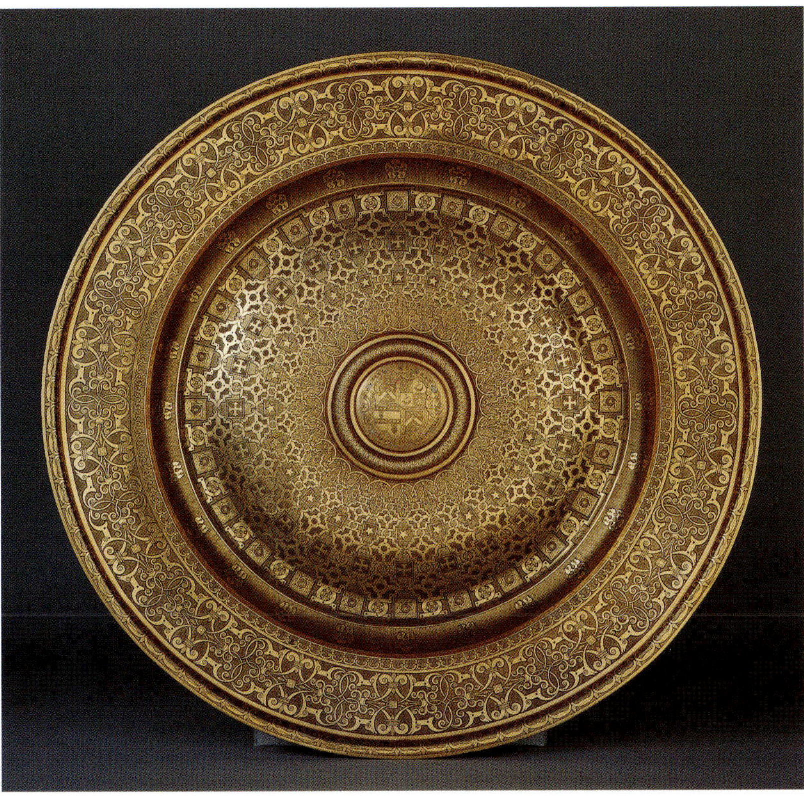

Fig. 11-5. Dish. London hallmarks for 1814–15. Maker's mark of Samuel Whitford II; arms and center plate with mark of William Burwash. Silver-gilt. Trustees of the Victoria and Albert Museum, London, M.47-1980.

ist silver, although it does incorporate asymmetrical motifs which are purely Islamic.

The next year saw the appearance of the first recorded members of a large group of pieces, in which, in the Renaissance tradition, porcelain, hardstones and other rare materials were mounted in silver or gold. They are closely related to objects of type characteristic of *Schatzkammern* of the sixteenth and seventeenth centuries, and were obviously intended to be shown with older objects in Beckford's collection. They are an expression of Beckford's obsession with hardstones and porcelain, so evident in his correspondence with Gregorio Franchi.[46] Although similar in general appearance to their Renaissance models, their imaginative and even playful treatment lifts them out of the realm of pastiche into something new, and very different from improvement by the addition of few simple elements to which Beckford subjected some of his older pieces.

Among the earliest objects in this group is a cup in which an agate bowl and lid of Indian outline (not originally belonging together) have been combined with two chalcedony compressed spherical knops (or knobs) to form a covered cup of Renaissance outline (see fig. 11-1). While some of the elements in the ensemble, such as the basketwork calyx are of conventional Renaissance type found both on surviving metalwork and design prints, the elegant trumpet-shaped foot is very finely flat-chased with a Moresque pattern against a matted ground, which very likely was adapted from a print.[47] This may account for its

identification as the "Persian" cup in the accounts and sales.[48] The foot enhances the exotic character suggested by the knops and shaping of the lid and pulls the whole group of disparate elements together.

A similar, but more adventurous process has taken place in the design of a ladle made in the same hallmarking year, 1815–16 (see cat. no. 56). In this case the finial is an Indian nephrite carved as a leaf and flower, its base set with rubies. The finial clearly suggested the form of the rest of the ladle, made of gold, in which a curved stem terminates in a flower-shaped bowl springing from the Beckford cinquefoil. Cups and spoons, established forms of *Schatzkammer* objects, appear several more times in Beckford's mounted wares. While many of the cups known from the sale catalogues, illustrated invoices, and designs have not reappeared for inspection, those that have reveal that they followed the same imaginative approach of the "Persian" cup. Sketches on bills and designs in a drawing book linked to the maker of the "Persian" cup, James Aldridge, suggest that in its basic shape it is the commonest single type of cup Beckford had mounted. On the evidence of the drawing book, however, most of the cups of this form had slightly domed feet in hardstone, rather than a trumpet-shaped metal foot. In form and decoration the designs show a confident handling of Renaissance design. The stem elements and finely engraved ornamental detail have a distinctly German character. While this could have been derived from actual German cups, it could also have been taken from prints, such as the engraved series of cups in the Nuremberg idiom of the 1550s attributed to the carver, goldsmith, and engraver Matthias Zuendt. One of these very likely provided the design for the border of the dish of 1812. On the other hand, some of the forms could also have come from other sources. A case in point is a characteristic type of bulbous gadrooned knop, present in drawings in the design book. The same type of knop also appears on the stem of a Dutch nautilus cup, the shell engraved by C. Bellekin, once in Beckford's collection.[49] The Aldridge design book also shows that some cups were decorated with enamel in the sixteenth-century German manner.

Among the most interesting of these cups is a very late example, made in 1826–27 by John Harris, in which pieces of lapis lazuli are made into a cup, with handles in the form of snakes and armorial herons' heads (see cat. no. 39). In this case, although the basic form is Renaissance, the ornamental details are neoclassical and once included a finial in the form of a vase of fruit, now lost.[50] These features no doubt reflect the general shift to classicism which followed Beckford's move from Fonthill Abbey, possibly inspired by the more classical surroundings in Bath. Classical detailing can also be found on an agate cup and cover with gold mounts of 1816–17, by James Aldridge, a variant of which also appears as a drawing in the design book (see cat. no. 117). In this earlier case, however, the classical acanthus and bound reed on the foot and finial are combined with a bossed border in the Renaissance style—similar to borders on the wooden robe chests from Fonthill (now in the Wallace Collection, London)—and pointed pierced elements suggestive of India, the traditional origin of the finest agate.

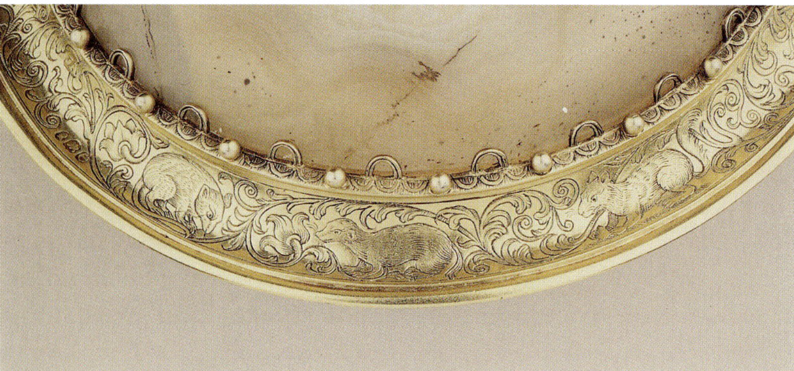

Fig. 11-6. Detail of the edge of the lid made for a cup and cover, London hall-marks for 1820–21. Maker's mark of James Aldridge. Agate, coral, chalcedony, enamel, mounted in silver-gilt. Private collection. *See cat. no. 119.*

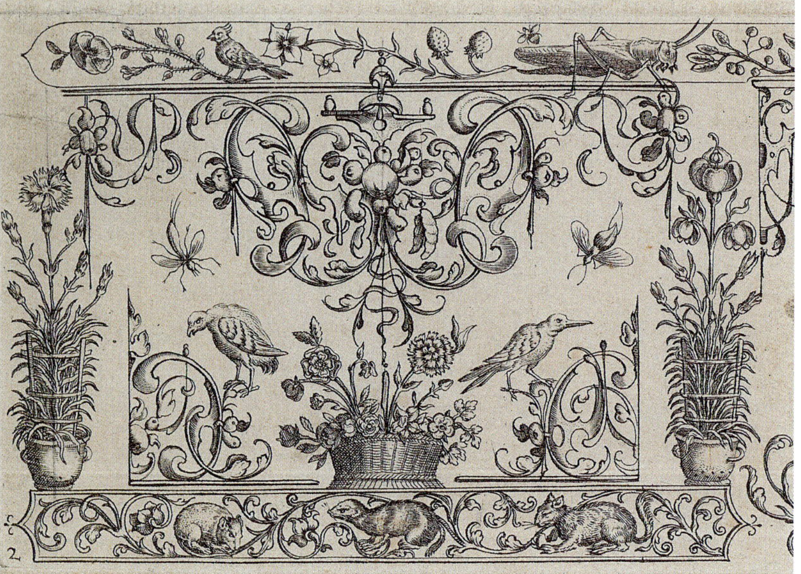

Fig. 11-7. Michel LeBlon. Design for ornament. Engraving. From *Somige Eenvooldige Vruchten En Spitsen Voor Dancomen* (1611). Trustees of the Victoria and Albert Museum, London, E.2946–1914.

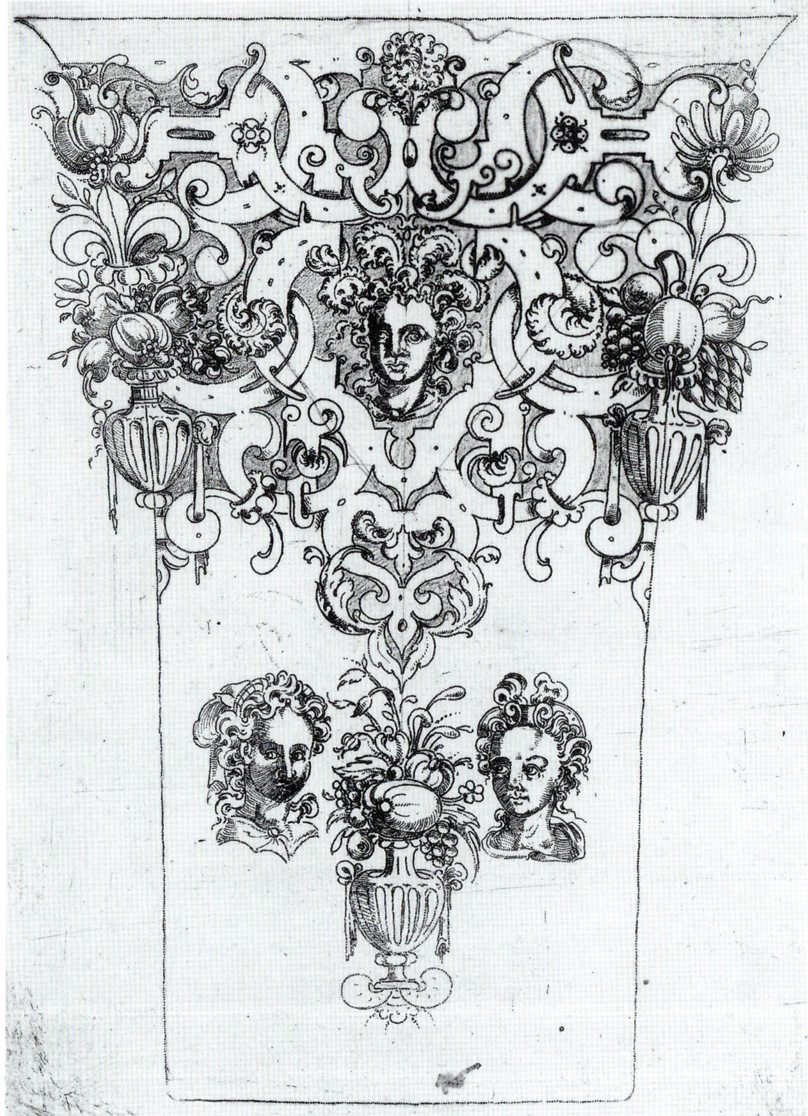

Fig. 11-8. Design for the decoration of a beaker, ca. 1580. Etching with added pencil lines. Trustees of the Victoria and Albert Museum, London.

An even more imaginative approach is shown in the mounted hardstone bowls. Although put together different makers, they share significant features as a group. Two, made respectively by Paul Storr in 1816–17 and James Aldridge in 1820–21, are supported on feet formed as chimeras (see cat. nos. 116, 119). Although such chimeras were known as stem decorations on Renaissance cups their use here, set on a ring and a solid base is more reminiscent of sixteenth-century furniture, as shown in the printed designs of Hans Vredeman de Vries or Jacques Androuet Ducerceau. The engraved moresque pattern on the base of the Storr example is similar to the inlaid moresques on Beckford's base made for the "Holbein" cabinet (now in the Victoria and Albert Museum, London) suggesting that both emerged from the same process of design, independent of their makers. The Aldridge cup, with its seventeenth-century coral figure of Hercules placed on

twelve scrolls, is a tour de force of design on the theme of open-work forms. This extends even to the underside of the base, which reveals another set of open scrolls, as well as flat-chased armorial cinquefoils. The rim of the cover is engraved with a pattern of scroll work enclosing a mouse, squirrel, and otter (possibly), taken with slight variations from a print of 1611 by Michel le Blon and executed in a technique identical to that in the cup (figs. 11–6 and 11–7; and see cat. no. 119).

Engraving and flat-chasing forms the main decorative theme of another bowl and cover, made by John Harris a year or two earlier (see cat. no. 118). While the general shape and the satyr-head handles are neoclassical[51] (as well as perhaps reflecting Beckford's acquisition of the "Rubens" cup in 1818), the flat-chased strapwork and fruit and flowers on the foot and lid are from a type of ornament found on late-sixteenth-century German cups. The sixteenth-century examples are often decorated using an etched or punched technique; in this case a similar effect has been conveyed through flat chasing and engraving, as in the "Persian" cup. A year or two earlier, William Burwash had made a salver in which a variant of the same pattern was flat chased and engraved. The result was one of the most extraordinary of Beckford's pieces (see cat. no. 108). From a heraldic cinquefoil at the center a strapwork pattern bursts with immense energy, in a manner without parallel in the Renaissance. The method of its design is suggested by a printed design for strapwork engraving in the Victoria and Albert Museum, upon which a fan-shaped section has been demarcated in pencil, isolating very similar decorative elements (fig. 11-8). This interest in small-scale flat decoration in different techniques, in all its variety and inventiveness, which plays such a major role in Beckford pieces, distinguishes them from most other historicizing metalwork of the time, which emphasized bold and crudely embossed three-dimensional forms.[52]

Mounted ceramics

Beckford's mounted ceramic pieces were more numerous than the mounted hardstones. While these included a considerable number of display pieces set in classicizing mounts similar to those made for Thomas Hope and other collectors, such pots were outnumbered by the smaller useful wares, in particular pieces of East Asian porcelain mounted as cream jugs, cups, and bowls. Their immense variety of treatment defeated the descriptive powers of Beckford's sale catalogue and inventory authors: among the packing cases removed from Fonthill in 1822 were twenty mounted cream jugs and twenty-three mounted sugar basins simply described by Gregorio Franchi as "all different."[53] To judge by those that have survived, they followed the same design approach as the mounted hardstones, the mounts taking imaginative hints from the form and decoration of the mounted original. The historicizing process was evidently not used immediately, however, for the earliest datable examples, made in 1812–13, have completely plain or classical mounts.[54] It was not until 1815 that the first suggestion of historicism appeared, in the form of a jug by Aldridge formed from a Chinese piece.[55] As with most of Beckford's jugs, the original handle has been ground away and in this case replaced with a curled scroll handle attached to simple strapwork-shaped plates. Another jug of the same date, by John Robins, has heavily modeled neoclassical mounts on famille-rose porcelain (see cat. no. 126).

The Renaissance theme properly enters the scene with another Aldridge jug, made in 1816–17. In this case the jug is of Meissen porcelain and completed an unmounted tea set (see cat. no. 110).[56] The lavish rocaille ornament on the mounts, the only known surviving example of the neo-Rococo style in Beckford's modern metalwork, was no doubt thought appropriate for the body. The stepped and cut-back formation of the pouring lip, however, is the first of several jugs with a form linked by Franchi (and Beckford) with the name of Holbein, and which evidently had considerable resonance as an indicator of Renaissance design.[57] Another jug, of 1817–18, has a different form of

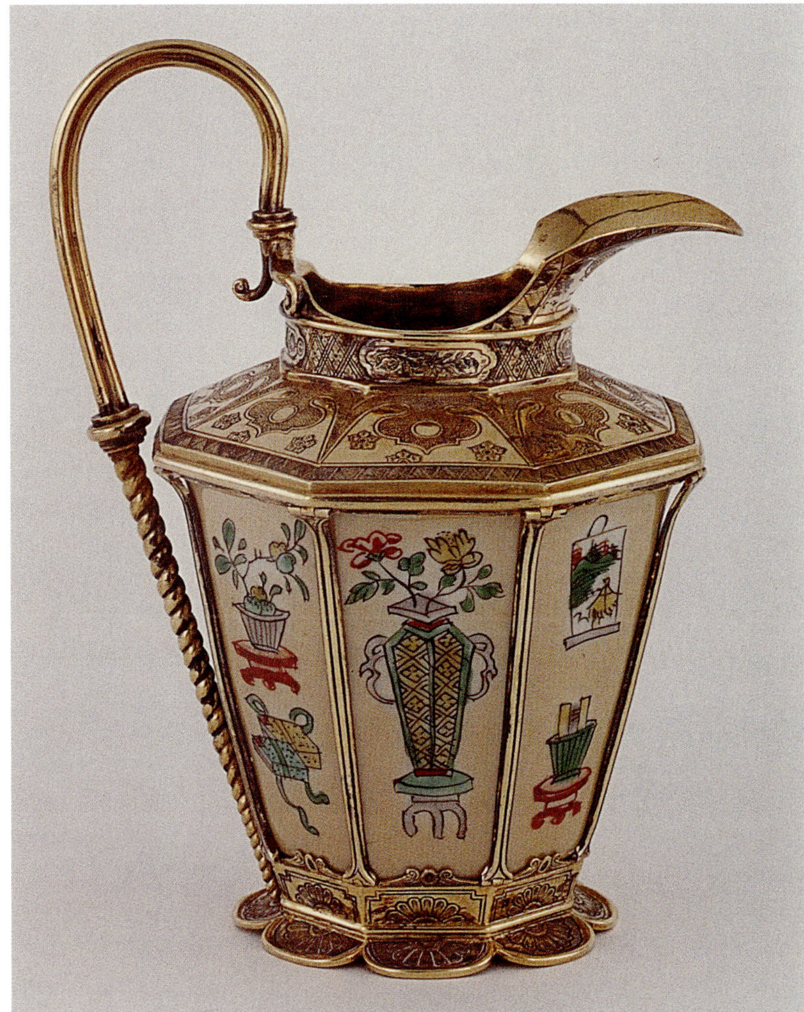

Fig. 11-9. Cream jug, London hallmarks for 1820–21. Maker's mark of James Aldridge. Famille verte Chinese porcelain in silver-gilt mounts. National Trust for Scotland, Brodick Castle.

Renaissance pouring lip, formed as scroll.[58] As so often, with Beckford's metalwork, the story is not as simple as it seems. Such lips are not generally to be found on Renaissance precious-metal ewers. The first type is characteristic of nautilus cups, of which Beckford owned a number of historic examples, while the second type is to be found on base-metal ewers. A less extreme version of the first type is used on an octagonal cup formed into a cream jug by James Aldridge in 1820–21 (fig. 11-9). It is an especially elegant example of the mixed design approach to such mounted wares. The engraved decoration, including half chrysanthemums on the scalloped foot base, echo the body decoration, but the upper portion also carries heraldic cinquefoils and a foil with eight lobes. The tendril-shaped handle would perhaps have matched the wirework handles of accompanying teaspoons.

In addition to these mounted hardstones and porcelains, there is another small group of mounted material to be considered. The first is a hookah associated with Tippoo Sahib, the "spout" mounting of which carries the mark of James Aldridge, who may have been responsible for the stem and the spout (see cat. no. 55). While the base, which is rather different in finish from the rest, carries curved panels apparently adapted from Rococo snuff boxes, the jeweled upright stem and top, in their finish and diaper ogee pattern, suggest that the designer had been looking at Persian or Turkish dagger sheaths of the type collected in *Schatzkammern* since the sixteenth century.[59] Horace Walpole owned two such daggers and sheaths and believed that they had belonged to Henry VIII. This treatment added what seemed to be a historical gloss to the presentation of the hardstone base, creating a new object.

The Oriental theme seems also to lie behind a pair of glass bottles exquisitely mounted in gold and set with agate finials made by James Aldridge in 1820–21 (see cat. no. 125). These small bottles form a fitting conclusion to the consideration of the design of Beckford's Fonthill metalwork. The splayed open feet are the most exaggerated examples of a number of such a foot treatments in Beckford's metalwork, where they were probably intended to give the objects an exotic feel, as is suggested by a design by Beckford for a "Turkish" table with similar feet.[60] That apart, the bottles are a distillation of Renaissance forms into completely new creations, *Schatzkammer* objects unmistakably of the nineteenth century.

AFTER FONTHILL

When he moved to Bath in 1822, Beckford took at least nine cases of his metalwork, hardstones, and other objets d'art, as well as mounted ceramics.[61] He also bought back a number of pieces from the Abbey sale of 1823. His ordering of this type of mounted object, however, seems almost to have ceased after the move, partly because he already had so much,[62] partly because his taste in objects had returned to the classical, matching the new interiors at Bath. The few dated examples of mounted ware reflect this change: the heron-handled cup; a bloodstone bowl of 1824–5 supported on heavily modeled dolphins by Paul Storr (see cat. no. 139); and two blanc-de-chine cups mounted in a simple guilloche gold band, probably in the 1840s (see cat. no. 142). Although Beckford had left a good deal of his neoclassical useful plate behind at Fonthill, he immediately set about adding to the remainder. Most of the pieces matched the style of the 1780s and 1790s, the exception being an elegant hot-water jug in a Grecian style close to that promoted by of Thomas Hope (see cat. no. 138).

In the 1840s Beckford's metalwork entered a short final phase. The pieces commissioned probably reflect changes to the interior of Lansdown Tower begun after 1841: a small classical salt cellar that was made in 1843–44 (see cat. no. 143), and candlesticks that were made in 1844–45 (see cat. no. 149). The candlesticks are particularly significant. They were made in London but, according to their inscriptions, modeled by Alfred Short, a Bristol silver retailer,[63] and designed by Edmund English, the Bath auctioneer who helped to furnish the tower and later published a series of chromolithographs in *Views of Lansdown Tower*. Two candlesticks are shown standing atop one of the cabinets made for the refurnishing of Lansdown Tower. In their large and simple overall forms—which are classical except for the curiously curling feet—their

emphatic modeling, and heavy proportions, they evidently reflect the new furniture. The feet may be an echo of the curling legs of a side table made for the tower and can indeed be seen as the last in a long line of such bases on Beckford's metalwork. They are also strikingly similar to the multiple curling feet on some contemporary French silver, in which they are a Renaissance element in vessels otherwise classical in form.[64]

METALWORK IN ITS CONTEXT

Little is known about how metalwork was used at Fonthill House, but enough details have survived to show that certain features characteristic of the later display of metalwork at Fonthill Abbey were already in place by the 1790s at Fonthill Splendens. In the Great Gallery, for example, in 1801, "candelabra of silver, gilt" helped to produce a "stately and palace like effect."[65] In the adjacent apartment two Vulliamy cabinets were "filled with a collection of rare old japan, antique cups of onyx, an ivory tankard, carved by Fiammingo, and the communion plate of solid gold, most exquisitely chased, which belonged to Louis the Sixteenth's private oratory at Versailles."[66] In the State Dressing Room, a white marble slab bore "vases and cups of gold" by Auguste.[67]

While much more is known about the furnishing of Fonthill Abbey, information about the position of individual pieces there should be treated with care, as objects were often moved about. This was especially the case between Beckford's departure in 1822 and the sale of 1823. The lack of locations in the 1822 sale catalogue means that the exact position of most of smaller metalwork is unknown, but accounts such as Rutter's *Description of Fonthill* (1822) make it possible to draw clear conclusions about Beckford's attitude to his metalwork, and its use and position. Of significance is the manner in which old and new pieces are mixed together, suggesting that for Beckford the new shared something of the status of the old. This notion is supported by the mix of old and new in a vignette in Rutter's *Delineations* (1823), which combines several of Beckford's most famous ancient objects with modern neoclassical pieces, including an Auguste gold tazza, a pair of modern mounted hardstone cups, and an imitation Chinese bronze or porcelain vase in silver.[68]

Rutter's account also shows that certain rooms were devoted to particular types of objects. The dining room (or "cabinet" room) in the East Wing, for example, in 1822 contained the greatest concentration of metalwork, possibly because some of Beckford's most important pieces of carcase furniture, including the two great Boulle armoires and the Curtius Cabinet, were in this room. One of the armoires held most of the large pieces of English and continental sixteenth- and seventeenth-century plate, including a series of great standing cups and dishes, as well as more modern pieces, such as the Auguste ewers and tazze and the pair of Boileau ewers. By 1822 hardstone cups of the type commissioned by Beckford were also in the armoires. The Curtius cabinet seems to have contained even more precious, and generally smaller pieces. These included a Limoges enamel dish and the Auguste gold tazze as well as the "Rubens" and Cellini vases. Also in the dining room was an ebony and pietre-dure armoire, which supported the two Romer cups and contained a number of hardstone and other pieces.[69]

For Beckford the impact of the carefully arranged contents of these and other cabinets was clearly a highlight of the Abbey. His own profound understanding of the arrangement objects within such cabinets and elsewhere—and the pleasure this gave him—is clear; he also treasured denying access to others. In 1817, for instance, he prevented Samuel Rogers from seeing the "great plate or the inside of the ebony cabinet or a thousand other things."[70] "Everything depends, my dear Gregory," he wrote to Franchi in 1817, "where things are placed. An object which looks like nothing on earth in the Brown Parlour is transformed when placed in the Lancaster Gallery, where I've put the strange candlesticks, which produce a wonderful effect there."[71] In 1819 he described the combined effect of the Cellini vase and a nautilus cup, at that time arranged in the Bouchardon cabinet:

> if anything could enchant such a timid and religious soul, it would be the incredibly rich and sublime effect produced by Cellini's stupendous dragon alongside the conch in the Bouchardon cabinet: diamonds, Topaz and enamel-everything glitters in a magical way. The little piece of scarlet leather, on which this sublime objet d'art rests, looks so well, and the height of the vase is so correct when it is grouped with the conch, that I see no need to despatch the lapis lazuli.[72]

In the other principal rooms of the Abbey metalwork and mounted pieces were apparently less numerous, but nonetheless a significant impact. In King Edward's Gallery, lit by rows of neoclassical candlesticks, some of the larger and more sculptural and older mounted pieces were shown on tables, notably the most important mounted ivories, which were placed on the so-called Borghese table (see figs. 10-5 and 10-6).[73] On a "toilette table" in the gallery in 1822 was the nautilus cup engraved by Bellekin, described as "one of the most noble and picturesque objects of this valuable collection," as well as a cup of yellow agate in enameled gold mounts.[74] Saint Michael's Gallery, like King Edward's Gallery, was principally devoted to books, but it also contained a number of the most important examples of older metalwork.[75] In 1822 the modern pieces included the Burghley Casket (see cat. no. 84) and the "Holbein" candlesticks (see cat. no. 107), the latter matching the black furniture believed to be sixteenth century, as well as the neo-Tudor cabinets on the side tables. By 1823, the Auguste Gothic candlesticks, minus their branches, had also been placed there.[76] Mounted porcelain was another important feature. The ten glazed display cabinets carried silver-mounted East-Asian porcelain vases and contained books or "valuable specimens of oriental china."[77] This probably included some of the huge quantity of mounted porcelain taken to Bath in the following year. On one of the cabinets stood the celebrated "Gaignières Ewer" (now in the National Museum, Dublin; see fig. 9-6).[78]

Metalwork was usually less evident in the remaining public rooms, except for the China Closet, which in 1823 contained "vast quantities of oriental and other specimens, displayed in twelve oak recesses,"[79] including, it seems, the "Persian" cup. The Crimson Drawing Room next door contained a Japanese lacquer or porcelain bowl on an Auguste ormolu base, standing on an Auguste lacquer cabinet.[80] In 1823 the adjacent Grand Drawing Room contained the Tippoo Sahib hookah and the Storr silver baskets (see cat. nos. 55 and 26), placed on ebony consoles on either side of the fireplace.[81] The more private rooms of the Abbey also contained metalwork, but in relatively small quantities. In 1823, in the Lancaster and Hamilton bedchambers, there were, fittingly enough, late-seventeenth-century toilet sets as well as baroque sconces. A small group of modern silver and mounted ceramics located in 1823 to the picture-hung Lancaster Gallery and Tribune Room may suggest that such pieces were also in the more private rooms. Finally, a small group of small objets d'art is recorded in a glazed case in the diminutive but richly decorated Green (or Gothic) Cabinet.

Later, in Bath, Beckford's metalwork was also often on the move between Lansdown Crescent and Lansdown Tower. By the 1844 inventory, made immediately after Beckford's death,[82] more examples of metalwork, both old and new, were contained in the Lansdown Crescent houses than in the tower. Of the pieces assigned to specific rooms,[83] by far the biggest group was contained in a series of oak cabinets in the drawing room of 19 Lansdown Crescent. The range of materials in the group is conveyed in a Maddox still lifes, in which five of the objects from the room are shown.[84] Also in the room were the "Rubens Vase" and the Valerio di Vicenza tazza.[85] The next biggest group was apparently in the small library, in which drawers were seemingly filled with plate. There were far fewer objects at the tower, at any rate after the alterations of 1841–44, but Maddox's illustrations of the rooms give for the first time a clear picture of how Beckford's metalwork collections were displayed. Mounted porcelain and hardstones were shown carefully arranged in and on glazed cabinets. The perfectly judged relationship between objects, paintings, and furniture in the interiors at Bath was remarked upon by visitors, including the German art historian Gustave Waagen in 1835.[86] Another visitor, three years later, noted in an anteroom at Lansdown Crescent two cabinets "containing china and small golden vessels. . . . I counted in one cabinet ten vessels of gold and in another five: these were small teapots, caddies, cups saucers, plates. I am told that they are used occasionally at tea-time."[87] Observations of this sort perhaps led to the claim by the *Bath Chronicle* in 1845 that "Mr Beckford's custom was to have different arrangement for every day in the year. The cup and saucer he used to-day at his breakfast were placed in a cabinet until the revolving year brought them into request."[88]

DESIGN AND SUPPLY

Who designed Beckford's historicizing modern metalwork? The answer is complex and often uncertain, but some things are clear. Beckford was quite capable of designing furniture and buildings. The Beckford papers contain a number of Beckford drawings of and for metalwork.[89]

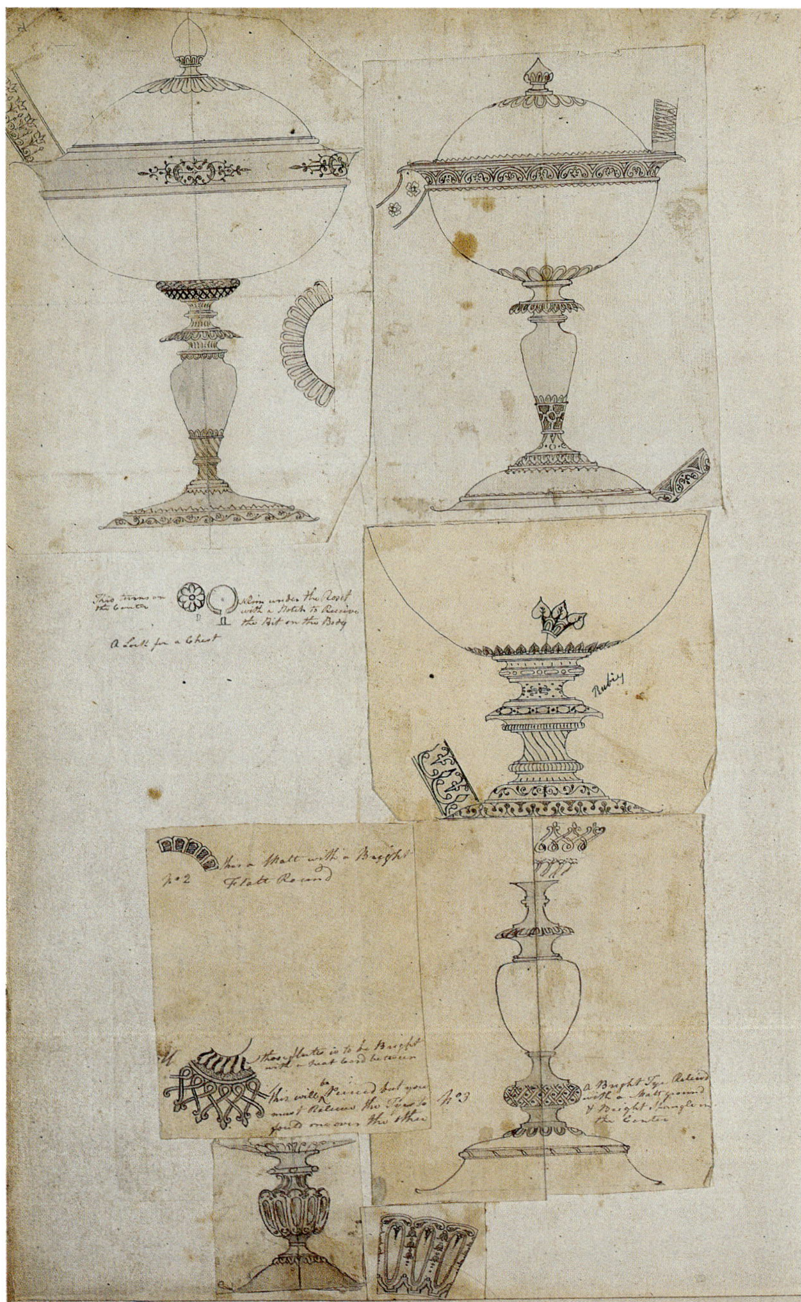

Fig. 11-10. Page from a design book assembled by James Aldridge, showing pieces made for William Beckford, 1815–20. The drawings are by Gregorio Franchi; the inscriptions, giving detailed instructions to the chaser, are probably by Aldridge. Pen and ink and wash. Trustees of the Victoria and Albert Museum, London, E.38-1972.

A handful of metalwork pieces was attributed to Beckford's own design in his lifetime, namely the sanctuary lamp, a "Persian" casket, and a pair of candlesticks, the last three of unknown appearance.[90] Beckford must himself have played a leading role in the design process of most of his commissions, however, for although several other people are known to have had a hand in the detailed drawings, the designs display a consistent approach over some forty years, strongly suggesting the influence of a single controlling mind. In addition, Beckford, for a

person in his social position, was remarkably well informed about metalwork designers in general, as seen in the case of Moitte and Boileau.[91] From his correspondence with his agent and factotum Gregorio Franchi, it is evident that Beckford was unusually knowledgeable about the makers of his pieces, ranging from major figures like Edmund Rundell and Paul Storr to obscure smallworkers like John Harris. It also seems certain that the metalwork would not have reached its imaginative heights without Franchi's contribution. Their correspondence illuminates an interchange of ideas in which Franchi was at least Beckford's equal in the production of design ideas, while surviving drawings show that he was considerably better at putting them down on paper. Franchi, frequently in London, also controlled the production process. Although the retailers of Beckford's pieces included Vulliamy and the leading supplier of the time, the royal goldsmiths Rundell, Bridge and Rundell, most of his historicist metalwork was made by a network of obscure jewelers, plateworkers, smallworkers, and engravers.[92] While it is possible to distinguish specialties among them, such as the heavy cast work of John Robins (see cat. no. 109), it is clear that the Beckford pieces were well outside the normal production of these artisans. A surviving book of design drawings belonging to the most prolific of the makers, James Aldridge, shows that the Beckford metalwork was very different from his normal production of trinkets and jewelry in the neoclassical style, and that Aldridge could not have devised the complex historicism of Beckford's pieces on his own. Inserted into the book are detailed drawings for mounted wares by Franchi, and possibly Beckford himself, in which almost nothing is left to chance (fig. 11-10).[93]

Franchi was also linked to such makers on his own account, for he was himself collecting and commissioning pieces of exactly the same type as Beckford. The contents of a sale of his collection in 1827 included not only complete pieces, but also many fragments of pieces ready for assembly into new objects.[94] The collection of older "small sculptures, carvings, and chasings . . . collected in Italy and other parts of Europe since 1802" included a celebrated French Renaissance casket now in the Louvre.[95] The new metalwork included "coffers and jewel caskets of silver chasings, agate, and jaspar, mounted in exquisite taste, after the original designs and under the immediate direction of proprietor."[96] One surviving example (see cat. no. 128), with its panels of Moresque interlace shows that they were very much like the pieces made for Beckford. Franchi's relationship to the craftsmen was evidently very close. Among the four people at his funeral was "Webster, his silver Castor," while Beckford was giving special assistance to "poor Coulson the engraver" at the same period.[97] Franchi's attitude toward the metalworkers was no doubt similar to that which he showed to wood carvers who worked for him, as recalled in 1854 by wood carver William Gibbs Rogers: "He [Beckford] had a caterer for his house in the person of Mons. Franchi, a man of taste. He would come into the carvers' workshops with a volume of Holbein or Aldegrever, select a spoon or a handle, and have them executed in ivory or ebony as high as he could get talent to bring them, would watch the progress of the work day by day, and the question would often be: 'If you spent another day on it, could you get it finer?'."[98]

From these sources it is possible to imagine how Beckford and Franchi between them might have conceived the metalwork. For mounted pieces, Franchi made illustrated suggestions in his letters, based on pieces he had seen, for example, at a London dealer: "of a large jasper one can make a beautiful thing in this way."[99] Such ideas would be outlined in greater detail, possibly with Beckford. At this stage the paper design sources in the Oak Library or "Board of Works," as they called it, at Fonthill might be consulted. These sources included engraved ornament as well as drawings.[100] In addition, both Beckford and Franchi would use their own profound knowledge of historic pieces. The small size and folds of Franchi's final drawings in the Aldridge design book suggest that they were sent to Beckford through the post for approval. Even then elements were not always satisfactory, details being added during manufacture.[101]

The gradual withdrawal of Franchi from Beckford's orbit after Beckford moved to Bath is matched by the reduction in the production of new historicist metalwork. Later pieces, such as the bowl in the Barber Institute, were within the orbit of the manufacturer to design. The start of new phase, cut off by Beckford's death in 1844, is suggested by the candlesticks of 1844–45. While little is known of Edmund English junior's activities as a silver designer, it is known that Alfred Short of Bristol, who made the model for casting and usually retailed entirely conventional pieces, occasionally had pieces made to his own design in London.[102]

The Beckford legacy

Beckford's historicizing metalwork was revolutionary, yet it was made up of intensely private pieces for private enjoyment. It was not made to impress or influence others, nor did it; it became public too late to promote a new approach to historicism. By the mid-1820s a heavy historicism had become acceptable in metalwork, confirmed by that most historicizing of all events, the coronation of George IV in 1821. Beckford's metalwork was very different from that made for the coronation, not only because it was much more delicate and imaginative as well as less ceremonial, but also because it was designed to be seen with older objets d'art. The complete lack of comment on it as specifically modern in the accounts and sale catalogues of Fonthill, as well as Hazlitt's blanket condemnation, show that Beckford had been entirely successful in his endeavor.

By the time much of this metalwork reappeared to public view in the mid-1840s, after Beckford's death, the situation had changed; historicism had been promoted from a peripheral style into one rapidly taking over from classicism. At the same time, design reform was in the air. The perfection of Beckford's metalwork was noted, and perhaps even over-praised, as the high finish of the "Holbein" candlesticks convinced people that they really were made of gold.[103] Significantly, in 1845 the *Illustrated London News* chose to illustrate not the older masterpieces, but a group of mounted hardstone cups almost all of which were modern.[104] The architect and designer Charles James Richardson, who had been employed to illustrate *Views of Lansdown Tower,* took a more serious attitude, in line with his active promotion of the Renaissance style and interest design reform. In 1851 in his *Studies of Ornamental Design*, he included Beckford's pieces of some thirty years earlier as exemplars of good modern design. They had become "Art Objects." Beckford's historicism, however, was only briefly in tune with design reform. Disappearing into Hamilton Palace, the metalwork was not seen again until the Hamilton Palace sale of 1882, by which time the mood had again changed. Years after the sale, the South Kensington Museum (now the Victoria and Albert Museum), on finding that it had paid £562–4s for a "Renaissance" cup that had actually been made in 1815, quietly put it out of sight. Rediscovered in storage in 1971, the same cup helped launch today's revaluation of the Beckford achievement in metalwork.[105]

1. This article is based on Michael Snodin and Malcolm Baker, "William Beckford's Silver," parts 1 and 2, *Burlington Magazine* 122, no. 932 (1980): 735–48; no. 933 (1980): 820–34 (hereafter cited as Snodin and Baker). The appendices of part 2 (hereafter cited as "appendix") list all the metalwork in the Beckford sales and inventories, as well as all the datable Beckford silver known in 1980. Since then a number of additional pieces have been identified. The most significant for this study are: the Storr wheat-ear bread basket ("appendix," E 20, cat. no. 26), the Auguste jewel coffer (ibid., C 8, cat. no. 52), the Auguste Gothic candelabra (ibid., C 10, cat. no. 2), the ormolu Gothic candlesticks (cat. no. 82), the Meissen cream jug with rococo-style mounts mounts (cat. no. 110), the agate covered bowl with Hercules finial of 1820–21 (ibid., G 121, cat. no. 119), the lapis-lazuli cup of 1826–27 (ibid., G 136, cat. no. 139), the candlesticks of 1844 (ibid., G 8, cat. no. 149), the agate cup with Bacchante finial (ibid., E 47, cat. no. 115), and the hookah of Tippoo Sahib (cat. no. 55). Another discovery of great significance is the Franchi box (cat. no. 128). In writing this article I have been much indebted to Bet McLeod, who made her researches available, and to Philip Hewatt-Jaboor, who generously allowed access to the PHJ–Beckford Database.

2. W. Hazlitt, *Criticisms of Art* (London: C. Templeman, 1844): 284, originally published in the *London Magazine* (November 1822).

3. Thomas Hope, *Household Furniture and Interior Decoration, Executed from Designs by Thomas Hope* (London, 1807): 3–4.

4. Ibid., p. 4.

5. E.g., George IV and his brother the Duke of York. See J. Culme, *Nineteenth-Century Silver* (London: Hamlyn for Country Life Books, 1977): 67–74; S. Bury, A. Wedgwood, and M. Snodin, "The Antiquarian plate of George IV: A Gloss on E. A. Jones," *Burlington Magazine* 121, no. 915 (1979): 343–53.

6. The dates given for London silver in this article follow the hallmarking year, which begins in May; thus a piece described as "1815–16" would have been brought to the Assay Office to be assayed and marked between May 1815 and May 1816.

7. For a discussion of the candlestick type, originated by Robert Adam, see M. Snodin, "Adam Silver Reassessed," *Burlington Magazine* 139 (January 1997): 23.

8. A. G. Grimwade, *London Goldsmiths, 1697–1837: Their Marks and Lives* (London: Faber, 1976): 653, 655.

9. E.g., a teapot stand in the English style made in Paris in 1788 for a London teapot of 1782–83 ("appendix," A14, C14).

10. Chancery Masters Exhibits C104/57 et seq., Public Record Office, Kew, London (hereafter cited as PRO).

11. Order Record Book 30, p.165, C 104/58 part 1, PRO.

12. See R. J. Campbell, "Jean-Guillaume Moitte: The Sculpture and Graphic Art" Ph.D. thesis, Brown University, 1982 (University of Michigan Microfilms): esp. pp. 178–197; G. Gramaccini, *Jean-Guillaume Moitte: Leben und Werk* (Munich: Berlin: Akademie Verlag, 1993).

13. W. Beckford, *Italy with Sketches of Spain and Portugal* (London, 1834): 362. He may have realized the significance of Moitte and Auguste after 1787, as their names do not appear in the manuscript of the Portuguese journal, from which the printed entry was adapted: *The Journal of*

William Beckford in Portugal and Spain, 1787–1788, ed. Boyd Alexander (London: Hart-Davis, 1954): 301.

14. "Appendix," C13, C14; and a pair of traveling table candlesticks of ca.1789, *European Silver*, sale cat., Sotheby's Geneva, 15 May 1995, lot 73.

15. *The Hamilton and Nelson Papers*, vol. 1, *1756–1797* (1893), The Collection of Autograph Letters and Historical Documents formed by Alfred Morrison, 2d ser. (Privately published, 1882–93): 165. The "gold vase" is a gold ewer marked in 1789, but engraved "1790" ("appendix," C3, ill. H. Nocq, *Orfevrerie civile Francaise*, vol 2, [Paris: A. Levy, 1927]: pl. 66); present whereabouts unknown.

16. The dates of Moitte–Auguste pieces in the Beckford sale descriptions record dates engraved on the objects.They are often several years after the time of manufacture.

17. "Appendix," C1–7, of which C.2 and C.6 are now in the Gilbert Collection; see T. B. Schroder, *The Gilbert Collection of Gold and Silver* [Los Angeles: L. A. County Museum of Art, 1988]: cat. no. 168). The gold tazze have not been recorded since 1823, when each was described as "a handled tazza and liner of gold, on plinth, supported by four winged chimeras, designed by Moiette, and executed by Auguste, 1793, at Paris, ornamented by a border of arabesque figures and Cupids, with mask and snake handles."

18. For the cabinet see *Hamilton and Nelson Papers*, vol. 1, (1893): 165; and John Rutter, *A Description of Fonthill Abbey* (Shaftesbury, 1822): 41: "A superb cabinet of gold Japan, and various foreign woods, on a stand ornamented with or-molu, the frieze most exquisitely chased and gilt, surmounted by an Egyptian granite slab, made by Auguste, supporting a many sided bowl, a rare specimen, on mosaic or-molu pedestal, after the antique, by Moette and Auguste, formed of winged chimeras, and rim, on ebony plinth." Both pieces are currently unidentified. For the candlestick: "A superb candelabrum or candlestick with 3 branches for 4 lights of elegant silver plate, the stem embraced by foliage, the scrolls of the branches formed of foliage and serpents executed by Auguste from a design of the celebrated artist Moitte" [and companion]: Christie's sale, 6 upper Harley Street, 10 May 1817, lots 63, 63*. Bought by Makepeace, probably for the Earl of Shrewsbury; see letter from Beckford to Franchi, 10 May 1817, quoted in *Life at Fonthill, 1807–1822, with interludes in Paris and London, from the correspondence of William Beckford*, ed. Boyd Alexander (London, R. Hart-Davis, 1957): 204. These have not so far been traced, but they probably resembled a Moitte design for a candelabrum, itself a more complex version of the Auguste candlesticks from the collection of the Duke of York (see n. 21 below); see also Gramaccini, *Moitte* (1993): cat. no. 159.23, fig. 229. Beckford also owned two pairs of ormolu tazze by Moitte and Auguste, "with ram's heads, in the finest taste" (Christie's sale, 6 upper Harley Street, 10 May 1817, lots 50, 52)

19. Unlike that of Auguste, Moitte's name was not engraved on the pieces. Beckford's interest in Moitte extended to acquiring from him his statues of Hebe and Ariadne; see Gramaccini, *Moitte* (1993): 62, cats 155, 156. The Hebe was sold at the Fonthhill House sale, Phillips 22 August 1807, lot 624.

20. Fonthill Abbey sale, Phillips 1822, lots 80, 81 (silver tazze of 1787, engraved date 1802; see appendix," C6,7); Christie's sale, 10 May 1817, lot 75 (the Morpheus jewel coffer; see "appendix," C8, cat. no. 52); Fonthill Abbey sale 1822, lots 78,79 (silver-gilt ewers of 1787, engraved date 1802; see "appendix," C1,C2, cat. no. 51); Fonthill Abbey Sale 1822, lots 60, 61 (gold tazze, dated 1793, present whereabouts unknown; see "appendix," C7).

21. E.g., a set of candelabra by Auguste in The Metropolitan Museum of Art, New York, once owned by the Duke of York and dated 1789, which have number of features characteristic of Moitte's style; see F. Dennis, *Three Centuries of French Silver* (New York: Metropolitan Museum of Art, 1960): 32; and Campbell, "Moitte" (1982): 87. There is also a tureen by Auguste of 1798, acquired by the royal household from Rundells in 1803; see Schroder, *Gilbert Collection* (1988): 362, fig.80.

22. M. Snodin, "J. J. Boileau: A Forgotten Designer of Silver," *Connoisseur* (June 1978): 124–33; H. Young, "A Further Note on J. J. Boileau, ' A Forgotten designer of silver'," *Apollo* 124, no. 296 (October 1986): 333–38; H. Roberts, "Beckford, Vulliamy and Old Japan," *Apollo* 124, no. 296 (October 1986): 338–341; Schroder, *Gilbert Collection* (1988): cat. nos. 89, 90, 93, 95, 98, 99.

23. A pair of silver-gilt ewers, "appendix," E15: "on tripod goats legs, winged snake and ebony handles, made by Green and Ward, from a design of Boilieu," Fonthill Abbey Sale, Phillips 1823, lots 817, 818.

24. For other probable Boileau-designed pieces see "appendix," D7, 9, 17, 25, E17.

25. E.g. a race cup of 1798/9 retailed by Jefferys and Gilbert (Snodin,"J. J. Boileau" (1978): 124–33.

26. Hope, *Household Furniture* (London, 1807): pls 15, 47, 49, 50, 52; D. Watkin, *Thomas Hope and the Neo-Classical Idea* (London: Murray, 1968): 54–57.

27. Victoria and Albert Museum, London, Department of Prints, Drawings and Paintings, nos. 8390.1, 8390.2, 8390.3, D.2196–1885. See also the Hope baskets with one on a Boileau-designed centerpiece made by Philip Cornman for Rundell, Bridge and Rundell, 1803 (*English and Continental Silver,* sale cat. Sothebys, London, 5–6 February 1987, lot 152).

28. E.g., a candlestick made in Sheffield 1773–74 by Samuel Roberts & Co.; see M. Snodin and

M. Howard, *Ornament, A Social History Since 1450* (London, and New Haven: Yale University Press, 1996): fig. 88.

29. "Delivered a pair of Silver candlesticks, extremely highly finished and Chased almost all over with very rich arabesque ornaments consisting of Birds leaves and flowers and mounted in several pieces in order to keep the burnish and dead parts neat from each other the whole gilt and finished in so perfect a manner as exactly to resemble a pair of highly finished Gold Chased Candlesticks at 60 guineas and 6 guineas the chased pattern: £69 6s.," PRO C104/57 part 2, p. 330.

30. The wooden examples were made in Nancy, by members of the Foulon family and other craftsmen; see H. Demoisne, "Bois de Bagard," *Connaisance des Arts* 191 (January 1968): 91–93.

31. C. Wainwright, *The Romantic Interior: The British Collector at Home, 1750–1850* (New Haven and London: Yale University Press, 1989): 90; A. Jaffer, *Furniture from British India and Ceylon: A Catalogue of the Collections in the Victoria and Albert Museum and the Peabody Essex Museum* (London: Victorian and Albert Publications, 2001): 130–42.

32. See n. 5 above. Old plate was being collected by 1786, apparently prompted by the need for appropriate furnishings in rooms decorated "in old Gothic style"; see C. Williams, ed.., *Sophie in London, 1786* (London: Jonathan Cape, 1933): 172.

33. For Pitts, a dish of 1809 with the border ornament partly taken from drawings by Giulio Romano' see *The Glory of the Goldsmith, Magnificent Gold and Silver from the Al-Tajir Collection* (London: Christie's, 1989): no. 127. For Storr, e.g. a punch bowl and stand of 1812 modeled on a lobed floral dish of about 1680, see ibid., no. 134.

34. Snodin and Baker, part 1, n. 53.

35. Fonthill Abbey sale, 1822.

36. Snodin and Baker, part 1, pp. 740–41.

37 Lady Ann Hamilton, notebook, MS. Beckford e. 4, fol. 49, Bodleian Library.

38. *Important Silver*, sale cat., Sotheby's, London, 3 May 1990, lot 16.

39. For a discussion of these candlesticks in the context of Empire ormolu, see H. Ottomeyer and Peter Proschel, *Vergoldete Bronzen, Die Bronzearbeiten des Spatbarock und Klassizismus* (Munich, 1986): 324. Their overall form is close to a candelabrum by Pierre-Philippe Thomire of 1815 (ibid., fig. 5.16.10).

40. Mark of James Aldridge. Victoria and Albert Museum Museum, M.289–1976; Snodin and Baker, part 1, fig. 23.

41. Both designed by John Flaxman and made by Rundell, Bridge and Rundell; see D. Bindman ed., *John Flaxman RA* (London: The Royal Academy of Art, 1979): 143–44, 145–47; S. Bury and M. Snodin, "The Shield of Achilles by John Flaxman RA," *Sotheby's Art at Auction* 19884/5, pp. 274–83.

42. E.g., a ewer engraved by Virgil Solis; see I. O'Dell-Franke, *Kupferstiche und Radierungen aus der Werkstatt des Virgil Solis* (Wiesbaden: Steiner, 1977): i 32.

43. Snodin and Baker, part 1, fig. 41; and "appendix," B38.

44. Beckford owned several Veneto-Saracenic pieces, both at Fonthill and at Bath.

45. From a set dated 1551. The Victoria and Albert example is E.2984–1910; see R. Bergau, *Wentzel Jamnitzers Entwurfe zu Prachtgefasse in Silber und Gold* (Berlin: Paul Bette, 1879): A.17.

46. See chap. 9, by Bet McLeod, in this volume.

47. E.g., a circular Moresque woodcut by Peter Flotner, from his Kunstbuch; see O'Dell-Franke, *Kupferstiche und Radierungen* (1977): ex 110.

48. Eg, ref. to "Coulson Pella Coppa Persana" in Gregorio Franchi's list of expenses ending 4 May 1818, with a sketch closely resembling the cup (Beckford MS c.37, fol. 80v). Coulson, an engraver, may have been responsible for the decoration. It is probably the cup and cover "delicately engraved in the Persian style" offered only in the Fonthill sale of 1822, lot 26 ("appendix," E.42).

49. Present whereabouts unknown: Fonthill Sale, 1823, lot 1148; for an illustration, see *Connoisseur* 11 (1905): 178–79.

50. *Snodin and Baker*, part 1, fig. 35.

51. See Hope, *Household Furniture* (London, 1807): pl. 47, a covered tazza with rams' head handles with curling horns; and N. M. Penzer, *Paul Storr 1771–1844: Silversmith and Goldsmith* (Feltham, NY: Spring Books, 1971): pl. 39, a centerpiece by Storr for the Duke of Wellington, 1811–12, of identical outline.

52. There are, however some examples of historicising engraving being added to older pieces, such as the engraved later cover of a mounted mid-sixteenth-century earthenware pot once in the collection of Fredrick Augustus, Duke of York; see P. Glanville, *Silver in Tudor and Early Stuart England* (London: Victoria and Albert Publications, 1990): cat. no. 39.

53. Franchi case list, Beckford MS c.37, fol. 94.

54. "Appendix," A45, A47.

55. Ibid., A53

56. Fonthill Abbey Sale, 1822, Day 9, lot 12, "Twelve Royal Dresden Tea-cups and Saucers, Sugar and Slop-basons pale green ground, rich gold borders and landscapes, inside and out, of a very superior quality, a Cream-ewer to correspond, massively mounted, and richly covered in silver-gilt, in a gilt glass dish." Fonthill Abbey Sale, 1823, lot 1051, 1052 (ewer).

57. Franchi accounts, MS Beckford c.37, fol. 82; there is a reference in a list of work done by Aldridge: "Huma leiteira Za ala Holbeins com pe novo." The accompanying sketch may show the present ewer.

58. "Appendix," A69; Snodin and Barker, part 1, fig. 45.

59. *Kuntskammer und Kronjuwelen* (Stuttgart: Wuerttemburgisches Landesmuseum, 1977): fig.76.

60. For a pencil sketch signed 'WB', showing an octagonal table with pointed legs, carrying a bowl and bottle, see Beckford MS c.84, fol. 109.

61. Beckford MS c.37, fols. 92–96; see also "appendix," F.

62. The inventory made at his death lists 105 pieces of mounted ceramic tea ware.

63. Short also sold the salt cellar and the blanc de chine cups (cat. no. 142).

64. E.g. a tea service of 1835–45 by Marc-Auguste Lebrun, Paris, for the family of La Tour du Pin; see P. Ennes, G. Mabille, and P. Thiebaut, *Histoire de la Table: les arts de la table des origines a nos jours* (Paris: Flammarion, 1994): figs 339–41.

65. John Britton, *The Beauties of Wiltshire* vol. 1 (London, 1801): 219.

66. Ibid., p. 227

67. Ibid., p. 231

68. Of 1820–21, mark of William Burwash; see "appendix," E.2; and M. Clayton, *Christies Pictorial History of English and American Silver* (Oxford: Phaidon, Christie's, 1985): 245, illus. I am indebted to Bet McLeod for this information. They are curiously paralleled by a design by Moitte for a vase of similar form; see Gramaccini, *Moitte* (1993): cat. no. 159.30, fig. 237.

69. For the Romer cups, see "appendix," G.173/4.

70. Alexander, *Life at Fonthill* (1957): 229.

71. Ibid., p. 184.

72. Ibid., pp. 323–24.

73. A mounted ivory cup attributed by Beckford to Magnus Berg ,Fonthill Abbey Sale 1822, Day 5, lot 47; and 1823 sale, lot 573 (now in the Royal Collection). Two ivory vases of ca.1700, attributed to François Langhemans, the silver mounts by David Willaume, Fonthill Abbey Sale 1822, Day 5, lots 1, 2; and sale 1823, lot 575 (now in the British Museum). A nautilus cup on an ivory stand attributed by Beckford to Benvenuto Cellini, Fonthill Abbey Sale 1822, Day 4, lot 7; and Sale 1823, lot 571; see also H. R Forster, *The Stowe Catalogue* (1848): lot 570, attributed to Fiammingo; and Snodin and Baker, part 1, n. 92.

74. Rutter, *Description* (1822): 57; Snodin and Baker, part 1, n. 92; and "appendix," E.56.

75. Wainwright, *Romantic Interior* (1989): 133–34.

76. The thirteen pairs of library candlesticks, two with branches for three lights, sold from the gallery in 1823 (lots 922–934) were presumably moved there from King Edward's Gallery for the sale.

77. Rutter, *Description* (1822): p. 60.

78. See A. Lane, "The Gaignières-Fonthill Vase: A Chinese Porcelain of about 1300," *Burlington Magazine* 103 (April 1961): 124–32.

79. Rutter, *Delineations of Fonthill Abbey* (London, 1823): p. 47.

80. See n. 18 above.

81. Rutter, *Delineations* (1823): 26.

82. MS Beckford b. 2.

83. The location of much of the material, including most of the plate and ceramics, is unspecified.

84. See cat. no. 156. In the drawing room were the ivory pedestals (Hamilton Palace sale, 3 July 1882, lots 872, 873), the filigree basket (cat. no. 154), the mounted shell (cat. no. 152), the satyr-headed agate bowl (cat. no. 118), and the silver gilt cup by Hans Petzold.

85. Attributed by Beckford to Valerio Belli, called di Vicenza; see Alexander, *Life at Fonthill* (1957): 241 (now in The Metropolitan Museum of Art, New York).

86. G. F. Waagen, *Works of Art and Artist in England*, vol. 3 (London, 1838): 120.

87. Henry Venn Lansdown, *Recollections of the Late William Beckford* (Bath, 1893): 22.

88. Quoted in *Illustrated London News*, 29 November 1845, p. 344.

89. Two designs for a neoclassical lamp and candelabrum (MS Beckford c.14, fol. 29r). Two rough sketches by Beckford seem to show pieces after they were made: a candlestick of cat. no. 149 type, dated 22 June 1843 (MS Beckford c.30, fol.90v., and c.34, fol.77), a conical-shaped cup on a square base, dated 30 May 1835 (ibid., fol. 108v) For an example of Beckford's designing abilities in general, see his sketch and instructions for a bird-footed table (MS Beckford c.14, fol.134v).

90. A "very massive silver gilt jewel casket on 10 cornelian feet, in the Persian taste . . . from a drawing of Mr Beckford' ("appendix," E 40) and pair of silver candlesticks, "designed by M Beckford" (Rutter, *Delineations of Fonthill* [1823]: 11).

91. He had met Edmund Rundell, who was honored with a nickname ("Fiume") and was aware that Rundells' silver was made by Paul Storr (Alexander, *Life at Fonthill* (1957): 180). The correspondence with Franchi also shows that he was aware of the identity of smallworkers such as John Harris VI (ibid., p.312).

92. James Aldridge, William Burwash, John Robins (plateworkers), John Harris VI, (smallworker), John Cuttel (lapidaryand jeweller), Samuel Coulson (jeweller and, probably, engraver), all working close to each other in the West End of London. See Snodin and Baker, part 2. The last two have no marks, but all appear in a series of meticulous accounts, illustrated with sketches, made up by Franchi between 1813 and 1818 (ibid., p.821, fn. 19, fig. 18; and MS Beckford c.37, fols.73–83).

93. Victoria and Albert Museum, Department of Prints, Drawings and Paintings, E.1–180–1972 (see Snodin and Baker, part 2, p. 822, n. 26). There are twenty-five drawings for Beckford metalwork, as well three drawings of antique plate, including the nautilus cup in n. 73 below, which Aldridge may have had in for repair. The rest of the book shows medals, jewellery, Jewish ritual plate, and a design for the back of the ormolu binding, designed by J. B. Papworth, of an extra-illustrated copy of Rudolph Ackermann, *History and Antiquities of the Cathedral church of St Peter's Westminster* (London, 1812; now in Westminster Abbey); see C. Fox, ed., *London: World City, 1800–1840* (New Haven and London: Yale University Press, 1992): cat. no. 179.

94. Franchi sale, Christie's, London, 16 and 17 May 1827.

95. Quoted description from ibid., the casket by Pierre Mangot of Paris, 1532–33; see Snodin and Baker, part 2, p. 823, n. 34; and M. Bimbenet-Privat, ed., *L'Orfevrerie parisienne de la Renaissance, Tresors disperses* (Paris: Commission des travaux historiques de la Ville de Paris, 1992): cat. no. 73a).

96. Franchi sale, Christie's, London, 16 and 17 May 1827.

97. Boyd Alexander, *England's Wealthiest Son* (London: Centaur, 1962): 231; Snodin and Baker, part 2, p. 821, n. 231.

98. *A List of the Carvings and Other Works of Art Collected by W. G. Rogers* (London, 1854): 26. This reference was communicated to me by the late Clive Wainwright.

99. MS Beckford c.12, fol.55.

100. Snodin and Baker, part 2, p.822, n32. Beckford's collection included ornament prints by many of the leading masters of the sixteenth and seventeenth centuries as well as Renaissance design drawings. Beckford's personal interest in design sources is suggested by a letter to Franchi of 24 June 1815 in which he complains of a volume by Jean Berain missing from the shelves of the library; see Alexander, *Life at Fonthill* (1957): 180.

101. Franchi to Beckford, 11 September 1815, MS Beckford, c.12, fol.54v, 53. There is a reference to a milk jug from Aldridge improved by Franchi by adding a detail. The letter begins: "You are right in wishing that these objects that are being made should be finished by now. At present Coulson is leaving with all his finished pieces for the small cup. Your excellency knows well it is not worth sending you pieces that are not well finished" (translation by Bet McLeod).

102. E.g., a pair of "Indian" (also described as "Chinese") candlesticks made by Barnards in 1845 (Victoria and Albert Museum, Archive of Art and Design, Barnard Day book (X), AAD 5/63–1988, p.768). Barnards also regularly made conventional small tablewares for Short. The Beckford candlesticks of 1842, billed on 29 August, are described as "altar candlesticks" and as being made to "his [Short's] design." They weighed 102 oz and 18dwt and were engraved beneath with two crests and names (ibid., p.2). The pair of 1844–45 were made for Beckford but never delivered. Beckford's sconces in the baroque style hallmarked 1842–43 ("appendix," A103) were billed in on 25 May1843, (ibid., p.180). Short also supplied twenty-one mourning rings at Beckford's death (Hamilton Muniments, NRA(S) 2177, vol. 1224, p. 13, Nov. 5, 1844). Information kindly supplied by Bet McLeod.

103. E. F. English, *Views of Lansdown Tower, Bath* (Bath, 1844): 8; C. Redding, *Memoirs of William Beckford* vol. 2 (London, 1859): 274; Lansdown, *Recollections* (1893): 28.

104. *Illustrated London News*, 6 December 1845, pp. 364, 365.

105. C. Wainwright, 'Some Objects from William Beckford's Collection now in the Victoria and Albert Museum," *Burlington Magazine* 113, no. 818 (1971): pp. 263–64.

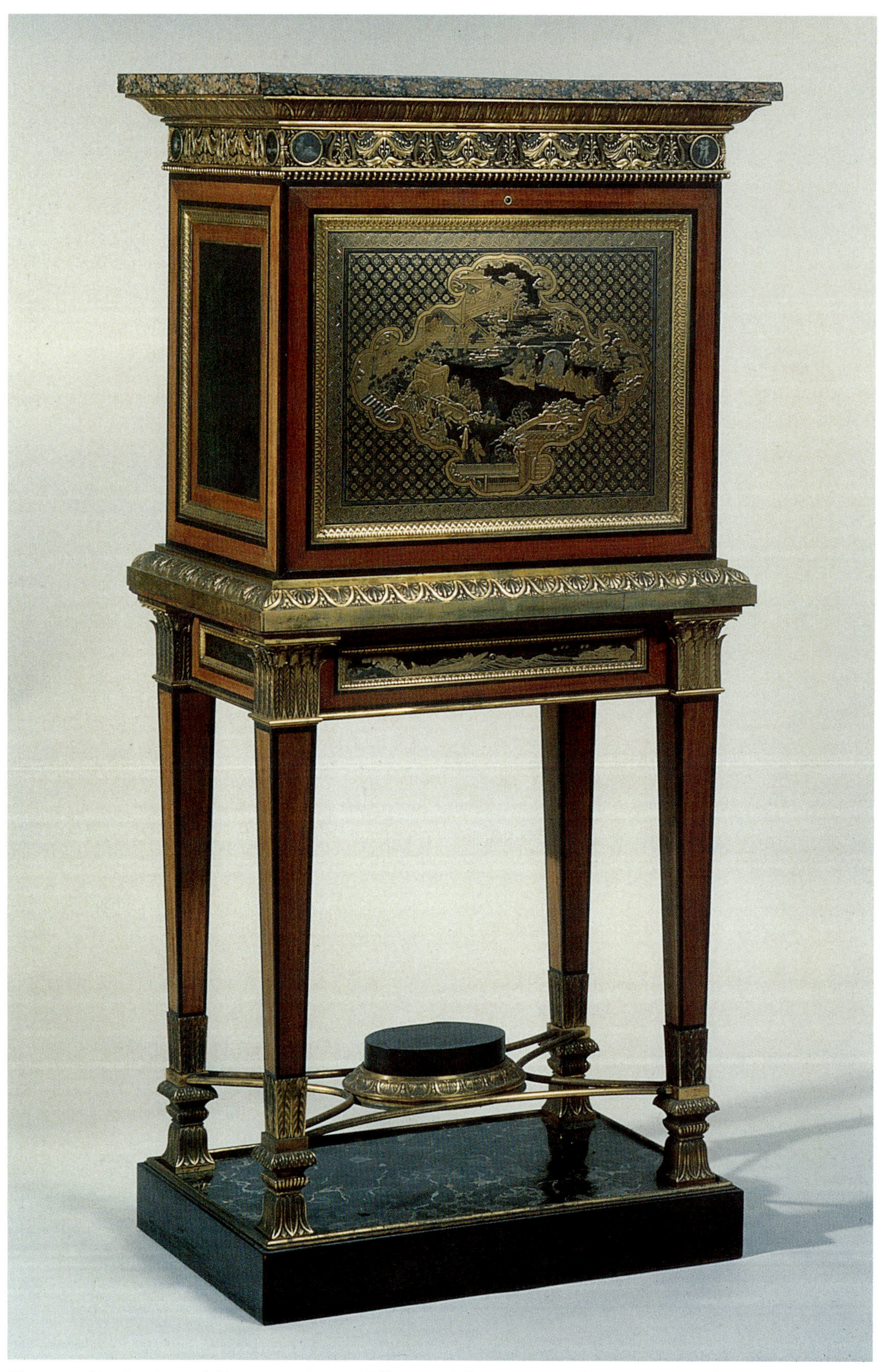

Fig. 12-1. Benjamin and Benjamin Louis Vulliamy. Cabinet-on-stand, ca. 1803. Mahagony, ebony, gilt bronze, Japanese lacquer. The "Buys" box, ca. 1635, a renowned piece of early Japanese lacquer, was disassembled and incorporated as panels in this piece. Elton Hall, Huntington.

CHAPTER XII

OBSERVATIONS ON JAPANESE LACQUER IN THE COLLECTION OF WILLIAM BECKFORD

OLIVER IMPEY AND JOHN WHITEHEAD

William Beckford, though an Englishman, emulated the French in the way he collected Japanese lacquer, following the taste and connoisseurship of the ancien régime. Buying mostly in France, Beckford collected pieces that had formed part of earlier collections, with whose owners he could identify. Especially appealing to him was the pleasure of owning pieces that had belonged to celebrated persons such as Madame de Pompadour or Cardinal Mazarin. His collection eventually included several examples of Japanese export lacquer of the highest quality. His treatment of some of these, however, was also influenced by French custom; he was not averse to having a particularly fine box disassembled, for example, and used as elements in a pair of cabinets (fig. 12-1), a practice well established by the time Beckford first visited Paris in 1781.

A few years earlier, in 1777, the collection of Pierre Louis-Paul Randon de Boisset, one of the greatest of all Parisian *amateurs* of the eighteenth century, had been sold. In the sale catalogue, the Paris *marchand-mercier* Claude-François Julliot summed up the reasons for collectors amassing quantities of fine Japanese lacquer:

> Precious old Japanese lacquer objects are a perfect match for porcelains, through the originality of their shapes, the ingenious and particular taste of their designs, the fine color of the gold and the quality of the workmanship; therefore connoisseurs consider these objects essential to the harmony of their collection.[1]

Japanese lacquer was recognized as superior in quality and beauty to other lacquers, delicately exotic and harmonizing perfectly with porcelain and other precious objects. It understandably prompted collectors to compete with each other in assembling sizable collections of such pieces.

For Beckford, the appeal described by Julliot was strong and easy to appreciate. Although Beckford does not appear to have mixed socially with other such collectors in Paris, at least he came into close contact with the dealers who provided these objects.[2] Their language and selling techniques, to judge by Julliot's statement, were extremely persuasive, especially to one eager to own the very best of what was available. In addition, Beckford's employment of the goldsmith Henri Auguste, both as a commercial intermediary and as a craftsman, bears witness to an aesthetic sensibility as fine as any in Paris at the time. The manner of furniture commissioned by Beckford was similar to that retailed by Dominique Daguerre, utilizing the cabinetry executed by the workshops of Martin Carlin or Adam Weisweiler, with gilt-bronze mounts made by various *bronziers*, such as François Rémond, and embellished with either Sèvres plaques or fine Japanese export lacquer panels cut up from cabinets. As far as it is known, and perhaps surprisingly, Beckford owned few pieces of such furniture, to which Japanese lacquer boxes and bibelots formed almost necessary companions.

Although his taste was based upon French models, there was a personal element that set him apart from his contemporaries. The essentially Parisian decorative taste of other owners of Japanese lacquer objects and mounted furniture is an elegant but specific one, not for those who were romantics or seasoned travelers; unlike the English, few Frenchmen were Grand Tourists. Like French collectors, however, Beckford employed Japanese lacquer boxes of exotic shapes as accompaniments for furniture—seventeenth-century furniture in his case, either real or imitation, decorated with ebony, Boulle marquetry, or with pietre dure plaques. The dark mysterious look of such furniture found a ready place in interiors fashioned by the author of *Vathek*.

The use of souvenirs as decoration was another fascination for Beckford, revealed through his personal association with (in his eyes at least) significant historic figures, such as Madame de Pompadour, Randon de Boisset, and Marie-Antoinette. Inevitably the dealers played upon Beckford's interest in provenance, and, while he was probably immune to such suggestions, nevertheless he may not have checked such putative origins as rigorously as collectors and their agents do today.[3]

Japanese Export Lacquer of the "Fine Period"

Japanese lacquer, or "old japan" as it is known, had been a staple trade material for Europe for nearly two centuries before William Beckford's birth.[4] The first European contact with Japan was made by the Portuguese in 1542 or 1543, and trade in lacquered furniture probably began in the 1570s. The Dutch arrived in Japan and competed with the Portuguese for the monopoly of the Japanese trade until 1639, when the Portuguese were expelled by the Japanese. Thereafter, the Dutch and Chinese shared a monopoly on trade with Japan, which lasted for the next two hundred-odd years.

From their early years, the Dutch had bought lacquer in the "namban" (exotic, non-Japanese) style, based upon inlay in pearl-shell but had found it hard to sell in other markets. Not until the expulsion of the Portuguese did the Dutch again purchase Japanese lacquer, but now in a very different style. This was a style of careful decoration in the *maki-e* ("sprinkled picture") technique in shades of gold and occasionally of other colors, such as red and silver, on a very fine gold ground. This technique, much used in Japan, was to be increasingly adapted to Dutch demand over the next sixty years.

The stimulus to trade in lacquer may have occurred around 1635–40 when a now unknown Japanese official presented lacquer boxes to Maria van Diemen and Pieternella Buys Lucasz, the wives of two officials—the Governor-General in Batavia, Antonio van Diemen, and his second-in-command, the Director-General Philips Lucasz.[5] Both of these boxes, known as the "van Diemen" box and the "Buys" box—perhaps the most celebrated of all "export" lacquers—belonged at one time to William Beckford. Significantly, they were made not to European but to Japanese order, as gifts to Europeans. Their forms are

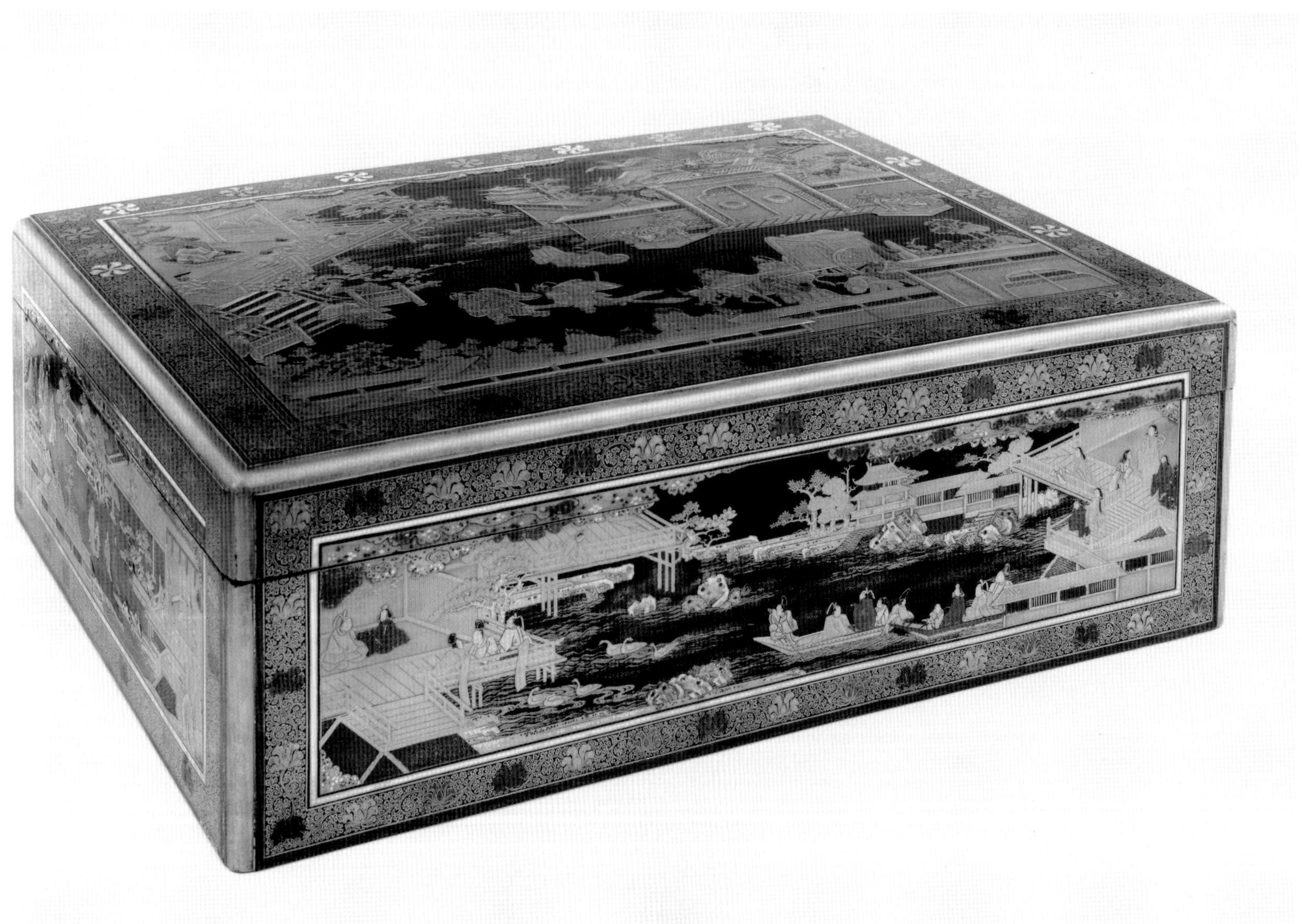

Fig. 12-2. The "van Diemen" box, ca. 1635. Japanese lacquer. The Victoria and Albert Museum, London, W.49-1916.

Japanese not European. What happened subsequently, and almost certainly immediately, was that the Dutch recognized this material as a new type of lacquer that might be salable in Europe. At first, all of the lacquer ordered by the Dutch was of the same very high quality as the van Diemen and Buys boxes, but made in complex European shapes using the most sophisticated lacquer techniques, and therefore very expensive. This was soon found to be impractical, and standards and prices were progressively lowered. Thus the very finest of the Japanese export lacquer wares those that were made in the first burst of export, in the late 1630s and the early 1640s.

Today, few examples of Fine Period Japanese export lacquer survive; only eight complete pieces (depending upon what is included) are known. There are also extant remnants of other pieces, some of which were cut up in the eighteenth century and used as panels in furniture (as Beckford did with the Buys box).[6] Of the complete or almost complete pieces, Beckford certainly owned three and probably two others. He definitely owned both the van Diemen and the Buys boxes; of the two great chests, he certainly owned one, the Mazarin chest (now in the Victoria and Albert Museum; the other, the Lawrence chest,[7] is now lost); of the two known jewel boxes of this type he probably owned one (now in the Victoria and Albert Museum; the other is in the Tokyo National Museum); of the two known caskets he also probably owned one, the Chiddingstone Castle casket (now on loan to the Ashmolean Museum, Oxford; the other is in the Museum für Angewandte Kunst, Vienna). Of two other boxes, Beckford attempted but failed to buy one, now in the Weston Collection, and the other is now in the Victoria and Albert Museum.[8]

The van Diemen Box

The box given to Maria van Diemen, probably before 1639, is a typical Japanese shape (fig. 12-2): the lid still fits exactly to the sides and there is a fitted drop-in tray. The external decoration is mostly in fine silver and gold *hiramakie* (flat decoration) and *takamakie* (raised decoration), within complex borders in fine Japanese style, with Japanese subject matter. A scene from *The Tale of Genji* covers the entire surface area within the borders. On the inside of the lid is the name of the recipient in *kimpaku*, thick gold inlay, "MARIA,UAN,DIEMEN," the only concession to European taste. The interior tray has a cartouche containing a landscape in an altogether different technique, resembling an ink painting on a gold ground. This is markedly different from the appearance of the lid; thus as Beckford wished to utilize one of the boxes for the panels of a pair of cabinets, it was logical to dismember the Buys box, where the scenes on lid and tray resemble each other.

The van Diemen box had belonged in the eighteenth century to Madame de Pompadour, who kept it in an ormolu-framed glass case. After her death in 1764, it was inventoried as "A very fine lacquer casket, with a black ground tray with pagods, in its glazed case with gilt-bronze mounts; valued at two thousand eight hundred pounds."[9] It was sold to Randon de Boisset, at whose sale in 1777 it was described as

A precious black ground casket, with beautiful and varied designs on the top and the sides. Inside the cover is a black-ground panel with an inscription in big gilt letters, which says: MARIA, VAN DIEMEN. . . . This casket, which may be unique, has achieved a reputation which would be difficult to describe. Every connoisseur is full of admiration for the great and precious richness of its work. It comes from the marquise de Pompadour.[10]

At that sale it was bought for the huge sum of 6,901 *livres*, by the dealer Lange for the duc de Bouillon. As it is not itemized in the list of lacquer purchased by Darnault for Beckford at the de Bouillon sale in 1801, it has been suggested that it was bought by Beckford on another occasion.[11]

At Fonthill the van Diemen box was kept in the Crimson Drawing Room (1823),[12] and at Lansdown Tower it was in the "Great Drawing Room" (1844)[13]; there is no mention of the ormolu and glass case. At the canceled sale of the contents of Fonthill of 1822, the box appears only in the third edition of the catalogue.[14] This suggests that Beckford had not initially intended to sell it.[15] In the 1823 Fonthill Abbey sale, where it was repurchased by Beckford through one of his agents for £50.18s.6d, it was described as:

A LARGE COFFER, with lid and tray, of the VERY FINEST JAPAN, representing on the top the arrival of Ambassadors at a Palace, and various landscapes on the sides. On the tray, is a neatly pencilled landscape, within a Scalloped gilt and enriched border. This rare Specimen was made for MARIA VAN DIEMEN, the daughter of the celebrated GOVERNOR OF BATAVIA. Her name is in capitals of gold within the lid. Mme de Pampadour [sic] became the possessor of it, and at her death it was purchased by the Duc de Bouillon.[16]

The box does not appear in the 1855 manuscript, "Deed of Entail at Hamilton Palace," for presumably it belonged to Beckford's daughter.[17] It clearly remained at the palace, however, where it was included in the Hamilton Palace sale of 1882, under the rubric, "Old Japan Lacquer," and described as "A FINE OBLONG BLACK AND GOLD BOX AND COVER, with landscapes, figures, and buildings in gold, inscribed inside 'Maria Van Diemen'—glass shade and stand."[18]

The Buys Box

The Buys box has the same early history as the van Diemen box, being presented to Pieternella Buys, wife of Philips Lucasz, the Director General in Batavia, at the same time. Clearly both boxes are from the same workshop, but beyond that, little of their history is known. It is not known where or when Beckford acquired it, though it was certainly before 1803, the date of Vulliamy's bill, in which Vulliamy stresses the extreme risk involved in dismembering such a piece.[19]

Before it was cut up, the Buys box was identical in size to the van Diemen box, with both measuring around 6⅜ inches high, 19 inches long, and 10½ inches deep (16 by 48 by 26.7 cm), with edges slightly rounded and recessed. The interior of its lid has, in the same lettering as the van Diemen box, the name "PIETERNELLAE,BUYS" as well as "ANTON:VERNATTY" and "WILL:DRINKWATER," both names certainly added later, their identities unknown. Beyond the similarity in size and lettering, the decoration of the two boxes has little in common. The lid of the Buys box has a somewhat similar scene but within a complex shaped cartouche, with spandrels of the *hanabishi* (flower-diamond) pattern. The interior tray of the Buys box bears another similar scene, but without human figures in the landscape, within a cartouche similar to that on the lid, but with more complex spandrels within the borders.

At first glance the two cabinets made with fragments of the Buys box look a true pair (for one of the cabinets, see fig. 12-1). A comparison of the lacquer area of the fall-front, however, to the one fitted with the original lid is marginally larger than that of the other, fitted with the tray. Within, the sides and the front and back of the original box are arranged as drawer-fronts, with some extra lacquer strips, possibly from the sides of the tray, as further decoration. Some lacquer from extraneous sources has been added, to form the fronts of the drawers of the stands; on one stand a scene of bamboo has been mounted upside down, as Vulliamy's craftsmen were not familiar with bamboo. What is interesting is that these interpolated pieces are almost of the same high quality; they must have been supplied by Beckford, well aware of the different qualities of lacquer.[20]

In 1812 James Storer was most likely referring to the Buys cabinets when he wrote that at Fonthill Abbey, "two inestimable cabinets of the rarest old japan enriched with bronzes by Vulliamy," stood in the small octagon tower in "an apartment devoted to the use of such artists as are employed in directing the works now carrying on at Fonthill."[21] They were sold together at the Hamilton Palace sale in 1882 and were described in the sale catalogue as "A CABINET OF EBONY AND MAHOGANY, the front formed of a large panel of Japan lacquer, with a landscape and figures in gold on a black ground, with border of mother-o'–pearl, trellis, and flowers, enclosing numerous drawers panelled with slabs of Japan lacquer, richly mounted with ormolu friezes and ornaments of classic design, and painted medallions by Auguste, surmounted by a rose granite slab, on high open stand and marble plinths—2 ft. 3 in. by 1 ft. 6 in., 4 ft. 11 in. high," and "THE COMPANION CABINET AND STAND."[22]

The Elephant Cabinet

At least five cabinets were apparently made for Beckford in 1792–93. In about 1792, he may have commissioned Henri Auguste to supervise the *ébéniste* Weisweiler in the making of a grand cabinet-on-stand, using a panel, divided, representing the Yatsuhashi bridge on a gold ground, as the doors. The shape of the panel in its original form is unknown. Two cabinets, made in Paris, were set with paintings by Piat-Joseph Sauvage on various supports including ivory, porcelain, paper

and parchment, while the other three were decorated with Japanese lacquer.[23] Of these, the two cabinets made from the Buys box by the firm of Vulliamy (now at Elton Hall) have been discussed above. There was another one, however, as confirmed by entries in both the canceled Fonthill sale of 1822 and the Hamilton Palace sale sixty years later. In the Fonthill sale catalogue, the piece was described as: "A superb Cabinet of Gold Japan, and Various Foreign Woods, on a stand ornamented with ormoulu, the frieze most exquisitely chased and gilt, surmounted by an Egyptian granite slab, made by Auguste."[24] The Hamilton Palace sale catalogue described: "A Cabinet, the frame of mahogany, with panels of gold japan lacquer, with richly chased metal-gilt mounts by Auguste, ornamented with medallion portraits and paintings by B. West—on stand, the top and base of black and gold marble—3 ft. 4 in. by 1 ft. 4 in., 2 ft. 5in. high."[25]

Probably through his continental European connections and interests, William Beckford developed the idea of having some lavishly decorated cabinets designed and made especially for him. This was in part a Baroque Anglo-Italian collecting tradition which saw its apogee in such pieces as the Badminton cabinet, and also a French one best shown by the commission from Daguerre in 1786 of a *sécretaire* for Louis XVI and dressing table for Marie-Antoinette which were made by Adam Weisweiler reusing a Japanese lacquer close stool taken out of the Royal Collection specially for the purpose.[26]

It is known that the royal goldsmith Henri Auguste worked for Beckford in a variety of ways, and a letter from Beckford to Sir William Hamilton in Naples in 1792 mentioning "furniture I am having made under his [Auguste's] directions," with "bronze friezes &c.," would seem to probably apply to the cabinet in the two sale catalogue entries quoted above.[27] The "Elephant" cabinet (now in a private collection), so-called here because of the extraordinary heads on the capitals of its legs, may be the piece commissioned by Beckford from Auguste, referred to in a letter to Hamilton in 1792, and later offered for sale at Fonthill Abbey and Hamilton Palace.[28] As well as sharing features in common with the cabinets at Elton Hall, it is close to a design by Jean-Guillaume Moitte, which is known to have belonged to Auguste. So it forms a significant new addition to the connection between Beckford and France at the end of the ancien régime.

Inevitably, the story is complicated by various discrepancies. Some of the features of this cabinet are extremely close to a design attributed to Jean-Guillaume Moitte (now in the Victoria & Albert Museum).[29] As in the case of another cabinet owned by Beckford, however, there are major differences between the design and the piece as it exists today.[30] The cabinet itself is of the same basic box shape as the drawing, with the same division into panels, although the edges of the cabinet in the drawing show the start of further similar panels, perhaps indicating it was to have rounded ends. The drawing shows the panels filled with sparse landscape scenes which are quite plausibly the very fine gold-ground Japanese lacquer panels there today. The two central panels in the drawing show what are probably intended to be gilt-bronze reliefs, the larger upper panel of a woman in classical drapery, and the lower with scrolls issuing from a patera. On the cabinet itself, there are no visible nail holes where such plaques might originally have been fixed.[31]

The gilt-bronze frieze and edgings on the "Elephant" cabinet are apparently very similar to those on the Buys cabinets at Elton Hall. The elaborate open frieze of the Buys cabinets consists of three separate elements, two alternating leaf motifs, with circular medallions at each end of the frieze enclosing little painted heads. The "Elephant" cabinet introduces a third leafy motif, and has four circular medallions. From photographic evidence it appears that these motifs are not made in exactly the same way (i.e. from the same molds) on the Buys and "Elephant" cabinets. It could therefore be that they are interpretations of the same designs but executed in different workshops, probably to match. At any rate, the Moitte drawing has a frieze that is different to any of the cabinets. The lower gilt-bronze molding and upper cornice seem to be very similar but again not absolutely identical, while the moldings that frame the lacquer panels seem to be nearly identical. The foregoing slight differences are easily explained by the fact that the "Elephant" cabinet and the Buys pair were not made in the same workshop. Although the "Elephant" cabinet is stamped by Adam Weisweiler, it is unusual that it should share no common feature with any surviving work by this well-documented *ébéniste*, apart possibly from the gilt-bronze cornice below the marble top.

Problems arise with the stand design too. The stand of the "Elephant" cabinet has nothing in common with the stand in the drawing but is broadly similar to those on the Buys cabinets, except that it lacks a frieze, stretcher and base, and its capitals are not plain leaf ones but have extraordinary and wholly un-French elephant heads with trunks and tusks surmounted by Ionic volutes.[32] As to the medallion portraits by "B. West," perhaps they bear a signature. If the black and gold marble top (on the cabinet described in the Hamilton Palace sale catalogue and the "Elephant" cabinet) and base were replacements, then did the Egyptian granite slab match the Buys ones? Why do the dimensions apparently exclude the stand, although its existence is mentioned?

If the "Elephant" cabinet really is the one that William Beckford had made in Paris under Auguste's direction, it may have been ordered during his stay in Paris from November 1791 to May 1793, although stylistically it could date from 1792 to the early nineteenth century. Weisweiler continued to use his *ébéniste*'s stamp even after the legal requirement for this ceased during the Revolution. It would presumably have to have been delivered before 1803, for it is in that year that the Buys cabinets were provided by the Vulliamy firm. In his design for Beckford, Vulliamy must have copied various elements of the "Elephant" cabinet, changing the scale to accommodate the lacquer panels from the Buys box.[33] As for the stand of the "Elephant" cabinet it could be French, but in this case why does it not match the drawing, and in the Buys cabinets, why did Vulliamy not copy the "Elephant" cabinet capitals? Both the preliminary drawing and the words "making the design" included in the Vulliamy bill imply that the firm of

Vulliamy had a design role in the creation of the Buys cabinets. This could have been to do with scale and models, however, rather than general design.

In conclusion it seems likely that the "Elephant" cabinet is the one supplied to Beckford by Auguste, but the stand may have been altered, possibly by Vulliamy. Unless further evidence comes to light, the exact date of its manufacture, and its relationship with the Buys cabinets, must remain a mystery.

The Chiddingstone Casket

The Chiddingstone casket (fig. 12-3) and the Vienna casket (not owned by Beckford) are the only known examples of Japanese lacquer work copied from a European form, such as a precious metal or mounted hardstone casket of the late Renaissance; this would have appealed to Beckford.[34] The record of Beckford's ownership of the Chiddingstone casket depends on whether or not the description of a cabinet in the Fonthill Abbey sale of 1823 applies to this piece:

> An exceedingly rare and beautiful small jewel cabinet of raised Japan, the model of a pavilion of Italian architecture, with a double roof, each constructed with hinges to open; at the corners of the building are columns supporting a cornice, in the front a central niche concealing a drawer, and a drawer on each side. The Japan is richly encrusted, also studded with silver, and in many parts bordered with mother of pearl.[35]

It is quite likely, if Beckford's judgment of lacquer was as good as it seems, that the "lacquer cabinet with a silver key"[36] that he

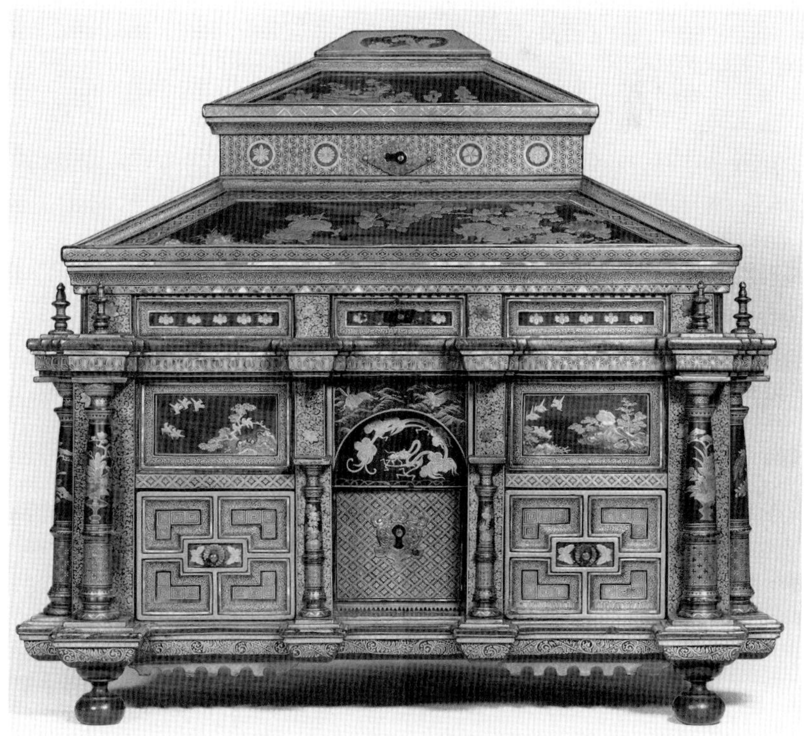

Fig. 12-3. Casket, ca. 1635. Japanese lacquer. The Denys Eyre Bower Bequest, Chiddingstone Castle, Kent, on loan to the Ashmolean Museum, Oxford.

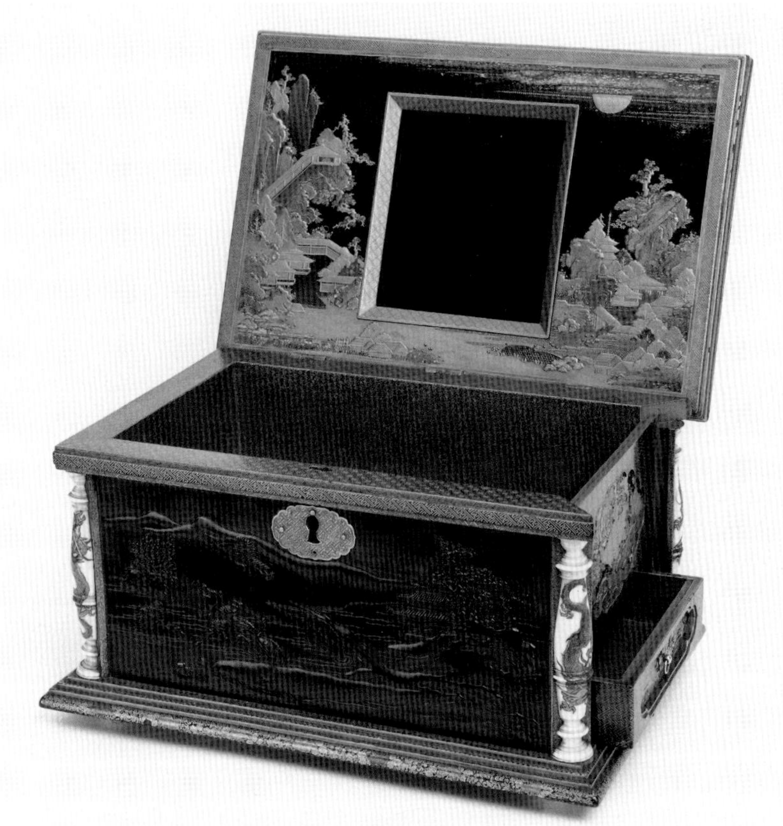

Fig. 12-4. Jewel casket, ca. 1635. Japanese lacquer. The Victoria and Albert Museum, London, 628-1868.

bought in 1814 could be this one, because of Beckford's qualification in the Fonthill Abbey sale catalogue (1823): "The lacquer is at least as fine as Maria van Diemen's." Few other pieces could fit this description, and the Buys box had already been dismembered. If this is so, then the "cabinet" had belonged to the Shah of Persia between 1736 and 1747, for "on this key is a Persian engraved plate which runs 'Saheb-Nadir-Pad Chah'."[37]

The Victoria and Albert Jewel Box

Beckford's ownership of the jewel box in the Victoria and Albert Museum (fig. 12-4), or at least his attempt to purchase a very similar box, is confirmed by a letter dated April 19, 1826, to Beckford from Gregorio Franchi, who was acting as Beckford's agent in Paris:

> Your casket [and?] tray is in good condition and not "fruste" [?] "Je crois que je vois la berbue, a son sujet, until yesterday I had it in my hands, we must buy it. The great [object?] of ebony and ivory is very curious; one of the ebony panels is cracked, the other warped and the rest is perfect. Every element can be con-

sidered perfect in its type. Inside is a drawer decorated on the exterior with cartouches, on the interior with rich mosaics. This drawer once had a box which I suspect is no. 1225 (read the catalogue description). The type of work is exactly the same as the casket. At the centre of the interior base are two silver letters which make me think that this piece was for some relative, like Maria Vandiemen's. The lacquer is of the same quality . . . although more delicate and its enrichments [?] are full of particular details that both of us can understand and appreciate. For example, in some parts, instead of the gold powder [*nashiji*], we find the ground decorated like the interior of your coral casket, and in other parts Japanese arms [*mon*]. It is impossible to see even one inch of undecorated background, red or black. The fronts [of the drawers? / interior of the lids?] is the same shape more or less that we find here [refers to drawing]. The type of carving in ebony is of the most artistically refined; one side? with a scene with cranes, the other side with two magical chimeras, and the sides with flowers and plants. On top more flowers and everything in the best possible taste.[38]

The description is remarkably close to the Victoria and Albert jewel box. The only difference appears to be in the mention of Japanese *mon*, which are not present in the Victoria and Albert box. The ebony panels on the front and back do bear cranes and "chimera," *shishi*; on the sides are flowers and plants, although the two human figures are not mentioned. The top has plants, and Franchi can be forgiven for not identifying the phoenix. When the side panel is raised, the secret drawer does indeed have a cartouche. Franchi's letter, however, does not clearly indicate exactly which piece has "lacquer . . . of the same quality" as the van Diemen box.

The jewel boxes in the Victoria and Albert and in the Tokyo National Museum compare closely with the Chiddingstone and Vienna caskets. The jewel box in Tokyo is lacquer-decorated like the Chiddingstone casket, while the Victoria and Albert casket has carved wood (possibly ebony) much like the exterior of the Vienna casket.[39] These four pieces, as well as the van Diemen and Buys boxes, were almost certainly made in the same workshop, perhaps that of the Koami family of Kyoto.[40]

The Mazarin Chest

There has been some confusion over the identity of the Mazarin chest (fig. 12-5), and its relationship to a very similar but slightly larger chest that was purchased from the Hamilton Sale of 1882 by Sir Trevor Lawrence, a renowned collector of Japanese art.[41] The cognomen "Mazarin" is used here to apply only to that chest now in the Victoria and Albert Museum. The "Mazarin" association is based upon the fact that the key of the chest bears the coat of arms of the Mazarin-Meilleraye family.[42] The Mazarin and Lawrence chests are so similar that they must have come from the same source, though this is unconfirmed by the documents. It was almost certainly the Mazarin

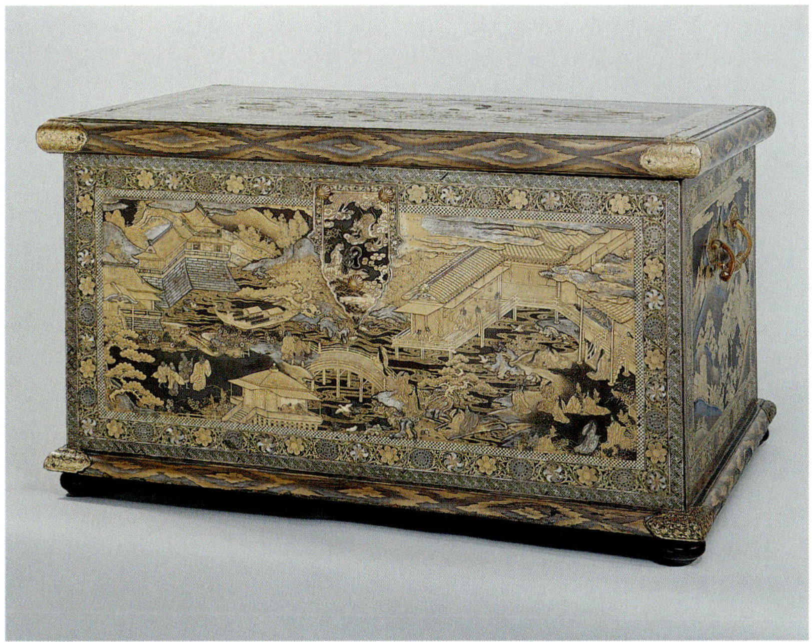

Fig. 12-5. The "Mazarin" chest, ca. 1635. Japanese lacquer. The Victoria and Albert Museum. 412-1882.

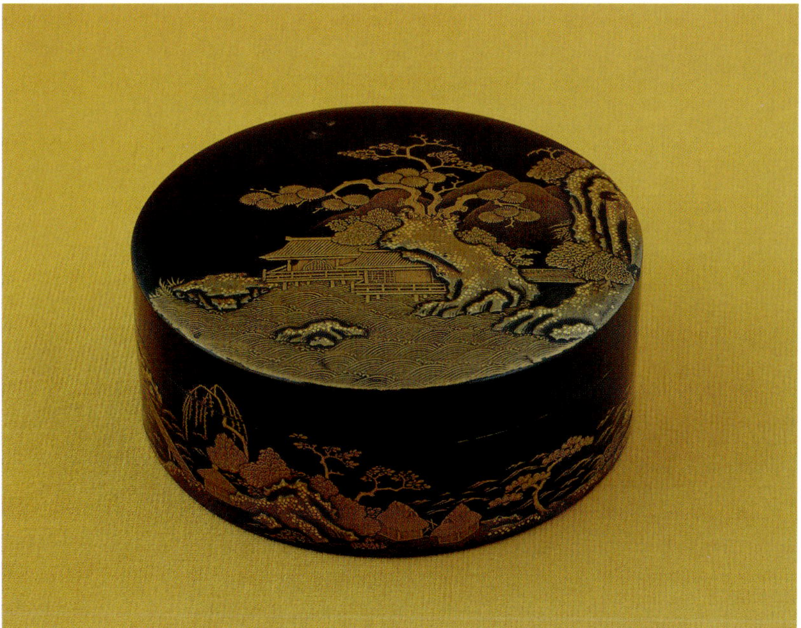

Fig. 12-6. Japanese box, late 17th century. Gold lacquer in *maki-e* ("sprinkled picture") technique with some *kirikane* (inlay), on a black ground. The National Trust, Charlecote Park.

chest that was bought for Beckford by the *marchand-mercier* Darnault at the sale of the collection of the Duc de Bouillon on 2 Thermidor, year 9 (20/21 July, 1800) for 1,280 livres; the sale catalogue described it as:

> A large chest three feet long, two feet wide and two feet high. The panels show landscapes with figures and animals, all encrusted with gold and silver in relief, the frames of the panels with motifs and rosettes encrusted with gold and mother-of-pearl, with its glazed case with gilt-bronze mounts, all in the finest condition.[43]

The identification with the Mazarin chest, as opposed to the Lawrence chest, made here, hinges upon the size; the size is given by Damault in *pieds* as 3 by 2 by 2; this, an approximate measurement, is the equivalent of 38⅜ by 25⅝ by 25⅝ inches (97.5 by 65 by 65 cm). The measurements of the Mazarin chest are 39⅜ inches wide, by 22¼ inches high by 25 inches deep (100.3 by 56.5 by 63.5 cm). The measurements of the Lawrence chest, as calculated from the Hamilton Palace sale catalogue, are 54 inches wide, by 27⅛ (137 by 69 cm). Clearly the Darnault bill refers to the Mazarin chest.

Logically, it would seem that in the 1823 Fonthill Abbey sale, lot 576 must be the Mazarin chest; in the sale catalogue, which was prepared under Beckford's supervision, it is described:

> A SUPERB COFFER OF RAISED JAPAN, presumed the largest specimen known of this *superior quality,* the LID, without and within, as also the FRONT and SIDES are covered with representations of buildin*gs and landscapes,* of the finest *raised and spangled Japan,* and with animals of SOLID *gold* and *silver. This unique specimen of Japanese art was formerly the property of* CARDINAL MAZARIN, and belonged subsequently to the DUC de BOUILLON.[44]

Describing this as a "unique specimen" and "the largest specimen known of this superior quality" suggests that the other chest, the Lawrence chest, which was larger and of equal quality, was not known to Beckford. The reference probably reflects more on its relation to the van Diemen and Buys boxes, and the other pieces described here, than to a piece so alike as to render the word "unique" absurd. The photograph of the Lawrence chest demonstrates its close similarity to the Mazarin chest in all but proportion and size.

James Storer recorded in 1812 that the Mazarin chest stood in the gallery at Fonthill Abbey,[45] where John Rutter also placed it in 1822, giving both the Mazarin and de Bouillon provenance.[46] It was included in the Hamilton Palace sale of 1882 as lot 147.[47] The Mazarin chest and

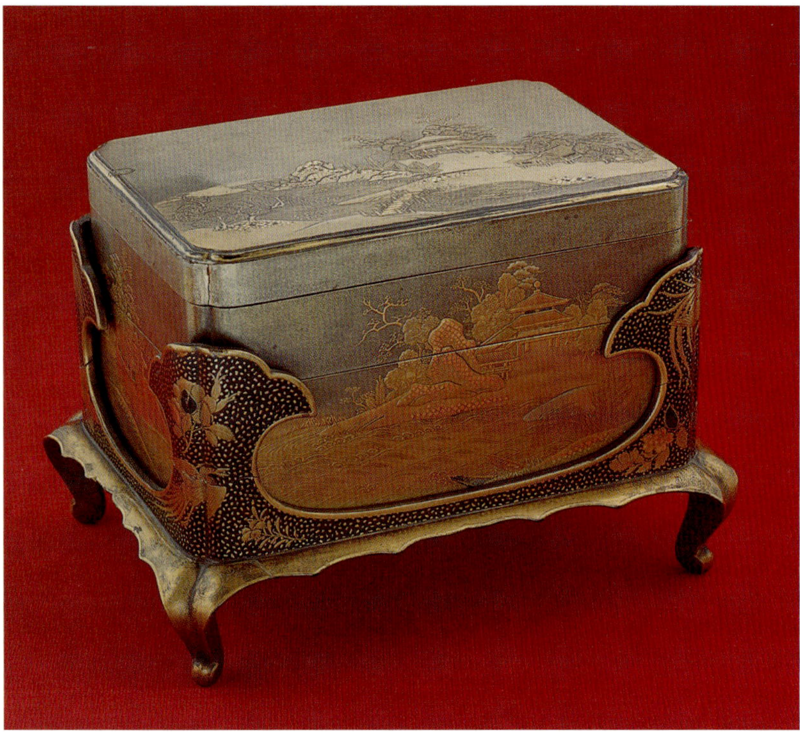

Fig. 12-7. Japanese *jubako* (tiered box) on a fitted stand, late 17th or early 18th century. Box: gold lacquer in *maki-e* ("sprinkled picture") technique, with some *kirikane* (inlay), on a black ground; stand: gold-speckled black ground. The National Trust, Charlecote Park.

the Lawrence chest are not like the other six pieces of the Fine Period that have been discussed, and they probably came from a different Kyoto workshop. The proportions of the smaller of the two, the Mazarin chest, are somewhat odd, by European standards, for a chest with a flat lifting lid; it is too narrow for the height and the depth.[48]

The Weston Box

In Franchi's letter of April 19, 1826, describing Beckford's jewel box (probably that now in the Victoria and Albert Museum), he also referred to a box with two silver letters. On May 7, 1826, wrote again to Beckford; "about the Mon Faux casket with CF letters, I have already told the Duke that your Excellency has let go his interest."[49] This suggests that the box with the two silver letters bore the monogram "CF" or "FC". The only known box with letters of this type is in the Weston Collection, New York. Franchi also suggests that Beckford either had ceased to be interested or that he had failed to buy it from the unnamed duke.

The box is a flattened rectangular form, some 8⅜ inches long (21.2 cm), with a close-fitting lid on which in raised gold lacquer is a tray-landscape with pine and plum trees within a formal border of flower-filled lappets. The interior of the box is decorated with a fine

landscape with birds, while the interior of the lid has lappets similar to those on the outside, around the monogram "CF" or "FC" in heavy silver, not inlaid as in the van Diemen and Buys boxes, but attached.[50]

Japanese Lacquer for the Domestic Market

Beckford did not only own export lacquer, that is, lacquer made specifically for the export market, but also lacquer in non-export styles and shapes that happened to be exported. Throughout the seventeenth and eighteenth centuries, the Dutch were clearly buying small items of Japanese lacquer on the open market in Japan and shipping them to Europe. In 1662 the Dutch authorities in Batavia wrote to the Chamber of Seventeen, Amsterdam (headquarters of the Dutch East India Company): "we have recommended [to the Principal in Deshima [a Dutch official] to fill the chests-of-drawers with small lacquered boxes, porcelain *poppegoet* [perhaps small figures or ceramics for dolls' houses] and other curiosities."[51] These circulated in Europe, and in the eighteenth century were collected as "old japan."

The *marchand-mercier* Edmé-François Gersaint wrote in the introduction to the sale of the collection of the Chevalier Antoine de la Rocque in 1745 "les morceaux de choix, sont de même, extrêmement rares à trouver, particulierement quand ils sont anciens. ils sont quelquefois portez à des prix qui étonnent, même en Hollande."[52] Choice pieces passed from collection to collection as the owners died and the pieces were bequeathed, sold or auctioned. Occasionally such pieces can be traced in more than one collection, but usually the descriptions are so laconic as to make this extremely unreliable.

Several eighteenth-century collections survive—perhaps not intact, but with a considerable number of pieces—in Germany at Dresden, Braunschweig, and Gotha, for instance; in Sweden at Drottningholm; and in Denmark in the Royal Collection. The best-documented of the collections in France, although scattered, is that of Marie-Antoinette. Several pieces in the Louvre or the Musée Guimet today can be traced to her ownership.[53] In England collections were at Drayton House and are at Burghley House]. Many of the pieces in these collections can be compared with pieces known to have been owned by Beckford, such as those now at Charlecote Park (figs. 12-6 and 12-7), which had been bought at the Fonthill Abbey sale in 1823 by George Hammond Lucy.[54]

Japanese lacquer not made especially for export to Europe was much more common in Europe than has usually been recognized. Bought on the open market in Japan, it was shipped as private trade by servants of the Dutch East India Company, usually perfectly legally, throughout the second half of the seventeenth century and the whole of the eighteenth century, apparently in large quantities. Because of its origin, the quality of these pieces varies from the extremely fine to the truly mediocre. And because of the quantity of this lacquer, it is extremely difficult to attempt to identify the usually terse or laconic contemporary descriptions with any known piece, unless there is additional evi-

dence. Even drawings such as those by Gabriel de Saint Aubin in the margins of his copy of the catalogue of the Gaignat sale of 1768, should not be relied upon to relate to a known example; there are simply too many pieces that may be similar.[55] An exception to this rule may be the piece shaped as a pomegranate bought for Beckford by Darnault from the de Bouillon sale that had been in the Gaignat sale, probably as lot 171 which was drawn by Saint Aubin.[56] Thus shapes for certain objects found in the various Beckford sale catalogues and other documents can be suggested, but few are certain and only those because of further documentation. Far the most important of these are the pieces pre-served at Charlecote Park, purchased by George Hammond Lucy at the 1823 Fonthill Abbey sale.

William Beckford, having established his collecting habits in France, where he acquired much of his lacquer, went on to form a extraordinary collection of Japanese export lacquer, owning at one time or another most of the finest pieces on record. He also possessed an assortment of lesser lacquers, which he valued for their decorative potential in the equally extraordinary interiors he created at Fonthill and Lansdown.

Acknowledgments: The authors would like to thank Alexandre Pradère, Bet McLeod, the PHJ/Beckford Archive, and Pedro Moura de Carvalho for help and advice, and for permission to use their work in this text.—OI and JW

1. [Les ouvrages precieux d'Ancien laque du Japon s'assortissent parfaitement avec les porcelaines, par la singularité des formes, le goût aussi ingénieux que particulier des dessins, le beau ton del'or, & I 'excellent fini du travail: ainsi les Amateurs ont-ils regardé comme essentiel d'en avoir les morceaux les plus rares pour le bel accord de leur Cabinet.] "Effets d'ancien laque du Japon," *Catalogue raisonné des Marbres, Jaspes Agathes . . . faisant partie du Cabinet de feu M. Randon de Boisset, Receveur General des Finances. Par C. F. Julliot, Marchand, rue S. Honore, pres celle du Four,* sale cat., Paris, 1777, p. 95.

2.Close examination of numerous English and French diaries and memoirs of the period reveals no mention of his name.

3. Francis Watson discussed this aspect of Beckford's collecting nearly forty years ago, describing his acquisition of the Duc de Bouillon's collection, and thus trying to match surviving pieces with descriptions in the sales document. This process is fraught with difficulty, and Watson's pairings do not all survive scrutiny. See Francis J. B. Watson, "Beckford, Mme de Pompadour, the Due de Bouillon and the taste for Japanese lacquer in the eighteenth century," *Gazette des Beaux Arts,* 61 (1963): 101–27.

4. See Oliver Impey, "A brief Account of Japanese Export Lacquer of the Seventeenth Century, and Its Use in Europe," in *Japanese Lacquers and their European Imitations,* Arbeitshefte des Bayerischen Landesamtes fur Denkmalpflege, 96 (Munich, 2000): 14–30. The substance lacquer, a form of varnish, derives from the sap of the lacquer tree, *Rhus vernicifera,* which is tapped from the tree like maple syrup. The best quality sap was imported into Japan from Cambodia. The sap has a toxic vapor, is very sticky, and dries in a damp atmosphere to a very hard finish, impervious to hot water, alcohol, and woodworm. The sap is colorless but is easy to color by the addition of various pigments. It is applied in increasingly fine layers with a brush, each layer being polished between coats. This process may take months, which makes the production of lacquer prolonged and expensive. The upper coats may accept inlay or may be raised by the addition of gesso. When polished and covered with a clear lacquer, this will be visible, providing the ground for decoration. "Namban" lacquer was overpainted in gold lacquer with a brush, but later Japanese lacquer was usually decorated in *maki-e* (literally "sprinkled picture"), whereby powdered pigments are scattered onto wet lacquer to form a pictorial decoration. This is a very difficult and slow procedure, and it is hardly surprising that it was little understood in Europe. Japanese lacquer usually had a black background, but later lacquer sometimes had a gold or other colored ground.

5. Joe Earle, "Genji meets Yang Guifei; a group of Japanese Export Lacquers," *Transactions of the Oriental Ceramic Society,* 47 (1984): 45–76.

6. Hugh Roberts, "Beckford, Vulliamy and Old Japan," *Apollo,* 124, no. 296 (October 1986): 338–41.

7. The, chest, now known only from a photograph was in the Hamilton Palace sale (Earle, "Genji" [1984]): fig. 18). A panel in the Victoria and Albert, cut from a Japanese cabinet or chest, came with the Salting Bequest and is said, without apparent foundation, to have come from the Hamilton Palace sale; supposedly it was formerly in Beckford's possession. It is frequently included in this "Fine Quality" group, but should not be so; the lacquer is not of the same high standard.

8. See Julia Meech, *Lacquerware from the Weston Collection,* exh. cat., Christie's, New York. 1995, no. 3.8; and Julia Hutt, "A Japanese Lacquer Chest in the Victoria and Albert Museum", *Apollo,* 147, no. 433 (March, 1998): 3–9.

9. [Une très belle cassette de lacque, avec un plateau fond noir à magots, dans sa cage de glace, garny en bronze doré; prisé deux mille huit cens livres.] Jean Cordey (ed.), *Inventaire des biens de Madame de Pompadour rédigé après son décès* (Paris: Société des Bibliophiles de France, 1929): no. 712.

10. [Une precieuse casette fond noir, dont le dessus et les battes forment aulant de tableaux ravissants par la variété . . . sur le dedans du couvercle est un cartouche fond noir avec inscription en gros caractères d'or, parlant ces mots: MARIA, VAN DIEMEN... Le Mérite de cette cassette, peut-être unique en son genre, est plus connu pour sa réputation, que l 'on ne pourroit le rendre: elle saisit d'admiration tout connoisseur par l'immense et precieuse richesse de son travail; elle vient de Madame la Marquise de Pompadour.] Quoted by Watson, 1963, op. cit.

11. Quoted in ibid.

12. John Rutter, *Delineations of Fonthill and its Abbey* (Shaftesbury and London, The Author, 1823).

13. Inventory of 1844, MS Beckford c.58, fol. 36, Bodleian Library, Oxford (cited hereafter as "MS Beckford").

14. *Magnificent Effects at Fonthill Abbey, Wilts. . . . Tuesday, October 7, 1822 and nine following days,* sale cat., Christie's, London, 1822, lot 93.

15. Clive Wainwright, "Some Objects from William Beckford's Collection now in the Victoria and Albert Museum," *Burlington Magazine* 113, no. 818 (1971): 254–64.

16. *The Fonthill View, the sale . . . the costly furniture, China and Unique & Splendid Effects, 23 September–2 October, 16 October–22, 1823,* sale cat., Phillips', Fonthill, 1823, lot 1365.

17. Draft deed of entail of the marbles [etc] in Hamilton Palace, 1855, MS Beckford c.60.

18. *Catalogue of Pictures, Works of Art and decorative objects, the property of His Grace the Duke of Hamilton, KG, June 17, 19–20, 1882,* sale cat., Christie, Manson and Woods, London, 1882, lot 146; sold for £315 to Sir Trevor Lawrence, who bequeathed it to the museum in 1916.

19. Roberts, "Beckford, Vulliamy" (1986).

20. Both a preliminary drawing for one of the cabinets, presumably by one of the Vulliamys or by their designers, and the original bill submitted by the firm of Benjamin and Benjamin Lewis Vulliamy to William Beckford in 1803 survive. The work was complex and difficult, and the price consequently high. See ibid.

21. James Storer, *A Description of Fonthill Abbey, Wiltshire* (London: Storer et al., 1812).

22. Hamilton Palace Sale, 1882, lots 172 and 173. They were bought by Christopher Beckett Denison for a combined price of 920 guineas (about half what they had cost to make up). On 11 July 1885 at the Denison sale at Christie's they were sold as lots 687 and 688, again together, for 795 guineas to Lord Carysfort, ancestor of the present owner.

23. See chap. 10, by Adriana Turpin, in this volume.

24. Fonthill Sale, 1823, lot 96; quoted by Roberts, "Beckford, Vulliamy" (1986): 340.

25. Hamilton Palace Sale, lot 293.

26. Oliver Impey and John Whitehead, "From Japanese Box to French Royal Furniture," *Apollo*, 132, no. 343 (September 1990): 159–65.

27. Quoted by Roberts, "Beckford, Vulliamy" (1986). Also see chap. 6, by Anne Eschapasse, in this volume.

28. Now in a private collection. Its existence was apparently unknown to Beckford scholars until the cabinet was reproduced by Alexandre Pradère in *Les Ebénistes Français de Louis XIV à la Révolution* (Paris, 1989): 42. A statement is made claiming a Beckford provenance. The cabinet is also reproduced in Thibaut Wolvesperges, *Le meuble français en laque au XVIIIe siècle* (Paris and Brussels, 2000): fig. 3. Wolvesperges confirms that it is stamped by Adam Weisweiler (personal communication, 2000).

29. Moitte's design was included in an auction in 1979 of a group of drawings from the collection of the goldsmiths Odiot, who had apparently purchased it and others after the Auguste bankruptcy in 1810. *Importants Dessins et Tableaux Anciens*, sale cat., Sotheby's, Monaco, 26 November, 1979, lot 619, design for the cabinet; ibid., lot 620, design for its frieze. The statement about the Auguste provenance comes from the introduction to the section devoted to the collection.

30. The cabinet sold at Sotheby's Monaco, 14 June 1997, lot 137; and the design sold Sotheby's Monaco, 22 February 1986, lot 181. In his catalogue notice for the cabinet, Alexandre Pradère discusses the problem of Beckford's cabinets at length.

31. The central panels are apparently of plain aventurine lacquer, but the very slight variations in shade visible in the illustration perhaps indicate they originally had something applied onto the surface. They could have been sufficiently well restored for such traces not to be easily discernible.

32. An examination of the cabinet by Chantal de Spot and Derek Ostergard on 6 April 2001 revealed that the piece did at one time have stretchers, which have been removed.

33. Stylistic argument for attribution to Vulliamy is impossible since they derived their models from outside sources including French sources and employed French craftsmen to manufacture some of the elements of their production. On this subject see Geoffrey de Bellaigue, "The Vulliamys and France," *Furniture History* (1967): 45–53.

34. Of two stages in height, roughly pyramidal in form, they open in the two registers to reveal shallow wells, the lower one above a single line of three drawers. They have pilasters at the corners, and flanking the central drawer on the front, of lacquered wood (Chiddingstone) or painted ivory (Vienna). Both caskets have multiple borders and moldings, with minute inlay of pearl-shell. The Vienna casket has panels of black wood veneer, probably ebony, finely carved in relief to give the appearance of black *takamakie;* the Chiddingstone casket has panels of gold and silver lacquer *takamakie* scenes of landscape, animals, birds and flowers, some with metal studs to give shine, though the lower panels, the flanking drawer-fronts, have quartered paneling with geometric patterns. Each casket has a recessed centre drawer of arched shape, and a loose fitting to cover this drawer.

The interiors of the lids (one above the other) of each casket are decorated with landscapes in *takamakie* on a black ground. The interior is in red lacquer and has or would have had a drop-in tray (the Chiddingstone tray is missing); the Vienna tray has red lacquered small open compartments around a central rectangular well in black lacquer in which is a diamond-shaped cartouche containing a landscape in the ink-painting technique used on the interior tray of the van Diemen box. The interior of the drawers are also in red lacquer while the outside of the drawers are decorated with flower-work in gold lacquer.

35. Fonthill Abbey Sale, 1823, lot 908.

36. Watson, "Beckford" (1963).

37. Saheb-Nādir-Pad Chah is the Indian title of Nādir Shah, the Afsharid Emperor of Persia who ruled from 1736 to 1747. In 1739 he invaded India and looted and sacked Delhi. It seems likely that it was at this time that he acquired the casket, for the Dutch had frequently made presents of grand pieces of Japanese lacquer to the various Moghul emperors and to their court. This is just the sort of piece that might have been used for such a presentation. It was already an antique at the time, being nearly a century old, and may well have been highly esteemed by the shah. If this is this casket, which seems likely, just how it reached Europe is unknown. The whereabouts of the key and its history are largely unknown; it was bought shortly after the Second World War by Denis Eyre Bower who set up the Trust at Chiddingstone Castle in Kent; see Joe Earle, *Japanese Lacquer; the Denys Eyre Bower Collection at Chiddingstone Castle* (London. 2000): no. 14.

38. Franchi to Beckford, 19 April 1826, fol. 80, 80v. MS Beckford c. 12. Translation from the Portuguese by Pedro Moura de Carvalho. *Mon* are *armas* in the original Portuguese. The comment, "this drawer once had a box," probably refers to the Weston box.

39. The shape is a simpler version of the caskets, having a rectangular body with ivory pilasters at the corners, and with a single hinged lid with coved sides, the upper panel of the lid sliding to reveal a compartment within the lid. At one side the wall lifts to allow access to a concealed drawer under the main recess. The wooden panels on the Victoria and Albert jewel box represent on the front, a water landscape with cranes, and on the back two *shishi* and a peony bush. One side has two woodcutters among trees and the other a tray-landscape; the top panel of the lid has two phoenix among stylized plants; the coved sides have cartouches. This shape is, in fact, not uncommon in Japanese export lacquer (unlike the caskets which appear to be unique), and is found in examples of lesser quality (e.g. at Belton House and at Burghley House). Just such a jewel box is represented in a painting by Simon Renard de Saint-André, who died in 1677, now in the collection of the Staatsgemaldesammlungen, Munich (displayed at Schloss Aschaffenburg); see Peter Thornton, *Seventeenth-Century Interior Decoration in England, France and Holland* (New Haven and London: Yale University Press, 1978): 421 and fig. 239.

40. Earle, "Genji" (1984): 45–76.

41. The Lawrence chest was presumably bought by the duke, an avid collector himself, after 1823, or Beckford would have known about it and would not have described the Mazarin chest as unique. It is likely that the Lawrence chest is that mentioned in the Deed of Entail of Hamilton Palace as "A large antique Japan chest (belonged to Cardinal Mazarin on a gilt stand, and Plate Glass cover in brass frame for ditto" (see n. 17 above).

The confusion between the Lawrence and Mazarin chests seems to have arisen between 1855 and 1882, long after Beckford's death. No secure reference can be found to a second chest of this quality in any of the Beckford or related papers, except in the Deed of Entail, until the Hamilton Palace sale. By 1882, the Lawrence chest seems to have been viewed as the important one, and its provenance had become confused with that of the smaller chest. As observed earlier, however, the chests are so similar in all ways except for size, that is likely that they had a common source at some point; this may well have been ownership by the Duc de Mazarin-Meilleraye. The assumption must be that, contrary to general opinion, it was the Mazarin chest that was owned by Beckford; apparently the only Beckford connection of the Lawrence chest is its inclusion in the Hamilton Palace sale. It was sold at the Lawrence sale of 1916 and since then its whereabouts are unknown.

42. Lucy Norton, ed., *Historical Memoirs of the Duc de Saint-Simon,* vol. 2 (London, 1968): 276–77 and 516. This does not mean that it necessarily belonged to Cardinal Mazarin, who, according to Saint-Simon, was an uncle of the Duc de Mazarin-Meilleraye.

43. [Un grand coffre de 3 pieds de long sur deux de large et deux de hauteur. Les panneaux représentent Paysages avec figures et animaux &c. le tout incrusté en or et argent relief, encadrements des dits panneaux représentant ornements et rosaces incrusté en or et en nacre-de-perle. avec sa cage de glace garnie de bronze doré le tout dans le plus parfaite conservation.] Quoted by Watson, "Beckford" (1963): 114. The confusion between the two chests is apparent in ibid.; and in Clive Wainwright, *The Romantic Interior,* (New Haven and London: Yale University Press, 1989): 121.

44. Fonthill Abbey Sale, 1823, lot 576.

45. Storer, *Description of Fonthill* (1812).

46. Rutter, *Delineations* (1822).

47. In the Hamilton Palace sale, the Lawrence chest was lot 1165, and the Mazarin chest, lot 147, which was described as "A VERY FINE OBLONG CHEST, of black lacquer, with raised landscapes in gold, and studded with animals, birds, and other objects in silver and gold, and with a large Medallion similar inside the lid. Formerly the property of Napoleon I." No measurements are given. The Napoléon provenance is pure fantasy. It was bought by the South Kensington Museum (later to be the Victoria and Albert Museum) for £772. The Lawrence chest, appears as "A VERY FINE OBLONG COFFER, OF OLD JAPAN LACQUER, with a large landscape, buildings, trees, and a river, with a bridge and figures in the foreground, in border of birds and scrolls, animals and birds in gold and silver in relief, similar landscapes on the front and ends and inside the lid, black and gold trellis-border, with circular ornaments, inlaid with mother-o'–pearl, chased with metal-gilt mounts—on carved and gilt wood stand—4ft. 6in. by 2 ft. 3 in.—*From the Collections of the Cardinal Mazarin, the Duc de Bouillon and Fonthill.*" It was sold to Sir Trevor Lawrence, the great collector of Japanese art for £682. 10s. It seems very strange that the similarity between the two chests was not commented upon by the cataloguer. It is worth noting that the Mazarin chest, the smaller of the two, was more expensive than the Lawrence chest.

48. The decoration is of superb quality, quite comparable to that on the other pieces we have been discussing, but in a style, pallette, and technique different enough to set it apart. The lid, and the interior of the lid have strongly depicted cartouches, with borders of dragons and birds in relief, within which are landscape scenes, with considerable use of red lacquer. Set into the landscapes are small metal animals in solid metal (probably silver or a silver alloy). These do not appear on the other pieces we have discussed; nor does the red lacquer in the pictorial parts. The front of the chest has a similar landscape without the cartouche. The wide borders are of a type that

resembles those on the van Diemen box, which are to become almost standard in later productions. The back has a charming surprise; it bears a flamboyant painting in gold lacquer of a tiger and bamboo in Kano style, asymmetrical and off-centre; no concession to a foreign client.

49. Franchi to Beckford, 7 May 1826, MS Beckford c. 12, fol. 84v. Translation by Pedro Moura de Carvalho.

50. It has been suggested that these letters refer to François Caron, who served the Dutch East India Company in Japan in the 1620s and 1630s, but this is unproven; see Meech, *Lacquerware* (1995): no. 3.

51. T. Volker, "Porcelain and the Dutch East India Company," *Mededelingen van het Rijksmuseum voor Volkenkunde* 2 (1954): 145.

52. [les morceaux de choix, sont de même, extrêmement rares à trouver, particulierement quand ils sont anciens. Ils sont quelquefois portez à des prix qui étonnent, même en Hollande.] Quoted in Watson, "Beckford" (1963): 103.

53. For Braunschweig, see Gunther Rudolf Diesinger, *Ostasiatische Lackarbeiten,* catalogue of the Herzog Anton Ulrich Museum (Brunswick, 1990); for Drottningholm, see Åke Setterwall, Stig Fogelmark, and Bo Gyllensvård, *The Chinese Pavilion at Drottningholm* (Malmö, 1974); for Denmark, see Joan Hornby, "Japan," in Bente Dam-Mikkelsen and Torben Lundbaek, *Ethnographical objects in the Danish Royal Kunstkammer, 1650–1800* (Copenhagen, 1980): 221–53. For Marie Antoinette's collection, see Meiko Nagashima, "Mid-Edo Period Lacquer: The Collection of Marie Antoinette," *Shikoshi* 22 (November, 1999): 24–57 (in Japanese).

54. At Charlecote Park there are several pieces of Japanese and other lacquer, bought by George Hammond Lucy at the Fonthill Abbey Sale of 1823. These include lot 554, a writing box (*suzuribako*); lots 547 and 548, two stacks of boxes (*jubako*) on stands; lots 549 and 550, two very similar *lac burguaté* incense burners; lot 992, a nest of boxes with cover; lot 997, a lobed box (*mokko* shape) with fruit and some others. See also Wainwright, *Romantic Interior* (1989): chap. 8.

55. E. Dacier, *Catalogues de ventes et livrets de salons illustrés par gabriel de Saint Aubin,* vol 2 (Paris, 1921).

56. Quoted by Watson, "Beckford" (1963).

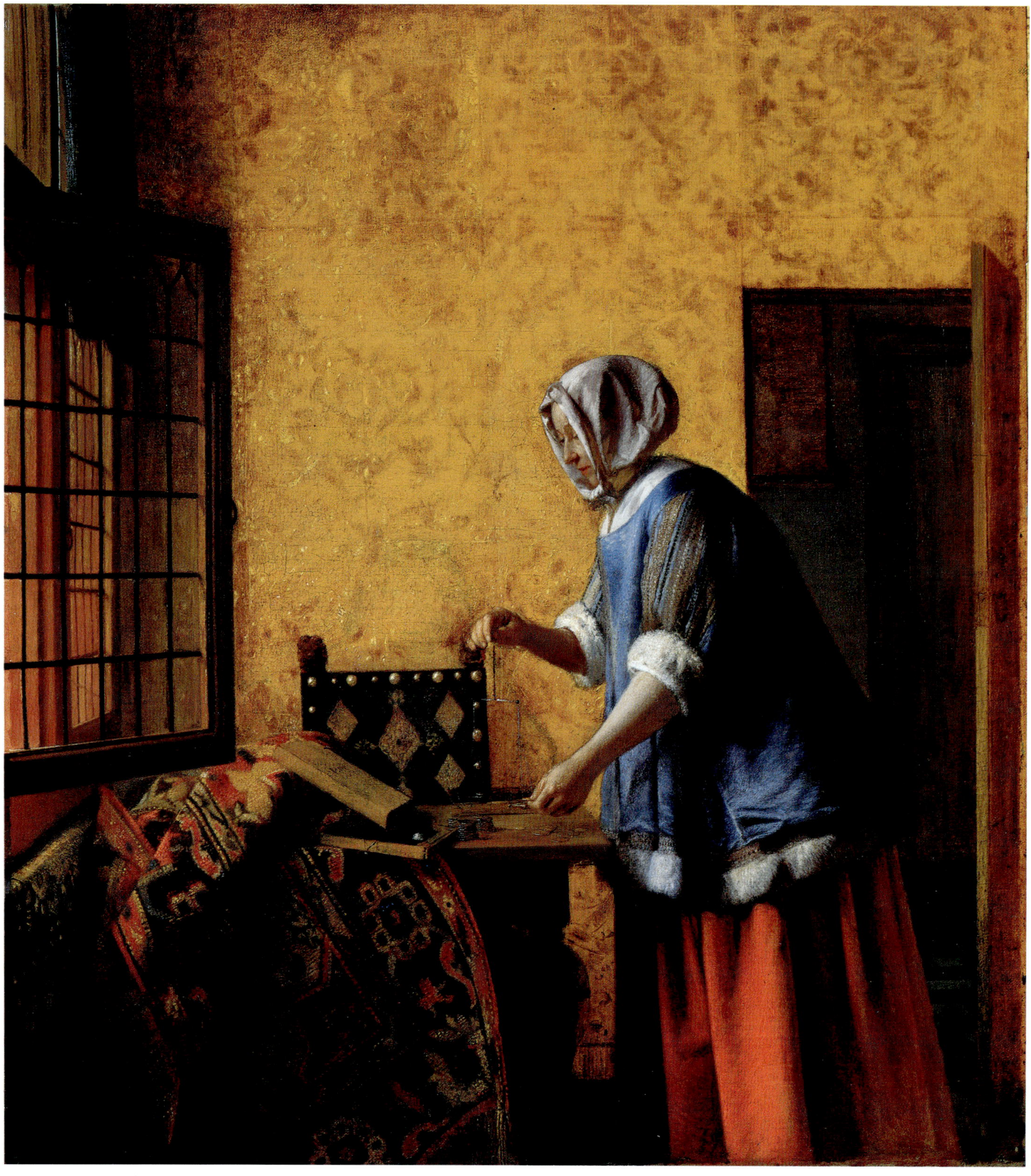

Fig. 13-1. Pieter de Hooch. *A Woman Weighing Coins (Die Goldwägerin)*, ca. 1664 or later. Oil on panel. Staatliche Museen zu Berlin, Gemäldegalerie

Chapter XIII

WILLIAM BECKFORD: COLLECTOR OF OLD MASTER PAINTINGS, DRAWINGS, AND PRINTS

Jeannie Chapel

From the beginning of his long lifetime of collecting, Beckford established for himself a sensational reputation as a distinguished and erudite connoisseur. This was intentional, for he apparently saw himself as a great patron of the arts in general and thought of his shrine as one where after his death his devoted following would come and worship.[1] Beckford was certainly ahead of his time with his pioneering passion for collecting early Italian Renaissance paintings—"Primitives" or "goldbacks"—and as such led the way for other collectors in the nineteenth century, such as Prince Albert. One of his early biographers wrote that Beckford had "secured a fame as a collector that will preserve his memory for many generations to come" and this has proved to be the case as his reputation is indeed widespread; the very existence of a Beckford Society also gives credence to this statement.[2] Some years after this prognostication Sacheverell Sitwell called him, "One of the greatest collectors" and "a real and peculiar genius."[3] Sitwell also pointed out that Beckford, like many of his contemporaries, such as Goya, was someone who perched on the divide between the ancien régime of the eighteenth century and the new world of the nineteenth century, a divide caused by the upheaval of the French Revolution and the enormous changes brought about by the Industrial Revolution.

William Beckford's life spanned the most important period of picture collecting in British history. The outbreak of the French Revolution in 1789 and the subsequent sales of numerous aristocratic French collections in London—notably the collection of the duc d' Orléans dispersed in a series of auctions in London in the 1790s, initiated a transformation in patterns of art ownership across Europe.[4] Aristocratic and Church owners, especially in France, Italy, and Spain, found themselves under pressure, sometimes to the point of compulsion, to part with collections acquired over generations. In France this process led in part to the establishment of public art museums and particularly the Musée Napoléon in the Louvre, which was to be a wonder of the world. In Britain, on the other hand, the importation of vast numbers of paintings by Old Masters (a term not in current use until the 1790s), through auctions or the activities of such art dealers as William Buchanan, created a number of magnificent private collections in the hands of noblemen, bankers, and other plutocrats. This was the beginning of changes in patronage and collecting that took place as a result of the new balance of wealth. At the close of the Napoleonic wars in 1815, Old Masters belonged to a wide variety of collectors, among others, the Prince Regent, the first Marquess of Stafford, the second Earl Grosvenor, the Duke of Wellington, the fifth Earl of Carlisle, the artistic patron Sir George Beaumont, and the banker John Julius Angerstein. Their collections were of outstanding quality.

In this distinguished assembly Beckford took a prominent place. The collector with whom perhaps he can be most closely compared is the Prince Regent, the future George IV. The two men were equally lavish and discriminating, equally interested in quality and attracted to French eighteenth-century works of art. For both men paintings were part of much broader collecting interests and contributed to the creation of a series of exquisite ensembles in their residences. Beckford thoroughly enjoyed his collections and had entertaining times at Fonthill and in Bath, hanging and rehanging the pictures within the elaborate furnishing schemes. This passion was similar to the Prince Regent's almost obsessive fondness for the constant rearranging and redecorating of the interiors of his palaces.

Many leading collectors during this period felt impelled by a sense of duty to make their possessions available to at least a limited public. Although aristocratic houses in the country had for many years been shown to visitors, there were very few opportunities for artists or connoisseurs to view private collections in London. Inspired by the Musée du Louvre and provoked by the absence of a National Gallery until 1824, a group of enthusiasts set up the British Institution in 1805.[5] The institution showed both contemporary work and Old Master paintings lent by private owners, Beckford included. This pioneering establishment offered important opportunities to display works of art not normally available, and it proved to be highly influential leading to a new awareness of the role of the Old Masters in didactic terms.[6]

At this time both Lord Stafford and Lord Grosvenor opened picture galleries in their houses in London to visitors and provided curators and catalogues, while attempts were made to arrange the pictures by school and period on museum lines. This interest in the transition from private to public gallery, however, was not shared by Beckford. Although a believer in the creation of a national collection of works of art, he remained a quintessentially private owner, admitting only a few visitors to his houses. Beckford's life was fundamentally solitary and private, and he would not have thought it important for his collection to be exemplary. This is borne out by the enormous variety of paintings in his collection, in both style and date. The collection was put together with a sense of pleasure, even when funds were short. It changed constantly and was arranged according to visual and romantic, rather than academic, criteria.

BECKFORD'S EARLY LIFE

From birth Beckford benefited from exceptional advantages. He possessed an independent spirit and, at times, huge financial resources. His extraordinary childhood and upbringing enabled him to develop his natural gifts for learning to acquire a sophisticated and extensive knowledge of the arts. He possessed an acutely observant and outstanding eye, and his love of book collecting contributed greatly to his understanding of art of all periods and in all media.[7] His inherited wealth gave him freedom to buy what he liked and his judgment and respect for paintings allowed him to take full advantage of the extraordinary opportunities of the time. Beckford had all the characteristics of a born collector. Often reluctant to part with pictures, he would regret a decision to sell and change his mind. He liked to be told of the movement of pictures that had once belonged to him.[8] He was continually inconsistent in his methods and unconventional in his selection. He was persevering and ruthless, competitive and determined, secretive and cunning. He refused to negotiate with anyone and demanded cash on payment. This applied even to the Prince Regent, who in May 1817 was interested in buying from Beckford Gerrit Dou's *The Poulterer's Shop* (now in the National Gallery, London). "The sum must be paid in cash down, either in bank notes, or by a draft at sight convertible into bank notes," wrote Beckford, "This is how I was paid for the Claudes and the Gaspar Poussins, and this is how I shall be paid for the Gerard Dou; otherwise it must come back . . . And no bargaining: either the cash in hand or the picture at Fonthill . . . I beg you . . . to establish the clearest understanding on this point . . . otherwise I shall go mad with grief and rage." The Prince Regent did not buy.[9]

From early in his life Beckford studied constantly, and his breadth of knowledge of the history of the fine arts is witnessed in his precocious satirical work, *Biographical Memoirs of Extraordinary Painters*. He had begun to write this extraordinary work when he was sixteen, and it was published anonymously in 1780 when Beckford was aged twenty. Idiosyncratic to a degree, this display of connoisseurship revealed Beckford's particular brand of humor and a clever use of his extensive scholarship. It was described as "a series of sharp and brilliant satires on the Dutch and Flemish schools—the language polished and pointed—the sarcasm at once deep and delicate—a performance in which the buoyancy of juvenile spirits sets off the results of already extensive observation, and the judgements of a refined (though far too fastidious and exclusive) taste."[10] The publication contained imaginary biographies of painters of the Dutch and Flemish schools of painting. The tone certainly indicated his disdain toward them, but Beckford, throughout his many years of collecting, owned examples of both schools in large numbers, including some important works. Contrary by nature, Beckford frequently and characteristically countered his own deeds and statements. *Biographical Memoirs* retained its popularity and in 1824, in light of the publicity surrounding the Fonthill sale, was reprinted by William Clarke, son of George Clarke, both of whom were booksellers on New Bond Street; it was further reprinted in 1834.

THE ALDERMAN'S PICTURES

Beckford grew up surrounded by pictures. His father, the Alderman, died in 1770, when Beckford was nine. There is not a great deal of information about the collection of paintings that his father had accumulated at Fonthill House and later at Fonthill Splendens, but it is evident that he had put together a fine assortment of Old Masters and contemporary paintings. He is known to have bought paintings at auction throughout the 1740s and 1750s.[11] These assorted works included mostly Dutch and Flemish landscapes, some Italian pictures, and paintings by Watteau. In 1754, for example, the Alderman had bought pictures at the three-day sale of Dr. Richard Mead of Great Ormond Street, London, physician to King George I.[12] Among these were the later version after Elsheimer of *Tobias and the Archangel Raphael Returning with the Fish* (then thought to be by Elsheimer; see cat. no. 7), *The Italian Comedians* (now attributed to Watteau and in the National Gallery, Washington), and a Steenwyck, *Interior of the Great Church at Antwerp by Daylight*.[13]

In 1755 a fire destroyed Fonthill House and seriously damaged or destroyed some of the pictures. Four of Hogarth's series, *The Harlot's Progress*, were damaged.[14] *The Sermon on the Mount* by Claude (now in the Frick Collection, New York), and its possible pendant, *Landscape with Queen Esther approaching the Palace of Ahasuerus* (the left third of the painting survived and is now at Holkham Hall, Norfolk), were also damaged.[15] After the fire Beckford's father built what came to be known as Fonthill Splendens, a grand house with palatial and sumptuous interiors. This house was later described in detail by a German visitor, C. A. G. Goede, who mentioned "splendid works of art, which the rich owner almost entirely had acquired from well-known, great galleries at amazing expense."[16] This conclusion was reinforced by the account of a visit made in September 1803 by Lady Ann Hamilton, the sister of the tenth Duke of Hamilton, Beckford's future son-in-law. She recorded that "the lower apartments which are fitted up, to set off abt 50 of the finest Pictures ever seen."[17] Many of these works were on a grand scale and must have impressed the young Beckford; they played a crucial role from the outset in his enthusiasm as a collector and formed the nucleus of his own collection.

Beckford's Travels

Beckford's travels began with a visit to Switzerland in 1777. In 1780 he was in France and Italy on a Grand Tour, and seven years later he made his first journey to Portugal and Spain, all at a crucial period in the history of Europe. Given Beckford's knowledge of and appreciation for works of art, it is surprising to find that he committed so few observations on paintings to writing. This is even more curious as the letters from his travels, which were later published, were supposedly addressed to Beckford's mentor, the landscape-painter Alexander Cozens, and the reader would expect to find Beckford eager to exchange views and references to works of art in general.[18] Certainly Beckford's romantic approach enabled him to appreciate the landscape through the eye and mind of the painter. He noted, for example, a scene that "Zuccarelli loved to paint" or "craggy pinnacles, crowned by mouldering towers . . . just such scenery as Polemburg [one of Beckford's favorite painters] and Peter de Laer introduce in their paintings."[19] He had dreams of conversations with painters, "with none but Albano and Claude Lorrain."[20]

Despite his love of Dutch and Flemish pictures, Beckford thought little of the Low Countries, but he was exhilarated by his first visit to Venice, where in the Palazzo Ducale he admired the work of Tintoretto and Veronese. In Florence on that same Italian tour in 1780 Beckford was more impressed with the sculpture, "ranks of statues, such treasures of gems and bronzes," and only specifically noted a Medusa's head by Leonardo and "a great many Polemburgs."[21] During Beckford's visit to Paris in 1783–84 he made contact with the landscape painter, "peintre des ruines," Hubert Robert (who was later first keeper of the new Louvre). Beckford visited the studios in the Louvre "hunting out the Artists in harbours."[22] Robert himself was an enormously successful painter, well known to many important private buyers, such as the duc de Choiseul.[23] These visits to studios were perhaps unsurprising in that Beckford always found painters particularly companionable, and later there were many who were welcome at Fonthill and in Bath. Beckford himself drew and sketched, about which Redding wrote: "He sketched exceedingly well with pen and ink, much in the manner of Rembrandt's coarser drawings."[24]

There are also few references to works of art in Beckford's journal from the journey made in Portugal and Spain in 1787–88. He noted a Rosa da Tivoli landscape at the Carmelite Church, and, at the Duke of Infantado's Palace, also in Madrid, he commented that pictures by "Rubens and Velazquez are glorious." Also admired at the Escorial were a Raphael *Holy Family* (now in the Prado), a Barocci, and a van Dyck.[25] Sparse evidence survives of picture transactions, although he is known to have bought paintings in Spain. Beckford wrote from revolutionary Paris in 1793 that the situation there was increasingly difficult. Determined to extend his stay, he was attempting to obtain

another passport, and it was proving to be a problem. He stated that he had "long since done with purchasing . . . finding it impossible to send my pictures home. I parted with 10 or 11 of them."[26] He was able to buy again in Paris between May 1801 and May 1803, which was a crucial time for opportunities of observing and buying works of art. When he was there in late 1814 Beckford made contact with the dealer Guillaume-Jean Constantin who had advised on the establishment of the Louvre and was keeper of pictures at Malmaison. He introduced Beckford to available paintings—"I expect I'll do some good business with him"— and urged Beckford to visit Malmaison, where the late Empress Joséphine's pictures were displayed. Beckford found that these made "a tolerably fine and harmonious effect," but again he was particularly taken more by the sculpture, such as Canova's *Paris*, than by the paintings.[27]

Beckford The Collector

Beckford was different from other collectors in a variety of ways, owing to the circumstances of his birth and his character. Such was his reputation as a buyer of paintings that to later generations any painting with a Beckford provenance was of great interest and remains so today. The problems that beset the history of Old Master paintings also apply to Beckford's large collection. For a variety of reasons paintings were continually bought and sold throughout his life. Identification has been made more difficult by changes in attributions and titles, vague descriptions in catalogues, or the lack of dimensions or dates. As the history of art has become increasingly specialized and precise, not one of the nineteenth-century or earlier attributions remains in Beckford's collection; Dürer, Holbein, van Eyck, Vermeer, or Leonardo, for example, have all received new attributions.[28] Characteristic of a true collector, Beckford appeared intent on obscuring his actions, frequently buying back paintings from his own sales, as well as using many agents and dealers.

Paintings were one of Beckford's passions in which he took immense pleasure. He bought them not as trophies to be envied by visitors, but for his private enjoyment. As he remarked, "Collections are made from ostentation by people of wealth, who do not know a good from a bad picture."[29] Visitors to Fonthill or to Lansdown Crescent were rare, so that few contemporary accounts of his collections survive. The published works of Storer, Rutter, Britton, and Neale of the first two decades of the nineteenth century provide an enormous amount of information about Fonthill, both of the interior arrangements and contents. Later, the works of Lansdown, Redding, Waagen, and English in the 1830s and 1840s serve as an invaluable record of Lansdown Crescent and Lansdown Tower.[30] These, however, contain few illustrations of what the interiors actually looked like, and given the huge traffic in paintings while Beckford was collecting Old Masters, it is frustrating that so little documentary evidence is available to substantiate how he bought and sold such large number of works or how he installed them in his residences.[31]

Beckford maintained a constant vigil on the activities of the art market, whether he was able to buy or not. "I'm very impatient to know the result of the great sale at Christie's, especially whether Lord Yarmouth (who swallows up everything) has swallowed up the fine Leonardo da Vinci."[32] The perusal of sale catalogues was a lifelong obsession, and Melville recorded that Beckford, in his last years in Bath, "to judge from his correspondence, seems unceasingly to have studied catalogues, and himself never overlooking anything great or small."[33] Beckford remained an enthusiastic collector until the end of his life, and made continual and relentless demands of his long-suffering agents. Two letters survive that were written in 1844, ten days before he died at the age of eighty-four. Both were to Henry George Bohn, the bookseller of 47 York Street, Covent Garden, urging Bohn to send the Nodier catalogue: "I must have that Cat[alogue] by any means—and at any cost—you have carte blanche to procure it," Beckford wrote in one, and urgently again "have it I must, if only for an hour Monday."[34] He could not always afford to buy; in 1833 he wrote in frustration to his bookseller, George Clarke, "We are deluged with famous sales, and Christie has his full share of them . . . . With such a thunder cloud hanging over my Jamaica properties, I could ill afford sunshiny purchases. Some good pictures may, probably enough, offer at Lady de Grey's sale, but I must shut my eyes."[35]

Beckford's methods of buying were unconventional and yet always unwavering. "When in Spain," he wrote, "I saw a Murillo (the subject of which was St John asleep, with angels in the background tending his sheep) in a distinguished prelate's collection . . . . I returned to England; found a pile of books of a very curious kind in one of my lumber-rooms; took them back with me to Spain, and the holy man could not resist them. We made an exchange. I got the Murillo, and he the books."[36] This memory of Beckford's gives an insight into how his mind worked and the dogged determination with which he achieved what he wanted. Beckford bought pictures as he did books and described this as a "fatal, expensive, ruinous, perfidious, cursed activity." He also had a reputation for being extravagant and was known among the dealers as such: "I am Sir Pay-Well."[37]

BECKFORD'S COLLECTIONS OF PICTURES

The large numbers and fluctuation of pictures in Beckford's collection at any one time make it difficult to ascertain exactly how many and which paintings Beckford actually owned. One source of possible confusion is the sale held at Christie's on January 23, 1789, of the collection of another William Beckford (died 1799), a historian who resided at Somerley Hall, Suffolk, and who lived much in Jamaica, an illegitimate son of Beckford's uncle, Alderman Richard Beckford. Confusion is likely particularly since both William Beckfords seemingly appreciated very similar works, including paintings of dwarfs.[38]

Today, paintings supposedly with a "Beckford" provenance may have come from the Farquhar Fonthill sale of 1823, where additional works that had no connection with Beckford were introduced by the auctioneers. It is not known exactly how many of the pictures had actually belonged to him.[39] Beckford himself claimed, "I sold but little

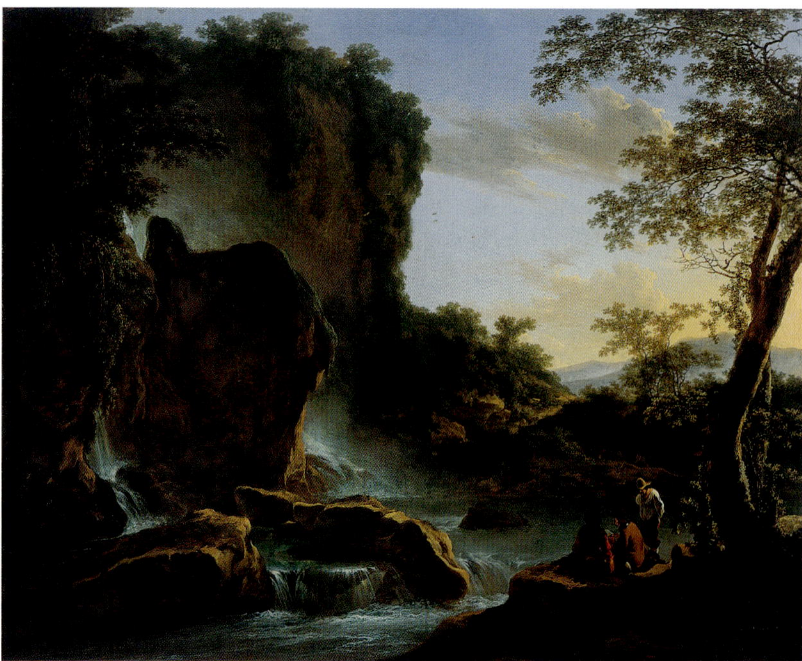

Fig. 13-2. Jan Both. *Italian Landscape with Artist Sketching a Waterfall,* ca. 1645–50. Oil on canvas. Cincinnati Art Museum, Mr. and Mrs. Harry S. Leyman Endow, 1981.413.

of what I valued . . . . Do not suppose that more than half of what was sold at Fonthill was mine."[40]

It is fascinating but difficult to try to categorize any of Beckford's collections at any one time. Henry Venn Lansdown of Bath wrote to his daughter in August 1838: "I have this day seen such an astonishing assemblage of works of art, so numerous and of so surprisingly rare a description that I am literally what Lord Byron calls 'Dazzled and drunk with beauty'. I feel so bewildered from beholding the rapid succession of some of the very finest productions of the great masters that the attempt to describe them seems an impossible task; however, I will make an effort."[41] There was an enormous breadth, scope, and variety in Beckford's choice of pictures, and he was innovatory in his propensity for collecting early Italian Quattrocento works. Beckford's deep religious convictions account for the numerous devotional works, which included many representations of the Madonna and Child.[42] One of the earliest altarpieces in the collection was the exquisite fourteenth-century Crucifixion, formerly attributed to Orcagna from the Campo Santo at Pisa.[43] There was a Crucifixion attributed to Rembrandt and many paintings of the *Adoration of the Magi*.[44] The collection included numerous depictions of the Holy Family and of the Infant Savior, such as one then thought to be by Leonardo, and an Infant Christ sleeping, then thought to be by Murillo.[45] Paintings of saints included those of Saint Jerome, who was a favorite saint of Beckford's, by Guercino, Domenichino, Cima, and Veronese.[46] Beckford owned numerous paintings of another favorite saint, Saint Anthony, such as *The Temptation of Saint Anthony* by Teniers (now at Brodick Castle,

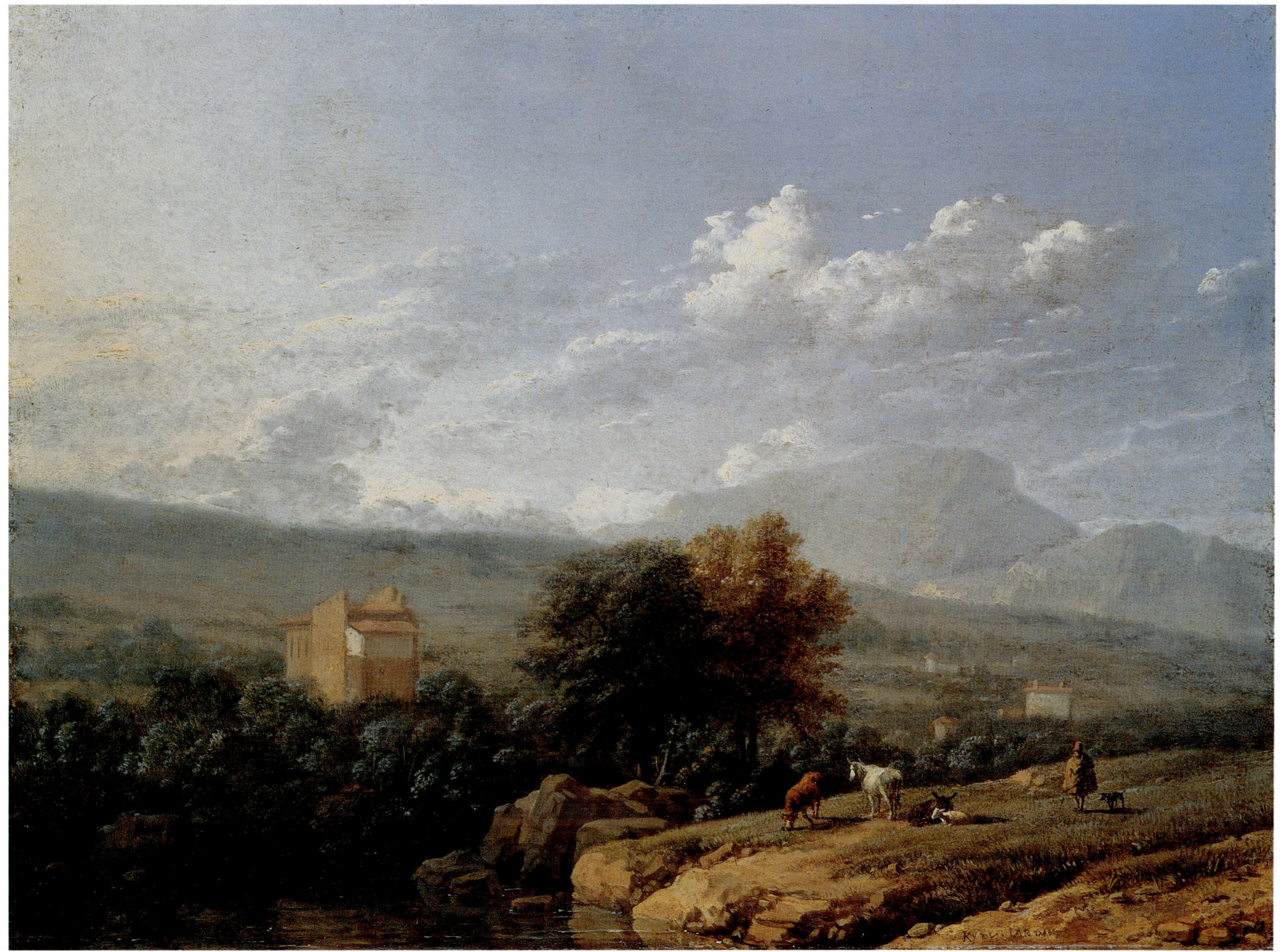

Fig. 13-3. Karel Dujardin. *Italian Landscape,* ca. 1642. Oil wood. Fitzwilliam Museum, Cambridge.

Scotland) and *Saint Anthony Preaching* by Salvator Rosa (now in a private collection).

Beckford's choice of secular works was considerably varied and idiosyncratic, ranging from the sophisticated and informed, to the more popular genre pictures by Dutch and Flemish painters. Given his love of architecture, it is not surprising to find that this is reflected in the many interior views of churches, particularly on a minute scale, such as those by Pieter Neefs (see cat. nos. 89 and 90). Interior views generally appealed to him, as can be seen in the many scenes illustrating domesticity, mostly of the seventeenth century, such as the de Hooch, *A Woman Weighing Coins* (*Die Goldwägerin*) (fig. 13-1) and *The Lady Drinking, Cavalier Asleep* by ter Borch (now in the Frau Bertha

Krupp von Bohlen und Halbach Collection, Essen). In view of Beckford's own passion for collecting, the van Opstal *Interior of a Grand Saloon of Pictures* (see cat. no. 94) was a particularly appropriate choice. Flemish and Dutch landscapes and seascapes featured prominently—by Cuyp, Backhuysen, Berghem, Ruysdael, van der Cappelle, Both (fig. 13-2), Dujardin (fig. 13-3), and particularly favorite artists, including Poelenburgh, van Ostade, Wouvermans, Brueghel, and Teniers. Beckford's love of drama and the exotic is seen in the choice of subjects, such as *The Seven Wonders of the World* by Brueghel and *The Building of the Tower of Babel* by van Valkenborch (whereabouts unknown, formerly thought to be the one in Museum of London).[47]

Beckford also owned paintings of the Elements, one set by

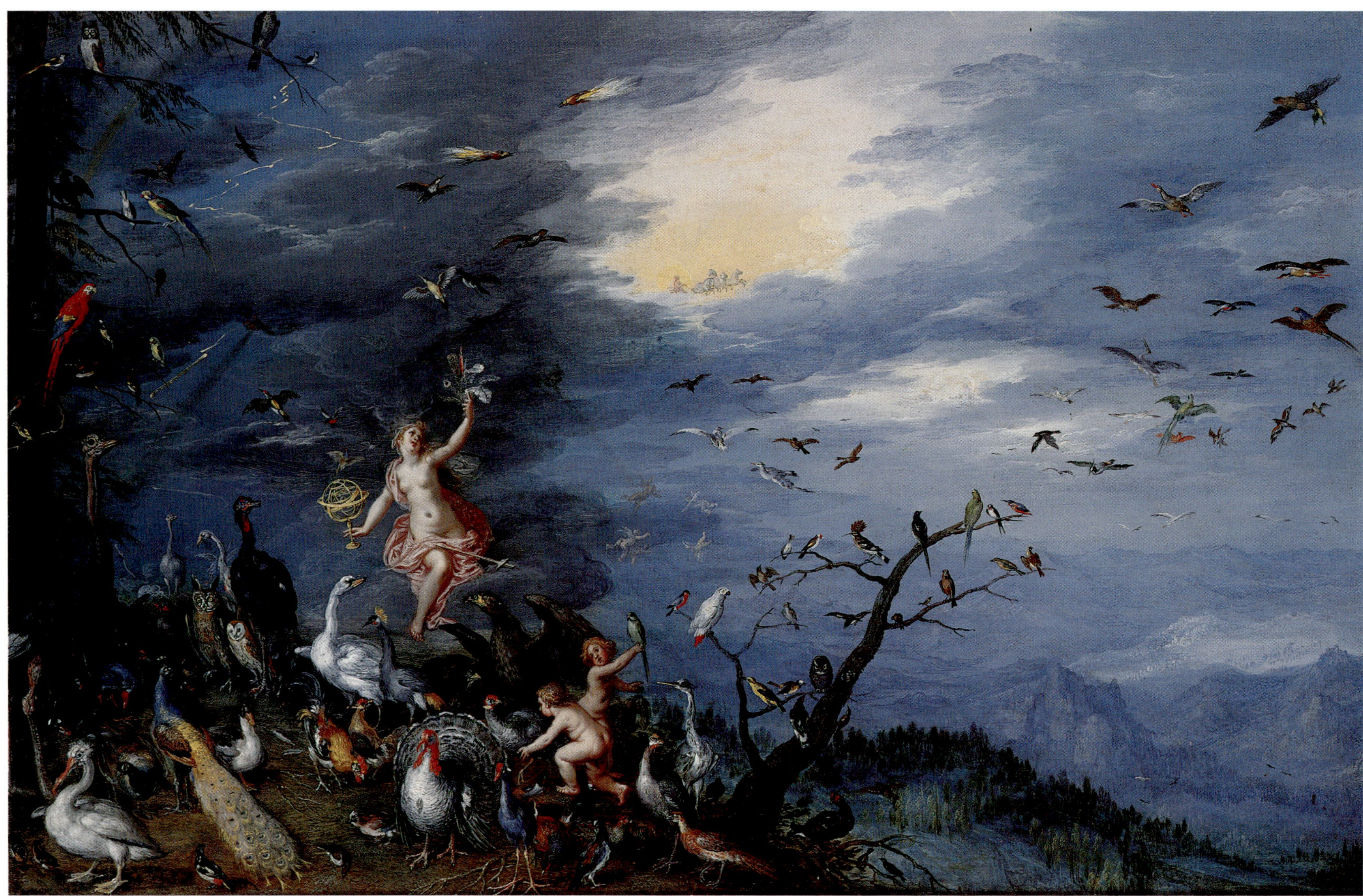

Fig. 13-4. Jan Brueghel. *The Element of Air,* 1611. Oil on copper. Private collection.

Brueghel (figs. 13-4 and 13-5) and the other by Bassano. His love of animals and birds is evident in the number of hunting scenes (despite his disapproval of that activity and his refusal to allow the local hunt over his land at Fonthill): for instance, *Stags and Bear Hunt* by the studio of Cranach (now in the Royal Collection, Sandringham), and *The Poultry Yard* by Hondecoeter (now in the National Gallery of Victoria, Australia). A favorite painting of Beckford's was a spectacular flower piece by Jan van Huysum (now in a private collection), which had been in the Praslin collection and was one of only a few flower paintings that Beckford owned.[48] There were a number of works by those painters fashionable throughout the period in which Beckford was collecting. Italian landscape painters were well represented by at least seven works by Salvator Rosa and three views of Venice by Canaletto. Beckford also admired French landscape painters and possibly owned nine works by Claude and six by Gaspar Dughet. He also owned a selection of charming French cabinet pictures, by Watteau, Lancret, and Fragonard (see cat. no. 45).

Beckford had an eye for portrait paintings, a genre he particularly admired. He owned some spectacular examples: *Doge Leonardo Loredan* by Giovanni Bellini (now in the National Gallery, London) and *Doge Giovanni Mocenigo* by Gentile Bellini (formerly identified as the Doge Andrea Vendramin and attributed to Giovanni Bellini; now in the Frick Collection, New York). Beckford also had works by Bronzino, such as the *Portrait of a Young Man*, once identified as Saint Louis Gonzaga (now in a private collection, on loan to the National Gallery, London) and *Eleonora di Toledo* (now in the National Gallery of Art, Washington). There was a random element to Beckford's choice, which ranged from masterpieces such as the *Vincenzo Capello* by Titian (fig. 13-6)—formerly attributed to Tintoretto and entitled *Constable Montmorency*—to a small portrait of Edward VI attributed to Guillim Stretes (or Scrots; now in the Royal Collection) and the flamboyant *Highland Chieftain, Lord Mungo Murray* by John Michael Wright.[49]

Other remarkable portraits that Beckford purchased include

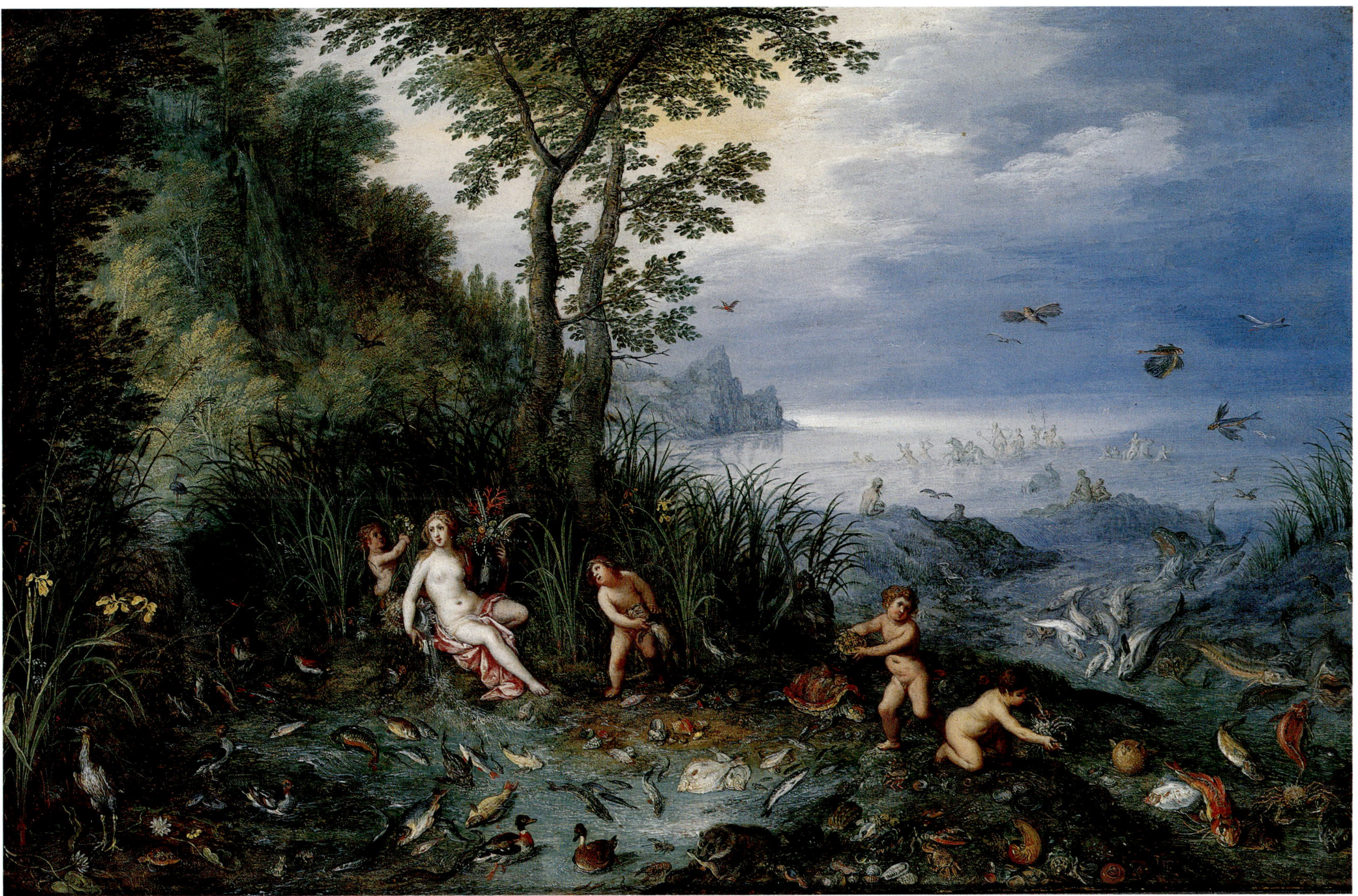

Fig. 13-5. Jan Brueghel. *The Element of Water,* 1610. Oil on copper. Private collection.

the *Portrait of a Canon* by Massys (now in collection of the Princes of Liechtenstein), formerly attributed to Holbein and entitled *Bishop Stephen Gardiner*. He also owned *Duc d'Alençon* by Clouet (now at Brodick Castle, Scotland) and the exquisite *Young Man at Prayer* by Memling (fig. 13-7).[50] Beckford had portraits by Velasquez, the Spanish artist most admired at the time: he bought at least three works—a version of *Philip of Spain in Brown and Silver* (possibly the one now in the National Gallery, London), a portrait of Pope Innocent X, and *A Knight of Malta* from the Marquess of Lansdowne. He also owned a portrait that was then considered to be of the Duke of Alva, then attributed to Sánchez Coello (see cat. no. 130). Beckford's admiration for his friend Nanibus, a dwarf who lived at the Abbey with Beckford, is reflected in paintings such as the *Portrait of a Dwarf* by William Dobson and *Philip II and his Dwarf* by Gaspar de Crayer (neither location known) as mentioned by Henry Venn Lansdown in one of his visits to Lansdown Crescent.[51]

Drawings and Prints

Beckford was as avid a collector of drawings and prints as he was of pictures and books and attended to them with the same minute attention and detail. When money was scarce he bought prints, about which he also possessed a considerable knowledge. He took a precise and specialist interest, writing in 1833: "as, is in pictures, as well as prints, I have learnt to trust no eyes but my own."[52] In a letter to his bookseller Bohn about a sale of engravings in 1842, which had been overlooked, Beckford wrote "If reasonable—recover them—they are of more consequence to me than to collectors in general on account of impression—which few are so nice about as myself."[53] He had no personal identification mark for the prints and drawings in his collection, which makes it more difficult to trace works belonging to him.

There was a four-day sale of Beckford's drawings and prints in March 1824, with a total of 632 lots including books of prints, a collection he had assembled over a period of thirty years from France,

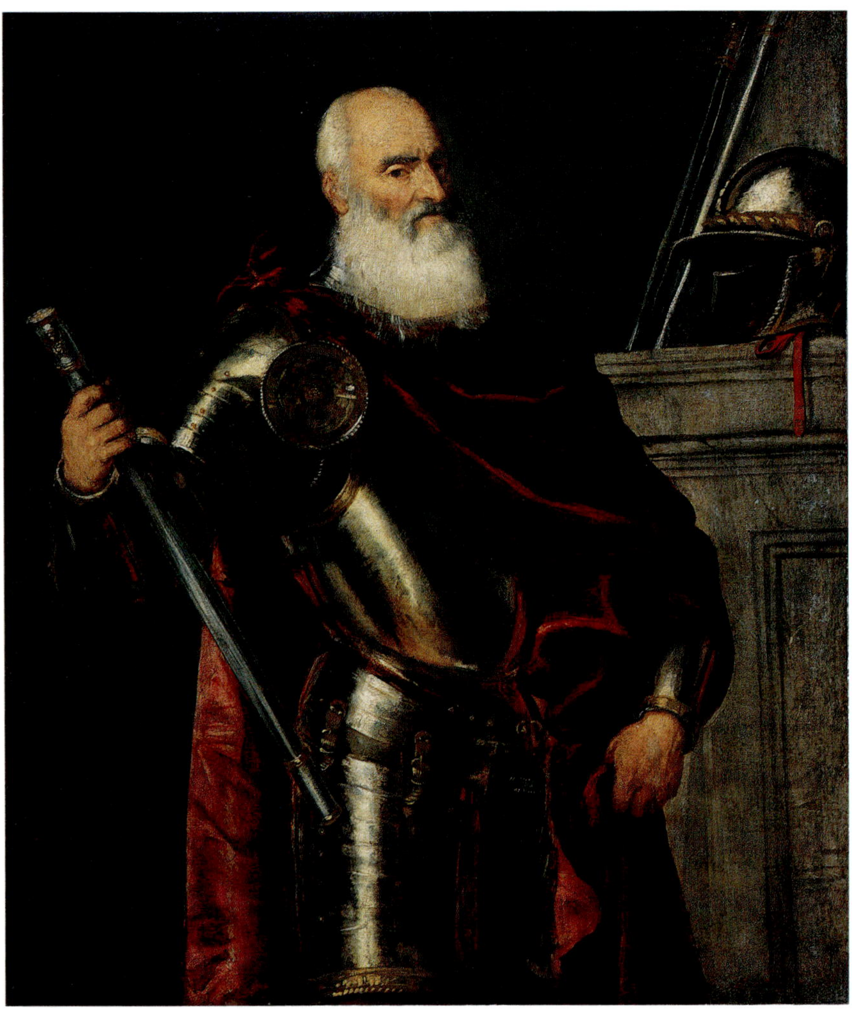

Fig. 13-6. Titian. *Portrait of Vincenzo Capello,* ca. 1540. Oil on canvas. National Gallery of Art, Washington, Samuel H. Kress Collection, 1957.14.3.

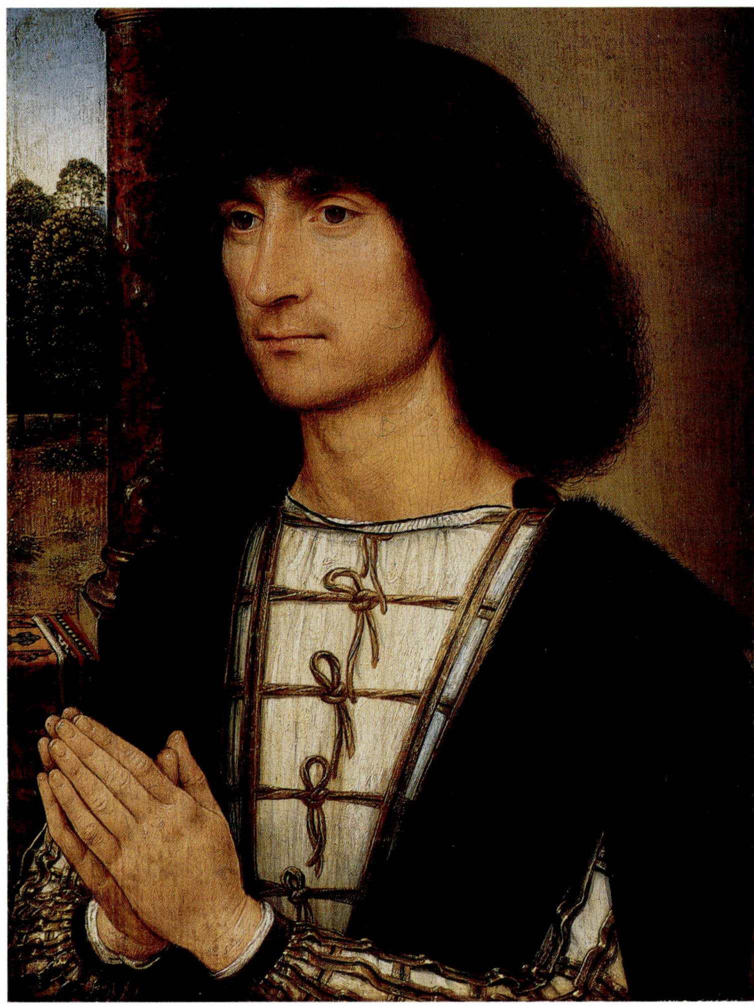

Fig. 13-7. Hans Memling. *Young Man at Prayer,* ca. 1485–90. Oil on oak panel. Fundación Colección Thyssen-Bornemisza, Madrid.

Italy, and England, "materially assisted by the great Events which have occurred during that period, on the Continent."[54] The many categories encompassed Beckford's vast range of interest and knowledge, from Chinese and botanical to Old Italian School and Rembrandt. Despite this dispersal and another in 1830 he continued both to buy and to sell prints and drawings, as he did paintings.[55] For instance, in the year following the first sale, he purchased ninety-six lots of prints at the sale of George Baker, a lace merchant, using the bookseller William Clarke of New Bond Street, London, as his agent.[56]

Presumably for reasons of provenance, Beckford was determined to buy from the sale of the well-known banker and collector of prints and drawings, William Esdaile of Clapham Common, London. Esdaile had a celebrated collection of Claude drawings that had been bought at the sales of Sir Thomas Lawrence's collection of Old Master drawings, which were mostly dispersed in 1836–37 by the dealer Samuel Woodburn. The catalogue for Esdaile's sale is annotated with information that the printseller, William Smith acting for Beckford, had offered £4,200 for the prints which had been rejected.[57] Beckford,

intent on acquiring some of Esdaile's drawings, had written to William Smith from Bath that the Rembrandt drawings were exquisite, "the Clauds [sic] . . . I beg must be reported minutely as we must carry off a few—even at high prices."[58] Beckford wrote to Smith, sometimes almost daily, between June 1840 and April 1844, indicating in great detail exactly what he wanted, as he did when buying books. In 1840, in one letter, he wrote from Bath with great frustration, "There wd by rare pickings for me [at a forthcoming sale] I make no doubt, but what can I do at this distance.—the rail road not likely to be finished before AD 1842," and on the same day he wrote again, "we must buckle on our armour in order to attack the Clauds [sic] etc."[59] Redding's description of a vast quantity of engravings in Lansdown Crescent, "scattered all over his house in drawers, without the slightest attempt at arrangement," is evidence of this relentless activity.[60]

The Collection in Situ at Fonthill

Given the constant changes made in Beckford's collection, particularly before his move to Bath, it is not easy to reconstruct the hanging and the grouping of the paintings at Fonthill. It was quite usual at this time for country houses to be visited, with or without an appointment. Mrs. Lybbe Powys was at Splendens in August 1776 and recorded in her diary, "there are many good pictures and many very indifferent . . . . the best at Fonthill are of the small kind, fit only for lady's cabinets; of these there are many capital ones," which was strange given other reports of opulent grandeur and important large scale paintings.[61] Two years later another visitor to Splendens, Richard Joseph Sulivan, wrote, "The whole, however, is rich, and has been fashionable in its day," and he listed what he considered to be the best of "a variety of paintings," among which were two by Salvator Rosa— *The Witch of Endor* (possibly a copy of the Louvre picture) and *Socrates in the Act of Swallowing Poison.*[62] Also mentioned were *Descent from the Cross* by Rembrandt (now attributed to the studio of Rembrandt and in the Hessiches Landesmuseum, Darmstadt), three paintings by Rubens, and two by Poussin.[63]

During the 1780s Beckford had begun to add to the collection, buying in particular paintings by Dutch artists and grand Italian landscapes, such as the Claudes and Salvator Rosas. In order to accommodate the increased number of paintings, he had to consider creating more gallery space. In April and May 1787 he employed John Soane to convert a corridor on the attic floor of Fonthill Splendens to house a double row of pictures, apparently to be framed by heavy drapery, which would be toplit by an innovative "canopy" dome. The scheme was abandoned, but had it gone ahead, it would have been the first such space that Soane designed.[64]

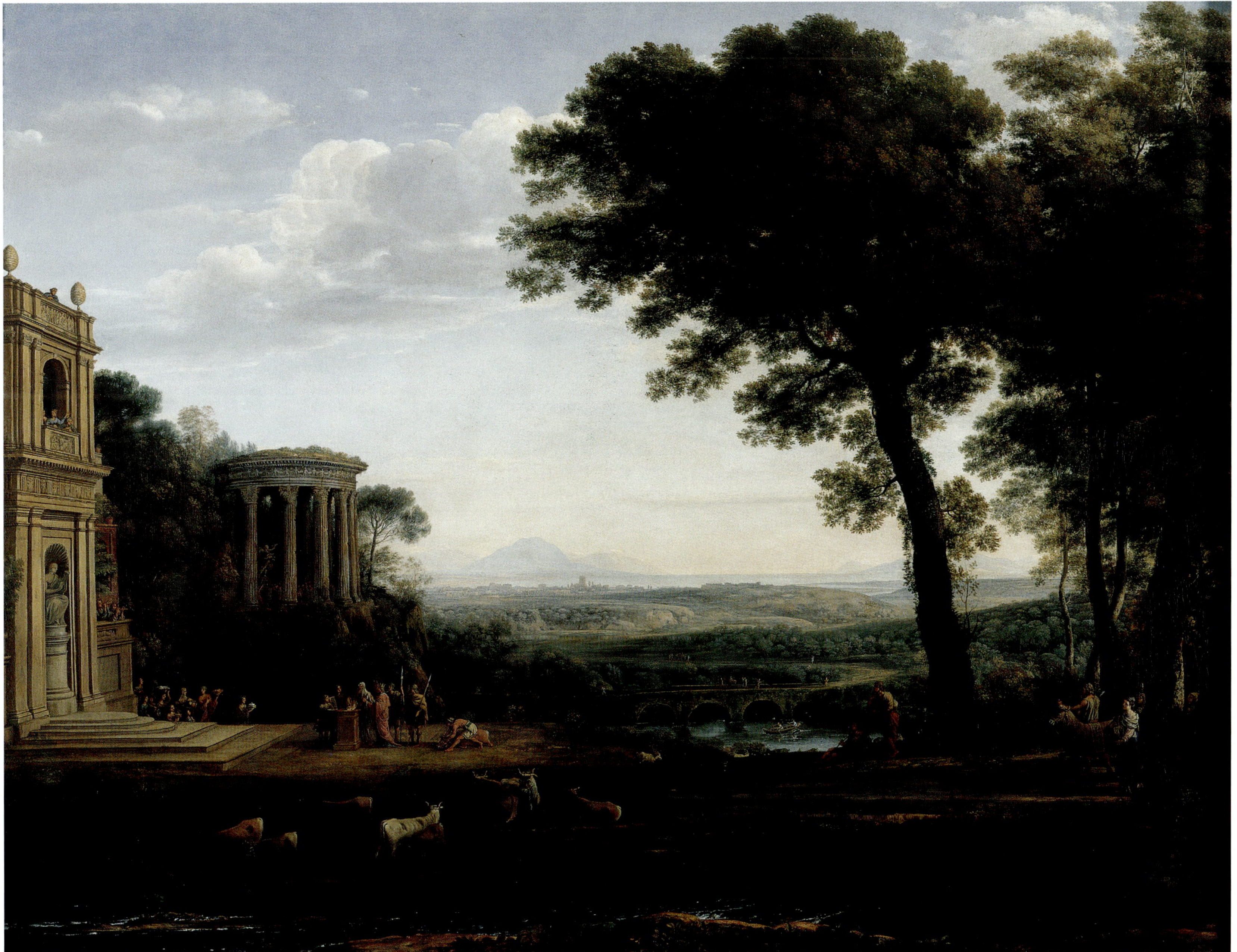

Fig. 13-8. Claude Gellée, known as Claude (Lorraine). *The Father of Psyche Sacrificing at the Temple of Apollo*, 1663. Oil on canvas. The National Trust, Fairhaven Collection, Anglesey Abbey, Cambridgeshire.

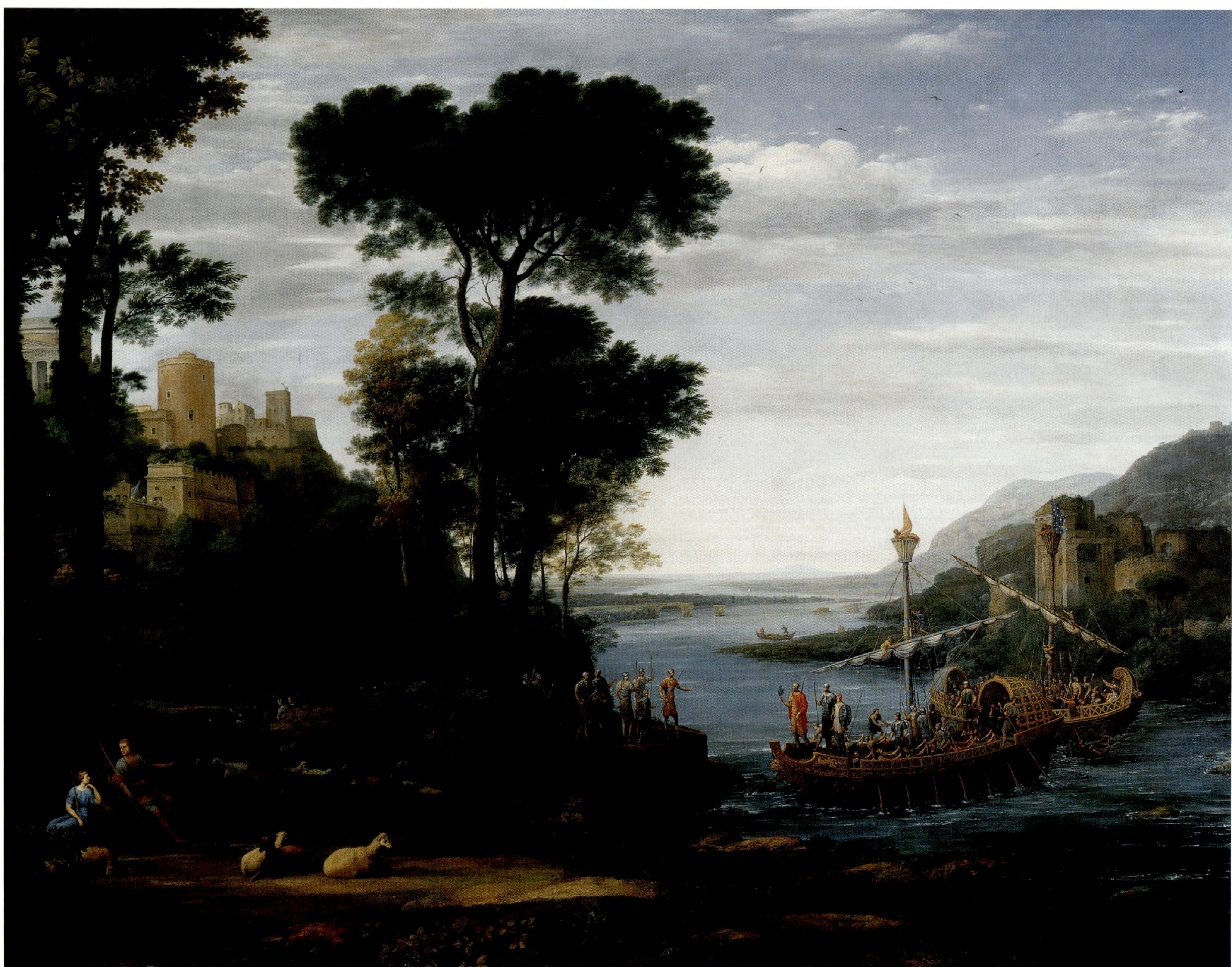

Fig. 13-9. Claude Gellée, known as Claude (Lorraine). *The Landing of Aeneas at Pallanteum*, 1675. Oil on canvas. The National Trust, Fairhaven Collection, Anglesey Abbey, Cambridgeshire.

A good account of the paintings at Splendens was made by the Rev. Richard Warner who, visited the house on September 5, 1800. He was not allowed into the new building of the Abbey, "till it be completed," but he wrote of the extravagances of Splendens, where "expense has reached its utmost limits in furniture and ornaments; where every room is a gold mine, and every apartment a picture-gallery."[65] In each room, but mostly in the ballroom, he saw paintings, which he listed in some detail: landscapes, interiors, genre pictures, religious subjects, portraits, and in particular the famous Altieri

Claudes, which Beckford had bought the previous year and hung in the saloon with the family portraits. The antiquary and connoisseur John Britton, who was as interested in promoting contemporary painters, given the "extravagant prices that are often given for the productions of an old master," as he was in older paintings, also wrote informative descriptions of Splendens. These constitute a valuable record of Beckford's collection prior to the sales of the early 1800s.[66]

In 1796 Beckford wrote to Sir William Hamilton: "harmony is everything in pictures, furniture etc. I have been trying to harmonize

Fonthill,—no easy attempt, I can assure you—wealth having done a confounded deal of mischief."[67] This letter, written before the sales in 1801, 1802, and 1807 of some of the contents from the opulent and lavish interiors of Fonthill Splendens, illustrates Beckford's continual concern for order and his striving to find pleasing arrangements of his much-prized possessions. A few years later the German visitor Goede pointed out: "with the decoration of each room, a certain plan had been followed, attempting to give each one a certain individual beauty, where every time tone, colour, and the stronger or weaker glow of the decoration perfectly correspond."[68] At Fonthill Abbey it is also evident that Beckford greatly enjoyed moving paintings and objects to gain the best effect of the whole, probably without much regard as far as the paintings were concerned for school, subject, or scale, or the design of the frame (see fig. 7-10). On June 29, 1818, Beckford wrote to his loyal friend Gregorio Franchi from Fonthill: "Here we spend our life putting up and taking down pictures . . . . A great pity not to have more pictures or the money to buy them."[69] This was written at a time when the Beckford finances were becoming more constrained. Unfortunately, no visual records exist of the interiors of Splendens, and those that exist of the Abbey and of Lansdown Tower (there are none of Lansdown Crescent) give little indication as to any special arrangement.

As with his books, Beckford cared deeply for his pictures and their transport and condition. The majority of the pictures that came from Beckford's collection and are now in the National Gallery, London, and elsewhere, are in extremely good condition. Beckford had a passionate dislike for restoration, overpainting, and overvarnishing, and could instantly recognize paintings that had been so treated. When he visited the Louvre in 1814, he commented on paintings by Raphael, Titian, and Correggio that were "all coloured like the rainbow, enough to give one the horrors and make one weep," the earlier pictures "re-gilded and re-painted, without value and without apparent authenticity."[70] It upset him greatly when later he had to witness the varnishing of some of his own pictures, which he had sold to the National Gallery, and on the death of William Seguier, the first keeper, Beckford wrote to William Smith of 24 Lisle Street, Leicester Square: "The powers above have done a handsome thing by me—they have finally removed from the varnishing world (notorious resort of Sharks, Cormaronts and Land-gulls) the great president of cheats and picture-skinners, the merciless be-dauber of my Raphael, and Mazzolino di Ferrara."[71] He was not alone in his feelings—the varnishing policies (which later resulted in having to clean pictures) of the National Gallery were heavily attacked at the time.[72]

Beckford and His Advisors

Beckford benefited enormously from a succession of knowledgeable advisors or agents, who were necessary for his style of collecting and to keep him informed of the art market when he was living in Wiltshire and Bath. He also relied on his friends. Among contemporary painters who acted on his behalf were the well-known American painter Benjamin West, president of the Royal Academy, and Henry Tresham, also a painter and member of the Royal Academy, both of whom were collectors and also dealt in pictures on behalf of others. West himself was a considerable collector and was instrumental in helping to form many other collections.[73] As Painter to His Majesty, West also appealed to Beckford's ambition for royal connections and was considered to have "real power" as "the most important catch and presented the least difficulties" among the advisors to those forming collections.[74] West was well acquainted with the Beckford family. He painted a posthumous portrait of Beckford's mother, Maria Hamilton Beckford, in about 1799 (see cat. no. 2).[75] Beckford made regular payments to West in exchange for paintings supplied, but West was also known by the dealers to exert significant influence on Beckford in buying and selling pictures. West reported from London to Beckford in Paris in December 1801: "The picture commerce of the sweepings of Italy, and Flanders go on this winter, nearly the same as the last, so that the works of Raphael, Correggio, and Leonardo da Vinci, are as plenty as when you were here."[76] Joseph Farington recorded in his diary that Beckford asked for West's help in disposing of paintings and drawings in late 1807, even though Beckford had had the opportunity to dispose of them at his own sale in that August.[77]

There was a great rivalry between West and Tresham, an Irishman and a pivotal character in Beckford's dealings, who owned a gallery in which works attributed to the greatest Old Masters were always available for sale.[78] "Tresham you know hates West as he does Hell. They have both a good deal to say with Beckford," reported the dealer William Buchanan.[79] By 1798 Tresham had been "introduced to Beckford to propose to him to purchase some of Lord Cawdors works of Art," and while Beckford was in Portugal in April and May 1799 it was Tresham who acted as his principal advisor for the purchase of the Altieri Claudes: *The Father of Psyche Sacrificing at the Temple of Apollo* of 1663 and its later pendant, *The Landing of Aeneas at Pallanteum* of 1675 (see figs. 13-8 and 13-9).[80] Beckford had seen these paintings at the Palazzo Altieri in Rome. He had written in July 1797 from Fonthill to his steward Captain Nicholas Williams, who was in Paris acting on Beckford's behalf: "obtain, I particularly desire, the best information and proposals you can concerning them. I have set my heart upon them."[81] They had been bought in Rome for about £500 for the pair by the painter-dealers, Robert Fagan and Charles Grignion the Younger, who had taken them to Naples in a wagon and from there by boat to Palermo, where Lord Nelson organized to bring them under armed escort on the *Tigre* to Falmouth.[82] With no known owner (they were in Palermo) and unlabeled, the paintings were put up for auction there but were soon taken to London and exhibited privately at Lincoln's Inn Fields by Charles Long (later Sir Charles Long and then Lord Farnborough). There they were purchased for Beckford by Tresham. In April 1799 he had written to Beckford in Portugal that "their preservation is extraordinary," and they were for sale at £7,000 without frames, but had been valued by Fagan and Grignion at £4,000 and were so highly priced as a result of the Orléans sale. Tresham intended "bidding a very handsome price, but nothing like his demand."[83] A week later

Tresham had advanced the offer to 5,000 guineas and finally paid 7,000 guineas for the pair and four smaller pictures.[84] Farington, who had followed the whole event with much interest, recorded that Beckford had written from Portugal "to have them purchased, without mentioning any Sum."[85] On his return to Fonthill later in 1799, the delighted Beckford wrote that the Claudes were "magnificently framed [the frames were designed by James Wyatt for £400] well-placed, and tenderly washed by Tresham, appear in the utmost Glory and perfection."[86] For reasons that are unclear, Beckford sold them for 10,000 guineas in 1808. It has been speculated that having startled the world with this purchase, he then became tired of being considered fashionable, but it was more likely to have been as a result of financial constraints given that he had written in late 1807: "Little by little I am suspending all work on the Abbey: in two months we shall have quiet in this place. But if the cursed Claudes aren't sold I shan't know which way to turn . . . ."[87]

A month after the purchase of the Claudes, Tresham bought six pictures for 2,000 guineas for Beckford from the collection of William Young Ottley, the writer and collector and later keeper of prints at the British Museum, who had been in Italy since 1791 buying Italian paintings and drawings.[88] Ottley and the Liverpool collector William Roscoe were important for their early interest in the Italian Primitives.[89] Beckford acquired pictures that Ottley had purchased and brought from Rome in the late 1790s.[90] They had been highly recommended to Beckford, at a suggested price of £2,000 for six pictures, in a letter in June 1799 from Tresham to Williams, with the promise from Tresham that if he buys them "he will possess, the first Clauds [sic], G Poussins and Salvators in the Kingdom."[91] The paintings were exhibited privately and on Beckford's exhibition list he had marked two ex-Colonna landscapes by Gaspar Dughet at £1200 for both and two Raphaels—*Charity* and *Dancing Figure*—in one frame, from the Borghese at £450.[92] Also marked at £400 each were two Salvator Rosas, also from the Colonna collection: *Saint Anthony Preaching*, also called *Saint John Preaching* (now in a private collection), and *A Landscape with Figures*, or *Banditti on the Banks of a River* (now in a private collection).[93] Tresham was also responsible for exhibiting the thirty-six paintings brought from Roman palazzi by the painter and dealer Alexander Day at his gallery at 20 Lower Brook Street, Mayfair, London between February and May 1800. This exhibition included *Saint Catherine of Alexandria* by Raphael (now in the National Gallery, London), which was later bought by Beckford and was one of his most important and much treasured paintings.[94]

Another important figure in Beckford's collecting activities and in his capacity as advisor on furnishings and the decorative arts was Edward Foxhall, "The Blockhead" (as Beckford called him), partner in Foxhall & Fryer, Upholsterers and "Carvers Gilders and Picture Frame Makers" of Old Cavendish Street, London. Foxhall had worked at Splendens through a connection with Soane and had been known to Beckford since at least 1787.[95] Foxhall also provided and made frames for Beckford.[96]

In June 1795 Foxhall had offered to negotiate for Beckford, who was in Portugal, for the collection of the French ambassador, Charles-Alexandre de Calonne, which the dealer Michael Bryan sold at Skinner & Dyke in March of that year. The previous month, Beckford had written from Lisbon to Thomas Wildman, his solicitor, agent, and "fleecer" (Beckford's description): "Never in my life was I more cruelly tantalized than by the splendid advertisement of Calonnes pictures . . . . I would almost give one eye . . . for a chance of viewing them with the other . . . even half an eye wd. do for me . . . O Lord . . . what Berghems, what Vanderveldes, what Teniers are eluding my grasp . . . perhaps forever . . . . on some more fortunate day I may have a chance of making them my own—at present . . . I must sit quiet in this dull corner of Europe and bite my fingers and gnash my teeth." The paintings, he continued,—"the purest I suppose ever offered to sale in London" and "a true select Paris collection in the nicest preservation"—were so highly priced that he wondered how anyone would be able to afford them at "this critical period big with invasion of Bankruptcy . . . at the rate we are governed our collections and curiosities stand a very likely chance of lining the walls of the grand national gallery at the Tuilleries . . . before 1796 is far advanced in its mysterious and melancholy progress."[97]

Until his death in 1815 Foxhall continued to work for Beckford, buying and selling pictures. It is possible that Foxhall was also actively selling pictures under his own name for Beckford. These included paintings that Beckford had inherited from the Alderman. At the Christie's sale of January 17, 1800, for example, Soane acquired his first "Beckford" picture, a landscape by Zuccarelli for 16 guineas, which was listed as Foxhall's property.[98] Foxhall also bought many pictures for Beckford, such as *The Exhumation of Saint Hubert* by a follower of Rogier van der Weyden (now in the National Gallery, London), at the sale of the second Earl of Bessborough.[99] He also bought *Laughing Boy* or *Boy with a Puzzle* by Luini (now in the Elton Hall Collection), a much-heralded picture then attributed to Leonardo, in the important sale of Beckford's friend and relation, Sir William Hamilton.[100] Beckford was clearly determined to own it, as a note in the Christie's archive catalogue reads, "Sir Wm Hamilton insured this Picture to Mr Beckford before the sale for 1500 gns.," one of the highest prices at the time; the picture was not sold again by Beckford.[101]

Gregorio Franchi was also crucial in Beckford's collecting activities. Often acting as agent in buying works of art for Beckford both on the Continent and in England, Franchi also formed his own collection of paintings on a modest scale. This was sold mostly in 1827, the year before Franchi's death and in two further sales in 1829 and 1832.[102] Writing in French or Portuguese, Franchi was the most important correspondent with Beckford on matters to do with the art world and would have known Beckford's collections better than any of the agents working for him.

Robert Hume, cabinetmaker, mostly at 65 Berners Street, London, began to work for Beckford around 1808 and played an important role in Beckford's collecting activities in the 1820s and

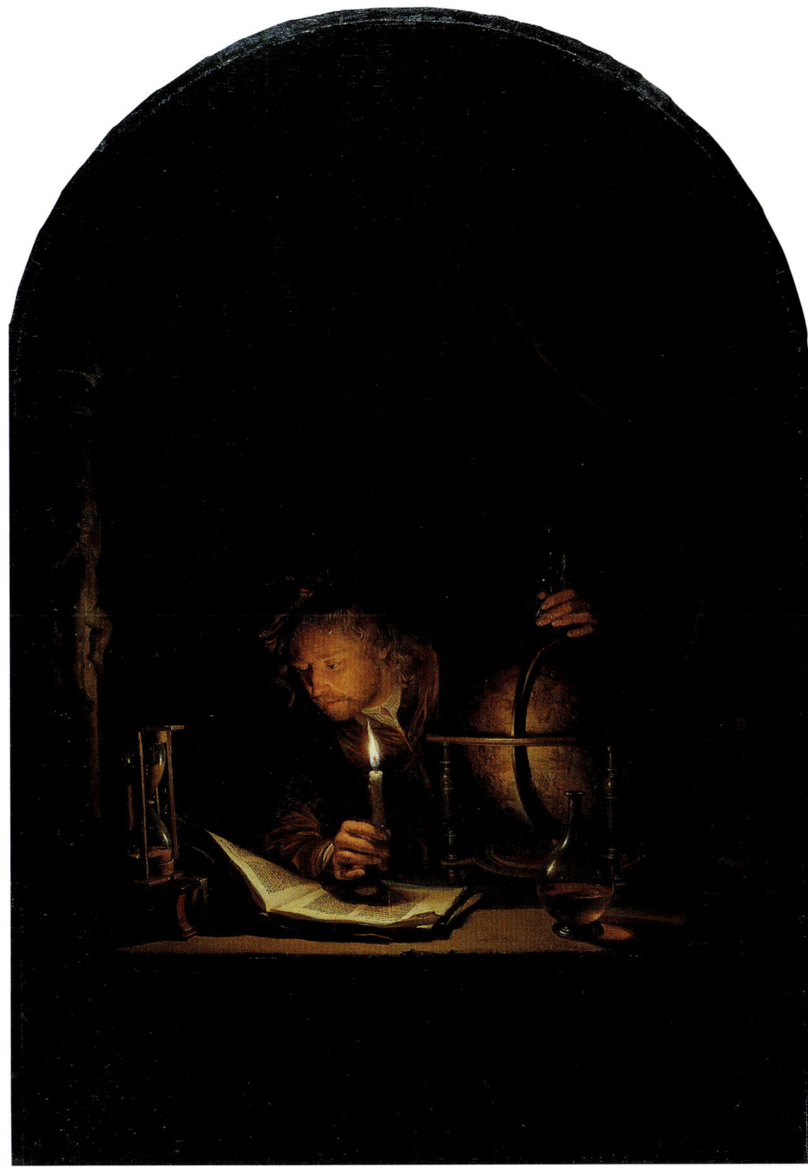

Fig. 13-10. Gerrit Dou. *Astronomer by Candlelight,* late 1650s. Oil on wood. The J. Paul Getty Museum, Los Angeles.

1830s.[103] Hume took over from Foxhall, and in turn, was later replaced by the bookseller and publisher Henry George Bohn of 47 York Street, Covent Garden, London, as Beckford's principal buying agent.

Throughout the 1823 sale at Fonthill, Hume kept Beckford in Bath regularly informed as events progressed, as he was to do later from London, sending him sale catalogues, news and details of pictures, as well as wine. Hume was involved in the controversy over the disposal of Old Master drawings belonging to the portrait painter and former president of the Royal Academy, Sir Thomas Lawrence. On Lawrence's death this collection—one of the most important collections of Old Master drawings ever to have been assembled—had been offered for sale and considered by the Crown and the British Museum but refused. A petition was circulated, signed by artists and collectors, proclaiming

that the drawings should be bought by the nation "rather than they should fall into the hands of our continental rivals."[104] Beckford himself had been unable to raise the necessary £22,000, but on July 30, 1836, his signature was added to the petition on his behalf by the leading London art dealer Samuel Woodburn, who was the major figure in the protest.[105] Woodburn had been instrumental in forming Lawrence's collection, as well as one of the main parties responsible for its dispersal. Furious with the decision not to buy the collection, Beckford wrote: "The Government is not sensible, in the true point of view, of the value of art to the nation . . . . It is shameful the country does not buy them."[106] The collection was dispersed.

Beckford and Dealers

Beckford did a large amount of business through the established art dealers of the time although few records have survived. One of the most invaluable contemporary sources of art world information and gossip was the Scottish dealer William Buchanan of Oxendon Street, London. Buchanan was a leading dealer in Old Masters, many of which he imported from war-ravaged Italy, France, and Spain.[107] Through him Beckford had access to the remains of the Orléans collection, which had been dispersed in separate sales, mostly through the dealer Michael Bryan, from 1792 to 1800, and to the Talleyrand collection of Dutch and Flemish pictures, which Buchanan bought in Paris in 1817.[108]

Opportunities were missed. Farington reported that Beckford, with his steward Williams and with Foxhall, had attended the last day of the Orléans exhibition in Pall Mall on July 31, 1799, but "owing to some bungling West had not purchased for him [Beckford] several pictures for which He wd. have given any price. - The 3 Marys - A Carrach [sic] - Moses striking the Rock, N. Poussin, - last Judgement, L. Bassan, The Circumcision, G Bassan etc."[109] Beckford did buy two Teniers later, however—*The Ale House and Smokers* and *The Cabaret* —for which he paid 500 guineas in 1800.[110]

Buchanan's letters reveal how the dealer tried to tempt Beckford with pictures, using West or Tresham as intermediaries for this purpose. Dealings between them were clearly complex and competitive, which is not surprising, given that Beckford was considered a major potential buyer. Such was his reputation that in May 1800 Robert Fagan, then the British Consul General in Sicily, sent a list of fifty-five pictures, "of the first class which you can to send to Mr Penn, Mr Beckford and others."[111]

Buchanan continued to circulate information about pictures and sales to possible collectors of Old Masters, but by January of 1805 a certain gloom had set in. In a letter to James Irvine, the Scottish painter who collaborated with him on importing pictures from France and Italy, Buchanan reported that there was "at present no spirit whatever in this Country to purchase works of any kind . . . . The old spirited collectors have either died out, or are blind; and the more modern and recent collectors have either filled their Collections, or from the pressure of times have given over purchasing till peace

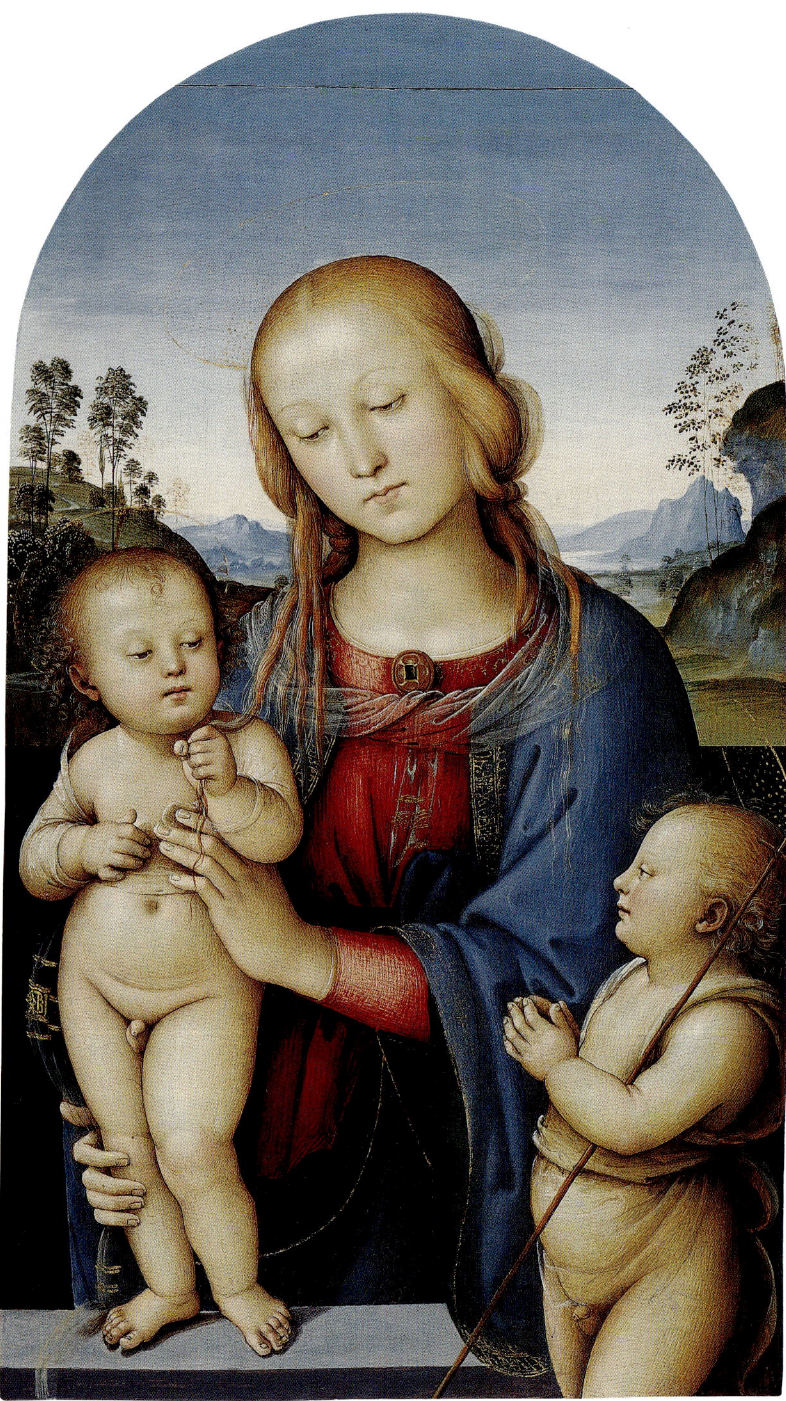

Fig. 13-11. Pietro Perugino. *The Virgin and Child with Saint John*, after 1500. Tempera on poplar. The National Gallery, London.

returns."[112] He had a large Domenichino altarpiece, *Madonna and Child with St Mauro*.[113] Despite its size he thought this painting was ideal for Beckford but he wrote that Beckford "is not purchasing much at present, or can afford much" and a few weeks later he wrote again, Beckford "is not now purchasing."[114] By this time Beckford's income

was a fifth of what it had been in the last years of the 1790s, and much of that had gone on the building of the Abbey. Presumably, in any event, he was not interested in paintings of such large dimensions.

The day books of the talented specialist dealer John Smith are extremely informative.[115] Through Hume, Smith worked for Beckford from 1829 until 1841. The account for April 1829 includes the first part of his own catalogue raisonné at £8 11s. 9d., a ham weighing 17 lbs. at 9d., a drawing design for a ceiling, and travel expenses to Penshurst and Eltham. Smith provided not only hams but also frames, books, and Dutch and Flemish landscape and genre paintings. These included works by Berghem, Wynants, Lingelbach, de Witte (possibly *The Interior of the Oude Kerke, Amsterdam, During a Sermon*; now in the National Gallery, London), and an *Interior with a Gentleman Playing the Piano and a Lady in Black Silk* by Gonzales Coques (present whereabouts unknown). Perhaps the most significant painting purchased was *A Geographer Pursuing his Studies by Candlelight*, also called *Astronomer by Candlelight* by Gerrit Dou (fig. 13-10).[116] Beckford bought *A Poulterer's Shop* (now in the National Gallery, London) in Paris in 1814 and also owned Dou's *Old Woman*, sometimes called *The Painter's Aunt* (now at Brodick Castle, Scotland).[117] Apparently from the profit raised by selling his letters to Richard Bentley to publish, Beckford bought a fourth painting by Dou, *A Dutch Girl Gathering a Pink*. This was bought for £500 in 1834 from an exhibition of Dutch and Flemish Masters belonging to the Elysée Bourbon collection held at the private house of James Christie, the auctioneer, in King Street, London.[118]

BECKFORD AND OTHER COLLECTORS

As well as buying and selling through the dealers, Beckford negotiated privately with other collectors, as was customary at this period. He mentioned in a letter of December 16, 1807, that he was happy to discuss the sale of "two or three small pictures" with Lord Grosvenor, who became the first Marquess of Westminster and was a well-known picture collector who later purchased a large part of the estate of Fonthill Abbey.[119] Another major collector, Lord Northwick, second Baron, of Northwick Park, Gloucestershire, and Thirlestane House, Cheltenham, bought at the 1802 sale, for instance, *A Gentleman's Portrait* by Cornelius Johnson, and he sold *Saint Catherine* by Raphael (now in the National Gallery, London) to Beckford some time between 1816 and 1824, when it was recorded by Buchanan.[120]

Beckford appeared not to have very close connections with other collectors. He was, however, an executor and trustee of the estate of the relatively little known marchand-amateur, William Gordon Coesvelt, a British subject, of Carlton Gardens, London, who lived in Italy at the end of his life and was a merchant and banker with connections with the house of Hope and Company of Amsterdam. Coesvelt collected mostly Italian and some Spanish pictures from about 1815, and Beckford was instrumental in buying for Coesvelt.[121] Through the printseller William Smith, Beckford purchased pictures and sculpture for Coesvelt, including a Rembrandt and a Claude. In turn Beckford bought from him such pictures as a *Virgin and Child with Saint Joseph* by Marcello Venusti (an "exquisite little painting") and *Madonna and Child with the Infant Saint John the Baptist* by Parmigianino (now in a private collection and attributed to Bedoli), each of which cost Beckford £25.[122] Coesvelt had bought these paintings in partnership with William Buchanan and his agent in Spain, the painter George Augustus Wallis, sometimes called "the English Poussin." In 1836 Coesvelt offered his entire collection for sale at £40,000 to the Emperor Nicholas I of Russia, who purchased only seven works, the rest being sold at various sales at Christie's until 1847.[123]

Robert Stayner Holford began collecting Old Masters in the 1830s. Like Beckford, Holford was a most energetic and knowledgeable collector with huge funds, chiefly the result of family investments in the New River Company. He had a million-pound inheritance at the age of thirty from an uncle and built two houses—Westonbirt House in Gloucestershire and Dorchester House in Park Lane, London—in which he displayed a rich collection of objects and pictures.[124] Beckford was, however, particularly scathing about him, referring to him as a "poor rich man" and "Mr Holdforth"—he had turned down the opportunity to buy some of Beckford's rather expensive pictures. In 1841, displaying what has been described as "unmitigated intolerance," Beckford ranted against Holford, describing him as one who had "no true feeling, no just appreciation of the unquestionable merits" of Beckford's *Virgin and Child with Saint John* by Perugino (fig. 13-11), a favorite and important painting, which Beckford tried to sell him.[125]

In 1839, however, when Beckford had begun to have dealings with Holford, he sold him one of his earliest Italian paintings, *Madonna and Child with Six Saints* by Pesellino (now in The Metropolitan Museum of Art, New York), dating to the late 1440s.[126] In another 1839 transaction, Beckford sold Holford three paintings for a total of £2,625: *A Strong Breeze at Sea* by Ludolf Backhuysen, *Ships Unloading on a River* ('*Embarquement des vivres*') by Wouvermans, and *An Extensive Winter Landscape* by Aert van der Neer.[127] A year later, Beckford sold Holford, through Buchanan, seven pictures for 4,500 guineas: landscapes by Claude, Berchem, Gaspar Dughet (*A Valley After a Shower*, now in the Ringling Art Gallery, Sarasota, Florida), Both, and Wouvermans, and interiors by van Steen and Adriaen van Ostade (*An Interior with Six Boors Smoking*).[128] Holford also bought Beckford's *Goatherd in the Sabine Hills* by Dughet (now in the Shizuoka Museum, Japan) and owned two Teniers that had once belonged to Beckford, *Villagers Merrymaking* and *Skittle Players*. This sale was completed despite, as Beckford's Bath agent Edmund English wrote, Beckford was not to be "induced separating the pictures and spoiling the arrangement of the hanging of a room, without an enticing offer to do so," what he called his "rules of non mutilation."[129] This last phrase is indicative of Beckford's enduring and meticulous attention to the arrangement of pictures and his habitual reluctance to sell, despite the overwhelming need to do so.

This necessity to sell certain pictures did arise, and by the spring of 1841 it was becoming increasingly evident that Beckford needed the money to redecorate Lansdown Tower, and he was intent

on selling his *Virgin and Child with Saint John* by Perugino. Beckford had bought this painting in about 1820 from the dealer Urbino Pizzetta of Foley Place, London, who claimed to have brought it from Perugia, but he had actually bought it from the Panné sale in 1819 in London.[130] In May of that year, Beckford wrote that if neither Holford nor Lord Crewe bought it, "I shall treasure up the picture and finish the tower in the cheapest manner we can devise."[131] Correspondence at this time indicates Beckford's increasing fury and impatience with Lord Crewe and Holford concerning this sale. Beckford wrote about the latter, "I doubt your [presumably Edmund English] doing anything to good purpose with such a coldblooded, pragmatical—prig as this conceited unconscious dupe of many a notorious member of the swell mob of London dealers."[132] Beckford sold the painting later that year to the National Gallery for £800.[133]

Melville recorded that "Beckford hated Horace Walpole as only one collector can hate another, and his feelings towards him never underwent any change" and that Beckford claimed "Walpole hated me."[134] Walpole died in 1797, but his collection was not sold until 1842, when Beckford joined in the excitement surrounding the sale at Strawberry Hill, which lasted for twenty-four days, and which he referred to as "this high-puff sale."[135] Beckford was then aged eighty-two, and there is much evidence of his interest in the Walpole sale throughout his correspondence. In March 1842 he wrote to the printseller William Smith, "You will find me all agog for S. Hill—*all ardour, all intrepidity*" [these four words have double underlining].[136] After months of "Strawberriana" correspondence, which sometimes reached fever pitch, Beckford claimed "Not a spark of Strawberry Hill mania remains in my bosom."[137] It has been aptly stated that Walpole's "highly individual taste would have been regarded as merely curious . . . by almost everyone except William Beckford."[138] Despite all that he wrote, Beckford may have bought paintings and drawings through Hume or William Smith, who were buying, although evidence is scant.[139]

The Fonthill Sales

The first sale, which took place in August 1801 in the Great Hall of Fonthill Splendens, comprised mostly furniture of the highest quality as well as eighteen decorative paintings. It was for the sale of February 1802, at Christie's in Pall Mall, that Beckford would have decided which paintings he wished to hang at Fonthill Abbey and which to dispose of by auction. Some of his father's paintings as well as some he had recently bought himself were sold. He also sold a few paintings that belonged to West and to John Trumbull, the American painter, possibly in a partnership with the two artists, an arrangement that was not unusual at that time.[140] Eighty-two pictures in all were sold, or failed to sell, on that day.[141] The last lot, his father's set of Hogarth's eight paintings, *The Rake's Progress* (now in Sir John Soane's Museum, London) was bought by Soane for £598 10s. It is likely that the provenance of these and other "Beckford" pictures in the collection was important to Soane, who was known to purchase items for their inherent association.[142]

Another sale at Splendens was held over seven days in August 1807, prior to the demolition of the house. Presumably this was a further process of reducing the collection to a manageable size despite the fact that Beckford was still buying pictures.[143] The *Gentleman's Magazine* reported "the total produce of the sale very far exceeded the appraisement."[144] The pictures were sold on the sixth day in forty-seven lots, some were sold, others failed to sell.[145] Given the numbers sold, it was evident that Beckford was having to reconsider his collection because of the difficulties of adjusting to the new spaces within the Abbey. Soane, who had long known Fonthill, expressed the view that "the costly abbey at Fonthill which, being partly finished and the mansion house in consequence pulled down, the pictures by ancient and modern masters were sold, being found too large, and unsuitable to the decoration of a modern Gothic abbey."[146]

Shortly before 1807 Beckford had moved into the Abbey. Some time after 1800 he had built onto the north wing with materials from the demolished pavilion of Fonthill Splendens, creating more hanging space for pictures and other works of art. In the Eastern Transept the visitor would proceed from the Great Portal through the Octagon to a suite of rooms, whose "main purpose was to house many of the chief treasures and pictures"; the last room was the Grand Drawing Room, where paintings hung in a conventional manner, as in any country house of that period.[147] With the exception of the three principal rooms—the Great Dining Room, the Crimson Drawing Room, and the Grand Drawing Room—the remaining huge and grandiose spaces, more long rectangles than ideal galleries, were not particularly suited for the hanging of pictures but were intended rather to make an impact as architectural wonders, with surprise scenic illusions, mirrors, dramatic curtains, stained glass, and bookcases. In 1812 John Storer mentioned only a few paintings in these rooms, such as works by Brueghel, Bronzino, Veronese, Zuccaro, van Eyck, and Benjamin West, which may have been noted by Storer under the guidance of Beckford as being among his favorite paintings.[148] From this account it can be seen that the Old Master paintings were hung beside works by contemporary painters bought or commissioned by Beckford; they were not displayed as works in a schematic arrangement.[149]

Throughout this period of Beckford's residence at the Abbey he continued to buy paintings to add to his collection, but by May 1817, owing to financial pressure, he had to sell paintings from Fonthill. These were sent to London to join the contents of Beckford's house at 6 Upper Harley Street, which he had been obliged to leave, and its contents were to be sold by Christie's. Two of the Fonthill pictures— *Sibylla Lybica* by Ludovico Carracci and *Job and his Friends* by Salvator Rosa (now in the Uffizi, Florence)—had fairly substantial reserve prices of £800 and £600, respectively, which indicated that Beckford was reticent about selling them. These reserves were not met, and the rest of the sale was not particularly successful, possibly reflecting the state of the market following the end of the Continental wars.

At this time it was becoming increasingly evident that Beck-ford was in financial difficulties, owing to the poor sugar market in Jamaica and the huge amounts of money spent on building the Abbey, and would not be able to remain at Fonthill. In January 1820 he wrote sadly that unless costs could be cut, "it will be impossible for me to continue at Fonthill."[150] Despite the urgent need for restraint in purchasing paintings, it seems that Beckford was unable to resist the temptation. For example, at the sale of the well-known London-based dealer Alexis Delahante in July 1821 Beckford purchased several pictures.[151]

A year later the decision was made to sell the Abbey and its contents. John Rutter published his *Description*, presumably under Beckford's direction, "as a Guide to the Visitor, and to convey Information to the more distant Enquirer," with elegant passages on the paintings and footnotes about the painters. Christie's printed their sale catalogue, thousands of which were sold for a pound each, which included admission. Crowds flocked to Fonthill to see for the first time the accumulation of Beckford's treasures. Franchi wrote to the Duke of Hamilton in Scotland, recommending that he not attend—"the sight of it would break your heart"—and sending him a list of prices, "for the objects which he [Beckford] wishes to reserve," which included paintings, furniture, and vases.[152]

The sale was abruptly canceled when Beckford unexpectedly decided to sell the property privately to John Farquhar, a Scottish gunpowder manufacturer, who would hold a sale on his own account a year later through the auctioneer, Harry Phillips. The agreement with Farquhar, dated October 5, 1822, included a proviso giving Beckford or his nominee the first choice of individual works in the sale.[153] These included the family portraits, thirteen lots of decorative objects, sixteen lots of pictures (out of a total of 115), and the first choice of a third of the prints and drawings, bound books, manuscripts, and books of prints. The lots were numbered against the Christie's catalogue in each day's sale. The exempted paintings were a curious mixture, mostly Dutch and Flemish landscapes, with, only a few major works, including *The Madonna and Child*, then attributed to Cima (now in The Metropolitan Museum of Art, New York, and attributed to the workshop of Giovanni Bellini).[154] Furthermore, Beckford was also intent on reinstating more of his own collection. Seemingly not content with reclaiming the few agreed pictures, Beckford had another change of heart: on the twenty-fourth day of the great Fonthill Farquhar sale of October 1823, he began to buy back his own pictures through his agents.[155] Four months earlier, in June 1823, he had also bought at least eight pictures from the sale of another collection, that of his fellow victim of diminished West Indian revenues, George Watson Taylor of Erlestoke Park, near Devizes in Wiltshire, who was selling pictures from his London residence. Beckford's interest was an indication that he was still actively changing the collection which had been moved to Lansdown Crescent.[156]

Beckford in Bath

Beckford had problems in accommodating his collections in Bath but with the purchase of the neighboring house, some judicious alterations, and the building of Lansdown Tower, he was able to continue his passion for collecting. He maintained a constant pressure on his agents in London to keep him informed of the market there; his letters sometimes expressed bursts of frustration, fury, and excitement in his demands for information. Paintings were bought and sold according to his irrepressible desire to purchase regardless of the soundness of his actions. In 1841 in order to finish redecorating the tower, he sold privately, to such buyers as Holford and the National Gallery, and there was also a sale of paintings from the tower conducted by Messrs English & Fasana, the Bath auctioneers.[157] By the time of Beckford's death in 1844, the inventory made by English & Son and Hume, listed over 350 works in Lansdown Crescent and in the tower, with a separate inventory of over 400 drawings and a huge amount of engravings.[158]

There were few visits to Beckford's Bath residences that have been recorded, those of Henry Venn Lansdown being the most notable.[159] Nevertheless, two distinguished German art historians, Johann David Passavant, a painter and later the director of the Städel Museum, Frankfurt, and Gustav Waagen both visited Beckford's collection in Bath in the 1830s. Passavant came to England in the early 1830s to see collections all over the country and to visit archives. His account of his visit to Bath is short, concentrating on Raphael's *Saint Catherine* and leaving no space for the Dutch pictures, except to comment on their high quality.[160]

Waagen, however, who visited in 1835, hugely admired the collection and wrote: "Mr. Beckford unites, in a very rare degree, an immense fortune with a general and refined love of art and a highly-cultivated taste."[161] He was admitted to the tower by ticket for a hurried two hours on a September morning and viewed the collection with precision and delight. In the afternoon he was irritated to have to make another hurried visit to Lansdown Crescent. He wrote a lyrical passage beginning, "I shall never forget the dining-room, which, taken all in all, is perhaps one of the most beautiful in the world," and ending "many things here meet in a culminating point, which, even singly, are calculated to rejoice the heart of man."[162] Here hung six of the many paintings which are now in the National Gallery in London from Beckford's collection: *Saint Catherine* by Raphael; *The Holy Family with Saints John the Baptist, Elizabeth, Zacharias and (?) Francis* by

Garofalo (see cat. no. 132); *The Trinity with the Madonna, Saints Joseph and Nicholas of Tolentino* and *Christ and the Woman Taken in Adultery* by Mazzolino; *The Adoration of the Kings* by Lippi; and the "large" *Tobias and the Archangel Raphael Returning with the Fish*, now known to be a later version after Elsheimer (see cat. no. 7). These paintings formed an astonishing group of works of superb quality, which were curiously admired by so few in Beckford's lifetime, but which eventually became accessible to all. In 1839 Beckford sold the Raphael, Garofalo, and the Mazzolino *Trinity* to the National Gallery for £7,350. He soon regretted it, considered that the "mongers and their satellites" had a bargain, and felt "contempt . . . unbounded . . . in deceiving me—have deceived themselves."[163] Two years later, however, he sold the National Gallery his much-loved *Virgin and Child with Saint John* by Perugino. In 1844 following the sale of the *Doge Loredan* by Bellini for £630, there was argument again with the trustees concerning the price, the controversial correspondence being continued by the Duke of Hamilton after Beckford's death that year. An attempt to buy it back failed, and the painting remained at the National Gallery, which now houses twenty-eight pictures with a Beckford provenance.[164]

Beckford can be seen as inconsistent, impulsive, demanding and innovatory. He was often obsessed with having to possess a certain object: "think of me when any drawings of this kind turn up—I have some already of this class very fine . . . [one of which] *I must have . . .* MISS IT NOT," Beckford wrote two years before his death in 1844.[165] He must have been an impossibly difficult man to please. His passion for works of art throughout his life is borne out by his correspondence. After his death the inventory made of the remaining paintings, prints and drawings in his collection (which were valued at over £16,000) is evidence of a hugely varied and discerning mind.[166] These works, which were left in Bath, were bequeathed to his younger daughter, Susan Euphemia, the Duchess of Hamilton. Some were sold in the sale at Lansdown Crescent of 1848, and the rest became part of the collection at Hamilton Palace in Lanarkshire, her husband's Scottish residence (now demolished). On the eventual dispersal of the Hamilton treasures at the great sale in 1882, these paintings were sold, with some remaining in the hands of the family, a selection of which can be seen at Brodick Castle on the Isle of Arran in Scotland.

Acknowledgments: I owe an enormous debt of gratitude to Giles Waterfield who gave me the opportunity of writing and researching this fascinating subject, and, with Philip Hewat-Jaboor and Bet McLeod, has given me constant help throughout the project. Alastair Laing very kindly read my typescript and I am extremely grateful to him for his most helpful comments. Others who have been especially generous with information, guidance or support include Sidney Blackmore, Duncan Bull, Hugo Chapman, Helen Dorey, Mireille Galinou, Charlotte Gere, Elisabeth Grant, Frank Herrmann, Michael Hirst, Helen Hoare, Niall Hobhouse, Luke Hughes, Brian Ivory, Pippa Mason, Janie Munro, Niel Rimington, Francis Russell, Rosalind Savill, Jonathan Scott, Charles Sebag-Montefiore, J. Peter Spang III, Thomas Tuohy, Adriana Turpin, Malcolm Warner, and Christopher Woodward.—JC

1. For a discussion of Beckford's belief that Fonthill would become a kind of shrine to the arts, see David Watkin, *Thomas Hope 1769–1831 and the Neo-classical Idea* (London: John Murray, 1968):151. Watkin also draws some interesting parallels between Hope and Beckford, two extraordinary men (ibid., pp. 15–16).

2. Lewis Melville, *The Life and Letters of William Beckford of Fonthill* (London: W. Heinemann, 1910): 289.

3. Sacheverell Sitwell, *Beckford and Beckfordism, An Essay* (London: Duckworth, 1930): 8 and 22.

4. For this period, see in particular Francis Haskell, *Rediscoveries in Art, Some Aspects of Taste, Fashion and Collecting in England and France* (Oxford: Phaidon Press, 1980): 38–84.

5. For further reading on the history of the British Institution, see Peter Fullerton, "Patronage and Pedagogy: The British Institution in the Early Nineteenth Century," *Art History* (March 1982): 59–72.

6. Beckford had been among a group of collectors and connoisseurs who had been contacted in 1802 and 1803 by the painter and engraver Josiah Boydell with a proposal to establish a national museum. Although not a subscriber to the British Institution, Beckford lent paintings to their 1818 exhibition: Ludovico Carracci, *Sybilla Lybica* (exhib. no. 13; on loan to the Walker Art Gallery, Liverpool, 1954–63, present location unknown) and Gerrit Dou, *A Poulterer's Shop* (exhib. no. 27; now in the National Gallery, London); and in 1821, Leonardo da Vinci (now Luini), *A Boy Shewing a Trick* (exhib. no. 14; now in the Elton Hall Collection). For a detailed discussion of the role of Old Master exhibitions at this time, see Francis Haskell, *The Ephemeral Museum: Old Master Paintings and the Rise of the Art Exhibition* (New Haven and London: Yale University Press, 2000).

7. He described himself as having "microscopic eyes" (Robert J Gemmett, ed., *The Consummate Collector: William Beckford's Letters to His Bookseller* [Wilby, Norwich: Michael Russell, 2000]: 144).

8. For instance, Hume reported Beckford's sale of *A Dutch Girl Gathering a Pink* by Dou to Lord Ashburton, letter dated 16 August 1839, MS Beckford c.22, fol. 194. Also see below, n. 118.

9. Letter to Franchi, 12 May 1817, quoted in *Life at Fonthill, 1807–1822, with interludes in Paris and London, from the correspondence of William Beckford*, trans. and ed. Boyd Alexander (London, R. Hart-Davis, 1957): 206.

10. This quote was taken from an unsigned and lengthy review of *Italy, with Sketches of Spain and Portugal*, *Quarterly Review* 102 (June 1834): 426; reprinted (with minor changes) in the 1834 edition of *Biographical Memoirs*.

11. See transcripts of sales compiled by Richard Houlditch between 1711 and 1759, Victoria and Albert Museum Library, Mss 86.00.18–19. Of sixteen sales between 1744–45 and 1759, "Beckford," "Whood, Beckford," and "Hood for Beckford" are recorded as purchasing a total of sixty-three paintings. It is possible that some of these may refer to William Beckford of Somerley Hall, Suffolk, Beckford's illegitimate cousin. In particular some paintings from "Mr Batts Sale" of 1756 (listed in Mss 86.00.18, p. 79), do correspond to works in the 1789 Christie's sale catalogue of the other William Beckford.

12. *Dr. Richard Mead*, sale cat., Langford, London, 20–22 March 1754; some lots are marked "Whood for Beckford." as the buyer.

13. The other, smaller Elsheimer of the same subject came into the young Beckford's collection later and is now thought to be circle of Elsheimer, was exhibited; see *The William Beckford Exhibition*, ed. Diana Keith Neal (Tisbury, Wiltshire: Compton Press, 1976): cat. no. G13; also see *The Estate of Walter P. Chrysler Jr.*, sale cat., Sotheby's, New York, 1 June 1989, lot 39.

14. There is some confusion about these paintings but two of the series survived.

15. The Alderman also owned *A Doctor of Law* (now in the Staatliche Museen Berlin, Gemäldegalerie) and *A Doctor of Physic in his Study* (present location unknown) by Ostade. These were purchased at the sale of John de Pesters of Hanover Square, London, Prestage, London, 1–2 April 1756, lots 27 and 28, together with *Landscape with Figures* by Brueghel and Rottenhammer (possibly the *Holy Family with the Infant Saint John*, lot 17 (now at Brodick Castle, Scotland) and *Venus Sleeping with Cupids in a Landscape* by Titian, lot 32 (present location unknown).

16. Christian August Gottlieb Goede, *England, Wales, Irland und Schottland: Erinnerungen an Natur und Kunst aus einer Reise in den Jahren 1802 und 1803*, vol. 5 (Dresden, 1804–5): 118.

17. Lady Ann Hamilton diary and account of Fonthill, 1803, MS Beckford e.4.

18. William Beckford, *Dreams, Waking Thoughts and Incidents*, ed. Robert J. Gemmett (Rutherford [N.J.]: Fairleigh Dickinson University Press, 1971): 223, n.121.

19. Ibid., p. 34.

20. Ibid., p. 91.

21. Ibid., pp. 157–59.

22. J. W. Oliver, *The Life of William Beckford* (London: Oxford University Press, 1932): 166.

23. Beckford may have bought works from Robert while in Paris as he owned *Ruins*, sold in the Fonthill Mansion sale, Phillips, Fonthill, Wiltshire,17 August 1807, lot 580, and *Albano Peasants in a Landscape*, which was placed in a mixed anonymous sale at Christie's, London, 22 May 1830, lot 40, but failed to sell. This was curiously the only painting Beckford submitted for that sale.

24. Cyrus Redding, ed. *Memoirs of William Beckford of Fonthill, author of "Vathek,"* vol. 2 (London: C. J. Skeet, 1859): 284.

25. *The Journal of William Beckford in Portugal and Spain, 1787–1788*, ed. Boyd Alexander (London: Hart-Davis, 1954): 293 and 312.

26. Letter to Thomas Wildman, 3 May 1793, MS Beckford c.37, fol. 20.

27. Beckford, *Life at Fonthill* (1957): 165–67.

28. For example, in 1850 Mrs Jameson identified the van Eyck, *The Entombment of a Cardinal* as *The Exhumation of Saint Hubert* by a follower of Rogier van der Weyden (now in the National Gallery, London) and the Memling *Young Man at Prayer* (now in the Thyssen-Bornemisza Collection, Lugano) formerly identified as such by Friedlander in 1937. The Ghirlandaio panels of Saint Catherine and of Saint Ursula in Beckford's sale at Christie's, London, 12 May 1817, lot 24, bought by Wadmore for 16 guineas, are in fact the side panels of the Withypoll triptych by Solario (now on loan to the Bristol City Art Gallery by the National Gallery, London), see Dorothy Lygon and Francis Russell, "Tuscan Primitives in London Sales: 1801–1837," *Burlington Magazine* 122, (February 1980): 116. I am most grateful to Francis Russell for bringing this important article to my attention.

29. Melville, *Life and Letters* (1910): 295.

30. See the bibliography in this volume for works by these authors.

31. The primary sources of information are the collections of Beckford manuscripts in the Bodleian Library, Oxford University (hereafter cited as Beckford MS), and in the Beinecke Rare Book and Manuscript Library, Yale University (hereafter referred to as Beinecke Library). Secondary sources include the catalogues of sales that contained his pictures and the inventories made after his death in 1844. Beckford, *Life at Fonthill* (1957) remains the major published source for details of the paintings in Beckford's collection, gleaned mostly from Beckford's letters to Franchi, now in the Bodleian Library.

32. Letter to Franchi, 22 June 1811, referring to the future third Marquess of Hertford (1777–1842) possibly buying at the sale of the Duke of San Pietro, quoted in ibid., p.99.

33. Melville, *Life and Letters* (1910): 309.

34. Both letters of 22 April 1844 in Victoria and Albert Museum Library, MSS 48.F.67 Forster Collection and 86.NN. Box II. Beckford died on 2 May 1844.

35. Beckford, *Consummate Collector* (2000): 226.

36. Quoted in Melville, *Life and Letters* (1910): 291–92. The painting is now in the Arnot Art Museum, Elmira, New York, and attributed to the school of Murillo. This much-mentioned painting was one of eighteen bought at the Hamilton Palace sale in 1882 for a total of £2,415 by Matthias H. Arnot (1833–1910), whose Scottish father, John Arnot, had emigrated to America in 1803. He bequeathed his house and collection of European paintings and sculpture to the town of Elmira.

37. Beckford, *Life at Fonthill* (1957): 169.

38. For instance, the portrait, *Architect Antonio dal Ponte* by Jacopo Bassano, illustrated by Gavin Hamilton in *Schola Italica Picturae* (1773) as in the collection of "Beckfort," came to be assumed to belong to Beckford but was in fact owned by his cousin.

39. Clive Wainwright surmised that Beckford may have let Farquhar have further pictures to sell: see Stanley Jones, "The Fonthill Abbey Pictures: Two additions to the Hazlitt Canon," *Journal of the Warburg and Courtauld Institutes* 41 (1978): 281, n.14.

40. Quoted in Melville, *Life and Letters* (1910): 320.

41. Henry Venn Lansdown, *Recollections of the Late William Beckford* (1893; reprint, Kingsmead Reprints, Bath, 1969): 5.

42. These included works by Andrea Agi, Bellini and workshop, formerly attributed to Cima (now in The Metropolitan Museum of Art, New York), Catena (now in the collection of the Earl of Harewood), and van Orley (formerly attributed to Dürer; now in the National Gallery, Ottawa).

43. Now called "in the style of di Cione" (in the National Gallery, London).

44. The *Crucifixion* is now "studio of" (in the Hessiches Museum, Darmstadt). The Adoration paintings include one by the school of van Cleve, formerly Mabuse (now in the Fitzwilliam Museum, Cambridge) and another by Lippi, formerly school of Botticelli (now in the National Gallery, London).

45. The Leonardo is now attributed to Luini (in the Musée Condé, Chantilly) and the Murillo is now "school of" (in the Arnot Art Museum, Elmira, New York).

46. The Cima is now in the National Gallery, London; and the Veronese was from the Monastery of Saint Benedict in Malta.

47. It is now known that the van Valkenborch was definitely not in Beckford's collection as cited in Boyd Alexander, "Fonthill, Wiltshire," part 3, "William Beckford as Collector," *Country Life* (8 December 1966): 1574. I am greatly indebted to Mireille Galinou for her help in this matter. Given Beckford's love of drama represented in this particular subject, it is not unexpected to find that he owned other Babel subjects, one by Paul Bril (present location unknown) and two panels by unknown painters incorporated in an ebony cabinet from the Royal Palace in Madrid, which were in the Lansdown Tower sale, English and Fasana, Bath, 5 January 1841, lot 13; present location unknown.

48. This was one of at least nine paintings in Beckford's collection once owned by Louis-César-Renaud de Choiseul-Praslin, whose family paintings were among those sold during and after the French Revolution.

49. The Stretes painting was purchased by Queen Victoria from the Hamilton Palace sale; see *The Collection of Pictures, Works of Art, etc., from His Grace the Duke of Hamilton KT*, sale cat., Christie's, London, 17 June 1882, lot 43. It was sold as by Holbein for £798. The Wright painting was formerly called *The Regent Murray in Highland Costume* and attributed to George Jamesone; see *Important British Art*, sale cat., Christie's, London, 14 June 2000, lot 2; now in a private collection.

50. The former was attributed to Zuccaro in the inventory dated 13 September 1844 of the contents of 19 and 20 Lansdown Crescent, the tower, and farm (MS Beckford c.58). The latter was orginally attributed to Dürer.

51. Lansdown, *Recollections* (1893/1969): 17.

52. Beckford to Clarke, 17 September 1833, quoted in Beckford, *Consummate Collector* (2000): 261.

53. Beckford to Bohn, 17 June 1842, V & A MSS 48.F.67.

54. *Fonthill Abbey* (William Beckford), sale cat., Phillips, London, 1–4 March 1824. The principal buyers were Lord Northwick, Sir William Keppel and the London print dealer, Paul Colnaghi.

55. For the second drawing sale see *The Property of a Distinguished Connoisseur*, sale cat., Sotheby's, London, 19–20 March 1830. Beckford's name does not appear on the catalogue but the collection is listed by Lugt as Beckford's; it contained 236 varied lots from Old Masters to "Modern" and others.

56. *George Baker deceased*, sale cat., Sotheby's, London, 16–27 June 1825.

57. *William Esdaile deceased*, sale cat., part 4, "Engravings," Christie's, London, 26–27, 29 June 1840.

58. *William Esdaile deceased:Drawings*, sale cat., Christie's, London, 30 June 1840. The sale included seventy-eight Claudes and fifty-seven Titians; Smith bought ten lots. Letter dated 5 June 1840, Gen. Mss 102, Box 3, f.50 (2), Beinecke Library.

59. Letters of 21 June 1840, Gen Mss 102, Box 3, f.8 and f.9, Beinecke Library.

60. Redding, ed., *Memoirs*, vol. 2 (1859): 371–72.

61. *Passages from the Diaries of Mrs Philip Lybbe Powys, of Hardwick House, Oxon., AD 1756 to 1808*, ed. Emily J. Climenson (London: Longman & Co., 1899): 166–67.

62. Last recorded at Christie's, London, 5 July 1991, lot 26.

63. Richard Joseph Sulivan, *A Tour through Parts of England, Scotland, and Wales, in 1778*, 2d ed., vol. 1 (London, 1785): 126–28. Of those paintings mentioned—*Abraham Offering up his Son Isaac, Belshazzar's Feast*, and *Mary Magdalen* by Rubens, and *Our Saviour in the Pharisee's House* and *The Woman Taken in Adultery* by Poussin—none has been traced.

64. The design for this corridor is in Sir John Soane's Museum, London; see Christopher Woodward, "William Beckford and Fonthill Splendens: Early Works by Soane and Goodridge," *Apollo*, 147 i (February 1998): 31–40. Soane's bill, dated April 1787, for this proposed work, which includes the introduction of prints of the Vatican, is in Gen Mss 102, Box 6, f.109, Beinecke Library. A colored set of forty-two impressions by Panini of "Loggie of the Vatican," included in the 1807 sale; see *Fonthill Mansion*, sale cat., Phillips, Fonthill, Wiltshire, 22 August 1807, lot 596; it sold for the handsome sum of 630 guineas.

65. Richard Warner, *Excursions from Bath* (Bath: R. Crutwell, 1801): 119–27.

66. John Britton, *The Beauties of Wiltshire*, vol. 1 (London, 1801): 210–39; for Britton's notes see MS. Eng misc. d.222, Bodleian Library.

67. Letter dated 15 April 1796, in *Catalogue of The Collection of Autograph Letters and Historical Documents formed between 1865 and 1882 by A. Morrison: The Hamilton and Nelson Papers*, vol. 1 (London: privately printed, 1893–94): 219.

68. Goede, *England, Wales, Irland*, vol. 5 (1804–5): 116–17.

69. Beckford, *Life at Fonthill* (1957): 244.

70. Ibid., p.161.

71. Letter of 14 November 1843, MS Beckford c.35, fol.48.

72. Alastair Laing has kindly pointed out that the policy of that time was to varnish pictures with an oil-based varnish that superficially enhanced the surface but soon darkened and subsequently required cleaning. Beckford was already furious with the National Gallery. After the death in 1823 of John Julius Angerstein he had offered either £16,00 or £20,000 depending on the source (Whitley recorded £16,000) for the *Raising of Lazarus* by Sebastiano del Piombo from the Orléans collection. It was eventually sold to the National Gallery the following year for £8,000 through the offices of the much despised Seguier.

73. See Helmut von Erffa and Allen Staley, *The Paintings of Benjamin West* (New Haven and London: Yale University Press, 1986): 20 and 156n.25 for the list of his sales in 1820, 1824, and 1836.

74. Haskell, *Rediscoveries*, (1980): 50. West also bought paintings on behalf of the Prince Regent who particularly liked Dutch and Flemish pictures.

75. For West's decorative and other works at Fonthill, see Albert Ten Eyck Gardner, "Beckford's Gothic Wests," *The Metropolitan Museum of Art Bulletin* (October 1954): 41–49.

76. West to Beckford, 22 December 1801, MS Beckford c.36, fol. 80; in another letter West informed him that Lawrence had a Parmigianino for sale: Lord Abercorn's altarpiece, *Madonna and Child with Saints John the Baptist and Jerome* (now in the National Gallery, London), which Beckford did not buy at £3,000 (letter of 25 June 1808, ibid., fol. 84).

77. Entry for 14 December 1807, *The Diary of Joseph Farington*, ed. Kathryn Cave, vol. 8 (New Haven and London: Yale University Press, 1978–84): 3167.

78. Tresham was also a major source of pictures at this time for Sir Richard Worsley, another important collector, mostly of statuary and gems.

79. Buchanan to Stewart, 21 April 1804, in Hugh Brigstocke, *William Buchanan and the 19th Century Art Trade: 100 Letters to his Agents in London and Italy* (New Haven: The Paul Mellon Centre for Studies in British Art, 1982): 268.

80. Entry for 22 December 1798, Farington, *Diary*, vol. 3 (1978–84): 1117. Colonel John Campbell, first Baron Cawdor, had owned the *Doge Leonardo Loredan* by Bellini (now in the National Gallery, London), which was in Beckford's collection by 1814.

81. Quoted in Melville, *Life and Letters* (1910): 247.

82. For a fuller account and history of the pictures, see Frank Herrmann, *The English as Collectors* (New Castle, Delaware: Oak Knoll Press / London: John Murray, 1999): 163–67; Hermann includes quotes from William T. Whitley, *Artists and their Friends in England, 1700–1799*, vol. 2 (London and Boston: Medici Society, 1928): 224–26 and 357–59.

83. Tresham to Beckford, MS Beckford c.36, fol. 24.

84. These were *Holy Family* by Garofalo (possibly that now in the National Gallery, London), *Saint Jerome* by Guercino (listed by Warner in September 1800 in the ballroom at Splendens and possibly the one in the Hamilton Palace sale, 24 June 1882 (lot 350) entitled *The Vision of Saint Jerome*, which was bought by Knowles for £16 16s.), *Adoration* by Guido Reni, which he thought was by Ludovico Carracci and which is possibly the small *Nativity* listed by Warner, and a *Christ and Saint John as Children* by Leonardo (also listed by Warner as "Two boys kissing" and presumably the Infant Saviour and Saint John sold at Jeffrey's Gallery, Salisbury, 1 May 1809, [not numbered, but lot 7] (letter of 21 April 1799, MS Beckford c.36, fol.26).

85. Entry for 8 May 1799, Farington, *Diary*, vol. 4 (1978–84): 1219.

86. Quoted in Melville, *Life and Letters* (1910): 259.

87. See James Lees-Milne, *William Beckford* (Tisbury Wiltshire: Compton Russell, 1976): 101; and Beckford, *Life at Fonthill* (1957): 55. They were bought by a dealer called Harris who sold them to Richard Hart Davis (1766–1842), MP for Bristol, for 12,000 guineas with two other Beckford pictures, both by Gaspar Dughet, *Storm: Moses and the Angel*, formerly entitled *The Calling of Abraham* (now in the National Gallery, London) and a large landscape, *The Cascatella of Tivoli* (now in the Museo de Arte de Ponce, Puerto Rico). Both Dughets and the companion of the latter, *View of Tivoli* (now in the Seattle Art Museum), all from the Palazzo Colonna, Rome, were later in the Miles collection at Leigh Court, near Bristol.

88. Entry for 17 June 1799, in Farington, *Diary*, vol. 4 (1978–84): 1240.

89. For further information on Ottley and Roscoe, see J. A. Gere, "William Young Ottley as a Collector of Drawings," *British Museum Quarterly* 28, no. 2 (June 1953): 43–53; and Michael Compton, "William Roscoe and Early Collectors of Italian Primitives," *Liverpool Bulletin* 9, Walker Art Gallery Number, (1960–61): 26–51. Roscoe never visited Italy.

90. MS Beckford c.36, fol. 22. A small sheet entitled "Private View" lists twenty-six pictures "purchased at Rome in December 1798 brought to England by Purchaser and Proprietor and now for sale by Private Treaty at 31 Margaret Street, Craven Square" in March 1799.

91. Tresham to Williams, 11 June 1799, MS Beckford c.36, fol. 27.

92. These were two small figures, later sold as *Charity* and *Nymph*; see *Fonthill Mansion,* sale cat., Phillips, Fonthill, Wiltshire, 17 August 1807, lot 20; sold to Walsh Porter for 105 guineas (present location unknown); for a report of the sale, see *Gentleman's Magazine* (September 1807): 880.

93. Only three years later Beckford sold the *Saint Anthony* (*Fonthill,* sale cat., Christie's, London, 27 February 1802, lot 81); it was bought by Lord George Cavendish, later the Earl of Burlington, for £199 10s., and the landscape also sold in 1802 sale for £105.

94. See William Buchanan, *Memoirs of Painting, with a chronological history of the importation of pictures by the great masters into England since the French Revolution*, vol. 2 (London: R. Ackermann, 1824): 7 n.22.

95. See Clive Wainwright, *The Romantic Interior: The British Collector at Home, 1750–1850* (New Haven and London: Yale University Press, 1989): 120. Also see chap. 3, by Philip Hewat-Jaboor, in this volume.

96. See Jacob Simon, *The Art of the Picture Frame* (London: National Portrait Gallery Publications, 1996): 122. There is little evidence of Beckford's preferences for frames, and it does appear that he did not favor one particular style to standardize the framing of his pictures.

97. Beckford to Wildman, 20 February 1795, MS Beckford c.37, fol. 22.

98. *Collection of Cabinet Pictures lately consigned from the Continent also a small collection of capital pictures the property of a Gentleman of Fashion*, sale cat., Christie's, London, 17 January 1800, lot 81.

99. *The Earl of Bessborough deceased*, sale cat., Christie's, London, 7 February 1801, lot 73 (then attributed to van Eyck).

100. *Sir William Hamilton KB*, sale cat., Christie's, London, 28 March 1801, lot 75.

101. Ibid. The attribution to Luini was made by Waagen who saw the picture at Hamilton Palace; see G. F. Waagen, *Treasures of Art in Great Britain,* vol. 3 (London: John Murray, 1854): 300.

102. *Chevalier Franchi,* sale cats., Christie's, London, 16–17 May 1827 and 22 May 1829; and a further sale, of Count Rossi, Franchi and others, conducted by Fosters, London, 11 May 1832, when many lots were sold at very low prices.

103. There is possible confusion with the name Hume, in that Sir Abraham Hume, the collector and author of a monograph on Titian, was cited as "an amateur dealer who acted for Beckford" in Gerald Reitlinger, *The Economics of Taste,* vol. 1 (London: Barrie & Rockliff, 1961): 31 This seems unlikely, and no further references to him acting on behalf of Beckford can be found.

104. Hume to Beckford, 15 July 1836, MS Beckford c.22, fol.159.

105. Hume to Beckford, 30 July 1836, MS Beckford c.22, fol.163.

106. See Boyd Alexander, *England's Wealthiest Son* (1962): 250.

107. See Buchanan, *Memoirs of Painting* (1824).

108. As cited in Herrmann, *English as Collectors* (1999): 135 and 193–98.

109. Entry for 31 July 1799, Farington, *Diary*, vol. 4 (1978–84): 1259. The purchase of Annibale Carracci's *Three Marys at the Tomb* (now in the National Gallery, London) would have been a triumph as it had the highest value of any of the paintings, see Haskell, *Ephemeral Museum* (2000): 26. For a contrary view of the effect of the Orléans collection sales in London, see Jordana Pomeroy, "The Orléans Collection: Its Impact on the British Art World," *Apollo* 145 (February 1997): 26–31.

110. Buchanan, *Memoirs of Painting,* vol. 1 (1824): 189. Beckford owned at least thirteen works by Teniers.

111. Possibly William Penn who wrote for the *Gentleman's Magazine* although Alastair Laing suggests that it was more likely to have been John Penn of Stoke Park, Buckinghamshire, a client of James Wyatt and major patron and collector. Fagan was anxious that the list was "published in the different papers" (quoted in Herrmann, *English as Collectors* [1999]: 162–63).

112. Brigstocke, *William Buchanan* (1982): 363.

113. Present location unknown; it was stolen from the church at Garlenda in 1979.

114. Brigstocke, *William Buchanan* (1982): 364 and 382.

115. John Smith day books, MSS 86.cc.1–6, Victoria and Albert Museum Library.

116. This was bought for £315 by John Smith; see *Joseph Barchard*, sale cat., Christie's, London, 6 May 1826, lot 6; it was sold by Smith to Beckford in the same month, and Beckford exchanged it with Hume by 1829. See John Smith, *A Catalogue Raisonné of the Works of the Most Eminent Dutch, Flemish, and French Painters*, vol. 1 (London: Smith & Son, 1829): 33.

117. Or, *Portrait of his Mother*, according to the 1844 Inventory, MS Beckford c. 58.

118. The exhibition was held on 3 and 4 April; see *Literary Gazette*, 19 April 1834, p. 284. The painting was later destroyed by a fire at Bath House, Lord Ashburton's residence in London.

119. Beckford, *Life at Fonthill* (1957): 59–60.

120. Buchanan, *Memoirs of Painting*, vol. 2 (1824): 7.

121. In a letter of 22 July 1839 from Florence, Coesvelt wrote to Beckford referring to "articles I begged you to buy for me and I shall want in the fall" (see the correspondence of 1839, 1841, and 1844, in Osborn Mss 17745 and 17747, Beinecke Library). It is obvious from these letters that Beckford and Coesvelt knew each other well. For instance, there are instructions to Beckford to burn Coesvelt's letters unopened in the event of his death and later, concerns as to the payment of his debts. They presumably knew each other through Beckford's illegitimate brother John who had worked at Hope and Company.

122. *Collection of Pictures of W. G. Coesvelt Esqre of London. A Descriptive Catalogue by the owner, with plates drawn and engraved by J. F. Joubert*, with an introduction by Mrs Jameson (London: J. Carpenter & Son, 1836): viii–xi. This volume of ninety pictures contains engravings for these paintings. They also appear with a Claude *Tobias and Angel* from the Colonna collection and a Salvator Rosa of the same subject on a list dated 17 May 1841 made by Coesvelt in Florence, Osborn Mss 17745, Beinecke Library.

123. See Buchanan, *Memoirs of Painting,* vol. 2 (1824): 231.

124. I am greatly indebted to Charles Sebag-Montefiore who very kindly supplied much information concerning Holford and Beckford.

125. Melville, *Life and Letters* (1910): 346 and 347.

126. Until 1870 it was attributed to Fra Angelico. Beckford also owned two exquisite panels by Fra Angelico: *Head of the Angel Gabriel* and a *Head of the Virgin* (now in the Detroit Institute of Arts), which probably formed part of an altarpiece and were from the collection of Baron Dominique Vivant-Denon.

127. All of which are untraced, the Backhuysen was last recorded with Paul de Boer in 1958; the Wouvermans was in *Old Master Paintings*, Sotheby's, London, 9 July 1975, lot 9; and the van der Neer was sold in *Important Old Master Pictures*, Christie's, London, 4 July 1997, lot 11 (the property of the late Sir Harold Wernher, Bt.).

128. The others are untraced, the Ostade was last recorded in *Sir George Holford*, sale cat., Christie's, London, 17 May 1928, lot 29 (bought Buttery for £1,890).

129. English to Holford, 4 March 1840, with a note added by Beckford on the same letter, MS Beckford c.30, fol.21.

130. Beckford described Pizzetta as "a famous picture scraper" who "told me it came directly from Perugia, but from what church or collection—took decent care not to certify" (letter to William Smith of Lisle Street, 22 July 1841, Gen Mss 102, Box 3, f.16, Beinecke Library).

131. Quoted in Melville, *Life and Letters* (1910): 347. This was a reference presumably to Hungerford, third Baron Crewe of Crewe Hall, Cheshire, whose family already owned a good collection of paintings, many bought in Italy in the eighteenth century.

132. Beckford to an unknown recipient but presumed to be English in Bath, 6 May 1841, Gen Mss 102, Box 2, f.33, Beinecke Library.

133. See David Bomford, "Perugino's *Virgin and Child with Saint John*," Technical Bulletin Number 1 (London: The National Gallery, 1977): 29–34.

134. Quoted in Melville, *Life and Letters* (1910): 299.

135. Ibid., p. 303. *The Classic Contents of Strawberry Hill, collected by Horace Walpole*, sale cat., George Robins, 25 April and 23 following days, 1842.

136. Beckford to Smith, 3 March 1842, Gen Mss 102, Box 3, f.17, Beinecke Library.

137. Beckford to Bohn, 30 July 1842, MSS 448.F.67, Victoria and Albert Museum Library.

138. Herrmann, *English as Collectors* (1999): 435. For a contemporary and somewhat pithy comparison of the two men, see Beckford, *Consummate Collector (2000)*: 269 (n. 2 quotes an article from the *New Monthly Magazine* of August 1833 by Edward Lytton Bulwer).

139. He certainly bought books of engravings, some of which are now in the Lewis Walpole Library, Farmington, Connecticut, and, for instance, a Teniers *Temptation of Saint Anthony* (now at Brodick Castle, Scotland). See *Lansdown Crescent, Bath*, sale cat., 26 July 1848, lot 37; the Teniers is stated as from Strawberry Hill, as is a drawing by Goupy *Assumption of the Virgin*, after A. Carracci in the same sale, but 28 July 1848, lot 16.

140. In 1795 Trumbull had been an attaché at the American Legation in Paris, and had bought pictures there. Beckford had placed five pictures of his own in Trumbull's sale, *Superb and distinquished collection of Italian, French, Flemish and Dutch pictures*, Christie's, London, 17–18 February 1797, lots 76, 86, 87, 88, and 89; they are not identified as belonging to Beckford. Two paintings from this sale reappeared in Beckford's sale, *A Gentleman . . . Fonthill in Wiltshire*, Christie's, London, 27 February 1802, lots 82 and 86: *Lucretia* by Guido Reni (present location unknown) and *Deianira and the Centaur Nessus* by Padovanino (now in the Ringling Art Gallery, Sarasota).

141. Two more paintings, which had arrived too late to be included in the February sale, were sold in a mixed sale, *Lately consigned from Paris*, Christie's, London, 26 March 1802. These were *An Incantation* by Salvator Rosa (lot 100; bought Lord Kinnaird for £32 11s.) and *The Visitation of Elizabeth* by Sebastiano del Piombo (lot 101; bought Zachary for £29 8s.).

142. See Robin Middleton, "Soane's Spaces and the Matter of Fragmentation," in *John Soane: Architect Master of Space and Light*, ed. Margaret Richardson and MaryAnne Stevens, exhib. cat. (London: Royal Academy of Arts, 1999): 35.

143. For instance he bought a Rembrandt *Portrait of a Rabbi* (now school of; in the Staatliche Museen Berlin, Gemäldegalerie) and a Claude *View in Rome* (now attributed to; in the National Gallery, London).

144. *Gentleman's Magazine* (September 1807): 880.

145. Among the Old Masters were *Woman Taken in Adultery* by Poussin and *Geese, birds* by Hondecoeter, which were bought with others by a local dealer, Mr. H. Jeffrey of Salisbury, who accumulated "Fonthill" pictures to sell privately at his establishment in the Market Place at Salisbury in May 1809. This is an early example of the awareness of the importance of the Beckford provenance and is particularly interesting that this was so in Wiltshire, Beckford's county, Fonthill being only about fifteen miles away from Salisbury.

146. In his fifth Royal Academy lecture; see David Watkin, *Sir John Soane: Enlightenment Thought and the Royal Academy Lectures* (Cambridge University Press in association with Sir John Soane's Museum and the Bank of England, 1996): 556. Soane bought another "Beckford" painting, the magnificent *The Riva degli Schiavoni, a View of Venice looking west with Saint Mark's in the Background* by Canaletto of 1736 (now in Sir John Soane's Museum, London) at the sale, *Fonthill Mansion*, Phillips, Fonthill, Wiltshire, 17 August 1807, lot 605.

147. See Boyd Alexander, "Fonthill, Wiltshire," part 2, "The Abbey and its Creator," *Country Life* (1 December 1966): 1433. Alexander described it as more like an "overhung room in a modern museum, judging by Rutter's illustration of it."

148. James Storer, *A Description of Fonthill Abbey, Wiltshire* (London: Storer et al., 1812): 11–20.

149. An interesting comparison of the building ground plan and display of Old Masters can be made with that at Alton Abbey, now Alton Towers in Staffordshire, belonging to the fifteenth and sixteenth Earls of Shrewsbury. I am grateful to J. C. R. King for drawing my attention to this comparison, see also Michael J. Fisher, *Alton Towers: A Gothic Wonderland* (Stafford: M. J. Fisher, 1999). Alton Abbey housed a large number of paintings, recorded by G. F. Waagen, *Works of Art and Artisits in England,* vol. 3(London: John Murray, 1838): 246–60; he called it Alton Tower.

150. Beckford to an unknown recipient (probably English), 28 January 1820, Mss Gen. 102, Box 3, f.55, Beinecke Library.

151. *Alexis Delahante, London, who has imported them to the Country for the purpose of Sale*, sale cat., Phillips, London, 14 July 1821. Beckford's purchases included *A Flock of Sheep with Shepherds* by Cuyp (lot 107; now in the Städel Galerie, Frankfurt), *Boy fishing* by Slingeland (lot 72; possibly that in the Staatliche Museen Berlin, Gemäldegalerie), and a *Portrait of Charles I* by van Dyck (lot 57; now school of van Dyck; in the collection of the National Trust, Great Britain). This was one of many sales. A much-respected dealer, Delahante settled in London from Paris having been exiled by Napoléon and after the Restoration imported pictures in large numbers from the Continent.

152. Franchi wrote "Ce spectacle vous brisait le coeur" and "pour les objets qu'il veut reserver," in a letter of 23 September 1822 from Fonthill to the Duke of Hamilton at Hamilton Palace, MS Beckford c 39, fol.89. This list included fourteen paintings, the highest prices for which were a Leonardo at £1,500 and the Berghem *Embarquement des vivres* at £1,200.

153. Sale agreement with Farquhar, dated 5 October 1822, MS Beckford b.8, fol.19–20.

154. The proposed sale, *Magnificent Effects etc. . . . Fonthill Abbey*, to be held by Christies's. Christie's clerk's copy of the catalogue for 16 October is also marked against certain reserved lots

of a further ten major pictures, with the names of Hume, Smith, Bentley, Jupe, the Duke of Hamilton (all acting for Beckford in some capacity), and Beckford himself. There was one picture common to both lists, the Berghem *Sea Port* (*Embarquement des Vivres*) (present location unknown).

155. It is possible that Beckford had commissioned a descriptive catalogue raisonné of his collection at the time of the 1823 sale. There is a reference to such a work in P. G. Patmore's rather grudging description of the "Fonthill Gallery," in "British Galleries of Art, No. IX," *The New Monthly Magazine* 8, Original Papers (1823): 403–8. Quoting a passage about a Teniers *Village scene*, (known as *The Sign of Teniers*) Patmore wrote that it came from "a Catalogue Raisonné of this collection, which has been printed but (I believe) not published." This of course could also be a reference to one of the many editions of Rutter's *Description* (or *Guide*) of 1822, produced to promote the sale. Patmore's description of the Teniers, however, is close to that which Hazlitt wrote in the *Morning Chronicle*, in August and September, 1823. It would seem likely that Patmore was quoting Hazlitt, who described the paintings at Fonthill, some of them in great detail. As Stanley Jones pointed out in his fascinating article on Fonthill and Hazlitt ("Fonthill Abbey Pictures" [1978]: 281), they had both been at Fonthill together in 1823 for the purpose of studying the pictures for publication. This series of articles had been commissioned by Phillips for fifty guineas to promote the Farquhar sale.

156. *George Watson Taylor of Cavendish Square*, sale cat., London, Christie's, London, 14 June 1823. Hume bought for Beckford, an unidentified version of the Velazquez *Portrait of Pope Innocent X*, *Embarquement des Vives* by Wouvermans, *The Effects of Intemperance* by Steen, *Self Portrait* by Poelenburg (now at Brodick Castle, Scotland) and *Portrait of Cardinal Mazarin* by Mignard. For further reference to Watson Taylor, see Hugh Roberts, "'Quite appropriate for Windsor Castle': George IV and George Watson Taylor," *Furniture History* 34, (2000): 115–37.

157. Beckford's sale, *Lansdown Tower, Bath*, English & Fasana, 4 January 1841, included twenty lots of pictures, sold reluctantly presumably, as some had been in his possession for a long time. Edmund English of Milsom Street, Bath, the auctioneer and dealer, had acted as an agent for Beckford since his move from Fonthill.

158. The total value of the works of art was £16,468, 1844 inventory, MS Beckford c.58. These were later either sold, sent to London, taken to Hamilton Palace in 1845 or sent to Easton Park up to 1848, Hamilton MSS Mis.M.12.50.

159. For Lansdown's visit of 1838, see Lansdown, *Recollections* (1893/1969). However, following the obituary of Beckford in the *Athenaeum*, 11 May 1844, p. 430, there was an account of both Lansdown Crescent and the tower interiors in the subsequent issue, 18 May 1844, pp. 455–56, initialled "I. W."

160. J. D. Passavant, *Tour of a German Artist in England,* vol. 1 (London: Saunders and Otley, 1836): 314–18. This was first published in German in 1833. Passavant had a special interest in Raphael, which resulted in a later publication: *Rafael von Urbino und sein Vater Giovanni Santi*, 2 vols. (Leipzig, 1839).

161. G. F. Waagen, *Works of Art and Artists in England*, vol. 3 (London: John Murray, 1838): 129.

162. Ibid., pp. 121 and 122.

163. Beckford to Hume, 26 May 1839, MS Beckford c.22, fol. 186.

164. G. Saunders Thwaites to the Duke of Hamilton,14 May 1844, MS Beckford c.39, fol.123. For a more detailed analysis of Beckford's collections and further discussion particularly on the paintings now in the National Gallery in London, see Thomas Tuohy, "William Beckford's Three Picture Collections: Idiosyncrasy and Innovation," *British Art Journal* 2, no.1, (Autumn 2000): 49–53.

165. Beckford to William Smith, concerning an item in the Strawberry Hill sale, 13 April 1842, Gen Mss 102, Box 3, f.18, Beinecke Library.

166. Inventory of 1844, MS Beckford c.58.

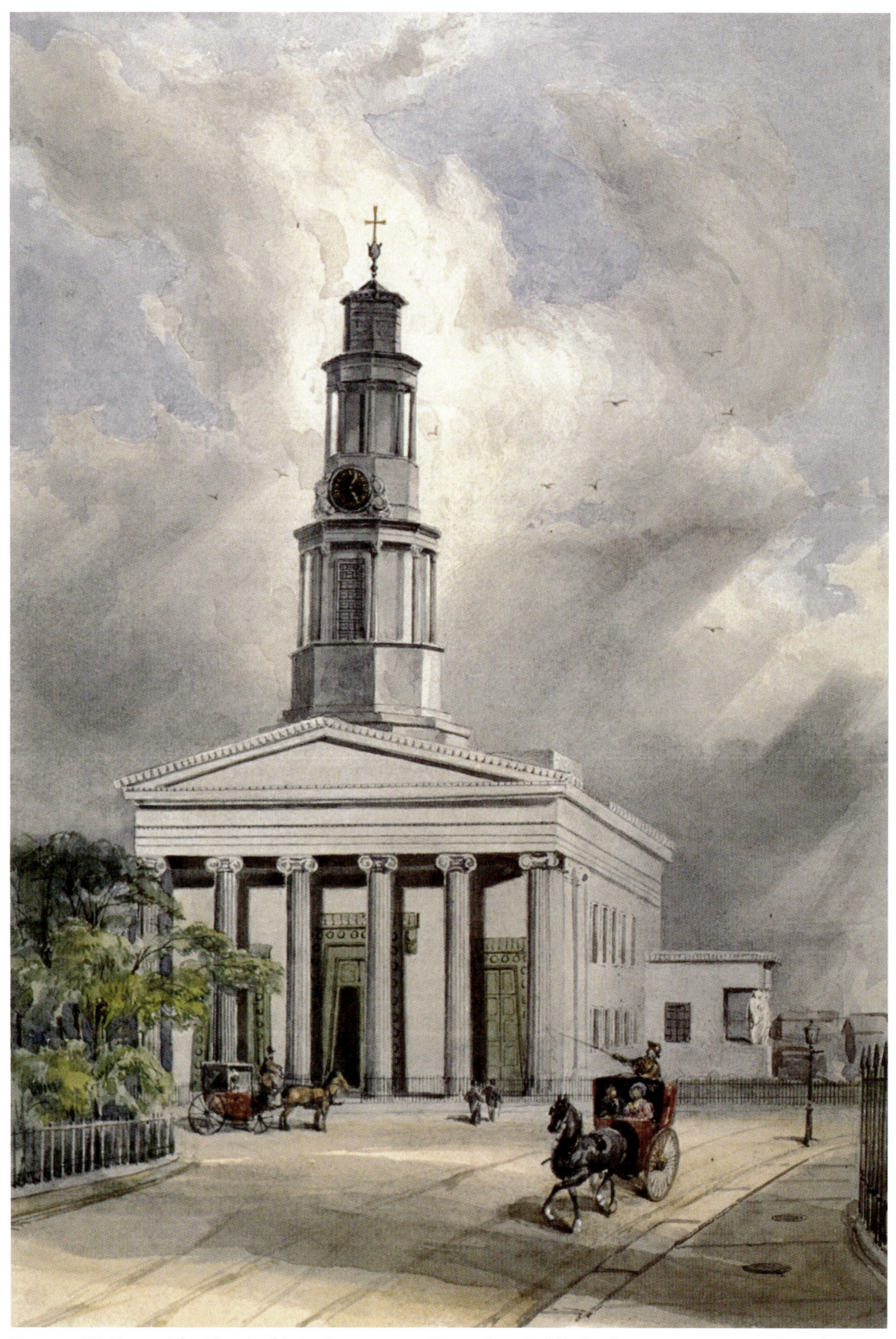

Fig. 14-1. W. Guest. *The Church of Saint Pancras*, 1855. Watercolor. Guildhall Library, Corporation of London.

CHAPTER XIV

WILLIAM BECKFORD IN LONDON

SIDNEY BLACKMORE

All London not withstanding ten thousand malevolent insinuations is at my feet . . .

William Beckford, March 1, 1782

William Beckford, son of an Alderman and Sheriff of the City of London, was born in the last year of the reign of George II (1760) and died when Queen Victoria had been on the throne for six years (1844). This was a period of considerable change in the capital, which grew from a population of about 650,000 to almost 2 million. It was a time of unprecedented building, with the construction of many residential districts, streets, and squares on the London estates of great landowners.[1] Many new churches were built (fig. 14-1). The court itself relocated from Saint James's to Buckingham House. The great architectural schemes of John Nash for the Prince Regent, linking Regent's Park with Carlton House, with their sweeping stucco facades, brought further changes to the face of the capital. There were also cultural innovations: the British Museum was established, for example, just before Beckford's birth and its present building erected during the final decades of his life; the National Gallery was founded in 1824 and moved into its new building in 1838. In the 1830s the railways arrived, bringing physical and social upheaval and accelerated growth to the city.

SOCIAL LIFE

Beckford claimed that George II saw him "when I was an infant in arms at my Aunt Effingham's apartment in Saint James's Palace."[2] Only much later, however, in 1782, did Beckford make a conspicuous mark on London society when, just after his coming-of-age, he was in demand in every fashionable house in the capital, displaying his talents as a singer and mimic. In April of that year he assisted Lady Craven, later Margravine of Ansbach, with the production of an operetta, "a faraggo of her Ladyship's—the music a faraggo of mine," which was performed at Queensberry House. In middle and later years of his life, however, when memories of the Powderham scandal still prevented his reception into English society, London was very much a place where Beckford, the compulsive and acquisitive collector, could visit booksellers, galleries, dealers, and auction rooms. The city also gave him the opportunity of keeping in direct contact with his long-suffering and faithful agents, who could expect censure or praise depending on their success or failure in executing his endless stream of commissions. In addition to their main tasks of purchases in the art market, his agents were expected to deal with other problems including accommodation. Also, for two periods, Beckford served as a Member of Parliament and, although a reluctant politician, had business of sorts to attend at Westminster.[3] He had a great love of music, opera, and the theater and could indulge these interests in the city.[4] His visits to London followed the established pattern of many members of the upper class, who traveled there each year, from their country estates, to participate in, or at least observe, the social season and life of the capital.

All of Beckford's London houses were in streets and squares laid out during the development of the great landed estates in the late eighteenth century, when the capital spread away from the old focuses of social and civic life and flowed toward Hyde Park in the west and what is now Regent's Park in the north. In renting or leasing a house for a number of years, Beckford was following contemporary custom practiced by the aristocracy, gentry, and affluent. The survival today of so many terraces and squares is due to the leasehold system operated by the ground landlords in which long-term investment was paramount to short-term gain. There was a ready market in rented properties. Richard Rush, the envoy extraordinary from the United States (1817–25), described his search for a suitable house, and how furnished houses were available from 400 to 1,000 guineas a year in the district where Beckford lived.[5] The first two houses that Beckford occupied after coming of age were in prime residential squares, Portman and Grosvenor, where the inhabitants possessed high social status, placing these among the smartest addresses in the capital. Beckford's later houses, although somewhat smaller, were still in very respectable streets mainly occupied by the nobility and gentry, together with some members of the professional class. From his various houses it was always an easy distance to the auction rooms; to dealers in books, paintings, and prints; and to theatres—places where his main interests lay.

Beckford would usually stay in London for two or three months at a time, frequently in the winter, when the main social season took place. At those times when, due to limited finance, he did not own or rent a town house—"Sedan chair I have none. House I have none. What remains to me is the gulph of the Abbey"—he would often stay at an hotel.[6] Occasionally, when within the vicinity of London, he stayed at the Black Dog Inn at East Bedfont, a village to the west of the city, about twelve miles from Hyde Park corner. At other times he based himself more centrally at Brunet's Hotel in Leicester Square.[7] The square had been a fashionable address in the eighteenth century, but gradually over the next century its appearance and reputation changed as hotels and shops moved in. Beckford may have chosen this particular hotel because it gave him a certain freedom and saved the cost of having to engage a retinue of servants that a rented house would have entailed.

Through Beckford's letters to Gregorio Franchi, his factotum and friend, it is possible to follow him in 1819, when he made one of his lengthy stays in the capital.[8] He arrived in London on January 13 and remained for three months. He traveled up from Fonthill, staying overnight in Marlborough at the Castle Inn. The London days were filled by inspecting medals, buying books, visiting his various agents, including the cabinetmaker Robert Hume: "almost everyday now I see Hume . . . little commissions and then one makes little purchases."[9] He went three times to see John Martin's *Capture of Babylon*, "O what a sublime thing!", which was on exhibition at the British Institution in Pall Mall.[10] There was also some parliamentary business to attend to. He went to the theater, a pantomime at Covent Garden on the evening he arrived in London, and performances at Drury Lane a few days later. Even when Beckford had no London house to maintain, weeks in the capital were expensive: "its cruel when you think that, without house, carriage, or splendour I'm spending £100 a week."[11]

On those evenings when he did not go to the theater he often spent his time reading and reviewing the ever-growing accumulation of books that filled his hotel room, a "delightful collection which in consequence . . . is not to be despised, and being composed not only of books to look at but also to read."[12] He was constantly being tempted to purchase objects, paintings, furniture, and books and prints: "I was right in thinking I wouldn't escape a few little purchases. I trusted—I had a look and there already in a tiny corner of my little cupboard at Jaunay's [hotel] are the divine gold-mounted little chest painted in the Hindu style."[13]

Whether in the country or the city, Beckford sought regular, concerted exercise, which he obtained through long rides on horseback. On February 17 he "went on one of my famous rides through the countries of Surrey and Kent. I was more than four hours on horseback, Nephew [his dog] running beside me the whole time never stopping for a rest."[14] That day he covered some thirty miles; it was a characteristic Beckfordian exploit.

In later years, Beckford day's would follow a fairly strict pattern. His lifelong love of flowers meant that he generally visited a nursery in the morning to select the finest blooms. It was a custom that provoked comment.[15] Flowers were also sent up to London from his Bath garden. Then he would pay a series of visits to his agents, dealers, and the auction houses before returning home at six-thirty. The artist W. P. Frith recorded seeing Beckford one day at Phillips, in Bond Street, when a painting said to be by Raphael was on view: "I stood close to the picture and studied Mr Beckford, who proceeded to criticise the work in language which my respectable pen can give my readers but a faint idea. It must not be thought that the remarks were addressed to me or anybody but the speaker himself. "That d—d thing a Raphael! Great heavens! think of that now! Can there be such d—d fools as to believe that a Raphael! What a d—d fool I was to come here!' and without a further glance at other pictures, the critic departed."[16] Cyrus Redding, Beckford's first biographer, gives a similar picture of Beckford trotting through an exhibition at the Society of British Artists, "stopping occasionally and grunting out an exclamation of contempt . . . 'Good heavens! this is the most cursed of them all! The face of badness can no further go, let's be off', and he ran hurriedly down the stairs to his carriage."[17] As part of his daily ritual he would also call at the house of his daughter, the Duchess of Hamilton, when the family was in residence.

Soho Square

In 1760, at the time of William Beckford's birth, his father Alderman Beckford occupied a townhouse, No. 22, on the east side of Soho Square, a residential development which in the first half of the century had been one of the most fashionable places in the capital. Although several writers have stated that the younger William was born at this house, there has been disagreement among Beckford's biographers.[18] Beckford himself delivered a typical rebuke to John Britton, the antiquarian: "I was born at Fonthill and cannot help being a little surpriz'd that amidst such an infinity of knowledge, you should happen to be ignorant of that all important circumstance."[19] He earlier wrote of "the deep-rooted affection I bore to Fonthill, the happy scene of my childhood and place of my nativity."[20]

Alderman Beckford's house, a typical townhouse of three bays, had been built in 1680. The Alderman lived here from 1751, and tax returns indicate that he did little to improve the property. Horace Walpole recorded that when John Wilkes, the journalist, politician, and "lover of liberty," was released from prison in April 1770, the Beckford residence "was embroidered with 'Liberty', in white letters three feet high. Luckily the evening was very wet, & not a mouse stirred."[21] It was here that the Alderman died on June 21, 1770, a few weeks after delivering his celebrated harangue, when presenting a petition to George III.

Alderman Beckford's house has not survived. It was replaced by an office block in 1913/14. One house in the square with a Beckford family connection, however, still stands. A few doors away, at 1 Greek Street, on the southeast corner of the square, is the house where Alderman Beckford's brother Richard resided from 1751 until his death two years later.[22] The house, containing fine interiors and rich plaster-work created for Richard Beckford, gives an indication of the wealth and standards of the family. The building, which since 1861 has belonged to The House of Saint Barnabas, a charity for homeless women, is a remarkable survival in an area of London that has seen so many changes over the last two centuries.

WIMPOLE STREET

In 1771, shortly after Alderman Beckford's death, his widow is listed as the occupant of 12 Wimpole Street, a house on the Cavendish/Harley estate about three-quarters of a mile northwest of Soho Square. Mrs. Beckford's house, dating from about 1770, was on the eastern side of the street in the block between Wigmore Street in the south and Queen Ann Street in the north. The street was a smart residential address, and her house, which she occupied until 1782, was one of the most valu-able properties. Occupants of the street in the 1780s included the Earl of Aberdeen (No. 4). Sir John Napier (No. 90), Sir Justinian Isham, Bt. (No. 11), Lady Williams Wynn (No. 14), and Sir Philip Gibbs, Bt. (No. 18). It was here, in his mother's house, that the young Beckford first met Dr. John Lettice who was to be his own tutor and eventually serve in the same capacity to his daughters. From this house, when in London, Beckford would as a young man go off to dancing, fencing, and riding lessons. Cyrus Redding recorded that when in London, Beckford had lessons from a French language tutor two or three evenings a week.

WEST END HOUSE

Although only about three miles from the center of London, West Hampstead in the late eighteenth century was still a small hamlet, a place with a few cottages and several more-substantial houses owned by householders of independent means. One such property was West End House, a house occupied by members of the Beckford family from 1775 to 1812, primarily by Beckford's mother, until her death here on July 22, 1798, and his daughters.[23]

The property was purchased in 1775, presumably on behalf of the Beckfords, by Thomas Wildman, the Beckford family's solicitor. The value of the house as recorded in tax returns increased consider-ably and suddenly in 1796, suggesting that substantial alterations or rebuilding was made around this date, possibly to provide additional accommodation for Beckford's daughters. Through additional pur-chases, the extent of the estate increased to about twenty acres. The house was approached by a carriage drive with a pair of lodges on West End Lane. An engraving made around 1858 (fig. 14-2) shows the side of the house, where blind arcading articulates the external walls of a single-story wing, possibly for servants. It continued on a high "covered way," possibly an elaborate porte cochere. A plan of the house made in the 1870s, indicates a fairly conventional five-bay Georgian villa, the main facade having a central doorway with two windows on either side.[24] One can assume that the house would have received some Beckfordian embellishments, but there is little information about its

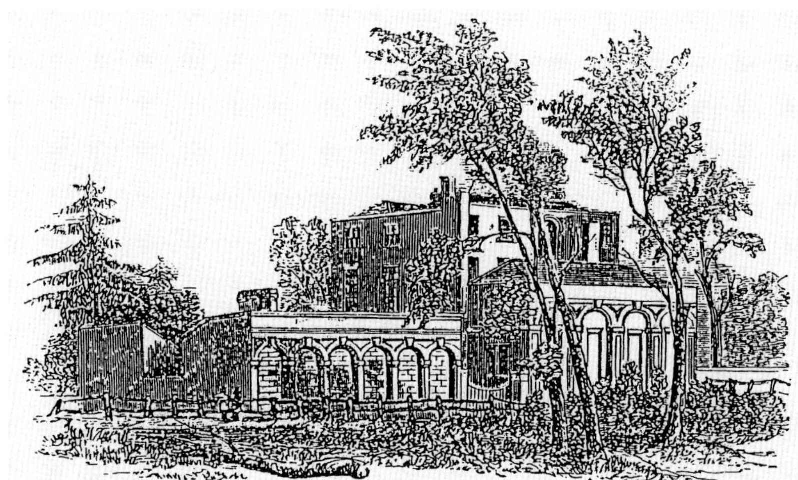

Fig. 14-2. "West End House," ca. 1858. Wood engraving. Camden Local Studies Archive

interior or contents. Mrs. Beckford, in her will, makes reference to "two vases in my best room," bequeathing them to her son who had always admired them; the house itself was left to Margaret Beckford, her eldest granddaughter.

In June 1781, Beckford wrote from West End to the first Lady Hamilton shortly after returning from his first Grand Tour. His mind was still filled with thoughts of his travels, and he was out of love with London: "I sit in a tent with my eyes half closed and fancy I discover your labyrinth in the base of Vesuvius." He longed to be back in Italy, but "I find myself so near that ugly word 'London'!"[25] Later, he seems to have used the house from his mother's death until 1811, when his elder daughter, Margaret, eloped with Col. James Orde, a soldier who was, in Beckford's eyes, totally unsuitable. On the occasion when Sir William and Lady Hamilton were staying at his house in Grosvenor Square Beckford retreated to West End.[26]

The house was lived in from 1838 to 1841 by Beckford's son-in-law, and there are recollections of Queen Victoria making visits there to General Orde and his second wife. The property was sold by Beckford's granddaughter Margaret Julia Orde in 1842. Later, after being used as a Girls Laundry School, the property was purchased by the Midland Railway Company, who laid out a railway line in front of it. The house was demolished in 1871.

PORTMAN SQUARE

In 1783, after completing his second Grand Tour, William Beckford leased his first independent London house, 9 Portman Square. This house was part of a new and fashionable development on the northern edge of London, on land belonging to the Portman family. Two houses in the square, Montagu and Home, were particularly celebrated. The first was built by Athenian Stuart for Mrs. Elizabeth Montagu, the famous

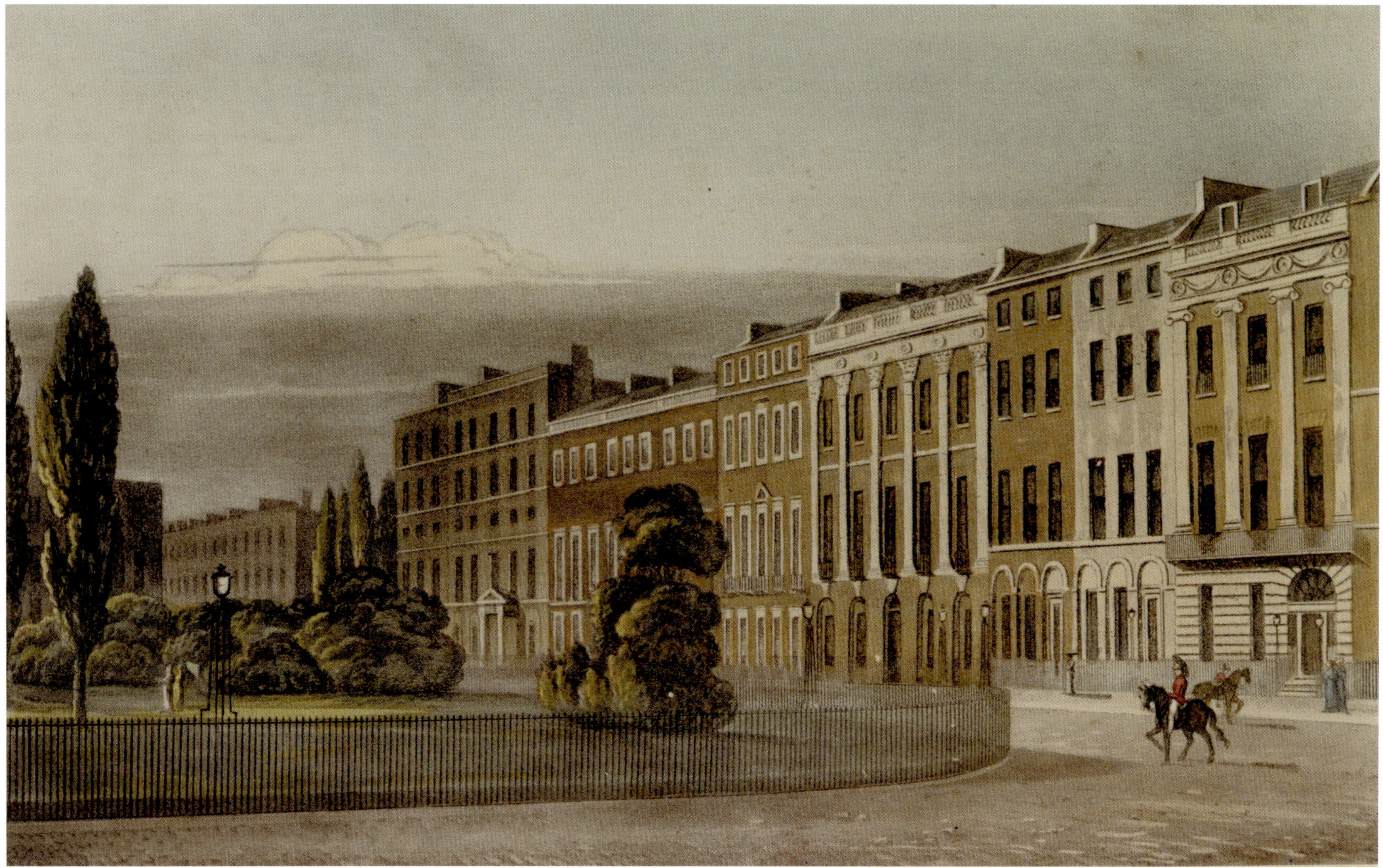

Fig. 14-3. George (or Thomas Hosmer) Shepherd. *Portman Square, North Side*, 1813. Aquatint. Beckford's House, No. 9, is the first house on the right. Westminster City Archives.

bluestocking, writer, and leading hostess. At No. 20, on the north side, was the palatial town mansion built in 1773–77 by Robert Adam for Elizabeth, Countess of Home, whose fortune, like Beckford's, came from sugar plantations. Home House with its delicate stucco decoration, circular staircase hall, and Etruscan room remains one of London's finest eighteenth-century interiors.[27]

Beckford's house (fig. 14-3), also on the north side, had been built in 1777 with a lease being granted in the following July to Beckford's kinsman the Honorable Charles Greville, son of the Earl of Warwick. (Greville is best remembered for passing on his mistress Emma to his uncle Sir William Hamilton, the envoy and antiquary.[28]) The house had an elaborate facade with rustic masonry on the ground floor and four Ionic pilasters below a garlanded frieze. Beckford, who was always happiest when in the country, delighted in the fact that the house had views over open countryside. He wrote in 1783: "Don't you remember telling me last year how much you were pleased with Charles Greville's house, its finely proportioned rooms, with their low

Grecian chimney pieces formed of real antique friezes and of the unlimited view it commands over green fields, Harrow in the one side, Hampstead on the other; well, I have purchased this smiling, well ventilated abode and, the more I examine it, the better I am contented with my bargain. With a few of Wyatt's touches, a bust here and a vase there, it will become thoroughly classical."[29]

The arrival of Beckford's "caravans from Fonthill laden with furniture and superfluities of all kinds" caused a stir in the neighborhood and brought Beckford to the attention of the square's most celebrated residents. He accepted an invitation from the Countess of Home, "known amongst all the Irish chairmen and riff-raff of the metropolis by the name, style, and title of the Queen of Hell. Aware of my musical propensities she determined to celebrate my accession to Portman Square by a sumptuous diner and a concert of equal magnificence . . . . last evening it took place and you never beheld so splendidly heterogeneous a repast as the dinner nor ever heard such a confounded jumble of good and bad Music—such a charivari in fact

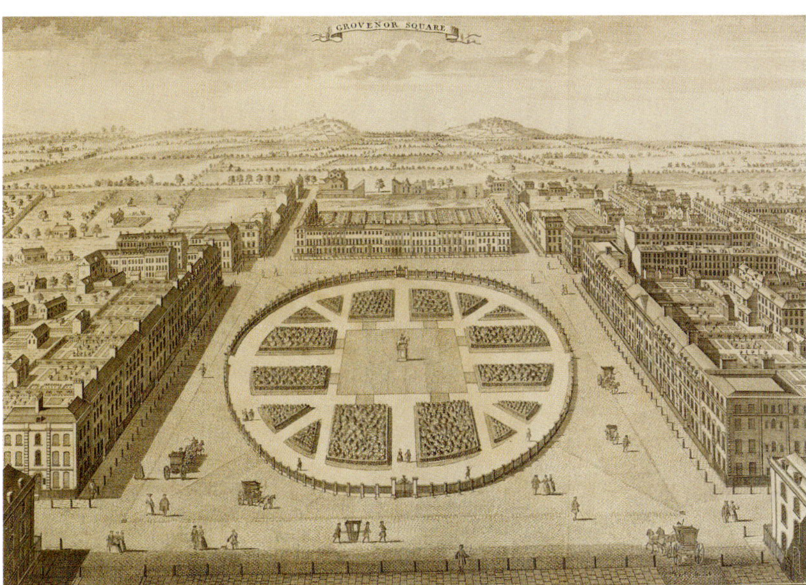

Fig. 14-4. Sutton Nicholls. *Grosvenor Square*, ca. 1731. Engraving. Westminster City Archives.

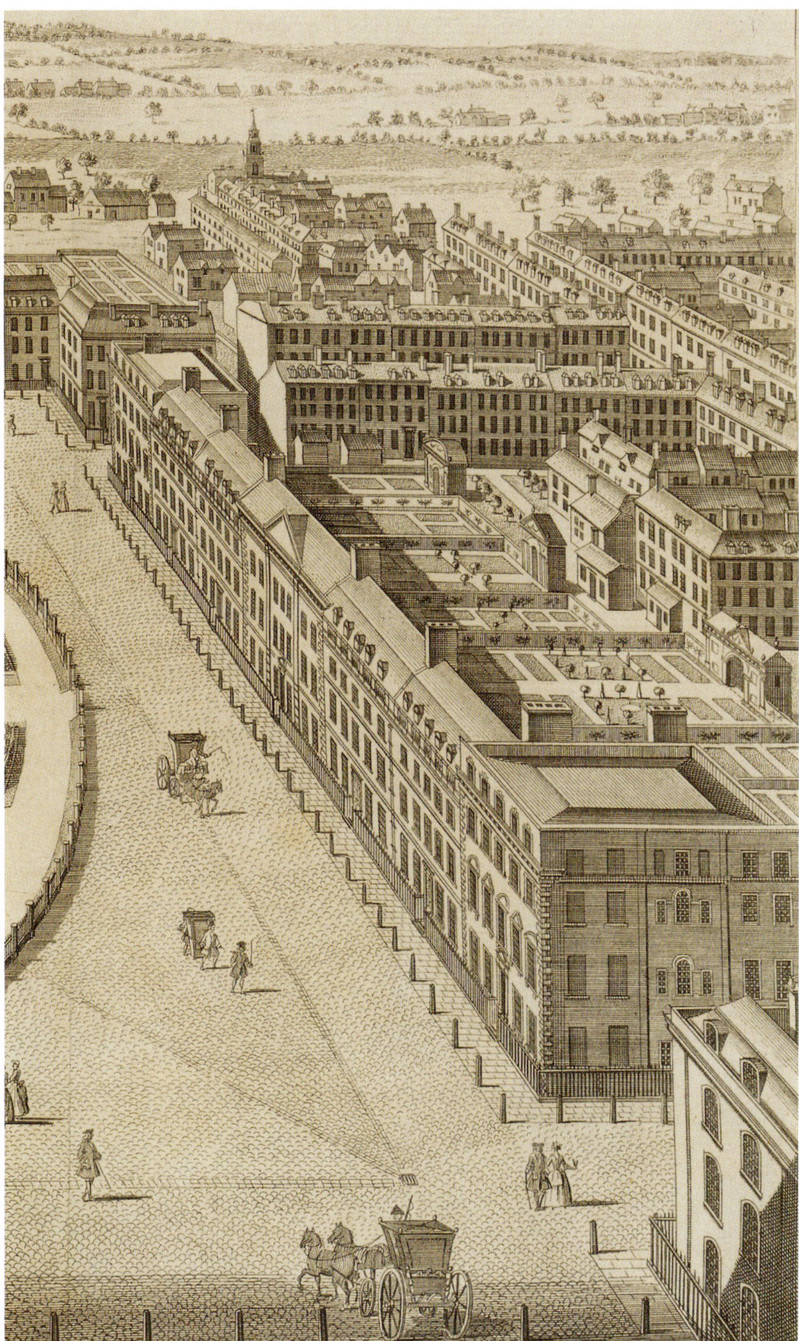

Fig. 14-5. The east side of Grosvenor Square (detail of fig. 14-4). Beckford's house, No. 2, is the second house from the corner; the rear gardens and stables are visible. Westminster City Archives.

as the concert." Mrs. Montagu was also seeking Beckford's company: she "desires me to name a day for meeting at dinner certain *Savii grandi* whom she promises to introduce to me."[30]

Other residents of the square included the Earl of Arundel, the Earl of Tankerville, Viscount Middleton, and the Dowager Countess of Egmont. Portman Square was a suitable address for a young man passing as "England's wealthiest son," determined to find a place among fashionable and aristocratic society.[31] The house may well have been chosen as a residence befitting married status, for on May 5, 1783, Beckford was married to Lady Margaret Gordon. A long honeymoon and the Powderham scandal, however, meant that he was not to enjoy his grand townhouse for long. In the last years of his life, Beckford would return to Portman Square to visit the town residence of his son-in-law and daughter, the Duke and Duchess of Hamilton. Beckford's own house was demolished in 1965.

Grosvenor Square

Beckford was abroad for much of the period 1785–95, but in 1796 he took possession of a new London residence. His house was in Grosvenor Square, the centerpiece of the Grosvenor Estate.[32] The square (fig. 14-4), developed between 1725 and 1731, had always attracted residents of a high social status. For four years Beckford rented No. 2, on the east side of the square, from Robert Scott, city merchant and Member of Parliament. The house had five bays with the entrance set between two pairs of windows (fig. 14-5). There were fine interiors; an early occupant, Sir Edward Turner of Ambrosden, wrote to Sanderson Miller, in 1743: "I have cornices which would draw your eyes out of their sockets."[33] Later occupants give an indication of the status of the house; these included the "Welsh Maecenas" Sir Watkin Williams Wynn, who lived here from 1768 to 1774, before moving to his new house designed by Robert Adam at 20 Saint James's Square, and the Marquess of Carmarthen, later fifth Duke of Leeds, from 1774 to 1795.

It was to this house in 1799 that the young J. M. W. Turner, as well as other artists and dilettanti, flocked to see Beckford's latest acquisition: two paintings by Claude Lorraine, known as the Altieri Claudes after the Roman princes who commissioned them. The experience of

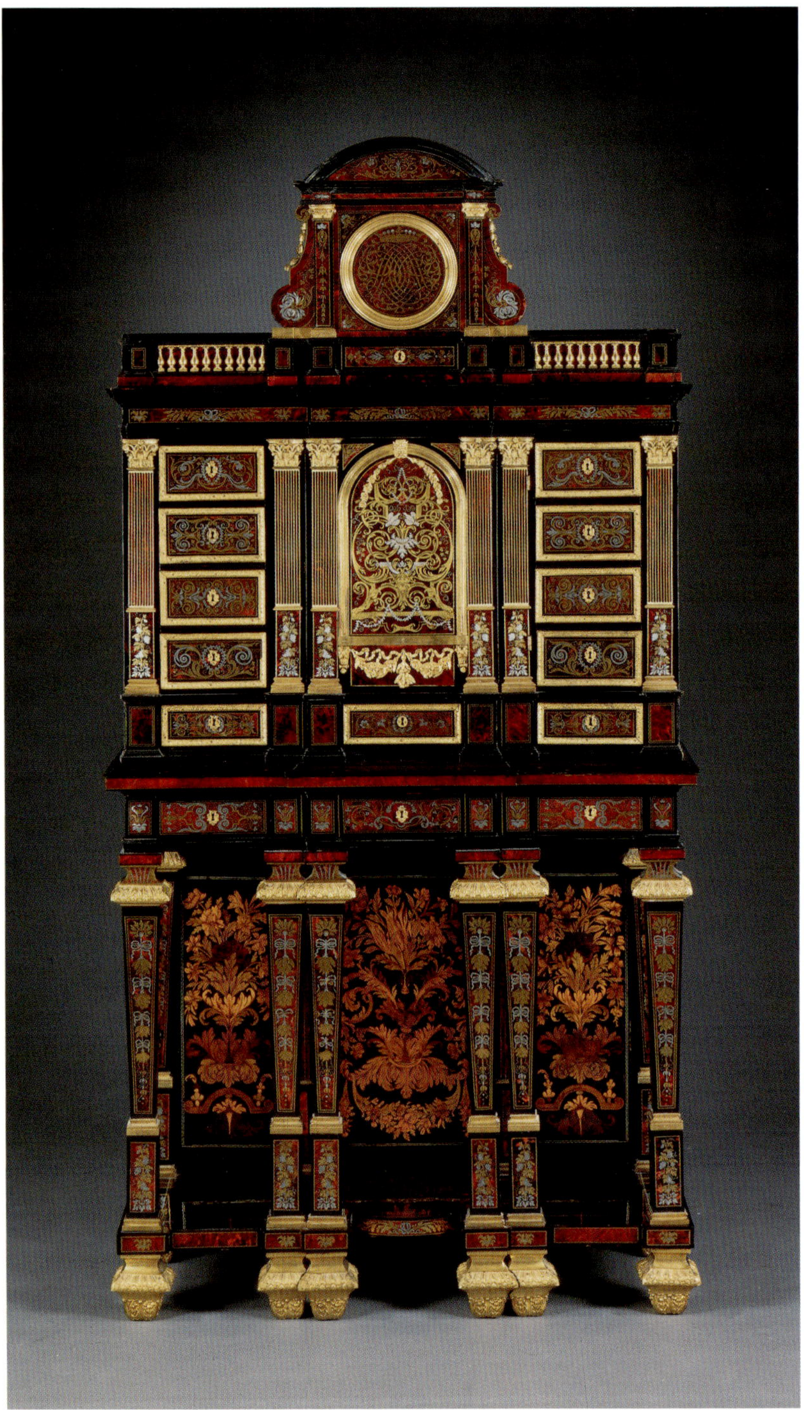

Fig. 14-6. Boulle cabinet-on-stand, ca. 1690. Inlaid ebony, tortoiseshell and marquetry, gilt bronze, pewter, and brass. Private collection.

seeing the Claudes had a profound effect on Turner, who was "both pleased & unhappy" as the painting "seemed beyond his power of imitation."[34] Beckford put his house at the disposal of Sir William and Lady (Emma) Hamilton in November 1800, when they returned to England upon Sir William's retirement as British envoy to Naples. From Grosvenor Square, the Hamiltons accompanied by Lord Nelson,

by then the hero of the Nile, set out for the celebrated Christmas visit to Fonthill, the only grand occasion in the Abbey's troubled history. The Hamiltons stayed at Grosvenor Square until January 1801, when they moved to a house in Piccadilly. Beckford himself was to remain in the house for only a few months more after his guests' departure. The house itself was demolished in 1858.

UPPER HARLEY STREET

Harley Street is today synonymous with doctors, but the profession's association with this area of London only commenced in the mid-nineteenth century; before then it was a fashionable residential street constructed in the 1750s as part of the Harley estate's development north of Oxford Street. On the east side of this long street, which runs north to south across the estate, William Beckford rented 6 Upper Harley Street (now 100 Harley Street) from 1811 until September 1817.

Beckford's house was typical of many London townhouses of the period: three bays wide, entered through a doorway framed with Coade stone rustication, and a keystone decorated with a classical female head.[35] Although the house externally may have appeared identical to many of its neighbors, the interior bore all the hallmarks of Beckford's very individualistic taste using his favored decorative features, such as fabric hangings across the full width of certain walls and mirrors placed to enhance the light and to reflect objects. As always, furniture and objects were of the finest quality.[36]

The entrance hall was furnished in a fairly conventional way, with a pair of solid mahogany benches of "handsome design—6 feet long" and an old blue and gold Japanese jar and cover, 36 inches high. Beckford appears to have introduced wooden partitions to separate the inner hall. On the ground and first floors were five main reception rooms: the principal bow room, back and front drawing rooms, and back and front dining rooms. The main colors used throughout the house were Beckford's favorite crimson and scarlet. In the front dining room and front drawing room, walls were covered with curtains extending across the width of the walls, a scheme Beckford was to use later in Bath. Beckford was not, however, unique in using fabric in this way, for it had been feature, as early as 1807, in Thomas Hope's house in Duchess Street.[37] Also, in the front drawing room he made much use of pier glasses to give an added sense of space and illusion. The bow room differed from Beckford's usual color scheme by having festoon window curtains of "remarkably strong & richly flowered green silk damask."[38] There were French curtains of striped clay-colored cloth, with inner French curtains of scarlet moreen. The twelve chairs in imitation satinwood and ebony with cane seats had loose stuffed cushions covered in yellow cloth. Overall the room possessed a vaguely Chinoiserie atmosphere, with a screen with Chinese figures and framed Chinese relief carvings.

The collection of plate gives an indication of the air of luxury exuded by Beckford's establishment.[39] For dining there were dozens of silver-gilt plates with oak-wreath edges; a grand dessert plateau almost twelve feet in length, consisting of seven square mirrors, semicircular ends, with silver-gilt border and feet; and for the center of the table, four elegant, tall candelabra each with three branches. Also a pair of tazza in ormolu with rams' heads and glass shades designed by Jean-Guillaume Moitte and executed by Henri Auguste.[40] There were agate cups, much porcelain, and many objets d'art. Useful as well as decorative was an ormolu letter weight, the stem of which was formed "of a group of boys on a foot of cupids sporting on the waters."[41]

Throughout his life Beckford was very conscious of the dramatic effects of lighting.[42] At Harley Street, the scarlet fabrics of the front drawing room were brought to life by two pairs of sumptuous candalabra reflected in the room's pier glasses. One pair was in the form of bronze winged figures of Apollo and Diana, bearing torches of ormolu for eight lights, each standing on a hemisphere of gold upon pedestals of serpentine.[43] The other of silver-gilt, designed by Moitte and executed by Auguste, was of five branches, each holding four lights, the stems embraced with foliage and the branches of foliage and serpents.[44]

The house contained furniture of the highest quality and was particularly rich in cabinets, wonderful containers for Beckford's treasury of precious objects. There were cabinets of Persian ebony, Japan lacquer, and a superb Louis XIV Boulle cabinet-on-strand (fig. 14-6) which was later owned by George Watson Taylor, another great collector of the Regency period.[45] Smaller pieces included a Boulle and tortoiseshell jewel case, and a nine-drawer cabinet of lacquer, "from bagatelle, a villa of the Comte d'Artois nr Paris."[46] Pictures included Lodovico Carracci's *Sibylla Lybica* (formerly in the Lansdowne Collection, present location unknown), Salvator Rosa's *Job and his Friends* (now in the Uffizi, Florence) and works attributed to Van Leyden, Rubens, Breughel, and Benjamin West.[47] There were also landscape views of Wiltshire by J. M. W. Turner and Indian scenes by William and Thomas Daniell.

In addition to having a passion for pictures, Beckford considered himself an accomplished musician, expecting to find a piano for his use in every house he occupied, however short the stay. The Harley Street house had a Broadwood grand pianoforte with additional keys and forty-two pedals. One can imagine Beckford and Gregorio Franchi playing on this instrument. Britton wrote that Beckford could play well but was far surpassed by Franchi "whose execution was so remarkably fine that his master's seemed flat and insipid in comparison."[48]

The house had extensive accommodations for servants, including a steward's hall, footman's room, cook's bedroom, and confectioner's room. Modern convenience was catered for by the "highly polished" register stoves in the front and back drawing rooms.

A permanent London house burdened Beckford's increasingly constrained finances brought about by a declining income from his West Indian estates and general economic difficulties in the United Kingdom. As early as 1815, Beckford asked Franchi whether White, Beckford's solicitor, counseled abandoning "the London house or Fonthill Abbey."[49] In May 1817 Christie's sold the main contents of the townhouse including furniture, plate, porcelain, and pictures

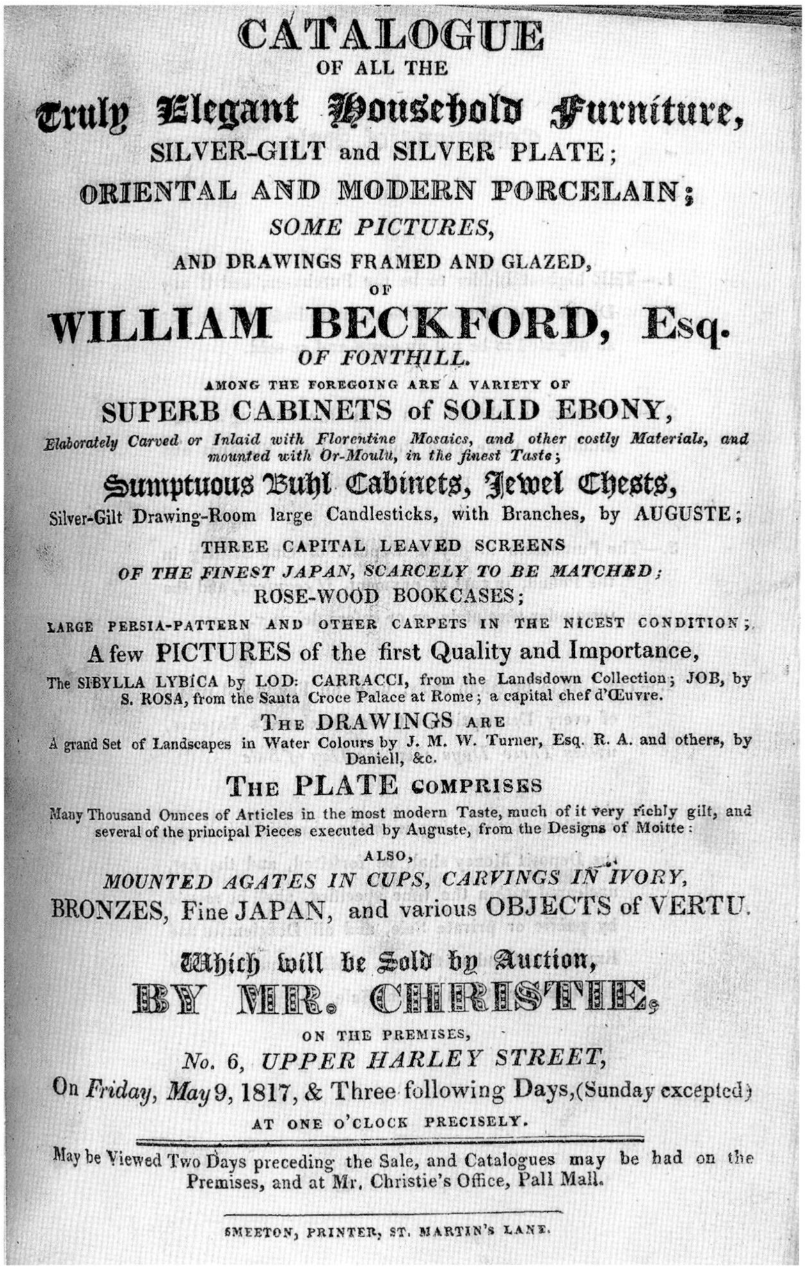

CATALOGUE

OF ALL THE

Truly Elegant Household Furniture,

SILVER-GILT and SILVER PLATE;

ORIENTAL AND MODERN PORCELAIN;

SOME PICTURES,

AND DRAWINGS FRAMED AND GLAZED,

OF

WILLIAM BECKFORD, Esq.

OF FONTHILL.

AMONG THE FOREGOING ARE A VARIETY OF

SUPERB CABINETS of SOLID EBONY,

Elaborately Carved or Inlaid with Florentine Mosaics, and other costly Materials, and mounted with Or-Moulu, in the finest Taste;

Sumptuous Buhl Cabinets, Jewel Chests,

Silver-Gilt Drawing-Room large Candlesticks, with Branches, by AUGUSTE;

THREE CAPITAL LEAVED SCREENS

OF THE FINEST JAPAN, SCARCELY TO BE MATCHED;

ROSE-WOOD BOOKCASES;

LARGE PERSIA-PATTERN AND OTHER CARPETS IN THE NICEST CONDITION;

A few PICTURES of the first Quality and Importance,

The SIBYLLA LYBICA by LOD: CARRACCI, from the Landsdown Collection; JOB, by S. ROSA, from the Santa Croce Palace at Rome; a capital chef d'Œuvre.

THE DRAWINGS ARE

A grand Set of Landscapes in Water Colours by J. M. W. Turner, Esq. R. A. and others, by Daniell, &c.

THE PLATE COMPRISES

Many Thousand Ounces of Articles in the most modern Taste, much of it very richly gilt, and several of the principal Pieces executed by Auguste, from the Designs of Moitte:

ALSO,

MOUNTED AGATES IN CUPS, CARVINGS IN IVORY,

BRONZES, Fine JAPAN, and various OBJECTS of VERTU.

Which will be Sold by Auction,

BY MR. CHRISTIE,

ON THE PREMISES,

No. 6, UPPER HARLEY STREET,

On *Friday, May 9, 1817,* & Three following Days, (Sunday excepted) AT ONE O'CLOCK PRECISELY.

May be Viewed Two Days preceding the Sale, and Catalogues may be had on the Premises, and at Mr. Christie's Office, Pall Mall.

SMEETON, PRINTER, ST. MARTIN'S LANE.

Fig. 14-7. Title page of the Christie's catalogue issued for the sale of the contents of Beckford's Upper Harley Street house in 1817. Courtesy of Christie's Archives.

(fig. 14-7).[50] Beckford remained at Fonthill during the view and sale, writing to Franchi: "A thousand times a day I chafe at being chained down here without having had the pleasure of seeing what so many unworthy idiots have seen—the spectacle of the house arranged by you . . . my dear Gregory, how difficult and how long is the path of true taste."[51] The Prince Regent and other members of the royal family attended a private viewing on the evening before the sale. General household goods were sold on the final day of the sale.[52] The penultimate lot reflected two of Beckford's other passions, dogs and flowers— "2 deal dog kennels, sundry flower pots."[53] The proceeds of the four days of sales netted £7,304. 8s. 2d.

Today, the house, like so many in the street, has been taken over by the medical profession.

Gloucester Place

In the 1750s a new thoroughfare was created from Paddington to Islington to provided easier access from Middlesex to Essex. The road, known then as New Road, partly formed the south boundary of Regent's Park, and would eventually be renamed as Marylebone Road. In early 1823 Beckford acquired a new London house in Gloucester Place, a development on the northern side of New Road. His financial situation had improved following the sale of Fonthill Abbey in the previous year, which prompted him to remark: "I am rid of the Holy Sepulchre . . . For twenty years I have not found my self so rich, so independent or so tranquil."[54] He could once more afford the luxury of a London residence.

Various objections were raised to the construction of the New Road and consequently a clause in the Parliamentary Bill stipulated that no buildings were to be erected within 50 feet of the road itself. Buildings were set back with gardens between the houses and the road. Marylebone Road is today a traffic-clogged artery, but in the early nineteenth century, the gardens gave "a pleasing and picturesque appearance." Beckford's house, 23 Gloucester Place, was the end house in a block of thirteen, with a narrow space or alley dividing it from the next group of six houses to the east. No image of Beckford's terrace has survived, but the next group to the east, Allsop's Buildings, was of four-story houses, two bays wide, with stucco decoration at ground floor level on alternate houses. Beckford's house was probably of similar format.

At the end of 1830 Beckford wrote: "Bad as today may appear, tomorrow promises to be still worse. I shall therefore lose no time in disposing of my house in the New Road."[55] A few months later, Beckford was virtually overwhelmed by the innumerable parcels of books and chattels arriving in Bath from Gloucester Place. Beckford described them as being "as bad as the Nightmare. They quite oppress me."[56] He finally left Gloucester Place in April 1831.

As Beckford rode along the New Road he would have passed the various churches that had been built in the preceding two decades; all exhibited to some degree the then current fashion for neoclassicism. One is tempted to surmise whether the initial inspiration for the lantern of Lansdown Tower came from the experience of seeing the tower of Saint Pancras New Church (see fig. 14-1), rather than from the engravings in his copy of Stuart and Revett's *Antiquities of Athens*. Beckford would have been particularly interested in this church with its caryatids of terracotta, modeled by Rossi, the sculptor, who had made the statue of Saint Anthony which Beckford had at Fonthill and took with him to Bath.

Gloucester Place was demolished in the early 1890s when the Great Central Railway arrived in London, sweeping away some 70 acres of residential property and gardens belonging to the Portman Estate. The Great Central Hotel, today the Landmark Hotel, occupied part of the site on which Gloucester Place once stood.

Park Street

Beckford's final London residence was 127 Park Street, situated on the Grosvenor Estate in a street that runs parallel to Park Lane. The street was developed between the 1720s and 1750s and had a mixture of social classes: some of the houses toward the north were small, often occupied by tradesmen; those toward the south, where Beckford's house was situated, were larger and on the western side, like Beckford's, had gardens looking towards Hyde Park. Residents of houses at the south end of Park Street included Lady Lord (No. 123), Lady Julia Howard (No. 124), Lord Methuen (No. 128), and Sir Adolphus Dalrymple (No. 129).

Throughout the summer of 1832, Beckford debated the possibility of a visit to London. There were various difficulties, however; Farratt, his steward, was unwell, so it might be necessary to stay in an hotel. As the year advanced, however, he was still making plans: "I bring no cook and only 3 attendants."[57] Finally, he rented the house at 129 Park Street, for the three winter months, from Mrs Pettiward (later Lady Hotham). Farratt was sent in advance to ensure that everything was in order. Beckford enquired of George Clarke, his London bookseller, about the piano: "As I cannot endear [sic] an indifferent piano forte, I wish to know what sort of instrument the Park St[reet] lady is so kind to leave open for it. Should it not be a superior one, I must supply its place with a better. I can tolerate nothing inferior in this line."[58] He was also concerned about the state of the bed and ordered his own to be sent up from Bath.

Beckford, despite certain misgivings (in typically Beckfordian manner many letters were addressed from "Cesspool House"), must have found the house convenient, for directories and other records show Beckford as the occupant of this house throughout the period 1835 to 1841. A financial statement prepared by Beckford's solicitor shows that he was paying £350 a year rent for the house in 1839/40.[59]

It was in this house on a gloomy February day that Beckford read from the manuscript of *The Episodes of Vathek* to Cyrus Redding: "He sat back from the window at least two thirds of the depth of the room. The light was indifferent, and yet with no difficulty he read . . . . He stopped but rarely, to make remarks upon particular passages. He was then, I believe seventy-eight years old, yet wore no spectacles and read a full hour and a half. He pronounced French with the old court accent."[60]

In March 1840 Beckford became fully determined to relinquish the property. He warned Edmund English that as a result of his decision there would be an inundation of pictures arriving at Lansdown Crescent, his Bath residence. One can only assume that Beckford, through the introduction of pictures and other objects, had turned Mrs. Pettiward's house into an interior reflecting his own taste. His decision to give up the London house, though no doubt due to financial constraints, also resulted from the recognition that he was coming to the end of his life, a reflection of Samuel Johnson's much quoted epigram: "When a man is tired of London, he is tired of life; for there is in London all that life can afford."

Beckford's house was later occupied by Viscount Casterleagh, who became fourth Marquess of Londonderry (resident, 1842–46), Sir John Lowther (resident, 1847–66), and Sir Charles Lowther (resident, 1866–69). The block that included Beckford's house was demolished, and Aldford House built in the 1890s for Alfred Beit the South African magnate. This in turn was replaced by Aldford House, a block of apartments and offices, in 1931–32.

For Beckford in his final decades, London may well have been a place containing ghosts from the past, including memories of his father, that larger-than-life Alderman and Lord Mayor, as well as recollections of the young Mozart and music lessons—fact or fiction—with the composer. Long past were the half-days and holidays spent entertaining the schoolboy William Courtenay and his Hamilton cousins, and the months of Beckford's own glittering social success in Portman Square. For Beckford the collector, however, the shelves and drawers of the dealers in prints and books, the rare acquisitions unearthed by his agents, the rooms of Mr. Christie in Pall Mall, and the picture dealers of the capital offered endless temptation. To someone whose enthusiasm for adding to his collections—even if it was only some "lost" Fonthill book—never dimmed with the passing years. The thrill of the collector's chase with its various ritualistic stages: expectation, pursuit, and finally possession—was a sport to banish ghosts, however old.

In the later years of his life Beckford is said to have often ridden up the Edgware Road to West End House: "to pull up his horse and gaze upon the old family habitation for some time, as if lost in thought or travelling back to bygone times."[61] One wonders if on his London rides he ever stopped or paid any attention to Saint John's Wood Chapel and its burial ground. Inside the chapel, then patronized by a large number of Anglo-Indians, is the memorial, complete with coat-of-arms and a profile portrait to "John Farquhar Esquire of Fonthill Abby[sic] in the County of Wilts and of this parish." The East Indian gunpowder merchant, who had purchased Beckford's Wiltshire estate, died in July 1826, seven months after the Abbey's tower had so gracefully collapsed. Laid to rest in much simpler style, in the burial ground itself, was Gregorio Franchi who died in 1828.[62] In recent years many monuments have been removed, but Franchi's grave survives in a small oasis designated as a nature reserve by the local council. The stone's inscription has all but vanished but, when the light is good, it is possible to guess at the wording: "Chevalier Gregorio Franchi, Portuguese Order of Christ," final monument to Beckford's greatest friend. "A few words will suffice, my beloved Gregory," Beckford had once written, "to assure you that my heart beats in perfect union with yours."[63] A mercurial character, Franchi like Beckford, was equally devoted to the pursuit of all that was rare and precious.

Acknowledgments: Dedicated to the memory of James Brister. My work owes much to the resources of the City of Westminster Archives Centre. I am also very grateful to Lynda McLeod, Librarian of Christie's, London.—SB

1. For the architectural development of Georgian London and the great estates see John Summerson, *Georgian London*, 3d ed. (London: Barrie and Jenkins, 1978).

2. Cyrus Redding, *Memoirs of William Beckford of Fonthill* (London: C. J. Skeet, 1859): 299.

3. He represented Wells (1784–90) and Hindon (1790–December 1794; and 1806–20). For his political career see R. G. Thorne, *The House of Commons 1790–1820: Members A–F* (London: Secker & Warburg, 1986): 170–71.

4. On one visit to the opera in June 1834, Beckford came face to face with Benjamin Disraeli who noted in his diary, "Conversation of three hours; very bitter and *malin,* but full of warm feelings for the worthy," quoted in Brian Fothergill, *Beckford of Fonthill* (London: Faber & Faber, 1979): 350.

5. See Richard Rush, *Memoranda of a Residence at the Court of London* (Philadelphia: Key and Biddle, 1833).

6. *Life at Fonthill, 1807–1822 with Interludes in Paris and London, from the Correspondence of William Beckford,* ed. Boyd Alexander (London: Rupert Hart-Davis, 1957): 269.

7. Louis Brunet, wine and brandy merchant, opened his hotel in 1800. It was taken over by Francis Jaunay in 1819.

8. Alexander, *Life at Fonthill* (1957): 265–302.

9. Ibid., p. 301.

10. Ibid., p. 279.

11. Ibid., p. 296.

12. Ibid., p. 301.

13. Ibid., p. 302.

14. Ibid., p. 286.

15. Lord Holland on one occasion in the 1830s observed Beckford returning to his house with a nosegay (Notebook of J. Mitford, Add MSS 32566, fol. 38, British Library).

16. W. P. Frith, *My Autobiography and Reminiscences* (London, 1888): 2, 131–32.

17. Redding, *Memoirs* (1859): 2, 392.

18. In this section I describe the main houses associated with William Beckford in London. Various writers have linked his name with other London properties, but his stay in these was usually short, or in some cases (such as 12 Manchester Square) is based on misunderstanding. In relation to Soho Square, Guy Chapman and Boyd Alexander state that Beckford was born here, while Cyrus Reading and J. W. Oliver give Fonthill as the birthplace.

19. Beckford to Britton, 31 December 1840, Wiltshire Archaeological and Natural History Society, Devizes.

20. William Beckford, *The Journal of William Beckford in Portugal and Spain 1787–1788*, ed. Boyd Alexander (London: Rupert Hart-Davis, 1954): 184.

21. Horace Walpole, *The Yale Edition of Horace Walpole's Correspondence,* ed. W. S Lewis, vol. 23 (London and New Haven, Yale University Press, 1967): 205.

22. See John Cornforth, "The House of St. Barnabas in Soho: 1 Greek Street, London W1," *Country Life* 130 (6 July 1961): 18–21.

23. See Dick Weindling, "West End House and the Beckford Scandal," *Camden History Review* 20 (1996): 19–23.

24. West End House, ground floor plan, London Borough of Camden Local History Collection.

25. Lewis Melville, *Life and Letters of William Beckford of Fonthill* (London; William Heinemann, 1910): 114.

26. Farington records the painter Benjamin West dining with Beckford here in 1804.

27. Home House is now a private club.

28. See Brian Fothergill, *Sir William Hamilton: Envoy Extraordinary* (London: Faber and Faber, 1969): passim.

29. Quoted by J. W. Oliver, *The Life of William Beckford* (London; Oxford University Press, 1932): 106.

30. Ibid.

31. Byron referred to Beckford as "England's wealthiest son"(*Childe Harold,* Canto I, Stanza 22). Beckford later commented: "We know what swarms of flatterers a grand reputation for riches has always engendered, and, as at this period I had the honour of passing for 'England's wealthiest son', the exaggerated praise I received may be easily accounted for" (quoted in Boyd Alexander, *England's Wealthiest Son* [London: Centaur Press, 1962], title-page).

32. For Grosvenor Square see F. H. W. Sheppard, *Grosvenor Estate in Mayfair: Part II,* Survey of London Series (London: University of London, 1980); and A. I. Dasent, *A History of Grosvenor Square* (London: Macmillan, 1935).

33. L. Dickens and M. Stanton, eds., *An Eighteenth Century Correspondence* (London, 1910): 93

34. Joseph Farington, *The Farington Diary,* ed. James Greig, vol. 2 (London: Hutchinson, 1922): 270.

35. Coade stone is artificial (cast) stone made by Coade and Sealy in London in late eighteenth and early nineteenth century.

36. The description of the interior and its contents is based *A Catalogue of the Useful Household Furniture of William Beckford, Esq. of Fonthill at his Dwelling House, 6 Upper Harley Street . . .* sale catalogue, Christie's, London, 13 May 1817.

37. Beckford and Hope were acquaintances; at one stage the latter was making assiduous love to Beckford's daughter Susan in expectation of marriage. For illustrations of Hope's house see his *Household Furniture and Interior Decoration . . .* (London: Longman, Hurst, Rees and Orme, 1807); for Hope see David Watkin, Thomas Hope and the Neo-Classical Idea (London: John Murray, 1968).

38. *Catalogue of all the Truly Elegant Household Furniture, Silver-gilt and Silver Plate . . . of William Beckford, Esq. of Fonthil . . .* on the premises No. 6, Upper Harley Street . . . , Christie's, London, 10 May 1817, lot 3.

39. The first day of the Christie's sale (9 May) was devoted to plate, the sale of 133 lots produced £2643.os.8d. For Beckford's silver collections see Michael Snodin and Malcolm Baker, "William Beckford's Silver," parts 1 and 2, *Burlington Magazine* 122, no. 932 (1980): 735–48; no. 933 (1980): 820–34.

40. *Catalogue of . . . Elegant Household Furniture,* 10 May 1817, lot 50 (sold to Davies for £15).

41. Ibid., lot 58 (sold to Baldock for £8.12s).

42. Beckford's fascination with interior lighting and its theatrical potential dates back to the occasion when P. J. de Loutherbourg produced "strange, necromantic light" for the Christmas party given at Fonthill Splendens in 1781. Later, at Fonthill Abbey, silver-gilt or gold candlesticks were placed at regular intervals along the length of the long galleries. Candles were a great expense; in 1819 Beckford wrote, "the weekly expenses continue . . . £38 for wax candles." Alexander, *Life at Fonthill* (1957): 294.

43. *Catalogue of . . . Elegant Household Furniture,* 12 May 1817, lot. 50 (sold for £101.17s).

44. Ibid., lot 63 (sold for £120.15s); lot 63* (sold for £116.11s.).

45. For Watson Taylor see Edward Lennox-Boyd, *Masterpieces of English Furniture: The Gerstenfeld Collection* (London: Christie's Books, 1998): 148–61; and Hugh Roberts, "Quite Appropriate for Windsor Castle: George IV and George Watson Taylor," *Furniture History* 30 (2000): 115–37.

46. *Catalogue of . . . Elegant Household Furniture,* 12 May 1817, lot 77.

47. Some of the pictures may have been brought from Fonthill for the 1817 sale. Of twenty-two paintings sold on 12 May (lots 209–39), three were not Beckford's: Van Eyck (lot 20); L. Carracci, (lot 22), V. Staveren (lot 29), but the property of Mr Pittar.

48. John Britton, *The Auto-Biography*, (London: the author, 1850): part 1, 231.

49. Alexander, *Life at Fonthill* (1957): 189.

50. *Catalogue of . . . Elegant Household Furniture,* 9–13 May 1817. Included in the sale may have been some items belonging to Gregorio Franchi, as Christie's annotated copy has a 'F' against certain lots. Beckford was far from pleased with the catalogue: "a poor affair, my dear Gregory, a very poor affair . . . Anachronisms, vulgarity etc.; it stinks . . . it is disgusting for me to read these platitudes . . . in a catalogue where my name is so conspicuous' (Alexander, *Life at Fonthill* [1957]: 203).

51. Alexander, *Life at Fonthill* (1957): 204.

52. *Catalogue of . . . Useful Household Furniture . . .* , 13 May 1817, was issued separately.

53. Ibid., lot 114 (flower pots etc.).

54. Alexander, Life at Fonthill (1957): 340.

55. *The Consummate Collector: William Beckford's Letters to His Bookseller*, ed. Robert J. Gemmett (Wilby: Michael Russell, 2000): 47.

56. Ibid., p. 71.

57. Ibid., p. 264.

58. Ibid., p. 173.

59. MS Beckford c.30, fol. 161, Bodleian Library, Oxford.

60. Redding, *Memoirs* (1859): 2, 341.

61. From Cyrus Redding's manuscript, quoted in Alexander, *England's Wealthiest Son* (1969): 233.

62. Franchi died in August 1828; his burial was paid for by the Duchess of Hamilton, Beckford's daughter. See Boyd Alexander, *From Lisbon to Baker Street* (Lisbon: British Historical Society of Portugal): 1977.

63. Alexander, *Life at Fonthill* (1957): 54.

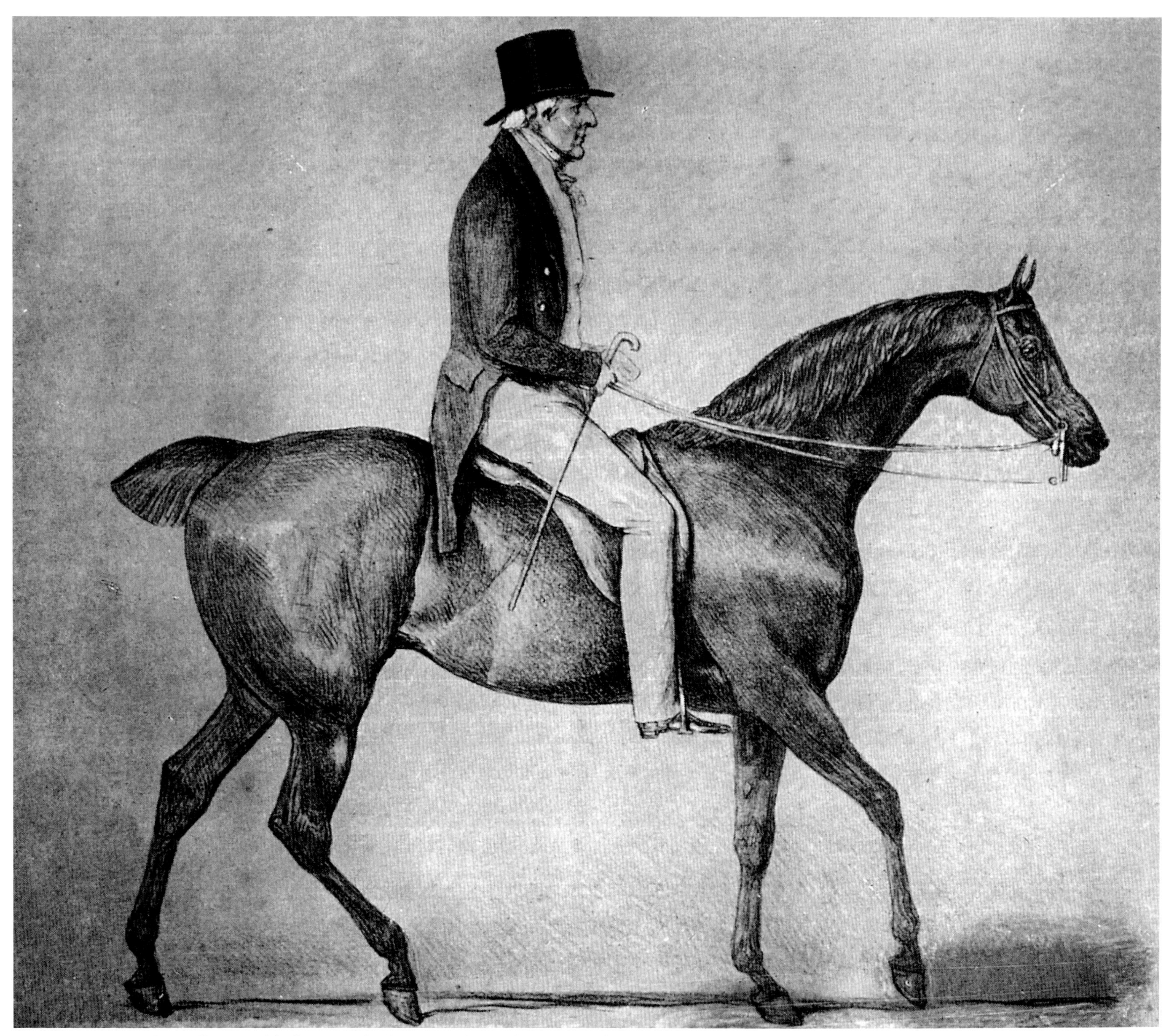

Fig. 15-1. John Doyle. *William Beckford on Horseback,* 1842. Lithograph. Private collection.

CHAPTER XV

THE BATH YEARS: 1822–44

SIDNEY BLACKMORE

> But Bath does not please me. After the great spectacle of the Abbey it seems to me incredibly dingy and the infamous old men and youths carried in chairs and mechanical carriages round the smoking bath horrify me— a horror not softened by the tender glances of certain old women clad in flounces supremely *à la mode,* who come and go eternally in this paradise of idlers and corpses.
>
> —William Beckford, September 22, 1817

In 1822, having disposed of Fonthill Abbey—"I am rid of the Holy Sepulchre"—William Beckford moved to Bath, the Somerset spa city some twenty-six miles from his Wiltshire estate.[1] At the beginning of the preceding century, Bath had been constrained within its medieval walls, but as the eighteenth century progressed, the city had expanded to become the most fashionable place outside London.[2] The nobility and upper-classes flocked to Bath to take the waters and participate in the social life. By the end of the century, however, Bath was in a period of transition. This is the city described by Jane Austen in the pages of *Persuasion,* a place where Sir Walter Elliot could live cheaply: "He might be important there at comparatively little expense." Bath had become a place of genteel retirement, where military officers on half-pay, retired clergy, members of the merchant classes, and spinsters of modest means could pass their final years.

SOCIAL LIFE

After leaving Fonthill, a place resonant for Beckford with nostalgic and romantic associations, it was inconceivable that he would purchase any other country house or estate. No other seat could live up to the fame of Fonthill, or its intimate associations with Beckford's taste, judgment, and reputation. A town residence offered the only option. Despite his earlier disparaging comments on Bath, he appreciated the advantages the city afforded: the expense of living there would not be as great, nor the temptations so many, as those in London. Beckford was following the example of his great-uncle Charles Hamilton, who had also moved to Bath for the last years of his life, after selling his estate in Surrey.[3] Bath's setting—in a bowl surrounded by green hills, giving the impression of the countryside intruding into the townscape—would also have appealed to the part of Beckford's temperament that delighted in the countryside and nature.

In his first months in Bath, Beckford lived at 66 Great Pulteney Street. He had, according to his first biographer, Cyrus Redding, expressed some interest in purchasing Prior Park, Ralph Allen's grand Palladian-style mansion then on the market, but he finally settled on a house in Lansdown Crescent, a more modest habitation on the other side of the city. In letters to Edmund English, who was negotiating on his behalf, Beckford declared that Lansdown was the only spot that interested him. In choosing this location, Beckford was retracing the steps of his great-uncle, who had made a garden behind his house in the Royal Crescent and later carried out other landscaping schemes on the lower slopes of Lansdown in the vicinity of Rock (now Hope) House. Beckford saw Hamilton's gardens and landscaping when he had visited "our holy uncle" in the summer of 1781. At that time he wrote to Lady Hamilton, first wife of his second cousin Sir William Hamilton, the envoy and antiquary, of the "everlasting C- H- who, it seems, is building a house to his garden and adding peach house to grape house and pinery to pinery on the slope of the crescent hill which is more than half embroidered with his vagaries."[4]

Many of Beckford's neighbors saw Bath as the place for their final years, where they could decline gently, but for Beckford the city was to be the setting for the third and final act in a life which was already legendary. Beckford's was a long life and his biographers have tended to concentrate on the Fonthill years and, whether from exhaustion or impatience, to rush through the final decades. The Bath years, however, can be seen as Beckford's Indian summer in which he created the extraordinary Lansdown Tower and published his acclaimed travel writings. By his death in 1844 he had fulfilled the prediction made so many years before: "I fear I shall never be so sapient, nor good for anything in this world, but composing old airs, building towers, forming gardens, collecting old Japan, and writing a journey to China or the moon."[5]

The enormous interest shown by the public, who flocked to view Fonthill Abbey in 1822 and 1823 during the sale views, coincided with Beckford's first years in Bath. In the city he could not hide from public gaze behind a wall twelve feet high, as he had done at Fonthill. In Bath he was a figure of celebrity and curiosity seen by residents as he rode through the city (fig. 15-1). He could enjoy the fame that the positive public exposure of the Abbey brought, although incidents from his past, in particular the Powderham scandal, occasionally returned to haunt him as when workmen building his tower, "suddenly struck work & insulted him by saying that they would not work for a ——r."[6] Gossip and scurrilous stories circulated about him: that his house was full of dwarfs, coins had to be washed before he would handle them, and that he had an income of one guinea a minute. In reality, despite the public perception, Beckford's life in Bath was one of fairly regular routine, as were the retirement days of other residents.

Beckford made one attempt to break from his usual routine, in 1826, when he planned to journey to Rome. Detailed preparations were made, carriages and new liveries for the servants ordered, and in August the journey began. Marlborough some thirty-two miles from Bath, where the party intended to stay for the first night, was reached. By now, owing to the heat of the August weather, Beckford was exhausted, suffering from a fever, and in a foul temper. He continued to London but then quickly returned to Bath. Italy was never reached. On an earlier occasion in 1795, he had made arrangements to go to Naples from Spain, but storms and a chase by Barbary pirates, or so he claimed, sapped his enthusiasm. Perhaps the reason for these aborted journeys was his recognition that he could not face revisiting a country that had meant so much to him on his first Grand Tour but two years later, had been the site of what can only be described he Grand Tour from hell. On that second visit, he caught a fever and experienced the tragedies of the deaths of his particular confidante, the first Lady Hamilton, and John Burton, his musician-in-attendance.[7]

Another event occurred in the summer of 1828 that Beckford was not prepared to face: the chevalier Gregorio Franchi whom Beckford had known for over forty years died.[8] From London, Robert Hume, Beckford's faithful agent, wrote to say that Franchi was ill, but Beckford did not see Franchi during his last illness nor attend the funeral. Beckford's daughter, the Duchess of Hamilton, paid for Franchi's grave. Beckford had first set eyes on Franchi when the young boy was in the choir of Lisbon's Patriarchal Seminary. In time Franchi became the intimate friend, confidant, and art agent to the rich Englishman. Correspondence shows the strength of their friendship, a relationship in which Beckford could for once express his feelings without the need of a mask to conform to the expectations of English society.[9] With Franchi there was no need to adopt that superior, sardonic attitude he so often displayed. To Franchi, Beckford was able to talk, gossip, or write about any subject: family, purchases of paintings, objects, and furniture, and even titillating speculation about young men, such as a circus performer named Saunders. Franchi's death meant that hereafter Beckford had no true confidant, with whom he could share his thoughts without the need of artifice. Years earlier Beckford had written, " I have no one to speak to in my own language, whichever way I turn, none presents themselves in whom I can place the least confidence or to whom I can express my sensations."[10]

For the last fifteen years of his life, Beckford was thrown back into a private world of his own. There would be short visits from his younger daughter and her family, and he would spend a number of months in London each year, but generally his days followed a strict routine.

In Bath, after taking some broth, he would ride at a fairly early hour to Lansdown Tower, his study-retreat, one mile away. He would then return to his house, take breakfast and read until noon. Next he would transact business with his steward and then read and write until two o'clock. This would be followed by a ride for two or three hours. John Britton, the writer and antiquary, recalled that whenever planting or building was taking place, Beckford "passed the larger part of the day where the work was proceeding."[11] He was affable to artists or writers who visited Bath. Britton wrote: "Meals were always served up on rare and fine china, whilst all the appendages were silver, gold or gilt. The wines and desserts were in character and harmony, being rich and costly, and cooked by the most skilful professors."[12] To visitors, such as Cyrus Redding, he would relish the opportunity of acting out the incidents of his earlier life, and to a certain extent embellishing them. Much information about Beckford's life comes from Redding, who possibly saw himself as Boswell to the older man.[13] Britton commented, like others, on the brilliance of Beckford's conversation: "poignant, witty, original, and occasionally eccentric."[14]

In 1823, after the highly publicized Abbey sale, a new edition of Beckford's celebrated Oriental tale, *Vathek*, first published in 1786, appeared.[15] In the following year, Beckford's youthful work, *Biographical Memoirs of Extraordinary Painters* (1780), was also reissued. The success of these publications and the leisure and solitude of the Bath years caused Beckford to re-examine the letters and journals of the travels made in his early life. He revised *Dreams, Waking Thoughts and Incidents*, the long-suppressed account of his travels based on letters from his Grand Tours of 1780 and 1782, and added material relating to his later Iberian journeys, producing *Italy, with Sketches of Spain and Portugal* by "the author of Vathek," which was published in two volumes in 1834. This work was received with considerable critical acclaim. "Telleyard" described it as "the book of the century," and Beckford was delighted when one reader compared his work to *Robinson Crusoe*. Such was its success that editions appeared in Paris and Philadelphia. The following summer he published *Recollections of an Excursion to the Monasteries of Alçobaca and Batalha*, his account of a Portuguese visit made almost forty years earlier. Although based on earlier notes it was very much an original work, described as being by "someone who saw sharply, beautifully, with the artist's eye."[16]He was also hopeful, given the current "Vathek mania," that *The Episodes of Vathek* would appear. For years he had entertained his friends with selected readings, and some had even seen his manuscripts. "Now the propitious hour," he wrote, "for sharpening the public appetite for more powerful episodes—which if ever they emerge from the Hades into day light will reduce Byron's Corsair and Victor Hugo's monsters and scoundrels to insignificance."[17] It was not to be. *The Episodes* would not be published until 1912.

Beckford's overwhelming passion as a collector during the

Bath years was for books and engravings.[18] He left Fonthill with one third of his original book collection, and thereafter was on the lookout for "lost" Fonthill volumes. His library was rich in works on travel, history, memoirs, and religion. His desire for books was an addiction that could not be cured: "The want of room here is disturbing—still, like the sea, and something else mentioned in Scripture I keep on craving and calling out—more!"[19] His long-suffering agents in London—William and George Clarke, and later Henry G. Bohn—were bombarded with letters almost daily. Having seen a periodical review or advertisement of a new book, Beckford would not be satisfied until the book or engraving had been delivered into his hands. On many occasions he would notice a new work in the booksellers' windows in Bristol and Bath: "I think I have seen some such in the shop windows here and in Bristol," he would write, but it was his London agents who had to find a copy and ensure that it was of the finest impression.[20] He pursued books at auction with similar vigor. From his bookbinders he demanded the highest quality and attention to detail. His favorite binder was Charles Lewis, nicknamed "the Angel." For the binding of an early French translation of Bunyan's *Pilgrim's Progress*, Beckford gave precise instructions: "Let it be bound in some choice, little scrap of genuine, rough grained blue morocco—no gold, except in the lettering…[title]—true and straight, accent over the last e correct and accurate. Inside red, with a broad border of blue mor[occo] said border with tooled fillets somewhat antiquated….The book deserves joints and every attention."[21] On those occasions when his agent failed to respond to his letters by return post, or when binders failed to match his exacting demands, they could be sure of receiving the full blast of Beckford's invective: "You have been making, no doubt, a pretty mess, a capital hash, an admirable stew. This I can easily imagine. Indeed, I was partly led to expect it, but that in the intervals of COOKERY you should not have found a few stray moments to send me, if not books, at least excuses….it is deplorable, shameful, halfwitted, and owlish to an excuse I never conceived possible."[22] In reality Beckford's bark was worse than his bite. Despite the threats and continuous stream of demands, whether for books or assistance on some minor domestic matter, his agents served him faithfully until either death or disaster overtook them.

When not haranguing his agents, Beckford spend much time reading. He had good eyesight and was a fast reader: "How lucky that I have a quick eye and can read a whole atlas column of newspaper advertis[ments] etc. at one glance!"[23] He often made notes as he read, usually simple listings of points that had caught his attention, though occasionally he made a specific comment or criticism or jotted down an anecdote. The notes were sent off with the book to be bound in at the front of the volume. He once embarked on a catalogue of the tower's "snug little collection," despite declaring on another occasion: 'What do I want with a catalogue? I know every book in my possession, and where to put my finger upon it.'[24] This was not always the case, however, particularly when hundreds of books were waiting for shelving, which resulted in him spending many frustrated hours searching in vain for a particular book. He was a great reader of newspapers and the periodical press and would mark and clip reports that caught his interest: accounts of homosexual crimes and trials, auctions, the foreign travels of the young Queen Victoria, and many other subjects. These would be carefully kept in little packets, which he created by folding sheets of paper.[25]

Beckford's personal archive records one unexpected opportunity that he seized with relish. In 1842, some forty-five years after Horace Walpole's death, a sale took place at Strawberry Hill, which enabled Beckford to get even with "the cursed pest of Strawberry Hill," whom he believed had entailed his estate to prevent Beckford from obtaining any items. Newspapers compared the Strawberry Hill sale with that of Fonthill two decades earlier. The same "fever" was gripping the public. Beckford was spotted at the presale viewing: "the late owner of Fonthill is ringing the Cellini-Bell in his ear."[26] Beckford purchased extravagantly, acquiring many items, from classical gems to a bronze bust of Caligula and old Chelsea porcelain. He also purchased dozens of books, including Walpole's own copy of *Historical Doubts on the Life and Reign of Richard III.* Beckford kept newspaper cuttings about the sale, marking any reference to himself. He also made calculations as the sale proceeded, to both assess how much money he had spent and was likely to lay out. At the end, he declared to Bohn: "We have paid quite dear enough for *every* article. The Banquet being over—now comes the reckoning….I wish to forget the egregious follies committed at this high-puff sale."[27]

Beckford continued to be obsessed by the fact that he had once been so close to a peerage, which the Powderham affair had denied him. His absense from the pages of the *Peerage*, although he was included in Burke's *Commoners,* was a great source of frustration and anger, particularly when others, descended from mere brewers or medical practitioners, had overtaken him to sit in the House of Lords. His rage on reading the *Annual Peerage* (1829) edited by the Norroy King of Arms with the assistance of "the Misses Innes of ——, I recollect not of what ilk…," led him to produce his own commentary on "our female nobility" and those elevated to the peerage during the reigns of George III and George IV.[28] Although his *Liber Veritatis* was not published during his lifetime, he entertained visitors over many years by reading vituperative passages from his manuscript.

Beckford's household staff at Fonthill had always been the subject of speculation and gossip, but except for Pierre, the Savoyard dwarf, his Bath servants escaped censure or comment. The 1841 census shows four male and eight female servants living at 20 Lansdown Crescent, while others were housed in the garden and stable cottages. From Fonthill Beckford brought with him his faithful gardener James Vincent, who was to outlive his master. Vincent would work miracles by planting fully grown trees to turn a bare landscape into woodland. Theirs was a relationship in which each realized his dependency on the other, although occasionally Beckford's temper would get the better of him. One visitor saw Vincent rushing for shelter to escape the blows of Beckford's cane. Next day, Beckford sent his gardener five pounds.

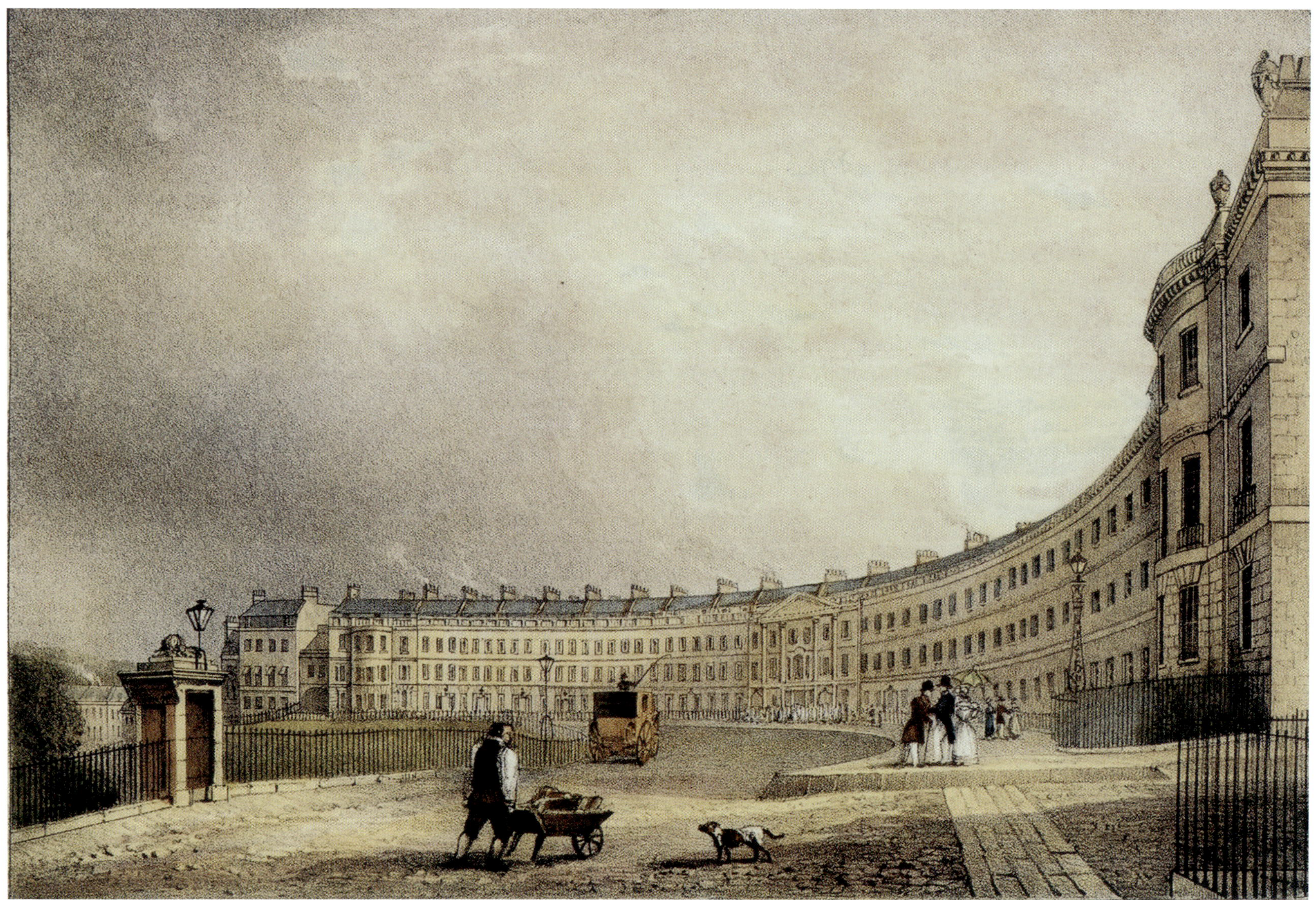

Fig. 15-2. *Lansdown Cresent*, 1828. Lithograph after A. Woodroffe. Courtesy of Bath Central Library.

Andrew Farratt, served for many years as Beckford's steward, showing concern about his employer's health. Farratt wrote on one occasion to Beckford, then in London, recommending that to ease gout Beckford should put a little grease and then spittle on his foot. Farratt then remembers that Beckford's dog Tout could have administered to Beckford's foot. The mention of the dead dog caused an outpouring of emotion from Beckford who wrote on the back of Farratt's letter: " He was my all in all, the comfort, charm of my life…his little shroud was cast off prematurely—& I cannot weep—& I cannot die—the greater my misery."[29]

Some years before leaving Fonthill, Beckford had disposed of his estates at Saint Pancras, Eaton Bray, and Witham, but even after the disposal of Fonthill, and despite the legends about the Beckford family's great wealth, Beckford had financial difficulties throughout his last two decades. Although he continued to live in a grand style, money

was limited. The disposal of his London houses (in 1831 and 1841) and the sale of pictures throughout this period were partly precipitated by the need for money. A statement from Beckford's solicitor in June 1840 showed that annual net proceeds from the remaining Jamaican estates amounted to £1,536, but even allowing for this income, Beckford owed £6,614 on his account.[30] He resolved to sell the Jamaican estate to get rid of "the cancer root & branch. I can endure no longer a species of gangrene which murders my peace."[31] He also disposed of his treasured pictures. He sold to the National Gallery his Raphael *Saint Catherine*, and paintings by Lodovico Mazzolino and Garofolo in 1839; a Perugino in 1841; and in the year of his death, 1844, the Giovanni Bellini portrait, *The Doge Leonardo Loredan*. In the spring of 1840, Edmund English was negotiating on Beckford's behalf to sell a group of pictures to Robert Holford of Westonbirt. Beckford's letters to English in which he huffs and puffs in typically Beckfordian fashion about Holford's slowness in coming to a decision reveals the depth of Beckford's anxiety to secure a sale.

Beckford would summon up a slight illness as an excuse for not making a journey or rushing to London to attend a sale, but generally, despite his increasing age, he was fairly robust: "I slap and dash about, walk through thick and thin as usual."[32] Daily he would go for his ride, except when there was an east wind. He dressed in the somewhat old-fashioned style of a Regency squire with top-boots, knee britches, green or brown coat, buff waistcoat, and white neck cloth. One obituary notice stated that: "to a stranger [he] might seem like a good old Zomersetzeer farmer."[33] When riding, he was often attended by a small cavalcade; at the head rode his steward, then two mounted grooms with long whips, followed by Beckford with his favorite dogs, and, bringing up the rear of the little procession, two more grooms.

On one occasion he made an offer to purchase Summer Hill Place, a house a little distance from Lansdown Crescent, demanding an acceptance within twenty-four hours. As the owner asked for time to consider the offer, Beckford in his usual impetuous way dropped the matter. In April 1843, "Having been most grievously disturbed early this morning by the noise of dogs I shall most probably remove from Bath in the course of the ensuing Summer."[34] Noise was not, however, the only cause for his threats to quit the city. He had been frustrated in his long-held intention that the tower should be his mausoleum, and so in April 1843 he applied for a faculty to be buried in the grounds. This was refused by the ecclesiastical authorities. Enraged, Beckford declared that he would leave Bath for Milford, his estate near Salisbury, and be buried in the cathedral. In June he threatened to sell his Lansdown estate and on its site build 1,500 hovels. Despite his threats—made with typically Beckfordian gestures and caliph-like anger— he remained at Lansdown Crescent.

Lansdown Crescent

Lansdown Crescent (fig. 15-2), set on the slopes of Lansdown Hill, with sweeping views across the valley to Prior Park, was designed by the Bath architect John Palmer and built between 1789 and 1793. Beckford's house, No. 20, which he purchased from Sir Walter James, for a sum reported to be £10,000, was the grandest and best positioned, being at the west end of the crescent and having a wide, bow-fronted facade.

A single Bath townhouse, however grand, was not large enough for the former owner of Fonthill Abbey and his many possessions. Soon he acquired 1 Lansdown Place West (then known as West Wing), the house to the west of his, the first in the adjacent terrace across a narrow lane.[35] Beckford linked the two houses by an enclosed bridge, designed by the young architect Henry Edmund Goodridge, at first floor level (fig. 15-3). Beckford sold 1 Lansdown Place West in March 1831 to Captain Arthur Lysaght, later a rear admiral.[36] The reason for selling was that the house was "not upon a level with my apartments and very inconvenient."[37] Beckford told George Clarke that he was advanced in a treaty for another house, but it was another five

years before he acquired 19 Lansdown Crescent, in March 1836, the house next to his on the eastern side. He claimed that " had I not bought this house, I would have been perpetually annoyed by the ticking of some cursed jack, the jingling of some beastly piano, horrid toned bells tinkling, and so on."[38] Although averse to noise, he purchased the house as a matter of necessity, to accommodate his evergrowing book collection and items transferred from his London house. No. 19 was the perfect house into which Beckford and his possessions could spread. Identical floor levels between the two properties enabled the two houses to be linked by the simple insertion of doors in the party walls.[39]

Early in his life, in a letter to his half-sister, Beckford wrote: "There is nothing I should dislike more than not having…a spot I call my own and an habitation however simple that I could shut myself up in when I please and in which I could change one thing and alter another just as my fancy suggested."[40] This nest building, whether in Portugal, at Fonthill, or in London, was a life-long compulsion. Whatever the space, he would take it over and make it his own. He described his delight in arranging his Portuguese house at Ramalhão, where he had transformed the lantern room into a tentlike space: "Half its curtains admit no light and display the richest folds, the other half are transparent and cast a mild glow on the mat and sofas.… The glasses multiply this profusion of drapery, and like a child I am not yet tired of running from corner to corner to view the different groups of objects reflected in them, and fancying myself admitted into a series of magic saloons."[41] Throughout his life Beckford used drapery—as at Ramalhão, in the great galleries at Fonthill, and later at Bath—to create a series of magic saloons.

At Lansdown Crescent, Beckford again adopted the formula used at Fonthill of having rich hangings of scarlet, crimson, purple, and blue. Crimson had a symbolic as well as visual impact: being the color of the Hamilton family, it indicated Beckford's aristocratic maternal lineage. Hangings were used not only at windows and in doorways, but also draped across an entire wall in some rooms. He had first observed the effects created by drapery in Madame de Aranda's Madrid boudoir: "I have often wondered architects and fitters-up of apartments have not more availed themselves of the powers of drapery. There is no ornament I like so well or that admits of more variety."[42] When a visitor to Lansdown Crescent commented on the use of drapery, Beckford replied that he was "very fond of drapery," but this was nothing compared to Fonthill where in the octagon there were "purple curtains fifty feet long."[43] Drapery hung at doorways to help control drafts and across walls to reduce noise. In many of the Bath interiors, tables were covered with cloths in rich Beckfordian colors. There was also much use of marble for the tops of cabinets and other surfaces.

Mirrors were expertly placed to enhance perspectives; one at the end of the gallery, for example, reflected both the gallery itself and the Great Drawing Room beyond. Henry Venn Lansdown commented on Beckford's use of mirrors and open doorways to give an illusion of spaciousness: "We paused an instant before leaving the dining room to

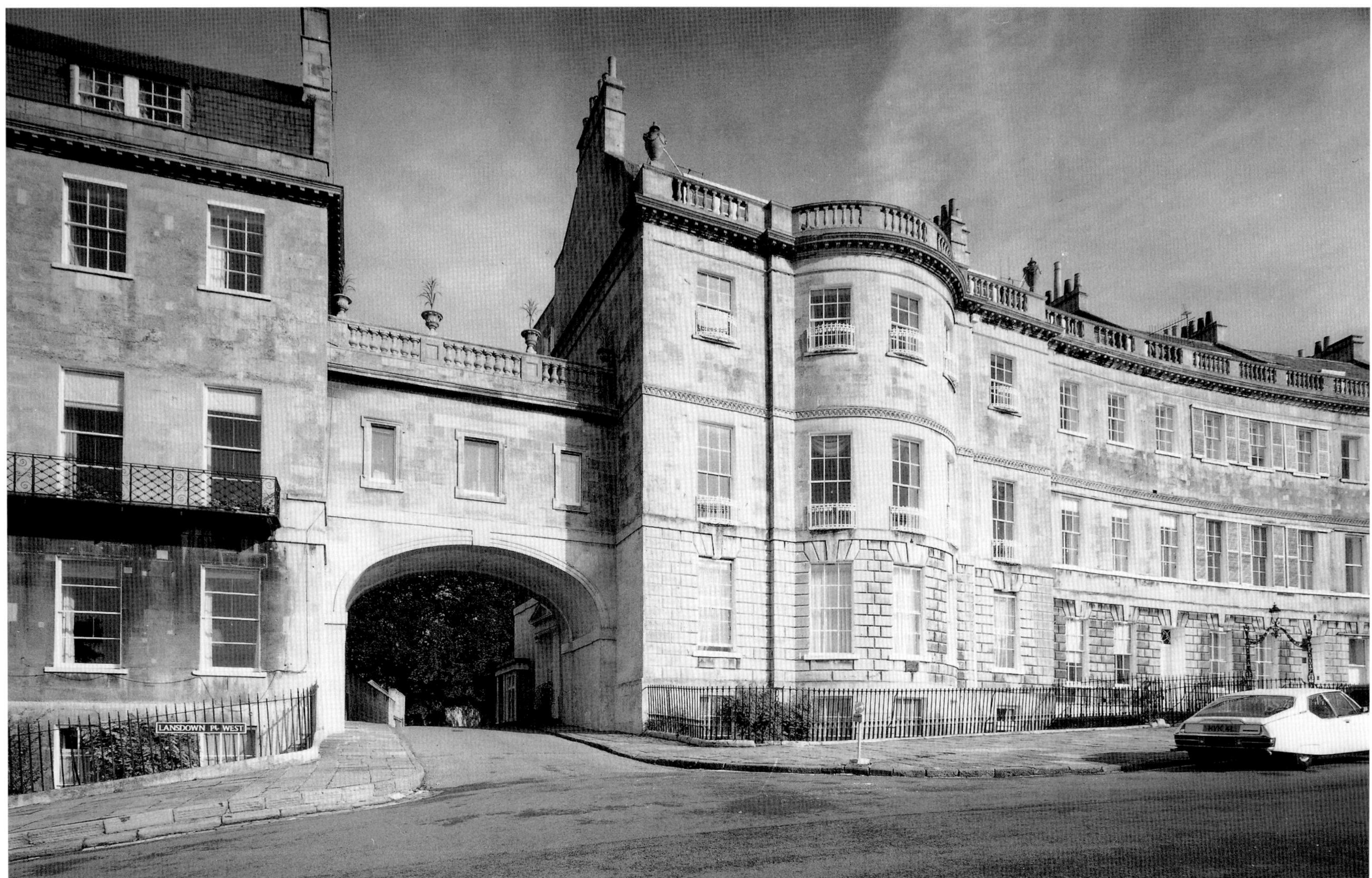

Fig. 15-3. Beckford's houses in Bath (fom left): 1 Lansdown Place West, connected by bridge to 20 Lansdown Crescent and the adjacent 19 Lansdown Crescent. Photographed in 1976. Courtesy of Country Life Picture Library.

admire a lovely bit of perspective. It is a line of open doors, exactly opposite each other…piercing and uniting the three lower rooms. The effect is vastly increased by a mirror placed in the lobby…which terminates the view."[44]

All the main rooms at Lansdown Crescent housed substantial parts of Beckford's book collection: "At least 5,000 volumes (most of which I wish to refer to) are lying piled up behind two ranks deep of others," he wrote in 1831, when his books from London began to arrive.[45] In the great galleries of Fonthill, row upon row of sumptuous bindings had contributed substantially to the overall richness of the interiors. Many of Beckford's bindings were in scarlet leather, the spines glittering with his gilded heraldic emblems, creating an effect of princely magnificence.

Beckford's main agents in Bath were the architect Henry Edward Goodridge and the Bath firm of English and Son, cabinetmakers, upholsterers, auctioneers, and undertakers.[46] Much of the furniture commissioned for his Bath residence was designed by Beckford himself with assistance from Goodridge and made by English and Son. Beckford, who had earlier designed certain pieces at Fonthill Abbey was not the only collector-designer of his time: Thomas Hope had designed neoclasssical furniture for his house in Duchess Street in London. The most surprising feature of the Lansdown Crescent furnishings was the extensive use of oak. Beckford clearly had a predilection for this wood. He had earlier used it, "the outlines slightly touched with gold," for brackets in the Oratory at Fonthill and also for the new base of the great Borghese pietre dure table. In going against the general taste of the day for mahogany and rosewood, Beckford was, as always, being both perverse and original. Oak allowed for gilding in a novel way. Many of the pieces, often with strong architectural elements, were conceived as cabinets and containers for his most precious books and objects.

The various decorative schemes were supervised by English. As a client, Beckford had to be approached with great caution, his agents and craftsmen learned through experience to pay attention to his every whim and his fastidiousness, often carrying out work when he was away in London. On one occasion, writing about plans to redecorate the dining room, Edmund English explained that he was fully aware of Beckford's great antipathy to the smell of paint but to overcome this the painter "will take the precaution of mixing spirit of Lavender with oil, instead of spirits of wine."[47]

20 Lansdown Crescent

Visitors to Lansdown Crescent would encounter Beckford's dwarf, Pierre de Grailly (fig. 15-4), who was employed by Beckford for over forty years, in the entrance hall: "The visitors were admitted by the hall porter and passed on to a servant in the interior while this wretched looking object sat in his armchair grinning."[48] Like some great frontispiece, the entrance hall and stone staircase prepared the visitor for the main interiors of the house. The scarlet curtains and carpets introduced the color scheme that would be followed in many of the principal rooms. Beckford's obsessive pride in his ancestry was indicated by a framed genealogical table complete with coats of arms (now in Brodick Castle). The themes of ancestry and dynasty were continued in the family portraits, where four generations were depicted, starting with the owner's father in a full-length portrait by Joshua Reynolds (see fig. 3-2) and George Romney's swagger portrait of Beckford himself, a picture painted in the period when Beckford attained his majority (see cat. no. 8). The next generation of the family was represented by Romney's portrait of Beckford's daughters, Margaret and Susan, when young, painted against a Fonthill landscape background (now at Huntingdon Library and Art Collection, San Marino, California). Finally, the fourth generation, was represented by Beckford's noble grandson, the Marquis of Douglas, shown in two portraits: one by Henry William Pickersgill, the other by the Bath artist Thomas Barker, painted when the boy was ten years old. Among other paintings were landscapes by two contemporary Bath artists, Benjamin Barker and Willes Maddox, the latter a young artist patronized by both Beckford and his daughter, the Duchess of Hamilton.[49]

On the ground floor at the front of the house was the dining room, which contained Beckford's most valuable pictures. Gustav Waagen, the German art historian who visited Bath in 1835, during his survey of English collections, was generous in his praise of the south-facing room:

I shall never forget the dining room, which, taken all in all, is perhaps one of the most beautiful in the world. Conceive a moderate apartment of agreeable proportions, whose walls are adorned with cabinet pictures, the noblest productions of Italian art of the time of Raphael, from the windows of which you overlook the whole paradisaical valley of the Avon, with the whole city of Bath, which is now steeped in sunshine. Conceive in it a company of men of genius and talent, between the number of the Graces and Muses, whose spirits are duly raised by the choicest viands, in the preparation of which the refined culinary art of our days has displayed its utmost skill, by a selection of wines such as nature and human care produce only on the most favoured spots of the earth, in the most favourable years, and you will agree with me that many things here meet in a culminating point, which even singly, are calculated to rejoice the heart of man.[50]

Beckford's most celebrated picture of his Bath period, Raphael's *Saint Catherine* (fig. 15-5) was hung in this room, "on the right as you enter," together with a Claude, Garofalo, and two Ferrara pictures. Redding relates how Beckford "took a key from his pocket

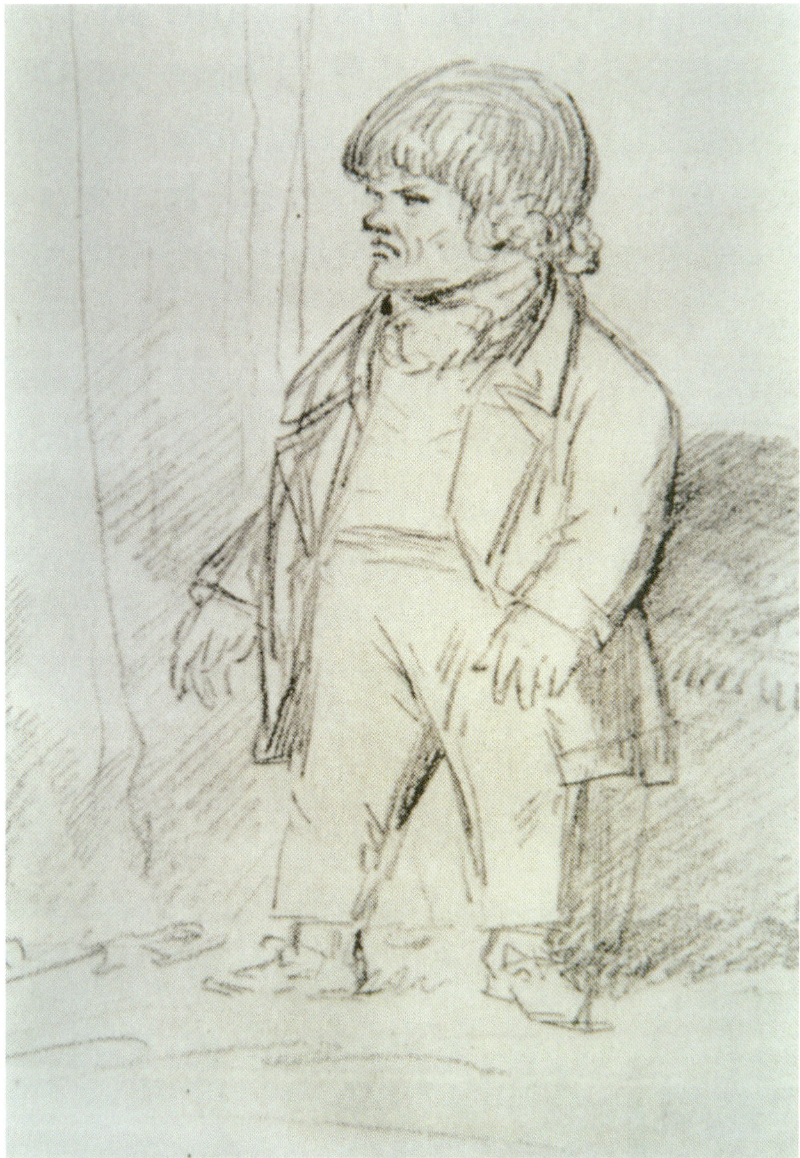

Fig. 15-4. Benjamin West. *Beckford's Dwarf*, n.d. Pencil on paper. Collection of Swarthmore College, Swarthmore, Pennsylvania.

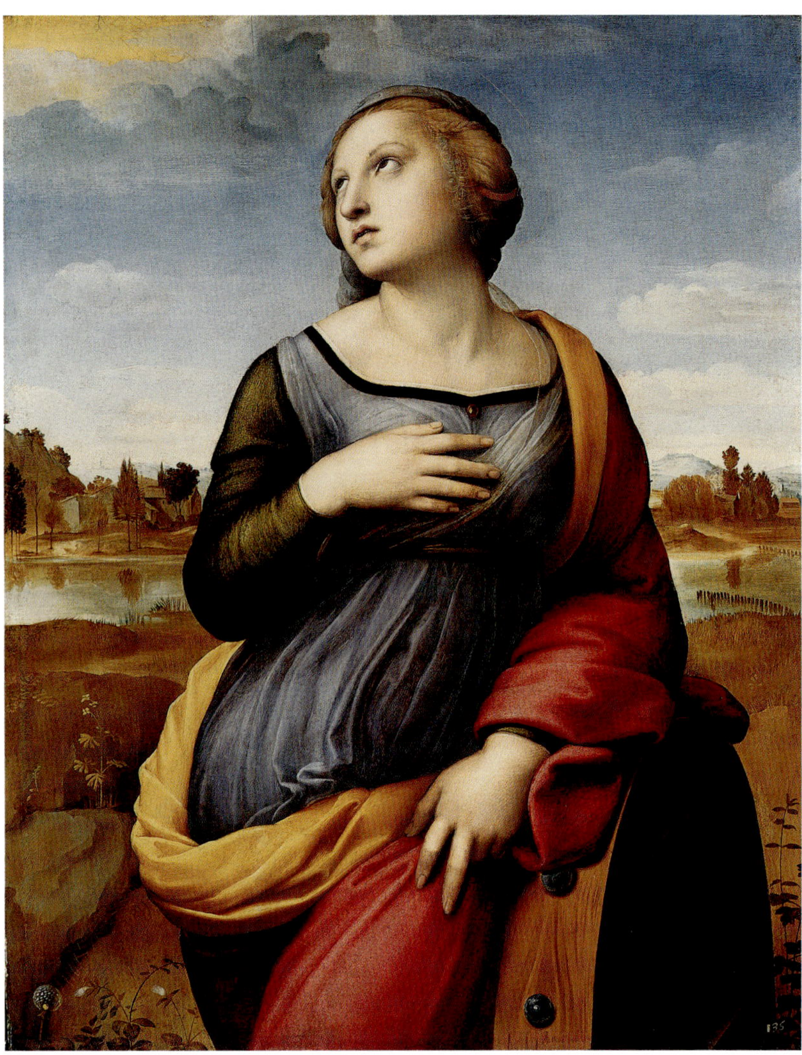

Fig. 15-5. Raphael. *Saint Catherine of Alexandria,* ca. 1507–8. Oil on wood. The National Gallery, London.

superb plates placed on the carpet containing its dinner and at desert two more equally valuable were placed on the table…& Tiny was then seated in a chair."[53] No space was wasted in the room, for mahogany bookcases and cabinets were fitted into a doorway and also recessed into the wall. One visitor commented that the room "in point of brilliancy and cheerfulness has more the character of a drawing than a dining room."[54] This atmosphere was created in part by the bookcases and in part by the presence, opposite the window, of an upright grand piano by Broadwood, "the largest ever made."[55] Over the chimneypiece hung a large mirror with a gilt frame. A scarlet moreen curtain covered one wall of the room; the three windows had similar curtains together with roller and muslin blinds. From the center of the room hung a Grecian lamp, with glass bowl and three lights. The floor was carpeted with a bordered Brussels carpet. Lansdown records seeing on a small table "an elegantly cut carafe of carnations of every variety of colour that you can possibly imagine."[56] Beckford's love of flowers, a lifelong passion, was often noted: "There is nothing in which Mr Beckford is more choice than in his bouquets. At every season the rarest living flowers adorn the house."[57]

Close to the dining room was the "small" library furnished with mahogany bookcases and cabinets, which covered the walls of the room. To make the best use of available space, a cabinet had been installed in the opening "where the grate originally was" and another of nine drawers was in the window recess. A small mahogany occasional table was covered with a scarlet cloth. Window and door curtains were of scarlet serge. A glass vase-shaped lamp with line and balance hung from the center of the ceiling. The paintings were a pair of Watteau garden scenes, Poelenburgh's *Italian Ruins and Figures,* panels by Fra Angelico entitled *Virgin* and *Announcing Angel,* and a small Gerrit Dou portrait, *The Artist's Mother.* The Marchioness of Santa Cruz, a romantic figure from Beckford's earlier days, was depicted in a small painting, possibly by Senguin. The floor was covered by a Turkey carpet.

The grandest room in Lansdown Crescent was the Great Drawing Room, on the first floor, with five windows looking south over the Bath landscape. The room continued into the gallery, contained within the bridge designed by Goodridge between 20 Lansdown Crescent and 1 Lansdown Place West (even after the sale of 1 Lansdown Place West, Beckford retained this space). The narrow gallery was lit by three windows, which also had crimson silk roller blinds. Crimson serge curtains, "laced, with valances fringed," hung from all windows. Mirrors were used to give a sense of space and perspective, with the one on the gallery's end wall being described as a "noble mirror, beautiful single-plate."[58]

Despite being called a drawing room, the main room was in reality like so many of Beckford's interiors, a library. The walls were lined with oak bookcases and cabinets to a height of eight feet. Even the main entrance door was covered with trompe l'oeil book spines to intensify the overall effect of the room. The gallery's wall facing the windows was also lined with bookcases and cabinets, with doors in the

unlocked the inner frame, and had me look at the picture without the glass."[51] There was also a Titian *Virgin,* two paintings by Van der Meulen, and a version of Benjamin West's *King Lear in a Storm* (now in the Detroit Institute of Arts). Above these hung two Vernet seascapes. One of Beckford's paintings by Canaletto, *Capriccio of Roman and Venetian Buildings,* was in this room. Beckford told the artist Lansdown that the painting was genuine because it had been purchased from the artist through Consul Smith. Over the square sofa with cushions and two bolsters covered in scarlet serge, hung " constellation of beauties" including paintings by G. Poussin, Wouvermans, Berchem, Van Huysum, and Poelenburgh.[52]

The furniture to fulfill the room's function as a dining room included a Spanish mahogany sideboard with marble top, matching side tables, and a mahogany circular table covered with a purple cloth. If we are to believe contemporary gossip, it was in this room that Beckford generally dined alone except for a favorite dog, Tiny: "two lower part, decorated with pilasters inlaid with pollard oak that was enriched with gilding.[59]

A total of eighteen portraits once hung above the bookcases in the drawing room, as recorded in the inventory made at Beckford's death. These included portraits said at the time to be by Benjamin West: *Edward IV, Henry VII, John of Brittany*, and *Alfonso of Spain*, which had come from King Edward's Gallery at Fonthill. Among others were Velazquez's *Spanish Nobleman*, Passerotti's *Pope Gregory XIII*, and a Rembrandt self portrait. *Cosimo Medici* by Bronzino, was over the door. Furniture included a pair of oak sofas and fourteen "carved and inlaid pollard oak" chairs with seats covered in crimson moreen.[60] There was also an ebony upright cabinet inlaid with panels of Florentine mosaic framed in water-gilt molding. In the gallery, a pair of "very neat oak hanging cabinets for bijouterie, with plate glass doors and gilt enrichments." These were similar in design to the small hanging cabinets shown in Willes Maddox's illustration of the tower's furniture (see fig. 9-7). A few of Beckford's choice objects were displayed in the main room, including the bloodstone cup supported on the tails of silver-gilt dolphins by Paul Storr (see cat. no. 139) and the celebrated Van Diemen Japanese lacquer box (now in The Victoria and Albert Museum, London). Brussels carpet close covered the floor while in the center was a "Persian bordered carpet," described as "so sumptuous that one is afraid to walk on it."[61] From the center of the main room hung an ormolu chandelier for six candles; four other "oak and gold candelabra" lit the room.

Adjoining the Great Drawing Room was a second reception room known as the Duchess's Drawing Room, because a portrait of Beckford's daughter, the Duchess of Hamilton, by Thomas Phillips, painted in about 1810, hung over the fireplace. This room was another gallery of family portraits, and was also lined with the customary bookcases, here in oak. Those on either side of the chimneypiece with carvings of Beckford's heraldic emblems (fig. 15-6). Lansdown described the room as being a "truly Royal room, the colour of the curtains, carpet, furniture being crimson, scarlet and purple."[62] The family portraits were a reminder to Beckford of his ancestors and the ghosts in his own life. Here were portraits by Benjamin West: of Beckford's mother, depicted in front of Fonthill Splendens (see cat. no. 2), Beckford's great-grandparents, Peter Beckford, the Governor of Jamaica, who laid the foundations of the Beckford family's fortune (now in The Metropolitan Museum, New York); and of Beckford's aunt, the Countess of Effingham, one of the "Methodistical dowagers" of his childhood (now in The National Gallery of Art, Washington).

Memories of Beckford's youth would have been rekindled by Reynolds's full-length portrait of Louisa, wife of his cousin Peter Beckford, "represented approaching an altar partially obscured by clouds of incense that she may sacrifice to Hygeia" (now in the Lady Lever Art Gallery, Port Sunlight).[63] Even Lansdown recognized her as the "Nouronihar" of *Vathek*. There was also a portrait of the Duke of Hamilton, aged about thirteen, "a sweet child, with the hair cut straight along the forehead, as worn by children some fifty years ago,

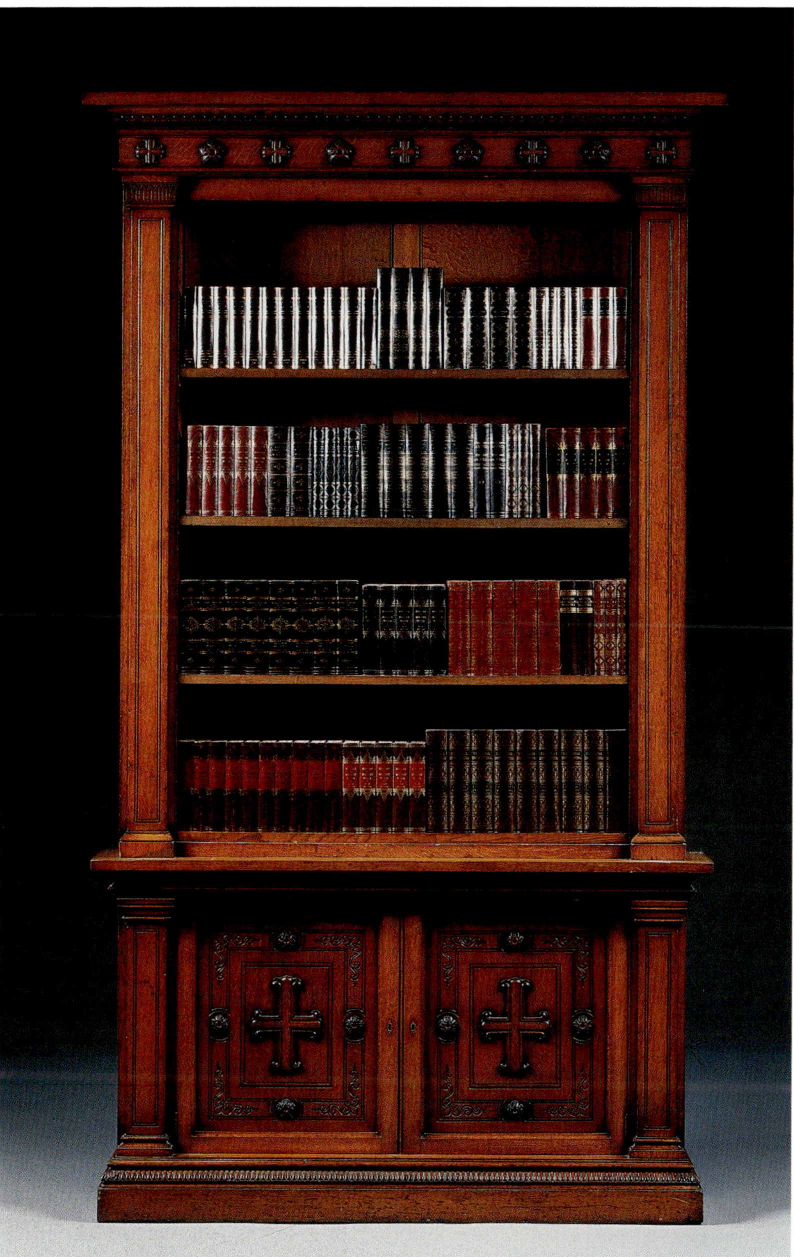

Fig. 15-6. Bookcase, one of a pair from the Duchess's Drawing Room, ca. 1825. Oak. This was probably designed by William Beckford. Private collection.

and hanging luxuriantly down his neck," a boy who had been present all those years before, like Louisa and William Courtenay, at Beckford's Christmas festivities in 1781.[64] Also hanging in the room was Reynolds's portrait of Beckford painted at about the time of his coming of age (now in the National Portrait Gallery, London), a portrait that Beckford used as the frontispiece of *Excursions to the Monasteries of Alçobaca and Batalha.*

Surprisingly Beckford appears to have owned no portrait of Lady Margaret, his wife.[65] Another portrait was missing from those that hung in the main reception rooms: George Romney's full-length portrait of William Courtenay (now in the Nemours Mansion,

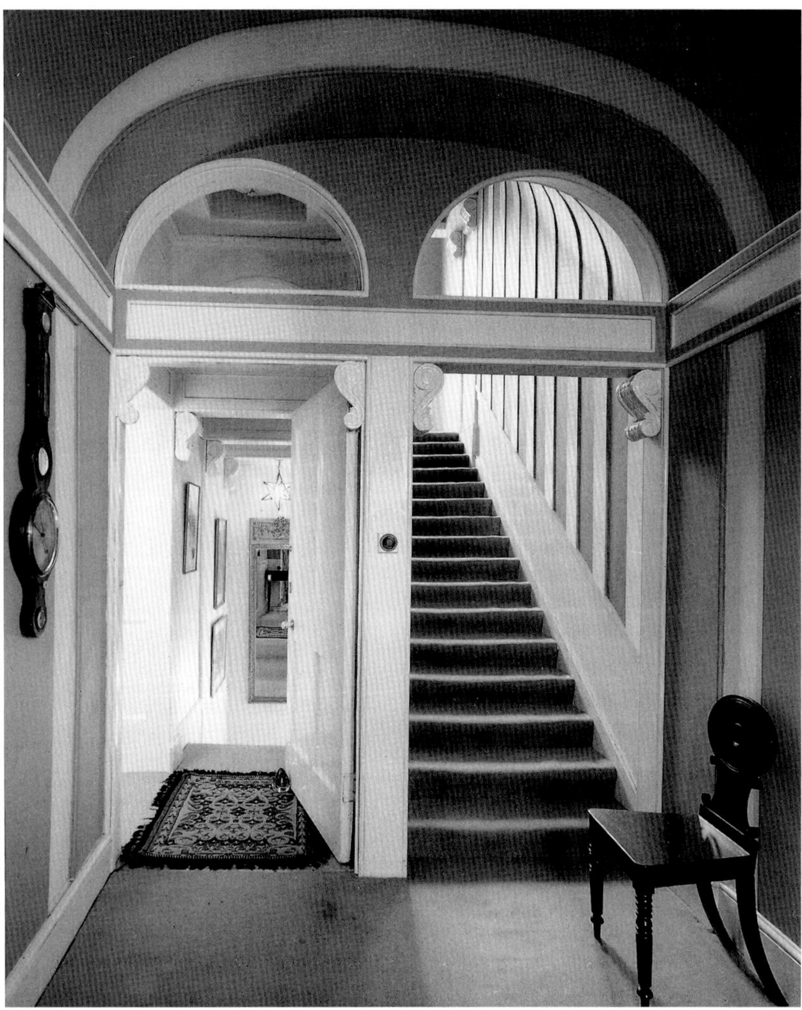

Fig. 15-7. The Entrance Hall and staircase, 19 Lansdown Crescent, Bath. Designed by Henry Edmund Goodridge, ca. 1837. Photographed in 1976. Courtesy of Country Life Picture Library.

Wilmington, Delaware), the picture painted for Beckford of the youth whose fatal attraction had caused him to lose his expected peerage and face six decades of social ostracism. The inventory of pictures, taken after Beckford's death, shows the portrait as being in the Ladies Maid's Room.

In 1838, Henry Venn Lansdown saw in the room a bronze of the Laocoon, behind which was hung a sketch by Veronese and two small, upright Bassanos. At the time of Beckford's death, however, the only picture in the room other than the family portraits was an *Allegory of Saint Anthony of Padua* by Sigueira. The room also contained a Broadwood grand piano.

On Beckford's death, Willes Maddox was commissioned by the Duchess of Hamilton to paint the death-bed scene (see cat.

no. 150). In the picture, Beckford lies in his narrow bed, beside which are a pair of cabinets on stands and a stool supporting an open book; it is described as "an austere, pictureless room, hung with lugubrious crimson curtain."[66] The inventory made in 1844, however, shows that Beckford's bedroom was anything but austere. It was crammed with numerous cabinets, many stuffed with precious objects. Nor was it pictureless; there were twenty-five paintings hanging on its walls. Beckford's oak bedstead with carved feet, headboard covered with scarlet cloth, was set within an alcove of scarlet serge hangings hung across brass rods and supported by four pillars. Among the profusion of furniture were two oak bookcases with carved cornices ornamented with the Beckford's heraldic emblems of the Latimer cross and cinquefoil. There were also the two cabinets shown in Willes Maddox's painting, one owned by Beckford since childhood (now at Brodick Castle), in which he kept the letters received from Alexander Cozens, "All your letters were deposited in a drawer lined with blue, the colour of Aether," letters which had filled his head with dreams and fantasies that had irreparably shaped his destiny.[67]

19 Lansdown Crescent

Upon acquiring No. 19 in 1836, Beckford connected it to his main house by creating doors through the party walls. Thereafter, the usual entrance to both houses was by means of the main door and staircase of No. 20. The street door of No. 19 now served no real purpose, and the entrance passageway was turned into a "sort of vestibule leading to a staircase, which from its mysterious and crimson light, rich draperies, and latticed doors seemed to be the sanctorum sanctorum of a heathen temple."[68] Beckford achieved the desired effect by covering the fanlight of the outer door with crimson silk. The original stairwell and balusters were removed, and in their place a tunnellike staircase was constructed, with bands running from the dado across the vault. Just before the staircase, the relatively small space was given a sense of greater space by subdividing it with two semicircular arches (fig. 15-7). Consequently, "in an amazingly small compass, there is a curiously Soanic feeling of inverted and intricate space division and space exploitation."[69] Legend has it that this arrangement was created to protect Beckford from being observed from above by his servants, but its true purpose more likely was to exploit fully the available space in as imaginative way as possible. It would have also provided some protection from drafts.

The main room on the entrance floor at the front of the house was a library, known as the Grecian or Scagliola Library (fig. 15-8) with walls adorned with nineteen yellow scagliola pilasters and broad arched recesses. The ceiling "belted across and enriched with bands of Grecian tracery in relief, delicately painted and slightly touched in gold. On the walls are some gilded ornaments, enough to give to the whole richness of effect without heaviness."[70] The main bookcases, of Spanish mahogany, filled the recesses. Between the windows a hanging bookcase, "manufactured in Bath from drawings by Mr Goodridge" in oak for small (duodecimo) books supported by "trusses with grecian figure

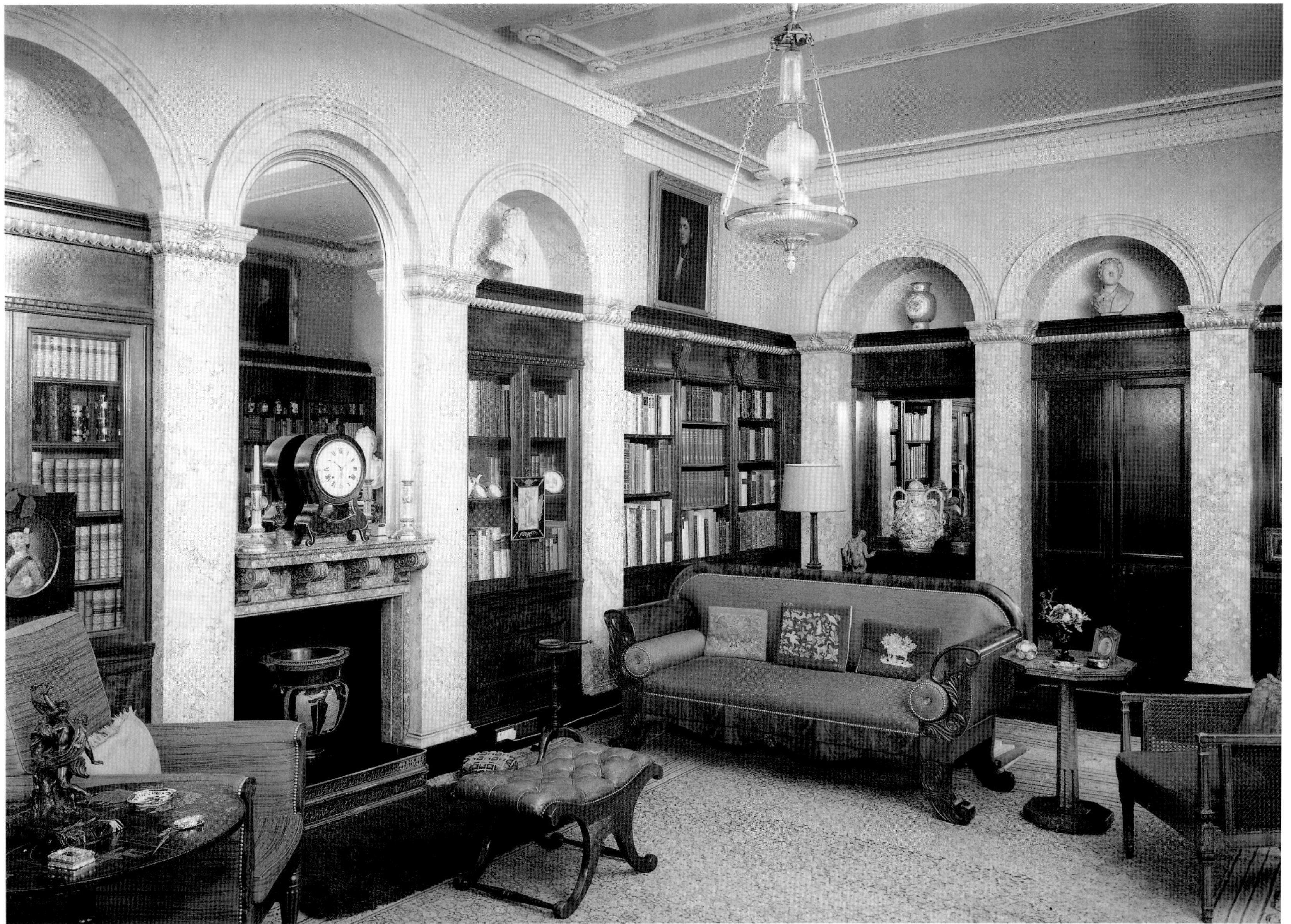

Fig. 15-8. The Grecian Library, 19 Lansdown Crescent, Bath. Designed by Henry Edmund Goodridge, ca. 1837. Photographed in 1976. Courtesy of Country Life Picture Library.

heads."[71] The Grecian theme was continued in the two Grecian elbow chairs, "Hopes pattern" with gilt moldings, and nails, and a silk fringe.[72] Close to the window was a table of *verde antico* marble on gilt-bronze supports with griffin heads and eagle claws on a *verde antico* plinth. The room had no pictures, being entirely given over to books. The chaste atmosphere was further enhanced by five vases: three of porphyry, one of *verde antico*, and a large one of Devonshire marble. There was also a sarcophagus of *giallo antico* marble. "The room in which I study," Beckford told a visitor, " is that…which you most properly call a Grecian library, for so it is."[73] Except for the gallery of No. 20, the room, despite war damage in 1942, is the only Beckfordian interior to survive virtually intact.[74]

At the rear of the entrance floor was another library, the Scarlet Room, furnished with oak bookcases and cabinets on black or ebony plinths. The ranges of bookcases included full-size, dwarf, and hanging. Several of the pieces are described in the 1844 inventory as having "arch recesses above, Ionic pilasters, trusses, carved mouldings, dentals, cornice carved blocking". From such descriptions the furniture would appear to have the same architectural quality of the pieces designed by Beckford and Goodridge for Lansdown Tower. Chairs were covered in scarlet leather, and curtains of purple cloth covered either the whole of the window wall or that facing it. Door curtains were of blue and crimson cloth. In this room hung Etty's *Prodigal Son*, Holbein's *Portrait of Protector Somerset*, a Perugino *Virgin*, and a seaport scene by Van der Ulft. On the floor was a bordered cut-pile carpet.

The first floor contained two rooms referred to as drawing rooms, but doubling as libraries and picture galleries for Beckford's collection. The smaller of the two rooms was the Back Drawing Room furnished with oak bookcases and cabinets, one of which was inset into the wall, possibly into an unused door opening. Like the furniture in the Scarlet Room, many pieces are described as being elaborately carved. In the window recesses were a pair of dwarf bookcases with three drawers, pollard oak tops, and twisted columns. Among the chairs were four X-shaped chairs, but with elbows, backs, and seats covered in scarlet leather, with silk fringes. Window curtains were of scarlet serge and buff worsted damask with a valance that was laced and fringed. Door curtains were of scarlet serge. Three paintings hung in the room: Hondecoeter's *Dead Game*, Stothard's *Tom O'Shanter*, and Fragonard's *Lady in a White Satin Dress*. From the ceiling, suspended by a crimson cord, was the silver-gilt lamp from the Oratory at Fonthill.[75] The floor was carpeted with a Brussels carpet.

After the artist Lansdown visited the house in 1838, he wrote: "Mr Beckford drew aside another curtain, and we entered the front drawing room.…The first thing that caught my eye was the magnificent effect produced by a scarlet drapery, whose ample folds covered the whole side of the room opposite the three windows from ceiling to the floor."[76] On either side of the fireplace were oak cabinets, the lower sections having open arches while above were glazed cupboards for books and objects. David Roberts's *Church Interior with Tombs of Ferdinand and Isabella of Spain*, Velazquez's *Innocent X*, Bembi's *Holy Family*, and Magnard's *Cardinal Mazarin* were the only pictures hanging in this room.

The main reception rooms at Lansdown Crescent displayed Beckford's preferences for crimson and scarlet hangings; the guest rooms in No. 20, however, allocated to members of his family, had much lighter and more conventional decorative schemes. The bedroom used by Beckford's daughter had a four-poster bedstead with chintz drapes and a Marseilles quilt. The square sofa, easy chairs, and window curtains were also covered in chintz. Like other rooms, the duchess's bedroom had to provide some space for books and objects. There was a long, dwarf bookcase of oak, enclosed with paneled doors, and a pair of Italian inlaid cabinets. The Duke of Hamilton's bedroom also had a four-poster bedstead with chintz hangings. There were mahogany bookcases and a pair of Italian cabinets part enclosed by glazed doors. The bedroom of Lady Lincoln, Beckford's granddaughter, had a field bedstead with pink cotton hangings and rosewood easy chairs covered in pink cotton. Framed and glazed drawings, including a view of Fonthill by Wyatt, adorned the walls of these rooms.

The Disposal of Beckford's Collections at Bath

In April 1844 Beckford caught a chill when out riding. A few days later George Beckett wrote to advise the dealer Smith that "Mr Beckford is labouring under a very severe attack of influenza & he is very ill indeed [so much so] that he wishes you *not* to send him any Prints whatsoever

for the present as he cannot possibly inspect them."[77] That Beckford, the insatiable collector, could no longer cast his eye over prints, books, and auction catalogues was a sign that the end was approaching. The Duchess of Hamilton, summoned to Bath, suggested that her father might like to see a priest, but he refused. Finally, the doctor was sent to talk to him, while in the next room the duchess and her family said prayers. Beckford died on May 2, 1844.

In his last will and testament William Beckford named his daughter Susan Euphemia, the Duchess of Hamilton, as the sole beneficiary of his estate except for a bequest to his lawyer and the provision of life annuities, equal to their wages and board, to five servants. For four months after Beckford's death, Edmund English and Son and Robert Hume made an inventory of his possessions.[78] The total valuation, excluding the book collection, was £47,339.2s. The duchess sent many choice paintings, items of furniture, and other objects to her London house and to the family seats at Easton in Suffolk and Hamilton Palace in Scotland. Annotations in the inventory reveal the distribution of certain other items. In the tradition of the time, Beckford's clothing and his gold repeater watch with enameled case, gilt key, and ribbon were given to his valet. In the drawings section of the inventory is an annotation suggesting that much of the primary documentation of Beckford's two great architectural creations was wantonly destroyed: alongside the entry, "Many drawings by Mr Wyatt, Mr Goodridge &c. respecting Fonthill and Lansdown Tower tied up in a roll," is the single word, "burnt."

Beckford sold certain paintings and furniture from Lansdown Tower in January 1841, just before embarking on the tower's final decorative scheme.[79] After his death, a sale of the Lansdown Tower, its grounds and contents, together with some items from Lansdown Crescent, was held in November 1845.[80] The townhouse at 20 Lansdown Crescent and its contents were offered to the public in a nine-day sale in July 1848.[81] The wine sold included: "Malmsey—Bin 15—Twelve bottles of great age and choice, from Fonthill; Mr Beckford's crest is on each bottle."[82]

Beckford's library was the one element of his collection not dispersed. The inventory valued the books and manuscripts at £26,614.12s.[83] Beckford's son-in-law, the Duke of Hamilton, was suspicious of this large valuation, but the sum was confirmed when Bohn, the bookseller, offered £30,000 for the collection. The duchess refused to sell, however, and eventually the thousands of volumes were taken to Hamilton Palace, where a special library, designed by Beckford's faithful architect Goodridge, was built to house them. From the end of the library, Reynolds's *Alderman Beckford* kept watch over his son's prized collection.

In the early 1880s Beckford's great-grandson, the twelfth duke, faced financial difficulties and decided to sell much of the contents of Hamilton Palace, including objects, pictures, and furniture that had once been in Beckford's collection.[84] Beckford's treasured library was sold, in four sales (some 9,837 lots) in 1882–83, for the princely sum of £73,551.[85] A further sale of paintings and portraits was held in 1919.[86]

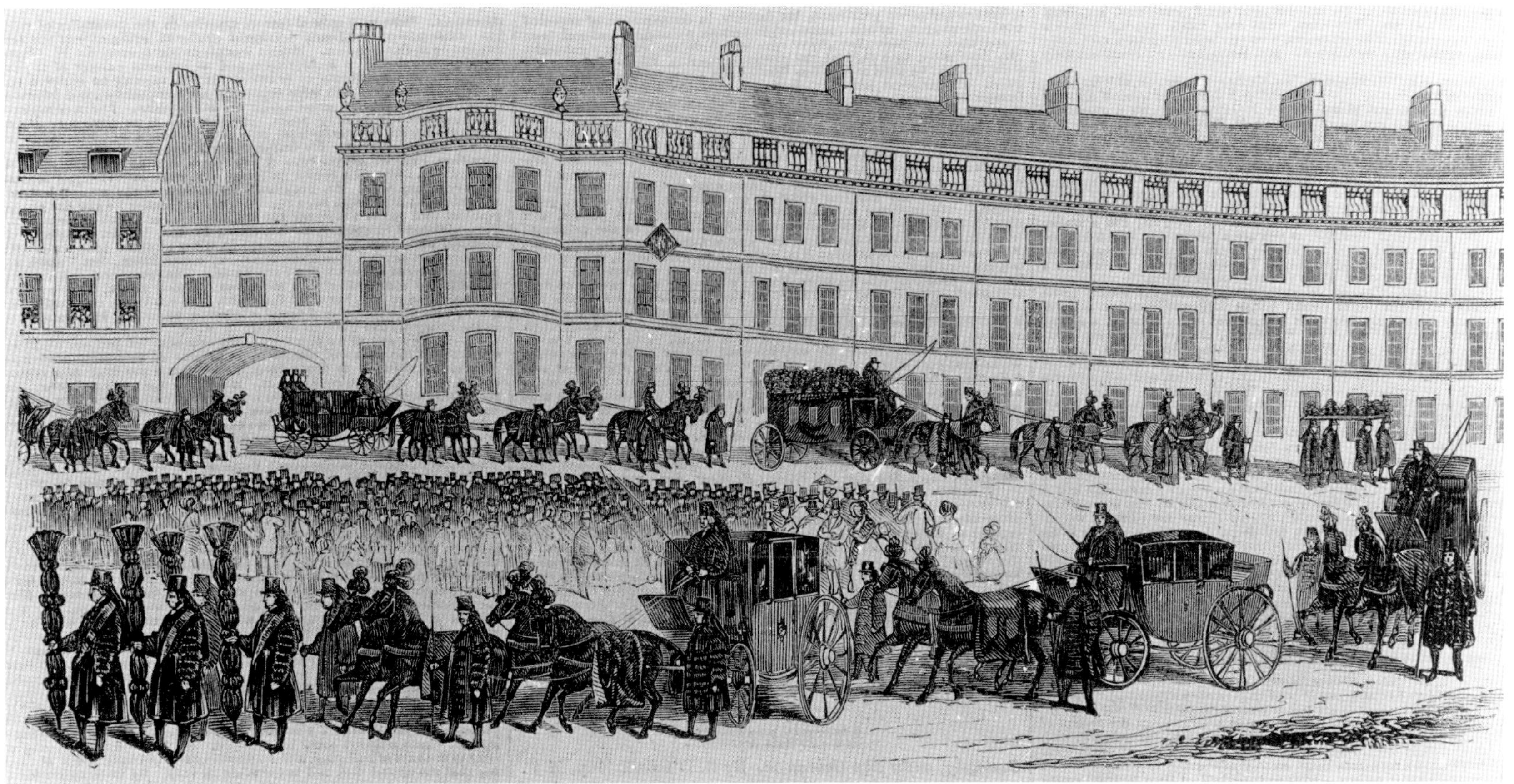

Fig. 15-9. Beckford's funeral procession leaving Lansdown Crescent. Wood engraving. From *Pictorial Times*, May 25, 1844. Courtesy of Bath Central Library

EPILOGUE

On May 19, 1844, Beckford's funeral cortege set out on what was expected to be his final journey (fig. 15-9). At Lyncombe Vale Cemetery, Beckford was entombed within the pink granite sarcophagus that he had originally planned for the grounds of Lansdown Tower. In death as in life, however, Beckford's path was never straight. Gregorio Franchi had once remarked: "If ever I see M. de Beckford on a path that is *not tortuous*, I shall be astonished; and still more so if I ever see him on one what could be called a straight one."[87] Four years after his death, Beckford made another journey up the slopes of his beloved Lansdown Hill, when his sarcophagus was finally placed in the shadow of Lansdown Tower, following his daughter's gift of the building and its grounds for use as a public cemetery.

In the last years of his life, Beckford would sometimes ride from Bath as far as Fonthill. "The woods are still magnificent," he wrote, "and one point of the ruins sublime. Mephistopheles himself could not have contemplated the whole scene more impartially and with greater composure."[88] In about 1843, Alfred Morrison saw the old gentleman, mounted on a sturdy cob, gazing at the ruins of the Abbey. "He had ridden over from Bath to look for a last time.... The old man and the young man looked at it in silence, and then returned to his own place."[89]

Acknowledgments: My work owes much to the resources of the Bodleian Library, Oxford; the Beinecke Rare Book and Manuscript Library, Yale University; and Bath & North East Somerset Libraries, Arts & Archives Service (Bath Central Library). I am grateful to Philip Hewat-Jaboor, Derek Ostergard, and the editorial staff of the Bard Graduate Center for helpful comments and suggestions. Material from the Beckford papers at the Bodleian Library are cited by shelf number as MS Beckford.—SB

Dedicated to the memory of Brian Fothergill, biographer of Sir William Hamilton, envoy extrordinary, and his second cousin William Beckford of Fonthill.

For an excellent overview of Beckford's years in Bath, see Philippa Bishop, "Beckford in Bath," *Bath History*, 2 (1988): 85–112.

1. Beckford to Dr. Schöll, 7 October 1822, quoted in *Life at Fonthill, 1807–1822, with Interludes in Paris and London, from The Correspondence of William Beckford*, ed. Boyd Alexander (London: Rupert Hart-Davis, 1957): 340. The epigraph that begins this essay is quoted in ibid., p. 222.

2. For Bath's social history, see R. S. Neale, *Bath, 1680–1850: A Social History* (London, Routledge & Kegan Paul, 1981). For architecture and townscape, see Walter Ison, *The Georgian Building of Bath from 1700 to 1830* (London: Faber & Faber, 1948); and Neil Jackson, *Nineteenth Century Bath: Architects and Architecture* (Bath: Ashgrove Press, 1991).

3. Hon. Charles Hamilton, ninth son of sixth Earl of Abercorn, created a famous landscape garden, between 1738 and 1773, at Painshill near Cobham, which has recently been restored. Hamilton also advised Henry Hoare on aspects of the landscape at Stourhead, Wiltshire, and he designed the cascade and grotto at Bowood, Wiltshire.

4. Lewis Melville, *Life and Letters of William Beckford of Fonthill* (London: William Heinemann, 1910): 116.

5. Beckford to Lady Hamilton, 2 April 1781, quoted in ibid., p. 105.

6. John Fisher to John Constable, 17 January 1825, quoted in John Constable, *Correspondence: The Fishers*, ed. by R.B. Beckett (Suffolk Record Society, 1986): 6, 198.

7. Brian Fothergill, *Beckford of Fonthill* (London: Faber and Faber, 1979): 134–40.

8. See Boyd Alexander, *From Lisbon to Baker Street: The Story of the Chevalier Franchi, Beckford's Friend* (Lisbon: British Historical Society of Portugal, 1977).

9. See, in particular, Alexander, *Life at Fonthill* (1957).

10. Beckford possibly to Alexander Cozens, 6 February 1780, Beckford's Red Copy Book, MS Beckford e. 1, p. 36. I am grateful to Dick Claesson for providing the source of this quotation. See also Melville, *Life and Letters* (1910): 92.

11. John Britton, *Auto-Biography* (London: the author, 1850): part 1, 230.

12. Ibid., p. 228.

13. Cyrus Redding, journalist and author of many miscellaneous books, was editor of the *Bath Guardian* (1834–35) when he first met Beckford. He was commissioned by Henry Colburn to write a biography of Beckford, but the publisher sold the manuscript to the Duchess of Hamilton (now MS Beckford c.85–6). Redding later rewrote his text and published it in 1859. For Redding's relationship with Beckford, see Jon Millington, "Cyrus Redding: Beckford's First Biographer," *Beckford Journal* 2 (1996): 26–33.

14. Britton, *Auto-Biography*, part 1 (1850): 232.

15. For early editions of Beckford's works see Robert J. Gemmett, "An Annotated Checklist of the Works of William Beckford," *Papers of the Bibliographical Society of America* 61 (1967): 243–55.

16. Rose Macaulay, *They Went to Portugal* (London: Jonathan Cape, 1946): 135.

17. Letter dated 10 July 1834, quoted in *The Consummate Collector: William Beckford's Letters to his Bookseller*, ed. Robert J. Gemmett (Wilby: Michael Russell, 2000): 290.

18. For Beckford as a book collector see Anthony Hobson, "William Beckford's Library," *The Connoisseur* 191 (April 1976): 298–305. For Beckford's correspondence (1830–34) with his bookseller George Clarke, see Gemmett, *The Consummate Collector* (2000).

19. Letter dated 23 April 1833, quoted in Gemmett, *The Consummate Collector* (2000): 203.

20. Letter dated 26 September 1830, in ibid., p. 35.

21. Letter dated 3 December 1831, in ibid., p. 104.

22. Letter dated 31 August 1834, in ibid., p. 313.

23. Letter dated 24 April 1831, in ibid., p. 71.

24. Catalogue of the books at Lansdown Tower, 1831, in Beckford's hand, arranged by room, bookcase, and shelf, MS Beckford f. 2.

25. The young Princess Victoria (later Queen) and her mother, the Duchess of Kent, visited Bath in October 1830. On their final day, Saturday, 23 October, the duchess and presumably her daughter, visited Lansdown Tower. At the end of their visit to the city, the royal party went on to Erlestoke near Devizes, the residence of George Watson Taylor. From a report in the *Bath Chronicle*, 28 October 1830. Watson Taylor was another distinguished collector, and Beckford visited Erlestoke in June 1832, when Watson Taylor, facing financial ruin, was forced to sell the contents of his house.

26. *Morning Post*, 20 April 1842, newspaper clipping, MS Beckford c.81, fol. 28.

27. Cyrus Redding, *Memoirs of William Beckford of Fonthill*, vol. 2 (London: C. J. Skeet, 1859): 303.

28. For Beckford's copy of *The Annual Peerage of the British Empire,* vol. 1 (London: Saunders and Oatley, 1829), see Beckford 269, Beinecke Rare Book and Manuscript Library.

29. MS Beckford c.30, fols. 58–59.

30. Ibid., fol. 161.

31. Ibid., fol. 162v.

32. Ibid.

33. Undated newspaper quoted in Boyd Alexander, *England's Wealthiest Son* (London: Centaur Press, 1962): 236.

34. Letter to Goodridge, 7 April 1834, GEN MSS 102/1/18, Beinecke Rare Book and Manuscript Library.

35. Beckford's original lease was dated 19/20 August 1823.

36. In selling the neighboring house Beckford was determined to preserve his privacy and shield himself from noise. The agreement with Lysaght states that no window openings are to be made in the eastern wall nor is the house to be used as a school or academy (MS Beckford c.29).

37. Letter dated 21 January 1831, quoted in Gemmett, *Consummate Collector* (2000): 54.

38. Redding, *Memoirs* (1859): 2, 363–64.

39. In the last year of his life Beckford is listed in the local ratebooks as the occupant of 18 Lansdown Crescent, but probably kept the property empty, for there is no reference to this house in the inventory made after his death (Walcot Ratebooks, Bath City Archives).

40. Letter to Mrs Hervey, undated (ca. 1778), quoted in Melville, *Life and Letters* (1910): 45.

41. *Journal of William Beckford in Spain and Portugal 1787–1788,* ed. Boyd Alexander (London: Rupert Hart-Davis, 1954): 192.

42. Ibid., p. 301.

43. Henry Venn Lansdown, *Recollections of the Late William Beckford of Fonthill, Wilts and Lansdown, Bath,* (Bath: Kingsmead Reprints, n.d.): 19.

44. Ibid., p. 22.

45. Letter dated 2 July 1831, in Gemmett, *Consummate Collector* (2000): 78.

46. Goodridge, the son of a Bath builder, was in practice in the city from 1819. He worked for Beckford throughout his years in Bath and later carried out commissions for the Duke and Duchess of Hamilton. Three generations of the English family traded as cabinet makers, upholsterers, auctioneers, and undertakers in the city from the 1770s. Acting as Beckford's agent in the purchase of property, furniture making, and interior decoration. Edmund Francis English represented Beckford in the disposal of various pictures, in particular the prolonged negotiations with Robert Holford. He was the author of *Views of Lansdown Tower* published shortly after Beckford's death. In December 1852 a "painful sensation [was felt] throughout the entire city of Bath," when the Englishes, senior and junior, disappeared without trace. Their business was bankrupt, and there had been various forged financial transactions. A public appeal was launched for Mrs English and her daughters. The Duchess of Hamilton told Goodridge that she was "much shocked to hear of the failure of the Englishes and hoped that something may be done by the friends of poor Mrs Edmund English to relieve her anxiety about her five unfortunate children" (letter dated 7 February 1853, AL 1848. B&NES, Bath Central Library).

47. Edmund English to William Beckford, 13 April 1839, MS Beckford c.30, fol. 11.

48. W. Gregory, *The Beckford Family, Reminiscences of Fonthill Abbey and Lansdown Tower* 2d ed. (Bath: Bath Chronicle, 1898): 102. There are no known illustrations of the rooms at Lansdown Crescent. The description that follows is based on the inventory (MS Beckford c.58) made in 1844 after Beckford's death, and catalogues of sales held in 1845 and 1848. I have also used the published account of visits made in 1835 by the German art historian Gustav Waagen, (*The Works of Art and Artists in England* [London; John Murray, 1838]: 3, 114–30; and in 1838 by the Bath artist Henry Venn Lansdown (*Recollections of the late William Beckford* [Bath: privately printed,1893]). Lansdown's book was in an edition of 100 copies, published by his daughter Charlotte.

49. Willes Maddox was born in Bath, worked in London and Italy 1841–42, and died in Constantinople, where he had painted a portrait of the Sultan.

50. Waagen, *Works of Art* (1838): 3, 121–22.

51. Redding, *Memoirs* (1859): 2, 312.

52. Lansdown, *Recollections of the Late William Beckford* (1893): 14.

53. J. Mitford Notebook, MSS Add 32567, fol. 315, British Library.

54. Lansdown, *Recollections of the Late William Beckford* (1893): 10.

55. Ibid.

56. Ibid., p. 14.

57. Ibid., pp. 14–15.

58. Sale catalogue, 31 July 1848, lot 82.

59. The furnishings of the gallery remain in-situ.

60. Sale catalogue, 31 July 1848, lot 52.

61. Lansdown, *Recollections of the Late William Beckford* (1893): 6.

62. Ibid., p. 8.

63. Ibid., p. 9.

64. Ibid., p. 11.

65. No portrait of Lady Margaret is recorded among either the Fonthill or Bath pictures. The only known image of her is a miniature by Maria Cosway (reproduced in Boyd Alexander, *England's Wealthiest Son* [London: Centaur Press, 1962]: facing page 54.

66. James Lees-Milne, *William Beckford* (Tisbury Wiltshire: Compton Russell, 1976): 116.

67. Melville, *Life and Letters* (1910): 37.

68. Lansdown, *Recollections of the Late William Beckford* (1893): 16.

69. H. A. N. Brockman, *The Caliph of Fonthill*, (London: Werner Laurie, 1965): 187.

70. Lansdown, *Recollections of the Late William Beckford* (1893): 16.

71. For "drawings by Mr Goodridge" see ibid.; for "trusses" see inventory of 1844, MS Beckford c.58.

72. Inventory of 1844, MS Beckford c.58.

73. Redding, *Memoirs* (1859): 2, 363.

74. The library at 19 Lansdown Crescent was owned for a number of years by the architectural historian and writer James Lees-Milne, here he wrote his biography of Beckford, published in 1976.

75. Illustrated in John Rutter, *Delineations of Fonthill and its Abbey*, (Shaftesbury: the author, 1823): 65.

76. Lansdown, *Recollections of the Late William Beckford* (1893): 19.

77. Letter dated 29 April 1844, GEN MSS 102, 3, 50 (no 43), Beinecke Rare Book and Manuscript Library.

78. MS Beckford c.58.

79. *Valuable Paintings, Magnificent Cabinets and Splendid Furniture from Lansdown Tower…*, sale cat., English & Son, Bath, 4–5 January 1841.

80. *Lansdown Tower, Bath*, sale cat., English & Son, Bath, 20–19 November 1845.

81. *Valuable and Costly Effects at 20, Lansdown crescent, Bath, the property of the Late William Beckford, Esq…*, sale cat., English & Son, Bath, on 24 July–1 August 1848.

82. Ibid., 28 July 1848, lot 21 (wines).

83. MS Beckford b.2.

84. *Pictures, Works of Art and Decorative Objects the Property of His Grace the Duke of Hamilton…*, sale cat., Christie's, 17 June 1882; and *The Hamilton Palace Collection: Illustrated Priced Catalogue* (London: Remington, 1882). The seventeen day sale realized £397,562.

85. *Beckford Library removed from Hamilton Palace*, sale cat., Sotheby, Wilkinson & Hodge part 1, 30 June–13 July 1882; part 2, 11–23 December 1882; part 3, 2–14 July 1883; part 4, 27–30 November 1883.

86. *Family Portraits Works by Old Masters and Modern Pictures the Property of the Trustees of his Grace the late Duke of Hamilton.*, sale cat., Christie, Manson & Woods, 6–7 November 1919.

87. Letter to the Duke of Hamilton, quoted in Alexander, *England's Wealthiest Son* (1962): 195.

88. Beckford draft letter dated 19 July 1835, quoted in J. W. Oliver, *The Life of William Beckford* (London: Oxford University Press, 1932): 315.

89. Anecdote recorded in Edith Olivier, *Four Victorian Ladies of Wiltshire* (London: Faber & Faber, 1945): 47.

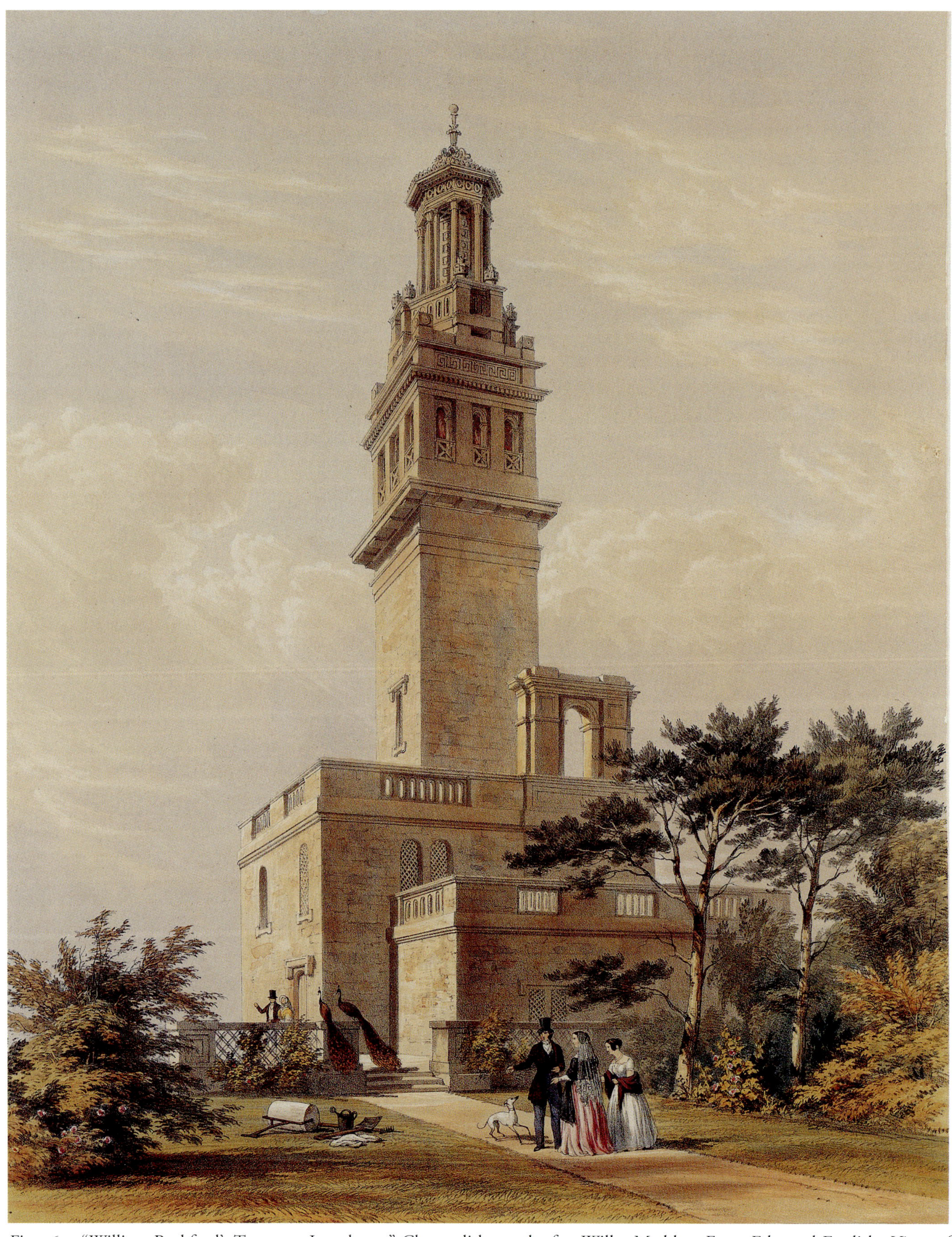

Fig. 16-1. "William Beckford's Tower on Lansdown." Chromolithograph after Willes Maddox. From Edmund English, *Views of Lansdown Tower* (1844).

CHAPTER XVI

BECKFORD'S TOWER IN BATH

CHRISTOPHER WOODWARD

The late proprietor of Fonthill Abbey, William Beckford Esq., arrived last week at his mansion in Lansdown Crescent, in this city, and we are informed that he has concluded the purchase of the land extending from the back of his residence to the top of Lansdown, which he intends to lay out with the same classic taste that he has already imparted with such enchanting [results] to the Wiltshire hills.

—Bath and Cheltenham Gazette, July 1, 1823

The Greco-Italian tower that William Beckford erected on the hills above the spa resort of Bath beginning in 1826 was far more than a postscript to Fonthill Abbey. While he lived, Lansdown Tower (fig. 16-1) would be a place where he could read, write, and reflect in absolute solitude; at his death, he intended to be buried in a sepulchral chamber within its walls. The tower is diminutive in comparison to the Abbey, its neo-Greek lantern rising to less than half the height of the Gothic spire, but its architecture was a more direct expression of Beckford's personal taste. At Fonthill James Wyatt had reinterpreted Beckford's wishes in his own idiom but in Bath Beckford employed a local architect, Henry Edmund Goodridge, to be his amanuensis. The tower's decoration and furnishing busied Beckford's imagination for the last twenty years of his life, and the result was one of the most original and beguiling buildings to be erected in early nineteenth-century Britain and a splendid finale to Beckford's career.

Beckford moved to Bath in the summer of 1823, at the age of sixty-two. He wrote: "At present I only have to distribute my funds prudently and await the outcome of events. For twenty years I have not found myself so rich, so independent or so tranquil."[1] In considering Beckford's choice of city it is most important to appreciate that William Beckford's Bath was not the gregarious spa resort of promenades, card parties, and balls that Thomas Gainsborough and Jane Austen had depicted in the previous century. Not only had fashionable society departed by the Regency period, but Beckford chose to live high on the hillside where he could ignore the city's existence. The land below Lansdown Crescent falls so steeply that from Beckford's windows the only sign of the Circus, Pump Room, and Assembly Rooms was the smoke from their invisible chimneys. Beckford did not enjoy the city's Georgian terraces; their uniformity of appearance and insistent horizontality were the antithesis of the Picturesque qualities of variety, surprise, and changing perspectives that would be embodied in the tower's design. As the German architect, Karl Friedrich Schinkel wrote when he visited Bath in 1826, the architecture is "rather boring and wholly in the mean English style."[2] He could enjoy, however, south-facing views across the valley to the wooded hills. Light glinted on villas built in the local white limestone, and the play of light on the folds of pasture during the course of the day was a study in the Picturesque.[3]

From the beginning the terraced house in town and the tower on the hill were conceived in tandem, and Beckford divided his time—and his collection of works of art and books—between the two. The tower stands 800 feet above sea level, on the flat summit of Lansdown, the hill that rises to the north of the city. From its belvedere 154 feet high it is possible to see 30 miles; King Alfred's Tower at Stourhead is a distinct, dark finger on the skyline 18 miles away, and the light on the distant, purple hillsides reminiscent of Claude's horizons. When asked what reconciled him to Bath after the vastness of Fonthill, Beckford indicated the panoramic view: "This! This! The finest prospect in Europe!"[4] The plateau was a "bare, shrubless tract of land" grazed by sheep when Beckford arrived and notorious even today for being cold, misty, and windswept.[5] Beckford was reminded of the desolate, flat Campagna around Rome: "I shall never forget how I passed over that land of the Dead, strewed with ruins and covered with green turf. . . . This scene [Lansdown] recalls to me my dreams and meditations there. The surface is smoother but it has the same dun colour, the same 'death-like stillness' and 'dread repose'."[6] The only human intrusions into this view were a few farmers and shepherds; there are few places in the neighborhood of English cities where one can see so far, but see so few people.

Life in Bath was a constant struggle for solitude. Beckford was frequently forced to descend from Vathekian heights of isolation to argue with neighbors over their barking dogs, with farmers over footpaths and fences, and with the local municipality about leaking water pipes. At Fonthill he had been a Caliph, the owner of a domain with rides 20 miles in length. In Bath he was the tenant of a strip of land approximately one mile in length from house to tower, and varying in width from 200 to 1,500 feet. His proud isolation was created by art-

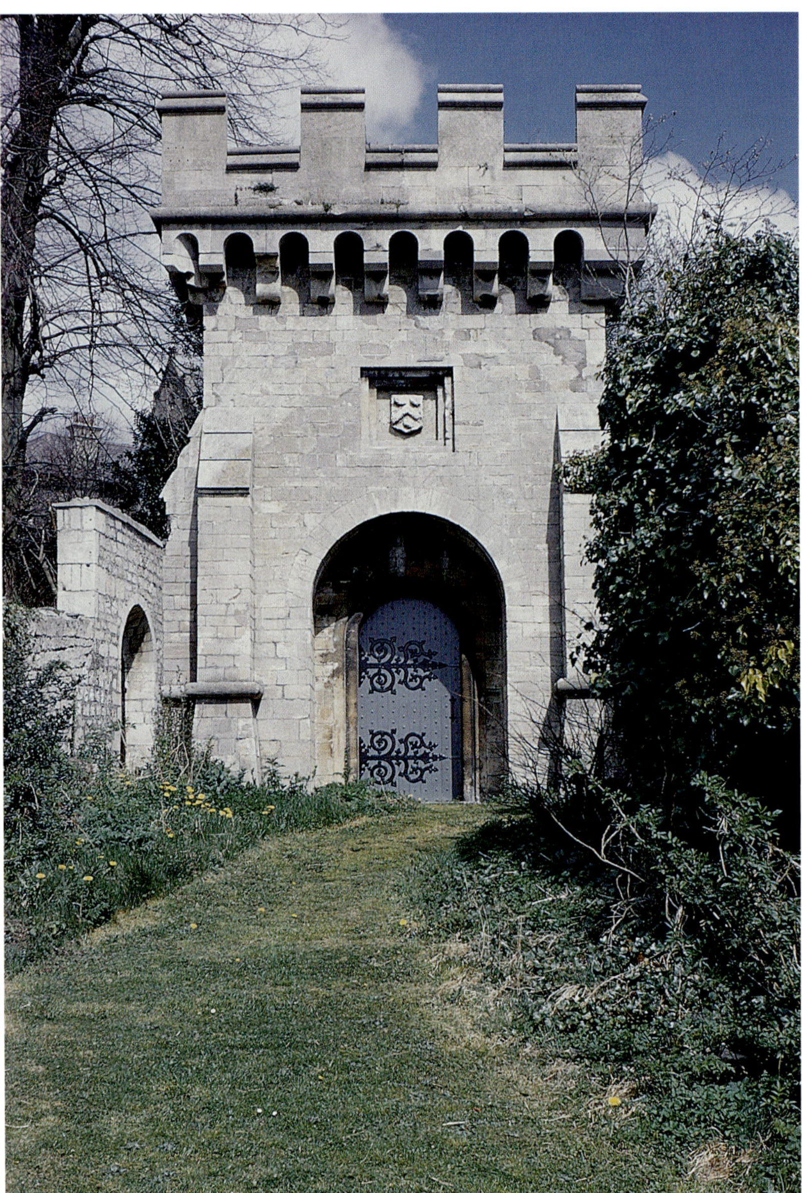

Fig. 16-2. The Embattled Gateway, Bath. Designed by H. E. Goodridge, ca. 1826. Photographed in 1970.

ful optical illusions, whether this was to plant trees, to bury his private path known as the Ride under a public road, or to erect a castellated gateway in order to hide from view an irritating eyesore on a neighbor's property (fig. 16-2).[7] As when he began to build Fonthill Abbey, his first action at Bath—six months after he arrived—was to enclose his land with a stone wall 10 feet high. This was a new impediment to the local lads who "beat the bounds" in 1828, the traditional custom of walking the boundary of the parish every seven years. As the *Bath Chronicle* of May 22, 1828, reported, "A curious feature of this cere-mony was that Mr Beckford's battlemented porch at the entrance to

his grounds happening to divide the two parishes of Walcot and Charlecombe, ladders were procured & three or four young men were sent over the top of it. A similar occurrence took place at the newly erected walls about that gentleman's tower which happens to divide that parish from Weston."[8] One can only imagine Beckford's splutter-ing anger at this deliberate violation of his privacy.

THE MAUSOLEUM

One of the earliest designs for the tower is a drawing in the Wiltshire Archaeological Museum and Natural History Society at Devizes with four elevations and a plan on a folded sheet of paper, which was later annotated by John Britton, "Mr Beckford–for Mausoleum at Fonthill." It is certainly for Lansdown, however, and can be dated to September or October 1823. The intention of burial is corroborated by several later letters: in 1834 he instructed his architect to "Form a marble panel in the centre of the present floor—conceal this pave-ment under a rich carpet—and keep the Tomb in a packing case until wanted."[9] Beckford's plan revived his earlier concept of being buried high inside the tower at Fonthill Abbey, and when news of the prospec-tive Lansdown Tower reached London, a hostile critic in the *Sunday Times*, October 5, 1823, reminded readers: "A lofty tower was the first ingested plan [at Fonthill], on the airy summit of which he wished his ashes to slumber . . . And since Fonthill has passed from him, it is believed he is planning another work on which the wrecks of his for-tune will be cast." No one in early nineteenth-century Britain rivaled Beckford in the splendor of his sepulcher, except for the Duke of Hamilton, who expended more energy and money on the construction of a neoantique mausoleum than did many princes of the age.

When Jean-Jacques Rousseau was buried in a sarcophagus on an island of poplars at d'Ermenonville in 1774, he was the first man to be buried in a garden since antiquity. This practice became a neoclas-sical cult, and in England pyramidical mausolea were built in Arcadian settings in the grounds of Cobham Hall, Kent, in 1782, and Blickling Hall, Norfolk, in 1794. At Trentham, Staffordshire, in 1807–8 the fam-ily mausoleum was built beside the main road in a deliberate echo of the Appian Way. Burial outside a churchyard required a special consent from the ecclesiastical authorities, however, and at Cobham the Bishop of Rochester refused to consecrate the Darnley mausoleum which, con-sequently, has lain empty ever since.[10] The Bishop of Bath and Wells would also refuse to consecrate Beckford's garden for private burial.

Beckford's wish to be buried in a garden may not have been particularly unusual by the 1820s, but two aspects of the plan were unique to the period. Noone chose to live inside a structure that would later become their tomb, and no tomb occupied such a commanding position in the landscape. In addition to its panoramic views, the site reminded Beckford of the Campagna, the malaria-ridden wilderness around Rome whose only inhabitants were shepherds and cattle-drovers and the dead, whose mausolea lined the Appian Way in the thousands. Most Grand Tourists hastened their carriages toward the distant glint of Saint Peter's dome, but in 1778 Beckford halted his retinue to explore, as he described in a famous meditation in *Dreams, Waking Thoughts and Incidents*. Crossing a brook he found:

> the shepherds huts on its banks, propped up with broken pedestals and marble friezes. I entered one of them, whose owner was abroad, tending his herds, and began writing upon the sand and murmuring a melancholy song. Perhaps, the dead listened to me from their narrow cells. The living I can answer for; they were far enough removed. You will not be surprised at the dark tone of my musings in so sad a scene; especially as the weather lowered; and you are well-acquainted how greatly I depend upon blue skies and sunshine . . . Heath and furze were the sole vegetation which covers this endless wilderness. Every slope is strewed with a the relics of a happier period; trunks of trees, shattered columns, cedar beams, helmets of bronze, skulls and coins.[11]

This was the imaginative background to the mausoleum on Lansdown. The mood of future oblivion was deepened by Beckford's participation in the widespread foreboding about the doom of British civilization. As expressed in, for example, Mary Shelley's novel, *The Last Man* (1826), there was in the 1820s and 1830s a greater sense of Millennialist foreboding than in any period since the late Middle Ages.[12] Beckford was the most outstanding example of an educated patron of apocalyptic art in Britain; in 1828, for example, he bought *The Opening of the Sixth Seal* by Francis Danby after its exhibition at the Royal Academy.[13] Struck by this picture, Beckford also commissioned Danby to paint scenes from the Book of Revelations as overdoors in the Sanctuary of the tower.[14] In the years leading up to the Great Reform Bill of 1832 Britain came closer to revolution than at any time since the seventeenth century, and Beckford shared the Millennialist belief that these disturbances were the signs foretold in the Book of Revelation. From the tower he could see the fires burning in Bristol in October 1831, when the mob destroyed the prisons, tax offices, and Bishop's Palace. In a letter of April 27, 1833, he discussed the increased emigration with his bookseller: "I do not wonder at the process of emigration [to America]. Flee from the wrath to come is sounding through the atmosphere like a blast from the dread trumpet of the Apocalypse. . . . The vision of the trunk-less seems to have warned the Prime Minister to little purpose. He keeps on-on-on—as if advancing to a gulph [sic] of ruin, of despair!"[15]

With characteristic solipsism, however, the end of the world had been brought home to Beckford with a bang in April 1832 when—with the fear of revolution at its height—robbers armed with a blunderbuss attempted to burgle the tower, and Beckford wrote, "Some of the Bristol connoisseurs, it is suspected, paid the Tower a domiciliary visit t'other night, quite à la garde nationale and would have carried off a capital booty, had not my people been raised from their slumbers. Guns were fired, sackfulls of good things dropped in the hurry of escape, and excepting two articles of more curiosity than value, nothing is missing."[16]

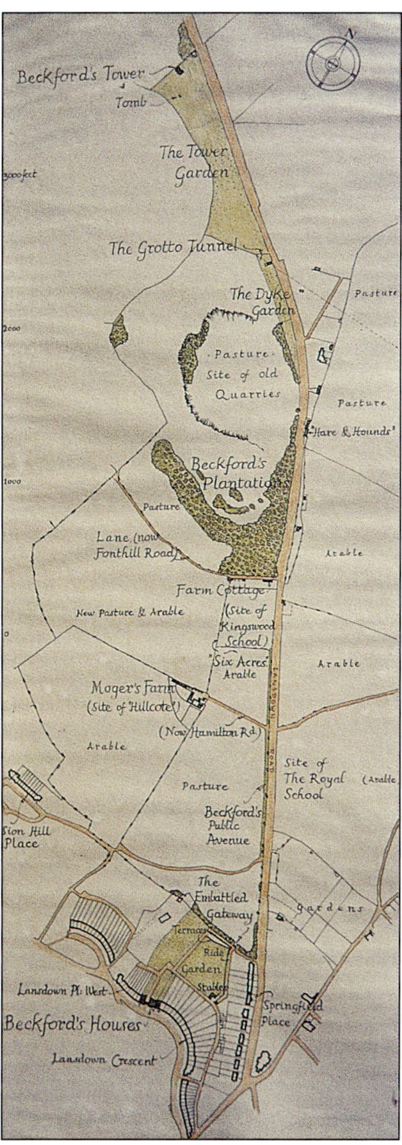

Fig. 16-3. Map of Beckford's Ride, based on an 1838 tithe map of the parish of Charlcombe. Drawn by Hugh Crallan for *William Beckford*, an exhibition held at the Holburne Museum, Bath, in 1966.

BECKFORD'S RIDE

Bath is encircled by hills, but as early as February 19, 1823, Beckford had decided to live on the slopes that rose to the north, which were named Lansdown: "Have the goodness therefore to turn all your attention to *Lansdowne* [sic] the *only* spot in the neighbourhood of Bath for which I entertain a decided predilection," he wrote to Edmund English, a Bath upholsterer and auctioneer whom Beckford used as his intermediary from the beginning to the end of his time in Bath. By March 1, 1823, Beckford had begun negotiations to buy the land for the tower and Ride from the Gunning family,[17] and on March 25, 1823, he signed the lease of three fields, plus thirty-nine acres of down and common. The Gunnings' estate was entailed, and he was only able to lease the land for ninety-nine years. The Ride (fig. 16-3) was therefore a patchwork of tenancies, and the only plot he was ever able to buy freehold was the kitchen garden immediately behind 20 Lansdown Crescent.[18]

The tower was built at the furthest tip of the leased property. The Ordinance Survey map of 1817 shows a building on the site of the tower and also a cottage by the road, and either one of these must be the "upstart house,"[19] mentioned by Beckford when he declared his intention of "converting the upstart house into a picturesque tower" as soon as possible.[20] By July 1, 1823, his plan to create an extensive garden was reported in the local newspaper, and in September the Quarter Sessions—an arm of the local judicature—agreed to the closure of footpaths across his land. In compensation, it was reported on September 16, Beckford "proposes giving an ample gravelled walk at least twelve feet wide, on which it is intended to plant an avenue of trees and place seats thereon . . ."[21] The surveyor signed the plan "H E Goodridge Archt, 1823"[22]; this is the first evidence of the involvement of the young man who was to become Beckford's architect. The map shows the site crisscrossed with footpaths leading from the city to Moger's Farm, the race course, and the Blathwayt Arms on the far rim of the plateau. Beckford was later to remark that the tower's gilded lantern was "a famous landmark for the drunken farmers on their return from market."[23] The *Observer* of October 13, 1823, gave the fullest report to date:

> Lansdown Hill is now the scene of most active labours. . . . From sunrise to sunset there are to be seen 300 or 400 workmen, in different directions, attended by immense numbers of carts &c., busily engaged in building walls about ten feet high with Bath stone, levelling irregularities or hillocks on the summit or about the hill, forming roads, and laying out grounds for the plantation of upward of 200,000 young trees. The summit of the hill is preparing for the erection of a Saxon tower, from the top of which will be seen Fonthill Abbey, a distance of 35 miles!

Construction did not begin until 1826, however, and by then the spire of Fonthill Abbey had collapsed. The *Bath Guide* of 1825 notes that the works of the estate "are apparently at a stand-still for the present." In May of that year Beckford leased ten acres beyond the tower, but his intention to "convert every acre of this field into wood" as a green backdrop to the structure when seen on the approach from Bath was prevented by the owner's insistence that only one acre could be planted with trees; any more would have to revert to field or pasture at the end of the tenancy.[24] In August 1826 Beckford bought, at a cost of £5,250, the garden directly behind 20 Lansdown Crescent, on two sides of which stood a terrace raised on stone vaults. This was a significant purchase, because not only was it freehold land, but he was now able to ride from his house to the tower without once stepping on to the public highway.

The best guide to Beckford's daily ride is the local artist with the confusing name—in this context—of Henry Venn Lansdown. He obtained an entrée to Beckford through his friend Goodridge in 1839 and many years later recalled his experience in a letter to his daughter.[25] The freehold land behind the house had become a "spacious kitchen garden, containing, I believe, 7 or 8 acres" and the adjoining vaulted terrace a "broad gravel walk bordered by lovely flowers and fruit trees" leading to "an archway of massive proportions erected chiefly to shut out the view of an unpicturesque object." This unidentified object was no doubt a structure on a neighbor's land. The gateway—which was in place by April 10, 1827, when it was drawn by John Buckler—was built in the "Saxon style" in which the tower was conceived.[26] It is a splendid piece of stage scenery: despite its overbearing, battlemented brow, the stone structure is only a few feet in depth. Passing under this archway, decorated with Beckford's coat-of-arms, Lansdown passed through a seven-acre plantation of trees and on to the curving shoulder of the downs. Here Beckford had placed seats from which to enjoy what he had described as the "finest prospect in Europe": the hills of Wales in the distance, the spired silhouette of Bristol, the plain of the Avon River below.

Returning to the plateau Venn Lansdown arrived at an "immense [stone] quarry" that had become a flower garden. It was "most picturesque"; "at a little distance they [the excavations] seem to present the wrecks of stately buildings, with rows of broken arches, and vividly recall the idea of Roman ruins. I afterwards mentioned my impressions on seeing them to Mr Beckford, who replied 'They do indeed put one in mind of the Campagna of Rome, and are vastly like the ruins of the Baths of Caracalla'."[27] These baths stood outside the center of the city and were the wildest ruins in Rome, a tumbling, scented jungle which to a Romantic imagination seemed to represent the triumph of Nature over the achievements of man. To Shelley, who wrote the first acts of *Prometheus Unbound* in the Roman ruins,[28] the scene represented the triumph of natural liberty over the monuments of tyranny; to Beckford they may have been a more melancholy *vanitas*, deepening the memory of the Campagna.

The Ride was a sequence of designed vignettes, and the next episode was the Ditch of Dyke Garden, sunk 12 feet below the level of the plateau. This stretch of land, 400 feet in length and 80 feet wide, was acquired from a farmer named Mr. Ennever in 1834 and five years later was bordered with flowers and apple trees. Venn Lansdown asked the gardener: "'I understood Mr Beckford had planted everything on the Down, but you surely found these apple trees here. They are fifty years old'. 'We found nothing here but an old quarry and a few nettles. Those apple trees were great trees when we moved them, and moving them stopped their bearing. They blossom in the spring, and look pretty, and that is all the master cares about'."[29] This is intended, one presumes, as a simile of Beckford's view of his own time on earth.

Ennever's house was extended and reconstructed in the style of an Italian farmhouse. Its archway led not into a farmyard, but into a grotto and tunnel, 70 feet in length. This saved Beckford from crossing the road leading to Chelscombe Farm, a public right-of-way he was unable to have closed. The last stage of the Ride was the Alpine Garden in the sunken ground at the base of the tower, and it was here that Beckford waited in order to continue Venn Lansdown's tour inside.

Building The Tower

The first evidence of construction is a report in the *Bath and Cheltenham Gazette* on October 5, 1826, that "one hundred men [are] employed in the erection of a splendid and ornamental building, of which a magnificent tower will form a part."[30] A sketch by Beckford inscribed "Nov. 1826" showed the tower built as high as the cornice above the belvedere, and a drawing by John Buckler dated April 10, 1827, shows that the octagonal story immediately above was in place by that date.[31] The *Gazette* of July 27, 1827, reports that the lantern was in place, but its pillars not yet gilded. In December 1827 the heating system was ordered, and the interiors seem to have been installed in the course of the following year. The *Bath Guide* of 1829 announced that the "interior of this Tower is furnished in a style of almost regal splendour." That year Goodridge traveled to Italy, a trip he could hardly have made unless Beckford was satisfied that the job was done.

There was a significant complication, however. In the memoir of H. E. Goodridge which his son Alfred published in 1864, it is reported that in twenty-eight days the tower was built up to the block cornice "where it was intended to be roofed. Then the belvedere was added, again with the intention of finishing the roof at this stage, but again Mr Beckford, cried 'Higher!', and the lantern was added to crown the summit."[32] This is not just another myth of Beckford's impulsiveness. The physical evidence uncovered in the 1999 restoration of the tower confirmed that Beckford had not one, but two, after-thoughts. The tower was conceived as a plain rectangle of masonry with a few slit windows, as austere and fortresslike as a tower in San Gimignano, Italy. After this was built, Beckford decided to add the belvedere. The sketch he made in November was not a survey but, most probably, his own design for this next stage. This first vertical addition was not a problem; the second—the cast-iron lantern "added to crown the summit"—was a greater challenge to the architect. Goodridge was required to place ten tons of iron on a tower whose uppermost stone walls had diminished to a width of 4 inches. With great ingenuity, at a lower level he inserted a grid of oak timbers inside the hollow core of the tower, and this wooden raft supported the base of the lantern. His sense of responsibility when faced with Beckford's whims was indeed a contrast to that of James Wyatt at Fonthill Abbey.[33]

The Architect

Henry Edmund Goodridge was a local builder's son who was to become Beckford's protégé and closest confidant in Bath.[34] James Goodridge, his father, was a successful developer and also for fifty years the agent to the Darlington estate which included Great Pulteney Street and Bathwick Hill. Henry had trained as an architect and visited Paris, but was only twenty-four years old when he was commissioned

by Beckford and had built almost nothing to impress his new client.[35] His own son, Alfred Goodridge, claimed that Beckford requested designs for a tower from numerous architects in London and Bath, but there are no records of these designs in the Drawings Collection of the Royal Institute of British Architects or in the catalogues of Royal Academy exhibitions at that time. Closer to the truth is the son's claim that Beckford, "who could not get on with anyone who in this respect was not like himself, was impressed with his [Henry's] great quickness and readiness of manner."[36] Goodridge's first commission was to survey the boundaries of Lansdown, and—given his father's local connections—he may have been recommended by Edmund English for this task. The relationship of Goodridge's measured drawings to Beckford's sketches for the "Saxon Tower" confirm that Goodridge began as an executant to his client's ideas. Beckford required an architect who was attentive, acquiescent, and reliable, prompt in fulfilling his impulsive demands, and available at the snap of his fingers—in short, the very antithesis of James Wyatt.

How good an architect was Goodridge? His earliest designs, such as The Corridor (1825) and Cleveland Bridge (1827) show a subtle and handsome adaptation of the monuments illustrated in Stuart and Revett's *Antiquities of Athens* (published from 1762 onward) to the streetscape of Bath. In the next decade his unfinished designs for two Catholic Cathedrals in a rich "Corinthian" style at Clifton (1838) and Prior Park in Bath (1834), show him to be one of the finest architects outside London working in the neoclassical style. Beckford approved the latter as "one of the happiest and most striking [designs] I ever beheld," showing that he continued in the role of mentor.[37] Goodridge's foothold in every textbook of nineteenth-century architecture, however, is owing to his interaction with Beckford; it was the patron's imagination that elevated Lansdown Tower to the status of a masterpiece. Goodridge applied the lessons to Montebello, a villa he designed for his own family shortly after his visit to Italy in 1829. Designed in a style which has been dubbed "Italianate" by many writers,[38] but which Goodridge himself called "Greco-Italian," this austere and asymmetrical villa has attracted attention for its so-called proto-Modernism.[39]

A codicil to the relationship is that Goodridge was commissioned by the Duchess of Hamilton to design the library at Hamilton Palace, where Beckford's books were moved after 1844, and made the design for the first mauseleum but was replaced by David Bryce. A French employee of the Hamiltons remarked of Alfred Goodridge, who traveled as an assistant to his father, "this young man is even more gossipy than his father, and has even less talent. But both possess plenty of cunning."[40] Perhaps the Frenchman was piqued, but if Henry were indeed a "gossip" it would explain the stories that appeared in the newspapers, such as an account of the "Saxon tower" in the *Observer* of October 1823.

Architectural Style

Although the tower was far less daring in conception and achievement than Fonthill Abbey, its architectural style was perhaps more novel than

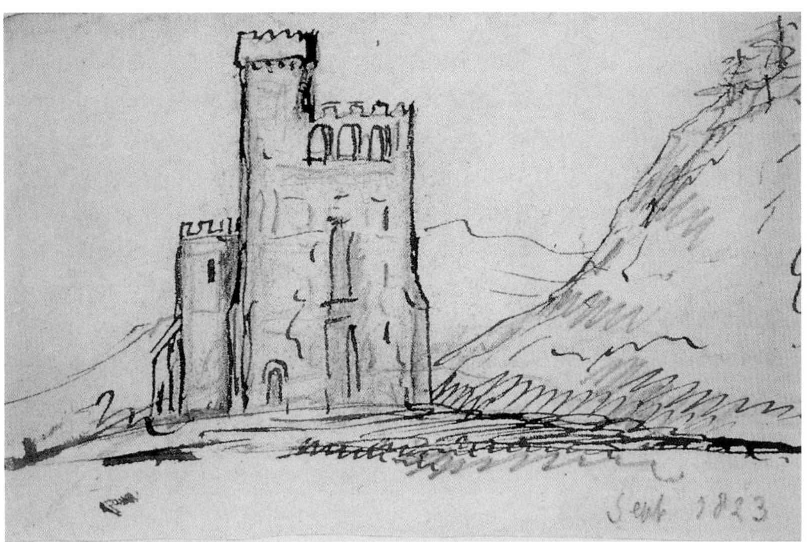

Fig. 16-4. William Beckford. Sketch of a "Saxon" tower, 1823. Pencil on newspaper. The Bodleian Library, Oxford, MS Beckford c.84, fol. 123.

Wyatt's neo-Gothic. A direct expression of Beckford's personal taste, it was unclassifiable in the stylistic terminology of the time; it was instead "a new style, mostly Beckford's own. It has been described variously as Tuscan, Roman, Byzantine, and Italo-Greek," and also Greek Revival.[41] The tower has been considered the "one English building [which] above all symbolizes the different strands which make up the Greek Revival . . . a unique combination of Classic and Romantic, Greek and Italianate, Picturesque and Sublime."[42]

Goodridge himself has explained the style, fortunately.[43] As recorded by his son, he said it "may be termed Greco-Italian, a style Mr Goodridge greatly adopted as he considered therein the purity of the Greek and the freedom of the Romanesque were best combined."[44]

The "purity of the Greek" refers not only to the archaeological exactitude of its ornamentation but also to the general chasteness of the exterior. By the "freedom of the Romanesque" the architect meant the Picturesque asymmetry and irregularity of early medieval architecture. The term *Romanesque* was common currency by 1864, when Alfred came to write his father's obituary, but was first coined by the Reverend William Gunn in a pamphlet published in 1819. In the 1820s "Saxon" was the accepted term for early medieval architecture,[45] and was applied to the first designs for the tower.

In an age of stylistic pluralism William Beckford, Thomas Hope, and John Soane were the three outstanding examples of individuals who synthesized the picturesque qualities of the medieval with elevations in the classical style. Hope did so by his asymmetric groundplans, and Soane by his abstraction of Gothic "effects" of illumination and verticality into classical interiors.[46] As for Beckford, from his earliest youth, his eye for pictorial "effect" had dissolved the established

boundaries between architecture styles.[47] As he declared in *The Long Story* of 1777, in the hero's palace the pillars "supported neither frieze nor cornice, nor any ornament consistent with the rules of architecture we observe on the surface of the earth."[48] Beckford was quite exceptional in his ability to capture the dramatic essence of a building. His suggestion that Ledoux's designs were "very like what Sir John Vanbrugh would have invented had he lived at the present period" was an aperçu worthy of the great modern critic Sir John Summerson.[49] Passing under the Bridge of Sighs in Venice in 1778 induced memories of Piranesi's *Carceri*, and this reverie was the first recorded instance in Europe of a writer making the imaginative leap of comparing an actual scene to a print by the artist.[50]

Unlike Soane or Hope, however, Beckford's synthesis of classical and Gothic was the consequence of an abrupt change of style midway through the design. The earliest design for a tower is a tiny squiggly sketch in Beckford's hand on newspaper, inscribed "Sep. 1823," with a notional landscape background (fig. 16-4). This was expanded into the drawing in the collection of the Wiltshire Archaeological and Natural History Society at Devizes, which in turn was worked up by Goodridge into a measured drawing now in the Hornby Art Library, Liverpool, dated to October 1823, when news of the "Saxon tower" appeared in the press for the first time.[51]

The second design is more expressive of "the freedom of the Romanesque." The compact donjon of the first sketch became more complex and asymmetric in plan and lively in silhouette; the deep recessions and bold, overhanging battlements cast strong shadows on its surface. These Picturesque qualities were translated into the neoclassical tower which was begun in 1826. More specific features that were "lifted" included the panoramic belvedere inside each tower and the triple-arched loggia.

Why Beckford changed to a neoclassical style at some point between autumn 1823 and autumn 1826 has yet to be explained. It might have been a delayed response to Thomas Hope's criticisms of Fonthill Abbey made in 1804, when his pamphlet promoting the Greek Revival argued that in Wiltshire a mock-Gothic tower could only ever be a poor neighbor to Salisbury Cathedral: "had the Grecian orders been employed, a mansion might have arisen, unrivalled in the most distant parts of the island."[52] Beckford admitted to Benjamin West that "Tom Hope was right in His remarks . . . a Gothic design was ill placed within view of Salisbury Cathedral,"[53] but that only Gothic windows allowed him the necessary space to display the heraldry delineating his ancestral lineage. (At Lansdown, incidentally, there was far less heraldry than at Fonthill.) One biographer was not convinced by this theory, however, suggesting that it was not in Beckford's nature to follow the advice of a rival connoisseur.[54] In all likelihood, the change was the consequence of some whim that will never be explained.

The moldings used in the interior decoration were textbook Greek Revival, as is best seen inside the belvedere, where the anthemion or Grecian honeysuckle, the lotus, and other standard motifs are found. The gilded lantern is the circular Choragic

Monument of Lysicrates transposed to an octagonal plan. This monument erected in Athens in the fourth-century B.C. was a canonical source for neoclassical architects, and had been adapted by the Inwoods in their design for the octagonal tower of Saint Pancras Church, London in 1819, and Beckford probably saw this tower after its construction began in 1822 (see fig. 14-1). In a student design for a monument to Princess Charlotte made in 1817, however, Goodridge had already proposed placing the same monument on an octagonal plinth.[55] Alternatively, Beckford might have suggested the source, as he had done when commissioning his bed from Soane at Fonthill House in 1786.[56] The choice of cast iron can safely be attributed to Goodridge, however, for in 1827 he was building Cleveland Bridge with a handsome balustrade in the same material.[57]

There is a third and final element to the Greco-Italian, however, and that is Beckford's pictorial approach to design. Furthermore, "Greco-Italian" has to be disentangled from the "Italianate" style that flourished in the 1820s and 1830s and is sometimes applied to the tower. This is not the ornate "Italianate" of Charles Barry's Travellers' Club (begun 1829), a style that chose as its model the urban *palazzi* of the Renaissance with their richly layered symmetrical facades. The tower has been placed in the context of the rustic variant of the Italianate, a style characterized by asymmetry, loggias, verandahs, campaniles, tiled roofs, and spreading eaves, as popularized in pattern books, such as J. G. Jackson, *Designs for Villas* (1828); R. F. Robinson, *Designs for Ornamental Villas* (1827); Robert Wetten, *Designs for Villas in the Italian Style of Architecture* (1828); Frederick Hunt, *Architettura Campestre* (1827); and Charles Parker, *Villa Rustica* (1832–33). The key building was The Deepdene, a country house near Dorking, Sussex, which was remodeled by Thomas Hope in 1818–23.[58] Hope built a tower topped by a loggia, probably the first of its type in Britain, "a curious open tower, constructed in the Tuscan or Lombard taste," according to a contemporary commentator.[59] It was to become a ubiquitous feature of Victorian villadom. The Deepdene was also the first house to demonstrate that picturesque asymmetry could be achieved not just in the neomedieval style but also in the neoclassical, as first explored by Hope in sketches made for his *Essay on Gardening* around 1807.[60] Even if the tower at Lansdown was not a direct response to Hope's criticisms of Fonthill, there is no doubt that Beckford recognized Hope's abilities as a collector and connoisseur.

On English soil the seed-acorn of the rustic Italianate was the little villa of Cronkhill which John Nash built on Lord Berwick's estate at Attingham, Shropshire, around 1802. The style was not invented in England, however, but in France around 1790.[61] The new approach to structures in the Italian countryside was initiated by painters such as Jean-Joseph Bidauld and Jean-Honoré Marmont de Barmont who traveled to Italy, and whose landscapes combined a deliberate evocation of Poussin with a delight in the play of light upon terracotta tiles and rough surfaces of flaking stucco, characteristics of the plein-air school of painters led by Henri de Valenciennes. It was a painter's style, introduced to architectural composition in the last years of the ancien

régime by E. Boullée and F.-J. Bélanger, and reaching its fullest and most delightful expression in the ensemble of towers, farmhouses, and villas created by the sculptor Frederic Lemot and the brothers Cacault, artists and collectors, at the town of Clisson, near Nantes, after 1805.

Beckford designed—but did not execute—a screen of offices to conceal the tower from the public road in a very similar rustic Italian style, which was also represented at Mr. Ennever's Cottage, reconstructed after 1834.[62] The tower itself was diametrically opposed in spirit, its austere and all-but-blind stone elevations unrelieved by welcoming verandas, spreading eaves or warm clay tiles. Moreover, at Clisson and at The Deepdene, Lemot and Hope chose wooded, hilly landscapes that were reminiscent of Italy—Tuscany perhaps—at its most verdant and benign. Beckford's inspiration, as noted, was the flat, desolate heathland around Rome. It is interesting that, nonetheless, Beckford did praise Charles Parker's *Villa Rustica* in a letter to his bookseller on August 9, 1832: "The work is itself so clever and elegant, the backgrounds touched in with taste and spirit so that when a 5th part comes forth I shall be happy to receive it."[63] While Parker's influence can be seen in the designs for offices and farmhouse mentioned above, Beckford might also have approved of a style which is "varied in the general outline and simple in the component details."[64] The tower's belvedere is constructed in a similar way to many of the loggias designed by Parker: an architrave placed on undecorated upright monoliths with no suggestions of a classical order. J. B. Papworth noted in *Designs for Rural Residences* (1818) that if a poet can move his audience by the composition of simple words, then so can an architect by his rearrangement of units which are basic in themselves.

Beckford's true empathy with the Italianate was not in the articulation of elevations, however, but in its Picturesque approach to composition. It was, as Papworth said "the painter's style of buildings." Not only did artists recognize the beauties of such structures in the actual landscape, but architects quoted from the buildings depicted by Claude and Poussin. Nash's Cronkhill might have been "lifted" from the background of a painting by Claude, while in 1827 Gilbert Meason published *The Landscape Architecture of the Great Painters of Italy*, in which he reprinted vignettes from the backgrounds of paintings as a design guide for the English villa builder. This is the most interesting point of contact with Beckford; an undated pencil sketch in his hand shows such a vignette: a tiny drawing of a tower annotated "Domenichino," after the creator of classical landscape, and predecessor of Claude and Poussin.[65] The architectural backgrounds of paintings such as Domenichino's provided the inspiration for Beckford's tower as it was first conceived, a vertical stone fortress with slit windows and no ornamental finial. In its choice of source, it was a design unprecedented in nineteenth-century Europe.

A tower was a critical feature in "the painter's style of buildings," and The Deepdene and Goodridge's Montebello had two apiece. A picturesque house was not designed to be approached on a straight, central axis, but to be viewed from a variety of points on a curving arc of approach. Beckford's tower is seen across a curving contour of

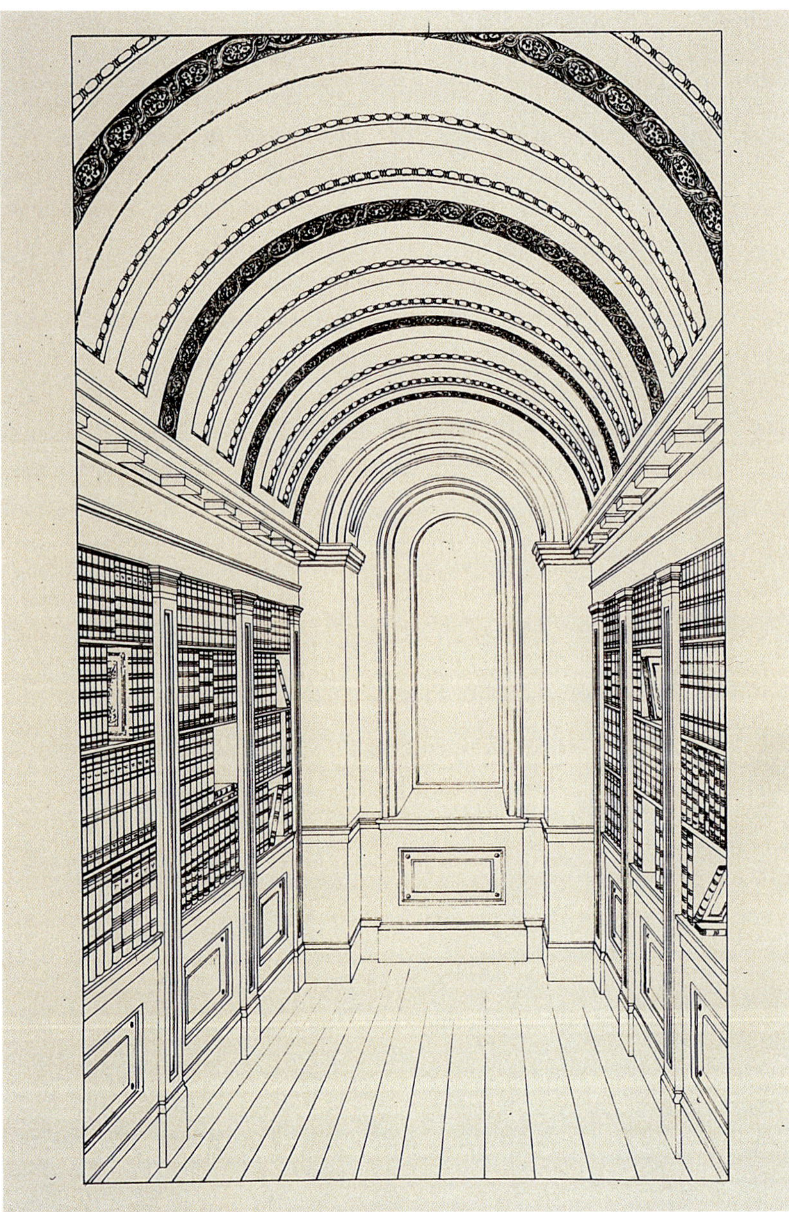

Fig. 16-5. Drawing of the Book Room, 1828. Pen and ink. Bath Reference Library.

the plateau, and it revolves in the viewer's eye like an object spun on a potter's wheel. When J. C. Loudon visited Charles Barry's Italianate Trentham House in Staffordshire in 1840, he described the role of its tower in the terminology of the time: "The effect of the tower at one angle, in forming a centre to the general mass, carrying it off, as artists say, or in artistical philosophy, communicating an axis of symmetry, is most satisfactory."[66]

The closest tower in Europe to that on Lansdown was one designed by Schinkel for Schloss Glienicke, near Potsdam, in 1832 which—unlike Schinkel's tower at Charlottenhof built three years

earlier, or those at Clisson or The Deepdene—is not an imitation of an Italian model.[67] This is how an architect in ancient Greece might have designed a tower; square in plan it rises bare of decoration to a belvedere with three windows on each side and piers supporting a low roof with a gleaming bronze finial. It is astonishingly similar to Beckford's tower before the lantern was added in the spring of 1827. Schinkel visited Bath on July 28, 1826, and rode on the downs. What might he have seen? The thought of a connection with the greatest architect in Europe is irresistible but, sadly, must be dismissed: Beckford did not begin construction until later that year, and there is no mention in Schinkel's thorough diary of meeting either Beckford or Goodridge.

A final illustration of how Beckford's scenic imagination synthesized different styles of architecture is the design of the windows of the tower. Each opening was an abstraction of the "effect" of medieval architecture, an approach that was unique for the time. As in a donjon, the masonry is pierced by small, round-headed openings, guarded by iron grilles and glazed with single, large sheets of plate glass. Beckford insisted on the clearer view provided by this avant-garde material—which was installed at Lansdown Crescent as well—but also wished to create, one presumes, the illusion of an unglazed opening behind the grille. As seen in Maddox's view of the Scarlet Drawing Room, the openings were narrow and deep to intensify the ingress of light, the iron grilles were gilded, casting latticed shadows onto the surface of the embrasures. The visitor would have the impression he was not in Georgian England but rather in some oriental or medieval fantasy; when Henry Venn Lansdown tried to describe the scene he could only make a comparison to interiors in Sicily or Malta.

INTERIOR DECORATION

On the ground floor of the tower were a vestibule and the Scarlet Drawing Room; on the first floor the Crimson Drawing Room and the Sanctuary dedicated to Saint Anthony of Padua. Placed above the entrance loggia were two small libraries and a water closet. The single-story block extending to the east (visible in fig. 16-1) contained bedrooms for servants, a kitchen, and services, but there was no bedroom for Beckford himself. Several inconsistencies between exterior and interior indicate that the design of the rooms had not been decided when the shell of the structure was completed in 1827. A first-floor window was blocked when it was decided to line the Book Room with shelves, for example, and the mirrored recess in the Crimson Drawing Room probably had been designed as a doorway.

The interiors were gutted in a fire of 1931, but their appearance can be reconstructed from four sources. First, shortly before his death, Beckford commissioned a local artist named Willes Maddox to paint the interiors. These watercolors were published as colored lithographs in Edmund English's *Views of Lansdown Tower* (1844), and reprinted as wood engravings in the *Illustrated London News* of November 29, 1845. Second, there are written descriptions of the handful of visitors who were permitted to visit, notably Henry Venn Lansdown and Cyrus

Redding. Third, English prepared two inventories of the contents: for an auction of furniture and fittings in January 1841, the preliminary to a major redecoration in May of that year, and for the sale after Beckford's death in 1844. The only visual evidence for the appearance of the interiors prior to the 1841 redisplay are a sequence of architectural drawings, which include the only image of the Book Room (fig. 16-5).[68] The purpose of these drawings is uncertain. They show the interiors midway through their fitting-out, so could not have been intended for publication; moreover, their draftsmanship is far too poor for this. Nor could they have been intended for the client's information, because Beckford was able to visualize an interior from the simplest sketch. The methodical technique—the equal width of every line, for example—suggests that they are some form of training exercise for a young assistant in Goodridge's office.[69]

The vestibule (fig. 16-6) was entered either by a door from the garden or by a door from the loggia on the roadside elevation to the north. This windowless room was illuminated by reflection, with daylight coming from the bow-window in the adjacent Scarlet Drawing Room, shining onto the mirror above the sideboard, and glimmering on the mirror-panels of the doors. Importantly, no fixed lamps are visible in any of the views of the interior, and it must be assumed that if Beckford lingered at the tower into the evening, portable lamps were brought from the servants' quarters. Reflected light was a specialty of Beckford's: at Fonthill House he mused over what one visitor described as a "Dormitory which he [Beckford] proposed to light by reflection."[70] The sideboard was of Siena marble and its shelf a glassy surface of light spilling down from the mirror above. It is now in the hallway of 10 The Circus, Bath, and the moldings are similar in profile to the sarcophagus in the churchyard. Between the Doric columns Beckford placed porcelain vases; to display objects at a level just above the floor seems to have been an idiosyncrasy of his.

In each corner of the vestibule were stools described as "Roman seats of Riga and Pollard oak."[71] Each is based upon the form of a Roman cinerary urn, with acroteria at the corners and a leather-covered seat supported by four piers incised as pilasters. A lion's mask was in the center of an X-shaped stretcher, a neo-Grecian detail that Goodridge applied to the balustrade which runs around the exterior of the belvedere. Architectonic and archaeological, they exemplify the style of the furniture designed in 1828.

The visitor turned right from the vestibule into the Scarlet Drawing Room (fig. 16-7); there were no doors in the opening. The room was 12 feet high, 17 feet 3 inches wide, and 29 feet 9 inches long, to the bow-window at the west end. To Henry Venn Lansdown, "The effect of this . . . room from the vestibule, illumined by the rays of the glorious sun was more beautiful than any thing of the sort I had ever witnessed."[72] The darkness of the windowless vestibule was intended to enhance the splendor of the sunlight streaming through gilded windows on to crimson hangings, gilding, and objets d'art. The sills in the bow window were slabs of marble,[73] and in the two-light window to the west Beckford placed a "large table formed of a block of Egyptian

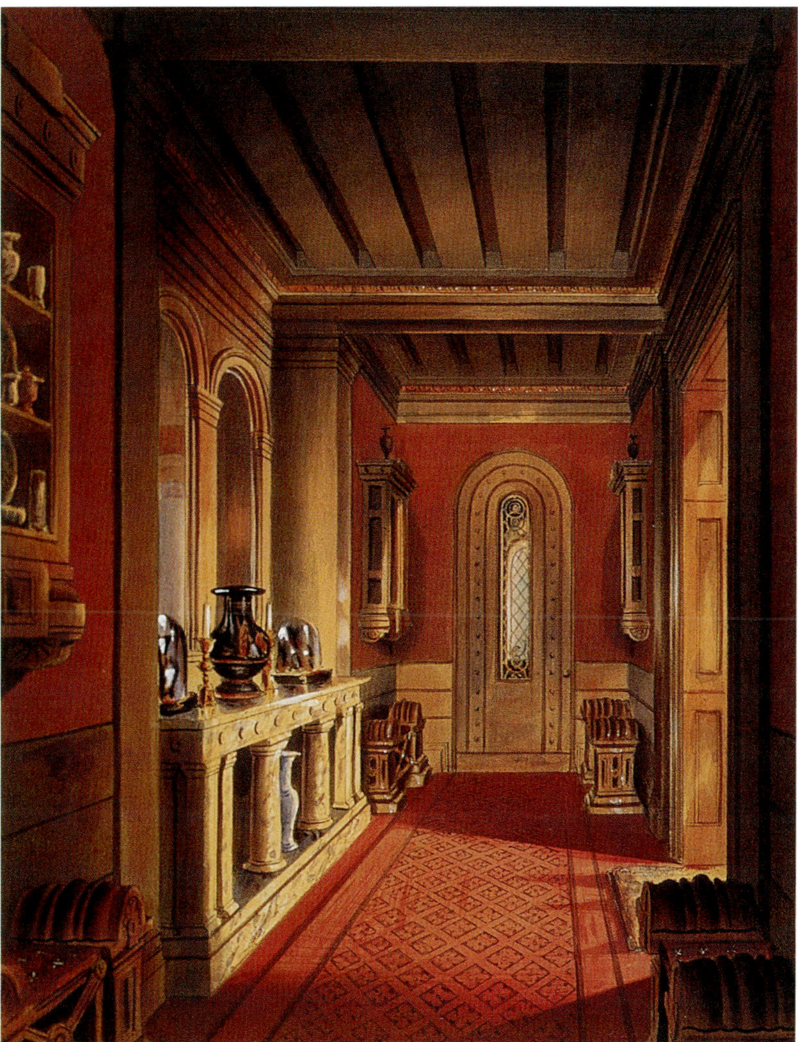

Fig. 16-6. "The Vestibule." Chromolithograph after Willes Maddox. From Edmund English, *Views of Lansdown Tower* (1844), plate 3. Courtesy of the Beckford Tower Trust, Bath.

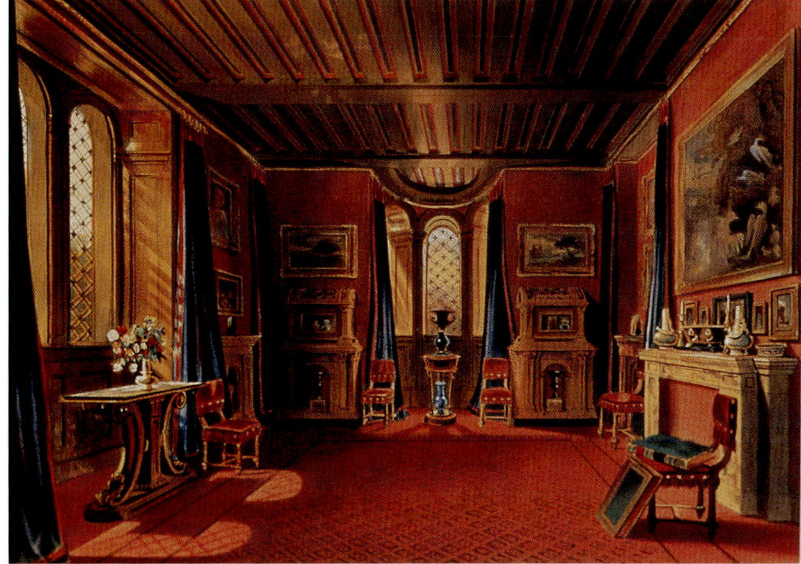

Fig. 16-7. "The Scarlet Drawing Room." Chromolithograph after Willes Maddox. From Edmund English, *Views of Lansdown Tower* (1844): plate 4. Courtesy of the Beckford Tower Trust, Bath.

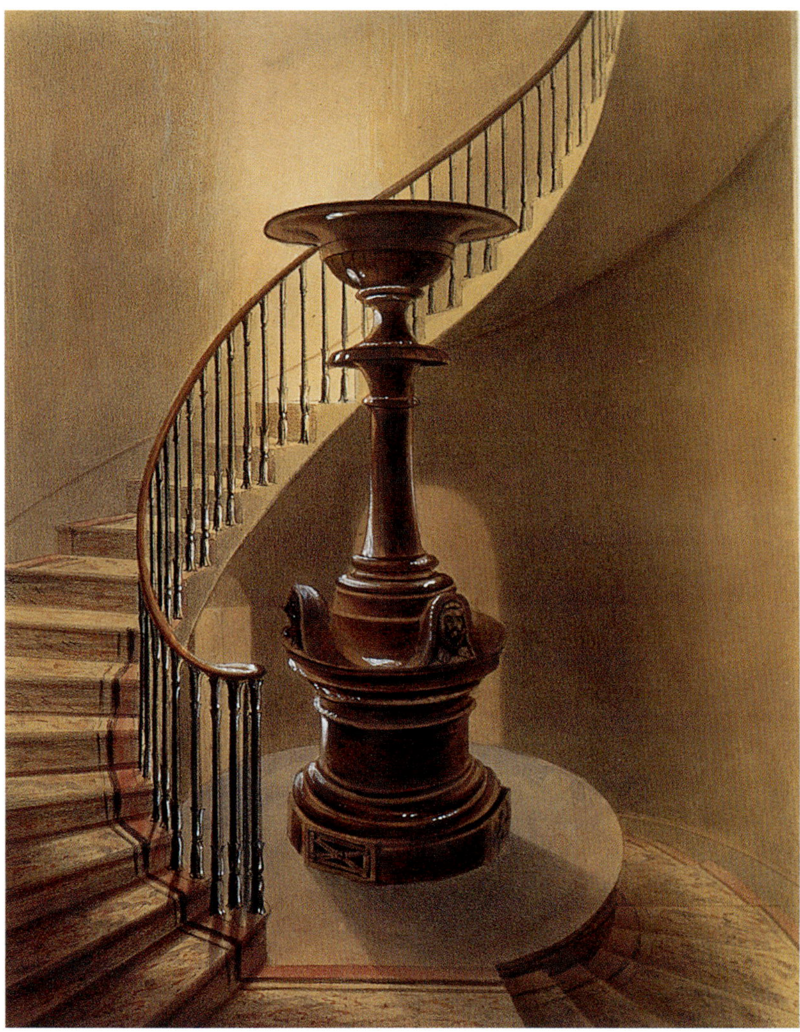

Fig. 16-8. "Staircase and Granite Vase." Chromolithograph after Willes Maddox. From Edmund English, *Views of Lansdown Tower* (1844). Courtesy of the Beckford Tower Trust, Bath.

porphyry."[74] These horizontal surfaces of reflected light were as personal a touch as the flowers in the ivory vase, which he would fuss into shape on arrival at the tower each morning.

How might one characterize the interior decoration of these rooms? First, the joinery was of stained or varnished oak with the moldings picked out in gilt, a decorative scheme that is preserved inside the bridge gallery connecting 20 Lansdown Crescent to 1 Lansdown Place West. To expose the natural grain of wood was highly avant-garde after a century in which all exposed joinery in fashionable interiors had been painted. No less "un-Georgian" was the exposure of the ceiling beams, although with Beckford's blurring of sources it is impossible to say whether this is a reference to the interior of an English Tudor or Italian Renaissance house, or indeed to a Grecian temple, where beams spanning the space were depicted in numerous archaeological publications of the time. The interstices between the beams were painted in a color that Redding remembered as "scarlet," Lansdown as "purple and red," and the *Illustrated London News* as "crimson, purple, and gold."

Each floor was covered with a crimson Wilton carpet interwoven with black quatrefoils[75] with a two-foot border of scarlet druggett 'to close cover the room.'[76] The walls were hung with a fabric which an advertisement in the *Illustrated London News* recorded as "scarlet moreen," and "Bordered with Gold Mouldings and Silk Lace."[77] Curtains were hung not to cover the windows—which had shutters on the exterior—but rather to shelter the paintings on the walls to each side. The fact that the upper drawing room was called "crimson" and the lower "scarlet" implies that there was a recognized distinction between the two colors. It is hard for the historian to add any clarification to the views by Willes Maddox, particularly as visitors were so dizzied by the splendor before their eyes. Redding recalled "A rich and dazzling effect arose from the predominance of the scarlet colour over everything else in this room,"[78] while to Henry Venn Lansdown "the curtains on each side of the window embrasures being a deep purple produce a striking contrast; the colouring of the ceiling, crimson, purple, and gold is admirable."[79]

The tower's curtains were replaced in 1841—they were thirteen years old, after all—and while English's 1844 inventory described them as "blue cloth" but the *Illustrated London News* of the following year as "purple and scarlet." Purple is possible but blue unlikely; it may even have been a lining, a mistake made by the auctioneer glancing at the folds of cloth.[80] Whether scarlet, purple or crimson the impression must have been of the changing play of light as it was absorbed by deep-colored folds of fabric and shimmered on marble, gilded picture frames, and sparkling objets d'art.

On each side of the bow window stood two "sarcophagus-headed coffers" (see cat. no. 148) displaying "Rare China" in a silk-lined cabinet behind a glazed door.[81] Each coffer is a miniature shrine to *vertu*, which is better compared to a religious reliquary than to a museum display case; few collectors have ever commissioned such elaborate and reverential display cases for secular objects. The coffers are neo-Renaissance aedicules in miniature, and, although designed in 1833, they epitomize the architectonic character of the initial phase of decoration. The lid is a barrel-vault, and at each end is an arch decorated with a pattern of five circular studs, a quotation from the pierced arch of the internal facade designed by Bramante at Santa Maria della Grazie, Milan. This device was borrowed by architects from Palladio through to Soane.[82] The semicircular lid is patterned with diamond-shaped studs, and in the interstices are the Hamilton cinquefoils, as tiny as cuff links. It was English who called them "Sarcophagus headed coffers" in the sale catalogue of 1841, and presumably this description was supplied by either Beckford or Goodridge.

The coffers also epitomize Beckford's quixotic nature as a client. When they were delivered, Beckford wrote to his bookseller George Clarke, on September 17, 1833: "The coffers are in their places in the Tower and fully answer my hopes and expectations. Never did I behold any piece of furniture half so striking and original."[83] In January 1841 they were offered for sale through English as lots 26 and 27 but in the event were not sold; by May their reinstatement and alteration was suddenly a matter of the greatest urgency. The frame of the door to the casket was already "ormolu gilt," but now the pattern of the lid needed to be gilded, perhaps to harmonize with a redecoration that intensified the theme of oak furniture picked out with gilt. While in London Beckford wrote to English on May 19, 1841: "the gilt mouldings studs &c of the Coffers to your most perseverant attention – it would therefore be provoking indeed to be delayed on account of them – therefore – pray exert yourself and get this cursed metalwork finished."[84] And two days later: "Allow me to tell you that you ought to have spurred on the metal mongers long ago – I will not wait for them – it wd be better to finish all in wood – hoops, studs and moulding than wear out my soul in this manner – I must have the coffers in their places [illeg.] my return."[85] On May 25 he repeated that such was the urgency he was now indifferent as to whether they would be gilded wood or gilded metal, and ultimately the former was used.[86]

To reach the first floor from the Scarlet Drawing Room, the visitor returned through the vestibule and passed outdoors through the external loggia to ascend thirty steps to an intermediate landing at the foot of the main staircase. Here stood a tazza vase carved from the same Aberdeen granite as the sarcophagus, with hot air pumped toward the belvedere through the vents in the base (fig. 16-8). These vents were covered with grilles of the Grecian X-shaped pattern, and the pedestal was decorated with lions' masks. The rim of the tazza had "bronze ornamented cornices."[87] It was installed in 1841, replacing a simple bronze grille in the floor, but its current location is unknown.

The Sanctuary dedicated to Saint Anthony of Padua (fig. 16-9) was an "apartment for devotional purposes," dedicated to the patron saint in Beckford's revenue, 16 feet 6 inches in length and 6 feet 6 inches wide.[88] The most introspective room in the tower, it was the only space to have the religious "gloomth" of the Revelation Chamber, which Beckford had considered creating as a mausoleum high inside the tower at Fonthill Abbey. "That is the true light of devotion," Beckford wrote ". . . the dim religious light of the sanctuary. It was that light which they intended to pervade the old cathedrals. The Bath Abbey church is of the late Gothic—too light for such an effect."[89] In the recess at the far end, spotlit by a skylight above, stood the statue of Saint Anthony of Padua, the patron saint in Beckford's personal retinue. Carved by J. C. Rossi the statue (now in Lisbon) stood on a plinth of Siena marble inscribed "DOMINUS ILLUMINATO MIO." Behind him was "a large slab of porphyry . . . surrounded by an elegant inlay of Sienna verd, antique border surrounding the whole figure of the saint," and while the border was a mosaic, the background was scagliola in imitation of porphyry.[90] The Sanctuary was illuminated by two skylights of ground, colored glass. The domes were elevated in height in order to focus the light into a small, intense circle on the compartments directly below and onto the figure of the saint. The bookshelves and barrel-vaulted corridor remained in shadow. This interior was the one space in the tower that showed the influence of Soane's subtle, theatrical manipulation of light in his interiors.[91]

In the semicircular lunettes below the dome in the entrance

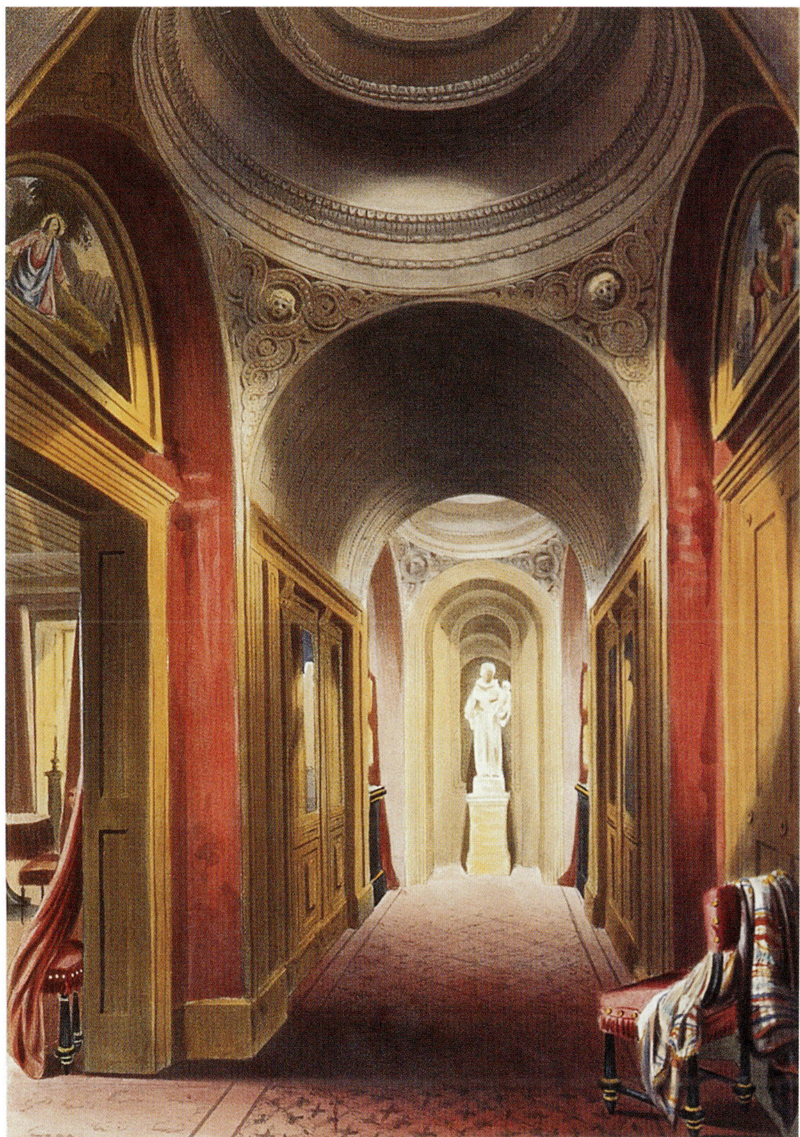

Fig. 16-9. "The Sanctuary." Maddox's scenes from the New Testament are visible inside the dome in the foreground. Chromolithograph after Willes Maddox. From Edmund English, *Views of Lansdown Tower* (1844). Courtesy of the Beckford Tower Trust, Bath.

were paintings of New Testament scenes commissioned from Willes Maddox, while in the compartment by the statue a circular-headed bookcase faced Francesco Mola's *Magdalene in the Desert* across the corridor. In 1841 the bookcase was sold, and replaced by the round-headed Perugino of the *Virgin and Child with Saint John*. Beckford had bought the picture two decades before,[92] and in May 1841 he tried to sell it in order to raise money for redecoration. The two potential buyers did not agree with his estimation of the picture, however, and he announced he would not sell: "I shall treasure up the picture and finish the tower in the cheapest manner we can devise," he warned.[93] A few weeks later he wrote: "The Doge shall replace Ostade, and the Perugino the semicircular shelves in the Jerusalem-looking lobby at the Tower."[94] Later that year, however, the Perugino was sold to the National Gallery for 800 guineas.

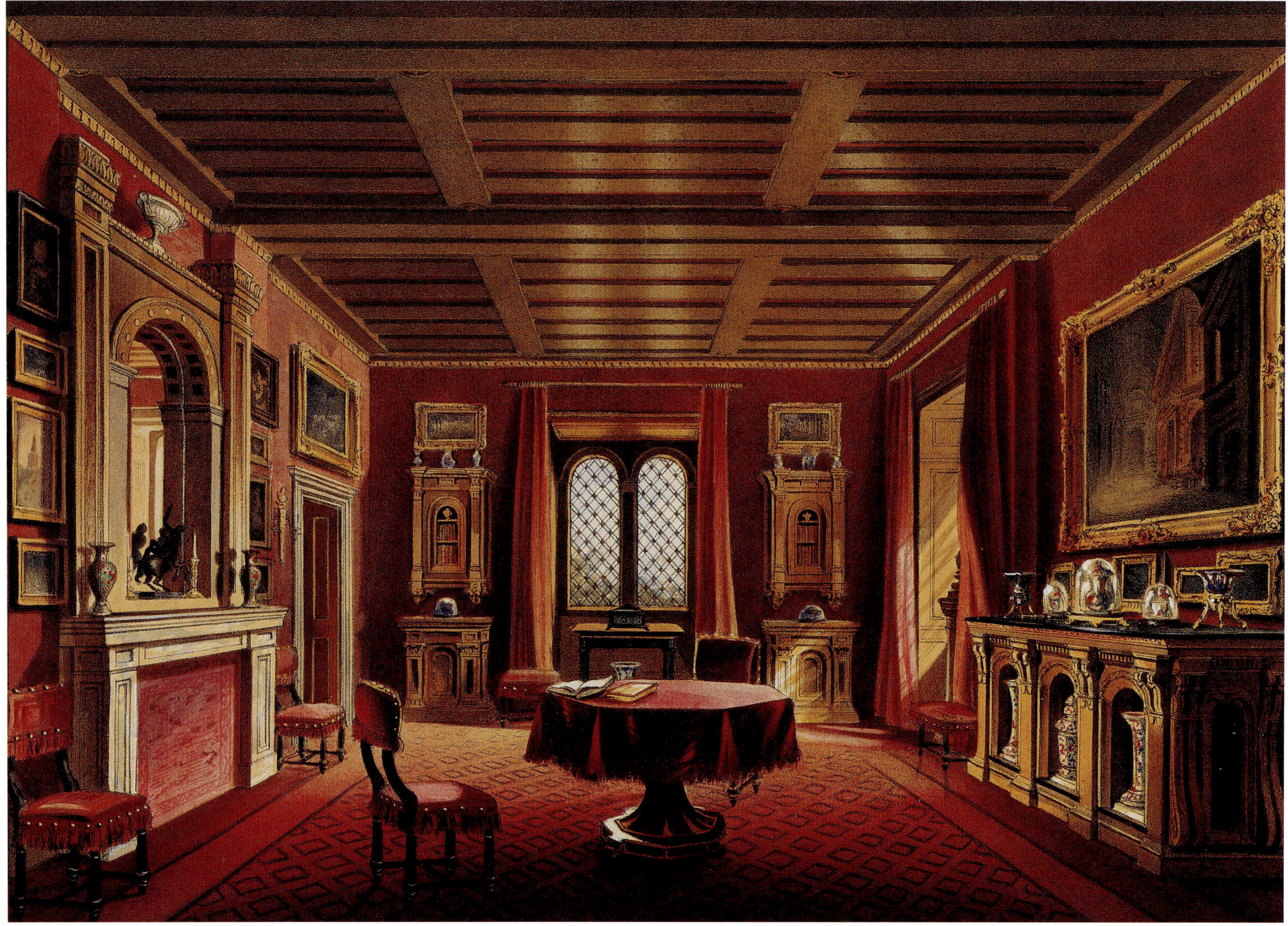

Fig. 16-10. "The Crimson Drawing Room." Chromolithograph after Willes Maddox. From Edmund English, *Views of Lansdown Tower* (1844): plate 9.

Willes Maddox's painting showed the view from the Sanctuary into the Crimson Drawing Room (fig. 16-10). The window at the far end looked back over the Ride, and perhaps Beckford would stand there to watch his visitors approach. This room was the same size as the drawing room below—but without the bow-window—and was decorated to the same specification. In Redding's eyes it "outdid in beauty the room below."[95] He must have been impressed by the greater profusion of objects, the mirrored overmantel, whose "apostrophe" form echoed the chimney-stack, and the arched recess lined with a mirror. This arched recess was the subject of a separate vignette by Maddox showing an ebony display cabinet (fig. 16-11). Originally intended to be a doorway, no doubt, it was converted into a recess when Beckford chose to realign the axis of the Sanctuary.

Unlike the drawing room on the floor below, the appearance of this room changed significantly in 1841. The chimneypiece was the only fixture in Maddox's view to survive this refurbishment, although the chairs of the "Fonthill pattern" seem to have remained unsold.[96] Beckford did sell a number of the impressive "collector's pieces" at the 1841 sale, including cabinets attributed to Bernini (lot 20) and "in the richest style of Holbein" (lot 24), and from the Etruscan Library a cabinet (lot 13) "originally in the Royal Palace of Madrid . . . enriched both in the exterior and interior with paintings by Old Franks" of biblical subjects including Adam and Eve, Noah, and the Tower of Babel.[97] Opposite the chimneypiece in the Crimson Drawing Room was "a superb ebony armoire" (lot 10), which was "in the style of those at El Escorial," 8 feet, 9 inches long and 6 feet, 6 inches high.

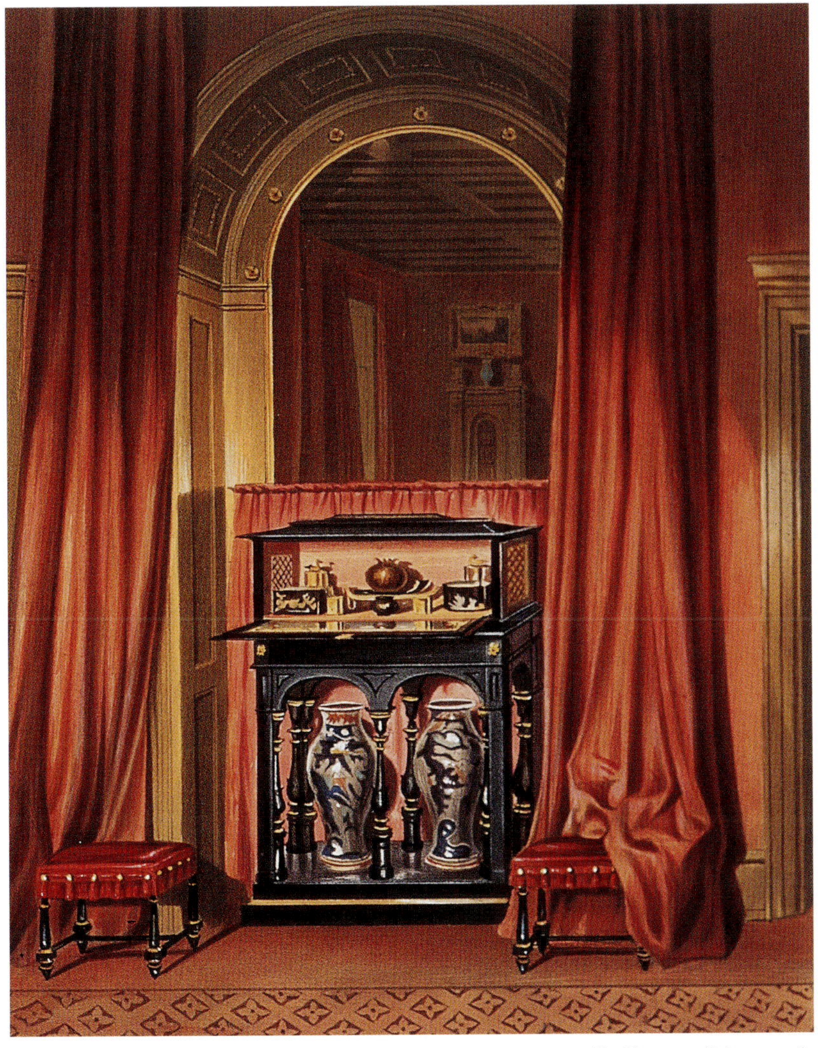

Fig. 16-11. "Black Cabinet in Crimson Drawing Room." Chromolithograph after Willes Maddox. From Edmund English, *Views of Lansdown Tower* (1844): plate 10. Courtesy of the Beckford Tower Trust, Bath.

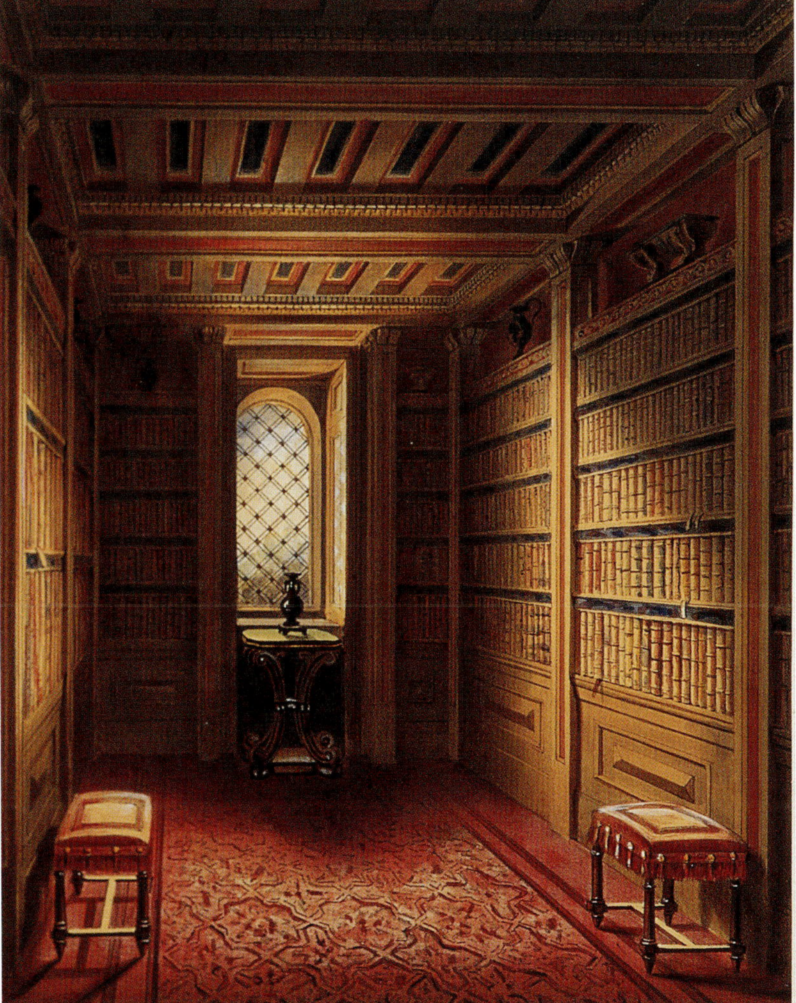

Fig. 16-12. "The Library." Chromolithograph after Willes Maddox. From Edmund English, *Views of Lansdown Tower* (1844). Courtesy of the Beckford Tower Trust, Bath.

What was the motive for the redecoration in 1841? Beckford may have been short of cash: his comments after failing to sell the Perugino suggest as much. The octagonal oak table, for example, was worthy to be in English's auction rooms but not to be the centerpiece of the drawing room of one of the greatest private collectors of the age. It is also evident that in selling the historic pieces Beckford had the intention of unifying the style of the interior decoration through new commissions to Hume and Goodridge. Finally, it may simply be that he was bored: whenever a style he had pioneered became more widely fashionable he sought a new challenge.

Typical of the new pieces introduced in 1841 was the sideboard that replaced the armoire opposite the chimneypiece. On May 21, Beckford had written: "I agree with you in [illeg.] the long side table wd produce a fine effect—provided (that is to say) proper brocatello and perfect black marble for border can be instantly procured—black marble above—ebony below."[98] On May 25, 1841, Beckford demanded that English hurry with the "long side table, with its black marble slab

of *extraordinary good quality* brocatelle, should be completed *as fast as possible*."[99] With its scrolling consoles and row of fancy, curving brackets, this piece is very different to the austere, rectilinear marble sideboard in the vestibule. No less expressive of the second phase in the decoration are the sidetables placed in front of the windows in the Scarlet Drawing Room and Etruscan Library. Each was a marble slab on scrolling legs, based on a slight sketch by Beckford.[100] The furniture in the earlier phase, by contrast, had Goodridge's architectural principles to give to the design a more rigid, architectonic structure.

Also on the first floor, two libraries were installed in the space above the loggia. The door visible on the left in figure 16–11 led into the Book Room (see fig. 16-5). Doric piers supported a fully articulated entablature, and bands of a guilloche pattern sprang from its cornice to divide the ceiling into five compartments. The design was all but identical to that of the shelving in the Sanctuary.

The Library (fig. 16-12) could only be entered by returning to the stairwell. If the sarcophagus-headed coffers in the Scarlet Drawing

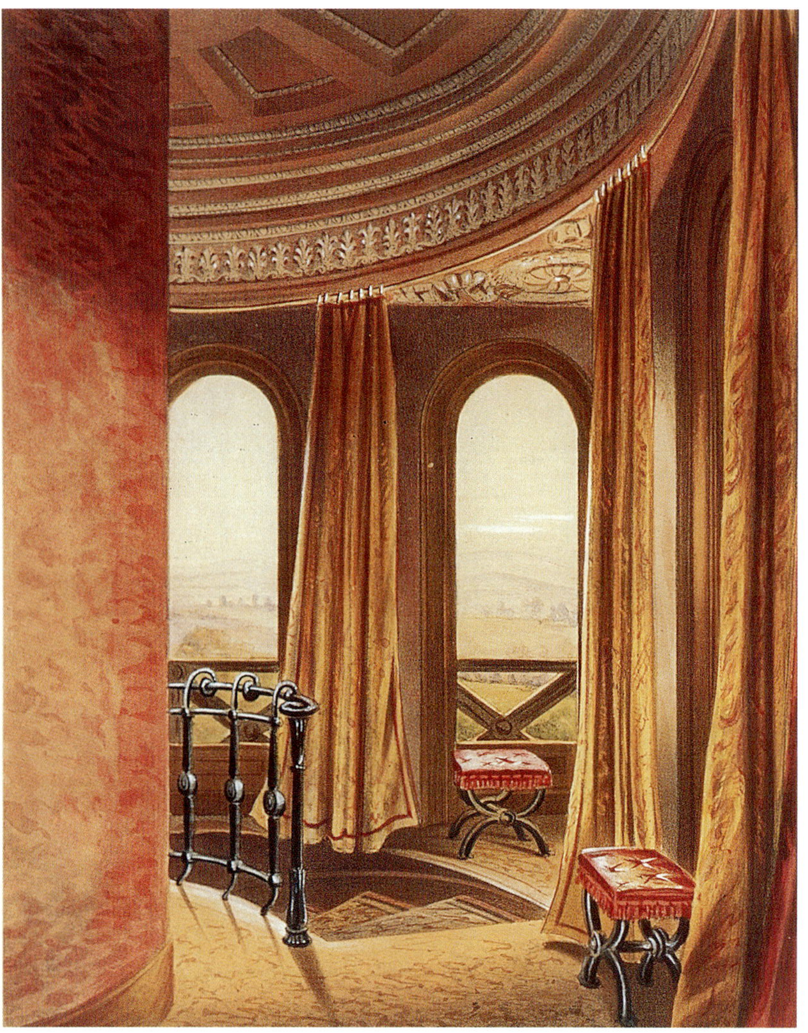

Fig. 16-13. "The Belvedere." Chromolithograph after Willes Maddox. From Edmund English, *Views of Lansdown Tower* (1844). Courtesy of the Beckford Tower Trust, Bath.

Room can be described as architecture in miniature, then this room was a walk-in bookcase. Shelves and ceiling formed a self-supporting structure, which was fitted inside the shell of the room and could be removed as a piece: the inventory of 1844 refers to "bookcases forming the room" and the "Portable Oak Ceiling." Decorative objects, including urns and sarcophagi, were displayed on the top shelf of the bookcase, a type of display that Beckford may have seen in the designs Soane prepared for the picture gallery at Fonthill House (see fig. 3-12), or in Soane's Dining Room at 13 Lincoln's Inn Fields.[101]

In this and the adjacent library, the visitor would have been most struck by the array of bindings of superlative quality. The sobriety of Beckford's taste was indicated by his dismissal of many bindings offered to him for sale as "excessively goldified,"[102] and his high stan-

dards are suggested by the insistent, even hysterical, letters to booksellers regarding his own bindings, distinguished by the Latimer Cross and Hamilton cinquefoil stamped in gold on their spines. He was ecstatic to discover the bookbinder Charles Lewis, and in 1831 Beckford compared him to the finest of the French binders in a letter to his bookseller George Clarke: "Lewis was, and is, I hope will continue to be the first artist in this line that Europe can boast of. His works alone are worthy to range in the Tower of Lansdown with Padeloup, de Seuil, de Rome &c &c."[103]

One imagines that each day Beckford ascended to the belvedere (fig. 16-13) with a pile of books under his arm, to read and reflect while seated at a Grecian stool. The cantilevered stone staircase was carpeted with a Brussels carpet, with a brass rod for each of the 156 steps. The margins of the stone treads were painted red and black, and the iron balusters the fashionable green that imitated patinated bronze. The circular drum in the center contains a timber spiral staircase climbing another forty steps inside the lantern to a crow's nest viewing point close to the soffit of the cast-iron lid.

The square room itself was astonishingly transparent, with three floor-length plate-glass sashes on each side. Here the curtains did change color in 1841 from the "crimson" described by Venn Lansdown to the "fawn" mentioned in the 1844 sale catalogue.

A squabble about public rights-of-way on his land was sufficient provocation for Beckford, even at the age of eighty-three, to consider leaving Bath. On June 27, 1843, he wrote in a fury to a neighbor's solicitor, threatening to build a crowded slum in the kitchen garden as his revenge on the city's respectable society:

I beg you will inform Mr Taylor that if I continue to be annoyed with complaints about paths I shall have recourse to a sweeping remedy. I shall quit Bath & immediately upon my departure all my Fences upon Lansdown shall be removed the whole thrown open & a town of not less than 1500 hovels erected upon the freehold property behind my present habitation.[104]

By this date he had abandoned the idea of being buried inside the tower and instead had commissioned a tomb to be placed in the garden directly adjacent. In April 1843 Beckford applied for the necessary dispensation from the ecclesiastical authorities, announcing that he would give the garden to the church. The Diocese refused to consecrate the land and, infuriated, Beckford announced he would leave Bath and buy an estate at Milford, near the city of Salisbury, where he could be buried in the cathedral.[105] His solicitors began to investigate the purchase, and Goodridge was instructed to design a house on the basis of Beckford's sketches. These drawings continued the style that Goodridge described as "Greco-Italian,"[106] with an strong inkling of the neo-Romanesque that would become so distinct a flavor in Goodridge's design for the gateway to the cemetery. Mr. Blathwayt of Dyrham Park offered £30,000 for the tower, but this was too little to fund a new mansion. Moreover, added Goodridge, the house would not be ready to live in for two years. Beckford stayed in Bath, and a year later he died at Lansdown Crescent at the age of eighty-four.[107] In a private collection is a sketch design for a tower in a monumental neo-Roman style, which later in the nineteenth-century was inscribed as made 'by the author of Vathek in his 83rd year'. Beckford never stopped dreaming of towers.

On May 11, 1844, he was buried in Bath's Abbey Cemetery, a new burial ground on the slopes on the opposite side of the city, in the granite sarcophagus which had been made for Lansdown. The contents of the tower were auctioned in 1845, and the tower itself and its gardens were offered for sale by English in April 1847. They were sold to a publican. No bedrooms existed, of course, and English exhibited a design by Goodridge to convert the tower into a villa suitable for a family, by doubling its size with a two-story extension to the east. Fortunately, this was never executed.

When, in 1847, the Duchess of Hamilton heard that the publican intended to open the grounds as a tea garden, she reacquired the property and presented the tower and its garden to the Rector of Walcot as a mortuary chapel and cemetery.[108] Beckford's sarcophagus returned in 1848, and Goodridge designed a cemetery gateway in what a contemporary called the "Byzantine style."[109] In return for Beckford being buried in the setting he had chosen, his garden became the cemetery for the parishioners wealthy enough to afford the expensive interment fees.[110]

In life, Beckford was aloof from the city; in death, he was unable to escape the good citizens of Bath and was surrounded by the tombs of shopkeepers and retired Naval officers. The ditch dug around his red granite sarcophagus was a final act of defiance. On the one hand, the gesture is trivial: an agile man can jump across the ditch. On the other hand, one is mesmerized by the absolute conviction displayed in its design and its choice of setting: this is surely the grave of a genius. When the clouds on Lansdown part, the surface becomes a slab of light, and high above, the tower's gilded belvedere sparkles like a genie's magic lantern (fig. 16-14).[111] Lansdown was Beckford's last stand in a lifelong struggle to protect the realm of childhood fantasy against the encroachment of the ordinary world. Inscribed on the tomb were words of his own composition:

Eternal Power!
Grant me through obvious clouds one transient gleam
Of thy bright essence in my dying hour.

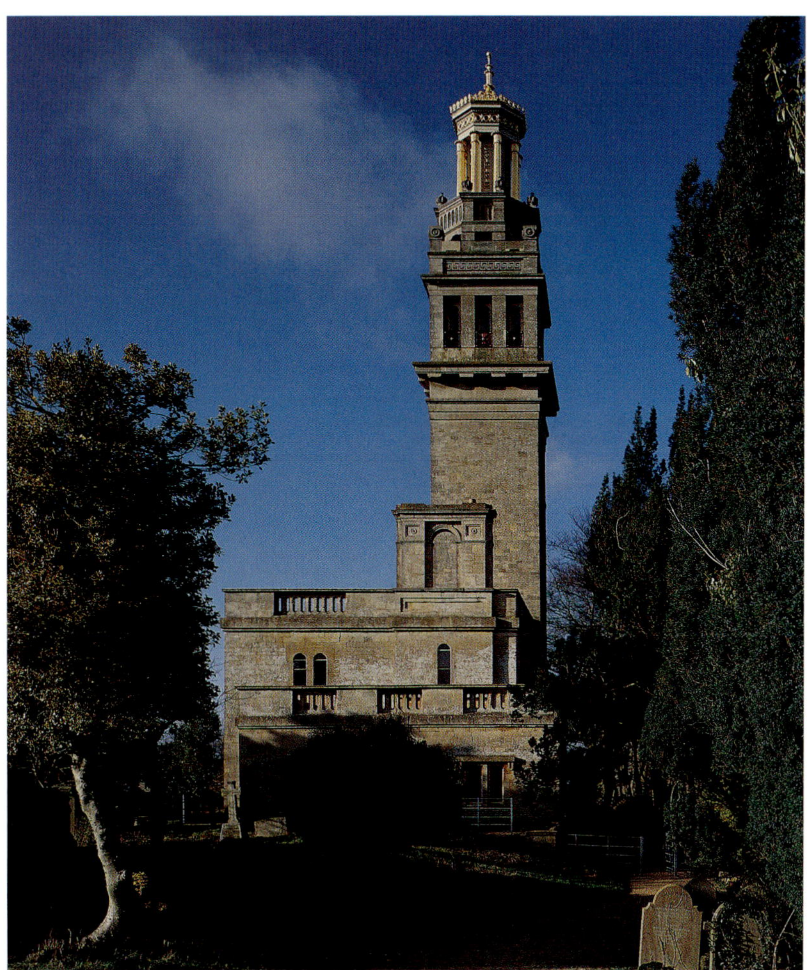

Fig. 16-14. Lansdown Tower, Bath. Photographed in 2000.

Acknowledgments: I am deeply indebted to the report prepared by Pat Hughes, the archaeologist commissioned by Bath Preservation Trust in their restoration of the tower. The report (which is on file at 1 Royal Crescent, Bath BA1 2LR) is an unusually good combination of research into primary sources and the study of physical evidence that survived the tower's conversion into a chapel and damage by fire in 1931. Kirsten Elliott's studies into Beckford's ownership of land, which have shown that he was the tenant and not the owner, significantly changed our understanding of the Ride. The distinguished Surveyor to the Restoration, Theo Williams, has resolved the complexities of the tower's construction, and with Jesca Verdon-Smith at the helm of the project, the restoration has been a pleasure to watch.—CW

1. Beckford to Dr. Schöll, n.d., quoted in *Life at Fonthill, 1807–1822, with interludes in Paris and London, from the correspondence of William Beckford*, trans. and ed. Boyd Alexander (London, R. Hart-Davis, 1957) 340.

2. Journal entry for 28 July 1816, quoted in David Bindman, ed., *The English Journey*, (London and New Haven: Yale University Press, 1993): 195.

3. See, for example, J. C. Ibbetson, *Picturesque Guide to Bath, Bristol &c* (London, 1793): 102–103.

4. Cyrus Redding, ed., *Memoirs of William Beckford of Fonthill, author of "Vathek,"* 2 vols. (London: C. J. Skeet, 1859).

5. John Britton, *Anstey's New Bath Guide* (Bath, 1829): 65.

6. Quoted in Boyd Alexander, *England's Wealthiest Son*, (London: Centaur, 1962): 226–27; for the Campagna see also Henry Venn Lansdown, *Recollections of the Late William Beckford* (1893; reprint, Bath: Kingsmead Press, 1980): 24.

7. Venn Lansdown describes this "archway of massive proportions" as "erected chiefly to shut out the view of an unpicturesque object" (*Recollections* [1893/1980]: 23).

8. Unless otherwise noted, the Bath newspapers cited are in the Bath Reference Library.

9. Gen Mss 102, Beinecke Rare Book and Manuscript Library, Yale University. Sidney Blackmore first drew my attention to this letter and demonstrated that the tower was conceived as a burial place (personal communication, 1998).

10. Roger Bowdler, "The Mausoleum at Blickling," *Apollo* (April 1998): 13.

11. Beckford, *Dreams, Waking Thoughts and Incidents*, ed. Robert Gemmett (Rutherford, N.J.: Fairleigh Dickinson University Press, 1971): 190. It is possible that in Mme de Staël's *Corinne, or Italy* (1807), the scene where the lovers explore the same area was inspired by *Dreams*; Gemmett (pp. 26–27) notes that de Staël had access to a copy after the book had been suppressed.

12. For this context, see Christopher Woodward, *In Ruins* (London: Chatto & Windus, 2001), chap. 9.

13. See David Bindman, "The English Apocalypse" in *The Apocalypse*, ed. Frances Carey, London, 1999; and ibid., pp. 251, 269. *The Opening of the Sixth Seal* is now in the National Gallery of Ireland, Dublin; the sketch is in the Victoria Art Gallery, Bath.

14. See Francis Greenacre, The Bristol School of Artists, 1810–1840 (Bristol City Art Gallery, 1975): 65.

15. Beckford to George Clarke, 27 April 1833, quoted in *The Consummate Collector*, ed. Robert Gemmett (Norwich: Michael Russell, 2000): 206.

16. Beckford to George Clarke, 27 April 1832, quoted in ibid., p. 142. Three days later he informed Clarke that he had doubled the garrison of the tower but removed any articles of great value; these are not specified, however (ibid., p. 143).

17. Letter from Beckford to Edmund English, 1 March 1823, AL248 Bath Reference Library.

18. Mrs Kirsten Elliott, personal communication, 2000.

19. Patricia Hughes, "Beckford's Tower," study commissioned by the Bath Preservation Trust, 1998, p. 2.

20. MS Beckford c.4, Bodleian Library, Oxford.

21. *Bath and Cheltenham Gazette*, 16 September 1823. This avenue of trees survives beside the main road as does a section of Beckford's boundary wall.

22. For the Quarter Sessions map, see QS/R 430, Somerset Record Office.

23. Quoted in Lewis Melville, *The Life and Letters of William Beckford of Fonthill* (London: W. Heinemann, 1910): 324.

24. Quoted in ibid., p. 323.

25. Lansdown, *Recollections* (1893/1980): 23.

26. Buckler drawing dated 10 April 1827, Add MSS 36382/157, British Library.

27. Lansdown, *Recollections* (1893/1980): 24.

28. Richard Holmes, *Shelley: The Pursuit* (London: Weidenfeld and Nicolson, 1974): 489–589.

29. Lansdown, *Recollections* (1893/1980): 24.

30. Quoted in Hughes, "Beckford's Tower" (1998): 5.

31. For Beckford's sketch, see MS Beckford c.84, fol. 124, insc. "Nov. 1826" in Beckford's hand. Reproduced in Christopher Woodward, "William Beckford and Fonthill Splendens," *Apollo* (February 1998): 40. For Buckler's drawing, see Add 36619 158/9, British Library.

32. Alfred S. Goodridge, *Brief Memoir of the Late Henry Edmund Goodridge . . .* , RIBA Sessional Papers, 1864–65, pp. 3–5.

33. When I published the Bodleian sketch ("William Beckford" [1998]: 40), I did not fully understand what happened and was further confused by the Buckler sketch (see Hughes, "Beckford's Tower" [1998]). Theo Williams, surveyor to the tower, solved the riddle and explained the sequence that is described in this essay.

34. Philippa Bishop, "Beckford in Bath," *Bath History* 1 (1988): 106.

35. For a discussion of Goodridge's training and early career see Christopher Woodward, "The End of the Terrace and the Rise of the Villa," in *The Picturesque in Late Georgian England*, ed. Dana Arnold (London: The Georgian Group, 1994); and idem, "Aerial Boudoirs of Bath," *Country Life* 4 (September 1997).

36. A. S. Goodridge, *Brief Memoir* (1864): 4.

37. Ibid.

38. For "Italianate" see Tim Mowl, "The Williamane: Architecture for the Sailor King," in *Late-Georgian Classicism* (London: The Georgian Group, 1987): 93–106.

39. The late architect Sir James Stirling considered purchasing Montebello in the 1960s (Lady Stirling, personal communication, 1999).

40. Quoted in A. A. Tait, "The Duke of Hamilton's Palace," *Burlington* 963 (July 1983): 394–402 n.35. The original French reads "ce jeune homme est encore plus bavard que son père, et a encore moins de talent. Mais tous les deux possedent beaucoup d'entregent."

41. James Lees-Milne, *William Beckford* (Tisbury, Wiltshire: Compton Russell, 1976): 91.

42. Joe Mordauant Crook, *The Greek Revival* (London: John Murray, 1972): 102.

43. See A. S. Goodridge, *Memoirs* (1864).

44. Ibid., p. 4.

45. For a study of the nomenclature of medieval architecture, see Tina Bizzarro, *Romanesque Architectural Criticism* (Cambridge University Press, 1992). William Gunn introduced the term *Romanesque* to English in 1819 in *An Introduction into the Origin and Influence of Gothic Architecture* (see ibid., p. 134).

46. Christopher Woodward, "Soane's Designs for Domes," in *Sir John Soane: Master of Space and Light*, ed. Margaret Richardson and MaryAnne Stevens (London: Royal Academy of Art, 1999): 62–67.

47. They intended to use the singular, "effect." See chap. 2, by David Watkin, in this volume.

48. "The Long Story," *The Beckford Reader* (1995).

49. Beckford to Louisa Beckford, Paris, 1784, quoted in J. W. Oliver, *The Life of William Beckford* (Oxford University Press, 1932).

50. Beckford, *Dreams* (1971): 124. J. Scott noted the significance of Beckford's observation; see Scott, *Piranesi* (London: Academy Edition, 1975): 55.

51 *Observer,* 13 October, 1823.

52. Thomas Hope, *Observations on the Plans and Elevations designed by James Wyatt, Architect, for Downing College* (London, 1804): 15; this theory was suggested by David Watkin who also quotes Beckford's remarks (*Thomas Hope and the Neo-classical Idea* [London: John Murray, 1968): 141.

53. Quoted in Watkin, *Thomas Hope* (1968): 141.

54. Lees-Milne, *William Beckford* (1976): 91.

55. For Goodridge's design see no. E 954–196 SS13, Department of Prints and Drawings, Victoria and Albert Museum, London.

56. Woodward, "William Beckford" (1998): 40.

57. William Vaughan of Bathwick was, incidentally, the masonry contractor for both the Cleveland Bridge and Lansdown Tower.

58. For an analysis of The Deepdene see Watkin, *Thomas Hope* (1968): passim. This is still the finest study of taste in this period.

59. Ibid., p. 173.

60. Ibid., p. 138.

61. Jean-Marie Perous de Montclos, Claude Allemand-Cosneau, et al., *Clisson, ou le retour d'Italie* (Paris: Imprimerie Nationale, 1996). The best study of the Italianate in continental Europe, this focuses on the *locus classicus* of the style, Clisson, a hilltop town in the curve of the Garonne River, where after 1805 the sculptor Lemot and the brothers Cacault, artists and collectors, created a Picturesque ensemble with belltowers, villas, and ruins in the woods. Lemot's Maison de Jardinier (1809–18) was an imitation of a courtyard farmhouse in Tuscany, with a dovecote as the necessary

vertical feature.

62. MS Beckford c.84, fol.127, reproduced in Woodward, "William Beckford" (1998): 40. The design is undated, and was probably a response to some intrusion on his privacy.

63. Gemmett, *Consummate Collector* (2000): 158.

64. Charles Parker, *Villa Rustica* (London: J Weale, 1848).

65. MS Beckford c.84, fol. 136.

66. J. C. Loudon, *Travels* (London: National Trust, 1990): 208.

67. Michael Snodin, ed., *Karl Friedrich Schinkel: A Universal Man* (New Haven and London: Yale University Press, 1991): 133–35. The tower at the Charlottenhof was an element of the Court Gardener's House and, in the architect's words, was "conceived in a picturesque style . . . in the style of country houses" (quoted in ibid., p.151).

68. The drawings are in the Bath Reference Library and were discovered by Pat Hughes during research into the recent restoration.

69. John Soane's pupils, for example, drew the interiors of 13 Lincoln's Inn Fields for this same purpose (Jill Lever, former curator of the RIBA Drawings Collection, personal communication, 2000).

70. John Bacon to Joseph Farington, in *The Diary of Joseph Farington*, ed. K. Garlick and A. Macintyre, vol. 3 (London and New Haven: Yale University Press, 1979): 756, entry dated 23 January 1797.

71. *Illustrated London News*, 29 November 1845.

72. Lansdown, *Recollections* (1893/1980): 31.

73. Inventory of 1844, prepared by Edmund English & Son, Bath, and Robert Hume, London, MS Beckford c. 58.

74. Lansdown, *Recollections* (1893/1980): 31–32.

75. Venn Lansdown called them "crimson Wilton carpets" (ibid., p. 31).

76. Inventory of 1844, MS Beckford c. 58.

77. Advertisement of sale in 1847, *Illustrated London News*, 28 April 1847.

78. Redding, *Memoirs,* vol. 2 (1859): 271.

79. Lansdown, *Recollections* (1893/1980): 29.

80. This suggestion was made by Bet McLeod (personal communication, 2000).

81. Lots 26 and 27 in *Catalogue of valuable paintings, magnificent cabinets, and Splendid Furniture for Lansdown Tower . . . ,* sale cat., English and Fasana, Bath, 4–5 January 1841, MS Beckford d.27, fol. 2.

82. David Watkin, "Rooms that Speak of Memory: Gonville and Caius College, Cambridge," *Country Life* (2 April 1998): 48–53.

83. Beckford to Clark, 17 September 1833, Gemmett, *Consummate Collector* (2000): 243.

84. Beckford to English, 19 May 1883, quoted in Bishop, "Beckford in Bath" (1988): 101.

85. Letter dated 21 May 1841, Box 3, folder 55, Beinecke Library.

86. Beckford to English, 25 May 1841, quoted in Melville, *Life and Letters* (1910): 348.

87. Redding, *Memoirs,* vol. 2 (1859): 272.

88. Ibid., p. 76.

89. Quoted in Melville, *Life and Letters* (1910).

90. For "a large slab of porphyry . . . ," see Lansdown (1893/1980): 30; for the scagliola background, see 1844 inventory, MS Beckford c. 58.

91. Soane spoke of the "dim religious light" of the mausoleum at Dulwich Picture Gallery (quoted in David Watkin, *Sir John Soane: Enlightenment Thought and The Royal Academy* [Cambridge University Press, 1966]: 415). The colored skylight in the passage to the Etruscan Library might also be attributed to Soane's influence, and a similar example survives at Fiesole, a villa built on Bathwick Hill by Goodridge in 1846.

92. Beckford to H. G. Bohn, 6 July 1840, quoted in Melville, *Life and Letters* (1910): 300.

93. Letter of 7 May 1841, quoted in ibid., p. 346.

94. Letter of 25 May 1841, quoted in ibid., p. 348.

95. Redding, *Memoirs,* vol. 2 (1859): 273.

96. "Six Ebonised Chairs Fonthill Pattern," *Catalogue . . . Lansdown Tower,* 4–5 January 1841, lot 17. Examples remain at Lansdown Tower.

97. Lot numbers and quotations are from ibid. For more on "collectors' pieces," see chap. 10, by Adriana Turpin, in this volume.

98. Letter dated 21 May 1841, Box 3, folder 55, Beinecke Library.

99. Beckford to English, 25 May 1841, quoted in Melville, *Life and Letters* (1910): 348.

100. MS Beckford c. 84, fols. 118–19.

101. Beckford called there on 5 December 1813, Soane Note Book 1813, Sir John Soane's Museum, London.

102. Gemmett, *Consummate Collector* (2000): 17.

103. Beckford to Clarke, 1 December 1831, in ibid., p. 103.

104. Letter dated 27 June 1843, MS Beckford c.14, fol. 102.

105. Hughes, "Beckford's Tower" (1998): 36.

106. MS Beckford c.84, fol. 33.

107. See Hughes, "Beckford's Tower" (1998): 37.

108. *Bath Chronicle*, 9 September 1847.

109. Ibid., 4 May 1848.

110. It was later discovered that the Reverend Widdington had been charging excessive burial fees and thus restricting access to include only his wealthier parishioners; see Hughes, "Beckford's Tower" (1998).

111. The tower continued as a mortuary chapel for the cemetery but was gutted by a fire in 1931. In 1969 the parish decided to sell it, and a heroic local couple, Dr. and Mrs. Lesley Hilliard, bought, restored, and opened the building to the public. In 1977 a separate trust was established, and in 1993 Bath Preservation Trust became the sole trustee and its chairman, Michael Briggs, resolved to restore the tower. The trust's surveyor, Theo Williams, discovered that the structure was leaning dangerously and, like Fonthill Abbey, in danger of collapse. The culprit was the lantern: ten tons of cast iron were supported on the timber framework improvised by Goodridge when Beckford had cried 'Higher!' and demanded an extra story. Goodridge's oak beams had been replaced by steel girders after the 1931 fire, but these had rusted away, and the lantern was liable to be toppled by the strong winds which blow across Lansdown. Bath Preservation Trust raised the funds for the extensive repairs, with 70 percent being a grant from the Heritage Lottery Fund. Next, the Landmark Trust joined the project and acquired the ground floor as an apartment to lease to tourists. They have re-created the 1844 appearance of the Vestibule and Scarlet Drawing Room. The first-floor rooms now contain a Beckford Museum and the Belvedere has been restored to its appearance in Willes Maddox's painting. For the first time since Beckford's death it is possible to climb the spiral staircase and, opening pleats of rich drapery, to enjoy the sun setting on the distant horizon with a purplish glow reminiscent of the paintings of Claude Lorraine. Nowhere else in Britain is Beckford's genius such a vivid presence.

Catalogue of the Exhibition

Derek E. Ostergard, Editor

Philip Hewat-Jaboor and
Bet McLeod, Assistant Editors

The objects in the exhibition have been grouped in nine thematic sections that explicate important aspects of Beckford's life. These groupings augment the essays by focusing on specific aspects of the objects in Beckford's collections. The text serves both the general reader, uninitiated to Beckford studies, and the specialist for whom a close examination and interpretation of objects remains highly significant. The authors have approached their subjects from a variety of connoisseurial and interdisciplinary perspectives. Some have sought new interpretations for objects already well catalogued, while others have focused on pieces that have been given scant attention until now. The authors were given the mandate to address the source of a design, its maker, the genesis of a commission or its fabrication, or even the use of a particular piece by Beckford and where it may have been positioned in his home. Related pieces in other collections are discussed as well.

For numbered source notes and information about an object's provenance, exhibition history, literature, and marks, signatures, and inscriptions, see the appendix. The following objects were displayed at just one of the exhibition's two venues: cat. nos. 54, 84, 94, and 129, at The Bard Graduate Center, New York, only; cat. no. 8, at the Dulwich Picture Gallery, London, only.

Contributors

Megan Aldrich — M. A.

Ellenor M. Alcorn — E. M. A.

Fabienne Audebrand — F. A.

Sidney Blackmore — S. B.

Barbara Drake Boehm — B. D. B.

Maureen Cassidy-Geiger — M. C-G.

Stefano Carboni — S. C.

Charles Cator — C. H. C.

Jeannie Chapel — J. C.

Rachel E. Church — R. E. C.

Aileen Dawson — A. D.

Layla S. Diba — L. S. D.

Rachel Layton Elwes — R. L. E.

John Hardy — J. H.

Christopher Hartop — C. H.

William Hauptman — W. H.

Henry Hawley — H. H.

Philip Hewat-Jaboor — P. H-J.

Malcolm Jack — M. J.

Ian Jenkins — I. J.

Ulrich Leben — U. L.

Martin P. Levy — M. P. L.

Jon Millington — J. M.

Bet McLeod — B. M.

Elisabeth Mitchell — E. M.

Jeffrey Hoyt Munger — J. H. M.

A. R. E. North — A. R. E. N.

Julia E. Poole — J. E. P.

Henry Potts — H. P.

Anna Somers Cocks — A. S. C.

Timothy Schroder — T. S.

Jeanne Sloane — J. S.

Eleanor Tollfree — E. T.

Beth Carver Wees — B. C. W.

Annette Wickham — A. W.

Christopher Woodward — C. W.

The Early Years, 1760–81

William Thomas Beckford was born on September 2, 1760, at Fonthill Splendens in Wiltshire. He was the great-grandson of Peter Beckford (d. 1710), Governor of Jamaica, whose immense sugar fortune would fuel the family's ambitions well into the nineteenth century. Beckford was the son of Alderman Beckford, twice Lord Mayor of London. A leading member of the Whig party, the Alderman was a forthright champion of the people and their cause for freedom of speech. In 1756, Alderman Beckford's advantageous marriage to the widowed Maria Marsh, a granddaughter of the sixth Duke of Abercorn, allied his mercantile fortune to one of the leading aristocratic Scottish families. William was proud of his mother's distinguished lineage, and he had a lifelong obsession with genealogy, heraldry, and antiquarian interests.

At the Alderman's death in 1770, William, as his only legitimate son, inherited his fortune, reputedly one of the largest in England. This legacy included the lucrative Jamaican estates as well as the magnificent neo-Palladian family seat of Fonthill Splendens. Set in an extensive park, the house had been furnished by the most fashionable artists and craftsmen of the day. These opulent surroundings were to fire the imagination of this precocious child who was educated at home under his mother's protective eye. Guided by his drawing master Alexander Cozens and with access to his father's extensive library, Beckford acquired a taste for the Orient, which was reflected both in his writing and in his obsession with exotic works of art. His father's collection of paintings was to be the source of inspiration for Beckford's inventive parody on Dutch and Flemish artists, published in 1780.

In 1777 Beckford was sent to continue his education in Geneva where he lived for eighteen months. While there he visited the Carthusian monastery of La Grande Chartreuse, its romantic mountain setting an inspiration for his future residence, Fonthill Abbey. In June of 1780 he embarked on his first Grand Tour, de rigueur for all British gentlemen at that time. Traveling by way of the Netherlands, Germany, and Austria, he spent six months in Italy, returning through Augsburg, Strasbourg, and Paris, and he arrived in London in April of 1781.

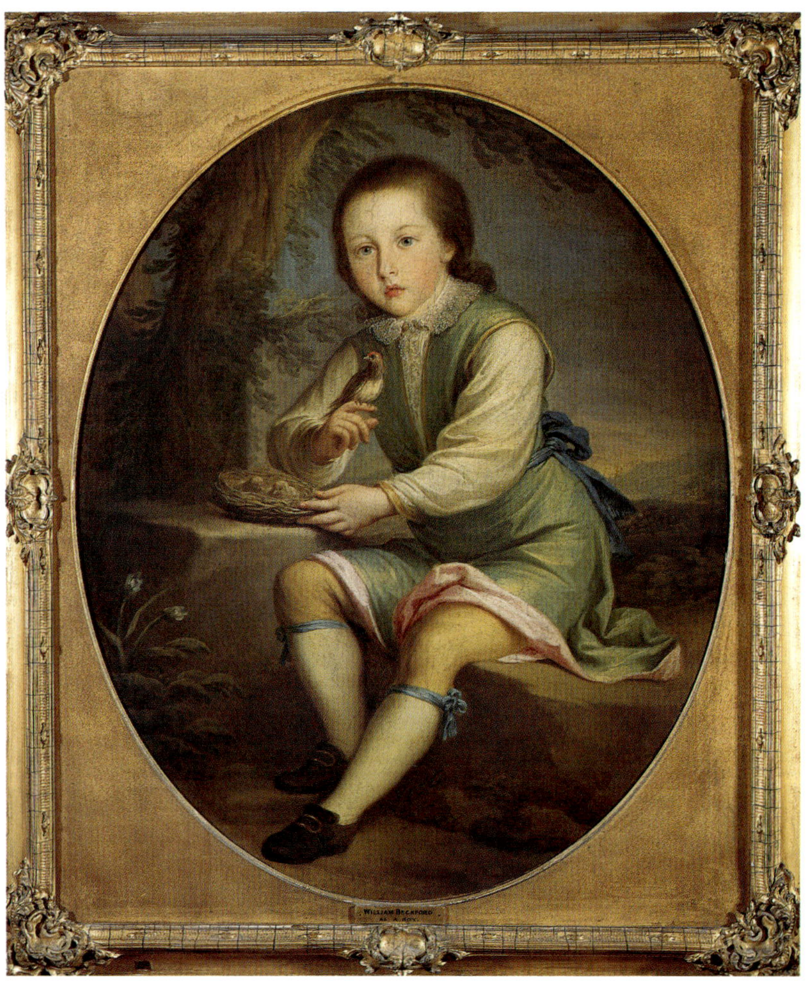

1. William Beckford
Andrea Casali (1705–1784)

ca. 1766; England
Oil on canvas
36¾ x 30 in. (93.35 x 76.2 cm)
The Hamilton Collection,
Lennoxlove, East Lothian

Andrea Casali's portrait of the young William Beckford, an image of a small boy, between six and eight years of age, staring straight ahead with a determination, confidence, and interest almost beyond his years, certainly agrees with accounts of Beckford at that age. His first tutor, the young Scot, Robert Drysdale, described the eight-year-old William as being "exceedingly sprightly. . . . He has been accustomed to speak and read French since he was 3 or 4 years old, and had begun the Latin about a year before I came here. He is of a very agreeable disposition, but begins already to think of his being master of a great fortune, I am apprehensive that both his father and mother contrary to their own desire and inclination may hurt him by their indulgence."[1]

Andrea Casali, an Italian artist who carried out extensive decorative schemes at Fonthill Splendens for Alderman Beckford (see chap. 3), executed portraits of Alderman Beckford, his wife Maria, as well as his son William and stepdaughter Elizabeth Marsh. Drysdale recounts Elizabeth Marsh's description of her half-brother's oval portrait, then in the State Dressing Room: "an excellent portrait of my Brother by Casali in an oval of an elegant ornamental Glass. Casali has taken the strongest resemblance of my Brother, and it is a sweet pretty picture."[2]

It is appropriate that the young Beckford is portrayed with a bird on his finger; he had a strong affinity with nature throughout his life. Unlike his cousin, the famous huntsman Peter Beckford, author of

Thoughts on Hunting (1781), William would have nothing to do with the sport. To stop the hunting activities of "the rivalling Nimrods of the vicinity" as well as to assure his own privacy, he built a wall many years later around his Fonthill estate. He also later told his biographer Cyrus Redding: "Your country gentlemen . . . will take no denial when they go hunting in their red jackets. . . . I found remonstrance in vain, so I built the wall to exclude them. I never suffer an animal to be killed except through necessity. In early life I gave up shooting because I consider we have not rights to murder animals for sport. I am fond of animals, the birds in the plantations of Fonthill seemed to know me— they continued their songs as I rode close to them; the very hares grew bold. It was exactly what I wished."[3]

Beckford claimed in later life, that on a visit to Paris in 1784, he formed a friendship with a lioness in the Jardin du Roi and, entering the cage, "smoothed down the enormous paw . . . leisurely and deliberately touching one after the other the terrific talons with which it was adorned."[4] It is a typically Beckfordian tale that demonstrates his predilection towards animals. Even in old age, he would feed the birds on the slopes of his beloved Lansdown Hill in Bath. —S. B.

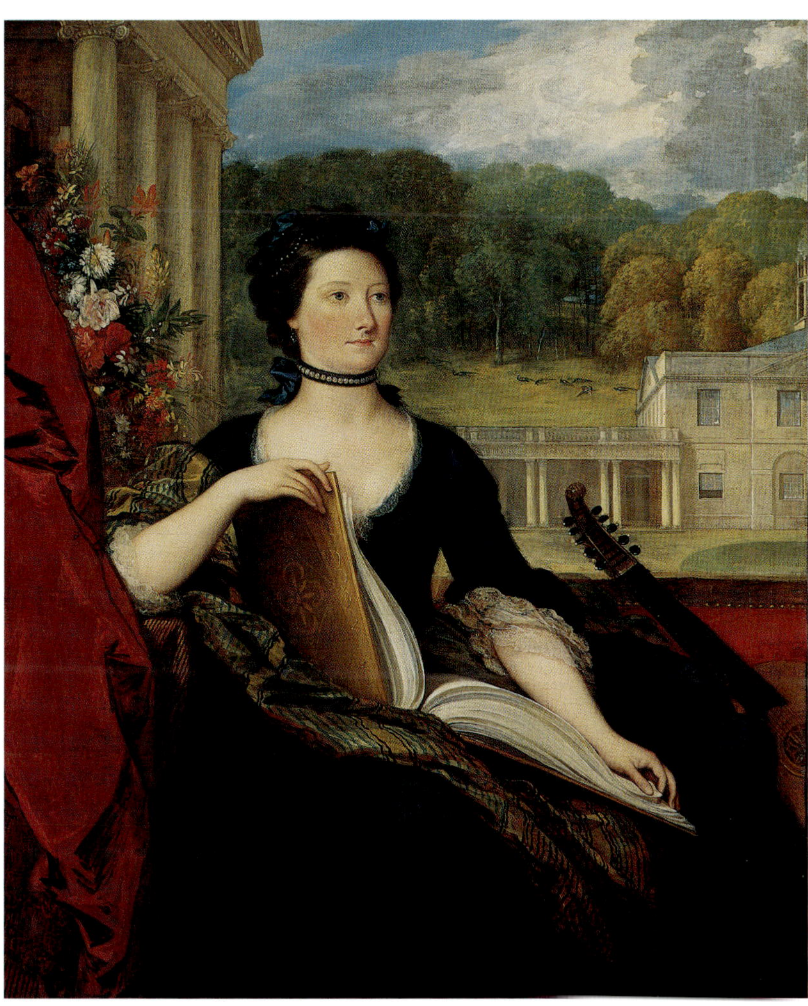

2. *Maria Hamilton Beckford*
Benjamin West (1738–1820)

1799; England
Oil on canvas
57½ x 45¼ in. (146 x 115 cm)
National Gallery of Art, Washington, Andrew Mellon Collection
(1947.17.23)

Maria Hamilton (1724–1798) was the daughter of the Honorable Charles Hamilton, son of the sixth Earl of Abercorn, and Bridget Coward, daughter of a prominent family established in Wells, Somerset, for a number of generations. Maria's first husband was a city merchant, Francis Marsh, by whom she had one daughter, Elizabeth, who was to gain fame as novelist.[1] In 1756, after the death of her first husband, Maria married Alderman William Beckford (cat. fig. 2A).

The Beckford marriage appears a curious union. Despite education at Westminster school and Oxford, the Alderman was something of a rough diamond. Mrs. Beckford was of different material, able to trace her descent through three lines from King Edward III, and she was of a somewhat religious, evangelical turn-of-mind.[2] As her son William was to write in his novel, *Azemia,* of Lady Arsinoe Arrogant, "she never seemed entirely able to forget that she had married a Commoner, though he was a man of family not very inferior to her own. The Arrogant blood, however (in spite of the elegant refinement of her mind, and a *tint* of Methodism, which teaches perfect humility) continually reminded her, at the head of this magnificent and well-furnished table, that Lady Arsinoe was *deplace.*"[3]

After her husband's death in 1770, Mrs. Beckford challenged her husband's will to set aside the executors who had power over the property and revenues of the estate and were also guardians of her young son. Consequently, William was declared a Ward in Chancery, which meant that she effectively controlled her son's future, as the court seems to have offered no opposition to her plans. At that time the decision was made that Beckford would not be sent away to school but would be tutored at home. One senses that at an early stage, she realized that in William she had a child who, although showing talent, even genius, was also given to melancholy and fantasy. For his part, William did not find the companionship and

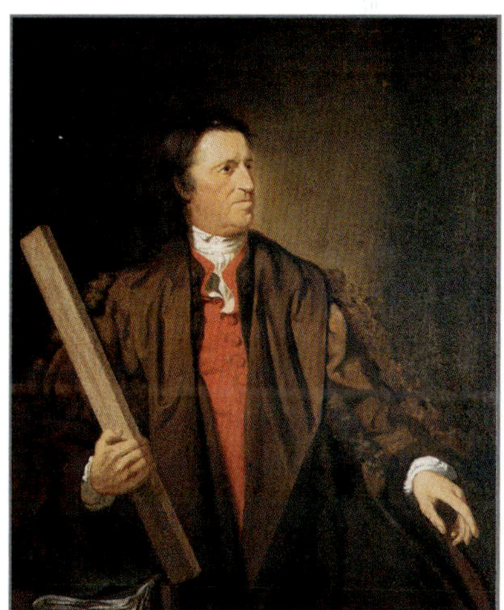

Cat. fig. 2A. *Alderman William Beckford*, ca. 1765. Attributed to Tilly Kettle (1735–1786). Oil on canvas; 49⅝ x 39¾ in. (126 x 101 cm). Palace of Westminster, London.

intellectual life that he sought in her during his youth. Mrs. Beckford had no time for the rhapsodical letters that flowed from her son's pen. Just two years before her death, he apologized in the course of a long letter for not having "concluded for your sake who have no affection for long Letters."[4] It is a revealing statement, which illuminates the essential difference in character and outlook between mother and son.

Mrs. Beckford may well have indulged her only son from an early age, but in adolescence and as he approached his majority, her evangelical strength must have been sorely tested to provide sufficient support for the various family crises her son generated. Beckford referred to his mother as the "Begum" and her friends as "Methodistical dowagers." On one occasion, he declared, "The Begum is raving at a rate, the prince of the abyss himself has no conception of, whilst Aunt Effingham blows up the flames, and declares it shall no longer be *her* fault."[5]

Benjamin West's portrait of Mrs. Beckford, painted in 1799, was one of four posthumous portraits of family members that Beckford commissioned from the painter.[6] A Pennsylvanian-born artist, West set up a studio in London in 1763 and received considerable patronage from George III, including a series of paintings to decorate the new chapel at Windsor Castle. In the 1790s, William Beckford, however, was West's most significant patron. The artist received £1,000 a year for paintings and sketches for the Revelation Chamber at Beckford's house, Fonthill Abbey. Beckford owned at least eighteen works by West.[7] West also acted as an art agent for Beckford, attending the Duke of Orleans's sale in May 1799. Beckford was persuaded by West and a fellow American artist, John Trumbull, to invest in a large tract of land on the Genesee River, New York, but after West's son Raphael visited America and discovered that a "set of swindlers were endeavouring to impose on Mr Beckford," Beckford hastily withdrew from the transaction.[8]

This portrait may be based on a painting or sketch by Andrea Casali, who was working on the decoration of Alderman Beckford's house, Fonthill Splendens, seen in the background. Mrs. Beckford, who is depicted in early middle-age,[9] is shown with a book, possibly a music score, and a stringed musical instrument. Beckford, late in life, recorded that his mother had learned the guitar from Collins, brother of the Countess of Abingdon.[10]

Mrs. Beckford died at her house at West End, Hampstead, in 1798. In her will she stipulated that she was to be buried in the family vault at Fonthill and that her funeral expenses should not exceed two hundred pounds. This sum may well have been exceeded for her remains were brought to Salisbury where the body lay in state at the White Hart Inn, before the funeral procession set off for Fonthill. At the park gates were "300 poor men, women and children in deep mourning . . . volunteers, ranged on either side of the road received the procession with reversed arms, drums muffled, fifes bound round with black crape, playing the Dead March in Saul."[11] Each of the poor received a gift of five shillings.

The picture was inherited by Beckford's daughter, the Duchess of Hamilton, and remained at Hamilton Palace, until it was sold in 1919, when it was mistakenly identified as portrait of Lady Elizabeth Gordon.[12] —S. B.

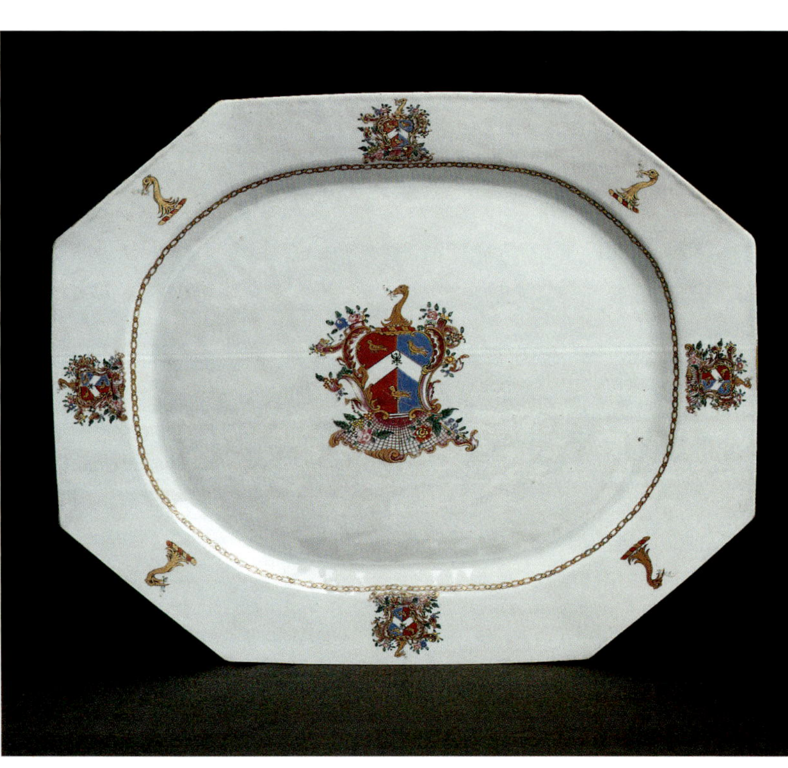

3. Plate

Maker unknown

ca. 1755; China
Porcelain
15 x 18½ in. (38 x 47 cm)
Private collection

This plate is part of a large service commissioned by Alderman William Beckford, probably at the time of the reconstruction of his house at Fonthill which was partially destroyed by fire in 1755. This led to the building of the neo-Palladian Fonthill House later to be inherited by his son William and which became known as Fonthill Splendens.

Armorial dinner services began to be commissioned by Europeans at the end of the seventeenth century and this service is typical of those ordered by the English nobility and merchant classes. Engravings or drawings showing coats of arms were sent to China as models, but in this instance the arms are thought to have been copied from a bookplate. The normal practice was for the polychrome coats of arms to be placed in the center of each piece. This elaborate service is unusual in that the border is also painted with the Beckford arms alternating four times with the Beckford crest—a heron's head erased, or, in the beak a fish, argent and arms—rather than the more typical Chinese flowers, no doubt to emphasize the importance of its owner.[1] The arms of Beckford of Jamaica and later of Fonthill— Per pale gules and azure, on a chevron argent, between three martlets or an eagle, displayed sable—are painted in the center, within an elaborate shell and scrollwork cartouche.

The forms of these armorial services were based on contemporary European designs for porcelain and silver; this service included the standard range of tureens, dishes, plates, bowls, juglets, and cups and saucers. The majority of the surviving portion of this service is now in the collection of the Alderman's descendants. —P. H-J.

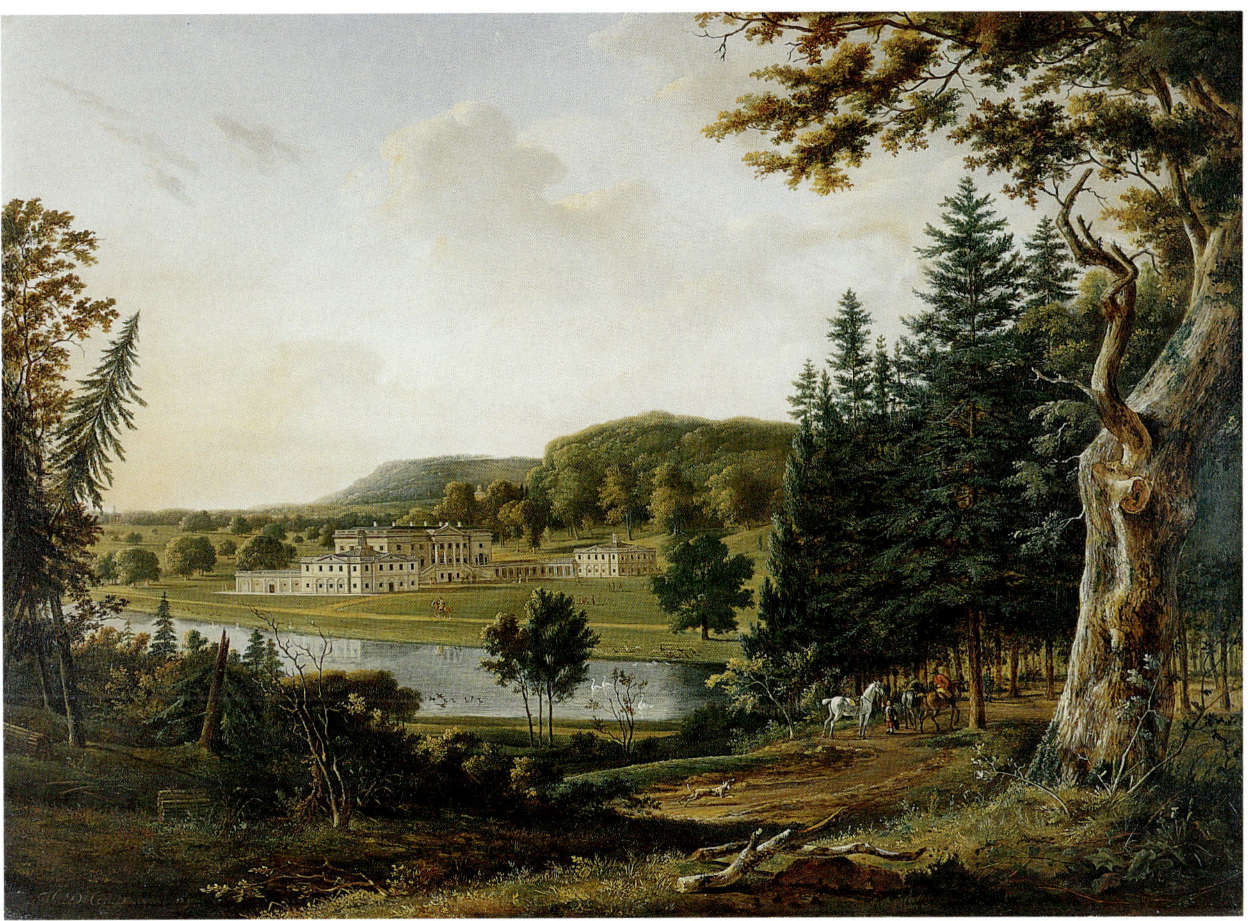

The Fonthill estate, originally owned by the Mervyn family, was purchased by Alderman Beckford in 1744 from Francis Cottington. This view shows Fonthill House, later known as Fonthill Splendens, from across the water looking toward the southwest. It was this magnificent house that was built for Alderman William Beckford around 1755–70 after fire had destroyed his remodeled Elizabethan house that had stood on the site. Modeled on the plan of Houghton Hall in Norfolk, the new Fonthill House was built in the Palladian manner with a central block and flanking pavilions linked by colonnades. The Alderman employed leading artists and craftsmen to furnish the opulent interiors in the latest style. The Italian artist Andrea Casali (see cat. nos. 1 and 6) was commissioned to paint ceilings and large mythological paintings with which to embellish the interiors.

The house was set in an extensive park close to a winding stretch of water, complete with grottoes and a splendid boathouse. The hill to the west was enhanced with a pagoda and a temple building, as well as an old parish church, which the Alderman had remodeled.

Under construction at the time of William Beckford's birth, Fonthill House was completed at the time of his inheritance in 1770, with the exception of some of the furnishings, including magnificent Gobelins tapestries and a crimson velvet state bed. Although Beckford was traveling extensively in the late 1780s and 1790s he asked the architect John Soane to make plans for an avant-garde top-lit picture gallery. This was not carried out, however, and Soane only completed relatively minor work. Beckford's great passion for French neoclassical furnishings and works of art encouraged him in the mid-1790s to modernize some of the interiors of Fonthill House. He employed a group of artists and craftsmen, such as Jean-Jacques Boileau, to impart a strongly franco-phile sense to the new interiors, which paralleled the work being carried out at Carlton House for the Prince Regent by Henry Holland.

At the same time as these remarkable interiors were being formed, Beckford had begun work on the building of Fonthill Abbey, which would eventually become his home and lead to the demolition of Fonthill House in 1807.

Beckford seems to have employed Hendrick de Cort shortly after the artist's arrival in England in 1790. It would seem he was a regular visitor to Fonthill, spending Christmas there in 1796,[1] and making sketching visits almost up until the time of Fonthill House's demolition.[2] Beckford also possessed views of both Salisbury and Exeter cathedrals by de Cort, which hung in the picture gallery that was decorated by Boileau and led off the corridor on the bed chamber storey at Fonthill House.[3]

Of Flemish origin, de Cort studied in Antwerp, becoming a member of the Guild of Saint Luke in 1770. Appointed painter to Archduke Maximilian in 1774, he went to Paris after 1776, where he was received into the Académie Royale in 1779. Two views of Chantilly (now in the Musée Condé) were painted for the Prince de Condé before de Cort returned to Amsterdam in 1781. He arrived in London in about 1790 where he remained until his death. He traveled extensively throughout England and Wales, cultivating prominent patrons for whom he executed paintings of their houses.[4]
—P.H-J.

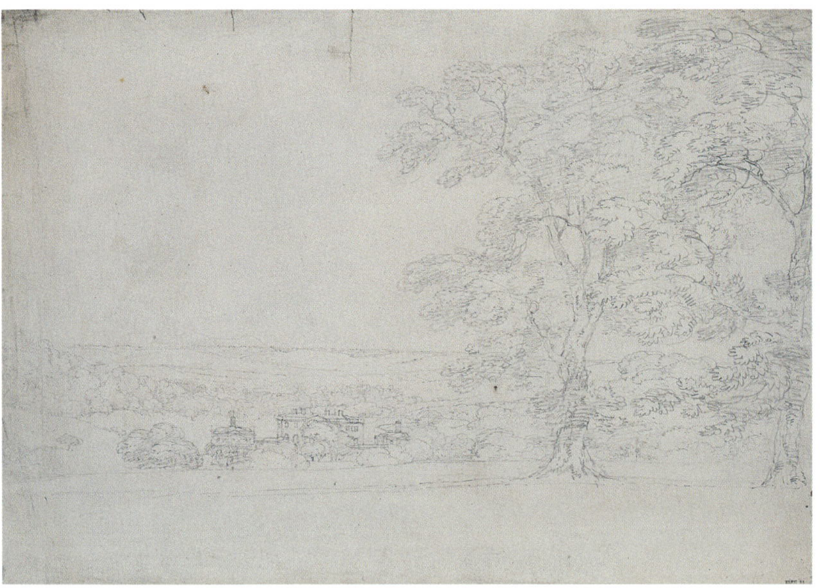

5. *View of Fonthill Splendens
from the West*
J. M. W. TURNER (1775–1851)

1799; England
Pencil on paper
13¾ x 17 in. (33.5 x 43.3 cm)
Tate Gallery, London, bequeathed by
the artist 1856 (D02202)

In 1799, when Turner was sketching at Fonthill, Beckford still resided at Fonthill Splendens, the neo-Palladian mansion he inherited from his father and the place where he grew up. Its rich furnishings and the art collections it housed made it famous even during Alderman Beckford's day, when it was seen as a rival to Houghton Hall, the palatial mansion of Sir Robert Walpole, the British prime minister to George II and the father of Horace Walpole. Later Beckford spent much time and money "improving" and updating the house, although its damp location was a continuing problem. He came to the decision to demolish it in stages, beginning with the east wing in 1801. Beckford continued to live at Fonthill Splendens until early in 1804, when he made the nearby Abbey his permanent home. It was at Fonthill Splendens that the party of Admiral Nelson stayed in December 1800. A torchlit drive through the woods led them up the hill to the Abbey, where they attended what became known as the famous "Nelson Banquet."

After Beckford left Fonthill Splendens, it provided useful guest accommodation, and his daughters evidently lived there for a time.[1] It was mostly taken down in 1807. By demolishing the house, Beckford was able to realize some money from salvaged materials and was saved the expense of maintaining it. He needed funds at this point, for the magnificent north range of the Abbey was begun in 1806, and the building's exterior was being faced in stone to replace the earlier, crumbling cement work – a legacy of its initial purpose as a garden "folly."
—M. A.

6. *Summer*
Andrea Casali (1705–1784)
ca. 1765; England
Oil on canvas
35⅞ x 28 in. (90.8 x 71.1 cm)
The Trustees of the Holburne Museum
of Art, Bath (A76)

Casali, who was born and died in Rome, came to work in England in 1741, having escorted visiting British "milordi" who were in Rome on the Grand Tour. He had previously worked in Rome and Spain. In England he worked as a dealer, a decorative painter, and a painter of religious subjects. He became fashionable and was employed in country houses, for instance at Hovingham Hall in North Yorkshire. There he painted a copy of *Aurora* by Guido Reni from the Casino Rospigliosi in Rome, one of many which he executed of this hugely popular work, which he also did for Alderman Beckford in the Great Hall at Fonthill.[1] Casali worked at Holkham Hall for the Earl of Leicester but it was Alderman Beckford, William's father, who was his greatest patron and for whom he painted a vast scheme of works at Fonthill House (later known as Fonthill Splendens), the Alderman's new house, built after the fire which destroyed the former house in 1755. The Alderman commissioned Casali, who only painted in oil, to execute a large number of ceiling compartments, for instance, in the Grand Entrance Hall, the Picture Gallery, the Saloon, the Grand Staircase, and the Great Dining Room.[2] Some of these were commented on in 1801 by Britton, albeit in a somewhat disparaging manner.[3] The Alderman also owned a variety of freestanding works by Casali, of religious, allegorical, and mythologi-

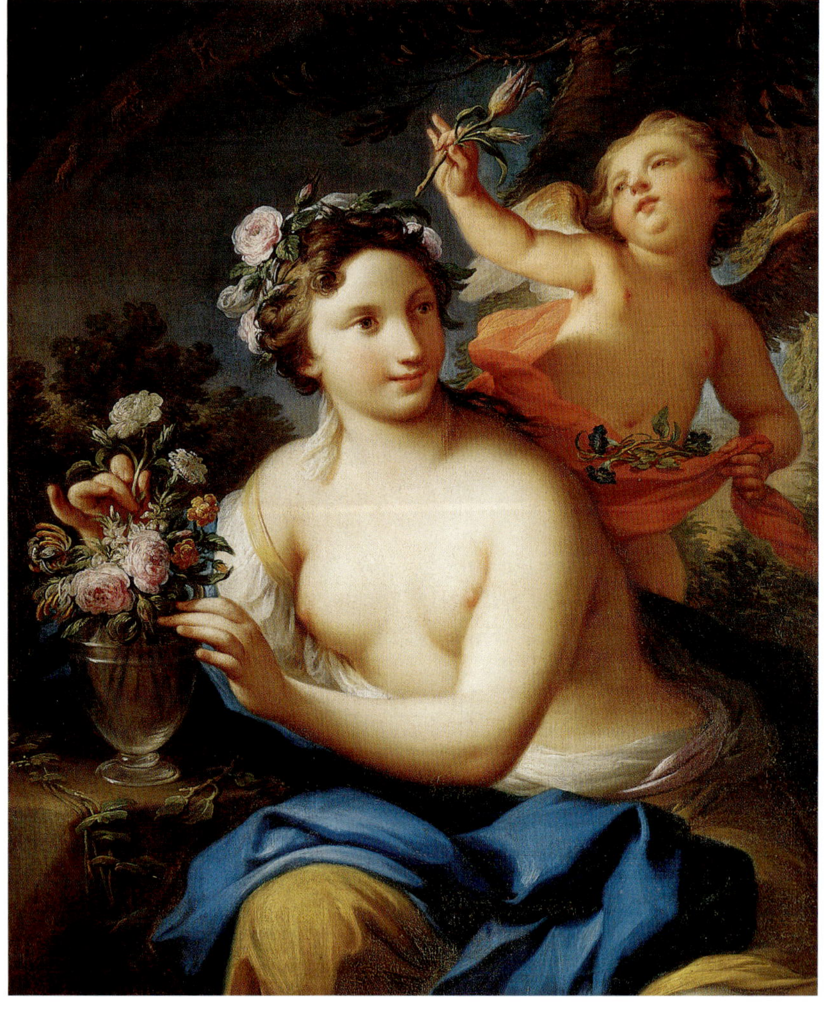

cal subjects. These were mostly purchased from Casali's sale, held in London in April 1766, the year he left England to return to live in Rome where he remained as a relatively obscure painter.[4]

Contemporary descriptions of the Alderman's house dwell on the lavish and sumptuous extravagance of the interiors and the richness of the materials used.[5] The large decorative works, considered by William Beckford to be old-fashioned and which he referred to as "dauberies," were swept out and sold with the contents of Splendens when Beckford decided to demolish the old house and concentrate solely on the building of the Abbey.[6] The contents of the two sales of items from Splendens give an indication of how dominant Casali's presence must have been, for in the first sale held in the Great Hall at Splendens in August 1801 there were twenty works by him and in the later dispersal sale of August 1807, eighteen works by Casali were included.[7] Some of these paintings from the staircase reappeared in 1809 in the sale held in Salisbury by Mr H. Jeffrey who collected paintings with a Beckford provenance with an intent to sell them, an early example of the awareness of the importance of Beckford as a collector.[8]

One of a set of four paintings representing the Seasons, this painting of *Summer* was purchased, along with *Autumn,* by the family of the Bath collector, Sir William Holburne (1793–1874). Holburne had a particular interest in objects owned by Beckford and had bought some items from the Lansdown Tower sale of 1845 after Beckford's death. Holburne's collection was established as a museum by his sister in the former Sydney Hotel in Bath and was opened in 1916.

There is some confusion surrounding these two paintings, owing to the presence of painted signs of the Zodiac for spring, Aries, Taurus, and Gemini, in the upper left corner, which may have been painted later. Regarded by Holburne as *Summer* and *Autumn* and by Casali, they hung in his study and were listed there in 1867.[9] By 1927, however, they were attributed to J. J. Lagrennée.[10] In 1976 they were reattributed to Casali and entitled *Spring* and *Summer.*[11] Another painting of *Autumn* is at Temple Newsam, Leeds, and is possibly one of another series of paintings. Paintings of *Winter* are lost. There are other paintings by Casali from Fonthill, which remained in the Bath area, at the Bath Reference Library and at Dyrham Park in Gloucestershire. Those paintings of around 1754 were purchased by Colonel George Blathwayt after 1845 from the Theatre Royal in Bath; three represent the Arts on the ceiling in the Great Hall and two others hang on the staircase. —J. C.

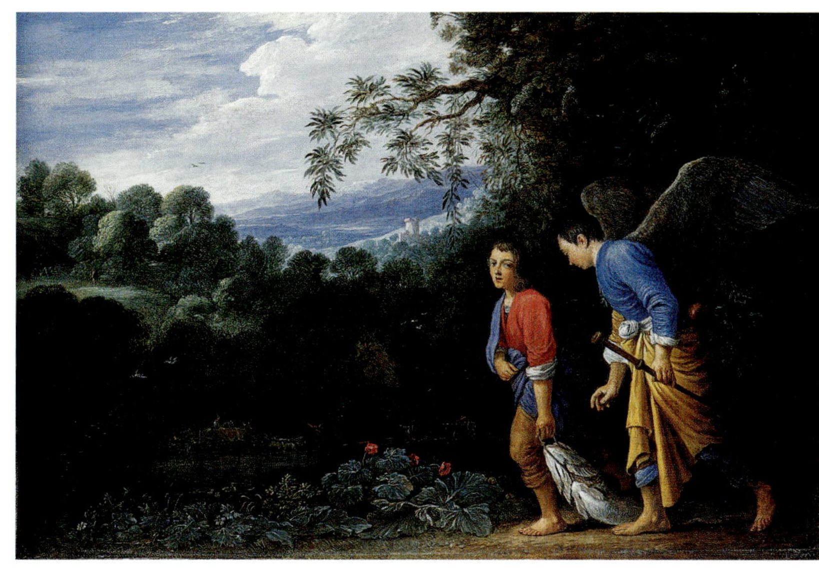

7. *Tobias and the Archangel Raphael Returning with the Fish*
AFTER ADAM ELSHEIMER
(BAPTIZED 1578–1610)

ca. 1750; The Netherlands
Oil on copper
7⅞ x 10⅞ in. (19.3 x 27.6 cm)
©The National Gallery, London (NG 1424)

Beckford owned two versions of this subject, referred to as the "large" and the "small" Tobit, both of which were considered to be genuine works by Elsheimer and were evidently much treasured by him. The "small" Tobit was seen by both Passavant and Waagen on their visits to Bath where it hung in the dining room at Lansdown Crescent.[1] This smaller version was retained by Beckford's daughter after his death and was sold in the Hamilton Palace sale in 1882.[2]

Elsheimer painted a number of compositions of this subject taken from the Book of Tobit in the Apocrypha, but this "large" version is now thought to be by a Flemish painter, one of many copies after the original work by Elsheimer.[3] It is painted on a thick copper plate on which had previously been engraved some heraldic patterns and a chain of a Maltese cross. The original of this painting is now lost but it is known (reversed) from the engraving of 1613 by Hendrick Goudt, a Dutchman who lived with the Elsheimer family and who made a number of engravings after Elsheimer's work. There is a contemporary copy of the work of about 1609 in the Statens Museum für Kunst, Copenhagen.[4]

Beckford possibly inherited the painting from his father, the Alderman, who had purchased it in the sale of the royal physician, Dr. Richard Mead, in 1754. It was recorded by John Britton in 1801 as hanging in an anteroom at Fonthill Splendens. Britton commented on its state of "high preservation."[5] The following year Beckford sold the picture and it was purchased at auction by William Seguier, a dealer and later keeper of the National Gallery. It was later bought by George Watson Taylor whose wife's huge wealth had also come from sugar in Jamaica. Similar in many ways to Beckford's collection, the Watson Taylor collection included Old Masters, eighteenth-century French decorative objects, and furniture. It was later much admired by Beckford on the occasion of the sale of Erlestoke Park in Wiltshire in 1832.[6] The painting later belonged to the Hon. Edmund Phipps, the younger brother of the Marquess of Normanby and Sir Charles Beaumont Phipps, keeper of Her Majesty's Privy Purse, and it was in the Phipps collection when Waagen saw it in 1854.[7] In 1859 Sir Charles Eastlake (1793–1865), director of the National Gallery, intended to purchase this picture at the Phipps sale and was prepared to pay £150 for it. He was outbid, however, by the dealer Henry Farrer (d. 1866), who had been paid a guinea by Eastlake for his opinion of the picture.[8] The painting was finally bequeathed to the National Gallery, London, in 1894. —J. C.

Coming of Age, 1781–1800

Beckford returned to England from his first Grand Tour in 1781 to celebrate his coming-of-age with a lavish party at Fonthill Splendens between September 28 and October 1. This event was followed several months later by the renowned Christmas party, when the house was transformed by the artistry of Philippe Jacques de Loutherbourg, an experience that may have contributed to the shaping of Beckford's semiautobiographical novel *Vathek*, which he was to write shortly afterward.

In May 1782, the restless young Beckford continued his education with a second Grand Tour, traveling on the Continent in regal splendor accompanied by a large retinue of servants. Taking a route similar to his first tour, he spent time in Venice, Rome, and especially Naples, where he stayed with a distant cousin, Sir William Hamilton, the British envoy. Beckford returned home in November having passed through Geneva and Paris on the return journey.

Beckford's obsession with a younger man, William "Kitty" Courtenay (see fig. 1-4), prompted concern over his complex private life, and his mother and her advisors felt it imperative that a suitable marriage be arranged. With an unimpeachable background, Lady Margaret Gordon, daughter of the Earl of Aboyne, was chosen, and the marriage took place on May 5, 1783. The honeymoon was spent in Switzerland and Paris, where Beckford purchased works of art, and books for his library, which was to become one of the most important of the time.

Back in England in the spring of 1784, Beckford became a Member of Parliament in pursuit of a political career for which he was temperamentally unsuited. This, coupled with his quest for a peerage, made him particularly vulnerable to political enemies. His liaison with Kitty Courtenay was used in a campaign to discredit Beckford, and as news of it became increasingly public, Beckford and his wife set out for Switzerland, after the birth of their first child in 1785. In this tranquil setting their second daughter was born, but Beckford's wife succumbed to puerperal fever and died. Distraught by his loss, Beckford received an additional blow when he learned that his novel *Vathek* had been published in London with neither his permission nor with his name.

In the midst of these tragedies, Beckford was encouraged to visit his sugar plantations in Jamaica, but the early part of the voyage was uncomfortable, and he disembarked in Lisbon, the first port of call. Rich beyond the measure of most Portuguese, Beckford was sufficiently captivated by the country to extend his stay. Many aspects of Portugal provided him with religious and aesthetic inspiration, which he later used in the building of Fonthill Abbey. During this time he met Gregorio Franchi, who was to be his companion and agent for most of the next thirty years. An additional six months were spent in Madrid, which Beckford would later recall in his writings as a particularly happy period.

Despite his travels, Beckford kept Fonthill Splendens as his principal residence, and in 1790 he employed the architect James Wyatt to undertake improvements to the house and park. Beckford also maintained a residence in Paris from the late 1780s until forced to flee in 1793 during the French Revolution. He was able to take advantage of the considerable social and economic upheaval in France to purchase and commission extraordinary works of art from the fiscally troubled royal manufactories and private workshops.

A second and more extensive stay in Portugal took place from 1793 until 1795, during which time Beckford began to formulate the idea of a picturesque tower to embellish the park at Fonthill. This would evolve into the legendary Abbey.

8. *William Beckford*
George Romney (1734–1802)

1781–82; England
Oil on canvas
93 x 57 in. (239.2 x 144.8 cm)
Upton House, Warwickshire, The Bearsted
Collection (The National Trust), UPT.P.68

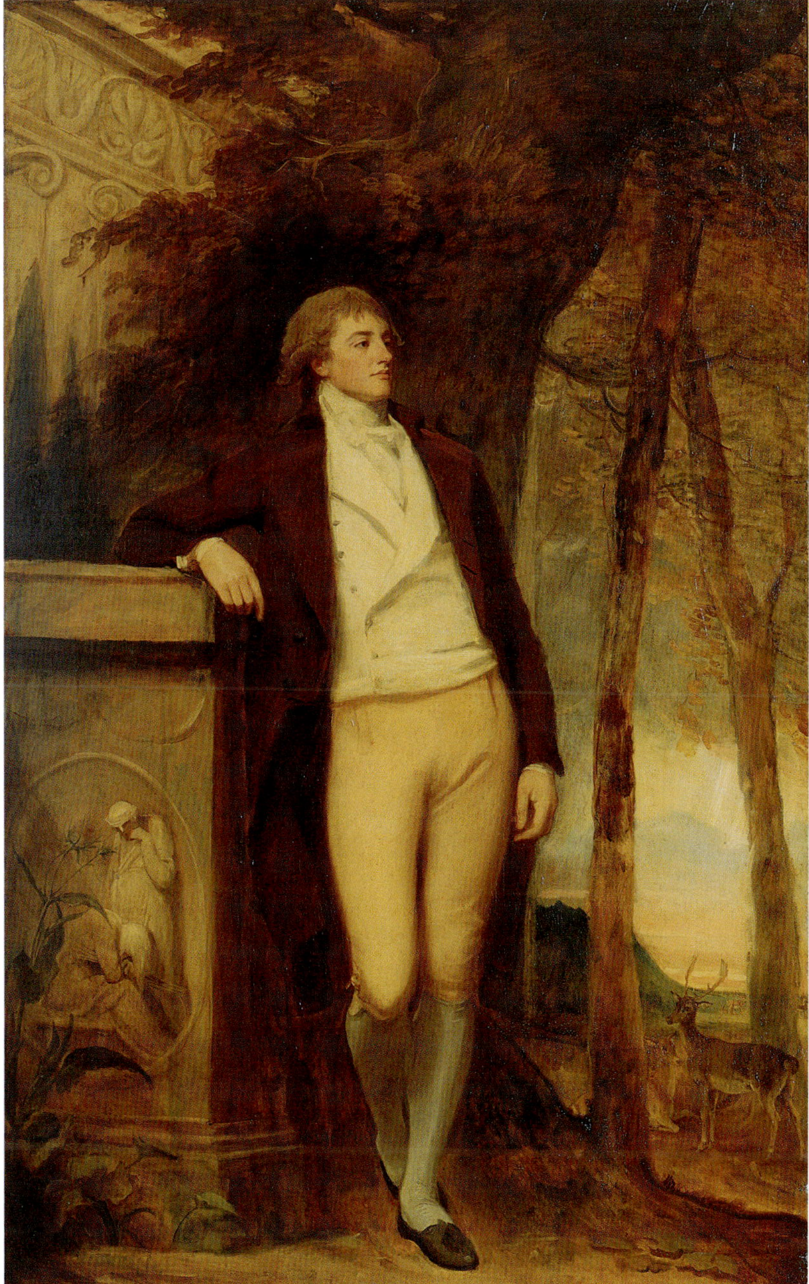

Romney's portrait of Beckford was begun in the summer of 1781, just after Beckford had completed his first Grand Tour, and before the celebrations, held at Fonthill in late September, to mark his coming-of-age.[1] Beckford was about to gain possession of his fortune and would soon be master of his own destiny. He is portrayed in a pose of almost nonchalant arrogance: the hauteur of an immensely rich young man on the threshold of public life.

Beckford's birthday celebrations—"A tumult of balls, concerts and illuminations," he told Lady Hamilton—were held during the last weekend in September. The Lord Chancellor headed two hundred guests who were entertained in the state rooms of Fonthill Splendens. Two famous Italian singers, Pachierotti and Tenducci, "sang like superior beings" a specially composed pastoral cantata by Rauzzini. Meanwhile in the park hundreds of tenants, "farmers and substantial tradesmen were feasting in tents." When night came, "at intervals mortars were discharged and a girandola of rockets burst into the bluish stars that cast a bright light for miles!"[2]

At Christmas that year, Beckford organized a more private party for his intimate friends, including William Courtenay, Louisa (wife of his cousin Peter Beckford), and his young cousins Alexander and Archibald Hamilton. The artist and scenery painter Philippe Jacques de Loutherbourg devised special lighting. The Italian musicians who had sung at his birthday celebration were again present. Years later, Beckford looked back with deep nostalgia on those three days and nights: "Even this long, sad distance from these days and nights of exquisite refinements . . . I still feel warmed and irradiated by the recollections of that strange, necromantic light which Loutherbourg had thrown over what absolutely appeared a realm of Fairy, or rather, perhaps a Demon temple deep beneath the earth set apart for tremendous mysteries—yet how soft, how genial was this quiet light."[3]

It had been suggested that this portrait was painted to satisfy Beckford's conventional and evangelical mother rather than the sitter himself.[4] Curiously, Romney was not paid for the portrait until May 1798, a few months before Mrs Beckford's death. Beckford is shown leaning on a classical plinth, a device used in the portraits of many eighteenth-century Grand Tourists painted in Rome. The landscape here is neither Rome nor its *campagna*, but English parkland, to indicate that Beckford is the master of the great estate of Fonthill. The carving on the plinth, which shows an old man bent with grief, clutching a bundle of sticks, watched by a younger man, has not been identified. The figures may represent King Lear and his fool, or Job and a comforter.[5] If the figure does represent Job, then the presence of the comforter, one who sympathizes with grief, while saying it is self-inflicted, would seem to have an almost prophetic vision if applied to Beckford's life. Another, so far unexplained element in this painting, which is also present in the portrait of William Courtenay (see fig. 1-4), commissioned by Beckford, is the teasel, or fuller's thistle, just in front of the plinth. It cannot be by chance that this plant appears in both portraits, but its presence has so far defied explanation.

The artist George Romney was, with Gainsborough and Reynolds, one of the most fashionable English portrait painters in the late eighteenth century. Born in Lancashire, he practiced in Kendal, before establishing himself in London in 1763. He was in Italy between 1773 and 1775 where he studied old masters, in particular Raphael, and antiquities. He painted a portrait of Beckford's young daughters in 1787 (now in the Henry E. Huntingdon Library and Art Gallery, San Marino).[6] Emma Hart, later Lady Hamilton, second wife of Beckford's cousin Sir William Hamilton, first sat for Romney in 1782 and in the following years the artist made some fifty portraits of her, often illustrating classical subjects.

This portrait remained in Beckford's possession until his death. In his Bath house it hung on the staircase. It then was taken by his daughter, the Duchess of Hamilton, to Hamilton Palace. At the 1919 sale of Hamilton portraits and pictures, it was wrongly identified as a portrait of Alderman Beckford, rather than his son.[7] —S. B.

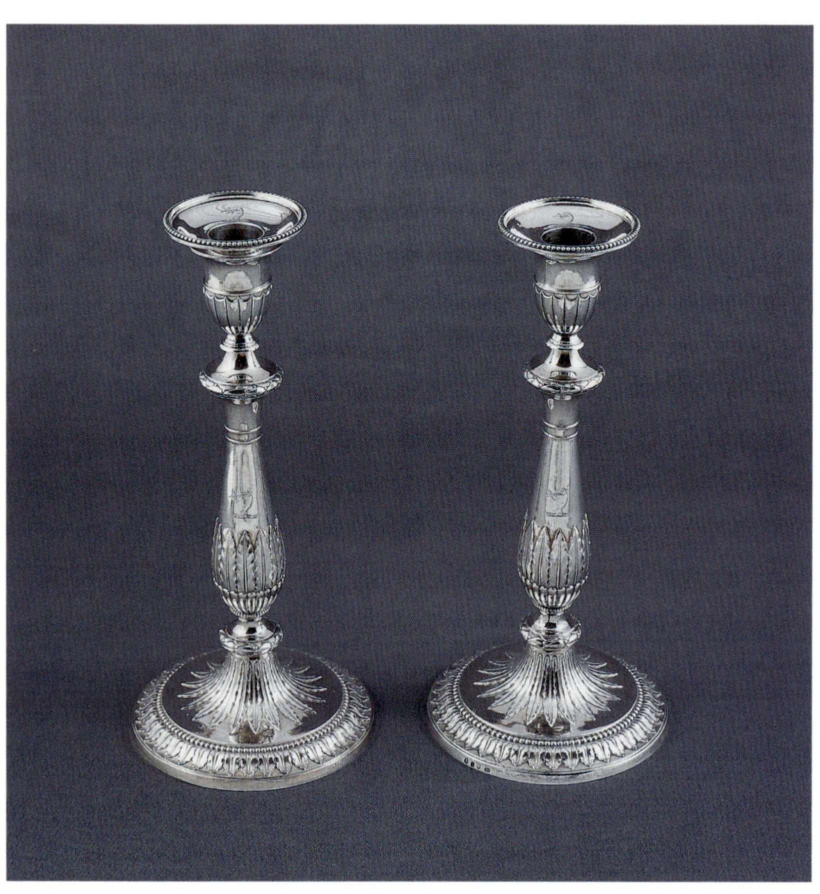

9. *Pair of Candlesticks*
JOHN SCOFIELD
(FL. 1776–1803)

1791–92; England
Silver
13⅜ x 7 in. (34.5 x 15.7 cm)
Beckford Collection, Brodick Castle,
National Trust for Scotland (58.597)

Like the candlesticks bought in 1781 (cat. no. 31) these larger versions, purchased to extend the set that Beckford already owned, were also supplied by John Scofield. There are, however, some slight variations: they lack the border of acanthus on the stem and have bats-wing decoration rather than stiff foliage on the sockets. Beckford may have given the silversmith exacting demands to improve on the design of the earlier candlesticks, but it is more likely that they were purchased from stock from a London retailer such as Jeffreys and Jones after Beckford's return from France in the spring of

1791. That summer he entertained Lady Craven and the German prince she was to marry and, a few weeks later, Sir William Hamilton and his former mistress, Emma, whom Hamilton had married earlier that year. Beckford continued to add to this set for the next twenty-five years.

The Beckford crest of a heron holding a fish in its beak, engraved on the stems and nozzles, barely intrudes on the elegant lines of these candlesticks; it provides identification rather than decoration. On August 11, 1791, Beckford was granted the right to add a tressure to his arms by the College of Arms,[1] the first of a series of augmentations over the next twenty years as his interest in his own genealogy became a passion. This manifested itself in the increasing use of heraldic motifs, as well as a more dramatic interpretation of these elements on his silver, porcelain, and interior decoration.
—C. H.

10. *Snuffer Tray*
JOHN SCOFIELD
(FL. 1776–1803)

1793–94; England
Silver gilt
1⅞ x 4¼ x 10¾ in. (4.7 x 11 x 27.4 cm)
Glasgow Museums
(E.1977-74-8)

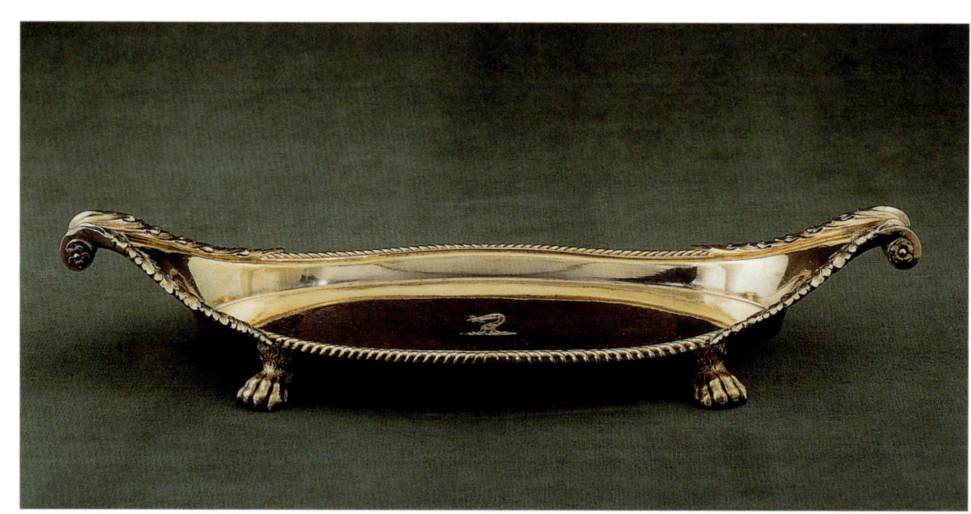

Beckford continued to add to the silver ordered at his coming-of-age throughout the 1780s and 1790s. This tray, one of a pair, was the stand for scissor-form candle snuffers (now lost); it matches the rich neoclassical candlesticks and tablewares supplied by Scofield and others in the early 1780s. It shows how a minor functional object can be made into

a lavish decorative object, and one can imagine the magnificent effect created by quantities of silver-gilt like this in the interiors of Fonthill Splendens, exceptional even by late eighteenth-century standards.

The heavy ropetwist borders and bold acanthus leaves at each end are gilded in a different color from that used on the plain field, which is

enlivened only by the engraved crest of Beckford. The expensive feature of gilding "in two colours" appears regularly in contemporary accounts, such as the ledgers of the retailers Wakelin and Tayler and their successors Wakelin and Garrard.[1] It was used to highlight engraved or chased decoration on gilt pieces. Interestingly, Beckford's tray and its com-

panion were evidently supplied from stock and not made to a special order, as close examination reveals that the crest was engraved after the gilding had been applied. While superb examples of neoclassical silver, these trays are by no means unique and give no hint of Beckford's later interest in innovative designs for silver. —C. H.

11. *Bowl*
JOHN SCOFIELD
(FL. 1776–1803)

1786–87; England
Silver gilt
4¼ x 5½ in. (11 x 14.1 cm)
Trustees of the National Museums
of Scotland, Edinburgh (1980.981)

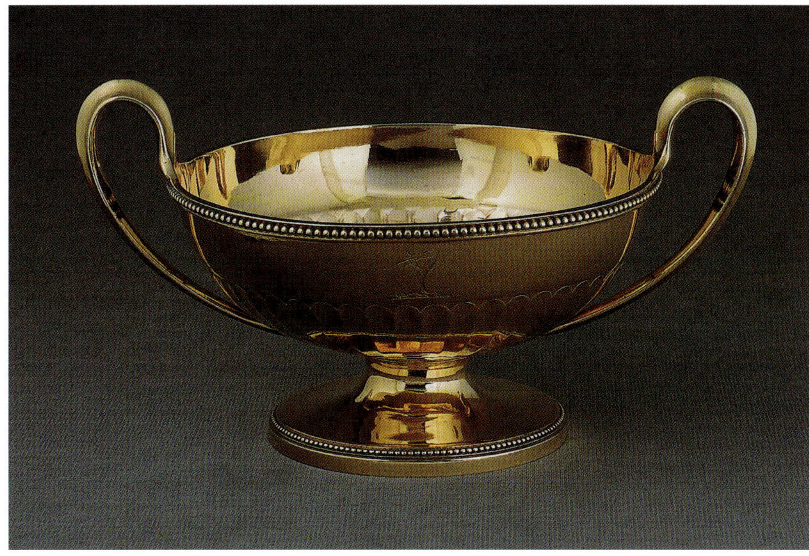

This bowl was evidently purchased during Beckford's visit to England after the death of his wife in May of 1786 and before his departure, in March 1787, for Jamaica, which instead took him to Portugal. The brevity of his visit to England precluded special commissions and this bowl, like so much of his silver purchased during the late 1780s and 1790s, is a stock item of a type readily available in the best London retailers of the period. Like the rest of his neoclassical silver from the Scofield workshop, however, it is of the highest quality, both in design

and workmanship. It follows the form of conventional neoclassical sauceboats of the 1780s, both circular and oval, which take the shape of Robert Adam's vases with their characteristic slender upswept handles, and adds to them panels of vertical fluting. The effect of these facets animates an otherwise plain surface. There is no indication, however, that this bowl or its companion piece, made by Robert Sharp ten years later, ever had a cover, and it may be that they were purchased as decorative vases rather than functional sauceboats.

Unlike the snuffer tray (cat. no. 10) or the gold teapot (cat. no. 20) these bowls have little plain surface area on account of their fluting, and Beckford's heron crest has been engraved unobtrusively on the side of the body. Together with much of Beckford's neoclassical silver-gilt

from this period, the piece evidently remained with Beckford throughout his life and passed on his death to the Hamilton family, from whom it was purchased, with its mate, in 1980 by the National Museums of Scotland. —C. H.

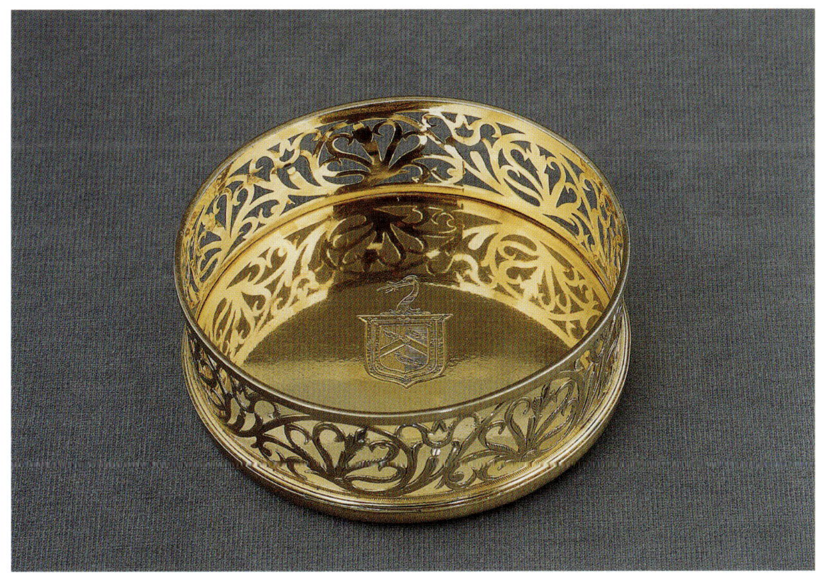

12. *Wine Coaster*
ROBERT SHARP
(FL. 1757–1803)

1793–94; England
Silver gilt, walnut, felt
1½ x 4⅜ in. (4.2 x 11 cm)
Trustees of the National Museums
of Scotland, Edinburgh (1977.216)

Beckford, although abstemious in his habits, enjoyed wine, which he purchased from the leading merchants. This wine coaster, one of four, is intended to hold a glass decanter. It is a typical late-eighteenth-century form, but its diameter is smaller than most. The felt covering the base allowed it to be pushed across a mahogany tabletop after the tablecloth had been removed and port or other dessert wines began their circuit. The form lent itself to mass-production, and the pierced sides of most late eighteenth-century coasters are fly-punched on a steam press. Interestingly, however, traces of fret-saw marks in the scrolling anthemion show that the decoration on Beckford's coasters is hand done, and overall the quality is superior to most examples. The engraved coat-of-arms and crest in the center is a conventional late eighteenth-century depiction; the arms show the double-tressure, or border, which Beckford was granted by the College of Arms in 1791.[1]

Evidently purchased, like the

snuffer tray (cat. no. 10) and the gold toasting fork (cat. no. 25), during his brief visit to England in 1793, the coaster bears the mark of Robert Sharp, formerly in partnership with Daniel Smith (see cat. nos. 20, 141) who made silver for Jeffreys and Jones, the royal goldsmiths. Sharp's work, like that of his contemporary Scofield, is distinguished by its high quality, and both workers are known to have been supplying silver, through the royal goldsmiths, to the Prince Regent at Carlton House. Sharp's mark, for example, appears on a pair of Régence-style candlesticks made in 1795–96 and engraved with the badge of the prince; a further identical set of the same year was supplied to John, the first Marquess of Bute.[2] While both these patrons were already looking to previous ages for inspiration, it was to be some years before Beckford's own interest in eclectic and revivalist silver manifested itself. —C. H.

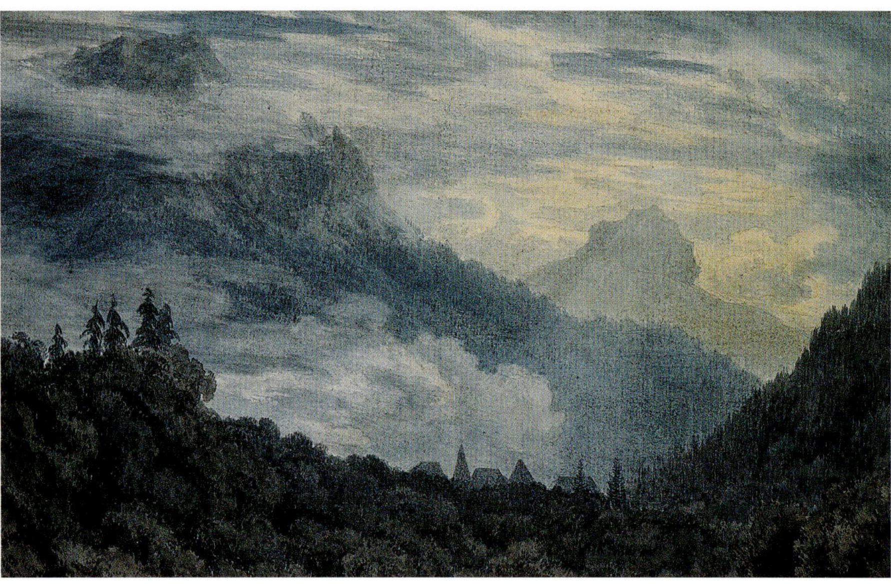

13. *La Grande Chartreuse*
JOHN ROBERT COZENS
(1752–1797)

ca. 1783–85; England
Watercolor
10 x 14⅛ in. (25.2 x 36 cm)
Private collection

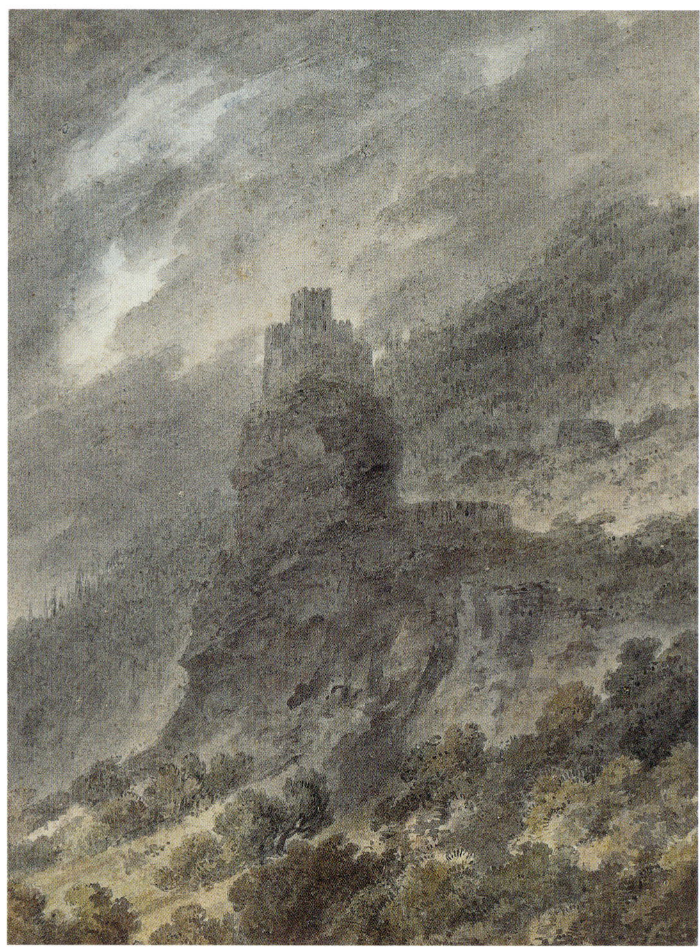

14. *Schloss Hadernburg between Bolzano and Trent*
JOHN ROBERT COZENS (1752–1797)

ca. 1783–85; England
Pencil and watercolor
18⅛ x 12 in. (45.9 x 30.6 cm)
The Victoria and Albert Museum, London
(DYCE 713)

13–19. BECKFORD AND COZENS

Beckford is frequently associated with his collection of prime Old Masters, but he was also an enthusiastic patron and collector of modern English art, a role that is often overlooked.[1] Besides commissioning works from such eminent figures as West and Turner, both of whom worked at Fonthill in the latter years of the eighteenth century, he regularly added to his collection through diverse acquisitions and commissions that included a host of paintings by such luminaries as Landseer, Gainsborough, and Romney.[2] Beckford's purchases did not neglect drawings and watercolors, and he incorporated works into his collection by Bonington, Copley Fielding, the Daniell brothers, and others.[3] Even in his last years in Bath, Beckford continually bought paintings by the younger generation, among whom were such lesser painters as Cope, Vickers, and Willes Maddox.[4] Of these artists, there is little documentation that he maintained an intimate relation with any of them or followed their careers actively, with certain exceptions. His acquisition of their works generally followed the standard procedure of employing agents, buying what struck his sensibilities directly through the exhibitions he attended, or in some instances through direct commissions for specific purposes.

Beckford's association with Alexander and John Robert Cozens, however, was considerably different. He was extremely devoted to both father and son, a decisive factor in forming some aspects of his artistic sensibilities for contemporary painting. The elder Cozens returned from Italy in 1749—he was one of the first British artists to travel there, following Richard Dalton by several years[5]—and began his long teaching career at Eton, where, despite his unconventional methods, he became a respected figure.[6] Beckford was fifteen when he first mentioned Cozens as a friend, having met him through his cousin George Douglas Morton, who was a pupil of Cozens at the time. It is known that Cozens would equally provide Beckford with some form of informal drawing instruction, but the extent of it has never been fully documented, and from the extant documents there is little indication that Beckford's talents were ever geared in this direction.[7]

There is no doubt that Beckford attached himself personally to Cozens in a way that he could not with others, except perhaps Lady Catherine Hamilton.[8] Cozens became a trusted friend to whom Beckford could express his feelings in a confident manner, sharing his deepest secrets, as he did about his interest in William Courtenay.[9] Cozens was also a correspondent with whom Beckford could share interests in the literature that ignited his imagination.[10] Beckford once wrote to him: "I long to see you to tell you a thousand things I cannot write. Indeed, you are the only Being upon this Planet in whose bosom I can deposit every thought which enters mine."[11] At the base of this relationship was Beckford's high regard for the painter's broad mind and unique character, which he described as "almost as full of systems as the Universe."[12] It was in a sense this consummate respect for Cozens' character, openness, and intellect that led Beckford to correspond with him regularly until the artist's death in 1786.

Beckford's alliance with John Robert Cozens was even more productive in artistic rewards than his relationship with Alexander had been. Credited with stimulating the transition of watercolor painting from strict topographical depiction of a specific site to one in which Romantic sensibilities and expression assert equal ground, John Robert was highly esteemed by such interpreters of landscape as Constable, and Turner.[13] The younger Cozens

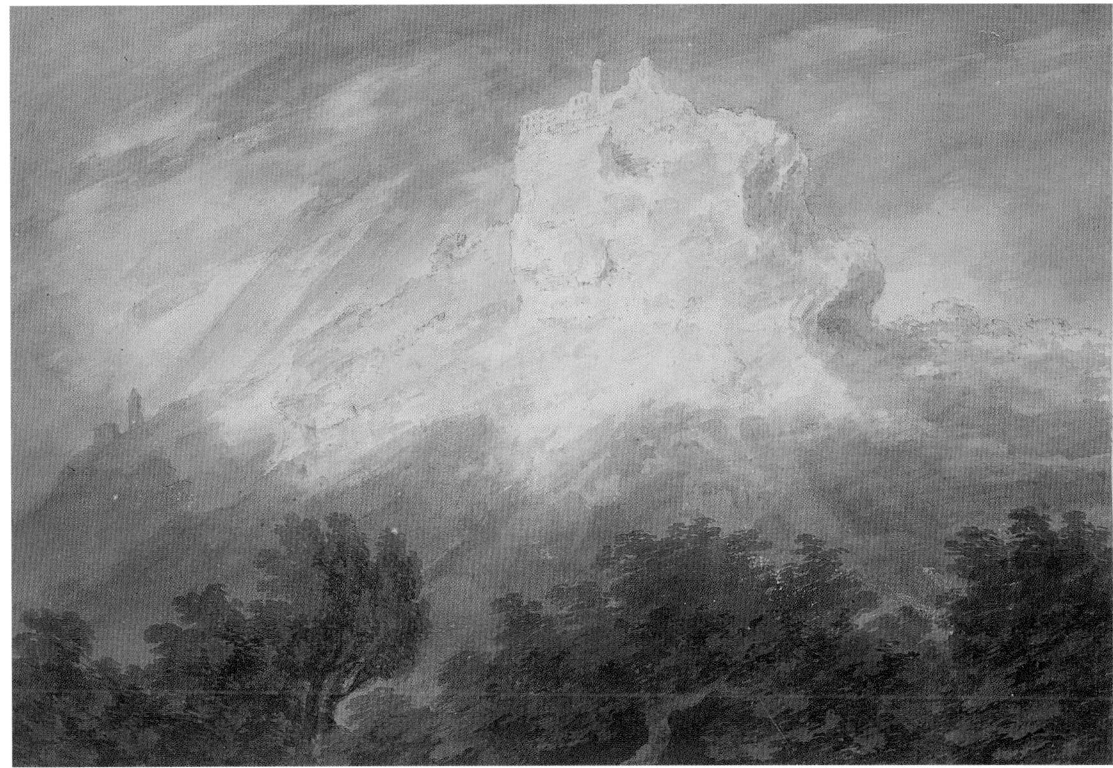

began working for Beckford from about 1780, by which time he had already fully developed his characteristic approach to landscape. His style had matured significantly when in 1776 he accompanied the young connoisseur Richard Payne Knight on his prolonged tour of the Continent. In their wanderings through the Swiss Alps, only several years after William Pars exhibited the first Alpine scenes in London,[14] Payne Knight's ideas on the Sublime served to influence the future direction of Cozens' art,[15] projecting a dimension to his studies made from nature that would find no artistic parallels until the nineteenth century. Beckford must have known some of these works, probably through the intermediary of the elder Cozens; in 1780, when Beckford was in Naples, he had asked Alexander whether his son continued with his drawings: "I hope he does—he cannot make too many. Having seen Italy I value them more than ever if that be possible."[16] When Beckford wrote these words, he was in the process of completing his own European tour, from which he returned to England hastily in April 1781.

The following year, Beckford made a second visit to the Continent, this time engaging John Robert to

accompany him and thus stimulate and ensure the continuity he hoped the younger Cozens would maintain. Traveling in a retinue of three carriages that included his physician, Dr. Ehrhart, his musician, John Burton, his former tutor, John Lettice, and Cozens, the party, sometimes mistaken for that of the Emperor of Austria who was traveling incognito on the same continental route, made the Channel crossing at Dover on May 16—where "Cozens climbed up the cliff and fell a-drawing."[17] Much of the route Beckford's group followed can be documented through Beckford's own letters as well as seven sketchbooks—now in the Whitworth Art Gallery, Manchester—that Cozens maintained throughout the voyage. Fundamentally, they traveled a conventional northern route through Belgium to Cologne before heading south to Innsbruck, traversing the daunting Brenner Pass toward Beckford's goal of Italy.

Cozens was sketching all the time and apparently pleased Beckford with the results. During a halt in Augsburg on June 2, 1782, Beckford informed Alexander that "Your son is well and grows every day in my esteem,"[18] clear evidence that Cozens' recording of the landscape

was fully in accord with Beckford's expectations and tastes. Cozens would gain his stride in the mountainous region of Tyrol, a romantic landscape that must have reminded him of the Swiss scenes he had already recorded with brio for Payne Knight and which accorded itself better with Cozens' artistic temperament. It was through the catalyst of this landscape that the work Cozens provided for Beckford now took on a more singular style. An almost quixotic, blatantly romantic character that was at the aesthetic heart of patron and painter became significant.[19]

Two views near Trent and Bolzano (cat. nos. 14 and 15)—the latter the castle perched on the craggy cliffs between Brixen (known today as Bressanone) and Bolzano; the former the Hadernburg Castle nearby—represent the break in Cozens' approach to landscape that occurred in Beckford's company and typify the best in Cozens' most mature works. The dispiriting weather—which disturbed Beckford, while Cozens' seemed to revel in it—and the eerie mood of each watercolor are clearly the central aesthetic foundations that galvanized Cozens' eye and hand. Although Cozens' work with Payne Knight demonstrated a

similarly sketchy method, capturing mood as much as place, few of the earlier works were as openly daring or abstracted as those he produced here with Beckford's endorsement. The forms of the rocks, structures, and surrounding landscapes are indicated with furious brushstrokes that literally sweep in steep angles across the paper, creating surface patterns that look forward to Turner's most extravagant watercolors decades later. Beckford, who had an eye for originality in all its forms, must have recognized that Cozens had effectively abandoned the topographical tradition in favor of a dramatically emotive interpretation, perhaps applying here his father's blot methods as a portal to the quintessential of each scene. If there is no pretense of pure recording on Cozens' part, nonetheless the results show how his imagination and fluid technique elucidate the rudimentary components of respective sites, atmosphere, and structures in a manner that stands singly in the history of watercolor of the eighteenth century.

When Beckford and Cozens followed the Adige River to Verona and then to Padua, they passed from the sensational landscape to the sedate, and accordingly became entranced by the calm of Italian plains under

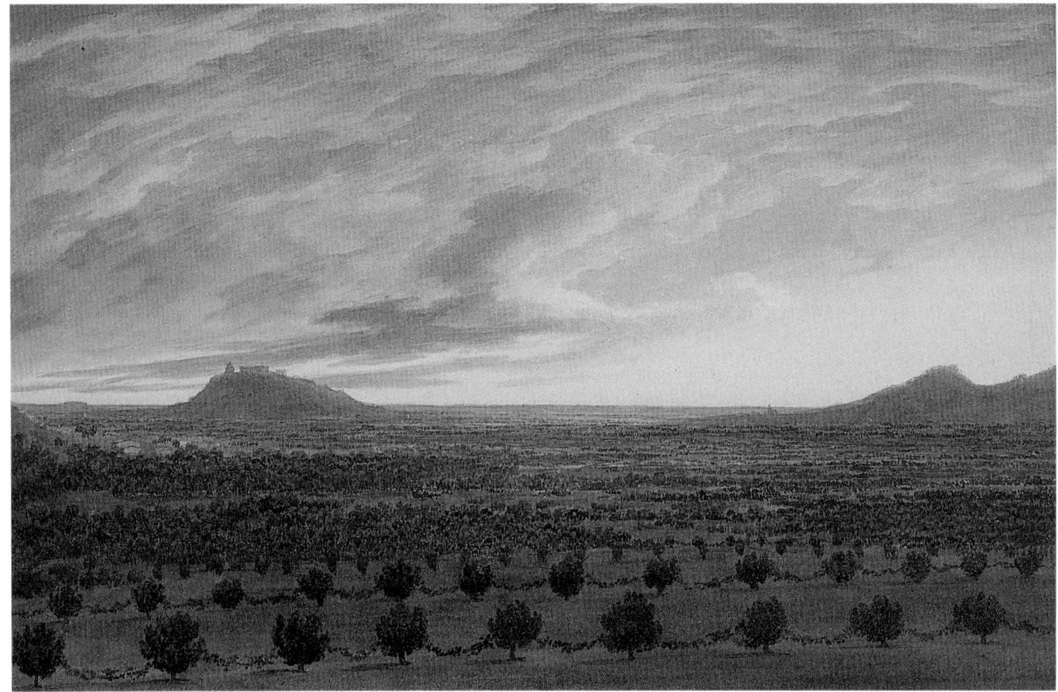

sunlit skies, a welcome relief after the dramatic conditions they had encountered in the north. Beckford was at first delighted with the change, but then grew excessively uncomfortable in the heat,[20] escaping to Mirabella where Cozens provided antipode images to the ones he had painted in the Tyrol (cat. no. 16). In a letter to Lady Hamilton, Beckford described "a boundless Scene of Towers" with "shrubby hilocs [sic] rising like Islands out of a Sea of Corn and Vine."[21] If Cozens was moved by the sublimity of the Tyrolean mountains as a stimulus for his most charismatic works, on the Paduan plain, and later in Rome and Naples, he discovered the catalyst for a poetic side that equally found a place in his unique idiom. The composition is a tour-de-force, "a labyrinthe of lines repeated to infinity with a pulsation which is felt but cannot be caught."[22]

Cozens and Beckford reached Rome in late June when the city was in the throes of the Feast of Saint Peter and Saint Paul (June 29). Beckford was quickly overcome by the noises of revelry — "the Pandemonium," as he described it[23] — and the stifling heat, this time retreating with Cozens to the outskirts of the city. From the vantage point of the Vatican and the Pamphili gardens,

Cozens provided Beckford with various views, one of the most eloquent of which is this dreamy, vaporous panorama of the Vatican (cat. no. 18). As in the works near Padua, the watercolor shows Cozens' lyrical side in the depiction of exceptional calm and beauty, with the parched Roman sky bathed by the delicate glow of the setting sun and perhaps the fireworks that Beckford and Cozens witnessed.[24] Beckford, like many others before him, was enthralled by this spectacle of the *Girandole*, noting that "five thousand rockets" created the illusion of "a flame of fire and filled the air with millions of stars."[25] Cozens' framing device of rhythmic trees serve as a particularly articulate foil against the structure of the church, throwing cast shadows into the viewer's space that create a hauntingly original conception of a much painted scene.

When they proceeded to Naples in the first week of July, Beckford's entire party came down with malaria. The entourage was taken in charge by Sir William Hamilton, who offered shelter and medical attention in his villa at Portici at the foot of Vesuvius; Cozens, who received the painter Thomas Jones there, would remain in bed here for a month.[26] About a week later John Burton died from malaria in deplorable condi-

tions. Beckford, already prone to dispiriting fits of melancholy which were exacerbated in Italy, could no longer stand the strain and left Naples on September 10, making his way to Switzerland by mid-October, where he met with his old friend Jean Huber and paid a visit to the Château de Prangins.[27] Cozens, on the other hand, remained behind, working in Vietri, Salerno, and Paestum, but now under different conditions; as Thomas Jones noted, Cozens was "Once more a free agent and loosed from the Shackles of fantastic folly and Caprice."[28]

Jones's remark implies that Cozens had in fact been fettered by Beckford's pictorial needs, but there is no reason to believe that Beckford's requirements as patron and benefactor were inhibiting for Cozens' art, even in its most expressive phase. In fact when Beckford left Naples, Cozens continued to scour the countryside for diverse scenes that would accord with Beckford's tastes, creating images that would respond to Beckford's ideals. In a sense he was still painting for Beckford *in absentia*.[29] The results included typical stormy coastal scenes, placid depictions of castle and ruins, and one of the most significant of all, the unearthly view of sepulchers in the Campagna (cat. no. 17). Recalling the mood of

the scene from Mirabella, Cozens lowered the horizon line considerably so that the tomb structures contrasted with the long diagonal of the distant aqueduct and take on surreal proportions. The effect is enhanced by the remarkable arrangement of clouds and shrouded light, creating what Oppé referred to as "probably the most poignant of all English landscapes [made in Italy]," a composition "that surpasses itself."[30] Further evidence that such a scene was geared for not only Cozens' particular vision of landscape but also Beckford's is the fact that the image Cozens created reflects Beckford's own writing. Brooding over the despondency that often affected him in Rome and Naples, Beckford referred to "vast wastes with here and there a shepherd's hut or neglected Sepulchre," as images on which he "mused away whole hours by the evening light."[31]

In the last months of 1782, Cozens remained in Rome and continued to make drawings for Beckford (such as cat. no. 19) until he left Italy in September 1783. His efforts, however, were questioned by Hamilton who wrote to Beckford that Cozens "has made some charming sketches but I see by his book that he is indolent as usual."[32] When Cozens met with his patron, now married, in Geneva in

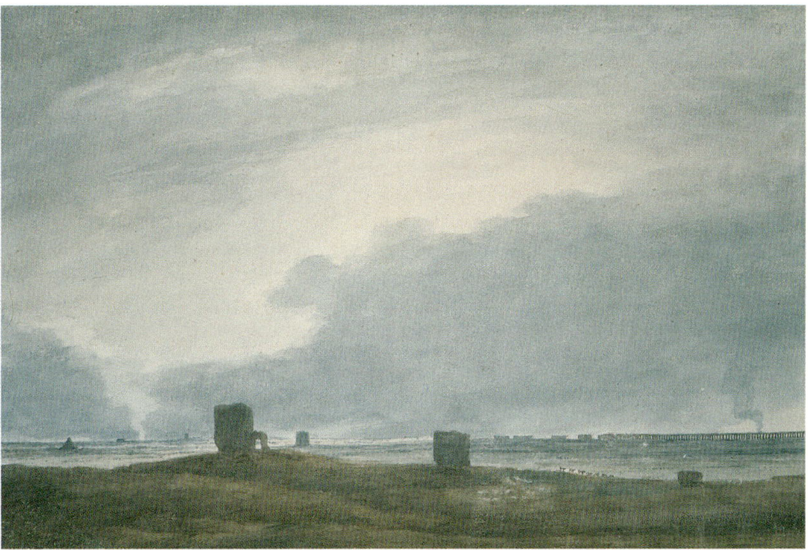

17. *Sepulchral remains in the Campagna near Rome*
John Robert Cozens (1752–1797)

ca. 1783–85; England
Watercolor and bodycolor over graphite
10⅞ x 14⅝ in. (26.0 x 37.2 cm)
Ashmolean Museum, Oxford (WA 1934.91)

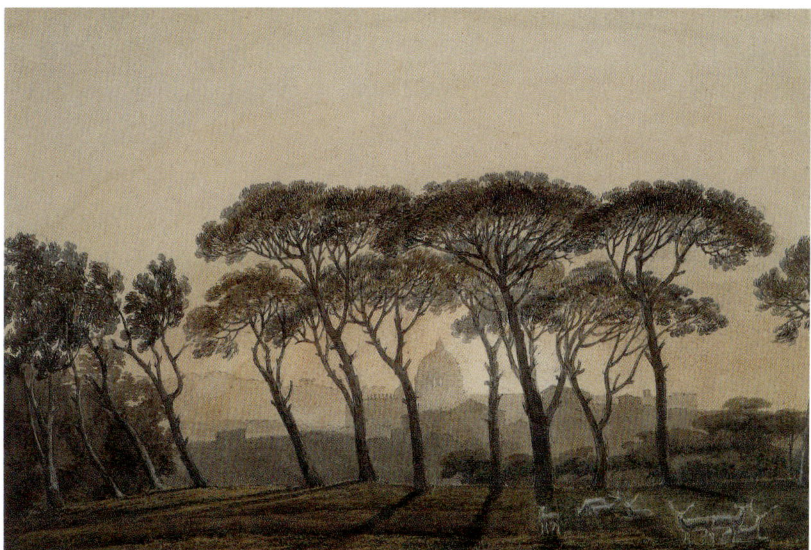

18. *St. Peter's from the Villa Borghese, Rome*
John Robert Cozens (1752–1797)

ca. 1783–85; England
Pencil and watercolor
10⅛ x 14½ in. (25.7 x 37cm)
The Whitworth Art Gallery, University of Manchester (D.1984.5)

October or early November, however, there seems to be no indication that Beckford concluded the same or reproached Cozens for laxity on his part.[33] By mid-November, Cozens was firmly ensconced in London, where he would reside for the next decade in circumstances that have remained nebulous, but he continued to correspond with Beckford and presumably refined and made copies of many of his sketches from Italy.

The relationship between patron and painter began to erode sometime in the 1790s under circumstances that are not recorded. Before 1794, Cozens' health deteriorated perceptively, and he displayed a mental illness for which he was placed under the guidance of the physician and amateur artist Thomas Munro.[34] A year later, Sir George Beaumont

organized a fund to assist Cozens' family in defraying extensive medical costs, to which Cozens' earlier patron, Payne Knight, contributed, but not Beckford. In the summer of 1797 Beckford was so at odds with Cozens that, while commending his father, he dismissed the son as "an ungrateful scoundrel."[35] Munro, on the other hand, established his informal "Academy" just before Cozens' death, inviting young artists to sketch from his collection of Cozens' work. In doing so, Cozens' landscape vision became imparted and highly influential on two students, Girtin and Turner, who carried Cozens' innovative approach to landscape painting, and presumably Beckford's, into the next generation where it would be exploited with mastery.
—W. H.

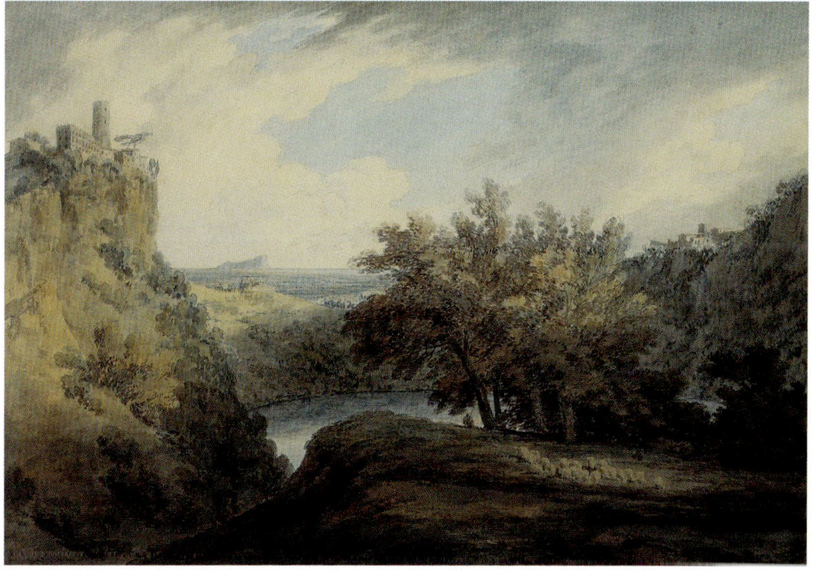

19. *The Lake of Nemi*
John Robert Cozens (1752–1797)

ca. 1783–85; England
Graphite and watercolor on wove paper
14⅝ x 21½ in. (37.1 x 53.5cm)
Yale Center for British Art, Paul Mellon Collection
(B.1975.4.1481)

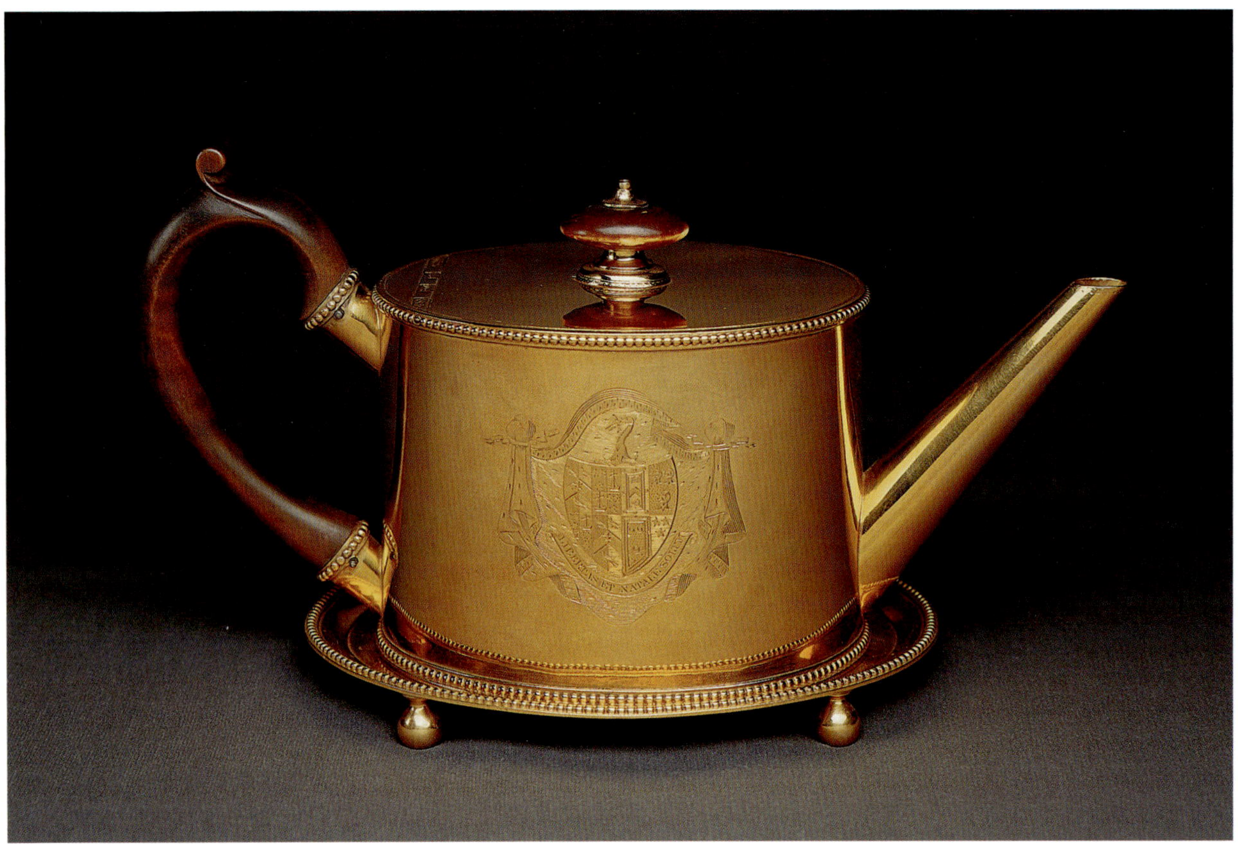

20. *Teapot and Stand*

ROBERT SHARP (FL. 1757–
1803) AND DANIEL SMITH
(FL. 1753–?1796)

1785–86; England
Gold, fruitwood
Teapot: 5⅝ x 9⅝ in. (14.3 x 24.45 cm);
Stand: ⅝ x 6¼ in. (1.7 x 15.9 cm)
The Trustees of The Barber
Institute of Fine Arts, The
University of Birmingham (48.18)

This teapot and its stand are part of a small group of functional objects in gold commissioned by Beckford. By his mid-twenties, Beckford's passion for opulence and precious objects was beginning to manifest itself, but this teapot, like his gold toasting fork (cat. no. 25) and the three gold objects by Henri Auguste that he owned, is a fascinating Beckfordian play on design and materials.[1]

This piece was indistinguishable from the silver-gilt teapots purchased as part of his coming-of-age plate in 1781,[2] and only its owner would have known that it is made of gold and not silver gilt. Even allowing for the vicissitudes of time, gold objects from this period are exceedingly rare and are mostly confined to racing trophies and other presentation pieces. Utilitarian objects are virtually unknown, largely because the softness of the alloy makes them impracticable.[3]

Beckford's conceit goes even further with this piece. Teapots and stands in this severe, neoclassical form were made in large quantities during the period, as the design was readily adapted to a production methodology allowing bulk manufacture. In addition, as a special commission in gold, the borders and other components of the teapot had to be handmade rather than made by machines used for producing identical elements in silver, further enhancing the precious version of a utilitarian object.

The teapot and stand can be dated precisely to the few weeks prior to Beckford's departure with his wife for Switzerland in the summer of 1785, and it is evident that these pieces either accompanied the Beckfords on their journey or were sent to them shortly thereafter. This is verified by the fact that in addition to the London hallmarks used between May 1785 and May 1786, the teapot and stand are struck with a tax mark known as the "duty drawback" mark.[4] The tax paid on all newly-wrought objects in silver and gold could be refunded on export. For a brief period between December 1, 1784, and July 24, 1785, a separate mark of the standing figure of Britannia was added to wares at the port of export to show that the duty had been refunded. The mark was discontinued "in view of the injury to the export trade occasioned by the delay and incon-

venience of the procedure and the fact that the mark on finished wares could not be struck without damage."[5] Only a handful of silver objects are known with this mark; and this teapot and stand appear to be the only surviving gold vessels and can be dated precisely between May 30 and July 24, 1785.

The armorials engraved on the teapot are depicted, in conventional eighteenth-century manner, against ermine mantling. Beckford had not yet discovered the decorative possibilities of heraldry. Beckford's pride in his Hamilton ancestry, however, which was later to become an obsession, has manifested itself with the inclusion of those arms quarterly with his own. His pride in his wife's ancestry, too, is shown by the inclusion of her many quarterings on the right side of the shield. This appears to be the only instance of his wife's arms impaled by his. It may be that as a memento of his brief marriage, which he recalled with increasing fondness as the years passed, Beckford kept this teapot to the end of his life. In Bath it was in Lansdown Tower where, in 1838, it stood on an oak cabinet. The intensity of these pieces must have been heightened by the contrast provided by the scarlet silk wall covering of the room. After Beckford's death, the teapot and stand passed to the Hamilton family and were sold in the sale of silver and gold from Hamilton Palace at Christie's in 1919. —C. H.

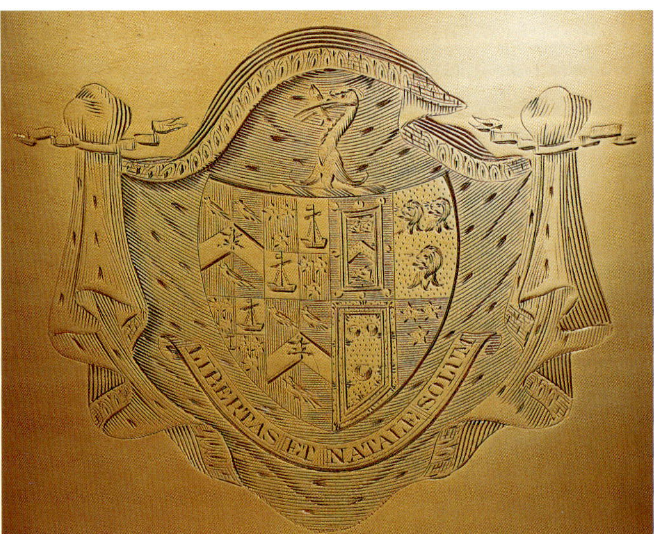

Detail of cat. no. 20.

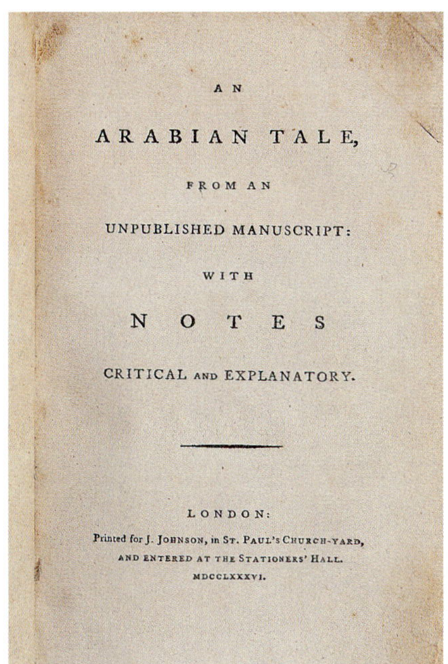

21. *An Arabian Tale, from an Unpublished Manuscript: with Notes Critical and Explanatory,* 1st London Edition
Author, William Beckford;
publisher, J. Johnson

1786; England
Paper, calfskin
8vo
Private collection

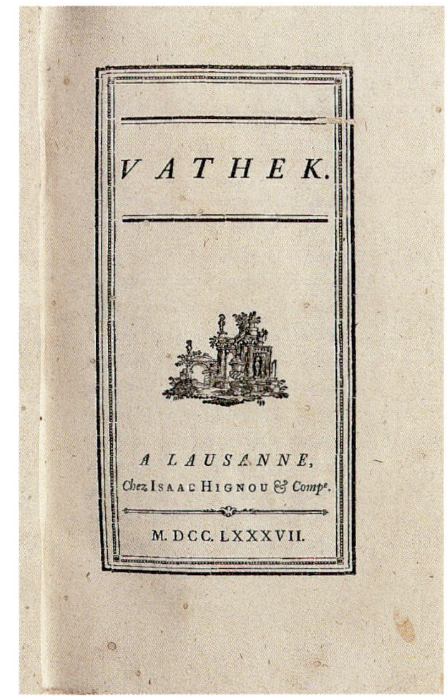

22. *Vathek, Conte Arabe,* 1st Lausanne Edition
Author, William Beckford;
publisher, Isaac Hignou

1787; Switzerland
Paper, vellum
8vo
Private collection

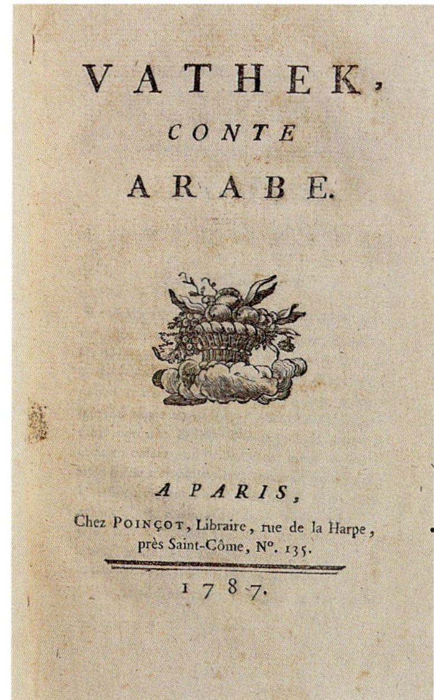

23. *Vathek, Conte Arabe,* 1st Paris Edition
Author, William Beckford;
publisher, Poinçot

1787; France
Vellum, calfskin
8vo
Private collection

21–24. Beckford and Vathek

Beckford began writing *Vathek* after the notorious Christmas party for his close friends at Fonthill Splendens in 1781. He worked on it for most of the following year, contrary to his biographer Cyrus Redding's credulous account. Redding claimed that Beckford had told him: "I wrote 'Vathek' when I was barely twenty-two years of age. I wrote it at one sitting, in French. It cost me three days and two nights of hard labour."[1]

Among those at the Christmas party was the tutor to Beckford's young cousins, the Reverend Samuel Henley, who shared Beckford's interest in Arabic and Persian literature. Afterwards, Beckford acknowledged his influence in a letter: "The spirit has moved me this Eve, and shut up in my Appartment as you advised, I have given way to fancies and inspirations. What will be the consequences of this mood I am not bold enough to determine. Good night—pray for the Soul of William Beckford." A week later, Beckford wrote again, "You are answerable for having set me to work upon a Story—so horrid that I tremble whilst relating it, and have not a nerve in my frame but vibrates like an Aspen." The choice of Vathek as hero may have been inspired by the Comtesse de Genlis, whose play, *Vathek. A Comedy in Two Acts*, had recently appeared in French, and then in an English translation.[2]

Beckford had written his first draft of *Vathek* in French, and asked Henley to revise it for him. At about this time Beckford decided to include a series of *Episodes*, and in January 1783 told Henley: "I go on bravely with the episodes of Vathec [sic], and hope in a few weeks to wind up his adventures." These would provide "the finishing touches of Oriental-ism."[3] Only three tales survived, and they remained unpublished until they were discovered by Lewis Melville among the Beckford Papers; they appeared in book form in 1912.[4] It was these *Episodes* that Byron so much wanted to see after having been greatly impressed by *Vathek*.

The idea of translating *Vathek* into English was quite possibly Henley's. Beckford wrote in November 1783 to remind him that he had "proposed likewise to translate Vathec [sic], which I left in your hands." Writing to Henley from Paris the following January, Beckford was becoming impatient: "I long to hear if you have finished Vathec, and when I may have an opportunity of introducing you to his other relations."

That Henley's involvement went beyond merely translating *Vathek* was confirmed when Beckford wrote to him from Fonthill in April 1785, "I shall sit down immediately to revise Vathec, and much approve y^r idea of prefacing the tale with some explanation of its costume." Later in the month he wrote, "The Arabian Nights will furnish some illustrations (particularly as to Goules, etc.) but much more may be learnt from Herbelot's Bib[liothèque] Orient[ale]. and Richardson's Diss[ertations]."

Writing in February 1786 from the Château de la Tour, near Vevey in Switzerland, Beckford told Henley: "The publication of Vathec must be suspended at least another year. I w^d not upon any account have him precede the french Edition. . . . The Episodes to Vathec are nearly finished, and the whole work will be compleated within a twelve month."

Henley, having seen his efforts to edit *Dreams, Waking Thoughts and Incidents* wasted in 1783, was proba-

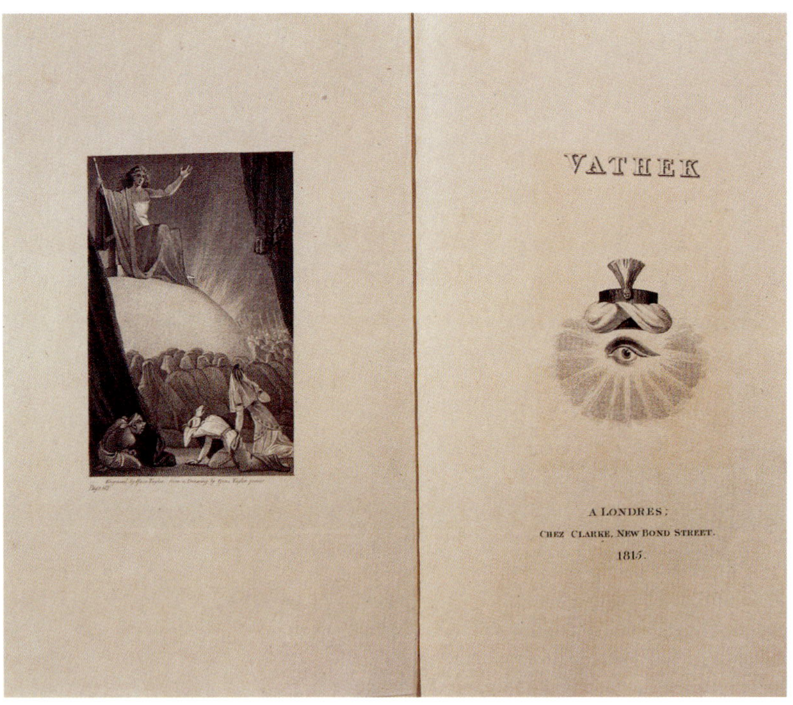

24. Vathek
AUTHOR, WILLIAM BECKFORD;
PUBLISHER, CLARKE

1815; England
Boards
large 8vo
Private collection

bly worried that *Vathek*, with his extensive notes at the end, might meet the same fate. So, in June 1786, he advertised the book in the *Morning Chronicle* as *"The History of the Caliph Vathek: An Arabian tale from an unpublished Manuscript with Notes Critical and Explanatory."*[5] It was well received by monthly magazines such as the *Critical Review, English Review, European Magazine, Gentleman's Magazine* and *Monthly Review*, yet Beckford had been robbed of his masterpiece. Because Beckford might well have delayed publication indefinitely, however, Henley, despite his betrayal, deserves credit for the appearance of *Vathek.*

When Beckford, in Switzerland and prostrate with grief over his wife's death in May, heard the unpleasant truth, he rushed out his French text in Lausanne (cat. no. 22) at the end of 1786 (the title page is actually dated 1787) with the help of Jean-David Levade, a professor of theology. In a preface to the work the publisher, Hignou, established Beckford's claim to authorship.[6] Beckford brought out a more idiomatic version in a lighter style but, owing to his absence in Portugal and delays by the publisher Poinçot, it did not appear until July 1787 (cat. no. 23). Compared with the Lausanne edition with only a few words at the end, it contained

twenty-three pages of Henley's notes. Three editions in German were to follow in 1788, while in 1791 the Lausanne edition was reissued in London with a cancel title page which read *Les Caprices et les Malheurs du Caliphe Vathek*, "Traduit de l'Arabe."[7] *Vathek* appeared in Dutch in 1837.

Richard Garnett noted in his preface to the 1893 edition of *Vathek* that reissues in French in Beckford's lifetime were based on the Paris edition, which must therefore represent his approved text.[8] In 1928 Marcel May assumed that because there were so many Anglicisms in the Lausanne edition, Beckford could not have had a copy of his manuscript with him in Switzerland. Thus he must have obtained a copy of Henley's published version and hastily retranslated it into French.[9] With some reservations, A. O. Hunter[10] and John Carter[11] supported May's theory.

In 1960, André Parreaux pointed out that there were passages in the Lausanne edition that did not appear in Henley's.[12] Therefore this could not be the source of the Lausanne edition, which, Parreaux found, closely resembled the unfinished manuscript in English begun in 1782 by Beckford's tutor, the Reverend John Lettice. So Parreaux concluded that Beckford must after

all have had a copy with him, most probably his original French manuscript (now lost), perhaps in an earlier form than the one Henley used or, failing this, Lettice's English translation. This eighty-two-page manuscript, now among the Beckford Papers in the Bodleian Library,[13] contains nearly the first half of *Vathek.* Parreaux's generally accepted theory means that the Lausanne edition is the closest to Beckford's earliest unrevised text, whether this is his manuscript or Lettice's translation.

However much Beckford must have resented Henley's treachery, he was happy enough about the quality of the 1786 edition to reissue the unsold sheets in 1809 with a cancel title page. At the time, he was busy settling into Fonthill Abbey, having finally demolished his father's house, Fonthill Splendens. Once construction of the grandiose Eastern Transept began in 1812, he prepared new editions of *Vathek* for his publisher, William Clarke. Both the French edition of 1815 (cat. no. 24) and the English one of 1816 are regarded as definitive since they were produced under Beckford's supervision; they were finely printed on good paper. As Roger Lonsdale observed,[14] there were many differences between the 1815 and 1816 texts; further, some errors from the previous editions remained uncorrected. A revised ver-

sion of the 1816 edition appeared in the same year.

In 1819 a curious retranslation into French of Henley's translation of *Vathek* was published in Paris. Only two other French editions appeared during Beckford's lifetime: a reissue in about 1828, possibly the sheets of the 1815 edition with a cancel title, and a reprint of this edition to coincide with the publication of *Italy; with Sketches of Spain and Portugal* in 1834. At the same time the English edition of 1816 was reprinted—with Walpole's *Castle of Otranto* and "Monk" Lewis's translation of *The Bravo of Venice*—in Bentley's Standard Novels series.

To cash in on the enormous interest in the 1823 Fonthill Abbey sale, Beckford reissued the 1816 revised English edition of *Vathek* with a few minor changes, the last he was to make. This means that all subsequent editions are based on one of seven versions: three in French, those of 1787 (Lausanne), 1787 (Paris), and 1815 (London), and four in English, 1786 (Henley's), 1816, 1816 revised, and 1823. From 1815, the 11 000 steps of Vathek's tower were reduced to 1,500, and this edition was also the first with an engraved frontispiece. It depicted Vathek and Nouronihar before Eblis, and it was reused in both 1816 editions and that of 1828. —J. M.

25. *Toasting Fork*
MAKER UNKNOWN

1793–94; England
Gold, ebony
L. 38¾ in. (98.4 cm)
Private collection

Like his gold teapot (cat. no. 20), William Beckford's gold toasting fork is also an extravagant conceit. Exquisitely chased with stiff foliage on a matted ground, its double-baluster form echoes Scofield's silver candlesticks (see cat. nos. 9 and 31). Silver toasting forks, with or without wood handles, are common utilitarian objects from the later Georgian period (Beckford owned three silver examples, all articulated[1]), but this gold example appears to be unique. Gold chasing of this quality was done by specialists who worked usually on watch cases and snuff boxes and many of them did not have a registered mark, which may explain why this fork lacks a maker's mark but is struck with hallmarks on one tine.

Beckford returned to England from Paris at the end of May 1793 and appears to have purchased this toasting fork during the summer before setting off for Portugal in the autumn, no doubt taking such a personal and extravagant item with him. Breakfast in the eighteenth century tended to be a private affair, eaten in one's bedchamber and, as one Swedish visitor observed, toast was essential as English houses were so cold that butter could not be spread on bread.[2] The same no doubt was true of the cold and damp residences of Lisbon in the winter months and certainly in later years his bedchamber in the Abbey at Fonthill. Like so many of the precious, personal items with which Beckford surrounded himself, this object passed to his descendants and was sold by the Hamilton family in the late 1980s. —C. H.

26. *Basket*
PAUL STORR (1771–1844)

1797–98; England
Silver gilt
5⅜ x 20⅜ x 15¼ in. (13.6 cm x 51.8 x 38.7 cm)
Gilbert Collection, Somerset House, London (1996.12)

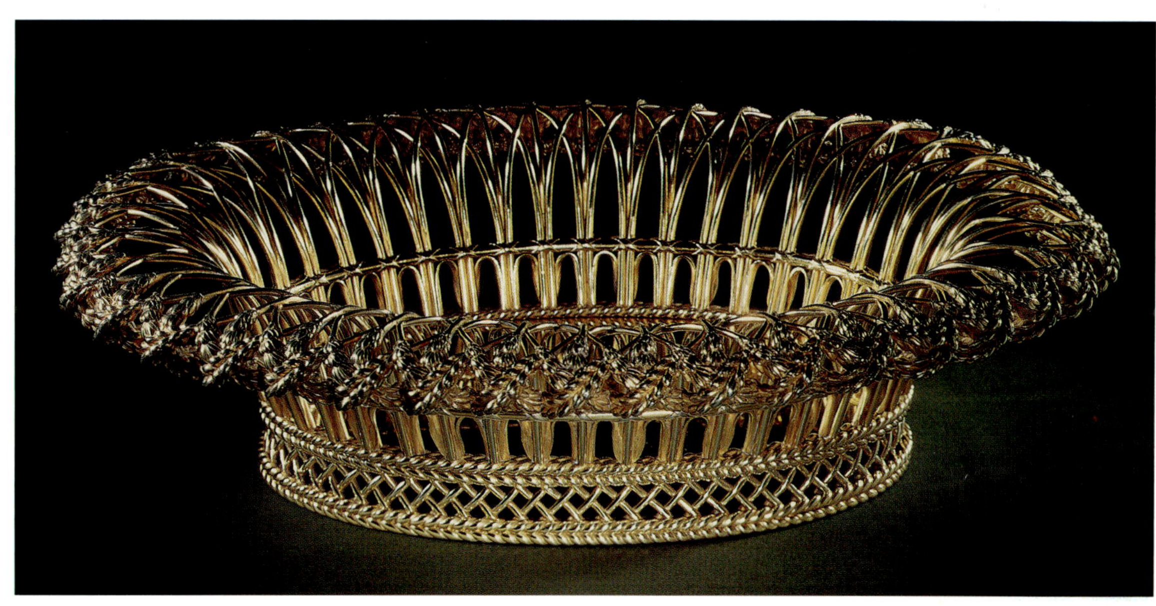

This monumental basket, one of a pair owned by Beckford,[1] is exceptional for the boldness of its design and the quality of its execution. Although at the time of its purchase Beckford was in the middle of the first, frantic phase of building Fonthill Abbey, it is clear that he had not lost his penchant for neo-classical silver. Moreover, one of the problems facing connoisseurs like Beckford and Horace Walpole, who sought to decorate in the "Gothick" style, was the dearth of medieval silver that could be used as models for their utilitarian plate.

Service à la française and the newly fashionable *service à la russe* both required quantities of tureens and entrée dishes—forms introduced in the eighteenth century. Cyrus Redding, describing the entertainment given by Beckford to Nelson and the Hamiltons on their visit to the partially completed Abbey in 1800, wrote, "a superb repast was served up in a long single line of enormous silver dishes. These dishes were wholly in the massy style and fashion of the ancient abbeys,"[2] although what form these dishes took, or what happened to them, is not known.

Gilt baskets appear also to have featured in the Nelson-Hamilton festivities: ". . . after various entertainments, a collation was provided in the library, consisting of various sorts of confectionery, served in gold baskets . . . after which Emma Hamilton performed some of her celebrated attitudes."[3] Silver baskets, often chased to represent basket-weave, are traditionally symbolic of hospitality. A common feature of eighteenth-century examples is a grain-wreathed female head representing Ceres, the goddess of the harvest. These masks are often found in conjunction with symbols of Bacchus to illustrate the classical author Terence's celebrated line, *"Sine Cerere et Tempero friget Venus"* (love withers without the stimulus of wine and the produce of the harvest). In the later expressions of rococo, wheat ears were occasionally used to decorate the sides of silver baskets,[4] alluding not to their function as bread baskets as is often supposed, for they were used for a variety of functions, but to Ceres and the hospitality invoked by the harvest.

On the Beckford basket, carefully modeled everted ears of wheat form the sides above plaited borders. These features, together with the basket's crisp lines, are reminiscent of a series of drawings for silverware in the Victoria and Albert Museum carried out in the Grecian style by J. J. Boileau. A French émigré designer, Boileau was clearly influenced by, and had possibly worked with, Jean-Guillaume Moitte, chief designer of the Paris royal goldsmith Henri Auguste, from whom Beckford commissioned a number of pieces (cat. nos. 51 and 52).[5] Beckford clearly knew of Boileau, for in the early 1790s Boileau worked at Fonthill Splendens as a ceiling painter. In the 1801 sale catalogue of its contents a pair of tripods is

described as being "designed by Boilieu," while later the Fonthill sale catalogues include a pair of "silver-gilt ewers, on tripod goat's legs winged snake and ebony handles, made by Green and Ward, from a design by Boileau," which evidently date from about 1800.[6] Interestingly, in the 1822 Christie version of the catalogue these lots are followed by: "A MAGNIFICENT BASKET, formed of ears of wheat, of the finest workmanship" and "A DITTO, DITTO." Although no mention is made of Boileau in the description in the catalogue, which was produced under the direction of Beckford and Franchi, it seems likely that he was the designer of the Beckford baskets. Moreover, virtually all of the Boileau-designed silver that has been identified bears Paul Storr's mark.[7]

The Boileau drawing that is closest to the Beckford baskets, however, lacks the everted wheat ears around the rim, which impart the massiveness so loved by Beckford. This more austere Boileau design was used

for a set of baskets made by Storr for Thomas Hope the year after the Beckford examples; one of the baskets was illustrated by Hope in one of the plates of silverware in his *Household Furniture and Interior Decoration*, published in 1807.[8]

Grand baskets, usually in pairs or sets of four, featured commonly on sideboards at the end of the eighteenth century. Their original function all but forgotten, they were foremost display pieces, their flat interiors providing an opportunity for the grand depiction of heraldic devices against decorative mantling. Perhaps surprisingly, therefore, the center of Beckford's basket is plain, and his solitary heron crest is engraved under the base.

The Beckford baskets, listed in the Grand Drawing Room at the Abbey, were purchased in the 1823 sale by Robinson and sold shortly thereafter to Nathan Meyer Rothschild (1777–1836), the banker, who had them mounted on ebony stands applied with elaborate foliate silver-

gilt mounts and, on the front of each, with cast versions of the Rothschild armorials. Rothschild, whose collecting habits were quite different from Beckford's, nonetheless shared Beckford's taste for rich silver gilt, using it for grand entertaining rather than the intensely personal gratification Beckford sought. Prince Pückler-Muskau described a dinner at Rothschild's house in 1827: "we had a great exhibition of splendor. The table service was of vermilion and silver; that of the dessert, I think, all gold,"[9] quite a different aesthetic from what one would have encountered at Fonthill.

The baskets descended in the family to Victor Rothschild who sold them at Sotheby's in 1937.[10] The pair was split up, and this basket, without its stand, was acquired by Francis Stonor. Subsequently in the Plohn Collection in New York,[11] it was purchased by Arthur Gilbert in 1970; the other basket is in a private American collection. —C.H.

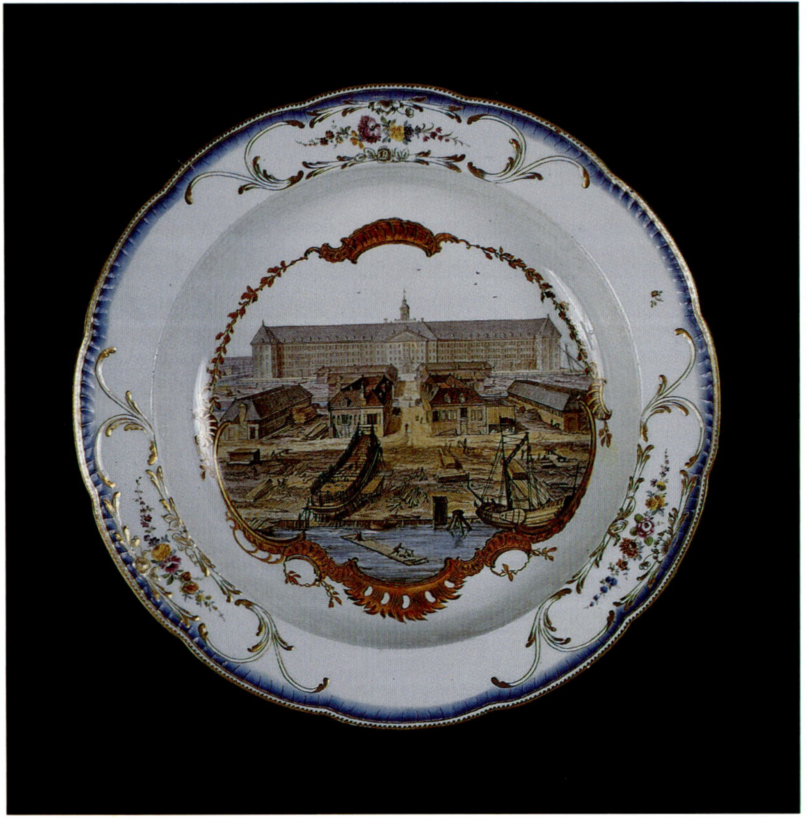

27. *Charger*
MEISSEN FACTORY

ca. 1772–74; Germany
Hard-paste porcelain
17⅟ in. (44.5 cm)
Trustees of the National Museums
of Scotland, Edinburgh (1869.62.4)

27–28. THE STADHOLDER SERVICE

These pieces belong to the Meissen dinner and dessert service produced around 1772–74 for the Stadholder of Holland, Willem V, Prince of Orange. Probably acquired by Beckford during the Prince's exile in England between 1795 and 1801/2, part of the service was displayed at Fonthill Abbey in the Oak Parlour, the remainder in the Western Corridor.1 With the sale of the eVects of Fonthill Abbey in 1823, 435 pieces passed to Mr. F. Hodges

of London. The service was next sold by Christie's, minus thirteen pieces, in 1868, divided into seventy-Wve lots. This allowed for the wide dispersal of the service, and it is thus known today in dozens of public and private collections in Europe and North America. The large plate (cat. no. 27) was the Wrst piece to be acquired by a museum when it entered the Royal Museum of Scotland in 1869.

Although the connection to

28. *Tureen*
MEISSEN FACTORY

ca. 1772–74; Germany
Hard-paste porcelain
Tureen, 13¼ x 16½ in. (33.7 x
41.9 cm); Stand (not in exhibition),
13⅞ in. (35.3 cm)
The Metropolitan Museum of Art,
New York, gift of Alfred Duane Pell,
1902 (02.6.128-9)

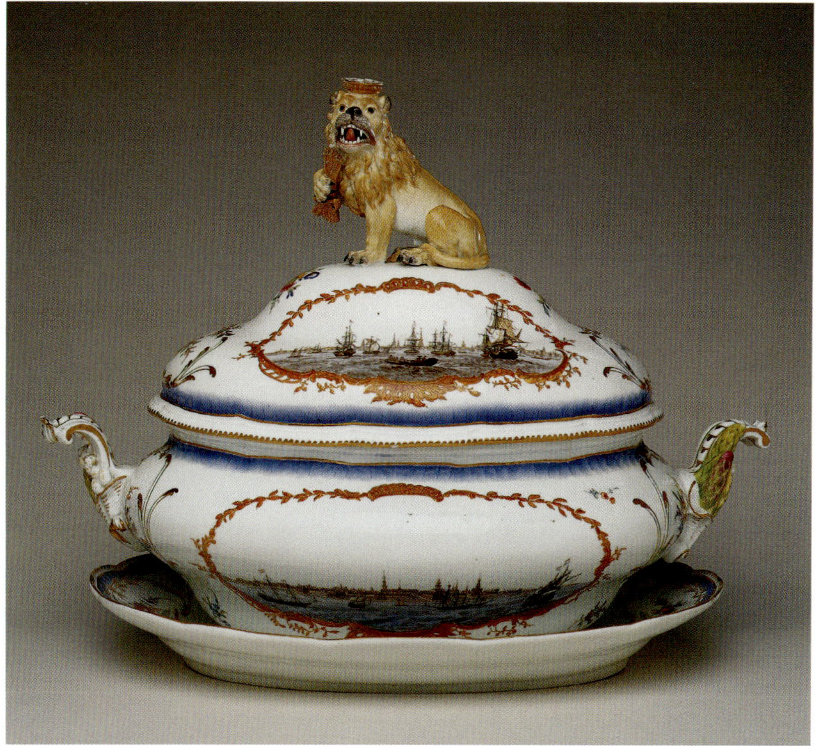

Willem V was expressly stated in both the 1823 and 1868 sale catalogues, this history was somehow lost until an account was published from the Meissen factory archives.[2] This account reported the modeling of the lion handle for the covers of the large tureens in October 1772, by the factory's chief modeler, Johann Joachim Kändler (1706–1775): "Einen ziemlich groszen Löwen, welcher auf eine ovale Terrine, welcher Servic vor den Stadthalter nach Holland bestellet worden ist, modelliret. Es ist solcher sitzend vorgestellet, halt in seiner rechten Pfote die zusammen gebundenen Pfeile, hat auf seinem Kopfe eine Crone, worauf die Worte in Lateinischen Buchstaben stehen: Ostindianische Compagnie. Solches Modell auch zerschnitten und zum abformen gegeben."[3] The lion derives from the Stadholder's coat of arms, which features a crowned rampant lion clutching seven arrows in his raised right paw, one for each of the Dutch provinces. On the two known tureens, the original porcelain crowns have been lost; the third tureen to the service was last recorded in a Dutch sale in 1904.

The circumstances of the production of the service and its acquisition by Beckford are not altogether clear. It is suggested that it was commissioned by the Dutch East India Company (VOC, or Verenigde Oostindische Compagnie) as a gift for Willem V, chief governor of the company from 1766 until his exile.[4] The prince was a noted connoisseur of topographical prints and drawings. The primary decoration is comprised of views of towns and properties with some relevance to the VOC, namely those within the Republic of the United Netherlands which also included Java. There are 152 known views, some of which copy drawings by Johannes Rach (1720–83)

and others, but most derive from seventeenth- and eighteenth-century engravings, a number of which are still at the Meissen manufactory today.[5] On each example of the service, the two-dimensional monochrome source has been translated into full color. The title of the view has been inscribed in black enamel on the underside of the porcelain, a feature in common with some Sèvres services of the period painted with natural history specimens.

The three tureens, covers, and stands owned by Beckford were each painted with views of the six towns where the VOC had its offices, always in pairs: either Amsterdam and Middelburg, Delft and Rotterdam, or Enkhuijzen and Hoorn. This tureen (cat. no. 28) shows Hoorn after a view published first in Pierre van de Aa's *La galerie agreeable du monde* (Leiden, 1729) and Enkhuijzen (source unidentified), while the cover depicts a view of Amsterdam after P. van den Berge (copying J. Kip) and Middelburg after J. C. Philips copying C. Shouman. The only known stand for the tureens, now in the Westfries Museum in Hoorn, has other views of Enkhuijzen and Hoorn. It seems possible that the covers were switched in the nineteenth century, just as the stands were separated from the tureens. What is not clear is whether each set was originally devoted entirely to two towns, or whether each set comprised all six views.

The Stadholder service was produced just prior to a period of great stylistic change at Meissen, brought about largely by the appointment of Camillo Marcolini as director in 1774. The old-fashioned "*neu Spanisch*" design of the porcelain predates the Seven Years War (1756–63) but seems to have been personally selected by Willem V,

who already possessed a dozen or more plates in the same pattern, painted with the arms of the House of Orange, which were a gift to him on his investiture in 1766. The rim ornament and flower painting similarly reflect rococo tendencies that lingered after the end of the Seven Years War, during Carl von Nimptsch's brief tenure as director of the manufactory (1763–73).[6] The subject matter of the decoration, however, is entirely new for porcelain table services and points to emerging neoclassical tastes and ideals. Before the Seven Years War, accurate topographical views on porcelain were restricted to porcelain snuffboxes, but they begin to appear on porcelain services produced at Fürstenberg and Meissen after the war's end.[7] The vogue for topographical subjects quickly spread over Europe and England and peaked during the Empire period. This, combined with Beckford's passion for landscape, may explain Beckford's purchase of the Stadholder service, as he was not fond of the country of Holland itself.

How the service came to the market or to Beckford's attention is unknown. Willem V fled Holland in early 1795, taking with him his most precious possessions, his cash, and seventy-eight family members and retainers who eventually resided with him at Hampton Court, where

they enjoyed the protection and support of his cousin, George III.[8] Records show that the Meissen service was not auctioned in Holland in the sales of the Stadholder's requisitioned property held in 1795 and 1796, nor does it appear in the Dutch royal inventories for these years, so it is assumed the prince brought it to England and sold it there before returning to the Continent in 1801 or the following year. Apparently Willem V traveled extensively during his time in England, despite Ernest Law's account to the contrary: "the life of himself and of his family, during the eight years they spent at Hampton Court, must have been dull and uneventful in the extreme—enlivened by nothing more exciting than an occasional visit from George III."[9] It is possible, although unlikely, that the prince visited Beckford or vice-versa. The prince endured a period of financial hardship following the bankruptcy of one of his bankers in London in 1797, perhaps forcing him to sell some of his possessions before being granted an allowance by the English crown in 1799. There is the further possibility that James Wyatt, who worked at Hampton Court in 1798, served as the go-between for Beckford's acquisition of the service, though Beckford was on the Continent from July 1798 until July 1799.[10] —M.C-G.

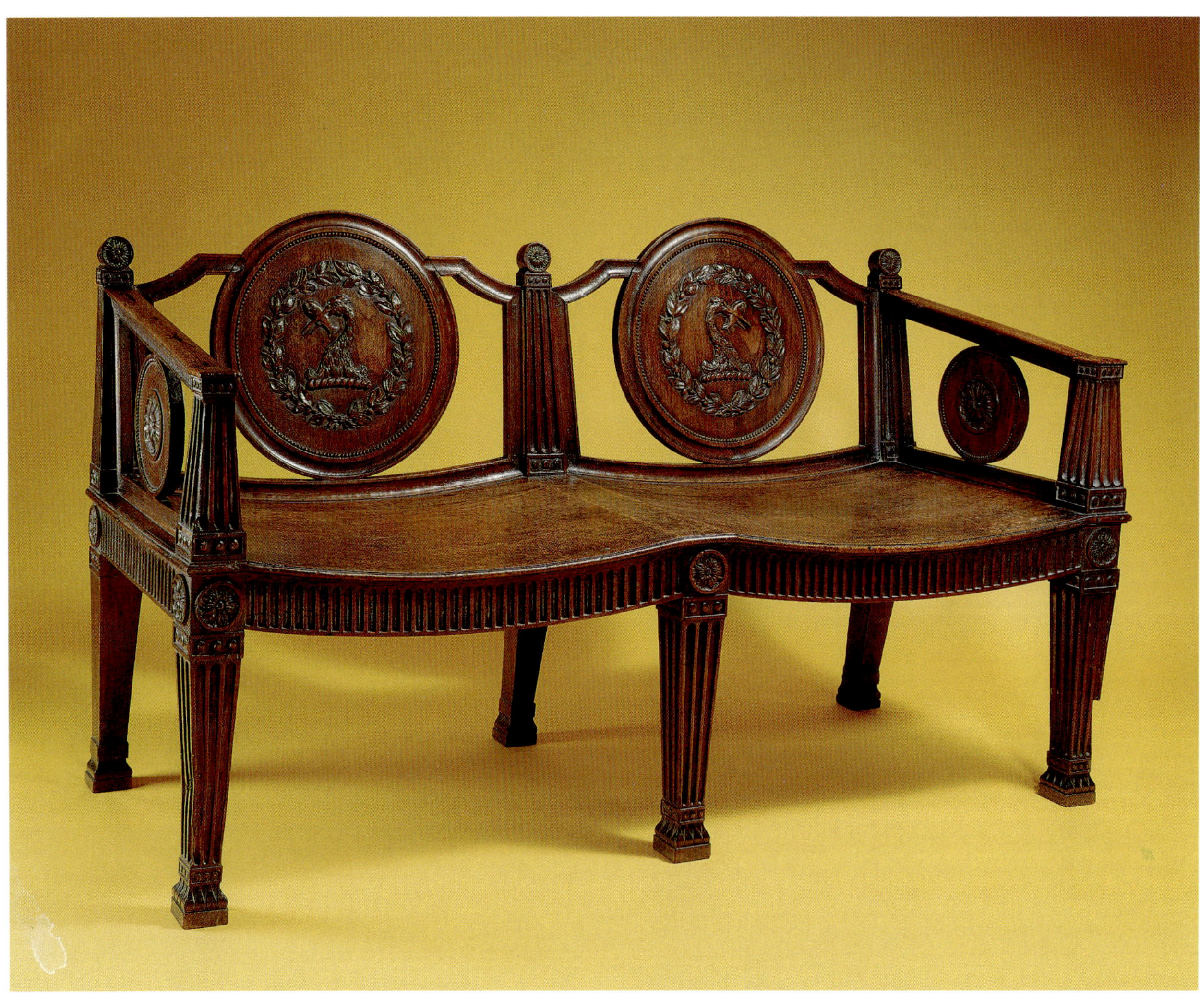

29. *Hall Settee*

Maker unknown

ca. 1775–1780; England
Mahogany
32 x 54 x 19½ in. (81 x 138 x 50 cm)
Saint Andrew's, Trent, Church
Council

This "Roman" seat was almost certainly commissioned by William Beckford, as it displays the heron that served as the armorial crest honoring his family. The heron is related to the stork, famed by classical authors for filial piety, and also to the "vigilant" crane; its powerful fish-hunting beak provided the *bec fort* rebus for some of Beckford's prime furnishings as well as his silver, porcelain, and other objects. This mahogany seat was intended to harmonize with the antique architecture of his banqueting hall at Fonthill Splendens, the house built by his father. The mansion's Vitruvian architecture had been inspired by the work of Andrea Palladio and by publications such as Robert Castell's *Villas of the Ancients Illustrated* (1729), while its principal decorations featured pagan deities from classical mythology. The seat was appropriate for a Roman *vestibulum*, which marked the transition between the exterior and interior of the house,

and its form evokes Roman altars, such as the one depicted on the Marlborough family's famous gem celebrating "Love" with the marriage of Cupid and Psyche. The prototype for the bench, however, with its antique-fluted and paterae-capped pilasters, derives from a Roman antiquity that was much admired by eighteenth-century artists and architects, such as Charles Heathcote Tatham, who visited Rome in the mid-1790s. There he gathered ideas and prototypes for Henry Holland's furnishing of Carlton House for the Prince of Wales, and included the ancient marble altar-seat in his *Etchings of Ancient Ornamental Architecture* (1799–1800). The Beckford crest on the "double-chair" back of this mahogany seat is borne on "shield" medallions, and these serve as wall-trophies to evoke the Virgilian concept that agriculture flourishes when arms and armor are laid aside.

The seat design is likely to date from the 1770s, and can be com-

pared to the elegant antique-fluted and medallion-backed seats featured in the garden-temple pattern-book, *Designs in Architecture*, issued by the brilliant architect John Soane in 1778, the year that he ceased working in Henry Holland's office to make a study visit to Rome.[1] Beckford employed Soane at Fonthill Splendens during the 1780s, and Soane may have played a role in suggesting the prototype for the seat. It could have been supplied by one of the fashionable London firms such as that of Thomas Chippendale Junior of St. Martin's Lane or John Linnell of Berkeley Square. —J. H.

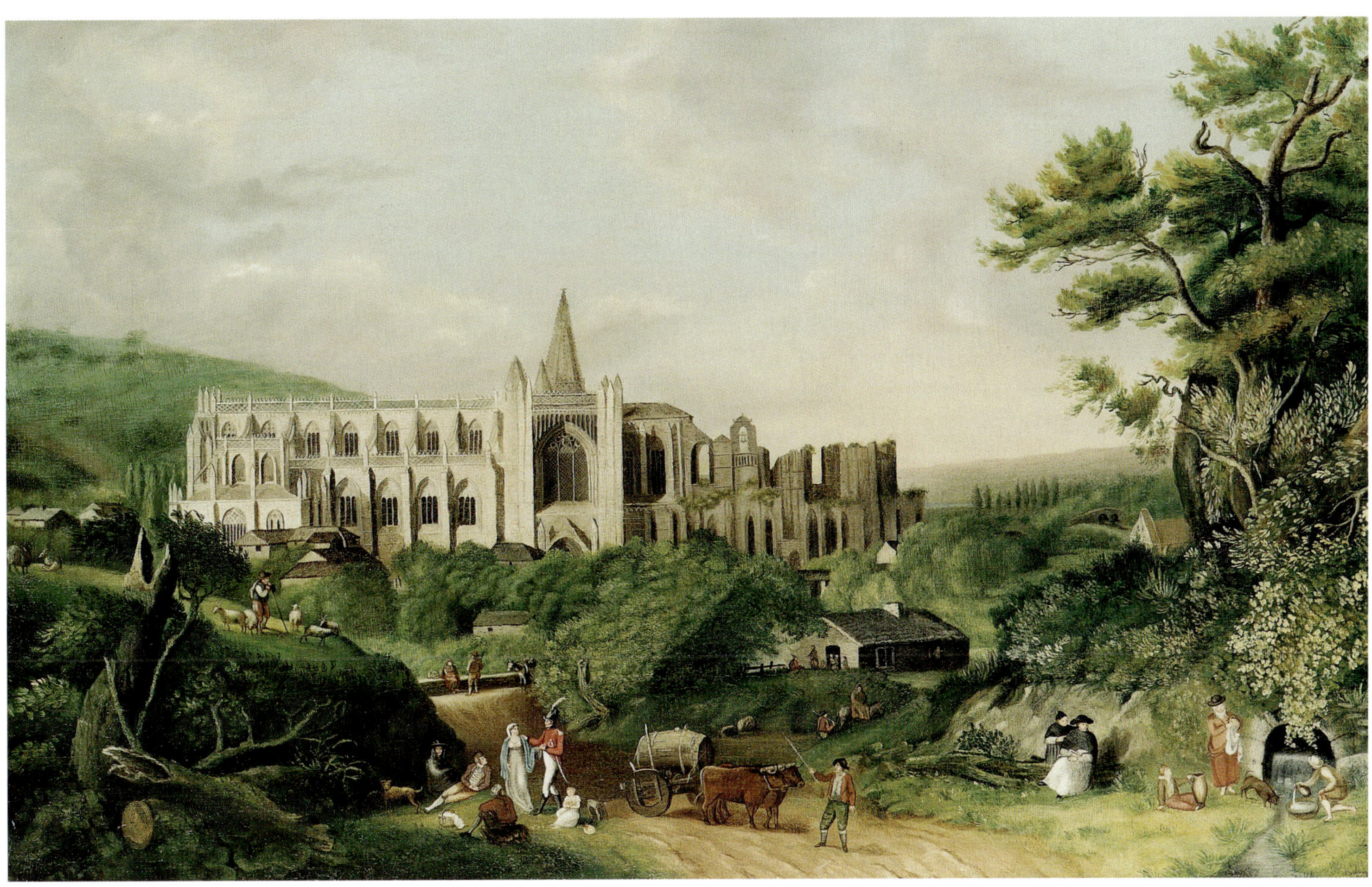

30. *View of the Monastery of Batalha, Portugal*
HENRI L'EVEQUE (1769–1832)

ca. 1807; Switzerland
Oil on canvas
25⅝ x 38⅝ in. (65 x 98 cm)
Collection of David Vyvyan-Robinson

L'Eveque's pastorally set view of the Monastery of Batalha is painted from the south, emphasizing the dramatic "ruins" of the unfinished chapels (Capelas Imperfeitas) to the right of the picture. Dedicated to Our Lady of the Victory, the church and monastery were commissioned by King João I to commemorate the Portuguese victory over the Castilians in the nearby field of Aljubarrota in 1295. Because of this origin, Batalha has a highly symbolic status in the history of the Portuguese nation, even now serving as the location of the tomb of the Unknown Soldier. The original architect was Afonso Domingues whose building imitated the English Perpendicular style. The presence of English taste is very evident in the Founder's Chapel, where King João and Philippa of Lancaster, his queen, together with their distinguished offspring who included Prince Henry the Navigator, lie buried, hand in hand, amid symbols of the English royal family including the Order of the Garter, the Leopard, and the Fleur-de-lis. The great octagonal Chapter House was begun in the fifteenth century, but the additional Manueline structures (the unfinished chapels) were never completed at the beginning of the sixteenth century. At that time other elaborate Manueline features, such as can be seen in the florid motifs of the Great Portal or in the cloisters, were added by Mateus Fernandes who had worked at Saint Jerónomos in Belém and at the Monastery of the Order of Christ at Tomar.

Beckford was captivated by Batalha from the first moment he saw it, by moonlight, in 1794. He had crossed the battlefield of Aljubarrota, his mind full of deeds of ancient knightly glory to describe the effect of the cluster of abbatial buildings, with buttresses, pinnacles, and spires surrounded by dense green foliage as we see in L'Eveque's representation.[1] The arches and moldings of the nave of the church reminded Beckford of Winchester Cathedral, while its lofty dimensions brought Amiens Cathedral to mind. He speculated on a connection with Winchester through the disciples of William of Wyeham who accompanied Philippa of Lancaster when she came to Portugal. The play of colors and shadow created by the light passing through the stained glass windows delighted him. He was also enthused by the Founder's Chapel, with its delicate gray, fluted stonework, fan-vaulted ceiling, and fine stained-glass windows. The Chapel's English royal associations appealed to Beckford's snobbish association of his own pedigree with that of the royal family. He admired the stately, octagonal Chapter House and Mateus Fernandes' elaborate Great Portal.

Writing to Sir William Hamilton on July 4, 1802, at the time of the building of Fonthill Abbey, Beckford had Batalha's "little turrets, flying buttresses, pinnacles and gothic loopholes" much in his mind.[2] He also attempted to convert his architect, James Wyatt, to his foreign tastes, and the influence of Batalha can be seen in Fonthill Abbey's central octagon. Wyatt studied James Murphy's drawings of Batalha, although he was also influenced by the octagonal tower at Ely Cathedral where he had worked on restoration.[3] The stained-glass windows, whose refracted light so dazzled Beckford, were reproduced in the stained glass windows of Saint Michael's Gallery in the south wing of Fonthill Abbey. Above all, however, Batalha inspired Beckford with a vision of the Gothic as Romantic scenery.[4] He left Portugal determined to re-create an effect that reminded him of a vision of Ariosto in the deepest recesses of his native Fonthill. —M. J.

Beckford and Heraldry

In the class-dominated society of Britain in 1760, rank, title, and social precedence were of singular importance. Beckford, a nouveau riche born of a union of colonial stock and a junior branch of the ducal house of Hamilton, could claim lineal descent from the blood royal of Scotland through his mother's family. This powerful combination of family heritage and vast wealth rightly led to Beckford's expectation of elevation to the peerage while still a young man. His affair with William "Kitty" Courtenay, the son of the Earl of Devon, however, led to scandal in 1784 and effectively denied him this great honor.

In part because of this humiliation and loss, Beckford became increasingly obsessed with his genealogy. For the remainder of his life, he would take refuge in family pride. Using the services of professional genealogists, Beckford sought to bolster his extraordinary claims of descent from almost all the royal houses of England and Scotland. This overwhelming obsession with his ancestry would help to shape the most important project of Beckford's life, the building of Fonthill Abbey. Beckford incorporated heraldic devices throughout the Abbey's ambitious scheme of decoration. Carpets were woven to incorporate the Latimer cross and the Hamilton cinquefoil, and the majority of curtains and furnishings were in crimson and scarlet, colors derived from the Hamilton livery. The use of heraldic emblems reached their greatest expression as decorative embellishments on furniture, textiles, metalwork, ceramics, and book bindings.

Beckford's full coat of arms (see frontispiece) is charged with thirty-six quarterings. As was traditional with any family having a right to a coat of arms, crests were a significant feature and were commonly shown on their own to demonstrate entitlement and status. Throughout his life, Beckford used the traditional Beckford family crest, a heron with fish in its beak, undoubtedly enjoying the pun on the heraldic designation, *bec fort*. The Beckford crest, however, was increasingly used in conjunction with an additional crest assigned to Beckford in 1798 to indicate his descent from the Abercorn branch of the house of Hamilton and to allude to his claim of descent from William, first Lord Latimer. This second crest is the familiar Hamilton ducal coronet bearing oak tree with saw, adapted for Beckford with a shield bearing the Latimer cross. Rather than use his father's motto, Beckford adopted the "De Dieu Tout" motto of the Mervyn family, who had owned the property of Fonthill in the sixteenth century.

The devices he most frequently employed, however, are combinations of those derived principally from his Beckford and Hamilton ancestors[1]: *Beckford*—Per pale (divided vertically) gules (red) and azure (blue) on a chevron between three martlets or (gold or yellow) an eagle displayed sable (black) within a bordure tressure fleury counterfleury of the first (a fleur-de-lys above and below the border); *Hamilton*—Quarterly: first and fourth, gules three cinquefoils pierced ermine, two and one; second and third, argent (silver or white) a lymphad with sails furled sable; *Roger de Bellemont*e—Gules a cinquefoil pierced ermine; *William Ist Lord Latimer*—Azure cross fleury between five martlets; or *Douglas (ancien)*—Azure three mullets in chief argent.

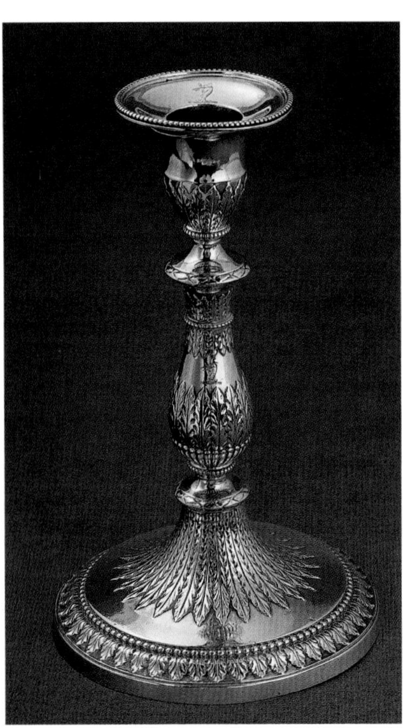

31. *Pair of Candlesticks (one shown)*
JOHN SCOFIELD
(FL. 1776–1803)

1781–82; England
Silver gilt
7⅞ x 4½ in. (19.5 x 11.5 cm)
Beckford Collection, Brodick Castle, National Trust for Scotland
(58.597)

Beckford's coming-of-age in 1781 was marked with the traditional "laying down" of new plate. Hardly any silver engraved with his father's arms has survived, and clearly much of it was used for its "melt value," being fashioned into his new dinner service, candlesticks, and household items executed in the latest style.[1] The silver, much of it gilt, bears the marks of leading silversmiths of the day, such as John Scofield, whose mark appears on these candlesticks, but as no invoices appear to have survived, it is not known which retailer actually supplied the service. It is likely that Beckford's plate came from London, from either Wakelin and Tayler of Panton Street, or Jeffreys and Jones of Cockspur Street, who succeeded to the royal warrant in 1783.[2] Scofield, whose workshop specialized in dinner services and candlesticks of the highest quality, is known to have worked for Jeffreys and Jones.[3]

At this early date, Beckford's interest in having a hand in the design of his own silver and in dealing directly with makers, rather than retailers, had yet to manifest itself. The silver ordered in 1781, while of the highest quality, is conventional in design. The graceful baluster form of these candlesticks is a Renaissance one to which Roman stiff foliage was applied. Based on designs by Robert (or possibly James) Adam, dating from the late 1760s, the final result is both elegant and eminently classical.[4] Candlesticks of this design appear as early as 1775; a suite of

"

them was supplied to Harewood House in 1779 and to the Duke of Cumberland in 1791.[5]

Beckford added larger examples to his set in 1791 (see cat. no. 9) and continued, despite the later demolition of Fonthill Splendens and his growing antiquarianism, to order more at intervals up to 1817. Beckford's passion for the rich and elegant classicism of his youth survived Fonthill Abbey. Part of the set appears, incongruously, on torchères with barleytwist supports in the view of King Edward's Gallery, where they must have injected a curious note of classicism into the Jacobean atmosphere of the long gallery. They also appear in the Grand Drawing Room in Rutter's *Delineations of Fonthill Abbey* (1823; see cat. fig. 88A).

It is not known how many candlesticks of this form Beckford owned; a total of eighteen have been traced, either at Brodick Castle or sold from the Hamilton Collection in the 1980s.[6]—C. H.

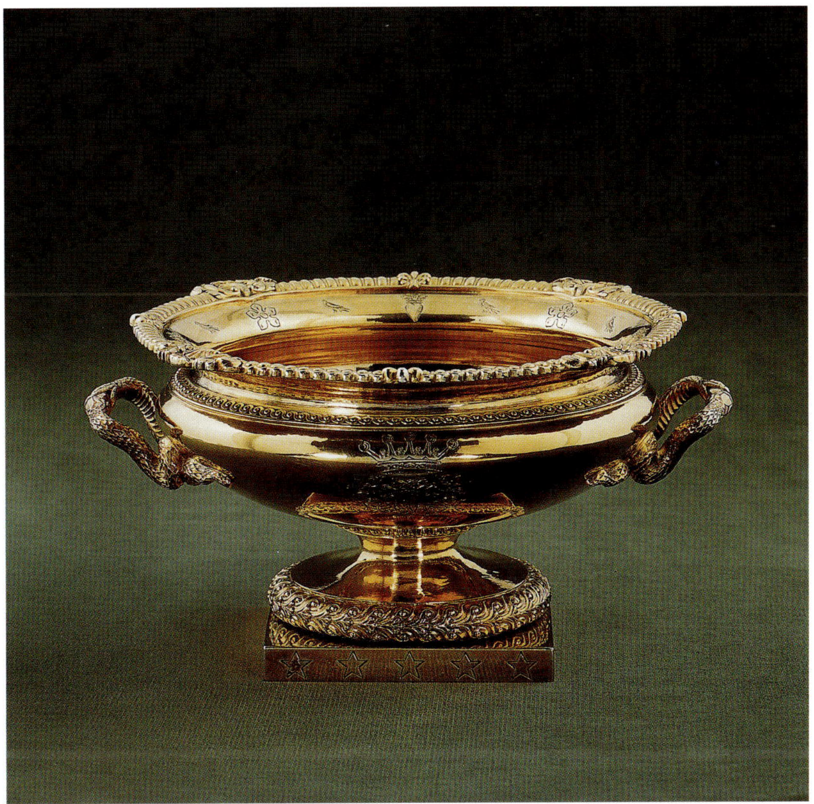

32. *Bowl*
PAUL STORR (1771–1844)

1809–10; England
Silver gilt
3¾ x 7¼ x 6½ in. (9.5 x 18.4 x 16.6 cm)
Glasgow Museums (E 1977.74–5)

On his grandson's first birthday, Beckford presented him with this bowl, inscribed under its base, "The Gift of William Beckford of Fonthill to his dear Grandchild and Godson William Alexander Anthony Archibald, Earl of Angus and Arran, on the 18 February 1812, the first anniversary of his birth." At the time, Beckford and Franchi were busy designing and commissioning from Storr the first of a series of highly individual silver objects for Fonthill Abbey. Remarkably, however, for this presentation piece Beckford chose to purchase a standard stock item, probably the sugar bowl from a tea service, from the royal goldsmiths. Its form is reminiscent of the celebrated Warwick vase which became the inspiration for a host of domestic silver articles during this period. The handles of this bowl, however, are based on double-snake handles that had appeared in Thomas Hope's *Household Furniture and Interior Decoration* (1807).[1]

The significance of this bowl lies in the addition of engraved heraldic motifs pertaining to Beckford's ancestry and that of his grandson. Inside the rim and again under the base, the martlet (bird) badge (Beckford), cinquefoils (Hamilton), and crowned hearts (Douglas) alternate as decorative borders. In the center of the interior, the Latimer cross is superimposed on the Hamilton cinquefoil. Strikingly, on each side of the pedestal foot is engraved a border of mullets (five-pointed stars), which is another Douglas badge. Beckford was particularly proud of his Douglas descent, but the use of the Douglas mullet is much rarer on his silver than his own martlet and the Hamilton cinquefoil.

Beckford's grandson William bore the courtesy title Earl of Angus and Arran until his father succeeded to the dukedom of Hamilton in 1819, after which he was known as Marquess of Douglas. He succeeded to the dukedom as eleventh duke in 1852, having married Princess Marie Amelie of Baden in 1843. Described in *Days of the Dandies* as having "inherited in some measure his father's *grandeeship* of manner," he lived most of his life abroad, in Paris or Baden.[2] His son, who succeeded as twelfth duke in 1863, was to sell most of the Hamilton and Beckford collections at auction in 1882. This bowl, however, was retained by the family and acquired by the Kelvingrove Museum in 1977. —C. H.

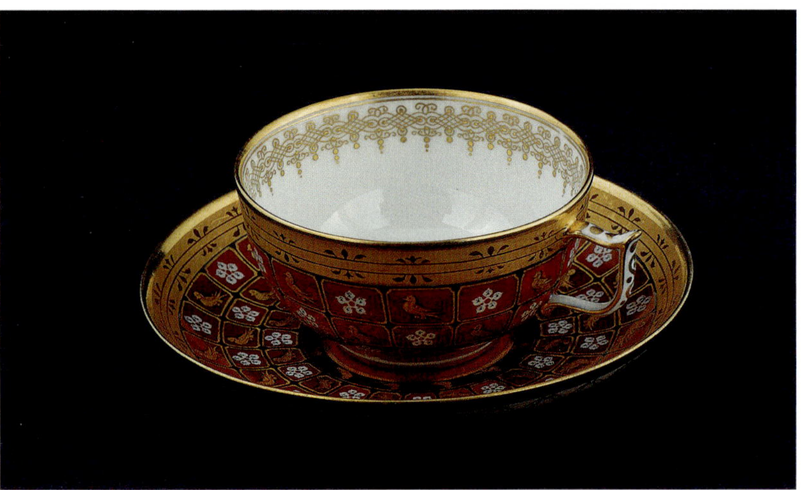

33. Cup and Saucer
BARR, FLIGHT AND BARR FACTORY

1810–13; England
Soft-paste porcelain
Cup: 1⅞ x 4 in. (4.8 x 10.2 cm); saucer: 5⅛ in. diam. (13 cm)
Beckford Collection, Brodick Castle, National Trust for Scotland (58.4001)

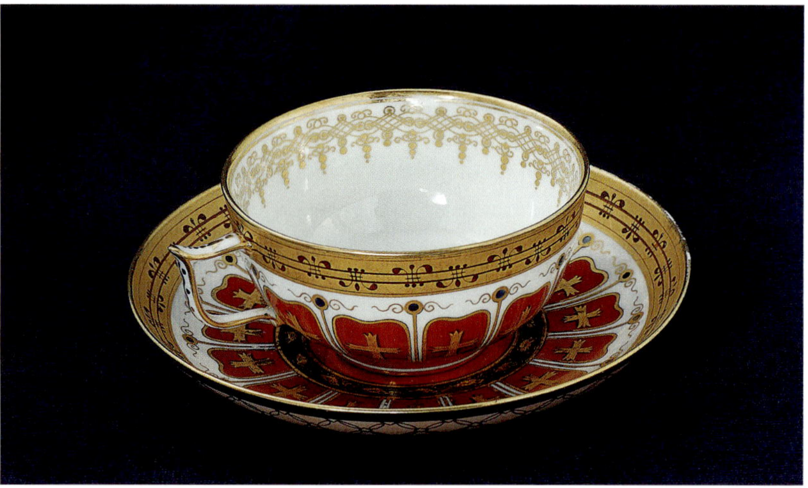

35. Cup and Saucer
BARR, FLIGHT AND BARR FACTORY

1810–13; England
Soft-paste porcelain
Cup: 1⅞ x 4 in. (4.8 x 10.2 cm); Saucer: 5⅛ in. diam. (13 cm)
Beckford Collection, Brodick Castle, National Trust for Scotland (58.4002)

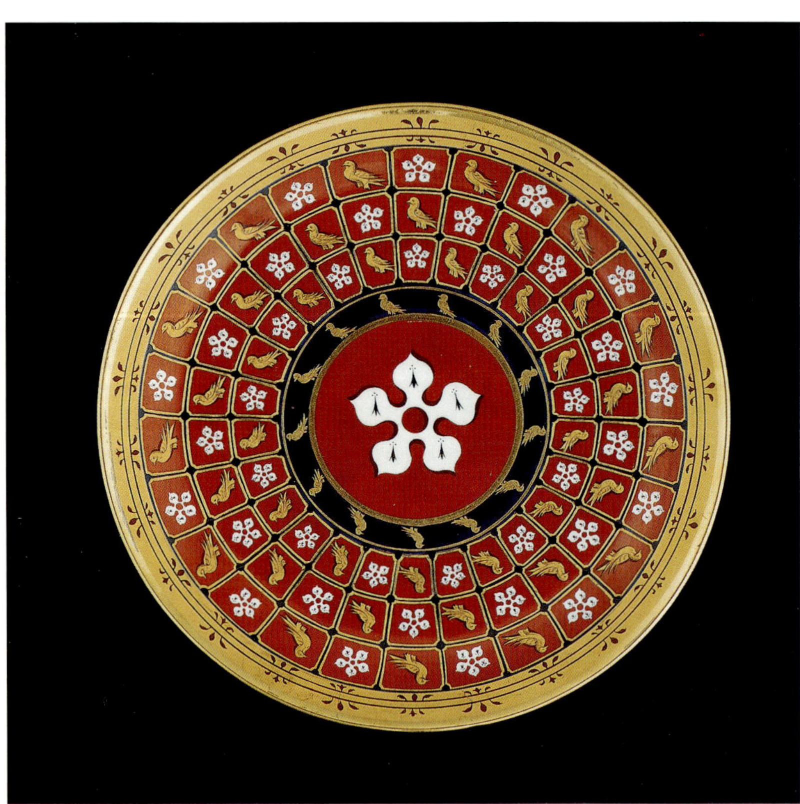

34. Plate
BARR, FLIGHT AND BARR FACTORY

1810–13; England
Soft-paste porcelain
7⅞ in. diam. (20 cm)
Beckford Collection, Brodick Castle, National Trust for Scotland (58.4001)

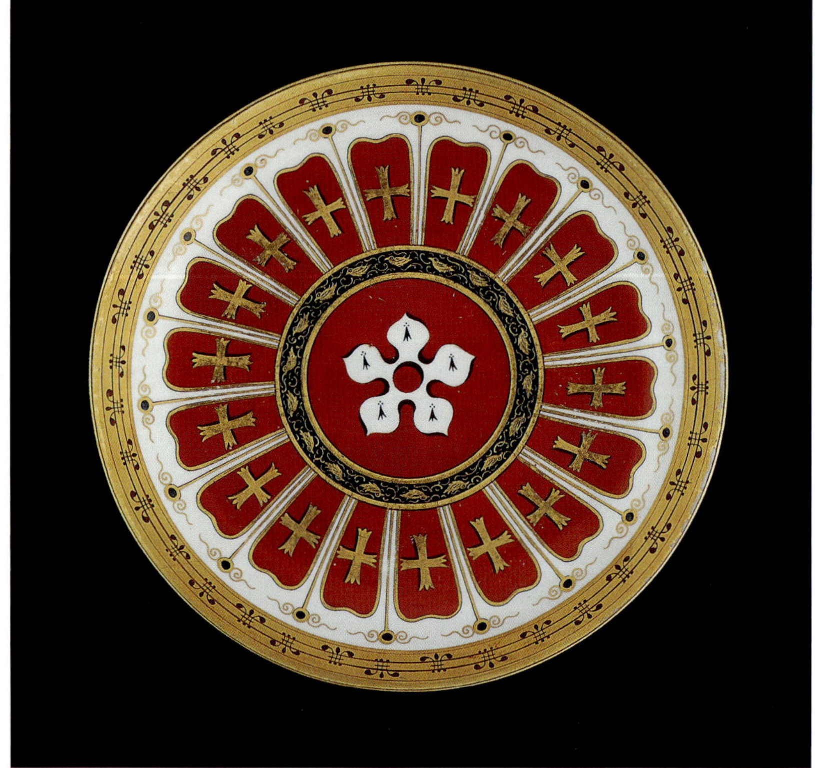

36. Plate
BARR, FLIGHT AND BARR FACTORY

1810–13; England
Soft-paste porcelain
7⅞ in. diam. (20 cm)
Beckford Collection, Brodick Castle, National Trust for Scotland (58.4002)

From the beginning of the nineteenth century, the Barr, Flight and Barr factory had become the most fashionable for the supply of armorial services, usually decorated with a standard Regency pattern and palette, with the individual's coat of arms prominently displayed either in the center or around the rim. Here, however, Beckford's favorite armorial devices of cinquefoil, martlet, and Latimer cross have completely taken over the field of decoration, in effect becoming the decoration. This extravagant, glamorous, and utterly unprecedented use of heraldic devices illustrates not only Beckford's obsession with his lineage, but also his status as a wealthy patron of much individuality. The successful working of the devices into patterns and the ironic use of shield-shaped lobes suggest a clever and somewhat irreverent eye for design, probably due to a combination of Franchi's design skills and Beckford's bitter determination to flaunt his lineage. As the Worcester factory had a substantial retail showroom in London, it is likely that from London Franchi supervised the production of this extraordinary set of porcelain.[1]

The circumstances of the commissioning of this service are unknown, although a completion date of 1813 can be adduced: the Barr, Flight and Barr partnership operated only between the years 1804 and 1813. Beckford increasingly used the combination of Beckford and Hamilton heraldic devices from 1810, the year of the marriage of his daughter Susan with Alexander, Marquess of Douglas, who was to succeed as tenth Duke of Hamilton in 1819. —B. M.

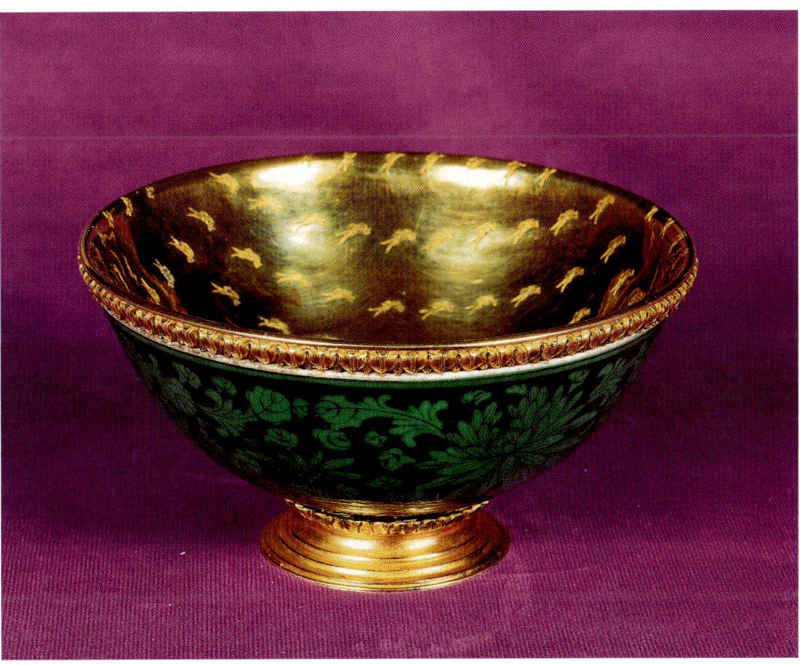

37. *Bowl*

JAMES ALDRIDGE
(FL. 1778–?1822)

Mounts, 1811–12, England; porcelain, 18th century, China Porcelain, silver gilt
2⅜ x 4½ in. diam. (6 x 11.5 cm)
Trustees of The Edward James Foundation, West Dean, Chichester (1163 OPT97)

This extraordinary object is the earliest known of a series of sugar basins and cream jugs, belonging to Beckford, created by applying silver-gilt mounts to Asian porcelain.[1] For the next nine years, Beckford and Franchi would collaborate on the design of the mounts, combining heraldic, Renaissance, and Asian motifs with an exuberance that heralds the exoticism of the ensuing decades.

With Asian porcelain arriving in Europe in ever-increasing quantities during the eighteenth century, the Paris *marchands-merciers* discovered the decorative possibilities of applying gilt-bronze, silver, or even gold mounts to relatively modest ceramic wares (or even fragments). This was a departure from the medieval and Renaissance practice of enshrining rare Asian ceramics with equally precious mounts. Beckford combined both traditions with this series of eclectic tea wares for Fonthill Abbey.

In contrast with the rest of the series, most of which are made from commonplace pieces of Chinese export porcelain, this bowl is an unusual example of the *famille noire* decoration that was perfected in the second quarter of the eighteenth century.[2] The style of the mounts is firmly classical, with finely chased stiff foliage borders on the rim and foot, giving no hint of the curious mixtures of Chinese and Mughal motifs with which Beckford and Franchi would experiment in the next few years. The foot is extremely heavy, occasioned by the extra weight of the silver-gilt lining to the interior, another unique feature. The most surprising feature of all, however, is the engraved decoration of this lining. The Beckford coat of arms appears in the center of the basin within a circular cartouche of scrolls similar to designs by Jacques Androuet Du Cerceau published in the sixteenth century. Here Beckford was no doubt drawing on his exhaustive library of design prints or even on some of the tooled patterns on his Renaissance bookbindings. The rest of the surface is covered in a continuous pattern of martlets, one of the heraldic badges used by Beckford (see cat. nos. 33–36, 40–44). In this Beckford was reviving a medieval tradition best seen in the repeated badges on surviving silver such as the Leigh cup belonging to the Mercers' Company and the Lady Margaret Beaufort cup at Christ's College, Cambridge.[3] The way in which the pattern of Beckford's martlets rise up the rim and seemingly cascade over it, however, reminds one of motifs in Japanese lacquer, another passion of Beckford's. —C. H.

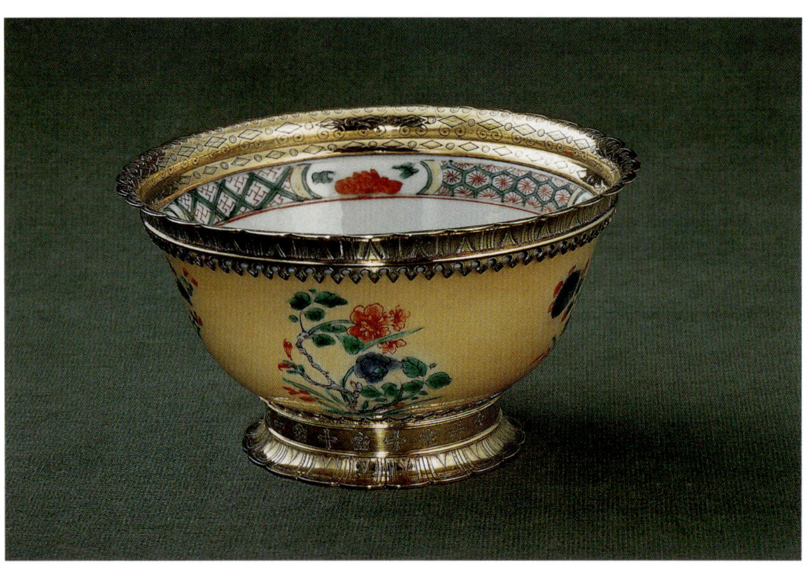

38. *Bowl*

JAMES ALDRIDGE
(FL. 1778–?1822)

Mounts, 1820–21, England;
porcelain, 18th century, China
Porcelain, silver gilt
3 in. (7.5 cm)
Beckford Collection, Brodick
Castle, National Trust for Scotland
(58.534)

In the early nineteenth century, the tradition of applying European-style mounts to Oriental porcelain, perfected in France under the ancien régime, gave way to a new fashion for mounts imitating the Chinese character of the porcelain. In England, perhaps the most striking examples of this trend are the mounts for porcelain designed by Frederick Crace from 1815 to about 1822 for the Chinese interiors of Brighton Pavilion.[1]

At the same time as this work was being carried out, however, Beckford and Franchi were designing mounts for modest pieces of Chinese porcelain in a completely different manner, enthusiastically combining Chinese, Mughal, and European motifs to create works of art which, in their careful groupings, would punctuate the eclectic interiors of the Abbey.

The work of designing and commissioning these objects continued as Beckford's financial situation worsened and even as plans were made for the eventual sale of Fonthill. Perhaps these small precious objects were intended to be taken by Beckford to enhance the interiors of his next home. An insight into the Beckford–Franchi design process is provided by the rare survival of a book of working drawings that belonged to James Aldridge,[2] whose mark appears on the mounts of this bowl. Among somewhat pedestrian designs for silverware, evidently by Aldridge himself, small drawings have been pasted into the book that are clearly by another hand, probably Franchi's own. They include details of decoration and reveal the restless design process that must have preceded Franchi's painstaking supervision of the work itself.

This Chinese export porcelain bowl, decorated with *famille verte* prunus trees on a *café au lait* ground, incorporates several motifs found in the Aldridge album. The spreading lobed foot, inspired by Mughal goldwork, appears in several versions, all enhanced, as on this bowl, with geometric engraving based on Chinese blue-and-white porcelain decoration.

Another key element in the Franchi drawings is heraldry. By the later Fonthill years, heraldic badges, rather than Beckford's crests, figure most frequently as decoration. On this bowl the Hamilton cinquefoil and the Latimer cross, the latter an allusion to Beckford's supposed descent from William, first Lord Latimer, alternate around the foot.
—C. H.

39. *Cup and Cover*

JOHN HARRIS (FL. 1818–1827)

Mounts, 1826–27, England;
hardstone, 18th century, Continental
Lapis lazuli, silver gilt
8¾ x 6⅞ in. (22.3 x 17.5 cm)
Lent by The Syndics of the Fitzwilliam Museum, Cambridge.
Bought from The Rylands, Gow, Leverton Harr and Marlay Funds, with Grants from The Regional Fund administered by The Victoria & Albert Museum, The National Heritage Memorial Fund, and The National Art Collection Fund, 1990 (M. 1&a-1990)

From the third quarter of the sixteenth century, carved lapis lazuli has often traditionally been associated with the Florentine court workshop of the Medici after Milanese and Roman craftsmen had been enticed to the court of Grand Duke Cosimo de Medici. Throughout the seventeenth and the eighteenth centuries, the pietre-dure workshop flourished in Florence until it was closed by Napoleonic forces in 1799.[1]

The stone used in this cup and cover may very well have originated in the Florentine workshop but probably, for stylistic reasons, not before the eighteenth century. This deep blue stone was mined from antiquity in the northern regions of Afghanistan. In the mid-sixteenth century, Afghanistan was divided between Persia and India with the province of Herat falling under Persian rule, hence the term *Persian lapis*.[2]

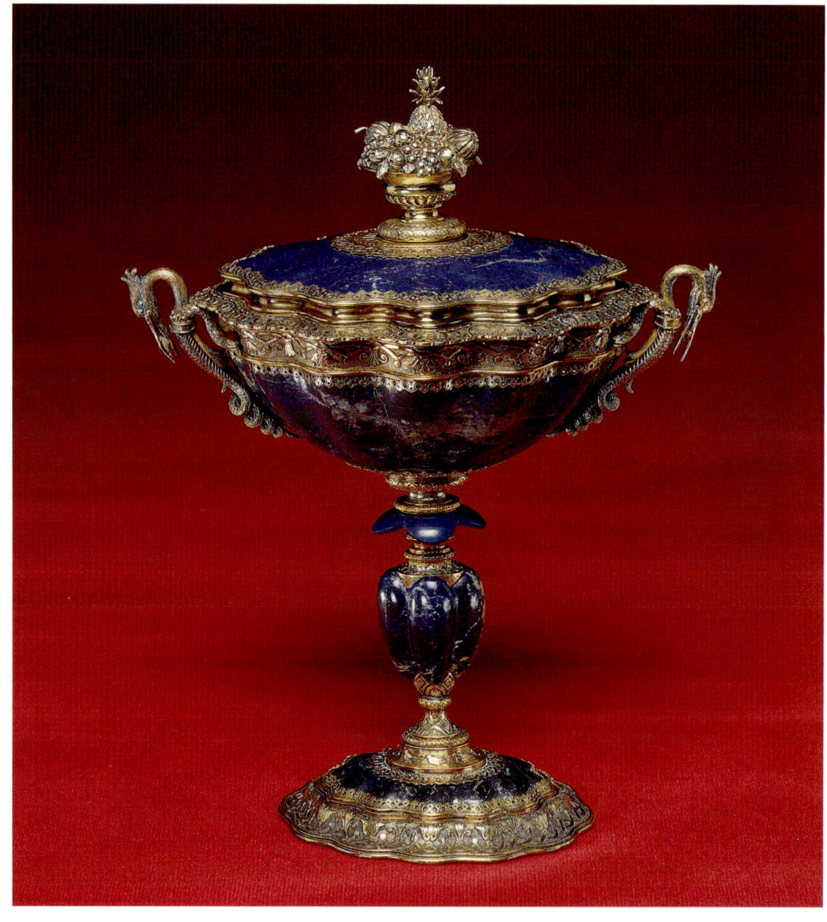

With the rediscovery of the lapis heron-handled cup and cover, thirteen mounted pieces by John Harris VI are known, with twelve of them dating to between 1818 and 1820.[3] The lapis cup, however, bears the date letter for 1826–27, which in itself is a mystery. Little information has so far come to light about Harris. His first mark was entered in May 1818, when he was based off Leicester Square, with a second mark entered in May 1821, by which time he had moved to Queen's Square off Golden Square. Both addresses are in Soho, which together with the West End were the main centers of silver manufacture. Interestingly, by September 1823 he had moved to Knightsbridge away from the mainstream of silver manufacture.[4]

That Harris was known to Beckford is documented in letters between the latter and Franchi. Beckford referred to Harris as the "Methodist"[5] and wrote in a letter to Franchi in June 1819: "Now that the Methodist has in his safe keeping the lapis lazuli and the gold, it wouldn't surprise me if he made off and if one heard no more of him until one read in the American papers: 'New York 21st Sept. 1819—Brother Harris, newly arrived from the Land of perdition, has gladdened our hearts with much spiritual discourse etc. etc.'."[6]

It is probable that "the lapis and the gold" that Beckford mentions refer to the materials used in the making of this object. The 1844 inventory made at Beckford's death describes a cup and cover in the drawing room in Bath as "Lapys Lazuli . . . richly mounted in gold".[7] That the cup has silver-gilt mounts, rather than gold mentioned in the inventory, does not necessarily imply that this is not "the lapis and the gold"; silver gilt and even electro-gilt have been erroneously listed as gold in early as well as later English inventories.[8] Further documentary evidence, however, may explain the delay between the presumed date for the commissioning of the piece and its completion.

The cup and cover was included in the Hamilton Palace sale catalogue of 1882 where it is illustrated and described.[9] The silver-gilt mounts by Harris with rather cumbersome handles, each wrought as a twisting serpent terminating in a heron's head, also include a broad foot and rim mount, which detract from the beauty of the polished stone. The cup and cover underwent further alterations after the Hamilton Palace sale. When the Fitzwilliam Museum acquired it, the original finial on the cover had been replaced by a pineapple, and the cinquefoil calyx joining the bowl with the stem was missing; these have now been replaced by a contemporary goldsmith. Once again the Beckford heraldry is further emphasized with martlets engraved around the upper foot mount as well as the presence of the herons' heads. —E. M.

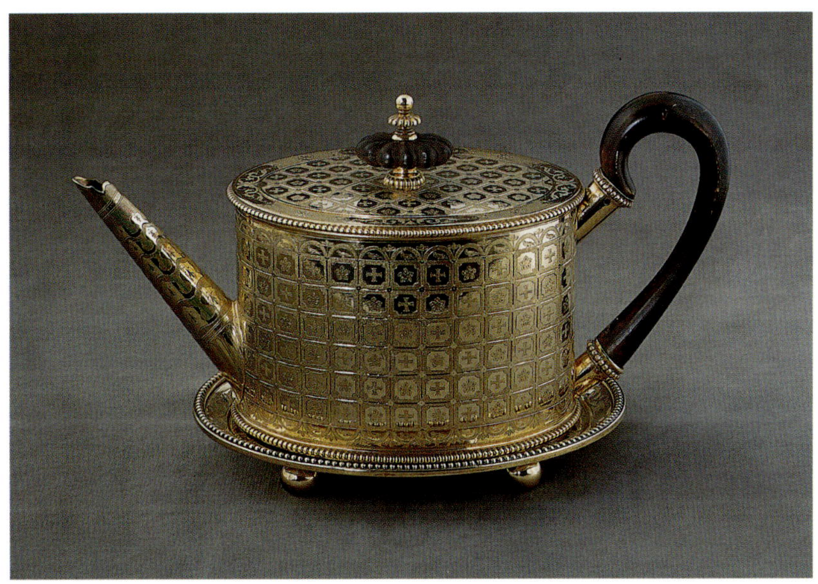

40. *Teapot and Stand*
PETER PODIO (FL. 1783–?)

1802–03; England
Silver gilt, ebonized wood
5 x 9⅜ x 3¾ in. (12.8 x 23.7 x 9.4 cm)
Trustees of the National Museums of Scotland, Edinburgh (1977.209)

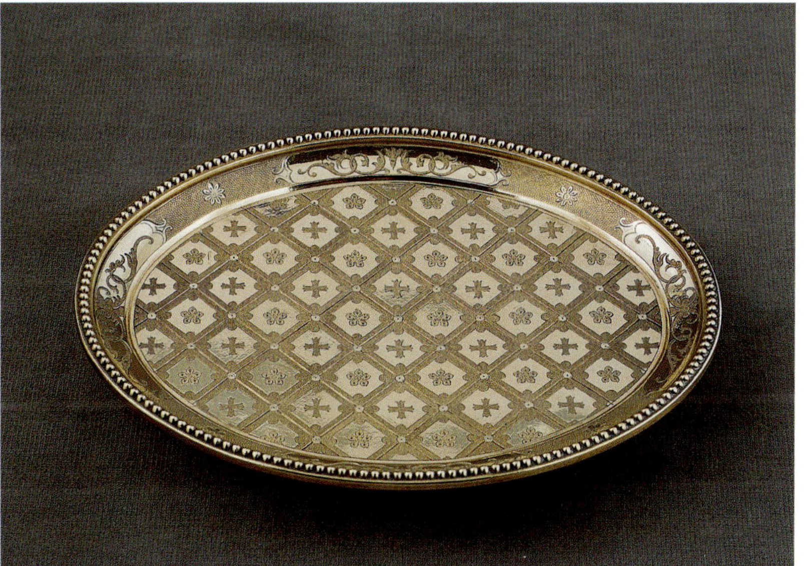

41. *Teapot Stand*
WILLIAM ELLIOT (FL. 1809–1818)

1817–18; England
Silver gilt
1 x 6⅜ x 5 in. (2.3 x 16.2 x 12.6 cm)
Trustees of the National Museums of Scotland, Edinburgh (1977.210)

40–44. TEA SERVICE

This service was created by combining a teapot, stand, and tea caddy (cat. nos. 40, 41, 44) of different dates and made by several silversmiths, but all in the conventional beaded oval style of Beckford's earliest silverware. Added to these, in 1819–20, were a sugar bowl and cream jug (cat nos. 42, 43), which are obviously a special commission given to the royal goldsmiths Rundell, Bridge and Rundell. Evidently the engraved pattern—geometric compartments containing heraldic badges covering all visible surfaces—was added to the components of the service at this time. The compartments in the decoration contain alternating Hamilton cinquefoils and Latimer crosses, while the borders have alternating cinquefoils, crosses, and martlets.

The use of heraldic badges, as opposed to coats of arms and crests, had died out in England in the sixteenth century, but Beckford was one of the first nineteenth-century patrons to recognize their decorative potential, especially when used, as they had been in the Middle Ages, in continuous, decorative patterns. Essentially these badges were a

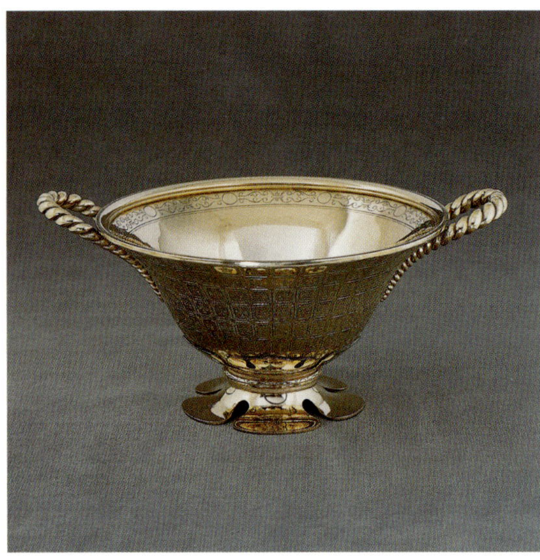

42. Bowl
PHILIP RUNDELL (1743–1827)

1819–20; England
Silver gilt
3⅝ x 7⅞ x 5¾ in. (9.2 x 19.3 x
14.7 cm)
Trustees of the National Museums of Scotland,
Edinburgh (1977.207)

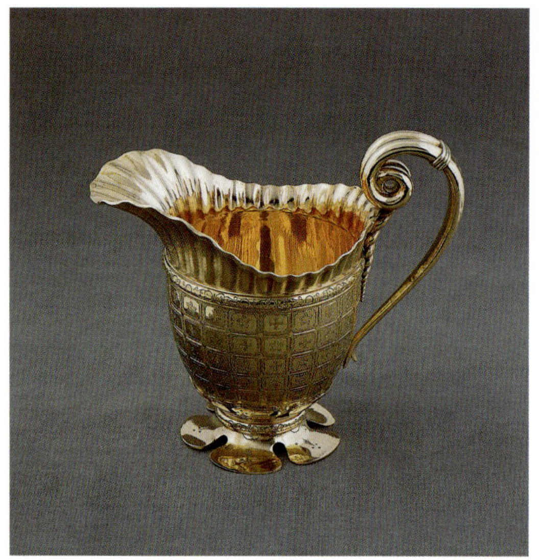

43. Jug
PHILIP RUNDELL (1743–1827)

1819–20; England
Silver gilt
5¼ x 5¾ x 3½ in. (13.2 x 14.5 x 9 cm)
Trustees of the National Museums of Scotland,
Edinburgh (1977.208)

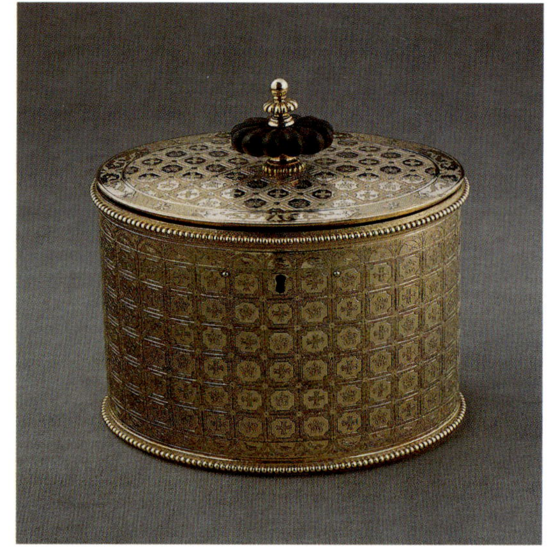

44. Tea Caddy
MICHAEL PLUMMER (FL. 1795–?)

1796–97; England
Silver gilt
5⅛ x 5⅛ x 3¾ in. (13 x 13.1 x 9.4 cm)
Trustees of the National Museums of Scotland,
Edinburgh (1977.211)

medieval device employed when the depiction of a complete shield was impractical, and they had developed separately from the charges that adorned coats of arms.[1] In this respect Beckford was at odds with the way heraldic decoration had evolved during the Georgian period, when the shield, with the addition of crest, supporters, motto, and ever more elaborate mantling, had grown in complexity and size. By the early nineteenth century such achievements had, at the hands of heraldic engravers like the Jackson family, assumed center stage as embellishments on silver and porcelain.

Beckford, however, usually avoided the use of large armorials and preferred instead to base decoration on single, or at the most two or three, small motifs. This tea service, dating from the last phase of work at Fonthill Abbey, is the apogee of this type of heraldic art, and it brilliantly shows the way in which his use of heraldry at Fonthill anticipated the great decorative schemes at Charlecote, Carlton Towers, and Arundel Castle.

While the three older pieces of this set are unusual only because of their heraldic decoration, the cream jug and sugar basin are of a unique form. The delicate everted bodies are raised on Asian scalloped spreading feet, flat-chased with Chinese scrolls. Similar feet appear in several of the drawings of small articles attributed to Franchi in the Aldridge scrapbook in the Victoria and Albert Museum (see fig. 11-10). The form of the cream jug, with a fluted lip reminiscent of those on Beckford's ewers by Auguste and Moitte, also appears in one of these drawings, although there the body has figural decoration.[2] —C. H.

Beckford as Francophile

As an ambitious young man with a considerable income, Beckford developed a refined and distinctive taste during his prolonged stays in Paris between 1777 and 1793. His frequent visits to the ateliers of noted Parisian artists, designers, and craftsmen gave him an intimate understanding of the creative process. During this formative period Beckford commissioned significant works of art, some of which would remain with him until the sale of his collection in 1822. This, together with his knowledge of the important collections in Paris and his attendance at many of the famous auctions, heightened his awareness of what would later come to be known as "French" taste.

Like many famous French collectors of the pre-Revolutionary era, Beckford acquired what was regarded as a specifically ancien régime taste for Dutch and Flemish cabinet pictures, objets d'art, mounted porcelains, hardstones, and cabinet bronzes. He shared the eighteenth-century French predelection for the finest Japanese lacquer, and furniture mounted with pietre-dure panels or made in the boulle technique.

Between 1788 and 1789, Beckford lived in Paris in one of the most celebrated townhouses of the era, the Hôtel d'Orsay. Its interiors, only recently completed in the latest neoclassical style, had a profound influence on the redecoration of Beckford's Fonthill Splendens in the 1790s. In spite of having to flee Paris during the Revolution and to suffer the seizure of a portion of his collection, Beckford would later return to Paris on several occasions. Although these visits occurred less frequently during the time he was building Fonthill Abbey, he maintained relationships with many of the artists and craftsmen he had known previously, and he would continue to make purchases in Paris through his agents for the remainder of his life. On his last visit in 1814, however, he expressed a general dissatisfaction with the state of the arts in Paris.

Although the French taste of his earlier years did not play as prominent a role in his collecting after his move to Bath in 1822, nonetheless the inventory of Beckford's collection after his death in 1844 reveals the legacy of a taste shaped by eighteenth-century French collecting traditions.

---

45. *Lady in a Red Corset and Satin Dress*
Jean-Honoré Fragonard (1732–1806)

ca. 1775–85; France
Oil on canvas
12¼ x 8⅞ in. (31 x 22.5 cm)
Private collection

Previously known from having been recorded in Beckford's collection in 1801 and from the 1882 Hamilton Palace sale catalogue, this painting has not been exhibited until now.[1] It is one of Fragonard's last works, probably from the period of the mid-1770s to late 1780s, few of which are recorded, and it reflects a new direction in Fragonard's stylistic development. It is quite remote from his earlier more flamboyant and sensuous style and subjects, and was possibly painted in collaboration with his pupil and sister-in-law, Marguerite Gèrard. Her style is very similar to this, and together they painted other subjects of the same genre with features common to this painting. The minute attention to detail and high finish is reminiscent of works by the seventeenth-century Dutch masters of genre subjects, such as Gerrit Dou, Gabriel Metsu, and Frans van Mieris, all painters much admired and collected by Beckford. He owned, for instance, *Woman Feeding a Parrot* by Frans van Mieris (now in the National Gallery, London), *Interior with a Lady in White Silk* (*Die Goldwägerin*) by Pieter de Hooch (now in the Staatliche Museen Berlin, Gemäldegalerie), and *Interior of a Chamber with a Lady Washing her Hands* by Eglon van der Neer (now in the Mauritshuis, The Hague). Beckford also admired contemporary French painters and owned works by Greuze and Claude Vernet, as well as a number of paintings by Lancret and Watteau, some of which had been inherited from his father.

It is likely that Beckford purchased this painting on one of his visits to Paris. In 1783–84 he met the painter Hubert Robert in his studio in the Louvre. Robert had worked and traveled with Fragonard from 1759.[2] Later, in 1792 Fragonard was involved in the establishment of the new Louvre, and from 1797 to 1800 he was similarly occupied at Versailles. Beckford may have known of him in this context.

The painting was at Fonthill Splendens by 1801 and was recorded

by the antiquarian John Britton as hanging in the upstairs gallery.[3] At Fonthill Abbey, it hung in the dining room (or "cabinet" room),[4] and at the time of Beckford's death in 1844, it was recorded as being in the back drawing room at Lansdown Crescent in Bath, among a rich mixture of paintings, including works by Domenichino, Hondecoeter, Rubens, Stothard, and Cope.[5]

Beckford's younger daughter, Susan Euphemia, the Duchess of Hamilton, who inherited his paintings, retained the picture and following its sale in the great dispersal of Hamilton Palace, it was later to be found again at Fonthill when the Shaw-Stewart family came into possession of the estate by marriage. It was listed in 1906 in a Fragonard catalogue but has not reappeared in any subsequent publication, even as a lost work.[6] It was recognized and authenticated by the scholar-dealer David Carritt, who, according to extensive notes among his posthumous papers, intended to include the painting in a publication on Fragonard in Italy. The picture had

come to his attention in 1978, when he consulted the Beckford historian James Lees-Milne.[7] Carritt was curious that the painting had not been acquired in 1882 by any of the passionate collectors of French eighteenth-century art, particularly the Rothschild family or any of the representatives of the many European museums who attended the Hamilton Palace sale. —J. C.

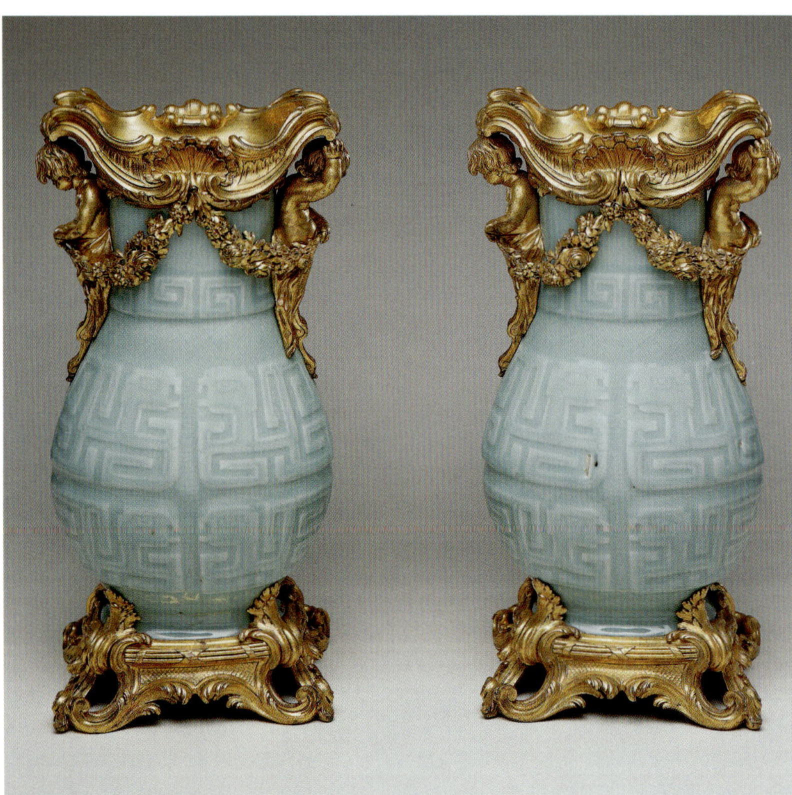

46. *Pair of Vases*
Maker unknown

Mounts, 1760–70; France;
porcelain, 18th century, China
Porcelain, gilt bronze
12¾ in. (32.4 cm)
The Metropolitan Museum of Art,
The Jules Bache Collection, 1949
(49.7.80–81)

This pair of vases corresponds very closely in detail to the single vase, one of a pair, depicted in the line drawing that accompanies lot 248 in the Hamilton Palace sale of 1882.[1] Because of this similarity, a Beckford provenance has long been hypothesized for the pair.[2] The 1844 inventory after Beckford's death lists a "Pair of Sea Green Vases mounted by Germain," with an inscription in the margin "Taken to HP Dec 1844."[3] In addition, the *List of Articles of Vertu Furniture etc. etc sent from Bath to Hamilton Palace* in the Hamilton Archives includes "A Pair of Sea Green Vases mounted by Germain."[4] These two references provide the definite linkage between the vases sold from Hamilton Palace and Beckford himself.

The Hamilton Palace vases are further connected with Beckford by the description of a pair of vases that was included in the canceled Fonthill Abbey sale of 1822. Lot 14 of the Tenth Day's sale lists "A pair of tooled and embossed old sea-green jars, magnificently mounted by Germain, with boys and festoon of flowers, scroll mouths and stands, chased and gilt – time of Louis XV."[5] This description aptly fits both the vase illustrated in the Hamilton Palace sale catalogue and this pair.

If it is accepted that the Metropolitan Museum's vases are the two sold as a pair from Hamilton Palace, their Beckford provenance is secure. A second pair of mounted vases, similar to this pair, however, existed in the late eighteenth century, one of

which can be seen on the mantel in a portrait of Pierre-Joseph-Victor de Besenval, Baron de Brunstatt, by Henri-Pierre Danloux.[6] If Danloux's depiction of the Besenval vase is accurate, it is not one of the pair acquired by Beckford, for the prominent molded vertical line very visible on the Besenval vase does not appear in the line drawing of the vase in the Hamilton Palace sale catalogue.[7] It is possible that other vases of this model with the same mounts existed, but the vases now at the Metropolitan are the only known examples that correspond to those owned by Beckford.

Interestingly, Beckford owned another pair of Chinese celadon vases of the same shape as these and with gilt-bronze mounts of the same design. The porcelain was differently decorated, however, with a peach in relief rather than the raised interlace ornament derived from archaic Chinese bronzes that is found on the Metropolitan's vases. The peach-relief–decorated vases also appear in the 1822 Fonthill Abbey sale catalogue, described as "A pair of oriental grey Jars of compressed shape, with the Sacred Peach in relief; the necks superbly mounted and the feet also of or moulu."[8]

Both pairs of vases must have seemed unusual in Beckford's collection. While it is well known that he was a passionate collector of richly mounted objects, it is clearly established that his taste was for objects with either Renaissance or Mannerist-style mounts, or for those with mounts executed in a rather severe neoclassical style.[9] The gilt-bronze mounts on the two pairs of celadon vases are in the full so-called Transitional style, in which rococo elements are fused with neoclassical ones and are employed with a certain symmetry and restraint. Symmetry notwithstanding, the richly sculptural garlands of flowers, the shell motifs centered on the undulating neck, and the curvilinear scrolls of the foot underscore the rococo qualities of the mounts, qualities which must have distinguished these vases from the vast majority of mounted objects that Beckford acquired or commissioned. In a letter to Gregorio Franchi, Beckford derisively comments on certain objects as having been "Pompadourised"[10]—presumably referring to their rococo aspects—so there must have been other qualities that drew him to the mounted celadon vases.

Chinese porcelains with French gilt-bronze mounts were among the most avidly sought-after objects by aristocratic and other illustrious collectors in France throughout the eighteenth century. The duc de Bourbon, Madame de Pompadour, the duc d'Aumont, and the famous collectors Randon de Boisset and Radix de Sainte-Foy are among those who owned mounted Chinese porcelains, as evidenced by posthumous inventories or contemporary sale catalogues.[11] It may be that Beckford, a devoted Francophile, was drawn to the romantic and historical associations of these mounted vases, which could be seen to epitomize a certain type of aristocratic taste prevalent in the third quarter of the eighteenth century.[12] The various royal and aristocratic provenances that he provided for his objects as described in the 1822 sale catalogue indicate the value that Beckford ascribed to this type of association. In addition, it is likely that it was Beckford who attributed the gilt-bronze mounts to "Germain", as stated in the 1822 sale catalogue.[13] Beckford presumably is referring to the silversmith and bronze worker François-Thomas Germain, whose name would have been impressive to Beckford due to his prominent stature among eighteenth-century French silversmiths, his title of *sculpteur-orfèvre du roi,* and his well-known, illustrious clientele.[14]

It is not known when and where Beckford acquired this pair of mounted vases. He may have purchased them in Paris during one of his numerous stays there in the 1790s or early 1800s, or through a London dealer at any point in the first two decades of the nineteenth century, if not earlier. In any case, the rococo aspect of the vases would have made them out of fashion when he acquired them, a fact which, when coupled with his own general dislike of the rococo, lends weight to the theory that considerations other than aesthetic prompted their purchase.

Whatever the basis for his appreciation, it is clear that Beckford highly valued the vases that eventually entered the collections at Hamilton Palace, and which presumably are those now in New York. While the vases were to have been auctioned at the canceled Fonthill Abbey sale of 1822, they were not sold subsequently to John Farquhar, the purchaser of Fonthill Abbey and much of its contents.[15] The vases were taken to Lansdown Crescent by Beckford where they remained until his death in 1844.[16] —J. H. M.

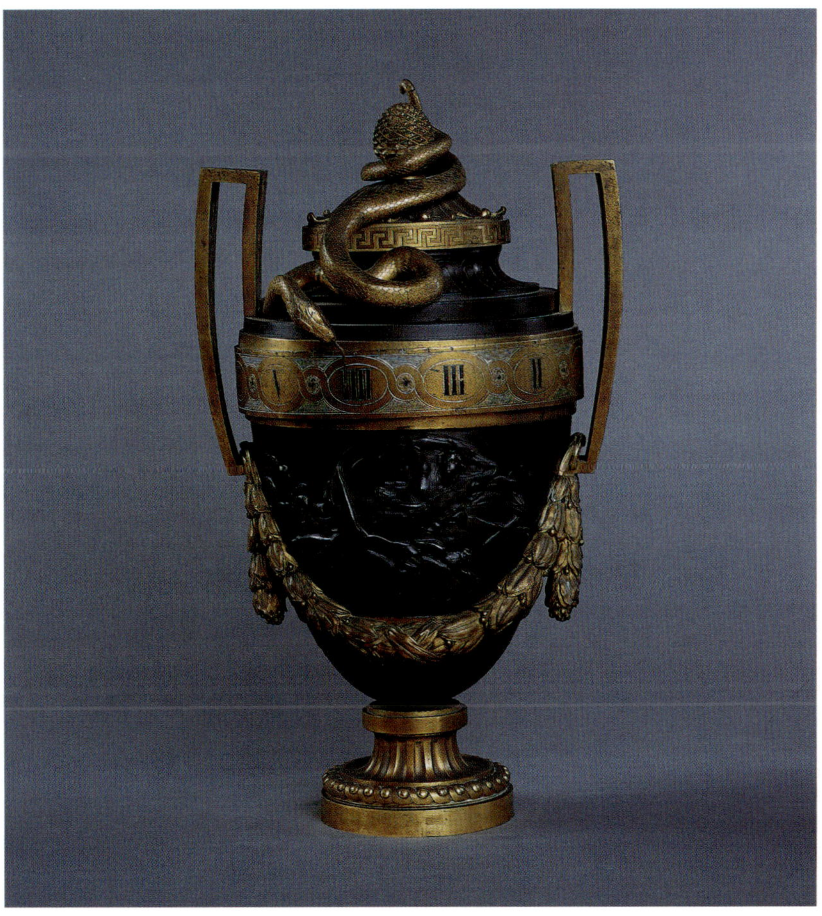

47. *Clock*
LOUIS DAUTHAIU (FL. 1735–1767)

ca. 1765; France
Gilt bronze, patinated bronze, enamel
28⅜ x 14¾ in. (73 x 37.5 cm)
Collection of the Hon. Lady Morrison, Malvern

The Grecian-urn (*vase grec*) clock reflects Beckford's taste for the elegant Louis XVI "antique" or "*gout grec*" style that had been introduced by the French architectural school in Rome and encouraged by David Le Roy's *Ruines des plus beaux monuments de la Grèce* (1758). The bronze cinerary urn would have served as a romantic garniture for a mantelpiece in one of Beckford's Parisian residences, and may have been intended to evoke his role as an "Apollo of the Arts." It recalls ancient sacrifices at love's altar, and in particular that of the Grecian heroine Andromache, the subject of Racine's celebrated tragedy *Andromaque*. This festive wine-krater urn has an egg-shaped body evoking Ovid's *Metamorphoses* (Loves of the Gods) and the story of Jupiter and Leda; while the laurels festooning its Grecian-fretted handles recall Apollo's poetic triumph as leader of the artistic muses of Mount Parnassus. Apollo's Pythian serpent here entwines its bacchic thyrsus-cone finial to mark the hours that are inscribed in Roman numerals on the ribbon-guilloche of the clock's revolving ring. Its figurative bas-reliefs depict Apollo as sun deity accompanied by the light-bearing dawn deity, Aurora, unveiling night's darkness.

The movement bears the signature of the clockmaker Louis Dauthaiu (*fl.* 1735–67), who was granted a court appointment in 1754 as "Horloger du Roy" under Louis XV. Among the most celebrated designers of urn clocks is the sculptor/bronze-founder Jean Louis Prieur, who was a member of the Paris Académie de Saint-Luc, and collaborated in the mid-1760s with the Rome-trained architect Victor Louis in the design of such clocks for the king of Poland's palace in Warsaw. His urn clocks were illustrated on "altar" pedestals comprised of truncated and antique-fluted columns.[1]

Along with the celebrated "Tippo Sahib" Indian jade hookah (see cat. no. 55), Beckford's urn clock may have been purchased at the 1823 Fonthill Abbey sale by Catherine Denne, first Countess Beauchamp. They were added to her collection of French furniture, Sèvres, and objets d'art assembled at Madresfield, Worcestershire, as part of its aggrandizement carried out by William Lygon, Baron Beauchamp of Powycke, first Earl of Beauchamp. —J. H.

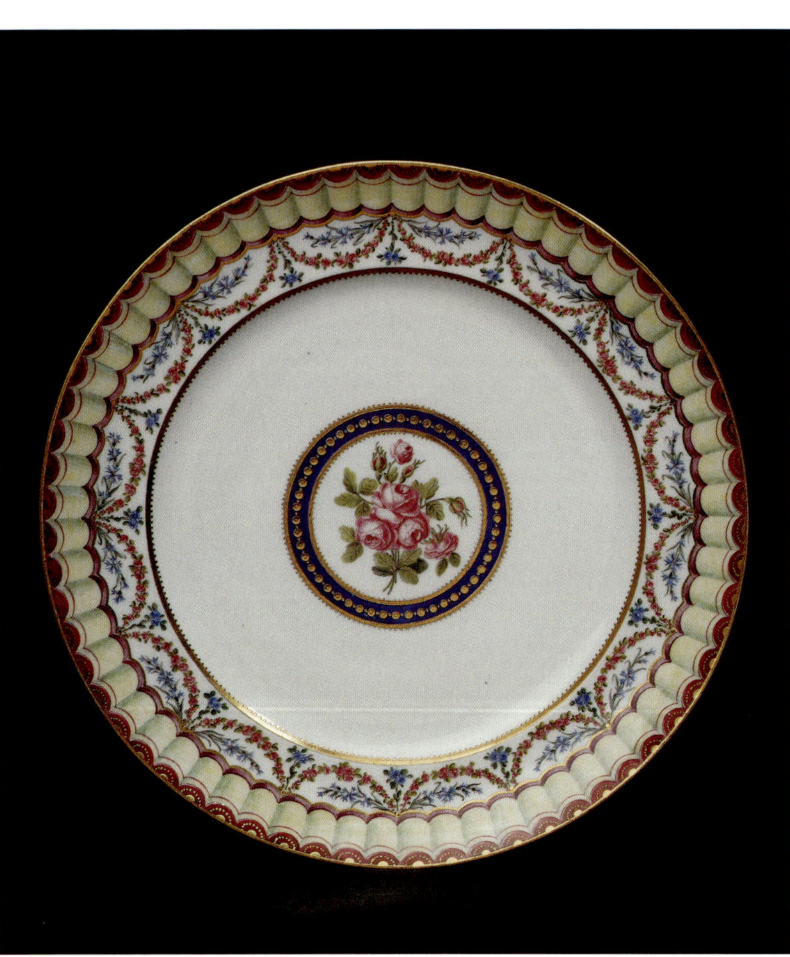

48. *Two Plates (one shown)*
SÈVRES FACTORY

1792; France
Soft-paste porcelain
9⅝ in. diam (24.29 cm)
Private collection

These soft-paste porcelain plates are part of a group of six from the same collection, all of which differ one from another in the colors and arrangement of the decoration, as well as in the quality of their manufacture. Both plates have numerous black specks and pinholes, suggesting either that the factory was experiencing production difficulties or perhaps was using up defective stock because shortages of raw materials and fuel prevented the making and firing of new pieces during the critical years of the French Revolution. In any case, such defects are fairly typical for the Revolutionary period. Nevertheless, the pink roses in the center of both plates are exceptionally well executed, notably on the plate painted by Jacques-François Louis de Laroche, a painter of flowers, ground colors, and patterns.[1] Guillaume Noël, who used the zodiacal sign of Libra as his mark, also painted flowers and patterns.[2] Both plates were gilded by Henri-Martin Prévost. All three men were experienced ceramics workers by 1792.

Floral designs for plates in a naturalistic and simple style consisting of small bouquets in the central well and swags or wreaths on the border were popular at all the French factories, especially those operating in Paris, toward the end of the eighteenth century. They have a freshness that appeals today, and there is no doubt that they were popular with British buyers both when they were made and in the mid-nineteenth century.[3]

The total of 120 plates purchased by "Milord Betford," as Beckford is designated in the Sèvres sales registers, cost the considerable sum, even accounting for galloping inflation at this time, of 4278 *livres*. Those Beckford purchased directly in March 1792 were priced at 33 *livres* each. Those bought for him in November that same year through the dealer Madame Lefebure cost 39 *livres*, the price that is marked on the watercolor drawing in the album still surviving at the factory which gives the name of the design.[4] It is possible that Beckford visited the factory and chose the pattern himself, since seventy-eight white plates were given to the factory's painters on January 10, 1792, to be painted with this pattern.[5] What he intended to do with this large quantity of plates is not entirely clear, since he was not apparently in the habit of entertaining. It is possible that they were used merely for display.[6]

The subsequent history of the plates is unclear. Although sixty "fine old Seve plates" were sold in several lots at Fonthill Abbey on September 9, 1823, neither of these two plates can be securely identified with the lots. It is not known whether they were included in the majority of the Beckford estate that went to Hamilton Palace in 1844, as no record of them in any of the surviving documents has yet been found. The first appearance of any from the set seems to be in the sale at Croxteth Hall, Liverpool, property of the late Earl of Sefton, when twelve were sold, and the catalogue fortunately included an illustration.[7] Seventeen additional plates from what was presumably a different source were sold in London in June 1980 as having belonged to Christian Dior. Further research remains to be done on the history of these plates after they left Beckford's possession, but their history may well never be fully established, or may come to light by chance. —A. D.

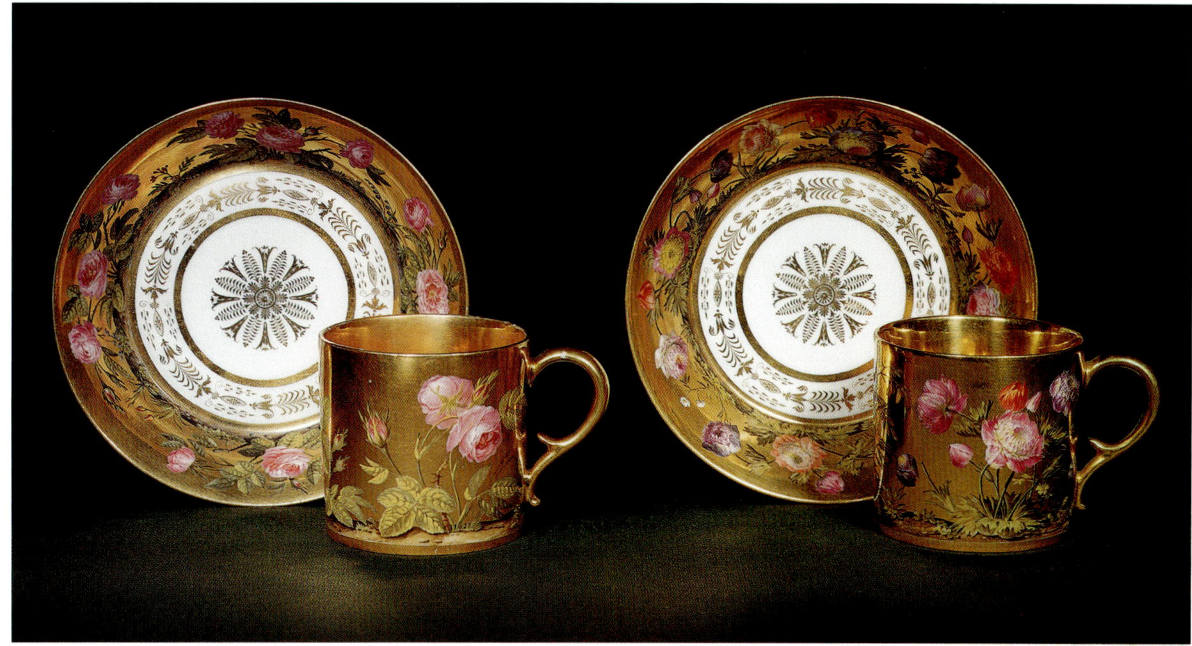

These two cups and saucers, from a group of four in the same collection, gilded on both exterior and interior surfaces and finely painted with naturalistic flowers, are among the most luxurious of all porcelain productions. Only three other examples from this set are known: one painted with marguerites is in the British Museum, London,[1] another painted with tulips in the Musée des Arts Décoratifs, Paris,[2] and a third in a private collection. Perhaps the closest in spirit and technique is a series of Chelsea beakers painted with flowers on a gold ground dating from the mid-1760s,[3] evidently intended as cabinet pieces, as were these examples. The Derby factory also sold cups with flowers on a gold ground in the 1790s.[4] As gilding is fired at a lower temperature than enamel colors, the gold ground on all the above pieces is likely to have been applied after the various firings needed for the flowers.

On the base of each cup and saucer is the highly unusual combination of the manufacturer's name and the Beckford armorial devices of heron and oak painted in freehand in gold within an oval.[5] It has been suggested that Beckford may have commissioned a set of twelve, even though the marks on surviving pieces differ.[6] The example in the Musée des Art Décoratifs is marked

with the manufacturer's name in red. The cup in this exhibition painted with full-blown roses and buds bears the factory mark stenciled in gray and the crests in gold. No explanation has been found for these variations in the marks of such clearly related pieces, but the hypothesis that the gilt device was added at Beckford's wish and that the firing of the gilding affected the factory mark is plausible. The addition of Beckford's devices is testament not only to his obsession with his lineage, but also to his reputation as a well-informed patron and connoisseur of immense wealth who, when in Paris, played an extremely active role in the commissioning of luxury works of art. Although initials are often seen on French porcelain of the late eighteenth and early nineteenth centuries, it is extremely unusual to find such armorial devices as these.

The flower painting on the cups and saucers is exquisitely executed. Although it was only in rather exceptional cases that the factory's painters signed their work, the caliber of those whose names we know, such as Etienne-Charles Le Guay, his wife Marie-Victoire Jacquotot, Piat-Joseph Sauvage, Martin Drölling, and Jacques-François Swebach as well as a member of the van Spaendonck family, demonstrates that the factory prided itself

on its painted decoration and was prepared to employ the leading painters.[7] On these cups the tulips, lily-of-the-valley, daisies, violas, bluebells, and pink roses and rosebuds shown on a naturalistic ground of soil, even if copied from models supplied by leading artists, are of excellent quality.[8] It is in tune with a West European taste for flower painting on porcelain during the early decades of the nineteenth century. Precisely painted gilt motifs in the classical style on the underside of the rim of the saucer also suggest a date in the early nineteenth century. It seems most likely that if the cups were purchased by Beckford in Paris, then it would have been at the time of his visit in 1814.[9]

Few records survive for the factory established by Christophe Dihl, Antoine Guérhard, and Guérhard's wife, Louise-Françoise Croizé, in 1781 in the rue de Bondy, Paris, but what survives can no doubt yield yet more information than has already been discovered.[10] No record of the production of gold-ground cups is known, nor of any order or payment by Beckford. The firm was commercially successful in the early nineteenth century, despite its fundamentally unsound finances and dependence on loans for survival, and it had long been viewed as second only to the Sèvres factory. It

operated at the top end of the market and had many distinguished clients over a period of several decades, including Benjamin Franklin, Gouverneur Morris, and George Washington.[11] All this would have exerted a natural attraction on Beckford, who may well have known of its products through their sale on the London market.[12]

The China Closet at Fonthill Abbey was described by Rutter as containing "Two French cabinet CUPS and SAUCERS, gold-ground, antique borders, painted with flowers by Van Spandonck, in a style of peculiar excellence," which, in all likelihood, refer to two of this set.[13] Eight of these cups and saucers were offered in four lots in the canceled sale of Beckford's collection at Fonthill Abbey in 1822.[14] The exceptional nature of these pieces has ensured their survival as prize examples of the high quality achieved by Paris porcelain makers. —A. D.

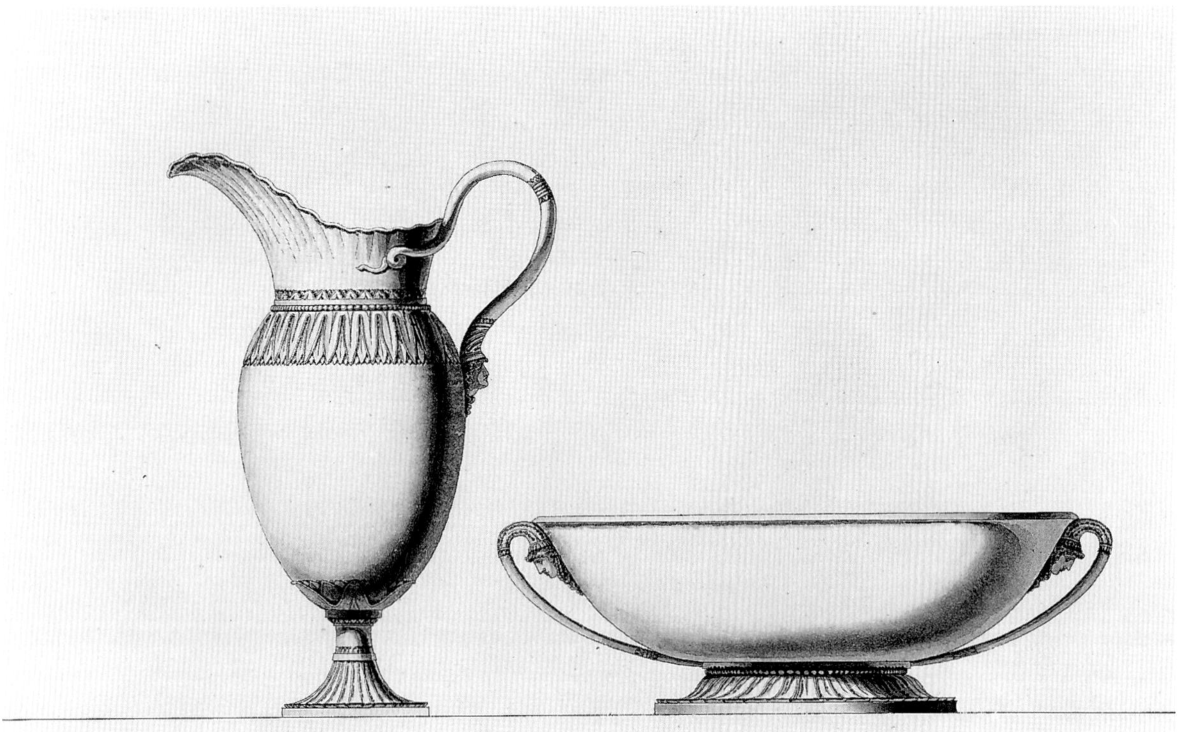

This design for a ewer and basin by Jean-Guillaume Moitte is similar to the designs by Moitte for a series of ewers and basins made by Henri Auguste for William Beckford (see cat. no. 51).[1] Moitte was born in Paris, the son of Pierre-Etienne Moitte, a Royal Academician and professional engraver.[2] In 1761 he entered the atelier of the highly influential sculptor and teacher, Jean-Baptiste Pigalle, who was a friend of his father. After three years, he transferred to the more centrally located studio of Jean-Baptiste Lemoyne, the favorite sculptor of Louis XV, and completed his apprenticeship there. Moitte's talent was evident at an early stage,[3] and by the 1780s, he had received various important commissions. For example, he was engaged by Claude-Nicolas Ledoux to sculpt the decoration for Parisian toll *barrières* that were built around Paris between 1785 and 1789 to raise revenue for the government.[4] Moitte's crowning achievement from the Revolutionary period, the pediment relief sculpture for the Panthéon, was pulled down at the order of Napoléon. Moitte was adaptable enough, however, to set aside his Republican beliefs and work on projects for the new regime. In the funeral oration for Moitte in 1810, Quatremère de Quincy already lamented the lack of surviving sculptural work by the artist.[5] At the same time, however, Quatremère drew attention to Moitte's achievement as a draftsman, in particular to the way in which his drawings were inspired by the antique.[6]

Perhaps the most significant period of Moitte's training was the time he spent in Rome as a *pensioner* at the Académie de France à Rome.[7] His sketches reveal that he studied ancient vases, urns, sarcophagi, and sculptures, paying particular attention to ornamental details and imperial Roman reliefs, including the frieze on Trajan's Column.[8] His observation of physical evidence as well as his consultation of various published sources on the art of antiquity greatly inspired Moitte in his work when he returned to France.[9]

This drawing of a ewer and basin was among the drawings of the Maison Odiot collection which came on the market in 1979.[10] Although none of the Odiot collection drawings are signed and dated, this one was probably executed some time between 1787 and 1795.[11] It is likely that Moitte and his assistants supplied Auguste with countless versions and variations of classical designs for ewers, basins, tazze, candelabra, as well as furniture mounts and furniture during this period, some of which might have been designed with particular clients in mind while others could be customized at a later date if necessary.

Moitte's use of a pronounced ink and wash technique to create strong highlights and shadows in his drawings may well have been inspired by Piranesi's engravings, which served as a major influence on the students of the Académie in Rome.[12] This drawing stands out from the many designs for metalwork that he produced, however, because of the particularly simple nature of the design and the restrained decoration of the pieces. The ewer is decorated with a simple leaf pattern around the top and is in the shape of a Greek jug or oinochoe, with a broad Renaissance-style lip. The basin is completely plain apart from the masks on the handles and the gadrooned foot.

Other designs by Moitte are for more elaborate ewers and basins. One design, for example, features a slim-necked ewer which is richly decorated with various foliated bands and an embossed figure of Lucretia sitting beside a pillar supporting a burning lamp.[13] In another design for a ewer and basin, the ewer is decorated with a winged dancing girl carrying a wreath.[14]

In his drawings for metalwork, Moitte displayed his love of simple classical forms. He often transformed the painted designs he saw on antique originals into decoration for metalwork and used Roman architectural ornament to decorate his designs. His tendency to employ architectural detail would certainly have been something Beckford admired, since Beckford attempted this in his own designs. Later on, Moitte produced more elaborate designs for Auguste, who by this time was one of the most important goldsmiths working for the new Emperor. Designs such as this one, however, show that in the 1780s and 1790s, Moitte preferred using linear classical forms and carefully restrained decoration. —E. T.

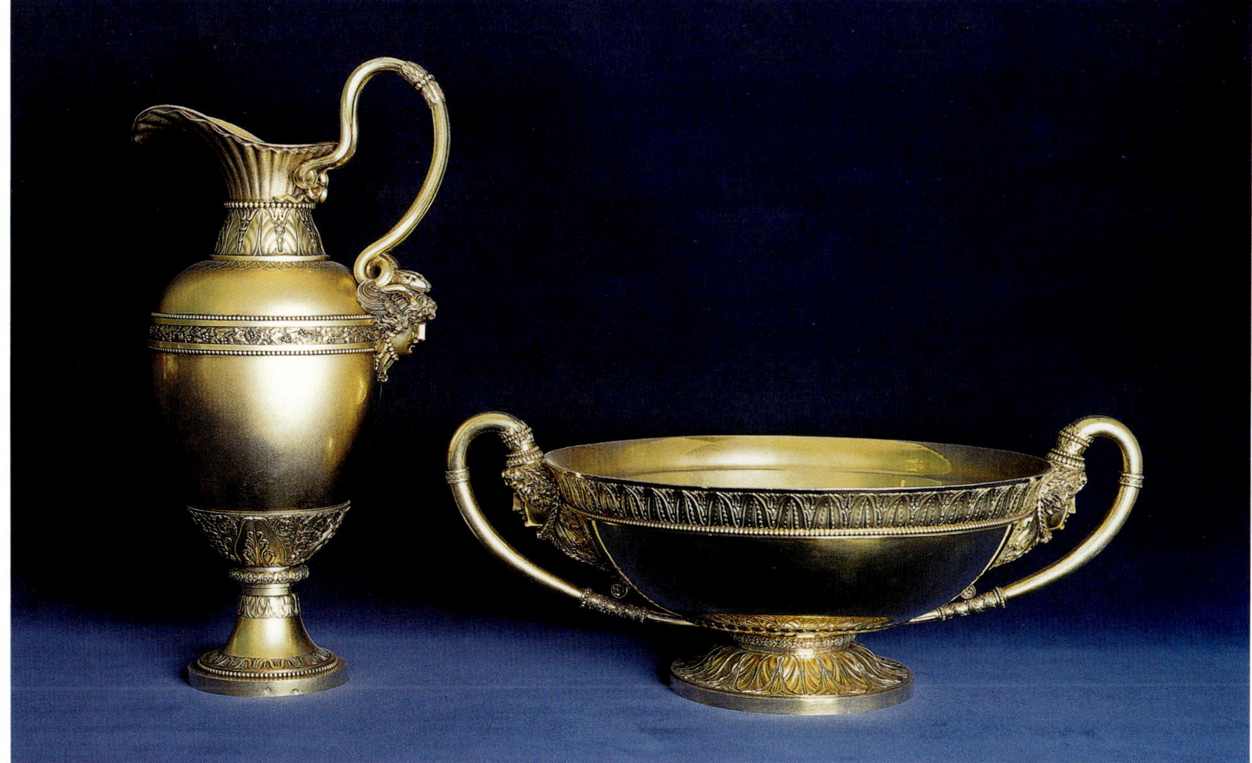

This ewer and basin and its companion set (now in the Gilbert Collection, London)[1] represent the epitome of the massive yet elegant classicism of late eighteenth-century silver made in Paris. Grandees from all over Europe appreciated the clean lines and superlative quality of Parisian silver, and in England both the Prince Regent and his brother the Duke of Cumberland, despite the highly charged political situation between their nation and France, were enthusiastic patrons of the best Paris silver of this period. It is a body of work that relies on line for effect, with richly burnished surfaces providing a strong contrast to the relief decoration. The elegant appearance of this ewer and basin gives little clue to their combined weight, which totals over 259 ounces (8054 grams). Even Beckford's love of heraldry was not allowed to interfere with the cool simplicity of these pieces—the Beckford and Hamilton crests are engraved discreetly under the bases.

Ewers and basins were used in earlier times for pouring rosewater over diners' hands, and they survived into the eighteenth century essentially as display pieces. The two sets must have fitted in well with the grand interiors of Fonthill Splendens, together with Beckford's other Auguste pieces and the London-made neoclassical silver, such as the gilt baskets from Storr (cat. no. 26). After the building of the Abbey, however, the ewers and basins were arranged with an eclectic mixture of objects in the Oak Parlour. Rutter describes the arrangement: "In the center of the east end is a pile of massy decorative gilt plate of various styles and ages. Amongst these magnificent articles are, two salvers with the initials of William and Mary; two ewers by Moiette [*sic*] and Auguste; two tazzas by the same artists; an ancient dish and cover in the Moorish taste, made at Granada; a pair of silver candlesticks designed by Mr. Beckford; an engraved silver cup by Wighels, date 1624. . . ."[2]

The fact that Rutter identified them as by Auguste and Moitte is significant. Beckford had first visited Henri Auguste's shop in the Place du Carrousel in 1788, beginning a relationship with the royal goldsmith that, even for Beckford, who was known for his irascibility to tradesmen, was tempestuous. Auguste supplied Beckford with furniture,[3] as well as a number of magnificent silver-gilt objects, a gold ewer, similar in outline to this ewer, and a pair of gold tazze.[4] Beckford's epithet for Auguste, "slippery eel," was well-deserved. In 1797, Beckford advised his agent in Paris, Nicholas Williams, that "you cannot pursue the shiny reptile . . . with too much caution and perseverance."[5] Auguste's unreliability and unorthodox business operations, as well as "his dissipations," as one contemporary added, would ultimately lead to his bankruptcy and flight from judicial proceedings in 1806.[6]

Beckford clearly regarded the sculptor Jean-Guillaume Moitte, the designer of these objects, as important as the supplier, and, unusually for the period, Moitte's name has been linked with these objects since the early nineteenth century. Beckford was one of the first patrons to respond to the lure of what has come to be known as "brand names." In both the 1822 and 1823 Fonthill Abbey catalogues (the 1823 Phillips version repeats the earlier description verbatim), the ewers are described as "noble and elegant . . . in the manner of the antique, by Moiette [*sic*] and Auguste; executed with a truth and feeling unexampled" and the tazze as being "after the antique, by the celebrated French sculptor Moiette and executed by H. Auguste (Paris, 1802) in a style of superior excellence."[7] The descriptions read as if dictated by the owner.

The early date of this ewer and basin is significant. Well before the turn of the nineteenth century, in the late 1780s, it is clear that Moitte and Auguste were collaborating on severely neoclassical works in a style that would later become known, erroneously, as "Empire." Just as importantly, they reveal what must be the earliest manifestation of Beckford's passion for the avant garde.

Exactly when Beckford first saw this ewer and basin is, however, open to conjecture. From their hallmarks, the components must have been submitted for marking sometime in 1787 or 1788.[8] According to the inscription, however, they were not delivered to Beckford until shortly after April 14, 1802. It has usually been conjectured that they, and their companion ewer and basin, which bear the tax agent Kalandrin's last marks, introduced in 1789, form part of an unidentified, canceled commission that Auguste sold to Beckford in 1802.

The story, however, is even more complex. The Gilbert set may well have been started as late as 1796. It has been suggested that "the system for hallmarking did not disappear with the demise of the monarchy [1792]."[9] While there were no new guild marks introduced between 1789 and 1796,[10] given the large number of surviving silver and gold objects struck with the last pre-revolutionary warden's mark, it is likely that hallmarking continued, perhaps spasmodically, in Paris for some years after 1789, but the warden's mark dated 1789 continued to be used.[11]

Among the Moitte drawings that have survived there are similar ewers and basins, but few provide a clue to the exact date of their execution. The largest group of drawings was acquired from Auguste's holdings after his bankruptcy, by his rival Jean-Baptiste-Claude Odiot,[12] and includes a ewer and basin similar in form to these examples. None of the Odiot group is dated, however, but a related drawing of silverware, sold in the auction of Moitte's own effects after his death, is in the Ecole des Beaux Arts, Paris.[13] It includes a basin virtually identical to the present example, and a ewer of the same outline, with identical spout and handle. It is signed and dated "l'an trois" (September 22, 1794–September 22, 1795). Another drawing of a ewer identical in form to the Beckford examples has a relief figure identified by Richard Campbell as Lucretia.[14]

Given Beckford's propensity for pairs and symmetry, it may be that he was shown the present ewer and basin in their unfinished state by Auguste sometime during one of his Paris stays in the early 1790s prior to his departure in 1793. He may have ordered a further pair, but only received the two sets from the silversmith on his return to Paris early in the following decade. Beckford's gold ewer of similar form was supplied by Auguste in 1791 according to its inscription and this date may provide a clue in dating Beckford's order for the two sets.[15] Auguste's ultimate tardiness in delivering the commission may well have been the cause of the dispute with him referred to above in the Beckford–Williams correspondence of 1797.[16] Beckford had similar difficulties over the delivery of a jewel casket that he ordered in April 1793 but did not receive until late in 1801.[17] —C. H.

52. *Casket*
Henri Auguste
(1759–1816)

ca. 1805; France
Silver gilt
8⅜ x 9⁷⁄₁₆ in. (21.3 x 31.4 cm)
The Toledo Museum of Art, Toledo, Ohio. Purchased with funds from the Florence Libbey Bequest in Memory of her Father, Maurice A. Scott (1969.301)

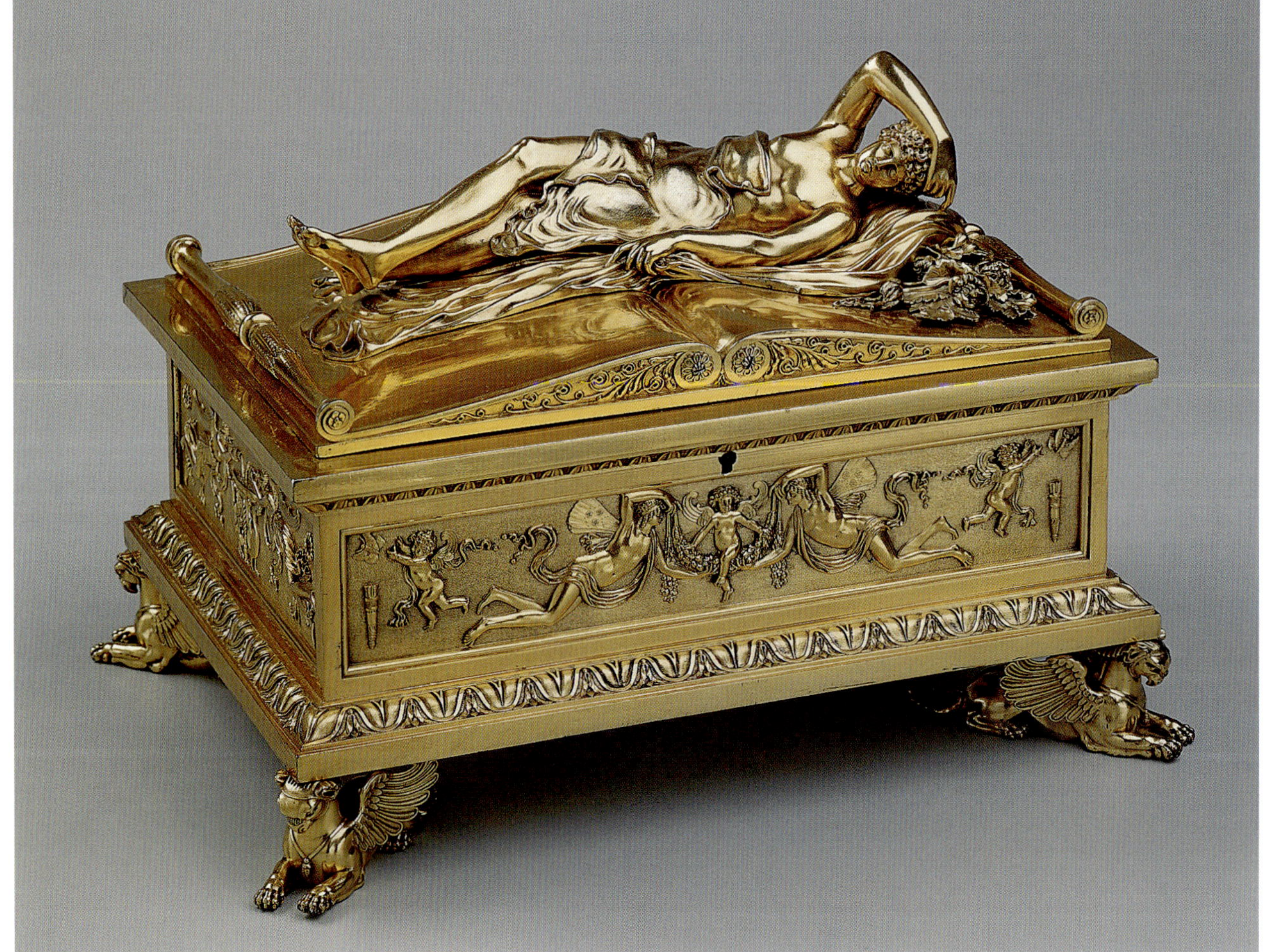

The subject of Morpheus, dreaming in "his lethargic state," was of particular fascination to Beckford, who referred to him as "my favorite subject." "You know my fondness for this drowsy personage. . . . Sleeping figures, with me, always produce the finest illusion . . . I can gaze whole hours upon them, with complacency. But when I see an archer, in the very act of discharging his arrow; a dancer, with one foot in the air; or a gladiator, extending his fist to all eternity; I grow tired. And ask, when will they perform what they are about? When will the bow twang? The foot come to the ground? . . . The wrestlers, for example, . . . filled me with disgust: I cried out, For heaven's sake! Give the throw, and have done."[1] These highly personal musings, a novelty in art criticism, were included in *Dreams, Waking Thoughts, and Incidents,* a series of letters based on Beckford's Grand Tour. In 1783 he completed the text, an evocative account of his restless emotional turmoil. The first lines of the work are "Shall I tell you my dreams?" and Morpheus is constantly invoked. Although he completed the manuscript and prepared it for publication, Beckford decided at the last moment not to release it, and it was not until 1834, after extensive revisions, that the text was

finally published as the first book of *Italy; with Sketches of Spain and Portugal.*

Beckford was a great admirer of Moitte's designs for silver, but whether any of his Moitte pieces were specially commissioned remains uncertain.[2] This box is the most unrestrained of all Beckford's pieces designed by Moitte. The figure on the cover, with its elongated limbs and twisted posture, is unusually large in proportion to the box, and quite unlike Moitte's other vessels, where the figures are rigidly classical and often minor ornamental components of the whole.[3] Some of Moitte's drawings for objects survived in the studio of Auguste's competitor Odiot.[4] Though the design for this box was not among them, the group includes two drawings for somewhat plainer boxes with smaller figures on the cover. For this figure of Morpheus, Moitte may have had a Mannerist source in mind. The arrangement of the limbs bears some resemblance to a drawing by Cellini for the Porte Dorée at Fontainebleau.[5] The frieze on the sides of the Beckford box, representing a pair of zephyrs carrying a putto on a garland, was reused by Auguste several years later. It appears as the central panel on Empress Joséphine's cadenas, part of the famous service of

746 pieces presented by the City of Paris to Napoléon three days after his coronation in 1804.[6] Here, the putti flanking the zephyrs are chasing bees, whereas on Beckford's "Morpheus" casket putti chase, appropriately enough, moths.[7]

When Beckford gave up his Harley Street residence in London, this box was among the pieces sold at auction in 1817. The catalogue included the information, doubtless provided by Beckford, that "this costly piece of art was executed by the celebrated Goldsmith Auguste, from a design of Moitte." The purchaser was the Earl of Yarmouth (later third Marquess of Hertford, 1777–1842), who was acting on behalf of the Prince Regent.[8] Lord Yarmouth had begun to buy pictures and French furniture on his own account around 1800, and between 1810 and 1819 he served as a saleroom agent for the prince, who was in the midst of the long process of outfitting Carlton House. The prince had been amassing a vast array of plate, much of it bought from Rundell, Bridge, and Rundell, who received an order in 1806 amounting to £70,000.[9]

Lady Hertford (1759–1834), in the meantime, was the prince's mistress, an arrangement that lasted until about 1820, by which time she was

in her sixties. She was succeeded by the Marchioness of Conyngham in 1820, when George IV ascended to the crown. The transition was recorded by Countess Lieven, wife of the Russian ambassador, in a letter to Metternich, ambassador to France, "I am going to do a really kind thing this morning. I am going to see the ex-favorite. Her fall from favor is official. She was never very nice to me during her reign: now I am going to revenge myself by being polite."

On November 3, 1820, the king sent the "Morpheus" box to his new mistress.[10] The marchioness was famously interested in enjoying the king's possessions, using his horses and carriages, and wearing the crown sapphires that Cardinal York had given to the king. During the infamous public trial of George IV's wife, Queen Caroline, Lady Conyngham was bitterly attacked: "'Tis pleasant at seasons to see how they sit/first cracking their nuts and then cracking their wit/then quaffing their claret—then mingling their lips/or tickling the fat about each other's hips." —E. M. A.

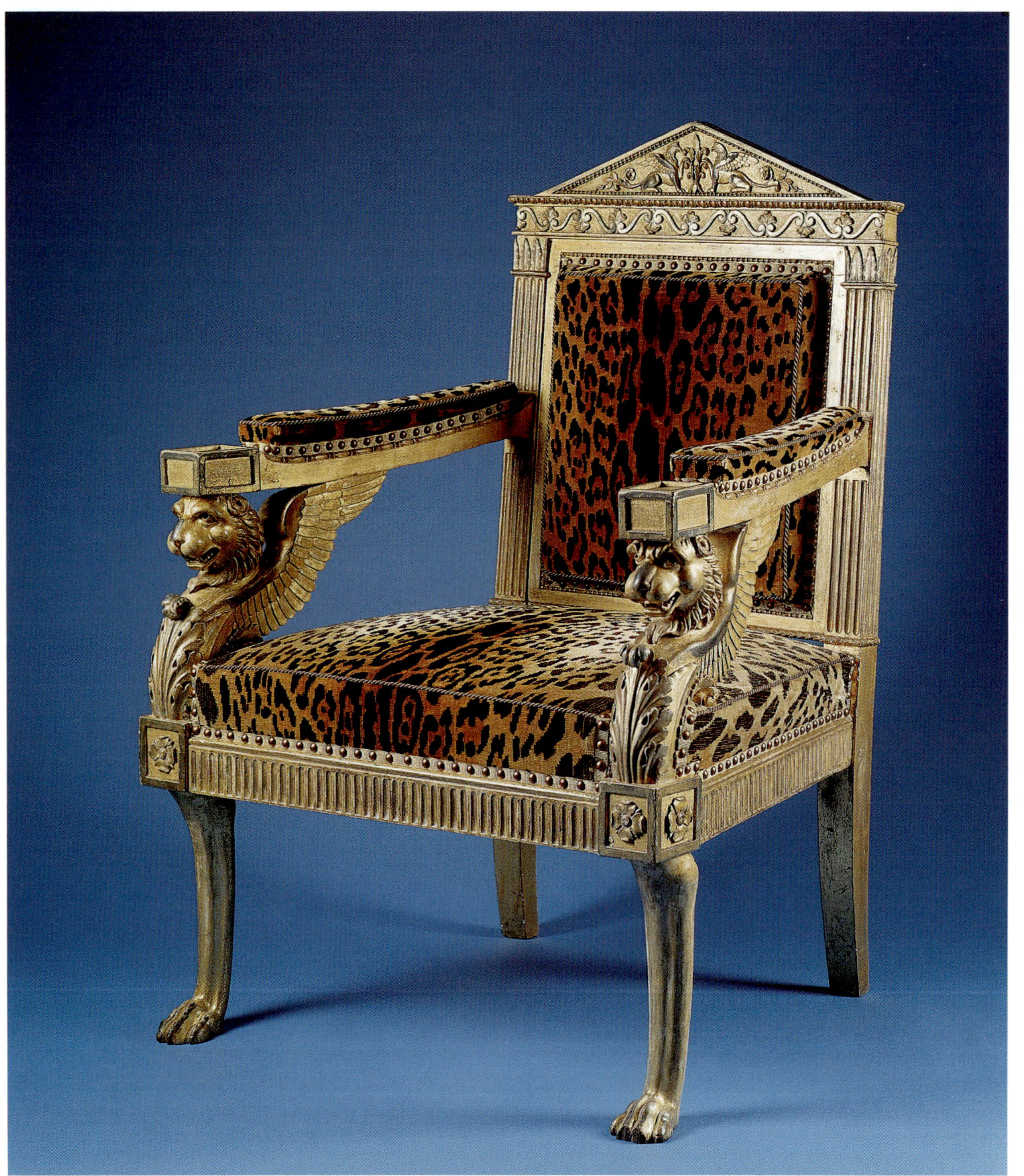

53. *Armchair*
MAKER UNKNOWN

1800–1810; Italy
Gilt wood, modern upholstery
42½ x 27⅞ x 26⅝ in. (108 x 70.3 x
67.8 cm)
Private collection

John Rutter's *Delineations of Fonthill*
included among its illustrations a
view of Beckford's Grand Drawing
Room (see cat. fig. 88A).[1] The picture shows part of a large, unusual
set of seat furniture consisting of a
settee, arm chairs, side chairs, and
stools. This suite of furniture constituted lots 1534 through 1540 of the
Fonthill sale of 1823, and included
sixteen fauteuils or armchairs, six

other chairs without arms, and six
"X stools, or window seats."[2] The
latter are of a common variety, to
judge from the illustrations, and
probably will never be identified
unless evidence of their Fonthill
provenance still accompanies them.[3]
On the contrary, the chairs are of an
unusual model and can be related
only to a limited number of extant
examples.[4] Their salient characteristics are front leg modeled on feline
legs and paws, fluted skirts, and
backs with flanking elements resembling pilasters topped with capitals
supporting pediments.[5] In addition,
the arm rests are supported by lion-
headed winged beasts. It is the rigid,
architecturally inspired backs, how-

ever, that distinguish these pieces
from most European furniture, associating them with a limited group
of chairs presumed to have been
designed and made about 1800 or
shortly thereafter. This group consists of two significant subgroups,
of which the first, like Beckford's
pieces, are crowned with triangular
pediments, while the second has
arched, segmental pediments decorated in the center with wreaths of
laurel and displayed eagles.
    Included in the auction sale of
the contents of the Parisian residence
of Cardinal Fesch, Napoléon's uncle,
were sets of seat furniture described
with both varieties of pediments.[6]
Furthermore, a published design

of 1828 by the Santi brothers is
related to one of these models.[7]
Dionesio Santi is known to have
been employed by Fesch.[8] The symbolism of the wreath and eagle
suggests that at least this variety of
chair was specifically associated with
Napoléon, and, in addition to
Cardinal Fesch, chairs topped with
pediments are known or reputed to
have been owned by persons closely
related to Napoléon.[9] Careful comparison of details of ornament on
chairs of both groups indicate
probable differences of their dates
and/or sites of manufacture.[10]
    In several respects, the Grand
Drawing Room and its furnishings,
as illustrated by Rutter and described
there and in the sale catalogue of
1823, differ from most of the state
apartments at Fonthill Abbey. The
style of its overmantel decoration is
clearly Gothic, but otherwise the
room is not of medieval inspiration,
and much of its contents were of
recent vintage, notably the seat furniture, as well as the marble-topped
table (see cat. no. 88), said to have
come from the Empress Joséphine's
residence at Malmaison, and the
large carpet, described as having
been made in 1814 at the Savonnerie
Factory for the imperial château
de St. Cloud near Paris and now in
the collection of the National Trust,
Kingston Lacey, Dorset. Unlike most
of the major interiors at Fonthill,
the Grand Drawing Room does not
include heraldic symbols related to
Beckford and his family among its
ornamentation. The furnishings are
chiefly French, several of them associated by date and provenance with
Napoléon. He had been defeated in
1815 and died in 1821. He was still
almost universally despised in
Britain in the 1820s, although among
his supporters was Beckford's son-in-
law, the Duke of Hamilton. It seems
possible that Beckford may have
intended the furnishings of the
Grand Drawing Room as a tribute
to Napoléon and as a suggestion of
his own relationship to the emperor
through the admiration in which
Napoléon was held by the Duke of
Hamilton.
—H. H.

An Eye to the East

The arts of the Orient, ranging from those of Turkey to those of Japan, were strongly represented in Beckford's collection, befitting the author of the acclaimed Orientalist novel *Vathek*. Beckford, who never traveled further east than Venice, was first introduced to the Orient by the painter Alexander Cozens. He was undoubtedly further stimulated in his romantic fascination for the fabled lands of Persia and the legendary East through his long sojourns in Lisbon, the center of the extended Portuguese colonial empire. In his pursuit of what is now known to be Indo-Portuguese carved ebony furniture, Beckford followed in the footsteps of antiquarian collectors such as Horace Walpole. One such casket-on-stand appears in his deathbed portrait (see cat no. 150). Beckford owned other caskets and cabinets, made of ivory, mother-of-pearl, and hardwoods, such as ebony, rosewood, and teak, and he particularly appreciated the skillful techniques and delicate mastery of exotic material revealed by these pieces.

Beckford owned pieces that were carved or inlaid with Islamic-inspired geometric, floral, or arabesque motifs, or with mythological themes from the cultures of the Indian subcontinent and Southeast Asia. Hardstones—principally quartz, jade, and rock crystal—were carved as bowls and lidded boxes. Some were mounted with gold and gemstones in a style and technique that makes them immediately identifiable as Mughal.

In terms of numbers, Chinese and Japanese ceramics formed the largest part of the collection, comprising ornamental vases and covers, as well as a substantial number of tea wares which were likely to have been used by Beckford on a daily basis. The ceramics ranged from Yixing stoneware to elegant monochrome and highly decorative polychrome enamels of the eighteenth and nineteenth centuries. Following a historic tradition in Europe of mounting precious and exotic materials in gold or silver gilt, Beckford commissioned a few highly significant examples of such mounted porcelains.

Much of Beckford's metalwork is described as Oriental or Persian, but many of these items were probably Venetian-Saracenic, decorated with Islamic-inspired strapwork and interlaced ornament. Beckford also owned Chinese silver and bronzes as well as carved Chinese and Coromandel lacquer. The leading connoisseur of Japanese lacquer of his time, Beckford amassed an extensive collection, including many of the very finest wares that had been produced for the export market in the seventeenth century.

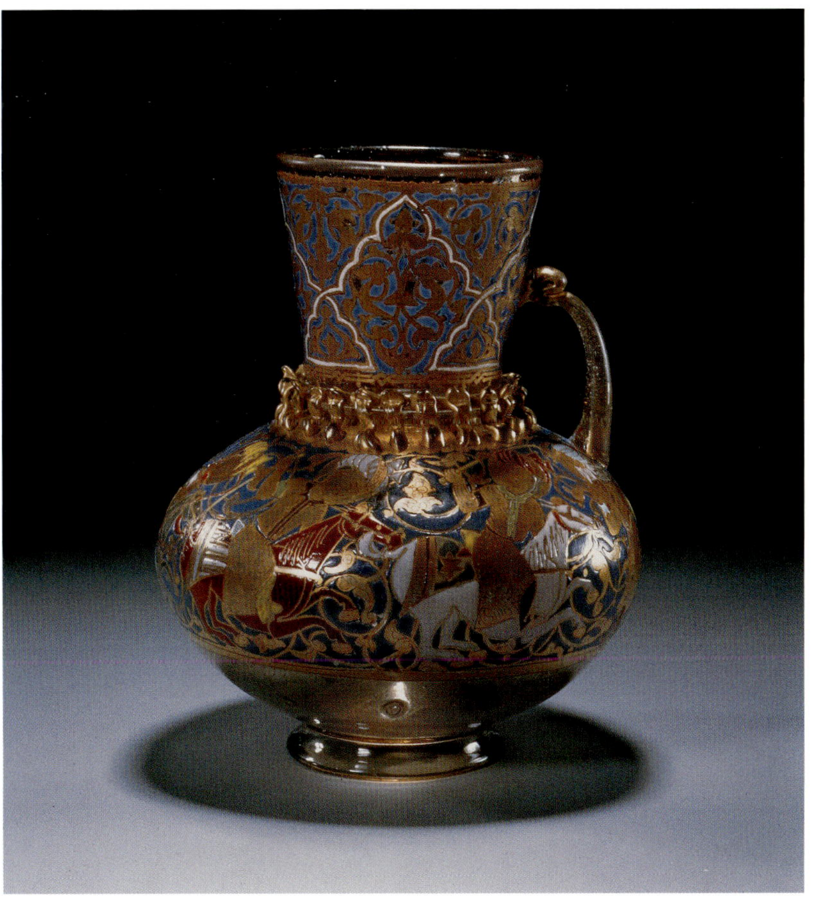

54. *Ewer*
Maker unknown

Second half of the 13th century;
probably Syria
Glass, enamel, gilding
7¼ in. (18.4 cm)
Private collection

This ewer is one of the most remarkable extant examples of a group of glass objects decorated with enamels and gilding that were produced in the Syrian and Egyptian regions from the late twelfth through the fifteenth centuries. Its near-perfect condition, unusual shape for a glass vessel, and flawless application of enamels create a dynamic and lively composition of six polo players against a lapis blue background filled with gold scrolls and make this ewer a unique work of Islamic art.

The technique used is difficult and time-consuming. The temperature in the kiln must be controlled carefully during the firing of enamels and gold so that there is no distortion of the glass vessel. This enameling technique had its golden age during the thirteenth and early fourteenth centuries and was successfully emulated by glassmakers in

Venice and Barcelona during the Renaissance, although they never achieved the same lavish refinement as their Near Eastern counterparts. Islamic enameled and gilded glass was later imitated in France, Austria, and Venice, not only as part of the discovery of Islamic art in the Orientalist fashion, but also as a fascinating technical challenge, during the second half of the nineteenth century.[1]

It is not known how Beckford acquired this ewer, which was first depicted in Willes Maddox's painting *Objects of Vertu* of 1844.[2] It is a matter of speculation whether the ewer traveled from Fonthill Abbey to Lansdown Tower or was added to Beckford's collection after 1822, the year he moved to Bath. In the Maddox painting (see cat. no. 157), it can be clearly identified in the group of nine objects, among which are two Chinese porcelains and the remainder of European manufacture.

In the context of this lifelong commitment to Orientalism, it can be suggested that Beckford acquired this ewer at an early stage of his life, making him a precursor to those scholars and collectors who admired Islamic glass in the nineteenth century. Enameled and gilded glass has long been appreciated in Europe. A bottle and vase, for example, had found their way into the *Wunderkammer* of Rudolf IV of Austria. Supposedly, the two vessels contained earth stained with the blood of the Innocents; they were bequeathed to the treasury of the Cathedral of Saint Stephen in Vienna in 1365.[3] A number of other vessels were turned into reliquaries and entered church treasuries or were later acquired by major museums.[4] During Beckford's lifetime, the only object of this type known to have been acquired before this ewer is a celebrated bottle depicting horsemen (now in The Metropolitan Museum of Art, New York), which was given by the vice-consul Champion to Francis I, the Hapsburg emperor shortly after 1825.[5] The so-called Cavour Vase, this unique dark blue glass vessel, documented for the first time in 1861, was apparently brought from the Holy Land and acquired by Camillo Benso, Count of Cavour, and, through his son-in-law, entered the collection of the king of Italy. Like the Mughal water pipe in Beckford's collection (cat. no. 55), a silver-gilt mount, a sort of cage for protection and display, was created for the Cavour Vase.[6]

It is unlikely, however, that Beckford was aware of his ewer's origin, and he most likely appreciated it simply as one of his innumerable European objets d'art. In the "Inventory after Death" by English & Sons of 1844, the ewer is described as "a Rare Venetian Glass Jug with various Figures, Horses and foliage richly enamelled."[7] Venice was indeed the putative origin of the majority of splendidly decorated glass objects at the time. Beckford was known for his own predilection for provenance and had he known of the Islamic origin of this piece, he would have most likely left a record of it. A few years later, provided it is one and the same vessel, it became "a Babylonian Vase," at least suggesting its "oriental" provenance.[8] It was only in Christie's Hamilton Palace sale of 1882 that the ewer was given an "oriental" attribution, and Schmoranz, Migeon, and Lamm included it later in their publications on Islamic art.[9]

Whether or not Beckford knew that the ewer was one of the rarest and most significant creations of the thirteenth-century Syrian glassmakers and glass painters,[10] it took pride of place in his collection. Its subsequent history of ownership, from the dukes of Hamilton to the barons de Rothschild, only confirms that it is an ideal object for the discerning connoisseur. —S. C.

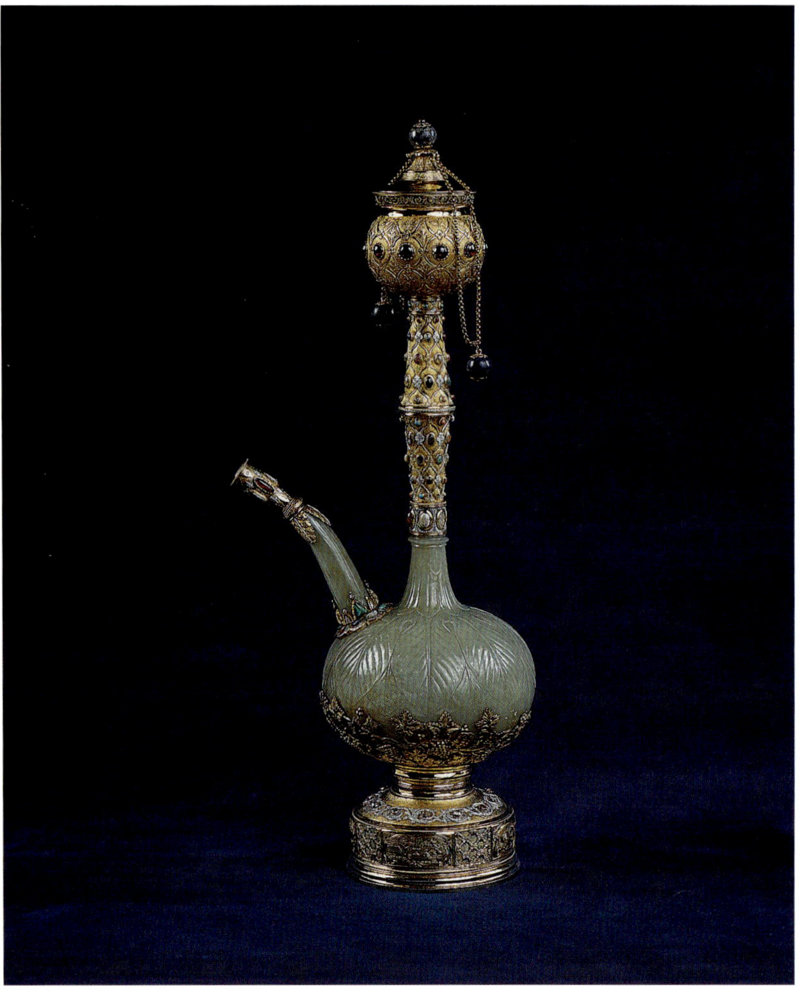

The silver-gilt circular base of this remarkable water pipe is fitted with rectangular panels of open trelliswork and rococo bas-relief panels, which appear to be "pulls" from mid-eighteenth-century European snuffboxes. The silver-gilt vine leaves around the base of the bowl closely resemble examples of work by Paul Storr. The silver-gilt elements are the work of James Aldridge and were made for William Beckford, probably to designs supplied by Beckford and Gregorio Franchi. The mounts may date from the period when Aldridge was producing similar works of art for Beckford, and the jade spout would have been added at this time.

The design of the stem suggests that the source may well have been Persian or Turkish dagger sheaths.[1] The use of platinum is unusual; unlike silver it does not tarnish and would have provided a permanent contrast to the silver gilt and gems. Included among the richly varied selection of gems are lapis lazuli, opal, turquoise, and bloodstone. The silver-gilt globular finial, which held the tobacco or opium, is set with a ring of what appear to be cabochon garnets or spinels, mounted on a different, but equally elaborate ground chased with florettes and quatrefoils. From the lapis-lazuli bead finial of the cover hang chains that end in further lapis-lazuli beads secured by silver-gilt Hamilton cinquefoils.

The tobacco pipe, sometimes interpreted as an opium device, is undoubtedly the ultimate Oriental fantasy object. This work is a particularly intriguing example of early Orientalizing taste. Here, an authentic Mughal carved nephrite ewer or water vase was remounted as a water pipe bowl with a mount devised for it in "Indian style." The style of carving has parallels in eighteenth-century Mughal and Deccani jades,[2] and the piriform shape with spout emanating from the side is common for metal water vases and ewers from the sixteenth century onward.[3]

Mughal water pipes were generally made of base metals, bidri, and glass. In addition to the standard globular and bell-shaped types that evolved from the seventeenth century onward, objects were sometimes adapted to create water-pipe bowls. Visual representations record water pipes of precious metals which are endowed with bowls of porcelain or coconut shell.[4] The rare extant jade water pipes are considered to be the most lavish examples of this production and are thought to have been made under royal patronage. The discovery of this work increases the number of extant jade water pipes of the period to six.[5] Two nephrite hookah bowls enameled with a trellis pattern and precious stones and set in elaborate French gilt and patinated bronze mounts, in the collection of the British Museum, have often been considered to be Beckford's, but are now known to have been acquired by Alexander, Marquess of Douglas, Beckford's son-in-law, himself a renowned collector.[6]

The 1823 sale catalogue of Fonthill Abbey gives the provenance of this piece as the collection of Tipu Sultan (r. 1767–99), the ruler of Mysore and Britain's principal adversary in India. Tipu Sultan, or Tippoo Sahib as he is known, acquired legendary status as the symbol of the last resistance to the British domination of India in the eighteenth century. His final defeat at the hands of Lord Arthur Wellesley, the future Duke of Wellington, at the battle of Seringapatam in 1799 and his subsequent suicide were celebrated in Britain with great pomp and ceremony. In what can only be described as a "Tipu Sultan" craze, plays and poetry celebrating the British victory were produced. Tipu Sultan's armor and regalia were exhibited at Carlton House and a life-size wooden figure of a tiger mauling a British soldier belonging to the defeated ruler was displayed in public to the amazed horror and delight of British audiences.[7] The impact of the defeat of Tipu Sultan was also felt in cultural terms since the ruler's immense treasures were divided among the victors. Ornaments from the golden jeweled throne, principally a hoopoe bird and tiger's head with rock-crystal tongue; as well as armor and costumes, were presented as gifts to the Prince Regent, later George IV, and are held today in the Royal Collection. The political significance of these relics was underscored by the display of the hoopoe at state banquets during the reign of William IV (1830–37).[8] Beckford would have been fully aware of these highly publicized events surrounding the British victory. His fascination with the Orient began in childhood with the discovery of the translations of the *Arabian Nights Entertainments,* on which his own novel *Vathek,* published in 1786, was modeled; it also borrowed freely from Herbelot's *Bibliothèque Orientale.*[9] Beckford was later to create a Turkish style room at Fonthill Splendens.[10]

Among other collectors, Robert Clive, first Baron Clive of Plassey, commonly known as "Clive of India," and his wife, formed perhaps the finest collection, much of which

still survives at Powis Castle. Significant numbers of army officers obtained relics of the siege at Seringapatam, such as daggers and small tiger's heads from Tipu's throne, which eventually came to enrich both royal and private collections in Britain.[11] Beckford purchased an important collection of Persian and Indian manuscripts from Tipu Sultan's library from Colonel Anthoine Polier, a Swiss architect and engineer to the court of Oudh in Northern India, and it is tempting to speculate that Beckford purchased other works of art from him.[12]

Beckford must have found the provenance of this work enticing. The sale catalogue of 1823 describes it as a "unique and princely object of luxury."[13] Stylistically, the nephrite bowl may be dated to the eighteenth century, but its royal provenance is more difficult to prove since the great majority of regalia, carpets, and costumes produced for Tipu's court were decorated with tiger stripes, the ruler's instantly recognizable emblem. The piece appears somewhat extravagant when compared with the refined classical jades Beckford acquired, such as the imperial lidded bowl (see cat. no. 57). The elegant decoration of stylized leaves, carved in the monochromatic celadon-colored nephrite, is framed by the richly worked mounts supplied by Aldridge. The intricate nature of the metalwork is enhanced by the subtle contrasts provided by the mounts, which are punctuated through the use of colored stones. The ambitious and cohesive design of the metalwork, however, would most likely not have been determined by Aldridge, but rather supplied by Beckford working in tandem with Franchi. The composite approach to the completion of this type of work was typical of the Orientalist approach by Europeans to non-Western art and reflected the "cultural colonialism" that characterized the period.

Beckford also believed strongly that the appropriate setting greatly enhanced the beauty of his artworks. The hookah was prominently displayed on a table of Egyptian marble (cat. no. 88) in the center of the

Grand Drawing Room at Fonthill Abbey (see cat. fig. 88A). In the history of collecting viewed through the lens of his Mughal holdings, Beckford was both prescient and a man of his time. In the case of the lidded bowl (see cat. no. 57) he may be compared to the greatest collectors such as the Mughal Emperors Jahangir (1569–1627) and Shah Jahan (1627–1658) or Rudolph II of Prague (1552–1612). In the case of the hookah, Beckford was following fashion trends rather than setting them. Given the prominent place given to the hookah in his collection, Beckford himself does not seem to have been aware of these distinctions. —L. S. D.

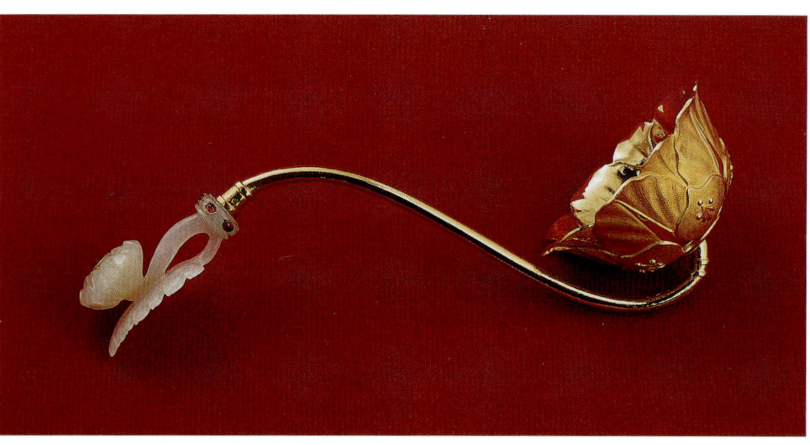

56. *Ladle*
Paul Storr (1771–1844)

Mounts, 1815–16, England;
nephrite (date unknown), India
Gold, nephrite, rubies
5⅛ in. (13 cm)
Beckford Collection, Brodick
Castle, National Trust for Scotland
(58.315)

As with Beckford's mounted hard-stone bowls, this ladle is made up from earlier components with the addition of inventive contemporary mounts, no doubt designed by Beckford and Franchi. The design of the carved jade finial is repeated in the gold bowl, which is in the classic form of a lotus flower, its exterior augmented with the Hamilton ermine. The jade finial is mounted with rubies reminiscent of those mounted on a cup and cover from Beckford's collection.[1] Although Indian in inspiration, the mounts are probably the work of John Cuttel, a lapidary and jeweler mentioned in Franchi's accounts, in which there are sketches of work for which he was paid in 1817.[2] These accounts also list amounts paid for "the workmanship on a cornelian spoon" and it is possible that Cuttel was respon-sible for some hardstone carvings. Because of the evidence of the large consignment of hardstones bought on Franchi's trip to Paris in 1814, it is unlikely that Cuttel was responsible for more than minor alterations.

The first recorded commission for Beckford from Paul Storr's work-shop was for some table candlesticks in 1800 made in a late-baroque northern style (cat. no. 107). Most of the commissions made for Beckford by Storr are for large pieces of silver-ware. Exceptions include an agate bowl on stand (cat. no. 116), a helio-trope bowl on a dolphin supports (cat. no. 139), and two mounted porcelain beakers in a private collec-tion. The 1844 inventory, made after Beckford's death, lists "a jade ladle . . . mounted with rubies" in an agate basin and gives its location as the dining room.[3] —E. M.

57. *Vase and Cover*
Maker unknown

17th century; India
Nephrite, gold, rubies, emeralds, enamel
4¾ in. (12 cm)
Beckford Collection, Brodick Castle, National Trust for Scotland (58.312)

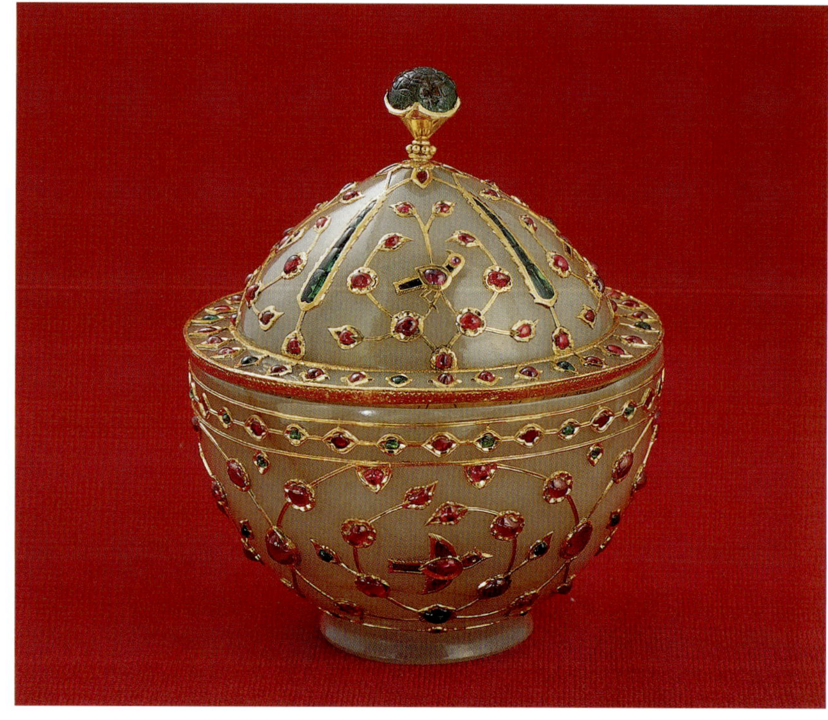

Based on its exquisite workmanship and possible provenance, this work, a fine example of early Mughal jade, amply justifies Beckford's reputation as a connoisseur. Delicate lidded cups of enameled gold, jade, and rock crystal were produced by local ateliers for the Indian courts in the seventeenth and eighteenth cen-turies. Comparable examples are depicted in illuminated manuscripts and albums produced for Mughal rulers.[1] The painted wall decoration, carved sandstone, and inlaid marble panels of Mughal palaces and tombs commonly featured such lidded cups, sometimes with matching saucers, as decorative motifs, along with ewers and rose-water sprinklers.[2] The Mughal Emperor Jahangir (1569–1627) was a notable aesthete who prided himself on his connois-seurship, and his artistic innovations included the introduction of floral designs and the development of jade carving.[3]

This cup is embellished with a graceful inlaid design of small-scale flowering stems, cypress trees, and birds. The design is executed in cabochon rubies and emeralds set into gold.[4] The carved cabochon emerald set as a finial was added by Beckford in the nineteenth century. Although the shape of this cup is derived from that of Chinese porce-lain and jade teacups which were imported by the court both for dis-play and for use as drinking cups, the elegantly executed jeweled deco-ration is purely Mughal, sumptuous yet restrained.

The proposed seventeenth-century dating and royal provenance of this work is supported by its exceptional quality, seventeenth-century stylistic features, and engraved inscription on the underside of the lid giving the weight of the cup. Such notations are extremely rare: the few recorded examples, all dating back to the seventeenth and eighteenth centuries, have been found on Chinese blue-and-white porcelain dishes from the royal Mughal stores or regalia from court workshops.[5] Close parallels for the decoration may be found in seventeenth-century jewelry, regalia, and ceremonial daggers.[6] Works of similar shape and decoration, which can be dated securely to the early to mid-seventeenth century, include a gold lidded cup with five-petaled flowers on a red enamel ground, from the Mughal treasury,[7] and an enamel cup with its original saucer featuring a radiating design of red crocuses and gold wave pattern.[8]

Beckford owned a number of gem-set nephrite and rock crystal vessels, whose description immediately identifies them as Mughal, although each is described as "Persian" in the Beckford archives. A rock-crystal Mughal vase and cover in this style, mounted on scrolled feet, is at Brodick Castle. That example was further embellished to Beckford's orders, probably in 1818. The Franchi "Accounts" detail what may be each of these pieces: A listing, the total of which is dated May 28, 1818, includes: "A Persian crystal vase with rubies and emeralds."[9] Another listing, the total of which is dated June 30, 1818, includes: "An emerald for the Persian cup. £12.12s."[10]

This example, or another extremely similar, was included in the 1822 and the 1823 Fonthill sale catalogues. Curiously, one of a similar type to this is included in the Franchi "Packing Lists" of items sent from Fonthill Abbey to Bath in 1822: "1 vase de jade enrichi de rubis et Emeraudes."[11] It also appears in the 1844 inventory taken after Beckford's death, noted as being in the dining room in Bath: "Jade . . . Persian, mounted in gold, rubies and emerald top."[12] The apparent discrepancy between the cup offered for sale in 1822 and in 1823 and that in the "Packing Lists" and inventory cannot be explained satisfactorily, unless Beckford had more than one cup and cover of this type.

This piece reflects the eighteenth-century taste for elaborately mounted exquisite works of art. In Fonthill Abbey it was displayed in Saint Michael's Gallery with other exotica and rarities. This piece was exhibited with examples of Japanese lacquerwork and statues, and precious agate vessels.[13]

—L. S. D.

58. *Teapot and Stand*
PAUL STORR (1771–1844)

1812–13; England
Silver gilt, ivory
Teapot: 5⅞ x 8⅝ x 5⅛ in.
(14.8 x 22 x 13 cm);
Stand: 6⅛ in. (15.5 cm)
Trustees of the National Museums of
Scotland, Edinburgh (1977.205, 206)

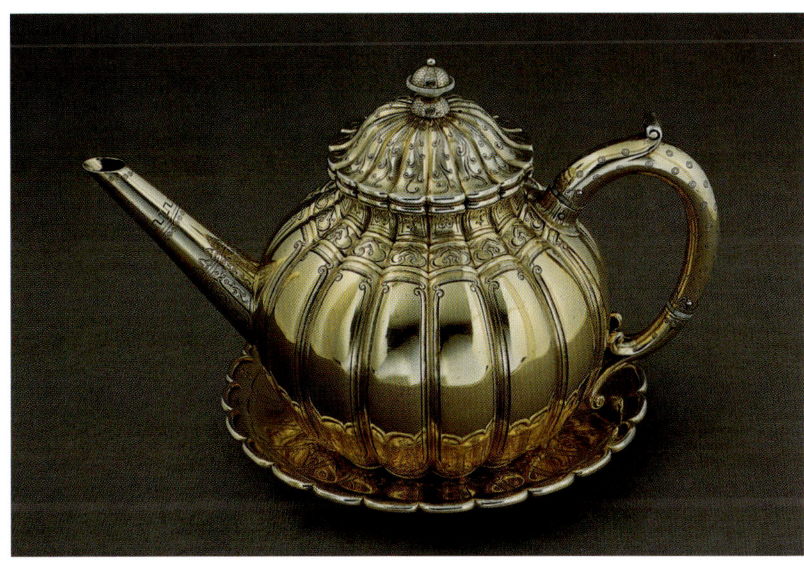

Chinese ceramics had been an important inspiration for many English silver tea wares since the end of the seventeenth century. In his commissions for tea equipage during his first years in Fonthill Abbey, Beckford went directly to Asian prototypes in ceramics, enamel, and even silver to create a new, exotic element in tea silver for his personal use. Together with the preserve pots purchased by Beckford in 1813–14 (cat. no. 68), this teapot and stand form part of a small group of tea wares produced by the Storr workshop.

The form of the pot is based on Yixing stoneware wine pots[1] with their high spouts (although here, for practical reasons, the spout has been lengthened), but the outline has been rounded in a thoroughly European manner. This pot reveals a curious mixture of sources: the distinctive bifurcated tendril base to the handle can be traced to handles on Chinese bronzes and porcelain, while it also appears on prints of Renaissance ewers as well.[2]

Under the base of the pot, in a typically Beckfordian manner, is a finely chased chrysanthemum motif, which is continued in the outline of the stand and is based on the rich monochrome dishes of the Yong-zheng period.[3] While the panels of engraved decoration, like those on the preserve pots, are also based on Chinese ceramics, this time blue-and-white porcelain, the pot and stand have additional motifs that are lacking on the other Storr pieces. They reveal a new and growing obsession on Beckford's part. The decorative possibilities of heraldry are exploited in the engraved decoration of both the pot and stand. The Hamilton cinquefoil appears boldly in the center of the stand and again, alternating with the Latimer cross, it appears around the edge of the stand and around the waisted rim of the teapot.

Beckford's precious tea wares seem to have been reserved for solitary use in his increasingly reclusive life at Fonthill, glimpsed by the occasional visitor. The public only gained access to the Abbey in 1822, when Mr. Christie, the auctioneer, held a viewing, and a year later when Phillips' finally conducted the sale. As a result they exerted little influence on commercially produced silver during the period.[4] This teapot and stand, along with most of Beckford's collection of exotic tea wares, went with him to Bath. It may have been part of the group seen by Henry Venn Lansdown in the lower anteroom at Lansdown Crescent in 1838: "Here are two cabinets, containing curious china, and small golden vessels. . . . I counted in one cabinet ten vessels of gold, in the other five: these were small teapots, caddies, cups, saucers, plates. I am told they are occasionally used at tea-time."[5] Taken to Hamilton Palace after Beckford's death, this teapot and stand remained in possession of the Hamilton family until purchased by the National Museums of Scotland in 1977. —C. H.

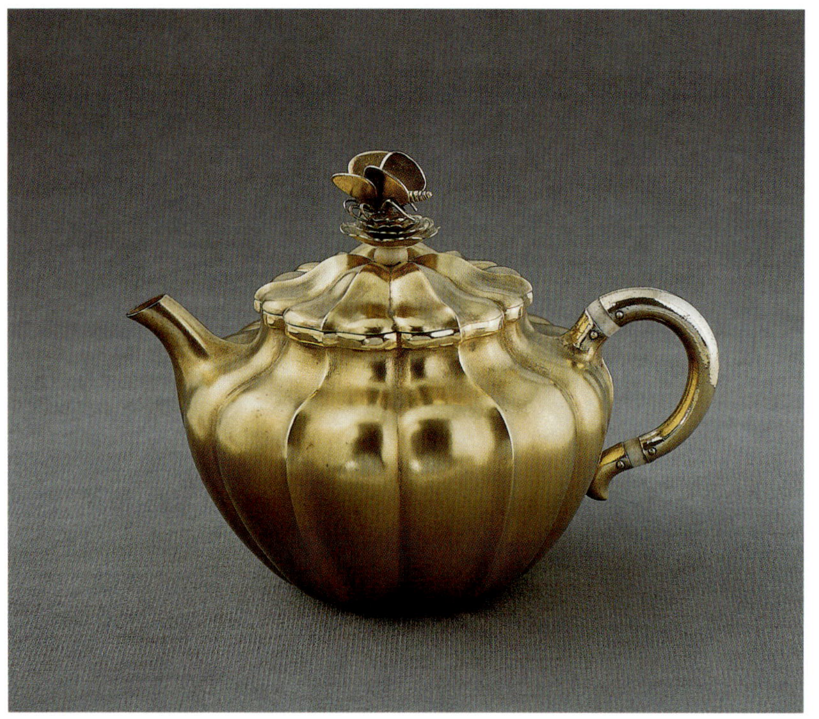

59. Teapot
JOHN PAGE (FL. 1813–?)

1817–18; England
Silver gilt
4½ x 5¾ x 4⅛ in. (11.5 x 14.7 x 10.5 cm)
Trustees of the National Museums of
Scotland, Edinburgh
(1980.977 a,b)

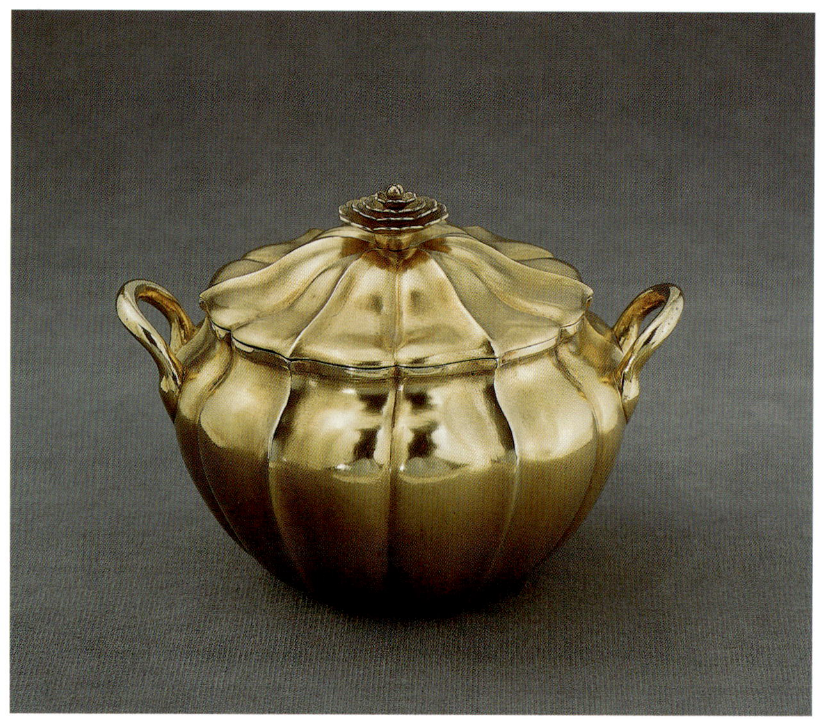

60. Sugar Bowl
JOHN PAGE (FL. 1813–?)

1817–18; England
Silver gilt
3¾ x 5 x 4⅛ in. (9.5 x 12.8 x 10.5 cm)
Trustees of the National Museums of
Scotland, Edinburgh
(1980.978 a,b)

59–62. TEA SERVICE

The individual pieces of this tea service, like the teapot and stand from Paul Storr (cat. no. 58), loosely follows similar forms employed for Yixing stoneware wine pots. The idea of rendering a utilitarian object in precious metal was not a new one: baskets and boxes chased to represent plaited straw date back to the early eighteenth century.[1] The tradition is considerably older, however, and a well-known Elizabethan silver tankard of 1597, modeled to represent wooden barrel-shaped examples of a type found in excavations, is a rare survivor of what must have been a common conceit.[2] Paradoxically,

though, like many Chinese ceramics, the stoneware form's own prototypes were silver examples, which have been excavated from tombs only in recent years, so Beckford and others would have been unaware of them.

The service is of small size, for solitary use, although it was augmented a year later by a much larger slop bowl (cat. no. 61), a rare form in English silver at this period but common enough in porcelain tea services of the time.[3] Beckford's two crests are engraved unobtrusively under the bases. Interestingly, the teapot has a silver handle (no doubt a wooden handle, more usual at this

period, was deemed too heavy in appearance) with ivory insulators, which were to become a standard feature of teapots some twenty years later. The innovative form and features of this service, however, were to have little influence on contemporary silver, as the set was inherited by Beckford's daughter, along with most of the rest of his tea wares, and not acquired by the National Museums of Scotland from her descendants until 1980.

The teapot, cream jug, and sugar bowl bear the mark of John Page, a maker about whom little is known. He registered his mark as a plate-

worker in 1813 with an address in Horseshoe Court, Ludgate Hill in London, which may suggest he supplied finished wares to the royal goldsmiths, Rundell, Bridge and Rundell, whose shop was around the corner. The mark on the slop bowl, "IB" with a pellet between, does not, as with Page's mark, appear on any other Beckford silver. It is similar to marks registered by several workers, but the most likely candidates are John Baddeley (mark entered as a plateworker October 1818) and James Barratt (entered as a smallworker in 1801).—C. H.

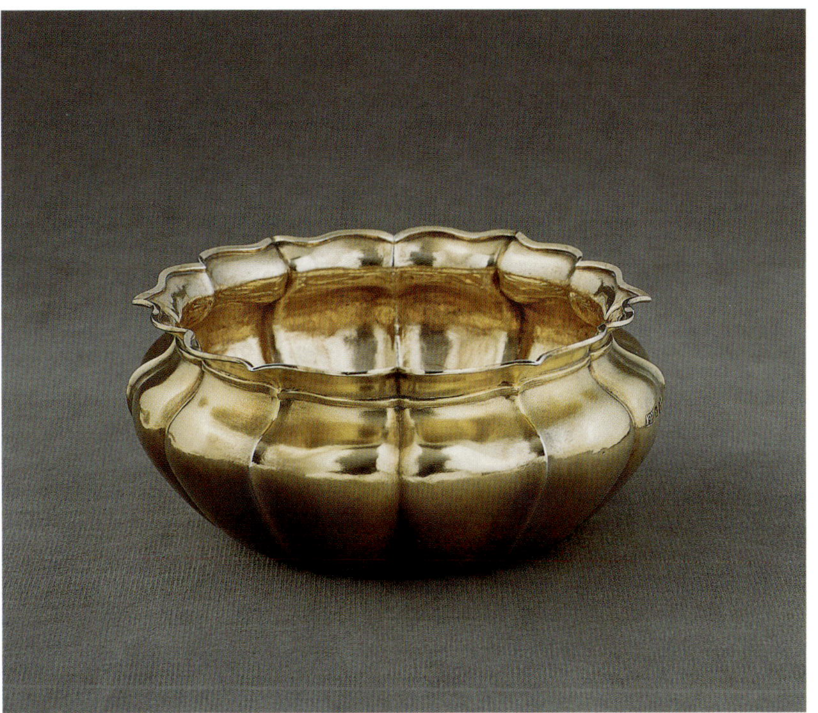

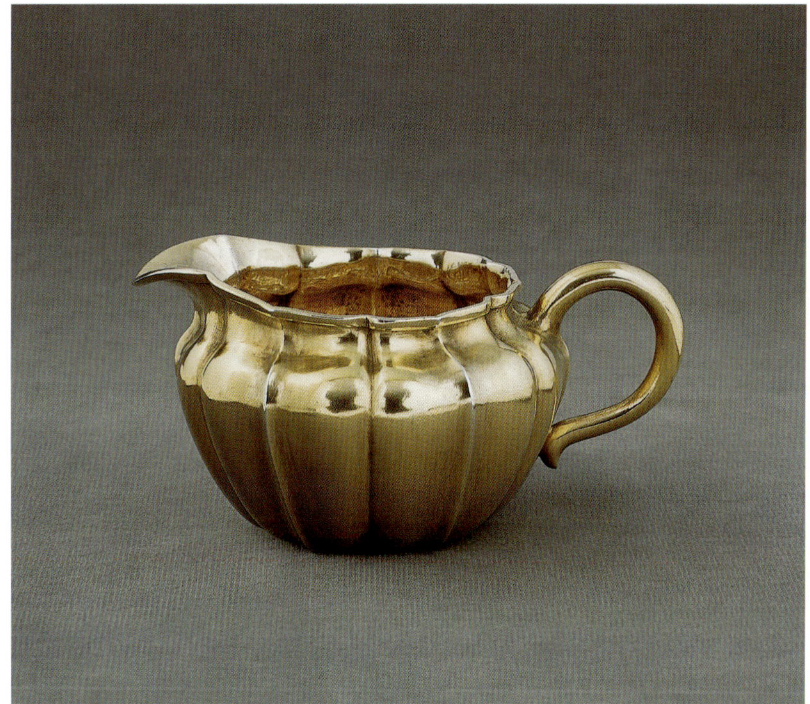

61. *Bowl*
JOHN BADDELEY (FL. 1818–?)
OR JAMES BARRATT (FL. 1801–POST 1816)

1818–19; England
Silver gilt
2⅜ x 5⅛ in. (6 x 13.1 cm)
Trustees of the National Museums of Scotland, Edinburgh (1980.980)

62. *Milk Jug*
JOHN PAGE (FL. 1813–?)

1817–18; England
Silver gilt
2½ x 5 x 3⅜ in. (6.5 x 12.6 x 8.7 cm)
Trustees of the National Museums of Scotland, Edinburgh (1980.979)

63. *Teapot and Cover*
SÈVRES FACTORY

Mounts, ca. 1815–20, England; porcelain, ca. 1780, France
Hard-paste porcelain, silver, silver gilt
5¾ in. (14.5 cm)
Beckford Collection, Brodick Castle, National Trust for Scotland (58.322)

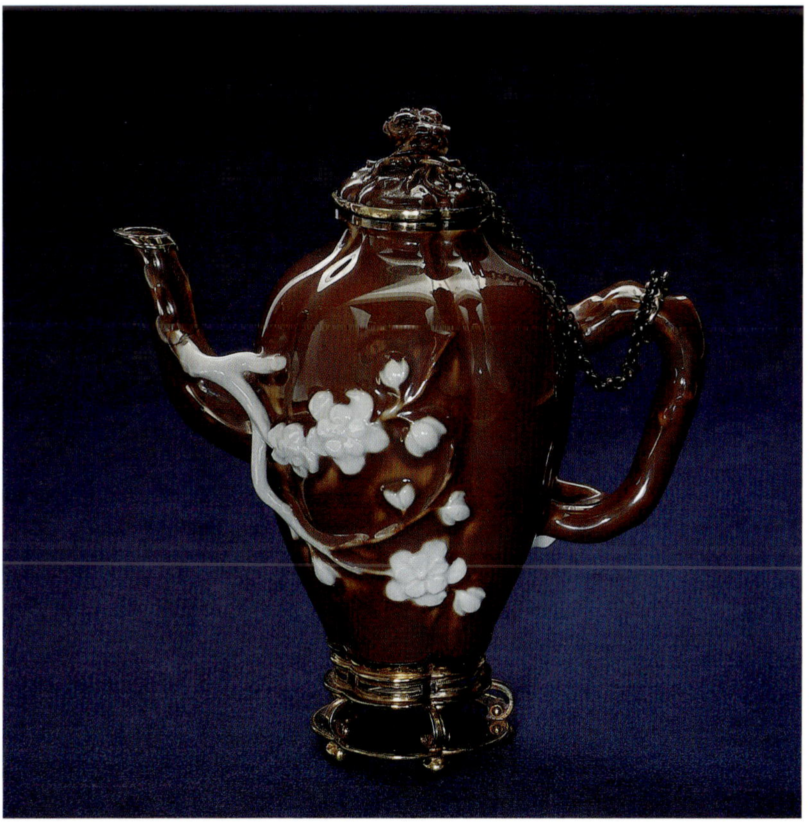

The hard-paste porcelain teapot is based on a Chinese *blanc-de-chine* wine ewer of the Kangxi period (1666–1722).[1] From the early 1770s when hard-paste porcelain was developed at Sèvres, there was a renewed vogue for chinoiseries,[2] which persisted for at least a decade.[3] Chinese-style motifs were often painted by Jean-Jacques Dieu (active 1777–90; 1794–98; 1801–11), who specialized in them.[4] It is unusual to find such faithfulness to Oriental forms, however, at the royal factory at this date.

Only one other teapot like this is known, also unmarked. So rare is it as a Sèvres production, that it was catalogued in 1896[5] by its then owner, the redoubtable collector and museum curator Augustus Wollaston Franks, as Meissen.[6] It does indeed bear a glancing similarity to pieces in a rather darker brown glaze (known as *Kapuzinerbraun*) invented in 1720 by the Meissen arcanist Samuel Stölzel, which in turn imitated a Chinese glaze based on iron oxide. The appearance on the London market in the mid-1980s of two marked Sèvres hard-paste porcelain cups dated 1781 which are related to this teapot, their prunus reliefs decorated in silver,[7] led to the correct attribution of the teapot and cover not long afterwards.[8] A cup and saucer with silvered reliefs bearing the Sèvres factory mark for hard-paste porcelain in the Musée des Arts Décoratifs, Paris,[9] should have permitted an earlier identification of the London piece, but the subject of hard-paste porcelain has only attracted scholarly attention in the last fifteen to twenty years, prompting a reexamination and reevaluation of this aspect of Sèvres production.

The Beckford teapot and cover were also misidentified (this time as Chinese porcelain) as recently as 1988 when the oil painting by Willes Maddox (cat. no. 155) in which it is depicted was exhibited.[10] The teapot was evidently considered as precious as the other, earlier, cabinet pieces shown in the painting. Beckford himself may not have known the piece was French, as he apparently did not purchase it directly from the factory.[11]

No design for this teapot and cover is known. A drawing for a matching milk jug and cover is in the Sèvres factory archive, as are a plaster model of a matching sugar bowl and two models of a milk jug, inscribed "*pot à sucre des Indes*" and "*pot à crème des Indes,*" respectively.[12] Since these items appear to have been in production for a short time only, as very few have survived, the name could well be the one given in the eighteenth century.

The teapot and cover were in Beckford's possession by 1822. The neo-gothic style of the mount forming the stand suggests a date of execution in the early nineteenth century. On the basis of its scroll and ball design common to other mounts on Beckford's Oriental porcelains, the design has been attributed to its owner's Portuguese companion, Gregorio Franchi.[13] The mounts are ample demonstration of the pride Beckford took in this exceptional teapot. —A. D.

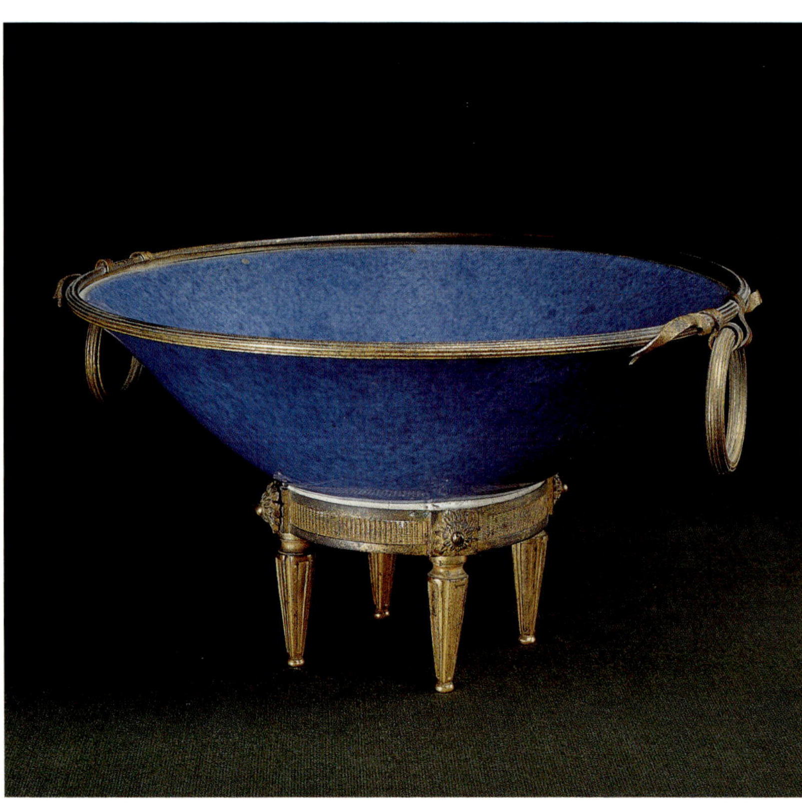

64. *Basin*

MAKER UNKNOWN

Mounts, ca. 1770, France; porcelain, 18th-century, China Porcelain, gilt bronze
4½ x 8 in. (11.43 x 20.32 cm)
Sir Edmund Fairfax Lucy, Charlecote Park (The National Trust), CHA.C.49

This eighteenth-century Chinese water-blue (cobalt) porcelain basin (one of a pair) has been transformed into an objet d'art—a miniature Roman bath—by the addition of ring-handles, in the Louis XIV "antique" style of the 1760s. It relates to the marble miniatures that were retailed in the eighteenth century by Roman bronze manufacturers to serve as decorative chimneypiece garnitures. The basin rims, like their ribbon-tied rings, are enriched with reeds, evocative of Ovid's *Metamor-phoses* and the love of the Arcadian fertility deity Pan for a water nymph. The basin is displayed on "tabouret" altar pedestals enriched with ribbons and supported on hermed and antique-fluted columnar legs. Such objects were particularly appropriate when used with the lavish furniture that was then being retailed by leading Parisian *marchands-merciers,* such as Dominique Daguerre (d.1792), who was patronized by the Prince of Wales following the opening of their London premises in the 1780s.

The pair of basins (one shown) were acquired at the Fonthill 1823 sale by George Hammond Lucy. They are likely to have been displayed in the "Elizabethan" drawing room in the state apartment at Charlecote House, Warwickshire, in one of the black cabinets-on-stand that were among the thirteen lots of furniture that Lucy purchased at the sale.[1] —J. H.

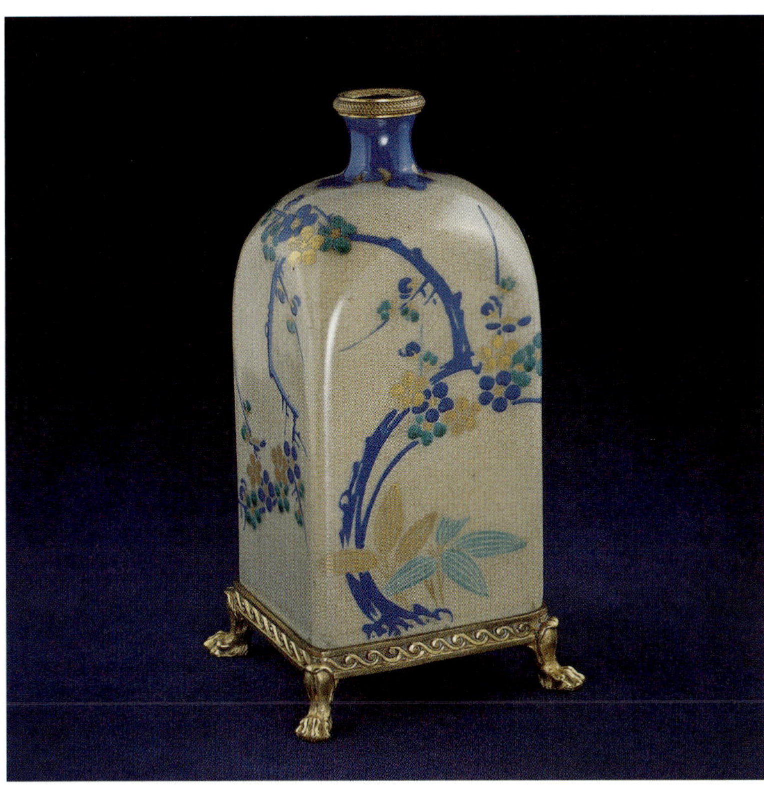

This eighteenth-century Japanese crackle-glazed porcelain "Kiyomizu" bottle (one of a pair) depicts ancient prunus trees, as well as pine and bamboo shoots. The decoration is picked out in blue against a light buff ground, while some of the blossoms are rendered in green or gold. This early nineteenth-century transformation into an objet d'art was achieved by bronze enrichments. The neck is wreathed by plaited reeds, while the plinth is fretted with Grecian wave-scrolls, evoking the triumph of the nature deity Aphrodite (Venus), and supported on triumphal palm-wrapped bacchic lion-monopodiae. Such ornament featured on the utensils in bronze, assembled around 1800 by the connoisseur Thomas Hope and illustrated in his *Household Furniture and Interior Decoration* (1807). The latter emulated Percier and Fontaine's *Recueil de decorations Interieures* (1801); and Hope's "animation" of such "furniture" expressed his wish to make it "speak" and contribute to the symbolical and narrative whole of each interior.

Related ormolu-enriched bottles and vases embellished the Carlton House interiors created for the Prince Regent and can be seen in W. H. Pyne's illustrations of the mansion in his *History of the Royal Residences* (vol. 3, 1819). These depict the change that took place in interior decoration around 1800 as the formal parlor was gradually replaced by the informal living-room. Seats were increasingly arranged around fireplaces and central tables, and their former position against the walls taken by bookcases, commodes, and tables. Whereas vases had tended to be displayed on mantelpieces or pier tables, they were now spread all round the room.

This pair of vases was acquired by George Hammond Lucy at the 1823 Fonthill sale for his home, Charlecote Park, Warwickshire.
—J. H.

65. *Bottle*
Maker unknown

Mounts, ca. 1810, England; porcelain, 18th-century, Japan
Porcelain, gilt bronze
8 x 3⅝ in. (20.32 x 9 cm)
Charlecote Park, The Fairfeax-Lucy Collection (The National Trust),-CHA.C.44a

66. *Vase*
Maker unknown

Mounts, ca. 1810, England; porcelain, 18th-century, China
Porcelain, gilt bronze
13¾ x 4¼ in. (35 x 10.85 cm)
Sir Edmund Fairfax Lucy, Charlecote Park, (The National Trust), CHA.C.37

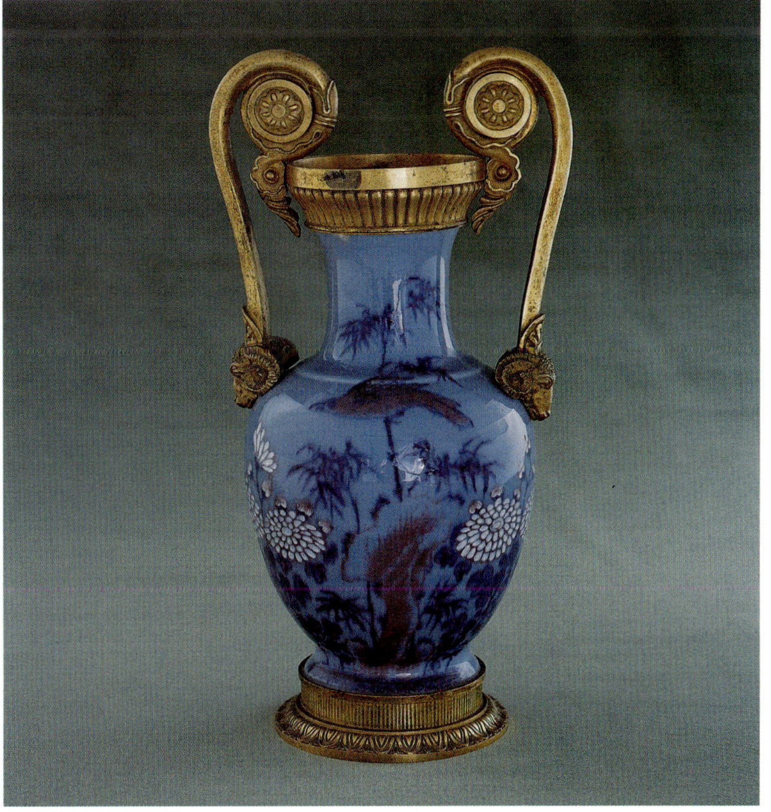

Such porcelain vases played an essential role in enlivening rooms since the later seventeenth century, and the establishment of European porcelain factories helped fuel what became a "vase" mania in the late eighteenth century. By then they were an essential element of decorating after the "antique" or Roman manner encouraged by a variety of pan-European publications.[1] Some of these vases were reissued in the *Collection of Antique Vases . . .* (1814) by Henry Moses; and the enthusiasm for them continued into the Regency period. Particular encouragement of this fashion for "Grecian" vases, however, was provided by the establishment around 1800 of the connoisseur Thomas Hope's mansion/museum in Duchess Street in London and his publication of *Household Furniture and Interior Decoration* (1807).

Slightly earlier, the London-based

establishment opened by the Parisian *marchand-mercier* Dominique Daguerre also played an important role in introducing the French court taste for metamorphosing colorfully flowered Asian porcelain into "antique" objets d'art with the aid of a *bronzier*'s enrichments. This sky-blue Kangxi baluster vase (one of a pair), displaying spring vignettes of Chinese gardens with birds perched among white prunus and peonies, has been transformed into an antique wine-krater vase with the addition of the gilt-bronze mounts. Displayed on Grecian palm-flowered plinths, their necks are wreathed with reeded palm-flowered ribbon-guilloches; while their Grecian-scrolled handles are supported by sacrificial rams' heads, evoking the festive wine-deity, Dionysus (Bacchus). These enrichments are likely to have been carried out by the Pall Mall firm of Benjamin Lewis Vulliamy, the royal clock-maker who also played the role of furniture supplier in the embellishment of objets d'art carried out for the Prince of Wales, later George IV. Many such vases, enriched by Vulliamy, were supplied by the dealer Robert Fogg, the prince's "China Man," who was also patronized by William Beckford. The pair of vases was acquired at Fonthill in 1823 by George Hammond Lucy for Charlecote Park, Warwickshire.[2]

—J. H.

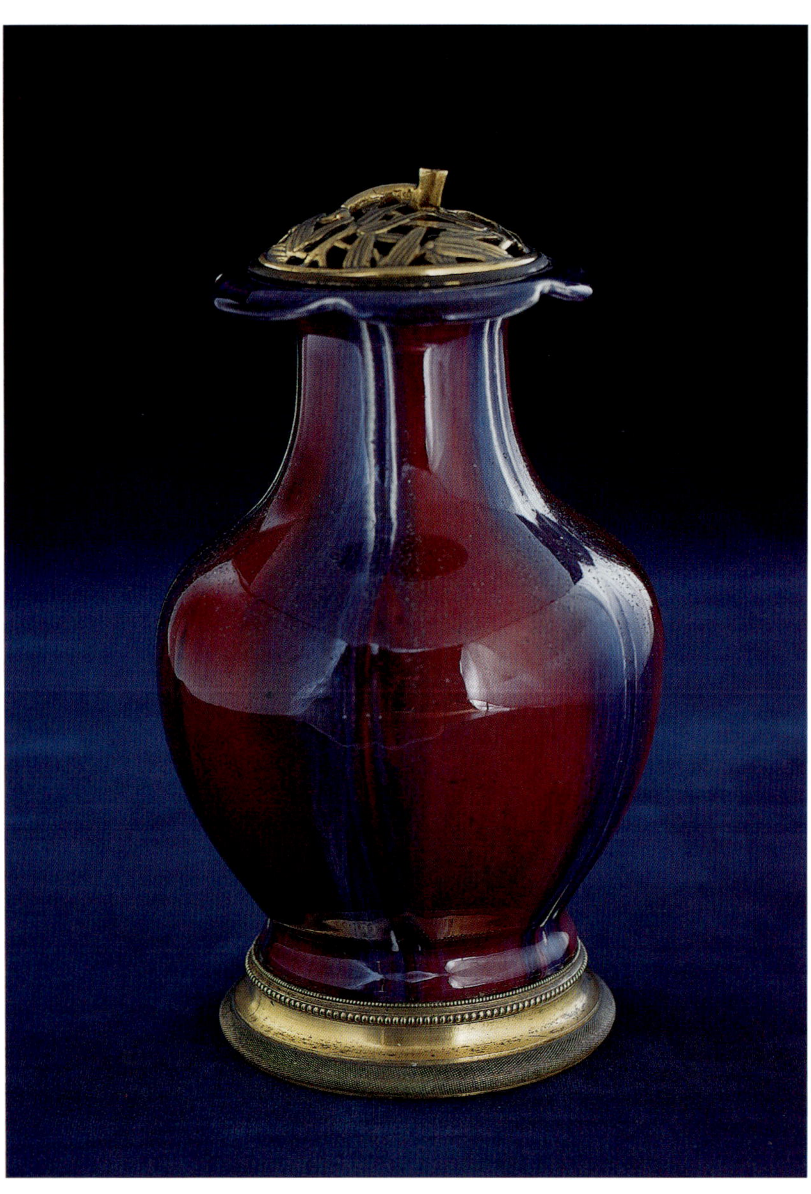

67. *Vase and Cover*
Maker unknown

Mounts, ca. 1800, England; porcelain, 18th-century, China Porcelain, gilt bronze
13 x 7 in. (33 x 18 cm)
Sir Edmund Fairfax Lucy, Charlecote Park (The National Trust) CHA.C.43a

This eighteenth-century red sang-de-boeuf and blue-shaded Chinese porcelain baluster vase is scalloped in flower-petaled form and fitted with a bamboo-like lid of fretted bronze. It has been transformed into a European objet d'art by the addition of a stepped and pearl-wreathed gilt-bronze plinth.

Beckford's acquisition of such objets d'art reflects his wish to establish Fonthill Abbey as one of the noblest residences in Europe. This aim was similarly shared and achieved by his son-in-law the tenth Duke of Hamilton in the embellishment of Hamilton Palace, Scotland. Follow-ing the duke's death in 1852, the *Illustrated London News* reported: "Hamilton Palace was made, by the taste of the nobleman, one of the noblest residences in Europe; and it probably contains a greater collection of precious curiosities and rare works of art than the abode of any man under the rank of a Sovereign."[1]

The pair of vases was among the thirty-one lots of Oriental ceramics purchased by George Hammond Lucy at the Fonthill 1823 sale. These pieces were mostly displayed in the drawing room of the state apartment at Charlecote Park, Warwickshire.[2]

—J. H.

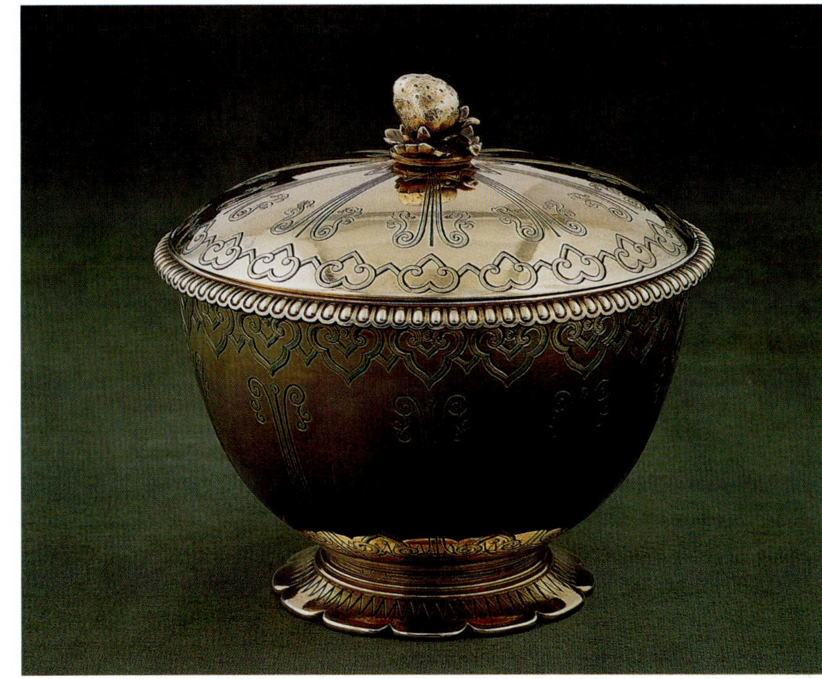

This pot and cover with a finial formed of strawberry leaves is one of a set of four, each surmounted by a different fruit to indicate the contents. They form part of a group of silver commissioned by Beckford from 1812 onward as he settled into the Abbey and turned his attention once more to items of very personal silverware, mostly tea wares. Unlike the silver he purchased in the 1780s and 1790s, however, these objects are completely different from conventional silver of the period. With their gilding giving them the richness that Beckford so admired, these exotic pots are a curious mixture of Chinese, Indian, and European features. It is evident that Franchi, or even Beckford himself, was responsible for their design. The Mughal spreading and scalloped foot is similar to some designs for mounted objects that have been attributed to Franchi, found in a album of drawings and prints belonging to James Aldridge.[1] While the plain hemispherical bowls and covers are reminiscent of Mughal enamels,[2] the applied tongue-and-dart border, a practical feature to give strength to the rim, is a generic feature of London-made silver of the period. The engraved decoration on the bowl and cover is inspired by Chinese blue-and-white porcelain, but the fruit-form finials, based on porcelain prototypes, are definitively European.

Paul Storr's workshop had also supplied the teapot and stand (cat. no. 58) in similar style the previous year. During this period Storr was manager of the workshops of Rundell, Bridge and Rundell through whom these orders must have been carried out. Before his association with the firm in 1800, Storr had made the "Holbein candlesticks" (cat. no. 107) ordered by Beckford through Vulliamy and Son. In general, Beckford enjoyed working with artisans and designers, and it is clear that he was used to dealing with Storr himself rather than the retailer, doubtless much to the annoyance of Edmund Rundell. In 1815 Beckford wrote to Franchi, "Advise Fiume [their nickname for Rundell], or rather Mr. Storr, not to let the candelabra languish too long."[3] —C. H.

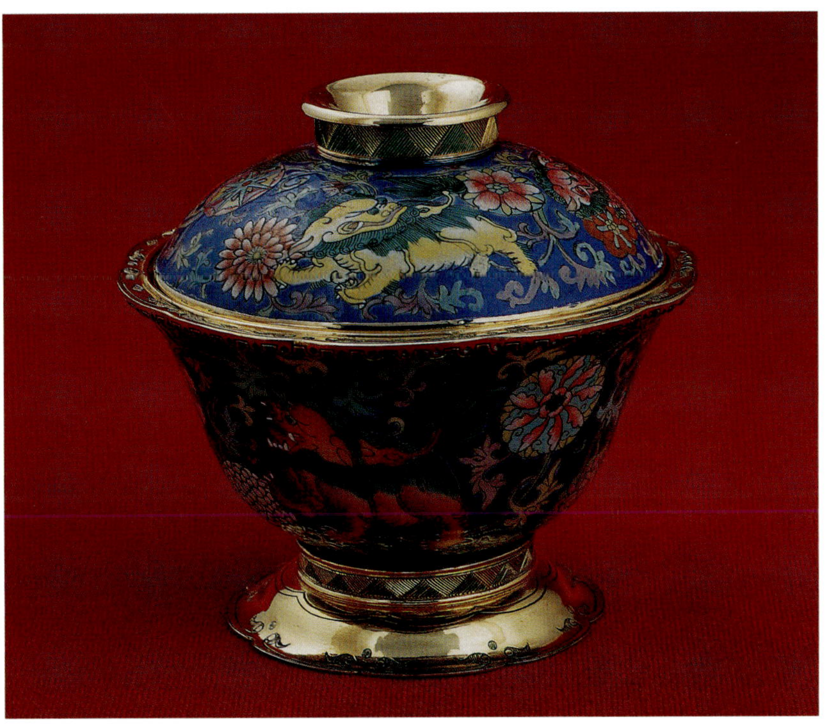

The lively polychrome decoration of this bowl and cover, with dragons amid elaborate foliage, provides an ideal foil for the richness of the silver-gilt mounts. It is quite different in feeling from the more restrained figural decoration of some of the cream jugs (see cat. no. 126), the *café–au-lait* floral bowl (cat. no. 38), and the Arita-ware bowl (cat. no. 127), suggesting that Beckford and Franchi devoted as much attention to the selection of suitable candidates for mounting as they did to the design and execution of the mounts themselves.

The spreading foot and scalloped rim follow the form of other bowls in the series, although each one has a different combination of Chinese and Mughal motifs. The basket-weave pattern engraved on the foot and cover has, like many of the other motifs found on the series of mounted pieces, its inspiration in Chinese blue-and-white porcelain.[1] The ring handle on the cover is also based on Chinese prototypes and, like its predecessors made in silver in London in the early eighteenth century, themselves based on Chinese porcelain models, it doubles as a foot, allowing the inverted cover to be used as a spoon tray. —C. H.

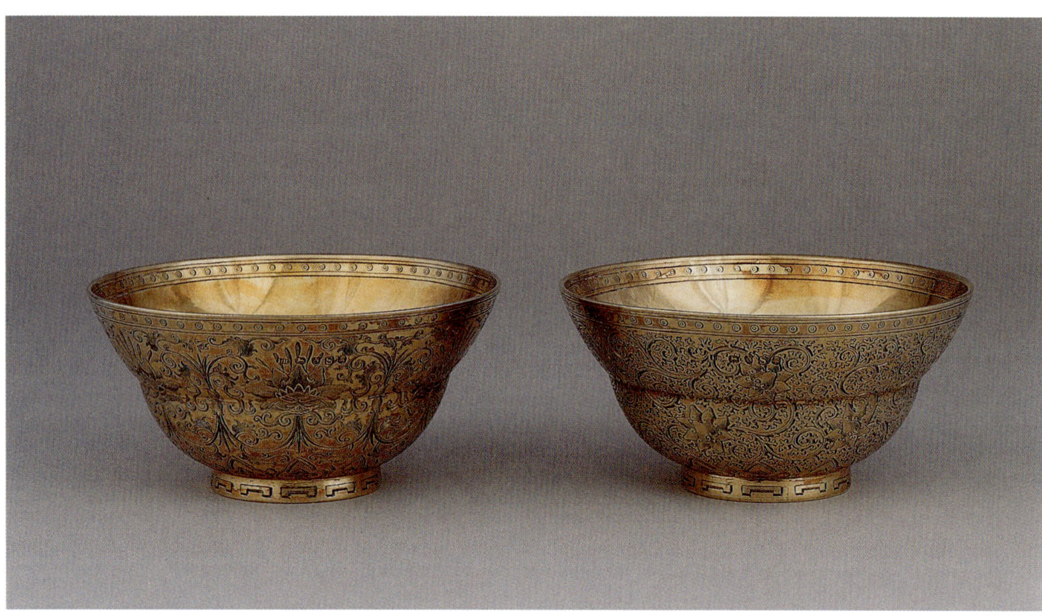

70. *Two Bowls*
JOHN ROBINS (FL. 1771–1831)

1813–14; England
Silver gilt
2¼ x 4⅜ in. diam. (5.6 x 11.1 cm)
Sterling & Francine Clark Art Institute, Williamstown, Massachusetts (1955.471)

The design and execution of these exquisite bowls reflect recurrent themes in Beckford's later, more innovative plate: his taste for Oriental art; his love of precious, finely detailed wares and gold and silver-gilt vessels; and his interest in heraldic devices. The vessels that survive from the early 1810s include a number of silver-gilt teawares, largely imitative of Chinese porcelains or enameled metalwork.[1] Their decoration accords with Beckford's passion for Chinese and Japanese works of art, evident in the quantities of porcelains and lacquers that he collected.[2] The elaborate strapwork, flowers, scrolls, and geometric borders, so painstakingly engraved on these bowls, echo the patterns found on enameled porcelains, cloisonné, and "Canton" enameled wares. The lotus flower ornament on one of these bowls is nearly identical to that on a larger silver-gilt bowl of 1812–13 marked by James Aldridge.[3] Other motifs, such as the dotted circles and the volutes and fretwork, are also found on a silver-gilt, melon-shaped teapot by Paul Storr (cat. no. 58).[4] Although marked by different goldsmiths, the engraving on these objects is consistently intricate and highly skilled, suggesting the work of a single hand. One possible candidate has been identified in the Beckford papers as "poor Coulson the engraver," whose name is associated with a superb mounted agate, chalcedony, and ruby standing cup marked by James Aldridge.[5] The engraving on each of these objects also reveals Beckford's lifelong obsession with his lineage, which is often evident in the decoration of his plate. The Robins bowls are engraved underneath with the two crests Beckford routinely used: the Hamilton oak tree, adapted for Beckford with a shield bearing the Latimer cross, and the Beckford heron grasping a fish in its beak.

The makers who marked Beckford's plate are an intriguing mix of prominent and lesser-known goldsmiths. The London firms he patronized included such prestigious names as Rundell, Bridge and Rundell, Paul Storr, and John Scofield. In Paris he purchased objects in silver gilt and gold from the fashionable shop of Henri Auguste.[6] His most inventive historicist plate, however, tended to be commissioned from less familiar craftsmen, such as John Robins, James Aldridge, John Harris VI, and William Burwash. John Robins, whose mark is struck on each of the present bowls, supplied some twenty objects to Beckford between 1812 and 1818.[7] These include the remarkable silver-gilt ladle (see cat. no. 109), a number of Beckford's prized porcelains (see cat. no. 126), and ivories.[8] Mounted wares were, in fact, far more numerous at Fonthill than were objects of solid silver or silver gilt. The desired effect, that of a sixteenth-century *Kunstkammer* or *Wunderkammer*, would certainly have favored the exquisitely mounted hardstones, porcelains, and ivories over the more domestic, utilitarian vessels more typical of Beckford's pre-Fonthill Abbey collecting.[9]

These bowls do not appear in the sales catalogues of 1822 and 1823, indicating that they may have been among the objects that Beckford took with him to Bath upon his departure from Fonthill Abbey. They are listed in the inventory of 1844, taken after Beckford's death, among a group of three slop basins and four sugar basins located in the "Small Parlour."[10] That they were probably used as tea wares is suggested both by this inventory reference and by the contemporary account of Henry Venn Lansdown, whose letter to his daughter Charlotte, written from Bath on August 21, 1838, includes the following passage: "We proceeded in the first place to the house, and I had an opportunity of examining the pictures and curiosities in the ante-room. Here are two cabinets containing curious china, and small golden vessels. . . . I counted in one cabinet ten vessels of gold, in the other five: these were small teapots, caddies, cups, saucers, plates. I am told that they are used occasionally at tea-time."[11] —B. C. W.

Fonthill Abbey, 1795–1822

Fonthill Abbey, originally conceived as a substantial folly to enhance the park at Fonthill Splendens, became one of the most spectacular and influential Gothic Revival buildings of its kind in Regency England. Inspired by his visit to the Portuguese monasteries of Alcobaça and Batalha in June of 1794, Beckford instructed his architect, James Wyatt, to draw up plans for an elaborate structure on the site of foundations for a commemorative tower that had been left incomplete at Fonthill at the time of Alderman Beckford's death in 1770. Wyatt, who was already carrying out renovations to Fonthill Splendens, was directed to include a mausoleum for Beckford in the building. Work began in 1796, and toward the end of the year, the building, by then some 200 feet in length, was sufficiently advanced to earn the name "Abbey," which Beckford had begun to call it. In December 1800, the partially completed Abbey was the setting for an elaborate banquet given for Admiral Nelson, the hero of the battle of Trafalgar, accompanied by his mistress Emma Hamilton and her husband, Sir William Hamilton, Beckford's distant cousin.

The decade of the 1790s was a period of financial instability for Beckford due to the mismanagement of his business affairs and the fluctuating price of sugar, the source of his income. In addition, his avid collecting, and the cost of remodeling Fonthill Splendens and building the Abbey, forced him to economize. In 1801 he demolished one wing of Fonthill Splendens. The remainder of the great mansion, with the exception of one pavilion, was taken down in 1807, following Beckford's decision in 1804 to finally inhabit the Abbey.

Throughout its short existence, the Abbey was expanded and altered to conform to Beckford's changing perception of the building's significance and use. It developed from a garden structure into a complex residence. Beckford's insistence on the Abbey being erected as quickly as possible, combined with the use of unsuitable materials and building techniques, led to the collapse of the Abbey's tower twice during construction.

Increasingly burdened by debt, Beckford came to the decision in 1822 to sell the Abbey and part of his collection. After unsuccessfully attempting to persuade his son-in-law, the Duke of Hamilton, to purchase the estate, Beckford asked the firm of auctioneers, Christie's, to compile a sale catalogue in that same year. Shortly before the intended auction, however, Beckford arranged a private sale of the house to the gunpowder millionaire John Farquhar, who sold the contents of the Abbey a year later, at an auction conducted by Henry Phillips, an event attended by thousands. Two years later, Farquhar was living in the Abbey when the tower collapsed for the final time on December 21, 1825, a event of such magnitude that it was commemorated in an engraving after a drawing by John Buckler (see fig. 7-1). Beckford, who had moved to the town of Bath, would visit the ruins of his Abbey on at least two occasions before his death in 1844.

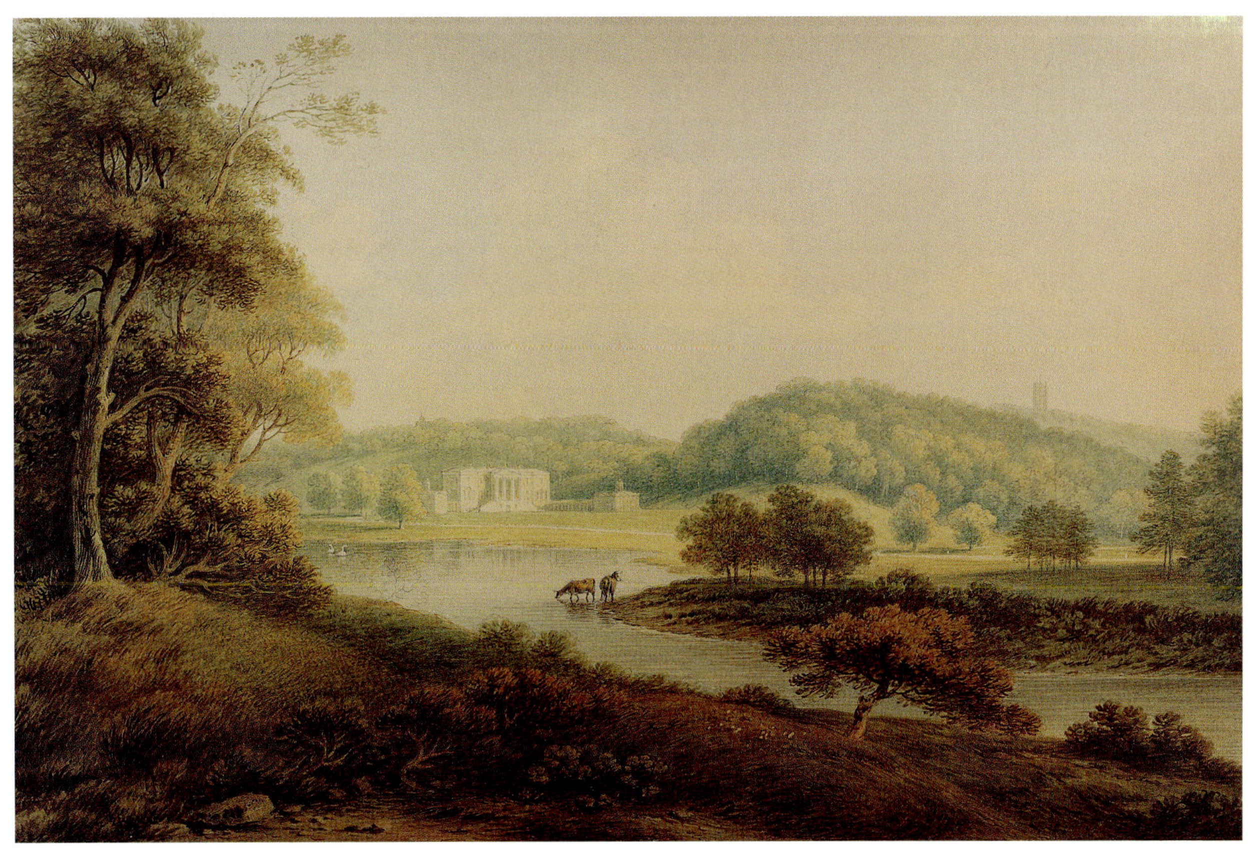

71. *Fonthill Splendens with a Distant View of Fonthill Abbey*
John Warwick Smith
(1717–1764)

ca. 1805; England
Pencil and watercolor
13⅜ x 20 in. (34.3 x 50.8 cm)
Collection of the Honorable Philip Smith

Fonthill Splendens is recorded in views by J. M. W. Turner, John Buckler, and Hendrik Frans de Cort, but this watercolor by Warwick Smith is the only known work to show the earlier house in relation to the Abbey.[1] This in itself raises problems, because Beckford started to demolish the colonnades and one of the wings in 1801, in search of building material for the Abbey. The tower was certainly under construction by then, as recorded in Turner's detailed drawings of 1799, but the distant view of the Abbey shows the tower completed, which was not the case by 1801. The building on the skyline above the house is the Church of Holy Trinity, built for Alderman Beckford, but replaced by T. H. Wyatt for the Marquess of Westminster in 1866.

It may be that Warwick Smith made this watercolor to show Beckford how the completed Abbey would look in relation to Fonthill Splendens, making use of Wyatt's designs. If not, it is a record taken before Splendens itself was pulled down in 1807, to show the Abbey as built, and reinstating the colonnade taken down earlier, perhaps based on Turner's view.

John Warwick Smith was so called either because of his patronage by the second Earl of Warwick, who sent him to Italy from 1776 to 1781 or, more likely, because he lived at Warwick beginning in 1781.[2] Smith, part of Beckford's close inner circle, was a frequent visitor to Fonthill and was given his own pet name there, "Father Bestorum," which may refer to his being older than the rest of the company, or, as has also been suggested, to his unattractive habits.[3] Beckford sometimes found Smith's melancholia annoying,[4] but he continued to invite him to the Abbey over many years. Smith exhibited views of Fonthill Abbey at the Old Watercolour Society in London in 1807, 1813, and 1815. In a letter of 1811 to his companion Franchi, Beckford wrote, "Father Bestorum is making pretty views of the Abbey and its surroundings, they will make a nice little volume like last years [sic] but much superior. I am not dissatisfied with him."[5]

Warwick Smith was president of the Old Watercolour Society in 1814, 1817, and 1818. His work was admired by his contemporaries for its depth and richness of color, although not by Turner who told Joseph Farington that he "reprobated the mechanically systematic process of drawing practised by Smith and from him so generally diffused. He thinks it can produce nothing but manner and sameness. . . . Turner has no settled process but drives his colours about till he has expressed the idea in his mind."[6] —H. P.

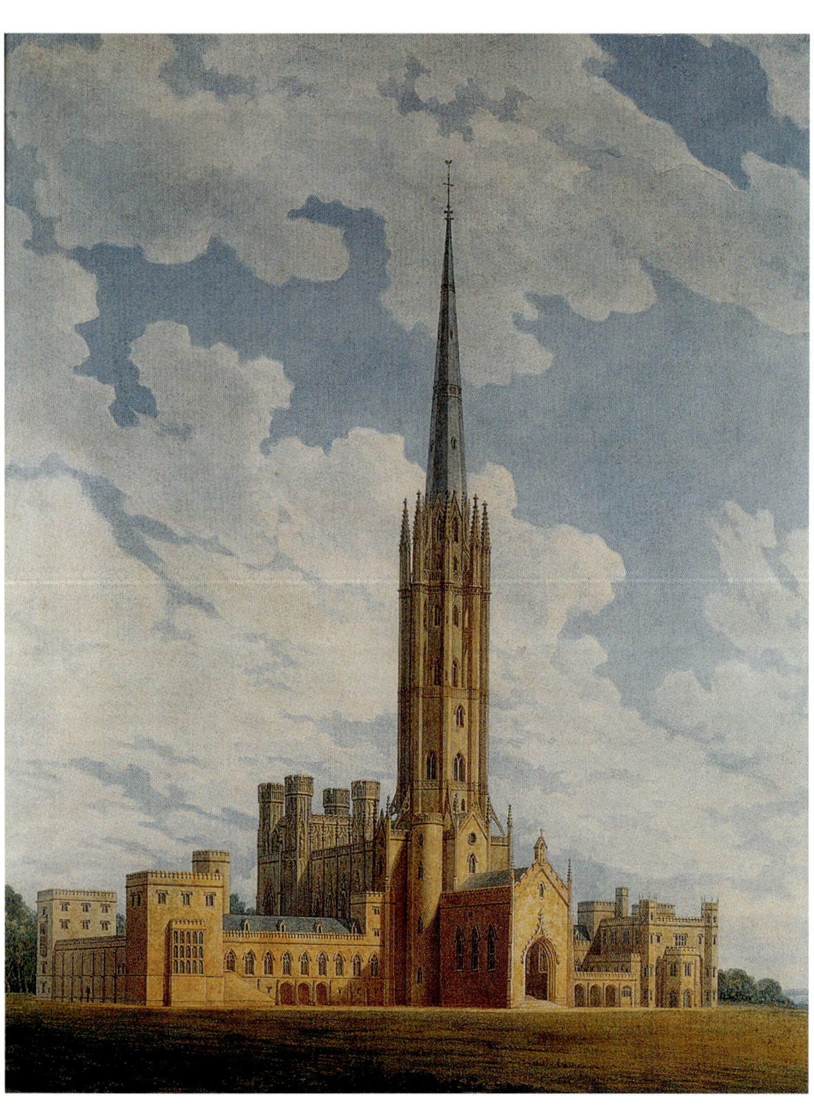

72. *Fonthill Abbey, Perspective Design from the North West*
CHARLES WILD (1781–1835)
TO THE DESIGN OF JAMES
WYATT, RA (1746–1813)

1799; England
Pencil and watercolor
21¼ x 15½ in. (54 x 39.4 cm)
Private collection

This drawing follows exactly James Wyatt's sketch design[1] and represents the third and last scheme for the spire of Fonthill, 1798–99.[2] The tower is shown to be considerably taller than the one in Wyatt's 1798 Royal Academy exhibit and closely resembles the structure as ultimately completed, minus the spire. No doubt the collapse of the upper part of the unfinished tower in May 1800 gave even Beckford, with his quest for ever greater height, doubts about the wisdom of adding such a spire to a structure that had been built in timber and Wyatt's compo-cement, and which would have to be rebuilt in stone.

Charles Wild was, like Turner before him, articled to Thomas Malton Jr., and he specialized in architectural subjects from the start. He was a natural choice to succeed Turner, who was already charging 35 guineas for his large finished watercolors, as perspectivist for Wyatt's Royal Academy exhibits. A smaller, but otherwise identical version of Wild's drawing is in the Victoria and Albert Museum, but no other renderings of this stage in the evolution of Fonthill are known.[3] This drawing is likely to have been included in Wyatt's 1799 exhibit at the Royal Academy as No. 1016, *View of a building now erecting at Fonthill in the style of a Gothic Abbey*. No design drawings or architect's perspectives of the later stages in the Abbey's development (the tower without the spire and the east wing) appear to have survived.

Wild continued to practice as an architectural draftsman and illustrator and it has been stated that "his minute truthfulness of form and perspective is apparent throughout all his work in colour."[4] He was an active member of the Old Watercolour Society and exhibited views of the English cathedrals, many of which were published as engravings. He was also one of the principal illustrators for Pyne's *History of the Royal Residences* (1820). Wild's sight began to fail in 1827, and he died blind in 1835. —H. P.

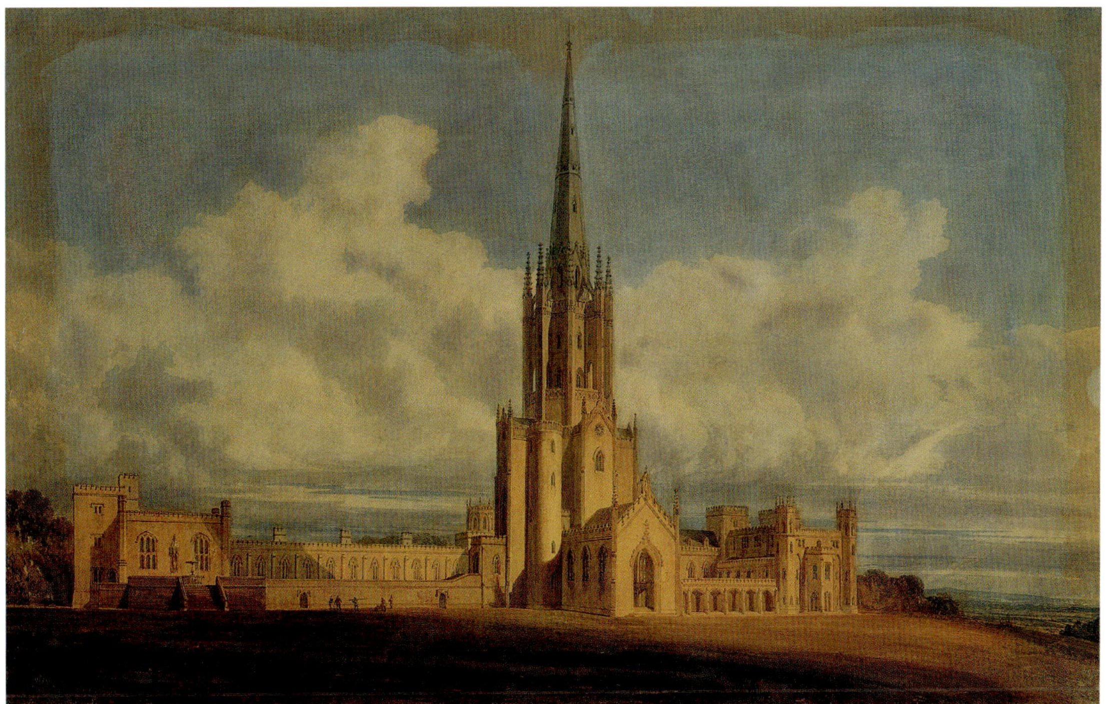

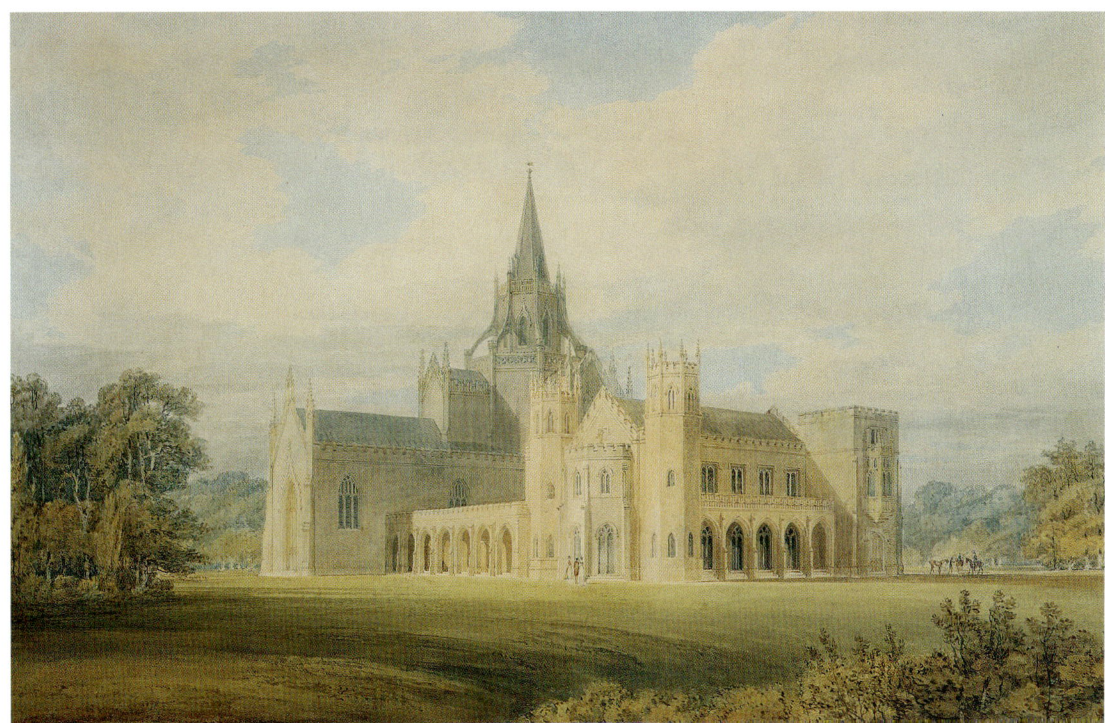

73–79. THE EVOLUTION OF FONTHILL ABBEY

One of William Beckford's outstanding achievements was the realization of his idea for a dramatic Gothic building to enhance the landscape of his estate at Fonthill, Wiltshire, in the west of England. At his death in 1770, Beckford's father had left the foundation of an unfinished commemorative tower on Stops Beacon, the highest point on the estate. By 1792 Beckford was discussing ideas with one of the leading architects of the day, James Wyatt, for building a Gothic "ruin" on an elevated site nearby, and by the summer of 1796 building work was underway. The ground floor was more or less complete by the end of the year.[1]

During 1797, in which year the early interiors of the Abbey were being planned, Wyatt exhibited the first of a series of designs for Fonthill Abbey, as it had come to be known.

Projected Design for Fonthill Abbey, Wiltshire, now in the collection of the Yale Center for British Art, was exhibited at the Royal Academy in 1798 under the name of Wyatt, but it is known that Wyatt commissioned the young artist J. M. W. Turner to execute the finished watercolor, perhaps as a presentation drawing for Beckford, showing the aesthetic possibilities for the Abbey.[2] The architecture represented is clearly that of Wyatt, however, and Turner would have relied upon Wyatt's now-vanished architectural drawings of the Abbey to prepare this watercolor.

In the Yale view, the western and southern ranges of the building are shown more or less as they appeared when finished, around 1803. The extended northern range of the Abbey, seen to the left in this view, with a raised terrace at the front, was

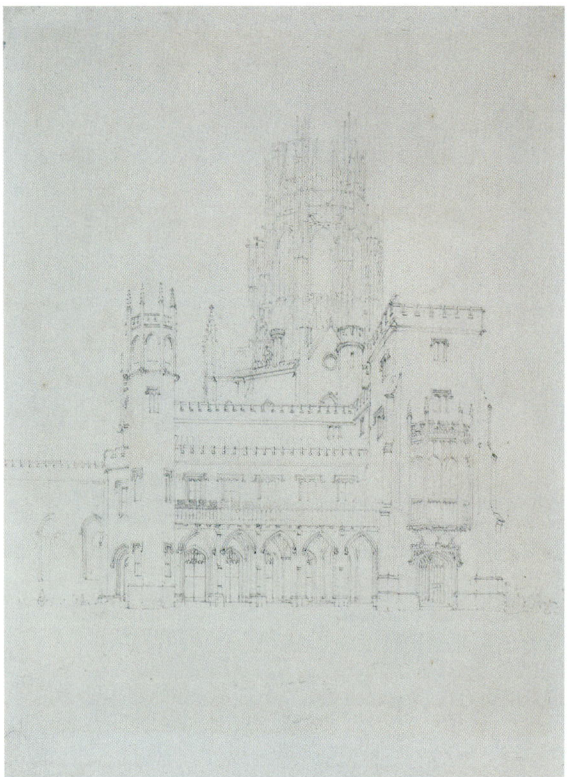

75. *Near View of the South Front of Fonthill
Abbey from the Lawn; Builders
at Work on the Tower*
J. M. W. Turner (1775–1851)

1799; England
Pencil on paper
18⅜ x 12⅞ in. (46.6 x 32.8 cm)
Tate Gallery, London, bequeathed by the artist 1856
(D02178)

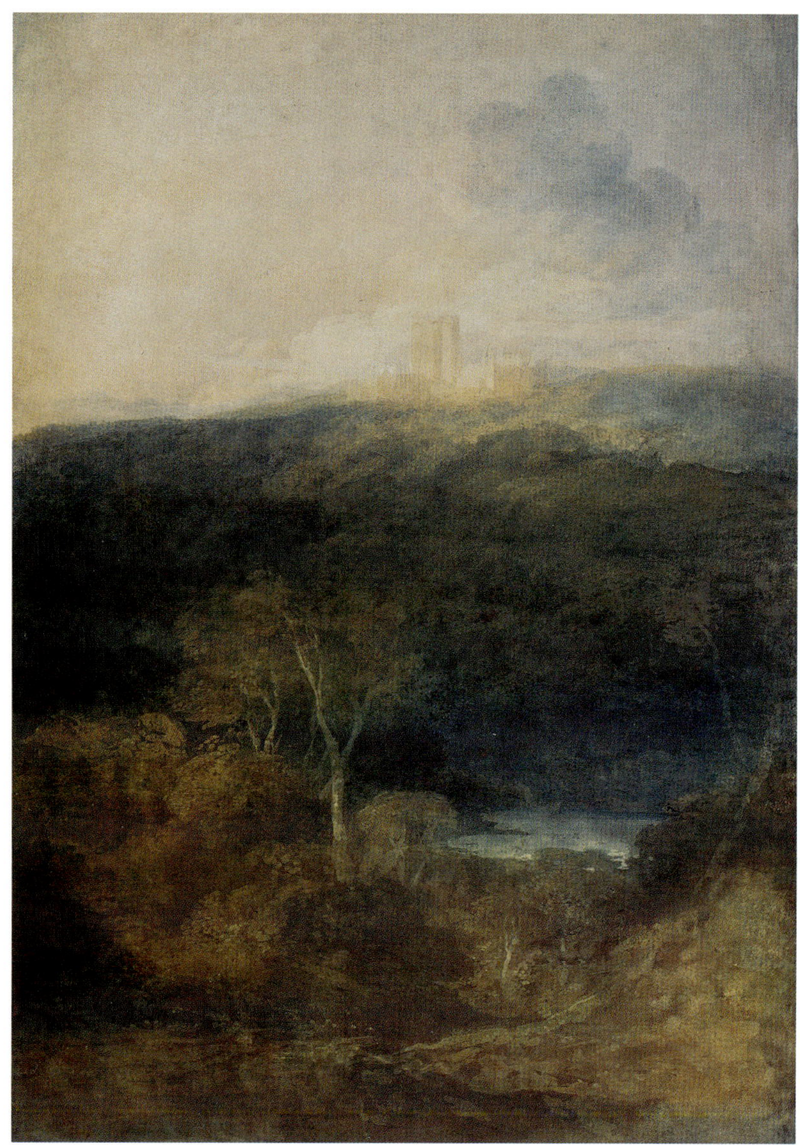

76. View of Fonthill Abbey
J. M. W. Turner (1775–1851)

1799–1800; England
Pencil and watercolor on paper
41¼ x 28 in. (104.5 x 71.2 cm)
Tate Gallery, London, bequeathed by the artist 1856
(D04167)

not built in this form. From 1806 to
1812 a more modest version of this
design was constructed, with lancet
windows and stepped buttresses on
the exterior of what was to be called
King Edward's Gallery, leading onto
the square "Lancaster Tower" with
its single oriel window. This range
terminated in a polygonal apse at the
extreme northern end of the Abbey,
the future location of Beckford's
much-discussed "sanctuary" dedicated to Saint Anthony of Padua, his
patron saint. None of this is visible
in the Yale view because, in 1798,
Beckford was intending to position
the sanctuary within the large octagonal space created by the central
tower.

This early view also shows an
elaborate central tower design with
enlarged crocketed pinnacles and
flying buttresses, neither of which
were used in the final tower design.
The elongated spire seen above the
central tower was never built, but
here it creates a silhouette that must
have been inspired by Salisbury
Cathedral, one of England's most
famous Gothic cathedrals which lay
to the southeast of the Fonthill
estate. Shortly before building
Fonthill Abbey, James Wyatt had
worked at Salisbury Cathedral on a
program of extensive restoration in
his capacity as Crown architect.

One of the most interesting if
puzzling Turner images, *Perspective
View of Fonthill Abbey* (cat. no. 74),
is now in the collection of the
Bolton Art Gallery in Lancashire.
It is not clear when this view was
taken, although it is generally dated
to around 1799. A good-sized watercolor, it shows the Abbey from the
southwest. The western hall, the
southwest and southern cloisters,
and the oriel window of the southeast tower, marking the terminus of
Saint Michael's Gallery, are depicted
in detail more or less exactly as they
were built (between 1796 and 1803).

*77. South-West View of a Gothic Abbey
(Morning), now Building at
Fonthill, the seat of W. Beckford,
Esq.*
J. M. W. TURNER (1775–1851)

1800; England
Graphite, watercolor and gum arabic on
wove paper
27¼ x 40½ in. (69.4 x 102.9 cm)
Art Gallery of Ontario, Toronto, Bequest of
John Paris Bickell, Toronto, 1952 (51/39)

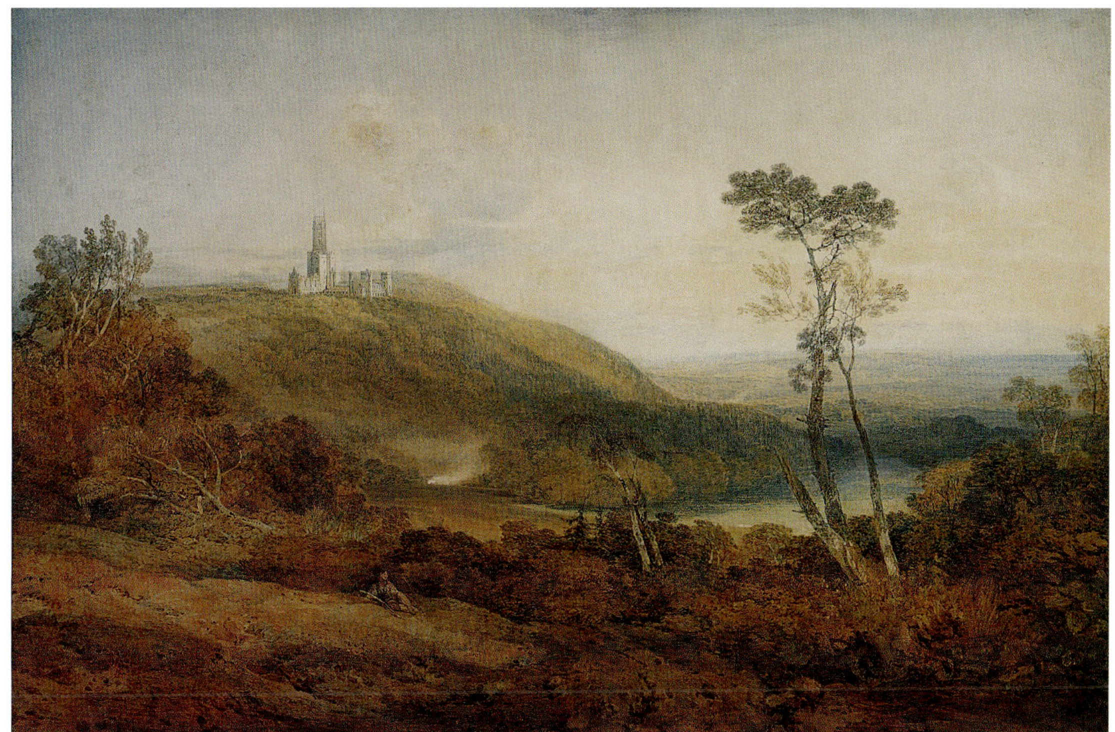

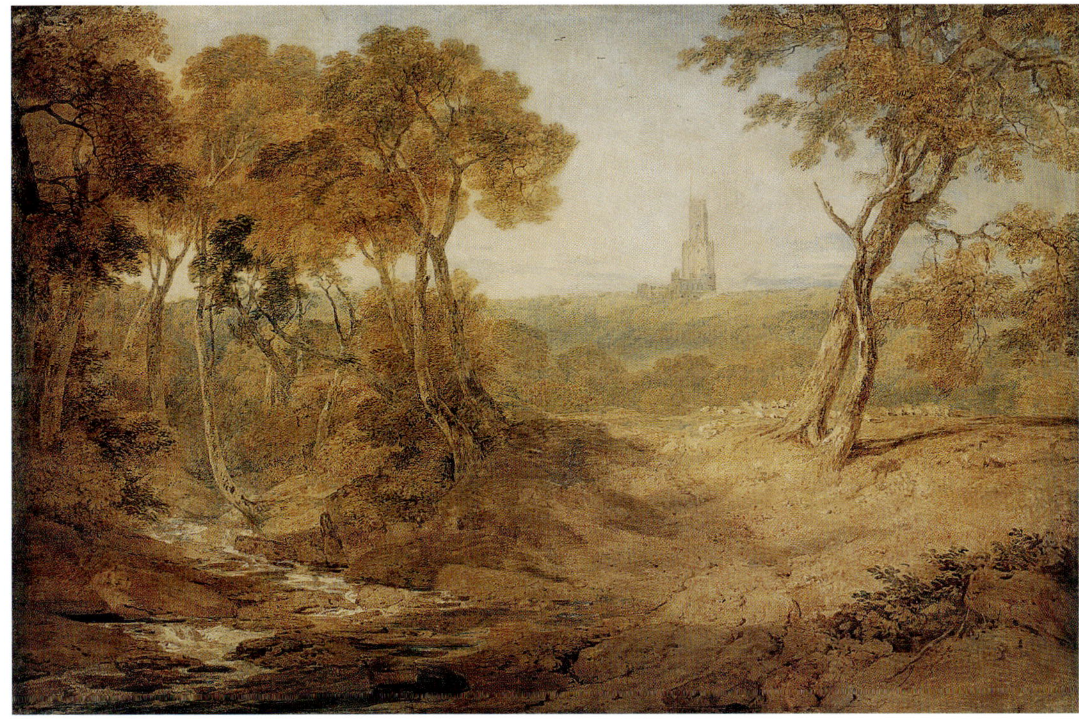

*78. South View of the Gothic Abbey
(Evening), now Building at
Fonthill*
J. M. W. TURNER (1775–1851)

ca. 1800; England
Watercolor
27¼ x 41 in. (70.5 x 104.4 cm)
The Montreal Museum of Fine Arts,
purchase, Horsley and Annie Townsend
bequest (1963.1385)

The architecture of the Conventual Abbey of Batalha in Portugal (see cat. no. 30), a subject of intense antiquarian interest during the 1790s, has supplied the inspiration for the design. The octagonal lantern with flying buttresses seen in the Bolton watercolor was taken almost without alteration from the Mausoleum of King John at Batalha, a building that James Wyatt would have known about by 1785 through a prominent Irish patron, William Burton Conyngham of Slane Castle, County Meath. Conyngham had sketched Batalha himself and promoted it in a publication prepared by the skilled architectural draftsman James Murphy in 1795. Both Wyatt and Beckford were subscribers to the volume, and Beckford visited the site during his third trip to Portugal between 1793 and 1796.

The Bolton Turner demonstrates that Beckford and Wyatt were seriously considering using Batalha as a model for the Octagon at Fonthill during the early stages of design, and logic would suggest that this view was done before the Yale view, where the central tower design is closer to the final version of the Abbey. The Yale view of 1798 retains the flying buttresses and elongated pinnacles of the Batalha mausoleum lantern, further suggesting that it is a development from it. This raises the possibility that the Bolton view of the Abbey may date to as early as 1797, preceding the Yale view. Perhaps because Wyatt had already used the Batalha model at two other Gothic houses (Lee Priory in Kent, and Cassiobury Park in Hertfordshire), or perhaps because the Portuguese building lacked the sublime height of the tower evident in the Yale version of the Abbey, Beckford ultimately decided not to use the Batalha mausoleum lantern as a model for the Abbey.

Turner's views of Beckford's Abbey

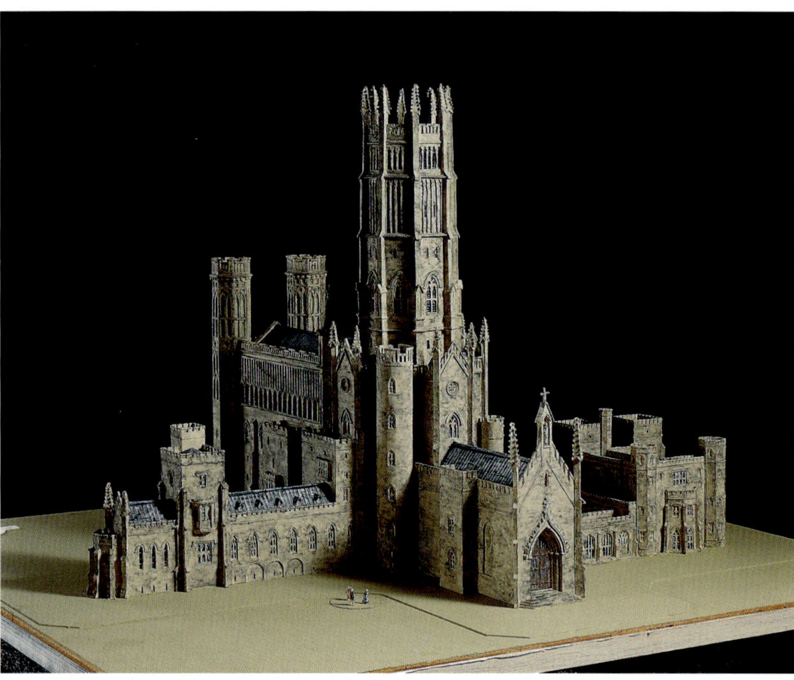

79. *Model of Fonthill Abbey*
MICHAEL BISHOP (AFTER THE ORIGINAL MODEL BY JAMES
WYATT, CA. 1798)

ca. 1981; England
Reinforced cardboard
25⅜ x 31½ in. (65 x 82.5 cm); scale, 1 inch to 12 feet
Beckford Tower Trust, Bath (Sole Trustee Bath Preservation Trust) (1981/3)

provide an invaluable record of some of the architectural ideas of James Wyatt, for Wyatt's own drawings and professional papers have nearly all disappeared. There is evidence of careful measurement of architectural detail in Turner's sketches, although his perspective is sometimes less than convincing. The architectural features are clearly depicted as they were built and can be related to other neo-Gothic work by Wyatt. This illustrates how closely Turner must have relied on Wyatt's architectural drawings. In 1799 Beckford commissioned Turner to prepare a series of watercolor views of Fonthill Abbey. Turner visited in the autumn to make preparatory drawings in his "Fonthill Sketchbooks," which were divided in the later nineteenth century and are now located principally at Tate Britain in London. One of these pencil sketches, *Fonthill Abbey with Workmen on Scaffold*, is interesting for its incidental detail, showing workmen and horse-drawn carts bringing building materials to

the Abbey, where the upper stories of the central tower are very obviously under construction.

Another Turner sketch (cat. no. 75) shows the octagonal tower in its unfinished state, along with a detailed rendering of the southern end of the building where the principal living rooms of the Abbey were located. To the right is visible the projecting oriel window of Saint Michael's Gallery; to the left of this structure, rendered with deep shadows, is the arcaded south cloister, which shaded the stained glass windows of the Oak Parlour, one of Beckford's main living rooms. Above this cloister are the smaller, lancet windows of the Eastern and Western Yellow Drawing Rooms, so-called because of the brilliant yellow silk damask with which they were hung. The Western Yellow Drawing Room had an oriel (seen here in the upper story of the polygonal bay) which contained large vases of Chinese porcelain given to Beckford by the prince of Brazil, a member of the

Portuguese royal family.[3] Some of Beckford's lacquer and ebony cabinets were also displayed in these rooms, and the black and gold contrast would have been accentuated by the sunlight that streamed into this southwest corner of the building.[4]

Turner's sketches of Fonthill, done in the autumn of 1799, were in preparation for a series of highly finished, watercolor views showing the Abbey as it was to appear by 1803. The five watercolors were exhibited at the Royal Academy in London in 1800, and they show the Abbey in the distance, from different directions and under different conditions of light. Perhaps because of the unfinished state of the building when he was sketching, Turner chose to depict it as a faraway point in the Fonthill landscape, rather than attempting to portray the architecture in detail.[5] The result is a series of glowing atmospheric views that reveal the highly picturesque, asymmetrical design of the Abbey as it would have appeared in 1803, when its first phase of building, consisting of the western hall, the southern range, and the central tower, was complete.

Fonthill Abbey (cat. no. 76) may have been a preparatory sketch for one of these five views. It shows the Abbey in the distance, seen from the southwest across the hollow in the landscape where Bitham Lake is situated. The Abbey, in common with the two trees which frame the lake, acts as the center point of the composition, and a contemporary publication on medieval architecture likened the qualities of Gothic to those of trees, suggesting that Gothic architecture arose from a system of building in timber.[6] In all of Turner's watercolor views of Fonthill, the Abbey dominates an empty landscape whose most prominent features are trees.

South-West View of a Gothic Abbey (Morning), now building at Fonthill, the seat of W. Beckford, Esq. (cat. no. 77) is perhaps the most beautiful and informative of these views. Here the hilly landscape rises above Bitham Lake, in the middle ground, to reveal the Abbey from the key southwest vantage point. The south range of the building, depicted in

detail in Turner's "Fonthill Sketchbooks," is clearly visible. To the left, in this view, lies the western hall with its pointed gable, while the central tower rises high above the structure in two stages. At this phase in its development, the Abbey had an irregular, L-shaped plan. Moreover, its shape and profile changed as it was observed from different directions. This, along with the differing lights Turner captured, makes his series of watercolors so interesting.

South View of the Gothic Abbey (Evening), now building at Fonthill (cat. no. 78) captures the building head-on from the south. This has the effect of emphasizing the height of the tower at the expense of the sprawling southern range of the Abbey, making it appear more vertical in silhouette than it actually was. Revealed in the distance through a parting of the trees, Turner suggests an almost poetic relationship between the surrounding landscape and the architecture of Fonthill Abbey.

Architectural models must have been a common feature of prestigious architectural commissions, but they rarely survive. Because of the clarity and detail with which the architecture of Fonthill Abbey is represented, this model (cat. no. 79), based on the original attributed to James Wyatt, shows the Abbey as it must have appeared in 1799, or later. Visible is the Eastern Transept, the largest range of the building, which was first illustrated in Wyatt's drawings shown at the Royal Academy in this year. The term *transept* is rather coyly and inaccurately used here. Beckford's transept was unfinished in 1822 when he sold the Abbey.

In 1800, when Turner created his series of watercolor views of Fonthill Abbey, it was an L-shaped building whose primary entrance was the western hall. The enormous oak formal entry door is clearly visible at the center of this model underneath the pointed gable. The south range, with its stout, battlemented towers and double polygonal bay, is visible towards the right of this model, while the looming tower, designed in two stages, has a squarish lower block (containing the Octagon Saloon) with an attached stair turret supporting an octagonal tower of four stories. The tower has slender stepped buttresses and truncated crocketed pinnacles developed from the octagonal lantern at Batalha Abbey. This was how the Abbey at Fonthill appeared from 1803, when the first phase was finished, to 1806, when the northern range was begun.

With the building of the northern arm of the Abbey, the L-shaped plan became T-shaped. To the left in the model can be seen the seven traceried windows of King Edward's Gallery, which—along with Saint Michael's Gallery to the south, to which it connected via the central Octagon—housed a great part of Beckford's library and collection of antiquarian objects and works of art.

To the north (left, in this illustration) lies the square Lancaster Tower, its oriel window marking the State Bedroom, and the extreme north of this range housed the sanctuary to Beckford's patron saint, Saint Anthony of Padua. This part of the Abbey was built by 1812, the year in which it was recorded in some detail by James Storer in *A Description of Fonthill Abbey, Wiltshire*.

The final part of the Abbey to be built was the Eastern Transept, which transformed the plan of the house into an asymmetrical cross. Begun in 1812 thanks to a temporary increase in Beckford's income, the great disparity in scale between this enormous block and the rest of the Abbey is made obvious by the model.

In 1812, the year before his death, James Wyatt had been much involved with designing architectural moldings and details for the transept, which he and Beckford had planned since 1799. The wing housed several large reception rooms, all decorated in crimson with heraldic emblems. The upper story was to have been a baronial hall dedicated to the knights who wrested the Magna Carta from King John. According to Beckford, he and his wife were descended from all of them.

The Eastern Transept was unfinished when John Farquhar purchased the Abbey from Beckford in 1822, and Farquhar was in the transept when the tower collapsed in 1825. As late as the 1840s, a large part of the

Abbey still stood, with much of its interior decoration still visible. Today all that survives is a small portion of the north range of the building. The key element in Beckford's early plans for the Abbey was a sanctuary to Saint Anthony, and it is this part of the building that has survived and was added to in the later nineteenth century. Perhaps Saint Anthony was, indeed, watching over his most famous devotee. —M. A.

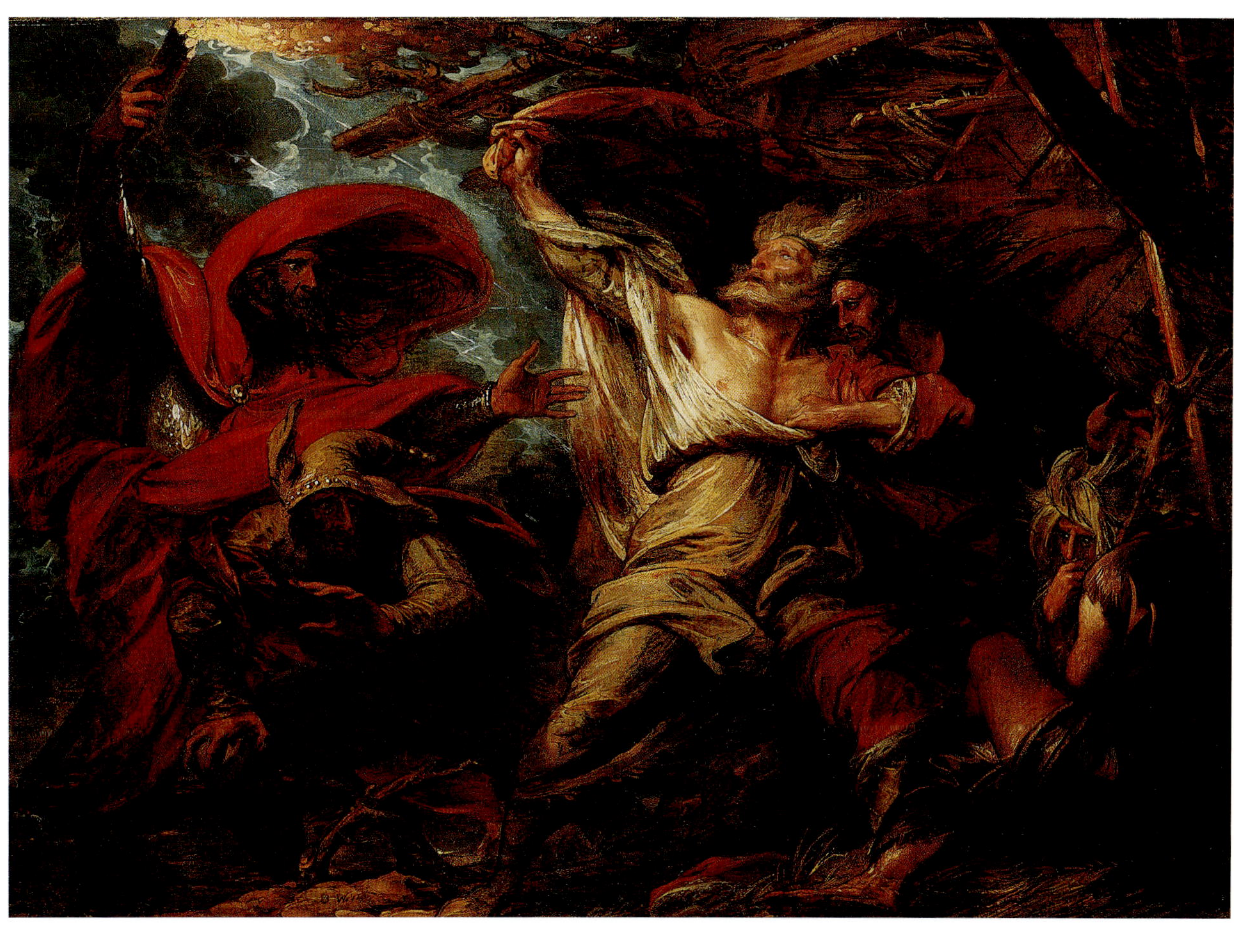

80. *King Lear*
Benjamin West (1738–1820)

ca.1788; England
Oil on canvas
20⅜ x 27½ in. (52.1 x 69.9 cm)
Founders Society Purchase, Gibbs-Williams Fund, The Detroit Institute of Art (77.58)

When Beckford was planning the decoration of Fonthill, he had Benjamin West in mind from the start. Beckford's interest in West was generated by the painter's enormous success and his importance as one of the leading lights of British history painters. As early as December 1796, Joseph Farington noted that Beckford had engaged "West . . . to paint a picture for him."[1] One picture became many, so that in the following May, Farington reported that Beckford had "ordered pictures from West of value £3000 and has paid him in advance £1000"—a sizable sum, but it was known that Beckford's annual income at a time came to £155,000.[2]

Farington's reference to the paintings Beckford ordered was to a series of Apocalyptic subjects conceived for the Revelation Chamber, which Beckford so scrupulously planned for Fonthill in 1798. This special room was designed to encase his coffin and remain a sacred spot in the building to which no entry was to be permitted.[3] West provided various decorative panels, but the series was never completed, and even when Beckford occupied Fonthill, the works that West had provided were never hung together as planned.[4]

While almost all of the paintings Beckford commissioned from West were portraits of his family or subjects related to the Fonthill site, Beckford's interest in West's paintings extended into the artist's religious and dramatic works.[5] This representation from *King Lear*, which was the only work, in this case an oil sketch, by West that Beckford acquired after the painter's death, had its origins in a commission West received in 1788 from John and Josiah Boydell for their Shakespeare Gallery.[6] The finished sketch, which West exhibited in the Royal Academy exhibition of 1789 (No. 88),[7] displays differences from the completed painting, which remained in the gallery until its acquisition by the Boston Athenaeum in 1828 (now in The Museum of Fine Arts, Boston). The provenance of this oil sketch is unaccounted for until Beckford acquired it sometime before 1838 when it was identified then as hanging in his dining room in Lansdown Crescent in Bath.

There is little doubt why such an effort should have appealed to Beckford. West's extraordinary mastery of drama and atmospheric effect, and the bold handling of color and form, were precisely the elements that Beckford thought desirable. The fact that it was a finished sketch, rather than a completed large painting, only enhanced its value for Beckford, since he thought it more demonstrative of West's genius than his completed efforts. As early as November 1, 1797, Beckford informed Farington that in regard to West's works, he "likes His sketches but not his pictures."[8] This was reaffirmed decades later when in front of this painting Beckford told Henry Venn Lansdown that having seen most of West's great pictures, "there is more genius in that sketch than in anything I ever saw of his."[9] —W. H.

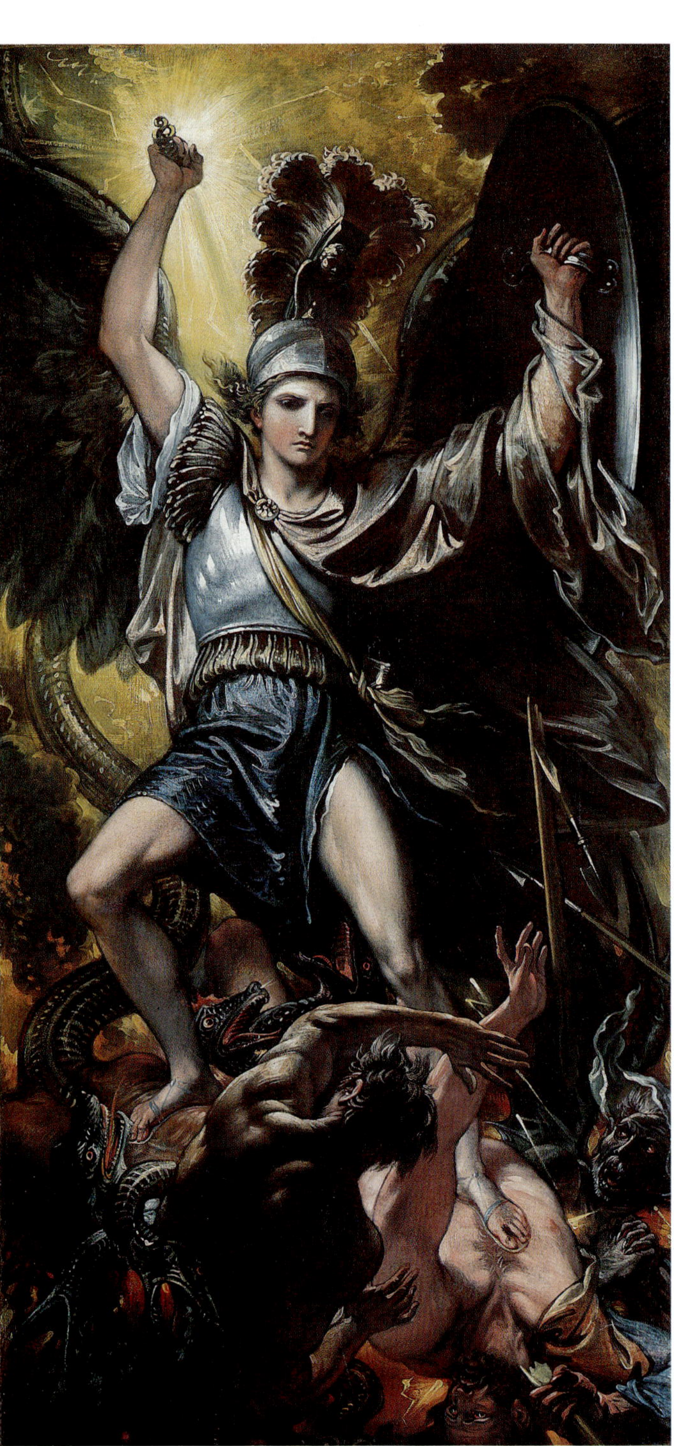

81. *Saint Michael and the Dragon*
BENJAMIN WEST (1738–1820)

1797; England
Oil on canvas
50⅜ x 23⁷⁄₁₆ in. (128.3 x 59.9 cm)
The Toledo Museum of Art, Toledo, Ohio; Museum Purchase Fund (1959.33)

One of the strangest aspects of Beckford's propositions for Fonthill Abbey was the so-called Revelation Chamber he planned in 1796. Detailed designs were already in place by the end of the following year and were known to Joseph Farington, who described the room as having walls five feet thick with recesses to accommodate coffins, including Beckford's own, as well as rich decorations that incorporated floors of colored stoneware with raised white decoration.[1] The room was intended to be seen from outside with no visitors allowed inside, a Beckfordian inner sanctum meant only for the unsullied select. West, who was approaching his sixtieth year, was engaged from the outset to provide pictorial decorations for the chamber in the form of wall paintings and window designs on Apocalyptic themes, some of which he began painting almost immediately after the commission was given. By September 1799, the plans were altered to the extent that now West was told not to begin work on the other paintings, and to terminate the works he had already begun, at that time amounting to four paintings.[2]

The idea of commissioning West for an image of Saint Michael came from Beckford.[3] The saint surely had personal associations for Beckford in at least two areas: the Feast of Saint Michael is September 29, Beckford's birthday, and Beckford probably saw analogies in Michael's celestial battles with his own terrestrial conflicts over tastelessness and ignorance. West's design, the first of the series to have been completed, was intended to be a stained-glass window, drawing upon an episode in the Apocrypha of John (Apoc. 12:7–9),[4] describing Saint Michael's defeat of the red dragon when it menaced the pregnant Virgin and the Child she would deliver.[5]

The composition West chose was necessarily an awkward one calling for Blakian imagination and Westian technique. Fundamentally it was an inharmonious composition, since the subject forced the juxtaposition of a grotesque Satanic creature with seven heads, seven diadems, and ten horns with a dauntless warrior-saint victorious in a celestial battle. The solution West chose, derived in part from Rubens's *Fall of the Rebel Angels*,[6] the composition of which West possessed four chalk studies,

hardly won the approval of Farington, who at the Royal Academy in 1797 thought the composition "very bad, ill drawn."[7] Beckford, however, apparently approved of the design and kept the painting for more than two decades. It would never hang in

the Revelation Chamber, which was not built, but may have hung in Saint Michael's Gallery in the south wing and then possibly in Beckford's Chintz Boudoir above the same gallery, where Beckford kept some of his most prized objects.[8] In 1823 it

was noted as hanging in the Tribune Room above the area which had been planned originally as the Revelation Chamber. —W. H.

---

82. *Pair of Candlesticks*
ATTRIB. TO BENJAMIN LEWIS VULLIAMY (1780–1854)

ca. 1800; England
Gilt bronze
14⅞ x 5¾ in. (36 x 14.61 cm)
Private collection

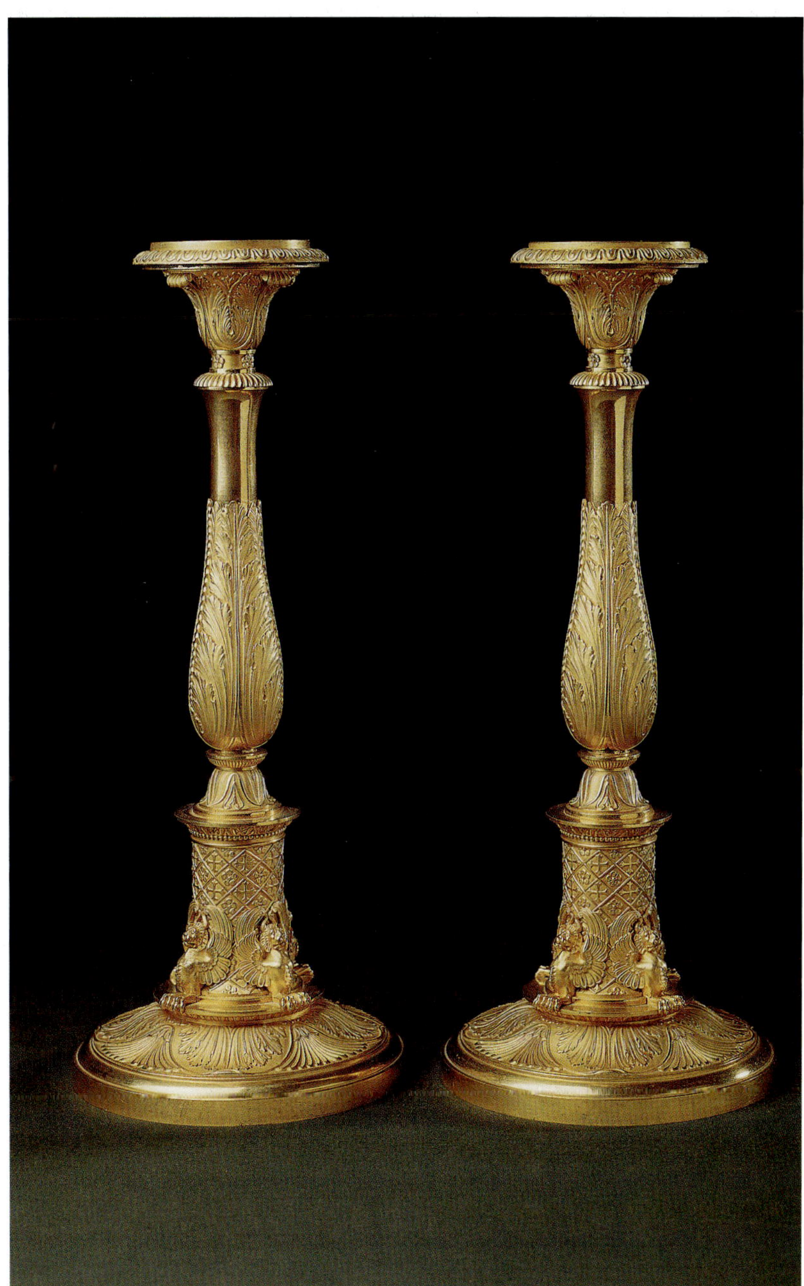

The candlesticks were designed around 1800 under the direction of William Beckford, and are executed in gilded bronze in a robust French antique manner that evokes Roman grandeur and celebrates Beckford's family achievements. Their multitier structure derives from the "Roman candelabra" featured in 1778 in the Italian publication, *Vasi, candelabri, cippi, sarcofagi, tripodi, lucerne, ed ornamenti antichi*, by architect G. B. Piranesi, published in Rome. Like elements in Beckford's Grecian-urn clock (see cat no. 47) the Homeric vase-capped pillars of these candlesticks also evoke the poets' concept of ancient sacrifices at Love's altar.

An overall pattern of cinquefoils

and Latimer crosses, all heraldic devices associated with Beckford, wreathe the "altar" pedestals in a diagonal, diaper pattern. The Hamilton cinquefoils inherited from Beckford's maternal side are checkered with his Beckford "cross moline," also called a Latimer cross, derived from the sixteenth-century Molinist, Hugh Latimer. Appropriately, their Grecian-stepped pedestals are guarded by chimerical eagle-winged lions that are sacred to the sun-deity Apollo and also symbolize the Element of Fire.

The choice of these griffins was further encouraged by the fact that they are derived from Piranesi's engraving of a tripod- altar pedestal

featured beneath a Roman krater vase in the collection of Cardinal Alessandro Albani.[1] This was one of two engravings that Piranesi dedicated to Beckford's cousin "Sign. Guglielmo Bekford" (William Beckford of Somerly Hall), who was

in Rome in 1770 while the architect was carrying out his grand project for *Vasi, candelabri, cippi, sarcofagi, tripodi, lucerne, ed ornamenti antichi*. More Beckford cinquefoils wreath the candle-nozzles, which are of wine-krater form wrapped by

Roman acanthus. More acanthus and triumphal palms are wrapped around their pillars.

The baluster form of these stems is likely to have been inspired by those of other candlesticks, wreathed by ancient "gothic" heads, that Beckford had commissioned from the celebrated Parisian goldsmith Henri Auguste. The latter were described as "of Gothic pattern by Auguste expensively chased and gilt."[2] Since the 1770s the firm of Auguste had employed the services of the brilliant Rome-trained sculptor-designer Jean-Guillaume Moitte, so the design of these candlesticks may be indebted in part to Moitte.

At Fonthill Abbey, Beckford celebrated his pride as a patriot and honored his ancestors' historic role in the defense of British liberty. Their achievements emblazoned his great library galleries and were splendidly lit by golden candlesticks. Some of these were placed upon rows of ebony-black gueridon-stands or torchères that combined an Elizabethan character with Louis XIV splendor. It is likely that Beckford's confidant and agent Gregorio Franchi supervised the design of the candlesticks as he was recognized by his contemporaries as "a man of taste"and known to have worked with various workshops in the design of objects for himself and Beckford. They are also likely to have been supplied by the Pall Mall firm of Benjamin Lewis Vulliamy, who held the appointment of Clockmaker to the Court and specialized in bronze manufactures. Vulliamy is especially celebrated for his role in supplying objets d'art to Carlton House for George IV as Prince of Wales and Prince Regent.

Formerly associated with a set of silver-gilt candlesticks which stood in Saint Michael's Gallery these gilt-bronze candlesticks are illustrated in Rutter's view of the Grand Drawing Room (cat. fig. 88A), standing on boulle torchères. —J. H.

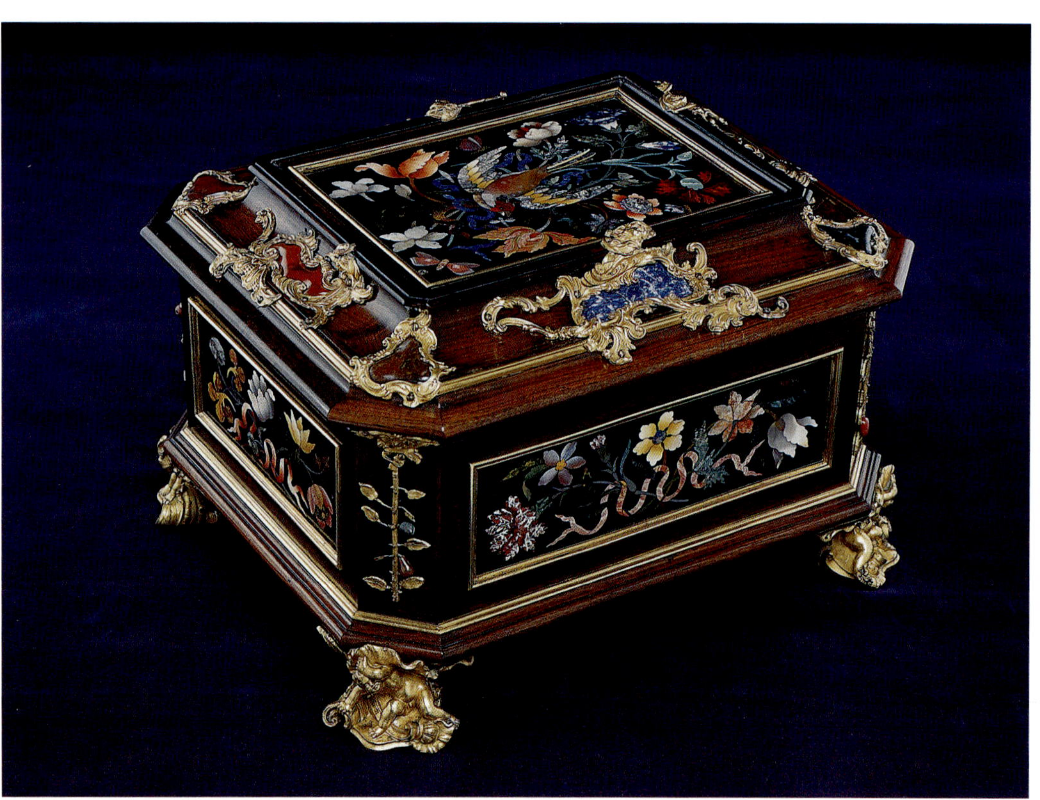

83. *Casket*

Maker unknown

ca. 1720; Italy
Ebony, pietre dure, semi-precious stones, gilt bronze
11⅝ x 19⅛ x 15 in. (29.5 x 48.5 x 38 cm)
Charlecote Park, The Fairfax-Lucy Collection (The National Trust), CHA.V.8

This ebony casket evokes the Renaissance magnificence of the Medici family. Appropriate for a jewel or dressing-box, its principal plaque displays a trompe l'oeil vignette of a bird seeking insects among flowers. The image serves to recall Flora, the Arcadian spring deity, and the Roman concept of an eternal spring, where love never grows cold. In addition, cupids and Venus-shell badges enrich its golden cartouches of Roman foliage, which are serpentined in the early eighteenth-century picturesque manner. The naturalistic treatment of the pietre dure reflects the Florentine style that was introduced at the Uffizi Palace's Gallerie dei Lavori of the Grand Duke Cosimo III (d. 1723), when it operated under the guidance of the sculptor and architect Giovanni Battista Foggini (1652–1725).

Pietre dure, together with rare marbles and mosaics, were much sought after by the eighteenth-century Grand Tourists. Among related caskets is one that belonged to the Prince de Beauvau Craon, who became Governor of Tuscany in 1737, and similar plaques feature on the monumental "Badminton" cabinet, which was commissioned from the Gallerie dei Lavori by Henry, third Duke of Beaufort around the time of his 1726 visit to Florence.[1]

It was probably during John Chute's tour of Italy in the 1740s that he acquired a Foggini casket, now at his home, The Vyne, in Hampshire.[2] Some of Foggini's greatest masterpieces are displayed in Rome at the Medici's Palazzo Pitti, from where this casket was reputed to have come.[3] Another related casket is in the Corsini collection, Rome.[4] Furniture comprised of ormolu-enriched ebony inlaid with either pietre dure or brass filigree comprised an important element of the Louis XVI court taste shared by Beckford and other English connoisseurs, such as the Prince of Wales. It later formed part of the Louis XIV revival that occurred during the reign of George IV (1820–30).

This casket, which was first recorded at Fonthill as part of the furnishings of the Great Dining Room, was acquired at the Fonthill auction in 1823 by George Hammond Lucy. He shared Beckford's "taste" and was recognized as "a lover of the fine arts, and a most excellent judge of all things rare and beautiful."[5] Lucy was one of the principal purchasers at the Fonthill sale, as he had just embarked on the aggrandizement of his recently inherited "Elizabethan" mansion of Charlecote Park, Warwickshire. His wife, Elizabeth, listed the sixty-four lots he purchased from the Fonthill sale, among which were a monumental sixteenth-century pietre-dure table from the Borghese Palace, a "Superb ebony commode, with panels of the fine ancient Florentine Pietre Commesse," and this "magnificent ebony coffer, the panels of beautiful Florentine mosaic . . . originally from the Pitti Palace, Florence."[6] —J. H.

84. *Casket*
Maker unknown

Late 18th century; Italy
Silver gilt, agate, jasper, lapis lazuli
8⅜ x 14½ x 11 in. (21.5 x 36.8 x 28 cm)
Burghley House Preservation Trust, Ltd., Lincolnshire (EWA08666)

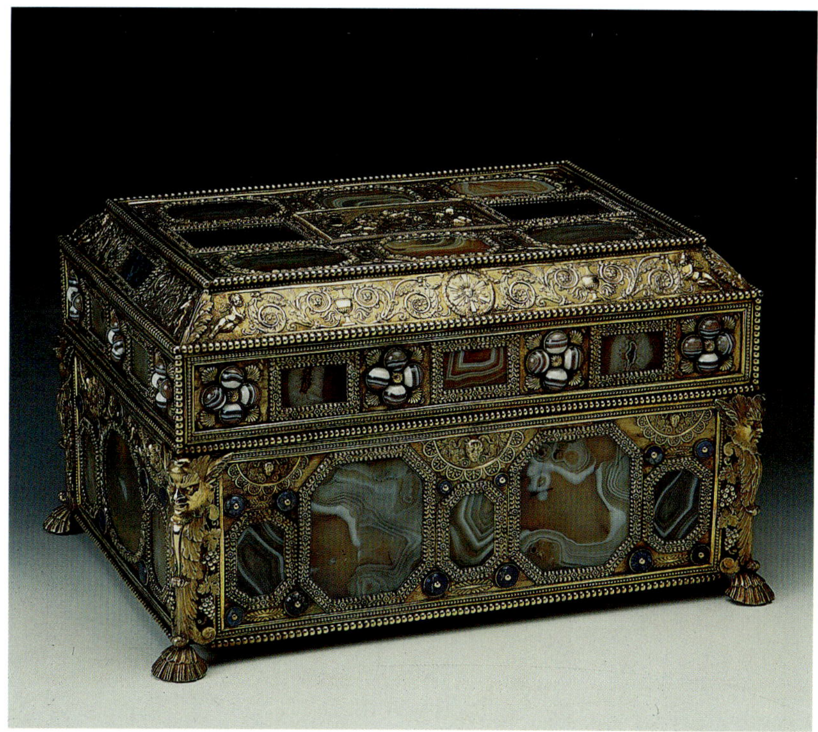

This casket is illustrated in "A Groupe of the rarest articles of virtu," which shows several objects from Beckford's collection displayed on a table (see fig. 9-2).[1] The use of rare agates and hardstones is reminiscent of the vogue for the specimen marble table-tops that were purchased in Rome by visitors on the Grand Tour. This casket is a magnificent display of rare agates mounted in a sophisticated and luxurious fashion. The form and decoration of the mounts represent an amalgam of styles and periods ranging from Byzantine, as seen in the granular bead decora-

tion and the stepped sloping lid, to Renaissance, with the grotesque-winged mask corner mounts. The Baroque style is represented by the inclusion on the lid of the rectangular silver relief of putti teasing a goat, after a design by the Italo-Flemish artist François Duquesnoy, who was known as "Il Fiammingo." Duquesnoy was sculptor to Pope Urban VIII in Rome, which may explain the reference to "devices from the Vatican" in the following description from Phillips' 1823 Fonthill Abbey sale catalogue (lot 1294): "A magnificent silver gilt

casket panelled with 36 of the most beautiful specimens of oriental & moss agates, jaspers, bloodstones &c. the friezes elaborately chased in arabesque devices from the Vatican." The casket was purchased for the considerable price of £137 by Kensington Lewis, a retailer who sold antique works of art as well as

modern pieces in an old style.[2] Subsequent to its purchase by Lewis it entered the collection at Burghley House, where the inventory lists it as having been bought in 1822, which is not accurate, as the casket was not sold until 1823. —E. M.

85. *Table*
Maker unknown

ca. 1816; England
Oak
29 x 34 x 20 in. (73.66 x 86.36 x 50.6 cm)
Charlecote Park, The Fairfax-Lucy Collection (The National Trust), CHA.F.7

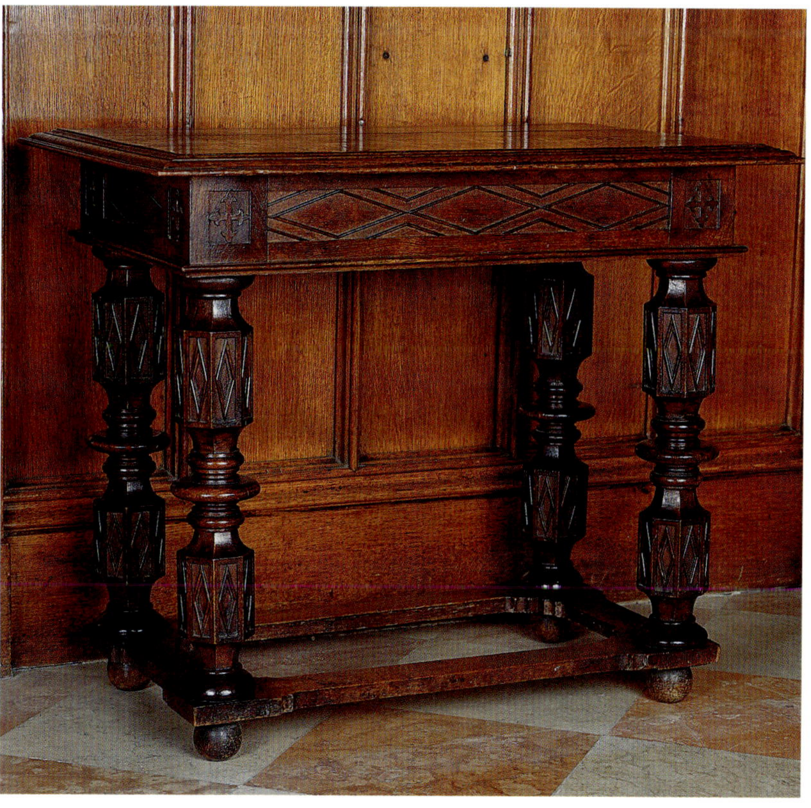

This is one of the "six oak stands" in "Edward the Third's Gallery" at Fonthill Abbey identified by John Rutter in 1822.[1] In *Delineations of Fonthill and its Abbey* (1823), Rutter described King Edward's Gallery as "a magnificent apartment embellished with a masterly and unsparing hand, superbly furnished, the ceiling covered with carving, and the walls nearly concealed by the ample and duplicated curtains of deep blue and scarlet."[2] The accompanying illustration (cat. fig. 85A) shows the

rich decoration, typical of Fonthill Abbey's interiors, filled with both old and contemporary furniture, including the famous "Borghese Table"[3] on a base made for Beckford, two massive oak cabinets,[4] some of the "twelve ebony fluted stands,"[5] and four of the "oak stands."

George Lucy was a major buyer at the Fonthill Abbey Sale of 1823, acquiring sixty-four lots for his home, Charlecote Park, for a total of £3,431.10.6d.[6] Included among Lucy's purchases were four of the six

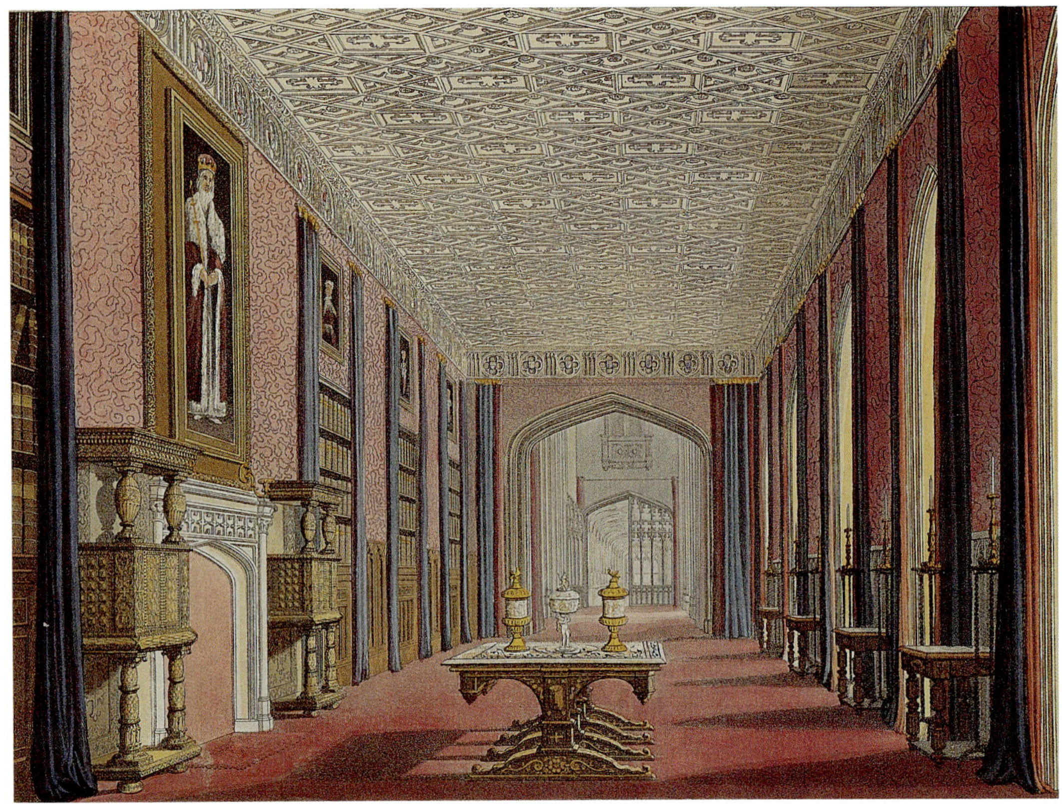

Cat. fig. 85A. "Fonthill Abbey: Interior of King Edward's Gallery, looking across the Octagon to Saint Michael's Gallery." From Rutter, *Delineations of Fonthill* (1823): plate 6.

tables from King Edward's Gallery, described as, "A pair of small GOTHIC TABLES, finely carved in oak" (day 14, lot 477), which sold for £16.5.6d., and the next lot, "A pair of ditto, en-suite," which sold for £16.16.0d. These are still at Charlecote Park.

The tables were conceived in the seventeenth-century style,[7] but are distinguished by their diamond carved frieze and correspondingly carved double tier octagonal and turned legs, with a Latimer cross in each top corner, signifying Beckford's commission. It is very likely that one of the Wyatts, either James or Jeffrey, was responsible for the design of the tables. Around 1810 chairs, for example, were supplied to Wyatt's design for Endsleigh House, Devon, the Duke of Bedford's quintessential Regency Picturesque, Tudor Gothic residence. The designs demonstrate the architect's ability to interpret the seventeenth-century style.[8] —M. P. L.

86. *Cabinet*

Attrib. Robert Hume Jr.
(fl. ca. 1815–50)

Cabinet work, ca. 1815–20,
England; pietre dure, 17th-
century, Italy
Ebony, gilt bronze, lacquer,
marble
50 x 61 x 18 in. (127 x 154.9 x
45.7 cm)
Charlecote Park, The Fairfax-
Lucy Collection (The National
Trust), CHA.F.72

The publications of John Rutter do much to bring alive the lost interiors of Fonthill Abbey. In *Delineations of Fonthill*, he wrote, "From the dining room the visitor is shewn into the NEW ROOM, which is fitted up with crimson hangings, and contains a very valuable collection of cabinets, paintings, &c. . . . A superb JEWEL CABINET of EBONY and other costly materials . . . Two fine BUHL COMMODES . . . A superb CABINET of GOLD JAPAN."[1] This cabinet or commode, then located on the west side of this

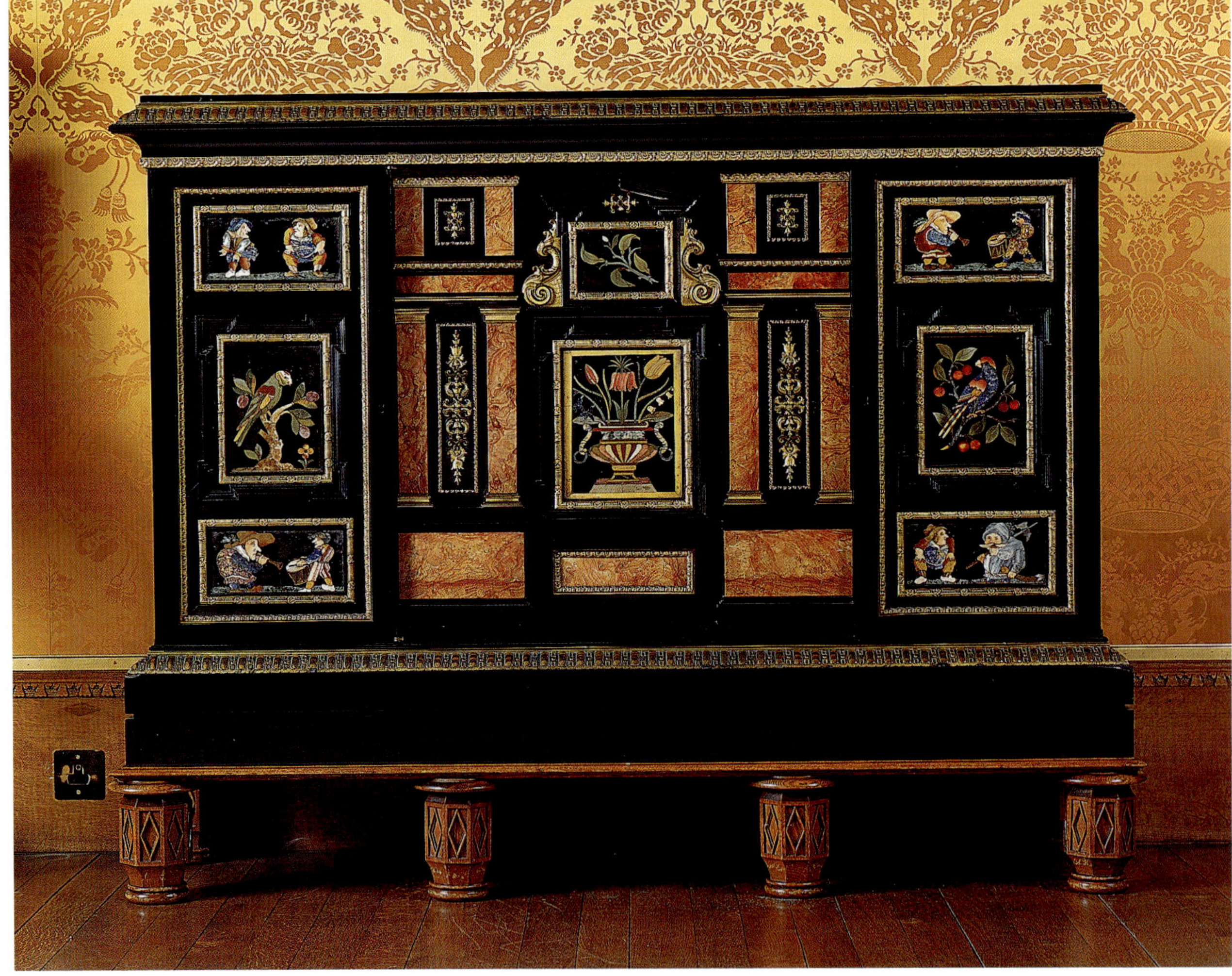

room, is described as the "fine
EBONY COMMODE, with mosaic
pannels, architectural centre and
wings, richly ornamented with
or-moulu, five feet three inches
long, with black marble slab." In
A Description of Fonthill Abbey (p. 29),
Rutter placed this "commode
of ebony, japan and Italian marble" in
the Great Dining Room. The commode can be identified in the canceled Fonthill Abbey sale, arranged
by Christie's in 1822, as lot 96 on the
third day. At the 1823 Philips' sale
at Fonthill Abbey, it was acquired
by George Hammond Lucy, from
the Crimson Drawing Room for
£156.10.0d (day 29, lot 1138); it was

described as "An EBONY COM-
MODE, with MOSAIC PANNELS,
architectural centre and wings, richly
ornamented with or-moulu, 5 feet 3
long, with black marble slab."

Beckford's companion and agent
Gregorio Franchi was passionately
interested in hardstones. He probably acted as an agent, finding materials to satisfy Beckford's admiration
for furniture and gilt-bronze
mounted objects using hardstones.
In 1814, for example, Franchi received
a shipment of hardstones from
Paris, which may have included
seventeenth-century pieces from
the Gobelins workshops, as well as
others from Italy.[2] This commode

may have been entirely constructed
in the early nineteenth century,
reusing earlier elements such as
pietre dure, "japan," perhaps the
marble pilasters, and some of the
central ormolu mounts.[3] The creation of this piece can be confidently
attributed to Robert Hume Jr., who
may have received the pietre dure
and marble pilasters from Franchi.[4]
The "Beckford" commode is closely
related to a group of commodes and
cabinets also attributed to Hume,
although it is arguably less successful
aesthetically than the other designs.[5]
The oak feet on the commode are
similar to the legs on the Fonthill
Abbey table (see cat. no. 85), but

they may have been added later by
Hume for Lucy.[6]

The configuration of the panels
and pilasters on the front of the
present commode is derived from
late-seventeenth- or early-eighteenth-
century models.[7] The four panels
depicting dwarfs are based on engravings published in Jacques Callot,
Varie Figure Gobbi (Florence, 1616),
top left and bottom right being
direct copies. The panels of flowers
and birds are typical of seventeenth-
and early-eighteenth-century Florentine work.[8] —M. P. L.

---

87. *Cabinet*

Attrib. Edward Holmes Baldock (1777–1845)

Cabinetwork, gilt bronze, ca. 1815,
England; ebony panel, 17th century,
France or The Netherlands
Ebony, gilt bronze
41 x 37⅞ x 16½ in. (104 x 95.2 x
42 cm)
Charlecote Park, The Fairfax-Lucy
Collection (The National Trust),
CHA.F.74 A and B

This commode, one of a pair, was
in the Crimson Drawing Room at
Fonthill Abbey, at one point situated
opposite the pietre-dure cabinet (cat.
no. 86). Rutter describes them as:
"A pair of EBONY COMMODES,
with carved doors, supported on
each side by ebony columns, with
or-moulu caps, bases and mouldings,
and with a black and gold marble
slab."[1] In the catalogue of the canceled Fonthill Abbey sale of 1822,
the cabinets are lots 55 and 56 on the
fourth day: "A SUPERB COM-
MODE of EBONY with carved
door.. ." and "A DITTO, the companion." On day 29 of the Fonthill
Abbey sale in 1823, lot 1144 was: "A
SUPERB CONSOLE of EBONY
with carved door, supported on
each side by ebony columns with
OR-MOULU caps, bases and
mouldings, and black gold MARBLE
SLAB." Lot 1145 was: "A DITTO,

the companion." They were sold
together, to Lucy, for £147.0.0d.,
and both commodes are still at
Charlecote Park.

During the second and third
decades of the nineteenth century,
there was a considerable vogue for
modern furniture incorporating old
ebony elements.[2] Robert Hume Jr.
supplied ebony furniture to Beckford, but this cabinet and its pair are
traditionally attributed to Edward
Holmes Baldock, one of Beckford's
favored suppliers.[3] Baldock is well
known for having fabricated furniture using seventeenth-century
carved ebony panels,[4] which seem to
have been something of a speciality
for him. When the contents of his
premises were auctioned in 1843,
there were several lots which must
have been similar in appearance to
the doors on the commodes at
Charlecote: "A pair of ebony doors,
richly engraved, the centre Boldly
carved in subjects . . . Mutius Scaevola
and Quintus Curtius . . . the story
of Galatea . . . Samuel denouncing
Saul," and so on.[5] The same sale
included "Fluted pillars" (May 26,
1843, lot 137) and many other ebony
elements. The door on this commode (cat. no. 87), depicting an
Adoration, would have come from
a seventeenth-century French or
Flemish cabinet.[6]

Other Beckford cabinets in this
catalogue display ormolu mounts of

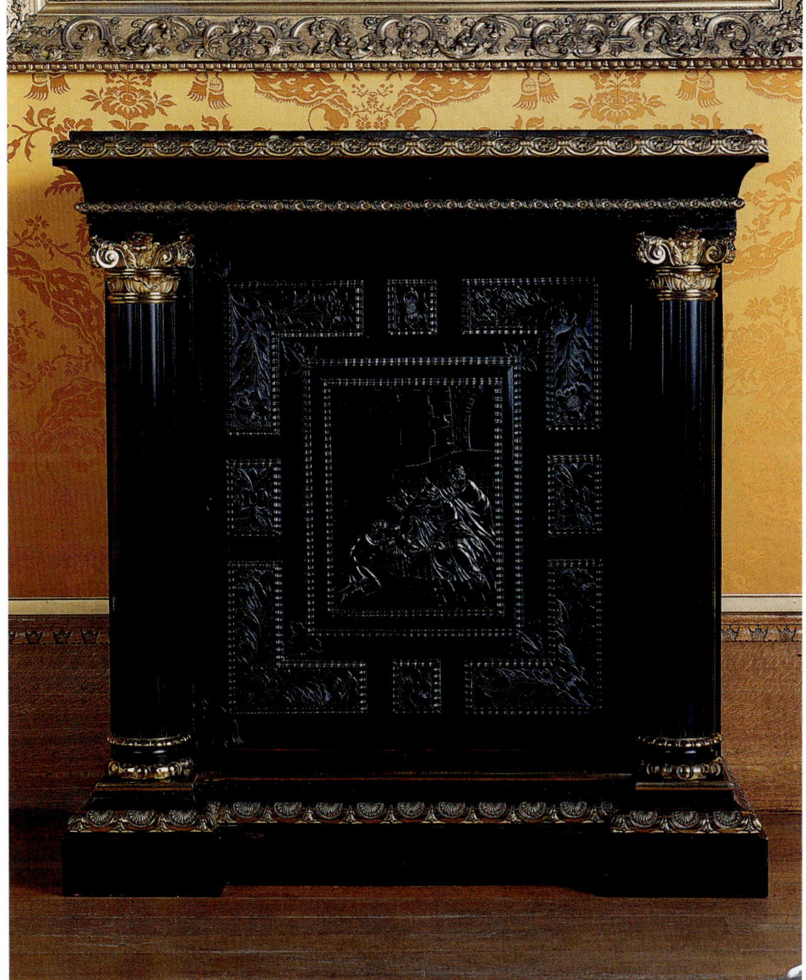

similar quality, although those on
the pietre-dure commode (cat. no. 86)
may be slightly superior to those on
this cabinet. In the context of this
piece and the pietre-dure commode,
it should be noted that Beckford

happily combined modern furniture
with furniture reusing old elements
and the grandest examples of ancien
régime *ébénisterie*.[7] —M. P. L.

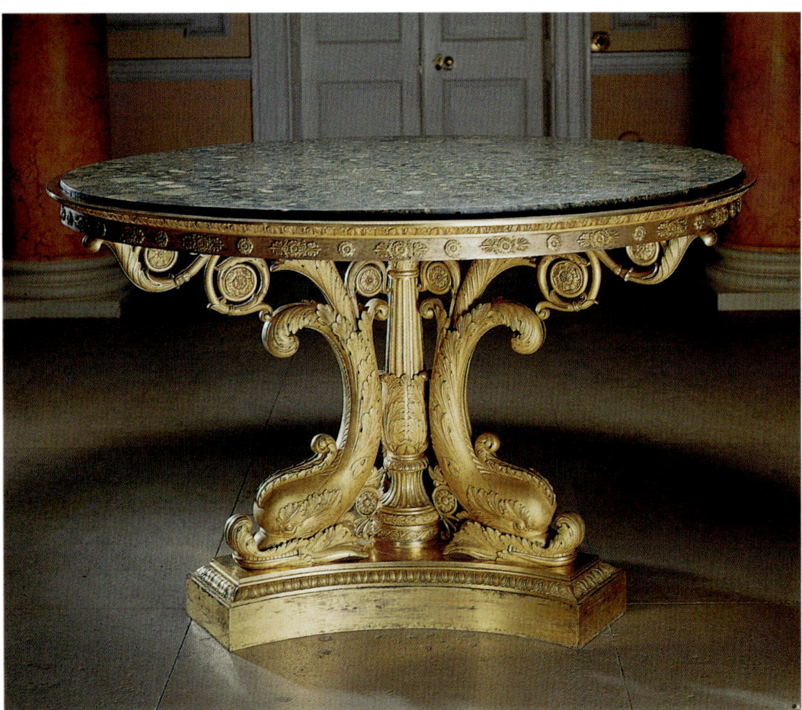

88. *Table*

Maker unknown

Base, ca. 1816, England;
marble, Africa
Gilt bronze, marble, oak
36¼ in. (92 cm), diam. 58½ in.
(148.5 cm)
Private collection

Of the many pieces owned by
Beckford, this table reveals his eye
for rare materials, his admiration for
superb contemporary craftsmanship,
and his fascination with provenance.
Rare marbles were highly prized
both in antiquity and in the eighteenth century. They were particularly appreciated by Beckford, who
may have been responsible for having
the gilt-bronze base made for this
rare marble top. In the posthumous
inventory of Empress Joséphine,
taken at Malmaison in 1814, the
gallery of the house is recorded as
having four tables—one pair and
two single semicircular consoles—
with tops of *breccia universale*
marble: "No. 1311 item à droite et
à gauche deux dessus de tables en
forme de consoles, brèche dure
universelle, formant jaspe, venant
d'Egypte, prisées cinq cents francs
ci . . . 500. . . . / No. 1378 item
ensuivant au coté droit de la grande
porte de la galerie, une table demi-
circulaire en brèche dure universelle,
formant jaspe, matière d'Egypte,
prisée deux cent cinquante francs

ci . . . 250. . . . / No. 1386 item en
suivant de l'autre coté de la porte
vitrée, une table demi-circulaire en
breche universelle formant jaspe,
matière d'Egypte, prisée deux cent
cinquante francs ci . . . 400."[1]

The circular top of this table is
composed of two mirror-figured
semicircular sections skillfully joined
together, and there is evidence of
the earlier configuration of the slabs
as tops for console tables. It seems
likely that Beckford acquired the
pair, listed as no. 1311, rather than
the two single console tops.

The hardstone *breccia verde
d'Egitto* (*lapis hecatontalithos*) from
Uadi Hammâmât (Mons Basanites)
on the west bank of the Red Sea
acquired the name *breccia universale*
because it is composed of numerous
fragments of other porphyritic and
granitic stones, principally green,
but also incorporating yellow, red,
white, and brown. Much admired
in the Roman Empire, it was
used for columns by Emperor
Constantine in the building of SS
Apostoli in Constantinople.[2]

The designer and maker of the
superb gilt-bronze base remain a
mystery. Beckford himself is likely to
have played a significant role in its
design and creation, but even where
it was made is not clear. The
extreme refinement of surface treatment with a strong emphasis on
matte surfaces, highlighted by spar-

ing use of burnishing suggests
French craftsmanship. This is echoed
by the ingenious construction,
which is a masterpiece of precision
engineering. The design, however,
suggests that it is more likely to have
been created in England than
France, but perhaps by French-
trained craftsmen. Although the Vulliamys are a possibility—the central
shaft is reminiscent of their work—
their records show no further commissions from Beckford after 1804.

The series of four massive chandeliers "of Grecian metal" supplied
by William Collins in 1823 to the
third Duke of Northumberland for
Northumberland House in the Strand
provides an interesting parallel. The
chandeliers were manufactured for
Collins by Johnston, Brookes and
Company, 32 New Street Square,
London, and demonstrate the scale
and quality of metalwork that was
being produced in England around
1820, a few years after the creation of
Beckford's spectacular table.

The table was located in the
Grand Drawing Room at Fonthill
Abbey (cat. fig. 88A) and was
described by Rutter in 1822: "In the
centre of the room upon a carpet of
extraordinary costliness, stands a
table of Egyptian marble, the largest
slab of the kind in Europe."[3] It is
shown with another of Beckford's
most prized possessions, the jeweled
hookah, another example of rare

Eastern materials embellished by
Western craftsmanship (see cat.
no. 55).

A year later, the Phillips' sale catalogue lists the table (lot 1140) in the
adjoining Crimson Drawing Room:
"A Splendid Saloon Table, formed
of a circular slab of the very rare
Breeche Universelle, of
extraordinary size, the diameter
being 4ft, 8, on a *grand and massive*
STANDARD, formed of THREE
BRONZE DOLPHINS, *sumptuously*
GILT, in or-mat, on a corresponding
PLYNTH and EBONY PEDESTAL,
and cover to ditto. his *extraordinary*
SLAB was brought from Egypt by
the EMPEROR BUONAPARTE,
and presented to the Empress
Josephine, and was purchased at the
sale at Malmaison, in 1816."[4]

Beckford's table was acquired at
the Fonthill sale by the "very wealthy
merchant and manufacturer" Philip
John Miles for his newly commissioned Leigh Court, Bristol. Miles
was also the owner of the famous
"Altieri" Claudes, paintings formerly
in Beckford's collection at Fonthill
Splendens.[5] —C. H. C.

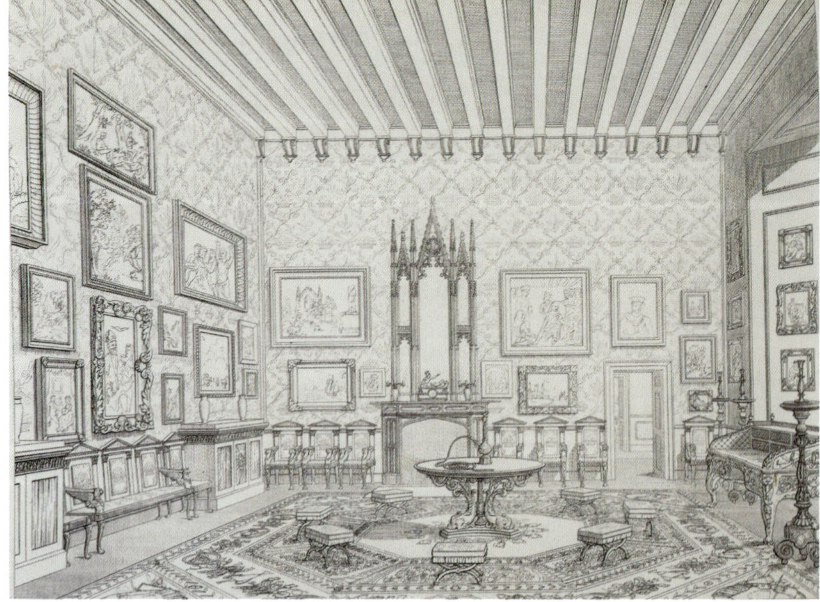

Cat. fig. 88A. "Fonthill Abbey: The Grand Drawing Room." From Rutter,
Delineations of Fonthill (1823): plate 5.

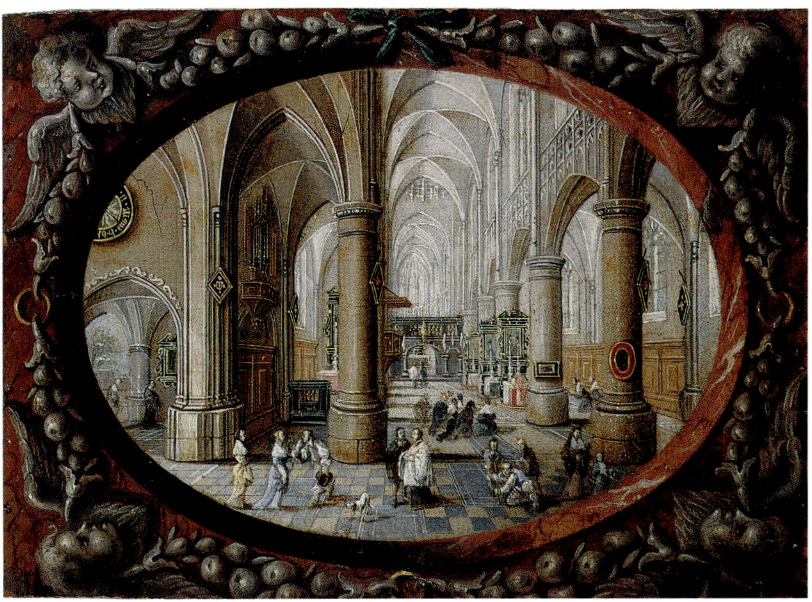

89. *Interior of a Gothic Church by Day*
PIETER NEEFS THE ELDER (AFTER 1577–1656/61)

ca. 1600–1650; The Netherlands
Oil on copper
4¾ x 6¼ in. (12.1 x 15.85 cm)
Private collection

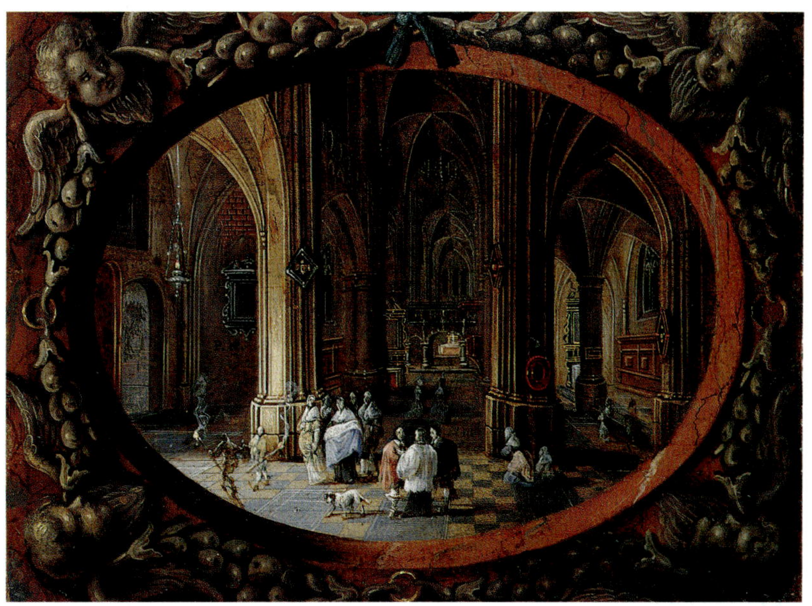

90. *Interior of a Gothic Church by Night*
PIETER NEEFS THE ELDER (AFTER 1577–1656/61)

ca. 1600–1650; The Netherlands
Oil on copper
4¾ x 6¼ in. (12.1 x 15.85 cm)
Private collection

89-90. CHURCH INTERIORS BY NEEFS THE ELDER

This pair of paintings appeared in the Beckford inventory, made after his death in 1844, as in the Belvedere at Lansdown Tower.[1] There they were displayed with *Young Man at Prayer,* then attributed to Dürer, and the "small" *Tobias and the Archangel Raphael Returning with the Fish* (cat. no. 7) then considered to be by Elsheimer.[2] They were further mentioned on an 1852 list of items sent from Bath to Easton Park (now demolished) in Suffolk, a residence of the Duke and Duchess of Hamilton.[3]

The oval shape is unusual in Neefs's work, but the paintings are similar in size and composition to a pair whose figures were painted by Frans Francken III and which also depict interiors by day and by night.[4] It was usual that the tiny figures in the interiors were painted by another hand, such as Francken, Teniers, Jan Brueghel, and Van Thulden, all of whom painted figures for Neefs. It is not known, however, who painted those in Beckford's pair of paintings.

Beckford's own passionate interest in architecture is evident in many of the paintings that he owned. In some cases the architecture was dominant, while in others it remained a backdrop for another subject. He was drawn to both the grand and the minute scale, and delighted in detailed architectural renderings, particularly of Gothic interiors of churches. Neefs was a particular favorite of his. Although it is difficult to ascertain exactly which other paintings by Neefs were owned by Beckford, given the problem of vague titles and descriptions, the collection certainly included *Interior of a Magnificent Cathedral*, with about fifty figures painted by Teniers, and *Interior of a Town House at Antwerp,* painted with the artist's son, Pieter Neefs II, and Gonzales Coques.[5] There are also numerous references to similar subjects by Dutch or Flemish painters that were owned by Beckford, such as *The Interior of the Oude Kerk, Amsterdam during a Sermon* by Emanuel de Witte (now in the National Gallery, London). Another very fine painting, *Interior of a Church* by Anthonie de Lorme, was commented on by Gustave Waagen during his visit to Lansdown Tower.[6] Two other interior views were at Fonthill Splendens: *Interior of a Church* by Jan van Nickelen and *Interior of the Great Church at Antwerp by Daylight* by Hendrik van Steenwyck, which Beckford had inherited from his father.[7]

Neefs was one of three brothers, all of whom were painters. He was probably a pupil of either the elder or younger Steenwyck, but his work demonstrates more obvious influence of the younger. A most distinguished architectural painter, Neefs concentrated mostly on interiors, particularly those of Antwerp Cathedral, often with slight variations in the composition or detail or sometimes with the introduction of imaginary elements. From 1609 to 1610 Neefs was a master in the Guild of Saint Luke in Antwerp, his home town. —J. C.

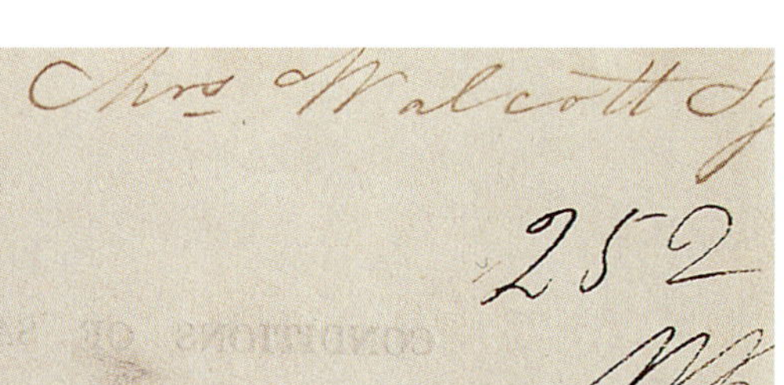

MAGNIFICENT

EFFECTS

AT FONTHILL ABBEY,

WILTS.

TO BE SOLD BY AUCTION,

By Mr. CHRISTIE,

ON THE PREMISES,

ON TUESDAY, OCTOBER 1, 1822, AND NINE FOLLOWING DAYS,

(SUNDAY EXCEPTED)

BEGINNING EACH DAY PUNCTUALLY AT TWELVE O'CLOCK.

The Abbey and Grounds may be Viewed after the 1st of July, by Cards, which, with Catalogues, may be had (at One Guinea each) of Mr. Clark, Bookseller, Bond Street, London: as also at the Beckford Arms, Fonthill: Lamb Inn, Hindon: of Messrs. Browdie and Dowding, Salisbury: at the Lord's Arms, Warminster: Deptford Inn, Wiley: York House, Bath: Bush Tavern, Bristol: New London Inn, Exeter: Crown, Blandford: Mr. Ruttee, Bookseller, Shaftsbury. Catalogues also may be had of Mr. Hitchcock, on the Single, at Amsterdam: at Mr. Nieuwenhuys's, Brussells: at Mr. Galignani's Office, Paris: and of Mr. Christie, Pall Mall, London.

*91. Fonthill Abbey Sale
Catalogue*
Christie's (second issue)

1822; England
Paper
7⅛ x 8¾ in. (19 x 22.2cm)
Private collection

The August 1822 announcement that Fonthill Abbey and its contents were for sale stimulated a "fever" of interest in seeing Beckford's Wiltshire estate. For twenty-five years, Beckford's building activities at Fonthill had attracted much speculation. Although the Abbey's tower was "so prodigiously tall that it is visible from a vast distance & is the principal, object to all the country around," very few people outside of Beckford's circle had actually visited the Abbey. A few brave trespassers, like William John Bankes, had climbed the boundary wall of the estate, but the general public was largely kept at bay, and the Abbey remained a subject of gossip and wonder.[1]

Beckford's financial position, despite the legends about his great wealth, worsened in the early 1820s. The price of sugar declined and with it the value of his Jamaican estates. He had high mortgages that demanded considerable annual interest payments. In 1822, he was hopeful that his son-in-law, the Duke of Hamilton, would come to his rescue by paying the most pressing debts, and in exchange for £80,000, Beckford would bequeath his entire estate to Hamilton and his heirs. After much haggling, conducted on Beckford's behalf by Gregorio Franchi—who said, "One of [Beckford's] whims is never to discuss business with the person concerned, and consequently I have to broach it"—the negotiations came to nothing.[2] Only one option remained, Fonthill had to be sacrificed.

The ten-day sale, to be arranged by James Christie, was first announced as starting on September 17, which date was changed to October 1 and again to October 8. Christie's catalogue, for which there are three issues, each bearing the respective date on the title page, was probably prepared with help by Beckford and Franchi. The public was admitted to view the Abbey and its grounds from July 1 by admission cards, which with the catalogue cost one guinea each (£46 in 2001).[3] The high cost of admission did not deter the public interest. So great was the curiosity that the London *Times* reported: "he is fortunate who finds a vacant chair within twenty miles of Fonthill. . . . Falstaff himself could not take his ease at the moment. . . . The beds through the county are literally doing double duty—people who come in from a distance during the night must wait to go to bed until others get up in the morning."[4] Among those who came to view Fonthill were the king's brother-in-law, the Duke of Gloucester, and the dukes of Beaufort, Buckingham, and Wellington. Altogether some 7,200 visitors were admitted.[5]

Illustrated guidebooks to the Abbey and its estate were issued by both Whittaker and John Rutter to meet the public hunger for information about Fonthill. In the following year further descriptions and illustrations were to appear, including Rutter's *Delineations of Fonthill and its Abbey* (1823), and John Britton's *Graphical and Literary Illustrations . . .* (1823).[6]

Beckford gauged the "fever" for his creation from the safety of Bath and London. "The rage is at its height," he wrote to the Duke of Hamilton on September 2. "They dream only of the Abbey, they talk only of it. I doubt whether since the beginning of printing they have ever uttered such extravagances."[7] Behind Christie's back, however, Beckford was conducting negotiations with a rival auctioneer Harry Phillips. The day after public viewing ended on October 5, just three days before the sale was due to commence, it was announced that negotiations were taking place to sell the whole estate by private treaty. —S. B.

92. *Fonthill Abbey Sale Catalogue*
Phillips'

1823; England
Paper
6⅛ x 9¼ in. (15.5 x 23.4 cm)
Private collection

During the final viewing days of Christie's proposed auction of 1822, Beckford was negotiating to sell Fonthill Abbey and its contents to an eccentric millionaire, John Farquhar, who gained his wealth by selling gunpowder to the East India Company. On retirement, he had increased his fortune by speculation. Unmarried and unkempt, he lived in squalor in London's Baker Street. On the day that Christie's auction should have begun, the agreement between Beckford and Farquhar was signed. Farquhar paid £275,000 for the Abbey and its estate, and a further £25,000 for the contents, except for a third of the library, manuscripts, drawings and prints, and some pictures and works of art already removed by Beckford to Bath.

Farquhar probably purchased Fonthill as a speculative venture. A year later, he instructed Phillips to sell the majority of the Abbey's contents, giving the public a second chance to see the celebrated estate. Accommodation was available at local hotels and inns, while refreshments and beds were offered in a dormitory at the Pavilion, the remaining wing of Alderman's Beckford's otherwise demolished Fonthill Splendens. Single beds were priced at 3s.6d. and double beds, 5s. John Constable, the artist, who visited on August 18, commented on the commercial nature of the view: "Mr Phillip's name (the Auctioneer) seemed here as great as Buonaparte's—cards of various kinds and board were put up—Mr P. desires this—Mr P. takes the liberty to recommend the following inns &c &c. . . ."[1]

Phillips' thirty-seven-day sale commenced on September 9 and ran until October 31, being much longer than that announced by Christie, as some twenty days were devoted to the sale of some 4,000 books. Phillips had also introduced into the sale books, furniture, and pictures that had not belonged to Beckford. John Constable felt sure that he had recently seen a battle scene by Wouvermans in London: "so that after all it is quite an auctioneer's

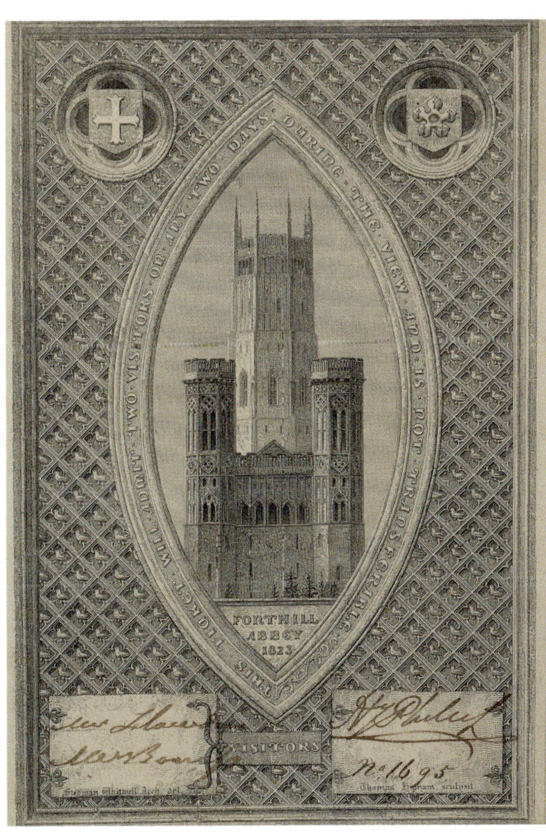

job."[2] Beckford himself declared to Cyrus Redding: "Do not suppose that more than half of what was sold at Fonthill was mine. . . . I would not disgrace my house with Chinese furniture—that was not mine—it was put in by the auctioneers."[3]
—S. B.

93. *Admission Ticket*
Phillips

1823; England
Paper
7⅞ x 5⅛ in. (20 x 13 cm)
Private collection

Admission tickets for viewing Fonthill in 1823 were available at various rates: for one person (half a guinea), two persons (one guinea), with admission allowed on any two days; and for three persons (five guineas), with admission every day of the view and sale. The ticket itself depicts the Eastern Transept of the Abbey with the central tower beyond. It bears Beckford's heraldic devices: the Latimer cross and cinquefoil. There are places for the names of the ticket-holders and the signature of the auctioneer, Harry Phillips. At the bottom were detachable tokens.

The *New Monthly Magazine* declared that "the world may just at present be divided into two classes; those who have seen Fonthill Abbey, and those who have not."[1] John Constable, one of those to fall into the first category, wrote to his wife after his visit: "It was very good of Fisher to take me to see that extraordinary place—the ticket to admit two persons is a guinea, beside impositions when you arrive."[2] Constable also commented on the large number of people present: "I counted more than 30 carriages, and half the number of gigs, & 2 stage coaches, so that in spite of the guinea ticket there was a great mix of company—very few genteel people."[3] Like many others, he was charmed by the place: "Imagine the inside of the Cathedral at Salisbury or indeed any beautifull Gothick building magnificently fitted up with crimson & gold, antient pictures, in almost every niche statues, large massive gold boxes for relicks, &c &c,. beautifull & rich carpets, curtains, & glasses—some of which spoiled the effect—but all this makes it one whole, strange, ideal, romantic place—quite fairy land."[4]
—S. B.

Antiquarian Taste

eckford's intense admiration for virtuoso works of art of an earlier period was reflected in his acquisition of objects that are masterpieces of technique, ornament, and materials. The diverse nature of Beckford's collection encompassed the art of the goldsmith, jeweler, lapidary, and ceramicist, and comprised a wide range of materials and styles. Well-known artists featured strongly in the collection, and, when accompanied by a significant provenance and romantic associations with the past, these pieces formed an important aspect of Beckford's taste.

That Beckford acquired many more Continental works of art than English pieces is possibly explained by his lifelong prejudice against a society that he considered had wronged him so badly. Nevertheless the lure of illustrious or sentimental provenance clearly outweighed any disdain for works of art from his own culture. Ironically, his celebrated "Cardinal Wolsey" ebony furniture, some of the historic pieces he claimed had English associations, is now known to be of Indo-Portuguese origin.

Although Beckford inherited a sizable fortune founded two generations earlier, he was still considered nouveau riche—and a colonial as well. By contrast with his aristocratic contemporaries, he had not inherited an impressive collection. His was almost entirely formed and dispersed, to a large degree, within his own lifetime.

Despite the antiquarian nature of the architecture and interiors that were so brilliantly realized at Fonthill Abbey and at Lansdown Tower, Beckford himself was first and foremost a romantic rather than an antiquarian collector. This aspect of his extremely diverse collection contained principally Renaissance and Mannerist works of art. This taste reflected the collections typically found in fifteenth-century Italian ducal courts or princely German *Schatzkammern* of the sixteenth and seventeenth centuries. Beckford's romantic sensibility quite consciously looked back to such aristocratic collecting traditions.

94. *Interior of a Grand Saloon of Pictures*
GASPARD JACOB VAN OPSTAL THE YOUNGER (1654–1717) AND OTHER MASTERS OF THE ANTWERP GUILD OF SAINT LUKE

ca. 1676–98; The Netherlands
Oil on canvas
53½ x 79⅛ in. (136 x 201 cm)
Private collection

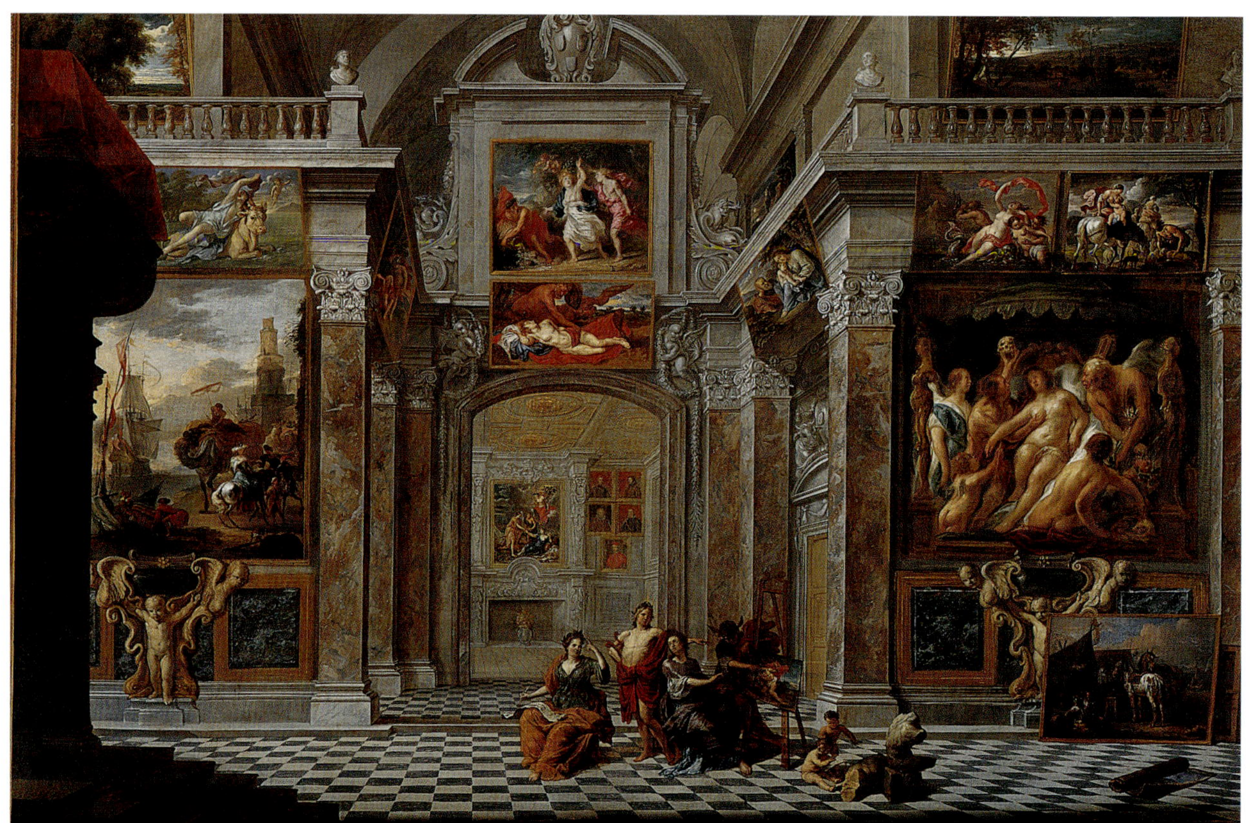

This painting hung at Fonthill Abbey, on the west wall of the "cabinet" or dining room, over the door.[1] After Beckford moved to Lansdown Crescent in Bath, it was in the anteroom or "small front parlour" where it was seen by Henry Venn Lansdown on his visit in 1838.[2] This location was also given in the inventory made following Beckford's death in 1844.[3] The painting hung with an assortment of pictures including: a portrait of Edward VI, then attributed to Holbein; the pair of Brueghel *Elements* (see figs. 13–4 and 13–5); and a watercolor of Fonthill Abbey by Turner.[4] More recently this painting was the property of Ray Livingston Murphy, an American collector, who was particularly interested in Beckford-related material, much of which was given to Yale University after his death. Other similar paintings of views of palace interiors in Beckford's collection included *Interior of a Palace Saloon* by Bartholomeus van Bassen, a Dutch painter and architect. This was described by Waagen as a "rather large, rich picture."[5] There was also *Interior of a Town House at Antwerp* painted by the Neefs, father and son, with Gonzales Coques, which shows a collection of identifiable paintings.[6]

The subject of this theatrical picture must have appealed greatly to Beckford as a collector, and he owned other examples in which an imposing architectural setting created a grand stage where the paintings within are identifiable.

Paintings of real or imaginary *Kunstkammern* or of picture galleries became fashionable from the beginning of the seventeenth century and were particularly popular in Antwerp, a city with rich merchants eager to display their wealth and possessions.

Although dated 1698, this painting was possibly begun in about 1663, the date of the founding by royal decree of the Academy of Saint Luke, under the direction of David Teniers. It is thought to be the presentation piece for the Antwerp Guild of Saint Luke, who retained control of the painters' Academy. The guild's coat of arms appears over the doorway. It is likely that this is a commemorative gift to the institution in which different painters collaborated with their own contributions of architectural background, figures, or miniature paintings. The group of allegorical figures representing the arts in the foreground of the painting are considered to be by van Opstal, while other elements are painted by several different individuals, some of whose initials or signatures appear but are barely decipherable.[7] The architecture is thought to have been painted by William Schubart von Ehrenburg.[8] Known works can be identified within the painting, although some are uncertain: in the upper left, *The Rape of Europa* by Titian, signed by Lumorlet (?); below it, *Coastal Scene* signed by Hendrik van Minderhout; just over the door, *Jupiter and Antiope* after Van Dyck and above it *Apollo and Daphne* by Theodor Boeyermans (signed with initials). In the background, the painting over the mantel has not been identified, but the portraits to the right are thought to be by Rubens and his school. To the top right is a large landscape possibly by Fouquier, with *Venus with Nymphs and Dolphins* in the style of Albani and *Flight into Egypt* possibly by Gentileschi or in the style of Simone Cantarini. The large center right painting is thought to be an allegory, a lost work by Jordaens, and possibly *Soldiers' Encampment,* signed with initials by Pieter van Bloemen, is propped against the wall.

Van Opstal was born in Antwerp and also painted portraits, as well as religious and allegorical subjects. He was Master of the Guild in 1676–77; his father, who had taught him to paint, had also been master. —J. C.

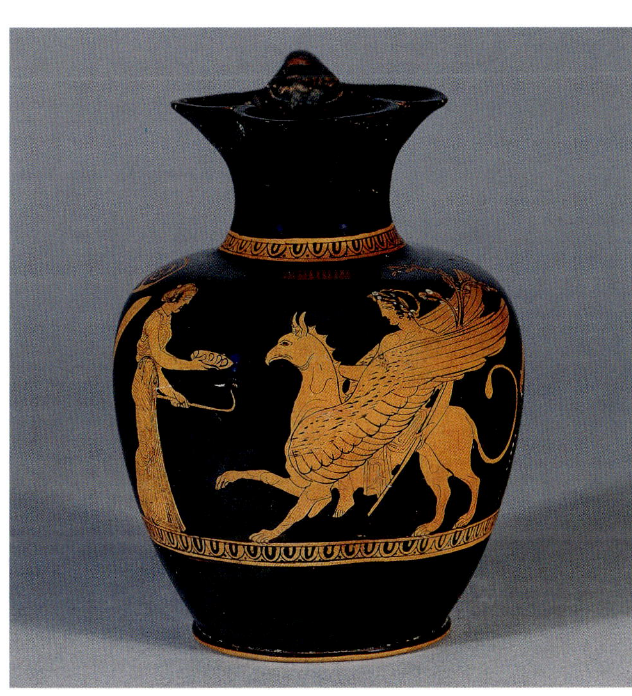

95. *Oinochoe (wine jug)*
THE NAME-PIECE OF THE PAINTER OF LONDON E543

ca. 420–400 B.C.; Greece
Ceramic
8¼ (21 cm), diam. at neck 5⅝ in.
(14.3 cm)
The British Museum, London
(E543)

After his birth on the Greek island of Delos, the god Apollo was carried by swans to the land of the Hyperboreans, beyond the north wind. He spent a year on this remote margin of the world before returning to Greece. Apollo is here shown carrying a long laurel branch, seated on a griffin. He is greeted by his sister Artemis holding a bow in one hand and a libation bowl in the other. Leto, the mother of these twins, follows with her scepter and beaded fillet. The subject is rare in Greek art, but the scenario of a deity riding a fantastic beast follows a pattern familiar for the epiphany of divine travelers in Greek vase-painting.[1]

Between 1828 and 1829 more than 3,000 Greek vases were found in tombs at Vulci, Italy, principally on land owned by the Prince of Canino (Napoléon's younger brother Lucien Bonaparte).[2] The discovery transformed contemporary understanding of such objects in bringing to light vases of the finest period of Greek vase-painting (ca. 550–450 B.C.), many of which had been imported into Etruria in antiquity from mainland Athens.[3] Before that discovery, collections such as that of Sir William Hamilton (1730–1803) had been assembled from excavations in southern Italy and Sicily,[4] where, in the fourth century B.C., migrant Greek potters manufactured provincial versions of painted Greek pottery.

When the Etruscan tombs at Vulci to the north were found, the contents proved to be rich in sixth- and fifth-century imports from Athens which made the south-Italian vases seem crude by comparison.[5] The Vulci vases were quickly sold into public and private collections, and their publication promoted interest in an entirely new repertoire of scenes depicting Greek daily life and stories from myth. Only in recent years have the south-Italian vases come to be appreciated once more.[6]

This vase was bought at the Canino sale in Paris by Beckford's son-in-law, the Duke of Hamilton.[7] He appears to have given the piece to Beckford, since it is included in the posthumous sale of Beckford's effects in Bath in 1845.[8] It was bought by Charles Empson, who sold it to the British Museum that same year.[9] The reason for the Duke of Hamilton's gift of the vase to Beckford is revealed by comparing the subject of this vase with that of another jug, formerly in Beckford's possession.[10] The subject is the epiphany from the Orient of a god, probably Dionysos. Dressed as a Persian, he arrives riding on a camel accompanied by his ecstatic retinue. This scene, facing right, made a pair with the image of Hyperboraean Apollo on this vase, facing left. Beckford must have acquired the other piece around the 1836 sale in Paris of the collection of Edmé-Antoine Durand.[11] The vase was listed in the Bath sale of 1845 as lot 419. It was bought by the Duke of Hamilton and came once more onto the market at the Hamilton Palace sale in 1882, when it entered the British Museum.[12] Made in Athens around 410–400 B.C., it had been found in the region of southern Italy known as Basilicata.

Both vases appear in the *Illustrated London News* in the description of the sale held in 1845 after Beckford's death.[13] Further "Etruscan" vases are also shown, although it cannot be certain from the engravings whether these are genuine or "Wedgwood Etruscan" pieces.[14] After Beckford's death "6 Imitation Etruscan Vases" were sent from Bath to Hamilton Palace.[15] It would appear that Beckford had many such vases at Lansdown Tower in Bath, where they were prominently displayed in the neo-Renaissance interiors of the Vestibule and, more appropriately, in the Etruscan Library. —I. J.

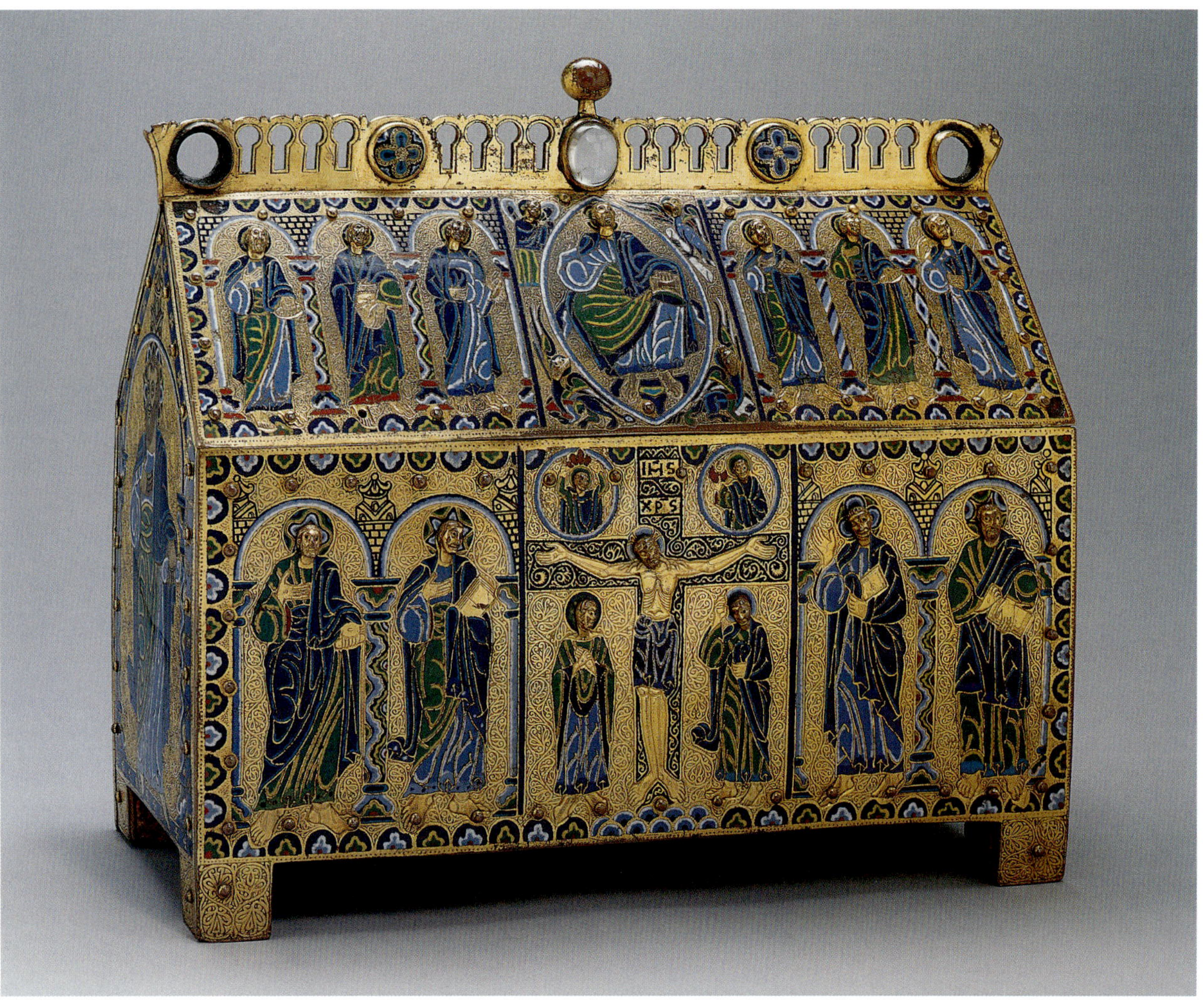

96. *Chasse*
MAKER UNKNOWN

ca. 1180–90; France
Copper, enamel, wood, paint
10⅜ x 11⅞ x 4½ in. (26.2 x 30.2 x
11.6 cm)
The Metropolitan Museum of Art,
New York, Gift of J. Pierpont
Morgan, 1917 (17.190.514)

When William Beckford owned this
enameled reliquary, he was ignorant
of its true attribution and misin-
formed about its history, although
he and his contemporaries accurately
perceived its rarity and quality. In
an engraving in John Rutter's *Delineations of Fonthill and Its Abbey*
(1823), this chasse is one of a select
few objects from Beckford's collection illustrated as part of "A Groupe
of the rarest articles of virtu (see
fig. 9-2)."

This chasse is among the finest
reliquaries created in Limoges, an
important center of medieval goldsmith's work, renowned from the
twelfth to fourteenth centuries in
particular for its enamels. Nine
different shades of enamel were used
in the chasse. Each of the apostles
wears a halo that is unique in design,
and each of the heads is separately
worked and applied to the reliquary,
giving it a sculptural aspect. The
engraving of the ground (known as
vermiculé, or wormlike) is as accomplished as it is rhythmic and bal-
anced, filling tiny spaces between the
legs of the figures as easily as broader
areas of ground. The carpeting of
the reverse with enameled quatrefoils
set in circles is a model of restrained
elegance.

Similar champlevé enamels on
copper, now recognizable as Limoges
work, were found in the collections
of English antiquarians by the mid-
eighteenth century. A reliquary very
similar to Beckford's and frequently
confused with it in earlier literature
belonged to Richard Bateman, perhaps as early as 1765.[1] Among the
earliest collectors of what are now
recognized as Limoges enamels were
clergy of the Church of England.[2]

An enameled reliquary of Thomas
Becket that Horace Walpole had
acquired from the auction of
Thomas Barrett's collection in 1755
had previously belonged to John
Batteley (d. 1708), archdeacon of
Canterbury.[3]

At the end of the eighteenth century, as treasures of the churches of
France were systematically inventoried and despoiled during the French
Revolution, objects in gold and
silver were melted down for the
inherent value of their metal. Less
precious works in copper were
passed over and either remained in
churches or came into a fortuitously
enhanced market. Like illuminated
leaves from choir books, which were
of little recuperable monetary value
but which were perceived as having
curious, exotic decoration, these
enamels met a burgeoning, English,
antiquarian taste.

It was at this time that William
Beckford acquired this enamel
chasse. In publications concerning
his collection, which depend heavily
on information supplied by Beckford
himself, the chasse is repeatedly discussed. It is singled out in John
Britton's *Illustrations, Graphic &
Literary, of Fonthill Abbey, Wiltshire*
as "an antient *Reliquary* . . . an article
of too much curiosity, antiquity, and
rarity to be passed with a slight
notice only."[4] It was further described
as "a Greek shrine of metal." Indeed,
Limoges enamels were frequently
referred to as "Byzantine" in early
studies and sale catalogues.[5]

The function of the chasse was
correctly noted as "for containing
relics." More important for Beckford,
however, appears to have been the
notion that these relics had been
"brought by St. Louis from Palestine"
and subsequently "deposited at St.
Denys, whence it was taken during
the French Revolution." Beckford
was a man obsessed with his own
putative royal lineage,[6] and so it is
not surprising that an object associated with French royalty and the
French royal abbey and necropolis of
the monarchy should have appealed
to him. The publications of Rutter
and Britton note in Beckford's collection, for example, an amber cabinet that had belonged to the queen
of Bohemia, as well as a "japan commode, formerly in the possession of
the late Queen of France. An armoir
of buhl and tortoiseshell, made for
Lewis XV," and a "purple silk quilt,
formerly belonging to Henry VII."[7]

Britton's text, however, citing the
catalogue printed for the sale that
was to have been conducted by
Christie's, does not claim that the
chasse was from Saint-Denis[8];
in any event, no inventory description corresponds to this piece.
(Only one Limoges chasse has been
identified from Saint-Denis; it has
been preserved in the Louvre since
December 5, 1793.[9]) These publications claim that the reliquary had
been brought to the abbey during
the French Revolution, but even this
association with the abbey is not
tenable. There is no indication that
the Abbey of Saint-Denis was used
as a temporary repository for precious works of art from locations
other than the Sainte Chapelle during the French Revolution.[10] Consequently, even though Beckford is
known to have purchased works of

art himself while he was in Paris for extended periods during the Revolution, it cannot be inferred that the information he supplied about the history of this reliquary is accurate. It is not clear whether Beckford himself or agents who purchased works for him are to be credited with supplying a suitably romantic history to accompany the magnificently crafted work of art. The fiction is consistent with the tastes of the time. Saint-Denis had become, after all, one of the premier tourist attractions of Europe.[11] In this context, it is interesting to note that in Beckford's own account of his visit to Batalha in Portugal, he saw "several golden reliquaries, as minutely chased and sculptured as any I ever saw at St. Denis."[12]

The Limoges enamel chasse is not mentioned in James Storer's *Description of Fonthill Abbey* (1812).[13] According to Rutter's 1822 publication of the same title, Britton's text, Britton's text, and the Christie's catalogue of 1822, Beckford kept the reliquary in Saint Michael's Gallery at Fonthill. A stylized image of it appears in plate 9 (though mentioned in the text as plate 10) of Britton's publication of Fonthill Abbey, set on the mantel and beneath a stained-glass window as the text describes. Even in the context of Fonthill Abbey, it is difficult to imagine a more appropriate location than Saint Michael's Gallery, where "all was in monastic taste, with shrines, reliquaries, and religious sculptures . . . illuminated with wax candles."[14] — B. D. B.

97. *Triptych: The Lamentation, The Prophet Daniel and an Apostle, probably St. Peter*
PIERRE REYMOND
(FL. 1530–1584)

1538; France
Enamel and gold on copper
Framed: 9 x 15¼ in. (22.9 x 38.7 cm)
Lent by The Syndics of the Fitzwilliam Museum, Cambridge
(M.l-1926)

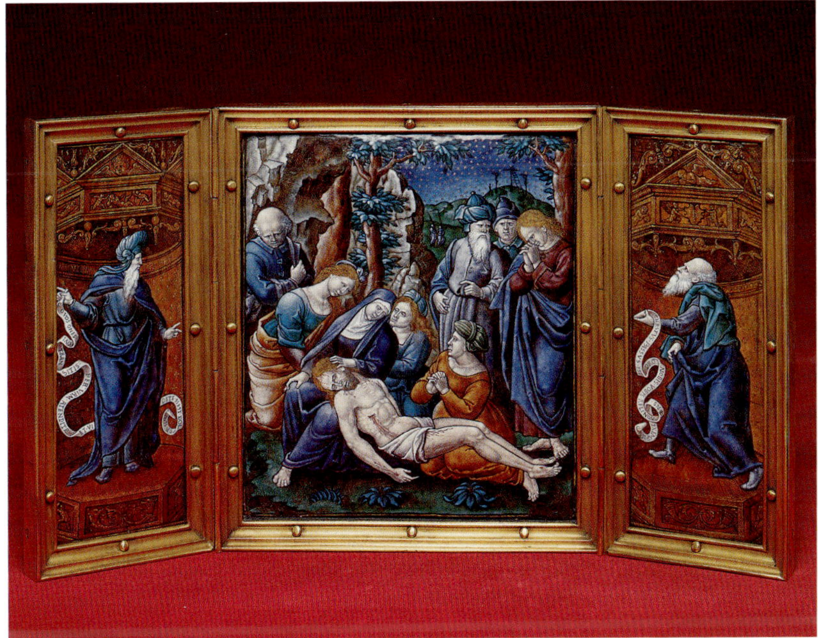

Pierre Reymond, recorded in Limoges between 1530 and 1584, was the proprietor of a prolific workshop in the rue d'Étaux, also known as rue Basse Manigne.[1] Throughout the period there was a demand for portable religious images, partly due to the peripatetic life of the nobility and high-ranking ecclesiastics. This triptych is one of a small group of polychrome enamels initialed "PR" and dated in the 1530s or early 1540s, which are generally acknowledged as by Reymond's own hand. The Lamentation, showing the four Marys grieving over the dead Christ, was derived from the engraving by Marcantonio Raimondi after Raphael.[2] On the left wing, the prophet Daniel holds a scroll with a Latin inscription from Lamentations 1:12 ("O all of you who travel by the road, wait and see if there is such sorrow"). The scroll, held by the apostle on the right wing, has an inscription from 1 Peter 2:21 ("Christ suffered for us, leaving for you an example"), which suggests that he could be Saint Peter, although he has no keys, Peter's usual attribute.

It is not known when this triptych came into Beckford's possession, possibly during one of his several visits to Paris between 1788 and 1814, when, as a result of the Revolution, many works of art came onto the market. Beckford was probably attracted to it on three counts: its superb quality, its High Renaissance style, and the moving subject of the central panel. He had immense admiration for Raphael and was drawn to Roman Catholicism through its visual and emotional impact since his visit to the shrine of Saint Anthony in Padua in 1780.

Beckford's small collection of Renaissance painted enamels included a polychrome triptych, now in the British Museum, comprising *The Descent from the Cross, The Entombment*, and *Christ Rising from the Tomb*, attributed to Nardon Pénicaud. The Reymond triptych descended to his son-in-law, Alexander, tenth Duke of Hamilton and was sold by the twelfth duke in 1882.[3] Vessels for the *dressoir* were represented by a basin of 1563 initialed "PR," and decorated with "a procession of Diana and Nymphs returning from the Chase,"' and a cipher and monograms associating it with Diane de Poitiers and Henri II.[4] The subject, *The Triumph of Diana,* after a design by Jacques Androuet du Cerceau, occurs on several vessels decorated *en grisaille* on a black ground, including a basin of 1558 with similar historical associations in the Kunsthistorisches Museum, Vienna.[5]

The Fitzwilliam's triptych was lot 87 in the canceled Fonthill sale of 1822 organized by Mr. Christie. It was described in the catalogue as "An extremely curious enamel on copper, in three divisions, the centre representing the Descent from the Cross, and Daniel and St. Paul in the side compartments, in an ebony frame." It did not appear in the 1823 sale held by Phillips, and it passed to the tenth Duke of Hamilton on Beckford's death. When next described in the *Catalogue of the Special Exhibition of Works of Art,* which was held at South Kensington in 1862, the central panel was identified differently, and correctly, as *The Marys Lamenting over Christ.* There seems little doubt, however, that it was the same object, for it is highly unlikely that both Beckford and his son-in-law owned Limoges triptychs of 1538 with the Prophet Daniel on one wing. When sold as lot 971 in Christie's Hamilton Palace sale of 1882, the triptych was illustrated in an ebony frame matching that of lot 977, the earlier triptych from Beckford's collection. In 1897 both triptychs were exhibited at the Burlington Fine Arts Club, by which time this one belonged to John Edward Taylor.[6] At the Taylor sale held by Christie's in July 1912, the Lamentation triptych (lot 142) was sold to the London dealer, Durlacher.[7] Its next owner, the politician Frederick Leverton Harris, bequeathed it to the Fitzwilliam Museum in 1926.[8] —J. E. P.

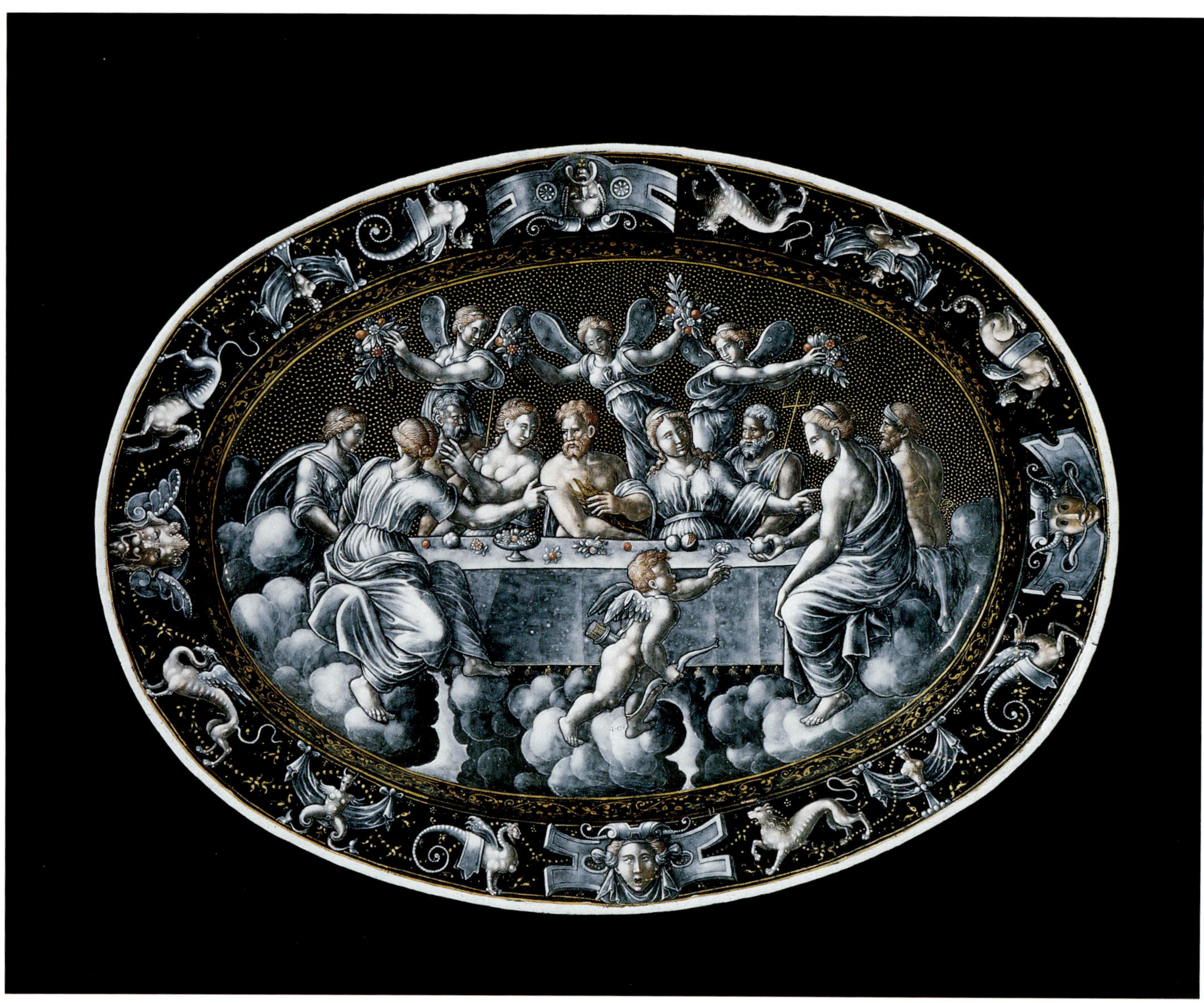

98. *Dish: The Wedding Banquet of Cupid and Psyche*
JEAN COURT ALSO KNOWN AS 'MASTER I.C.' (FL. 1553–85)

1560–80; France
Enamel and gold on copper
20⅛ x 15¼ in. (51.2 x 38.8 cm)
The Victoria and Albert Museum,
London, Salting Bequest
(C.2442-1910)

Beckford owned a substantial number of sixteenth-century painted Limoges enamels, probably acquired as examples of the *Schatzkammer* items he so judiciously collected. The autographed workmanship, the sophisticated, painterly technique, and highly decorative Mannerist vocabulary would have appealed to a collector such as Beckford. His love

of glittering, shimmering surfaces is exemplified in the jewellike qualities of Limoges enamels, as well as the large number of oil paintings on copper in his collection.[1]

This large oval dish can be positively attributed to Jean Court, also known as Master I.C.[2] It is painted in grisaille enamel with flesh tones and gilt on a black ground and depicts the wedding feast of Cupid and Psyche. A popular subject for large display pieces, the scene is based on the story of Psyche as recounted by Lucius Apuleius in the *Metamorphoses*, or *The Golden Ass* (book 5, chapter 24). The original iconographic source is the fresco cycle of the wedding feast of Cupid and Psyche, executed in 1518 at the Villa Farnesina, Rome, by Giulio Romano and Giovanni Francesco Penni, after designs by Raphael.[3] Two series of engravings by the Master of the Die

ensured the rapid dissemination of this design and its adaptation in different media.[4] The great popularity of this scene is attested to by the numerous examples, carried out by the best Limoges workshops, found in both public and private collections.

The rim of the dish is ornamented with strapwork and grotesque masks, caryatids, and fantastic beasts, a repertoire of decorative motifs used to great effect by the enameler. The reverse is decorated with a sophisticated design of bold strapwork ornament around an oval cartouche, flanked on two sides by male and female foliate busts, and on the two remaining sides by two grotesque masks. The decoration on the reverse is typical of the work of Jean Court.[5] Each side of this dish demonstrates a superb mastery of technique, particularly in the grisaille work, which is often incised. Jean Court was one of

a number of Limousin enamelers who specialized in producing display services and large-scale decorative items intended to dress the sideboard as an alternative to silver and gold.[6] Four other oval dishes painted by him with this scene are known.[7]

The esteem in which Beckford held Limoges enamels can be demonstrated by their inclusion in each of the three paintings by Willes Maddox that depict a selection of the most outstanding works of art in his collection (see cat. nos. 155–157). Beckford's collection was considered remarkably high in quality: he is now known to have owned nine of the twelve Limoges enamels belonging to the eleventh Duke of Hamilton which were selected for exhibition at the South Kensington Museum in 1862. —F. A.

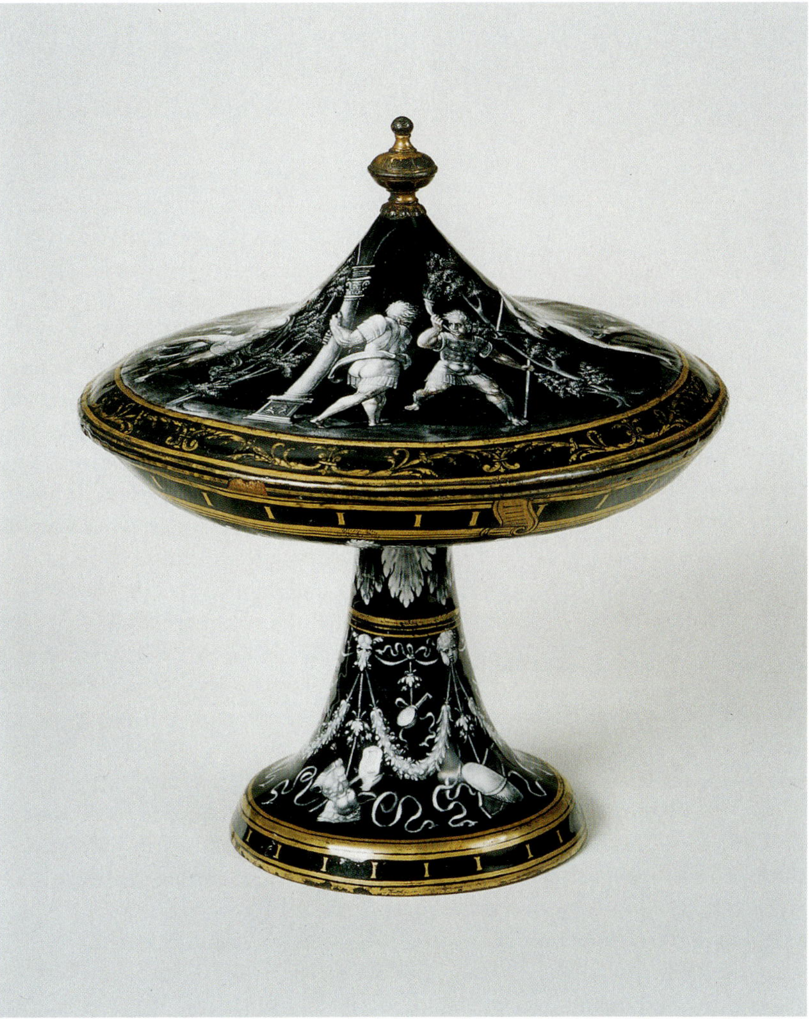

Painted in grisaille enamel with flesh tones and gilt, on a black background, the tazza and cover depict scenes from the life of Samson, taken from the Book of Judges: on the cover, Samson, the fox, and grain, a reference to Samson burning the fields of the Philistines; Samson slaying the lion; Samson carrying the Gates of Gaza; and Samson tearing down the pillars of the temple. The inside of the cover is painted with the marriage feast of Samson, and Samson slaying the Philistines with the jawbone of an ass. The inside of the tazza depicts Delilah shearing Samson's hair and his capture by the Philistines. The underside of the foot is painted with emblems of Christ's Passion (crown of thorns, nails, lance), indicating that Samson's trials prefigured those of Christ.

This is a fascinating and enigmatic piece, described by Horace Walpole in 1784 as: "A very fine standing cup and cover, enameled on copper with the story of Sampson [sic], from the designs of Parmigiano."[1] It has been suggested that the source for the scene of Delilah shearing Samson's hair is an engraving by Lucas van Leyden of 1508.[2] Another tazza is painted with a slightly modified version of the same scene.[3] The van Leyden source, however, must be discounted, as the engraving does not include the scene of the capture of Samson. A plaque with the same composition of Delilah shearing Samson's hair and the capture of Samson is evidence that another engraving, as yet to be identified, served as the model.[4] This same scene can also be found on two other plaques.[5] These extant examples, carried out by different painters and different workshops, confirm the relative rarity of the Samson iconography in Limoges enamels. This rarity is surprising when compared to the numerous examples of a similar theme, the Trials of Hercules, which is found on many different forms in Limoges enamels. The Samson cycle, however, can be seen in such other media as illuminated manuscripts. Samson carrying the Gates of Gaza is shown in the Gimani *Breviary* in Venice and the *Book of Hours* of Henri II.[6] Whatever the original source, it is clear the enamel painter has skillfully adapted the scenes to achieve an overall effect similar to that found on maiolica: this is particularly noticeable on the cover of the tazza, where the four isolated scenes are linked together by scrolling foliage.

This piece can be firmly attributed to the painter Jean II Pénicaud, even though the inscription on the foot bearing his name and date is probably part of a nineteenth-century restoration. Although his signed and dated works are few, Jean II Pénicaud's work is characterized by a particularly fine representation of the human face. He painted a number of profiles,[7] and paid great attention to the full face.[8] Eyes are often edged and cross-hatched with black to indicate the pupil, and this technique was employed to depict sadness or solemnity.[9] He showed a preference for the grisaille technique, using subtle pink highlights to outline flesh and taut muscles, which gives movement to the figures without having to alter the pose or use bold foreshortening.[10] Despite the rarity of his polychrome work,[11] Jean II Pénicaud was a master of color and used gold highlights to great effect. The gold *camaïeu* on the interior of the cover of this piece is exceptional in contemporary work and is similar to a medallion by Jean II Pénicaud which represents, on one side, a battle, and on the other, a large classical figure.[12]

A skilled painter in polychrome, and using grisaille with adroitness and subtlety, Jean II Pénicaud also reveals a delight in the portrayal of the natural world, which becomes an intrinsic part of his compositions. Unlike contemporary enamelers, he used lesser-known engraved models, from a number of different sources.[13] These strong individual traits could not help but attract the attention of such a passionate amateur as Horace Walpole, although it is not clear why Walpole described this piece as being after Parmigiano. Nonetheless, the original compositions and skillful treatment of the scenes on the interior and exterior of this covered tazza have given Jean II Pénicaud an assured place in the highest ranks of Limoges enamel painters.

Walpole had a number of significant pieces of Limoges enamels, although it is not known exactly when or how he acquired these. The sale of the contents of Strawberry Hill, offered in 1842 by Walpole's descendants, provided the last opportunity for Beckford to triumph over a long-dead collector whom he had particularly disliked, most probably out of jealousy.[14] Ironically, Beckford acquired this covered tazza entirely by chance. He had instructed Robert Hume junior to purchase a number of different lots, but this piece was not among them.[15] It would appear that Hume acquired this lot on a speculative basis, against stiff competition from the Parisian dealer, Roussel, and he later offered it to Beckford.[16] Hume wrote to Beckford from London on 18 May 1842: "Your letter was just in time to save Samson a journey to Paris – He is now yours and in your power perhaps more than ever He was in Delilah's."[17] —F. A.

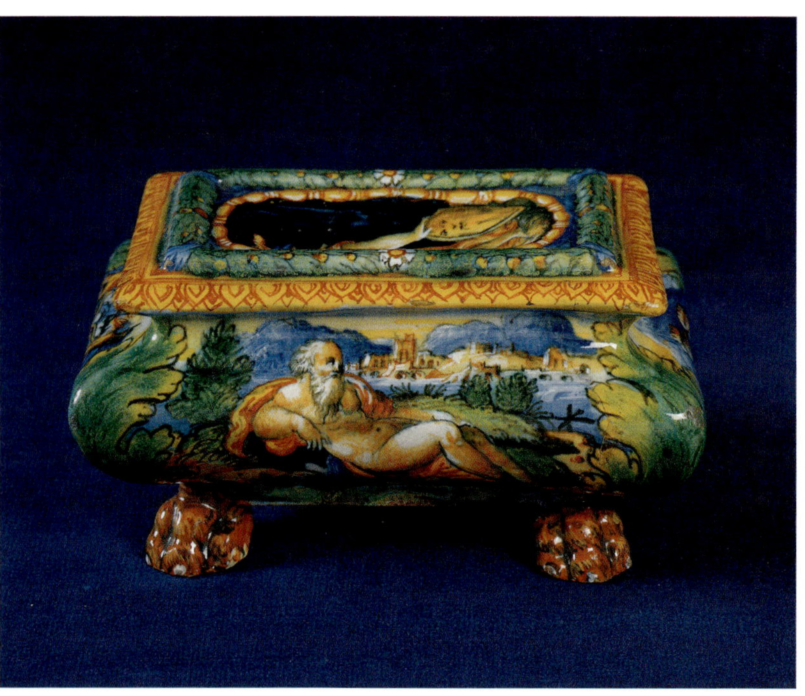

100. *Saltcellar*
PROBABLY WORKSHOP OF
GUIDO DURANTINO
(FONTANA; FL. CA. 1520–76)

ca. 1535–70; Urbino, Italy
Maiolica
3 x 5¾ x 3¾ in. (7.7 x 14.5 x 9.5 cm)
The Walters Art Museum,
Baltimore (48.1338)

Saltcellars often formed part of *istoriato* services that included plates and bowls of various sizes as well as matching basins and candlesticks. This saltcellar is in the form of a classical sarcophagus and is painted on each long side with a river god reclining in a landscape; on one short side with buildings in a landscape, on the other an unidentified

coat of arms surmounted by three turtles and a motto in Greek letters, "SLOWNESS." Each corner is painted with acanthus leaves rising from four lion's paw feet, the well depicts Minerva with a shield and helmet.[1] Two pilgrim flasks (now in the Musée des Arts Décoratifs, Lyons) bear the same arms.[2] A saltcellar of the same form and palette (now in the British Museum) is also painted with a reclining river god, while the well contains a naked, armed female, possibly Minerva.[3] A third example (now in the Wallace Collection) is painted all over with a landscape and the figures of Mercury, Zeus, and cupids, and the well with a figure of a naked female.[4]

Beckford appears to have owned very little maiolica. None is listed in his Harley Street sale of 1817, and of the pieces listed in the 1822 and 1823 Fonthill Abbey sale catalogues, all are generically described as "Raphael ware" and with "historic" figures or subjects, although these subjects are not identified. In addition, following the death of Beckford in 1844, the Bath sales of his possessions which occurred in 1845 and 1848 contain no

maiolica, nor is maiolica shown in any of the interior views of Fonthill Abbey or Lansdown Tower.

The inclusion of this piece in the Willes Maddox *Objects of Vertu* (see cat. no. 157) is somewhat curious and certainly not representative of Beckford's holdings of maiolica. It may have had some particular significance for Beckford, which his daughter Susan, Duchess of Hamilton, respected, because this saltcellar remained part of the Hamilton family collection until sold in 1882. Perhaps Beckford admired the coat of arms and the motto, or perhaps he was merely attracted to a heraldic piece of maiolica.

Two other pieces of maiolica in Beckford's collection that could also be associated with an individual family were acquired from the celebrated Strawberry Hill sale in 1842: a pair of pilgrim flasks with Medici arms and "portraits" in roundels. They were purchased for Beckford at that sale by Robert Hume junior and remained in the Hamilton family collection until sold in 1882.[5]
—B. M.

101. *Design for a Dagger*
PETER FLÖTNER
(CA. 1485–1546)

ca. 1540; Germany
Pen and ink on paper
13⅞ x 3 in. (34.7 x 7.6 cm)
The British Museum, London
(1848.11.25.8)

This design for the hilt and scabbard of a dagger is typical of the sixteenth-century taste for decorative armor inspired by classical forms.[1] The hilt shows a Roman breastplate and arms surrounded by stylized Renaissance motifs, while the scabbard is decorated with the *Triumph of Bellona*. This Roman goddess of war, equivalent to the Greek Enyo, has been variously described as the

wife, sister, or daughter of Mars, and in Roman art, Bellona was depicted in cult statues and reliefs.[2] The scene on this dagger is a variation on the theme of a classical triumphal procession, and was a highly appropriate subject for the decoration of weapons. A Swiss dagger decorated with the same scene exists in a Danish private collection, but it may date from the nineteenth century

and is likely to have been based on an intermediary drawing.[3]

This drawing was attributed to Hans Holbein the Younger when acquired by William Beckford in 1814 from William Ottley. Holbein depicted triumphal processions, such as *The Triumph of Riches*, and this may account for the original attribution.[4] The design is now thought to be by Peter Flötner as it is much

closer to his style and shares similarities with several other designs for hilts and daggers by this artist.[5] Best known for his small-scale sculpture, Flötner was also an accomplished medalist, cabinetmaker, printmaker, and designer.[6] His early life is sparsely documented, but he is thought to have been born in Thurgau, Switzerland, and may have trained in Augsburg. He settled in

Nuremberg in 1522 after a brief period in Ansbach.[7] Flötner made much use of ornament inspired by architectural forms, featuring grotesque figures, acanthus leaves, and scrolls, and he is known for his innovative interpretations of classical and Renaissance motifs. Flötner's prints and plaquettes were used as models by Nuremberg goldsmiths such as Wenzel Jamnitzer, and the *Kunstbuch das Peter Flötner*—a selection of his woodcuts—was published in 1546, contributing to the wide dissemination of his designs.

William Beckford's interest in this drawing must have rested, at least in part, on its attribution to Holbein, as inventories and sale catalogues of Beckford's collection give little indication that he took any interest in armor or weaponry.[8] Beckford demonstrated a particular interest in the style of ornament used by Holbein; he asserted that two candlesticks (see cat. no. 107) he had commissioned from Paul Storr in 1800 were derived from a design by Holbein.[9] Similarly, Beckford claimed that a South German cabinet of around 1550 in his collection had been designed by Holbein for Henry VIII, presumably due to its resemblance to a Holbein drawing.[10] He described the raised lip of a jug he had commissioned (Brodick Castle, Scotland) as "a la Holbeins" and he is known to have owned *Portrait of a Canon* then attributed to Holbein (now to Quentin Massys) and a design for the Seymour cup (cat. no. 102).[11]

Beckford was not alone in his zeal for work by Old Masters like Holbein. In the late eighteenth and nineteenth centuries, revolution and war in continental Europe brought unprecedented riches to the English market. While the emphasis was on painting, many collectors also turned their attention to graphic works, attracted by the immediacy of the medium and the insight it provided into the preliminary workings of the great artists. Sir Thomas Lawrence, William Roscoe, Samuel Rogers, Samuel Woodburn, and William Esdaile were among the dealers and collectors acquiring drawings and prints. Beckford's enthusiasm for drawings differed somewhat, however, from that of his contemporaries.

Significantly, this drawing was acquired during a period (ca. 1810–20) when Renaissance ornament was a distinctive feature of artwork made for Beckford. The paper has been carefully folded down the center of the hilt, while the scabbard area is untouched, suggesting that the hilt had been copied and attesting to the fact that this drawing's primary value for Beckford was as a design source.
—A. W.

---

102. *Design for a Cup*
HANS HOLBEIN THE YOUNGER (1497–1543)

1536–37; Germany
Ink on paper
17⅛ x 9⅜ in. (44.6 x 23.8 cm)
The British Museum, London
(1848.11.25.9)

This design was drawn after the appointment of Holbein as King's Painter to Henry VIII in 1536. It can be dated to the period between the marriage of Jane Seymour to the king on May 30, 1536, and her death in childbirth in 1537. A later version can be found in the Ashmolean Museum, Oxford.[1] A cup that fit this design—made by a court goldsmith of gold set with pearls and diamonds and decorated with love knots and the Queen's motto—was taken to Holland by the Duke of Buckingham in 1629 and subsequently melted down.[2]

The drawing was bought by William Beckford from the collection of the portrait painter, Sir Thomas Lawrence, although the exact date of purchase is unknown. Lawrence was the most celebrated collector of drawings of the period and accumulated an unparalleled

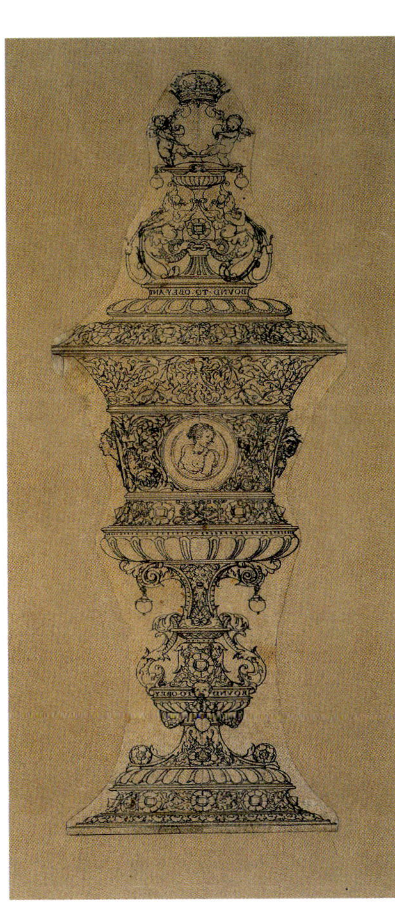

collection of Old Masters. At his death, his collection was offered to the nation, but the government was unwilling to purchase it. Beckford, though unable to buy the collection in its entirety, signed a petition protesting its dispersal.

Beckford's interest in Old Masters is well documented, and he certainly included Holbein among the artists whose work he valued. He owned a number of objects that he attributed, accurately or otherwise, to Holbein. Among these is the famous "Holbein" cabinet (see fig. 10-7) which Beckford believed to have been executed "from an original design of Holbein" for Henry VIII, along with a design for a dagger, now known to be by Peter Flötner (cat. no. 101). In 1800, he also commissioned the London goldsmith Paul Storr and the manufacturers Vulliamy and Co. to make copies from a pair of wooden candlesticks, which he claimed were by Holbein (cat. no. 107). The royal association would also have pleased Beckford due to his passionate interest in his own lineage. Among the objects sold from Fonthill Abbey in 1823 were "a set of chairs of ebony which belonged to Cardinal Wolsey" and a "magnificent state bedstead, of ebony with crimson damask hangings, and a rich purple silk quilt worked with gold which belonged to Henry VII."[3]

Another factor that may have attracted Beckford to this drawing was its depiction of gems. Many of Beckford's most prized objects were made of semiprecious stones, often set with gems in gold or silver-gilt mounts, such as the hookah carved in jade and set with jewels (see cat. no. 55). A rare visitor to Fonthill Abbey in 1817 described "another suite of apartments fill'd with fine medals, gems, enamelled miniatures, drawings old and modern, curios, prints and manuscripts."[4]

The stand on which the "Holbein" cabinet sits may have been designed by Beckford and most likely his companion Gregorio Franchi, using the Renaissance ornament that is shown in prints and drawings such as this one. Beckford's interest in Renaissance objects developed while the general fashion still leaned toward classicism. His collection comprised not only objects made for him in a historicist style, but also many original sixteenth-century objects, such as a cup (now in the Thyssen-Bornemisza Collection), which is similar to the lost Holbein original and was owned by Beckford while he lived at Lansdown Crescent, Bath[5] —R. E. C.

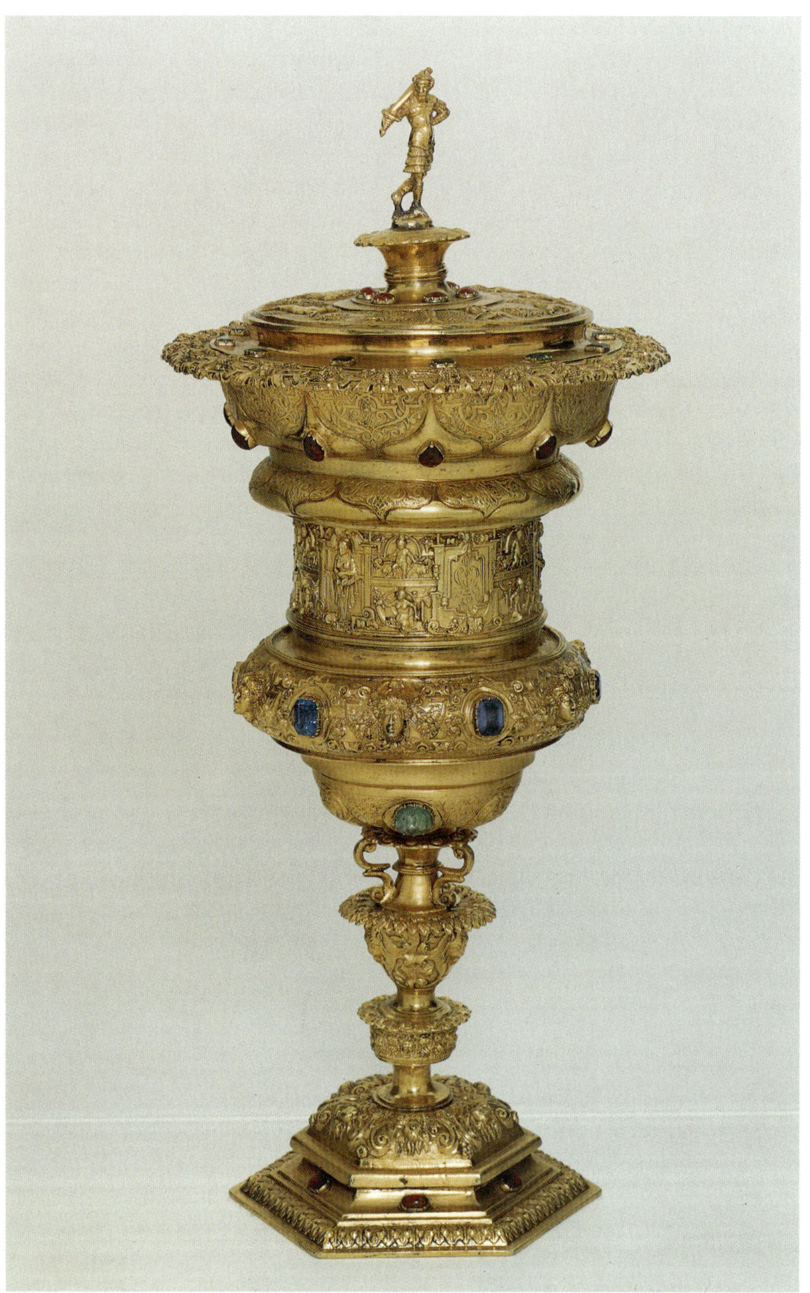

This ceremonial drinking cup was made for the welcoming rituals practiced in Germany from the Middle Ages to the eighteenth century. Nuremberg was the leading German center of fine goldsmithing at the time of the cup's creation. The cup makes a costly, virtuoso display of technical skill, with the chasing and embossing of the hunting scenes on the lid and the etched arabesques on the lobes of the lip. The strapwork frieze around the bowl is derived from goldsmithing models probably by the most famous Nuremberg goldsmith of the sixteenth century, Wenzel Jamnitzer. The cup originally had jewels only on the lower roll molding of the bowl, replaced in the early part of the nineteenth century, probably when the other jewels were added. The cup was already so decorated when it was described as being in the drawing room at Lansdown Tower in 1844, together with another exceptionally fine Nuremberg Mannerist standing cup of 1626 (now in the Thyssen-Bornemisza Collection).

Along with George IV, Beckford was a pioneer in the taste for the late-Renaissance style. He not only collected works from that period, but also had pieces made for himself "in the manner," such as a ladle (cat. no. 109) derived from an engraved spoon design of 1539 by the German metalworker Heinrich Aldegrever and a pair of candlesticks (cat. no. 107) of 1800 by Paul Storr, described wrongly by Beckford as being "from an original design by Hans Holbein." It was the northern Renaissance style, rather than the Italian which attracted Beckford, probably as a result of his having seen the still extraordinarily rich princely treasuries of Germany.

The etched arabesques on the lip of this cup would have appealed to Beckford's taste, as revealed by the number of pieces in his collection decorated with Veneto-Saracenic arabesques. The special significance of this standing cup to Beckford is reinforced by its illustration in Maddox's *Objects of Vertu* (cat. no. 155) and in its retention by his heirs until the late twentieth century.

This cup was probably given its extra jewels for Beckford, another example of the "ostentatious magnificance [sic] which is calculated to gratify the sense of property in the owner and excite the wondering curiosity of the stranger," described by the critic William Hazlitt.[1]
—A. S. C.

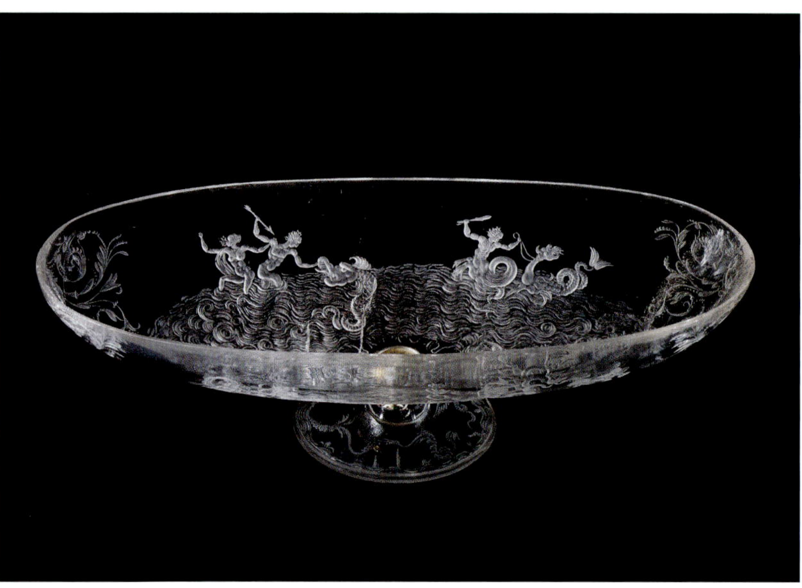

From the fourteenth century, the magical transparency of rock crystal and its mythical talismanic properties ensured that it was one of the most highly prized materials in European princely collections. Skilled techniques were required to carve, polish, and engrave this extremely hard material. Rock crystal was found in some quantity in Northern Italy, and Milan became one of a number of centers that produced specialist lapidary workshops in the sixteenth century. This footed bowl has been attributed to the Sarachi workshop of Milan based on similarities of the marine figures with examples identified with the work of the Sarachi, in particular the protruding foreheads and flaming hair.[1] The engraving of the foliage at each end of the bowl appears to be by a different hand and does not relate to the main composition, possibly being later in date. The foliate engraving may suggest that the original proportions of the bowl were rather different, and that it may have had handles or an upper section of some kind, now lost, the damage ground down to produce this current form.[2]

Hardstones were a lifelong and all-consuming passion for Beckford. No doubt first stimulated by the princely collections he saw in his travels on the Continent, this passion was shared by his companion, Gregorio Franchi, whose own love of hardstones and commercial trading in these items may have further encouraged Beckford's collecting activities in the field.[3] A reading of the documents shows that of the hardstones, quartz, either in its chalcedony or crystalline form, occurs most frequently. Rock crystal would appear to be of particular importance to Beckford, no doubt due to his appreciation of the purity and clarity of the stone and the virtuoso engraving with which most of his were decorated. Two extant examples of European rock crystal, and one example of Mughal rock crystal set with gold and gems, from Beckford's collection are at Brodick Castle. Other rock crystals from his collection have been recently identified as forming part of the Hamilton Palace collections and sold in 1882.[4]

The original mounts at the rim of the flanged foot on this bowl are missing; these mounts may well have been engraved with a Garde-Meuble registration number, thus allowing for its reputed provenance.[5] The foot mounts were missing since at least 1818, when the cup was acquired by Beckford. Gregorio Franchi wrote from London on 11 June 1818: "the box arrived this morning with all the things . . . the crystal cup is beautiful and still has part of its foot enamelled in gold of beautiful taste."[6] This letter enumerated the price as being 501 *livres*, and continued: "the crystal is very good and we must make an enamelled circle around the foot in order for it to be perfect. . . . the work is no doubt by Bolerius de Vicence [Valerio de Vicenza]."[7]

Beckford further detailed the acquisition in an immediate response to Franchi: "Up to now I've received no description of the divine packet just arrived from Paris and so well bought by Chardin, but I have the objects themselves, and they are certainly beautiful, really beautiful, and in the best taste. I know nothing of such Cinquecento purity as this Valerio di Vicenza. What inspiration! What genius! What a divine little piece of enamel, with little rubies and emeralds and a small garland, worthy to form a crown for the nymphs victorious in the games and races on Calypso's isle. . . . In short everything is good. Judging from these few items, what must the collection as a whole have been like! It does honour to Durand, and Fate was kind to you. . . . Enclosed you will find an order on Morland for £108. I find this lot a good bargain and the Valerio sublime."[8]

This extract shows that the collar mounts around the junction of the bowl and foot had, at least in 1818, what were described as precious gems, although Beckford could well have been praising mere enameled "jewels." It also confirms that the bowl was acquired as being by Valerio di Vicenza (Valerio Belli), which was probably an optimistic attribution to one of the most celebrated gem engravers of the Renaissance. The bowl was purchased on Beckford's behalf by his bookseller and art agent, Chardin, from the Chevalier Durand, a noted connoisseur and dealer in hardstones. The 1844 inventory of the contents of Lansdown Tower and 19 and 20 Lansdown Crescent, taken after Beckford's death, describes the bowl as being from the French Royal Collection: "Oblong Crystal Vase Engraved by Valerio di Vicinza and from the Garde Meuble."[9] This royal provenance was not, however, repeated in several subsequent Hamilton inventories, nor the Hamilton Palace sale of 1882, and further research needs to be undertaken to establish the validity of the claimed provenance.[10]

Beckford's taste for hardstones was decidedly aristocratic; it is notable that the majority of the sixteenth-century hardstones detailed in the several sale catalogues reputedly came from either French royal and noble collections or Italian ducal collections. In his overwhelming passion for hardstones, Beckford was quite unlike his collecting contemporaries in England, and this singularity in taste is a trait for which Beckford was renowned even in his own lifetime.

This bowl clearly engaged Beckford's emotions as well as his eye as a connoisseur of exotic material and virtuoso workmanship: "This evening all is the colour of mother-of-pearl and opal; the sea is covered with vessels and fishing barques; the coast of France is as visible as Wardour from Fonthill; there's a slight breeze which crisps the waves like those so delicately sculptured by Valerio di Vicenza."[11] —B. M.

---

105. *Casket*
MAKER UNKNOWN

ca. 1600; Italy
Rock crystal, verre eglomisé, lacquer, giltwood, metal
11 x 15⅜ x 11⅛ in. (28 x 39 x 29 cm)
Hanns Schell Collection, Graz, Austria

Quite apart from its sumptuousness, which was in perfect keeping with Beckford's overall predilection, this casket combines four of Beckford's interests: the Renaissance, semi-precious stones, lacquer, and Veneto-Saracenic arabesques. The 1823 Phillips' sale at Fonthill contained two such pieces, described: "These very curious reliquaries belonged to Pope Paul V of the Borghese family and are designed in the style of Camillo Maderno."[1]

This entry, confused and partly implausible, might give a clue to the origin of the caskets, which could indeed have come from the Borghese family. Camillo Borghese reigned as Pope Paul V from 1605 to 1621, which is also a possible date for this piece. On the other hand, it is unlikely that the head of the Fabbrica of Saint Peter's basilica, Carlo (not Camillo) Maderno, had a hand in designing it, as its general form was already well established some thirty years earlier, in Venice, its likely place of manufacture. Titian's second version of his portrait of Lavinia, formerly in the Cowper Collection, Panshanger, shows her holding up

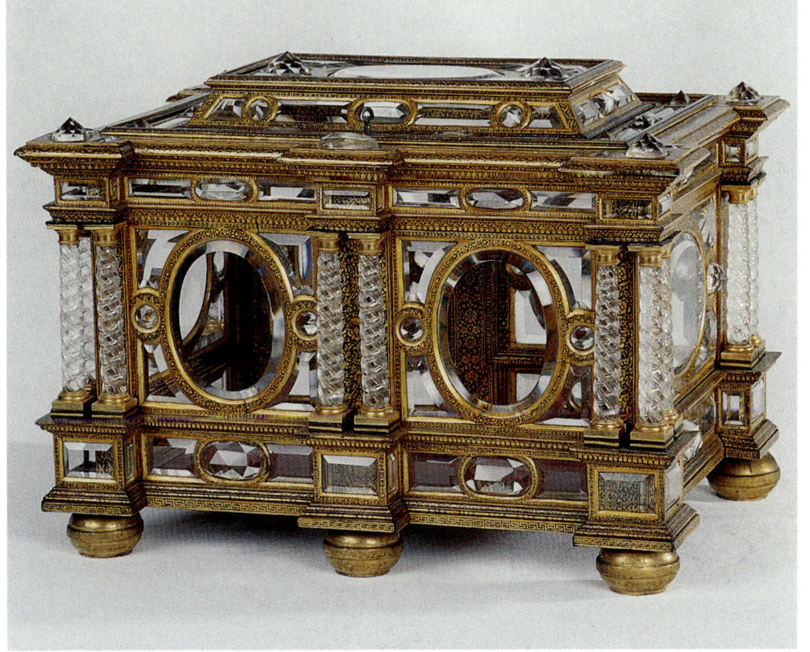

just such a casket. Finally, as to the suggestion that it is a reliquary, while there is no reason why it could not have been used as such, these caskets had a rather more interesting role in court diplomacy.[2] The popes had always given presents of a ritualized sort, such as the Gold Rose, to favored Catholic princes. This tradition was expanded beginning in 1601, when Queen Margaret of Spain, wife of Philip III, suggested to Clement VIII that the papacy give the first-born heirs of approved monarchs a set of baby clothes in a special casket. This would remain a

tradition until 1880. Because these were no ordinary garments, but made from silver thread and richly embroidered, and unlikely to have been worn, the caskets had crystal panels that allowed these pieces to be viewed.

The lacquer work strongly suggests that this casket was made in Venice, which, because of its close trading contacts with the Islamic world, had imported special skills and ornamental designs from the East. The lacquer, executed by craftsmen called *azziministi*, a word which reveals its Arabic origins,

came from Syria as early as 1300. It consists of a solution of three parts fir resin, called *colophonium*, dissolved in one part linseed oil to which color has been added. The Armoury of the Doge's Palace in Venice hold shields lacquered with moresques like those on this casket, and there is no doubt that such ornamentation came from the Muslim world and gained currency in Venice in the early sixteenth century. It appears on the sixteenth-century metalwork in the so-called Veneto-Saracenic style, of which Beckford had large quantities, and

on bookbindings.

Hans Huth lists nine caskets of lacquer with inset crystal panels, of which this is one.[3] He discovered a contemporary provenance for only one of them, the casket now in the Museu Nacional de Arte Antiga in Lisbon, which came from the Monastery de la Graça in Lisbon, to which it was given by Dom. Fr. Aleixio de Menedes, Primate of the Church of the Indies, residing at Goa 1606–1609. —A. S. C.

---

106. *Covered Cup*

David Willaume
(1658–1741); ivory
attributed to the circle
of Giovanni Battista
Pozzo (fl. 1697–1752)

Mounts, 1711–12, England; ivory,
early 18th century, Italy
Ivory, silver gilt
16⅞ in. (42.4 cm)
The British Museum, London,
Wilding Bequest
(M&ME1969,7-5.11a)

The mounting of carved ivory cylinders, or "sleeves," in silver or silver-gilt was fashionable in continental Europe during the seventeenth and eighteenth centuries, although it was not practiced in England. These sleeves were cut from an African elephant tusk and often carved with bacchanalian scenes; this vase (one of a pair) shows a continuous frieze of putti and child-satyrs probably copied from the antique. These sleeves were always intended for some form of mounting, and were mounted most commonly as tankards, for display purposes.

The mounts here are among the masterpieces of David Willaume, a Huguenot silversmith who lived in London from 1687.[1] The decoration is typical of the Huguenot style, with its thick-walled forms and cast ornament. The design is extremely unusual, and was probably developed together with the patron who commissioned the cups. Beckford devised a provenance that included

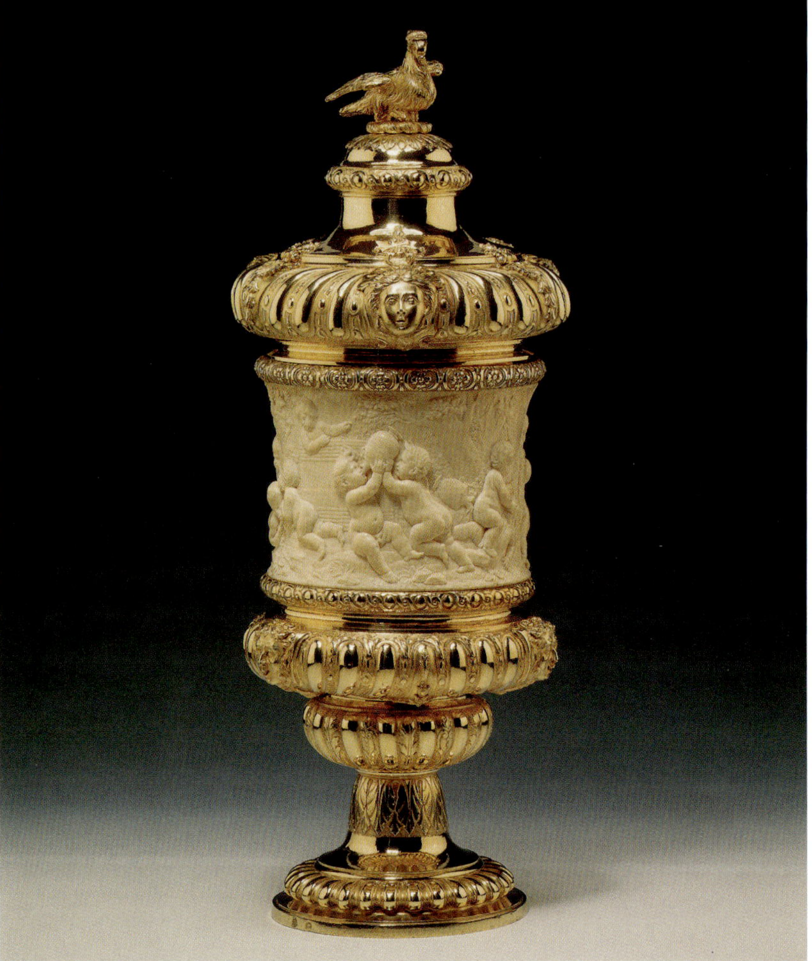

the Earl of Arundel. This was inspired partly by Beckford's penchant for titled pedigrees and by the knowledge that a previous owner, Lady Betty Germain, had inherited some of the antiquities from the great collection formed by Thomas Howard, second Earl of Arundel. There is no evidence, however, that Arundel commissioned the cups or that the large crest finials in the

form of a crouched eagle bear any relationship to a specific owner.

The ivory of these cups was thought by Beckford to have been carved by the celebrated sculptor "Fiammingo" (François Duquesnoy), but is now considered to have been executed by a member of the circle of Giovanni Battista Pozzo (fl. 1697–1752).[2] Pozzo is known to have worked in Rome, producing a num-

ber of carved ivories for visiting tourists. Beckford's enthusiasm for carved ivories prompted him to purchase a number of significant examples,[3] including the "Magnus Berg" cup (now in the Royal Collection) and the present pair sold from the Margravine of Anspach sale in London in 1818.[4] He also owned carved sleeve vases mounted as tankards.[5] One tankard in particular is described as being by Strous, with mounts by the royal goldsmiths, Rundell, Bridge and Rundell.[6] Carved ivory sleeve vases were also remounted by Beckford as plinths for other precious objects.[7]

The Willaume cups sit firmly at the center of Beckford's collection of *Schatzkammer* objects, reflecting the art of the goldsmith and the sculptor, as well as the virtuoso use of exotic and rare materials. Carved ivory sleeves with extravagant silver-gilt mounts in the antique taste suited the aesthetic of Fonthill. They are clearly visible flanking the "Magnus Berg" cup in King Edward's Gallery in John Rutter's *Delineations of Fonthill* (1823; see cat. fig. 85A). Although the Arundel provenance was wishful thinking by Beckford, it satisfied his desire to accumulate the kind of objects found in princely collections of the sixteenth and seventeenth centuries. —R. L. E.

Beckford, Franchi, and Design

Beckford's antiquarian interests are most clearly expressed in the works of art he commissioned in historicist styles. His avowed passion for historicism was interpreted, however, with a thoroughly modern eye and executed in the best of contemporary techniques. Beckford possessed a large number of sources from which he and Gregorio Franchi could draw inspiration, and principal among these were European ornamental prints, a traditional method for the dissemination of design ideas. His extraordinarily large and comprehensive library also contained ample source material appropriate for historicist and imitative styles. Many of the books and print sources would have been consulted in the Oak Library at Fonthill Abbey, also known as the "Board of Works," which served primarily as a study room for the artists and craftsmen working at the Abbey. Beckford's large collection of Renaissance and Mannerist works of art were themselves inspirational in the realization of historicist pieces.

In commissioning works of art Beckford was the visionary who conceived of the piece, and he was possessed by an unusual capacity for involvement in the production process, but it was Gregorio Franchi who brilliantly realized this historicist vision. Franchi worked closely not only with the established goldsmiths and retailers who supplied useful plate and decorative work for Fonthill Abbey, but also with the many "smallworkers" or independent jewelers who produced Beckford's mounted wares. Significantly, most of the extant designs for mounted work are attributed to Franchi, who had an outstanding eye for form and ornament and was an excellent draftsman. His designs show an understanding of Renaissance and Mannerist ornament that is often imaginatively used in conjunction with designs for forms imitative of heraldic motifs and Oriental materials and sources.

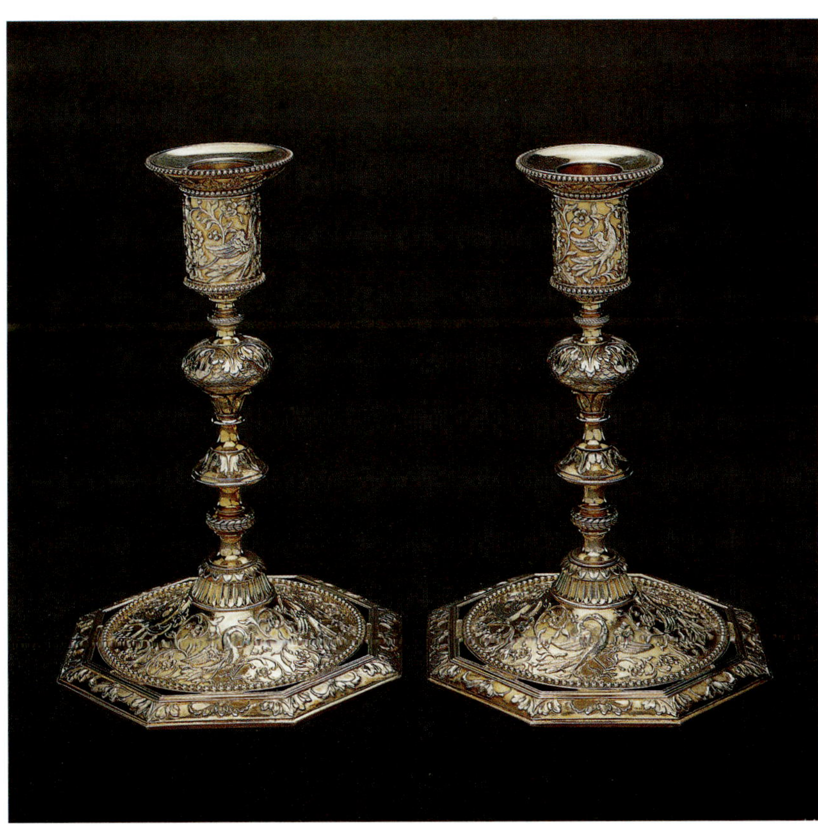

107. *Pair of Candlesticks*
PAUL STORR (1771–1844)

1800–1801; England
Silver gilt
6⅞ x 5 in. (17.4 x 12.7 cm)
Collection of Mrs. Jerome T. Gans

These silver-gilt candlesticks, made in 1800, mark a significant change in Beckford's taste in silver. They are the earliest examples of the refined and, on occasion, idiosyncratic historicist plate that was one of Beckford's great innovations. Unlike his earlier purchases of French or English plate in the neoclassical style, these candlesticks are copies of a late-seventeenth-century model. Beckford was able to put forth the claim that they were after a design by Holbein, as listed in the 1822 Christie's sale catalogue.[1] These candlesticks were among a large group of purchases that Beckford made in 1800 from Vulliamy and Son, London's most important supplier of luxury goods. Beckford's orders that year were for mainly furniture and clocks, Vulliamy's specialty.

For the manufacture of these unique candlesticks, however, the firm engaged Paul Storr, who was well established at this time, as an independent goldsmith. In addition to working for Vulliamy and Son, he executed work for the royal goldsmiths, Rundell, Bridge and Rundell, whom he would join as a partner in 1807.[2] These candlesticks exemplify the fine casting and meticulous finish for which Storr was admired, although the design is completely eccentric and unlike Storr's early austere classicism. The charge of £69 6s included six guineas "for the chased pattern." The fine surface finish was described at length in Vulliamy's accounts, which record

"a pair of silver candlesticks extreamly [sic] high finished in every part and chased almost all over with very rich arabesque ornaments consisting of birds, leaves, and flowers & mounted in several pieces to keep the burnish and dead parts extremely neat & clear from one another. The whole gilt & finished in so perfect a manner as exactly to resemble a pr of highly finished gold candles."[3] The inscription on the underside of the bases, "Made for the abbey at Fonthill by Vulliamy & Son 1800," was apparently engraved by Vulliamy at Beckford's behest, further evidence that both patron and retailer were aware of the originality of the commission.

The baluster stems of the candlesticks are made in four pieces, threaded for assembly, a construction required by the unusually slender stem. Vulliamy's interest in preserving the crispness of the "burnish and dead" areas is characteristic of their attention to workmanship. The reference to gold in the Vulliamy daybook is significant because Beckford, it seems, was in the habit of telling visitors that these pieces were not only after a design by Holbein, but that they were gold. One visitor to Lansdown Tower, Henry Venn Lansdown, wrote to his daughter in 1834 describing his tour of the house: "Holbein's candlesticks are really gold! The chasing is elegance itself; an inscription states that they were made in 1800 for the Abbey at Fonthill."[4] Perhaps Beckford had originally wanted the candlesticks to be executed in gold, and although he had economized with silver, he could not resist presenting them as gold.

The transport of these pieces to Fonthill (possibly with other plate) cost the remarkable sum of £22 7s due to the fact that the firm engaged a post coach with four horses for the delivery which took three days.[5] The candlesticks are modeled (and possibly even cast) from a group of carved fruitwood pieces made in France in the city of Nancy that are known as "Bois de Bagard," after their traditional attribution to the workshop of the monumental sculptor César Bagard (1620–1707). More recently the carvings have been associated with Nicolas-François Foulon (1628–1698) and others.[6] These decorative objects include the components of toilet services such as round and square boxes, mirrors, wall sconces, as well as candlesticks in the present and related forms. The plain, geometric shapes of these objects are decorated with panels of scrolling Berainesque foliage in low relief. The designs are loosely related to current French silver forms, though no silver candlesticks are known that can be clearly identified as a source for the wood models. The wood candlesticks often feature a pelican amidst scrolling foliage, and Beckford may have been struck by its similarity to a heron, a family crest that embellished much of his plate. Though Vulliamy's must have had a wooden candlestick to copy, it is not known whether Beckford was aware of it, nor is there any record that Vulliamy claimed that the design was associated with Holbein. The Holbein attribution is more likely a reflection of Beckford's own obsession. Holbein was one of a number of widely known Renaissance artists who had worked at the English court, and Beckford must have associated the elegant ornament on the candlesticks with the arabesques and geometric forms of Holbein's designs for silver, one of which he owned (cat. no. 102).

Rutter recorded the candlesticks in Saint Michael's Gallery, where they rested on buhl cabinets. Though listed in the canceled 1822 sale, they did not appear in the 1823 catalogue. Beckford took them with him to Bath, where they were recorded in the Crimson Drawing Room in Lansdown Tower. They were retained in the family until the 1919 sale of the Hamilton possessions.[7] No other examples of this model dated as early as 1800 have come to light, but another pair must have been in circulation, since copies were made later in the nineteenth century. Perhaps Storr or Vulliamy had retained the models which were then reused.[8]
—E. A.

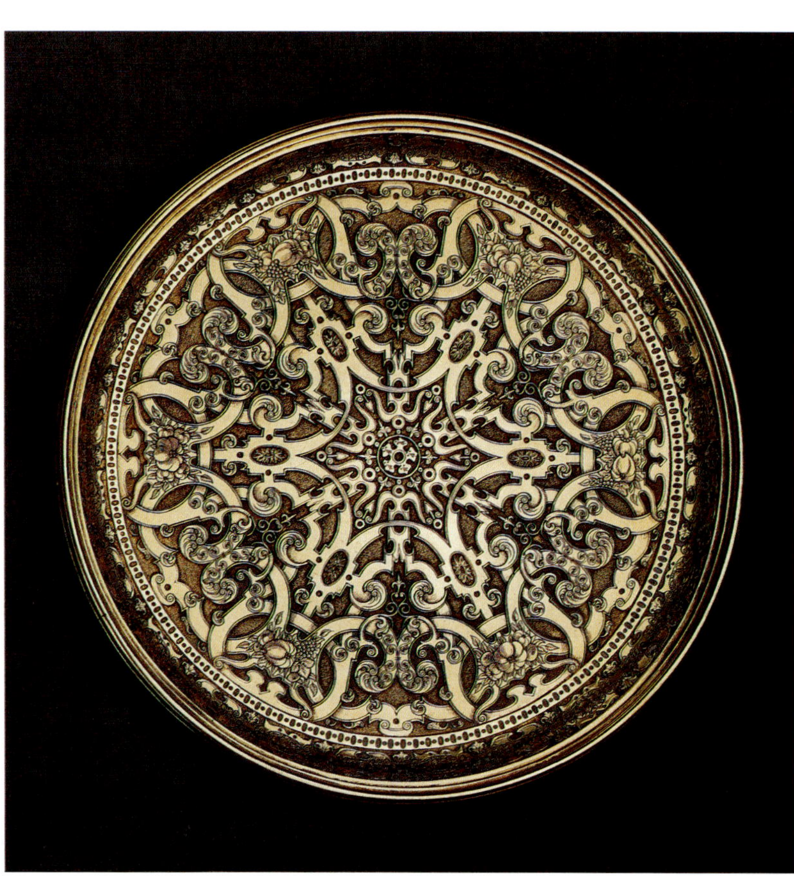

108. *Salver*
William Burwash
(fl. 1782–?1820)

1817–18; England
Silver gilt
Diam. 6⅞ in. (17.2 cm)
Private collection

This extraordinary salver, originally one of a pair, represents a startling departure in the historicist silver Beckford commissioned in the later Fonthill years. Of heavy gauge, suggesting that it may have been intended as a decanter stand rather than a card tray, its field was deeply etched and then finished with chasing and engraving in a radiating design of interlaced Renaissance-inspired strapwork, heightened with cartouches of engraved fruit. The straps are of varying thicknesses, woven together in a manner similar to patterns engraved by Théodore de Bry and George Wechter the Elder of Nuremberg.[1] The integration of paterae at intervals in the design, and the way the whole pattern bursts out of the salver, give the design an energetic three-dimensionality, completely unlike Renaissance ornament. The only other instance of this very distinctive strapwork occurs on John Harris's silver-gilt-mounted agate bowl and cover of 1818–19 at Brodick Castle (cat. no. 118). Unlike that bowl, however, this salver has even more idiosyncratic features. In the center is the Hamilton cinquefoil, while the border is decorated with Chinese motifs with clusters of engraved fruit. The whole is raised on eight small Chinese-style feet. The result is an original work of art, unlike any other objects commissioned by Beckford, and unique among silver produced during the Regency period in England.

The technique of combining etching with engraving for the field of a salver is also unknown in silver of the period. William Burwash, the son of a bricklayer, had begun his career as a maker of watch cases. By 1808 he was described as a silversmith, and by the time Beckford's salvers were commissioned, he had established himself as a specialist maker of high-quality salvers and platters.[2] Burwash's mark appears on the central boss, engraved with Beckford's arms, of a large silver-gilt dish of 1814–15, makers mark of Samuel Whitford II, now in the Victoria and Albert Museum, London.[3] The extravagant mixture of Islamic knotwork and Renaissance motifs is totally unlike the decoration on this salver.

Beckford's two crests are superbly engraved on the reverse of the salver, in a larger size than usually found at this period, and with the addition of his mottos inscribed on scrolling ribbons. The two salvers may be the ones described as "a Silver-Gilt Gothic Salver richly chased and engraved" and "A Ditto" in both the 1822 and 1823 Fonthill catalogues—typically for the period, "gothic" being used to mean "exotic."[4] If so, they were bought back by Beckford in the Phillips' sale, for they next appear in the 1882 Hamilton Palace sale, purchased by the dealer Durlacher for £78 15s.[5] —C. H.

109. *Ladle*

John Robins (fl. 1771–1831)

1812–13; England
Silver gilt
1½ x 4 x 1½ in. (3.8 x 10.1 x 3.7 cm)
Trustees of the National Museums of Scotland, Edinburgh (1980.983)

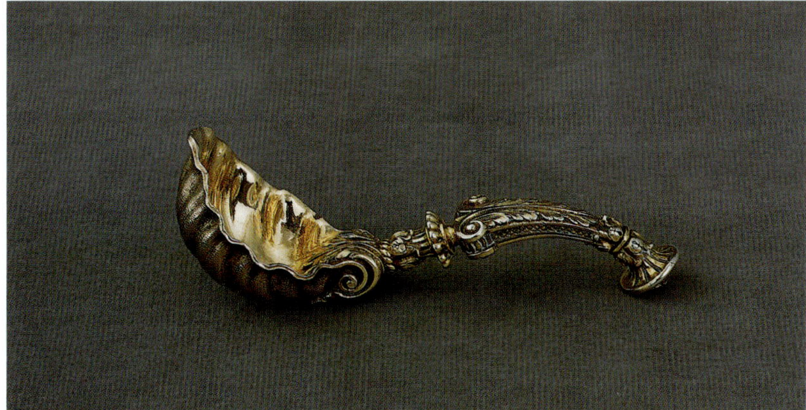

A group of small precious objects, ornamented with a variety of motifs from Asia and from Renaissance designs, were made under Franchi's direction for Beckford during the years when the latter was settled into the Abbey. Most of the objects were worked up by Franchi using Beckford's vast collection of ornamental prints and drawings.

This ladle, however, is the only known piece in the group that is copied directly from a print source, in this case an engraving of 1539 by Heinrich Aldegrever (1502–1558) of two ornamental spoons and a com-bined whistle and grooming tool.[1] The stem of the spoon in the foreground of the print, which is divided into sections of boldly modeled acanthus leaves, was copied almost exactly in silver gilt. On the terminal of Beckford's spoon, an element not visible in the engraving, the Hamilton cinquefoil has been applied, perhaps not surprisingly. The bowl of Aldegrever's spoon appears in the engraving to be joined to the stem with hinged acanthus leaves and was probably intended to fold as a traveling spoon. The Beck-ford spoon has been given a heavy cast shell bowl, matted on the exterior but with a plain interior, joined to the stem with heavy acanthus leaves. The ladle was perhaps intended as a sugar or preserve spoon, or merely as an objet d'art.

An idea of the exacting process for commissioning these objects can be gleaned from comments by William Gibbs Rogers, a wood-carver, who noted: "Mons Franchi, a man of taste. He would come into the carvers' workshop with a volume of Holbein or Aldegrever, select a spoon or handle, and have them executed in ivory or ebony as high as he could get talent to bring them, would watch the progress of work day by day, and the question would often be—'if you spent another day on it could you get it finer?'"[2]

John Robins was one of the group of small independent silver-smiths with whom Franchi appears to have dealt directly when placing commissions for small cabinet pieces for Fonthill. Although Robins's name does not appear in the corre-spondence between Beckford and Franchi, his mark appears on a num-ber of objects and mounts made for Beckford around this time.[3] The mark Robins registered at Gold-smiths' Hall, "IR" with a pellet between the initials,[4] appears on most of the other Robins pieces in the group, but this ladle bears the punch without a pellet. Similar marks without the pellet were in use at the time by John Reily and by John Robertson, both smallworkers. Given the existence of other work by Robins in the Beckford group, how-ever, it seems reasonable to suppose that this is a hitherto unrecorded version of Robins's mark. —C. H.

110. *Jug*

James Aldridge (fl. 1778–?1822), Meissen Factory

Mounts, 1816–17, England; porcelain, ca. 1740–45, Germany
Hard-paste porcelain, silver gilt
6⅞ x 4⅞ in. (17.5 x 12.5 cm)
Collection of Marian Walecki

This Meissen jug, with its exquisite silver-gilt mounts, belongs to the group of highly inventive mounted porcelains commissioned by Beck-ford and known to have been made between 1814 and 1820 for Fonthill Abbey. Just as Beckford's antique Chinese porcelain seemed to require silver mounts in Oriental style, this mid-eighteenth-century Meissen jug called for mounts in a Germanic rococo style. The bold relief decora-tion on these mounts, so different from the engraved geometric decora-tion on Beckford's Chinese wares, may have been inspired in part by the molded rococo decoration gener-ally found on the small "sparrow-beak" spouts of Meissen jugs of this type. The silver-gilt neck mount, expertly embossed and chased with a profusion of rococo ornament, com-pletely envelops the porcelain spout, and builds the height of the piece well beyond the original rim. The overlapping of rococo motifs and the density of the surface texture recall the distinctive goldwork produced in London by German immigrant craftsmen in the mid-eighteenth century.[1]

While the general idea of a mount sympathetic to the design of the object is typical of Aldridge's work for Beckford, rococo design is not. In fact, this jug is the only known surviving example of Fonthill silver in the rococo style. The only refer-ence to another object in this style among Beckford's silver is a pen-and-ink design in Aldridge's album of drawings attributed to Franchi.[2] The rendering shows a similar, but covered, Meissen jug with a robust silver-gilt handle in rococo style. It

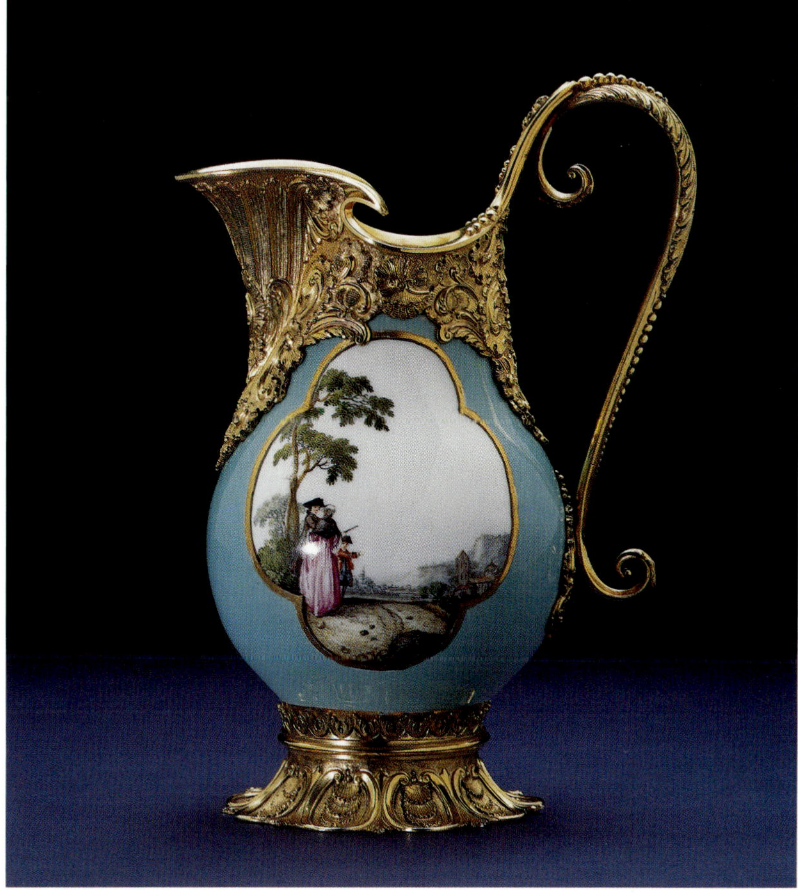

is unknown whether the design was executed, but the reference to a "Dresden cream jug and cover, sea green, with landscapes in compartments, the mounting of silver gilt" in Beckford's 1817 Harley Street auction suggests that it, or another one like it, had been made.[3] Most of Beckford's commissions in silver revived Renaissance, Islamic, or Oriental designs. These more exotic historicist styles were artistically avant-garde during the Fonthill years, while the rococo revival, on the other hand, was already an established style in English silver by 1816.

Despite this relatively conservative aspect of its design, this cream jug reveals the unique creative influence of Beckford and Franchi. The overall approach—that of setting off a precious object in equally precious mounts—is a Renaissance conceit adopted enthusiastically by Beckford in this period. Details of the mount design, such as the band of leaves that grip the foot and the beaded tendril handle, relate to mounts on Beckford's Renaissance revival hardstones and to a number of Franchi's pen-and-ink designs. Even the double-walled construction of the neck and its notched lip recall sixteenth-century objets d'art, such as the mounted nautilus cup in Beckford's collection.[4] Further, the handle of the jug incorporates Beckford's heraldic charges, the well-known Hamilton cinquefoil and Latimer cross. The workmanship is so detailed that even the correct heraldic "color" of the cinquefoil (ermine) is indicated by tiny ermine tails in relief on each of the five leaves.

Christie's catalogue of the contents of Fonthill of 1822 describes a Meissen service which almost certainly includes the present jug: "Twelve Royal Dresden Tea-cups and Saucers, Sugar and Slop-basins pale green ground, rich gold borders and landscapes, inside and out, of a very superior quality, a Cream-ewer to correspond, massively mounted, and richly covered in silver-gilt."[5] This description suggests that, rather than standing alone in a display cabinet with Renaissance objects or other kinds of mounted porcelains, this cream jug was part of a tea service that was actually used.

Why Beckford would select the cream jug alone from the set for mounting is unclear, but cream jugs in English silver were traditionally a vehicle for fanciful design. Since their first appearance in the early eighteenth century, they have been treated more sculpturally and imaginatively than sugar bowls or other tea wares. In the 1823 sale, the jug was separated from the tea service and sold as the next lot in the catalogue: "A Dresden cream ewer to correspond, massively mounted, and richly covered in SILVER-GILT, in a gilt glass dish." Surviving records indicate that Beckford owned a considerable number of such jugs; in 1822 Franchi described "20 Cream ewres [sic] mounted in silver gilt all different" among the property removed from Fonthill at that time.[6] After Beckford's death in 1844, the inventory of his much depleted collection still included thirty-four mounted porcelain jugs of unknown description.[7]

According to the newspaper reports on the auction held in 1845, after Beckford's death, there was general disbelief that one household could have contained so much porcelain. Buyers at the auction, conducted by Edmund English & Son of Bath, were so skeptical that the Bath *Chronicle* was compelled to explain the profusion of "matchless china" writing: "There is a general feeling of surprise at the quantity of china, and many are credulous as to the fact of its being the genuine property, and veritably having belonged to Mr. Beckford. For two reasons we place entire confidence in the announcement. In the first place, there is not one single piece of those ten thousand specimens but is remarkable for its beauty, quality, and costliness; and, secondly, because Mr. Beckford's custom was to have a different arrangement for every day in the year. The cup and saucer he used to-day at his breakfast were placed in a cabinet until a revolving year brought them into request; and such was the custom likewise at dinner, dessert, and tea."[8]

In light of such remarks, perhaps this cream jug, and the related Chinese porcelain cream jugs now at Brodick Castle, were not strictly treasures for the *Schatzkammer* but rather components of daily life during Beckford's years at Fonthill and afterward. —J. S.

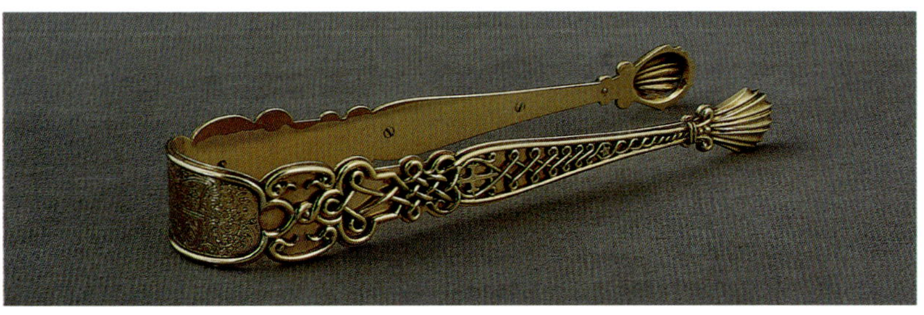

III. *Sugar Tongs*
Attrib. Joseph William Story and William Elliot (partnership fl. 1809–1818)

ca. 1812; England
Silver gilt
5¼ in. (13.3 cm)
Trustees of the National Museums of Scotland, Edinburgh (1977.215)

One of a group of eclectic sugar tongs created for Beckford under Franchi's direction, this example makes full use of Beckford's heraldic badges. The shaped stems are applied with panels of interlacing strapwork based on woodcuts by Albrecht Dürer, copied from designs believed to be by Leonardo which Dürer had seen on his second visit to Venice in 1505–57.[1] The strapwork is affixed to the arms with small rivets—a curious construction more suited to the fabrication of a gold snuff box than the making of a piece of silver. The Beckford badges of the Douglas star and the Latimer cross appear among the strapwork.

As with all of the sugar tongs in this group, the end is engraved with Beckford's coat-of-arms. In this instance the shield is divided into four quarters. In the first and fourth appear the arms of Beckford, within the double tressure which he had been granted by the College of Arms on March 20, 1810, to replace the single tressure he had added in 1791. The tressure, a decorative border, is found mostly in Scottish heraldry. It could be added to a coat of arms. At that time, heraldic scholars were divided as to whether it was a symbol of descent from the Scottish royal house, or merely a mark of distinction given to the grantee.[2] The College of Arms was a romantic backwater during Beckford's lifetime before its scientific revival in the second half of the nineteenth century. The institution probably cared little for such detail, and, as Beckford's biographer Cyrus Redding wryly commented, "the Herald's Office aided his fancy."[3] They were happy to grant Beckford whatever additional devices and badges he wished for, within reason, and in exchange for hefty fees. The College of Arms had confirmed his right to bear thirty quarterings.[4]

The arms have as the second quartering, the arms of Hamilton, and, for the first time, an additional quartering, the arms of Douglas as the third quarter of the shield. With the marriage of his daughter Susan Euphemia in April 1810 to the Marquess of Douglas, heir to the dukedom of Hamilton, Beckford was eager to reinforce his own claim to descent from the ancient Hamilton and Douglas families. About a month before the wedding, Beckford had been awarded the right to bear a special version of the Hamilton crest. The only other object engraved with Beckford's arms with the same quarterings is the large silver-gilt charger of 1814–15 (see fig. 11-5).[5]

The inclusion of so many quarterings on such a small engraved shield made the heraldic minutiæ unintelligible to all but the user of the tongs. —C. H.

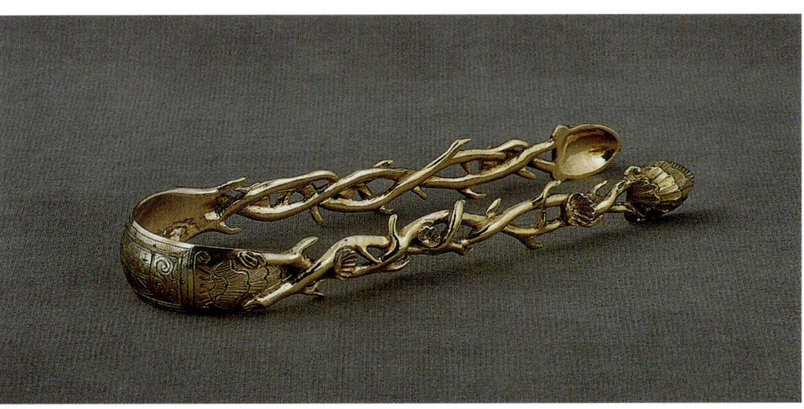

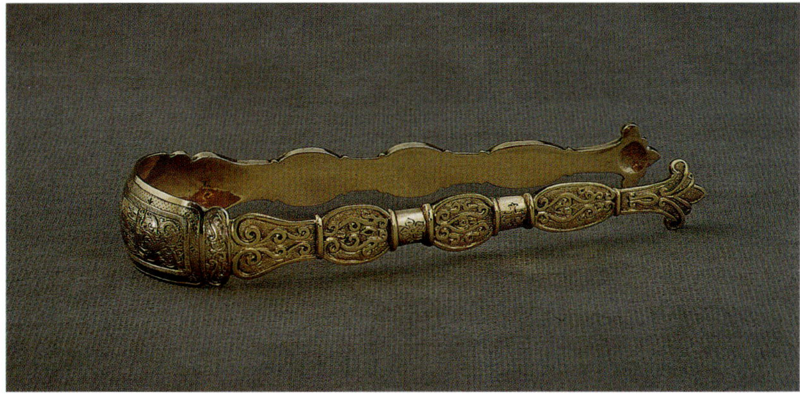

112. *Sugar Tongs*
Joseph William Story
and William Elliot
(partnership fl.
1809–1818)

1813–14; England
Silver gilt
¾ x 5⅜ x 1¼ in. (1.8 x 13.75 x 4.5
cm)
Trustees of the National Museums
of Scotland, Edinburgh (1977.213)

Ornamental sugar tongs, of the large size typical of the Regency period, provided the opportunity for Beckford and Franchi to intermingle Renaissance, naturalistic, and heraldic motifs to great effect. The National Museums of Scotland possess four of this series, purchased from the Hamilton family in 1977, of which three are included in this exhibition (see also cat. nos. 111 and 113). On this pair, the stems have been delicately modeled and cast in the lost-wax process as interlaced coral stems applied at intervals with small shells. The bow, or end, has been engraved with Beckford's arms within a conventional angular shield. Interestingly, however, the coat, which bears the quartered Beckford and Hamilton arms, is enclosed by the double tressure granted to Beckford in 1810, which is in contravention of the laws of heraldry as the tressure pertains to the Beckford arms only. —C. H.

113. *Sugar Tongs*
Joseph William Story
and William Elliot
(partnership fl.
1809–1818)

1812–13; England
Silver gilt
⅞ x 5¼ x 1¼ in. (2.3 x 13.3 x 4.5
cm)
Trustees of the National Museums
of Scotland, Edinburgh (1977.214)

On this pair of tongs, the stems have been shaped into oval compartments and chased (rather than applied as on cat. no. 111) with arabesques on a matted ground. The Hamilton cinquefoil and the Latimer cross are engraved in the links between the cartouches, and Beckford's arms, quartering Hamilton, are engraved on the end. As on the coral-stemmed version, the arms have been enclosed in their entirety by the double tressure granted to Beckford in 1810.

The partnership of Story and Elliot in Clerkenwell was one among the group of plateworkers who were used by Franchi to carry out the commissions for the small, intricate tea wares purchased by Beckford between 1810 and 1815.[1] The firm produced large quantities of conventional work, much of it involving lost wax casting and intricate chasing as here. —C. H.

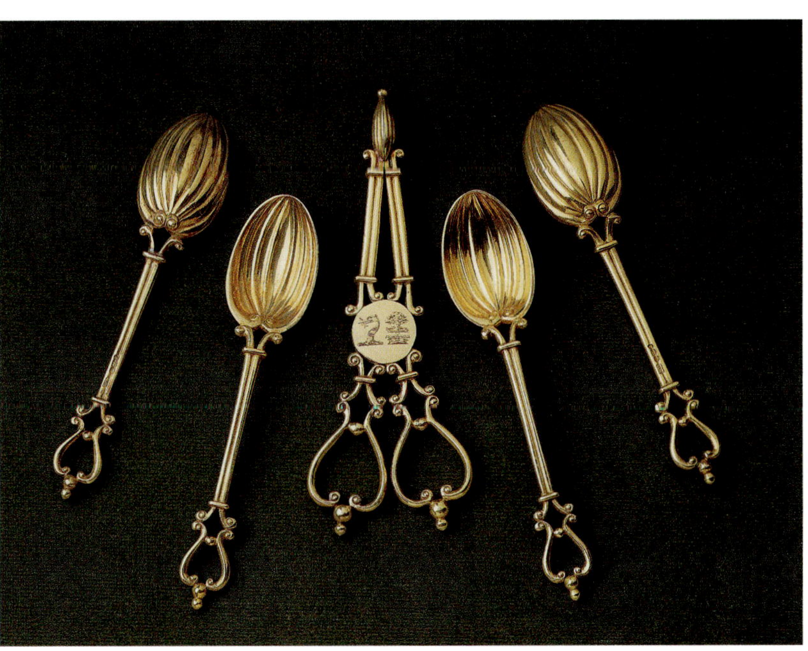

114. *Sugar Tongs and Four*
Teaspoons
John Robins (fl. 1771–1831)

1818–19; England
Silver gilt
Tongs: 5⅝ in. (14.3 cm);
teaspoons: 5¼ in. (13.5cm)
Private collection

Beckford must have taken great delight in mixing tea wares of varying styles at each tea time. These spoons and tongs are one of a series of sets, all different, that complemented the various tea services commissioned during this period (cat. nos. 40–44 and 59–62). The heart-shaped openwork terminals are reminiscent of late seventeenth-century fire tools, while the bowls of the teaspoons are fluted to resemble melons. Unlike some of Beckford's other sugar tongs, this example is of scissor form, a type in vogue in the middle of the eighteenth century that had all but died out by the Regency period. —C. H.

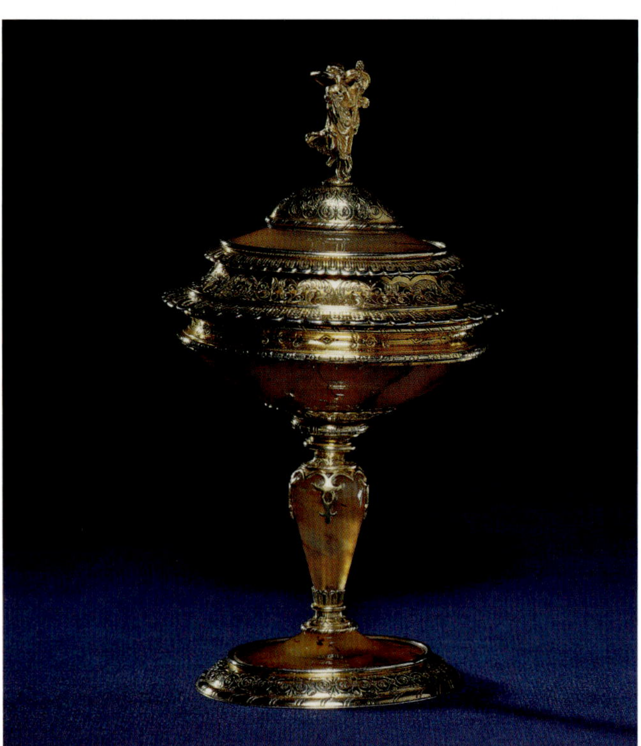

115. *Cup and Cover*
Maker unknown

Mounts, ca. 1820, England;
hardstone, date unknown,
Continental Europe
Agate, silver gilt
6 x 3¼ x 2 in. (15.2 x 8.2 x 5 cm)
Gilbert Collection, Somerset
House, London (1999.84)

From about 1815 until late in his life
Beckford commissioned London
goldsmiths to make a series of objets
d'art, many of which were mounted
pieces incorporating materials such

as rock-crystal, hardstones, and Chinese or European porcelain. The
goldsmiths employed by Beckford
included not only some of the leading London makers, but also a number of lesser-known craftsmen, such
as James Aldridge and John Harris.
The sophistication, quality, and individuality of the designs, however,
suggest a strong creative input from
Beckford and from surviving correspondence we know that the detailed
discussions with goldsmiths were
often conducted by his friend and
confidant Gregorio Franchi.

Some of this was quite comic.
The two friends devised a number of

nicknames for the goldsmiths. Philip
Rundell was referred to by Beckford
as "Fiume" and John Harris as "the
Methodist." In a letter of 1819 to
Franchi, Beckford wrote, "Now that
I recollect that the Methodist has in
his keeping the lapis-lazuli and the
gold, it wouldn't surprise me if he
made off and if one heard no more
of him until one read in the American papers: "New York, 21ˢᵗ Sept.
1819—Brother Harris, newly arrived
from the Land of perdition, has
gladdened our hearts with much
spiritual discourse."[1]

The ethos that Beckford was
seeking to evoke with these costly
and sophisticated objects was that of
the princely *Schatzkammer* of the
sixteenth and seventeenth centuries.
As beautiful as many of the objects
are, their character was quite out of
keeping with the grandeur of contemporary Regency taste and they
failed to arouse much enthusiasm
when exposed to the public in 1822
as the viewing of the canceled
Christie's sale at Fonthill. The critic
William Hazlitt perhaps summed up
the general response when he commented acidly that Fonthill was "a
Cathedral turned into a toy shop, an
immense Museum of all that is most
curious and costly and, at the same
time, most worthless in the productions of art and nature . . . Mr.
Beckford has shown himself an
industrious bijoutier, a prodigious
virtuoso, an enthusiastic collector
of expensive trifles; [but] the only
proof of taste (to our thinking) he

has shown in this collection is his
getting rid of it."

This cup represents all the qualities in his possessions that Beckford
sought and that Hazlitt disparaged.
Beckford is thought to have been
closely involved with the production
of Christie's sale catalogue. His
own opinion of the cup is probably
reflected in its fulsome description
as a "cup and cover, stand and foot,
small and choice, the Mocoa agate
elegantly mounted, elaborately
engraved and surmounted by a Baccante, all of silver-gilt."[2] Like many
of the mounted pieces he commissioned, its design draws on the
aesthetic of Renaissance pattern
books, which he had in his library.
The strapwork at the top of the stem
and the engraved arabesque ornament both look back to the sixteenth century, while the carefully
modeled Bacchante finial is a specifically Renaissance motif. Bacchante
was the female devotee of Bacchus;
she is usually depicted in swirling
drapery expressing physical abandonment while her attribute of the
Thyrsus, a wand tipped by a pinecone, is a symbol of fertility and a
reference to the prevalent worship
of the spirit of the pine.

The absence of hallmarks on the
mounts makes it difficult to date this
cup precisely, but comparison of it
with others, notably the mounted
pieces at Brodick Castle, suggests a
date of around 1816–20, with James
Aldridge or John Harris as the most
likely maker. —T. S.

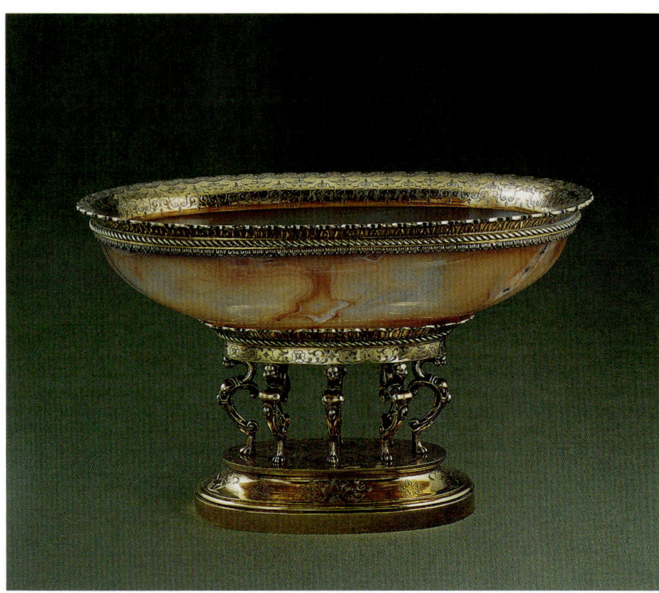

116. *Bowl*
Paul Storr (1771–1844)

Mounts, 1816–17, England;
hardstone, date unknown,
Continental Europe
Agate, silver gilt
5½ x 8½ in. (14 x 21.5 cm)
Beckford Collection, Brodick
Castle, National Trust for
Scotland (58.325)

While in Paris during the summer of
1814, Gregorio Franchi arranged for
an enormous shipment of hardstones
which included agates, lapis lazuli,
jade, and cornelian, both mounted
and unmounted. As a number of

the hardstone-mounted pieces in
Beckford's collection were made up
shortly after that time, it is probable
that the hardstones were the ones
included in this shipment. This
might explain the large number of
unmounted hardstones that were in
the Fonthill Abbey sales catalogues
of 1822 and 1823. Their source in
Paris is not clear, but some were
probably purchased from M. Durand
and others from the sale of stock
owned by Henri Auguste, following
his prosecution for criminal bankruptcy.[1] Auguste, the preeminent
goldsmith in Paris, had been a major
supplier to Beckford. Moreover,
Paris had for some time been the

source for unmounted hardstones, especially after 1789 when the French Royal Collections were dispersed. A considerable number of them entered the Louvre in 1796.[2] In 1800 the French mineralogist C. P. Brard remarked on the trade in these most desirable agates.[3]

Franchi himself had a great knowledge and love of hardstones as is evidenced by his letters to Beckford: "the agates are all cohesion and one in particular is of such quality that I've never seen another in a particular collection."[4] He was also a collector, and a large number of hardstones were included in the sales of his collection in 1827 and after his death in 1828.

The mounts Beckford commissioned from Paul Storr for this bowl are in a Renaissance revival style. This can be seen in the delicate engraved arabesque decoration on the rim around the lip and on the scalloped foot mount. The edge of the stand is engraved with Hamilton cinquefoils as well as the Beckford heron and Hamilton oak tree crests. The agate bowl rests on a tray, supported by eight classically inspired caryatids. Another version of this support is also found on the "Hercules" cup with mounts by James Aldridge (cat. no. 119). The caryatids are reminiscent of Netherlandish Mannerist silver of the late sixteenth century, where they were used only as ornaments and not as supports. These caryatids suggest table legs and indeed Vulliamy and Son, for whom Paul Storr had worked in 1801, had supplied bronze legs in the form of chimeras for a table in the very same year as Storr's first documented piece for Beckford.[5] —E. M.

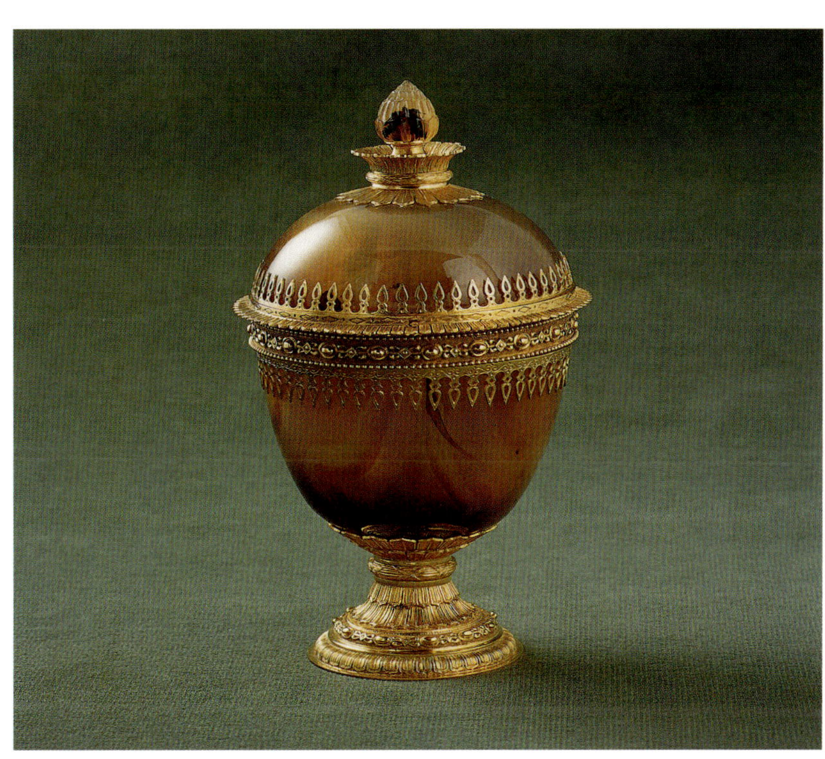

117. *Cup and Cover*
JAMES ALDRIDGE
(FL. 1778–?1822)

Mounts, 1816–17, England; hardstone, date unknown, Continental Europe
Agate, gold
5½ x 3⅛ in. (14 x 8 cm)
Beckford Collection, Brodick Castle, National Trust for Scotland (58.305)

Of all the goldsmiths associated with Beckford's silver- and gold-mounted hardstones and porcelain, James Aldridge has provided the clearest link between goldsmith and client. Many of Franchi's designs for Beckford's mounted hardstones are included in a book of designs now in the Victoria and Albert Museum, London.[1] Unlike the designs in the rest of the book, the renderings of Beckford's silver are on separate sheets of paper attached to the book along with annotated drawings for mounts by Franchi. One of these is a drawing for mounts similar to those used on this agate cup and cover. Further evidence is supplied in Franchi's detailed accounts in which there is also a small drawing.[2]

The Aldridge family had been prolific plateworkers from the 1720s to the 1780s and well-known members of the trade. James Aldridge was the son of James Aldridge of Plaistow, Essex. He was apprenticed to Charles Aldridge of Aldersgate Street London on April 8, 1778, and released from his apprenticeship in May 1785. James Aldridge entered his first maker's mark on February 22, 1798, giving his London address as 20 Strand. He worked as a smallworker, a maker of small items such as the mounts on the Beckford pieces or even for small gold work such as rings and snuff boxes. From about 1807, he is recorded at 11 Northumberland Street, Strand, and listed in various directories as a goldsmith or goldsmith and jeweler until 1845–46.[3]

Beckford's earliest silver commissions were for plate in 1781,[4] on the occasion of his coming-of-age. He continued to order a substantial number of pieces in the 1780s and 1790s, and it is possible that Aldridge's connection with Beckford arose at this time. One of the earliest of the pieces Aldridge made for Beckford, however, was executed in 1812: a bowl that imitates an eighteenth-century Chinese porcelain or enameled copper bowl, with engravings that suggest the various colors that would have been painted on.[5]

This agate cup and cover can possibly be identified with the "small . . . mammelated agate richly mounted in gold" that was located in the drawing room in Beckford's house in Bath.[6] The simply carved and highly polished stone has been sympathetically mounted to reveal the full glory of the natural inclusions that make it so fascinating. The mounts do not dominate the piece and in order to include Beckford's heraldic motifs these have been discreetly placed on the base on which the heron and oak tree crests and the mottoes *De Dieu Tout* and *Through* had been engraved. The pierced spearheads on the rims of both the cover and bowl together with the pineapple-shaped finial are evidence of Beckford's lifelong fascination with the Orient. In fact this jewellike cup and cover would not have looked out of place in the magnificence of the Prince Regent's creation, Brighton Pavilion. —E. M.

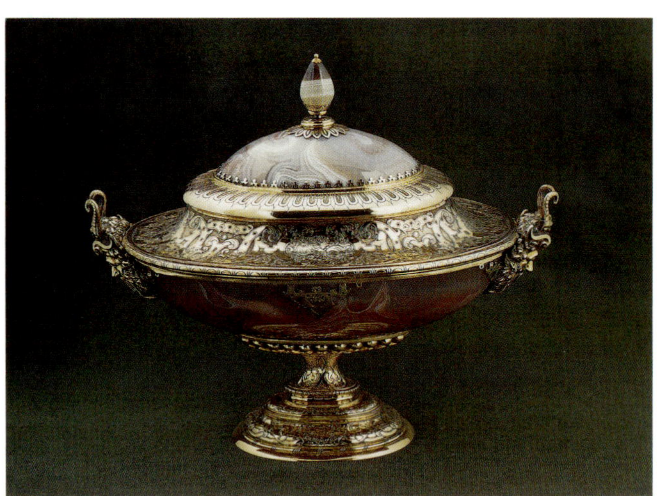

118. *Bowl and Cover*
JOHN HARRIS
(FL. 1818–1827)

Mounts, 1818–19, England;
hardstone, probably late 18th
century, Continental Europe
Agate, silver gilt
8⅝ x 9¾ in. (22 x 24.7 cm)
Beckford Collection, Brodick
Castle, National Trust for
Scotland (58.306)

This bowl and cover is described in
the Fonthill Abbey 1822 sale catalogue as "A Magnificent large oval
cassolette, of Hungarian Agate, massively mounted in silver, engraved,
chased and gilt, ornamented with
masks of satyrs modelled, and of the
first workmanship."[1] It is the second
hardstone mounted piece by John
Harris included in this catalogue (for
the other, see cat. no. 39).

Although the term *Hungarian* is
used, the agate was probably mined
in the hills around Idar-Oberstein in
the valley of the Nahe in the German Rhineland where the agate-
cutting industry is thought to have
emerged in the fifteenth century.
This same stone of pink agate with
white and purple banding is found
on a group of South German, late-
Gothic vessels, dating to around
1500, an example of which is in the
Victoria and Albert Museum.[2] For
stylistic reasons, the cutting of the
stone in Beckford's cup and cover,
however, precludes a date earlier
than the late eighteenth century.
That Franchi was aware of German
agate is confirmed by a letter to

Beckford in 1822 in which he said
that they had become too expensive.[3]

The silver-gilt mounts by Harris
derive much of their inspiration from
Mannerism. The incurved broad rim
mount can be found on silver from
the sixteenth century and can be
closely compared with the drawing
of a bowl and cover attributed to the
Florentine Francesco Salviati of the
mid-sixteenth century.[4] The satyr's
masks again are Renaissance, but
after the antique as in the drawings
of Agostino dei Musi of the 1530s.[5]
Indeed the masks may very well
have been inspired by the masks on
Beckford's "Rubens" vase, which he
bought in 1818, as the hallmarks on
Harris's bowl and cover are 1818/19.
The "Rubens" vase (now in the
Walters Art Museum, Baltimore; see
fig. 9-3) is Romano-Byzantine dating
to around A.D. 400 and was carved
from a single agate.[6] It was regarded
by Beckford as one of the most
important works of art in his collection. "It is truly beautiful," Franchi
wrote to Beckford's son-in-law, Lord
Douglas, "and I repeat it is the finest
object in the Abbey."[7]

The design for the intricate strapwork engraving is taken from a late-
sixteenth-century South German
source and is close to that found
on a Beckford silver-gilt salver by
W. Burwash of 1817–18.[8] As the
engraved ornament is close to that

found on the Burwash dish, it is
probably the work of the engraver
Coulson, whose collaboration on the
pieces is noted in lists of Franchi's
accounts and whose name is mentioned in a letter to Beckford in
August 1828.[9] There appears to be
some confusion as to whether this
is Samuel Coulson, a jeweler first
recorded in 1818 but not in the
directories as a jeweler and goldsmith until 1822, or Samuel Couldon
who was apprenticed as an engraver
to W.N. Hughes from 1819 to
1826. The names of enamelers and
engravers in the eighteenth and
nineteenth centuries are legion.
Because heraldry played such a
prominent part in the decoration
of plate, engravers were especially
numerous, and it is usually impossible to connect surviving work with
any of the names listed in directories.

Although the agate bowl and
cover was listed in Christie's 1822
sale catalogue, they were retained by
Beckford when he moved to Bath in
that year. It was illustrated in an
engraving after Willes Maddox in
English's *Views of Lansdown Tower*
(1844), where it was listed as being
in the drawing room.[10] It subsequently passed into the Hamilton
collection and is now part of the
National Trust for Scotland's collection at Brodick Castle. —E. M.

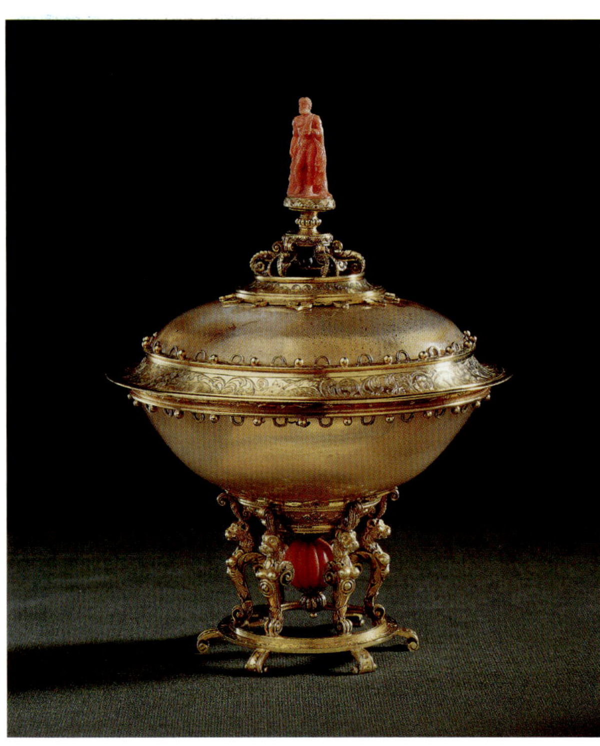

119. *Cup and Cover*
JAMES ALDRIDGE
(FL. 1778–?1822)

Mounts, 1820–21, England;
hardstone, probably late 18th
century, Continental Europe;
coral, 18th century, Italy
Agate, silver gilt, coral
6½ x 4¾ in. diam. (16.5 x 12 cm
diam.)
Private collection

This cup and cover was shown in the
Illustrated London News, where it was
described as: "A Tazza of botryioidal
[sic] chalcedony mounted on six
chimeras, with coral pendant, and
cover of precious agate, exhibiting an
entire fortification, with rim of
chased and engraved gold; the border

with animals and arabesques, and
the cover surmounted by a finely
sculpted Hercules in coral: This was
knocked down to Mr Raven for 74
guineas."[1] The newspaper's interesting use of the word *botryoidal,*
meaning shaped like clusters of
grapes, sheds light on the use of the
term *mammelated agate,* which
occurs a number of times in the 1844
inventory taken after Beckford's
death.

This cup is listed in the inventory
as a "mammelated cup and cover
with coral Hercules" and as being
located in one of the oak hanging
cabinets in the dining room at 19
Lansdown Crescent.[2] The agate bowl
displays within it clusters of inclusions, reminiscent of nipples or
breasts and similar to an agate used
in an enameled gold-mounted cup

in the Medici Collection in Florence, described simply as an oriental agate.[3] The cover, on the other hand, is carved from a different type of agate containing inclusions of other minerals which appear like dendritic forms (treelike) in the stone. Both the shape of the bowl as well as the saucerlike cover indicate that the carving of the stone is likely to date from the late eighteenth century.

The finial of Hercules standing with his club and lion's pelt is a type of coral (*Corallum rubrum*) dredged from the Mediterranean off the coasts of Naples, Southern Italy, and Sicily. The figure, inspired by the antique, dates from the eighteenth century and was made in Southern Italy, most probably in Naples, which,

after the closure of the Trapani workshop in Sicily at the end of the seventeenth century, was the primary source of carved coral. Suspended from the bowl is a carved and fluted eighteenth-century coral knop.

The silver-gilt mounts contain many of the features characteristic of Beckford's historicist silver. The rim mount is decorated with a continuous frieze of animals, including a mouse, squirrel, and an otter, connected by intricate foliate scrollwork. The design is taken almost directly from an early seventeenth-century German print (see fig. 11-7).[4] Beckford's extraordinary library contained a comprehensive collection of ornamental prints and drawings, including examples by such established

Renaissance artists as Holbein (see cat. no. 102), Schongauer, and Aldegrever (see cat. no. 109).

This piece bears the Beckford heraldic devices typical of many of Beckford's works of art. The armorials, however, were cunningly designed so as to be visible only by handling the piece. The Beckford martlets are concealed under the rim of the cover and the Hamilton cinquefoils are unusually cast and applied in a band at the top of the base supporting the bowl. The appeal of small-scale, ingeniously designed objects is characteristic of Beckford's taste and underlines his fascination with such *Schatzkammer* objects.

The importance of this cup and

cover to Beckford is apparent by its inclusion in the fanciful strapwork designs illustrating the title page to Edmund English's volume dedicated to Lansdown Tower.[5] It is the only heraldic piece recorded in Willes Maddox's *Objects of Vertu* (cat. no. 155). C. J. Richardson, who produced the chromolithographs for English's volume, later published a series of ornamental designs.[6] A preface illustration shows a number of objects from Beckford's collection, perhaps indicating the esteem in which Beckford's objects were held, and this cup and cover feature prominently. —E. M.

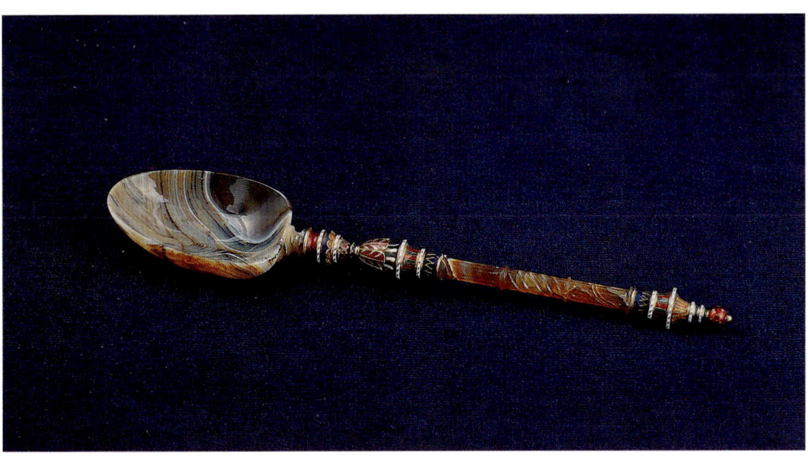

120. Spoon
Maker unknown

Mounts, ca. 1815–20, England; hardstone, date unknown, Continental Europe
Agate, gold, enamel
7⅞ in. (18 cm)
Beckford Collection, Brodick Castle, National Trust for Scotland (58.366)

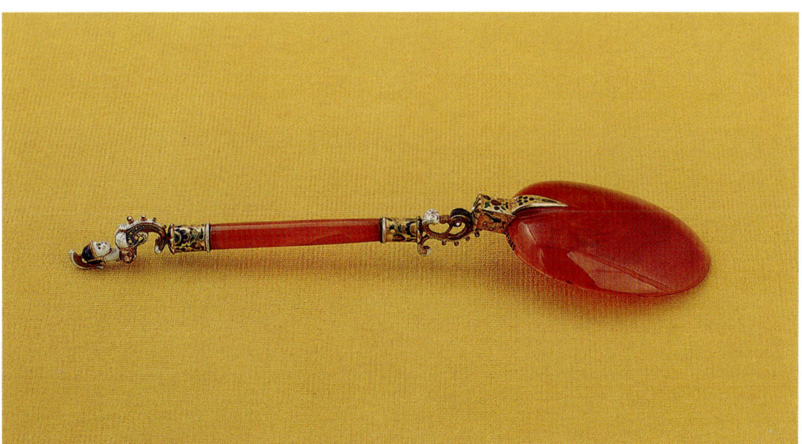

121. Spoon
Maker unknown

Mounts, ca. 1815–20, England; hardstone, date unknown, Continental Europe
Agate, gold, enamel
6¼ in. (16 cm)
Beckford Collection, Brodick Castle, National Trust for Scotland (58.335)

120–24. Hardstone spoons

Beckford's fascination with hardstones may well have originated when he was twenty, during his Grand Tour visit to Florence in 1780. On October 15, in a letter to Alexander Cozens, he wrote: "I beheld such ranks of statues, such treasures of gems that I fell into a delightful delirium and unable to check my rapture flew madly from bust to bust and cabinet to cabinet like a Butterfly bewildered in a Universe of Flowers."[1] Certainly all his life he

appears to have retained this fascination as is demonstrated by the number of hardstone pieces that were still in his collection upon his death.

The hardstone spoons reflect aspects of taste that were evident in the great *Kunstkammers*. In the sixteenth century such pieces were never intended for use but were diplomatic gifts or designed simply to be displayed in cabinets where they would be seen and handled by the privileged few. Rock crystal,

ivory, agate, coral, and shell were all used to fashion such spoons. It is not surprising that on all the Beckford hardstone spoons the mounts are gold or enameled gold. Where Beckford placed the spoons in his own residence certainly suggests that he perceived of them as "treasures of gems." According to the 1844 inventory, in the drawers of the small library were "2 agate spoons-gold and enamel mounting" and in the drawers of his bedroom "4 agate

spoon bowls . . . .a lapis lazuli spoon gold mounted" and a "cornelian spoon with enamel mounting."[2]

Of the five spoons exhibited here, the one of orbicular jasper (cat. no. 122) is most likely to be a remounted late-Renaissance piece, as demonstrated by the shallow broad bowl. The intricate metalwork, which continues alternatively up the stem, may hide traces of old mounts and even breaks in the stem. At the junction with the bowl, the mount is engraved

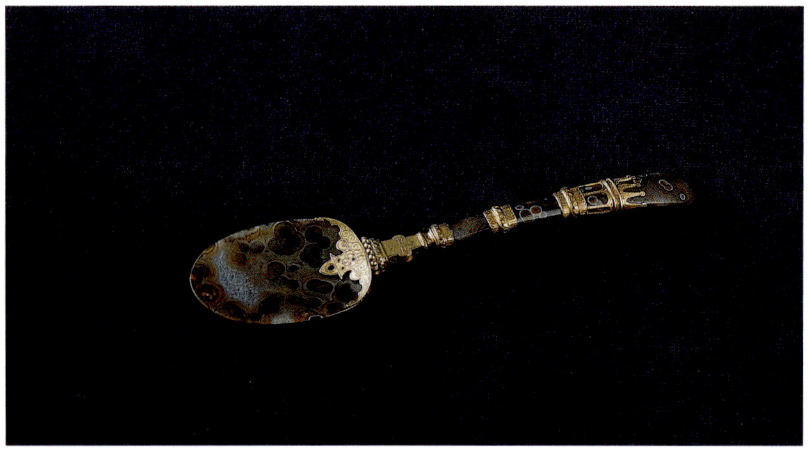

122. *Spoon*
MAKER UNKNOWN

ca. 1815–20
Mounts, ca. 1815–20, England; hardstone, date unknown,
Continental Europe
Agate, gold
5⅛ in. (13 cm)
Beckford Collection, Brodick Castle, National Trust for Scotland (58.336)

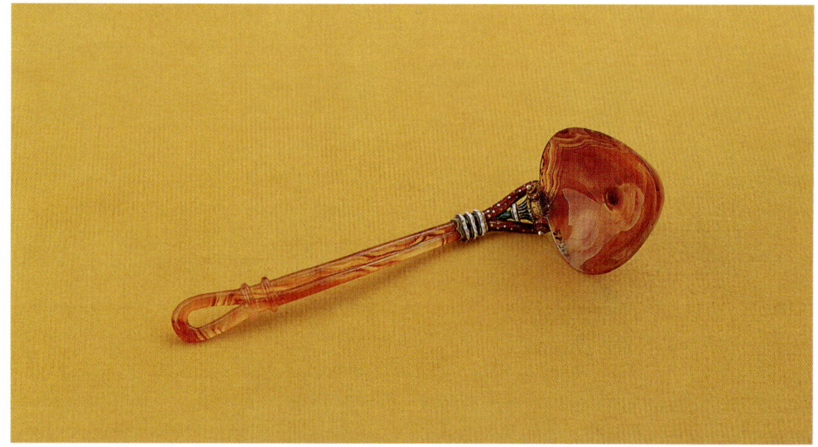

123. *Ladle*
MAKER UNKNOWN

Mounts, ca. 1815–20, England; hardstone, date unknown,
Continental Europe
Agate, gold, enamel
4¼ in. (11 cm)
Beckford Collection, Brodick Castle, National Trust for Scotland (58.360)

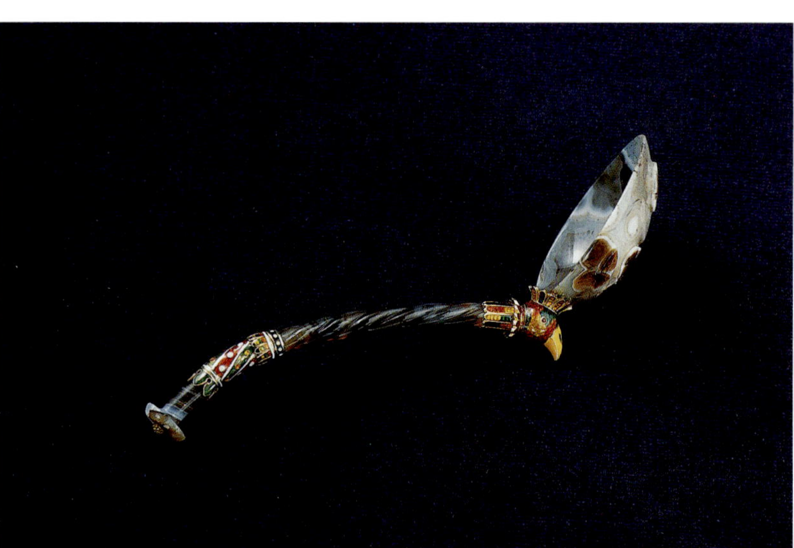

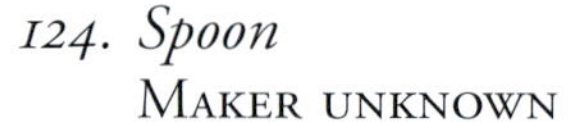

124. *Spoon*
MAKER UNKNOWN

Mounts, ca. 1815–20,
England; hardstone,
date unknown,
Continental Europe
Agate, gold, enamel,
5½ in. (14 cm)
Beckford Collection,
Brodick Castle,
National Trust for
Scotland (58.334)

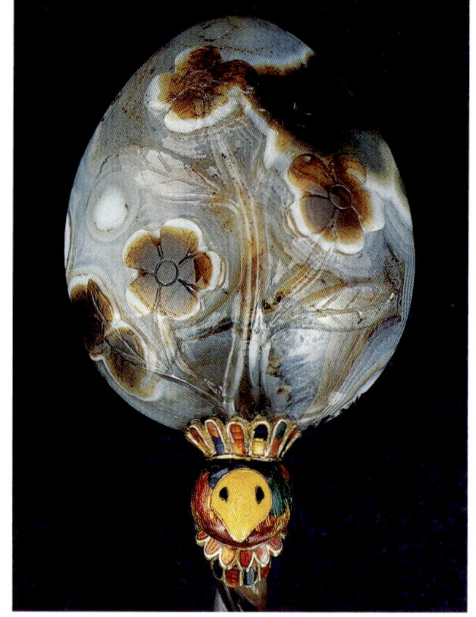

Underside of cat. no. 124

with the Latimer cross. The crown-like mounting is reminiscent of that used on the glass scent flasks by James Aldridge (cat. no. 125).

The four other spoons are of agate and have enameled gold mounts inspired by those found on late-sixteenth- to early-seventeenth-century hardstones as well as jewelery. The Franchi Account Books, which date from 1813 to 1818, include the mention, "To Cuttel for the workmanship on a cornelian spoon. £2–2s."[3] John Cuttell is listed as a lapidary and a jeweler in Johnstone's Commercial Guide for 1818. As the

Franchi accounts also have sketches of already mounted hardstone cups posted against Cuttell's name, he was certainly involved either directly or indirectly in the attachment of these bowls to their mounts.[4]

The underside of the bowl of the "parrot spoon" (cat. no. 124) is carved with cinquefoils arranged as a floral spray and it is more likely that this is the work of a London lapidary rather than an already imported piece. Historically, London was, from the seventeenth century, a center for the production of carnelian spoons and agate-handled

knives.[5] It may be that this earlier production of spoons was resurrected by Beckford and Franchi. Conversely, Franchi may have imported the spoon bowls in his 1814 shipment of hardstones to which handles were then attached. Certainly the presence of bowls without handles in the drawers of his bedroom supports this theory.

These spoons have finely worked enameled gold mounts, parallels for which can be found on a design for a hardstone cup with enameled mounts by Gregorio Franchi in the Aldridge design book. The spoon

with the finial in the form of a helmeted warrior (cat. no. 121) is the closest in style to those made during the Renaissance.[6]

The names of enamelers listed in the London trade directories in the eighteenth and nineteenth century are numerous, but their names were jealously guarded by the London retailers. To judge from the number of fine-quality enameled gold boxes that bear the marks of London gold-smiths, however, their work was generally excellent and Beckford would have had a wealth of choice among these craftsmen. —E. M.

125. *Scent Flask*
James Aldridge
(fl. 1778–?1822)

Mounts, 1820–21, England;
glass, agate, gold, dates unknown,
possibly England
5¼ in. (13.5 cm)
Beckford Collection, Brodick
Castle, National Trust for
Scotland (58.342)

This exotic flask, one of a pair, is one
of the last of the series of mounted
objects conceived by Beckford and
Franchi for Fonthill Abbey. The red
and black mottling of the glass body,
which was probably made in Birmingham, imitates sardonyx.[1] The
conceit of one material imitating
another is taken a step further, however, by the addition of the delicate
gold mounts from the Aldridge
workshop, which render the glass as
precious as the sardonyx it imitates.

The decorative properties of sardonyx had long been recognized as
an effective foil for mounts in precious metal, and it is possible that in
commissioning these bottles Beckford was remembering the celebrated
fourth-century sardonyx vase with
sixteenth-century mounts that he

had no doubt seen in the Medici
Treasury.[2] He had visited Florence
in 1780 and had written to Cozens
of "such treasures of gems" at the
treasury.[3]

The tall, waisted form of the flask
has an Islamic flavor, heightened by
the shaped and flared foot and
twisted wire handles. Similar slender
vessels are shown in Aldridge's
design album,[4] and some possess
trailing handles, as does the finely
engraved interlacing on the foot.
The *Kunstkammer* effect is enhanced
by the addition of carved agate
knops to the stopper, while under
the base, the Hamilton and Latimer
badges have been engraved in an
alternating pattern.

In the inventory prepared after
Beckford's death in 1844, these bottles were listed in the drawing room
in Lansdown Crescent, where they
are described as "Cornelian small . . .
mounted in gold, Moca stone tops."[5]
Like many of the objets d'art, these
flasks were taken to Hamilton Palace
and were ultimately given with the
contents of Brodick Castle to the
National Trust for Scotland in 1958.
The influence of Beckford's *Kunstkammer* objects on nineteenth-
century decorative arts was therefore

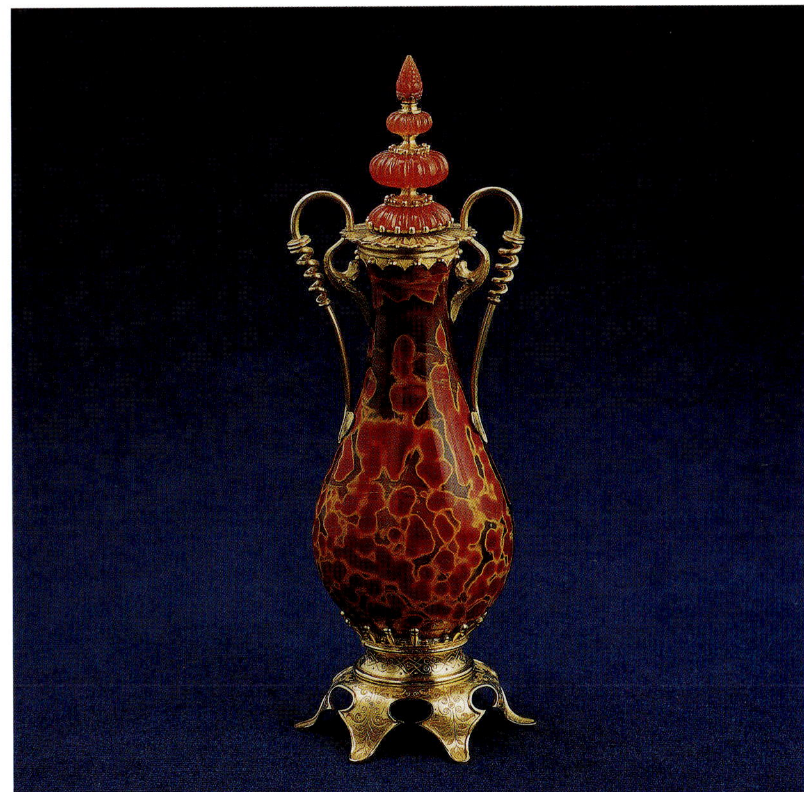

limited, although the artist C. J.
Richardson did make drawings and
rubbings of the decoration used on a
number of Beckford pieces during
the Lansdown years which he used
in his highly influential books on
design published in the middle years

of the century. One of these flasks
appears with other Beckford objects
as part of an ornamental frieze on
the title page of his *Studies of Ornamental Design* (1851). —C. H. and
E. M.

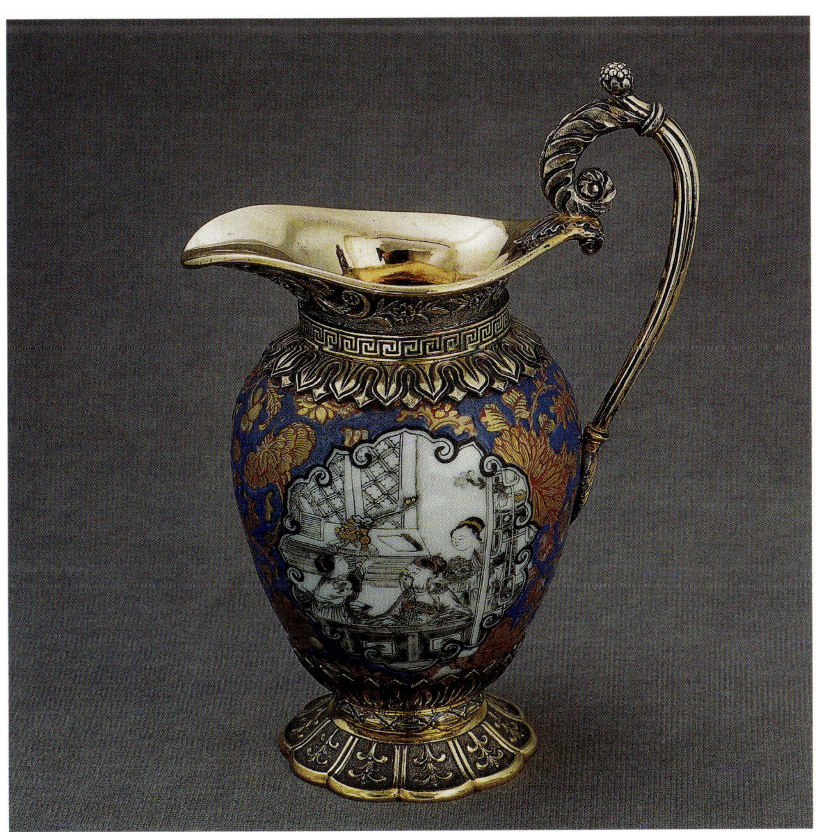

126. *Jug*
John Robins (fl. 1771–1831)

Mounts, ca. 1820, England;
porcelain, 18th-century, China
Porcelain, silver gilt
6⅛ in. (15.5 cm)
Beckford Collection, Brodick
Castle, National Trust for
Scotland (58.359)

The tradition of applying mounts in
precious metal to rare and costly
oriental porcelain dates to the Middle
Ages. Indeed Beckford owned what
is now regarded as the earliest documented example of this type of
European mounting: a celadon vase
with silver-gilt mounts applied about
1381.[1] More immediately, however,
Beckford also enthusiastically
embraced the tradition of mounting
decorative, rather than rare, porcelain and thus creating distinctive
works of art out of Chinese export
porcelain or Meissen (cat. no. 110).

This approach had been pioneered
by the eighteenth-century *marchands-
merciers* of Paris but had all but disappeared by the end of the century.
The form and decoration of the
mounts were given as much attention to detail and execution by
Franchi and Beckford as the silver
they commissioned for Fonthill
Abbey, using a broad range of styles
and motifs.

On the mounts of this typical
Chinese export porcelain vase, classical Greek key and tied laurel borders
are combined with a Renaissance-
inspired acanthus-clad handle, while
the delicate chasing enhances the
colors of the overglaze enamel decoration. The overall effect is a rich
and costly one, elevating the vase
into the status of an art object.
—C. H.

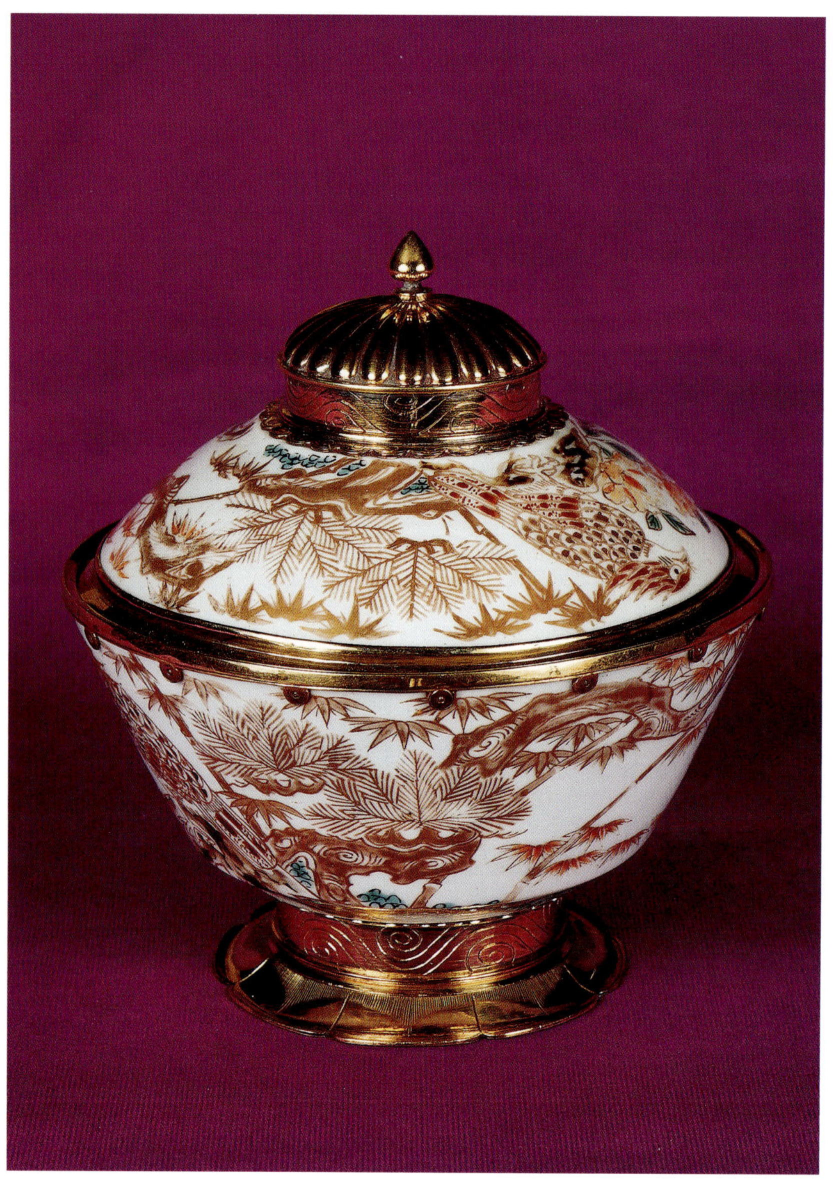

127. *Bowl and Cover*
JAMES ALDRIDGE
(FL. 1778–?1822)

Mounts, 1817–18, England;
porcelain, ca. 1680–1730, Japan
Porcelain, silver gilt
5⅜ in. (13.5 cm)
Trustees of The Edward James
Foundation (1163 OPT78)

Unlike most of the other mounted pieces in Beckford's series of exotic tea ware, this bowl is Japanese Arita ware rather than made from Chinese porcelain.[1] The difference was not always apparent to collectors at the beginning of the nineteenth century and, for example, some "Japanese bottles" that Beckford wrote about enthusiastically were in all likelihood Chinese. The silver-gilt mounts on this bowl and cover show the full flowering of the Beckford–Franchi collaboration with a mixture of motifs from Asia and Europe. The circles around the rim and the lobed Mughal-style spreading foot appear in some of the drawings in the Aldridge design book, while the engraved band of swirls is copied from Chinese blue-and-white porcelain.[2] The cover, however, is surmounted by a fluted dome and pointed finial that is entirely European in feeling. The final effect is one of exotic whimsy and quite different from Beckford and Franchi's earliest known commission, the *famille noire* bowl of 1811 (cat. no. 37).

This bowl, together with the *famille noire* example and three other mounted pieces, were purchased by the collector William James (1854–1912) of West Dean Park from the sale of the Christopher Beckett-Denison collection in 1885.[3] Much of that collection, including the Beckford pieces, had been purchased by Beckett-Denison only a few years before from the Hamilton Palace sale.[4] Beckford's mounted tea wares had gone to Hamilton Palace after his death and it appears the family chose to sell a few in the 1882 sale, retaining the rest, which were taken to Brodick Castle, another Hamilton house, on the Isle of Arran. The ones sold in 1882 appear to be those without heraldic decoration, the one exception being the *famille noire* bowl decorated with martlets (cat. no. 37). —C. H.

128. *Casket*

JOHN HARRIS
(FL. 1818–1827)

1820–21; England
Silver, parcel gilt
5⅞ x 12¾ x 10 in. (15 x 32.2 x
25.3 cm)
Theodora Wilbour Fund in
memory of Charlotte Beebe
Wilbour and Frank Brewer
Bemis Fund
The Museum of Fine Arts,
Boston (MFA 1994.89)

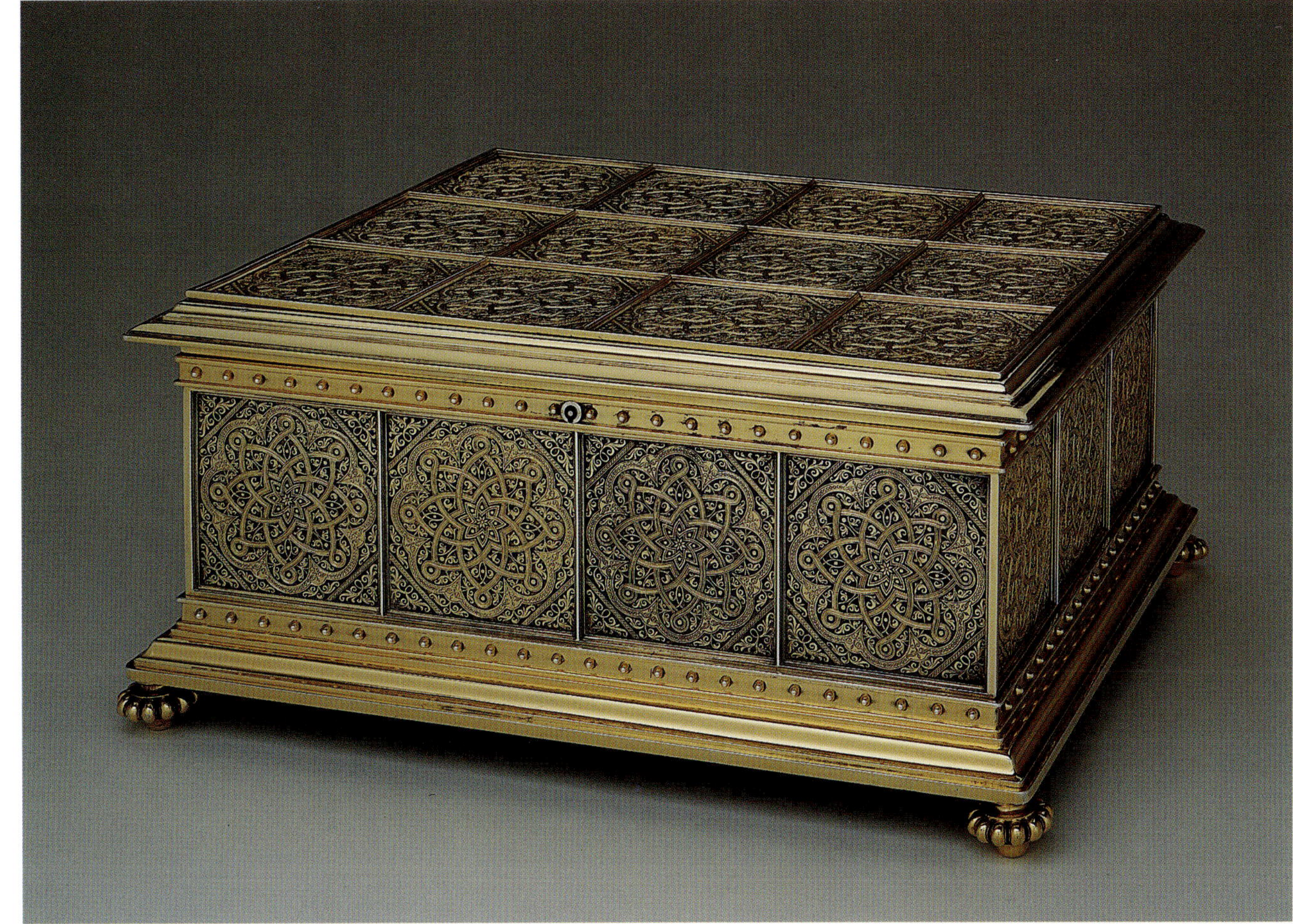

This casket is one of the most intrigu-ing and mysterious pieces of silver associated with William Beckford. It is not recorded in any of the Beck-ford inventories or sales, but it was among the property belonging to Gregorio Franchi that was sold by Christie's in 1827, a year before Franchi's death.[1] The casket has a second cover concealed in the lid that can be released with a second key. Like the body of the casket, the secret cover is divided into minutely cast square panels, but the ornament is in the form of interlaced ribbons surrounding a cipher and containing the motto, "Le tems [sic] peut nous detruire mais non pas nous detacher" (time can destroy us but never separate us). In the Franchi sale cata-logue the casket was described as having "within the outer lid . . . a very delicately gilt frame for a por-trait," now missing. Presumably the casket was a gift from Beckford to Franchi.

By 1820, the year this casket was made, Beckford and Franchi's joint endeavors in the production of his-toricist works had begun to taper off. Beckford was worried about finances, and in 1819 he wrote to Franchi: "Cups, goblets, the Queen's salvers, harpsichord, china for sweet-meats, massive objects from Ceylon, Cuttel, Coulson, Aldridge and Fogg [jewelers and goldsmiths]—all are crying out 'Pay me! Pay me!' And how to pay I no longer know."[2]

John Harris, who marked this casket, was a regular supplier to Beckford (see cat. nos. 38 and 118). The cast panels of geometric orna-ment represent great technical virtu-osity. Their design is reminiscent of the patterns of Arabic calligraphy, which Beckford and Franchi cer-tainly knew through Renaissance prints and possibly manuscript examples. The design of the casket has no precedent in English or Continental silver. This casket imi-tates the effect, if not the technique, of Indo-Portuguese filigree caskets

which feature tightly composed geo-metric panels made of wire spirals.[3] Beckford would have been familiar with such caskets from his several periods of residence in Portugal. The panels on the hidden cover are in the form of an interlaced knot, a symbol of divine revelation particularly appropriate to the pledge of eternal union that they enclose. The French phrase is distinguished by the spelling of the word *tems*, which sug-gests an early French text as a source. Beckford was also a collector and composer of epitaphs, which he published occasionally under the pen name Viator.[4] Though most of these are humorous or absurd, an epitaph may have been the source of the motto. Perhaps, the key to under-standing the circumstances of the commission of the casket is the cipher at the center of each knot. The initials might be G, F, V, stand-ing for Gregorio Franchi and Vathek or Viator, a pseudonym Beckford often used.[5] A more satisfying read-

ing of the letters, however, suggests that they might be F, D, and M. The cipher may refer to any of a host of pet names that Beckford and Franchi used to refer to each other, and its meaning remains elusive.

By the time of the 1827 sale, Franchi had withdrawn to his flat in Baker Street in London, impover-ished. Beckford had lost interest in his companionship, and Franchi made several appeals to Beckford, unheeded, for support for his wife in Portugal. The sale of Franchi's pos-sessions included objects of jasper, ivory, agate, maiolica, bronze, and marble. This casket brought the highest price in the sale, and the auctioneer noted the buyer as "Fles," possibly a code for Franchi himself or for Beckford. —E. A.

Bath: The Final Years, 1822–1844

In 1822, at the age of sixty-two, Beckford moved to the spa city of Bath after the sale of Fonthill Abbey. He acquired a substantial townhouse at 20 Lansdown Crescent, which he expanded with the purchase of another, immediately adjacent, but across a narrow lane. Beckford linked the two buildings with an enclosed bridge at the second floor, which would house part of his library. Several years later he sold the second house, retained the bridge, and purchased a third house immediately next to No. 20, where he would live until his death in 1844.

Through the ingenious assembly of several parcels of land extending from the back of the house into the countryside, Beckford was able to create a narrow, irregularly shaped garden of startling variety, nearly a mile long. Skillfully laid out with a grotto, sunken gardens, and picturesque structures, this comparatively small garden reflected the grand landscape he had created at Fonthill.

Beckford conceived the idea of constructing another tower, with the help of a young local architect, Henry Edmund Goodridge, at the farthest end of this garden, on top of Lansdown Hill with its spectacular views over the countryside. Built in a picturesque neoclas-sical manner between 1826 and 1828, the tower was the antithesis of the neo-Gothic Fonthill Abbey. Lansdown Tower and its interiors reflected a new aesthetic, an innovative form of classicism uniquely interpreted by Beckford. This tower would become the repository for many of his most important paintings, books, and works of art and would offer Beckford, on his daily visits, a place of retreat and contemplation.

With the security of his new financial resources, generated from the sale of Fonthill Abbey, Beckford continued to collect actively and commission works of art. In particular, he added to his extraordinary library and was constantly refining his collection of paintings. Toward the end of his life, when in his eighties, Beckford engaged in the refurbishment of the tower, commissioning new furniture as well as silver and other works of art. While out on his daily ride Beckford caught a cold and died on May 2, 1844. In compliance with his wishes, Beckford was buried above ground in a magnificent granite sarcophagus that he had designed. Virtually his entire estate was inherited by his second daughter Susan, Duchess of Hamilton. The choicest works of art and his library were removed from Bath and became part of the celebrated collection at Hamilton Palace in Scotland.

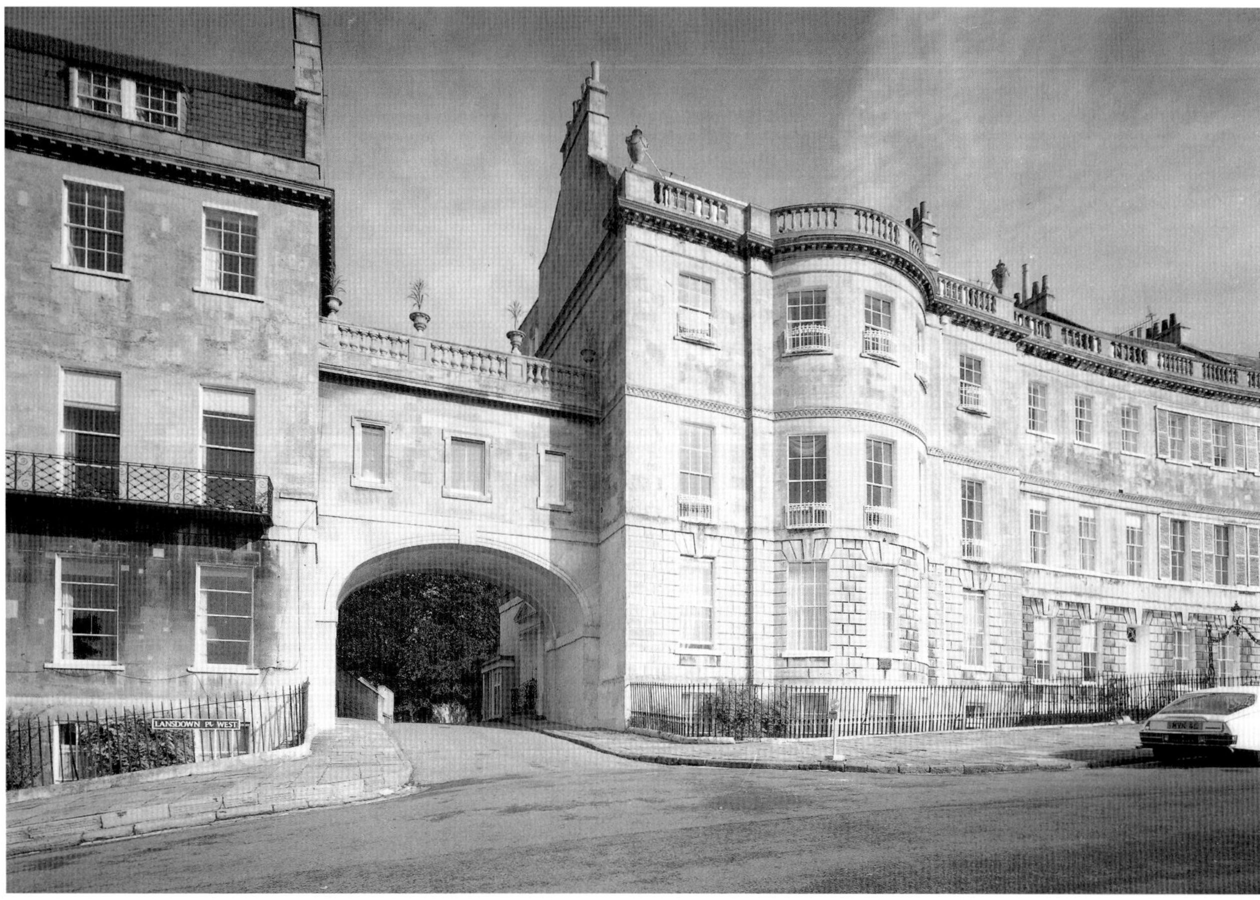

Cat. fig. 129A. William Beckford's houses in Bath: 1 Lansdown Place West (left of the bridge) connects via the bridge to 20 Lansdown Crescent and the adjacent 19 Lansdown Crescent. Photographed in the 1980s.

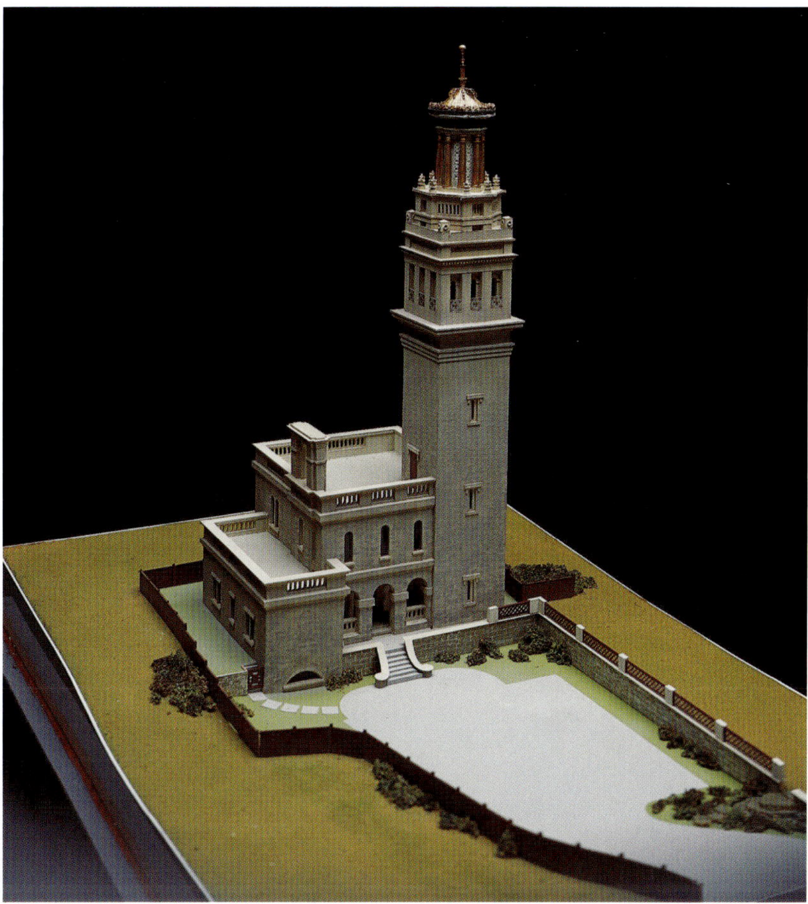

129. Model of Lansdown Tower
E. J. Matthews

1976; England
Wood, fiberglass
15 x 7 x 5¼ in. (38 x 18 x 13.5 cm)
Beckford Tower Trust, Bath (Sole
Trustee Bath Preservation Trust)
(1989/49)

In 1822 Beckford retired to Bath, and within weeks of his purchase of 20 Lansdown Crescent he began to dream of a second tower that would be no less remarkable than Fonthill Abbey.[1] The tower survives and stands 130 feet high on the summit of a hill rising 800 feet above sea level to the north of the city. Beckford enjoyed the solitude of the wind-swept, uninhabited plateau of Lansdown and described the views thirty miles into Wales to the west and Wiltshire to the south as "The finest prospect in Europe."[2]

On March 25, 1823, Beckford signed the lease for a narrow strip of land, approximately one mile in length, which ran from behind his residence at No. 20 to the tower. Immediately, he surrounded the land with a stone wall ten feet high and began to plant a sequence of framed, picturesque vignettes on the route. The construction of the tower, however, did not begin until three years later; the *Bath and Cheltenham Gazette* of October 5, 1826, reported that "one hundred men [are] employed in the erection of a splen-did and ornamental building, of which a magnificent tower will form a part."[3] Beckford conceived the structure as his mausoleum. His first designs, sketched in the autumn of 1823, indicated his concept for a neo-Romanesque tower (see fig. 16–4), asymmetric in plan and lively in sil-houette, with deep recessions and bold overhanging battlements that cast strong shadows on its surface. These picturesque qualities of form were merged with the classical language of ornamentation in the Greco-Italian tower which rose in 1826.

The tower that was begun in

October of that year was a bare rec-tangle of masonry pierced by four slit windows. Beckford's inspiration was the type of fortified tower found in Italian hill towns and often depicted in the background of Renaissance paintings, a source that was unique in early nineteenth-century European architecture. When this tower was built as high as the cornice, however, Beckford decided to add a belvedere, an aston-ishingly transparent room with three floor-length plate-glass sashes on each side. It was still not high enough, however, and in the spring of 1827 Beckford instructed his architect Henry Edmund Goodridge to build the gilded lantern, adding an extra ten tons of cast iron. His design transposed to an octagonal plan the Choragic Monument of Lysicrates, a circular structure erected in Athens in the fourth century B.C. There are 156 stone steps of the spiral staircase that ascend to the Belvedere (fig. 16–14); the circular drum in its center con-tains another spiral staircase, made of timber, with an additional forty steps inside the lantern to a "crow's-nest" viewing point.

Although the tower was far less modest in conception and achieve-ment than Fonthill Abbey, its archi-tectural style was perhaps more novel than Wyatt's neo-Gothic. It was unclassifiable in the stylistic termi-nology of the time, being a direct expression of Beckford's personal taste: Goodridge was a young and untested local architect, who was chosen as an able executant to Beckford's whims. As recorded by the architect's son, the tower's design "may be termed Greco-Italian, a style [in which] the purity of the

Greek and the freedom of the Romanesque were best combined."[4] The "purity of the Greek" refers to the general chasteness of its exterior in addition to the archaeological exactitude of the lantern, and the decoration of the interiors with text-book Greek Revival moldings. The "freedom of the Romanesque," by contrast, was the picturesque asym-metry and irregularity of early medieval architecture. This synthesis of classical and Gothic was the con-sequence of the abrupt change of style during the course of the design.

Beckford rode each day from his house at 20 Lansdown Crescent to the tower. There he could read, write, and reflect in absolute soli-tude, and enjoy the pictures, books, and objets d'art that were displayed in the building's six small rooms. Windows of gilded-iron latticework illuminated crimson and scarlet cur-tains and carpets, marble sills and tabletops, gilded cornices, and join-ery of stained and varnished oak. The most imposing entrance was through the loggia to the north, but the majority of visitors entered from the garden to the rear. On the ground floor, a vestibule led into

the Scarlet Drawing Room lit by a bow-window projecting to the west; on the first floor were the Crimson Drawing Room and top-lit Sanctu-ary dedicated to Saint Anthony of Padua. Placed above the triple-arch of the entrance loggia were two small libraries. The single-story block extending to the east contained bed-rooms for servants, a kitchen, and services, but there was no bedroom for Beckford himself.

After Beckford's death Lansdown Tower was sold to a publican, but in 1847 when Beckford's daughter the Duchess of Hamilton heard that he intended to open a tea garden to the public, she reacquired the property and presented the tower and its gar-den to the local parish as a mortuary chapel and cemetery.[5] Its interiors were gutted by fire in 1931; it now houses the collection of the Beckford Tower Trust. Recently the interior of the Belvedere has been restored to its appearance in 1844.

This model was commissioned for a Beckford exhibition in 1976, and shows the landscaping at that date; the original approach via the cemetery has recently been restored.
—C.W.

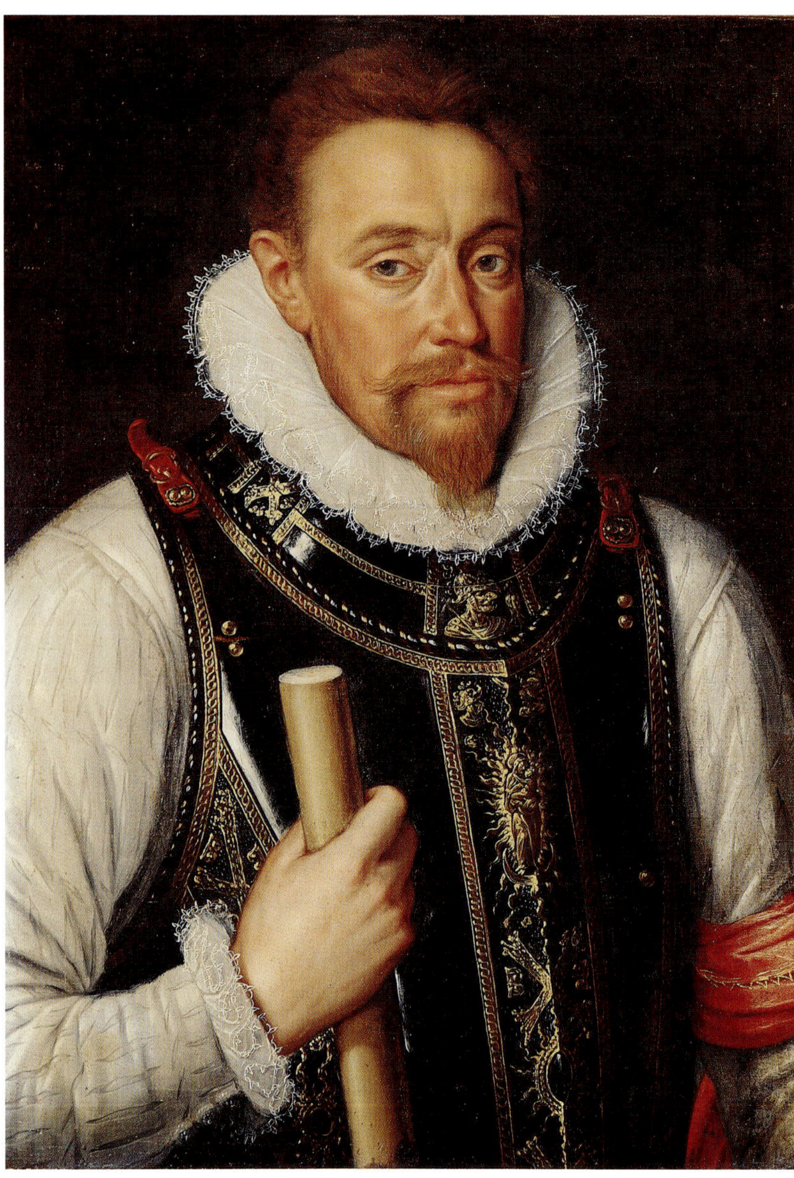

130. *Unknown Sitter, traditionally called The Duke of Alva*
ANONYMOUS, POSSIBLY FLEMISH

Late 16th century
Oil on canvas
28⅜ x 20⅛ in. (72 x 51 cm)
Private collection

This portrait has not previously been published or exhibited, but it has long been attributed to Alonso Sánchez Coello (1531/2–1588). At least since the time of Beckford's ownership it has been thought to portray Don Fernando Álvarez de Toledo, the third Duke of Alva (also Alba), born in 1507. It may have been reduced from its original dimensions.

It is not known how Beckford came to own the portrait which he was either given or purchased believing it to be of the Duke of Alva. Beckford was in Spain from November 1787 to June 1788 and again in December 1795. Beckford had a connection with the Alva family. In 1838, on a visit to Lansdown Crescent, Henry Venn Lansdown recorded, "Mr Beckford next pointed out a head in marble brought from Mexico by Cortes, which was for centuries in the possession of the Duke of Alba's family, and was given to the present proprietor by the Duchess."[1]

Although Beckford had been presented to the thirteenth Duchess of Alva in late 1787 in Madrid, it is unclear how well he knew the family.[2] Without doubt he would have welcomed the introduction and been proud to possess a portrait supposedly of a member of this famous and powerful dynasty. Doña María Teresa Cayetana de Silva, Duchess of Alva, died in 1802, leaving one of the most important private collections of paintings in Spain.[3] Her heirs, on the order of Charles IV, sold paintings to Don Manuel Goday, the Prince of Peace (Principe de la Paz). In turn his collection was ordered to be sold by the government in Madrid in 1808, and some of the paintings were purchased between that year and 1813 by George Augustus Wallis, the agent in Spain for the dealer William Buchanan in London.[4] Buchanan wrote in 1808 that the duke's collections were to be sold "very soon; and the present moment offers an opportunity that can never again return."[5]

This portrait may have arrived in England by this route. It is likely that it was the one put up for sale in 1820 in London by the dealer Urbino Pizzetta of Foley Place, with whom Beckford had dealings in that year.[6] Given that it was rare to find works by Sánchez Coello (as it was then considered to be) outside Spain at that time, it is curious that Gustave Waagen did not mention it when he visited Beckford's collection in Lansdown Crescent. The portrait hung in the back drawing room, with, among others, a Fragonard (see cat. no. 45).[7] Beckford owned other portraits by Spanish painters, including three by Velazquez— *Philip IV of Spain in Brown and Silver*, *Pope Innocent X* and *A Knight of Malta*.[8] He also owned *Portrait of Donna Juana of Austria* by Antonio Moro and *Portrait of a Young Lady*.[9]

Reservations as to the traditional identification of the painter and sitter have been expressed. Portraits of this kind are problematic due to the paucity of information, but it is certain that Beckford considered that he owned a portrait of the Duke of Alva by Sánchez Coello. This is a good example of the kind of problem which arises frequently in trying to ascertain the extent of Beckford's collection and identify the individual works.[10] The possibility that this work is by Juan Pantoja de la Cruz, whose style is similar and who painted in the Flemish tradition has been proposed.[11] He trained in the workshop of Sánchez Coello and painted with minute attention to detail and an emphasis on facial features. —J.C.

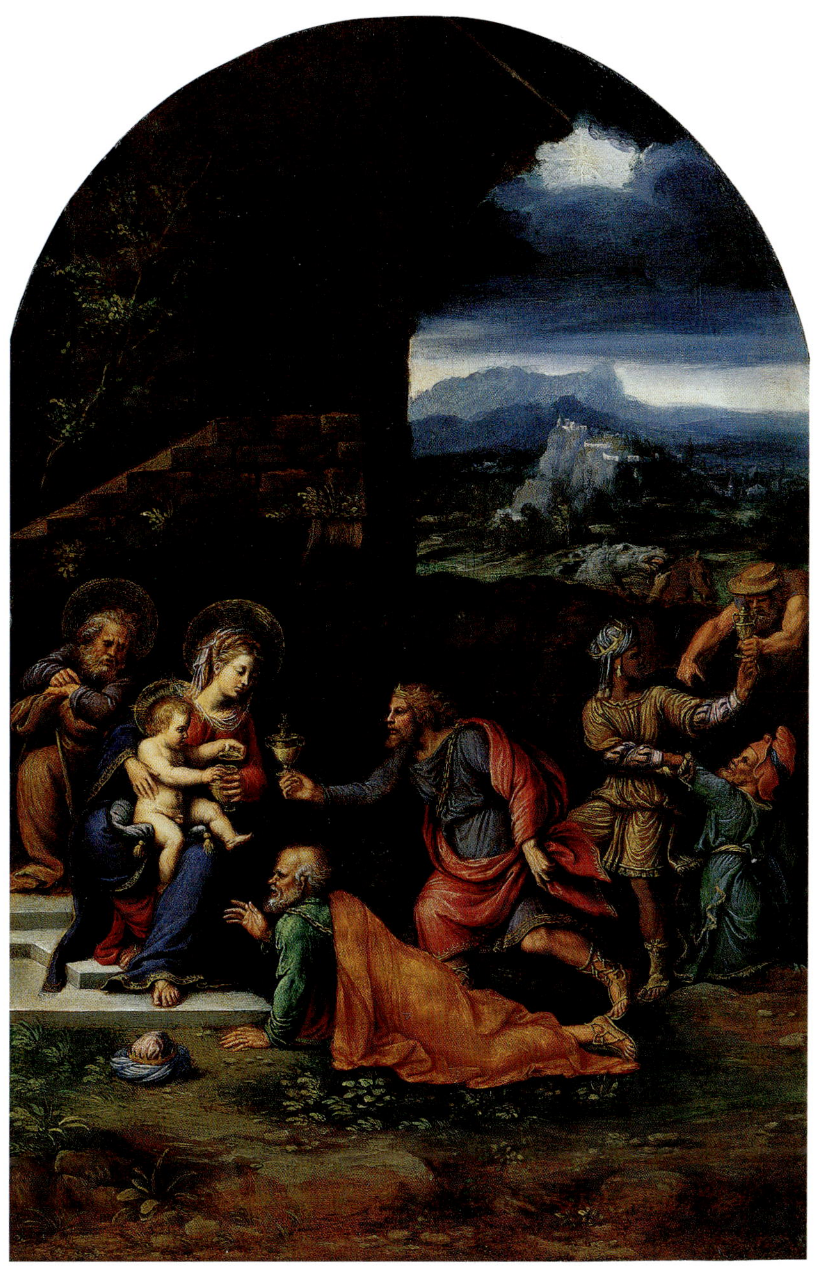

131. *The Adoration of the Magi*
GIROLAMO DA CARPI
(1501–1556)

before 1549; Italy
Oil on panel
20¼ x 13⅛ in. (51.1 x 33.3 cm)
Hall and Knight Ltd., New York
and London

Beckford owned a remarkable collection of Italian paintings and was one of the earliest collectors of Italian Primitives. He possessed an exceptional knowledge and had an unusually observant eye for paintings of all periods, and examples of outstanding quality, including works by Cima, Lippi, Bellini, and Raphael, hung both at Fonthill Abbey and in

Bath. This painting was in the dining room at Lansdown Crescent in Bath with more than forty others, some of which were distinguished pictures, including *The Holy Family with Saints John the Baptist, Elizabeth, Zacharias and Francis* by Garofalo (see cat. no. 132).[1] At that time this painting was considered to be a work by Marcello Venusti and was sold as such in 1882 at the Hamilton Palace sale. In 1835 Gustave Waagen visited Beckford's collection and was deeply moved particularly by the extremely high quality of the paintings in the dining room. He wrote that he would never forget the room, "which, taken all in all, is perhaps one of the most beautiful in the world . . . whose walls are adorned

with cabinet pictures, the noblest productions of Italian art of the time of Raphael."[2] Indeed there hung the *Saint Catherine* by Raphael, from the Borghese collection in Rome, *Christ and the Woman taken in Adultery* and *The Trinity with the Madonna, Saints Joseph and Nicholas of Tolentino and Angels* by Mazzolino, and *The Adoration of the Kings* by Lippi.[3]

This painting was attributed to da Carpi in 1983 and was compared to the slightly smaller version of it which is in the National Gallery in London.[4] Their painting differs in the detail and the overall treatment but the compositions are very similar. The National Gallery picture was catalogued from 1861 to 1912 as by Dosso Dossi, later as "Ferrarese

School, early XVI century," and in 1975 as "North Italian School," although favoring the attributions to da Carpi.[5]

Girolamo da Carpi was taught by his father and later worked in the workshop of Garofalo. In the 1530s and 1540s he was working for the Este court in Ferrara, often with Garofalo, and in Bologna. It is likely that this work was executed in the period just before da Carpi was called to Rome in 1549 by Cardinal Ippolito II d'Este. He remained there until 1553, working on the excavation of Hadrian's Villa at Tivoli and as an architect for Pope Julius III at the Vatican. —J. C.

132. *The Holy Family with Saints John the Baptist, Elizabeth, Zacharias and (?) Francis*
GAROFALO (BENVENUTO TISI, 1476–1559)

ca. 1520; Italy
Oil on canvas
23¾ x 18⅞ in. (60.3 x 47.8 cm)
© The National Gallery, London
(NG 170)

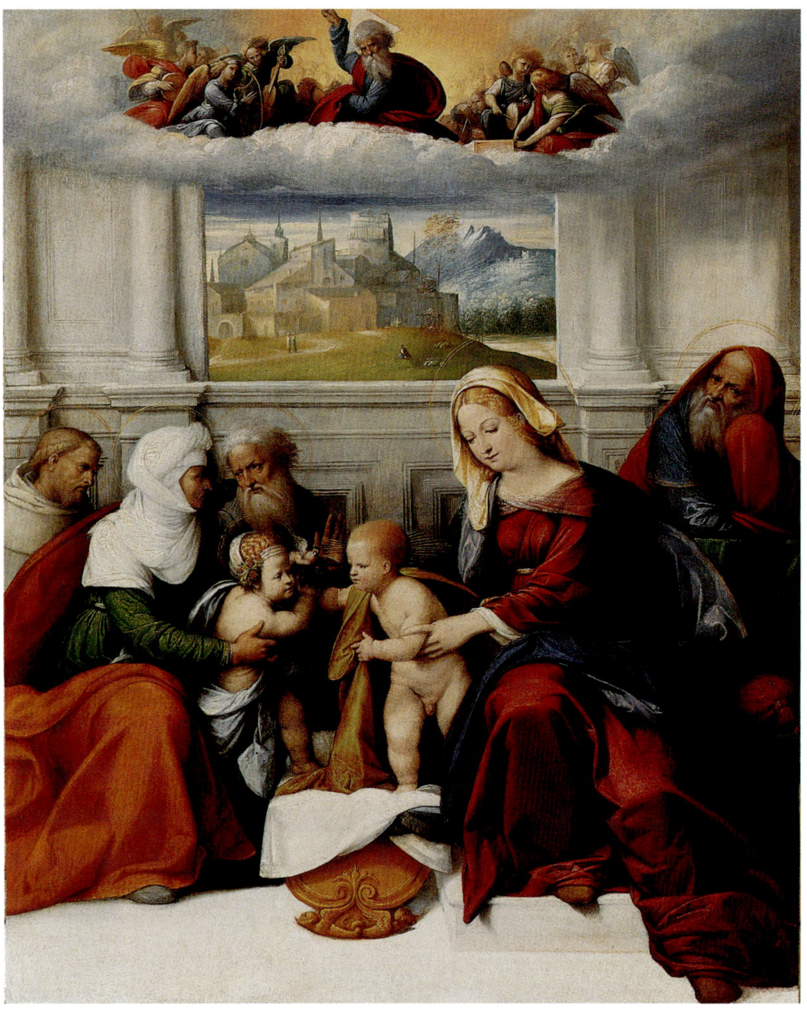

This painting was seen by Britton in 1801 in the "Great Gallery" at Fonthill Splendens. He described it as "in the highest preservation . . . the object of veneration in the Prince Aldobrandini's private chapel."[1] It is very likely to have been one of the four smaller pictures that Beckford purchased in 1799, with two Claudes from the Altieri collection (see figs. 13–8 and 13–9), all of which he bought from Henry Tresham, a painter, collector, and dealer, for a total of 7,000 guineas.[2] Rutter reported seeing the painting in the "New Room" at Fonthill Abbey in 1822.[3] It was one of Beckford's most treasured paintings and appeared on the list of fifteen specially reserved pictures from the proposed sale in 1822, with a price of £400.[4] Later after Beckford had moved to Bath both Waagen and Passavant commented on the painting's exceptional qualities and the influence of Raphael.[5]

In 1839, Beckford sold this painting, as well as *Saint Catherine* by Raphael and *The Trinity with the Madonna, Saints Joseph and Nicholas of Tolentino and Angels* by Mazzolino, Garofalo's contemporary, to the National Gallery for £7,350. The gallery already owned *Saint Augustine with the Holy Family and Saint Catherine of Alexandria* by Garofalo of about the same date, which had been bequeathed by the Reverend Holwell Carr in 1831. In 1841 Beckford sold to the National Gallery the *Virgin and Child with Saint John* by Perugino for 800 guineas, despite bitterly regretting having sold them the three paintings earlier. The painting is very likely from the collection of Cardinal Pietro Aldobrandini and was listed in his inventory of 1603.[6] He was the nephew of Pope Clement VIII, who founded the family fortune and who gave him a million scudi. Most of the family collection was sold by Giovan Battista Borghese Aldobrandini who died in 1802. Other paintings owned by Beckford with an Aldobrandini provenance are *Christ and the Woman taken in Adultery* by Mazzlino (also now in the National Gallery, London) and *The Adoration of the Magi* by da Carpi (see cat. no. 131).

Garofalo was born and died in Ferrara and spent most of his working life in that area. It is thought that he visited Rome around 1513 where he was influenced by Raphael as evidenced in Garofalo's work from that time onward. —J. C.

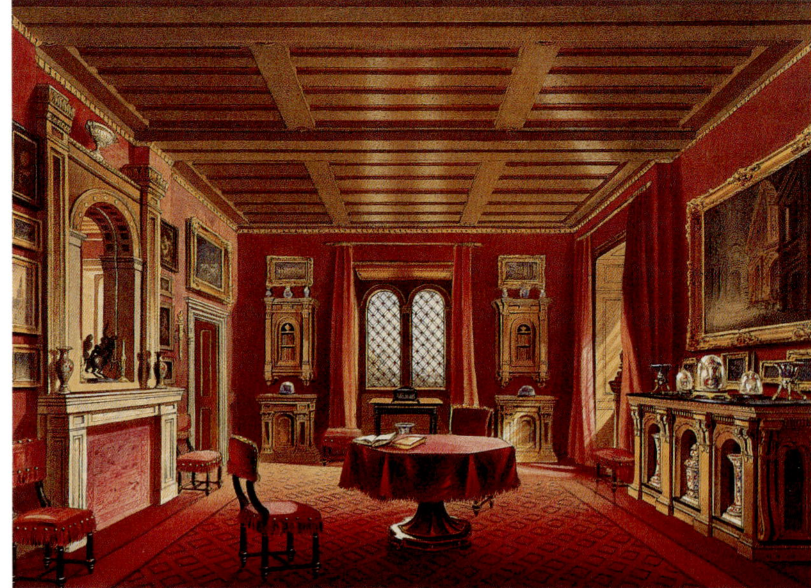

Cat. fig. 132A. "Lansdown Tower: Crimson Drawing Room." Chromolithograph after Willes Maddox. From English, *Views of Lansdown Tower* (Bath, 1844): plate 9.

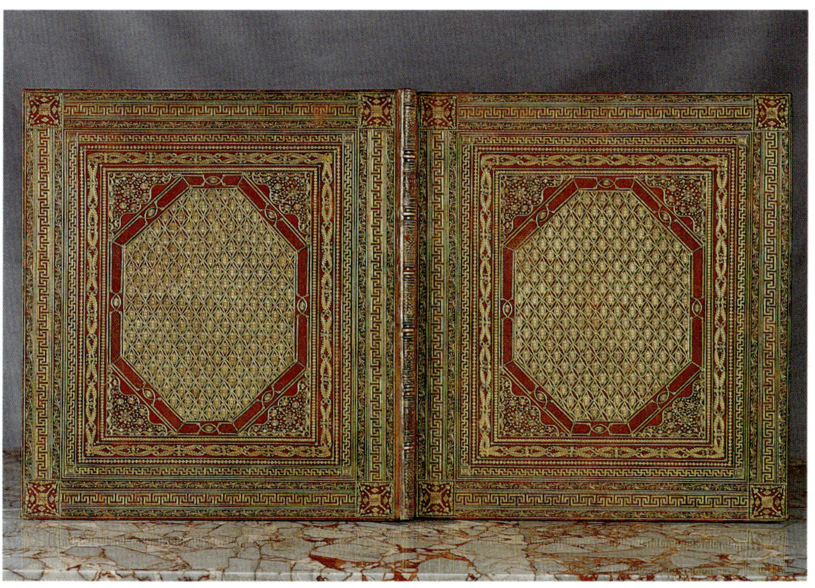

133. *Binding*

BINDER: CHRISTIAN
KALTHOEBER
(FL. CA. 1780–CA. 1880)

Binding, late 18th century,
England; book, 1704, Rome, Italy
Russia, gilt
17⅞ x 15 in. (45 x 38 cm)
Private collection

"Mr Beckford . . . was the greatest book enthusiast I ever knew," wrote H. G. Bohn, who acted as Beckford's book agent in the last decade of the collector's life. "[He] preferred Aldines, and other early books bearing the insignia of celebrities such as Francis I, Henri et Diane, and de Thou, and especially choice old morocco bindings by Desseuil, Pasdeloup, and De Rome. He closely watched all the great sales, both in London and Paris."[1]

Beckford's taste in bindings was generally for an understated elegance, with just a few lines in gold, and he usually rejected elaborate bindings. When the Duchesse de Berri's library came up for sale in 1831, he suspected that it contained "quite a blaze of gaudy bindings . . . not at all likely to tempt me."[2]

Beckford's exacting commissions for bindings were carried out by a number of craftsmen in both England and France. Christian Samuel Kalthoeber, a German immigrant working in London, was Beckford's favored English binder from about 1787 until the early 1800s. Beckford later used Charles Smith, and then Charles Lewis "not uncommonly called in our slang the Angel," with whom he placed many of his commissions over a ten-year period.[3] Other binders were sometimes used, but their work generally failed to match Beckford's high standards: Lewis "is . . . the only binder, or director of binding whose works I can admit upon my shelves. Cheapness cannot reconcile me to bungling, and the want of a certain masterly touch."[4] After Lewis's death in 1836, Beckford employed a number of English binders. In Paris, his agents used N.-D. Derome *le jeune*, and Jean-Claude Bozerian.[5]

Kalthoeber was described, in his time, as "the finest bookbinder in the world."[6] This binding does not exhibit the elegant restraint of Beckford's own Fonthill style (see cat. nos. 134–37) but is a bravura display of the craftsman's work, with Greek-key pattern and floral roll-tool borders around an octagonal panel. The book illustrates, in sixteen engraved plates by H. Frezza, the fresco decorative scheme carried out in 1617 by Francesco Albani for Palazzo Verospi, in Rome. At Fonthill Abbey, Beckford's large collection of books on architecture and the fine arts were kept mainly in the Oak Library, for the use of artists employed on the building designs for the Abbey. "On the shelves and in the armoires . . . Mr. Beckford had deposited an extensive and costly collection of works in the fine arts for their information and study".[7] This volume, *Picturae Francisci Albani in Aede Verospia* by Franciscus Albanus, has an interesting earlier provenance, having previously belonged to the painter Sir Joshua Reynolds and bears both his signature and stamp of ownership.
—S.B.

134. *Binding*

BINDER UNKNOWN

Binding, ca. 1816, England;
book, 1816, England
Half morocco
8½ x 5⅜ x 1 in. (21.5 x 13.5 x
2.5 cm)
Beckford Tower Trust, Bath (Sole
Trustee Bath Preservation Trust)
(BLIB/6)

135. *Binding*

BINDER: POSSIBLY BOZERIAN

Binding, early 19th century,
England; book, 1699, France
Half morocco
7 x 4⅛ x 1⅛ in. (18 x 10.5 x 3 cm)
Beckford Tower Trust, Bath (Sole
Trustee Bath Preservation Trust)
(BLIB/15)

136. *Binding*

BINDER UNKNOWN

Binding, ca. 1801, England;
book, 1801, England
Half morocco
10⅞ x 8⅝ x 1¼ in.
(27.6 x 22 x 3.1 cm)
Beckford Tower Trust, Bath (Sole
Trustee Bath Preservation Trust)
(BLIB/1)

137. *Binding*

BINDER UNKNOWN

Binding, ca. 1814, England;
book, 1814, England
Half russia, gilt
8⅜ x 5½ x 1 in. (22 x 14 x 2.5 cm)
Beckford Tower Trust, Bath (Sole
Trustee Bath Preservation Trust)
(BLIB/16)

134–37. THE ART OF THE BOOKBINDER

In December 1787, journeying toward Madrid and "having nothing to look at except dreary plain bounded by barren, uninteresting mountain[s]," William Beckford was reduced to "tumbling over the trashy collection of books"—some seven volumes of travel writing, two of biography, and two of letters—which he happened to have with him.[1] He threatened, on reaching Madrid, to throw the volumes into the river Manzandres, but at his death, over half a century later, the books remained in his collection.

Although a great collector of the decorative and fine arts, Beckford's unbridled, consummate passion was for books.[2] Pictures came and went, particularly when a profit could be made; but it was with the greatest reluctance that Beckford parted with books.[3] He was forced to surrender a substantial part of his library in 1822, owing to the terms of the Fonthill Abbey sale contract, but was thereafter always searching for any "lost" Fonthill volumes that might be retrieved. When he did not want a particular volume, he instructed his agents to run up the auction price: "if you appear very eager, they may be led on to something ridiculous."[4]

Through the bindings be commissioned, Beckford imposed his own very distinctive mark of ownership upon his books. As in all his collecting activities, quality was of utmost importance. He castigated as "brutes" craftsmen who failed to meet his exacting standards: "I have not even yet recovered from the shock the blue calf binding inflicted upon me. Observe how irregular the vile blind tooling is . . . curse on the bungling beast. His workmen (fellow brutes) have decidedly no eye."[5]

These four volumes display examples of the so-called "Fonthill" bindings, plain and sober in style. Nevertheless, they exhibit in the compartments of the spine, the cinquefoil from the Hamilton arms borne by his mother and the cross fleury from the coat of arms of the first Lord Latimer, from whom Beckford also claimed descent. Occasionally, although not in the examples shown here, the compartments also contain the crests of the Beckford family (the heron's head with the motto, "De Dieu Tout") and the Hamiltons (an oak tree from which hang the Latimer arms, with the motto, "Through"). The Jens Wolff volume (cat. no. 136), however, displays—as is sometimes found on his books—the Beckford and Hamilton crests in the corners of the covers.

Beckford often made notes as he read, sometimes on the front end papers or on loose sheets that he had bound into the volume. Often his notes give just the page number and a line or so about some point which interested or amused him. He made eleven notes on Scott's *Paris Revisited* (cat. no. 134); and seized on one of the author's comments which would have particularly appealed to his own sense of injured pride: "in England we have constituted portrait painting a regular branch of our manufactures—eminence which may lead a man to honor of knighthood as certainly as if he were eminent as a soap boiler or a cotton-spinner, or a vendor of lottery tickets." Unfortunately, there are no notes in Jens Wolff's *Sketches and Observations*, which is surprising as it includes a brief description of the town of Cintra and makes reference to Robert Walpole, the British Minister in Portugal, and Mr. Gildemeester, the Dutch consul, people with whom Beckford was acquainted during his time there.

After Beckford's death, his books were taken by his daughter to Hamilton Palace where they were housed in a special library designed by Beckford's architect, H. E. Goodridge. The collection was sold in a series of sales in 1882–83. Some

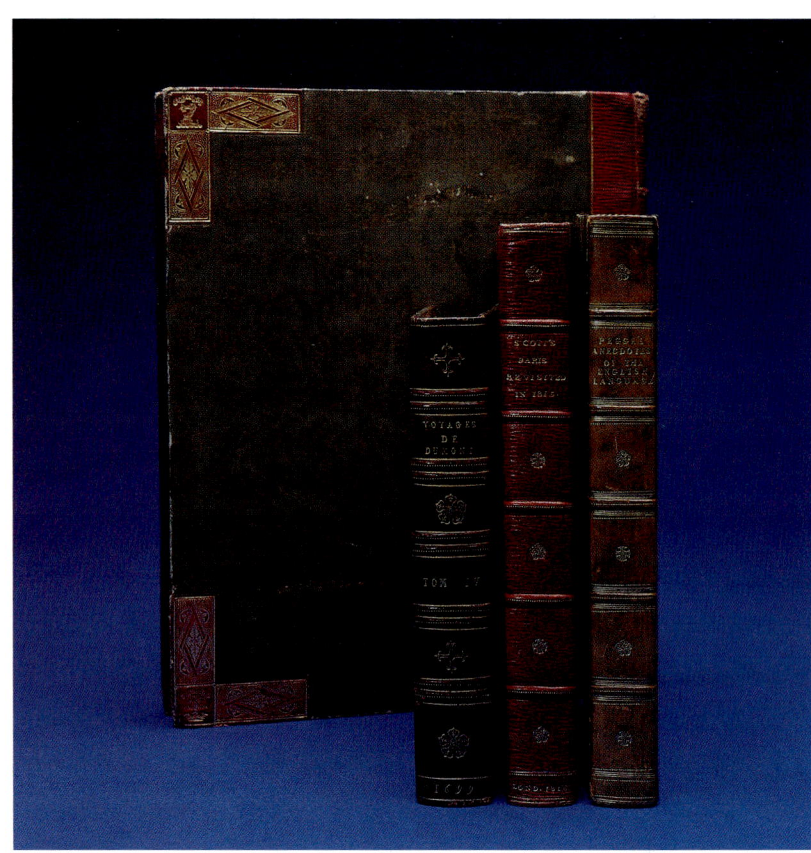

of these volumes were later in the collections of the fifth Earl of Rosebery, a significant purchaser at the Beckford library sale, and of one of Beckford's biographers, James Lee-Milne. The latter bequeathed his collection of Beckford volumes to the Beckford Tower Trust. —S. B.

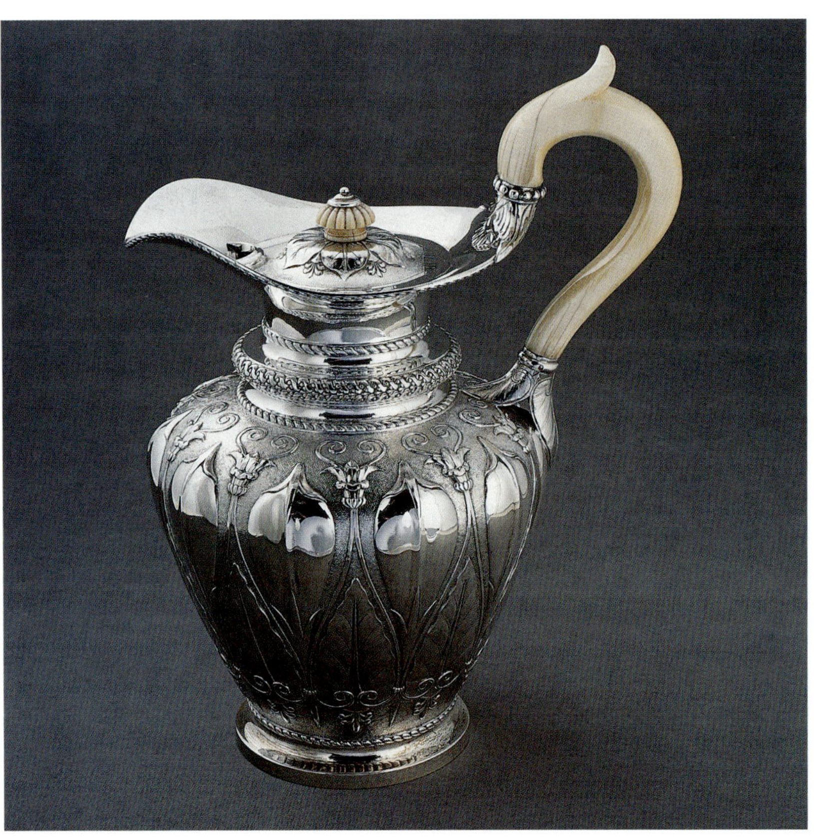

138. *Jug*
Cato Sharp for Philip Rundell (1743–1827)

1823–24; England
Silver, ivory
10¾ in. (27.5 cm)
Beckford Collection, Brodick Castle, National Trust for Scotland (58.871)

Beckford's appreciation for classicism never left him. At Fonthill Abbey he continued to illuminate the galleries with Scofield's neoclassical candlesticks (cat. nos. 9, 31), while Auguste's rich and monumental silver gilt was mixed with antiquarian and exotic pieces. Later, at his conventional Georgian townhouse in Bath, he once again turned to the classical world for his everyday silverware.

It may be that with Fonthill Abbey no longer a part of his life, he needed to simplify his surroundings with the elegant, if repetitive, streets of Bath and, indoors, with emphatically classical silver. It was not until later in life that his passion for the exotic would manifest itself again in his silver commissions.

This jug, typical of the heavy neo-Grecian style popularized by Rundell, Bridge and Rundell, is clearly not a special commission but was purchased, like much of the silver that Beckford bought as a youth, from stock. Paul Storr had left the employ of Rundell's in 1819 and from that time their workshops were directed by Cato Sharp, although the mark used by the firm was one registered by the senior partner, Philip Rundell. Beckford's earlier large-scale patronage of the leading silversmiths of the day was not revived in the 1820s. This jug is part of a very small

396

group of conventional silver, purchased from Rundell's following Beckford's new-found prosperity, after the sale of the Abbey, when, as he remarked, he had not for a long time felt "si riche, si independent ni si tranquille."[1]

With the Beckford and Hamilton crests engraved under the base, heraldry was once again reduced to a mark of identification rather than for ornament or display. On an equally classical cake basket purchased from Rundell, Bridge and Rundell at the same time, the engraved coat of arms in the center, with its drapery mantling, follows the conventions of the 1780s.[2]
—C.H

---

139. *Bowl*
Paul Storr (1771–1844)

Mounts, 1824–25, England; hardstone, possibly ca. 1600, Continental Europe
Heliotrope, jasper, silver gilt
9 x 4½ in. (22.8 x 11.4 cm)
The Trustees of The Barber Institute of Fine Arts, The University of Birmingham, Birmingham (54.5)

Of all the Beckford mounted hardstones, this heliotrope jasper bowl is among those most likely to be a remounted Renaissance piece. The shape of the bowl is consistent with those found on a number of hardstone and enameled gold-mounted tazzes that were made in the Milanese hardstone workshops around 1600. It also relates to others from the workshop of the Miseroni family in Prague. Stylistic comparisons can be found with pieces now in the Prado Museum, Madrid (formerly in the collection of the Dauphin of France, son of Louis XIV), as well as others from the Habsburg Imperial Collection in the Kunsthistorisches Museum, Vienna (formerly in Prague).[1] Indeed Beckford himself owned several mounted hardstones that had originally come from the French royal collections.[2]

Although the bowl was not mounted until 1824, it was most probably part of the 1821 shipment of hardstones which Franchi sent from Paris. This theory is confirmed by a letter written by Franchi from Rome in June 1821, in which he wrote that "it was pointless to buy cups whether mounted or unmounted as the German examples were as expensive as the oriental examples, and all were of mediocre quality."[3] The bowl may possibly be identified with the then unmounted "coupe ovale de jaspe sanguin Clanbaril" which was included in the case lists of 1822 when Beckford transferred many of his possessions from Fonthill to Bath.[4]

"A large blood stone cup, supported by silver gilt dolphins on a pedestal of bloodstone" is listed in the drawing room of 20 Lansdown Crescent in the 1844 inventory taken after Beckford's death, and this bowl, executed from heliotrope, or bloodstone, as it is more commonly called, was erroneously listed for a number of years as porphyry, a rare purple and white flecked stone. Storr executed mounts with a form of calyx beneath the stone and then an oval rim, and indeed the presence of the calyx certainly supports the theory that it is a remounted old piece; the mounts may possibly be covering signs of previous mounting.

In 1824, when these silver-gilt mounts are dated, Beckford was living in Bath. The mounts that Storr used are unlike the historicist style that Beckford favored for the agate bowl of 1816 for Fonthill (cat. no. 116); rather they are more in tune with the classicism of the Regency period and with the interior decoration of Lansdown Crescent. Dolphins and other marine motifs had been popular elements in English decoration from the beginning of the nineteenth century.[5]

By 1819 Storr's partnership with Rundell, Bridge and Rundell had ceased and yet Beckford continued to work with him. In Beckford's dealings with silversmiths, he apparently wished to talk to the craftsmen responsible for the workmanship of his pieces, certainly when it came to the important commissions. Indeed there is no other recorded instance of a Rundell's customer having direct contact with the metalworkers, and

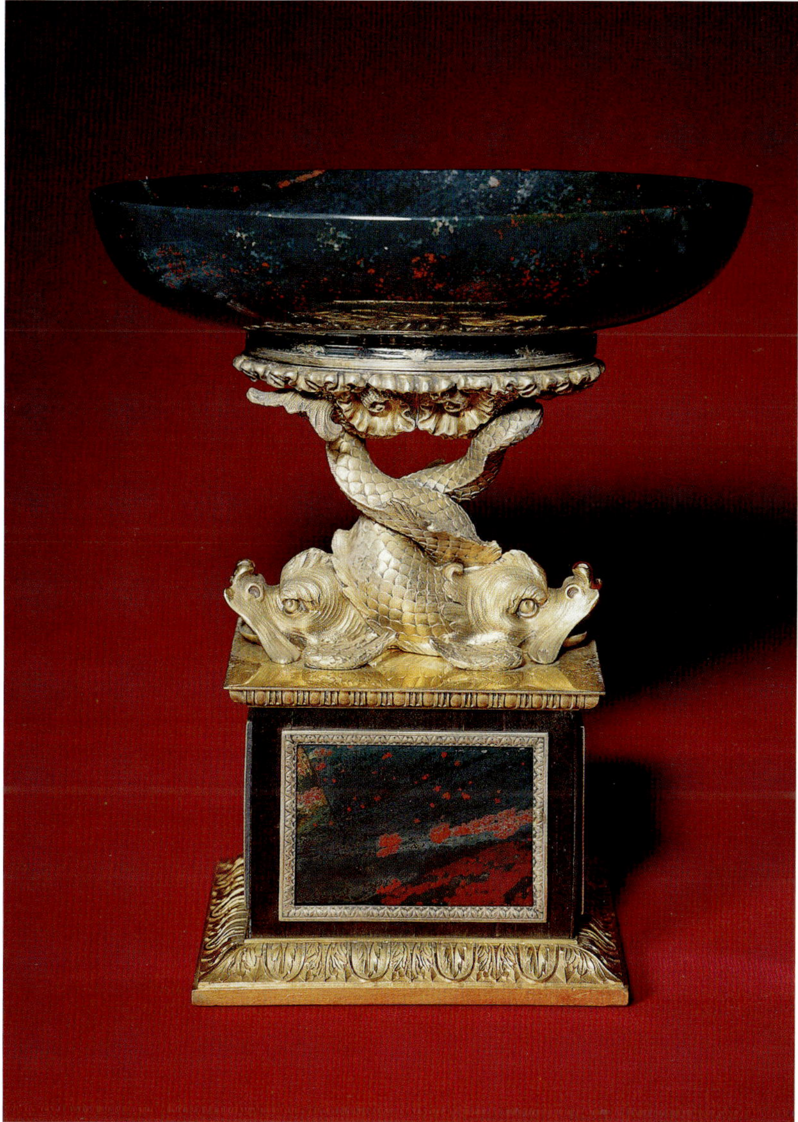

this interaction appears to have been actively discouraged, as undoubtably it would have been by other retailers. The chief designer, William Theed of Rundell's, had spoken of his wish to "have access to the Noblemen or Gentlemen who gave them commissions" and not have the retailers of the firm "intruding their opinions in matters of taste & design."[6]

The dolphin bowl passed to the Hamilton collection upon Beckford's death and was included in the Hamilton Palace sale of June 1882.[7]

It next appeared in the Sir Francis Oppenheimer sale in 1954.[8] The Storr dolphin bowl is now part of the collection of the Barber Institute of Fine Arts at the University of Birmingham in the United Kingdom and was included in the Birmingham Art Gallery's exhibition, *Gold and Silver* in 1963.[9] —E. M.

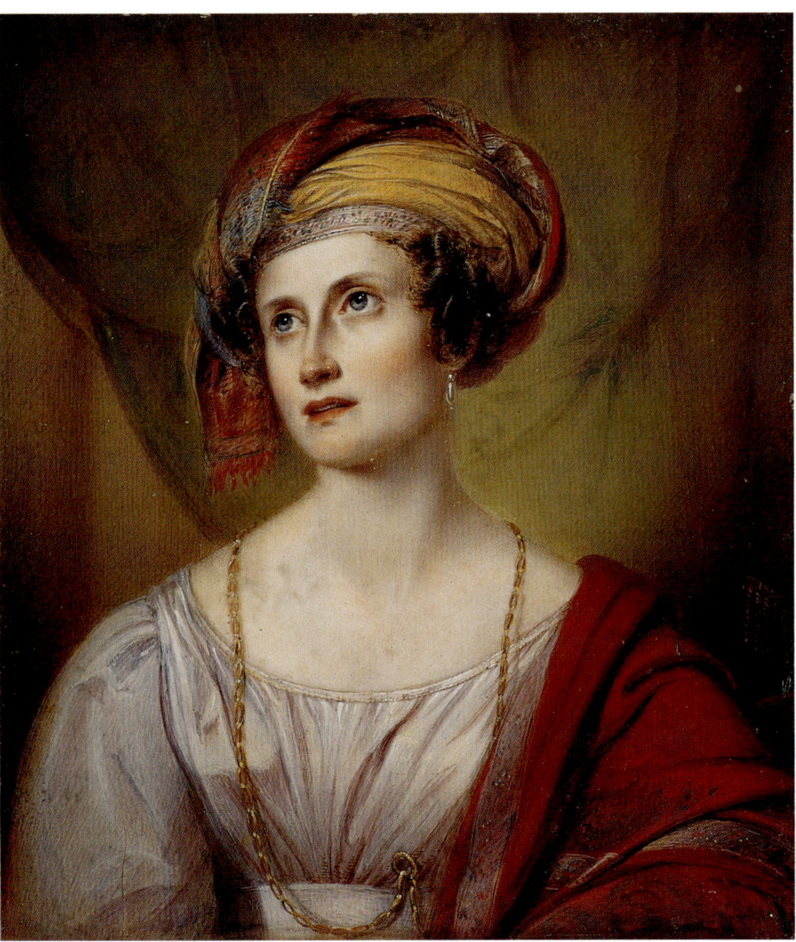

140. *Susan Euphemia, Duchess of Hamilton, as a Sibyl*
AUGUST GRAHL (1791–1866)

1827; Italy
Gouache on ivory
5½ x 4½ in. (14 x 11.4 cm)
The Hamilton Collection

Beckford's daughter Susan Euphemia and her husband Alexander, tenth Duke of Hamilton, traveled a great deal in Europe after their marriage in 1810. They were in Italy in 1818, when her father, fretting about her absence, remembered the trauma that had arisen during his own sec-

ond Grand Tour: "What an idea— gadding to Naples in the fevor of June & leaving the children to be muzzled by the pope & Mamselle! I wonder what we shall hear of next."[1] This portrait was painted in Rome in 1827 during one of the Hamiltons' long sojourns abroad.

August Grahl, a miniature painter, was born in Proppentin, Mecklenburg, and studied at the Berlin Academy. He visited Italy in 1817/18 and made further travels after the death of his first wife in 1821, going to Vienna, Venice, Florence, and Rome, where he remained until 1830. He was in England in 1831. He painted a portrait of Hans Christian Anderson in Dresden in 1846; the writer thought that the portrait "is quite splendid, resembles me, just as I wish to look."[2]

In portraying Susan as a sibyl, Grahl was following a long tradition. The sibyls were the wise women of the Classical world, who, inspired by Apollo, uttered prophesies. Adopted by the early Christian church, they were seen, like the Hebrew prophets, as prophets of the coming of Christ. The sibyls are represented in Filippo Lippi's Carafa Chapel in Santa Maria Sopra Minerva, Rome, and most famously in Michelangelo's Sistine Chapel ceiling, where five sibyls— the Delphic, Cumaean, Libyan, Erythrean, and Persian—are shown.

Among many artists to depict

sibyls were Guercino (*The Cumaean Sibyl with a Putto,* 1651) and Domenichino (*Cumaean Sibyl,* 1616; now in the Galleria Borghese, Rome), whose work may well have been seen by Susan Euphemia. Domenichino's painting, in turn, inspired Marie-Louise-Elizabeth Vigée-Le Brun's portrait of *Lady Hamilton as a Sibyl* (ca. 1791), which the artist showed throughout Europe to demonstrate her skills, resulting in other sitters such as Princess Dolgorouky insisting on being portrayed in a similar pose. Gavin Hamilton also painted Lady Hamilton as a sibyl.[3] Guido Reni's celebrated painting *Beatrice Cenci* also shows the sitter in the guise of a sibyl, wearing the traditional sibyl's turban. There are further examples of early nineteenth-century sibyl portraits in mosaic, which would have been produced for the tourist market,[4] and of sibyls in other media. Mary Shelley's novel, *The Last Man* (1826), opens with a visit to the cave of the Cumaean sibyl. More ephemeral representations occurred, such as an "amusement for evening parties," advertised in 1828, consisting of a pack of fifty-two playing cards, "the Sybil's Leaves," which in prophetic verse foretold the future.[5] —S. B.

141. *Pair of Tea Kettles, Lamp Stands, and Wind Shields*
DANIEL SMITH (FL. 1753–?1796), ROBERT SHARP (FL. 1757–1803), AND BENJAMIN PRESTON (FL. 1817–OB1887)

Stand and wind shield, 1781–82, England; Pair A, Kettle and lamp, 1796, England; Pair B, Kettle and lamp, 1832–33, England
Silver, ebony, leather
14½ in. overall (37 cm)
Beckford Collection, Brodick Castle, National Trust for Scotland (58.866, 58.867)

Like much of Beckford's silver from the 1780s and 1790s, these kettles are stock items of a standard design but, unlike his objects from the Scofield or Smith and Sharp workshops, in this case, the quality and design are not of the highest quality. Their bellied form is purely functional, and they are remarkable only for their large size. The kettles follow a bulbous form common during the last quarter of the eighteenth century, but the wind shields are a rare feature. Similar triangular examples were supplied by Edward Wakelin for four kettles made for Sir James Lowther in 1757–58.[1] By the 1780s such kettles and their shields, with their impracticable and odiferous lamps, were becoming obsolete and

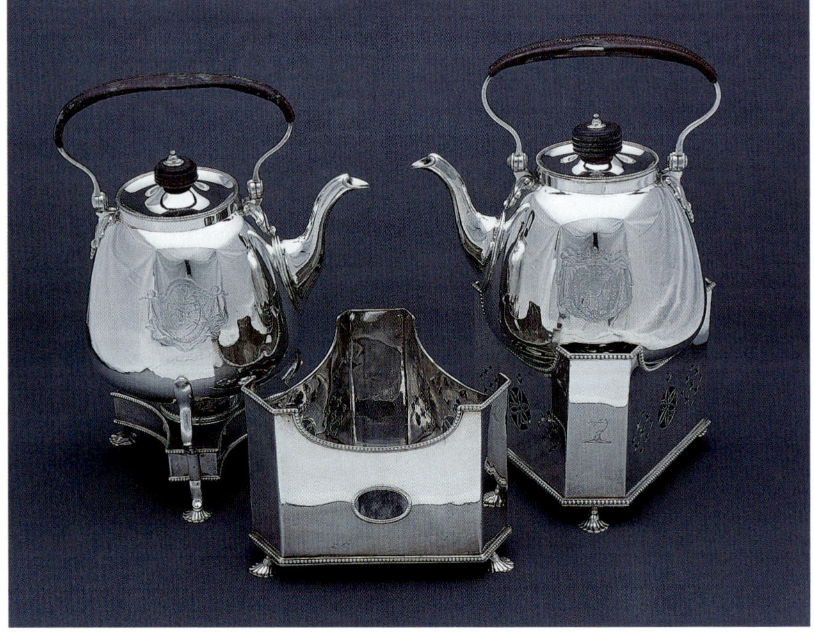

were replaced by tea urns, heated by hot coals or pre-heated iron elements. Given the different dates and makers' marks on the components of the earliest example, it is clear that Beckford owned an even larger set, starting with one or more examples in 1781 as part of his coming-of-age silver. He added identical kettles in 1796–97, as work on the Abbey got underway, and a pair again in 1832–33 while living in Bath. That Beckford chose to replicate the first kettle and lampstand nearly fifty years later is remarkable, especially in light of his unsurpassed familiarity with ornamental alternatives and his well-documented interest in innovative silver design. The size is equally provocative in light of Beckford's well-known reclusive nature, especially during his time in Bath. Why would he have needed additional utilitarian kettles of such large size?

The earlier kettle is engraved with Beckford's arms and crest, while the Bath example has in addition the version of the Hamilton crest Beckford was granted in 1810. This example has also been engraved after Beckford's death, with the arms of the tenth Duke of Hamilton, whose wife, Beckford's daughter, Susan, inherited it in 1844. Both kettles were acquired with other Beckford silver by the National Trust for Scotland and are displayed at Brodick Castle, one of the Hamilton houses. —C.H.

142. *Cup*
ALFRED SHORT
(FL. ?1837–?1845)

Mounts, ca. 1840–44, England; porcelain, early 18th century, China
Porcelain, gold
3⅜ in. (8.50 cm)
Beckford Collection, Brodick Castle, National Trust for Scotland (58.332)

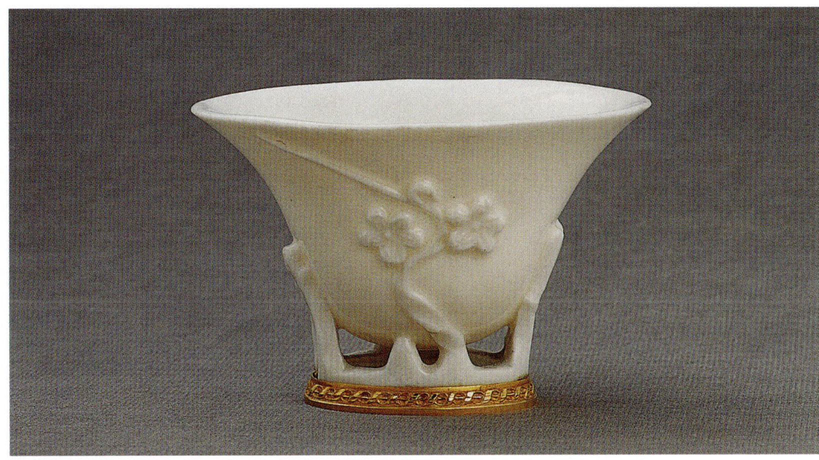

This delightful, if commonplace, Chinese export porcelain libation bowl is one of a pair at Brodick that have been enhanced through the addition of gold mounts to the foot. Like much of the porcelain that was mounted to Beckford's specifications some twenty years earlier, this piece follows a tradition devised in the eighteenth century by the great *marchand-merciers* of Paris. In fact, were it not for the signature (on the foot) of the Bristol jeweler and retailer Short, and a lack of delicacy to the chasing, it could be confused with mounted objects of the previous century. The Beckford cup should be compared with a Dehua-ware cup with similar prunus decoration that was given gilt-bronze mounts in Europe in the second half of the eighteenth century (now in the Peabody Essex Museum, Salem, Massachusetts).[1]

Produced in kilns in Fukien Province in southeast China, Dehua ware was a popular form of glazed but undecorated porcelain made in large quantities for export to Europe in the eighteenth century. It lent itself especially well to rich gold mounts, and Beckford must have been attracted to its stark whiteness as an effective foil to the crimson wall coverings he favored in his residence in Bath and in Lansdown Tower. —C. H.

143. *Saltcellar*
WATHERSTON & BROGDEN
(FL. 1841–1864)

1843–44; England
Silver gilt
1 x 3⅗ in. (2.6 x 9.0 cm)
Beckford Collection, Brodick Castle, National Trust for Scotland (58.316.3a)

During the final years of his life, Beckford commissioned a group of highly individual silver. With Franchi long dead, Beckford may have relied, out of his dwindling circle of acquaintances, upon Henry Edmund Goodridge, the young architect who designed Lansdown Tower, or Edmund English, the Bath decorator and auctioneer, to advise him on their design. The group, much of it now at Brodick Castle, Scotland,[1] was supplied by the Bristol jeweler Short and includes two ladles in similar style to this saltcellar (cat. no. 144) and a pair of monumental candlesticks (cat. no. 149). In addition, Short supplied gold mounts for a pair of blanc-de-chine cups (cat. no. 142) and copies of Beckford's late-seventeenth-century wall sconces, which had belonged to William and Mary and had been purchased by Beckford from Rundell's in their sale of outmoded royal plate in 1808.[2] Watherston and Brogden were, like Barnard and Sons (see cat. no. 149), a large firm of wholesale jewelers and goldsmiths in Covent Garden, London.[3] The workmanship of these later objects shows no diminution in quality, and the chasing of the handles of this salt is equal to work Beckford commissioned some twenty years earlier.

The bowl of the salt is a plain

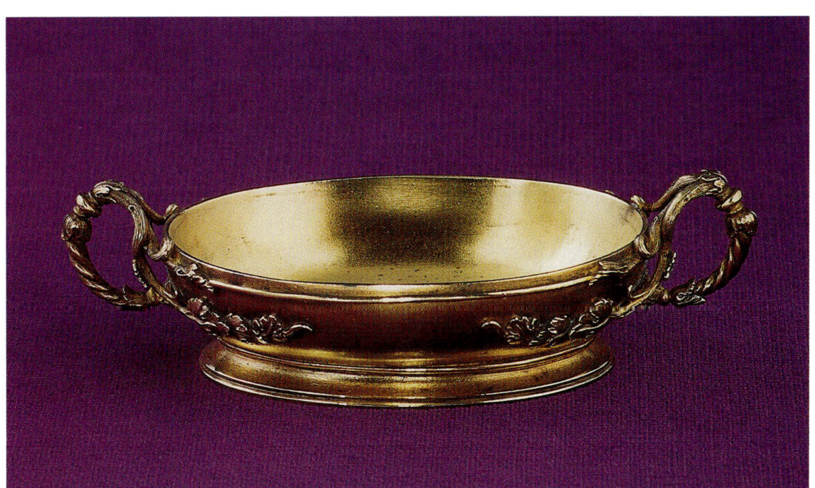

classical oval, decorated with rope and vine tendril handles. It has nothing of the Gothic, Renaissance, or Asian influences of the commissions of the previous twenty-five years. Late in life, Beckford discovered the decorative possibilities of the picturesque style, with its natura- listically depicted leaves and tendrils. The overall effect, however, is eminently symmetrical, with clearly defined lines, and ultimately, classicism returned as a theme at the end of Beckford's life. —C. H.

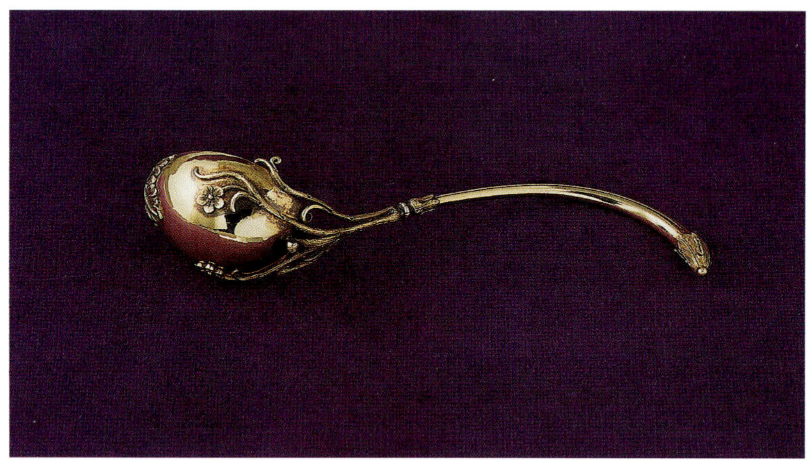

Like the saltcellar (cat. no. 143), these ladles shows Beckford's emerging interest in naturalistic motifs in the final years of his life, but the Asian aesthetic should also be compared with the jade and gold ladle from Storr's workshop of 1815–16 (cat. no. 56). With delicately curving stems reminiscent of Mughal jades, these ladles may have been intended as sugar or cream spoons. Although both are unmarked, they were clearly commissioned about the same time as the saltcellar, and were probably supplied by Short of Bristol and made by Watherston.
—C. H.

145. *Armchair*
MAKER UNKNOWN

ca. 1827–44; England
Ebonized beech(?), gilding, later leather, silk, brass
37¾ x 24 x 21½ in. (94.6 x 60.9 x 54.6 cm)
Private collection

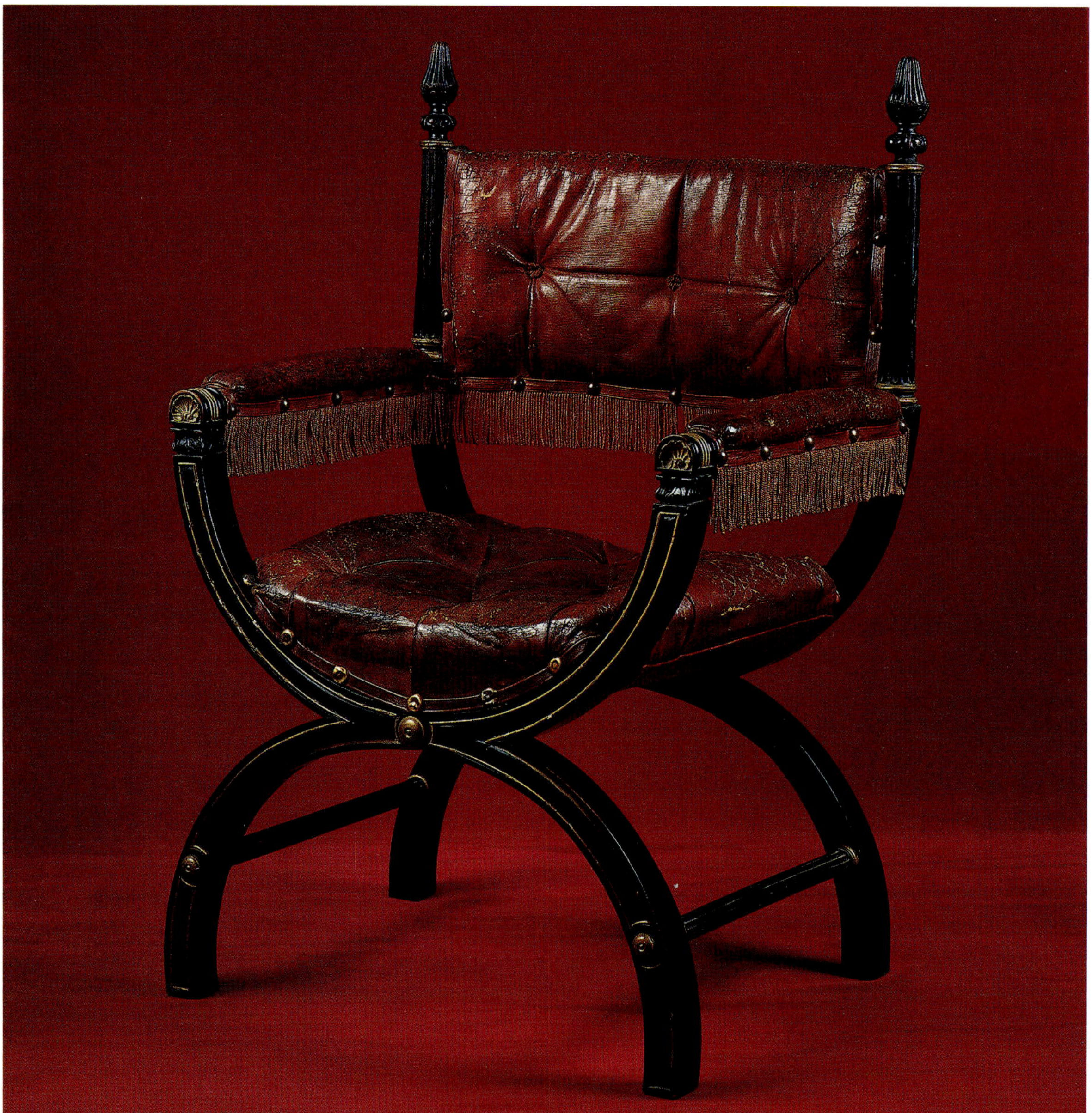

It may be that this chair is one of the "2 arm[chairs]" from the "Ebonized chairs" sent after Beckford's death to either Portman Square or Easton Park, houses belonging to his daughter and son-in-law, the Duke and Duchess of Hamilton. Although it is not known precisely where this chair was used by Beckford, nor how many examples of this model were made, it is possible that it was first supplied to him for Lansdown Tower. A chair of this pattern is illustrated by Willes Maddox in the group of "Ornamental Furniture."[1] Together with a parcel-gilt oak and marble stand of *athénienne* form in the same plate,[2] this chair is distinctly old-fashioned for its date, whether around 1827 or later. The description of "TWO BLACK ANTIQUE SHAPED ELBOW CHAIRS, with gilt ornaments, the backs and seats covered with crimson morine, with silk fringe" may refer to chairs like the one exhibited and suggests further uncertainty about when Beckford first owned such chairs.[3]

The direct source for the present chair, ultimately derived from ancient Roman prototypes, is clearly Thomas Hope.[4] In imitating Hope, Beckford may have been paying tribute indirectly to another great connoisseur collector. Although Hope expressed doubts about the architecture of Fonthill Abbey,[6] Beckford had once welcomed the possibility that the creator of the magnificent interiors at Duchess Street in London might become his son-in-law.
—M. P. L.

146. *Chair*

Maker unknown

ca. 1827–44; England
Ebonized beech (?), gilding, later
leather, silk, brass
34¾ x 18½ x 19½ in. (87 x 47 x
49.5 cm)
Private collection

Chairs of this pattern, probably the
so-called Fonthill pattern, were used
by Beckford in the Scarlet Drawing
Room (cat. fig. 146A), Crimson
Drawing Room (cat. fig. 132A), and
Sanctuary at Lansdown Tower.[1]
There seem to have been a number
of variations of this model. The *Illustrated London News* reviewed the
auction of 1845, held after Beckford's
death, and included rather imprecise
depictions of these chairs. The one
depicted in the view of the Sanctuary, for example, appears to suggest
that on some examples the legs were
somewhat bulbous.[2]

The sale of Lansdown Tower
included "Four ebonized chairs,
Fonthill pattern, seats and backs,
covered in crimson cloth, with silk
lace, bullion fringe, gilt annulets
and nails" (day 6, lot 385). These
chairs described as being in the
Crimson Drawing Room sold for
£16.10.0d. The next day of the sale
lot 496 (day 7), from the Scarlet
Drawing Room, contained "six oak
Fonthill pattern chairs, with carved
reeded legs, with gilt annulets, the
backs and seats stuffed and covered
in scarlet morocco, silk fringe, and
gilt nails" which sold for £34.16.0d.

This chair, with its fluted legs,
appears to be a variant of the two
lots described above; it is likely to be
either one of the "8 Fonthill chairs"
or from the "Ebonized chairs—
6 seats, 2 arm, 12 chairs" sent between
October and December 1846 by
English and Son to either Portman
Square in London or Easton Park,
Hamilton family homes.[3] It is not
known how many chairs were originally at Lansdown Tower, nor how
many different models existed. Two
chairs (lacking provenance) with
plain, bulbous legs and remnants
of their original "crimson cloth"
may have been part of lot 385; they
were acquired by the Beckford
Tower Trust for Lansdown Tower in
1993.[4]

The origin of the nomenclature
"Fonthill pattern" may have been the
1845 sale catalogue, although it is
conceivable that such chairs were
indeed first used at Fonthill Abbey.
Lot 746 (day 17) of the Fonthill
Abbey sale in 1823 contained, for
instance, "12 ebonized ditto [chairs],
backs and seats, stuffed with hair,
covered with red morocco and silk
fringe," which sold for £12.1.6d.
There is no firm documentation,
however, before the chairs were illustrated by Willes Maddox at Lansdown Tower in 1844. Although they
would have been very advanced in
conception, it is possible that such
simple chairs were designed earlier
for Fonthill Abbey.

There is some evidence that
chairs in the seventeenth-century

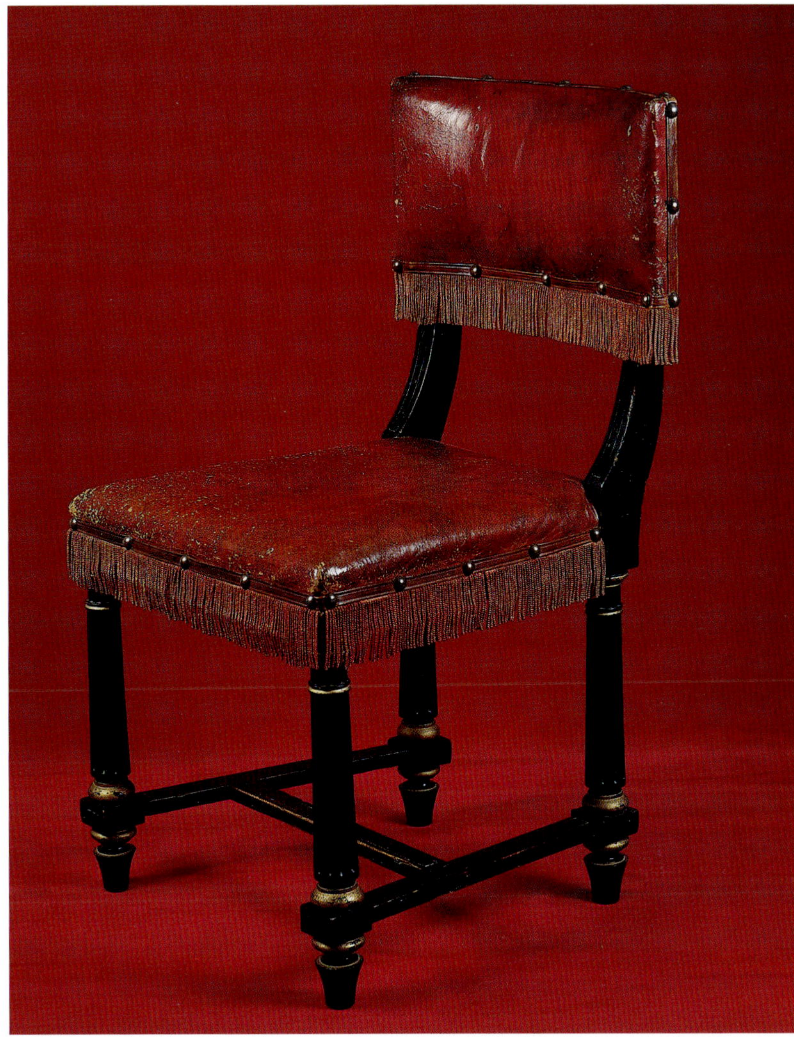

taste were being designed during the
second decade of the nineteenth century. Examples can be found in the
"Tracings by Thomas Wilkinson,
from the Designs of the late Mr
George Bullock 1820."[5] The distin-
guishing features of the "Fonthill
pattern" chairs—the upholstered
back and seat raised on turned
legs—appear to derive from English
and Dutch "back-stools" dating
from the first half of the seventeenth
century.[6]

Chairs and other furniture made
from ebony were frequently a feature
of antiquarian interiors, such as
those of Fonthill Abbey. Two Coromandel Coast chairs, thought to
have been given by Charles II
to Elias Ashmole, were presented in
1683 by Ashmole to the museum
in Oxford that now bears his name.
One of these chairs, and another
from the collection of Horace
Walpole at Strawberry Hill, were
later published in Henry Shaw's
influential *Specimens of Ancient Furniture*.[7] Part of the appeal of these

ebony chairs was doubtless the
myth, started by Walpole, that some
of his ebony chairs at Strawberry
Hill had originally been owned by
Cardinal Wolsey at Esher Place, which
he had occupied in 1519. Walpole's
legend dates the chairs nearly two
hundred years earlier than their
probable date of manufacture.[8]
Beckford himself later acquired some
of his own "Wolsey" chairs,[9] and
owned many others, similar to one
now in the Victoria and Albert
Museum, London.[10] These chairs
and other black furniture contrasted
dramatically with the rich interiors
at Fonthill Abbey, such as Saint
Michael's Gallery.[11] Even if the
"Fonthill pattern" chairs were not
first designed until around the date
that Lansdown Tower was completed
(1827) or soon afterward, rather than
for Fonthill Abbey, they would still
mark an early antiquarian exercise in
the seventeenth-century style.
—M. P. L.

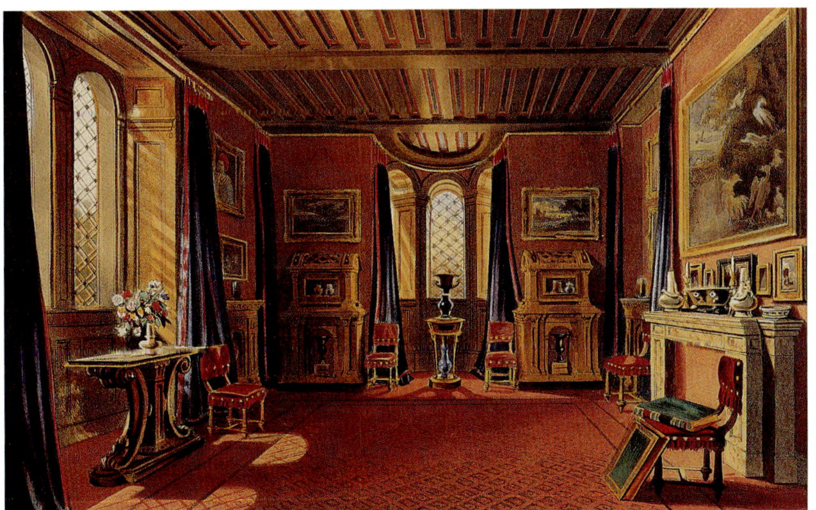

Cat. fig. 146A. "Lansdown Tower: The Scarlet Drawing Room." Chromolithograph
after Willes Maddox. From English, *Views of Lansdown Tower* (Bath, 1844): plate 4.

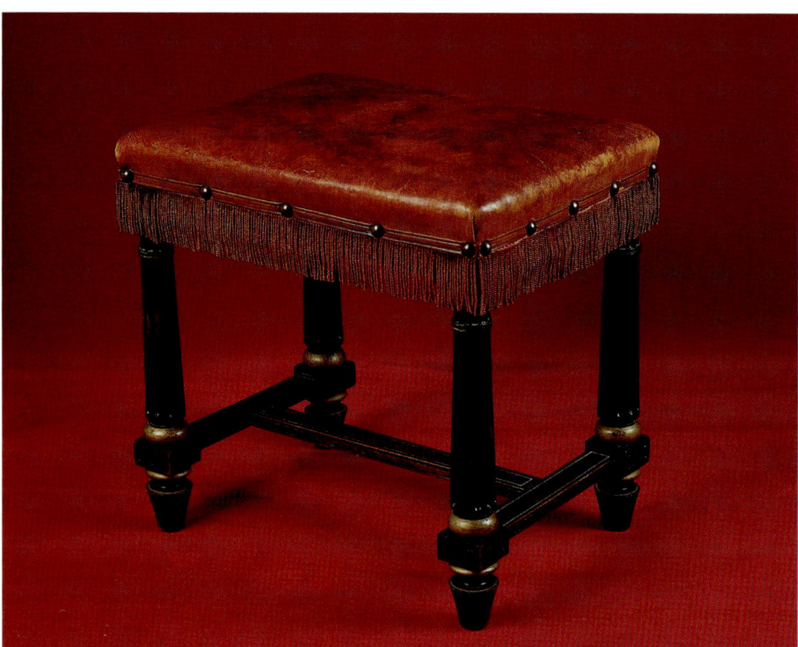

147. *Stool*
MAKER UNKNOWN

ca. 1827–44; England
Ebonized beech(?), gilding, later
leather, silk, brass
18 x 18¼ x 13 in. (45.7 x 46.4 x
33 cm)
Private collection

Stools of this pattern were used by
Beckford in the Crimson Drawing
Room at Lansdown Tower[1] (see cat.
fig. 132A). Lot 386 (day 6) in the
Lansdown Tower sale of 1845 contained "Two stools to match," referring to the four ebonized chairs sold
in the previous lot (see cat. no. 146).
Two more stools were offered as lots
387 and 388. The three lots each sold
for £4.16.0d.
Two similar stools, apparently
with turned, bulbous legs were in
the "Etruscan library."[2] Stools from
the Etruscan library were sold on
day 8 of the 1845 sale as lot 574, "A
pair of oak seats, Fonthill pattern,
covered in scarlet cloth, bullion
fringe, and fluted legs, with gilt
annulets"; they fetched £6.10.0d. As
with the sidechair (cat. no. 146), this
stool, which has fluted rather than
plain legs, may have been one of
the "6 [ebonized] seats" sent to the
Duchess of Hamilton at either Portman Square or Easton Park. It is not
known how many of these stools
were originally supplied.
Rutter's view of Saint Michael's
Gallery, for example, shows low
ebonized "foot stools," which appear
to have barley-twist legs in the
seventeenth-century taste. Taller
examples are identifiable in the view
of King Edward's Gallery published
by John Britton.[3] Stools of this model
were clearly designed en suite with
the "Fonthill pattern" chairs. Along
with the chairs, it is possible that
these stools may originally have been
at Fonthill Abbey. Black stools certainly formed part of the Abbey's
furnishing scheme.
In the absence of any accounts or
other documentation, and given that
the dates of supply are unknown, it
is impossible to be sure who was
responsible for the design or manufacture of this ebonized seat furniture. If there is an association with
Fonthill Abbey, it could have been
through the cabinetmaker Edward
Foxhall who was employed by Beckford from as early as 1787 until 1815.
Robert Hume, first father, then son,
were greatly involved in various
capacities, including the supply of
Beckford's grander furniture, both at
Fonthill Abbey and at Lansdown
Tower.[4]

These ebonized chairs and stools,
of more modest ambition, may have
come from a less august source. If
the ebonized seat furniture dates
from the period of Lansdown Tower,
however, then Beckford's architect,
Henry E. Goodridge, probably
directed by Beckford himself, could
have been responsible for their
design. A clue as to the maker might
be found in those cabinetmakers
who subscribed to Edmund English's
Views of Lansdown Tower. English's
family were involved in cabinetmak-
ing as well as other related endeavors.[5] Other Bath cabinetmakers who
subscribed included Charles Perry
and Thomas Perry, one of whom
appears to have supplied Beckford
with furniture.[6] London cabinetmakers, including William Smee,
Thomas King, and William Pocock,
as well as Robert Hume, were all
subscribers, and it is possible that
any of these cabinetmakers might
have supplied these pieces.
The design of this stool derives
from English seventeenth-century
prototypes and would have been
eminently suitable for Fonthill Abbey.
A particularly valuable demonstration of this source is a birchwood
stool, painted and covered with
fringed velvet, and dated to around
1610–20, at Knole Park, Kent.[7]
—M. P. L.

148. *Coffer*
MAKER UNKNOWN

ca. 1831–41; England
Oak, gilt bronze, glass, silk
28 x 33¾ x 19½ in. (71.1 x 85.7 x
49.5 cm)
Private collection

Robert Hume Jr. was a key figure in
the supply of furniture for Lansdown Tower.[1] This new information
makes an earlier suggestion that the
manufacture of the present coffer
might be attributed to Charles or
Thomas Perry of Bath less certain.[2]
The furniture for the tower, well
illustrated in *Views of Lansdown
Tower,*[3] strongly suggests a Beckford–
Goodridge collaboration. The design
of the coffer seems to derive from
the Roman sarcophagus form, the
fifth-century sarcophagus in the so-
called Mausoleum of Gallia Placidia,
Ravenna, for example.[4]
Hume might have made the four
coffers on stands, including this
example which is lacking its stand
and plinth. Evidence for Hume's
participation may be found in
Beckford's letter to Hume in which
he writes: "Your chastely beautiful
oaken cabinets are filled with the
rare gems of art."[5] Two of the coffers
on stands are illustrated by Willes
Maddox (cat. fig. 146A),[6] placed on
either side of the bow window; and
they are described as "carved oak
coffers contain[ing] numerous specimens of japan, elaborately inlaid
with pure gold and coral."
Either because of financial diffi-

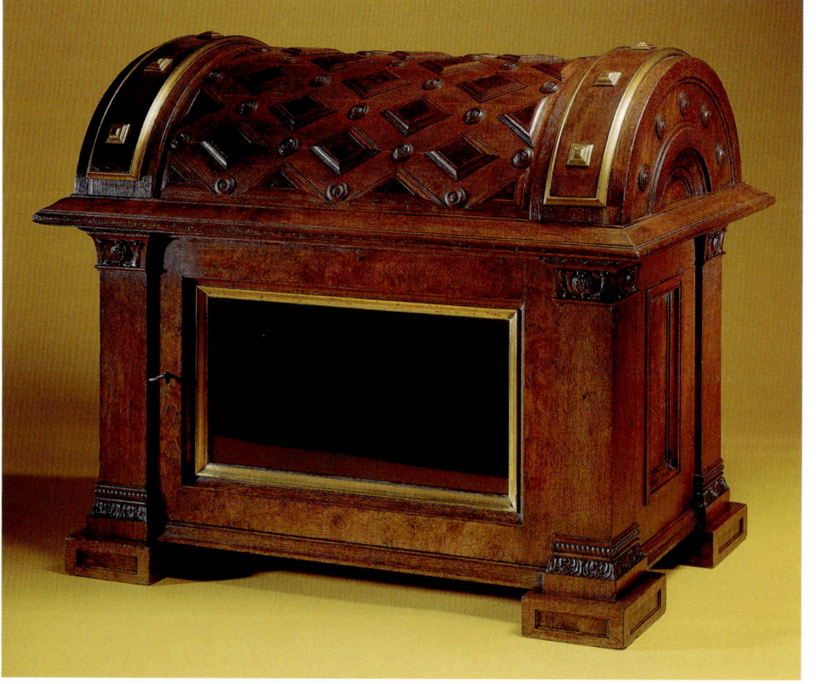

culties in 1841, or because he wished to refurnish the tower, Beckford offered part of the tower's contents for sale. On January 4, 1841, English and Fasana of Bath offered " . . . VALUABLE PAINTINGS, Magnificent Cabinets. AND SPLENDID FURNITURE, From LANSDOWN TOWER." Lot 26 in this auction was "A PAIR of SARCHOPHAGUS-HEADED COFFERS and Stands, of Riga and Pollard Oaks, 3ft. 4 wide and 5 ft. 5 high.—This pair of cabinets are singularly beautiful in design and workmanship, and every part is finished with the greatest possible care, and

the carving is most minute and exquisite. The Coffers are intended for rare China, and are lined accordingly with rich silk and each enclosed with a glazed door framed in or-molu gilt. The pedestals under Cabinets open, with shelves for Books, &c." Lot 27 in the sale was "A PAIR of DITTO—exactly to match."

Either they remained unsold or Beckford changed his mind and purchased them back. On May 19, 1841, he wrote to English about alterations to these coffers: "I must urgently recommend the gilt mouldings studs &c of the Coffers to your immediate

& most perseverant attention."[7] Following Beckford's death, some of the contents of Lansdown Tower were offered in 1845, by English & Son. This time the coffers and stands were sold on day 8, lots 520 and 521. The first lot was "A pair of superb trunk-headed coffers, of Riga and pollard oak. These cabinets are of singularly fine design—the tops are curiously pannelled, and studded with large square water gilt nails. . . . The pedestals on which they stand have arched recesses; the sides are intended for books; and are enclosed by doors. Five feet 9 inches high, by 3 feet 4 wide."

The discrepancy in height between the coffers offered in the two sales could be explained by the fact that either the marble plinths (see cat. fig. 146A) were not included with the stands in the first sale, or they were made after the sale held in January, 1841.[8] Despite the auction that was held after Beckford's death, however, it is not clear that these pieces immediately left Beckford's family. An inventory taken in 1852 of items belonging to Susan, Duchess of Hamilton, at a family residence, Easton Park in Suffolk, tantalizingly includes "Four oak Coffers, Dome tops."[9] —M. P. L.

---

149. *Pair of Candlesticks*
EDWARD BARNARD & SONS
(FL. 1829–1910)

1844–45; England
Silver
12⅞ x 6¼ in. diam. (32.5 x 16 cm)
Private collection

In 1841 Edmund English, the Milsom Street auctioneer and decorator, conducted an auction of furniture and decorative items from Lansdown Tower, "with a view of refurnishing the whole more classically, as it now stands," as he commented a few years later. With Franchi long dead and his own health failing, Beckford embarked on a last phase of designing and commissioning furniture, decorative objects, and idiosyncratic silver for the tower, much of it in a new ponderous classical idiom, using English and the architect Henry Goodridge as his collaborators. With the exception of the occasional visitor such as Cyrus Redding, Beckford's only companions, apart from his daughter and members of his staff, appear to have been English and Goodridge during these final, lonely years. Nevertheless, in his rather solitary existence, Beckford lost none of his earlier drive to create highly individual silver, the last of which was to be these monumental candlesticks.

None of these later commissions was given to any of the main London shops. This was no doubt due to the fact that by the early 1840s most of the ones Beckford had

patronized were gone: Ward and Green had long closed; Paul Storr had retired in 1838; and Rundell's, which had lost its royal warrant, was on the verge of closure. Without Franchi, moreover, Beckford no longer had a trusted agent in London to oversee his exacting commissions. Instead, the order for these candlesticks, as well as those for the saltcellar (cat. no. 143), the mounts for the pair of blanc-de-chine cups (cat. no. 142), and the copies of his 1688 wall sconces, were given to Alfred Short, a Bristol retail silversmith and jeweler.[1] Doubtless English was behind this patronage of a local colleague, although Short is not known to have supplied anything of comparable quality to any other client.

Short in turn placed the order for the candlesticks with Edward Barnard and Sons, a large firm of manufacturing silversmiths in Angel Street, Saint Martin's-le-Grand, London.[2] Many of the business records of Barnard's have survived and an entry in their Daybook "X" for August 29, 1842, includes an order from Alfred Short for a "Pair of altar Cand[lestic]ks., 12? ins. High, to his design, O.G. foot, finish'd in 5 Scrolls, chased water leaves upper part, acanthus and water leaves with scaling & leather money up stem, boss below do. chased cross's stars & ovolo edge Saucer chased Scale work to under, twisted leaves on upper boss, chased shaped chalice . . . [illegible], inner bissle [bezel], The

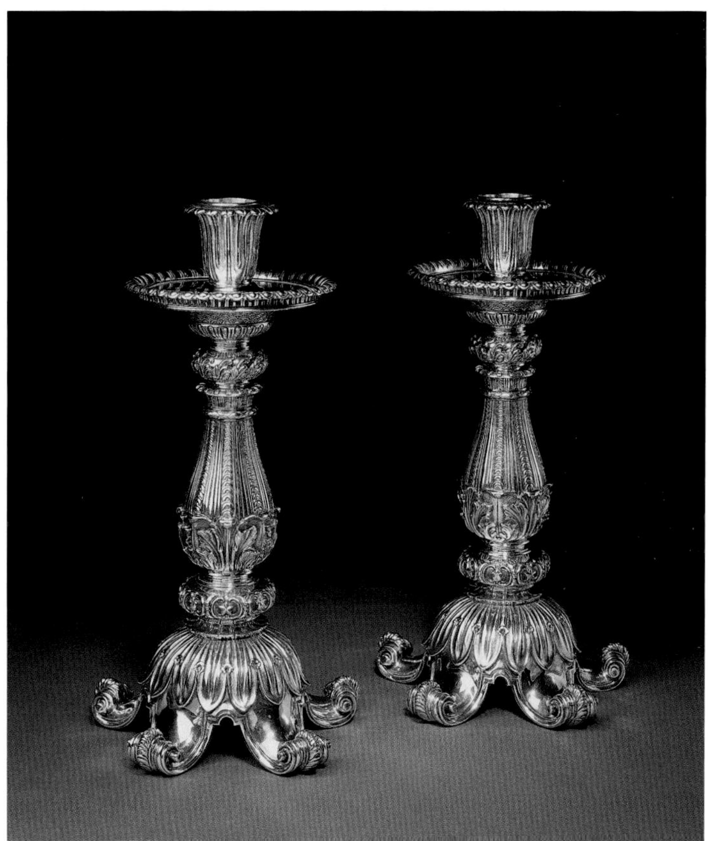

Saucer to lift off by slide, top of stem."[3] The total cost of £94 15s 8d included gilding, a packing case and "engraving two crests & names underneath." The two crests were presumably Beckford's heron and his version of the Hamilton crest; the names were those of Short as modeler and English as designer.

It was Beckford, however, who probably conceived the design for these candlesticks, perhaps relying on English to work up the drawings that Short gave to Barnard's.[4] Their

eclectic mixture of styles and motifs is typically Beckfordian, with Renaissance motifs combined with Grecian waterleafs and egg-and-dart patterns. While their extraordinary bell-shaped bases are reminiscent of Islamic hookahs, the scrolls and acanthus leaves on such bold outlines recall Giulio Romano's silverware.[5] It is not surprising that even with Beckford's last commission, heraldry still figures prominently, with the Douglas five-pointed star (mullet) chased around the base of the stem.

Edmund Francis English is not known as a designer. His father's firm of English and Becks had gone bankrupt in 1828, reemerging as English and Fasana, which from 1841 was known as English and Son. The firm, described a few years later as "masters of artistic effect in house-hold embellishment," organized Beckford's funeral in May 1844, described in newspapers as "the most magnificent ever seen in Bath."[6] Some months later, English copublished an impressive folio, *Views of Lansdown Tower, Bath: The Favourite Edifice of the late William Beckford Esq.*, with richly colored plates by Willes Maddox and text by English, which had clearly been written under Beckford's supervision. The candlesticks, not delivered until just after Beckford's death,[7] appear prominently on top of a cabinet in plate 12, no doubt placed there by English himself, perhaps following

Beckford's original intentions, but also no doubt as a subtle form of self-advertisement.

Following the publication of *Views of Lansdown Tower*, English organized two auctions of furniture, pictures, and objects, and Beckford's houses and the tower were sold.

The candlesticks were taken to Hamilton Palace,[8] where they appear in the duchess's sitting room in an 1876 inventory.[9] They were sold in the 1882 Hamilton Palace sale,[10] and shortly afterwards Beckford's crests were removed from under the base and replaced with the crest and motto of Stanhope under an earl's coronet, pertaining either to one of the earls Stanhope or earls of Chesterfield. Their subsequent provenance is unknown until they appeared at auction in 1987.[11]

—C. H.

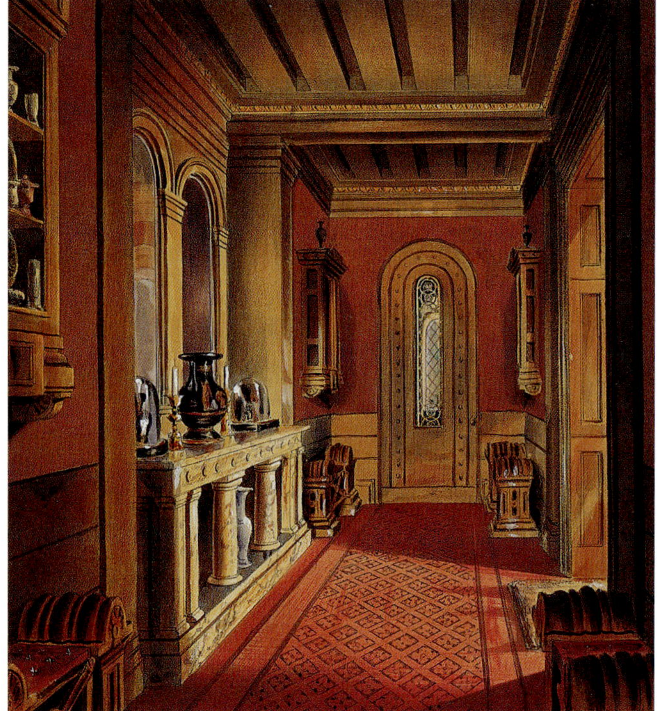

Cat. fig. 149A. "Lansdown Tower: The Vestibule." Chromolithograph after Willes Maddox. From English, *Views of Lansdown Tower* (Bath, 1844): plate 3.

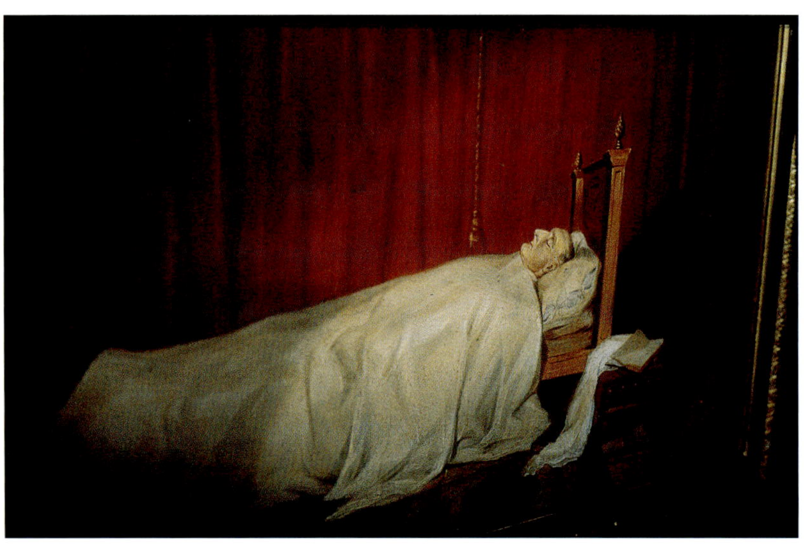

150. *William Beckford*
WILLES MADDOX
(1813–1853)

1844; England
Oil on canvas
11 x 13¾ in. (28 x 35 cm)
Beckford Collection, Brodick Castle, National Trust for Scotland (58.17)

"Beckford contemplated the closing scene of existence very frequently," Cyrus Redding wrote, "and wondered why he had been spared so long. He never disguised his age . . . exclaiming 'I am almost ashamed of being so old, really death seems to have forgotten me or has unintentionally passed me by; perhaps he means I shall be a centenarian. I have no objection . . . [but] I must submit to go when I am knocked for; still it is the common doom'."[1]

Willes Maddox's painting of Beckford on his deathbed gives an insight into the opposing elements of his character. Although he lies, as he did at Fonthill Abbey, on a narrow truckle bed, he is surrounded by the outward symbols of nobility and lineage; the curtains, stool, and bed-head are all of crimson, the family color of his Hamilton ancestors. A silver-gilt cup and ewer from his collection are in the background. Close to the bedhead is the ebony cabinet decorated with a double-eagle (now at Brodick Castle) that he had owned since the time of his youth in Geneva. In a drawer of this cabinet "lined with blue, the colour of the Aether," he kept the letters written to him by Alexander Cozens, the artist, who filled the young Beckford's mind with a yearning for the exotic.[2] On the stool is an open book, to remind us of his insatiable passion for books.[3] Finally, on the floor, rugs woven with heraldic devices are visible.

Deathbed paintings, although common in northern and eastern Europe, particularly in the sixteenth and seventeenth centuries, are fairly rare in English art. Van Dyck's *Venetia, Lady Digby* (1633) being a notable exception.[4] Given the cloud of ostracism that hung over Beckford for almost sixty years, it is tempting to conclude that his daughter, in commissioning this work, was attempting to demonstrate that her

father had died well, that despite refusing to see a priest, he had nothing on his conscience to wrestle with as death approached. There is much stage management and some distortion of scale and perspective employed in the picture. Beckford's bed is set within the serge hung space of his bed alcove, but it gives no impression of the Aladdin's-cave clutter of his bedroom, in which hung some twenty-five pictures and stood at least sixteen cabinets and chests, as well as other furniture. For Beckford's final years the limited space of his residence meant that objects and pictures had to crowd into his bedroom, for in Bath he could not afford the luxury of the austere monastic cell that he had enjoyed at Fonthill Abbey.

Willes Maddox, the son of a Bath grocer, was born in the city on August 23, 1813. A portrait and historical painter, he was the last artist to work for William Beckford.[5] Redding wrote that Maddox received Beckford's patronage, "from being imbued with a genuine feeling for Italian art, imbibed on a visit to that land of taste."[6] Beckford owned Maddox's *View near Rome with*

Monks in Procession and *Favourite Greyhound Belonging to the Pretender.*[7] Maddox also painted the three lunettes in the Sanctuary at Lansdown Tower for Beckford.[8] At the auction in 1845, the auctioneer declared that these paintings were "the very last things that Mr Beckford ordered & saw them on his death-bed."[9] Maddox also painted a series of oil paintings of Beckford's objets d'art (cat. nos. 155–57) and portraits of the Duke and Duchess of Hamilton (cat. nos. 158, 159).[10]

Maddox exhibited in London (1844–53) at the Royal Academy and the British Institution. He visited Constantinople in 1853, staying with his brother Dr. Richard Maddox in Pera, and was commissioned to paint a portrait of the Sultan but died a few months later on June 26 before completing his portrait.[11] —S. B

---

151. *William Beckford*
WILLES MADDOX
(1813–1853)

1844; England
Oil on canvas
Framed: 13½ x 14½ in. (34.3 x 36.8 cm)
Collection of Professor Bernard Nevill

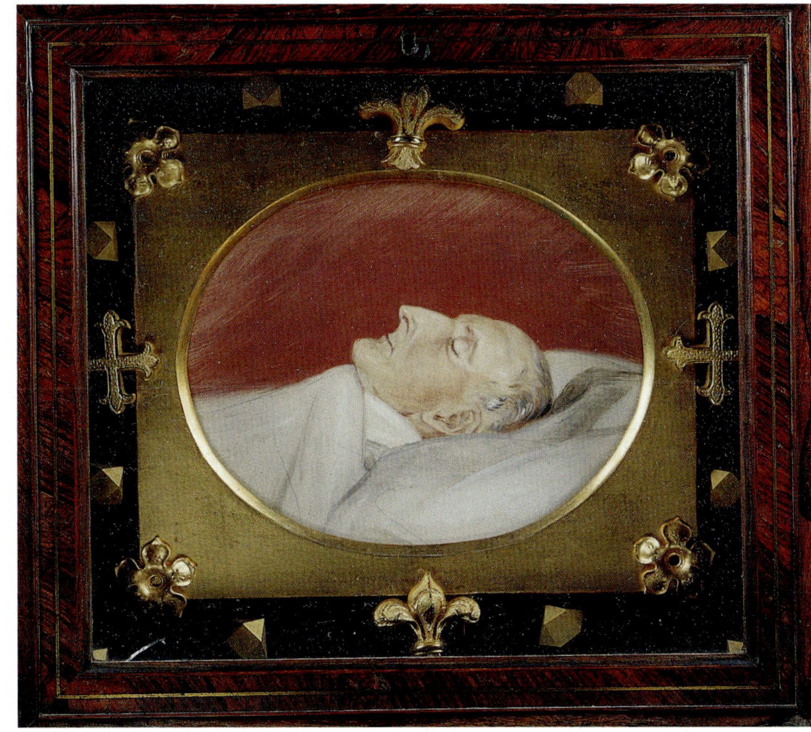

In April 1844, Beckford caught a chill when out walking in the cold east wind. His chill developed into a fever and influenza. He wrote to Bohn, his book dealer, demanding to see an auction catalogue for the Nodier sale: "send it to me by any means & at any cost—have it I must, if only for an hour."[1] Beckford's condition deteriorated so fast, that on the same day, he wrote to his daughter pleading for her to come to his bedside: "O shorten the distance!—I can bear it no longer."[2] He died on May 2, 1844.

Beckford was embalmed by English and Hiscox, surgeons of Bath. His elaborate coffin of Spanish mahogany, "embellished with superior mouldings and covered with purple Genoa velvet of the purest fabric," was put on public display at All Saints Church.[3] On the morning of the funeral, May 18, "the solemn knoll from all the churches announced the solemn event." The funeral cortege of ten mourning and nine other carriages (see fig. 15-8) made its way from Lansdown Crescent through the main streets of Bath to the cemetery. The chief mourners were the Duke and Duchess of Hamilton and their children. Crowds thronged the streets to watch the procession and at the cemetery "a strong body of police" were in attendance to prevent any disorder.[4]

This portrait is an enlarged version of Beckford's head as seen in the painting of Beckford by Maddox (cat. no. 150). Enclosed within a rosewood box-frame, with brass inlay, the gilt frame of the painting is surrounded by fleurs-de-lis and Beckford's heraldic emblems: the cinquefoil and Latimer cross. A contemporary account states that "The gilded metal ornaments even the nails" of Beckford's coffin were "all moulded and cast expressly for the purpose and of a massive and rich appearance."[5] The sides of the coffin were decorated with Latimer crosses and cinquefoils. If the heraldic emblems and nails enclosed within the frame are identical to those specially made to decorate Beckford's coffin, then this painting and its setting would have had a very special significance for Beckford's daughter: an object of veneration and remembrance, a small and portable shrine, for a father who throughout his life had been half in love with death.

For many years Beckford had been preparing for death. At Fonthill Abbey, partly inspired by the great Portuguese Abbey of Alcobaça with its "sepulchral chapel, where lie interred Pedro the Just and his beloved Inez," Beckford planned to be buried within a chamber decorated with pictures and windows based on the Book of Revelations.[6] The diarist Joseph Farington recorded that "Beckford's Coffin is to be placed opposite the door. The room is not to be entered by strangers, to be viewed through wire gratings."[7] The building of his final years, Lansdown Tower, was also conceived as a mausoleum, but he was frustrated in his burial plans by the ecclesiastical authorities.[8] Beckford's pink granite sarcophagus, costing £511.18s, was carved in 1842, and for the final years of his life stood in a grove of lilacs close to his tower. Nearby, was the marble tomb of his favorite dog, Tiny.

Beckford was fascinated by death and its associated rites: these were matters of serious interest, yet they could also be the subjects of his grotesque humor, and even fantasy. He invented a story, believed by his daughter, that he had been given permission to see the features of the Emperor Charles V in his sarcophagus in the Escorial.[9] When paying for his own sarcophagus, Beckford drafted a few lines saying that it would require a "tremendous apparatus and the labor of many men to remove the slab which covers it."[10] On judgment day "the chest containing my remains . . . will be found, directed most probably, as follows: 'To the blessed St. Anthony of Padua etc etc. Paradise Row, Apostles' Place, Heaven'."[11] —S. B.

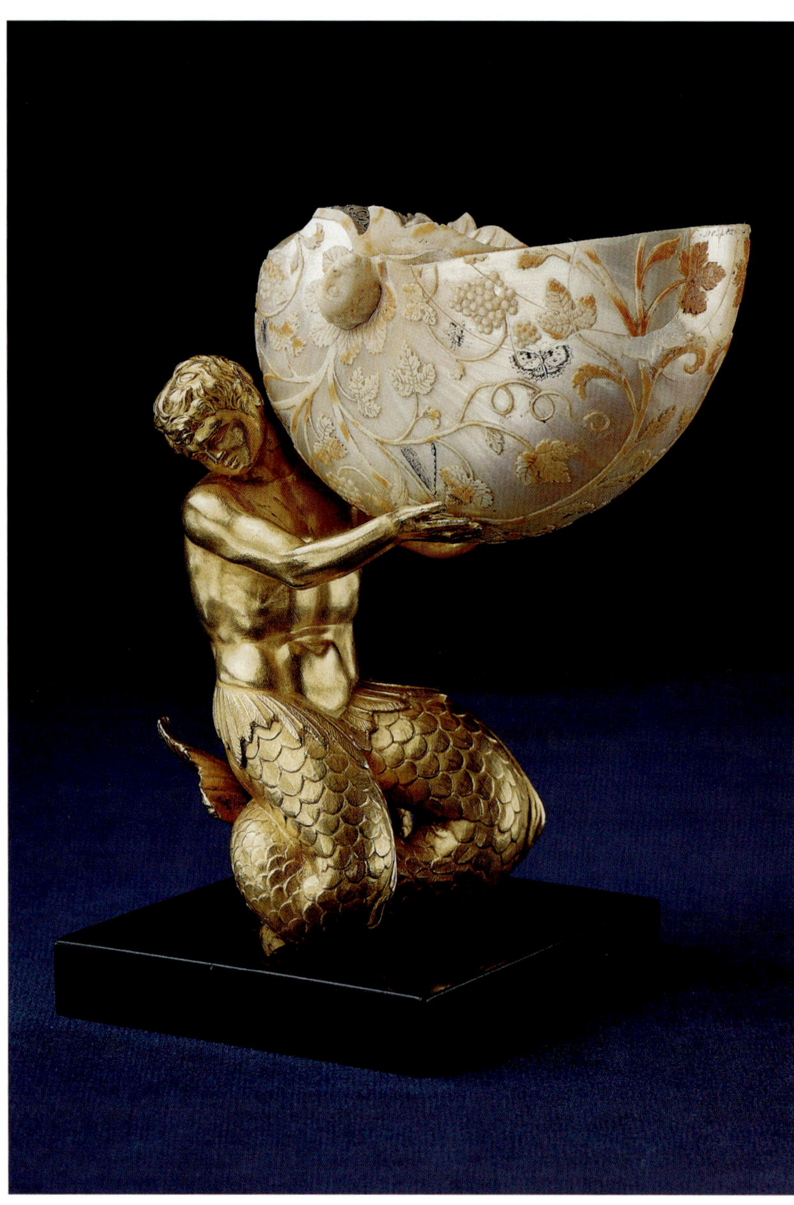

152. *Nautilus Shell*
MAKER UNKNOWN; SHELL CARVED AND ENGRAVED BY
CORNELIUS VAN BELLEKIN (D. AFTER 1711)

Mounts, late 18th/early 19th century, England [?];
shell (engraving), ca. 1700, The Netherlands
Nautilus shell (*Nautilius pompilius*), ivory, silver gilt, marble
4¾ x 3½ x 2 in. (12 x 9 x 5 cm)
Private collection

Nautilus shells, generally extravagantly mounted as sumptuous display items, were an essential component of princely *Kunstkammern* of the sixteenth and seventeenth centuries. This example is signed by Cornelius Van Bellekin (d. after 1711), a distinguished member of an eminent Amsterdam family of engravers of shell and horn.[1] It is engraved with butterflies, ladybirds, moths, and flies, depicted in a naturalistic manner reminiscent of the ornamental sixteenth- or seventeenth-century engravings of Jacob Hofnagel, Marten de Vos, or Francis Le Febvre. A characteristic of the Bellekin workshop is the visored helmet carved out of the shell, and the carved ivory masks serving as strap mounts. During the seventeenth century, Amsterdam was the principal trading center for the importation of exotic shells from the Indian Ocean: from here Bellekin sold his work to clients in France and Germany.[2]

The triton support and marble base were added to the shell at a much later date, possibly during either the second or third decade of the nineteenth century. The silver-gilt triton bears three indistinct marks, suggesting a casting from another model. Triton supports emphasized the marine theme of the shell itself and were well suited to the fluid sculptural movement of the Baroque style. They were often used as mounts in northern Europe in the seventeenth century, based on earlier triton figures used in Renaissance Italy, in fountains by Bernini, for example. A more immediate stylistic connection for this triton support may, however, be the nineteenth-century revival of Baroque figural supports, as seen in the triton and nautilus shell salt-cellars produced by the workshop of Paul Storr for the royal goldsmiths Rundell, Bridge and Rundell from 1810. These were themselves heavily influenced by earlier marine silver gilt supplied to Frederick, Prince of Wales, by Nicholas Sprimont from 1741.

Beckford was one of the greatest British collectors of nautilus cups, having had nine in his collection.[3] Only this example, however, and one other, presently at Brodick Castle, are currently known. The example at Brodick Castle is fitted with silver-gilt dolphin mounts on a coral foot. The rim mounts bear engraved decoration in the Renaissance manner and, although unmarked, are characteristic of the work commissioned by Beckford and designed by Gregorio Franchi. The quality and type of mounts on the other nautilus cups in Beckford's collection would appear to vary quite considerably, ranging from the finest silver gilt, set with gems and semiprecious stones, to a pair described in a private inventory as having Neptune and his trident on the top.[4] He also possessed less elaborate examples, one described in a sale catalogue simply as "chased silver."

Two other nautilus cups previously in Beckford's collection are known through illustrations. One can be seen in the very deliberate, staged view of a select number of objects depicted in John Rutter's "Groupe of the Rarest Articles of Virtu" (see fig. 9-2). This same cup is also seen in John Britton's view of King Edward's Gallery at Fonthill Abbey (see cat. fig. 85A) and was sold from Fonthill Abbey in 1823 to Richard Grenville, second Duke of Buckingham, later to be illustrated in the Stowe sale catalogue of 1848. The second cup is seen in a Westminster family portrait, now in a private collection.

Three nautilus shells appear in the 1844 inventory taken after Beckford's death, indicating that these types of exquisitely detailed, small-scale works of art continued to fascinate and delight him throughout his life. —U. L. and B. M.

Mounts, ca. 1815–20, England;
porcelain, ca. 1800, China
Porcelain, silver gilt
9 in. (23cm)
Beckford Collection, Brodick Castle,
National Trust for Scotland (58.532)

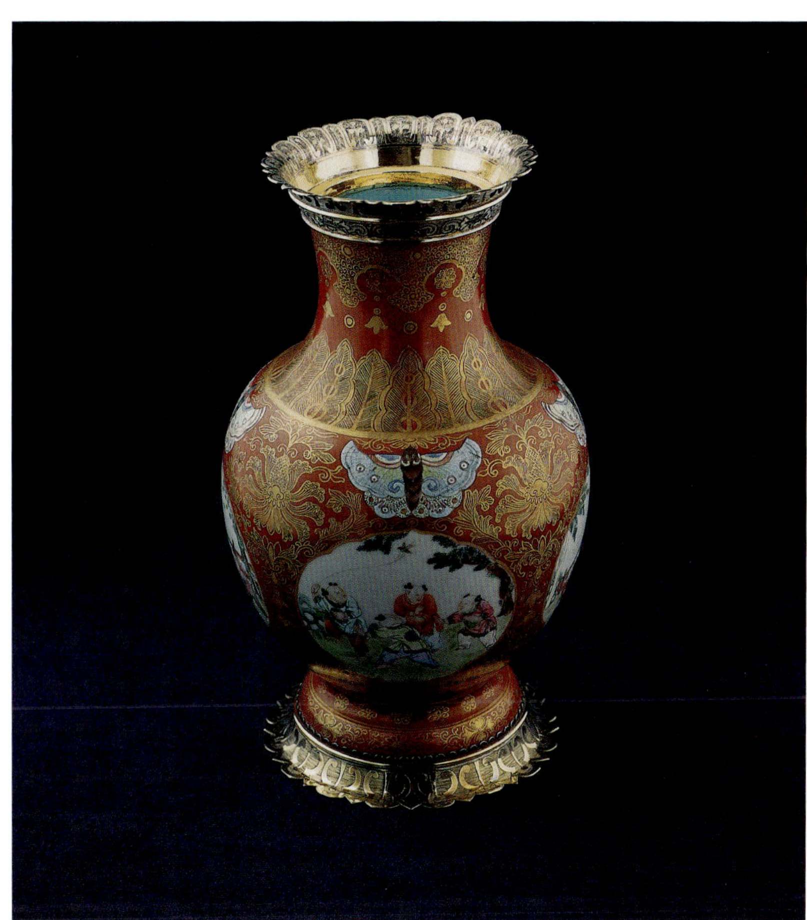

This Chinese porcelain baluster vase is the only mounted example of a set of three that are still at Brodick Castle. Decorated with butterflies and reserved panels on an iron-red ground, heightened with gilt motifs, the scalloped rim and foot mounts echo the gilt decoration of the vase. The mounts are characteristic of the work carried out for Beckford by James Aldridge (see cat. nos. 37, 38, 55, 69, 110, 117, 125, 127), and the vase is a further example of Beckford's acknowledgment of the intrinsic decoration of the piece itself. Beckford purchased mainly contemporary Chinese porcelains for mounting.

This piece is included in Willes Maddox's *Objects of Vertu* (cat. no. 156) in whose illustrations all the porcelains shown date from the eighteenth or nineteenth centuries.
—P. H-J. and B. M.

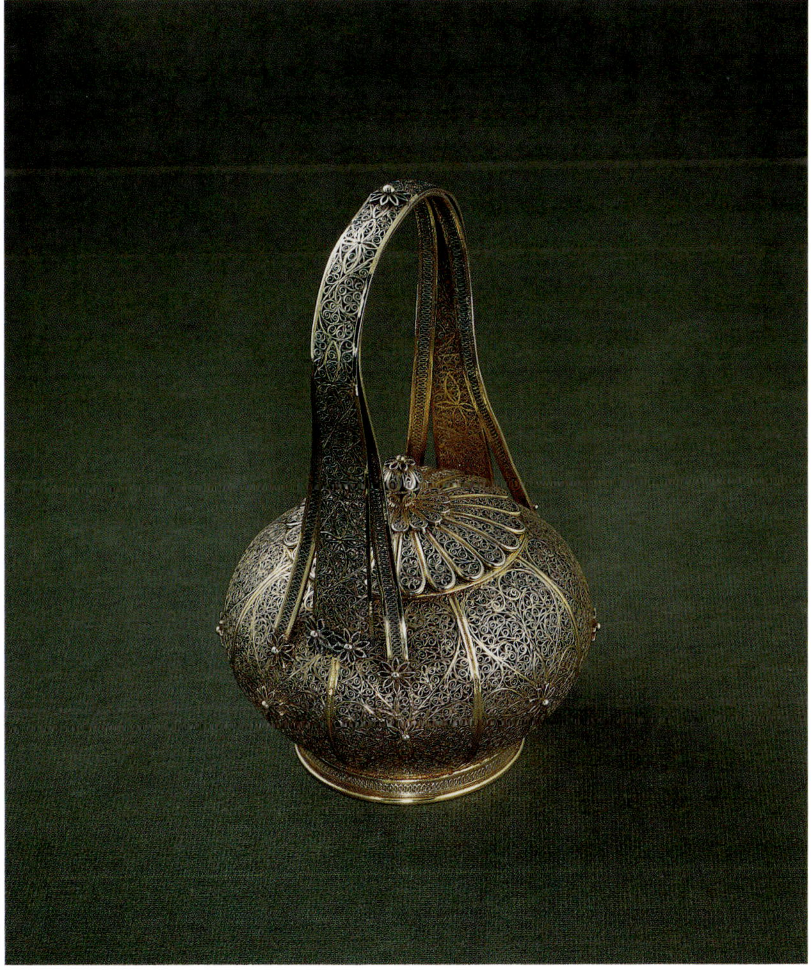

154. Casket and Cover
MAKER UNKNOWN

18th century; Turkey
Silver gilt
6¾ in. (17 cm)
Beckford Collection, Brodick Castle, National Trust for Scotland (58.308)

Filigree is a decorative technique used by metalworkers and jewelers in which twisted gold or silver wire, usually in the form of spirals or closely formed scrolls, is soldered within frames to make panels of ornament. The frames are made first, soldered together, then filled with the fine scrolls. This technique has been known since classical times and was especially popular in China, India, and Turkey.

The Beckford casket is in the form of a globular casket with cover and prominent strap handle. The body, cover, and strap are formed of dense scrolls set within narrow bands. This shape was well known in the East, where it is found in bronze and tinned copper wares from late medieval times. It is a model that was especially used in Persia, India, and Turkey. The prominent handle is an unusual feature and was intended to imitate fabric, leather, or even plaited straw. The applied silver petals with central droplets, used to decorate the body and handle, are also distinctive. These may have been filled with colored enamels— to provide a color contrast with the body of the vessel.

Filigree wares are notoriously difficult to date and localize. Very few are marked, as flat surfaces are usually not large enough to receive the makers stamp. Any attribution therefore must be based on shape and decoration. In Beckford's time, however, this casket was described as Persian, an attribution based more on his fascination with Persia than on real stylistic considerations. In describing his more exotic eastern wares, Beckford had a tendency to attribute them immediately to Persia. A filigree perfume-burner, set with turquoise, in his collection is almost certainly Indian but was also described as Persian.

In technique and decoration the casket has much in common with filigree work produced in Turkey. A Turkish rose-water sprinkler in the Victoria and Albert Museum, London, stamped with an Ottoman silver-mark, has panels of silver-gilt filigree similar in profile to those forming the cover of the Beckford casket, and like the casket the sprinkler has silver droplets set within the ornament.[1] Applied flowers on a filigree surface are also used on a Turkish amulet case in the Tradescant Collection of the Ashmolean Museum, Oxford. This is described as Turkish in the catalogue of the collection published in 1656.[2] The large strap handle is an unusual feature for caskets of globular form but

has a parallel in a silver-gilt filigree basket in the Wallace Collection that is also attributed to a Turkish workshop.[3] The decoration on some Turkish silver-gilt sleeve mounts also has links with the decorative treatment on the cover of the Beckford casket. Filigree was used extensively in Turkey for decorative wares such as bowls and for certain larger items of adornment such as belt-mounts.

An Indian origin for the casket must also be considered, as during the period William Beckford was forming his collection, India was the principal source for silver filigree work. Most if it was made in Cuttack, Orissa, and large quantities were brought to the West in the eighteenth and nineteenth cen-

turies.[4] An Indian origin for this piece, however, can be discounted, as the shape is not an Indian form. Moreover, most Indian filigree is treated with acid to produce a matte-white finish, and the upper surface polished.[5] This casket has been polished and gilt overall—a different technique. This casket could well date from as early as the second half of the seventeenth century, when much fine filigree was made in Turkey, although its condition suggests an eighteenth-century date.

The Beckford casket is shown in Willes Maddox's *Objects of Vertu* (cat. no. 156). The objects shown seem to have been selected as examples of different ornamental techniques.

They include carved ivory, rock crystal, and enameled wares, so this casket seems to have been a favorite piece. It is probably the "Vase-gilt filagree [sic] with a handle" listed in the Lansdown inventory of 1844 as being in the drawing room.[6]

Filigree work obviously appealed to Beckford. It looked exotic, and the density of ornament, so much a feature of his commissioned plate, would have pleased him. Other filigree wares in the collection include a seventeenth-century Spanish jewel casket, a Turkish bezoar-stone holder and an Indo-Persian perfume burner.
—A. R. E. N.

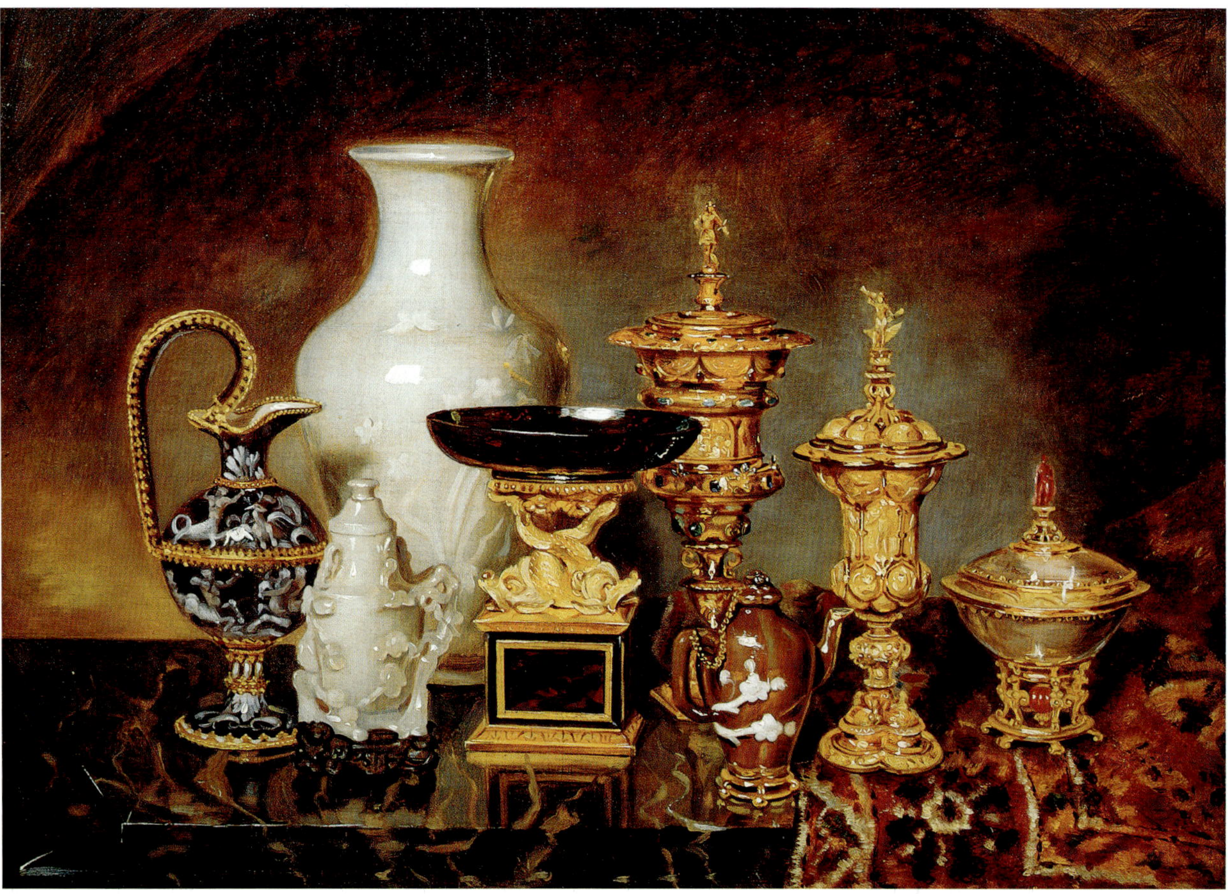

155. *Objects of Vertu*
WILLES MADDOX (1813–1853)

1844; England
Oil on canvas
23⅜ x 28⅜ in. (58.7 x 72.7 cm)
Beckford Tower Trust, Bath (Sole Trustee Bath Preservation Trust)
(1986/43)

From left: Limoges ewer (now in the Musée du Louvre, OA 6185); carved jade bottle and cover on carved wooden stand; Celadon glazed porcelain vase with white decoration; bloodstone bowl on dolphin support (cat. no. 139); silver-gilt standing cup and cover (cat. no. 103); Sèvres teapot and cover (cat. no. 63); silver-gilt standing cup and cover; agate cup and cover with silver-gilt mounts (cat. no 119). In the chromolithograph after this painting, "Objects of Vertu No. 1," the objects are shown in reverse order to the painting.

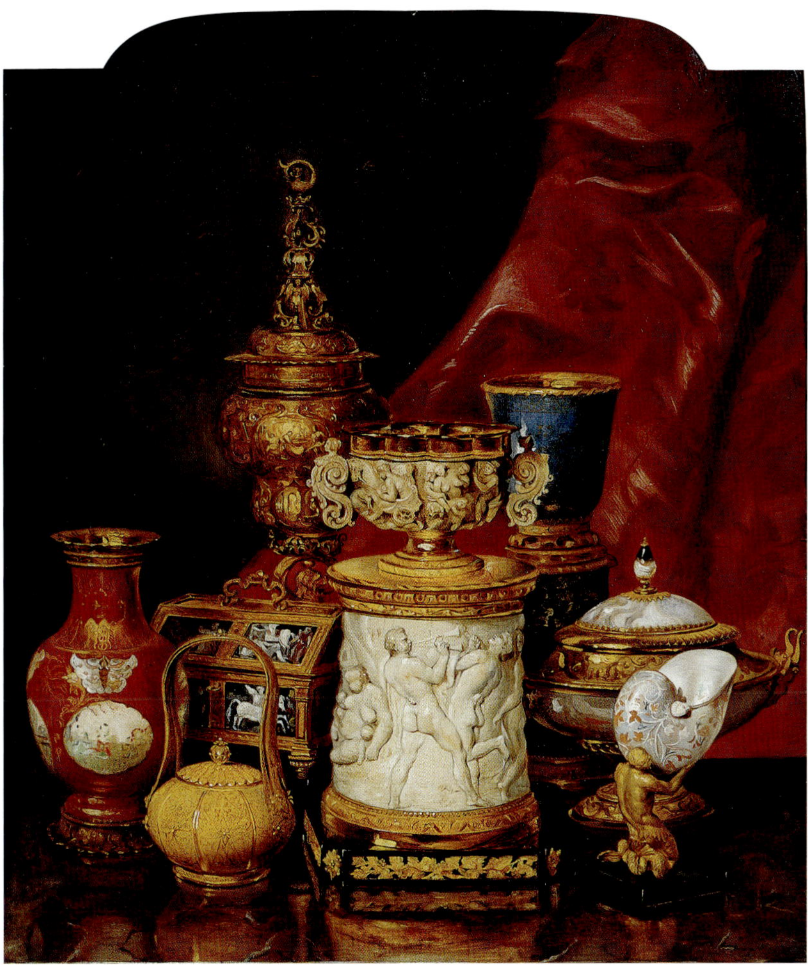

156. *Objects of Vertu*
Willes Maddox (1813–1853)

1844; England
Oil on canvas
29⅛ x 26⅜ in. (74.3 x 67 cm)
Beckford Tower Trust, Bath (Sole Trustee Bath Preservation Trust) (1986/44)

From left: porcelain vase with silver-gilt mounts (cat. no. 153); Limoges enamel chasse; globular filigree bowl and handle (cat. no. 154); covered standing cup (now in the Thyssen-Bornemisza Collection, K194b; see fig. 9-4); carved ivory bowl, mounted in silver gilt (now in Brodick Castle); mounted on ivory plinth with gilt-bronze mounts; powder blue porcelain beaker, lined with silver gilt and with silver-gilt mounts; plinth of mottled marble with silver-gilt mounts; agate bowl and cover with silver-gilt mounts (cat. no. 118); nautilus shell on triton support (cat. no 152). This painting corresponds to the chromolithograph, "Objects of Vertu, No. 2."

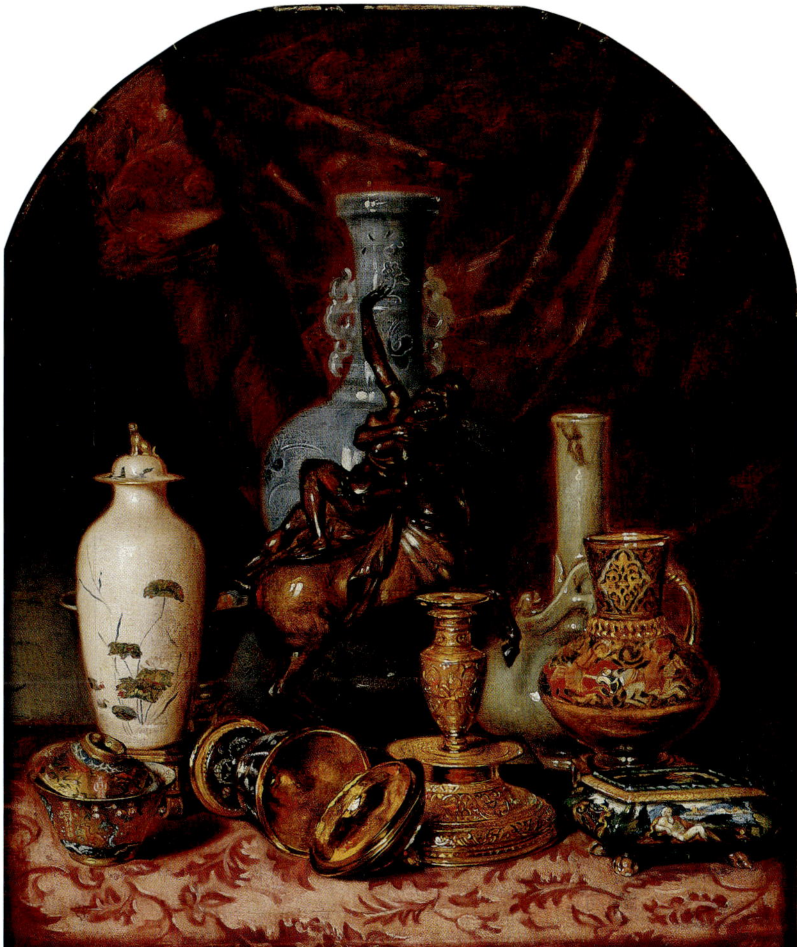

157. *Objects of Vertu*
Willes Maddox (1813–1853)

1844; England
Oil an canvas
30 x 26⅛ in. (76.2 x 66.3 cm)
Beckford Tower Trust, Bath (Sole Trustee Bath Preservation Trust) (1986/ 45)

From left: olive ground porcelain bowl and cover; pink crackle-glaze porcelain vase and cover; blue bowl with silver gilt mounts; Limoges vase and cover, lined and mounted with silver gilt (now at Brodick Castle); bronze statue by Giambologna of Nessus and Dejanira (now at the Huntington Art Gallery, 17.13); lavender ground porcelain vase with handles at the neck; Veneto-Saracenic candlestick; celadon ground porcelain vase with lizard at the neck; enameled glass ewer (cat. no. 54); majolica saltcellar (cat. no. 100). This painting corresponds to the chromolithograph, "Objects of Vertu, No. 3."

155–57. Objects of Vertu

These paintings depict a selection of some of the outstanding works of art in Beckford's collection at the time of his death in 1844. Willes Maddox was one of the artists commissioned by Edmund English for the preparation of *Views of Lansdown Tower*, published in October 1844. Maddox drew the illustrations, which were then printed as chromolithographs by C. J. Richardson. The circumstances under which this publication was commissioned remain unclear. English claims in his prefatory remarks that the publication was conceived to satisfy the demands of those visitors to the tower who "often expressed a desire to possess some memorial of that which had so attracted their attention."[1]

English further states that the illustrations were drawn "under Mr Beckford's own eye—a sufficient guarantee of their artistic fidelity."[2] That the drawings were certainly undertaken in Beckford's lifetime is indeed borne out by Beckford's letter, dated March 9, 1844, in which he writes about the artists being present at the tower: "English tells me that the artists are working 'with passion' on views of the holy Tower—actually I approve of the sketches that I've already seen."[3]

Although clearly commissioning "views" of Lansdown Tower, Beckford may not have intended to produce a guide for visitors that would include these views. It is more likely that his daughter Susan commissioned the posthumous publication from English, based on the drawings carried out in her father's lifetime.

The inventory dated September 13, 1844, taken by English and Son and Robert Hume, lists a number of paintings by Maddox in situ at the tower. *The Salutation, The Temptation,* and *Christ's Agony in the Garden* were hanging in the lunettes of the Oratory.[4] For these Maddox was paid 30 guineas apiece.[5] Maddox also supplied three more works for Beckford: *A View near Rome with Monks in Procession* is listed as being in the entrance hall of Nos. 19 and 20 Lansdown Crescent, where, tucked away in a Ladies' Maids' Room there, were *View in Venice* and *A Groupe of Bijouterie.*[6] This last work may have been the oil on canvas sold in 1855: "Articles of Vertu . . . from the

collection of William Beckford . . . by Willes Maddox."[7]

In the 1844 publication the chromolithographs are entitled, respectively, "Objects of Vertu No. 1, in Mr. Beckford's Collection" (plate 7); "Objects of Vertu No. 2, in Mr. Beckford's Collection" (plate 11); "Objects of Vertu No. 3, in Mr. Beckford's Collection" (plate 13). It is the three chromolithographs that are commonly illustrated in modern publication, rather than the oils themselves.

These three oils on canvas by Maddox were painted after his drawings for the chromolithographs. They were undoubtedly commissioned by his daughter Susan at the same time as she commissioned the deathbed portrait (see cat. no. 150) and the death portrait from Maddox (see cat. no. 151). Documents show that four oils depicting objects from his collection were in fact painted by Maddox, presumably these and one other.[8]

The fourth was still in the family's possession in 1864, but its present whereabouts is unknown. The three paintings in the exhibition have been assigned numbers corresponding to those of the chromolithographs.

The works of art depicted appear to be random in terms of material, style, and date, much as they were in Rutter's "Groupe of the Rarest Articles of Virtu" (see fig. 9-2). Some of the works of art depicted were embellished or mounted to Beckford's orders, others remain in their original state. The objects are usually thought to have been from Lansdown Tower, but a reading of the 1844 inventory taken after Beckford's death shows that some of the works of art were kept at Lansdown Crescent, at least at the time of his death. Only one item bearing Beckford's heraldic devices was selected (cat. no. 119) and this was so cunningly designed that the devices are not seen unless the mounted

bowl and cover are closely examined at first hand. Further assessment of the works of art selected reveals that Limoges enamels appear in each group, and that all of these were mounted pieces. Chinese porcelain also appears in each group, some pieces mounted, others not.

The works of art must have had especial significance for Beckford to warrant their selection. Whether this was in aesthetic terms, in order to create a *Kunstkammer* group, or in terms of a romantic association with the past, or an acknowledgment of provenance, is impossible to determine. Whatever their significance may have been to Beckford, his daughter Susan respected his selection, as she retained all items shown, except, curiously, for the "Hercules" mounted cup and cover (cat. no. 119).

It is their inclusion in these paintings that has allowed identification of many of the objects.
—B. M.

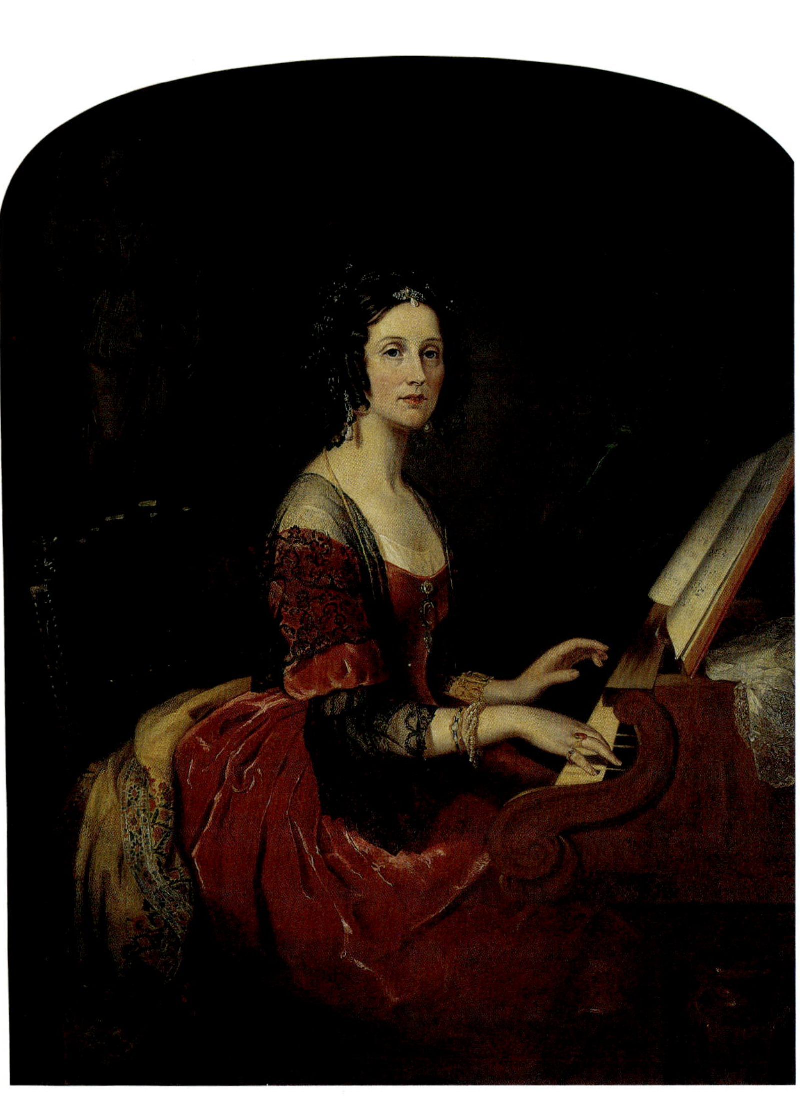

158. *Susan Euphemia, Duchess of Hamilton*
WILLES MADDOX (1813–1853)

1852; England
Oil on canvas
56 x 44 in. (142.3 x 111.7 cm)
Beckford Collection, Brodick Castle, National Trust for Scotland (58.5.2a)
Not exhibited†

Susan Euphemia Beckford (1786–1859), William Beckford's favorite daughter, was born at the Château de la Tour de Peilz near Vevey, Switzerland, when Beckford and his wife were in voluntary exile from England. Lady Margaret, Beckford's wife, died a few days after Susan's birth, and thereafter Beckford's daughters were raised in England by his mother and other relatives.

At one time, Lady Ann Hamilton, later to become Susan's sister-in-law, was in charge of Susan and her elder sister Margaret (1785–1818).[1] Lady Ann appears to have been an "amiable virgin" but possibly had the somewhat "Methodistical" outlook of Beckford's mother and her lady friends. Calvanistic Swiss governesses and the Reverend John Lettice, Beck-

ford's former tutor, were employed to give instruction to the girls.

In 1811 Beckford's elder daughter Margaret eloped with a soldier, Lieutenant-Colonel James Orde, of fairly modest family and fortune, which led to Beckford's estrangement from her until just before her early death in 1818. He held, however, great expectations for the marriage of Susan. At one stage, he suggested his friend the rich Spanish Count Fuentes y Egmont as a suitor, but this did not take place due to Susan's own objections and alarm raised by her mother's brother.[2] Another suitor, also rejected, was Thomas Hope, one of the great collectors of the Regency period. Eventually, a marriage was arranged between Susan and Alexander Hamilton, heir to the dukedoms of Hamilton and Brandon. Hamilton had been a close friend of Beckford's since the younger man's schooldays. Hamilton, then Marquess of Douglas, was eighteen years older than his bride. The marriage settlement cost Beckford £20.000, but from Beckford's point-of-view, the marriage provided him with an alliance with an old noble family. Beckford also hoped that his son-in-law might well be able to achieve for him the social rehabilitation and peerage that he greatly desired.

The Douglases spent much time abroad, and within the family they spoke and wrote in French. There are preserved a few impressions of Susan observed by her contemporaries. Lady Granville, for example, remarked that "she looks thin, but always beautiful. Her manner I think is very disagreeable, so forced in gaiety, making her so little available as a companion upon any subject. All my natural thoughts and movements abandon me when I am sitting with her, and I remain looking at her fine face, now all astonishment, and now all animation, and now all tenderness for [her husband], just as I sit looking at a diorama."[3]

Susan had two children—a son, William (1811–63), who married Princess Mary of Baden, a cousin of Napoléon III (a marriage that pleased the aging Beckford), and a daughter, Susan Harriet Catherine (who married the Earl of Lincoln, heir to the Duke of Newcastle). Lady Lincoln's marriage ended in scandal when she left her husband and children.[4] Susan also brought up her nieces, the daughters of her sister Margaret, although the Duke of Newcastle considered that her supervision was "not that to form a wife," and he saw the nieces as "poor creatures . . . more like waiting maids than anything else."[5]

Susan, like her father, had a great love of music. Early in her life, the diarist Joseph Farington recorded that she "sings exquisitely but it is a rule for Her not to sing in any House but that which she resides with Lady Ann Hamilton in Baker St."[6] Her father presented her with a Pleyel piano, and she owned a score of sonatas by Boccherini (both now in the Hamilton collection). It is appropriate, therefore, that Willes Maddox should show the duchess seated at a piano.[7]

Susan had great affection for her father, although at times he was critical of her lack of learning. He referred to his daughter and son-in-law as the "Arcadians," those least intellectual of the Greeks, but he looked forward to her visits to Fonthill and Bath. Father and daughter both presented a somewhat artificial mask in public; when in private, they acted somewhat differently. One anecdote records that "They used to amuse themselves in imitating the Peacocks in the woods. One day Beckford said to her – 'I called to the Peacocks today, and they answered me' 'Ah,' said she, 'it was *I*'."[8] —S. B.

---

159. *Alexander, 10th Duke of Hamilton*
WILLES MADDOX (1813–1853)

ca. 1852; England
Oil on canvas
56 x 44 in. (142.3 x 111.7 cm)
Beckford Collection, Brodick Castle, National Trust for Scotland (58.5.2b)
Not exhibited†

"Never was such a *magnifico* as the 10th Duke," recorded one of his contemporaries, "when I knew him he was very old, but he held himself straight as any grenadier. He was always dressed in a military laced undress coat, tights and Hessian boots &c."[1] Maddox's portrait, painted toward the end of the sitter's life, shows the Duke of Hamilton and Brandon seated and wearing the star of the Order of the Garter, the highest order of knighthood in Great Britain which he had been awarded in 1836.[2]

Alexander Hamilton Douglas was born on October 5, 1767, the elder son of Archibald, later ninth Duke of Hamilton, and Lady Alexander Stewart, fifth daughter of Alexander sixth Earl of Galloway. The Hamilton family had a long and proud history, holding lands in Lanarkshire from the late thirteenth century. Sir James Hamilton, the first baron (d.1479), married as his second wife Princess Mary Stewart, eldest daughter of James II of Scotland. On the death of James V, James second Earl of Arran and third baron (d.1575) was second in line of succession to the Scottish throne and acted as regent and tutor for the young Mary Queen of Scots.

Through his mother, William Beckford was a distant cousin of the Hamiltons, and he had established a close relationship with Alexander and his brother Archibald when they were still schoolboys at Harrow School. He entertained the brothers—whom in his letters he referred to as "the boys," "the urchins," and "the boobies"—at Fonthill and in his mother's townhouse in London's Wimpole Street.[3] After the Powderham scandal of 1784, Hamilton and his kinsman Sir William Hamilton, the antiquary and envoy, were the only British friends to remain loyal to Beckford. It is tempting to surmise that it was Beckford's obsession with noble and royal lineage that set his young cousin on a course that resulted in his being described as "the proudest man in England."[4] Hamilton came to believe that he was the descendant of the regent Arran and the true heir to the Scottish throne.

Hamilton's early years, after Oxford, were spent in Italy. He became Member of Parliament for Lancaster in 1802. At this time, Lady Stafford described him as being "so odd! so different from every other man! . . . His great coat, long *queue*, and fingers covered with gold rings . . . and he is in every particular as foreign as when he first came from abroad."[5] He was sent as ambassador to Saint Petersburg in 1807 but proved incompetent, almost to the point of endangering relationships between the two countries. After being replaced, he spent some time pursuing "an old battered beauty," the wealthy Countess Potocka, in the vain hope of marriage.[6]

Hamilton, then Marquess of

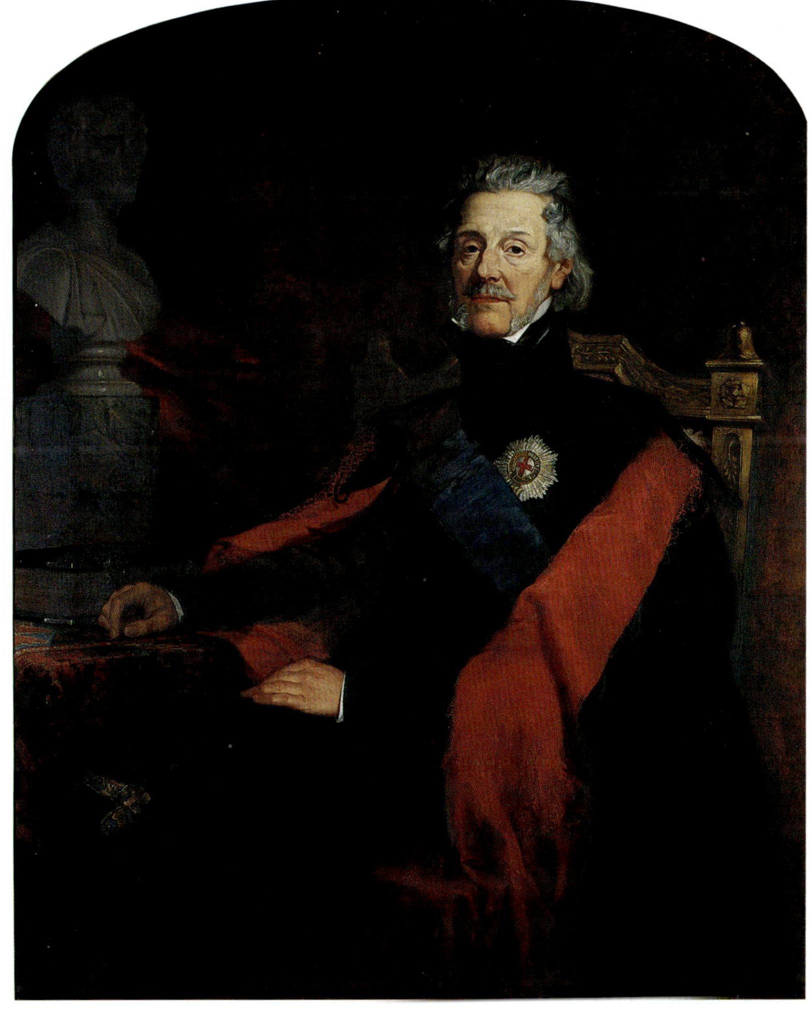

Douglas, married Beckford's youngest daughter, Susan, in April 1810, although the marriage had been suggested from at least 1804. Beckford pinned his hopes for social rehabilitation and a peerage on his son-in-law's influence, but a long period of Tory rule meant that Hamilton, a Whig, could do nothing to promote Beckford's cause.

Beckford was fully aware of Hamilton's enthusiasm for Napoléon, which included visiting the emperor when in exile on Elba, and considered that the marriage would pay dividends if Napoléon ever regained power.[7] Hamilton commissioned David to paint *The Emperor Napoléon in His Study at the Tuileries* (now in the National Gallery of Art, Washington). He was one of a circle of British gentlemen in Rome, in the 1810s, who paid devoted court to Napoléon's favorite sister, Princess Pauline Borghese. In her will, the princess left Hamilton her silver-gilt dressing case (now in the National Museums of Scotland, Edinburgh), two Sèvres vases to his wife, and to their daughter, a ring set with opals.

In 1819 Hamilton succeeded his father as tenth Duke of Hamilton, Marquess of Hamilton, Marquess of Douglas and Clydesdale, Earl of Angus, Arran, Lanark, and Selkirk, Baron Hamilton, Avon, Polmont, Mackanshire, Innerdale, Abernethy, and Jedburgh Forest, and premier peer in the peerage of Scotland; Duke of Brandon in Suffolk, and Baron Dutton, of Great Britain. He was also hereditary keeper of the Holyrood House in Edinburgh. Although Lord High Steward at the coronations of William IV (1830) and Queen Victoria (1837), the duke played little part in British public life, spending much time abroad. Lady Granville reported seeing him in Paris in 1836: "in green slippers because of his gout, and a cord round his throat like a *huissier de la Chambre*, nobody know[s] why."[8]

The architect David Hamilton was engaged by the duke to enlarge his main family seat at Hamilton (1822–30), adding a new north front some 264 feet in length, with a central portico supported by monolithic Roman Corinthian columns. The duke's proudest and grandest gesture was the huge mausoleum he built close by. Beckford's own architect Goodridge was one of the architects who submitted plans, but the design chosen was by David Bruce. Work began on the structure in 1842 and was still unfinished at the time of the duke's death in 1852. The duke was laid-to-rest in an ancient Egyptian sarcophagus, which he had purchased in Paris in 1836.

The duke, like his father-in-law, was a passionate collector and owned fine French furniture, including pieces from the collection of Marie Antoinette, Japanese lacquer, majolica illuminated manuscripts, and pictures. Like Beckford, he had a number of cabinets by Robert Hume which were mounted with pietre dure. Among his pictures were Rubens's *Daniel in the Lions' Den* (now in the National Gallery of Art, Washington) and Jacopa Bassano's *The Departure of Abraham for Canaan* (now in the National Gallery of Art, Ontario). The manuscript collection included Botticelli's drawings for Dante's *Divine Comedy* (now in the Kupferstichkabinett, Berlin). The Hamilton Palace collection was sold at Christie's in 1882 and realised £397,562.[9] The Hamilton Library was sold in 1882/83, and a further sale of portraits and pictures took place in 1919.[10]

Hamilton Palace was demolished in 1922. The duke's sarcophagus was transferred to Bent Cemetery, Hamilton, in 1921 when it was feared that land subsidence would undermine the mausoleum's structure. The great mausoleum still stands, very close to the M74 motorway, a remarkable survival and a symbol for a man who even in his own lifetime was seen as a relict from a previous age, as his obituary remarked, "in 1852 he nursed the prejudices which he had imbibed before 1789."[11] —S. B

† Due to the fragility of one of the Brodick portraits, both were replaced with similar portraits courtesy of the Hamilton Collection. The organizers of this exhibition would like to thank the Duke and Duchess of Hamilton for their gracious consent to lend the portraits of the 10th Duke and Duchess of Hamilton. The portrait of the Duke was painted circa 1842 by Sir Daniel Macnee (1806–1882), and the portrait of the Duchess was painted by Willes Maddox (1813–1853) in 1859.

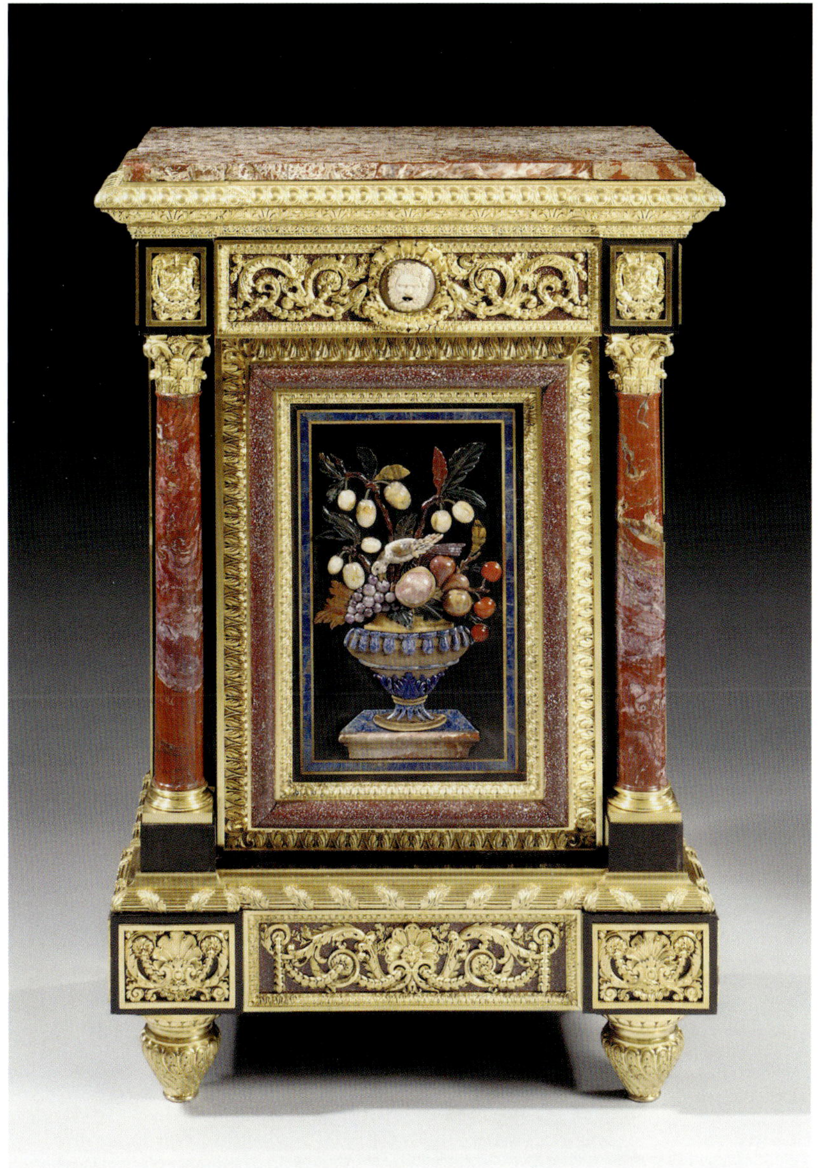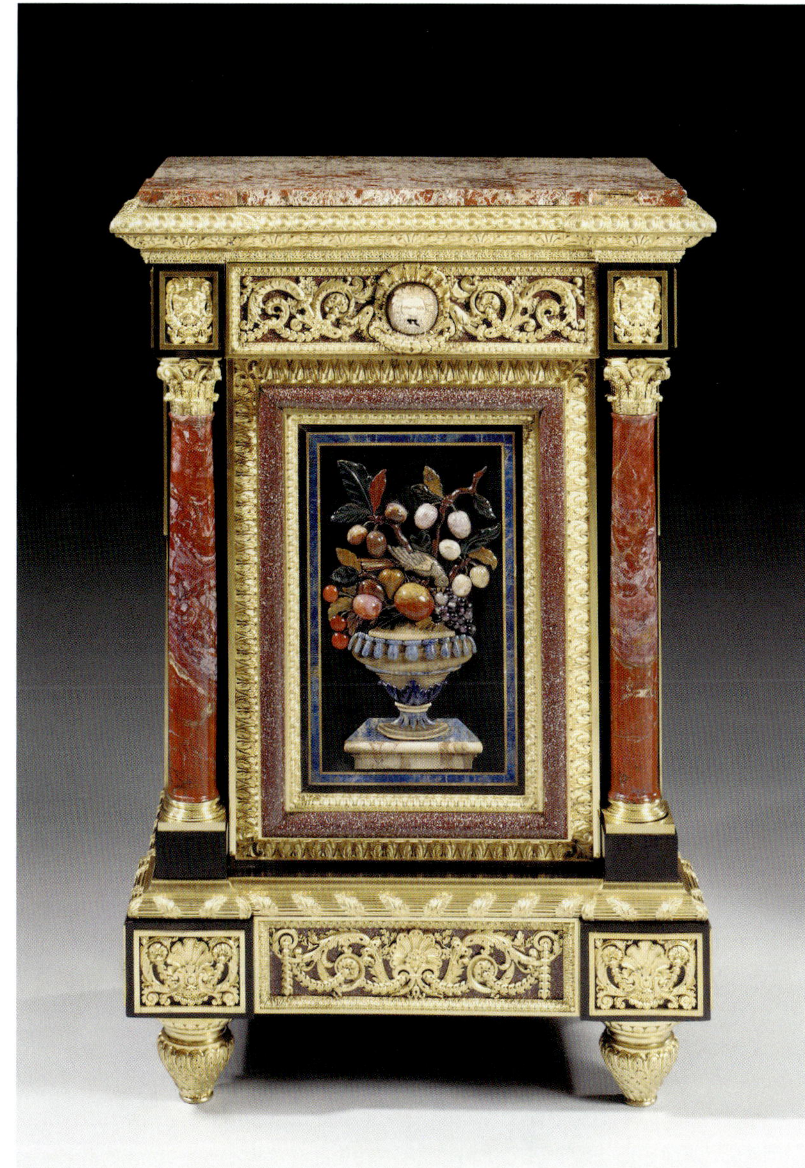

160. *Pair of Cabinets*
Maker unknown

Mounts, cabinetwork, 1825,
France; porphyry, jasper, cameos,
1825, Italy; pietre dure, late 17th
century, France, attributed to the
Gobelins workshop
Ebony, oak, maple, hardstones,
gilt bronze,
41 x 26 1/2 x 15 1/4 in. (104 x 67
x 38.5 cm)
Christie's

This pair of magnificent cabinets
were commissioned by Beckford at a
time when he was relieved from the
financial burden of Fonthill Abbey
which enabled him to enjoy a period
of renewed commissioning and collecting works of art. Beckford's taste
for highly finished metalwork and
richly colored materials is exemplified in these cabinets, which represent something of a departure from
the simpler pietre-dure cabinets that
he owned at Fonthill Abbey. Franchi
asserted, "Even if they are small,
they will be small and precious."[1]
Their richness reflects the revival in
taste for Louis XIV furniture that
was particularly strong in England in
the second quarter of the nineteenth
century as George IV refurnished
the State Rooms at Windsor Castle.

The cabinets were assembled in

Paris using a pair of late-seventeenth-
century pietre-dure panels.[2] The
work was actively overseen by
Franchi. In Rome he purchased the
jasper for the columns and the
Egyptian porphyry that served as a
frame for the pietre-dure panels and
provided the luxurious ground on
which to show off the gilt-bronze
mounts. He wrote to Beckford in
November 1824: "The two cabinets
that are being made in Paris cannot
be finished without bringing from
here the necessary porphyry and
slabs that are supposed to be the
background for the gilt bronze
mounts."[3] The carcases appear to
have been reused from an earlier
piece of furniture, and the gilt-
bronze mounts were made in Paris
by an unidentified but highly
accomplished *bronzier*. In January

1825 Franchi detailed their progress
in a letter to Beckford: "from Paris
I have news that the dealer has
the wood ready and that they are
finished. The bronzes are still being
made."[4] Also from Rome came the
pair of bacchic cameo masks that
served as key escutcheons: "the key-
holes are two magnificent masks of
agate, a milk-colour on a dark
ground, that are in the hands of a
disciple of Girometti."[5]

It is not known whether these
cabinets were housed in Lansdown
Crescent or in Beckford's London
house. They do appear to have fallen
victim, as with certain paintings,
to Beckford's need to raise funds
again in the 1830s, as they had
passed into the possession of the
Duke of Sutherland by 1839.
—P. H-J. and B. M.

Appendix

Key to Abbreviated Sources

In the source notes and the provenance appendix, the following shortened references have been used for oft-cited sources.

Alexander 1962
Boyd Alexander. *England's Wealthiest Son.* London: Centaur Press, 1962.

Bell and Girtin 1934–35
C. F. Bell and Thomas Girtin. "The Drawings and Sketches of John Robert Cozens: A Catalogue with an Historical Introduction." *Walpole Society* 33 (1934–35).

Britton 1801
John Britton, *The Beauties of Wilt-shire.* 2 vols. London: Vernor & Hood, 1801.

Britton 1823
John Britton. *Graphical and Literary Illustrations of Fonthill Abbey, Wiltshire; with Heraldical and Genealogical Notes.* London: Longmans, Green and Co., 1823.

Chapman 1937
Guy Chapman, *Beckford.* London: Jonathan Cape, 1937.

Charlecote Park **1996**
Charlecote Park. Guidebook. London: The National Trust, 1996.

Christie's 1817
Catalogue of all the Elegant Household Furniture . . . of William Beckford, Esq., of Fonthill. . . . Sale cat., Christie's, London. 9–13 May 1817

Christie's 1822
Magnificent Effects at Fonthill Abbey. . . . Sale cat., Christie's, Fonthill. Scheduled to begin 1 October 1822, the sale was canceled.

Christie's 1827
A Catalogue of a Select and Very Beautiful Assemblage . . . Collected in Italy and Other Parts of Europe, Since the Year 1802, by the Chevalier Franchi. . . . Sale cat., Christie's, London, 16–17 May 1827.

Christie's 1882
Catalogue of the collection of . . . the Property of His Grace the Duke of Hamilton. . . . Sale cat., Christie, Manson and Woods, 17 June–20 July 1882.

Christie's 1919
The Remaining Contents of the Palace. Sale cat., Christie's, Hamilton Palace, 12–14 November 1919.

English 1841
Valuable Paintings, Magnificent Cabinets, and Splendid Furniture from Lansdown Tower. . . . Sale cat., English and Fasana, Lansdown Tower, Bath, 4–5 January 1841.

English 1844
Edmund English. *Views of Lansdown Tower.* Bath, n.p., 1844. Three plates are often cited in the notes to the catalogue entries: pl. 7, "Objects of Vertu No.1"; pl. 11, "Objects of Vertu No.2"; and pl. 13, "Objects of Vertu No. 3." For the corresponding oil paintings by Willes Maddox, see cat. nos. 155–57.

English 1845
Catalogue of the Splendid Furniture, Cabinets, Paintings . . . the Property of the Late William Beckford, Esquire. . . . Sale cat., English and Son, Lansdown Tower, Bath, 20–27 November 1845.

English 1848
Catalogue of the Valuable and Costly Effects . . . the Property of the Late William Beckford, Esq. . . . Sale cat., English and Son, Lansdown, Bath, 24 June–2 July 1848.

Farington *Diary*
The Diary of Joseph Farington. 16 volumes. New Haven and London: Yale University Press, 1978–84.

"Inventory of 1844"
Inventory dated 13 September 1844, made by English Son of Bath and Robert Hume, of the contents of 19 and 20 Lansdown Crescent, tower and farm, MS Beckford c. 58, Bodleian Library, Oxford.

Beckford and Hamilton Silver **(Spink 1980)**
Malcolm Baker, Timothy Schroder, E. Laird Clowes. *Beckford and Hamilton Silver from Brodick Castle.* London: Spink and Son, 1980.

Beckford and Hamilton Silver **(Brussels 1992)**
Silver: National Trust for Scotland Treasures; Beckford and Hamilton Silver from Brodick Castle. Brussels: Bank Brussels Lambert, 1992.

Library sale 1882
Catalogue of the First Portion of The Beckford Library. Sale cat., Sotheby's, Wilkinson & Hodge, 30 June–30 November 1882

Life at Fonthill
Life at Fonthill, 1807–1822, with interludes in Paris and London, from the correspondence of William Beckford. Trans. and ed. Boyd Alexander. London, R. Hart-Davis, 1957.

Melville 1910
Lewis Melville. *The Life and Letters of William Beckford of Fonthill.* London: W. Heinemann, 1910.

MS Beckford
William Beckford papers in the Bodleian Library, Oxford.

Oliver 1932
J. W. Oliver. *The Life of William Beckford of Fonthill.* London: Oxford University Press, 1932.

Phillips' 1801
A Catalogue of Part of the Superlatively Elegant and Magnificent Household Furniture . . . the Genuine Property of William Beckford, Esq., of Fonthill. . . . Sale cat. Phillips', London, 19–22 August 1801.

Phillips' 1807
Fonthill Mansion . . . Sale cat. Phillips, Fonthill, 17–24 August 1807.

Phillips' 1823
The Unique and Splendid Effects of Fonthill Abbey . . . Sale cat., Phillips, Fonthill, 9 September–29 October 1823.

Redding 1859
Cyrus Redding, *Memoirs of William Beckford,* vol. 2 (London: Charles J. Skeet, 1859): 94–95.

Rutter 1822
John Rutter. *A Description of Fonthill Abbey and Demesne, Wilts; the Seat of William Beckford, Esq. Including a List of its Numerous and Valuable Paintings, Cabinets, and other Curiosities.* Shaftesbury: the author, 1822.

Rutter 1823a
John Rutter. *Delineations of Fonthill and its Abbey.* Shaftesbury and London, the author, 1823.

Rutter 1823b
John Rutter. *A new descriptive guide to Fonthill abbey and demesne, for 1823, including a list of its paintings and curiosities.* Shaftesbury: the author, 1823.

Sloan 1986
Kim Sloan. *Alexander and John Robert Cozens: The Poetry of Landscape.* New Haven and London: Yale University Press, 1986.

Snodin and Baker 1980
Michael Snodin and Malcolm Baker. "William Beckford's Silver," parts 1 and 2. *Burlington Magazine* 122, no. 932 (1980): 735–48; no. 933 (1980): 820–34.

Treasure Houses **1985**
The Treasure Houses of Britain. Exh. cat., Washington, D.C.: National Gallery of Art, 1985.

Venn Lansdown 1893
Henry Venn Lansdown. *Recollections of the Late William Beckford.* 1893; reprint, Bath: Kingsmead, 1969.

Waagen 1838
Gustave F. Waagen. *Works of Art and Artists in England.* 3 vols. London: John Murray, 1838.

Wainwright 1989
Clive Wainwright. *The Romantic Interior: The British Collector at Home, 1750–1850.* New Haven and London: Yale University Press, 1989.

William Beckford **(Bath) 1966**
Summers, Peter. *William Beckford. Some notes on his life in Bath, 1822–1844.* Exh. cat., Holburne of Menstrie Museum. Bath: n.p., 1966.

William Beckford **(Salisbury) 1976**
The William Beckford Exhibition. Exh. cat. Tisbury, Wiltshire: The Compton Press, 1976.

A. Source Notes

The Early Years

1. *William Beckford*

1. Robert Drysdale, quoted in Oliver 1932, p. 9.
2. Quoted in Guy Chapman and John Hodgkin, *A Bibliography of William Beckford of Fonthill* (London: Constable, 1930): 115.
3. Redding 1859, pp. 94–95.
4. Oliver 1932, p. 169.

2. *Maria Hamilton Beckford*

1. Elizabeth (1748–1820) married Col. William Thomas Hervey in 1774. Her novels include *Melissa and Marcia; or the Sisters* (1788), *The Church of St. Siffrid* (1797), and *Amabel: or, Memoirs of a Woman of Fashion* (1814).
2. Robert Drysdale, one of William Beckford's early tutors, wrote that Mrs. Beckford "prefers virtue and Religion to every other accomplishment; may Almighty God succeed her pious devices and contentions in the Religious Education of her son" (quoted in Oliver 1932, p. 5).
3. William Beckford, *Azemia*, vol. 2 (London: Sampson Low, 1797): 103–4. Boyd Alexander suggests that Lady Asinoe may well have had certain characteristics of Mrs. Beckford (Alexander 1962, p. 36).
4. Letter dated 29 November 1796, quoted in Melville 1910, p. 223.
5. Guy Chapman, *Beckford* (London: Jonathan Cape, 1937): 121.
6. The other portraits are of his aunt, Elizabeth, Countess of Effingham (now in the National Gallery of Art, Washington), and his Beckford great-grandparents (now in The Metropolitan Museum of Art, New York). See Helmut von Erffa and Allen Staley, *The Paintings of Benjamin West* (New Haven: Yale University Press, 1986): nos. 615, 592, and 593.
7. Ibid.
8. For further details of the land transaction see Alexander 1962, pp. 219–20.
9. A preparatory drawing, with a slighter sketch, by West for the portrait is in the Pierpont Morgan library, New York. See Ruth S. Kramer, *Drawings by Benjamin West and His Son Raphael Lamar West* (New York: Pierpont Morgan Library, 1975): 71–72, no. 158, pl. 86–87.
10. ". . . a tall, sallow Italian costumed like the portraits of Corelli and whom I remember perfectly well visiting my mother more than half a century ago in the capacity of her teacher of Guitar"; see William Beckford, *The Vision, Liber veritatis*, ed. Guy Chapman (London: Constable and Co., 1930): 94.
11. An account of Mrs. Beckford's death and funeral is given in *Gentleman's Magazine* 68 (July 1798): 637–39.

12. *Catalogue of Family Portraits Works by Old Masters and Modern Pictures the Property of the Trustees of his Grace the late Duke of Hamilton,* sale cat., Christie's, 6 November 1919, lot 74.

3. **Plate**

1. David Sanctuary Howard, *Chinese Armorial Porcelain* (London: Faber and Faber, 1974): 557, Q6.

4. *Fonthill Splendens*

The author would like to thank Gill Jerdan at Sudeley Castle for her help in the prepartion of this entry.

1. Farington *Diary*, vol. 3, p. 726.
2. A pencil and wash drawing by de Cort, very close in detail to the Sudeley painting, was sold at Christie's London, 8 July 1986, lot 46, together with a number of other views dated 1791–92. Two further views by de Cort, lot 45 of the same auction, show the portico at Fonthill House, one with an inscription, implying that the drawings date from 1806.
3. These were sold Phillips' 1807, day 6, 27 August, lots 573 and 574, respectively. Beckford also owned his *The Tomb of Asserius*. A further landscape was included in Christie's 1822, day 7, lot 29, "De Cort, *A Landscape with Ruins and Water*— painted with transparent and very pleasing effect." This reappeared the following year; see Phillips' 1823, day 25, lot 117, which sold for £15 –15 to Hume. It had hung in the Western Nunnery at the Abbey.
4. For further information on de Cort see Ellis Waterhouse, *The Dictionary of British 18th Century Painters* (Woodbridge: Antique Collectors Club, 1981); Luke Hermann, *British Landscape Painting of the Eighteenth Century* (London: Faber and Faber, 1973): 128; John Harris, *The Artist and the Country House* (London: Sotheby Parke Bernet, 1979): 333.

5. *View of Fonthill Splendens from the West*

1. Farington *Diary*, vol. 6 (1978): 2230, entry dated 1 February 1804.

6. *Summer*

The author is greatly indebted to Christopher Woodward and Lady Elizabeth White of the Holburne of Menstrie Museum in Bath, as well as James Lomax of Temple Newsam House, Leeds, for their help with this entry.

1. See Francis Russell, "The Stourhead Batoni and Other Copies after Reni," *National Trust Year-Book* (1975–76): 111.
2. See Edward Croft-Murray, *Decorative Painting in England, 1537–1837*, vol. 2 (Middlesex: Country Life Books, 1970): 182.
3. Britton 1801, vol. 1, pp. 214–15 and 219.
4. The sale of fifty lots was held in London

by Prestage: *Collection of pictures of Chevalier Andrea Casali who is going to reside in Italy*, 18 April 1766. A previous sale, *Chevalier Casali, peintre*, held by Prestage & Hobbs, London, 23–24 March 1762, included forty-two paintings and eight sculptures that Casali had acquired for his dealing purposes.
5. See, for example, *Passages from the Diaries of Mrs Philip Lybbe Powys, of Hardwick House, Oxon., A.D. 1756 to 1808*, ed. Emily J. Climenson (London: Longman & Co., 1899): 166–67. Powys commented on the smaller Casalis on her visit in 1776, as did Richard Warner in his letter from Bath, 5 September 1800, in Warner, *Excursions from Bath* (Bath: R. Crutwell, 1801): 119–27.
6. See *Life at Fonthill*, p. 42.
7. Phillips' 1801; and Phillips' 1807.
8. This sale held in May 1809 in the Market Place, Salisbury, and contained four works by Casali.
9. *Catalogue of the Pictures and Library of Sir Thomas William Holburne Bart.,* (Bath, 1867): nos. 89 and 90, as from Beckford's collection. They were catalogued again as *Figure of Summer* and *Figure of Autumn* by Casali in W. Chaffers, *Catalogue of the Holburne of Menstrie Art Museum* (Bath: Dryden Press, 1887): 70, nos. 1408 and 1409.
10. This attribution is repeated in *Catalogue of Pictures and Miniatures*, part 1 (n.p., 1927): 49; and *Catalogue of Pictures*, part 1 (n.p., 1936): 48–49.
11. This attribution was made by M. Olivier Michel, Librarian of the French School in Rome.

7. *Tobias and the Archangel Raphael Returning with the Fish*

1. J. D. Passavant, *Tour of a German Artist in England*, vol. 1 (London: Saunders & Otley, 1836): 318. The painting was particularly admired by G. F. Waagen, who called it "a real masterpiece in clearness, extreme delicacy in the gradation, and felt execution"; see Waagen 1838, vol. 3, pp. 124–25.
2. Christie's 1882, 17 June, lot 64. This is considered to be the best version of this work; see Malcolm Waddington, "Elsheimer Revised," *Burlington Magazine* 114 (September 1972): 610. It was most recently in *The Estate of Walter P. Chrysler Jr.*, sale cat., Sotheby's, New York, 1 June 1989, lot 39.
3. See Michael Levey, *National Gallery Catalogues: The German School* (London: The National Gallery, 1959): 40–42; and Keith Andrews, *Adam Elsheimer*, rev. ed. (Munich, Schirmer/Mosel, 1985): 33 and pl. 40. For earlier references, see Willi Drost, *Adam Elsheimer und sein Kreis* (Potsdam: Akademische Verlagsgesellschaft Athenaion, 1933): 87 and ill. no. 37 (as

after Elsheimer); Heinrich Weizsäcker, *Adam Elsheimer: Der Maler von Frankfurt* (Berlin, Deutscher verein für Kunstwissenschaft, 1936): and ibid., rev. ed. (1952) ed. Hans Möhle, cat. and sources, vol. 1, p.123 and vol. 2, pp. 13–14, no. 9.
4. See Keith Andrews, *Adam Elsheimer* (Oxford: Phaidon, 1977): 33; Andrews also gives the various former attributions for the painting exhibited here (ibid., p. 154, cat. no. 25).
5. Britton 1801, vol. 1, p. 218.
6. Beckford bought at least ten paintings from this sale in 1823, which occurred as the result of the Taylors' conspicuous overspending and bankruptcy; see Hugh Roberts, "'Quite Appropriate for Windsor Castle': George IV and George Watson Taylor," *Furniture History: The Journal of the Furniture History Society* 36 (2000): 115–37.
7. Waagen 1838, vol. 2, p. 229. Waagen wrote that it was "As powerful in colour as it is delicate and solid in execution."
8. To add to the insult Farrer then offered the picture to the National Gallery at a ten-percent profit, but it was refused. See David Robertson, *Sir Charles Eastlake and the Victorian Art World* (Princeton, N.J.: Princeton University Press, 1978): 187.

Coming of Age

8. *William Beckford*

1. Beckford first sat for the portrait between 4 June 1781 and 30 March 1782; see H. Ward and J. Roberts, *Romney*, vol. 2 (New York: Charles Scribner's Sons, 1904): 9.
2. Letter to Lady Hamilton, 14 October 1781, in Melville 1910, pp.121–22.
3. For Beckford's full account of the Christmas festivities, written in 1838, see Oliver 1932, p. 89–91.
4. A suggestion made by Alastair Laing, *In Trust for the Nation: Paintings from National Trust Houses* (London: National Trust, 1995): 34.
5. Ibid.
6. Beckford in December 1791 paid £105 for the portrait of his daughters.
7. *Catalogue of Family Portraits Works by Old Masters and Modern Pictures the property of the Trustees of his Grace the late Duke of Hamilton,* sale cat., Christie's, 6–7 November 1919, lot. 55.

9. **Pair of Candlesticks**

1. Rutter 1823a.

10. **Snuffer Tray**

1. For example, the Earl of Mount Edgecumbe's account with Wakelin and Garrard, 1800, charges £28 15s for "gilding . . . in the best manner in two colours" (Victoria and Albert Museum, Gentleman's Ledger, GL 21AS, f11).

11. Bowl

No notes.

12. Wine Coaster

1. For notes on the Beckford arms, see Rutter 1823a.

2. The Carlton House examples are now in a private collection; for the Bute examples see C. Hartop, *The Huguenot Legacy: English Silver 1680–1760* (London: Thomas Heneage, 1996): 382, illus.

13–19. Beckford and *Cozens*

1. Various references in Joseph Farington's diaries of 1796–97 note Beckford's interests in promoting and collecting contemporary English art; see Farington *Diary*, vol. 3, pp. 726 and 734; and ibid., vol. 4, pp. 739 and 821.

2. Others included Hoppner, De Loutherbourg, Danby, De Cort, Bonington, Etty, Stothard, Nasmyth, Roberts, and Palmer.

3. Among the other watercolorists that Beckford collected were Warwick Smith, Girtin, Prout, and Shotter Boys.

4. For a brief review of Beckford's collecting tastes, see Boyd Alexander, "William Beckford as Patron," *Apollo* 127 (July 1962): 360–64.

5. On Dalton, see Anne Lyles and Robin Hamlyn, *British Watercolors from the Oppé Collection*, exh. cat. (London: The Tate Gallery, 1997): 64, no. 14. Alexander Cozens' work in Italy was thought lost by Beckford, as he noted in a letter; see Alexander 1962, pp. 46–47. Nearly sixty of these survive, fifty-seven alone in the British Museum.

6. For a discussion of Cozens' teaching here, see Henry Angelo, *The Reminiscences of Henry Angelo*, vol. 1, (1828; reprint, London: Kegan Paul & Co., 1904), 212–15. Among his pupils was Sir George Beaumont who, it was said, was one of the few who made any sense of it.

7. Sloan 1986, p. 74.

8. In a letter to Lady Hamilton of 1777, Beckford remarked that in England he had "no friend like you to to sustain my spirits and receive my ideas except Mr. Cozens whom you have heard me frequently mention"; see Melville 1910, p. 30.

9. Brian Fothergill, *Beckford of Fonthill* (London: Faber and Faber, 1979): 77.

10. As he did in 1779, recommending Goethe's *The Sorrows of Werther*, which had been published only five years earlier: "Read it and tell me if every line is not resplendent with Genius"; Melville 1910, p. 76.

11. In a letter dated 6 February 1780, quoted in Melville 1910, p. 80.

12. A. P. Oppé, *Alexander and John Cozens* (London: Adam and Charles Black, 1952): 34.

13. In 1835 Constable called him "The greatest genius that ever touched landscape," for which see R. B. Beckett, ed., *John Constable's Correspondence: Patrons, Dealers, and Fellow Artists* (Ipswich, 1966),

p. 147. Turner's appreciation began when he and Girtin were employed by Thomas Munro to copy Cozen's works in his collection. Girtin drew the outlines while Turner "washed in the effects"; see Farington *Diary*, vol. 3, p. 1090, entry for 12 November 1798.

14. Pars traveled to Switzerland with Lord Palmerston in 1770, exhibiting the first Alpine views drawn in situ in the Royal Academy the following year, nos. 143–49; see Andrew Wilton, *William Pars' Journey Through the Alps* (Zurich: Clivo Press, 1979).

15. Sloan 1986, pp. 113–114. Cozens remained on the Continent until 1779.

16. Melville 1910, p. 95.

17. Bell and Girtin 1934–34, p. 17.

18. Melville 1910, p. 151.

19. See Oppé, *Alexander and John Cozens* (1952): 144–45.

20. Melville 1910, pp. 152 and 154.

21. Ibid., pp. 155–56.

22. Oppé, *Alexander and John Cozens* (1952): 147.

23. Melville 1910, p. 156–57.

24. Ibid., p. 156.

25. The spectacle was one that constantly intrigued tourists and artists alike, including Wright of Derby in 1776; for further information see Judy Egerton, *Wright of Derby*, exh. cat. (London: Tate Gallery, 1990): 172 and 175–6, nos. 104 and 106.

26. A. P. Oppé, "The Memoirs of Thomas Jones," *Walpole Society* 34 (1951): 113–14. Jones had missed Beckford who had gone to his studio to inspect his work, expressing "his great satisfaction and pleasure, in terms almost extatic [sic]." On the importance of the Jones' *Memoirs*, see Francis W. Hawcroft, *Travels in Italy 1776–1783, Based on the Memoirs of Thomas Jones*, exh. cat. (Manchester: Whitworth Art Gallery, 1988).

27. Melville 1910, pp. 163–64. On the Prangins visit, see chap. 4, by William Hauptman, in this volume.

28. Oppé, "Memoirs of Thomas Jones" (1951): 114.

29. Sloan 1986, p. 147.

30. Oppé, *Alexander and John Cozens* (1952): 148.

31. Melville 1910, p. 158. The reference to a "shepherd's hut" too may be to a watercolor by Cozens drawn between Naples and Portici, which is similar in its mood and color to the work exhibited here; it is now in the Victorian and Albert Museum. See Sloan 1986, p. 147.

32. Oliver 1932, p. 126; see also Sloan 1986, p. 149.

33. Bell and Girtin 1934–35, p. 17, refer to his seeing Beckford in October; Oppé, *Alexander and John Cozens* (1952): 114 notes November as the date.

34. See Oppé, *Alexander and John Cozens* (1952): 116.

35. Farington *Diary*, vol. 3, p. 855, entry for 17 June 1797.

20. Teapot and Stand

1. See cat. no. 51 for further information on these pieces. I am grateful to Paul Spencer-Longhurst of the Barber Institute for his help in preparing this catalogue entry.

2. An identical silver-gilt teapot and matching tea caddy by Aaron Lestourgeon, of 1781, was sold by the Duke of Hamilton and Brandon, Sotheby's, London, 14 July 1988, lot 136, and subsequently Sotheby's, New York, 16 April 1996, lot 268. A further pair by the same makers is in the Glasgow Museums. Another teapot of the same date, in silver, maker's mark of Charles Aldridge and Henry Green, is in the Hamilton Collection at Brodick Castle. Given its poor condition and the fact that it is accompanied by a stand made to match by the Parisian silversmith Henri Auguste in 1788, it appears to have accompanied Beckford on his travels.

3. Two other gold eighteenth-century teapots are known, both made in Edinburgh and given as race prizes. See E. Alfred Jones, *Old English Gold Plate* (London: Derby, Bemrose and Sons, 1907): 20; and A. Grimwade, "A New List of Old English Gold Plate," *Connoisseur* 127 (May 1951): 86–87.

4. Sir Charles Jackson, *English Goldsmiths and their Marks*, rev. ed. (Woodbridge, UK: Antique Collectors Club, 1989): 58.

5. Ibid., p. 86.

21–24. Beckford and *Vathek*

1. Cyrus Redding. "Recollections of the Author of 'Vathek'," *New Monthly Magazine* 71 (May–August 1844): 150.

2. In Stéphanie Félicité Brulart de Genlis, Marchioness de Sillery, *Théâtre à l'usage des jeunes personnes*, 4 vols. (Paris: Panckoucke, 1779–80); English trans., *Theatre of Education*, 4 vols. (London: T. Cadell, & P. Elmsly; T. Durham, 1781); German & Italian trans. in 1780, and Dutch in 1786–88; English trans. reissued in *The Beauties of Genlis* (Perth: Morison, 1787): 151–90.

3. Guy Chapman, *Beckford* (London: Jonathan Cape, 1937): 145.

4. William Beckford. *The Episodes of Vathek*, trans. Sir Frank Marzials (London: Swift, 1912).

5. Chapman, *Beckford* (1937): 202.

6. For a list of all Beckford's works published in his lifetime, see Guy Chapman and John Hodgkin, *A Bibliography of William Beckford of Fonthill* (London: Constable, 1930).

7. André Parreaux, "Beckford's *Vathek*, "Londres 1791," *The Book Collector* 7 (1958): 297–99.

8. William Beckford, *Vathek*, ed. Richard Garnett (London: Lawrence & Bullen, 1893): v, xix–xxiv.

9. Marcel May, *La jeunesse de William Beckford et la genèse de son "Vathek"* (Paris: Les Presses Universitaires de France, 1928).

10. A. O. Hunter, "Le *Vathek* de William Beckford: Historique des éditions françaises," *Revue de littérature comparée* 15 (January–March 1935): 119–26.

11. John Carter, "The Lausanne Edition of Beckford's *Vathek*," *The Library*, 4th series 17, no. 4 (March 1937): 369–94.

12. André Parreaux, *William Beckford, Auteur de Vathek (1760–1844)*, Etude de la création littéraire (Paris: Nizet, 1960).

13. MS Beckford c.49.

14. William Beckford, *Vathek*, ed. Roger Lonsdale (London: Oxford Univ. Press, 1970).

25. Toasting Fork

1. One of 1793, maker's mark of Phipps and Robinson, specialist makers of small utilitarian items, was sold by the Duke of Hamilton, Sotheby's, 24 June 1980, lot 278; a pair of silver-gilt examples, by the partnership of Phillips, Phipps and Robinson, 1813, remain at Lennoxlove.

2. Per Kalm, *Account of his Visit to England on his Way to America in 1748*, trans. Joseph Lucas (London: Macmillan, 1892).

26. Basket

1. This basket, unknown to Snodin and Baker in 1980 other than from its description in the Fonthill sale catalogues, was first identified as Beckford's by Timothy Schroder whose excellent 1984 catalogue entry has provided the basis for this entry; see Schroder, *The Gilbert Collection of Gold and Silver* (Los Angeles: Thames and Hudson, 1988): 324–27.

2. Redding 1859, p. 123. Redding was relying on contemporary, and probably erroneous, newspaper accounts.

3. W. Gregory, *The Beckford Family: Reminiscences of Fonthill Abbey and Lansdown Tower* (London: Simpkin, Marshall, Hamilton, Kent & Co., 1898): 38.

4. Cf. the example of 1750–51, maker's mark of Samuel Courtauld, in the Hartman Collection, Museum of Fine Arts, Boston, discussed in Christopher Hartop, *The Huguenot Legacy: English Silver 1680–1760* (London: Thomas Heneage, 1996): 230–31.

5. Michael Snodin first drew attention to the importance of Boileau. In his analysis of the Boileau designs he discussed the similarities between Boileau's design for silver-gilt ewers at Woburn Abbey and Moitte's designs for Beckford's gold ewer supplied by Auguste; see Snodin, "J. J. Boileau: A Forgotten Designer of Silver," *Connoisseur* (June 1978): 124–33.

6. Christie's 1822, day 9, lots 73 and 74; Phillips' 1823, day 17, "The Oak and Tapestry Dining Parlour," lots 817 and 818.

7. Snodin and Baker 1980, part 2, p. 820.

8. See David Watkin, *Thomas Hope and the Neo-Classical Idea* (London: Murray, 1968): 54; two baskets of similar form, engraved with the arms of Sir Alexander Grant, Bt. (died 1825) were formerly in

the Moss Collection and illustrated in *The Lillian and Morrie Moss Collection of Paul Storr Silver* (Memphis: Brooks Memorial Art Gallery, 1968): 220.

9. *A Regency Visitor: The English Tour of Prince Pückler-Muskau, Described in his Letters 1826–1828* (New York: Dutton, 1958): 211.

10. Sale of 26 April 1937, lot 20.

11. Sotheby's, London, 15 October 1970, lot 79.

27 and 28. **The Stadholder Service**

1. Much of the basic information for this entry is derived from Abraham L. den Blaauwen, *The Meissen Service of Stadholder Willem V* (Zwolle/Apeldoorn, 1993). Rutter stated: "fitted on one side with armoires and shelves, the latter of which carry part of the fine Dresden service which is in the oak parlour," Rutter 1823a, pp. 10–13. Information kindly supplied by Bet McLeod.

2. Den Blaauwen, *Meissen Service* (1992).

3. Ibid., p. 17.

4. Ibid.

5. For an example, see Maureen Cassidy-Geiger, "Graphic Sources for Meissen Porcelain: Origins of the Print Collection in the Meissen Archives," *Metropolitan Museum Journal* 31(1996): 117 (sheet 7. Het Dorp ZUYLEN: …).

6. During the same period, another large Meissen service of mixed rococo patterns, including the same model tureen but with a putto in place of the armorial lion, painted with a mélange of subjects, with no obvious unifying theme, was presented to Count Aleksej Grigorevitsch of Orlov-Tschesmenskij, a brother of Catherine the Great's favorite. See Gisela Reineking von Bock, ed., *Prunkvolles Zarenreich/ Eine Dynastie blickt nach Westen 1613–1917,* exh. cat. (Cologne, 1996): 235–37, cat. nos. 183–90.

7. For a general discussion of the subject, see Winfried Baer, "Veduta Painting on Porcelain in the Eighteenth-Century," in *Along the Royal Road,* exh. cat. (New York: Bard Graduate Center, 1993): 54–65.

8. I was greatly aided by Jan Daniël van Dam of the Rijksmuseum and Edward Impey of Historic Royal Palaces in the research presented in this section. For more on Willem V in exile, see W. Fritschy, "De financiën van de Oranjes tussen revolutie en restauratie," in *Jaarboek Oranje* (Nassau Museum, 1996): 35–65; and Thomas H. von der Dunk, "Een vorstelijke balling als tourist, De reizen van voormalig stadhouder Willem V in Engeland 1795–1801," in ibid. (References courtesy of J.D. van Dam and copied exactly from facsimile correspondence.)

9. Ernest Law, *The History of Hampton Court Palace,* vol. 3 (London: G. Bell and Sons, 1891): 319–23.

10. This idea was suggested to me by Edward Impey.

29. **Hall Settee**

1. E. White, *Pictorial Dictionary of British Eighteenth Century Furniture Designs* (Woodbridge, Eng.: Antique Collectors' Club, 1990):143.

30. *View of the Monastery of Batalha, Portugal*

1. William Beckford, *Recollections of An Excursion to the Monasteries of Alcobaça and Batalha,* ed. Boyd Alexander (London: Centaur Press, 1972): 66.

2. Letter 674, Hamilton/Nelson Papers, 1894, vol. 2, p.193, British Library, London.

3. See James Murphy, "Sketches of Batalha Abbey," ca. 1788, MS 260, Portugal, Society of Antiquaries, London.

4. See Kenneth Clark, *The Gothic Revival* (London, John Murray. 1962): 89.

BECKFORD AND HERALDRY

Introduction

1. Sir Bernard Burke, *The General Armoury of England, Scotland, Ireland and Wales, etc,* (London: Harrison and Sons, 1884); Alexander Nisbet, *A System of Heraldry Speculative and Practical with the True Art of Blazon, according to the most approved heralds in Europe, etc.,* 2d ed. (Edinburgh: Alex. Lawrie, 1804).

31. **Pair of Candlesticks**

1. A kettle on lampstand of 1742, maker's mark of George Wickes, engraved with the Alderman's arms, shows that his silver was of the highest quality but conventional in design.

2. See Major-General H. D. W. Sitwell, "The Jewel House and the Royal Goldsmiths," *Archaeological Journal* 117 (1960): 152.

3. A. Grimwade, *London Goldsmiths: Their Marks and Lives, 1697–1837,* rev. ed. (London: Faber and Faber, 1990): 766.

4. Three drawings in Sir John Soane's Museum, London, show candlesticks of similar form, although with spiral and straight fluting to the surfaces. Although this version was executed in silver by John Carter beginning in 1767, it seems likely that the plainer form of the Beckford version, in addition to being more elegant, was also easier to make and better at reflecting the light from the candles.

5. A set of four dating to 1775, maker's mark of Smith and Sharp, were advertised by Brand Inglis in 1988. Four from the Harewood House set, made by the partnership of Richard Carter, Daniel Smith and Robert Sharp,were sold by Christie's, London, 30 June 1965, lot 85. Four of the 1791 date by John Scofield, are on loan to the Victoria and Albert Museum; for an illustration see R. Rowe, *Adam Silver* (London: Faber and Fabr, 1965): pl. 96.

8. Snodin and Baker 1980, part 2, pp. 824–45.

32. **Bowl**

1. I am most grateful to Rosemary Watt of Glasgow Museum and Art Gallery for her help in preparing this catalogue entry.

2. V. Gibbs, ed., *The Complete Peerage,* vol. 6 (London, 1916–26): 275.

33–36. **Worcester and Heraldry**

1. I would like to thank Hilary Young for his assistance in the preparation of this entry.

37. **Bowl**

1. I am grateful to Sharon-Michi Kusunoki of the Edward James Foundation for her help in preparing this catelogue entry.

2. I am grateful to Catherine Delacour of the Musée Guimet, Paris, John Adamson and Colin Sheaf for their help in identifying the bowl.

3. For the Leigh cup see J. F. Hayward et al., *Historic Plate of the City of London* exh. cat. (London: Goldsmiths' Hall, 1951): plate 2; for the Beaufort cup see R. A. Crighton, *Cambridge Plate,* exh. cat. (Cambridge: Fitzwilliam Museum, 1975): B2.

38. **Bowl**

1. Sir Francis Watson, *Mounted Oriental Porcelain,* exh. cat. (New York: Frick Collection, 1986): 128.

2. Victoria and Albert Museum, Department of Prints and Drawings, E.3–1972. I am very grateful to Bet McLeod for her insights into these drawings.

39. **Cup and Cover**

1. The workshop reopened in the early nineteenth century but was not to regain its position until the second half of the century.

2. In a 1714 manuscript in the library of the Kunsthistorisches Institut, Florence, Giuseppe Toricelli notes: "From France we get lapis lazuli. It is different from the Persian lapis: the mine contains a lot of copper therefore the lapis is very green. It polishes well"; quoted in A. M.Massinelli, *The Gilbert Collection, Hardstones* (London: Philip Wilson Publishers in association with The Gilbert Collection, 2000): 225. Specialist mineralogists are unaware of a French source for this stone and it is likely that it was imported to France and then continued on to Italy.

3. Snodin and Baker 1980, part 2, p. 821.

4. John Culme (personal communication, 2001) has suggested that by then he could have been working for a retailer which raises further questions how Beckford came to commission him.

5. By 1819 this would not necessarily have been a term of disparagement as Methodism was by then an accepted part of the establishment.

6. Alexander, *Life at Fonthill,* p. 312.

7. Snodin and Baker 1980, part 2, p. 833, G136

8. John Culme came across instances of this in royal inventories as far back as Elizabeth I, where it was apparently quite usual for the silver gilt to be termed gold plate. Electrogilt metal has been called gold in reports of English visitors to maharajas' palaces, equipped by English manufacturers in the 1880s.

9. Christie's 1882, 19 July, lot 2028, bought by W. Massey-Mainwaring for £787.10s.

40–44. **Tea Service**

1. For an explanation of the badge, see T. Woodcock and John Martin Robinson, *The Oxford Guide to Heraldry* (Oxford: Oxford University Press, 1988): 197.

2. The drawing is pasted to the back of p. 103

BECKFORD AS FRANCOPHILE

45. *Lady in a Red Corset and Satin Dress*

I am most grateful to Christian Carritt for giving me permission to quote from David Carritt's papers. I also thank Colin Anson and Timothy Bathurst of Artemis Fine Arts Ltd. for their help and Francis Russell for his kind guidance.

1. Britton 1801, vol. 1, p. 239.

2. See the letters recording the meeting in Oliver 1932, pp.166–67.

3. See Britton 1801, vol. 1, p. 239.

4. John Rutter, *A New Guide to Fonthill Abbey* (1822): 39–40.

5. "Inventory of 1844," p. 29.

6. Pierre de Nolhac, *J-H. Fragonard, 1732–1806* (Paris: Goupil, 1906): 144; it is listed in the catalogue as from the Fonthill Collection, in this edition only.

7. As noted in his diary for the period 1975–78; see David Carritt, *Through Wood and Dale* (London: John Murray, 1998): 224.

46. **Pair of Vases**

1. Christie's 1882, lot 248, ill. p. 39.

2. The author is indebted to Bet McLeod for generously sharing not only her essay prior to publication, but also for her very helpful research notes and observations concerning the Metropolitan Museum's vases.

3. "Inventory of 1844," book 2, p. 48. I thank Bet McLeod for bringing this information to my attention.

4. "List of Articles of Vertu Furniture etc etc sent from Bath to Hamilton Palace," 1 February 1849, Hamilton MSS, NRA (S) 3438. This information was kindly provided by Bet McLeod.

5. Christie's 1822, day 10, lot 14.

6. *An Aspect of Collecting Taste* (New York: Stair Sainty Matthiesen, 1986): cat. no. 17.

7. This observation was first made by Bet McLeod. The present whereabouts of the Besenval vases are unknown.

8. Christie's 1822, day 3, lot 15*. It is almost certain that this pair can be identified as the pair sold at Christie's, London, 1953, lot 20, illus., purchased by Sangeorgi, present whereabouts unknown.

9. See chap. 9, by Bet McLeod, in this volume.

10. Ibid.; and *Life at Fonthill*, pp. 151–52.

11. See, for example, sale catalogue, Randon de Boisset, Paris, 27 February 1777, pp. 74–82; and *Le Cabinet du Duc D'Aumont*, sale cat., 1782 (facsimile reprint, New York: Acanthus Books, 1986).

12. I thank Bet McLeod for her insights and observations concerning Beckford's collecting tastes.

13. Attributions for the 1822 sale catalogue from Bet McLeod; see chap. 9 in this volume.

14. The attribution of the gilt-bronze mounts of the Metropolitan Museum's vases remains uncertain. François-Thomas Germain is, in fact, a plausible suggestion as a maker, but any number of metal-workers could have produced these mounts, which are of very high quality. Among the names that have been suggested is that of Jean-Joseph de Saint-Germain, who is known to have used boy terms on his clock cases somewhat similar to those found on the vases, and who often worked in a style that simultaneously employed both rococo and neoclassical motifs.

15. In contrast, the pair of mounted vases with the peach-relief decoration were sold to Farquhar; the vases appear in Philips' 1823, day 30, lot 1205, and were sold to the dealer Emmerson. I thank Bet McLeod for this information.

16. "Inventory of 1844."

47. Clock

1. See Hans Ottomeyer and Peter Proschel, *Vergoldete Bronzen,* vol.1 (Munich: Klinkhardt and Biermann, 1986): 166, no.3.4.1.

48. Two Plates

1. David Peters, *Decorators and Date Marks on 18th Century Vincennes and Sevres Porcelain* (London: privately published, 1997): 46.

2. Ibid., p. 55.

3. See Tamara Préaud, "Competition from Sèvres porcelain," *Derby Porcelain International Society Journal* 4 (2000): 38–48; see also David Peters, "The Decoration and Decorators of Late-Eighteenth-Century Sèvres Porcelain in the Bowes Museum," *Burlington Magazine* 1058, no. 133 (May 1991): 306–11. John and Josephine Bowes exemplify the British collectors at mid-century.

4. The large folio album was first published by Marcelle Brunet, "Sèvres: les grands acheteurs choisissaient dans cet album," *Connaissance des Arts*, no. 170 (April 1966): 102–9. Although the article includes fifteen illustrations, none shows the "parasol chinois, arabesques" design. However, it has been recently illustrated in color together with others; see Préaud, "Competition" (2000): 41, pl. 5.

5. John Whitehead, "Some French Purchases by William Beckford," *Beckford Journal* 2 (spring 1996): 41.

6. I am indebted to Bet McLeod, who has kindly discussed the history of the plates with me, for this suggestion.

7. Christie's, London, sale cat. Croxteth Hall, Liverpool, 17 September 1973, lot 888. I owe this reference to John Whitehead.

49. Two Cups and Saucers

1. Aileen Dawson, *A Catalogue of French Porcelain in the British Museum,* rev. ed. (London: British Museum, 2000), no. 270.

2. R. de Plinval de Guillebon, *Paris Porcelain,* trans. R. Charleston (London: Barrie and Jenkins, 1972): 142, fig. 102.

3. There are two examples in the British Museum collection, one marked with a gold anchor, both from Blenheim Palace; see E. Adams, *Chelsea Porcelain* (London, British Museum Press, forthcoming): figs 12.2 and 12.3.

4. Dawson, *Catalogue* (2000): 366.

5. For a discussion of these cups and saucers and their various marks, see Bet McLeod, "In Lucifer's Metropolis: Willam Beckford's Collection of French Porcelain," *Journal of the French Porcelain Society* 16 (2001).

6. Ibid.

7. Ibid.

8. This suggestion was made in ibid.

9. Ibid.

10. Much valuable work has been done by Régine de Plinval de Guillebon, principally in *La Porcelaine de Paris 1770–1850* (Fribourg: Office du Livre, 1972); idem, "La manufacture de porcelaine de Dihl et Guérhard rue de Bondy, et rue du Temple," *Bulletin de la Société de l'histoire de Paris et de l'Ile de France* 109 (1982): 177–212; idem, "La manufacture de porcelaine de Guérhard et Dihl dite du duc d'Angoulême," *The Journal of the French Porcelain Society, London* 4 (1988). For additional publications by this author, see the bibliography in Dawson, *Catalogue* (2000).

11. Dawson, *Catalogue* (2000): 357–58.

12. Services belonging to the Marquis de Luzerne, French ambassador in London, were sold from his house in Portman Square, London, in March 1792, see ibid., p. 357.

13. Rutter 1822, p. 48.

14. See Philip Hewat-Jaboor, "An Early Nineteenth Century Dihl and Guerhard Porcelain Cup and Saucer made for William Beckford," *Beckford Journal* 2 (spring 1996): 7–8.

50. Design for a Ewer and Basin

1. I would like to thank Bet McLeod, Christopher Hartop, and Michael Snodin for their assistance in preparing this entry. For works Beckford commisioned from Auguste, see Snodin and Baker 1980, part 1, pp. 736–38; for a useful list of Beckford's French silver, see ibid., part 2, appendix, pp. 826–27. For the catalogue record on the Gilbert ewer and basin, see Timothy B. Schroder, *The Gilbert Collection of Gold and Silver* (Los Angeles: Thames and Hudson, 1988): 617–21; it relates the pieces to Moitte's drawings.

2. For detailed accounts of Moitte's career and oeuvre, see Richard James Campbell, "Jean-Guillaume Moitte: The Sculpture and Graphic Art, 1785–1799," Ph.D. diss., Brown University, 1982 (University of Michigan Microfilms, Ann Arbor, 1983); and see also Gisela Gramaccini, *Jean-Guillaume Moitte,1746–1810: Leben und Werk,* 2 vols. (Berlin: Akademie Verlag, 1993).

3. In 1766, he won the Prix de la Tête d'expression and the second Prix de Sculpture for his bas-relief, *Alexandre buvan le breuvage que lui présente son médécin Philippe.*

4. For a detailed consideration of his work for Ledoux, see Campbell, "Moitte" (1983): 34–47.

5. See the Quatremère de Quincy, *Funerailles de M.Moitte* (1810): 495–96.

6. "M. Moitte se fit remarquer dès ses premiers pas dans la carrière, par des dessins nombreux qui, en manifestant son goût, répandirent aussi celui de l'antiquité, dont il se montrait le disciple. Sa manière en général respirait et inspirait le grand," in ibid.

7. In 1768, he was awarded the Prix de Rome for his bas-relief, *David portant la tête de Goliath en triomphe,* and from 1768 to 1771, he attended the Ecole Royale des Elèves Protegés, in preparation for his three-year sojourn in Rome. In the end, however, he only spent two years in Rome owing to his continuing ill health.

8. Examples of these sketches, which include depictions of monuments in Rome and the Roman campagna, are reproduced in Gramaccini, *Moitte,* vol. 2 (1993): 158–84. Most of the sketches are in the archives of the Institut de France and the Ecole des Beaux-Arts. His study of antique examples would also have been supplemented by a study of casts after the antique, which were displayed at the Académie at the Palazzo Mancini; see E. Tollfree, "Napoleon and the 'New Rome': Rebuilding Imperial Rome in Late Eighteenth- and Early Nineteenth-Century Paris," Ph.D. diss, University of Bristol, 1999, chap. 2, pp. 66–73.

9. One of the most important printed sources on ancient art which was available at this time was Le Comte de Caylus, *Recueil d'antiquités égyptiennes, étrusques, grecques, et romains* (1756–67). Other sources which would undoubtedly have assisted Moitte with his designs for metal-work later on were Vien's *Suite des vases* (1760) and Delafosse's *Nouvelle iconologie historique* (1768). Interestingly, on his return to Paris, Moitte joined the Paris Académie de Saint-Luc and became a colleague of Delafosse, who was already an academician there.

10. For the most recent catalogue record for the drawing, see Timothy Clifford, *Designs of Desire: Architectural and Ornamental Prints and Drawings, 1500–1850,* exh. cat. (Edinburgh: National Galleries of Scotland, 1999): 280, cat. no. 141.

11. Moitte's design for this basin, which was acquired by Beckford, has been dated to 1787 and several other of his designs for metalwork craters, vases, and basins have been dated to ca.1788–90 (see Gramaccini, *Moitte,* vol. 2 [1993]: 248–53, figs. 219–28). A drawing in the Ecole des Beaux-Arts, which was donated by the son of Edouard Gatteaux, a former pupil of Moitte, includes a basin similar to the two owned by Beckford and can be dated to 22 September 1794–22 September 1795; see Campbell, "Moitte" (1983): 182–83 and fig 38.

12. On the significance of Piranesi to students at the Académie in Rome from the 1740s, see Tollfree, "Napoleon" (1999): 27–28.

13. Gramaccini, *Moitte,* vol. 2 (1993): 252, fig. 227; and Campbell, "Moitte" (1983): 184.

14. Gramaccini, *Moitte,* vol. 2 (1993): 253, fig. 228.

51. Ewer and Basin

I am grateful to Lewis Smith and Michael Koopman of Rare Art (London) Ltd. for arranging for me to examine this ewer and basin.

1. Timothy B. Schroder, *The Gilbert Collection of Gold and Silver* (Los Angeles: Thames and Hudson, 1988): 617, no. 168.

2. Rutter 1823a, p. 11

3. A pair of lacquer cabinets with mounts by Auguste, probably designed by Moitte, were in Christie's 1882, 17 June, lots 172 and 173, and are now at Elton Hall, Cambridgeshire; a related, larger, cabinet is in a private collection; a jewel cabinet, based on a design by Moitte inscribed "diamantaire de Lord Beckford" and "Henri Auguste" was recently on the art market; see L. Morton, ed., *Partridge: Recent Acquisitions* (London: Partridge Fine Arts, 1998): no. 59.

4. This ewer appears in Willes Maddox's picture of Beckford on his deathbed; it was sold by the Duke of Hamilton, Christie's, London, November 4, 1919, lot 140 and is now in a private French collection; the pair of gold tazze do not appear to have surfaced since sold in 1823

5. Melville 1910, p. 248

6. Given eight years by his creditors to put his affairs in order, Auguste was caught in 1809 attempting to abscond with his stock to England. He fled and died in Haiti in 1816 (see C. Saunier, "Monsieur Auguste," *Gazette des Beaux Arts* 3 (1910): 441–60.

7. Christie's 1822, day 8, lots 78 and 79 (ewers), lots 80 and 81 (basins); Phillips' 1823, day 17, lots 827 and 828 (ewers), lots 829 and 830 (basins). The present set was sold Christie's, Geneva, 26 April 1977, lot 384.

8. M. Bimbenet-Privat and G. de Fontaines, *La Datation de l'Orfèvrerie Parisienne sous l'Ancien Régime* (Paris: Commission des travaux historiques de la ville de Paris, 1995): no. 538.

9. Charles Truman: *The Gilbert Collection of Gold Boxes* (Los Angeles: Los Angeles County Museum of Art and Harry N. Abrams, 1991): 25. I am very grateful to Charles Truman for his insights into Paris hallmarking during this period.

10. "The Chapelier Law of March 2, 1791, definitely abolished the guilds, but by a remarkable *volte-face* only twenty-nine days later the Constituent Assembly made an exception in favour of the goldsmiths' guilds, which were thereby re-established and thus survived all the other ancient guilds, retaining their legal status until finally abolished by the law of 19 Brumaire, An VI" (Louis Carré, *A Guide to Old French Plate* [New York:G. Scribner's Sons, 1931]: 173).

11. Bimbinet-Privat and de Fontaines (*Datation* [1995]: 29) have suggested that the 1789 mark may have been used until the first suppression of the guild in early March 1791. It seems unlikely that however volatile the political situation was between 1791 and 1796 no silver was made and offered for sale, and certainly no significant quantities of unmarked silver that can be dated to this period exist.

12. A significant portion of these was sold Sotheby's, Monaco, 26 November 1979.

13. *Le Neo-classicism français: Dessins des Musées de Province*, exh. cat. (Paris: Grand Palais, 1974): 101.

14. Richard James Campbell, "Jean-Guillaume Moitte: The Sculpture and Graphic Art, 1785–1799," Ph.D. diss., Brown University, 1982 (University of Michigan Microfilms, Ann Arbor, 1983).

15. On 27 February 1792, Beckford wrote to Sir William Hamilton: "Si le roi de Naples est désireaux d'avoir de beaux ouvrages d'or, d'argent ou de bronze, c'est à Auguste qu'il doit s'adresser" (Morton, *Partridge* [1998]: 141).

16. The correspondence refers to Auguste "making restitution," and it may be that Auguste had been given the choice of delivering the commission or returning Beckford's advance. By 22 October 1797, Williams was in prison, and he wrote to Beckford: "I am informed I was denounced by two different persons. I have a great suspicion one is Mr. Auguste."

17. "Beckford anglais de nation étans à Paris dans le mois d'avril 1793 demanda au citoyen Sauvage le project d'un meuble . . . " (Petition to the Commission des Monuments, 29th Brumaire, An II (October/November, 1793); Beckford paid an advance of 7,000 livres to the various workmen involved but, interestingly, nothing to Auguste who is not mentioned in the petition but who must have been involved in supplying the cabinet as a related drawing for it was among the Auguste–Moitte drawings (see footnote 4 above). Sauvage, a painter, advertised the completed cabinet in the Journal de Paris in September 1801 (Morton, *Partridge* [1998]: 142).

52. **Casket**

1. William Beckford, *Dreams, Waking Thoughts and Incidents,* ed. Robert J. Gemmett (Rutherford, NJ: Fairleigh Dickenson University Press, 1972): 156–58.

2. The casket was discussed in Snodin and Baker 1980 (part 1, p. 739) in the context of Beckford's other Moitte-designed work, though its location was not known. Michael Snodin later identified the box as in the Toledo Museum of Art.

3. See Gisela Gramaccini, *Jean-Guillaume Moitte, 1746–1810: Leben und Werk,* vol. 2 (Berlin: Akadamie Verlag, 1993): pls. 220–38; and Richard James Campbell, "Jean-Guillaume Moitte: The Sculpture and Graphic Art, 1785–1799," Ph.D. diss., Brown University, 1982 (University of Michigan Microfilms, Ann Arbor, 1983): 178–97.

4. Sold Sotheby Parke Bernet, Monaco, 26 November 1979.

5. National Gallery of Art, Woodner Collection, 1991.190.2; for an illustration see John Pope-Hennesy, *Cellini* (New York: Abbeville Press, 1985): pls. 70–71. I am grateful to Anne Poulet for this suggestion.

6. *Versailles et les tables royales en Europe,* exh. cat. (Paris: Musee National des chateaux de Versailles et de Trianon, 1993): 207–15.

7. They were interpreted in the 1961 sale catalogue as butterflies, symbols of Joséphine; Sotheby's, London, 15 June 1961. The butterfly is sometimes associated with Napoléon's sister, Pauline Borghese.

8. Christie's, London, 9–12 May 1817, lot 75. I am very grateful to Matthew Winterbottom of the Royal Collection, who shared the results of his research on this piece. The receipt and dispatch of the box are recorded in the Jutsham Delivery and Receipt Books, Royal Archives, Windsor.

9. *Carlton House: The Past Glories of George IV's Palace,* exh. cat. (London: Queen's Gallery, 1991): 44.

10. The casket was not among the pieces sold by her descendants at Christie's, London, 4–7 May 1908. I am grateful to Jennifer Pittman, Christie's silver department, New York, for her assistance.

53. **Armchair**

1. Rutter 1823a, pp. 30–311, pl. 5.

2. Phillips' 1823, p. 218.

3. Some stools formerly at Abercairny, Perthshire, were there associated with other seat furniture of a design similar to that of pieces from the Grand Drawing Room at Fonthill. To judge from the rather poor photograph included in an article on this house, in which one of these stools is pictured, it does not seem to represent a piece of the same structural design as those depicted by Rutter, which may themselves inaccurately reproduce Beckford's pieces, and its style suggests French work of the 1780s, rather than the Empire style of other examples in the Grand Drawing Room at Fonthill. Mark Girouard, "Abercairny, Perthshire, " part 2, *Country Life*, 129, no. 3341 (16 March 1961): 587, fig. 9.

4. It seems likely that the representation of the seat furniture in Rutter's plate 5 is not entirely correct. Their triangular pediments extend beyond the width of the backs and the winged chimeras which serve as arm supports rise to a higher level than that of the arms themselves. Neither of these characteristics can be observed in any of the known, extant versions of pieces of this design. Also included in plate 5 is the representation of a famous roll-top desk by J. H. Riesener; see Peter Hughes, *The Wallace Collection, Catalogue of Furniture,* vol 2 (London: Trustees of the Wallace Collection, 1996): 929–40; 191 (F102). Both the pictorial marquetry and the internal fittings of this desk are incorrectly represented in the Rutter illustration, putting into question the general accuracy of his drawings and making possible the assumption that the seat furniture of that room was, in fact, of the design of some of the surviving pieces, rather than precisely like that in Rutter's plate 5.

5. The only other chair that the author of this entry has discovered that includes a back flanked by pilasters and topped by, in this case, a segmental pediment with displayed eagle at its center is a throne in which Napoleon is shown seated. It is included in an engraving after a design by Moitte; see Gisela Gramaccini, *Jean-Guillaume Moitte, 1746–1810: Leben und Werk,* vol. 2 (Akadamie Verlag, 1993): 317, fig. 349.

6. Cardinal Fesch's name is not mentioned on the title page of the catalogue of the auction conducted in Paris by Thiessen-Creteil-Henry on 17 June 1816, but the location of his Parisian residence in the Chausée d' Antin is specified as the source of its contents. The relevant lots are as follows: "[Lot] 444. Douze chaises, seize fauteuils, avec deux canapés, en bois sculpté et doré, et bourrés de crin, sans être couvets; les bras des fauteuils sont soutenus par des chimères ailées, à tête de lion, et des dossiers entourés d' arabesques avec couronement cintré et orné de l' aigle romaine. [Lot] 445. Quatorze chaises, quatorze fauteuils et trois canapés, sans être couverts et semblables aux précédents, à cela pres que les dossiers se terminent en pointe au lieu d' être ronds, et qu' à la place de l'aigle il y deux griffons en regard. [Lot] 446. Six chaises, dix fauteuilles et deux causeuses non couverts, semblables à ceux qui précèdent, à cela près d'une différence d' ornement dans les bras des fauteuils." Since these chairs were in Fesch's Paris house, it seems likely that they were made in that city, though their place of manufacture is by no means certain, and many pieces of related design have been described as Italian. Unfortunately, none of the extant chairs of these described designs can today be certainly identified as having belonged to Fesch, although at least some of them, including Beckford's, probably did.

This entry was prepared before the publication of Lucy Wood, *Le Mobilier du Cardinal Fesch: Napoléon, les Bonapartes et l'Italie,* exh. cat., (Ajaccio: Musée Fesch, 2001). To judge from the quotation made from this catalogue recently by an auction house, the documents referring to furniture made in Rome for Cardinal Fesch describe only the variety of seat furniture decorated with splayed eagles and wreaths in their pediments, not to the variety with triangular pediments and griffins represented by some of the pieces sold in Paris from Fesch's residence there and by all of the pieces owned by Beckford and the chair in this exhibition.

7. Dionisio and/or Lorenzo Santi, *Modèles de Meubles . . .* (Paris: Banceainé, 1828): plate 41, no. 5. The chair illustrated here resembles those with segmental pediments crowning their backs.

8. Thieme-Becker, *Allgemeines Lexikon der Bildenden Künstler,* vol. 39 (Leipzig, 1935): 433.

9. Napoléon used the eagle as an emblem of the French empire he founded, following Roman precedent. A settee from the Sacombe Park Sale, Christie's, 11 October 1993, lot 169, bears a label saying that it belonged to Joachim Murat, King of Naples (1771–1815) who was married to one of Napoléon's sisters. Anatole Demidoff, married to Mathilde Bonaparte, had furniture of this design in the ballroom of his Villa San Donato; see Francis Haskell, *Anatole Demidoff: Prince of San Donato (1812–70)* (London: Trustees of the Wallace Collection, 1994): 24–25; *Palais de San Donato, Florence*, sale cat., Pillet, Le Roy, Mannheim, beginning 15 March 1880, lot 143. Two chairs were reputedly removed from Josephine's Malmaison by Earl Cowley, British Ambassador to Paris, 1852–67, now in the Lady Lever Art Gallery (acc. nos. 4162–3); see sale cat., Sotheby's, London, 14 June 1991, lot 150, and Percy Macquoid, *English Furniture . . . in the Lady Lever Art Gallery . . .* (London, n.d.): no. 410. Seat furniture at

the Dunimarle Museum, Culross, Fife was catalogued in the early twentieth century as having belonged to Napoléon himself; see *French Connections,* exh. cat. (Edinburgh: Her Majesty's Stationery Office and Royal Scottish Museum, 1985): 152, no. 60.

10. Some chairs of similar design but with cruder carving seem likely to have been made in Italy. Alvar Gonzalez-Palacios, *Il Tempio del Gusto,* vol. 2 (Milan: Longanesi, n.d.): 49, fig. 73. It seems entirely possible that purchasers of furniture from the Fesch sale may have expanded their suites by having pieces made to match locally in France or Britain, as well as Italy. A settee composed of four chair-back segments, illustrated in Frances Collard, *Regency Furniture* (Woodbridge, Eng.: Antique Collectors' Club, 1985), plate 14, and presumably that now owned by the Victoria and Albert Museum, London, is very likely a British example of such an imitation. The frieze beneath the pediments on this piece seems narrower and less clearly defined than those on other examples of seat furniture with triangular pediments. It is impossible today to identify with absolute certainty the seat furniture pictured in the Grand Drawing Room at Fonthill. Among the pieces identifiable through photographs, the most likely candidates seem to be those that belonged until recently to the marquesses of Londonderry, namely the armchair in this exhibition and its pair, and the six side chairs included in the 1996 catalogue of the Mallett firm, London, pp. 76–77. These chairs are said to have come from a Londonderry seat, Wynyard Park, Durham, and one is pictured in Giles Worsley, "Wynyard Park, County Durham II," *Country Life* 180, no. 4646 (4 September 1986): 669, fig. 12. Like Beckford, the third Marquess of Londonderry is known to have employed members of the Wyatt family's architectural partnership in the remodeling of both Wynyard Park and his London townhouse during the 1820s and 1830s, near the time of the Fonthill auction through which Beckford's pieces passed. It is possible that one of the Wyatts suggested the purchase of the Fonthill chairs by their new client, Londonderry, though this transference could also have been made later, through other currently unknown parties.

An Eye to the East

54. Ewer

1. The ewer was described and referred to as exhibited in Manchester in A.W. Franks, *Special Exhibition of Works of Art of the Mediaeval, Renaissance, and more recent periods* (London, South Kensington Museum, 1862): 389, Section 20, Glass, no. 4969.

2. Gaston Migeon, *Exposition des art musulmans* (Paris: Manzi Joyant, 1903), no. 988, ill. in the "Album," pl. 63, center.

3. The most successful glassmakers who either made straightforward copies of Islamic vessels or created objects inspired by Islamic enameled and gilded glass, beginning in the 1860s, are Philippe-Joseph Brocard (d. 1896) in Paris, Émile Gallé (1846–1904) in Nancy, Josef and Ludwig Lobmeyr (1828–64 and 1829–1917) in Vienna, and the Salviati Company in Venice. See Stephen Vernoit, *Occidentalism: Islamic Art in the 19th Century, The Nasser D. Khalili Collection of Islamic Art,* vol. 23 (Oxford and London: Oxford University Press, 1997): esp. 220–27; and Stefano Carboni and David Whitehouse, *Glass of the Sultans,* exh. cat. (New York: The Metropolitan Museum of Art and The Corning Museum of Glass, 2001): 297–301 and 306–11.

4. Published in *The Collection of the Late Baroness Batsheva de Rothschild,* sale cat., Christie's, London, 14 December 2000, lot 15, pp. 58–65, esp. 63. The comprehensive entry establishes, for the first time, the provenance of this ewer beginning with Beckford and reconstructs the history of its ownership since 1844.

5. The entries on the two Mughal jades (cat. nos. 55 and 57) deal more extensively with this issue.

6. Published most recently in Carboni and Whitehouse, *Glass of the Sultans* (2001): 249–53, cat. nos. 124, 125. For a general survey, see Stephen Vernoit, "Islamic Gilded and Enamelled Glass in Nineteenth-Century Collections," in Rachel Ward, ed., *Gilded and Enamelled Glass from the Middle East* (London: The British Museum, 1998): 110–15.

7. Two such examples are a handled vase in the Basilique de Sainte-Anne at Apt (Vaucluse) and a beaker, now in the Louvre (inv. no. MAO 6131), which was found under the altar of the Church of Santa Margherita in Orvieto. For the vase, see Michael Rogers, "European Inventories as a Source for the Distribution of Mamluk Enamelled Glass," in R. Ward, *Gilded and Enamelled Glass* (1998): 69–73, fig. 17.2; and Stefano Carboni, *Glass from Islamic Lands. The Al-Sabah Collection* (New York: Thames and Hudson, 2001): 356–59, cat. no. 98. The beaker is illustrated in *Europa und der Orient,* exh. cat. (Berlin: Martin-Gropius-Bau, 1989): cat. no. 4/54, colorpl. 213.

8. The Metropolitan Museum of Art, inv. no. 41.150; see Carboni and Whitehouse, *Glass of the Sultans* (2001): 254–56, cat. no. 126.

9. The vase is now in the Museum of Islamic Art, Qatar; see ibid., pp. 260–63, cat. no. 129.

10. Book 5, p. 77, Drawing Room, as reported in *Collection . . . Rothschild* (2000): 65.

11. Hamilton Muniments, List of Pictures, Furniture, Ornaments, China, etc. sent from Bath to Easton Park up to August 1848, Hamilton MSS. misc. m. 12.50.

12. Gustave Schmoranz, *Old Oriental Gilt and Enamelled Glass Vessels* (Vienna and London: G. Norman and Sons, 1899): pl. 30; Migeon, *Exposition* (1903); Carl Johan Lamm, *Mittelalterliche Gläser und Steinschnittarbeiten aus dem Nahen Osten* (Berlin: D. Reimer, 1929–30): 328 and pl. 126:19.

13. Space does not permit a comparative art-historical analysis of this work. Suitable parallels are the bottle in the Metropolitan Museum mentioned above and the objects discussed in the catalogue entry quoted in note 9. Large-figure horsemen are also evident on: a canteen in the British Museum (see Carboni and Whitehouse, *Glass of the Sultans* [2001]: 247–49, cat. no. 123); a bottle in Vienna (see above, n. 7); beaker in the Louvre (see above n. 8); and another beaker in the Grünes Gewölbe in Dresden (Lamm, *Mittelalterliche Gläser* [1929–30]: pl. 129:3). A fragmentary bottle or bowl in the Al-Sabah Collection in Kuwait is the only comparable object that also shares the blue background with the Beckford Ewer (Carboni and Whitehouse, *Glass of the Sultans* [2001]: 339–39, cat. no. 89a).

55. Water Pipe *(Hookah)*

1. As suggested by A. R. E. North

2. Carved jade dish, Dar al Athar al-Islamiyyah, LNS 320 HS, probably Deccan third quarter seventeenth century; for a comparable eighteenth-century Indian carved jade described as a "lamp-stand," see *Catalogue of a Special Exhibition of Hindustan Jade in the National Palace Museum* (Taipei, 1983), pl. 65. Robert Skelton (personal communication) has suggested that an Ottoman or Turkestan origin for this piece cannot be discounted, since the carving of the ewer also presents similarities with these lesser know traditions.

3. See Mark Zebrowski, *Gold, Silver, and Bronze from Mughal India* (London: Alexandria Press in association with Laurence King, 1997): pls 189–97 and 352–53.

4. Ibid., pls. 361–166, 402–5.

5. Basil Gray, ed., *The Arts of India* (Oxford: Phaidon, 1981): 185; and Robert Skelton, *The Indian Heritage Court Life and Arts Under Mughal Rule,* exh. cat. (London, Victoria and Albert Museum, 1982), no. 366 for descriptions of the corpus.

6. Information supplied by Bet McLeod.

7. *Tigers Round the Throne: The Court of Tipu Sultan* (London: Zamana Gallery, 1990): 14.

8. Ibid., p.38.

9. Timothy Mowl, *William Beckford: Composing for Mozart* (London: J. Murray, 1998): 30–31, 122.

10. See chap. 3, by Philip Hewat-Jaboor, in this catalogue.

11. See Mildred Archer, Christopher Rowell, and Robert Skelton, *Treasures from India: The Clive Collection at Powis Castle* (New York: Meridith Press and The Clive Museum, 1987); and *Tigers* (1990), passim.

12. The collection is now in the Berlin Museum. See Skelton, *Indian Heritage* (1982): 51, no. 90. For a full discussion of the relationship bewtween Beckford and Polier, see William Hauptman, "Beckford, Brandoin, and the 'Rajah': Aspects of an Eighteenth-Century Collection," *Apollo* 143 (May 1996): 30–39. My thanks to Philip Hewat-Jaboor for this reference.

13. Philips' 1823, lot 1541. The provenance must still be treated with caution, due both to the uncertainty of the place of production of the jade component and to Beckford's unfortunate tendency to manufacture evidence, see Mowl, *Beckford* (1998): 1.

56. Ladle

1. An agate cup and cover by James Aldridge, 1815–16, The Victoria and Albert Museum

2. Snodin and Baker 1980, part 2, p. 821, n.19, Sheet 6.

3. "Inventory of 1844."

57. Vase and Cover

1. Robert Skelton, *The Indian Heritage Court Life and Arts Under Mughal Rule,* exh. cat. (London, Victoria and Albert Museum, 1982), nos. 40 and 49. I wish to thank Robert Skelton and Manijeh Bayani-Wolpert for discussing these two pieces with me and for assistance in reading the inscription.

2. See Mark Zebrowski, *Gold, Silver, and Bronze from Mughal India* (London: Alexandria Press in association with Laurence King, 1997): pls.269, 273, 274, 695, 697.

3. Skelton, *Indian Heritage* (1982): 15.

4. There is the possibility that that the "rubies" may be foil-backed colored glass. This suggestion, made by Derek Ostergard who examined the piece at Brodick Castle on 6 January 2001, is based on the fact that where the red elements taper in plan and elevation towards the points of their bezel set patterns, the color remains consistent and equal to the other, square-cut and thicker red elements.

5. For Chinese porcelains see Basil Gray, "The Export of Chinese Porcelain to India" in *Transactions of the Oriental Ceramic Society, 1964–66* (London: Oriental Ceramic Society, 1967): 21–37; Skelton, *Indian Heritage* (1982), nos. 401 and 402; Regina Krahl *Chinese Ceramics in the Topkapu Saray Museum, Istanbul,* vol. 1 (London: Sotheby's Publications in association with Directorate of the Topkapu Saray Museum, 1986): 135; for a seventeenth–eighteenth-century Mughal nephrite jeweled bottle with lid, see Skelton, *Indian Heritage* (1982), no. 367.

6. For a white nephrite pendant with similar decoration and an unpublished rock crys-

tal dagger for cypress tree design in cut emeralds, see Susan Stronge, *A Golden Treasury, Jewellery from the Indian Subcontinent* (London: Victoria and Albert Museum, 1988); for a gold enameled lidded betel-nut container and saucer, see A. A. Ivanov, V. G. Lukonin, and L. S. Smesova, *Inverlirnuye izdeliya Vostoka: Drevniy Isrednevekovuy periody* [Oriental Jewelry: Ancient and Medieval Periods] (Moscow: Iskusstvo, 1984): 213, no. 99, pl. 163.

7. Ivanov, Lukonin, and Smesova, *Inverlirnuye* (1984): 213, no.103, pl. 167.

8. Dar al Athar al Islamiyya, Kuwait, no. LNS 2191J

9. MS Beckford c. 37, fols. 73–99, sheet 6, vii. All information from the Beckford archives kindly supplied by Bet McLeod.

10. Ibid., sheet 6, xi

11. Franchi "Packing Lists," MS Beckford c. 37, "Caisse No. 1."

12. "Inventory of 1844."

13. Rutter 1823a, p.54

58. Teapot and Stand

1. The Chinese wine pot, with its loop handle and spout, provided the model for European teapots; in Asian tea ceremonies, tea is made in the cups, not in a pot.

2. Snodin and Baker 1980, part 1, p. 743.

3. Cf. the set of twelve in the Palace Museum, Beijing, illustrated in *Kangxi, Yongzheng, Qianlong: Qing Porcelain from the Palace Museum* (Hong Kong, 1989): 316, pl. 145.

4. A few objects inspired by Asian prototypes were sold in the 1817 sale of Beckford's London townhouse, including a hexagonal silver teapot, sugar basin, and tea caddy, all chased with panels of Chinese landscapes. These were based on seventeenth-century Chinese ceramic wine pots which in turn were based on silver examples such as the rare example of around 1680 in the Peabody-Essex Museum, Salem, Massachusetts. Of Beckford's pieces, the bowl at least appears to have been the example made in 1812–13 by Paul Storr, sold Christie's, London, 13 December 1967, lot 21. Storr also made a similar covered bowl in 1810–11, illustrated in V. Brett, *The Sotheby's Directory of Silver, 1600–1940* (London: Sotheby's Publications, 1986), no. 1273; the design was used for teapots by Storr and lesser makers into the 1830s.

5. Venn Lansdown 1893: 22.

59–62. Tea Service

1. Cf. a pair of covered boxes, London, 1713, mark of Gabriel Sleath, sold Christie's, London, 3 May 1995, lot 90.

2. See C. Hartop, "A Elizabethan Rarity," in *Christie's Review of the Season (*London, 1985): 307.

3. Slop basins do, however, figure in the pattern books of Barnard Brothers, the large-scale manufacturing silversmiths (cat. no. 149), from 1808 onwards, where they

are categorized as "pint, pint + ?, and quart" (Archive of Art and Design, Victoria and Albert Museum, London, AAD5/63–1988).

63. Teapot and Cover

1. I am grateful to my colleague at the British Museum, Jessica Harrison-Hall, for this information.

2. See Aileen Dawson, 'Sèvres porcelain in the V & A, new light on some eighteenth-century hard-paste rarities," in Hugh Casson, *Victoria and Albert Album 5* (London: De Montfort, 1986): 343–52. It should be noted that the new palette of colors for use on hard-paste permitted more faithful reproduction of Oriental decorative motifs.

3. A *bouillote* or teapot dated 1778 in the British Museum is decorated with chinoiseries in two colors of gold and silver on a brown ground; other pieces of the same form are recorded with different chinoiserie decoration, see Aileen Dawson, *A Catalogue of French Porcelain in the British Museum,* rev. ed. (London: British Museum, 2000), no. 122. Black-ground pieces decorated with chinoiseries in two colours of gold and platinum include a teacup dating from 1792–93 also in the British Museum, see ibid., no. 130.

4. These dates are given in D. Peters, *Decorator and Date Marks on 18th Century Vincennes and Sèvres Porcelain* (London: n.p., 1997): 29.

5. A. W. Franks, *Catalogue of a Collection of Continental Porcelain*, exh. cat. (London: Bethnal Green Museum, 1896), no. 73.

6. For Franks and his European ceramic collecting, see Aileen Dawson, 'Franks and European Ceramics, Glass and Enamels', in M. Caygill and J. Cherry, *A. W. Franks, Nineteenth-Century Collecting and the British Museum* (London: British Museum Press, 1997): 200–219.

7. Sotheby's, 5 March 1985, lot 120, two cups and saucers dated 1781, now in a private collection.

8. This emerged in discussions with Robert Williams and Anton Kristensen, to whom I remain indebted.

9. Inventory number unknown.

10. It was a loan exhibition at the Silver and Jewellery Fair, London, 1988.

11. Bet McLeod, "In Lucifer's Metropolis: Willam Beckford's Collection of French Porcelain," *Journal of the French Porcelain Society* 16 (2001).

12. Manufacture National de Sèvres, Archives de Sèvres, R.I., liasse 2, dossier 9, fol. 2, illustrated in Dawson, *Catalogue* (2000): 146, fig. 123a.

13. See chap. 9, by Bet McLeod, in this volume.

64. Basin

1. See Wainwright 1989.

65. Bottle

1. David Watkin, introduction to *Thomas Hope; Regency Furniture and Interior Decoration* (London: Dover Publication, 1971): ix.

66. Vase

1. These publications include G. B. Piranesi, *Diverse Maniere d'Adornare I Cammini* (Rome, l769); idem, *Vasi ,Candelabri . . .* (Rome, l778); Pierre-François Hugues d'Hancarville, *Collection of Etruscan, Greek and Roman Antiquities* (Naples, 1766–67); and William Tischbein, *Collection of Engravings from Ancient Vases* (Naples, 1791–95).

2. For further information see Wainwright 1989.

67. Vase and Cover

1. *Scotland and the Arts of France*, exh. cat. (Edinburgh: Royal Scottish Museum, 1985): 92.

2. For further information see Wainwright 1989.

68. Pot and Cover

1. Victoria and Albert Museum, Department of Prints and Drawings, E.1–80–1972.

2. Stuart Carey Welch, *India: Art and Culture, 1300–1900*, exh. cat. (New York: The Metropolitan Museum of Art, 1985): 274.

3. Letter of 2 June 1815, in Italian, quoted in *Life at Fonthill*, p. 180.

69. Bowl and Cover

1. See Sir Harry Garner, *Oriental Blue and White* (London: Faber and Fabr, 1954), pl. 43.

70. Two Bowls

1. Snodin and Baker 1980, part 1, 743. For comparable Chinese metalwork, see B. W. Robinson, *Chinese Cloisonné Enamels* (London: Her Majesty's Stationery Office, 1972), n.p. For related porcelain decoration, compare for example a Qing dynasty bowl with Yongzheng mark illustrated in Louise Allison Cort and Jan Stuart, *Joined Colors: Decoration and Meaning in Chinese Porcelain*, exh. cat. (Washington, DC: Arthur M. Sackler Gallery, 1993) cat. no. 26.

2. For Beckford's Chinese porcelains and mounted wares, see Malcolm Baker, Timothy Schroder, and E. Laird Clowes, *Beckford and Hamilton Silver from Brodick Castle*, exh. cat. (London: The National Trust for Scotland, 1980): cat. nos. B29–B38.

3. Victoria and Albert Museum, illustrated in Snodin and Baker 1980, part 2, p. 738, fig. 23.

4. The teapot, now in the National Museums of Scotland, Edinburgh, is dated 1812–13. See ibid., fig. 24.

5. Now in the collection of the Victoria and Albert Museum, London. See ibid.,

p. 747, note 80, and ibid., part 2, p. 821.

6. See Timothy Schroder, "George Booth and William Beckford: A Study in Patronage," in *The International Silver and Jewellery Fair and Seminar* (London: The Fair, 1989): 25; and Snodin and Baker 1980, part 1, pp. 736 and 739. Beckford's French silver is itemized in ibid., part 2, appendix C, pp. 826–27.

7. Snodin and Baker 1980, part 2, pp. 820–21.

8. Now in the National Museums of Scotland, Edinburgh; illustrated in ibid., part 1, p. 738, fig. 26.

9. Baker, Schroder, and Clowes, *Beckford and Hamilton Silver* (1980): cat. nos. B31 and B32.

10. Snodin and Baker 1980, part 1, p. 744.

11. Ibid., part 2, p. 830, G33.

FONTHILL ABBEY, 1795–1822

71. *Fonthill Splendens with a Distant View of Fonthill Abbey*

1. Turner, engraved for William Angus, *The Seats of the Nobility and Gentry, in Great Britain and Wales: in a collection of select views* (Islington: W. Angus, 1787); Buckler, engraved for Colt Hoare, *Modern Wiltshire* (1829); deCort, engraved for *Aedes Fonthillianae* (1793).

4. Martin Hardie, *Water-Colour Painting in Britain,* vol. 1 (London: Batsford, 1967–68): 113.

5. *William Beckford* (Salisbury) 1976, p.39

6. *Life at Fonthill*, pp. 113, 259

7. Ibid., pp. 109, 110.

8. Farington *Diary*, vol. 3, entry for 16 November 1799.

72. *Fonthill Abbey, Perspective Design from the North West*

1. Cat. no. WYJA (8) 3, Royal Institute of British Architects, London.

2. John Wilton-Ely, "The Genesis of Fonthill Abbey" in *William Beckford* (Salisbury) 1976.

3. Cat. no. 2952–1876, Victoria and Albert Museum, London.

4. Martin Hardie, *Water-Colour Painting in Britain,* vol, 3 (London: Batsford, 1968): 15.

73–79. *The Evolution of Fonthill Abbey*

1. John Wilton-Ely, "Beckford the Builder" in *William Beckford* (Salisbury) 1976, pp. 40–41.

2. James Hamilton, *Turner and the Scientists* (London: Tate Gallery, 1998): 24–25.

3. James Storer, *A Description of Fonthill Abbey, Wiltshire* (London: Storer et al, 1812): 14.

4. Faringon *Diary*, vol 4 (1978): 2230.

5. Hamilton, *Turner* (1998): 25.

6. James Hall, *Essay on the origin and principles of Gothic architecture* (Edinburgh,

1797); an expanded and revised edition was published in London in 1813.

80. *King Lear*

1. Farington *Diary*, vol. 3, p. 726.

2. Ibid., p. 840. Farington reported on 4 October 1797 (ibid., p. 901) that this was Beckford's income *that* year, but even in a bad year, when his revenues were off, Beckford could count on at least £55,000 from his Caribbean holdngs and £18,000 from his English estates; see ibid., p. 916.

3. A description appears in ibid., p. 1117.

4. For West's paintings, see Helmut von Erffa and Allen Stanley, *The Paintings of Benjamin West* (New Haven and London: Yale University Press, 1986): 102–7. For West and Beckford see Robert C. Alberts, *Benjamin West. A Biography* (Boston: Houghton Mifflin, 1978): 244f.

5. Beckford would eventually own eighteen of West's paintings, including four portraits of Beckford's family. The last work of West's that Beckford bought in the painter's lifetime was his *Abraham and Isaac*, which was exhibited in the Royal Academy exhibition of 1801 (no. 134), for which see Erffa and Staley, *West* (1986): 291, no. 241.

6. Ibid., no. 210. On the Boydell project, see Winifred H. Friedman, *Boydell's Shakespeare Gallery* (New York and London: Garland Publishing, 1976).

7. Frederick Cummings identified the sketch exhibited in London in 1789 as the one in the Museum of Art, Rhode Island School of Design; see *Romantic Art in Britain: Paintings and Drawings, 1760–1860*, exh. cat (Detroit Institue of Art, 1968), cat. entry for West's *Lear*; Erffa and Staley note that Detroit picture was in fact the one (*West* [1986]: no. 211).

8. Farington *Diary*, vol. 3, p. 912.

9. Venn Lansdown 1893, p. 13. Lansdown, himself a painter, was befriended by Beckford in Bath and wrote letters about their conversations to his daughter, who privately published these in a series of 100 copies.

81. *Saint Michael and the Dragon*

1. Farington *Diary*, vol. 3, p. 1117, entry for 22 December 1798.

2. For these, see Helmut von Erffa and Allen Stanley, *The Paintings of Benjamin West* (New Haven and London: Yale University Press, 1986): nos. 400, 404, 405, and 409. Nevertheless, Beckford would acquire other paintings associated with Apocalyptic themes, particularly from Danby in 1828 and again in 1829.

3. Millard Rogers, Jr., "Benjamin West and the Caliph: Two Paintings For Fonthill Abbey," *Apollo* 52 (June 1966): 420–25.

4. When the painting was shown in the Royal Academy exhibition of 1797 (no. 242), the catalogue described it as "Michael casteth out the Dragon and his Angels, for a window at the new abbey, Font Hill." The painting was sold in

Phillips' 1823, p. 259, lot 250, along with *St. Thomas à Becket* (lot 251), as "a design for stained windows."

5. The subject itself was one of the most popular in British Apocalyptic painting, frequently employing Milton's writing as a direct source. See Marcia Pointon, *Milton and English Art* (Manchester: Manchester University Press, 1970). For a revealing discussion of Apocalyptic themes, see Morton D. Paley, *The Apocalyptic Sublime* (New Haven and London: Yale University Press, 1986), where West's *St. Michael* is discussed on pp. 42–44.

6. Rogers, "Benjamin West" (1966): 422, however, cites Reni's *Archangel St. Michael* in Rome which seems unlikely since West had seen it more than three decades earlier.

7. Farington *Diary*, vol. 3, p. 828, entry for 28 April 1797.

8. See von Erffa and Staley, *West* (1986), no 408, citing James Storer's account. See too Rogers, "Benjamin West" (1966): 423.

82. Pair of Candlesticks

1. J. Wilton-Ely, *Piranesi* (London: Arts Council of Great Britain, 1978): 987, no. 909.

2. Snodin and Baker 1980, part 2, appendix C, p. 827.

83. Casket

1. Alvar Gonzales-Palacios, *Il Gusto dei Principi*, vol. ii (Milan: Longanesi, 1993): figs 754–67; and the *Badminton Cabinet*, sale cat., Christie's, London, 5 July 1990, where the "Craon" casket is illustrated fig. 6.

2. Anna Maria Giusti, *Pietre Dure* (London: Philip Wilson, 1992): pl. 44.

3. E. Cole, *Il Mobile di Palazzo Pitti, 1537–1737* (Rome, 1996).

4. Alvar Gonzalez-Palacios, *Il Tempio del Gusto*, vol. ii (Milan: Longanesi, 1986): fig 63.

5. J. Hardy and C. Wainwright, "Elizabethan-Revival Charlecote Revived," *The National Trust Year Book* (London: Europa Publications, 1976): 16.

6. Ibid., pp.12–9; Wainwright 1989, pp. 290–40.

84. Casket

1. *Four Centuries of Decorative Arts from Burgley House*, ed. Oliver Impey, exh. cat. (Alexandria, Va.: Art Services International, 1998): 124, cat. no. 37.

2. Information kindly supplied by Philip Hewat-Jaboor and Bet McLeod.

85. Table

1. Rutter 1822, p. 55.

2. Rutter 1823a, p. 33.

3. See cat. fig. 85a.

4. Phillips' 1823, lots 447 and 448.

5. Rutter 1822.

6. Wainwright 1989, p. 215.

7. See, for example, Jonathan Marsden, 'The Chastleton Inventory of 1633,' *Furniture History: The Journal of the Furniture History Society* 36 (2000): 22–42, fig. 10.

8. See Simon Jervis, "Cottage, Farm and Villa Furniture," *The Burlington Magazine* 117 (December 1975): 848–59, fig. 98; and John Cornforth, "Endsleigh House, Devon," part 2 *Country Life* (16 October 1997): 62–65, fig. 9.

86. Cabinet

1. Rutter 1822, pp. 40–41; and Rutter 1823a.

2. For further information, see chap. 9, by Bet McLeod, in this volume.

3. Examined at Charlecote Park on 23 February 2001.

4. For further information, see chap. 9, by Bet McLeod, in this volume.

5. For a commode from Erlestoke, see Edward Lennox-Boyd "Patronage and Collecting: George Watson Taylor" in Edward Lennox-Boyd, ed., *Masterpieces of English Furniture: The Gerstenfeld Collection* (London: Christie's Books, 1998): 148–61; the pair to the Gerstenfeld commode is on loan from the Brooklyn Museum of Art to The Metropolitan Museum of Art, New York. Four further Watson Taylor pieces, from his London home, are now in the Royal Collection (see Hugh Roberts, "'Quite Appropriate for Windsor Castle': George IV and George Watson Taylor," *Furniture History: The Journal of the Furniture History Society* 36 (2000): 115–37, figs. 3 and 4.

6. This distinctive feature, which appears supporting an different Italian seventeenth-century ebony and pietre dure cabinet, also at Charlecote, is not mentioned in the sale catalogue descriptions. It is, furthermore, quite different to the terminations on the other commodes and cabinets, attributed to Hume, cited above.

7. For example, a seventeenth-century cabinet on nineteenth-century stand owned by Beckford at both Fonthill Abbey and Lansdown Tower, sold by Sotheby's, New York, 7 December 1991, lot 87. Monique Riccardi-Cubitt, *The Art of the Cabinet* (London: Thames and Hudson, 1992) illustrates other examples, including John Evelyn's cabinet (p. 75) and a cabinet given by Cosimo III to the Earl of Exeter (p. 19). Also worthy of comparison is a "Gobelins" cabinet in the Palais Rohan, Strasbourg.

8. See Clive Wainwright, "Charlecote Park, Warwickshire," part 2, *Country Life* (28 February 1985): 508.

87. Cabinet

1. Rutter 1822, p. 41.

2. A pair of cabinets, similar in design to the pair at Charlecote, but lacking the distinctive stylized linen-fold side panels, was sold by Phillips', Oxford, 6 September 1985, lot 352, and a smaller, less elaborate pair by Phillips', Cardiff, 24 July 1991, lot 54. Other examples include a desk,

erroneously described as Anglo-Indian (Christie's, London, 23 February 1984, lot 138) and another, more correctly described (Christie's, London, 10 October 1990, lot 81).

3. For further information, see chaps. 9, by Bet McLeod, and 10, by Adrianna Turpin, in this volume.

4. See Geoffrey de Bellaigue, "Edward Holmes Baldock," parts 1 and 2, *The Connoisseur* (August 1975): 290–99; (September 1975): 18–25.

5. Ibid., part 2, pp. 20–21.

6. See, for example, Guilaume Janneau, *Le Meuble d'ébénisterie* (Paris: Edition Jacques Freal, 1974), fig. 3.

7. See Philippe Jullian, "La fause abbaye de Fonthill et les collections de l'extravagent William Beckford," *Connaissance des Arts* (March 1963): 95–103.

88. Table

1. Serge Grandjean, "Les Collections de l'Imperatrice Josphine à Malmaison et leur dispersion," *La Revue des Arts* 4 (1959): 193–98; idem, *Inventaire après décès de l'Impératrice Joséphine à Malmaison* (Paris: Reunion des Musees Nationaux, n.d.).

2. R. Gnoli, *Marmora Romana*, rev. ed., (Rome: Edizioni dell'Elefante, 1988): 117–21. Gnoli identifies a pair of columns, now in the Archaeological Museum in Istanbul, as probably those admired by Constantine the Rhodian around A.D. 940, which measure approximately 49 in. (125 cm) in circumference.

3. Rutter 1823a.

4. Phillips' 1823, lot 1140.

5. The Member of Parliament for Bristol, Miles engaged Thomas Hopper around 1814 to design Leigh Court in the heavy Grecian taste. His antiquarianism is clearly evident in the 1845 watercolor of the Morning Room (City of Bristol Museum and Gallery), where Miles happily juxtaposed "fashionable" Regency furniture (for instance, the set of armchairs attributed to George Smith, one of which is now at the Royal Pavilion, Brighton, and illustrated in *Treasure Houses* 1986, no. 526) with the finest Georgian giltwood furniture (for instance, the set of eight George I gilt-gesso open armchairs acquired at the Wanstead sale in 1822).

89–90. *Church Interiors by Neefs the Elder*

1. "Inventory of 1844," fol. 40.

2. The former is now attributed to Hans Memling and is in the Thyssen-Bornemisza Collection, Lugano; the latter is now called circle of Elsheimer and was sold in *The Estate of Walter P. Chrysler Jr.*, Sotheby's, New York, 1 June 1989, lot 39.

3. NRA(s), MSS Hamilton. Misc. M 12.50, listed as "a pair of interiors."

4. In The Metropolitan Museum of Art, New York, acc. no. 30.58.21 and 22.

5. In neither case is the current location known, the former was in Phillips' 1807, lot 609, "from the Orléans Collection," and is possibly the same as the one in the Beckford sale of Lansdown Tower, Bath, 25 November 1845, lot 321, which was dated 1654. The Antwerp painting was sold as "The Property of a Lady," in *Old Master Paintings*, sale cat., Christie's, London, 16 April 1999, lot 55. Another, *Interior of a Gothic Church, with a stonemason in the foreground* of 1654 was sold in the sale of Mrs John Beckford, Sotheby's, London, 18 November 1959, lot 128.

6. For this and comments on other interior views in Beckford's collection see Waagen 1838, vol. 3, pp. 112–30.

7. This painting was bought by 'Whood' for Alderman Beckford from the sale of Dr. Richard Mead, Langford, 20 March 1754, lot 45, and was described in 1838 as "one of the most wonderful finished pictures I ever beheld" by Henry Venn Lansdown, see Venn Lansdown 1893, p. 28.

91. Fonthill Abbey Sale Catalogue (Christie's)

1. For the public and press response to Fonthill Abbey see Robert Gemmett "The Critical Reception of William Beckford's Fonthill," *English Miscellany*, 19 (1968) pp. 133–51. For the Fonthill sales and books, prints and objects associated with the public interest in the Abbey, see Jon Millington, *Souvenirs of Fonthill Abbey* (Bath: Bath Preservation Trust, 1994). Bankes (1786–1855) of Kingston Lacy, Dorset, a friend of Byron, climbed the wall of Fonthill disguised as a "poor labourer" in a frock smock and ragged hat just before he went off on a lengthy Grand Tour (1812–20), during which he began his distinguished picture collection. For his letter to his grandmother describing his visit in 1811, see "William Bankes' Account of his Surreptitious Visit to Fonthill," *Beckford Journal* 1 (1995): 47–50. The quotation "so prodigiously tall…" in ibid., p. 47.

2. *Life at Fonthill*, pp. 330–31.

3. For the Christie's entrance ticket see Millington, *Souvenirs* (1994): 9 (E1).

4. *Times*, 30 September 1822, p. 3.

5. See *Gentleman's Magazine*, 92, part 2 (October 1822): 291.

6. See Millington, *Souvenirs* (1994).

7. *Life at Fonthill*, p.337.

92. Fonthill Abbey Sale Catalogue Phillips')

1. John Constable, *Correspondence*, ed. by R.B. Beckett (Ipswich: Suffolk Record Society, 1964): 284, 29 August 1823,

2. Ibid.

3. Quoted by Melville 1910, p. 320.

93. Admission Ticket

1. Quoted in Robert J. Gemmett, "The Critical Reception of Beckford's Fonthill," *English Miscellany* 19 (1968): 138.

2. John Constable, *Correspondence*, ed. by R. B. Beckett (Ipswich: Suffolk Record Society, 1964): 284, 29 August 1823.

3. Ibid.

4. Ibid., p.285.

ANTIQUARIAN TASTE

94. *Interior of a Grand Saloon of Pictures*

1. Rutter 1822, p.38; and Rutter 1823a, p.29.

2. Venn Lansdown 1893, p. 22, where it was described as "a fine interior . . . representing a noble picture gallery" and erroneously called van Ostade.

3. "Inventory of 1844," p.22.

4. The portrait of Edward VI is now attributed to Guillim Stretes (or Scrots) and is in the Royal Collection at Hampton Court.

5. Waagen 1838, vol. 3, p.115.

6. Sold as "The Property of a Lady," *Old Master Pictures*, sale cat., Christie's, London, 16 April 1999, lot 55.

7. For a full discussion of the painting see S. Speth-Holterhoff, *Les Peintres Flamands de Cabinets d'Amateurs au XVII ième Siècle* (Brussels: Elsevier, 1957): 190–93 and pl. 74.

8. The painting has been compared to the *Picture Gallery of Antoine van Leyen* by Gonzales Coques with William Schubart von Ehrenberg (The Mauritshuis, The Hague) in which the same architecture and similar composition are seen; see *Estate of Ray Livingston Murphy*, sale cat. Christie's, New York, 15 January 1986, lot 111.

95. Oinoche (wine jug)

1. For this (no. 364) and other representations of the subject, see W. Lambrinudakis, "Apollo über Tiere herrschend," in *Lexicon Iconographicum Mythologiae Classicae* II.1 (Zurich and Munich, 1984): 229–30.

2. A. de Angelis, "Ceramica Attica della Collezione Bonaparte da Vulci," *Archeologica Classica* 42 (1990): 29–53.

3. I. Jenkins, "La vente des vases Durand (Paris 1836) et leur réception en Grande-Bretagne," in *L'Anticomanie, La collection d'antiquités aux 18 et 19 siècles*, ed. Annie-France Laurens and Krzysztof Pomian (Paris: Ecoles des hautes études en sciences sociales, 1992): 269–78.

4. I. Jenkins, "'Contemporary Minds': Sir William Hamilton's affair with Antiquity," in I. Jenkins and Kim Sloan, *Vases and Volcanoes: Sir William Hamilton and his Collection* (London: British Museum Press, 1996): 40–64.

5. Jenkins, "La vente des vases Durand" (1992).

6. The revival in their fortune may be attributed principally to the work of the late Professor A. D. Trendall.

7. J. de Witte, *Description d'une collection de vases peints et bronzes antiques provenant des fouilles de l'Etrurie* (Paris: Firmin Didot, 1837): 1, no. 1. Bought by the Duke of Hamilton for 755 francs.

8. English 1845, lot 636.

9. "Acquisitions, Greek and Roman Antiquities, 1840–45," British Museum, Department of Greek and Roman Antiquities Library, 367, 1845, 11–28. 1.

10. Ceramic red-figured squat lekythos (H. 9¼ in.), British Museum Catalogue of Vases, E695.

11. J. de Witte, *Description des antiquités et objets d'art qui composent le cabinet de M. le chevalier E. Durand* (Paris: Firmin Didot, 1836): lot 97.

12. Christie's 1882, lot 86a, purchased for £168. The duke had paid £200 for it at the Beckford sale.

13. *Illustrated London News*, 6 December 1845, p. 365.

14. Ibid., 29 November 1845, p. 344.

15. "List of Articles of Vertu, Furniture etc., etc., sent from Bath to Hamilton Palace," Hamilton District Library, NRA(S)3438; information kindly supplied by Bet McLeod.

96. Chasse

1. Marie-Madeleine Gauthier, *L'Epoque romane*, vol. 1 of *Catalogue international de l'Oeuvre de Limoges* (Paris: Editions du centre national de la recherche scientifique, 1987): 184–85, cat. 211.

2. Simone Caudron, "Emaux champlevés de Limoges et amateurs britanniques du XVIIIe siècle," *Bulletin de la société archéologique et historique du Limousin* 103 (1976): 147–48.

3. See Barbara Drake Boehm, "A Pair of Limoges Candlesticks in The Cloisters Collection," *The Cloisters: Studies in Honor of the Fiftieth Anniversary*, ed. Elizabeth C. Parker and Mary B. Shepard (New York: The Metropolitan Museum of Art, 1992): 159.

4. John Britton, *Illustrations, Graphic & Literary, of Fonthill Abbey, Wiltshire* (London, 1823): 55.

5. A Limousin chasse was explained as the work of "A party of Greeks who visited the country in the reign of Henry III"; see *Proceedings of the Society of Antiquaries of London*, vol. I, 2d. series (1860): 149–52.

6. See the discussion in Albert ten Eyck Gardner, "Beckford's Gothic Wests," *The Metropolitan Museum of Art Bulletin* (October 1954): 49.

7. Rutter 1823a, p. 30.

8. Wainwright 1989 tries to argue a provenance from Saint-Denis itself.

9. See Danielle Gaborit-Chopin, *Le Trésor de Saint-Denis*, exh. cat. (Paris: Réunion des musées nationaux, 1991): 226–27, no. 42.

10. Danielle Gaborit-Chapin, Musée du Louvre, personal communication, 2001.

11. See Gaborit-Chopin, *Trésor de Saint-Denis* (1991): 12–13.

12. Cited by Gardner, "Beckford's Gothic Wests" (1954): 48.

13. Published as an appendix in Melville 1910, pp. 355–66.

14. Wainwright 1989, p. 128.

97. Triptych: *The Lamentation, The Prophet Daniel and an Apostle, probably St. Peter*

1. For biographical details see, Susan L. Caroselli, *The Painted enamels of Limoges: A Catalogue of the Collection of the Los Angeles County Museum of Art* (Los Angeles: The Museum, 1993): 80–83.

2. S, Boorsch, ed., *The Illustrated Bartsch: 29, formerly 15 (part 2) Italian Masters of the Sixteenth Century* (New York, Abaris Books, 1982): 26, 37.

3. J. J. Marquet de Vasselot, *Les Émaux Limousins de la fin du XVe siècle et de la première partie du XVIe. Étude sur Nardon Pénicaud et ses contemporains* (Paris: A. Picard, 1921): 278–79, and pl. 38.

4. Christie's 1822, p. 40, lot 41.

5. Philippe Verdier, *The Walters Art Gallery, Catalogue of the Painted Enamels of the Renaissance* (Baltimore: Walters Art Gallery, 1967): 325–27, under no. 175, see fig. 34. Verdier cites further pieces.

6. *Catalogue of a Collection of European Enamels from the Earliest Date to the End of the XVII Century* (London: Burlington Fine Arts Club, 1897): 42, no. 148, and pp. 42–43, no.150 and pl. 1.

7. Christie's, 1–4 and 9–10 July 1912, *Catalogue of the Renowned Collection of Works of Art . . . formed by the late John Edward Taylor*.

8. Tancred Borenius, *The Leverton Harris Collection* (London, 1931): 10, and pl. 8. A. Borenius reverted to identifying the centre panel as the Deposition.

98. Dish: *The Wedding Banquet of Cupid and Psyche*

1. All Beckford/Hamilton information has been kindly supplied by Bet McLeod. English translation of the authors' French text by Bet McLeod.

2. For a thorough discussion of the problem of the identification of 'I.C.,' "I.C.D.V.," and "I.D.C.," see: S. Baratte, *Les émaux peints de Limoges* (Paris, Reunion des musées nationaux, 2000): 317.

3. Bartsch 15, no. 69, p.223, pl. 31; see also S. Boorsch, ed., *The Illustrated Bartsch: 29, formerly 15 (part 2) Italian Masters of the Sixteenth Century* (New York, Abaris Books, 1982): 194–225.

4. The stained-glass windows of the Galerie de Psyché, château d'Ecouen, carried out in 1542 and now in the Galerie d'Aumale, château de Chantilly, are based on the engravings.

5. For an example of the characteristic decoration on the reverse of dishes by Jean Court, see S. Netzer, *Maleremails aus Limoges: Der Bestand des Berliner Kunst-*

gewerbemuseums (Berlin, Kunstgewerbe-museum, 1999): 104–5, no. 14.

6. *Le dressoir du Prince: Services d'apparat à la Renaissance*, exh. cat. (Ecouen: Musée national de la Renaissance, 1995–96): 104–5.

7. Victoria and Albert Museum (Acc. No. C. 80–1885); British Museum (Acc. No. 85,5–8,16); see *Norfolk and the Grand Tour*, exh. cat. (Norwich: Castle Museum, 1985): 105–6, no. 34. Walters Art Gallery (Acc. No. 44–201); see: P. Verdier, *Catalogue of the Painted Enamels of the Renaissance*, (Baltimore: Walters Art Gallery, 1967): 309–12, no. 170. Private collection; see: *Emaux de Limoges de la Renaissance*, exh. cat. (Paris: J. Kugel, 1994): 88–91, no. 19.

99. Tazza and Cover: *Scenes from the Story of Samson*

1. Horace Walpole, *A Description of the Villa . . . at Strawberry Hill* (Strawberry Hill, Eng.: Thomas Kirgate, 1784): 10.

2. P. Verdier, *The Taft Museum: European Decorative Arts* (New York: Hudson Hills Press, 1995): 347. For the engraving, see M. Hébert, *Inventaire des gravures des Ecoles du Nord, 1440–1550: Bibliothèque Nationale, Cabinet des Estampes*, vol. 2 (Paris: Bibliothèque Nationale, 1983): 240, no. 2937.

3. Cincinatti, The Taft Museum, Inv. No. 1931–276

4. Dijon, Musée des Beaux-Arts, Legs. Trimolet, Cat. No. T 1302, attributed to Jean III Pénicaud. For other versions of the Samson cycle, attributed to the Master 'I.P.', see S. Netzer, *Maleremails aus Limoges: Der Bestand des Berliner Kunstgewerbemuseums* (Berlin: GundH, 1999): 150, cat. no. 3, K4985, K4986, K4987, K4988.

5. Paris, Musée du Louvre, Inv. No. OA 951, attributed to Master "KIP"; see S. Baratte, *Les émaux peints de Limoges* (Paris: Réunion des musée nationaux, 2000): 91; Ecouen, Musée national de la Renaissance, Inv. No. E.Cl. 898 A–E, attributed to the workshop of Jean III Pénicaud.

6. For details, see *Livres d'heures royaux*, exh cat. (Ecouen: Musée national de la Renaissance, 1993): 33–35, cat. no. 4, ill. p. 34.

7. For examples, see *Saint Luke*, dated 1549 and signed "I.PENICAULT" (Victoria and Albert Museum, C.475–1873); *Saint Mark* (London, Victoria and Albert Museum, C. 483–1873); *Saint Matthew* (London, British Museum, M.240, reproduced in: *Illustrated catalogue of European Enamels*, exh. cat. [London: Burlington Fine Arts Club, 1897]: pl. 33, no. 154).

8. For example, the bearers of the instruments of the Passion (Oxford, Ashmolean Museum, 1947–191–240, ex. coll. Gambier-Parry, monogrammed "P. I."

9. For example, a plaque of the Virgin and Child mounted on a pax (Paris, Musée des Arts décoratifs, Inv. 16741)

10. For examples, see Ecouen, Musée national de la Renaissance, covered cup (Inv. E.Cl; 11270); Paris, Musée du Louvre, "Saturn" (Inv. OA 951, see Baratte, *Les émaux* [2000]: 91); Toulouse, Fondation Bemberg, "Saturn" (see: Philippe Cros, *Guide des collections: Fondation Bemberg*, 1995, p.11).

11. For polychrome examples, see Baratte, *Les émaux* (2000): 88–89.

12. See C. Briend, "Les objets d'art," *Musée des Beaux-Arts de Lyon: Guides collections* (Lyon: The Museum, 1993): 59.

13. For example, see a plaque showing the Entombment (Oxford, Ashmolean Museum) taken from an engraving of the Master of the Sforza Hours.

14. All Walpole/Beckford/Hamilton information has kindly been supplied by Bet McLeod. Translation of the authors' French text by Bet McLeod.

15. MS. Beckford c. 22, fols. 198–202.

16. MS. Beckford c. 22, fols. 209–11.

17. MS. Beckford c. 22, f. 216.

100. Saltcellar

1. The author has not examined this piece, and is most grateful to Timothy Wilson for his assistance in the preparation of this entry. Information on the salt is taken from the files of the Walters Art Museum.

2. Inv. 1889/1–2. Information kindly supplied by Carola Fiocco and Gabriella Gherardi.

3. British Museum, MLA 1852, 11–29, 4. See T. Wilson, *Ceramic Art of the Italian Renaissance* (London: British Museum, 1987): 62, cat. no. 87.

4. Wallace Collection, C136. See A.V.B. Norman, *Wallace Collection: Catalogue of Ceramics*, vol. 1 (London: Wallace Collection, 1976): 271–72, cat. no. C136, ill., p. 272.

5. Strawberry Hill Sale, 1842, day 23, lot 53, bought by Hume for £29.8.0.; Christie's 1882, lot. 824, bought by E. Joseph for £ 110.5.0., present whereabouts unknown.

101. Design for a Dagger

1. This drawing is fully catalogued in J. Rowlands, *Drawings by German Artists in the Department of Prints and Drawings in the British Museum* (London: British Museum Press, 1993): cat. no. 285, pl. 186.

2. *Enciclopedia dell'arte antica, classica e orientale*, vol. 2 (Rome: Instituto della enciclopedia italiano, 1958–66): 47.

3. Rowlands, *Drawings* (1993).

4. See J. Rowlands, *Holbein: The Paintings of Hans Holbein the Younger* (Oxford: Phaidon, 1985).

5. For example see that of 1539 in the Berlin-Dahlem Kupferstichkabinett illustrated in *Gothic and Renaissance Art in Nuremberg, 1300–1500* (New York and Munich: The Metropolitan Museum of Art and Prestel Verlag, 1986): 448, pl. 259.

6. The Apollo Fountain, Nuremberg, for example.

7. J. Chipps Smith, *Nuremberg: A Renaissance City, 1500–1618* (Austin: University of Texas Press, 1983): 224.

8. Snodin and Baker 1980, part 2, appendices A–G, pp. 824–33.

9. Ibid., part 1, p. 743 and n.57.

10. The cabinet is in the Victoria and Albert Museum (No. 27–1869) and the drawing is in the British Museum (No. 1854-7-8).

11. For a discussion of the jug see Snodin and Baker 1980, part 1, p. 747. Information on "Portrait of a Canon" kindly supplied by J. Hobhouse.

102. Design for a Cup

1. Karl T. Parker, *Catalogue of the Collection of Drawings from the Ashmolean Museum*, vol.1, *Netherlandish, German, French and Spanish Schools* (Oxford: Clarendon Press, 1938): 134, under no. 299.

2. See full catalogue entry in John Rowlands, *Drawings by German artists in the Department of Prints and Drawings in the British Museum* (London: British Museum Press, 1993): 149–50, cat. no. 326.

3. Extract from George Redford's *Art Sales*, vol.1 (1888), quoted in Frank Hermann, *The English as Collectors* (London: John Murray 1999): 190–92.

4. From a letter by Lady Bessborough to Lord Granville Leveson Gower recounting the visit of Samuel Rogers to see William Beckford, quoted in ibid., pp. 214–17.

5. Hannelore Müller, *European Silver: The Thyssen-Bornemisza Collection* (London: Sotheby's Publications, 1986): 136–39, cat. no. 36.

103. Cup and Cover

1. Hazlitt, quoted by Snodin and Baker 1980, part 1, p.738.

104. Bowl

1. An attribution to the Sarachi workshop is detailed on the catalogue files for this object at The Metropolitan Museum of Art, New York.

2. The author has not examined this bowl, and thanks Hugh Tait for his assistance in the preparation of this entry, and for his suggestions, based on the photographic evidence, regarding the composition and form of this bowl.

3. For further details of Beckford, Franchi and the acquisition of hardstones, see chap. 9, by Bet McLeod, in this volume.

4. Ibid.

5. Suggested by Clare Vincent, personal communication, 5 January 2001.

6. Letter in Portuguese, MS. Beckford c.12, fol. 55, transcribed and translated by Pedro Mauro de Carvalho for the PHJ/Beckford Database

7. Ibid., fol. 55v.

8. Letter from Beckford to Franchi, 13 June 1818, cited in *Life at Fonthill*, pp. 241–42.

9. "Inventory of 1844," Book no. 2, p. 53, in Oak side Cabinet in the Drawing Room, No. 19 Lansdown Crescent.

10. This author has not examined the Durand sale catalogue, nor the French archives.

11. Letter from Beckford to Franchi, 22 May 1819, cited in *Life at Fonthill*, p. 307.

105. Casket

1. The casket was purchased for Lord Grosvenor (later the Marquess of Westminster) at the Phillips' 1823 sale; see Robert Hume to the Duke of Hamilton, 4 November 1823, NRA[s], 2177, Bundle 602. Hume wrote: "I purchased many lots for Lord Grosvenor . . . two crystal Italian coffers."

2. Hans Huth, *Lacquer of the West: The History of a Craft and an Industry, 1550–1950* (Chicago: University of Chicago Press, 1971).

3. Ibid.

106. Covered Cup

1. See H. Tait, "Huguenot Silver, The Wilding Bequest," part 1, *Connoisseur* (August 1972): 270–74; and idem, "London Huguenot Silver," in *Huguenots in Britain and Their French Background, 1500–1800*, ed. I. Scouloudi (Basingstoke: Macmillan, 1987).

2. Attribution courtesy of Christian Theuerkauff, 1987.

3. For further information on this interest of Beckford's, see chap. 9, by Bet McLeod, in this volume.

4. *Carlton House: The Past Glories of George IV's Palace*, exh. cat. (London: Queen's Gallery, 1991): 186, no. 160, illus.

5. Phillips' 1823, day 12, lot 183, "An Ivory Tankard and Cover, finely sculptured, representing the Battle of the Centaurs, Satyrs, etc. in old mounting of silver, chased and gilt."

6. Ibid., day 14, lot 469, "An ivory vase, mounted by Rundell and Bridge, in chased silver gilt. It is in alto-relievo, sculptured by Strous. The subject, a marine Venus, attended by Tritons and Sirens."

7. Ibid., day 15, lot 571, "A Magnificent Ivory Plynth, most elaborately chased in basso relievo by B. Cellini, with or-molu base and top." One of these plinths is affixed with a nautilus shell and appears in the alternate view, by Britton, of King Edward's Gallery with one British Museum vase and a hardstone vase and bowl on stand. This same ivory sleeve vase with nautilus shell is seen in Willes Maddox's *Objects of Vertu* (cat. no. 156); H. R. Foster, *The Stowe Catalogue* (London, 1848), day 5, lot 570; and Christie's 1882, lot 872.

BECKFORD, FRANCHI, AND
DESIGN

107. **Pair of Candlesticks**

1. Christie's 1822, lot 58.

2. As manager of Rundell's workshops and London's leading goldsmith, Storr supervised the production of a high volume of superbly executed domestic plate in the antique taste. See N.M. Penzer, *Paul Storr, the Last of the Goldsmiths* (London: Batsford, 1954).

3. London, Public Record Office (PRO) C104/58, 268, 20 December 1800. Also see Helen Clifford, "The Vulliamys and the Silversmiths 1793–1817," *Silver Society Journal* 10 (fall 1998): 96–102.

4. I am very grateful to Christopher Hartop for bringing this to my attention; see Venn Lansdown 1893, p. 31.

5. PRO C104/58, 268, 20 December 1800; also see Helen Clifford, "The Vulliamys and the Silversmiths, 1793–1817," *Silver Society Journal* 10 (fall 1998): 96–102.

6. Helene Demoraine, "Bois de Bagard," *Connaissance des Arts* 191 (January 1968): 90–93; see also Edward H. Pinto, *Treen and other Wooden Bygones* (London: G. Bell & Sons, 1969): 119–20, 366–67, figs. 123, 387.

7. Christie's 1919, lot 75; subsequently sold at Christie's New York, 24 May 1977, lot 121, and again at Christie's, New York, 19 April 1997, lot 273.

8. For example, see a pair marked for 1865/7 by John Figg, sold Sotheby's, New York, 21 October 1998, lot 178. The ornament on Beckford's candlesticks was recorded in rubbings by C. J. Richardson, preserved in albums in the Victoria and Albert (E.3308.B.196). I am grateful to Christopher Hartop for this information. The Victorian examples may have been inspired by such records of the Beckford examples.

108. **Salver**

1. See especially Wechter's design for a goblet, one of thirty engravings published in 1579 (VAM E.4281.1910)

2. A. Grimwade, *London Goldsmiths: their Marks and Lives 1697–1837*, rev. ed. (London: Faber and Faber, 1990): 739.

3. Snodin and Baker 1980, part 1, p. 741, illus. 31.

4. Christie's 1822, day 6, lots 52 and 53, and Phillips' 1823, day 17, lots 825 and 826.

5. Lot 617, "A Pair of Circular Trays, of silver-gilt, covered with ornaments of elaborate flat-chasing – *7 in. diam. From the Beckford Collection".*

109. **Ladle**

1. For discussions of the print see Janet S. Byrne, *Renaissance Ornament Prints and Drawings* (New York: The Metropolitan Museum of Art, 1981): 117; and *Ornemanistes du XV au XVII siècle*, exh. cat. (Paris: Musée du Louvre, 1987): no. 44.

2. William Gibbs Rogers, *A List of Carvings and other Works of Art…*(London, 1854): 26, quoted in Wainwright 1989, p. 139.

3. Snodin and Baker 1980, part 2, p.821.

4. A. Grimwade, *London Goldsmiths, their Marks and Lives 1697–1837*, rev. ed. (London: Faber and Faber, 1990): no. 1623.

110. **Jug**

1. German silversmiths Augustin Heckel, George Daniel Gaab, and Peter Glazier, all probably from Augsburg, designed and chased gold snuffboxes in London in the 1750s. It is often impossible to distinguish German and English goldwork in this period. See A. Kenneth Snowman, *Eighteenth Century Gold Boxes of Europe* (London: Faber and Faber, 1990): 273.

2. The contents of the album, now in the Victoria and Albert Museum, are described in Snodin and Baker 1980, part 2, p. 822. This rendering (f7) belongs to the group of silhouetted drawings in the album associated with Beckford rather than Franchi, but definite attribution is not possible. The detailed working drawings in the album, on the other hand, are accepted as the work of Franchi.

3. Christie's 1817, day 2, lot 35.

4. A drawing for a nautilus cup mount in Franchi's design album (f12) has both beading and a notched lip. Michael Snodin and Malcolm Baker have remarked on the similarity of the lips on Beckford's cream jugs to those on the mounted nautilus cup at Fonthill. See Snodin and Baker 1980, part 1, pp. 747–48.

5. Christie's 1822, day 9, lot 12.

6. Snodin and Baker 1980, part 2, 829–30.

7. Ibid., p. 833. The only other known Meissen cream jug in Beckford's collection is a silver-gilt mounted beaker at Brodick Castle. The cylindrical beaker is more geometric than the present cream jug and has suitably simple mounts with a snake handle of Franchi's renaissance type.

8. As quoted in "Sale of the Beckford Collection," *Illustrated London News*, 29 November 1845, p. 344.

111. **Sugar Tongs**

1. See Janet S. Byrne, *Renaissance Ornament Prints and Drawings* (New York: The Metropolitan Museum of Art, 1981): 30–31.

2. See A. Fox-Davies, *The Art of Heraldry: an Encyclopædia of Heraldry* (London: T. C. and E. C. Jack, 1904): 98–99.

3. Redding 1859, p. 150.

4. See Thomas Woodcock and John Martin Robinson, *The Oxford Guide to Heraldry* (Oxford University Press, 1988): 134; ten of these quarterings were disallowed in 1879 not because of an fraudulent claim on Beckford's part, but because the genealogy on which they were based was found to be incorrect.

5. I am very grateful to Bet McLeod for her insights into this aspect of Beckford's heraldry.

112. **Sugar Tongs**

No notes.

113. **Sugar Tongs**

1. A set of six silver-gilt circular dishes recently on the market, approximately 8¼ inches in diameter, were also supplied by Storey and Elliot to Beckford in 1813–14. They are in the George II style, but have the Beckford arms engraved in the center within an elaborate cartouche; the borders are applied with the Hamilton cinquefoil and the Latimer cross.

114. **Sugar Tongs and Four Teaspoons**

No notes.

115. **Cup and Cover**

1. Snodin and Baker 1980, part 2, p. 821.

2. Christie's 1822, day 8, lot 43.

116. **Bowl**

1. Letter in Portuguese from Franchi to Beckford, Ms. Beckford c. 12, fol. 46v., translated by Pedro de Moura Carvalho for the PHJ/Beckford Archive.

2. *La collection de gemmes de Louis XIV*, exh. cat. (Paris: Musee du Louvre, 2001).

3. C. P. Brard, "Traité des Pierres Precieuses," noted: "Il circule dans le le commerce des calcédonies taillees en maniere de tasses et de soucoupes qui sont extrement recherchees par les amateurs" [Circulating in the trade there are chalcedonies carved as saucers and bowls which are extremely sought after by collectors].

4. See chap. 9, by Bet Mcleod, in this volume.

5. Snodin and Baker 1980, part 1, p.747.

117. **Cup and Cover**

1. Inventory no. E.1–89–1972.

2. Snodin and Baker 1980, part 2, n.19 and fig.18.

3. James had retired on 30 September 1843 but was later in partnership with his son Edward Aldridge who continued the business under the name of James Aldridge until his move to new premises at 46 Gerrard Street, Soho. This information has been provided by John Culme compiled from Arthur G. Grimwade, *London Goldsmiths, 1697–1837: Their Marks and Lives*, 3d ed. (London: Faber and Faber, 1990): 421; and John Culme, *The Directory of Gold and Silversmiths, Jewellers and Allied Traders, 1838–1914* (Woodbridge: Antique Collector's Club, 2000): 8.

4. A substantial amount of these early commisons are at Brodick Castle see Malcolm Baker, Timothy Schroder, and E. Laird Clowes, *Beckford and Hamilton Silver from Brodick Castle*, exh. cat. (London: The National Trust for Scotland, 1980): cat. nos. B1–B13.

5. Victoria and Albert Museum (No.C86–1913).

6. "Inventory of 1844"; Snodin and Baker 1980, part 2, p.833, G122.

118. **Bowl and Cover**

1. Christie's 1822, day 5, lot 58; Snodin and Baker 1980, part 2, p.828, E61

2. Inv. no. 389.1854.

3. Snodin and Baker 1980, part 1, p.747, note 79. The letter is quoted below, in cat. no. 139.

4. J. F. Hayward, *Virtuoso Goldsmiths* (London: Sotheby Parke Bernet, 1977): fig.77.

5. Ibid., figs. 11 and 12.

6. The history of the "Rubens Vase" is extraordinary: It was apparently looted by the Crusaders in Constantinople and then passed into the French Royal Collection. Looted again by Huguenot forces in 1590 it was subsequently sold and passed into the collection of Sir Peter Paul Rubens. He then shipped it to the Orient with a view to selling it to a Mughal Prince, but it was shipwrecked off the Australian coast in 1629; see Boyd Alexander, "Fonthill Wiltshire II" in *Country Life* (8 December 1966): fig. 9.

7. *Life at Fonthill*, p. 255.

8. Note the design for a cup originating from Nuremberg around 1580; illustrated in Snodin and Baker 1980, part 1, fig. 30.

9. Beckford Papers, the English Accounts, sheet 6, referred to in Snodin and Baker 1980, part 2, n. 19.

10. "Objects of Vertu, No. 2."

119. **Cup and Cover**

1. *Illustrated London News,* 6 December 1845, p 364, vignette p. 365.

2. "Inventory of 1844," p. 49.

3. A. M. Masinelli and F.Tuena, *Treasures of the Medici* (London: Thames and Hudson, 1992): 114.

4. From a print, with slight variations, by Michel le Blon, 1611. As suggested by Michael Snodin (see chap. 11, in this volume).

5. English 1844, title page.

6. C. J. Richardson, *Studies of Ornamental Design* (London: John Weale, 1851). Information kindly supplied by Philip Hewat-Jaboor and Bet McLeod.

120–24. **Hardstone Spoons**

1. Melville 1910, p. 351.

2. "Inventory of 1844," p. 54.

3. Beckford Papers, the English Accounts, sheet 6; the list is dated 26 February 1818.

4. Snodin and Baker 1980, part 2, p. 821.

5. For examples of such spoons see K. Marquardt, *Eight Centuries of European Knives, Forks and Spoons* (Stuttgart: Arnoldsche, 1997): 164.

6. Compare with the finial on the enamelled gold agate spoon in the Rosenborg Palace Collection, Copenhagen, illustrated in *Die Renaissance im Deutschen Sudwesten zwischen Reformation und Dreissigjärigem Krieg*, exh. cat., vol. 2 (Karlsruhe,

Badischen Landesmuseum, 1986): 622, no. L13.

125. Scent Flask

1. We are grateful to Charles Truman for this suggestion.

2. See A. M. Masinelli and F. Tuena, *Treasures of the Medici* (London: Thames and Hudson, 1992): 38–39.

3. Quoted in Brian Fothergill, *Beckford of Fonthill* (London: Faber and Faber, 1979): 89.

4. Victoria and Albert Museum, Department of Prints and Drawings, E.3–1972.

5. Snodin and Baker 1980, part 2, G132.

126. Jug

1. The mounts are now lost, and the vase is in the National Museum of Ireland; see A. Lane, "The Gagnières-Fonthill Vase: A Chinese Porcelain of about 1300," *The Burlington Magazine* 103, no. 697 (1961): 124–32. See fig. 9-6, in this volume.

127. Bowl and Cover

1. I am grateful to Catherine Delacour of the Musée Guimet, Paris, John Adamson, and Colin Sheaf for their help in identifying the origin of the porcelain.

2. Sir Harry Garner, *Oriental Blue and White* (London: Faber and Faber, 1954): pl. 16. The Aldridge sketchbook is in the Victoria and Albert Museum, London, Department of Prints and Drawings, E.3–1972.

3. For a discussion of William James and his son Edward as collectors see Sharon-Michi Kusunoki, "Surrealism and 'The Golden Age'," *Apollo* (June 1999): 3–10.

4. The press reported that on average the prices were approximately two-thirds what had been paid in the Hamilton Palace sale (Christie's 1882; see W. Roberts, *Memorials of Christie's: a Record of Art Sales from 1766 to 1896,* vol. 2 [London: G. Bell, 1900]: 80–82).

128. Casket

1. Christie's London, May 16th 1827, and following day, second day's sale, Lot 99. This entry is based on a longer text in Ellenor M. Alcorn, *English Silver in the Museum of Fine Arts, Boston,* vol. 2, *Silver from 1697* (Boston: Museum of Fine Arts, 2000): 270–73.

2. *Life at Fonthill,* p. 323.

3. I am grateful to Philip Hewat-Jaboor for this suggestion. See *Ourivesaria Portugesa no Museu de Arte Antiga* (Lisbon, 1984), fig. 15.

4. *Literary Gazette,* 8 March and 5 April 1823.

5. Originally suggested by Clive Wainwright.

Bath: The Final Years, 1822–1844

129. Model of Lansdown Tower

1. For a detailed discussion of the tower, see chap. 16, by Christopher Woodward, in this volume.

2. Quoted in Venn Lansdown 1893, p. 24.

3. *Bath and Cheltenham Chronicle,* 5 October 1826.

4. "Memoir of Mr Henry Goodridge, FRIBA" in *RIBA Sessional Papers 1864–65,* extra pagination p.4, by A. S. Goodridge.

5. *Bath Chronicle,* 9 September 1847.

130. *Unknown Sitter, traditionally called The Duke of Alva*

1. Venn Lansdown 1893, p. 20.

2. See William Beckford, *The Journal in Portugal and Spain 1787–1788,* ed. by Boyd Alexander (London: Rupert Hart-David, 1954): 297.

3. The Alva family owned, for instance, two important paintings now in the National Gallery, London: *Mercury Instructing Cupid before Venus* ("The School of Love") by Correggio which was seen in 1776 in the Alva collection by Henry Swinburne (*Travels through Spain* [London: Elmsly, 1779]: 353), and *The Adoration of the Name of Jesus* by El Greco which was later owned by Sir William Stirling-Maxwell (1818–1878), the pioneer writer on Spanish art and major collector of Spanish paintings.

4. *The Toilet of Venus* ("The Rokeby Venus") by Velazquez (now in the National Gallery, London), the "Alva" Madonna by Raphael (now in the National Gallery of Art, Washington) were among those which were purchased and sent to England at this time.

5. William Buchanan, *Memoirs of Painting, with a chronological history of the importation of pictures by the great masters into England since the French Revolution,* vol. 2 (London: R. Ackermann, 1824): 230.

6. *Sale of A Collector of Taste and A Merchant of Respectability*, Christie's, London, 26 May 1820, lot 89. Also in this sale was a "small" *Tobias and the Archangel Raphael* by Elsheimer, which may have been the one that Beckford bought (see cat. no. 7). He purchased the *Virgin and Child* by Perugino (now in the National Gallery, London) from him around 1820. Pizzetta had possibly bought the portrait from the *Sale of A Gentleman, Mr. Norman of Plymouth Dock, Devon,* John Hickman, London,16 May 1818, lot 26a.

7. "Inventory of 1844," p. 29.

8. The *Philip IV* is possibly the one in the National Gallery, London; *Pope Innocent X* was purchased at the George Watson Taylor sale, Christie's, London, 14 June 1823, lot 23; and sold in the Christie's 1882, 8 July, lot 1136, bought by F. Davis £110 5s. *The Knight of Malta* was bought at the *Sale of the Property of the late Most*

Noble the Marquis of Lansdowne deceased, Coxe, Burrell & Foster, London,19 March 1806, lot 37, for 185 guineas. It is possibly the same as the *Portrait of a Youth*, sold at Hamilton Palace sale, as above, lot 1137, bought Arnot £283 10s. (as from Fonthill and the Marquess of Lansdowne) and now in the Arnot Art Museum, Elmira, New York as by Simone Stone.

9. The former was in the *Sale of the Property of Rose Campbell Esq., deceased, late of Cadiz,* Christie?s, London, 9 July 1814, lot 39, bought Foxhall for Beckford. The latter was thought to be by Antonio Moro and entitled *Jeanne d'Archel* (or d'Arkel) of the House of Egmont. It is now in the National Gallery, London, attributed to Nicolas de Neufchâtel and known to portray Susanna Stefan. It was recorded by James Storer, *A Description of Fonthill Abbey, Wiltshire* (London: Storer et al., 1812): 19.

10. Many scholars have been consulted about this picture and I am most grateful to David Edge, Rosemarie Mulcahy, Joanna Woodall, Aileen Ribeiro, and Robert Oresko for their help.

11. My thanks to Margaret Scott who has proposed this attribution.

131. *The Adoration of the Magi*

1. "Inventory of 1844," p. 25.

2. Waagen 1838, vol.3, p.121.

3. All these paintings are now in the National Gallery, London.

4. See Francis Russell, "A Late Work by Girolamo da Carpi," *Burlington Magazine* 125 (June 1983): 359 and fig. 53. See also Nicholas J. Hall, "Girolamo da Carpi," in *The Adoration of the Magi,* exh. cat. (London and New York: Hall & Knight Ltd., 2001): 82–85.

5. See Cecil Gould, *National Gallery Catalogues: The Sixteenth-Century Italian Schools* (London: The National Gallery, 1975): 176–77.

132. *The Holy Family with Saints John the Baptist, Elizabeth, Zacharias and (?) Francis*

1. Britton 1801, vol. 1, p. 226.

2. Letter of 21 April 1799, MS Beckford c.36, fol.26. One was described as a Holy Family by "Garofali." The three other paintings mentioned were: a *Saint Jerome* by Guercino, listed by Richard Warner in September 1800 in the ballroom at Splendens (*Excursions from Bath* [Bath: R. Crutwell, 1801]: 122), and possibly the one in the Hamilton Palace sale; an *Adoration* by Guido Reni, which Tresham thought was by Ludovico Carracci and which is possibly the small *Nativity,* listed by Warner; and *Christ and Saint John as Children* by Leonardo, also listed by Warner as "Two boys kissing" and presumably the same as *The Infant Saviour and Saint John* sold at Jeffrey's Gallery, Salisbury, l May 1809 (not numbered but the seventh lot in that sale).

3. Rutter 1822, p. 44.

4. Letter of 23 September 1822, in French, from Franchi to the Duke of Hamilton, MS Beckford c.39, fol. 89.

5. Waagen 1838, vol. 3, p.123. Waagen wrote: "The graceful composition in the spirit of Raphael, the felt execution, the warm, brownish, and yet clear colouring, make this one of the most pleasing pictures of the master. It was formerly in the domestic chapel of the Aldobrandini family at Rome." See also J. D. Passavant, *Tour of a German Artist in England,* vol. 1 (London: Saunders & Otley, 1836): 316.

6. See Cecil Gould, *National Gallery Catalogues: The Sixteenth-Century Italian Schools,* (London: The National Gallery, 1975): 92–93.

133. Binding: *Picturae Francisci Albani in Aede Verospia*

1. Letter to *The Times,* 19 January 1882.

2. Letter to George Clarke, 15 March 1831, quoted in *The Consummate Collector,* ed. Robert J. Gemmett (Wilby: Michael Russell, 2000): 63.

3. Letter to George Clarke, 27 November 1831, in ibid., p. 101.

4. Ibid.

5. For Beckford's binders see A. R. A. Hobson, "William Beckford's Binders," *Festschrift Ernst Kyriss* (Stuttgart: Max Hettler, 1961): 375–81.

6. "The famous Kalthoeber, who is undoubledly now the finest bookbinder in the world, produced a binding which cost thirty guineas. Its fame spread immediately and many people paid visits to his shop to see it; lords and ladies were among the visitors and the king himself heard so many reports of it that he ordered it to be brought to Buckingham House" (J. C. Huttner, *Englische Miscellen* 6 [1802]: 5, quoted in H. M. Nixon, *The German Binders in London in the Late Eighteenth Century,* in *Twelve Books in Fine Bindings from the Library of J. W. Hely-Hutchinson* [Oxford: for the Roxburghe Club, 1953] 69.

7. Rutter 1823a, p.14.

134–37. The Art of the Bookbinder

The four volumes in the exhibition are: John Scott, *Paris Revisited in 1815, by way of Brussels: Including a Walk over the Field of Battle at Waterloo* (London: Longman, Hurst, Rees, Orme, and Brown, 1816); Du Munt, *Voyages de M. du Mont, en France, en Italie, en Allemagne, a Malthe, et en Turquie,* vol. 4 of 4 (La Haye, France: Foulque et l'Honoré, 1699); Jens Wolff, *Sketches and Observations taken on a Tour through a Part of the South of Europe* (London: Wilson, 1801); and Samuel Pegge, *Anecdotes of the English Language, Chiefly Regarding the Local Dialect of London and its Environs,* 2d ed. (London: J Nicols, Son and Bentley, 1814).

1. William Beckford, *The Journal in Portugal and Spain, 1787–1788,* ed. by Boyd Alexander (London: Rupert Hart-David,

1954): 285–86.

2. For an account of Beckford as a book collector see Anthony Hobson, "William Beckford's Library," *Connoisseur* 191 (April 1976): 298–305.

3. Beckford sold duplicate books from his collection in 1801. For Beckford book sales see *Sale Catalogues of Libraries of Eminent Persons*, vol. 3, ed. by Robert J. Gemmett (London: Mansell with Sotheby Parke-Bernet Publications, 1972).

4. Letter to William Clarke, 5 August 1833, quoted in *The Consummate Collector*, ed. Robert J. Gemmett (Wilby: Michael Russell, 2000): 247

5. 4 April 1833, in ibid., p. 197.

138. Jug

1. Brian Fothergill, *Beckford of Fonthill* (London: Faber and Faber, 1979): 318.

2. The basket, also at Brodick Castle, is illustrated in Malcolm Baker, Timothy Schroder, and E. Laird Clowes, *Beckford and Hamilton Silver from Brodick Castle*, exh. cat. (London: The National Trust for Scotland, 1980): B39.

139. Bowl

1. See in particular the heliotrope jasper tazza illustrated in D. A.Iniguez, *Catalogo de las Alhajas del Delfin*, exh. cat. (Madrid: Museo del Prado, 1989): no 12 (no. 79 in the 1776 inventory).

2. These include Phillips' 1823, lots 468, 1049, 1050, 1062, and 1065.

3. Snodin and Baker 1980, part 1, p. 747, n. 79.

4. Ibid., part 2, appendix F, p. 829, caisse no 1.

5. Thomas Sheraton's Directory for 1803 had many similar ideas. For an recent article on such decorative elements see J. Gleeson, "John Fish and the Dolphin Furtniture at Brighton Pavilion," *Apollo* 146 (September 1997): 9–13.

6. Joseph Farington, *The Farington Diary*, ed. James Grieg, vol. 7 (London: Hutchinson, 1927): 147; for an illustration see J. Culme, *Nineteenth Century Silver* (London: Hamlyn for Country Life Books, 1977): 65.

7. Lot 487, purchased by F. Davis for £525.

8. Sale, 25 June 1954, lot 135.

9. Illustrated in *Objects of Vertu* (see cat. no. 155). The dolphin bowl is also illustrated in *William Beckford* (Salisbury) 1976, p. 87.

140. *Susan Euphemia, Duchess of Hamilton, as a Sibyl*

1. H. C. Anderson, *Dagbøger, 1825–75*, vol. 3 (Copenhagen: Det danske Sprog-og Litteraturselskab, 1971–76): 303. For a discussion of Grahl's portrait see Jackie Wullschläger, *Hans Christian Anderson: The Life of a Storyteller* (London: Allen Lane, 2000): 272.

2. William Beckford to Margaret Orde, his eldest daughter ,17 June 1817, quoted in

Howard B. Gotlieb, *William Beckford of Fonthill: Writer, Traveller, Collector, Caliph . . .* (New Haven: Yale University Library, 1960): 40.

3. For portraits of Lady Hamilton see Patricia Jaffe, *Lady Hamilton in Relation to the Art of her Time* (London: Arts Council, 1972).

4. An example was in the collection of Gianni Versace (see *Collection of Gianni Versace,* sale cat., Sotheby's, New York, 5 April 2001, lot 17).

5. Advertisement, *The Athenaeum,* 9 Jan 1828, p. 31. Susan Euphemia was painted as a youngster with her sister Margaret by George Romney in 1789 (oil on canvas, now in the Huntingdon Library and Art Gallery, San Marino, California). For a pencil and watercolor sketch, ca. 1800–1805, by Richard Cosway, see Stephen Lloyd, *Richard & Maria Cosway,* exh. cat., (Edinburgh: Scottish National Portrait Gallery, 1995): 127, no.155. Cosway's *Unknown Lady as a Sibyl,* which also resembles Susan Beckford and, in view of its provenance, is likely to be a portrait of Beckford's daughter, see ibid., no.163, For a portrait by Thomas Phillips, R.A., see *Family Portraits, Works by Old Masters . . . property of Trustees of his Grace the late Duke of Hamilton*, sale cat., Christie's, 6 November 1919, lot 41; reproduced in Melville 1910, facing page 90 (where it is wrongly described as Hon. Mrs. Peter Beckford by Sir Joshua Reynolds). For a portrait miniature of the duchess by Mrs. Ann Mee, see *Objects of Vertu and Miniatures,* sale cat., Christie's, South Kensington, 30 July 1991, lot 7.

141. Pair of Tea Kettles, Lamp Stands, and Wind Shields

1. George Wickes: Gentleman's ledger, Victoria and Albert Museum, VAM GL2, ff100, 104.

142. Cup

1. Accession no. E75.106.

143. Saltcellar

1. I am very grateful to Ken Thorburn and Bill Cowell of the National Trust for Scotland for their help in preparing the entries for this and other objects from Brodick Castle.

2. Malcolm Baker, Timothy Schroder, and E. Laird Clowes, *Beckford and Hamilton Silver from Brodick Castle*, exh. cat. (London: Spinks, 1980): B41.

3. The mark struck on this saltcellar was unidentified until the publication of John Culme's *Directory of Gold and Silversmiths: Jewellers and Allied Traders 1838–1914,* (Woodbridge: Antique Collectors' Club, 1987).

144. Pair of Ladles

No notes.

145. Armchair

1. English 1844, pl. 14.

2. English 1845, day 7, lot 500, sold for £30.17.0d; tentatively identified in a private collection.

3. Phillips' 1823, lot 1171, and lots 1172–74 offering two more each.

4. Thomas Hope, *Household Furniture and Interior Decoration* (London: Longman, Hurst, Rees and Orme, 1807), pl. 20: "No. 3 and 4. Front and side of an armchair, after the manner of the ancient curule chairs."

5. See David Watkin, *Thomas Hope and the Neo-Classical Idea* (London: Murray, 1968): 141.

146. Chair

1. For the Sanctuary, see English 1844, pl. 8.

2. *Illustrated London News*, 22 November 1845, p. 324.

3. NRA (S) Hamilton Muniment, 2177, bundle 2715, both Hamilton residences.

4. See National Art Collections Fund Review (1993), p. 45, no. 3873.

5. City Museums and Art Gallery, Birmingham, M.3.74, for example, on pp. 3 and 5.

6. See Peter Thornton, "Back-stools and Chaises à Demoiselles," *The Connoisseur* (February 1974): 99–105.

7. Henry Shaw, *Specimens of Ancient Furniture* (London: W. Pickering, 1836), pls. 12 and 13.

8. See Clive Wainwright, "'Only the True Black Blood'," *Furniture History: The Journal of the Furniture History Society* 21 (1985): 250–57.

9. Phillips's 1823, day 13, lots 341–43.

10. See Amin Jaffer, *Furniture from British India and Ceylon* (London, Victoria and Albert Museum, 2001): 141–42.

11. See John Britton, *Graphical and Literary Illustrations of Fonthill Abbey, Wiltshire* (London: The Author, 1823): 9.

147. Stool

1. English 1844, pl. 9.

2. See *The Illustrated London News*, 6 December 1845, p. 364.

3. John Britton, *Graphical and Literary Illustrations of Fonthill Abbey, Wiltshire* (London: The Author, 1823): viii.

4. See chap. 9, by Bet McLeod, in this volume.

5. Edmund English's father was recorded as a cabinetmaker in 1787 but was declared bankrupt in 1828; for a history of the English family see Jean English, *The History of the English Family in Bath, 1770–1890* (Bristol: n.p.,1995). Later, however, English & Son was at 21 Milson Street, Bath trading as "auctioneers, undertakers, carvers and gilders, estate and house agents" (Geoffrey Beard and Christopher Gilbert, eds, *Dictionary of English Furniture Makers 1660–1840* [Leeds, Furniture History Society, 1986]: 281.

6. See Martin Levy, "A Coffer from Lansdown Tower," *The Beckford Journal* 3 (spring 1997): 25–26, and n. 4.

7. See Ralph Edwards, *The Shorter Dictionary of English Furniture* (London, Country Life Books, 1974): 500, no. 3.

148. Coffer

1. For further information on Hume and Beckford, see chap. 9, by Bet McLeod, in this volume.

2. Martin Levy, "A Coffer from Lansdown Tower," *The Beckford Journal*, vol. 3 (spring 1997): 25–29.

3. English 1844; the chromolithographs in the book were after paintings by Willes Maddox.

4. For further architectural references to the coffer, see chap. 16, by Christopher Woodward, in this volume.

5. Beckford to Hume, 18 August 1837, MS Beckford c.22, fol. 175.

6. English1844, pl. 3.

7. Beinecke Rare Book and Manuscript Library, Yale University; see Levy, "Coffer" (1997): 29.

8. The author is grateful to Philip Hewat-Jaboor and Bet McLeod for this suggestion.

9. Hamilton Muniments, Hamilton MSS, misc. M. 12/52.1.

149. Pair of Candlesticks

1. Alfred Short is listed in the 1845 Bristol directory as a silversmith and jeweler at 37 Corn Street.

2. J. Culme, *The Directory of Gold and Silversmiths, Jewellers & Allied Traders, 1838–1914*, vol. 2 (Woodbridge, Antique Collectors Club, 1987): 29; see also J. Banister, "Identity Parade: the Barnard Ledgers," *Proceedings of the Society of Silver Collectors, 1974–76* (London, 1980): 165–69.

3. Daybook, AAD5/63–1988, Archive of Art and Design, Victoria and Albert Museum, London.

4. No designs or other documentary evidence of English's work as a designer survives, or records of his firm, due no doubt to English's subsequent bankruptcy and disappearance. A newspaper account headed "Failure and Flight of Messrs. English & Son" appeared on 8 December 1852 (I am grateful to Toby English for drawing this to my attention).

5. See, for example, Romano's design for a candlestick, perhaps for Ferrante Gonzaga, in the Strahov Library, Prague.

6. Jean English, *The History of the English Family in Bath, 1770–1890* (Bristol: n.p., 1995): 10.

7. Although the entry in Barnard's Daybook is dated 29 August 1842, the candlesticks were not submitted for assay and hallmarked until after the introduction of the date letter H on May 29, 1844, several weeks after Beckford's death. The delay is unexplained. The weight given in the 1842 Daybook entry is over five ounces greater than the current weight of these candlesticks. This can be explained by loss

due to wear, the erasure of Beckford's crests, and the removal, at some point between 1882 and 1987, of their gilding. The 1842–45 Barnard Daybook (AAD5/63–1988, Victoria and Albert Museum), which appears complete, includes a number of orders from Short for modest silverware during this period, as well as the copies of Beckford's 1688 wall sconces.

7. They may be the "2 very rich Solid Silver Candlesticks" in the "List of Articles of Vertu, Furniture etc. etc. sent from Bath to Hamilton Palace," dated 1 September 1848 (Hamilton Public Library, Hamilton Palace Inventory 1835, tipped in).

8. "A pair of very richly chased Silver Gilt candlesticks on five scroll feet. Designed for Wm. Beckford Esq. By English of Bath, and Manufactured by Short of Bristol" (Hamilton Muniments: 1876 Inventory of Hamilton Palace NRA(S) 3438). I am grateful to Bet McLeod for this reference.

9. Lot 622: "A Pair of Silver-gilt Candlesticks on five feet, chased with foliage, designed for the late W. Beckford, Esq."

10. Christie's, New York, 27 April 1987, lot 262. I am grateful to Charles Truman who, during the preparation of that catalogue, identified their Beckford provenance.

150. *William Beckford*

1. Alexander 1962, p. 137.

2. Melville 1910, p. 37.

3. The book may be *Remarks on Custine's Russia,* said by Cyrus Redding to be the last book Beckford read.

4. Ann Sumner, ed., *Death, Passion and Politics Van Dyck's Portraits of Venetia Stanley and George Digby* (London: Dulwich Picture Gallery, 1995).

5. Maddox's first name is spelled in various ways. The form "Willes" is used on both the title page of *Views of Lansdown Tower* (1844) and the Lansdown Tower sale catalogue (1845).

6. Redding 1859, p. 276.

7. The paintings were hung in the entrance hall/staircase at Lansdown Crescent ("Inventory of 1844").

8. *The Temptation in the Wilderness, Christ's Agony in the Garden,* and *The Annunciation,* lots 334–35. A manuscript annotation in English 1845 comments that "there is truly considerable merit in these works but the impression is German" (B&NES: Bath Central Library).

9. Ibid.

10. Six works by Maddox, including three gouaches for *Views of Lansdown Tower,* are now in the Victoria Art Gallery, Bath. His *Music shall play wherever they go* (formerly *The Golden Age*) is in the Guildhall Art Gallery, London.

11. "Mr. William Maddox of our city has been commissioned to paint a portrait of the Sultan, who watches the progress of the work with extreme satisfaction and interest" (*Bath Chronicle,* 24 March 1853).

151. *William Beckford*

1. Letter postmarked 22 April 1844. National Art Library, Victoria and Albert Museum, London.

2. Letter in French, see Oliver 1932, p.328

3. From Bath newspaper reports cited in W. Gregory, *The Beckford Family* (Bath: Bath Chronicle, 1898): 104–9.

4. Ibid., p.107.

5. Ibid., p.108.

6. Beckford, *Recollections of an Excursion to the Monasteries of Alcobaça and Batalha* (London: John Murray, 1835): 36.

7. Farington *Diary,* vol. 3, p. 1091.

8. In 1843 Beckford contemplated building at mausoleum at his estate at Milford near Salisbury. See Timothy Mowl, *William Beckford* (London: John Murray, 1998): 302.

9. Brian Fothergill, *Beckford of Fonthill* (London: Faber and Faber, 1979): 248–49.

10. Beckford draft, see Oliver 1932, p. 321

11. Ibid.

152. Nautilus Shell

1. All the information on the shell and the triton has been provided by Ulrich Leben, who first identified the triton at Waddesdon Manor through its illustration in Willes Maddox's *Objects of Vertu* (see cat. no. 155). Leben suggests a Baroque source for the triton figure. We would like to express my gratitude to Sandra Davison of the Thame Conservation Studio and to Rupert Harris who worked on the conservation of the shell and the triton. Also to Linda Homfray and Robert Selbie for editorial assistance.

2. Comparable shells engraved by Bellekin are to be found in: the Rijksmuseum, Amsterdam; Grünes Gewölbe, Dresden; Kunstgewerbemuseum, Berlin; Musée du Louvre, Paris; Wadsworth Atheneum, Hartford. For further information on nautilus shells and their supports, see: W. H. van Seters, "Oud nederlandse Parelmoerkunst, het werk van leden der familie Belquin parelmoergraveus en schilders in de 17eew," *Nederlands Kunsthistorisch Jaarboek* 9 (1958): 173; H. U. Mette, *Der Nautiluspokal: Wie Kunst und Natur miteinander spielen* (Munich, 1995). Information supplied by Ulrich Leben.

3. The information on Beckford's collection of nautilus shells has been provided by Bet McLeod. See chap. 9, by Bet McLeod, in this volume.

4. Mary Elizabeth Lucy, *Biography of the Lucy Family of Charlecote Park in the County of Warwick,* vol. 2 (n.p., 1862): 37. Lucy wrote: "A pair of most beautiful Nautilus Shells, mounted in silver gilt, richly chased; with Neptune and his Trident on the top." These were in the sitting room at Charlecote Park but were stolen in 1850 and not recovered.

153. Vase

No notes.

154. Casket and Cover

1. Victoria and Albert Museum, No. L. 311.1.

2. Elias Ashmole and Dr. Thomas Wharton, *Musaeum Tradescantianum* (London: John Grismond, 1656). The authors described it as a "Turkish alkoran in a silver box."

3. Wallace Collection, No. XXIIA 25.

4. G. C. M Birdwood, *The Industrial Arts of India* (London: Chapman, 1880): 193.

5. For Indian filigree see *Treasures from India* (London: National Trust, 1987): no. 87.

6. Snodin and Baker 1980, part 2, p.833.

155–57. *Objects of Vertu*

1. English 1844, preface.

2. Ibid.

3. [English me dit que ses artistes travaillant 'con amore' aux vues de la Tour sacré – effectivement, j'ai bonne opinion des equisses qu'on m'a deja montre.] MS. Beckford c.21, fol. 269 v.

4. MS. Beckford c. 58, p. 40.

5. Bill addressed to the Executors of Beckford's Estate, dated 19 April 1844, NRA[S], 2177, Bundle 2745.

6. Ibid., p. 23, 30.

7. Messrs. Rainey, Bath, 22 December 1855, "The property of Henry Lawson, FRS, at 7 Lansdown Crescent," Lot no. 97. Information kindly supplied by Sidney Blackmore.

8. NRA[S] M.4/79, p. 84.

158. *Susan Euphemia, Duchess of Hamilton*

1. Lady Ann Hamilton was lady-in-waiting to the Princess of Wales, later Queen Caroline. Beckford's elder daughter was known as Margaret. Sir Richard Colt Hoare recorded, from the Fonthill Parish Register, her full names as being Maria Margaret Elizabeth, while Mrs. Beckford in her will names her eldest grandaughter as Maria Elizabeth Margaret.

2. "It is not true that Mr Beckford endeavoured to force his daughter into a union with Comte D'Egmont, contrary to her inclinination." Newspaper clipping dated 26 July 1804 in Beckford's cuttings book, Beckford 409, Beinecke Rare Book and Manuscript Library, Yale University.

3. Harriet, Countess Granville, *Letters,* vol. 2 (London: 1894): 335.

4. See Virginia Surtees, *A Beckford Inheritance: the Lady Lincoln Scandal* (Wilton: Michael Russell, 1977).

5. Quoted in ibid., p. 35.

6. Farington *Diary,* vol. 8, p.1844. Samuel Rogers commented on her ability, like her father, to extemporise on the piano, see Melville 1910, p. 239.

7. There are two version of the portrait. Another, now at Lennoxlove, shows a difference in piano and background, and the duchess is wearing different jewellery, including bracelets with cameo portrait profiles, possible of her children.

8. J. Mitford Notebook, Add MS 32566, fol. 34, British Library.

159. *Alexander, 10th Duke of Hamilton*

1. Lord Lamington, "Days of the Dandies," *Blackwood Magazine* (1890), quoted in *The Complete Peerage . . .* , vol. 6 (London: St. Catherines Press, 1926): 274.

2. Willes Maddox exhibited a portrait of the duke at the Royal Academy exhibition in 1852 (no 439).

3. See Beckford's letters to Rev. Samuel Henley in *The Collection of Autograph Letters and Historical Documents formed by Alfred Morrison,* 2d series (London: n.p. 1893):1.

4. *The Times,* 20 August 1852, p. 6(a).

5. Quoted in R. G. Horne, *The House of Commons, 1790–1820,* vol. 4 (London: Secker & Warburg, 1986): 127.

6. Earl of Malmesbury, *Diaries and correspondence of First Eal of Malmesbury* (London: Richard Bentley): 4, 392.

7. Alexander 1962, pp. 222–23.

8. *Letters of Harriet, Countess Granville,* ed. F. Leverson-Gower, vol. 2 (London: Longmans Green, 1894): 210.

9. *Pictures, Works of Art and Decorative Objects: the Property of His Grace the Duke of Hamilton . . .* sale cat., Christie's, 17 June 1882; and *The Hamilton Palace Collection: Illustrated Priced Catalogue* (London: Remington, 1882).

10. *The Hamilton Palace Libraries…,* sale cat., Sotheby, Wildinson & Hodge, London, 1 May 1884; and *Catalogue of Family Portraits Works by Old Masters and Modern Pictures the property of the Trustees of his Grace the late Duke of Hamilton,* sale cat., Christie, Manson & Woods, London, 6 November 1919.

11. *The Times,* 20 August 1852, p. 6(a).

160. Pair of Cabinets

1. Letter in Portuguese from Franchi to Beckford, Rome, 6 January 1825, MS Beckford c.13, fol. 37v. With thanks to Pedro de Moura Carvalho his translation.

2. For a full description of these cabinets, see *Important English Furniture and Carpets,* sale cat., Christie's, London, 14 June 2001, lot 100. An article on the cabinets by Philip Hewat-Jaboor and Bet McLeod is planned for a forthcoming volume of *Furniture History: The Journal of the Furniture History Society.*

3. Letter in Porguese from Franchi to Beckford, Florence, 20 November 1824, MS Beckford c.13, fol. 35v. With thanks to Pedro de Moura Carvalho his translation.

4. Letter in Portuguese from Franchi to Beckford, Rome, 29 January 1825, ibid., fol. 44v. With thanks to Pedro de Moura Carvalho his translation.

5. Ibid.

B. Provenance, Exhibitions, Literature, Marks, Signatures, and Inscriptions

This section includes additional data on the history of the objects in the exhibition.

Provenance: Tracing the history of Beckford's objects after his ownership is often difficult because of the manner of cataloguing objects in the eighteenth and nineteenth centuries and because Beckford himself was often secretive about the works of art from his collection. In addition, the complexities of inheritance (entitlement) within the Beckford/Hamilton family have added to this problem. Gaps in the known provenance are indicated by a dash in brackets: [—].

Exhibitions and Literature: The varying degrees of information available for individual objects may be readily noted. Specific sales of works of individual items from Beckford's collection are sometimes listed under *Literature, Exhibitions,* and *Provenance* when they provide evidence of all three circumstances. A sale such as the canceled 1822 Christie's sale would not represent a change in ownership and is therefore not listed under *Provenance,* but its catalogue is cited under *Exhibitions,* because Beckford's collections were on view, and also in the *Literature* section. The Phillips' 1823 sale at Fonthill Abbey is listed under all three headings because title for the objects did transfer (although frequently the next owner is not known) and the works of art were both on exhibition and listed in the sale catalogue. In some cases this history is unknown and is so indicated.

Marks, Signatures, and Inscriptions: In many cases these are given as "unknown," indicating that the curators have been unable to examine the objects personally before publication and there is no mention of marks, signatures, and inscriptions in the literature.

For a key to oft-cited sources, see page 414. Full citations for other sources can be found in the bibliography.

The Early Years, 1760–81

1. *William Beckford*

Provenance: William Beckford; by descent; Hamilton Collection.

Exhibitions: Unknown.

Literature: Unknown.

Marks, Signatures, Inscriptions: Unknown.

2. *Maria Hamilton Beckford*

Provenance: William Beckford; by descent to the 12th Duke of Hamilton; Christie's 1919; National Gallery of Art, Washington, Andrew Mellon Collection, 1947.

Exhibitions: Christie's 1919.

Literature: Christie's 1919; Martha Hamilton-Phillips, "Benjamin West and William Beckford: Some Projects for Fonthill," in *The Metropolitan Museum of Art Journal* (New York, 1981), pp. 157–74, illus. fig 5; Helmut von Erffa and Allen Staley, *The Paintings of Benjamin West* (New Haven and London: Yale University Press, 1986), p. 493, fig 594.

Marks, Signatures, Inscriptions: Unknown.

3. Plate

Provenance: Alderman William Beckford; by descent; private collection.

Exhibitions: *William Beckford* (Bath) 1966, p. 26, no. 73; *William Beckford* (Salisbury) 1976, p. 80, no. 1 (for similar plates).

Literature: Jon Millington, *Beckford's Tower, Bath: An Illustrated Guide* (Bath, 1996), p. 9 (for another plate from this service).

Marks, Signatures, Inscriptions: None.

4. *Fonthill Splendens*

Provenance: William Beckford; John Farquhar; Phillips' 1823, day 27, lot 328, £23.12.06 to Nixon; James Morrison, possibly purchased at the sale or later acquired by him; by descent; Sudeley Castle.

Exhibitions: The Royal Academy, 1791, no. 421, *A View of Font-Hill*; Phillips' 1823, day 27, lot 328; 111th National Loan Exhibition, The Grosvenor Gallery, London, 1914/15, no. 111; Sotheby's, *The Artist and the Country House*, 1995–96, no. 91.

Literature: Phillips' 1823, day 27, lot 328.

Marks, Signatures, Inscriptions: signed and dated "H. De. Cort, Antwertpiensis, 1791" and with label pasted on the reverse, apparently in the artist's hand: *Aedes Fonthillianae* / Quod Genio optimaque sua dextra potuit,/ Nobilissimo ingeniosissimo Domino, /Domino Wlmo. Beckford, / Liberlium Artium Judici, Cultori, Patrono / Dedicat Henricus de Cort, / Antwerpianus, Galliaei Regis Academiae, / Serenissimique Principis Condai Pictor, 1791 [*The Fonthill Mansion* / That which he was able to accom- plish by his Genius and his own good right hand, / To the Most Noble, Most ingenious Lord, / Lord William Beckford. / The Judge, Cutlivator and Patron of the Liberal Arts, / Henry De Cort dedicates, / A native of Antwerp, Painter of the Royal French Academy, and of the most serene Prince of Condé, 1791]; signed and dated "H. De. Cort, Antwerpiensis, 1791."

5. *View of Fonthill Splendens from the West*

Provenance: J. M. W. Turner, by whom bequeathed to the Tate Gallery, 1856.

Exhibitions: Unknown.

Literature: A. J. Finberg, *A Complete Inventory of the Drawings of the Turner Bequest*, vol. 1 (National Gallery, London, 1909), pp. 120–21, 176.

Marks, Signatures, Inscriptions: Unknown.

6. *Summer*

Provenance: Alderman Beckford, ca 1766; William Beckford; Sir William Holburne of Menstrie before 1808; by descent; Holburne of Menstrie Museum.

Exhibitions: *William Beckford* (Bath) 1966, nos. 66, 67; *William Beckford* (Salisbury) 1976, p. 89, no. 45.

Literature: Unknown.

Marks, Signatures, Inscriptions: Unknown.

7. *Tobias and the Archangel Raphael Returning with the Fish*

Provenance: possibly the one in Dr. Richard Mead sale, Langford, London, 21 March 1754, lot 49, bought 'Whood' for Alderman William Beckford £31 10s.; William Beckford; his sale Christie's, London, 27 February 1802, lot 26, bought William Seguier £27 16s. 6d.; George Watson Taylor, by 1819; his sale Christie's London, 14 June 1823, lot 31, bought Thwaites (or bought in) £74.11s.; the Honorable Edmund Phipps, by 1854; his sale Christie's, London, 25 June 1859, lot 40, bought Henry Farrer £162 15s.; Samuel Sandars, by 1879, bequeathed by him to the National Gallery, London, 1894.

Exhibitions: Christie's, London, 27 February 1802, lot 26; British Institution, 1819, no. 20; Christie's, London, 14 June 1823, lot 31; British Institution, 1851, no. 108; Christie's, London, 25 June 1859, lot 40; Royal Academy, 1879, no. 239.

Literature: Christie's, London, 27 February 1802, lot 26; Christie's, London, 14 June 1823, lot 31; Christie's, London, 25 June 1859, lot 40.

Marks, Signatures, Inscriptions: Unknown.

Coming of Age

8. *William Beckford*

Provenance: William Beckford; by descent to the 12th Duke of Hamilton; Christie's 1919, lot 55, incorrectly as Alderman Beckford by Romney, purchased by [?Charles] Davis on behalf of Marcus Samuel, first Viscount Bearsted; by descent; The National Trust, Upton House, 1948.

Exhibitions: *Works of Old Masters & Scottish National Portraits*, Royal Scottish Academy Building (Edinburgh, 1883), no. 16; *Loan Exhibition of Old Master and Scottish National Portraits* (Edinburgh, 1866), no. 1470; *International Exhibition* (Glasgow, 1888), no. 128; Christie's 1919, lot 55; *The Bearsted Collection* (London: Whitechapel Art Gallery, 1955), no. 13 (illus. pl. 2); *English Pictures* (London: Agnews, 1965), no. 61; *William Beckford* (Bath, 1966); *La peinture romantique anglaise* (Paris: Petit Palais, 1972), no. 216; *Europalia* (Brussels, 1973), no. 55; *Portugal e o Reino Unido: A aliança revisitada,* (Lisbon: Gulbenkian Museum, 1994–95), no. 150; *In Trust for the Nation, Paintings from National Trust Houses* (London: The National Gallery, 1995), no. 9, and illus.

Literature: Christie's 1919, lot 55.

Marks, Signatures, Inscriptions: Unknown.

9. Pair of Candlesticks

Provenance: William Beckford; by descent to Mary Louise, Duchess of Montrose; acquired by the Treasury in lieu of death duties in 1958; transferred to the National Trust for Scotland, Brodick Castle.

Exhibitions: Unknown.

Literature: *Beckford and Hamilton* (Brussels 1992), B9 or B10; *Beckford and Hamilton Silver* (Spink 1980), B8; Snodin and Baker 1980.

Marks, Signatures, Inscriptions: London hallmarks for 1791–92; maker's mark of John Scofield (Grimwade no. 1670).

10. Snuffer Tray

Provenance: William Beckford; by descent to the 15th Duke of Hamilton; Glasgow Museums, 1977.

Exhibitions: Unknown.

Literature: Unknown.

Marks, Signatures, Inscriptions: Maker's mark of John Scofield (Grimwade no. 1670).

11. Bowl

Provenance: William Beckford; by descent to the 15th Duke of Hamilton; Trustees of the National Museums of Scotland, 1980.

Exhibitions: Unknown.

Literature: Unknown.

Marks, Signatures, Inscriptions: London

hallmarks for 1786–87; maker's mark of John Scofield (Grimwade no. 1670).

12. Wine Coaster

Provenance: William Beckford; by descent to the 15th Duke of Hamilton; Trustees of the National Museums of Scotland, 1977.

Exhibitions: Unknown.

Literature: Unknown.

Marks, Signatures, Inscriptions: London hallmarks for 1793–94; maker's mark of Robert Sharp (Grimwade no. 2436).

13. *La Grande Chartreuse*

Provenance: William Beckford; his sale 10 April 1805, lot 32, purchased by Seguier; A. Anderdon Weston; his sale 16 February 1922, lot 100; Victor Rienaecker; S.A. Morrison; private collection.

Exhibitions: Burlington Fine Arts Club 1923 (52).

Literature: Bell and Girtin 1934–35, no. 429B.

Marks, Signatures, Inscriptions: Unknown.

14. *Schloss Hadernburg Between Bolzano and Trent*

Provenance: William Beckford; sold Christie's 1805; [—]; Victoria and Albert Museum.

Exhibitions: Unknown.

Literature: Bell and Girtin 1934–35, p. 206; Sloan 1986, p. 141.

Marks, Signatures, Inscriptions: Unknown.

15. *View Between Brixen and Bolzano: Storm Effects*

Provenance: William Beckford; sold Christie's 1805; [—]; Victoria and Albert Museum.

Exhibitions: Unknown.

Literature: Bell and Girtin 1934–35, p. 206; Sloan 1986, pl. 154, p. 141.

Marks, Signatures, Inscriptions: Unknown.

16. *View from Mirabella, the Villa of Count Algarotti on the Euganean Hills*

Provenance: William Beckford; sold Christie's 1805; [—]; Victoria and Albert Museum.

Exhibitions: Unknown.

Literature: Bell and Girtin 1934–35, p. 216; Sloan 1986, pl. 158, p. 145.

Marks, Signatures, Inscriptions: Unknown.

17. *Sepulchral Remains in the Campagna near Rome*

Provenance: William Beckford; sold Christie's 1805; [—]; Victoria and Albert Museum.

Exhibitions: Unknown.

Literature: Bell and Girtin 1934–35, p. 370; Sloan 1986, pl. 166, p. 149.

Marks, Signatures, Inscriptions: Unknown.

18. *St. Peter's from the Villa Borghese, Rome*

Provenance: William Beckford; sold Christie's 1805; [—]; The Whitworth Art Gallery.

Exhibitions: Unknown.

Literature: Bell and Girtin 1934–35, p. 361; Sloan 1986, pl.161, p. 148.

Marks, Signatures, Inscriptions: None.

19. *The Lake of Nemi*

Provenance: William Beckford; Christie's 1805; Sir Thomas Barlow; by descent Sir Thomas D. Barlow; Colnaghi; Paul Mellon, 1961; Yale Center for British Art, 1975.

Exhibitions: Christie's 1805; *English Drawings from the Collection of Mr. and Mrs. Paul Mellon* (Washington, DC: National Gallery of Art, 1962), no. 21; *Painting in England, 1700–1850* (Richmond, VA.: Museum of Fine Arts, 1963), no. 64; *English Drawings and Watercolors, 1550–1850* (New York: Pierpont Morgan Library, and London, Royal Academy, 1972–73), no 63, illus.; *English Landscape, 1630–1850* (New Haven: Yale Center for British Art, 1977), no. 75, illus.

Literature: Christie's 1805; Bell and Girtin 1934–35, no.142 and pl.12a.

Marks, Signatures, Inscriptions: Unknown.

20. Teapot and Stand

Provenance: William Beckford; by descent to the 12th Duke of Hamilton; Christie's 1919; [—]; Barber Institute.

Exhibitions: Christie's 1919.

Literature: Christie's 1919.

Marks, Signatures, Inscriptions: London hallmarks for 1785–86 and "duty drawback" mark used between 1 December 1784 and 24 July 1785; maker's mark of Daniel Smith and Robert Sharp (Grimwade no. 506).

21. *An Arabian Tale . . .*, 1st London Edition, 1786

Provenance: [—]; private collection.

Exhibitions: Unknown.

Literature: Unknown.

Marks, Signatures, Inscriptions: Unknown.

22. *Vathek*, 1st Lausanne Edition, 1787

Provenance: [—]; private collection.

Exhibitions: Unknown.

Literature: Unknown.

Marks, Signatures, Inscriptions: Unknown.

23. *Vathek*, 1st Paris Edition, 1787

Provenance: [—]; private collection.

Exhibitions: Unknown.

Literature: Unknown.

Marks, Signatures, Inscriptions: Unknown.

24. *Vathek*, 1815

Provenance: William Beckford; by descent to the 12th Duke of Hamilton; Library sale 1882, lot 728; [—]; private collection.

Exhibitions: Library sale 1882, lot 728.

Literature: Library sale 1882, lot 728.

Marks, Signatures, Inscriptions: Unknown.

25. Toasting Fork

Provenance: William Beckford; by descent to 15th Duke of Hamilton; Sotheby's, London, 14 July 1988, lot 122 (withdrawn by owner); Spink and Son, Ltd., London; Sotheby's, New York, 24 April 1998; private collection.

Exhibitions: Sotheby's, London, 14 July 1988, lot 122; Sotheby's, New York, 24 April, 1998.

Literature: Sotheby's, London, 14 July 1988, lot 122; Sotheby's, New York, 24 April, 1998.

Marks, Signatures, Inscriptions: London hallmarks for 1793–94.

26. Basket

Provenance: William Beckford; John Farquhar; Phillips' 1823, day 32, lot 1543; purchased Robinson; Nathan Meyer Rothschild; by descent to the family of Victor Rothschild; Sotheby's, 26 April 1937; Francis Stonor Plohn Collection; Sotheby's, London, 15 October 1970, lot 79; Arthur Gilbert 1970.

Exhibitions: Christie's 1822, day 9, lot 75 or 76; Phillips' 1823, day 32, lot 1543; Sotheby's, 26 April 1937; Sotheby's, London, 15 October 1970, lot 79.

Literature: Christie's 1822, day 9, lot 75 or 76; Phillips' 1823, day 32, lot 1543; Sotheby's, 26 April 1937; Sotheby's, London, 15 October 1970, lot 79; Timothy Schroder, *The Gilbert Collection of Gold and Silver* (Los Angeles, 1984), pp. 324–27.

Marks, Signatures, Inscriptions: London hallmarks for 1797–98; maker's mark of Paul Storr (Grimwade no. 2235).

27. Charger

Provenance: The Stadholder of Holland, Willem V, Prince of Orange; William Beckford; John Farquhar; Phillips' 1823; Mr. F. Hodges; Christie's 1868; Royal Scottish Museum, 1869.

Exhibitions: Phillips' 1823; Christie's 1868.

Literature: Rutter1823a, pp. 10–13; Phillips' 1823; Christie's 1868; Abraham L. den Blaauwen, *The Meissen Service of Stadholder Willem V* (Zwolle/Apeldoorn, 1993).

Marks: Unknown.

28. Tureen

Provenance: Phillips' 1823, 435 pieces to Mr. F. Hodges; Christie's 1868, 418 pieces sold in 75 lots; [—]; Alfred Duane Pell; The Metropolitan Museum of Art, 1902.

Literature: Unknown.

Marks, Signatures, Inscriptions: Unknown.

Exhibitions: Phillips' 1823, Christie's 1868.

Literature: Phillips' 1823; Rutter 1823a, pp. 10–13; Christie's 1868; Abraham L. den Blaauwen, *The Meissen Service of Stadholder Willem V* (Zwolle/Apeldoorn, 1993).

Marks, Signatures, Inscriptions: Unknown.

29. Hall Settee

Provenance: William Beckford; Phillips' 1801, lot 47, 48, or 49; [—]; St. Andrew's, Trent.

Exhibitions: Phillips' 1801, lot 47, 48, or 49.

Literature: Phillips' 1801, lot 47, 48, or 49; Phillippa Bishop, "Settees from Fonthill Splendens," *The Beckford Journal* 1 (Spring 1995), p. 15–17, illus. p 16 (discusses a second pair).

Marks, Signatures, Inscriptions: None.

30. *View of the Monastery of Batalha, Portugal*

Provenance: [—]; Charles Jones, New York 1963; Doyle's New York, 13 May 1998; David Vyvyan-Robinson.

Exhibitions: Doyle's New York, 13 May 1998.

Literature: Doyle's New York, 13 May 1998; *Country Life* (26 December 1963), p. 1729; engraved by *B. Comte*, 1810, and published by Messrs. Colnaghi, 23 Cockspur Street, London 1812.

Marks, Signatures, Inscriptions: Unknown.

Beckford and Heraldry

31. Pair of Candlesticks

Provenance: William Beckford; by descent to Mary Louise, Duchess of Montrose; acquired by the Treasury in lieu of death duties in 1958; transferred to The National Trust for Scotland, Brodick Castle.

Exhibitions: Unknown.

Literature: *Beckford and Hamiltion Silver* (Spink 1980), B6; Snodin and Baker 1980, illus. 12; *Beckford and Hamilton Silver* (Brussels 1992) B7.

Marks, Signatures, Inscriptions: London hallmarks for 1781–82; maker's mark of John Scofield (Grimwade no. 1670)

32. Bowl

Provenance: William Beckford; his grandson, The Earl of Angus and Arran; by descent to the 15th Duke of Hamilton; Glasgow Museums, 1977.

Exhibitions: Unknown.

Literature: Unknown.

Marks, Signatures, Inscriptions: London hallmarks for 1809–10; maker's mark of Paul Storr (Grimwade no. 2235) for Rundell, Bridge and Rundell.

33–36. Two Cups and Saucers, Two Plates

Provenance: William Beckford; by descent,

Mary Louise, Duchess of Montrose; acquired by the Treasury in lieu of death duties in 1958; transferred to the National Trust for Scotland, Brodick Castle.

Exhibitions: *William Beckford* (Salisbury) 1976, no. 31, p. 86, for two pieces from the same service; *Beckford and Hamilton Silver* (Spink 1980), B16, B17; *Beckford and Hamilton Silver* (Brussels 1992), B18, B19, pps. 66–67, illus. p. 67.

Literature: Unknown.

Marks, Signatures, Inscriptions: around the footrim of each piece, in gilt, variously, "Barr Flight & Barr, Worcester Porcelain Manufacturers, to their Majesties"; or "Barr, Flight & Barr – Worcester, Porcelain Manufrs. & Co." Each pattern bears on the reverse of each plate and saucer either: a polychrome Hamilton crest of oak issuing from ducal crown, the saw differenced for Beckford by a shield bearing the Latimer cross, below the Hamilton motto "THROUGH"; or, the Beckford crest of heron with fish in its beak, below the eckford motto "DE DIEU TOUT" (Information kindly supplied by Bill Cowell and Kate Mitchell). The 1844 Inventory details the set in Lansdown Tower, and described as: "A Tea Set of Worcester Red and Gold consisting of 11 Cups and Saucers Basin and 9 Plates Basin 5 Plates and 4 Cups and Saucers" ("Inventory of 1844, p. 41). The 1854 inventory of the Hamilton residence at Portman Square, London, detailing items from Bath, lists "12 Bread and Butter Plates, 16 Cups & Saucers, and 2 Slop Basins with the Armorial bearings of the Duchess of Hamilton and Wm Beckford Esq." (NRA[S], Hamilton MSS, Misc, M. 12/51).

The set now in the ownership of the National Trust for Scotland comprises: Pattern A—6 plates, 1 slop bowl, 7 breakfast cups with wishbone or "Dresden" handles, 7 saucers; Pattern B—6 plates, 1 slop bowl, 7 breakfast cups with wishbone, or 'Dresden' handles, 7 saucers. More pieces of the set survive in private collections.

37. Bowl

Provenance: William Beckford; by descent to the 12th Duke of Hamilton; Christie's 1882; Christopher Beckett-Denison; his sale 1885; William James; by descent; Trustees of the Edward James Foundation.

Exhibitions: Christie's 1882; Christopher Beckett-Denison; his sale 1885.

Literature: Christie's 1882; Christopher Beckett-Denison; his sale 1885. Snodin and Baker 1980, pt. 2, F3.

Marks, Signatures, Inscriptions: mounts, London hallmarks for 1811–12; maker's mark of IR, apparently for John Robins (for a discussion of this maker's mark, see cat. no. 109).

38. Bowl

Provenance: William Beckford; by descent to Mary Louise, Duchess of Montrose; acquired by the Treasure in lieu of death duties in 1958; transferred to The National Trust for Scotland, Brodick Castle.

Exhibitions: Unknown.

Literature: Unknown.

Marks, Signatures, Inscriptions: mounts, London hallmarks for 1820–21; maker's mark of James Aldridge (Grimwade no. 1768).

39. Cup and Cover

Provenance: William Beckford; by descent to the 12th Duke of Hamilton; Christie's 1882, p. 221, lot 2028, purchased by W. Massey-Mainwaring for £787 10s.; [—]; private collection, Australia; Christie's, London, 6 December 1989, *Important Silver and Objects of Vertu*, lot 208, £143,000, Fitzwilliam Museum.

Exhibitions: Christie's 1882, lot 2028; Christie's London, 6 December 1989, lot 208; *Principal Acquisitions of the Past Seven Years*, Fitzwilliam Museum, Cambridge, 21 May–26 August 1990; *Fifteen Years of the National Art Collections Fund*, Christie's, London, 6 January–26 January 1997; *William Beckford's Buildings, held by the Beckford Tower Trust*, Christie's, 15 January–3 February 1998.

Literature: Christie's 1882, lot 2028; Christie's, London, 6 December 1989, lot 208; Snodin and Baker 1980, pt.1, fig. 35; ibid., pt. 2, G 136; Michael Jaffé, "William Beckford's Lapis-Lazuli Cup," *National Art-Collections Fund Review* (1990), pp. 124–27.

40. Teapot

Provenance: William Beckford; by descent to the 15th Duke of Hamilton; National Museums of Scotland, 1977.

Exhibitions: Unknown.

Literature: Unknown.

Marks, Signatures, Inscriptions: London hallmarks for 1802–3; maker's mark of Peter Podio (Grimwade no. 2215).

41. Teapot Stand:

Provenance: William Beckford; by descent to the 15th Duke of Hamilton; National Museums of Scotland, 1977.

Exhibitions: Unknown.

Literature: Unknown.

Marks, Signatures, Inscriptions: London hallmarks for 1817–18; maker's mark of William Eaton (Grimwade no. 3105).

42. Bowl

Provenance: William Beckford; by descent to the 15th Duke of Hamilton; National Museums of Scotland, 1977.

Exhibitions: Unknown.

Literature: Unknown.

Marks, Signatures, Inscriptions: London hallmarks for 1819–20; maker's mark of Philip Rundell (Grimwade no. 2228).

43. Jug

Provenance: William Beckford; by descent to the 15th Duke of Hamilton; National Museums of Scotland, 1977.

Exhibitions: Unknown.

Literature: Unknown.

Marks, Signatures, Inscriptions: London hallmarks for 1819–20; maker's mark of Philip Rundell (Grimwade no. 2228).

44. Tea Caddy

Provenance: William Beckford; by descent to the 15th Duke of Hamilton; National Museums of Scotland, 1977.

Exhibitions: Unknown.

Literature: Unknown.

Marks, Signatures, Inscriptions: London hallmarks for 1796–67; maker's mark of Michael Plummer (Grimwade no. 2058).

BECKFORD AS FRANCOPHILE

45. *Lady in a Red Corset and Satin Dress*

Provenance: William Beckford; by descent to the 12th Duke of Hamilton; Christie's 1882, lot 1107, bought Agnew £472 10s.; sold by them 8 July 1882 to Sir Michael Robert Shaw-Stewart, Ardgowan, Greenock, Lanarkshire, Scotland; Walter Richard Shaw-Stewart, Fonthill Abbey, Tisbury, Wiltshire, by 1903; by descent; private collection.

Exhibitions: Christie's 1822, lot 32; Christie's 1882, lot 1107.

Literature: Christie's 1822, lot 32; Christie's 1882, lot 1107; Pierre de Nolhac, *J-H Fragonard 1732–1806* (Paris, 1906), p. 144.

Marks, Signatures, Inscriptions: signed "fragonard" (lower left).

46. Pair of Vases

Provenance: William Beckford; by descent to the 12th Duke of Hamilton; Christie's 1882, lot 248, purchased by Duncan, £850 10s; [—]; Jules Bache; The Metropolitan Museum of Art, 1949.

Exhibitions: Christie's 1822, day 10. lot 14; Christie's 1882, lot 248.

Literature: Christie's 1822, day 10, lot 14; Book no. 2, "Inventory of 1844," p. 48; *List of Articles . . . from Bath to Hamilton Palace,* Hamilton MSS. NRA (S) 3438; Christie's 1882, lot 248.

Marks, Signatures, Inscriptions: None.

47. Clock

Provenance: William Beckford; John Farquhar; Phillips' 1823, lot 1560, £42 12s 6d, possibly purchased at this sale by Catherine Denne, first Countess Beauchamp; by descent; the Honorable Lady Morrison, Madresfield Court.

Exhibitions: Phillips' 1823, lot 1560.

Literature: Phillips' 1823, lot 1560; catalogue of Madresfield, 1895, p. 15, no. 56

Marks, Signatures, Inscriptions: the movement signed Louis Dauthiau.

48. Two Plates

Provenance: William Beckford; [—]; private collection.

Exhibitions: Unknown.

Literature: John Whitehead, "Some French Purchases by William Beckford," *The Beckford Journal* 2 (spring 1996), p. 41.

Marks, Signatures, Inscriptions: illustrated plate, decoration painted by Guillame Noël (1755–1800), gilder, Henri-Martin Prévost (1757–1797); unillustrated plate, decoration painted by Jacques-François Louis de Laroche (1758–1802), gilder, Henri-Martin Prévost.

49. Two Cups and Saucers

Provenance: William Beckford; by descent to the 15th Duke of Hamilton; private collection.

Exhibitions: Unknown.

Literature: Philip Hewat-Jaboor, "An Early Nineteenth Century Dihl and Guerhard Porcelain Cup and Saucer Made for William Beckford," *The Beckford Journal* 2 (spring 1996), pp. 7–8.

Marks, Signatures, Inscriptions: cup A, (decorated with pink roses) Manuf. de MM. Dihl & Guerhard a Paris, and with the Beckford heron and Hamilton oak devices in an oval (in gilt); saucer A, (decorated with pansies) stencilled in grey MF. de Dihl et Guerhard a Paris, and with the devices of the beckford heron and Hamilton oak in an oval (in gilt); cup and saucer B, (decorated with marguerites) Manuf. de MM. Dihl & Guerhard a Paris, and with the devices of the Beckford heron and Hamilton Oak in an oval (in gilt).

50. Design for a Ewer and Basin

Provenance: Maison Odiot; Sotheby's Monaco, November 1979; Jacques Fischer, Paris; National Galleries of Scotland.

Exhibitions: Sotheby's Monaco, November 1979.

Literature: Sotheby's Monaco, November 1979.

Marks, Signatures, Inscriptions: [lower right in pencil] "C.468"; red collector's stamp "Collection/J.B.C./Odiot/no." with the number "468" added in black pen.

51. Ewer and Basin

Provenance: William Beckford; John Farquhar; Phillips' 1823, day 17, ewers lots 827, 828, basins lots 829, 830; [—]; Christie's Geneva, 26 April 1977, lot 384; private collection.

Exhibitions: Christie's 1822, day 8, ewers lots 78, 79, basins lots 80, 81.; Phillips' 1823, day 17, ewers lots 827, 828, basins lots 829, 830; Christie's Geneva, 26 April 1977, lot 384.

Literature: Christie's 1822, day 8, ewers lots 78, 79, basins lots 80, 81; Phillips' 1823, day 17, ewers lots 827, 828, basins lots 829, 830; Christie's Geneva, 26 April 1977, lot 384.

Marks, Signatures, Inscriptions: Paris hallmarks

for 1787–78 (struck with the charge marks of the *régisseur général des droits de marque* François Kalandrin in use between 1782 and possibly as late as 1796, and the Paris warden's mark used between July 1787 and November 1788) and 1798–1809; the bases engraved *H. Auguste F Paris 14 Avril 1802*; maker's mark of Henri Auguste (1759–1816), in use between 1785 and ca. 1796 (Nocq, I, p. 33).

52. Casket

Provenance: William Beckford; Christie's 1817 lot 75, £107.10; purchased by the Earl of Yarmouth (9 July 1817) on behalf of the Prince Regent, Carlton House; given by him 3 November, 1820 to the Marchioness of Conyngham; [—]; Frank Partridge and Sons; The Toledo Musuem of Art, 1969.

Exhibitions: Christie's 1817, lot 75.

Literature: Christie's 1817, lot 75; The Toledo Museum of Art, "Treasures for Toledo," *Museum News*, n.s. 12, no. 4 (winter 1969), illus; "Accessions," *Art Quarterly* 33, no. 1 (spring 1970), p. 92; Ruth Davidson, "Museum Accessions," *Antiques* 99, no. 1 (January 1971), p. 42, illus., "Recent Acquisitions," *Art Quarterly* 34, no. 1 (spring 1971), p. 133; "Le Chronique des Arts," *Gazette des Beax-Arts*, vol. 81, no. 1249, illus. p. 131; *The Toledo Museum of Art: A Guide to the Collections* (Toledo, 1976), illus. p. 83; Gisela Gramaccini, *Jean-Guillame Moitte (1746–1810): Leben und Werk* (Berlin, 1993), 2:63, fig. 238, p. 257.

Marks, Signatures, Inscriptions: Located in center of inside bottom: maker's mark (after 1793); unofficial assay mark (1794–97); official assay mark (1798–1809); Paris excise mark (1798–1809)

53. Armchair

Provenance: Probably Cardinal Fesch; probably William Beckford; probably John Farquhar; probably Phillips' 1823, lots 1534–1540 inclusive; the 3rd Marquess of Londonderry; by descent; private collection.

Exhibitions: probably Phillips' 1823, lots 1534–1540.

Literature: probably Phillips' 1823, lots 1534–1540; Lucy Wood, *Le Mobilier du Cardinal Fesch: Napoléon, les Bonaparte et l'Italie*, exh. cat. (Ajaccio: Musee Fesch, 2001).

Marks, Signatures, Inscriptions: Unknown.

An Eye to the East

54. Ewer

Provenance: William Beckford before 1844; by descent; Christie's 1882, day 8, 3 July 1882, lot 857; Baron Alphonse de Rothschild, inv. no. P48; Baron Edouard de Rothschild, inv. no. E.de R. 252; Baroness Batsheva de Rothschild; her sale, Christie's London, 4 December 2000, lot 15; private collection.

Exhibitions: Manchester, 1858 (for reference to the Manchester exhibition, see *Special Exhibition of Works of Art of the Mediaeval, Renais-*

sance, and more recent periods [London: South Kensington Museum, 1862], 389, no. 4969); Christie's 1882, day 8, 3 July 1882, lot 857; Gaston Migeon, *Exposition des art musulmans* (Paris: Musée des Arts Decoratifs, 1903), no. 988, illus. in the *Album*, pl. 63, center; Irit Ziffer, *Islamic Metalwork*, exh. cat. (Tel Aviv: Eretz Museum, 1996), 53, fig. 32; Christie's London, 4 December 2000, lot 15.

Literature: English 1844, pl. 7; Christie's 1882, day 8, 3 July 1882, lot 857; Christie's, London, 4 December 2000, lot 15.

Marks, Signatures, Inscriptions: None.

55. Water Pipe (*Hookah*)

Provenance: [—]; William Beckford; Phillips' 1823, lot 1541, sold 209gns., possibly purchased by Catherine Denne, first Countess Beauchamp; first recorded at Madresfield, 1876; by descent; the Honorable Lady Morrison, Madresfield Court.

Exhibitions: Phillips' 1823, lot 1541.

Literature: Phillips' 1823, lot 1541.

Marks, Signatures, Inscriptions: the maker's mark for James Aldridge (Grimwade no. 1768).

56. Ladle

Provenance: William Beckford; by descent to Mary Louise, Duchess of Montrose; acquired by the Treasury in lieu of death duties in 1958; transferred to the National Trust for Scotland, Brodick Castle.

Exhibitions: *Treasure Houses 1985*, no. 513, p. 576, illus.

Literature: Unknown.

Marks, Signatures, Inscriptions: London hallmarks for 1815–16, maker's mark of Paul Storr (Grimwade no. 2235).

57. Vase and Cover

Provenance: William Beckford; by descent to Mary Louise, Duchess of Montrose; acquired by the Treasury in lieu of death duties in 1958; transferred to the National Trust for Scotland, Brodick Castle.

Exhibitions: Unknown.

Literature: Snodin and Baker 1980, pt. 2, A73; *Treasure Houses 1985*, no. 513, p. 576

Marks, Signatures, Inscriptions: 29 tolas . . . 6 . . . rizvan (approx 134 grams).

58. Teapot and Stand

Provenance: William Beckford; by descent to the 15th Duke of Hamilton; National Museums of Scotland, 1977.

Exhibitions: Unknown.

Literature: Unknown.

Marks, Signatures, Inscriptions: London hallmarks for 1812–13; maker's mark of Paul Storr (Grimwade no. 2235).

59. Teapot

Provenance: William Beckford; by descent

to the 15th Duke of Hamilton; National Museums of Scotland, 1980.

Exhibitions: Unknown.

Literature: Unknown.

Marks, Signatures, Inscriptions: London hallmarks for 1817–18; maker's mark of John Page (Grimwade no. 1593).

60. Sugar Bowl

Provenance: William Beckford; by descent to the 15th Duke of Hamilton; National Museums of Scotland, 1980.

Exhibitions: Unknown.

Literature: Unknown.

Marks, Signatures, Inscriptions: London hallmarks for 1817–18; maker's mark of John Page (Grimwade no. 1593).

61. Bowl

Provenance: William Beckford; by descent to the 15th Duke of Hamilton; National Museums of Scotland, 1980

Exhibitions: Unknown.

Literature: Unknown.

Marks, Signatures, Inscriptions: Maker's mark of "IB" with pellet between, probably for John Baddeley (Grimwade no. 1167) or James Barratt (no. 1158).

62. Milk Jug

Provenance: William Beckford; by descent to the 15th Duke of Hamilton; National Museums of Scotland, 1980.

Exhibitions: Unknown.

Literature: Unknown.

Marks, Signatures, Inscriptions: London hallmarks for 1817–18; maker's mark of John Page (Grimwade no. 1593).

63. Teapot and Cover

Provenance: William Beckford; by descent to Mary Louise, Duchess of Montrose; acquired by the Treasury in lieu of death duties in 1958; transferred to the National Trust for Scotland, Brodick Castle.

Exhibitions: Unknown.

Literature: English 1844, pl. 7.

Marks, Signatures, Inscriptions: Unknown.

64. Basin

Provenance: William Beckford; John Farquhar; Phillips' 1823, lot 361, George Hammond Lucy, £2 15s; by descent; Sir Edmund Fairfax Lucy, on loan to The National Trust, Charlecote Park.

Exhibitions: Phillips' 1823, lot 361.

Literature: Phillips' 1823, lot 361. Wainwright 1989, p. 236, fig. 204; *Charlecote Park 1996*, p. 25.

Marks, Signatures, Inscriptions: Unknown.

65. Bottle

Provenance: William Beckford; John Farquhar; Phillips' 1823, lot 1211, George Hammond Lucy, £4. 0. 0; by descent; The National Trust, Charlecote Park.

Exhibitions: Phillips' 1823, lot 1211.

Literature: Phillips' 1823, lot 1211; Wainwright 1989, p. 238, fig. 206; *Charlecote Park 1996*, p. 22.

Marks, Signatures, Inscriptions: Unknown.

66. Vase

Provenance: William Beckford; John Farquhar; Phillips' 1823, lot 1240, lot 1241, George Hammond Lucy; by descent; Sir Edmund Fairfax Lucy, on loan to The National Trust, Charlecote Park.

Exhibitions: Phillips' 1823, lot 1240, lot 1241; *William Beckford* (Salisbury) 1976, no. 30.

Literature: Phillips' 1823, lot 1240, lot 1241; Wainwright 1989, p. 286, fig. 206; *Charlecote Park 1996*, p. 22.

Marks, Signatures, Inscriptions: Unknown.

67. Vase and Cover

Provenance: William Beckford; John Farquhar; Phillips' 1823, lot 333, George Hammond Lucy, £14.3.6; by descent; Sir Edmund Fairfax Lucy, on loan to The National Trust, Charlecote Park.

Exhibitions: Phillips' 1823, lot 333.

Literature: Phillips' 1823, lot 333; Wainwright 1989, p. 237, fig. 205; *Charlecote Park 1996*, ill. p.24.

Marks, Signatures, Inscriptions: Unknown.

68. Pot and Cover

Provenance: William Beckford; by descent to the 15th Duke of Hamilton; National Museums of Scotland, 1977.

Exhibitions: Unknown.

Literature: Unknown.

Marks, Signatures, Inscriptions: London hallmarks for 1813–14; maker's mark of Paul Storr (Grimwade no. 2235).

69. Bowl and Cover

Provenance: William Beckford; by descent to Mary Louise, Duchess of Montrose; acquired by the Treasury in lieu of death duties in 1958; transferred to the National Trust for Scotland, Brodick Castle.

Exhibitions: Unknown.

Literature: Unknown.

Marks, Signatures, Inscriptions: The mounts with London hallmarks for 1817–18; maker's mark of James Aldridge (Grimwade no. 1768).

70. Two Bowls

Provenance: William Beckford; by descent to the 12th Duke of Hamilton; Christie's 4 November, 1919, lot 62; [—]; Sterling and Francine Clark.

Exhibitions: Christie's 4 November 1919, lot 62.

Literature: Christie's 4 November 1919, lot 62; Beth Carver Wees, "English Silver in an American Museum: The Sterling and Francine Clark Art Institute," *Silver Society Journal* 4 (fall 1993), p. 121, fig. 7; idem, *English, Irish & Scottish Silver at the Sterling and Francine Clark Art Institute* (New York: Hudson Hills Press, 1977), cat. no. 280.

Marks, Signatures, Inscriptions: Hallmarks for 1813–14, maker's mark of John Robins; engraved on the underside with the Beckford heron and the Hamilton oak.

FONTHILL ABBEY, 1795–1822

71. *Fonthill Splendens with a Distant View of Fonthill Abbey*

Provenance: [—]; the Honorable Philip Smith.

Exhibitions: Unknown.

Literature: Unknown.

Marks, Signatures, Inscriptions: signed and inscribed on verso.

72. *Fonthill Abbey, Perspective Design from the North West*

Provenance: [—]; Sotheby's London, 13 November 1997, lot 38; private collection.

Exhibitions: probably Royal Academy, 1799, no. 1016; Sotheby's London, 13 November 1997, lot 38.

Literature: Sotheby's London, 13 November 1997, lot 38.

Marks, Signatures, Inscriptions: None.

73. *Projected Design for Fonthill Abbey, Wiltshire*

Provenance: [—]; Paul Mellon; Yale Center for British Art, 1975.

Exhibitions: Unknown.

Literature: Unknown.

Marks, Signatures, Inscriptions: None.

74. *Perspective View of Fonthill Abbey from the South-West*

Provenance: William Beckford; by descent to the 12th Duke of Hamilton; Christie's 1919; Ralph Brocklebank; Fine Art Society, London; Bolton Museum and Art Gallery, 1948.

Exhibitions: Christie's 1919.

Literature: Christie's 1919.

Marks, Signatures, Inscriptions: Unknown.

75. *Near View of the South Front of Fonthill Abbey from the Lawn; Builders at Work on the Tower*

Provenance: J. M. W. Turner by whom bequeathed to the Tate Gallery, 1856.

Exhibitions: "Turner and the Scientists," Tate Gallery, London, March–June 1998.

Literature: A. J. Finberg, *A Complete Inventory of the Drawings of the Turner Bequest*, vol. 1 (National Gallery, London, 1909), pp. 120–21, 176; James Hamilton, *Turner and the Scientists*, (Tate Gallery: London, 1998), pp. 24–26.

Marks, Signatures, Inscriptions: None.

76. *View of Fonthill Abbey*

Provenance: J. M. W. Turner by whom bequeathed to the Tate Gallery, 1856.

Exhibitions: "Young Turner: Early Work to 1800; Watercolours and Drawings from the Turner Bequest," no. 46, Tate Gallery, January–March 1988.

Literature: A. J. Finberg, *A Complete Inventory of the Drawings of the Turner Bequest*, vol. 1 (London: National Gallery, 1909), pp. 120–21, 176; Anne Lyles, *Young Turner: Early Work to 1800, Watercolours and Drawings from the Turner Bequest, 1787–1800* (London: Tate Gallery, 1989), p. 41.

Marks, Signatures, Inscriptions: "J" and "99" or "86" in ink in corner.

77. *South-West View of a Gothic Abbey (Morning), now Building at Fonthill, the seat of W. Beckford, Esq.*

Provenance: William Beckford; [—]; John Paris Bickell; The Art Gallery of Toronto, 1952.

Exhibitions: Unknown.

Literature: Unknown.

Marks, Signatures, Inscriptions: Unknown.

78. *South View of the Gothic Abbey (Evening), now Building at Fonthill*

Provenance: William Beckford; J. Allnutt, 1862; Frederic Nicholls, 1906; Sir Henry Pellatt; Gordon C. Edwards; [—]; The Montreal Museum of Fine Arts.

Exhibitions: *Exhibition at the Royal Academy of Arts* (London: Royal Academy of Arts, 1800); *19th Loan Exhibition of Water-Colours and Pastels* (Montréal: Musée des beaux-arts de Montréal, 1897); *Loan Collections of Paintings of the English, Old Dutch, Modern Dutch, French and Other European Schools* (Toronto: Art Gallery of Ontario, 1909); *Canada Collects, 1860–1960: European Painting from famous Canadian Collections of the past and from Contemporary Collections in various parts of Canada* (Montréal: Musée des beaux-arts de Montréal, 1960).

Literature: *Exhibition at the Royal Academy of Arts, London* (London: Royal Academy of Arts, 1800); *19th Loan Exhibition, Water-Colours and Pastels. In the Art Gallery, Phillips Square* (1897); *Loan Collection of Paintings of the English, Old Dutch, Modern Dutch, French and Other European Schools Contributed by Private Collectors in the City of Toronto and held in the Public Library, College Street* (Toronto: Art Gallery of Toronto, 1909); *Canada Collects, 1860–1960: European Painting from Famous Canadian Collections of the Past and from Contemporary Collections in Various Parts of Canada* (Montreal:

1960); "Accessions of American and Canadian Museums," *The Art Quarterly* 27, no.2 (1964); Andrew Wilton, *J.M.W. Turner: His Art and Life* (1979); Hélène Lamarche, *Looking at the Collections of the Montreal Museum of Fine Arts* (1992, English edition); Katharine Baetjer, *Glorious Nature—British Landscape Painting–1750–1850* (1993).

Marks, Signatures, Inscriptions: Unknown.

79. Model of Fonthill Abbey

Provenance: Beckford Tower Trust.

Exhibitions: Unknown.

Literature: Unknown.

Marks, Signatures, Inscriptions: None.

80. *King Lear*

Provenance: William Beckford, before 1838; by descent to the 12th Duke of Hamilton; Christie's 1882, lot 1068, by H. Graves and Co., £31.10.0; Thomas B. Walker; Walker Art Galleries, 1927; Frank Gunter; Detroit Institute of Art, 1977.

Exhibitions: "Art in Britain. Paintings and Drawings 1761–1860," Detroit Institute of Art, 1968.

Literature: *Art in Britain. Paintings and Drawings 1761–1860,* Detroit Institute of Art, (Detroit, 1968); Helmut Von Erffa and Allen Staley, *The Paintings of Benjamin West* (New Haven and London: Yale University Press, 1986), pp. 102–107, no. 210.

Marks, Signatures, Inscriptions: Unknown.

81. *Saint Michael and the Dragon*

Provenance: William Beckford; John Farquhar; Phillips' 1823, p. 259, lot 250; [—]; Foster's Auction House, London, 1941; Charles Mitchell, London and Bryn Mawr, Pennsylvania; The Toledo Museum of Art, 1959.

Exhibitions: London, Royal Academy, 1797, no. 242; Christie's 1822, lot 89; Phillips' 1823, p. 259, lot 250; Foster's Auction House, London, 1941; *The World of Benjamin West* (Allentown [PA] Art Museum, 1962), no. 25, illus.; *Revealed Religion: Benjamin West's Commission's for Windsor Castle and Fonthill Abbey* (San Antonio [TX] Museum of Art, 1983), no. 39, pp. 58, 69, illus. p. 60; *American Paintings from the Toledo Museum of Art* (New York: IBM Gallery of Science and Art, 1986); *Benjamin West: American Painter at the English Court* (Baltimore Museum of Art, 1989), no. 45, pp. 89, 91, 115, illus. p. 88.

Literature: *Public Characters of 1805* (London, 1805), 7:561; J. Barlow, *Columbiad, a poem* (Philadelphia, 1808), p. 398; "A Catalogue of the Works of Benjamin West, Esq.," *Supplement to Le Belle Assemblée* 4 (1 July 1808), p. 14; J. Galt, *The Life, Studies and Works of Benjamin West Esq.* (London, 1820), 2:219; Christie's 1822, lot 89; Phillips' 1823, p. 259, lot 250; Foster's Auction House, London, 1941; M. Rogers, Jr., "Benjamin West and the Caliph; Two Paintings for Fonthill Abbey," *Apollo* 83 (June 1966), pp. 420–25, fig. 2; Montgomery Art Gallery, Pomona College, *18th Century Drawings from*

California Collections (Claremont, California, 1976), p. 46, fig. 24 (cat. by D. Steadman); J. Dillenberger, *Benjamin West: The Context of His Life's Work* (San Antonio, 1977), pp. 109, 150, 194, 209, fig. 75; *The Toledo Museum of Art, American Paintings* (Toledo, 1979), pp. 110–12, fig. 7; "New Accessions," *The Toledo Museum of Art Museum News* 5, no. 3 (fall 1962), p. 66, illus.; "Accessions of American and Canadian Museums, April–June 1962," *Art Quarterly* 25, no. 3 (fall 1962), p. 263, illus. p. 270; Mahonri Sharp Young, "From Howling Wilderness to Queensborough Bridge," *Apollo* 86, no. 70 (December 1967), p. 496; Helmut Von Erffa and Allen Staley, *The Paintings of Benjamin West* (New Haven and London: Yale University Press, 1986), no. 408, pp. 388, 395–6, 400–1, illus.; Nancy Grubb, *Revelations: Art of the Apocalypse* (New York, 1997), illus. p. 109, (col.); [illus. p. 208 (col.) in Tiny Folio edition]; Gail E. Husch, *Something Coming: Apocalyptic Expectation and Mid-Nineteenth Century American Painting* (Hanover, NH, 2000), pp. 191, 193 fig. 61.

Marks, Signatures, Inscriptions: Unknown.

82. Pair of Candlesticks

Provenance: William Beckford; John Farquhar; Phillips' 1823, lot 1167, sold for £7. 7s.od. or lot 1168, sold for £7. os. od; Beatrice Lagrave Maltby; Christie's New York, *Important English Furniture and Objects of Art*, 16 April 1994, lot 15 (a set of four); private collection.

Exhibitions: Phillips' 1823, lot 1167 or 1168.

Literature: Rutter 1822, p.60; Rutter 1823a, pl. 7, illustrates these or a similar set; Rutter 1823b, p. 35; Phillips' 1823, lot 1167 or 1168; H. Ottomeyer and P. Pröschel, *Vergoldete Bronzen*, vol. 1 (Munich: Klinkhardt and Biermann, 1986), fig. 5.1.3., p. 324; Wainwright 1989, p. 134, pl. 114; Snodin and Baker 1980, pt.1, n. 51, ibid., pt. 2, E 8; John Hardy, "Candlesticks from Fonthill Abbey," *The Beckford Journal* 2 (spring 1996), pps. 62–23.

Marks, Signatures, Inscriptions: None.

83. Casket

Provenance: William Beckford; John Farquhar; Phillips' 1823, lot 1151, £105; purchased George Hammond Lucy; by descent; The National Trust, Charlecote Park.

Exhibitions: Christie's 1822, day 9, lot 95; Phillips' 1823, lot 1151; *William Beckford* (Salisbury) 1976, no. 5.

Literature: Christie's 1822, day 9, lot 95; Rutter 1822, p. 37; Phillips' 1823, lot 1151; Wainwright 1989, p. 236, fig. 203; *Charlecote Park* 1996, p. 25

Marks, Signatures, Inscriptions: None.

84. Casket

Provenance: William Beckford; John Farquhar; Phillips' 1823, lot 1294, £137, purchased by Kensington Lewis; Burhgley House.

Exhibition: Phillips' 1823, lot 1294; *Four Centuries of Works of Art from Burghley House* (1998), no. 37, p. 124

Literature: Rutter 1823a, vignette, "A Groupe of

the Rarest Articles of Virtu"; Phillips' 1823, lot 1294; Snodin and Baker 1980, pt. 2, C21.

Marks, Signatures, Inscriptions: None.

85. Table

Provenance: William Beckford; John Farquhar; Phillips' 1823, lot 477, 478, purchased by George Hammond Lucy, £16. 5s.6d.; by descent; The National Trust, Charlecote Park.

Exhibitions:; Phillips' 1823, lot 477; *Gothick 1720–1840* (Brighton Art Gallery & Museums, 1975), no. A23; *William Beckford* (Salisbury) 1976, no. 8.

Literature: Rutter 1822, p. 55; Rutter 1823a, illus. pl. 6; Rutter 1823b, p. 39; Britton 1823, illus. pl. 8;; Phillips' 1823, lot 477; *Charlecote Park* 1996, p.13

Marks, Signatures, Inscriptions: None.

86. Cabinet

Provenance: Fonthill Abbey; Christie's 1822, day 3, lot 96; Phillips' 1823, lot 1138, purchased by George Hammond Lucy, £199; by descent; The National Trust, Charlecote Park.

Exhibitions: Christie's 1822, day 3, lot 96; Phillips' 1823, lot 1138.

Literature: Rutter 1822, p. 41; Christie's 1822, day 3, lot 96; Rutter 1823a, p. 29; Rutter 1823b, p. 24; Phillips' 1823, lot 1138; Wainwright 1989, p. 237, fig. 205; *Charlecote Park* 1996, p. 25.

Marks, Signatures, Inscriptions: None.

87. Cabinet

Provenance: William Beckford; John Farquhar; Phillips' 1823, lot 1144, purchased by George Hammond Lucy, £147 10s; by descent; The National Trust, Charlecote Park.

Exhibitions: Christie's 1822, day 4, lot 55 and lot 56; Phillips' 1823, lot 1144; *Treasure Houses* 1985, no. 490, p. 553.

Literature: Christie's 1822, day 4, lot 55 and lot 56; Rutter 1822, p. 41; Phillips' 1823, lot 1144.

Marks, Signatures, Inscriptions: None.

88. Table

Provenance: the marble top, Empress Joséphine's collection at Malmaison, possibly her sale, 1816; the marble top and base, William Beckford; John Farquhar; Phillips' 1823, day 29, lot 1140, for £267 10s to Miles; Philip John Miles, Leigh Court, Bristol; his son, Sir William Miles, 1st Bt.; his seventh daughter, Florence Louisa, wife of the Rev. Hon. Francis Edmund Byng, later fifth Earl of Strafford; their son, Edmund Henry, sixth Earl of Strafford, who as Viscount Enfield succeeded his maternal grandfather, or uncle; by descent; private collection.

Exhibitions: Phillips' 1823, day 29, lot 1140.

Literature: Postumous inventory of Empress Joséphine, Malmaison 1814; Phillips' 1823, day 29, lot 1140; Rutter 1823a, p. 31 and illustrated; Rutter 1823b, p. 30.

Marks, Signatures, Inscriptions: Unknown.

89. *Interior of a Gothic Church by Day*

90. *Interior of a Gothic Church by Night*

Provenance: William Beckford; by descent to the 15th Duke of Hamilton; private collection.

Exhibitions: Unknown.

Literature: Unknown.

Marks, Signatures, Inscriptions [each painting]: initialed "P. N." (center left).

91. Fonthill Abbey Sale Catalogue (1822)

Provenance: [—]; private collection.

Exhibitions: Unknown.

Literature: Unknown.

Marks, Signatures, Inscriptions: inscribed in ink, "Mrs. Walcott Sympson 252".

92. Fonthill Abbey Sale Catalogue (1823)

Provenance: [—]; private collection

Exhibitions: Unknown.

Literature: Unknown.

Marks, Signatures, Inscriptions: None.

93. Admission Ticket

Provenance: [—]; private collection

Exhibitions: Unknown.

Literature: Unknown.

Marks, Signatures, Inscriptions: "no. 1695", in ink.

ANTIQUARIAN TASTE

94. *Interior of a Grand Saloon of Pictures*

Provenance: Presumed painted for the Guild of Saint Luke in Antwerp; Benjamin Shaw; Christie's, London, 7 June 1819, lot 67, Hume for William Beckford £21; John Farquhar; Phillips' 1823, lot 141, bought in ("Wright" in catalogue) £24. 13s. 6d.; William Beckford; English 1845, lot 341, bought in £44 2s; John Rhodes, by 1868; by descent to Col. Fairfax Rhodes of Brockhampton Park, Andoversford, Gloucestershire; Sotheby's, London, 11 July 1934, lot 144, bought Feldman; Henri Antoville Galleries, New York; Julius H. Weitzner, New York, by 1949; Estate of Ray Livingston Murphy sale, Christie's, New York, 15 January 1986, lot 111; private collection.

Exhibitions: Christie's, London, 7 June 1819, lot 67; Christie's 1822, lot 23; Phillips' 1823, lot 141; English 1845, lot 341; *National Exhibition of Works of Art* (Leeds, 1868), no. 877; Sotheby's, London, 11 July 1934, lot 144; *Pictures within Pictures* (Hartford, Connecticut: Wadsworth Atheneum, 1949), no. 33 and ill. pl. 7.; Christie's, New York, 15 January 1986, lot 111.

Literature: Christie's, London, 7 June 1819, lot 67; Rutter 1822, p. 38; Christie's 1822, lot 23; Rutter 1823a, p. 29; Phillips' 1823, lot 141; English 1845, lot 341; *National Exhibition of Works of Art* (Leeds, 1868), no. 877; Sotheby's, London, 11 July 1934, lot 144; *Pictures within Pictures* (Hartford, Connecticut: Wadsworth Atheneum, 1949), no. 33 and ill. pl. 7.; Christie's, New York, 15 January 1986, lot 111.

Marks, Signatures, Inscriptions: "J.J. van Opstal F. 1698" [signed and dated on a scroll over the knee of the figure in center left].

95. Oinoche (wine jug)

Provenance: Found in an Etruscan tomb at Vulci on the estate of Lucien Bonaparte, Prince of Canino; purchased at his sale by the Duke of Hamilton; presumed gift to his father-in-law William Beckford; English 1845, lot 636, purchased by Charles Hempson; by whom given to The British Museum, 1845.

Exhibitions: English 1845, lot 636.

Literature: English 1845, lot 636; J. de Witte, *Description d'une collection de vases peintes et bronzes antiques provenat des fouilles de l'Etrurie,* (Paris, 1837) 1, no. 1; "Acquisitions, Greek and Roman Antiquities, 1840–45," British Museum, Department of Greek and Roman Antiquities Library, 367, 1845.11–28.1; *London News,* 6 December, 1845, p. 365, illus.

Marks, Signatures, Inscriptions: Unknown.

96. Chasse

Provenance: William Beckford; John Farquhar; Phillips' 1823, lot 1263, sold £26.10.0; Anne, Countess of Newburgh; Hon. Robert Curzon, M.P.; Robert Curzon (14th Baron Zouche, in 1870), Parham, near Pulborough, Sussex; Robert Nathaniel Curzon (15th Baron, Zouche, 1873–1911); Georges Hoentschel, Paris, by 1911; Jacques Seligmann, Paris, 1912; J. Pierpont Morgan by whom gifted to The Metropolitan Museum of Art, 1917.

Exhibitions: Christie's 1822, day 9, lot 58; Phillips' 1823, lot 1263.

Literature: Christie's 1822; Britton 1823, frontispiece; Rutter 1823a, vignette, "A Groupe of the Rarest Articles of Virtu"; Phillips' 1823, lot 1263.

Marks, Signatures, Inscriptions: None.

97. Triptych: *The Lamentation, The Prophet Daniel and an Apostle, probably St. Peter*

Provenance: William Beckford; by descent to the 12th Duke of Hamilton; Christie's 1882, lot 971; [—]; Christie's, 1–4 July 1912, *Catalogue of the Renowned Collection of Works of Art . . . formed by the late John Edward Taylor,* lot 142; [—]; the Fitzwilliam Museum.

Exhibitions: Christie's 1822, p. 12, lot 87; Christie's 1882, lot 971; *Catalogue of a Collection of European Enamels from the Earliest Date to the End of the XVII Century* (London: Burlington Fine Arts Club, 1897), p. 42, no. 148; Christie's, 1–4 July 1912, lot 142; *Treasures from the Fitzwilliam* (Cambridge: Fitzwilliam

Museum, 1989), p. 43, no. 45.

Literature: Christie's 1822, p. 12, lot 87; J. C. Robinson, ed., *Catalogue of the Special Exhibition of Works of Art of the Mediaeval, Renaissance and More Recent Periods on loan at the South Kensington Museum, June 1862,* rev. ed. (London, 1863), pp. 165–66, no. 1750; Christie's 1882, lot 971; Christie's, 1–4 July 1912, lot 142; Tancred Borenius, *The Leverton Harris Collection,* (London: privately printed, 1931), p. 10, and pl. 18.

Marks, Signatures, Inscriptions: initialed and dated "P 1538 R" on the left wing, "P.R" on the central panel, below Christ, and "PR" spaced out on the right wing, all in gold.

98. **Dish:** *The Wedding Banquet of Cupid and Psyche*

Provenance: William Beckford; by descent to the 12th Duke of Hamilton; Christie's 1882, lot 970, £1218, purchased by W. Wareham; George Salting, his bequest to the Victoria and Albert Museum, 1910.

Exhibitions: J. C. Robinson, ed., *Catalogue of the Special Exhibition of Works of Art of the Mediaeval, Renaissance and More Recent Periods on loan at the South Kensington Museum, June 1862,* rev. ed. (London, 1863), pp. 165–66, no. 1810; Christie's 1882, lot 970; *Catalogue of a Collection of European Enamels from the Earliest Date to the End of the XVII Century* (London: Burlington Fine Arts Club, 1897), no. 72.

Literature: Christie's 1882, lot 970; Bet McLeod, "Some further objects from William Beckford's collection in the Victoria & Albert Museum," *Burlington Magazine* 143 (June 2001), pp. 367–70.

Marks, Signatures, Inscriptions: monogram "I.C" in gilt below the heel of Cupid.

99. **Tazza and Cover:** *Scenes from the Story of Samson*

Provenance: Horace Walpole; Robins, Strawberry Hill, 1842, lot 59, purchased by Hume for Beckford; William Beckford; by descent to the 12th Duke of Hamilton; Christie's 1882, lot 966, purchased by T. M. Whitehead for £2,100; George Salting, his bequest to the Victoria and Albert Museum, 1910.

Exhibitions: J. C. Robinson, ed., *Catalogue of the Special Exhibition of Works of Art of the Mediaeval, Renaissance and More Recent Periods on loan at the South Kensington Museum, June 1862,* rev. ed. (London, 1863), no. 1676; Christie's 1882, lot 966.

Literature: Christie's 1882, lot 966; Bet McLeod, "Some further objects from William Beckford's collection in the Victoria & Albert Museum," *Burlington Magazine* 143 (June 2001), pp. 367–70.

Marks, Signatures, Inscriptions: Unknown.

100. Saltcellar

Provenance: William Beckford; by descent to the 12th Duke of Hamilton; Christie's 1882, lot 817, purchased by J. E. Taylor for £141.15.0; Christie's, London, July 1912, lot 246; [—];

Henry Walters, The Walters Art Gallery.

Exhibitions: Christie's 1882, lot 817; Christie's, London, July 1912, lot 246.

Literature: English 1844, pl. 13; Christie's 1882, lot 817; Christie's, London, July 1912, lot 246; J. Prentice von Erdberg and M. C. Ross, *Catalogue of the Italian Maiolica in The Walters Art Gallery* (Baltimore: Walters Art Gallery, 1952), p. 32, pl. 40, cat. no. 62.

Marks, Signatures, Inscriptions: Unknown.

101. Design for a Dagger

Provenance: William Ottley; William Beckford, 1814; [—]; The British Museum.

Exhibitions: Unknown.

Literature: J. Rowlands, *Drawings by German Artists in the Department of Prints and Drawings in the British Museum* (London: British Museum Press, 1993), cat. no. 285, plate 186.

Marks, Signatures, Inscriptions: None.

102. Design for a Cup

Provenance: Sir Thomas Lawrence; William Beckford; Smith; The British Museum.

Exhibitions: Unknown.

Literature: J. Rowlands, *Drawings by German Artists in the Department of Prints and Drawings in the British Museum* (London: British Museum Press, 1993), cat. no. 326, pp. 149–50.

Marks, Signatures, Inscriptions: None.

103. Cup and Cover

Provenance: William Beckford; by descent to the 15th Duke of Hamilton; Sotheby's London, 25 October 1973, lot 126; the Museo Thyssen Bornemisza Collection.

Exhibitions: J. C. Robinson, ed., *Catalogue of the Special Exhibition of Works of Art of the Mediaeval, Renaissance and More Recent Periods on loan at the South Kensington Museum, June 1862*, rev. ed. (London, 1863), no. 6189; Sotheby's, London, 25 October 1973, lot 126; *Wenzel Jamnitzer und die Nürnberger Goldschmiedekunst 1500–1700* (Nuremberg: Germanisches Nationalmuseum, 1985), no. 31.

Literature: English 1844, pl. 7; I. Finlay, "Foreign Silver in the Collection of the Duke of Hamilton," *Connoisseur* 124: 83, ills. 3, 4, Sotheby's London, 25 October 1973, lot 126; Hannelore Müller, "Notes on Sixteenth-Century German Silverware," *Apollo* (July 1983), p. 51, fig 2; idem, *The Thyssen Bornemisza Collection: European Silver* (London: Sotheby's Publications, 1986), p. 36–39.

Marks, Signatures, Inscriptions: Unknown.

104. Bowl

Provenance: By repute, Garde-Meuble, 2.35; Chevalier Durand; Paris, 25–27 May, 1818, lot 93, purchased by Chardin for William Beckford, 501 livres; by descent to the 12th Duke of Hamilton; Christie's 1882, lot 2027, ill., purchased by Marks, Durlacher Brothers for £1,207.10s; F.O. Matthiessen Collection, gifted to The Metropolitan Museum of Art, 1904.

Exhibitions: Paris 25–27 May, 1818, lot 93; Christie's 1882, lot 2027.

Literature: Paris 25–27 May, 1818, lot 93; Christie's 1882, lot 2027; Olga Raggio, "Light and Line in Renaissance Crystal Engravings," *Metropolitan Museum of Art Bulletin*, n.s. 10 (March 1952), pp. 193–202, ill. p. 199.

Marks, Signatures, Inscriptions: Unknown.

105. Casket

Provenance: William Beckford; John Farquhar; Phillips' 1823, either lot 1143, sold for £56.14.0, or lot 1142, £54.10.0; Lord Grosvenor; by descent to the Marquess of Wesminster; Arturo Lopez-Willshaw; Baron de Redé; Sotheby's Monaco, 26 May 1975, lot no. 157; Sotheby's London, 7 December 1995, lot no. 254; Hanns Schell.

Exhibitions: Christie's 1822, day 3, either lot 101 or 102;; Phillips' 1823, either lot 1143 or lot 1142; Sotheby's Monaco, 26 May 1975, lot. no. 157; Sotheby's London, 7 December 1995, lot no. 254.

Literature: Christie's 1822, day 3, either lot 101 or 102; Rutter, 1822, p. 4; Rutter 1823b, p. 24; Rutter 1823a, p. 29; Phillips', 1823, either lot 1143 or lot 1142; Hans Huth, *Lacquer in the West: The History of a Craft and Industry, 1550–1950* (Chicago and London: University of Chicago Press, 1971), p. 7–10.; Sotheby's Monaco, 26 May 1975, lot no. 157; Sotheby's London, 7 December 1995, lot no. 254.

Marks, Signatures, Inscriptions: Unknown.

106. Covered Cup

Provenance: Henrietta Howard, Countess of Suffolk; bequest to Lady Elizabeth Germain, 1767; her sale, 1769, £163; Margravine of Anspach, Brandenburgh House, Phillips', 29 July, 1818, 465 gns; William Beckford; John Farquhar; Phillips' 1823, day 15, lots 574 (sold for £294.0.0), 575; Mrs. Walker, Blythe Hall, Nottinghamshire, bequest to the grandmother of Miss Sybil Weldon; Christie's, London, 9 July 1954; Crichton's; Peter Wilding Esq., bequest to the British Museum, 1969.

Exhibitions: Phillips', 29 July 1818; Christie's 1822, day 5, lots. 51, 52; Phillips' 1823, day 15, lots 574, 575; Christie's, London, 9 July 1954.

Literature: Phillips', 29 July 1818; Christie's 1822, day 5, lots 51, 52; Rutter 1822, p. 55; Rutter 1823a, p. 31 and pl. 6; Britton 1823, p. 8; Phillips' 1823, day 15, lots 574, 575; Christie's, London, 9 July, 1954; H. Tait, "Huguenot Silver, The Wilding Bequest Part I," *Connoisseur* (August 1972), pp. 270–74; and idem, "London Huguenot Silver" in *Huguenots in Britain and Their French Background 1500–1800*, ed. I. Scouloudi (Basingstoke: Macmillan, 1987).

Marks, Signatures, Inscriptions: Hallmarks for 1711–12; maker's mark for David Willaume.

BECKFORD, FRANCHI, AND DESIGN

107. Pair of Candlesticks

Provenance: William Beckford; by descent to the 12th Duke of Hamilton; Christie's 1919, lot 75; Lord Fisher; Sotheby's, London, 23 January 1964, lot 19; [—]; Christie's, New York, 24 May 1977, lot 121, purchased by Asprey; Christie's, New York, 15 April 1997, lot 273, Mrs. Jerome Gans.

Exhibitions: Christie's 1822, day 4, lot 58; Christie's 1919, lot 75; Sotheby's, London, 23 January 1964, lot 19; Christie's, New York, 24 May 1977, lot 121; Christie's, New York, 15 April 1997, lot 273.

Literature: Christie's 1822, day 4, lot 58; Rutter 1822, pp. 60–61; Rutter 1823a, p.66; English 1844, p. 8, pl. 7; Cyrus Redding, *Memoirs of William Beckford*, vol. 2 (London: C. J. Skeet, 1859), 274; Christie's 1919, lot 75; Sotheby's, London, 23 January 1964, lot 19; Christie's, New York, 24 May 1977, lot 121; Snodin and Baker 1980, pt. 2, A36, E1; Michael Clayton, *The Collector's Dictionary of the Silver and Gold of Great Britain and North America*, 2d ed. (London: Hamlyn, 1985), p. 60, illus. fig. 77; Vanessa Brett, *The Sotheby's Directory of Silver* (London: Sotheby's Publications, 1986), p. 247, no. 1111; Timothy Schroder, *The Gilbert Collection of Gold and Silver* (Los Angeles: Los Angeles County Museum of Art, 1988), p. 326; Charles Truman, ed., *Sotheby's Concise Encyclopedia of Silver* (London: Conran Octopus, 1996), illus. on dust jacket; Christie's, New York, 15 April 1997, lot 273.

Marks, Signatures, Inscriptions: London hallmarks for 1800–1801; maker's mark of Paul Storr (Grimwade no. 2235).

108. Salver

Provenance: William Beckford; John Farquhar; possibly Phillips' 1823, day 17, lot 825, or 826; possibly William Beckford; by descent to the 12th Duke of Hamilton; Christie's 1882, lot 617; private collection.

Exhibitions: possibly Christie's 1822, day 6, lot 52, or 53; Christie's 1882, lot 617.

Literature: possibly Christie's 1822, day 6, lot 52, or 53; Christie's 1882, lot 617.

Marks, Signatures, Inscriptions: London hallmarks for 1817–18; maker's mark of William Burwash (Grimwade no. 3047).

109. Ladle

Provenance: William Beckford; by descent to the 15th Duke of Hamilton; Trustees of the National Museums of Scotland, 1980.

Exhibitions: Unknown.

Literature: Snodin and Baker 1980, p. 821, illus. fig. 26.

Marks, Signatures, Inscriptions: hallmarks for 1812–13, lacking town mark but apparently London; maker's mark of "IR," apparently for John Robins.

110. Jug

Provenance: William Beckford; John Farquhar; Phillip's 1823, lot 1052 (ewer only), £14.0.0; Sir Michael Sobell; Sotheby's London, 9 June 1994, lot 244; Marian Walecki Collection.

Exhibitions: Christie's 1822, day 9, lot 12; Phillip's 1823, lot 1052 (ewer only); Sotheby's London, 9 June 1994, lot 244.

Literature: Christie's 1822, day 9, lot 12; Phillip's 1823, lot 1052 (ewer only); Sotheby's London, 9 June 1994, lot 244.

Marks, Signatures, Inscriptions: the mounts with London hallmarks for 1816–17; maker's mark of James Aldridge (Grimwade no. 1768).

111. Sugar Tongs

Provenance: William Beckford; by descent to the 15th Duke of Hamilton; Trustees of the National Museums of Scotland, 1977.

Exhibitions: Unknown.

Literature: Unknown.

Marks, Signatures, Inscriptions: None.

112. Sugar Tongs

Provenance: William Beckford; by descent to the 15th Duke of Hamilton; Trustees of the National Museums of Scotland, 1977.

Exhibitions: Unknown.

Literature: Unknown.

Marks, Signatures, Inscriptions: London hallmarks for 1813–14 (apparently lacking leopard's head); maker's mark of J. W. Storey and William Elliot (Grimwade no. 1762).

113. Sugar Tongs

Provenance: William Beckford; by descent to the 15th Duke of Hamilton; Trustees of the National Museums of Scotland, 1977.

Exhibitions: Unknown.

Literature: Unknown.

Marks, Signatures, Inscriptions: London hallmarks for 1812–13 (apparently lacking leopard's head); maker's mark of J. W. Storey and William Elliot (Grimwade no. 1762).

114. Sugar Tongs and Four Teaspoons

Provenance: William Beckford, by descent to the 15th Duke of Hamilton; private collection

Exhibitions: Unknown.

Literature: Unknown.

Marks, Signatures, Inscriptions: London hallmarks for 1818–19; maker's mark "IR," apparently for John Robins.

115. Cup and Cover

Provenance: William Beckford; [—]; Partridge Fine Art; Gilbert Collection.

Exhibitions: Christie's 1822, day 8, lot 43.

Literature: Christie's 1822, day 8, lot 43; *Silver at

Partridge's: Recent Acquisitions (October 1994), 42–43, no. 32.

Marks, Signatures, Inscriptions: Unknown.

116. Bowl

Provenance: William Beckford; by descent to Mary Louise, Duchess of Montrose; acquired by the Treasury in lieu of death duties in 1958; transferred to the National Trust for Scotland, Brodick Castle.

Exhibitions: *Beckford and Hamilton Silver* (Spink 1980), B 18; *Beckford and Hamilton Silver* (Brussels 1992), B 20, p. 68; *Treasure Houses* 1985, no. 513, p. 575; *William Beckford* (Salisbury) 1976, no. 52.

Literature: Snodin and Baker 1980, pt. 1, fig. 42, p. 745; ibid., pt. 2, p. A62.

Marks, Signatures, Inscriptions: mounts with London hallmarks for 1816–17; maker's mark for Paul Storr (Grimwade no. 2235).

117. Cup and Cover

Provenance: William Beckford; by descent to Mary Louise, Duchess of Montrose; acquired by the Treasury in lieu of death duties in 1958; transferred to the National Trust for Scotland, Brodick Castle.

Exhibitions: *Beckford and Hamilton Silver* (Spink 1980), B19; *Beckford and Hamilton Silver* (Brussels 1992), B21 p. 69.

Literature: English 1844, pl. 11; Snodin and Baker 1980, pt. 1, fig 40, p. 745; ibid., pt. 2, p. A59.

Marks, Signatures, Inscriptions: mounts with London hallmarks for 1816–17; maker's mark for James Aldridge (Grimwade no. 1768).

118. Bowl and Cover

Provenance: William Beckford; by descent to Mary Louise, Duchess of Montrose; acquired by the Treasury in lieu of death duties in 1958; transferred to the National Trust for Scotland, Brodick Castle.

Exhibitions: *William Beckford* (Salisbury) 1976, no. 21; *Beckford and Hamilton Silver* (Spink 1980), B20; *Beckford and Hamilton Silver* (Brussels 1992), B22, p.70; *Treasure Houses* 1985, no. 513, p. 575.

Literature: Snodin and Baker 1980, pt. 1, fig. 37, p.742.

Marks, Signatures, Inscriptions: London hallmarks for 1818–19; maker's mark of John Harris.

119. Cup and Cover

Provenance: William Beckford; English 1845, lot 514, £77 14s. purchased by Raven; [—]; private collection.

Exhibitions: None.

Literature: "Inventory of 1844," p. 49; Snodin and Baker 1980, pt. 2, G 121; English 1844, title page and pl. 11; *Illustrated London News*, 6 December 1845, p. 364, vignette p. 365; C. Richardson, *Studies in Ornamental Design* (London: John Weale, 1851), illus. frontispiece.

Marks, Signatures, Inscriptions: The mounts with London hallmarks for 1820–21; maker's mark of James Aldridge (Grimwade no. 1768).

120. Spoon

Provenance: William Beckford; by descent to Mary Louise, Duchess of Montrose; acquired by the Treasury in lieu of death duties in 1958; transferred to the National Trust for Scotland, Brodick Castle.

Exhibitions: *Beckford and Hamilton Silver* (Spink 1980), B27; *Beckford and Hamilton Silver* (Brussels 1992), B28.

Literature: Snodin and Baker 1980, pt. 2, A112.

Marks, Signatures, Inscriptions: None.

121. Spoon

Provenance: William Beckford; by descent to Mary Louise, Duchess of Montrose; acquired by the Treasury in lieu of death duties in 1958; transferred to the National Trust for Scotland, Brodick Castle.

Exhibitions: *Beckford and Hamilton Silver* (Brussels 1992), B30, p. 76.

Literature: Unknown.

Marks, Signatures, Inscriptions: None.

122. Spoon

Provenance: William Beckford; by descent to Mary Louise, Duchess of Montrose; acquired by the Treasury in lieu of death duties in 1958; transferred to the National Trust for Scotland, Brodick Castle.

Exhibitions: *Beckford and Hamilton Silver* (Spink 1980), B24; *Beckford and Hamilton Silver* (Brussels 1992), B 26, p. 74.

Literature: C. Richardson, *Studies in Ornamental Design* (London: John Weale, 1851).

Marks, Signatures, Inscriptions: None.

123. Ladle

Provenance: William Beckford; by descent to Mary Louise, Duchess of Montrose; acquired by the Treasury in lieu of death duties in 1958; transferred to the National Trust for Scotland, Brodick Castle.

Exhibitions: *Beckford and Hamilton Silver* (Spink 1980), B25; *Beckford and Hamilton Silver* (Brussels 1992), B26, p. 74.

Literature: Snodin and Baker 1980, pt. 2, A113.

Marks, Signatures, Inscriptions: None.

124. Spoon

Provenance: William Beckford; by descent to Mary Louise, Duchess of Montrose; acquired by the Treasury in lieu of death duties in 1958; transferred to the National Trust for Scotland, Brodick Castle.

Exhibitions: *Beckford and Hamilton Silver* (Spink 1980), B26; *Beckford and Hamilton Silver* (Brussels 1992), B28, p. 75; *Treasure Houses* 1985, no. 513, p. 576.

Literature: Snodin and Baker 1980, pt. 1, fig. 43, p. 475; ibid., pt. 2, A1.

Marks, Signatures, Inscriptions: None.

125. Scent Flask

Provenance: William Beckford; by descent to Mary Louise, Duchess of Montrose; acquired by the Treasury in lieu of death duties in 1958; transferred to the National Trust for Scotland, Brodick Castle.

Exhibitions: *William Beckford* (Salisbury) 1976, no. 14; *Beckford and Hamilton Silver* (Spink 1980), B21; *Beckford and Hamilton Silver* (Brussels 1992), B24, p. 72.

Literature: C. Richardson, *Studies in Ornamental Design* (London: John Weale, 1851), illus. frontispiece; Snodin and Baker 1980, pt. 2, A82.

Marks, Signatures, Inscriptions: The mounts with London hallmarks for 1820–21; maker's mark of James Aldridge (Grimwade no. 1768).

126. Jug

Provenance: William Beckford; by descent to Mary Louise, Duchess of Montrose; acquired by the Treasury in lieu of death duties in 1958; transferred to the National Trust for Scotland, Brodick Castle.

Exhibitions: *Beckford and Hamilton Silver* (Spink 1980), B32; *Beckford and Hamilton Silver* (Brussels 1992), B44, p. 88.

Literature: Snodin and Baker 1980, pt. 1, fig. 44. p. 746; ibid., pt. 2, A130.

Marks, Signatures, Inscriptions: The mounts with London hallmarks for ca. 1820; maker's mark of John Robins (Grimwade no. 1623).

127. Bowl and Cover

Provenance: William Beckford; by descent to the 12th Duke of Hamilton; Christie's 1882; Christopher Beckett-Denison; his sale 1885; William James; by descent; Trustees of the Edward James Foundation.

Exhibitions: Christie's 1882.

Literature: Christie's 1882.

Marks, Signatures, Inscriptions: The mounts with London hallmarks for 1817–18; maker's mark of James Aldridge (Grimwade no. 1768).

128. Casket

Provenance: William Beckford; Gregorio Franchi; Christie's 1827, lot 99; [—]; Asprey's; The Museum of Fine Arts, Boston.

Exhibitions: *Portugal e o Reino Unido: A alianca revisitade* (Lisbon: Gulbenkian Mueseum, 1994–5), fig. 21, p. 97

Literature: Ellenor M. Alcorn, *English Silver in the Museum of Fine Arts, Boston*, vol. 2, *Silver from 1697* (Boston, 2000), pp. 270–73.

Marks, Signatures, Inscriptions: London hallmarks for 1820–21; maker's mark of John Harris; cover inscribed, "Le tems [sic] peut nous detruire mais no pas nous detacher."

Bath: The Final Years, 1822–1844

129. Model of Lansdown Tower

Provenance: Beckford Tower Trust.

Exhibitions: *William Beckford* (Salisbury) 1976, no. A56.

Literature: Unknown.

Marks, Signatures, Inscriptions: None.

130. *Unknown Sitter, Traditionally called The Duke of Alva*

Provenance: Possibly in the sale of Urbino Pizzetta, Christie's, London, 26 May 1820, lot 89, bought in; William Beckford; John Farquhar; Phillips' 1823, lot 26, bought Swabey for Beckford £31 10s.; by descent to the 12th Duke of Hamilton; Christie's 1882, lot 1141, bought Agnew £420; sold by them 8 July 1882 to Sir Michael Robert Shaw-Stewart; Walter Richard Shaw-Stewart, by 1903; by descent, private collection.

Exhibitions: Christie's, London, 26 May 1820, lot 89; Christie's, 8 October 1822, lot 31; Phillips' 1823, lot 26; Christie's 1882, lot 1141.

Literature: Christie's, London, 26 May 1820, lot 89; Christie's, 8 October 1822, lot 31; Phillips' 1823, lot 26; Christie's 1882, lot 1141.

Marks, Signatures, Inscriptions: Unknown.

131. *The Adoration of the Magi*

Provenance: Supposedly from the Palazzo Aldobrandini, Rome; William Beckford; English 1848, lot 42, bought in (in catalogue bought "Worsley") £170 10s; by descent to the 12th Duke of Hamilton; Christie's 1882, 24 June 1882, lot 403, the Honorable William Frederick Barton Massey-Mainwaring £1218; Christie's, London, 24 April 1998, lot 127; Messrs Hall & Knight Ltd.

Exhibitions: Christie's 1822 lot 94; English 1848, lot 42; Christie's 1882, 24 June 1882, lot 403; Christie's, London, 24 April 1998, lot 127.

Literature: Christie's 1822 lot 94; English 1848, lot 42; Christie's 1882, 24 June 1882, lot 403; Christie's, London, 24 April 1998, lot 127; Nicholas J. Hall, "Girolamo da Carpi, *The Adoration of the Magi*," catalogue, (London and New York, Hall and Knight Ltd., 2001), pp. 82–85.

Marks, Signatures, Inscriptions: Unknown.

132. *The Holy Family with Saints John the Baptist, Elizabeth, Zacharias and (?) Francis*

Provenance: said to have been in the domestic chapel of the Aldobrandini family in Rome; probably therefore that listed in the inventory of Cardinal Pietro Aldobrandini 1603, lot 86; possibly bought by Beckford from Tresham in 1799; William Beckford by 1801; John Farquhar; Phillips' 1823, lot 189, bought Hume for Beckford £299 15s.; purchased from Beckford by the National Gallery, London, 1839.

Exhibitions: Christie's, 8 October 1822 lot 108; Phillips' 1823, lot 189.

Literature: Britton 1801, vol. 1, p. 226; Rutter 1822, p. 44; Christie's, 8 October 1822 lot 108; Phillips' 1823, lot 189; Waagen 1838, vol. 3, p. 123; J. D. Passavant, *Tour of a German Artist in England* (London: Saunders and Otley, 1836), vol. 1, p. 316; Cecil Gould, *National Gallery Catalogues: The Sixteenth Century Italian Schools* (London, The National Gallery, 1975), pp. 92–93.

Marks, Signatures, Inscriptions: Unknown.

133. Binding: *Picturae Francisci Albani in Aede Verospia*

Provenance: Sir Joshua Reynolds; William Beckford; by descent to the 12th Duke of Hamilton; Library sale 1882, lot 104; Frank Linsley James, by descent to Edward James; private collection.

Exhibitions: Library sale 1882, lot 104

Literature: Library sale 1882, lot 104

Marks, Signatures, Inscriptions: signature and small ownership stamp for Sir Joshua Reynolds on the title; William Beckford's penciled library number on the front free endpaper; Edward James' bookplate on inside cover.

134. *Paris Revisited in 1815, by way of Brussels: Including a Walk over the Field of Battle at Waterloo*

Provenance: William Beckford; [—]; James Lees-Milne; bequeathed to the Bath Preservation Trust, 1989

Exhibitions: Unknown.

Literature: Unknown.

Marks, Signatures, Inscriptions: Unknown.

135. *Voyages de M. du Mont, en France, en Italie, en Allemagne, a Malthe, et en Turquie*, volume 4 of 4

Provenance: William Beckford; by descent to the 12th Duke of Hamilton; Library sale 1882, part 1, lot 2684 purchased by Wickham 16s.; William Wickham; by descent to Charlotte, Lady Bonham-Carter; gifted to James Lees-Milne, 1975; bequeathed to the Bath Preservation Trust, July 1998.

Exhibitions: Library sale 1882, part 1, lot 2684.

Literature: Library sale 1882, part 1, lot 2684.

Marks, Signatures, Inscriptions: Unknown.

136. *Sketches and Observations taken on a Tour through a Part of the South of Europe*

Provenance: William Beckford; by descent to the 12th Duke of Hamilton; Library sale 1882, part 4, lot 562, purchased by Bain, £1; Rosebery Sale, Sotheby's, 28 October 1975, lot 507, purchased by Rosenkilde & Bragge, £104.50; James Lees-Milne, purchased from Traylen, 1989, £285; bequeathed to the Bath Preservation Trust, July 1998.

Exhibitions: Library sale 1882, part 4, lot 562; Rosebery Sale, Sotheby's, 28 October 1975, lot 507.

Literature: Library sale 1882, part 4, lot 562; Rosebery Sale, Sotheby's, 28 October 1975, lot 507.

Marks, Signatures, Inscriptions: Unknown.

137. *Anecdotes of the English Language, Chiefly Regarding the Local Dialect of London and its Environs*, 2nd edition

Provenance: William Beckford; by descent to the 12th Duke of Hamilton; Library sale 1882, part 3, lot 549 (part of lot); Rosebery Sale, Sotheby's, 28 October 1975, lot 268; James Lees-Milne, purchased from Traylen, cat. 91, 1980–81; bequeathed to the Bath Preservation Trust, July 1998.

Exhibitions: Library sale 1882, part 3, lot 549 (part of lot); Rosebery Sale, Sotheby's, 28 October 1975, lot 268.

Literature: Library sale 1882, part 3, lot 549 (part of lot); Rosebery Sale, Sotheby's, 28 October 1975, lot 268.

Marks, Signatures, Inscriptions: Unknown.

138. Jug

Provenance: William Beckford; by descent to Mary Louise, Duchess of Montrose; acquired by the Treasury in lieu of death duties in 1958; transferred to The National Trust for Scotland, Brodick Castle.

Exhibitions: Unknown.

Literature: Unknown.

Marks, Signatures, Inscriptions: London hallmarks for 1823–24; maker's mark of Philip Rundell (Grimwade no. 2228) but made under the direction of Cato Sharp in the workshops of Rundell, Bridge and Rundell.

139. Bowl

Provenance: William Beckford; by descent to the 12th Duke of Hamilton; Christie's 1882, lot 486, £550; Sir Francis Oppenheimer; [—]; The Trustees of the Barber Institute of Fine Arts.

Exhibitions: Christie's 1882, lot 486, £550; Sir Francis Oppenheimer; *Gold and Silver* (Birmingham Art Gallery, 1963); *William Beckford* (Bath) 1966, no. 74.

Literature: English 1844, pl. 7; Christie's 1882, lot 486, £550; Sir Francis Oppenheimer; *William Beckford* (Salisbury) 1976, p. 87 illus.; Snodin and Baker 1980, pt. 2, A101; Wainwright 1989, fig. 128, p.146; The Barber Institute of Fine Arts, *Handbook* (1993), p. 124.

Marks, Signatures, Inscriptions: London hallmarks of 1824–25; maker's mark of Paul Storr (Grimwade no. 2235).

140. *Susan Euphemia, Duchess of Hamilton, as a Sibyl*

Provenance: Susan, Duchess of Hamilton; by descent; the Hamilton Collection.

Exhibitions: Unknown.

Literature: Unknown.

Marks, Signatures, Inscriptions: "Roma/ Grahl/1827."

141. Pair of Tea Kettles, Lamp Stands, and Wind Shields

Provenance: William Beckford; by descent to Mary Louise, Duchess of Montrose; acquired by the Treasury in lieu of death duties in 1958; transferred to the National Trust for Scotland, Brodick Castle.

Exhibitions: *Beckford and Hamilton Silver* (Spink 1980), B9, B10; *Beckford and Hamilton Silver* (Brussels 1992), B11, B12.

Literature: Snodin and Baker 1980, pt. 2, A13, A29a, A102.

Marks, Signatures, Inscriptions: Stand and wind shield, London hallmarks for 1781–82; maker's mark of Daniel Smith and Robert Sharp (Grimwade no. 506). [Pair A, kettle and lamp:] London hallmarks for 1796–97; maker's mark of Rolbert Sharp (Grimwade no. 2436); [Pair B, kettle and lamp:] London hallmarks for 1832–33; maker's mark of Benjamin Preston (Grimwade no. 206).

142. Cup

Provenance: William Beckford; by descent to Mary Louise, Duchess of Montrose; acquired by the Treasury in lieu of death duties in 1958; transferred to the National Trust for Scotland, Brodick Castle.

Exhibitions: *Beckford and Hamilton Silver* (Spink 1980), B42; *Beckford and Hamilton Silver* (Brussels 1992), B47.

Literature: Snodin and Baker 1980, pt. 2, A133.

Marks, Signatures, Inscriptions: "James Short" inscribed on foot.

143. Saltcellar

Provenance: William Beckford; by descent to Mary Louise, Duchess of Montrose; acquired by the Treasury in lieu of death duties in 1958; transferred to the National Trust for Scotland, Brodick Castle.

Exhibitions: *Beckford and Hamilton Silver* (Spink 1980), B41; *Beckford and Hamilton Silver* (Brussels 1992), B48.

Literature: Snodin and Baker 1980, pt. 2, A104, fig. 17.

Marks, Signatures, Inscriptions: Bristol maker's mark of JHW.

144. Pair of Ladles

Provenance: William Beckford; by descent to Mary Louise, Duchess of Montrose; acquired by the Treasury in lieu of death duties in 1958; transferred to the National Trust for Scotland, Brodick Castle.

Exhibitions: *Beckford and Hamilton Silver* (Spink 1980), B41; *Beckford and Hamilton Silver* (Brussels 1992), B48.

Literature: Snodin and Baker 1980, pt. 2, A104, fig. 17.

Marks, Signatures, Inscriptions: Bristol maker's mark of JHW.

145. Armchair

Provenance: William Beckford; by descent to Mary Louise, Duchess of Montrose; private collection.

Exhibitions: Unknown.

Literature: Unknown.

Marks, Signatures, Inscriptions: None.

146. Chair

Provenance: William Beckford; by descent to Mary Louise, Duchess of Montrose; private collection.

Exhibitions: Unknown.

Literature: Unknown.

Marks, Signatures, Inscriptions: None.

147. Stool

Provenance: William Beckford; by descent to Mary Louise, Duchess of Montrose; private collection.

Exhibitions: Unknown.

Literature: Unknown.

Marks, Signatures, Inscriptions: None.

148. Coffer

Provenance: William Beckford; English 1841, lot 26 or lot 26, unsold or repurchased by William Beckford; English 1845, day 8, lot 520 or 521; [—]; Blairman's; private collection.

Exhibitions: English 1841, lot 26 or lot 26; English 1845, day 8, lot 520 or 521; *William Beckford's Buildings, held by the Beckford Tower Trust*, Christie's, 15 January–3 February 1998.

Literature: English 1841, lot 26 or lot 26; English 1845, day 8, lot 520 or 521; Martin Levy, "A Coffer from Lansdown Tower," *The Beckford Journal* 3 (spring 1997), pp. 25–29.

Marks, Signatures, Inscriptions: None.

149. Pair of Candlesticks

Provenance: William Beckford; by descent to the 12th Duke of Hamilton; Christie's 1882, lot 622; [—]; Christie's New York, 27 April 1987, lot 262; private collection.

Exhibitions: Christie's 1882, lot 622; Christie's New York, 27 April 1987, lot 262.

Literature: English, 1844, plate 12; Christie's 1882, lot 622; Christie's New York, 27 April 1987, lot 262.

Marks, Signatures, Inscriptions: Maker's mark of Edward Barnard and Sons (Grimwade no. 575); engraved under the bases, *ENGLISH BATH DELT.* and *SHORT BRISTOL SCULPT.*, and also engraved with the later crest and motto of Stanhope under an earl's coronet.

150. *William Beckford*

Provenance: Susan Euphemia, Duchess of Hamilton; by descent to Mary Louise, Duchess of Montrose; acquired by the Treasury in lieu of death duties in 1958; transferred to the National Trust for Scotland, Brodick Castle.

Exhibitions: Unknown.

Literature: *William Beckford* (Salisbury) 1976, illus. p. 72.

Marks, Signatures, Inscriptions: signed and dated 1844 on reverse.

151. *William Beckford*

Provenance: Susan Euphemia, Duchess of Hamilton; [—]; private collection.

Exhibitions: Unknown.

Literature: Unknown.

Marks, Signatures, Inscriptions: Unknown.

152. **Nautilus Shell**

Provenance: William Beckford; by descent to the 12th Duke of Hamilton; Christie's 1882, lot 481, purchased by Duncan, for £162.15s; Baron Ferdinand de Rothschild; Waddesdon Inventory, 1898, no. 1648; by descent to present owner.

Exhibitions: Christie's 1882, lot. 481.

Literature: English, 1844, pl. 11; Christie's 1882, lot 481; Snodin and Baker 1980, pt. 2, G164.

Marks, Signatures, Inscriptions: the shell signed by Cornelius Van Bellekin.

153. **Vase**

Provenance: William Beckford; by descent to Mary Louise, Duchess of Montrose; acquired by the Treasury in lieu of death duties in 1958; transferred to the National Trust for Scotland, Brodick Castle.

Exhibitions: Unknown.

Literature: English 1844, pl. 11.

Marks, Signatures, Inscriptions: Unknown.

154. **Casket and Cover**

Provenance: William Beckford; by descent to Mary Louise, Duchess of Montrose; acquired by the Treasury in lieu of death duties in 1958; transferred to the National Trust for Scotland, Brodick Castle.

Exhibitions: Unknown.

Literature: English 1844, pl. 11.

Marks, Signatures, Inscriptions: Unknown.

155. *Objects of Vertu*

Provenance: Susan Euphemia, Duchess of Hamilton, By descent to 15th Duke of Hamilton, Beckford Tower Trust.

Exhibitions: Unknown.

Literature: English 1844, pl. 7.

Marks, Signatures, Inscriptions: Unknown.

156. *Objects of Vertu*

Provenance: Susan Euphemia, Duchess of Hamilton, By descent to 15th Duke of Hamilton, Beckford Tower Trust

Exhibitions: Unknown.

Literature: English 1844, pl. 11.

Marks, Signatures, Inscriptions: Unknown.

157. *Objects of Vertu*

Provenance: Susan Euphemia, Duchess of Hamilton, By descent to 15th Duke of Hamilton, Beckford Tower Trust

Exhibitions: Unknown.

Literature: English 1844, pl. 13.

Marks, Signatures, Inscriptions: Unknown.

158. *Susan Euphemia, Duchess of Hamilton*

Provenance: Susan Euphemia, Duchess of Hamilton; by descent to Mary Louise, Duchess of Montrose; acquired by the Treasury in lieu of death duties in 1958; transferred to the National Trust for Scotland, Brodick Castle.

Exhibitions: Unknown.

Literature: Unknown.

Marks, Signatures, Inscriptions: signed and dated 1852.

159. *Alexander, 10th Duke of Hamilton*

Provenance: Susan Euphemia, Duchess of Hamilton; by descent to Mary Louise, Duchess of Montrose; acquired by the Treasury in lieu of death duties in 1958; transferred to the National Trust for Scotland, Brodick Castle.

Exhibitions: Unknown.

Literature: Unknown.

Marks, Signatures, Inscriptions: signed and dated 1852.

160. **Pair of Cabinets**

Provenance: William Beckford; the Dukes of Sutherland, probably George Granville Leveson-Gower, second Duke of Sutherland, for Stafford House, London, at the latest prior to 1839, where they are recorded in an inventory; by descent to Cromartie Sutherland-Leveson-Gower, fourth Duke of Sutherland (d. 1913), Stafford House; sold Knight, Frank & Rutley, 14 July 1913, lot 92; anonymous sale, Christie's London, 10 December 1959, lot 137 illus. (780 gns to Harrington); William Redford Antiques, London; Sotheby's London, 30 November 1984, lot 376; anonymous sale, Sotheby's London, 10 June 1988, lot 86 (£958,500); Christie's.

Exhibitions: Knight, Frank & Rutley, 14 July 1913, lot 92; anonymous sale, Christie's London, 10 December 1959, lot 137; Sotheby's London, 30 November 1984, lot 376; Sotheby's London, 10 June 1988, lot 86; Christie's London, 14 June 2001, lot 100.

Literature: Knight, Frank & Rutley, 14 July 1913, lot 92; anonymous sale, Christie's London, 10 December 1959, lot 137; Sotheby's London, 30 November 1984, lot 376; David Pearce, *London's Mansions* (London: B.T. Batsford Ltd., 1986), p. 200, fig. 154; Sotheby's London, 10 June 1988, lot 86; J. Yorke, *Lancaster House, London's Greatest Town House* (London: Merrell, 2001), p. 147, pl. 96.; Christie's London, 14 June 2001, lot 100.

Marks, Signatures, Inscriptions: None.

Bibliography Compiled by Jon Millington*

Editor's note: This bibliography is based a far more extensive compilation by Jon Millington. It represents only a small portion of the published material devoted to Beckford studies and related disciplines. It primarily includes published works, generally excluding manuscripts and university theses, as well as archival material; the main depository of Beckford papers is the Bodleain Library, Oxford University. An earlier bibliography is of invaluable assistance: Guy Chapman and John Hodgkin, *A Bibliography of William Beckford of Fonthill* (London: Constable, 1930).

As a subject bibliography, this bibliography has been organized to follow the chapters in the catalogue as closely as possible, with the addition of a list of selected publications by Beckford, including a separate section for his novel, *Vathek.*

References below to *The Times, Sunday Times Magazine,* and *Times Literary Supplement* are to the London publication. In many book citations below, page numbers are given for mention of Beckford.

1. Beckford's Life

Biographies

Alexander, Boyd. *England's Wealthiest Son*. London: Centaur, 1962.

Brockman, H. A. N. *The Caliph of Fonthill*. London: Werner Laurie, 1956.

Chapman, Guy. *Beckford*. London: Jonathan Cape, 1937.

Fothergill, Brian. *Beckford of Fonthill*. London: Faber and Faber, 1979.

Lees-Milne, James. *William Beckford*. Tisbury, Wilts: Compton Russell, 1976. Reprint, London: Century, 1990.

Melville, Lewis. *The Life and Letters of William Beckford*. London: Heinemann, 1910.

Mowl, Timothy. *William Beckford: Composing for Mozart*. London: John Murray, 1998.

Oliver, J. W. *The Life of William Beckford*. London: Oxford Univ. Press, 1932.

Redding, Cyrus. *Memoirs of William Beckford of Fonthill, Author of "Vathek"*. 2 vols. London: Charles J. Skeet, 1859.

Full-length Studies

Chadourne, Marc. *Eblis ou l'Enfer de William Beckford*. Paris: Pauvert, 1967.

Claésson, Dick. *William Beckford av Fonthill, Wilts., 1760–1844. En forskningsöversikt*. Gothenburg: Göteborgs universitet, 1995.

Farrell, John T. *A Reinterpretation of the Major Literary Works of William Beckford*. Ann Arbor, Michigan: University Microfilms, 1984.

Gemmett, Robert. J. *William Beckford*. Boston, Mass: Twayne, 1977.

Girard, Didier. *William Beckford, Terroriste au Palais de la Raison*. Paris: José Corti, 1993.

Gregory, W., ed. *The Beckford Family*. Bath: Queen Square Library, 1887.

Lansdown, Henry Venn. *Recollections of the Late William Beckford*. Bath: Privately printed, 1893. Reprint, Bath: Kingsmead, 1969.

Life at Fonthill, 1807–1822, with interludes in Paris and London, from the correspondence of William Beckford. Translated and edited by Boyd Alexander. London, R. Hart-Davis, 1957.

*I would like to thank Richard Allen, Sidney Blackmore, Dick Claésson, and, especially, my wife for their help in the preparation of this bibliography. —J. M.

Mahmoud, Fatma Moussa, ed. *William Beckford of Fonthill, 1760–1844: Bicentenary Essays.* Cairo, 1960.

May, Marcel. *La Jeunesse de William Beckford et la Genèse de son "Vathek."* Paris: Les Presses Universitaires de France, 1928.

Parreaux, André. *William Beckford, Auteur de Vathek.* Paris: Nizet, 1960.

Sitwell, Sacheverell. *Beckford and Beckfordism.* London: Duckworth, 1930.

Contemporary and Posthumous Accounts

[Announcement of birth.] *Gentleman's Magazine* 30 (October 1760): 489.

[Harrison, William Henry]. "Conversations with the late W. Beckford, Esq. Contributed by Various Friends." Parts 3–6. *New Monthly Magazine* 72 (September 1844): 18–24; (October 1844): 212–221; (November 1844): 418–427; (December 1844): 516–522.

Lettice, John. "William Beckford, Esq. of Fonthill." *European Magazine* 32 (September 1797): 147–150

Redding, Cyrus. "Recollections of the Author of 'Vathek'." *New Monthly Magazine* 71 (June, July 1844).

———. *Fifty Years' Recollections.* 3 vols. London: Charles J. Skeet, 1858, 3:83–120.

———. "Beckford's Life." In *Yesterday and To-day.* 3 vols. London: T Cautley Newby, 1863, 3:33–35.

———. "William Beckford." In *Past Celebrities whom I Have Known.* 2 vols. London: Charles J. Skeet, 1866, 1:249, 263 292–347.

Obituaries

Annual Register . . . for the Year 1844 86 (1845), Appendix to Chronicle: 236–238.

Gentleman's Magazine, n.s. 22 (August 1844): 209–213.

Gentleman's Magazine, n.s. 22 (December 1844): 659.

"The Late William Beckford." *Mirror of Literature,* n.s. 5 (11 May 1844): 294–296.

Literary Gazette 28 (11 May 1844): 308.

"Mr Beckford and Fonthill." *Chambers's Edinburgh Journal* n.s. 2 (17 August 1844): 101 103.

"W. Beckford, Esq." *Athenæum,* 11 May 1844, 430.

2. Aspects of Beckford

General

Alexander, Boyd. "The Decay of Beckford's Genius." In *William Beckford of Fonthill, 1760–1844: Bicentenary Essays,* edited by Fatma Moussa Mahmoud, 17–29. Cairo, 1960.

Alger, John Goldworth. *Englishmen in the French Revolution.* London: Sampson Low, 1889.

Anderson, Jorgen. "Giant Dreams." *English Miscellany* 3 (1952): 53–59.

Angelo, Henry. *The Reminiscences of Henry Angelo.* 2 vols. London: Kegan Paul, etc., 1904, 1:174–175.

Baridon, Michel. "La Modernité de Beckford." In *Cahiers Charles V. 9: Le Passé Présent,* 19–40. Paris: Centre National des Lettres: 1988.

———. "From Beckford to Mallarmé: The tradition of *L'Art pour l'Art.*" In *The Beckford Society Annual Lectures 1996–1999,* edited by Jon Millington, 55–80. Privately printed, 2000.

"Beckford, His Daughter, and the Cry of the Peacock." *Bath and County Graphic* 7 (September 1902): 53.

"Beckford's younger daughter cut off with a pittance." *Bell's Weekly Messenger* (6 January 1799).

Beer, Gavin de, ed. "Voltaire's British Visitors." *Studies on Voltaire and the Eighteenth Century* 4 (1957): 130–132.

Betsky, Aaron. *Queer Space: Architecture and Same Sex Desire.* New York: William Morrow, 1997.

Bishop, Franklin. "Masonic Rites and Architecture." *The Goth* (December 1992): 5–7.

Blackmore, Sidney, ed. *The Beckford Newsletter: An Occasional Newsletter of the Beckford Society.* Privately printed, 1996—.

Bowring, John, ed. *The Works of Jeremy Bentham.* 11 vols. Edinburgh: William Tait, 1843, 10:91, 97, 107.

Brion, Marcel. "Le Secret du Calife Beckford." *Revue des Deux Mondes* (1 July 1949): 156–165.

Browne, Robert Gore. *Chancellor Thurlow: The Life and Times of an XVIIIth Century Lawyer,* 131–132, 209, 212, 223–224. London: Hamish Hamilton, 1953.

Burke, John. "Beckford of Fonthill." In *A Genealogical and Heraldic History of the Commoners of Great Britain and Ireland,* 1:678–682. London: Henry Colburn, 1833.

Burke, John, and John Bernard Burke. "Beckford of Fonthill." In *A Genealogical and Heraldic Dictionary of the Landed Gentry of Great Britain and Ireland,* 1:77–78. London: Henry Colburn, 1849.

Carnero, Cuillermo. "William Beckford (1760–1844) o el Erotismo de Fina Estampa." *Insula* 24 (October–November 1969): 18–19.

Cave, Graham. "Beckford at the Salisbury Festival." *Beckford Tower Trust Newsletter* (spring 1992): 8.

Chadourne, Marc. "L'incroyable William Beckford." *Revue de Paris* 69 (1962): 43–58.

Claésson, Dick. "Författarskap och biografi: En diskussion kring det biografiska problemet 'Beckford'." *Tidskrift för litteraturvetenskap* [Magazine of Literature] (1999): 3–4, 109–128.

Cobbett, William. *Rural Rides.* Har-

mondsworth, Middlesex: Penguin Books, 1967.

Cholmondeley, Richard Hugh, ed. *The Heber Letters, 1783–1832,* 302. London: Blatchworth Press, 1950.

Delaney, Mary. *The Autobiography and Correspondence of Mary Granville, Mrs Delaney.* Edited by Lady Llanover. 2d series. 3 vols. London: Richard Bentley, 1862.

De Magny, Oliver. "L'Esthétique de l'Ennui." *Les Lettres Nouvelles* 5 (March 1957): 403–411.

Dorment, Richard. "Man of Mystery. Alexander Cozens at the V&A." *Country Life,* 27 November 1986, 1703.

Exposição. Exhibition: A Viagem de Uma Paixão, William Beckford & Portugal, An Impassioned Journey, 1787, 1794, 1798. In Portuguese and English. Palácio de Queluz: Instituto Português do Património Cultural, 1987.

Farington, Joseph. *The Farington Diary.* Edited by James Grieg. 8 vols. London: Hutchinson, 1922–28, 4:33, 197, 242–243, passim.

———. *The Diary of Joseph Farington.* New ed., prepared from the MS in the Royal Library at Windsor Castle. 16 vols. New Haven: Yale University Press, 1978–84, 1–6 (1978–79) covering July 1793–December 1804, edited by Kenneth Garlick and Angus Macintyre; 7–16 (1982–84) covering January 1805–December 1821, edited by Kathryn Cave; *Index,* 1998, edited by Evelyn Newby.

Flaubert, Gustave. *Correspondance.* 7th series, 302, 313. Paris: Conard, 1935.

Forgues, Paul Emile Daurand. *Originaux et Beaux-Esprits de l'Angleterre contemporaine.* 2 vols. Paris: Charpentier, 1860, 1:46–47.

Gallet, Michel. *Claude-Nicolas Ledoux, 1736–1806,* 24, 26, 254, 269–271. Paris: Picard, 1980.

Gemmett, Robert J. "The Birth Date of William Beckford." *American Notes and Queries* 6, no. 10 (June 1968): 149–150.

Girard, Didier. "Beckford in Paris, 1792: Unconcerned but not Indifferent (Man Ray's Epitaph)." *Beckford Tower Trust Newsletter* (spring 1993): 5–9.

Gotlieb, Howard B. *William Beckford of Fonthill, Writer, Traveller, Collector, Caliph, 1760–1844: A Brief Narrative and Catalogue of an Exhibition to Mark the Two Hundredth Anniversary of Beckford's Birth.* New Haven: Yale University Library, 1960.

Gray, Robert. *Letters During the Course of a Tour through Germany, Switzerland, and Italy in the Years MDCCXCI and MDCCXCII.* London, 1794.

Green, Martin. *Children of the Sun.* London: Constable, 1976.

Grigson, Geoffrey. *The Harp of Aeolus.* London: Routledge, 1947.

Gunn, J. A. W. et al., eds. *Benjamin Disraeli Letters.* 6 vols. Toronto: University of Toronto Press, 1982–1997. Letters to Beckford or references in other letters (cited by letter numbers), vol. 1, *1815–1834* (1982), 193 and n. 1, 242, 253 and n. 2, 255 & nn6,7, 282, 283, 327 and nn. 1,2, 329 and n. 3, ?330, 335 and n. 1, 332 and n. 4, 337 n. 8, 341, ?453x;

vol. 2, *1835–1837* (1982), 612 and n. 2; vol. 3, *1838–1841* (1987), 1026 and nn. 1, 2; vol. 4, *1842–1847* (1989), 1272 n. 6; vol. 5, *1848–1851* (1993), 1748; vol. 6, *1852–1856* (1997), 2300 and n. 1.

Haggerty, George E. "Beckford's Pæderasty." In *Men in Love: Masculinity and Sexuality in the Eighteenth Century,* 136–150. New York: Columbia University Press, 1999.

Heinemann, Elke, *Babylonische Spiele: William Beckford und das Erwachen der modernen Imagination.* Munich: Wilhelm Fink, 2000.

Hilliard, Elizabeth. "Annuities for Beckford's Servants." *Beckford Tower Trust Newsletter* (spring 1985): 2–3.

———. "Marquise de Santa Cruz: Love-Letters to William Beckford. Transcribed and Annotated by Roger Kann." *Beckford Journal* 2 (1996): 3–6.

Hillier, Bevis. "House Style. Case Study." *The Times Magazine* (29 April 1995): 42–43.

Huxley, Aldous. *Prisons, With the "Carceri" etchings by G. B. Piranesi: Critical study by Jean Adhémar,* 16. London: Trianon Press, 1949.

Jack, Malcolm. "How Wealthy Was 'England's Wealthiest Son'?" *Beckford Tower Trust Newsletter* (spring 1987): 4.

———. "The Professor of Paederasty." *Beckford Journal* 7 (2001): 45–46.

Jaloux, Edmond. *Johann-Heinrich Füseli,* 144. Montreux, 1942.

Janzen, Gerlof. "Strange Bedfellows or The Ambivalent Feelings and Attitudes of William Beckford toward Holland and the Dutch." *Beckford Journal* 6 (2000): 17–28.

Jean-Aubry, Georges. "Un original du xviiie siècle: Jean Huber ou le démon de Genève." *Revue de Paris* (1936): 593–626, 807–821.

Jouve, Severine. *Les décadents.* Paris: Plon, 1989.

Kann, Roger. "Marquise de Santa Cruz. Lettres d'amour à William Beckford." *Studies on Voltaire and the Eighteenth Century* 341 (1996): 239–332.

Larbaud, Valery and Georges Jean-Aubry. *Correspondance, 1920–1935.* Paris: Gallimard, 1971.

Lees-Milne, James. "Blake and Beckford: A Television Script." *Beckford Journal* 4 (1998): 5–17.

Lemaitre, Henri. *Le Paysage anglais à l'aquarelle, 1760–1851.* Paris: Bordas, 1955.

Lockhart, John Gibson. *Memoirs of Sir Walter Scott.* 5 vols. London: Macmillan, 1900.

Magny, Olivier de. "L'esthétique de l'ennui." *Les lettres nouvelles,* no. 47 (March 1957): 403–411.

Mérimée, Prosper. *Correspondance générale,* publiée par Maurice Parturier. 2d series, 4:112. Toulouse: Privat, 1956.

Millington, Jon, comp. *Beckford in the Gentleman's Magazine.* Privately printed by *The Beckford Society,* 2001.

Moore, Thomas. *The Journal of Thomas Moore.* Edited by Wilfred S. Dowden. Vol. 1, 1818–1820. Newark: University of Delaware Press, 1983.

Morgulis, Gregoire. "Un épisode de la vie de Beckford." *Revue de Littérature Comparée* 14 (1934): 690–694.

Mowl, Timothy. *Horace Walpole*. London: John Murray, 1996.

Norton, Rictor. "The Fool of Fonthill." *The Advocate* 23 (1973). Revised reprint, "The Fool of Fonthill: Rich, Gay, and Merrie in Perilous Times." *Gay News* 41 (28 February–13 March 1973): 9 and cover.

———. "Beckford of Fonthill" and "Beckford's Scrap Books." In *Mother Clap's Molly House: The Gay Subculture in England 1700–1830*, 221–231. London: Gay Men's Press, 1992.

Parreaux, André. "William Beckford (Principaux Problèmes Chronologiques)." *Bulletin des Etudes Portugaises* 1 (1931): 47–57.

Paul, Sir Balfour. "Robert Drysdale: Tutor to William Beckford." Parts 1–5. *Wiltshire Gazette*, 14, 21, and 28 February 1924; 6 and 13 March 1924.

Pitt, William. *Correspondence of William Pitt, Earl of Chatham*, edited by W. S. Taylor and J. H. Pringle. 4 vols. London: John Murray, 1838–1840, 2: 11–12; 4: 240, 290–291, 313–316.

Pückler-Muskau, Prince Hermann Ludwig Heinrich von. *Tour in England, Ireland and France in the years 1828 and 1829*, 2:210–213. Translated from *Briefe eines Verstorbenen* (1830). London: Effingham Wilson, 1832.

Raimond, Jean, and J. R. Watson, eds. *A Handbook to English Romanticism*. London: Macmillan, 1992.

Rolt, L. T. C. *Brunel*. London: Longmans, Green, 1957.

Rousseau, André–Michel. "L'Angleterre et Voltaire (1718–1789)." *Studies on Voltaire and the Eighteenth Century* 146 (1976): 287–288, 291, 321–322; ibid. 147 (1976): 606, 608, 626–628, 691, 787, 867.

Sadleir (Sadler), Michael. *Things Past*, 193. London: Constable, 1944.

Scott, Jonathan. *The Arabian Nights Entertainments*. London: Longman, etc., 1811.

Sizer, Theodore. "William Beckford and his American Property." *Yale University Library Gazette* 39, no. 1 (July 1964): 42–45.

Summers, Peter. *William Beckford: Some notes on his life in Bath 1822–1844 and a catalogue of the exhibition in the Holburne of Menstrie Museum*. Bath: Privately printed, 1966.

Thiebault, Marcel. "De Romain Gary à William Beckford." *Revue de Paris* 63 (December 1956): 159–163.

Thrale, Hester Lynch. *Thraliana: The Diary of Mrs Hester Lynch Thrale, later Mrs. Piozzi, 1776–1809*. Edited by Katharine Balderston. 2 vols. Oxford: Clarendon Press, 1942, 1:598; 2:640, 799, 969.

Vidler, Anthony. *Claude-Nicolas Ledoux: Architecture and Social Reform at the End of the Ancien Régime*, 337–340, 343, 346, 356, 379. Cambridge: M.I.T. Press, 1990.

Vidler, Anthony. "The Architecture of Lodges: Ritual Form and Associational Life in the Late Enlightenment." *Oppositions* (New York), no. 5 (summer 1976): 89–90, 97

(notes). Reprint, in idem, *The Writings of the Walls*, 100–101. Princeton, 1987.

Ward, Geoff, ed. *Romantic Literature: A Guide to Romantic Literature*, 81, 141. London: Bloomsbury, 1993.

Weightman, Jonathan. "Staging Beckford: The Theatre of Place and the Theatre of Self." *Beckford Journal* 6 (2000): 50–57.

Westland, Peter. *The Romantic Revival, 1780–1830*, 163–164. Based on the original work of Arthur Compton-Rickett. London: English Universities Press, 1950.

William Beckford Exhibition 1976. Exh. cat. Tisbury, Wilts: Compton Press, 1976.

Woolf, Virgina, and Lytton Strachey. *Letters*. Edited by Leonard Woolf and James Strachey, 16, 93. London: Hogarth Press, Chatto & Windus, 1956.

Religion

Darton, Eric. "William Beckford and Religion." *Beckford Journal* 4 (1998): 33–38.

[Hillier, Bevis]. "William Beckford and Islam." *Connoisseur* 191 (April 1976): 250–253.

Nolan, J. C. M. "The Devotee Glances at the Glorious One." *Beckford Journal* 4 (1998): 39–47.

Rope, H. E. G. "William Beckford and the Faith." *The Month* 176 (September 1940): 155–163.

Portraits of Beckford

Alexander, Boyd. "Fonthill and Portraits of William Beckford (1760–1844)." *Register of the Museum of Art*. University of Kansas 3 (Winter 1967): 2–13.

Chapman, Guy. *Times Literary Supplement*, 4 July 1929, 538.

———. "Un portrait inconnu de William Beckford." *Revue de Littérature Comparée* 27 (1953): 113–114.

Davis, Frank. "Talking about Salerooms." *Country Life* (14 February 1972): 296–297.

Gemmett, Robert J. "The Behnes' Portrait of William Beckford." *Études Anglaises* 19, no. 3 (1966): 261–262.

O'Donoghue, Freeman. *Catalogue of Engraved British Portraits preserved in the Department of Prints and Drawings in the British Museum*. Vol. 1, 152. London: Printed for the Trustees. 1908)

Piper, David. *The English Face*. London: Thames & Hudson, 1957.

3. Family and Beckford Associates

Alderman Beckford (1709–1770)

Beavan, Alfred B. *Aldermen of the City of London*, 198. London, 1908.

Bourne, Henry Richard Fox. *Famous London Merchants. A Book for Boys*. London: J. Hogg, 1869.

Glover, E. *A History of the Ironmongers' Company*. London: The Worshipful Company of Ironmongers, 1991.

Hackmann, W. K. "William Beckford's Profit from Three Jamaican Offices." *Historical Research* 63 (February 1990): 107–109.

Hammond, Norman. "Monastery gives up two 'lost' country mansions." *The Times*, 29 July 1996.

Knill, Lady Lucy. *The Mansion House*. London: Stanley Paul, 1937.

Literary Gazette 6 (24 August 1822): 540.

McGarvie, Michael. "The Beckford Family and Witham Friary." *Beckford Tower Trust Newsletter* (spring 1982): 2–4.

———. "A Seal with the Beckford Arms." *Beckford Tower Trust Newsletter* (spring 1985): 8.

Obituary. *Universal Magazine* 46 (June 1770): 334.

Pickford, John. *Notes and Queries* 6th series 3 (12 March 1881): 215.

Samuel, Arthur Michael. "Lord Mayor Beckford." *The Saturday Review*, 10 July 1920, 30–31. Reprint, in idem, *The Mancroft Essays*, 262–265. New ed. London: Cape, 1937.

[W. C. W.] Ald. Beckford's marriage, 8 June 1756, in parish register, Loughton, Essex. *Notes and Queries* 8th series 2 (15 October 1892): 304.

[Will of 19 June 1765.] *Universal Magazine* 47 (July 1770): 46–47, 49–50.

Wilson-North, Robert. "Witham. From Carthusian Monastery to Country House." *Current Archaeology*, no. 148 (June 1996): 151–156.

William Courtenay (1768–1835)

Courtenay, Sir Christopher. *The Courtenay Family*. Privately printed, 1967.

Lees-Milne, James. "The Powderham Castle Affair." In *Society Scandals*, edited by Harriet Bridgeman and Elizabeth Drury, 36–50. Newton Abbot, Devon: David & Charles, 1977.

[Nichols, John Gough]. *Gentleman's Magazine*, n.s. 4 (July 1835): 89.

Alexander (ca. 1717–1786) and John Robert Cozens (1752–1797)

Bell, C. F., and Thomas Girtin. *The Drawings and Sketches of John Robert Cozens*. Oxford: Walpole Society, 1935.

Binyon, Laurence. *English Water-Colours*, 39, 47, 51–52. London: A. & C. Black, 1933.

Clarke, Michael. *The Tempting Prospect*, 129–131. London: British Museum Publications, 1981.

"Cozens (1752–1797), J. R. Six Landscapes in Italy." *National Art-Collections Fund Review* (1985): 136–138.

Davis, Frank. "Talking about Salerooms." *Country Life*, 31 January 1974, 179.

Neve, Christopher. "Two Journeys in Monochrome. John Robert Cozens at the Whitworth." *Country Life*, 11 March 1971, 531.

Oppé, A. P. *Alexander & John Robert Cozens*. London: A. & C. Black, 1952.

Sloan, Kim. "Working for William Beckford:

'The Shackles of Fantastic Folly and Caprice,' 1780–4." In *Alexander and John Robert Cozens. The Poetry of Landscape*, 138–157. London: Yale University Press, 1986.

———. "Beauty, Beckford, and the Sublime 1775–86." In ibid., 73–79.

Wilton, Andrew. *The Art of Alexander and John Robert Cozens*, New Haven: Yale Center for British Art, 1980.

Gregorio Franchi (1770–1828)

Alexander, Boyd. *From Lisbon to Baker Street: The Story of the Chevalier Franchi, Beckford's Friend*. Lisbon, 1977.

Blackmore, Sidney. "Chevalier Franchi's Tomb." *Beckford Tower Trust Newsletter*, Pt. 2 (spring 1980): [4].

Darton, Eric. "Franchi's Last Days." *Beckford Tower Trust Newsletter* (spring 1982): 5.

———. "The Enigma of Chevalier Gregorio Franchi." *Beckford Tower Trust Newsletter* (spring 1993): 12–14.

Henry Edmund Goodridge (1797–1864)

Goodridge, Alfred S. "Brief Memoir of the late Henry Edmund Goodridge." *R.I.B.A., Sessional Papers*, 1864–1865.

"Funeral of the late William Beckford, Esq." *Bath and Cheltenham Gazette*, 22 May 1844.

Woodward, Christopher. "Aerial Boudoirs of Bath." *Country Life*, 4 September 1997, 68–71.

John Lettice (1737–1832)

Burney, Frances. *The Early Diary of Frances Burney, 1768–1778*. Edited by Annie Raine Ellis. Vol. 1, 151, 155–157, 155 n. London: George Bell, 1907.

Obituary. *Gentleman's Magazine* 102, Pt. 2 (November 1832): 477–480.

Cyrus Redding (1785–1870)

Millington, Jon. "Beckford's First Biographer." *Beckford Tower Trust Newsletter* (spring 1984): 6–8. Revised, "Cyrus Redding: Beckford's First Biographer." *Beckford Journal* 2 (1996): 26–32.

4. Fonthill: General

Burton, Elizabeth. *The Early Victorians at Home*, 55–57. London: Longman, 1972.

Chettle, Lt.-Col. H. F. "The Successive Houses at Fonthill." *Wiltshire Archæological & Natural History Magazine* 49 (June 1942): 505–512.

———. "The Background to the Beckfords." In *Two Centuries at Fonthill Gifford*, 1–15. Privately printed, ca. 1960.

The Cottington Family. *Wiltshire Archaeological & Natural History Magazine* 23 (1887): 337–339.

Crowley, D. A., ed. *A History of Wiltshire*. Victoria County Histories. Oxford: Oxford Univ. Press, 11:77–83, 98–103; 13:114–125; (155–169), 214, 236.

"Fonthill Abbey. The Estate and the Successive

Mansions." *Wiltshire Gazette*, 6 December 1923.

Hoare, Richard Colt. *A History of Modern Wiltshire. Hundred of Dunworth and Vale of Noddre*, 12–28, 195–196, 230–233, and 6 pls. London: Nichols, 1829.

"New Church at Fonthill Gifford." *Illustrated London News*, 29 September 1866, 303, & woodcut, 305.

Rogers, K. H. *Wiltshire & Somerset Woollen Mills*, 251–252. Edington, Wilts: Pasold Research Fund, 1976.

Sawyer, Rex. "The Fonthills." In *The Nadder Valley in Old Photographs*, 33–42. Stroud, Glos: Alan Sutton, 1994.

Sheard, Norah. *A Short History of Hindon*. Privately printed, 1970.

[W. T.] "Ill-Fated Fonthill and its Owners." *Bath and County Graphic* 8 (February 1904): 116–117.

Thacker, Christopher, et al. "Twin Towers." *Journal of the Georgian Group* (1995): 115–118.

5. Fonthill House and Fonthill Splendens

"Account of the magnificent Fete given by William Beckford, Esq. at his Seat at Fonthill, in Wiltshire, on the 6th of January, 1797." *Salisbury Journal*, ?17 January 1797. Reprint, in *West of England Miscellany* 29 (23 January 1797): 71–75. See Colt Hoare, *Dunworth* (1829), 25.

Angus, William. *The Seats of the Nobility and Gentry in Great Britain and Wales*. London: W. Angus, [1797].

Beamon, Sylvia P., and Susan Roaf. *The Ice-Houses of Britain*. London: Routledge, 1990.

Britton, John. *The Beauties of Wiltshire*. Vol. 1, 208–249, and 2 pls. London: Vernor & Hood, etc., 1801.

Brulé, André. "Une Visite à Fonthill en 1792." *Revue Anglo-Américaine* 10 (October 1933): 33–42.

[Brydges, Sir Samuel Egerton & Stebbing Shaw, comp.] *The Topographer* 4 (1791): 237.

Climenson, Emily J., ed. *Passages from the Diaries of Mrs Lybbe Powys . . . 1756 to 1808*. London: Longmans, 1899.

"Country News." *Gentleman's Magazine* 71, Pt. 2 (September 1801): 853–854.

"Country News." *Gentleman's Magazine* 77, Pt. 2 (September 1807): 880.

Elderton, John. "Tour into the lower parts of Somersetshire." *Gentleman's Magazine* 61 Pt. 1 (March 1791): 231.

Goede, Christian August Gottlieb. *England, Wales, Irland und Schottland*. 5 vols. Dresden, 1804–1805, 5:116.

[Gough, Richard]. "Excursions from Bath. By the Rev. Richard Warner." *Gentleman's Magazine* 71, Pt. 2 (October 1801): 915.

Hall, Michael. "Only a Picture of a House." *Country Life*, 11 January 1996, 28, 29.

Harris, John. "Fonthill, Wiltshire: Part 1—Alderman Beckford's Houses." *Country Life*,

24 November 1966, 1370–1374.

Meister, Jacques Henri. *Letters Written during a Residence in England*, 295–314, 315–324. Translation of *Souvenirs de mes voyages en Angleterre*, 1795. London: T. N. Longman, 1799.

Pococke, Richard. *The Travels through England of Dr. Richard Pococke*. Edited by James Joel Cartwright. London: Camden Society, 1888–1889. 2:47.

"Principal Front of the seat of the Late William Beckford, Esq." *Universal Magazine* 47 (September 1770): 113 (opposite).

[Sale of 1801, furnishings, organ, etc.] *Bell's Weekly Messenger*, 30 August 1801.

[Sale of 1807, pictures and porcelain.] *Bell's Weekly Messenger*, 30 August 1807.

Stroud, Dorothy. *Sir John Soane, Architect*. London: Faber and Faber, 1984.

[Sulivan, Sir Richard]. *Observations made during a Tour through Parts of England, Scotland, and Wales*, 50–51. London: T. Becket, 1780.

Warner, Richard. *Excursions from Bath*, 119–127. Bath: R. Cruttwell, 1801.

Wiltshire Archaeological & Natural History Magazine 44 (December 1928): 254.

Woodward, Christopher. "William Beckford and Fonthill Splendens." *Apollo* 147 (February 1998): 31–40.

Woolfe, John, and James Gandon. *Vitruvius Britannicus*. Vol. 4, 9 and pls. 82, 83, 84/85, 86/87. London, 1767. Reprint, New York, Blom: 1967.

6. Fonthill Abbey

Guidebooks

Bibliographicum (1819). London: William Clarke, 1817.

Britton, John. *Graphical and Literary Illustrations of Fonthill Abbey, Wiltshire*. London: The Author, 1823.

Rutter, John. *A Description of Fonthill Abbey and Demesne*. Shaftesbury: J. Rutter, 1822.

———. *Delineations of Fonthill and its Abbey*. Shaftesbury: The Author, 1823.

———. *A New Descriptive Guide to Fonthill Abbey and Demesne*. Shaftesbury: J. Rutter, 1823

Storer, James. *A Description of Fonthill Abbey*. London: W. Clarke, etc., 1812.

———. *Description of Fonthill Abbey*. Salisbury: Brodie, 1823.

Neale, John Preston. *Graphical Illustrations of Fonthill Abbey, The Seat of John Farquhar, Esq*. London: Sherwood, Jones, etc., 1824. Offprint from *Views of the Seats of Noblemen and Gentlemen*. 2d series, vol. 1. London: Sherwood, Jones, 1824.

Nichols, John Bowyer, ed. *Historical Notices of Fonthill Abbey, Wiltshire*. London: Nichols & Son, 1836.

Whittaker. *A New Guide to Fonthill Abbey*. London: G. & W. B. Whittaker, 1822.

Contemporary Accounts

"Abbey Open for Inspection & Described." *New Monthly Magazine*, n.s. 6 (1 August and 1 October 1822): 383, 479–480.

"Account of the Christmas Festivities at Fonthill." *European Magazine* 31 (January 1797): 4–6.

"Account of the Works Now Executing at Fonthill." *European Magazine* 31 (February 1797): 104–107.

[Adams of Shaftesbury]. An evocation of the ruinous state of the Abbey by "T. A. jun." *Gentleman's Magazine* 96, Pt. 1 (May 1826): 424.

d'Andrade, Mme C. "L'abbaye de Fonthill." *L'abeille* 2ᵉ année (1840), 250.

Britton, John. *Wiltshire*. The Beauties of England and Wales. Vol. 15, 265–268. London: Vernor & Hood, 1814.

———. *The Beauties of Wiltshire*. Vol. 3. London: Longman & J. Britton, 1825.

———. *Autobiography*, Pt. 2, edited by T. E. Jones, 6, 12, 20–31, 181, 210–211 and appendix, [189]. London: Printed for the Author, 1849. Bound with appendix, 1850.

Constable. Leslie. C. R. *Memoirs of the life of John Constable*, 105. London, 1951.

Cooke, George Alexander. *Topographical and Statistical Description of the County of Wilts*. London: Sherwood, Neely & Jones, ca. 1820.

"Country News." *Gentleman's Magazine* 66, Pt. 2 (September 1796): 784.

Crockery Jr. "The Fonthill Mania." *Literary Chronicle and Weekly Review* (1823): 603–604.

Cunningham, Alan, ed. *The Anniversary for 1829*. London: John Sharpe, 1828.

Dugdale, James. *The New British Traveller*. Vol. 4, 464–465. London: J. Robins, 1819.

"A Day at Fonthill Abbey." *New Monthly Magazine*, n.s. 8 (October 1822): 368–380.

"Domestic Occurrences. Intelligence from various parts of the country." *Gentleman's Magazine* 97, Pt. 2 (October 1827): 362.

J. E. [?Easton, J.] Interior of the Abbey from *Storer* (1812). *Gentleman's Magazine* 92, Pt. 1 (April 1822): 325–327.

Easton, J. *The Salisbury Guide*. New ed. Salisbury: J. Easton, 1824. 94 pp.

"Exclusive Intelligence. Reminiscences of an Elderly Member of the Fourth Estate. Fonthill Abbey." *Dublin University Magazine* 76 (August 1870): 196–199.

[Fall of the Tower.] *Gentleman's Magazine* 95, Pt. 2 (December 1825): 557.

[Fall of the Tower.] *Mirror of Literature* 7 (January–June 1826): 54–55.

[Fenton, Richard] under pseud. "A Barrister." *A Tour in Quest of Genealogy*. London: Sherwood, Nealy & Jones, 1811.

"Fonthill." *The Crypt, or Receptacle for Things Past* 1, no. 9, 19 December 1827, 220.

"Fonthill Abbey." *The Times*, 5 October 1822, 2e.

"Fonthill Abbey." *Mirror of Literature* 1 (23 November 1822): 49–52, w view (woodcut).

"Fonthill Abbey." *Ackermann's Repository of Arts*, 2d Series, 3, No. 8 (1 August 1823): 103–105 and lithograph.

"Fonthill Abbey." Parts 1–4. *Gleaner* 1, no. 23 (1 October 1823): 353–355 and sw view; no. 24 (8 October): 369–371 and Oratory (woodcut); no. 25 (15 October): 385–387 & Hall, etc (woodcut); no. 26 (22 October): 407–409.

"Fonthill Abbey. A Familiar Letter from a Visitor, August 18, 1823." *The Humorous Delineator; or Vehicle* 1, no. 10 (18 August 1824): 149–151. From *British Traveller Evening Paper*.

"Fonthill Abbey, South East View." *Mirror of Literature* 8 (15 July 1826): 25–26.

"The Fonthill Property." *The Times*, 30 September 1822, 3a.

"Fonthill Property." *The Times*, 4 October 1822, 3a.

Frith, William Powell. "The Fonthill Story." In *My Autobiography and Reminiscences*. Vol. 2, 131–137. London: Richard Bentley, 1887.

Gilpin, William. *Observations on the Western Parts of England Relative chiefly to Picturesque Beauty to which are added a few remarks on the picturesque beauty of the Isle of Wight*, 116–117. London: T. Cadell & W. Davies, 1798.

Goldsmith, Rev. J. [Sir Richard Phillips]. *The Natural and Artificial Wonders of the United Kingdom*. Vol. 2, 321–326 and illus. London: G. B. Whittaker, 1825.

Gomme, G. L. *Topographical History of Warwickshire, Westmoreland, and Wiltshire*, 233–258. London: The Gentleman's Magazine Library, 1901.

[Gothic improvements at Fonthill.] *Bell's Weekly Messenger*, 23 May 1802.

Gower, Granville Leveson (1st Earl Granville). *Private Correspondence, 1781–1821*. Vol. 2, edited by Castalia, Countess Granville, 544–545. London, 1916.

[W. G.] "Candid Critique on the Architecture of Fonthill Abbey." *Gentleman's Magazine* 92, Pt. 2 (December 1822): 491–494.

Havell, Robert. *A Series of Picturesque Views of Noblemen's and Gentlemen's Seats*. London: R. Havell & Son, 1823.

Hawker, Peter. *The Diary of Col. P. Hawker, 1802–1853*. Vol. 1, 26–27, 247–249. London: Longmans, 1893.

Hawkins, Desmond, ed. *The Grove Diaries. The Rise and Fall of an English Family, 1809–1925*. Wimborne, Dorset: Dovecote Press, 1995.

Hazlitt, William. *New Monthly Magazine*, February 1828.

[Hoare, Richard Colt]. "Fonthill Abbey. On its Close." *Gentleman's Magazine* 92, Pt. 2 (October 1822): 291.

———. [Fall of the Tower.] *Gentleman's Magazine* 96, Pt. 1 (February 1826): 123.

M. J. "Fonthill Abbey." *Literary Chronicle and Weekly Review*, (1822): 665–667.

Jerdan, William. *The Autobiography of W. J.* Vol. 3, 103–110. London: A. Hall. Virtue, 1853.

[Macquin, Abbé Dennis]. "A Visit to Fonthill Abbey." Parts 1–5. *Literary Gazette* 6 (17 August 1822): 520–521; (24 August): 527–528; (31 August): 555–556; (14 September): 585; (21 September): 602–603.

Olivier, Edith. *Four Victorian Ladies of Wiltshire*, 46–47. London: Faber and Faber, 1945.

[A Passer By.] Exterior of the Abbey. *Gentleman's Magazine* 91 Pt. 1 (December 1821): 495–496.

Patmore, Derek. *Portrait of My Family*, 27–29. London: Cassell, 1935.

———. *My Friends and Acquaintances*. Vol. 3, 60–61, 68–71. London: Saunders & Otley, 1854.

Peniston, John. *The Letters of John Peniston, Salisbury Architect, Catholic, and Yeomanry Officer 1823–1830*. Edited by Michael Cowan. Trowbridge: Wiltshire Records Society, 1996.

Sarisburiensis. "Fonthill's Warning." *The Crypt, or Receptacle for Things Past* 1, no. 5 (24 October 1827): 113–117.

[Tresham, Henry]. Nelson's visit. *Gentleman's Magazine* 71, Pt. 1 (March, April 1801): 206–208, 297–298, illus. opposite 289. Reprint, in *Wilts County Mirror*, 20 September 1907.

[Visitors to Fonthill.] *The Times*, 20 September 1822, 2d.

"William Bankes' Account of his Surreptitious Visit to Fonthill [in 1811]." *Beckford Journal* 1 (1995): 47–50.

Later Accounts

Alexander, Boyd. "Fonthill, Wiltshire. Part 2, The Abbey and its Creator." *Country Life*, 1 December 1966, 1430–1434.

Ashworth, Katharine. "Tisbury's Ancient Secrets." *Country Life*, 4 November 1954, 1590, 1592.

Barnes, Max. "a–z of West Ways. Fonthill Gifford." [Bristol] *Evening Post*, 5 July 1971, 25.

Barnes, Max. "Follies. A dream in ruins." [Bristol] *Evening Post*, 1 August 1978.

Bishop, Phillipa. "Beckford, William 1760–1844: British Antiquarian and Connoisseur." In *Encyclopedia of Interior Design*, edited by Joanna Banham, vol. 1, 111–114. London: Fitzroy Dearborn, 1997.

Blunt, Anthony. "Fonthill Abbey." *The Venture*, no. 2 (February 1929): 75–81.

Brewer, John. *The Pleasures of the Imagination*. London: Harper Collins, 1997.

"Building Fonthill Abbey." *Bath and County Graphic* 8 (May 1903): 11–12.

Butler, David B. "Visitors to Fonthill." *Country Life*, 3 January 1957, 25.

Byron, Robert, ed. *Shell Guide to Wiltshire*. London: Architectural Press, 1935.

Clarke, Stephen. "The Troubled Gestation of Britton's *Illustrations of Fonthill*." *Beckford Journal* 6 (2000): 58–74.

Craft, Adrian. "Subterranean Enlightenment at Fonthill." *Beckford Journal* 3 (1997): 30–33.

Cruickshank, Dan. "Ghost of Christmas Past." *The Guardian*, 22 December 1997, 12–13.

Darton, Eric. "Fonthill: John Farquhar and After." *Beckford Tower Trust Newsletter* (spring 1987): 6–7.

Dobson, Roger. "Living in a delusion of grandeur." *Weekend Telegraph*, 1 April 1995, 13.

Favret, Mary A. "A Home for Art." In *At the Limits of Romanticism. Essays in Cultural, Feminist and Materialist Criticism*, edited by Mary A. Favret and Nicola J. Watson, 79 n. 5. Bloomington: Indiana University Press, 1994.

Fisher, Michael. "In the Shadow of Fonthill—Pugin's Early Years at Alton Towers." *True Principles* (Pugin Society) 2, no. 1 (winter 2000): 7–9.

[Fonthill Abbey.] *Wiltshire Times*, 15 May 1909.

"Fonthill Abbey. Britton v Rutter." *Wiltshire Gazette*, 24 and 31 January 1924.

Gemmett, Robert J. "The Critical Reception of William Beckford's Fonthill." *English Miscellany* 19 (1968): 133–151.

Girard, Didier. ""Delineations" on the Fonthill Pageant." *Beckford Tower Trust Newsletter* (spring 1987): 2–3.

———. "William Beckford's Nostalgic Visions." *Beckford Tower Trust Newsletter* (spring 1988): 8–9.

Grigson, Geoffrey. *Wessex*. London: Thames & Hudson, 1957.

Heath, Frank R. "Fonthill Abbey." In *Wiltshire*. 7th ed., revised by R. L. P. Jowitt, 105–109. London: Methuen, 1949.

Headley, Gwyn and Wim Meulenkamp. *Follies*. London: Jonathan Cape, 1990.

Herrick, George R. "Fabulous Fonthill." *College Art Journal* 12 (1953): 128–131.

Hilliard, Elizabeth. "Fonthill Redivivus." *Beckford Tower Trust Newsletter* (spring 1989): 2–3.

Hutton, Edward. *Highways and Byways in Wiltshire*. London: Macmillan, 1917. pp. 187–191.

Jones, Margaret. "Nelson at Fonthill." *Country Life*, 28 February 1957, 389.

Kite, Edward. "Fonthill and the Beckfords." *Wiltshire Advertiser*, 30 September, 7 October, 21 October 1909.

Lewis, W. G. J. "Follies at Fonthill." *Country Life*, 14 March 1957, 485–486.

Longford, Elizabeth. "The Duke of Wellington's Search for a Palace." *Horizon* 11 (spring 1969): 106, 112, 113.

Luff, S. G. A. "The Romantick Abbey: A Consideration of Beckford's Folly." *The Aylesford Review* 6 (Winter 1963–64): 26–32.

Meehan, J. F. "Famous Buildings of Bath and District. No. 31, Fonthill Abbey: The Wiltshire Residence of William Beckford." *The Beacon* (Frome, Somerset), August 1900, 127–128.

[Michael, W.] "History of Fonthill Abbey." In *Important Spots in Wiltshire*. Westbury, Wilts: W. Michael, ca. 1880. Reprint, ca.

1886; as *Historic Spots in Wiltshire* [1901].

Millington, Jon. "Engravings of Fonthill." *Beckford Journal* 7 (2001): 47–59.

———. "Fonthill after Beckford." *Beckford Journal* 2 (1996): 46–59.

———. "A Transient Gleam." *Beckford Journal* 4 (1998): 64.

[Murray's], *Handbook for Travellers in Wiltshire, Dorsetshire and Somersetshire*. 2d ed. London: John Murray, 1859.

Nightingale, James E. *Objects of Interest in the Fonthill Excursion*, 15–24. Salisbury, Wilts: Wiltshire Archæological and Natural History Society, 1870.

Norton, Rictor. "A Visit to Fonthill." *Gay News* 133 (Christmas 1977): 32–33.

Rushton, Andrée. "The Fonthill Barrier." *Beckford Journal* 4 (1998): 65–70.

Schiff, Gert, "'Ich bin reich und entschlossen Türme zu bauen' Über William Beckford." *Du* (November 1961): 21–25.

Scott, T. G. "Fonthill Buildings." *Country Life*, 24 January 1957, 157.

Simpson-White, R. "Visiting Fonthill." *Country Life*, 10 January 1957, 67.

Skoggard, Carl. "William Beckford, Fonthill Abbey." *Nest* (New York) 4 (Spring 1999): 25–35.

Steegman, John. "Strawberry Hill and Fonthill." In *The Rule of Taste from George I to George IV*, 79, 83–85. London: Macmillan, 1936.

Stratford, Joseph. *Wiltshire and Its Worthies*, 76–77. Salisbury, Wilts: Brown, 1882.

Strong, Roy, "Collapsed Fonthill: Beckford's Grand Folly." *Sunday Times Magazine*, 19 November 1969, 70–72. Revised reprint as "The Fall of Fonthill." in idem *Lost Treasures of Britain*, 188–201. London: Viking—The Penguin Group, 1990.

Watkin, David. *Thomas Hope, 1769–1831, and the Neo-Classical Idea*. London: John Murray, 1968.

William Beckford: A Pageant of his life at Fonthill. Sunday 15 June at Fonthill Old Abbey. Fonthill: n.p., 1986.

Worth, R. N. *Tourist's Guide to Wiltshire*, 48–49. London: Edward Stanford, 1887.

Fonthill: Architectural Studies

Brockman, H. A. N. "Fonthill Abbey." *Architectural Review* 95 (June 1944): 149–156 and cover illus.

Brown, Roderick, ed. *The Architectural Outsiders*, 75, 126. London: Waterstone, 1985.

Clark, Kenneth. *The Gothic Revival*, 104–111, pls. 6, 7. London: Constable, 1928.

Cundall, Edward George. "Turner Drawings of Fonthill Abbey." *Burlington Magazine* 29 (April 1916): 16, 21 and pls. 1, 2.

Curl, James Stevens. *Georgian Architecture*. Newton Abbot, Devon: David & Charles, 1993.

Davis, Terence. *The Gothick Taste*, 14, 22, 48, 103, 106, 108–113, 117, 121–122. Newton

Abbot, Devon: David & Charles, 1974 [1975].

Eastlake, Charles. *A History of the Gothic Revival*, 61–65. London: Longmans, Green, 1872.

Germann, Georg. *Gothic Revival*, 71 and pl 15. London: Lund Humphries, 1972.

Harris, John. "English Country House Guides, 1740–1840." In *Concerning Architecture*, edited by John Summerson, 68–69. London: Allen Lane: The Penguin Press, 1968.

Hughes, G. Bernard. "Poor Man's Pottery Pictures." *Country Life*, 11 February 1971, 297.

Linstrum, Derek, ed. *Catalogue of the Drawings Collection of the Royal Institute of British Architects: The Wyatt Family*. Farnborough, Hants: Gregg, 1973.

Longbourne, David. "A Painting of Fonthill Abbey Discovered." *Beckford Journal* 3 (1997): 6–7.

Macaulay, James. *The Gothic Revival, 1745–1845*, 146–148 and pl. 80. Glasgow: Blackie, 1975.

Mayhew, Edgar deN. "A View of Fonthill Abbey." *Register of the Museum of Art, University of Kansas* (December 1957), reissued, 1 no. 9 (spring 1965): 16–21.

McCarthy, Michael. *The Origins of the Gothic Revival*, 2, 146. New Haven: Yale University Press, 1987.

Miller, Norbert. "William Beckford's Verwandlung von Fonthill / WB's Metamorphosis of Fonthill." *Daidalos. Berlin Architectural Journal* 4 (15 June 1982): 33–53.

Millington, Jon. "Francis Danby." *Beckford Tower Trust Newsletter* (spring 1985): 1, 3.

Pevsner, Nikolaus. "Fonthill Gifford." In *Wiltshire*. 2d ed., revised by Bridget Cherry, 246–249. Harmondsworth, Middlesex: Penguin Books, 1975.

Summerson, John. *Architecture in Britain, 1530 to 1830*, 244, 283–284, 290 and pls. 162A,B. 163. Harmondsworth, Middlesex: Penguin Books, 1953.

Summerson, John. *The Architecture of the Eighteenth Century*, 94 and fig. 104. London: Thames & Hudson, 1986.

Turnor, Reginald. *Nineteenth Century Architecture in Britain*, p. 4 and illus. opp. London: Batsford, 1950.

"Turner's Fonthill Abbey Drawings." *Times Literary Supplement*, 11 May 1916, 224.

Wilton-Ely, John. "The Genesis and Evolution of Fonthill Abbey." *Architectural History* 23 (1980): 40–51 and pls. 28–36.

———. "Beckford, Fonthill Abbey and the Picturesque." In *The Picturesque in late Georgian England*, edited by Dana Arnold, 35–44, 70–73. London, 1994.

———. "Beckford's Fonthill Abbey: A Theatre of the Arts." In *The Beckford Society Annual Lectures 1996–1999*, edited by Jon Millington, 3–22. Privately printed, 2000.

7. Beckford's Tower in Bath

"Arrival of Her Royal Highness the Duchess of Kent in this City." *Bath Journal*, 25 October 1830, 2.

"The Beckford Tower." *Illustrated London News* 11 (11 September 1847): 167.

"Beckford's Tower given to Walcot Parish by Duchess of Hamilton." *Gentleman's Magazine,* n.s. 28 (December 1847): 628a–b.

Beckford's Tower, Lansdown: Restoration. Bath: Walcot Parochial Church Council, 1954.

"Domestic Occurrences. Intelligence from various parts of the country." *Gentleman's Magazine* 97, Pt. 2 (August 1827): 171b.

[Elstob, Rev. Mr]. Tower one of the earliest examples of modern Italian. *Gentleman's Magazine* n.s. 13 (April 1840): 410.

English, Edmund. *Views of Lansdown Tower, Bath.* Illustrated by Willes Maddox. London: Edmund English Jr., 1844.

"Lansdown Tower." *Illustrated London News* 7 (22 November 1845): 324–325.

"Lansdowne Tower." *The Pictorial Times* 6 (22 November 1845): 328–330.

Millington, Jon. *Beckford's Tower, Lansdown, Bath.* Pamphlet. Bath: L. T. Hilliard, 1973. 6th ed., Bath: Bath Preservation Trust, 1996.

[Redding, Cyrus, signed "Nerke."] "The Tower of the Caliph." *New Monthly Magazine* 71 (August 1844): 457–466.

"Sale of Mr. Beckford's Property from Lansdown Tower." *Gentleman's Magazine,* n.s. 25(January 1846): 70a–72b.

[Sale of Beckford's Tower to a publican.] *Gentleman's Magazine,* n.s. 28 (August 1847): 195b–196a.

"Sale of the Beckford Collection." *Illustrated London News* 7 (29 November and 6 December 1845): 344–346 and 365.

"Saxon tower to be built on Lansdown." *The Courier.* 9 October 1823, 2, 3.

Reports

Bath Museums Service. *Bath Museums News* from 1988, biannually.

Bath Preservation Trust. *[Annual] Newsletter* & *Annual Report* from 1993.

Hughes, Pat. "Beckford's Tower, Lansdown, Bath." Pt. 1 [History], report commissioned by Bath Preservation Trust, 1999–99.

Sampson, Jerry. "Beckford's Tower, Lansdown, Bath." Pt. 2 [Archaeology], report commissioned by Bath Preservation Trust, 1998–99.

Beckford's Tomb

"The Colebroke Dale Company's Railing for a Tomb." *Illustrated London News* 18 (3 May 1851): 374 with woodcut.

Crystal Palace and its Contents. London: W. M. Clark, 1852.

[Meyler's] *Original Bath Guide*, 127–128. Bath: Meyler & Son, ca. 1846, 86.

Millington, Jon. "The Railings for Beckford's Tomb." *Beckford Tower Trust Newsletter,* Pt. 2 (spring 1980): 1–3.

Passingham, R. *Notes and Queries,* 4th Series 10 (17 August 1872): 138. Corrections by R. W. F., (12 October 1872): 301 & R. Passingham, 5th Series 1 (6 June 1874): 460.

"Tomb of the late Mr. Beckford, at Bath." *Illus-trated London News* 9 (29 August 1846): 140, with woodcut.

Tunstall, James. *Rambles about Bath,* 115–116, 222–223. London: Simpkin, Marshall, 1847.

8. Landscape Gardening

Boniface, Priscilla, ed. *In Search of English Gardens: The Travels of J. C. Loudon,* 13, 144–145, 149–153, 212–215. Wheathampstead, Herts: Lennard Publishing, 1987.

Châtel, Laurent. "The Mole, the Bat, and the Fairy or the Sublime Grottoes of 'Fonthill Splendens'." *Beckford Journal* 5 (1999): 53–74.

Debois Landscape Survey Group (John Phibbs). *Fonthill, Wiltshire. A Survey of the Landscape.* Privately printed reports commissioned by the owners of the Splendens site, 1991–93.

———. *Beckford's Tower: A Survey of the Landscape.* Privately printed reports commissioned by Bath Preservation Trust, November 1993. Revised March 1994.

Gemmett, Robert J. "Beckford's Fonthill: The Landscape as Art." *Gazette des Beaux-Arts* 80 (December 1972): 335–356.

Geoffrey Grigson. "Caves of Verdure." In *Gardenage,* 150–165. London: Routledge & Kegan Paul, 1952.

Hadfield, Miles. *A History of British Gardening,* 296–297. London: John Murray, 1979. First published as *Gardening in Britain,* 1960.

Hadfield, Miles, and John Hadfield. *Gardens of Delight.* London: Cassell, 1964.

Hadfield, Miles, Robert Harling, and Leonie Highton. *British Gardeners: A Biographical Dictionary,* 33. London: Zwemmer, 1980.

Harding, Stewart, and David Lambert. "Beckford's Ride." In *Parks and Gardens of Avon,* 70–71, Bristol: Avon Gardens Trust, 1994.

Honess, Keith A. "Beckford" and "Fonthill." In *The Oxford Companion to Gardens,* edited by Sir Geoffrey Jellicoe et al., 42, 195. Oxford: Oxford Univ. Press, 1986.

Hussey, Christopher. *The Picturesque,* 162–163, 197, 199, 214, 264. London: Putnam, 1927.

Hunt, John Dixon. *Gardens and the Picturesque,* 229, 237. Cambridge: M.I.T. Press, 1992.

Jacques, David. *Georgian Gardens,* 90, 156–159, 174, 179 and pl. 10. London: Batsford, 1983.

Loudon, John Claudius. "First-rate Residences: Fonthill Abbey." In *Encyclopaedia of Gardening,* 1246. London: Longman, etc., 1822.

———. "Notes on Gardens and Country Seats, visited . . . [in] 1833, during a Tour . . ." *Gardener's Magazine* 11 (September 1835): 441–449.

———. "Notes of a Gardening Tour in 1833." *Gardener's Magazine* 12 (1836): 503–506.

———. *Arboretum et Fruiticetum Britannicum.* Vol. 1, 128. London: A Spottiswoode, 1838.

Malins, Edward. *English Landscaping and Literature 1660–1840.* London: Oxford Univ. Press, 1966.

McGarvie, Michael. "Mr Beckford's Vanished Arcadia." *The Field* (20 May 1976): 912–914.

———. "Arcadia in Wessex: William Beckford and his Gardens." *Bath Evening Chronicle,* 5 June 1976.

———. "William Beckford, Gardener, at Witham and Fonthill." *Frome Society Yearbook* 7 (1997–98): 112–121.

Miller, Naomi. *Heavenly Caves: Reflections on the Garden Grotto,* 88. London: George Allen & Unwin, 1982.

Mayoux, Jean-Jacques. *Richard Payne Knight et le pittoresque,* 8. Paris: Les Presses modernes, 1932.

Mosser, Monique, and Georges Teyssot, eds. *The Architecture of Western Gardens,* 274, 276, 280 n. 29. Cambridge [Mass.]: M.I.T. Press, 1991.

Neal, James. "Survey of the Beckford Ride: Summary of the Draft Report produced by the Debois Landscape Survey Group. December 1993." *Beckford Tower Trust Newsletter* (spring 1994): 9.

Pook, Sally. "Tower trust in garden project." Report by Debois Landscape Survey Group. *Bath Chronicle,* 11 October 1994.

Quest-Ritson, Charles. *The English Garden Abroad,* 156–165. London: Viking, 1992.

Sieveking, Albert Forbes. *The Praise of Gardens,* 223–228. London: Dent, 1899.

Sladen, Gillian. "Beckford's Tower Garden." *Beckford Journal* 1 (1995): 11.

Thacker, Christopher. *Masters of the Grotto: Joseph and Josiah Lane,* 21, 23, 24–28, 29–31. Tisbury, Wilts: Compton Press, 1976.

Thacker, Christopher. *The Wildness Pleases,* 45–46, 187–192, 197–198, 203, 210–212. London: Croom Helm, 1983.

9. Beckford's Collections

General

Alexander, Boyd. "Fonthill, Wiltshire, Pt. 3— William Beckford as Collector." *Country Life,* 8 December 1966, 1572–1576.

Aslet, Clive, and Christopher Hartley. "Brodick Castle, Isle of Arran." Parts 1 and 2. *Country Life,* 10 February 1983, 322–325; 17 February, 380–383.

Barker, Nicolas. *Treasures from the Libraries of National Trust Country Houses.* New York: Royal Oak Foundation & Grolier Club, 1999.

Finley, William K. *William Beckford Collection. GEN MSS 102.* New Haven: Yale, 1991.

Foss, Arthur. *Country House Treasures.* London: Weidenfeld & Nicolson, 1980. Brodick, 69–70. Charlecote, 95–96. Dodington, 127. Dyrham, 133. Powerham, 272.

Furst, Herbert. "Two Famous Connoisseurs and Collectors – Beaumont and Beckford." Parts 1 and 2." *Apollo* 35 (March 1942): 59–61, 75, (April): 81–84.

Gothick 1720–1840. Introduction by Duncan Simpson Exh. cat., 7, 8, 12, 15, 16 and pls. 19, 20. Brighton, 1975.

Gow, Ian. "Treasures of the Country Life Library." *Country Life,* 25 September 1997, 130–133.

Hamilton Palace Collection. Illustrated Priced Catalogue. Paris: Librairie de l'art & London: Remington, 1882.

"Hamilton Palace Sale." *Illustrated London News* 80 and 81, 10 June 1882, 568, 569; 17 June 1882, 591, 593; 24 June 1882, 608, 609–610; 1 July 1882, 6; 8 July 1882, 31, 42; 15 July 1882, 66, 69, 72–73, 76; 22 July 1882, 86; 30 December 1882, 687.

Hawcroft, Francis W. *Travels in Italy, 1776–1783: Based on the "Memoirs" of Thomas Jones.* Manchester: Whitworth Art Gallery, 1988.

Herrmann, Frank. "The Beckford Collection Sold." In *The English as Collectors,* 210–219. London: Chatto & Windus, 1972.

———. *Sotheby's. Portrait of an Auction House,* 73–75, 78. London: Chatto & Windus, 1980.

Holbrook, Mary, and Sidney Blackmore. *The True Style.* Bath: Holburne Museum, 1972.

Jullian, Philippe. "La fausse abbaye de Fonthill et les collections de l'extravagant William Beckford." *Connaissance des Arts* 133 (March 1963): 95–103.

Millington, Jon. "Research for the 'Souvenirs of Fonthill Abbey' Exhibition." *Beckford Tower Trust Newsletter* (spring 1994): 9–10.

———. *Souvenirs of Fonthill Abbey.* Bath: Bath Preservation Trust, 1994.

Morley, John. *Regency Design, 1790–1840.* London: Zwemmer, 1993.

Redford, George. *Art Sales.* 2 vols. London, 1888.

Roberts, W. *Memorials of Christie's.* 2 vols. London: Bell, 1897.

Tait, A. A. "The Duke of Hamilton's Palace." *Burlington Magazine* 125 (1983): 394–402.

Tipping, H. Avray, "Hamilton Palace." Parts 1–3. *Country Life,* 7 June 1919, 662–671; 14 June 1919, 716–723; 21 June 1919, 748–755.

Wainwright, Clive. "William Beckford e La Sua Collezione." Parts 1 and 2. *Arte Illustrata* No. 37/38 (January/February 1971): 46–53; 39/40 (March/April 1971): 52–60.

———. "Some objects from William Beckford's Collection now in the Victoria and Albert Museum." *Burlington Magazine* 113 (May 1971): 254–264.

———. "Charlecote Park, Warwickshire–ii." *Country Life,* 28 February 1985, 506–510.

———. "Fonthill Abbey." In *The Romantic Interior: The British Collector at Home, 1750–1850,* 108–146 and passim. New Haven: Yale University Press, 1989.

———. "In Lucifer's Metropolis." *Country Life,* 1 October 1992, 82–84.

Beckford's Library

"The Beckford Library." Parts 1–7. *Athenæum,* 20 May 1882, 636; 23 December 1882, 849–850; 30 December 1882, 899; 2 June 1883, 701; 3 November 1883, 566; 1 December 1883, 703; 8 December 1883, 739.

[Beckford Library Sale.] Parts 1–9. *The Bibliographer* 1 (February 1882): 85–87; 2 (July 1882): 25–27; (August): 60–62; 3 (January 1883): 50; (February): 77–82. 4 (July): 51; (August): 83; (September):

III–II5; 5 (January 1884): 45–48; (June 1884): 13.

[Beckfordiana at Brodick.] *Book Collector* 9 (1960): 395.

[Beckford's library unfavourably compared with Sunderland library.] *Gentleman's Magazine*, 253 (September 1882): 381.

"Boyd Alexander Bequest." *Bodleian Library Record* 10, no. 5 (August 1981): 267.

British Museum. *List of Catalogues of English Book Sales 1676–1900 now in the British Museum*. London, 1915.

Brunet, Jacques Charles. *Catalogue des livres rares et précieux de feu M. Jacques-Charles Brunet*. Biographical introduction by A. J. V. Le Roux de Lincy. Paris: Potier, 1868.

Carter, John. "Two Beckford Collections." *The Colophon*. New Graphic Series No. 1 (March 1939): [67–74].

Carter, John. *Taste & Technique in Book-Collecting*. Cambridge: Cambridge Univ. Press, 1948.

[Clements sale of 329 Beckford books]. "News & Comment." *Book Collector* 15 (1966): 473–474.

De Ricci, Seymour. *English Collectors of Books & Manuscripts, 1530–1930*. Cambridge: Cambridge Univ. Press, 1930.

Hobson, A. R. A. "William Beckford's Binders." In *Festschrift Ernst Kyriss*, 375–381. Stuttgart: Max Hettler, 1961.

Gemmett, Robert J. "Beckford in the sale-room." *Times Literary Supplement*, 17 November 1966, 1056.

———. "The Beckford Book Sale of 1808." *Papers of the Bibliographical Society of America* 64 (Second Quarter 1970): 127–164.

———. "The Beckford Library Sale of 1817." *Library Chronicle* (Univ. of Pennsylvania) 37 (Winter 1971): 37–69.

———. "The Beckford Book Sale of 1804." *Bulletin of the New York Public Library* 77 (Winter 1974): 205–223.

———, ed. *Sale Catalogues of Libraries of Eminent Persons*. Vol. 3, *Poets and Men of Letters: William Beckford*. London: Mansell with Sotheby Parke-Bernet, 1972.

Hobson, Anthony. "William Beckford's Library." *Connoisseur* 191 (April 1976): 298–305.

Norman, Geraldine. "Beckford interest raises price of Rosebery books." *The Times*, 28 October 1975.

Norman, Geraldine. "Outstanding prices in book sale." *The Times*, 29 October 1975, 16.

Osborne, Eric. "Insatiable Bibliophile." *Books and Bookmen*, January 1973, 76–77.

Parreaux, André. "Note sur la partie Portugaise de la Bibliothèque de William Beckford." *Bulletin des Etudes Portugaises* 2 (1932): 87–93.

Quaritch, Bernard. *Contributions Towards a Dictionary of English Book Collectors*. London: Bernard Quaritch, 1892–1921.

Rosebery, Eva. "Books from Beckford's Library now at Barnbougle." *Book Collector* 14 (1965):

324–334 and pls. 1–4.

Smiley, P. O'R. "Beckford's Library." *Beckford Tower Trust Newsletter* (spring 1982): 7.

Wainwright, Clive. "The last of Beckford's library." *Times Literary Supplement*, 19 December 1975, 1525.

Beckford in list of subscribers

Britton, John. *The History and Antiquities of the Abbey, and Cathedral Church of Bristol*. London: Longman, 1830.

Dallas, R. C. *Miscellaneous Writings: consisting of Poems: Lucretia a Tragedy: and Moral Essays. With a Vocabulary Of The Passions in which their sources are pointed out, their regular currents traced, and their deviations delineated*. London, Longmans, 1797.

Richardson, George. *The New Vitruvius Britannicus*. 2 vols. London: Printed by W. Bulmer & Co. for the Author, 1802 & 1808.

Soane, John. *Plans, Elevations and Sections of Buildings Executed in the Counties of Norfolk, Suffolk, Yorkshire, Staffordshire, Warwickshire, Hertfordshire etc*. London, 1788.

Tatham, Charles Heathcote. *Etchings, representing the best known examples of Ancient Ornamental Architecture*. 1799.

Ceramics

"Chinese Armorial Plate." *Art Collectors Journal* (Spring 1990): 168.

Craig, Sir Algernon Tudor. *Armorial Porcelain of the Eighteenth Century*. London: Century House, 1925. p. 32.

Dawson, Aileen. *A Catalogue of French Porcelain in the British Museum*. London: British Museum Press, 1994.

Hewat-Jaboor, Philip. "An Early Nineteenth Century Dihl and Guerhard Porcelain Cup and Saucer made for William Beckford." *Beckford Journal* 2 (1996): 7–8.

Horvath, J. E. "The Pedigree of Louis the Great's Ewer." In *Louis the Great*, edited by S. B. Vardy et al., 325–338. Boulder, Colorado: East European Monographs Series, 1986.

Howard, David Sanctuary. *Chinese Armorial Porcelain*, 339, 366, 557. London: Faber and Faber, 1974.

Lane, Arthur. "The Gaignières-Fonthill Vase; A Chinese Porcelain of about 1300." *Burlington Magazine* 103 (1961): 124–132.

Watson, Sir Francis. *Chinese Porcelains in European Mounts*. New York: China Institute of America, 1980.

Whitehead, John. "Some French Purchases by William Beckford." *Beckford Journal* 2 (1996): 39–44.

Objets d'Art

Eisenberg, Jerome M. "The Rubens Vase in Baltimore: An Oriental copy?" *Minerva* 8, no. 2 (March/April 1997): 20–25.*

Jaffé, Michael. "William Beckford's Lapis-lazuli Cup." *Art Collectors Journal* (spring 1990): 124–127.

Millington, Jon. "A Lapis Lazuli Cup." *Beckford*

Tower Trust Newsletter (spring 1990): 8.

———. "The Barber Institute of Fine Arts, Birmingham University." *Beckford Tower Trust Newsletter* (spring 1994): 11–12.

———. "Beckford's Lighting." *Beckford Journal* 1 (1995): 56.

Robinson, William. "The Hamilton Jug." *Christie's Magazine* 17, no. 7 (December 2000): 32–35.

Ross, Marvin Chauncey. "The Rubens Vase—Its History and Date." *Journal of the Walters Art Gallery* 6 (1943): 8–39.

Stone, Richard E. "A Noble Imposture: The Fonthill Ewer and Early-Nineteenth-Century Fakery." *Metropolitan Museum Journal* 32 (1997): 175–206.

Stone, Richard E. "The Fonthill Ewer." *The Metropolitan Museum of Art Bulletin* (winter, 1997–98): 46–55, 56. Reprint, as *Appearance and Reality: Recent Studies in Conservation*, New York, 1998.

Furniture

Bishop, Philippa. "Settees from Fonthill Splendens." *Beckford Journal* 1 (1995): 15–17.

Cornforth, John. "Princely Pietra Dura." *Country Life*, 1 December 1988, 162, 164.

Country Life, 16 February 1995, 49.

Davis, Frank. "Talking about Salerooms." *Country Life*, 20 January 1972, 151–152.

Hardy, John. "A Beckford Bookcase." *Beckford Journal* 2 (1996): 60–61.

———. "Candlesticks from Fonthill Abbey." *Beckford Journal* 2 (1996): 62–63.

Hughes, Peter. *The Wallace Collection Catalogue of Furniture*. 3 vols. London: Trustees of the Wallace Collection, 1996.

Levy, Martin. "A Coffer from Lansdown Tower." *Beckford Journal* 3 (1997): 25–29.

Mallalieu, Huon. "Around the Salerooms." *Country Life*, 16 February 1995, 49.

Norman, Geraldine. "Reversal of fortune." *Telegraph Magazine*, 3 July 1999, 24, 26.

Wainwright, Clive. "William Beckford's Furniture." *Connoisseur* 191 (April 1976): 290–297.

Watson, Francis J. B. *Wallace Collection Catalogues: Furniture*. London: Trustees of the Wallace Collection, 1956.

———. "Beckford, Mme de Pompadour, the Duc de Bouillon & the Taste for Japanese Lacquer in Eighteenth-Century France." *Gazette des Beaux-Arts* 61 (February 1963): 101–127.

Metalwork

Argenteries. Le Trésor du National Trust for Scotland / Schatten in Zilver. Topstukken van de National Trust for Scotland. Brussels: National Trust for Scotland, 1992.

Baker, Malcolm, Timothy Schroder, and E. Laird Clowes. *Beckford and Hamilton Silver from Brodick Castle*. London: Spink, 1980.

Grimwade, A. G. "A New List of Old English Gold Plate: Part 3, 1750–1830." *Connoisseur* 128 (1951): 85–86.

Hayward, J. F. "Royal Plate at Fonthill." *Burlington Magazine* 101 (1959): 145.

Morison, Patricia. "Silver Freak." *Daily Telegraph*, 30 January 1988.

Oman, Charles. "Caddinets and a Forgotten Version of the Royal Arms." *Burlington Magazine* 100 (December 1958): 435.

Schroder, Timothy B. *The Gilbert Collection of Gold & Silver*. Los Angeles: Los Angeles County Museum of Art, 1988.

———. "George Booth and William Beckford: A Study in Patronage." *The International Silver & Jewellery Fair & Seminar* (April 1989): 21–28.

———, ed. *Heritage Regained: Silver from the Gilbert Collection*. London: Heather Trust for the Arts, 1998.

Snodin, Michael, and Malcolm Baker. "William Beckford's Silver." Parts 1 and 2. *Burlington Magazine* 122 (November 1980): 734–748; (December 1980): 820–831, 833–834.

Tipping, H. Avray. "The Hamilton Palace Collection of Silver." *Country Life*, 1 November 1919, 558–561.

Paintings and Drawings

Adams, Eric. *Francis Danby: Varieties of Poetic Landscape*. New Haven: Yale University Press, 1973.

Alexander, Boyd. "William Beckford as Patron." *Apollo* 76 (July 1962): 360–364.

Balston, Thomas. *John Martin, 1789–1854: His Life and Works*. London: Duckworth, 1947.

Boase, T. S. R. *English Art, 1800–1870*. Oxford: Clarendon Press, 1959.

Feaver, William. *The Art of John Martin*. Oxford: Clarendon Press, 1975.

Hamilton-Phillips, Martha. "Benjamin West and William Beckford: Some Projects for Fonthill." *Metropolitan Museum Journal* 15 (1981): 157–174.

Hardie, Martin. *Water-colour Painting in Britain*. 3 vols. London: Batsford, 1968.

Harris, Lucian. "Archibald Swinton: A New source for Albums of Indian Miniatures in William Beckford's collection." *Burlington Magazine* 143 (June 2001): 360–366 and figs 47–57.

Hauptman, William. "Beckford, Brandoin, and the 'Rajah'." *Apollo* 143 (May 1996): 30–39.

———. "William Beckford as Connoisseur and Collector: Some Remarks from the Art Historical Perspective." In *The Beckford Society Annual Lectures, 1996–1999*, edited by Jon Millington, 35–54.

Hazlitt, William. "Fonthill Abbey." *London Magazine* 6 (November 1822): 405–410; "Pictures at Fonthill." *London Magazine* 8 (October 1823): 357–360. Reprint, idem, *Criticisms on Art* (1843), 284–299; 103, 108–111.

Hilliard, Elizabeth. "Willes Maddox." *Beckford Tower Trust Newsletter* (spring 1987): 3.

Holbein. "Beckford: 'Extracts from a Journal'." *Notes and Queries* 209 (December 1964): 477–478.

Ingamells, John. *The Wallace Collection Catalogue of Pictures*. 4 vols. London: Trustees of the Wallace Collection.

Jones, Stanley. "The Fonthill Abbey Pictures: Two Additions to the Hazlitt Canon." *Journal of the Warburg and Courtauld Institutes* 41 (1978): 278–296 and pl. 37, 38.

Levey, Michael. *National Gallery Catalogues. German School.* London: National Gallery, 1959.

McLeod, Bet. "Some further objects from William Beckford's Collection in the Victoria and Albert Museum." *Burlington Magazine* 143 (June 2001): 367–370 and figs 58–65.

Millington, Jon. "Beckford's Pictures now in the National Gallery." *Beckford Journal* 1 (1995): 37–40.

Nolan, J. C. M. "'Ah Dear Comet…': Beckford and the Apocalyptic Art of West and Danby." *Beckford Journal* 3 (1997): 8–19.

Oppé, A. P. *Catalogue of an Exhibition of Drawings & Paintings by Alexander Cozens* 6, 12, 44, 52. Sheffield, 1946.

Paley, Morton D. *The Apocalyptic Sublime.* New Haven: Yale University Press, 1986.

Passavant, Johann David. "Collection of pictures belonging to W. Beckford, Esq." In *Tour of a German Artist in England, with Notices of Private Galleries, and Remarks on the State of Art.* Vol. 1, 314–318. London: Saunders & Otley, 1836.

[Patmore, Peter George]. "British Galleries of Art.—No. 9, *Fonthill.*" *New Monthly Magazine,* n.s. 8 (November 1823): 403–408. Reprint, as "The Late Fonthill Gallery." in idem, *British Galleries of Art,* 119–141. London: Whittaker, 1824.

Pressly, Nancy L. *Revealed Religions: Benjamin West's Commissions for Windsor Castle and Fonthill Abbey.* San Antonio, Texas: San Antonio Museum of Art, 1983.

Roberts, Hugh. "Beckford, Vulliamy and Old Japan." *Apollo* 124 (October 1986): 338–341.

Rogers Jr., Millard F. "Benjamin West and the Caliph: Two Paintings for Fonthill Abbey." *Apollo* 83 (June 1966): 420–425.

Tipping, H. Avray. "The Hamilton Palace Collection of Pictures." Parts 1–3. *Country Life,* 18 October 1919, 479–484; 25 October, 514–517; 1 November, 558–561.

Tuohy, Thomas. "William Beckford's three picture collections." *British Art Journal* 2, no. 1 (fall 2000): 49–53.

Von Erffa, Helmut, and Walter Staley. *The Paintings of Benjamin West.* New Haven: Yale, 1986.

Waagen, Gustav. *Works of Art and Artists in England.* Vol. 114–130. London: John Murray, 1838.

Watson, F. J. B. *Wallace Collection Catalogues: Pictures and Drawings.* London: Trustees of the Wallace Collection, 1968.

Sculpture

Gramaccini, Gisela. *Jean-Guillaume Moitte.* Berlin: Akademie Verlag, 1993.

Nares, Gordon. "Painshill, Surrey—Part 2." *Country Life,* 9 January 1958, 65.

10. Sale Catalogues: A Selection

Nineteenth-Century Sales

Phillips. Fonthill, 19–22 August 1801. *A Catalogue of Part of the Superlatively Elegant and Magnificent Household Furniture . . . the Genuine Property of William Beckford, Esq., of Fonthill . . .*

Christie. London, 27 February 1802. Pictures.

Christie. London, 26–27 March 1802. Pictures.

Leigh, Sotheby & Son. London, 24 & 26 May 1804. Books and prints.

Christie. London, 10 April 1805. Drawings by Cozens.

Phillips. Fonthill, 17–22 & 24 August 1807. Pictures, furniture, etc.

Phillips. Fonthill, 16–19 September 1807. Furniture, etc.

Leigh, Sotheby & Son. London, 9–11 June 1808. Books and prints.

Leigh, Sotheby & Son. London, 6–8 May 1817. Books and drawings.

Christie. London, 9–13 May 1817. *Catalogue of all the Elegant Household Furniture . . . of William Beckford, Esq., of Fonthill . . .*

Christie. *Magnificent Effects at Fonthill Abbey, Wiltshire.* London, 1822. Originally scheduled for 17 September 1822; rescheduled for 1 October and again for 8 October; canceled.

Phillips. *The Valuable Library of Books in Fonthill Abbey . . . The Unique and Splendid Effects of Fonthill Abbey . . . The Pictures and Miniatures at Fonthill Abbey.* London, 1823. 37-day sale. Days 1–10, Books, lots [1]–113; days 11–18, Unique Effects, lots [121]–175; days 19–23, Books, part 2, lots 291–342; days 24–27, Pictures, lots [228]–278; days 28–32, Unique Effects, part 2, lots 176–222; days 33–37, Books part 3, lots 343–391.

Phillips. Fonthill, 1–4 March 1824. Drawings and prints.

Phillips. London, 22–? June, 1825. *Costly Furniture, Bronzes, Marbles, Lathe, &c., of a Gentleman from the West of England . . .*

George Robbins. "Fonthill Park and Estate." London, 29 October 1829.

Sotheby. London, 19–20 March 1830 [attributed]. Drawings and prints.

Phillips. "The Fonthill Abbey Estate." London, 30 October 1838.

English & Fasana. Bath, 4–5 January 1841. *Valuable Paintings, Magnificent Cabinets, and Splendid Furniture from Lansdown Tower . . .*

English & Fasana. Bath, 20–29 November 1845. *Catalogue of the Splendid Furniture, Cabinets, Paintings… the Property of the Late William Beckford, Esquire*

Roussel. Paris, 22–24 February 1847. Objects from China and Japan, etc.

English. Bath, 24 July–2 August 1848. *Catalogue of the Valuable and Costly Effects . . . the Property of the Late William Beckford, Esq . . .*

The Hamilton Palace Libraries. Catalogue of The Beckford Library, removed from Hamilton Library. London: Sotheby, Wilkinson & Hodge, 1882–1883. Four parts, 30 June 1882—30 November 1883.

Christie. London, 17 June–20 July 1882. Pictures, furniture, etc. from Hamilton Palace.

Sotheby. London, 8 July 1884. Books returned from four-part sale.

Sotheby. London, 23 May 1889. Manuscripts.

Accounts of the Christie 1822 Fonthill Abbey sale

"Fonthill Abbey." Announcement in July of Christie's sale. *Gentleman's Magazine* 92, Pt. 1 (Suppl. 1822): 628.

"Fonthill Abbey." *Literary Gazette* 6 (12 October 1822): 653.

"The Fonthill Effects." *The Times,* 2 October 1822, 2a.

Accounts of the Phillips 1823 Fonthill Abbey sale

[Account of irregularities.] *Literary Gazette* 7 (30 August 1823): 555.

Brasbridge, Joseph. *The Fruits of Experience.* London: Printed for the Author, 1824.

Christie's sale advertisements. *Literary Gazette* 6 (1822). [Pictures on 24 September and silver and gilt plate to begin on 17 September] (10 August): 509; [Furniture to begin on 17 September] (17 August): 525; [sale postponed until 1 October, and pictures to begin on 8 October] (31 August): 558; [Silver and gilt plate to begin on 1 October] (7 September): 573.

Fairfax-Lucy, Alice. *Charlecote and the Lucys,* 255–256. London. Oxford Univ. Press, 1958.

"Fonthill Abbey." *The Times,* 15 August 1823, 3d.

"Fonthill Abbey." *Gentleman's Magazine* 93, Pt. 2 (October 1823): 364.

"Fonthill Sale." *Literary Gazette* 7 (20 September 1823): 602; (27 September): 617–618.

"The Fonthill Abbey Sales of 100 Years Ago." Parts 1–9. *Wiltshire Gazette* 30 August 1923; 6, 20, 27 September 1923; 4, 11, 18 October 1923; 1, 29 November 1923.

Haydon, Benjamin Robert. *B. R. H.: Correspondence and Table-talk.* Vol. 2, 79. London: Chatto & Windus, 1876.

Littlebury, Isaac. "Fonthill Campaign: A slight Sketch." *Literary Gazette* 7 (4 October 1823): 634–635.

Millington, Jon. "John Constable's Visits to Fonthill Abbey in 1823." *Beckford Tower Trust Newsletter* (spring 1983): 8–9.

Phillips, Harry. "The Sale at Fonthill Abbey." *Examiner,* 23 November 1823, 763.

Rawlence, Guy. "The Beckford Sale at Fonthill Abbey." *The Field* 5 (January 1946): 15.

"Sale at Fonthill." *The Times,* 11 September 1823, 2b.

Whitfield, Paul. "Fonthill Abbey." *Discovering Antiques,* no. 48.

Twentieth-Century Sales

Phillips. Fonthill, 17 August 1907. *A Catalogue of the Magnificent and Costly Household Furniture . . . of Fonthill Mansion . . .*

Christie. Hamilton Palace, 12–14 November 1919. *The Remaining Contents of the Palace.*

Sotheby. London, 4–6 July 1966. First part of Clements Library.

Sotheby. London, 18–20 October 1971. Lytton Strachey Library.

Sotheby. London, 25 October 1973. Early German and Dutch silver, lots 123–127.

Sotheby. London, 29 November 1973. Seven sketch books by John Robert Cozens.

Sotheby. London, 27–28 October 1975. Rosebery Library.

Sotheby. London, 6 July 1977. The Beckford Papers, lot 272.

Sotheby. London, 24 June 1980. Silver from Lennoxlove, lots 258–261, 276–278, 280.

Sotheby. London, 14 July 1988. Silver-gilt teapot & caddy, etc. 1781, sold by D. of Hamilton.

Christie. London, 17 November 1994. Important English Furniture, lot 107 (pair of settees displaying Beckford's crest).

Phillips. London, 12 December 1995, lot 31 & 18 June 1996, lot 21. Holbein portrait of the Protector, Duke of Somerset, Hamilton Palace sale, 17 June 1882, lot 8.

Sotheby. New York, 16 April 1996, lots from 14 July 1988 sold again.

Sotheby. Hadspen, Somerset, 29 May 1996, Lots 33, 34, looking glasses reputedly from Splendens; Dihl & Guerhard porcelain cup and saucer on second day.

Christie. London, 4 July 1996, lot 204, Louis XIV tortoiseshell casket, ?lot 289 or 889 in 1823 sale.

Christie. London, 6 November 1996, lot 120, George III christening bowl given to Thomas Wildman by Beckford's mother in 1788.

Sotheby. New York, 22 April 1998, gold toasting fork made in London in 1783.

Christie's. *Collection of the Late Baroness Batsheva de Rothschild.* 14 December 2000, lot 15, "A Mamluk Enamelled Glass and Gilded Clear Glass Jug."

11. Publications by Beckford: *Vathek* and *The Episodes*

Seven versions of *Vathek* were published in Beckford's lifetime: four in English—1786, 1816, 1816 (second issue), and 1823; and three in French—Lausanne 1787, Paris 1787 & Londres 1815.

In English

An Arabian Tale, from an Unpublished Manuscript: with Notes Critical and Explanatory. [Vathek]. London: J. Johnson, St. Paul's Church-yard, 1786.

An Arabian Tale, from An Unpublished Manuscript: with Notes Critical and Explanatory. A New Edition. London: Printed for W. Clarke, New Bond Street, 1809.

Vathek. Third Edition. London: Printed for W. Clarke, New Bond Street, 1816.

Vathek. Third Edition. London: Printed for W. Clarke, New Bond Street, 1816.

Vathek. From the Third London Edition, Revised and Corrected. Philadelphia: M. Carey, 1816.

Vathek. Fourth Edition. London: Printed for W. Clarke, New Bond Street, 1823.

Vathek. Fifth edition. London: George Clarke, Mount Street, Berkeley Square, 1832.

Vathek; An Arabian Tale. London: Richard Bentley, etc., 1834.

Vathek. Philadelphia: Carey, Lee & Blanchard, 1834.

Vathek. Translated from the French. Baltimore: Joseph Robinson, 1834.

Vathek: An Arabian Tale. Paris: Baudry's European Library, 1834.

Vathek; An Arabian Tale. London: Richard Bentley, etc., 1836. Reprint, 1949.

Vathek and Other Stories—A William Beckford Reader. London: Pickering & Chatto, 1993.

Vathek: An Oriental Romance. New York: Morris, Willis & Fuller, 1845.

Vathek; An Arabian Tale. London: George Slater, 1849. Reprint, 1850.

Vathek; An Arabian Tale. London: H. G. Bohn, 1852.

Vathek; An Arabian Tale. Philadelphia: Henry Carey Baird, 1854.

Vathek; An Arabian Tale. London: Ward & Lock, 1856.

Vathek. In *The Arabian Nights' Entertainments*, 541–580. London: Charles Griffin, 1866.

Vathek; An Arabian Tale. London: William Tegg, 1868.

Vathek; An Arabian Tale. New York: James Miller, 1868.

The History of the Caliph Vathek. Printed verbatim from the First Edition, with the Original Preface and Notes by Henley. London: Sampson, Low etc., 1868. 2d ed, New York: Scribner, Welford & Co., 1869.

Vathek. In *A Library of Famous Fiction Embracing the Nine Standard Masterpieces of Imaginative Literature*, 841–897. New York: J. B. Ford & Company, 1873.

Vathek: An Arabian Tale. Nashville, Tennessee: A. Setliff, 1880.

The History of the Caliph Vathek. London: Nimmo & Bain, 1883.

The History of the Caliph Vathek. New York: Thomas R Knox, 1886.

Vathek. An Arabian Tale. New York: John B. Alden, 1887.

Vathek. An Arabian Tale. New York: Hurst, n.d.

The History of the Caliph Vathek. New York: Cassell, 1886.

The History of the Caliph Vathek. London: Cassell, 1887.

The History of the Caliph Vathek. New York: F. M. Lupton, n.d.

The History of the Caliph Vathek. Printed verbatim from the First Edition, with the Original Preface and Notes by Henley. 8th ed. New York: Scribner, Welford & Co., Philadelphia: Porter & Coates; New York: William L Allison, ca. 1889.

The History of the Caliph Vathek. New York: Pollard & Moss, [1889].

The History of the Caliph Vathek; and European Travels. London: Ward, Lock, 1891.

Vathek: An Arabian Tale. London: Lawrence & Bullen, 1893.

The History of the Caliph Vathek. London: Newnes, [1897].

Vathek: An Arabian Tale. London: Gibbins, 1900.

The History of the Caliph Vathek. Printed verbatim from the First Edition, with the Original Preface and Notes by Henley. New York: James Pott, 1900.

The History of the Caliph Vathek. An Eastern Romance. London: Greening, 1900. Reprint, 1905.

The History of the Caliph Vathek. London: Methuen, 1901.

Vathek. London: Greening, n.d.

Vathek. Reprint of Greening (1900). London: Collins, n.d.

The Episodes of Vathek. Parts 1–3. *The English Review* 4, "Histoire de la Princesse Zulkaïs et du Prince Kalilah" (December 1909): 163–184; "Histoire du Prince Alasi de la Princesse Firouzkah," 6 (August 1910): 137–147; (September 1910): 309–322.

The Episodes of Vathek. Translated by Sir Frank Marzials. London: Stephen Swift, 1912.

Vathek. An Arabian Tale. London: Routledge, [1912].

Vathek. New York: Brentano's, 1921.

Vathek. London: Chapman & Dodd, [1922].

The Episodes of Vathek. London: Chapman & Dodd, [1922].

Vathek. London: Philip Allan, [1923].

Vathek: An Arabian Tale. London: William Glaisher, 1924.

Vathek. New York: John Day, 1928.

Vathek. Translation, introduction, and notes by Herbert B. Grimsditch. Translation of the Paris 1815 edition. London: Nonesuch Press, 1929.

Vathek. In *Shorter Novels. Eighteenth Century*, 193–306. London: Dent, 1930–1953.

Vathek. In *Three Eighteenth Century Romances*. New York: Scribner, [1931]. Reprint, 1963 & later.

Vathek: an Arabian Tale. Translation, introduction, and notes by Herbert B. Grimsditch. New York: Limited Editions Club, 1945.

Vathek. In *Shorter Novels of the Eighteenth Century*, 193–278. London: Dent, 1953 and later.

Vathek. Translation, introduction, and notes by Herbert B. Grimsditch. London: The Bodley Head, 1953.

Vathek. Translation, introduction, and notes by Herbert B. Grimsditch. London: The Folio Society, 1958.

Vathek. In *Three Gothic Novels*, edited with an introduction by E. F. Bleiler, 107–253. New York: Dover, 1966.

Vathek. An Arabian Tale. London: New English Library, 1966.

Vathek. In *Three Gothic Novels*, edited by Peter Fairclough, 149–255. Harmondsworth, Middlesex: Penguin, 1968 and later.

Vathek. Edited by Roger Lonsdale. Oxford: Oxford Univ. Press, 1970.

Vathek. Menston, Yorkshire: Scholar Press, 1971.

The History of the Caliph Vathek, including The Episodes of Vathek. New York: Ballantine, 1971.

Vathek. The English translation by Samuel Henley (1786) and the French editions of Lausanne and Paris (1787). Delmar, NY: Scholars' Facsimiles & Reprints, 1972.

The Episodes of Vathek. Rutherford, NJ: Fairleigh Dickinson University Press, 1975.

Vathek and Other Stories—A William Beckford Reader. Edited by Malcolm Jack. London: Pickering & Chatto, 1993. Reprint, Harmondsworth, Middlesex: Penguin Books, 1995.

The Episodes of Vathek. Edited by Malcolm Jack. Sawtry, Cambs: Dedalus, 1994.

Vathek In *Four Gothic Novels*, 81–154. Oxford: Oxford Univ. Press, 1994.

Vathek. London: Creation Books, 2000.

Vathek with The Episodes of Vathek. Peterborough, Ontario: Broadview, 2001. Edited By Kenneth W. Graham.

In French

Vathek. Lausanne: Isaac Hignou, 1787 [1786].

Vathek, Conte Arabe. Paris: Poinçot. 1787.

Les Caprices et les Malheurs du Calife Vathek. Translated from arabic. London, 1791.

Vathek. Londres: Clarke, New Bond Street, 1815.

Histoire du Calife Vathek. 2 vols. Paris: Anth^e Boucher. 1819.

Vathek. London: Clarke, ca. 1828.

Vathek. With Notes. Nouvelle Edition. London: Richard Bentley, 1834.

Vathek. Reprint from the original French. Paris: Adolphe Labitte, 1876.

Vathek. Reprint from the original French. Paris: Perrin, 1893.

Vathek, conte arabe. Paris: Les Exemplaires, 1928.

Vathek with The Episodes of Vathek. Edited by Guy Chapman. 2 vols. Cambridge: Printed at the University Press for Constable, 1929.

Vathek: Conte Arabe. Paris: José Corti, 1946 [1947].

Vathek et Les Episodes. Paris: Editions Stock, 1948.

Vathek et Les Episodes. Lausanne: Editions Rencontre, 1962.

Vathek: conte arabe. Paris: Le club français du livre, 1962.

Vathek. Paris: Cercle du livre précieux, 1962.

Vathek. Grenoble: Roissard, 1971.

Vathek. Histoire du Prince Alasi. Histoire du Prince Barkiarokh. Paris: Flammarion, 1981.

Vathek. Paris: Editions Slatkine, 1997.

In Dutch

Vathek, Gene Arabische Vertelling. Translated by J. Potgieter. Amsterdam: J.H. en G. van Heteren, 1837.

Vathek. Translated by Max Schuchart. Utrecht/ Antwerp: Uitgeverij het Spectrum, 1982.

In German

Der Thurm von Samarah . . . Aus dem Arabischen. Translation of Lausanne edition by Georg Schatz. Leipzig: Dykischen Buchhandlung, 1788.

Vathek, eine arabische Erzählung. Translation of Paris edition. Vienna, 1788.

Vathek, eine arabische Erzählung. Translated by Georg Christian Römer. Mannheim, 1788.

Vathek, eine arabische Erzählung. Translated by Otto Mohnike. Leipzig: Cnobloch, 1842.

Vathek. By "John Beckford'. Translated by Franz Blei. Leipzig: Julius Zeitler, 1907.

Vathek. Translation and introduction by Karl Toth. Zurich: Amalthea, 1921.

Vathek: Eine arabische Erzählung. Translated by Hans Schiebelhuth. Berlin: Fritz Gurlitt, [1924].

Vathek: Eine arabische Erzählung. Translated by Hans Schiebelhuth. Munich: Winkler, 1964.

Vathek mit der Episoden. *Vathek* translated from the French by Franz Blei, revised by Robert Picht. The *Episodes* translated by Ronald Weber. Preface by Stéphane Mallarmé translated by Max Hölzer. Frankfurt: Insel, 1964.

Die Geschichte vom Kalifen Vathek: mit der Episoden. Translated by Franz Blei, revised by Robert Picht. Leipzig: Insel, 1974.

Die Geschichte des Kalifen Vathek. Berlin: Wagenbach, 1975.

Vathek. Translated by Franz Blei. Leipzig: Insel, 1976–

Vathek. Translated by Hans Schiebelhuth. Stuttgart: Edition Weitbrecht, 1983.

Vathek: Eine orientalische Erzählung. Translated by Wolfram Benda. Bayreuth: Bear Press, 1985.

Vathek: Eine orientalische Erzählung. Translation and afterword by Wolfram Benda. Munich: Winkler, 1987.

Vathek. Translated by Wolfram Benda. Munich: Deutscher Taschenbuch Verlag, 1988.

Vathek. Translated by Franz Blei. Includes the *Episodes* (translator unknown). Frankfurt: Insel Taschenbuch, 1989.

Vathek. Translated from the French by Franz Blei. Suhrkamp Verlag KG., 1999.

In Italian

Vathek. Translated and edited by Giaime Pintor. Turin: Einaudi, 1946; reprint, 1973, 1989.

Vathek. Translated by Aldo Camerino. Milan: Franco Maria Ricci, 1978.

Racconti orientali [three tales from the *Episodes*]. Translated by L. Romito. Edited by G Servadio. Soveria Mannelli: Rubbettino (Il colibri), 1989.

Vathek e gli episodi. Translated by Aldo

Camerino (*Vathek*) and Ruggero Savinio (*Episodes*). Milan: Fabbri-Bompiani-Sonzogno-Etas, 1966. Reprint, 1974 (Club degli editori) and 1991.

Storia del principe Alasi e della principessa Firuzkah. Translation and introduction by Giandonato Crico. Palermo: Sellerio, 1992.

In Japanese

Vathek. Translated from mainly French versions by Yasuhiko Kisaichi. 2 vols. Tokyo: Kokusho Kankokai, 1990.

In Portuguese

Vathek—Conto Árabe. Translated by Albert Demazière. Lisbon: Os Amigos do Livro, n.d.

Vathek. Translation, introduction, and notes by Manuel João Gomes. Lisbon: Estampa, 1978.

Historia do Califa Vathek. Translated by Mário Cláudio. Porto: Edições Afrontamento, 1982.

Vathek. São Paulo: L & PM Pocket, 1997.

In Russian

Caliph Vathek. An Arabian Tale. Translated from the French. St Petersburg: St Petersburg Mining Institute, 1792.

Vathek—An Arabian Tale. Translated by Boris Zaitsev. Moscow: K. F. Nekrasov, 1912.

Vathek: *News on Foreign Literature* Translated by M. and E. Ramm.(St Petersburg), 1913.

Vathek. In *Fantasy Stories*, edited and annotated by V.M. Zhirmunsky and N.A. Sigal, 163–228. Leningrad: Nauka, 1967.

Vathek—An Arabian Tale. Translated by Boris Zaitsev from the Paris 1787 version. Moscow: Moscow State University, 1992–1993.

In Spanish and Catalan

Vathek; cuento arábe. Translation and introduction by Guillermo Carnero. Barcelona: Editorial Seix Barral, 1969.

Vathek. Translated by Guillermo Carnero. Madrid: Ediciones Siruela, 1984.

Vathek, cuento árabe. Translated by Manuel Serrat Crespo. 2d ed. Barcelona: Bruguera, S.A., 1985.

Vathek. Translated by Jorge Luis Borges. 3rd ed. Madrid: Hyspamerica Ediciones Argentina, S.A., 1988.

Los Episodios de Vathek. Translated by Claudia Monfils. Madrid: Valdemar, 1991.

Vathek, cuento árabe (Con sus tres Episodios). Translated from the Paris 1787 version, edited, and with introduction and notes by Javier Martín Lalanda. Madrid: Alianza, 1993.

Vathek: un conte àrab. Translated into Catalan from the 1786 version by Carles Urritz, Barcelona: Laertes, 1995.

In Swedish

Vathek eller Kalifen på Resa. Translated by Ragnhild Haglund. Stockholm: Wahlström & Widstrand, 1927.

12. Travel Writing and Other Publications by Beckford

Arranged in chronological order by the date of the first edition.

Biographical Memoirs of Extraordinary Painters (1780)

Biographical Memoirs of Extraordinary Painters. London: J. Robson, New-Bond-Street, 1780.

Biographical Memoirs of Extraordinary Painters. 2d ed. London: J. Robson, New Bond Street, 1780.

Biographical Memoirs of Extraordinary Painters. London: William Clarke, New Bond Street, 1824.

Biographical Memoirs of Extraordinary Painters. London: Richard Bentley, 1834.

Biographical Memoirs of Extraordinary Painters. Rutherford: Fairleigh Dickinson University Press, 1969.

Biographical Memoirs of Extraordinary Painters (1780). Cambridge: Oleander Press, 1977.

Memorias Biograficas de Pintores Extraordinarios. Madrid: Alfraguara Nostromo, 1978.

Vies authentiques de peintres imaginaires. Paris: José Corti, 1990.

Vite immaginarie di pittori straordinari. Introduction by Violetta Candiani, translated by Mariapaola Dèttore. Rome: Biblioteca del Vascello, 1994.

Memorie biografiche di pittori straodinari. Translated by M. Billi. Essay by G. Fossi. Florence: Guinti, 1995.

Dreams, Waking Thoughts and Incidents (1783)
(became *Italy, etc.* Vol. 1, 1834)

Dreams, Waking Thoughts and Incidents. London: J. Johnson, St. Paul's Church Yard, 1783.

Dreams, Waking Thoughts and Incidents. Edited, with introduction and notes, by Robert J. Gemmett. Rutherford, NJ: Fairleigh Dickinson University Press, 1971.

The Grand Tour of William Beckford. Edited by Elizabeth Mavor. Harmondsworth, Middlesex: Penguin Books, 1986.

Voyage d'un rêveur éveillé de Londres à Venise. Translated by Roger Kann. Paris: José Corti, 1988.

Voyage d'un rêveur éveillé de Venise à Naples. Translated by Roger Kann. Paris: José Corti, 1989.

Rheinreise. Translated by Wolfram Benda. Bayreuth: Bear Press, 1990.

Een dromer op reis; een Grand Tour. Translated and introduction by Gerlof Janzen. Amsterdam: Uitgeverij Contact, 1991.

Portuguese Journal (1787–1788)
(became *Italy, etc.,* Vol. 2 (1834)

The Journal of William Beckford in Portugal and Spain 1787–1788. Edited by Boyd Alexander. London: Hart-Davis, 1954.

Diário de William Beckford em Portugal e Espanha. Translated by João Gaspar Simões, edited by Boyd Alexander. Lisbon: Emprensa Nacionade Publicidade, 1957.

Journal Intime au Portugal et en Espagne 1787–1788. Translated by Roger Kann. Paris: José Corti, 1986.

Menuetten met de markies. Portugees dagboek 1787. Translated by Gerlof Janzen, edited by Boyd Alexander. Amsterdam: Uitgeverij Contact, 1992.

Italy; with Sketches of Spain and Portugal (1834)

Italy; with Sketches of Spain and Portugal. 2 vols. London: Richard Bentley, 1834.

Italy; with Sketches of Spain and Portugal. 2d ed. 2 vols. London: Richard Bentley, 1834.

Italy, with Sketches of Spain and Portugal. Paris: Baudry's European Library, 1834.

Italy, with Sketches of Spain and Portugal. 2 vols. Philadelphia: Key & Biddle, 1834.

Italy, Sketches. Paris: Cornon & Blanc, 1835.

Italy, pp. 1–202 in *Sketches of Italy* by Mrs Jameson. Frankfort: Charles Jugel, 1841.

A Côrte da Rainha D. Maria I. Translated by Zacarias d'Aça. Lisbon: Tavares Cardoso & Irmâo, 1901.

Lettres d'Espagne et de Portugal, 1787–1788. Translated by Madeleine Clemenceau-Jacquemaire. Paris: Eugène Figuière, [1936].

"Lettres de Venise." *Revue de Paris* 44 (1 August 1937): 520–548.

Un Ingles en la España de Godoy (An Englishman in Godoy's Spain). Translated by Jesús Pardo. Madrid: Taurus Ediciones, 1966.

Da Trieste alla laguna veneta con scrittori del passato. Translated by Franca Piazza. Florence: G Barbèra, 1968.

"Itali, com Descrições de Espanha e Portugal." In Maria Laura Bettencourt Pires. *Portugal visto pelos Ingleses*. Textos de literatura-9, 27–33. Lisbon: Instituto Nacional de Investigação Cientifica, 1981.

Un califfo a Venezia. Translated and edited by P. Pepe. Naples: Alfredo Guida Editore, 1994.

De Venezia alle Dolomiti con William Beckford. Translated by F. Piazza. Florence: Barbera.

Recollections of an Excursion to the Monasteries of Alcobaça and Batalha (1835)
(based on Beckford's 1794 Journal)

Recollections of an Excursion to the Monasteries of Alcobaça and Batalha. London: Richard Bentley, 1835.

Recollections of an Excursion to the Monasteries of Alcobaça and Batalha. Philadelphia: Carey, Lea and Blanchard, 1835.

Erinnerungen von einem Ausfluge nach den Klöstern Alcobaça und Batalha. Translated by S. H. Spiker. Berlin: Duncker & Humblot, 1835.

Alcobaça e Batalha (Recordações de uma excursão). Translated by Joaquim Lúcio Lobo & M. Vieira Natividade. Alcobaça: Tip. A. M. de Oliveira, 1914.

Excursion à Alcobaça et Batalha. Translated,

introduction & notes by André Parreaux. Paris: Société d'Editions "Les Belles Lettres," 1956.

Beckford's 1794 Journal. Edited by Boyd Alexander. In Howard B. Gotlieb, *William Beckford of Fonthill*. New Haven: Yale University Library, 1960.

Recollections of an Excursion to the Monasteries of Alcobaça and Batalha. Fontwell, Sussex: Centaur Press, 1972.

Recollections of an Excursion to the Monasteries of Alcobaça and Batalha. Watchung, NJ: Saifer, [1972].

Recollections of an Excursion to the Monasteries of Alcobaça and Batalha. Folcroft, PA: Folcroft Library Editions, 1974.

Recollections of an Excursion to the Monasteries of Alcobaça and Batalha. Norwood Editions, 1978.

Excursión a Alcobaca y Batalha. Translated by Luis Antonio de Villena. Barcelona: Laertes, 1983.

Souvenirs d'Alcobaça et Batalha. Translated by André Parreaux. Paris: José Corti, 1989.

Ricordi di viaggio ai monasteri di Alcobaca e Batalha. Translated by Domenico Cosmai. Bari: Ladisa, 1994.

The Vision (1930)

The Vision, Liber veritatis, by William Beckford of Fonthill. London: Constable and Co.,1930. Edited with an introduction and notes by Guy Chapman.

Collections

Italy, Spain, and Portugal, with an Excursion to the Monasteries of Alcobaça and Batalha. London: Richard Bentley, 1840.

Italy, Spain, and Portugal, with an Excursion to the Monasteries of Alcobaça and Batalha. 2 vols. in 1. New York: Wiley & Putnam, 1845, 1847, 1848.

The History of the Caliph Vathek; and European Travels. London: Ward, Lock, 1891.

The Travel-Diaries of William Beckford of Fonthill. Edited by Guy Chapman. 2 vols. London: Constable, 1928.

13. Commentary on Beckford's Travels and Travel Writing

Alexander, Boyd. "The Marquis of Marialva's Friendship with Beckford." *British Historical Society of Portugal. Second Annual Report and Review* (1975): 11–22.

Alexander, Boyd, "Beckford's Debt to Portugal." *British Historical Society of Portugal. Fifth Annual Report and Review* (1978): 21–36.

Alger, John Goldworth. *Napoleon's British Visitors and Captives: 1801–1815*. London: Constable, 1904.

Anderson, Patrick. "The Enchanted Garden: William Beckford in Italy and Portugal." In *Over the Alps*, 73–144. London: Hart-Davis, 1969.

Anglesey, Marquess of, (George Paget), ed. *The Capel Letters*. London: Jonathan Cape, 1955.

"Beckford, William por ocasião de um bicentenário 1787–1987." *O Estudo da História,* no. 3–4, 2d series (1987): 31–48.

Beer, Gavin R. De. "Anglais au pays de Vaud. v. William Beckford." *Revue historique vaudoise* 59 (December 1951): 165–180.

Borenius, Tancred. "A Footnote to Beckford." *Burlington Magazine* 78 (June 1941): 201–202.

Bombelles, Marc de. *Journal d'un Ambassadeur de France au Portugal, 1786–1788.* Edited by Roger Kann. Paris: Presses Universitaires de France, 1979.

Boxer, C. R. "Maria Laura Bettencourt Pires. *William Beckford e Portugal.*" ?, 9 December 1988.

Bullough, Geoffrey. "Beckford's Early Travels and His 'Dream of Delusion'." In *William Beckford of Fonthill, 1760–1844. Bicentenary Essays,* edited by Fatma Moussa Mahmoud, 31–50. Cairo, 1960.

Carnarvon, Earl of. *Portugal and Galicia.* 3d ed, 11. London: John Murray, 1848.

Castro, D. Luis de. "Beckford em Cintra." Parts 1–3. *Ilustração Portuguesa* no. 36 (1906):411–416; no., 37 (1906): 425–431; no., 38 (1906): 46?–472.

[Carrére, J. B. F.] *Voyage au Portugal, et particulièrement à Lisbon . . . ,* 119–127. Paris: Deterville, 1798.

Carvalho, João Pinto de. *Lisboa de outrora.* Vol. 1, 99–112. Lisbon: Edição do Grupo Amigos de Lisboa, 1938.

Chaney, Edward. *The Evolution of the Grand Tour: Anglo-Italian Relations since the Renaissance.* London: Frank Cass, 1998.

Claésson, Dick. "'Sinking Apace into the Bosom of Delusions': William Beckford's Earliest Narrative of Travel, An introduction to *Fragments of an English Tour.*" *Beckford Journal* 5 (1999): 6–13.

Costa, Francisco. *Beckford em Sintra no Verão de 1787. Narrativa literária seguida de—História da Quinta e Palácio do Ramalhão.* Sintra: Câmara Municipal de Sintra, 1982.

Costa, Francisco. *História da Quinta e Palácio de Monserrate.* Sintra: Câmara Municipal de Sintra, 1985.

Curley, Thomas M. "William Beckford and the Romantic Tradition of Travel Literature." *Studies on Voltaire and the Eighteenth Century* 305 (1992): 1819–1823.

Dewey, Clive. "Monserrate, Sintra, Portugal." *Country Life,* 1 November 1990, 88, 89, 91.

Flor, J. Almeida. *Sintra na literatura romântica inglesa.* Sintra: Câmara Municipal de Sintra, 1978.

Gordon, Pryse Lockhart. *Personal Memoirs or Reminiscences of Men and Manners.* 2 vols. London, 1830.

Gracias, J. A. Ismael. "Bocage na India." *Oriente Português* 14 (1917): 29 et seq.

Guerra, Oliva. "Sintra e Lord Beckford." *Colóquio* 46 (1967): 14–16.

Harrison, William Henry. *The Tourist in Portugal:* Landscape Annual Series. London: Robert Jennings, 1839.

Hibbert, Christopher. *The Grand Tour.* London: Weidenfeld & Nicolson, 1969.

Hilliard, Elizabeth. "Dr. and Mrs. Hilliard's Visit to Portugal." *Beckford Tower Trust Newsletter* (spring 1986): 7–8.

Hume, Martin. *Through Portugal,* 172–173, 188–192. London: Grant Richards, 1907.

Inchbold, A. C. *Lisbon & Cintra,* 156–158, 174–177. London: Chatto & Windus, 1907.

Ingamells, John, ed. *A Dictionary of British and Irish Travellers in Italy, 1701–1800.* New Haven: Yale University Press, 1997.

Jack, Malcolm. "Recollections of a Congress at Sintra." *Beckford Tower Trust Newsletter* (spring 1988): 3–4.

———. "Beckford and Portugal: a Review Essay." *Beckford Tower Trust Newsletter* (spring 1990): 2–3.

———. "William Beckford: traveller, artist, escapist." *Studies on Voltaire and the Eighteenth Century* 305 (1992): 1823–1824.

———. *William Beckford. An English Fidalgo.* New York: AMS Press, 1996 [1997].

———. "Ramalhão: Beckford's First Sintra House." *Beckford Journal* 3 (1997): 20–24.

———. "Monserrate: Beckford's Second Sintra House." *Beckford Journal* 4 (1998): 48–51.

———. "Portuguese Pilgrims and Irish Seminarians." *Beckford Journal* 6 (2000): 5–7.

Jaloux, Edmond. "Beckford." *Gazette de Lausanne,* 24 November 1945, 1.

Jaloux, Edmond. "Lettres de Beckford." *Gazette de Lausanne,* 8 December 1945, 1.

Jones, Thomas. *Memoirs.* London: Walpole Society, 1951.

Kingsbury, Ida, "Post Script to the Excursion. In Beckford's Footsteps to Alcobaça and Batalha." *British Historical Society of Portugal.*

Seventh Annual Report and Review (1980): 23–40.

———. "'Vathek' The First Caliph." In *Castles, Caliphs and Christians: a Landscape with Figures.* Monserrate, 25–36. Lisbon: British Historical Society of Portugal, 1994.

Kinsey, Rev. William Morgan. *Portugal Illustrated,* 133. London, 1828.

Lawless, Valentine Browne, Baron Cloncurry. *Person Recollections of the Life and Times, with Extracts from the Correspondence, of Valentine, Lord Cloncurry.* Dublin: McGlashan, 1849.

Macaulay, Rose. "Aesthete. William Beckford." In *They Went to Portugal,* 108–142. London: Jonathan Cape, 1946.

Mayoux, Jean-Jacques. "Note sur l'Excursion à Alcobaça et Batalha." *Critique* 13 (October 1957): 905–907.

Moore, Thomas. *Memoirs, Journal, and Correspondence of Thomas Moore.* Edited by Lord Russell. London, 1853

Morgulis, Grégoire. "Un Épisode de la vie de Beckford." *Revue de Littérature Comparée* 14 (October 1934): 690–694.

Nolan, J. C. M. "Beckford's Excursion to the Grande Chartreuse Revised." *Beckford Journal* 5 (1999): 33–42.

Oliver, J. W. "The Caliph of Fonthill." *Times Literary Supplement,* 17 November 1932, 859.

Parreaux, André. *Le Portugal dans l'œuvre de William Beckford.* Paris: Société d'Editions "Les Belles Lettres," 1935.

Parreaux, André. "Beckford et le Portugal. Du Nouveau sur Quelques Problèmes." *Bulletin des Etudes Portugaises,* n.s. 18 (1955): 93–130.

Parreaux, André. "Beckford et le Portugal." *Bulletin des Etudes Portugaises,* n.s. 21 (1958): 97–155. Reprint, Paris (1958).

Parreaux, André. "Etudes Portugaises sur William Beckford." *Bulletin des Etudes Portugaises* 2 (1932): 177–184.

Parreaux, André. "Précisions sur les séjours de William Beckford au Portugal." *Bulletin des Etudes Portugaises* 6 (1939): 45–49.

Perrochon, Henri. "Un ami de Gibbon." *Gazette de Lausanne,* 1 May 1932, 1.

Pires, Maria Laura Bettencourt. "A Reexamination of William Beckford's Life and Accomplishments in Portugal." *Beckford Tower Trust Newsletter* (spring 1986): 2–6.

Pires, Maria Laura Bettencourt. *William Beckford e Portugal.* Lisbon: edições 70, 1987.

Quillinan [neé Wordsworth], Dorothy. *Journal of a Few Months' Residence in Portugal, and Glimpses of the South of Spain.* Vol. 2, 56–57. London: Moxon, 1847.

Redford, Bruce. *Venice and the Grand Tour.* New Haven: Yale University Press, 1996.

Sewell, Gordon, "William Beckford on the Grand Tour." *Bournemouth Evening Echo,* 18 July 1969, 13.

Shaffer, E. S. "'To Remind us of China'— William Beckford, Mental Traveller on the Grand Tour: The Construction of Significance in Landscape." In *Transports, Travel, Pleasure, and Imaginative Geography, 1600–1830,* edited by Chloe Chard & Helen Langdon. New Haven: Yale University Press, 1996.

[Sherer, Moyle]. *Recollections of the Peninsular.* 5th ed., 39–40. London: Longman, etc., 1827.

Shore, H. N. *Three Pleasant Springs in Portugal,* 54–55, 60–65, 71–73, 86–87 and passim. London: Sampson Low, 1899.

Sitwell, Sacheverell. *Southern Baroque Art. A Study of Painting, Architecture and Music in Italy and Spain in the 17th and 18th Centuries.* 3rd ed. London: Duckworth, 1930.

———. *Portugal and Madeira,* 114–116 & passim. London: Batsford, 1954.

Soares d'Azevedo Barbosa de Pinho Leal, Augusto. *Portugal antigo e moderno.* Vol. 5, 436–438. Lisbon, 1875.

[Spain.] *Notes and Queries* 3rd Series 3 (16, 23 May 1863): 382–383, 401.

"The Spirit of Eighteenth-Century Madrid." *Times Literary Supplement,* 30 December 1955, 795.

Tuckerman, H. T. "William Beckford and the Literature of Travel." *Southern Literary Messenger* 16 (January 1850): 7–14.

Villiers, G. H. "Mr. Beckford in Portugal." *National Review* 74 (1920): 808–816.

Wahba, Magdi. "Beckford, Portugal and 'Childish Error'." In *William Beckford of Fonthill, 1760–1844. Bicentenary Essays,* edited by Fatma Moussa Mahmoud, 51–62. Cairo, 1960.

Walter, Felix. *La littérature portugaise en Angleterre à l'époque romantique,* 29. Paris: Honoré Champion, 1927.

Whaley, Buck. *Buck Whaley's Memoirs . . . Written by Himself in 1797.* Edited by Sir Edward Sullivan. London: Alexander Moring, 1906.

Photocredits: With the exception of the individual credits listed below, all photographic credits belong either to the institution, archive, or collector who provided the photograph, or to the author whose text it accompanies. **Michael Agee:** Cat. no. 70. **Jörg P. Anders:** Fig. 13-1. **From Beckford em Sintra no Verao de 1787 by F. Costa (Sintra: Câmara Municipal, 1982):** Figs 5-2 to 5-5. **Sidney Blackmore:** Cat. fig. 129A. **Bridgeman Art Library, London and New York:** Fig. 2-1. **Geremy Butler Photography:** Figs. 14-4, 14-5. **Richard Carafelli:** Fig. 1-3. **Christie's Images Inc.:** Figs. 3-10, 10-8, 14-5, 15-6. Cat. nos. 54, 105, 110, 157, 160. **Ken Cohen:** Cat. no. 94. **Country Life Picture Library, London:** Figs. 10-5 (Tim Imrie), 15-3, 15-7, 15-8. **DOWIC Fotografi:** Fig. 4-7. **Jérôme Letellier:** Figs. 6-2, 6-5, 6-6. **Montreal Museum of Fine Arts (Brian Merrett):** Cat. no. 78. **Derry Moore:** Fig. 2-11. **National Trust Photographic Library:** Figs. 10-6 (Andreas von Einsiedel); 13-8, 13-9 (John Hammond). **Photographie François Martin, Geneve:** Figs. 4-5, 4-6. **Photothèque des Musées de la Ville de Paris:** Fig. 6-1. **Prudence Cuming Associates Limited, London:** Cat. no. 30. **Sylviane Pittet:** Fig. 4-4. **RMN / K. Ignatiadis:** Fig. 10-4. **Antonia Reeve:** Figs. 12-6, 12-7. Cat. nos. 1, 9–12, 27, 31–36, 38, 40–44, 47, 55–63, 65–69, 83, 85–87, 109, 111–13, 116–18, 120–24, detail of 124, 125, 126, 138, 140–47, 153, 154, 158, 159. **Richmond and Rigg Photography:** Fig. 3-11. **Betsy Barlow Rogers:** Fig. 8-1. **Sotheby's Photographic:** Cat. no. 25. **Chris Titmus, Hamilton Kerr Institute:** Fig. 3-2. **Bruce White:** Figs. 1-2, 3-7, 3-15, 3-16, 3-17, 7-5, 7-6, 7-8, 7-9, 7-10, 9-2, 9-5, 9-7, 11-6, 16-1, 16-10, 16-14. Cat. nos. 3, 4, 6, 8, 20, detail of 20, 26, 29, 45, 48, 49, 53, 64, 71, 72, 79, 82, 88–90, 93, 107, 108, 114, 115, 119, 130, 133, 139, 148, 149, 151, 152, 155, 156. Cat. figs. 85A, 132A, 146A, 149A. **David Wiltshire Photography:** Figs. 3-4, 7-1, 8-2, 8-3, 8-5, 8-6. Cat. nos. 21–24, 51, 91, 92, 129, 134–37.

Index: Available on the Bard Graduate Center website at http://www.bgc.bard.edu/publications/catalog.html